2000 World Development Indicators

The World Bank

2000 World Development Indicators

Manufactured in the United States of America
First printing March 2000

This volume is a product of the staff of the Development Data Group of the World Bank's Development Economics Vice Presidency, and the judgments herein do not necessarily reflect the views of the World Bank's Board of Executive Directors or the countries they represent.

The World Bank does not guarantee the accuracy of the data included in this publication and accepts no responsibility whatsoever for any consequence of their use. The boundaries, colors, denominations, and other information shown on any map in this volume do not imply on the part of the World Bank any judgment on the legal status of any territory or the endorsement or acceptance of such boundaries. This publication uses the Robinson projection for maps, which represents both area and shape reasonably well for most of the earth's surface. Nevertheless, some distortions of area, shape, distance, and direction remain.

Photo credits: Curt Carnemark/World Bank, Jan Pakulski/World Bank.

If you have questions and comments about this product, please contact:

Development Data Center
The World Bank
1818 H Street, NW, Room MC2-812, Washington, DC 20433, USA
Hotline: (800) 590 1906 or (202) 473 7824; fax (202) 522 1498
Email: info@worldbank.org
Website: www.worldbank.org or www.worldbank.org/data

ISBN 0-8213-4553-2

Foreword

The past year brought the first signs of recovery from the financial crisis that swept the globe in 1997. It also brought a stronger and more focused commitment to reducing poverty in the world. These are both encouraging signs. Economic growth provides the resources needed to improve people's lives—creating new jobs, increasing productivity, and producing goods and services. But only growth with equity—growth that reaches the poor—can close the gap between the rich and the poor.

Low income is just one of poverty's many dimensions. The poor lack material goods, education, medical care, and information. They also lack security and the means to protect their families. And they suffer the indignity of being displaced and dispossessed, even in their own communities. So we cannot look for a single solution to poverty. Nor can we measure poverty by just one indicator. We must look at a range of indicators.

That is why the Development Assistance Committee of the Organisation for Economic Co-operation and Development (OECD) in 1996 selected seven international development goals from the resolutions of UN conferences. Then, in 1998 a joint meeting of the UN, the OECD, and the World Bank proposed 21 indicators to track progress toward those goals.

This year's *World Development Indicators* tells us that achieving those goals will be difficult but still attainable in many countries. Progress in reducing poverty rates stalled, especially in Asia, as a consequence of the financial crisis, and in Europe and Central Asia income distributions worsened. Even so, the goal of reducing poverty rates to half of their 1990 levels can still be achieved in most regions, if growth resumes without further increases in inequality.

Looking at other social indicators, we find that many countries will achieve equal school enrollments for girls and boys in the next five years. Overall, we may fall short of the goal, but the progress toward it will bring benefits that extend beyond the classroom to all society. Reaching full primary school enrolment in the next 15 years will be more difficult. It now appears that 75 million children will be out of school in 2015, two-thirds of them in Sub-Saharan Africa. Even harder will be reducing child mortality to two-thirds of its 1990 level by 2015. Only 13 countries are on track. Some are falling back. But many more could achieve this goal by increasing health services for the poor and stemming the HIV/AIDS epidemic.

These are only some of the enormous challenges we face in eliminating poverty—challenges we can begin to address only with knowledge, with energy, and with resolve. The beginning point is knowledge—knowledge of how far we have come and how far we have to go. And that is the purpose of the *World Development Indicators*, which we are pleased to offer now in its fourth year of publication.

James D. Wolfensohn
President
The World Bank Group

Acknowledgments

This book and its companion volumes, the *World Bank Atlas* and the *Little Data Book,* were prepared by a team led by Eric Swanson. The team consisted of Swaminathan Aiyar, Mehdi Akhlaghi, David Cieslikowski, Richard Fix, Amy Heyman, Masako Hiraga, M. H. Saeed Ordoubadi, Sulekha Patel, K. M. Vijayalakshmi, Amy Wilson, and Estela Zamora, working closely with other teams in the Development Economics Vice Presidency's Development Data Group. The CD-ROM development team included Azita Amjadi, Elizabeth Crayford, Reza Farivari, Angelo Kostopoulos, and William Prince. K. Sarwar Lateef served as adviser to the team and provided substantial inputs. The work was carried out under the management of Shaida Badiee.

The choice of indicators and textual content was shaped through close consultation with and substantial contributions from staff in the World Bank's four thematic networks—Environmentally and Socially Sustainable Development; Finance, Private Sector, and Infrastructure; Human Development; and Poverty Reduction and Economic Management—and staff of the International Finance Corporation and the Multilateral Investment Guarantee Agency. Most important, we received substantial help, guidance, and data from our external partners. For individual acknowledgments of contributions to the book's content, please see the *Credits* section. For a listing of our key partners, see the *Partners* section.

Bruce Ross-Larson was the principal editor, and Peter Grundy, the art director. The cover and page design and the layout were done by Communications Development Incorporated with Grundy & Northedge of London. Staff from External Affairs oversaw publication and dissemination of the book.

Preface

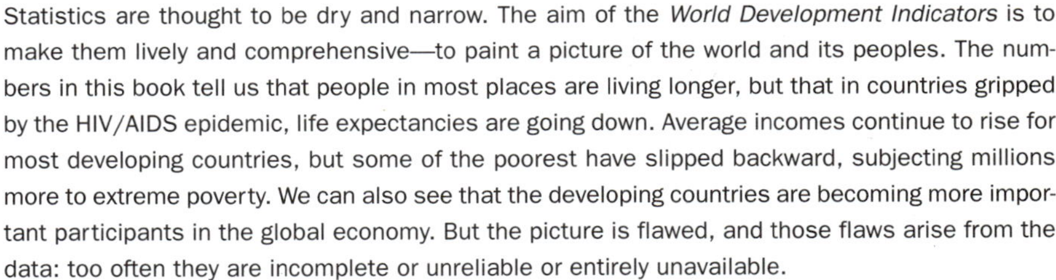

Statistics are thought to be dry and narrow. The aim of the *World Development Indicators* is to make them lively and comprehensive—to paint a picture of the world and its peoples. The numbers in this book tell us that people in most places are living longer, but that in countries gripped by the HIV/AIDS epidemic, life expectancies are going down. Average incomes continue to rise for most developing countries, but some of the poorest have slipped backward, subjecting millions more to extreme poverty. We can also see that the developing countries are becoming more important participants in the global economy. But the picture is flawed, and those flaws arise from the data: too often they are incomplete or unreliable or entirely unavailable.

Why do statistics matter? Put simply, they are the evidence on which policies are built. They help to identify needs, set goals, and monitor progress. Without good statistics, the development process is blind—policymakers cannot learn from their mistakes, and the public cannot hold them accountable. The World Bank's new poverty reduction strategy process calls for a country-driven, outcome-based approach to reducing poverty, and that approach depends on publicly accessible and reliable statistics.

Why are good statistics so hard to obtain? A cycle of underfunding has left many statistical agencies without the resources to carry out their tasks. Often the value of good statistics goes unappreciated. In some cases politicians, government agencies, and civil society—failing to understand their role in policymaking and democratic decisionmaking—fail to ask for the information they need. In other cases the demand for immediate answers leads to short-term responses—quick surveys and guesstimates—that take resources away from long-term development of the statistical system. Added to this, statisticians in developing countries need better training, better equipment, and better treatment to carry out the important work they are charged with.

Recognizing the many flaws in the statistical system and the need to address them directly by improving the capacity of countries to produce statistics, a consortium of more than 90 countries and international organizations has come together under the banner of Partnership in Statistics for Development in the 21st Century, or Paris21. The aim of Paris21 is to raise awareness of the value of good statistics—and to increase the resources for statistical capacity building in developing countries. The World Bank, as a member of Paris21, has pledged to work closely with all its development partners in this effort. Although the process of building strong statistical systems is slow, we hope that future editions of the *World Development Indicators* will reflect the new work that we embark on today.

As we work together toward improvements, we continue to be grateful for the support and cooperation of our many partners—the international organizations, statistical offices, nongovernmental organizations, and private firms that have provided their data and contributed to this product. We also appreciate the comments and responses from users—helping us measure how we are doing in continuing to make the *World Development Indicators* a useful tool. So please write to us at info@worldbank.org. And for more information on the World Bank's statistical publications, please visit our website at www.worldbank.org and select data from the menu.

Shaida Badiee
Director
Development Data Group

Contents

1 WORLD VIEW

2 PEOPLE

Boxes

Figures

Text tables

3 ENVIRONMENT

Boxes

Figures

Text tables

4 ECONOMY

Boxes

Figures

Text tables

5 STATES AND MARKETS

Boxes

Figures

6 GLOBAL LINKS

Partners

Defining, gathering, and disseminating international statistics is a collective effort of many people and organizations. The indicators presented in the *World Development Indicators* are the fruit of decades of work at many levels, from the field workers who administer censuses and household surveys to the committees and working parties of the national and international statistical agencies that develop the nomenclature, classifications, and standards fundamental to an international statistical system. Nongovernmental organizations and the private sector have also made important contributions, both in gathering primary data and in organizing and publishing their results. And academic researchers have played a crucial role in developing statistical methods and carrying on a continuing dialogue about the quality and interpretation of statistical indicators. All these contributors have a strong belief that available, accurate data will improve the quality of public and private decisionmaking.

The organizations listed here have made the *World Development Indicators* possible by sharing their data and their expertise with us. More important, their collaboration contributes to the World Bank's efforts, and to those of many others, to improve the quality of life of the world's people. We acknowledge our debt and gratitude to all who have helped to build a base of comprehensive, quantitative information about the world and its people.

For your easy reference we have included URLs (web addresses) for organizations that maintain websites. The addresses shown were active on 1 March 2000. Information about the World Bank is also provided.

International and government agencies

Bureau of Arms Control, U.S. Department of State

The Bureau of Arms Control, U.S. Department of State, is responsible for international agreements on conventional, chemical and biological weapons, and strategic forces; treaty verification and compliance; and support to ongoing negotiations, policymaking, and interagency implementation efforts.

For information contact the Public Affairs Officer, Bureau of Arms Control, U.S. Department of State, 2201 C Street NW, Washington, DC 20520, USA; telephone: (202) 647 6946; website: www.state.gov/www/global/arms/bureauac.html.

Carbon Dioxide Information Analysis Center

The Carbon Dioxide Information Analysis Center (CDIAC) is the primary global change data and information analysis center of the U.S. Department of Energy. The CDIAC's scope includes potentially anything that would be of value to those concerned with the greenhouse effect and global climate change, including concentrations of carbon dioxide and other radiatively active gases in the atmosphere; the role of the terrestrial biosphere and the oceans in the biogeochemical cycles of greenhouse gases; emissions of carbon dioxide to the atmosphere; long-term climate trends; the effects of elevated carbon dioxide on vegetation; and the vulnerability of coastal areas to rising sea levels.

For information contact the CDIAC, Oak Ridge National Laboratory, PO Box 2008, Oak Ridge, TN 37831-6335, USA; telephone: (423) 574 0390; fax: (423) 574 2232; email: cdiac@ornl.gov; website: cdiac.esd.ornl.gov.

Food and Agriculture Organization

The Food and Agriculture Organization (FAO), a specialized agency of the United Nations, was founded in October 1945 with a mandate to raise nutrition levels and living standards, to increase agricultural productivity, and to better the condition of rural populations. The organization provides direct development assistance; collects, analyzes, and disseminates information; offers policy and planning advice to governments; and serves as an international forum for debate on food and agricultural issues.

Statistical publications of the FAO include the *Production Yearbook, Trade Yearbook,* and *Fertilizer Yearbook.* The FAO makes much of its data available on diskette through its Agrostat PC system.

FAO publications can be ordered from national sales agents or directly from the FAO Sales and Marketing Group, Viale delle Terme di Caracalla, 00100 Rome, Italy; telephone: (39 06) 57051; fax: (39 06) 5705/3152; email: Publications-sales@fao.org; website: www.fao.org.

International Civil Aviation Organization

The International Civil Aviation Organization (ICAO), a specialized agency of the United Nations, was founded on 7 December 1944. It is responsible for establishing international standards and recommended practices and procedures for the technical, economic, and legal aspects of international civil aviation operations. The ICAO promotes the adoption of safety measures, establishes visual and instrument flight rules for pilots and crews, develops aeronautical charts, coordinates aircraft radio frequencies, and sets uniform regulations for the operation of air services and customs procedures.

To obtain ICAO publications contact the ICAO, Document Sales Unit, 999 University Street, Montreal, Quebec H3C 5H7, Canada; telephone: (514) 954 8022; fax: (514) 954 6769; email: sales_unit@icao.org; website: www.icao.int.

International Labour Organization

The International Labour Organization (ILO), a specialized agency of the United Nations, seeks the promotion of social justice and internationally recognized human and labor rights. Founded in 1919, it is the only surviving major creation of the Treaty of Versailles, which brought the League of Nations into being. It became the first specialized agency of the United Nations in 1946. Unique within the United Nations system, the ILO's tripartite structure has workers and employers participating as equal partners with governments in the work of its governing organs.

As part of its mandate, the ILO maintains an extensive statistical publication program. The *Yearbook of Labour Statistics* is its most comprehensive collection of labor force data.

Publications can be ordered from the International Labour Office, 4 route des Morillons, CH-1211 Geneva 22, Switzerland, or from sales agents and major booksellers throughout the world and ILO offices in many countries. Telephone: (41 22) 799 78 66; fax: (41 22) 799 61 17; email: publns@ilo.org; website: www.ilo.org.

International Monetary Fund

The International Monetary Fund (IMF) was established at a conference in Bretton Woods, New Hampshire, United States, on 1–22 July 1944. (The conference also established the World Bank.) The IMF came into official existence on 27 December 1945 and commenced financial operations on 1 March 1947. It currently has 182 member countries.

Partners

The statutory purposes of the IMF are to promote international monetary cooperation, facilitate the expansion and balanced growth of international trade, promote exchange rate stability, help establish a multilateral payments system, make the general resources of the IMF temporarily available to its members under adequate safeguards, and shorten the duration and lessen the degree of disequilibrium in the international balances of payments of members.

The IMF maintains an extensive program for the development and compilation of international statistics and is responsible for collecting and reporting statistics on international financial transactions and the balance of payments. In April 1996 it undertook an important initiative aimed at improving the quality of international statistics, establishing the Special Data Dissemination Standard (SDDS) to guide members that have or seek access to international capital markets in providing economic and financial data to the public. In 1997 the IMF established the General Data Dissemination System (GDDS) to guide countries in providing the public with comprehensive, timely, accessible, and reliable economic, financial, and sociodemographic data.

The IMF's major statistical publications include *International Financial Statistics, Balance of Payments Statistics Yearbook, Government Finance Statistics Yearbook,* and *Direction of Trade Statistics Yearbook.*

For more information on IMF statistical publications contact the International Monetary Fund, Publications Services, Catalog Orders, 700 19th Street NW, Washington, DC 20431, USA; telephone: (202) 623 7430; fax: (202) 623 7201; telex: RCA 248331 IMF UR; email: pub-web@imf.org; website: www.imf.org; SDDS and GDDS bulletin board: dsbb.imf.org.

International Telecommunication Union

Founded in Paris in 1865 as the International Telegraph Union, the International Telecommunication Union (ITU) took its current name in 1934 and became a specialized agency of the United Nations in 1947. The ITU is an intergovernmental organization in which the public and private sectors cooperate for the development of telecommunications. The ITU adopts international regulations and treaties governing all terrestrial and space uses of the frequency spectrum and the use of the geostationary satellite orbit. It also develops standards for the interconnection of telecommunications systems worldwide.

The ITU fosters the development of telecommunications in developing countries by establishing medium-term development policies and strategies in consultation with other partners in the sector and providing specialized technical assistance in management, telecommunications policy, human resource management, research and development, technology choice and transfer, network installation and maintenance, and investment financing and resource mobilization.

The *Telecommunications Yearbook* is the ITU's main statistical publication.

Publications can be ordered from ITU Sales and Marketing Service, Place des Nations, CH-1211 Geneva 20, Switzerland; telephone: (41 22) 730 6141 (English), (41 22) 730 6142 (French), and (41 22) 730 6143 (Spanish); fax: (41 22) 730 5194; email: sales.online@itu.int; telex: 421 000 uit ch; telegram: ITU GENEVE; website: www.itu.ch.

National Science Foundation

The National Science Foundation (NSF) is an independent U.S. government agency whose mission is to promote the progress of science; to advance the national health, prosperity, and welfare; and to secure the national defense. It is responsible for promoting science and engineering through almost 20,000 research and education projects. In addition, the NSF fosters the exchange of scientific information among scientists and engineers in the United States and other countries, supports programs to strengthen scientific and engineering research potential, and evaluates the impact of research on industrial development and general welfare.

As part of its mandate, the NSF biennially publishes *Science and Engineering Indicators,* which tracks national and international trends in science and engineering research and education.

Electronic copies of NSF documents can be obtained from the NSF's Online Document System (www.nsf.gov/pubsys/index.htm) or requested by email from its automated mailserver (getpub@nsf.gov). Documents can also be requested from the NSF Publications Clearinghouse by mail, at PO Box 218, Jessup, MD 20794-0218, or by telephone, at (301) 947 2722.

For more information contact the National Science Foundation, 4201 Wilson Boulevard, Arlington, VA 22230, USA; telephone: (703) 306 1234; website: www.nsf.gov.

Organisation for Economic Co-operation and Development

The Organisation for Economic Co-operation and Development (OECD) was set up in 1948 as the Organisation for European Economic Co-operation (OEEC) to administer Marshall Plan funding in Europe. In 1960, when the Marshall Plan had completed its task, the OEEC's member countries agreed to bring in Canada and the United States to form an organization to coordinate policy among industrial countries. The OECD is the international organization of the industrialized, market economy countries.

Representatives of member countries meet at the OECD to exchange information and harmonize policy with a view to maximizing economic growth in member countries and helping nonmember countries develop more rapidly. The OECD has set up a number of specialized committees to further its aims. One of these is the Development Assistance Committee (DAC), whose members have agreed to coordinate their policies on assistance to developing and transition economies.

Also associated with the OECD are several agencies or bodies that have their own governing statutes, including the International Energy Agency and the Centre for Co-operation with Economies in Transition.

The OECD's main statistical publications include *Geographical Distribution of Financial Flows to Developing Countries, National Accounts of OECD Countries, Labour Force Statistics, Revenue Statistics of OECD Member Countries, International Direct Investment Statistics Yearbook, Basic Science and Technology Statistics, Industrial Structure Statistics,* and *Services: Statistics on International Transactions.*

For information on OECD publications contact the OECD, 2, rue André-Pascal, 75775 Paris Cedex 16, France; telephone: (33 1) 45 24 82 00; fax: (33 1) 49 10 42 76; email: sales@oecd.org; websites: www.oecd.org and www.oecdwash.org.

United Nations

The United Nations and its specialized agencies maintain a number of programs for the collection of international statistics, some of which are described elsewhere in this book. At United Nations headquarters the Statistics Division provides a wide range of statistical outputs and services for producers and users of statistics worldwide.

The Statistics Division publishes statistics on international trade, national accounts, demography and population, gender, industry, energy, environment, human settlements, and disability. Its major statistical publications include the *International Trade Statistics Yearbook, Yearbook of*

Partners

National Accounts, and *Monthly Bulletin of Statistics,* along with general statistics compendiums such as the *Statistical Yearbook* and *World Statistics Pocketbook.*

For publications contact United Nations Publications, Room DC2 853, 2 UN Plaza, New York, NY 10017, USA; telephone: (212) 963 8302 or (800) 253 9646 (toll free); fax: (212) 963 3489; email: publications@un.org; website: www.un.org.

United Nations Centre for Human Settlements (Habitat), Global Urban Observatory

The Urban Indicators Programme of UNCHS (Habitat) was established to address the urgent global need to improve the urban knowledge base by helping countries and cities design, collect, and apply policy-oriented indicators related to urban development at the city level. In 1997 the Urban Indicators Programme was integrated into the Global Urban Observatory, the principal United Nations program for monitoring urban conditions and trends and for tracking progress in implementing the goals of the Habitat Agenda. With the Urban Indicators and Best Practices programs, the Global Urban Observatory is establishing a worldwide information, assessment, and capacity building network to help governments, local authorities, the private sector, and nongovernmental and other civil society organizations.

Contact Christine Auclair (guo@unchs.org), Urban Indicators Programme, Global Urban Observatory, UNCHS (Habitat), PO Box 30030, Nairobi, Kenya; telephone: (2542) 623694; fax: (2542) 624266/7; website: www.urbanobservatory.org.

United Nations Children's Fund

The United Nations Children's Fund (UNICEF), the only organization of the United Nations dedicated exclusively to children, works with other United Nations bodies and with governments and nongovernmental organizations to improve children's lives in more than 140 developing countries through community-based services in primary health care, basic education, and safe water and sanitation.

UNICEF's major publications include *The State of the World's Children* and *The Progress of Nations.*

For information on UNICEF publications contact UNICEF House, 3 United Nations Plaza, New York, NY 10017, USA; telephone: (212) 326 7000; fax: (212) 888 7465 or 7454; telex: RCA-239521; email: publications@un.org; website: www.unicef.org.

United Nations Conference on Trade and Development

The United Nations Conference on Trade and Development (UNCTAD) is the principal organ of the United Nations General Assembly in the field of trade and development. It was established as a permanent intergovernmental body in 1964 in Geneva with a view to accelerating economic growth and development, particularly in developing countries. UNCTAD discharges its mandate through policy analysis; intergovernmental deliberations, consensus building, and negotiation; monitoring, implementation, and follow-up; and technical cooperation.

UNCTAD produces a number of publications containing trade and economic statistics, including the *Handbook of International Trade and Development Statistics.*

For information contact UNCTAD, Palais des Nations, CH-1211 Geneva 10, Switzerland; telephone: (41 22) 907 12 34 or 917 12 34; fax: (41 22) 907 00 57; telex: 42962; email: reference.service@unctad.org; website: www.unctad.org.

Partners

United Nations Educational, Scientific, and Cultural Organization

The United Nations Educational, Scientific, and Cultural Organization (UNESCO) is a specialized agency of the United Nations established in 1945 to promote "collaboration among nations through education, science, and culture in order to further universal respect for justice, for the rule of law, and for the human rights and fundamental freedoms . . . for the peoples of the world, without distinction of race, sex, language, or religion. . . ."

UNESCO's principal statistical publications are the *Statistical Yearbook, World Education Report* (biennial), and *Basic Education and Literacy: World Statistical Indicators.*

For publications contact UNESCO Publishing, Promotion, and Sales Division, 1, rue Miollis F, 75732 Paris Cedex 15, France; fax: (33 1) 45 68 57 41; email: publishing.promotion@unesco.org; website: www.unesco.org.

United Nations Environment Programme

The mandate of the United Nations Environment Programme (UNEP) is to provide leadership and encourage partnership in caring for the environment by inspiring, informing, and enabling nations and people to improve their quality of life without compromising that of future generations.

UNEP publications include *Global Environment Outlook* and *Our Planet* (a bimonthly magazine).

For information contact the UNEP, PO Box 30552, Nairobi, Kenya; telephone: (254 2) 62 1234 or 3292; fax: (254 2) 62 3927 or 3692; email: oedinfo@unep.org; website: www.unep.org.

United Nations Industrial Development Organization

The United Nations Industrial Development Organization (UNIDO) was established in 1966 to act as the central coordinating body for industrial activities and to promote industrial development and cooperation at the global, regional, national, and sectoral levels. In 1985 UNIDO became the sixteenth specialized agency of the United Nations, with a mandate to help develop scientific and technological plans and programs for industrialization in the public, cooperative, and private sectors.

UNIDO's databases and information services include the Industrial Statistics Database (INDSTAT), Commodity Balance Statistics Database (COMBAL), Industrial Development Abstracts (IDA), and the International Referral System on Sources of Information. Among its publications is the *International Yearbook of Industrial Statistics.*

For information contact UNIDO Public Information Section, Vienna International Centre, PO Box 300, A-1400 Vienna, Austria; telephone: (43 1) 260 26 5031; fax: (43 1) 213 46 5031 or 260 26 6843; email: publications@unido.org; website: www.unido.org.

World Bank Group

The World Bank Group is made up of five organizations: the International Bank for Reconstruction and Development (IBRD), the International Development Association (IDA), the International Finance Corporation (IFC), the Multilateral Investment Guarantee Agency (MIGA), and the International Centre for Settlement of Investment Disputes (ICSID).

Established in 1944 at a conference of world leaders in Bretton Woods, New Hampshire, United States, the World Bank is a lending institution whose aim is to help integrate developing and transition economies with the global economy, and reduce poverty by promoting economic growth. The Bank lends for policy reforms and development projects and provides policy advice, technical assistance, and nonlending services to its 181 member countries.

Partners

For information about the World Bank visit its website at www.worldbank.org. For more information about development data contact the Development Data Center, World Bank, 1818 H Street NW, Washington, DC 20433, USA; telephone: (800) 590 1906 or (202) 473 7824; fax: (202) 522 1498; email: info@worldbank.org; website: www.worldbank.org/data.

World Health Organization

The constitution of the World Health Organization (WHO) was adopted on 22 July 1946 by the International Health Conference, convened in New York by the Economic and Social Council. The objective of the WHO, a specialized agency of the United Nations, is the attainment by all people of the highest possible level of health.

The WHO carries out a wide range of functions, including coordinating international health work; helping governments strengthen health services; providing technical assistance and emergency aid; working for the prevention and control of disease; promoting improved nutrition, housing, sanitation, recreation, and economic and working conditions; promoting and coordinating biomedical and health services research; promoting improved standards of teaching and training in health and medical professions; establishing international standards for biological, pharmaceutical, and similar products; and standardizing diagnostic procedures.

The WHO publishes the *World Health Statistics Annual* and many other technical and statistical publications.

For publications contact Distribution and Sales, Division of Publishing, Language, and Library Services, World Health Organization Headquarters, CH-1211 Geneva 27, Switzerland; telephone: (41 22) 791 2476 or 2477; fax: (41 22) 791 4857; email: publications@who.ch; website: www.who.ch.

World Intellectual Property Organization

The World Intellectual Property Organization (WIPO) is a specialized agency of the United Nations based in Geneva, Switzerland. The objectives of WIPO are to promote the protection of intellectual property throughout the world through cooperation among states and, where appropriate, in collaboration with other international organizations and to ensure administrative cooperation among the intellectual property unions—that is, the "unions" created by the Paris and Berne Conventions and several subtreaties concluded by members of the Paris Union. WIPO is responsible for administering various multilateral treaties dealing with the legal and administrative aspects of intellectual property. A substantial part of its activities and resources is devoted to development cooperation with developing countries.

For information contact the World Intellectual Property Organization, 34, chemin des Colombettes, Geneva, Switzerland; mailing address: PO Box 18, CH-1211 Geneva 20, Switzerland; telephone: (41 22) 338 9111; fax: (41 22) 733 5428; telex: 412912 ompi ch; email: publications.mail@wipo.int; website: www.wipo.int.

World Tourism Organization

The World Tourism Organization is an intergovernmental body charged by the United Nations with promoting and developing tourism. It serves as a global forum for tourism policy issues and a source of tourism know-how. The organization began as the International Union of Official Tourist Publicity Organizations, set up in 1925 in The Hague. Renamed the World Tourism Organization, it held its first general assembly in Madrid in May 1975. Its membership includes 138 countries and territories and more than 350 affiliate members representing local governments, tourism associations, and private companies, including airlines, hotel groups, and tour operators. The World Tourism Organization publishes the *Yearbook of Tourism Statistics,* the *Compendium of Tourism Statistics,* and the triannual *Travel and Tourism Barometer.*

For information contact the World Tourism Organization Capitán Haya, 42, 28020 Madrid, Spain; telephone: (34) 91 567 81 00; fax: (34) 91 567 82 18; email: omtweb@world-tourism.org; website: www.world-tourism.org.

World Trade Organization

The World Trade Organization (WTO), established on 1 January 1995, is the successor to the General Agreement on Tariffs and Trade (GATT). The WTO provides the legal and institutional foundation of the multilateral trading system and embodies the results of the Uruguay Round of trade negotiations, which ended with the Marrakesh Declaration of 15 April 1994. The WTO is mandated with administering and implementing multilateral trade agreements, serving as a forum for multilateral trade negotiations, seeking to resolve trade disputes, overseeing national trade policies, and cooperating with other international institutions involved in global economic policymaking.

The WTO's Statistics and Information Systems Divisions compile statistics on world trade and maintain the Integrated Database, which contains the basic records of the outcome of the Uruguay Round. Its *Annual Report* includes a statistical appendix.

For publications contact the World Trade Organization, Publications Services, Centre William Rappard, 154 rue de Lausanne, CH-1211, Geneva, Switzerland; telephone: (41 22) 739 5208 or 5308; fax: (41 22) 739 5792; email: publications@wto.org; website: www.wto.org.

Private and nongovernmental organizations

Currency Data & Intelligence, Inc.

Currency Data & Intelligence, Inc. is a research and publishing firm that produces currency-related products and undertakes research for international agencies and universities worldwide. Its flagship product, the *World Currency Yearbook,* is the most comprehensive source of information on currency. It includes official and unofficial exchange rates and discussions of economic, social, and political issues that affect the value of currencies in world markets. A second publication, the monthly *Global Currency Report,* covers devaluations and other critical developments in exchange rate restrictions and valuations and provides parallel market exchange rates.

For information contact Currency Data & Intelligence, Inc., 45 Northcote Drive, Melville, NY 11747, USA; telephone: (631) 643 2506; fax: (631) 643 2761; email: curncydata@aol.com; website: pacific.commerce.ubc.ca/xr/cdi.

Euromoney Publications PLC

Euromoney Publications PLC provides a wide range of financial, legal, and general business information. The monthly *Euromoney* magazine carries a semiannual rating of country creditworthiness.

For information contact Euromoney Publications PLC, Nestor House, Playhouse Yard, London EC4V 5EX, UK; telephone: (44 171) 779 8888; fax: (44 171) 779 8656; telex: 2907002; email: hotline@euromoneyplc.com; website: www.euromoney.com.

Partners

Institutional Investor, Inc.

Institutional Investor magazine is published monthly by Institutional Investor, Inc., which develops country credit ratings every six months based on information provided by leading international banks.

For information contact Institutional Investor, Inc., 488 Madison Avenue, New York, NY 10022, USA; telephone: (212) 224 3300; email: info@iimagazine.com; website: www.iimagazine.com.

International Road Federation

The International Road Federation (IRF) is a not-for-profit, nonpolitical service organization. Its purpose is to encourage better road and transport systems worldwide and to help apply technology and management practices that will maximize economic and social returns from national road investments. The IRF has led global road infrastructure developments and is the international point of affiliation for about 600 member companies, associations, and governments.

The IRF's mission is to promote road development as a key factor in economic and social growth, to provide governments and financial institutions with professional ideas and expertise, to facilitate business exchange among members, to establish links between IRF members and external institutions and agencies, to support national road federations, and to give information to professional groups.

The IRF publishes *World Road Statistics.*

Contact the Geneva office at 2 chemin de Blandonnet, CH-1214 Vernier, Geneva, Switzerland; telephone: (41 22) 306 0260; fax: (41 22) 306 0270; or the Washington, DC, office at 1010 Massachusetts Avenue NW, Suite 410, Washington, DC 20001, USA; telephone: (202) 371-5544; fax: (202) 371-5565; email: info@irfnet.com; website: www.irfnet.org.

Moody's Investors Service

Moody's Investors Service is a global credit analysis and financial opinion firm. It provides the international investment community with globally consistent credit ratings on debt and other securities issued by North American state and regional government entities, by corporations worldwide, and by some sovereign issuers. It also publishes extensive financial data in both print and electronic form. Its clients include investment banks, brokerage firms, insurance companies, public utilities, research libraries, manufacturers, and government agencies and departments.

Moody's publishes *Sovereign, Subnational and Sovereign-Guaranteed Issuers.*

For information contact Moody's Investors Service, 99 Church Street, New York, NY 10007, USA; telephone: (212) 553 1658; website: www.moodys.com.

PricewaterhouseCoopers

Drawing on the talents of 150,000 people in more than 150 countries, PricewaterhouseCoopers provides a full range of business advisory services to leading global, national, and local companies and public institutions. Its service offerings have been organized into six lines of service, each staffed with highly qualified, experienced professionals and leaders. These services include audit, assurance, and business advisory services; business process outsourcing; financial advisory services; global human resource solutions; management consulting services; and global tax services.

PricewaterhouseCoopers publishes *Corporate Taxes: Worldwide Summaries* and *Individual Taxes: Worldwide Summaries.*

For information contact PricewaterhouseCoopers, 1301 Avenue of the Americas, New York, NY 10019, USA; telephone: (212) 596 7000; fax: (212) 259 5324; website: www.pwcglobal.com.

The PRS Group

Political Risk Services is a global leader in political and economic risk forecasting and market analysis and has served international companies large and small for about 20 years. The data it contributed to this year's *World Development Indicators* come from the *International Country Risk Guide,* a monthly publication that monitors and rates political, financial, and economic risk in 140 countries. The guide's data series and commitment to independent and unbiased analysis make it the standard for any organization practicing effective risk management.

For information contact The PRS Group, 6320 Fly Road, Suite 102, PO Box 248, East Syracuse, NY 13057-0248, USA; telephone: (315) 431 0511; fax: (315) 431 0200; email: custserv@PRSgroup.com; website: www.prsgroup.com.

Standard & Poor's Rating Services

Standard & Poor's *Sovereign Ratings* provides issuer and local and foreign currency debt ratings for sovereign governments and for sovereign-supported and supranational issuers worldwide. Standard & Poor's Rating Services monitors the credit quality of $1.5 trillion worth of bonds and other financial instruments and offers investors global coverage of debt issuers. Standard & Poor's also has ratings on commercial paper, mutual funds, and the financial condition of insurance companies worldwide.

For information contact The McGraw-Hill Companies, Inc., Executive Offices, 1221 Avenue of the Americas, New York, NY 10020, USA; telephone: (212) 512 4105 or (800) 352 3566 (toll free); fax: (212) 512 4105; email: ratings@mcgraw-hill.com; website: www.ratings.standardpoor.com.

World Conservation Monitoring Centre

The World Conservation Monitoring Centre (WCMC) provides information on the conservation and sustainable use of the world's living resources and helps others to develop information systems of their own. It works in close collaboration with a wide range of organizations and people to increase access to the information needed for wise management of the world's living resources. Committed to the principle of data exchange with other centers and noncommercial users, the WCMC, whenever possible, places the data it manages in the public domain.

For information contact the World Conservation Monitoring Centre, 219 Huntingdon Road, Cambridge CB3 0DL, UK; telephone: (44 12) 2327 7314; fax: (44 12) 2327 7136; email: info@wcmc.org.uk; website: www.wcmc.org.uk.

World Resources Institute

The World Resources Institute is an independent center for policy research and technical assistance on global environmental and development issues. The institute provides—and helps other institutions provide—objective information and practical proposals for policy and institutional change that will foster environmentally sound, socially equitable development. The institute's current areas of work include trade, forests, energy, economics, technology, biodiversity, human health, climate change, sustainable agriculture, resource and environmental information, and national strategies for environmental and resource management.

For information contact the World Resources Institute, Suite 800, 10 G Street NE, Washington, DC 20002, USA; telephone: (202) 729 7600; fax: (202) 729 7610; telex 64414 WRIWASH; email: lauralee@wri.org; website: www.wri.org.

Users guide

1

Principal sections

Are signposted by these icons:

Section 1 World view 

Section 2 People 

Section 3 Environment 

Section 4 Economy 

Section 5 States and markets 

Section 6 Global links 

The tables

Tables are numbered by section and display the identifying icons of each section. Countries and economies are listed alphabetically (except for Hong Kong, China, which appears after China). Data are shown for 148 economies with populations of more than 1 million people and for which data are regularly reported by the relevant authority, as well as for Taiwan, China, in selected tables. Selected indicators for 58 other economies—small economies with populations between 30,000 and 1 million, smaller economies if they are members of the World Bank, and larger economies for which data are not regularly reported—are shown in table 1.6. The term *country,* used interchangeably with *economy,* does not imply political independence or official recognition by the World Bank, but refers to any territory for which authorities report separate social or economic statistics. When available, aggregate measures for income and regional groups appear at the end of each table.

2.4 Employment by economic activity

	Agriculture				Industry				Services		
	Male % of male labor force		Female % of female labor force		Male % of male labor force		Female % of female labor force		Male % of male labor force		Female % of female labor force
	1980	1992–97[a]	1980	1992–97[a]	1980	1992–97[a]	1980	1992–97[a]	1980	1992–97[a]	1980
Albania	54	22	62	27	28	45	17	45	18	34	21
Algeria	27	..	69	..	33	..	6	..	40	..	25
Angola	67	..	87	..	13	..	1	..	20	..	11
Argentina	17	2	3	0	40	33	18	12	44	65	79
Armenia	21	..	21	..	48	..	38	..	31	..	41
Australia	8	6	4	4	39	31	16	11	53	63	80
Austria	..	6	..	8	..	42	..	14	..	52	..
Azerbaijan	28	..	42	..	36	..	20	..	36	..	38
Bangladesh	67	54	81	78	5	11	14	8	29	34	5
Belarus	29	..	23	..	44	..	33	..	28	..	44
Belgium	..	3	..	2	..	41	..	16	..	56	..
Benin	66	..	69	..	10	..	4	..	24	..	27
Bolivia	52	2	28	2	21	40	19	16	27	58	53
Bosnia and Herzegovina	26	..	38	..	45	..	24	..	30	..	39
Botswana	6	3	3	2	41	38	8	18	53	60	89
Brazil	*34*	28	*20*	23	*30*	26	*13*	9	*36*	45	*67*
Bulgaria	..	..	..	..	..	..	..	..	..	..	..
Burkina Faso	92	..	93	..	3	..	2	..	5	..	5
Burundi	88	..	98	..	4	..	1	..	9	..	1
Cambodia	70	71	80	79	7	6	7	3	23	23	14
Cameroon	65	..	87	..	11	..	2	..	24	..	11
Canada	7	5	3	2	38	32	16	12	58	63	84
Central African Republic	79	..	90	..	5	..	1	..	15	..	9
Chad	82	..	95	..	6	..	0	..	12	..	4
Chile	22	19	3	4	27	34	16	14	51	47	81
China	..	..	..	..	..	..	..	..	..	..	..
Hong Kong, China	2	0	1	0	47	31	56	15	52	69	43
Colombia	2	1	1	0	39	32	26	21	59	66	74
Congo, Dem. Rep.	62	..	84	..	18	..	4	..	20	..	12
Congo, Rep.	42	..	81	..	20	..	2	..	38	..	17
Costa Rica	34	27	6	6	25	26	20	17	40	46	74
Côte d'Ivoire	60	..	75	..	10	..	5	..	30	..	20
Croatia	..	7	..	3	..	50	..	34	..	43	..
Cuba	30	..	10	..	32	..	22	..	39	..	68
Czech Republic	13	7	11	4	57	50	39	29	30	43	50
Denmark	*11*	5	*4*	2	*41*	36	*16*	15	*48*	58	*80*
Dominican Republic	40	..	11	..	26	..	16	..	34	..	73
Ecuador	44	10	22	2	21	27	15	16	34	64	63
Egypt, Arab Rep.	46	32	10	43	21	25	14	9	34	43	76
El Salvador	51	38	10	7	21	25	21	21	28	37	69
Eritrea	79	..	88	..	7	..	2	..	14	..	11
Estonia	19	16	12	8	50	39	36	27	31	44	52
Ethiopia	90	89	89	88	2	2	2	2	8	9	10
Finland	15	9	12	5	45	39	23	14	39	52	63
France	9	6	7	4	44	37	22	15	47	57	71
Gabon	59	..	74	..	18	..	6	..	24	..	21
Gambia, The	78	..	93	..	10	..	3	..	13	..	5
Georgia	31	..	34	..	33	..	21	..	37	..	45
Germany	..	3	..	3	..	46	..	19	..	51	..
Ghana	66	..	57	..	12	..	14	..	22	..	29
Greece	..	18	..	23	..	28	..	13	..	54	..
Guatemala	64	..	17	..	17	..	27	..	19	..	56
Guinea	86	..	97	..	2	..	1	..	12	..	3
Guinea-Bissau	81	..	98	..	3	..	0	..	17	..	3
Haiti	*81*	..	*53*	..	*8*	..	*8*	..	*11*	..	*39*
Honduras	63	53	40	7	17	19	9	27	20	28	51

55 | 2000 World Development Indicators

Indicators

Indicators are shown for the most recent year or period for which data are available and, in most tables, for an earlier year or period. Time-series data are available on the *World Development Indicators* CD-ROM.

2

PEOPLE

Employment by economic activity | 2.4

	Agriculture				Industry				Services			
	Male % of male labor force		Female % of female labor force		Male % of male labor force		Female % of female labor force		Male % of male labor force		Female % of female labor force	
	1980	1992–97[a]	1980	1992–97[a]	1980	1992–97[a]	1980	1992–97[a]	1980	1992–97[a]	1980	1992–97[a]
ıngary	24	11	19	5	45	40	36	25	31	50	45	71
dia	63	..	83	..	15	..	9	..	22	..	8	..
donesia	57	41	53	42	13	21	13	16	29	39	32	42
an, Islamic Rep.	36	..	50	..	28	..	17	..	35	..	33	..
ıq	21	..	62	..	24	..	11	..	55	..	28	..
eland	..	15	..	3	..	34	..	15	..	49	..	79
ael	8	3	4	1	39	38	16	14	52	58	80	84
aly	13	7	16	7	43	38	28	22	44	55	56	72
maica	47	31	23	11	20	27	8	12	33	42	69	77
pan	9	5	13	6	40	39	28	24	51	55	58	69
rdan	..	6	..	4	24	27	7	10	76	66	93	87
azakhstan	28	..	20	..	38	..	25	..	34	..	55	..
enya	23	19	25	20	24	23	9	9	53	58	65	71
orea, Dem. Rep.	39	..	52	..	37	..	20	..	24	..	28	..
orea, Rep.	31	10	39	13	32	38	24	21	37	52	37	66
uwait	2	..	0	..	36	..	3	..	62	..	97	..
rgyz Republic	35	48	33	49	34	12	23	7	32	31	44	38
o PDR	77	..	82	..	7	..	4	..	16	..	13	..
tvia	18	23	14	18	49	33	35	20	32	44	50	62
banon	13	..	20	..	29	..	21	..	58	..	59	..
sotho	26	..	64	..	52	..	5	..	22	..	31	..
bya	16	..	63	..	29	..	3	..	55	..	34	..
huania	26	23	29	18	47	35	30	21	27	42	41	61
acedonia, FYR	30	10	47	6	38	53	23	41	32	32	30	51
adagascar	73	..	93	..	9	..	2	..	19	..	5	..
alawi	78	50	96	73	10	25	1	7	12	25	3	20
alaysia	34	19	43	14	26	36	21	30	40	46	36	56
ali	86	..	92	..	2	..	1	..	12	..	7	..
auritania	65	..	79	..	11	..	2	..	24	..	19	..
auritius	29	15	30	13	19	39	40	43	47	46	31	45
exico	..	30	..	13	..	24	..	19	..	46	..	68
oldova	49	..	38	..	32	..	21	..	19	..	41	..
ongolia	43	..	36	..	21	..	21	..	36	..	43	..
orocco	48	4	72	3	23	33	14	46	29	63	14	51
ozambique	72	..	97	..	14	..	1	..	14	..	2	..
yanmar	..	..	..	..	..	..	..	..	..	..	..	..
amibia	52	..	42	..	22	..	10	..	27	..	47	..
epal	91	..	98	..	1	..	0	..	8	..	2	..
etherlands	..	4	..	3	..	32	..	10	..	62	..	85
ew Zealand	..	11	..	6	..	33	..	13	..	56	..	81
caragua	..	..	..	..	..	..	..	..	..	..	..	..
ger	7	8	6	5	69	51	29	24	25	41	66	71
geria	52	..	57	..	10	..	5	..	38	..	38	..
orway	10	7	6	3	40	35	14	10	50	59	80	87
man	52	..	24	..	21	..	33	..	27	..	43	..
akistan	..	[illegible]	..	67	..	20	..	11	..	36	..	22
anama	*37*	[illegible]	*6*	3	*21*	21	*12*	11	*39*	50	*81*	86
apua New Guinea	76	..	92	..	8	..	2	..	16	..	6	..
araguay	58	6	9	1	20	37	22	13	22	57	70	87
eru	45	10	25	5	20	27	14	12	35	63	61	83
hilippines	60	48	37	28	16	19	15	13	25	33	48	59
oland	..	21	..	20	..	41	..	21	..	38	..	59
ortugal	22	12	35	16	44	40	25	21	34	48	40	64
uerto Rico	8	5	1	0	24	26	29	15	67	70	70	84
omania	..	35	..	43	..	36	..	24	..	29	..	33
ussian Federation	19	..	13	..	50	..	37	..	31	..	50	..

2000 World Development Indicators | 56

Statistics

Data are shown for economies as they were constituted in 1998, and historical data are revised to reflect current political arrangements. Exceptions are noted throughout the tables.

On 1 July 1997 China resumed its exercise of sovereignty over Hong Kong. On 20 December 1999 China resumed its exercise of sovereignty over Macao. Unless otherwise noted, data for China do not include data for Hong Kong, China; Taiwan, China; or Macao, China.

Data for the Democratic Republic of the Congo (Congo, Dem. Rep., in the table listings) refer to the former Zaire. For clarity, this edition also uses the formal name of the Republic of Congo (Congo, Rep., in the table listings).

Data are shown whenever possible for the individual countries formed from the former Czechoslovakia—the Czech Republic and the Slovak Republic.

On 25 October 1999 the United Nations Transitional Administration for East Timor (UNTAET) assumed responsibility for the administration of East Timor. Data for Indonesia include East Timor.

Data are shown for Eritrea whenever possible, but in most cases before 1992 Eritrea is included in the data for Ethiopia.

Data for Germany refer to the unified Germany unless otherwise noted.

Data for Jordan refer to the East Bank only unless otherwise noted.

In 1991 the Union of Soviet Socialist Republics was dissolved into 15 countries (Armenia, Azerbaijan, Belarus, Estonia, Georgia, Kazakhstan, Kyrgyz Republic, Latvia, Lithuania, Moldova, Russian Federation, Tajikistan, Turkmenistan, Ukraine, and Uzbekistan). Whenever possible, data are shown for the individual countries.

Data for the Republic of Yemen refer to that country from 1990 onward; data for previous years refer to aggregated data for the former People's Democratic Republic of Yemen and the former Yemen Arab Republic unless otherwise noted.

In December 1999 the official name of Venezuela was changed to República Bolivariana de Venezuela (Venezuela, RB, in the table listings).

Whenever possible, data are shown for the individual countries formed from the former Socialist Federal Republic of Yugoslavia—Bosnia and Herzegovina, Croatia, the former Yugoslav Republic of Macedonia, Slovenia, and the Federal Republic of Yugoslavia. All references to the Federal Republic of Yugoslavia in the tables are to the Federal Republic of Yugoslavia (Serbia/Montenegro) unless otherwise noted.

Additional information about the data is provided in *Primary data documentation*. That section summarizes national and international efforts to improve basic data collection and gives information on primary sources, census years, fiscal years, and other background. *Statistical methods* provides technical information on some of the general calculations and formulas used throughout the book.

Discrepancies in data presented in different editions of the *World Development Indicators* reflect updates by countries as well as revisions to historical series and changes in methodology. Thus readers are advised not to compare data series between editions of the *World Development Indicators* or between different World Bank publications. Consistent time-series data for 1960–98 are available on the *World Development Indicators* CD-ROM. Except where noted, growth rates are in real terms. (See *Statistical methods* for information on the methods used to calculate growth rates.) Data for some economic indicators for some economies are presented in fiscal years rather than calendar years; see *Primary data documentation*. All dollar figures are current U.S. dollars unless otherwise stated. The methods used for converting national currencies are described in *Statistical methods*.

3

The World Bank's classification of economies

For operational and analytical purposes the World Bank's main criterion for classifying economies is gross national product (GNP) per capita. Every economy is classified as low income, middle income (subdivided into lower middle and upper middle), or high income. For income classifications see the map on the inside front cover and the list on the front cover flap. Note that classification by income does not necessarily reflect development status. Because GNP per capita changes over time, the country composition of income groups may change from one edition of the *World Development Indicators* to the next. Once the classification is fixed for an edition, using the most recent year for which GNP per capita data are available (1998 in this edition), all historical data presented are based on the same country grouping. Low-income economies are those with a GNP per capita of $760 or less in 1998. Middle-income economies are those with a GNP per capita of more than $760 but less than $9,360. Lower-middle-income and upper-middle-income economies are separated at a GNP per capita of $3,030. High-income economies are those with a GNP per capita of $9,361 or more. The 11 participating member countries of the European Monetary Union (EMU) are presented as a subgroup under high-income economies.

Aggregate measures for income groups

The aggregate measures for income groups include 206 economies (the economies listed in the main tables plus those in table 1.6) wherever data are available. Note that in this edition table 1.6 does not include France's overseas departments—French Guiana, Guadeloupe, Martinique, and Réunion—which are now included in the national accounts (GNP and other economic measures) of France. To maintain consistency in the aggregate measures over time and between tables, missing data are imputed where possible. Most aggregates are totals (designated by a *t* if the aggregates include gap-filled estimates for missing data; otherwise totals are designated by an *s* for simple totals), median values (*m*), or weighted averages (*w*). Gap filling of amounts not allocated to countries may result in discrepancies between subgroup aggregates and overall totals. See *Statistical methods* for further discussion of aggregation methods.

Aggregate measures for regions

The aggregate measures for regions include only low- and middle-income economies (note that these measures include developing economies with populations of less than 1 million, including those listed in table 1.6). The country composition of regions is based on the World Bank's analytical regions and may differ from common geographic usage. For regional classifications see the map on the inside back cover and the list on the back cover flap. See *Statistical methods* for further discussion of aggregation methods.

2.4 Employment by economic activity

	Agriculture				Industry				Services		
	Male % of male labor force		Female % of female labor force		Male % of male labor force		Female % of female labor force		Male % of male labor force		Female % of female labor force
	1980	1992–97[a]	1980	1992–97[a]	1980	1992–97[a]	1980	1992–97[a]	1980	1992–97[a]	1980
Rwanda	88	..	98	..	5	..	1	..	7	..	1
Saudi Arabia	45	..	25	..	17	..	5	..	39	..	70
Senegal	74	..	90	..	9	..	..	..	17	..	8
Sierra Leone	63	..	82	..	20	..	4	..	17	..	14
Singapore	2	0	..	0	33	34	40	25	65	66	59
Slovak Republic	15	11	13	6	38	49	34	28	48	41	54
Slovenia	14	12	17	13	49	49	37	31	38	38	46
South Africa	18	..	16	..	45	..	16	..	37	..	68
Spain	20	10	18	6	42	39	21	14	39	52	60
Sri Lanka	*44*	33	*51*	40	*19*	22	*18*	24	*30*	41	*28*
Sudan	66	..	88	..	9	..	4	..	24	..	8
Sweden	8	4	3	1	45	39	16	12	47	57	81
Switzerland	8	5	5	4	47	35	23	15	46	59	72
Syrian Arab Republic	..	23	..	54	..	28	..	8	..	49	..
Tajikistan	36	..	54	..	29	..	16	..	35	..	30
Tanzania	80	..	92	..	7	..	2	..	13	..	7
Thailand	68	49	74	52	13	22	8	17	20	29	18
Togo	70	..	67	..	12	..	7	..	19	..	26
Trinidad and Tobago	11	14	9	5	44	33	21	13	45	54	70
Tunisia	33	22	53	20	30	32	32	40	37	44	16
Turkey	45	30	88	65	22	29	5	13	33	41	8
Turkmenistan	33	..	46	..	32	..	16	..	36	..	38
Uganda	84	..	91	..	6	..	2	..	10	..	8
Ukraine	26	..	24	..	46	..	33	..	28	..	44
United Arab Emirates	5	..	0	..	40	..	7	..	55	..	93
United Kingdom	4	3	1	1	48	38	23	13	49	59	76
United States	5	4	2	2	40	34	19	13	55	63	80
Uruguay	..	7	..	2	..	34	..	17	..	59	..
Uzbekistan	35	..	46	..	34	..	19	..	32	..	36
Venezuela, RB	20	19	2	2	31	28	18	14	49	53	79
Vietnam	71	70	75	71	16	12	10	9	13	18	15
West Bank and Gaza	..	..	..	..	..	..	..	..	..	..	..
Yemen, Rep.	60	..	98	..	19	..	1	..	21	..	1
Yugoslavia, FR (Serb./Mont.)	..	..	49	..	..	..	19	..	..	..	32
Zambia	69	..	85	..	13	..	3	..	19	..	13
Zimbabwe	29	23	50	38	31	32	8	10	40	46	42
	.. w	.. w	.. w	.. w	.. w	.. w	.. w	.. w	.. w	.. w	.. w
L… ome	..	..	..	..	..	..	..	..	..	..	..
Excl. China & India	64	..	73	..	12	..	8	..	24	..	19
Middle income	33	..	31	..	33	..	25	..	34	..	45
L… iddle income	34	..	29	..	34	..	26	..	32	..	45
U… iddle income	..	24	..	22	..	30	..	15	..	46	..
Low & middle income	..	..	..	..	..	..	..	..	..	..	..
East Asia & Pacific	..	..	..	..	..	..	..	..	..	..	..
Europe & Central Asia	26	..	26	..	43	..	31	..	31	..	43
Latin America & Carib.	..	22	..	13	..	28	..	13	..	50	..
M… ast & N. Africa	39	..	47	..	25	..	14	..	37	..	40
So… sia	64	..	83	..	14	..	10	..	23	..	8
Sub-Saharan Africa	62	..	74	..	14	..	5	..	24	..	22
High income	8	5	7	3	41	37	22	16	51	58	71

a. Data are for the most recent year available.

57 | 2000 World Development Indicators

Footnotes

Known deviations from standard definitions or breaks in comparability over time or across countries are either footnoted in the tables or noted in *About the data*. When available data are deemed to be too weak to provide reliable measures of levels and trends or do not adequately adhere to international standards, the data are not shown.

Users guide

4

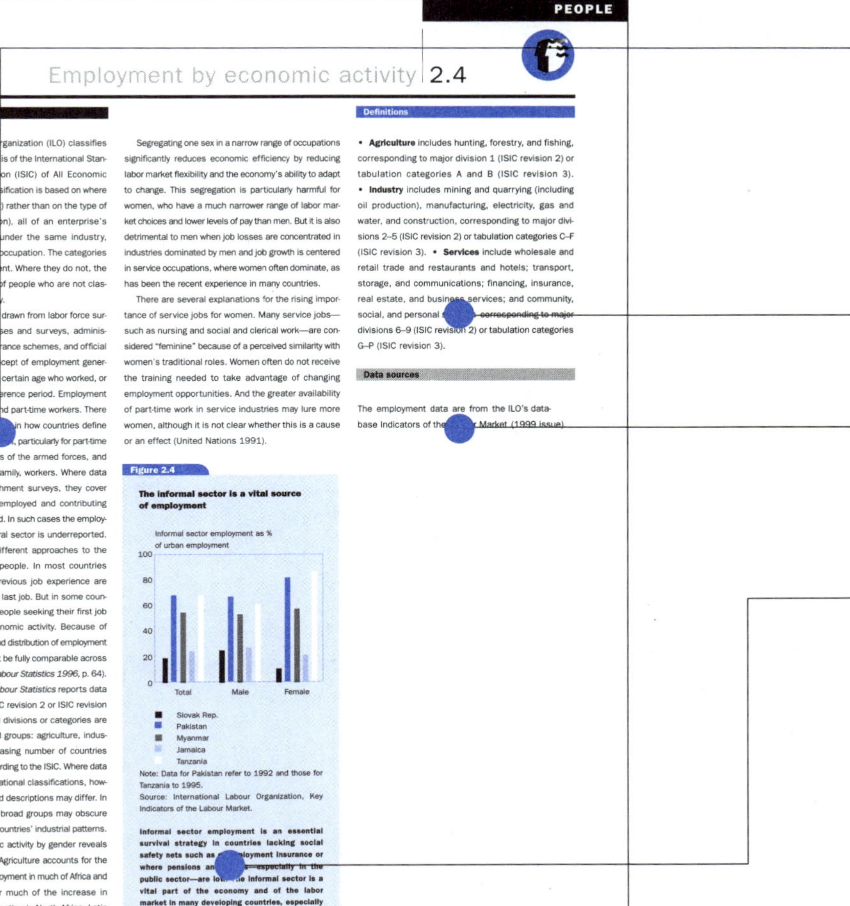
PEOPLE

Employment by economic activity 2.4

out the data

International Labour Organization (ILO) classifies nomic activity on the basis of the International Stan- Industrial Classification (ISIC) of All Economic vities. Because this classification is based on where k is performed (industry) rather than on the type of k performed (occupation), all of an enterprise's loyees are classified under the same industry, rdless of their trade or occupation. The categories uld add up to 100 percent. Where they do not, the rences arise because of people who are not clas- ble by economic activity.

Data on employment are drawn from labor force sur-, establishment censuses and surveys, adminis-ve records of social insurance schemes, and official onal estimates. The concept of employment gener- efers to people above a certain age who worked, or held a job, during a reference period. Employment include both full-time and part-time workers. There however, many differ in how countries define measure employment, particularly for part-time kers, students, members of the armed forces, and sehold, or contributing family, workers. Where data obtained from establishment surveys, they cover employees; thus self-employed and contributing ly members are excluded. In such cases the employ- t share of the agricultural sector is underreported. ntries also take very different approaches to the tment of unemployed people. In most countries nployed people with previous job experience are sified according to their last job. But in some coun- the unemployed and people seeking their first job not classifiable by economic activity. Because of e differences, the size and distribution of employment conomic activity may not be fully comparable across ntries (ILO, *Yearbook of Labour Statistics 1996*, p. 64).

he ILO's *Yearbook of Labour Statistics* reports data major divisions of the ISIC revision 2 or ISIC revision this table the reported divisions or categories are egated into three broad groups: agriculture, indus- and services. An increasing number of countries rt economic activity according to the ISIC. Where data supplied according to national classifications, how-, industry definitions and descriptions may differ. In tion, classification into broad groups may obscure lamental differences in countries' industrial patterns. distribution of economic activity by gender reveals e interesting patterns. Agriculture accounts for the est share of female employment in much of Africa and . Services account for much of the increase in nen's labor force participation in North Africa, Latin rica and the Caribbean, and high-income economies. dwide, women are underrepresented in industry.

Segregating one sex in a narrow range of occupations significantly reduces economic efficiency by reducing labor market flexibility and the economy's ability to adapt to change. This segregation is particularly harmful for women, who have a much narrower range of labor market choices and lower levels of pay than men. But it is also detrimental to men when job losses are concentrated in industries dominated by men and job growth is centered in service occupations, where women often dominate, as has been the recent experience in many countries.

There are several explanations for the rising importance of service jobs for women. Many service jobs—such as nursing and social and clerical work—are considered "feminine" because of a perceived similarity with women's traditional roles. Women often do not receive the training needed to take advantage of changing employment opportunities. And the greater availability of part-time work in service industries may lure more women, although it is not clear whether this is a cause or an effect (United Nations 1991).

Figure 2.4

The informal sector is a vital source of employment

Note: Data for Pakistan refer to 1992 and those for Tanzania to 1995.

Source: International Labour Organization, Key Indicators of the Labour Market.

Informal sector employment is an essential survival strategy in countries lacking social safety nets such as unemployment insurance or where pensions and ... especially in the public sector—are low. The informal sector is a vital part of the economy and of the labor market in many developing countries, especially in Asia and Sub-Saharan Africa.

Definitions

- **Agriculture** includes hunting, forestry, and fishing, corresponding to major division 1 (ISIC revision 2) or tabulation categories A and B (ISIC revision 3).
- **Industry** includes mining and quarrying (including oil production), manufacturing, electricity, gas and water, and construction, corresponding to major divisions 2–5 (ISIC revision 2) or tabulation categories C–F (ISIC revision 3).
- **Services** include wholesale and retail trade and restaurants and hotels; transport, storage, and communications; financing, insurance, real estate, and business services; and community, social, and personal services, corresponding to major divisions 6–9 (ISIC revision 2) or tabulation categories G–P (ISIC revision 3).

Data sources

The employment data are from the ILO's database Indicators of the Labour Market (1999 issue).

2000 World Development Indicators | 58

Notes about data

About the data provides a general discussion of international data standards, data collection methods, and sources of potential errors and inconsistencies. Readers are urged to read these notes to gain an understanding of the reliability and limitations of the data presented. For a full discussion of data collection methods and definitions readers should consult the technical documentation provided by the original compilers cited in *Data sources*.

Definitions

Definitions provide short descriptions of the main indicators in each table.

Sources

Partners are identified in the *Data sources* section following each table, and key publications of the partners drawn on for the table are identified. For a description of our partners and information on their data publications see the *Partners* section.

Figures

When appropriate, tables are accompanied by figures highlighting particular trends or issues.

Symbols

..	means that data are not available or that aggregates cannot be calculated because of missing data in the years shown.
0 or **0.0**	means zero or less than half the unit shown.
/	in dates, as in 1990/91, means that the period of time, usually 12 months, straddles two calendar years and refers to a crop year, a survey year, or a fiscal year.
$	means current U.S. dollars unless otherwise noted.
>	means more than.
<	means less than.

Data presentation conventions

- A blank means not applicable or that an aggregate is not analytically meaningful.
- A billion is 1,000 million.
- A trillion is 1,000 billion.
- Figures in italics indicate data that are for years or periods other than those specified.
- Data for years that are more than three years from the range shown are footnoted.

The cutoff date for data is 1 February 2000.

N
W
E
S

World View

A sixth of the world's people produce 78 percent of its goods and services and receive 78 percent of world income—an average of $70 a day. Three-fifths of the world's people in the poorest 61 countries receive 6 percent of the world's income—less than $2 a day. But their poverty goes beyond income. While 7 of every 1,000 children die before age five in high-income countries, more than 90 die in low-income countries. How do we bridge these huge and growing income gaps, matched by similar gaps in social living standards? Can the nations of the world work together to reduce the numbers in extreme poverty? This is the fundamental challenge of the 21st century.

Recent trends in poverty

New data from the World Bank suggest that the number of people in extreme poverty (living on less than $1 a day) has been relatively stable in the past decade, rising in the early 1990s to a peak of 1.3 billion and then falling slightly to 1.2 billion in 1998—roughly the same as in 1987 (table 1a).[1] But the regional picture is varied. In East Asia and the Pacific the number in poverty fell sharply from 452 million in 1990 to 278 million in 1998, mainly because of progress in China, with the rest of East Asia cutting its numbers by a third. Almost all other regions had their number in poverty increase. South Asia's rose from 495 million to 522 million, and Sub-Saharan Africa's from 242 million to 291 million.

The proportion of people living in extreme poverty—the poverty rate—went down modestly from 29 percent in 1990 to 24 percent in 1998. Here again East Asia took the lead, reducing its rate from 28 percent to 15 percent. South Asia, home to the largest number of the world's poor, saw a modest decline of four points to 40 percent over the same period. Sub-Saharan Africa (46 percent) and Latin America and the Caribbean (16 percent) had barely discernible reductions.

Some regional trends:

- While the overall trend in **East Asia and the Pacific** is impressive, much of this gain was made before 1997. The financial crisis of 1997–98 checked the strong momentum of growth. Data from national surveys, based on national poverty lines, suggest that Indonesia, the Republic of Korea, and Thailand had sharp increases in poverty. Vietnam seemed the exception—its poverty continued to decline. In China, where growth slowed but was still high, the pace of poverty reduction slowed sharply after 1996, and the numbers in poverty may even have increased.

Table 1a

Poverty in developing and transition economies, selected years, 1987–98

	Population covered by at least one survey	People living on less than PPP $1 a day (millions)					Headcount index (%)				
	%	1987	1990	1993	1996	1998[a]	1987	1990	1993	1996	1998[a]
East Asia and the Pacific	90.8	417.5	452.4	431.9	265.1	278.3	26.6	27.6	25.2	14.9	15.3
Excluding China	71.1	114.1	92.0	83.5	55.1	65.1	23.9	18.5	15.9	10.0	11.3
Europe and Central Asia	81.7	1.1	7.1	18.3	23.8	24.0	0.2	1.6	4.0	5.1	5.1
Latin America and the Caribbean	88.0	63.7	73.8	70.8	76.0	78.2	15.3	16.8	15.3	15.6	15.6
Middle East and North Africa	52.5	9.3	5.7	5.0	5.0	5.5	4.3	2.4	1.9	1.8	1.9
South Asia	97.9	474.4	495.1	505.1	531.7	522.0	44.9	44.0	42.4	42.3	40.0
Sub-Saharan Africa	72.9	217.2	242.3	273.3	289.0	290.9	46.6	47.7	49.7	48.5	46.3
Total	88.1	1,183.2	1,276.4	1,304.3	1,190.6	1,198.9	28.3	29.0	28.1	24.5	24.0
Excluding China	84.2	879.8	915.9	955.9	980.5	985.7	28.5	28.1	27.7	27.0	26.2

Note: The estimates in the table are based on data from the countries in each region for which at least one survey was available in 1985–98. Where survey years do not coincide with the years in the table, the survey estimates were adjusted using the closest available survey for each country and applying the consumption growth rate from national accounts. The number of poor in each region was then estimated using the assumption that the sample of countries covered by surveys is representative of the region as a whole. This assumption is obviously less robust in the regions with the lowest survey coverage. The headcount index is the percentage of the population below the poverty line. For more details on the data and methodology see Chen and Ravallion forthcoming.
a. Estimated.
Source: Chen and Ravallion forthcoming.

- **South Asia** continued to record solid per capita GDP growth. But the pace of poverty reduction slowed considerably, particularly in India, reflecting the drag on its overall performance from the populous and poorest states of north India (Bihar, Madhya Pradesh, and Uttar Pradesh). Bangladesh's performance has been much better, while Pakistan's low growth rates throughout the 1990s made poverty worse.
- The gains in growth recorded in **Sub-Saharan Africa** in the mid-1990s were reversed by lower commodity prices and reduced export demand, reflecting both the slackening of growth in world trade and increased competition from countries that had sharp exchange rate depreciations. Africa's aggregate performance conceals wide variations between the handful of steady reformers (Côte d'Ivoire, Ghana, Mauritania, Tanzania, and Uganda) and the countries in severe conflict (Burundi, the Democratic Republic of the Congo, Rwanda, Sierra Leone, and countries in the horn of Africa). In between lie a large number of countries having difficulty in making the transition to a path of sustained economic reform. Those enjoying good growth have seen poverty decline; the others have seen worsening income poverty and social indicators.
- While extreme poverty is confined to a relatively small share of the people in **Latin America and the Caribbean** (15 percent living on less than $1 a day, 36 percent on less than $2 a day), both the share and the numbers in poverty remain stubbornly stagnant, apparently immune to the growth in the 1990s because of high levels of inequality. There are exceptions. Data for Brazil suggest that the Real Plan helped poverty drop 30 percent in two years after the 1994 launch. But the global financial crisis wiped out a third of these gains.
- The economic depression in most transition economies in **Europe and Central Asia** through much of the 1990s may have hit bottom. But the combination of falling output and rising inequality led to large increases in the numbers in poverty, including those in extreme poverty. In 1990 very few in this region lived on less than $1 a day. Today there may be more than 24 million, 5 percent of the population—and as many as 93 million, or 20 percent of the population, now live on less than $2 a day.
- In the **Middle East and North Africa** only 2 percent of the population live on less than $1 a day, and some 22 percent on less than $2. Poverty has declined in the 1990s, helped in recent years by rising oil prices and stronger growth.

Halving poverty by 2015

What are the prospects for attaining the international development goal of halving the proportion of people in extreme poverty between 1990 and 2015?

Much depends on the pace and quality of growth, according to the World Bank's *Global Economic Prospects 2000.* With slow growth and rising inequality there likely will be little progress in reducing the total number of poor—much like the experience of the last decade. In the next decade the number of people living in poverty would remain virtually unchanged, with more than a billion people still living on less than $1 a day. Only with inclusive growth—only if the right combination of policies and interventions leads to sustained growth without increases in inequality—can we stay on track to reach the target.

This brighter picture requires policies that encourage economic stability and direct new resources toward poverty reduction, so that countries can grow out of extreme poverty. That should make it

Box 1a

The international development goals

An OECD–United Nations–World Bank conference (held in Paris on 16–17 February 1998) identified 6 social goals and 16 complementary indicators to be monitored by the development community as part of a new international development strategy. (The table numbers show where these indicators appear.)

Reduce poverty by half
- Headcount index (table 2.7)
- Poverty gap index (table 2.7)
- Income inequality: share of income accruing to poorest 20 percent (table 2.8)
- Child malnutrition (table 2.17)

Provide universal primary education
- Net primary enrollment ratio (table 2.10)
- Progression to grade 5 (table 2.11)
- Illiteracy rate of 15- to 24-year-olds (table 2.12)

Improve gender equality in education
- Gender differences in education and literacy (tables 1.3 and 2.13)

Reduce infant and child mortality
- Infant mortality rate (table 2.18)
- Under-five mortality rate (table 2.18)

Reduce maternal mortality
- Maternal mortality ratio (table 2.16)
- Births attended by skilled health staff (table 2.16)

Expand access to reproductive health services
- Contraceptive prevalence rate (table 2.16)
- Total fertility rate (table 2.16)
- HIV prevalence in pregnant 15- to 24-year-olds (table 2.17)[1]

1. These data are not yet available, but table 2.17 shows comparable indicators.

possible to reduce the number of people living on less than $1 a day to about 700 million by decade's end.

The fundamental message is that only with substantial policy change will the world achieve the goal. Now only East Asia and the Pacific is poised to meet the goal. With more inclusive growth the poverty reduction goal is attainable in South Asia as well. But only with even better growth effort and stronger reductions in inequality will Latin America and Sub-Saharan Africa be likely to attain it.

What of the social development goals?

Social development indicators generally improve as incomes rise. And most indicators continued to improve between 1990 and 1998. But progress does not warrant confidence that the international development goals can be attained (box 1a). Moreover, health gains are being eroded in countries suffering the AIDS epidemic, many of which are experiencing sharp reductions in life expectancy (Tanzania, Uganda, Zambia, and Zimbabwe). And the countrywide averages that are the focus of the international development goals conceal considerable differences in health and education—with the poor systematically having higher mortality rates and lower enrollment ratios.

Mortality rates

The international development goals call for a two-thirds reduction in infant and child mortality rates and a three-fourths reduction in maternal mortality ratios from 1990. Neither is likely on current trends. Infant mortality rates fell by 13 percent in South Asia, 9 percent in Sub-Saharan Africa—and 10 percent in developing countries as a group. Under-five mortality rates declined by 3 percent for Sub-Saharan Africa and 10 percent for all developing countries. To be on track for attaining the goals, mortality rates should have come down by roughly 30 percent.

These national averages conceal wide disparities between rich and poor families in some countries. Generally, children born into poor families have a higher chance of dying before their fifth birthday than children born into better-off families, but inequality varies by country. In Ghana and Pakistan the rates for the top and bottom fifths vary only slightly, with the poor having 1.1–1.2 times the rate of under-five mortality. But in South Africa the poor have twice the rate of the rich—and in Northeast Brazil 10 times (table 1b).

Equally difficult for the majority of developing countries is achieving the maternal mortality reduction target. This is especially so for countries with levels above 300 per 100,000 live

Table 1b

Under-five mortality rate in poorest and richest quintiles
Per 1,000 live births

	Period	Average	Poorest quintile	Richest quintile	Ratio of poorest to richest
Brazil[a]	1987–92	63	116	11	10.4
Ghana	1978–89	142	155	130	1.2
Pakistan	1981–90	147	160	145	1.1
South Africa	1985–89	113	155	71	2.2

a. Data refer to the Northeast and Southeast.
Source: Wagstaff 1999.

births in 1990 or later.[2] Countries can make a dent in maternal deaths with safe motherhood initiatives, such as those preventing and managing unwanted pregnancies. The most effective intervention is having personnel trained in midwifery attend the delivery, which can substantially reduce the number of women who remain at risk.

But the poor have a smaller percentage of births in the presence of trained health professionals. Evidence from 10 developing countries studied between 1992 and 1997 shows that only 22 percent of births were attended by medically trained health staff for the poorest fifth of the population, while for the richest fifth 76 percent of births were attended by trained staff (figure 1a). There were undoubtedly large variations in the quality of trained staff for the two groups.

A big factor in mortality in many developing countries: HIV/AIDS. In some countries in Sub-Saharan Africa infant and child mortality, after years of steady decline, has begun to rise again. And analysis by Hanmer and Naschold (1999) indicates that HIV/AIDS is strongly and positively correlated with maternal mortality.

Does this mean that the international development goals for health outcomes are unlikely to be attained? Much depends on containing the HIV/AIDS epidemic, improving delivery of health services to those in need, and realizing the benefits of continuing technological progress. Hanmer and Naschold's study suggests that in the best case the infant mortality target could be met for developing countries as a whole, with South Asia almost making the target and Sub-Saharan Africa reducing its rate by 44 percent. Even without improvements in health service delivery, all regions other than South Asia and Sub-Saharan Africa could still reach the target. But if HIV/AIDS continues to spread as projected by various epidemiological models, no regions except East Asia and the Pacific would meet the goal of a two-thirds reduction.

For under-five mortality, all regions other than Sub-Saharan Africa could reach the target if HIV/AIDS is contained and health services continue to improve. Without improved services, East Asia and the Pacific, Europe and Central Asia, and Latin America and the Caribbean could still meet the target. In the AIDS pandemic scenario East Asia and the Pacific and Europe and Central Asia would still make the target, but the developing world as a whole would see only a 23 percent reduction in under-five mortality, far short of two-thirds.

None of the regions would achieve the maternal mortality target, even assuming that 80 percent of births are attended by medically trained staff. Starting from its high current maternal mortality ratios, Sub-Saharan Africa could get close to the target under the better health services scenario, but the scenario's assumptions may be too optimistic for the region.

Figure 1a

The poorest have least access to maternal and child health services

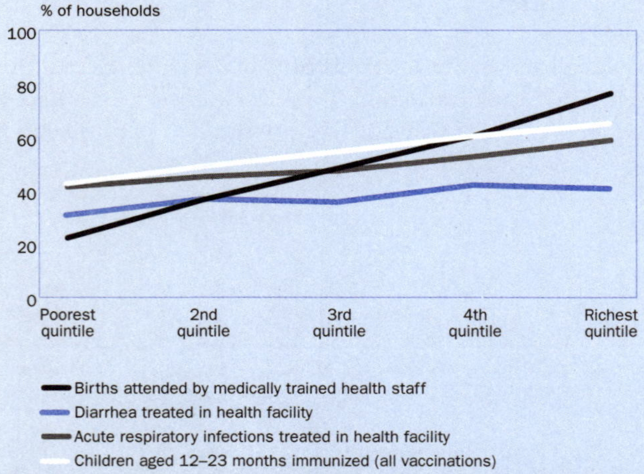

% of households

Poorest quintile, 2nd quintile, 3rd quintile, 4th quintile, Richest quintile

- Births attended by medically trained health staff
- Diarrhea treated in health facility
- Acute respiratory infections treated in health facility
- Children aged 12–23 months immunized (all vaccinations)

Note: The data are from 10 developing countries (Bolivia, Chad, Côte d'Ivoire, India, Malawi, Morocco, Peru, the Philippines, Tanzania, and Vietnam) for years between 1992 and 1997. Households are grouped into quintiles by assets.

Source: Analysis of demographic and health surveys conducted by the World Bank and Macro International.

Education outcomes

The international development goals aim at 100 percent net enrollment in primary school by 2015, and equal enrollment for boys and girls in primary and secondary school by 2005. Neither is likely. The exhaustive Oxfam study *Education Now* (Watkins 1999) estimates that 125 million children of primary school age were out of school in 1995. Of these, two-thirds were girls. In 1995 girls made up only 43 percent of those enrolled in primary school in low-income countries. By 2005 they are expected to make up only 47 percent of primary enrollment. While girls' enrollment in secondary school is rising faster than boys', they will make up only 47 percent of secondary enrollment by 2005. That last 3 percent is difficult to achieve.

The United Nations Educational, Scientific, and Cultural Organization (UNESCO) is more optimistic, suggesting that East Asia and the Pacific will meet the target, and that Europe and Central Asia and Latin America and the Caribbean are likely to (figure 1b). Progress will be slower in South Asia, Sub-Saharan Africa, and the Middle East and North Africa. Oxfam projects gradual progress, with 96 million still out of school in 2005 and 75 million in 2015, two-thirds of them in Sub-Saharan Africa.

Within countries the poor are systematically worse off than the rich. In many countries few children from poor households have schooling. In Benin, India, Mali, and Pakistan the majority of 15- to 19-year-olds from the poorest 40 percent of households have zero years of schooling. In India, by contrast, 15- to 19-year-olds from the richest 20 percent of households have an average of 10 years of schooling. In Brazil, where almost all children from the poorest households attend some school, only 15 percent actually complete primary school.

Responding to the challenge

Slow progress has led to growing consensus on what is needed to scale up and accelerate the efforts to attain the ambitious targets.

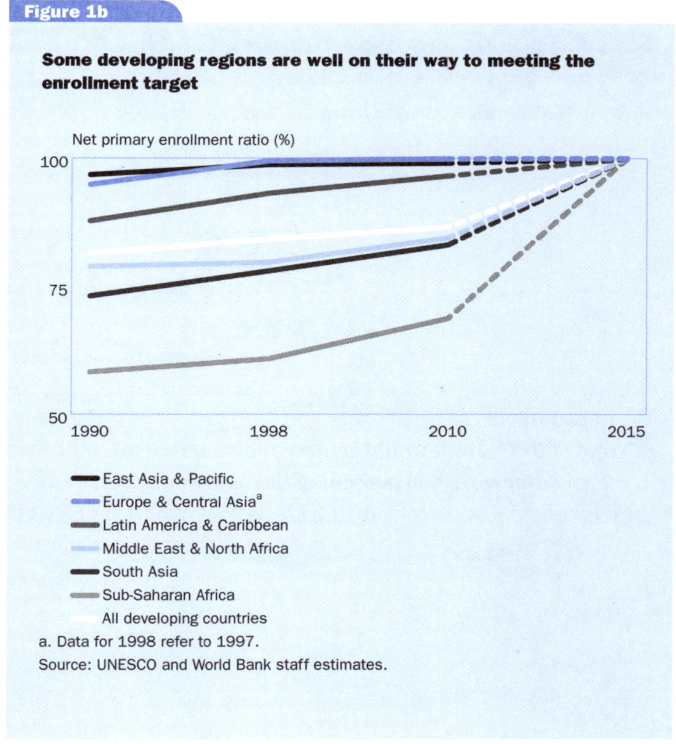

Figure 1b

Some developing regions are well on their way to meeting the enrollment target

a. Data for 1998 refer to 1997.

Source: UNESCO and World Bank staff estimates.

This consensus is based on general agreement that:

- Multidimensional societal transformation is the ultimate goal of development.
- We need to ensure that such transformation is country led rather than donor led.
- We need to work together through strategic partnerships to support countries anxious to move ahead.
- We need to focus such efforts on a clear set of monitorable development outcomes.

Building on this consensus, the annual meetings of the World Bank and the International Monetary Fund in Washington, D.C., in September 1999 set two priorities for action. First, greatly expand the debt relief granted to reforming heavily indebted poor countries and link such relief to their efforts to reduce poverty. Second, help indebted countries and all other recipients of concessional aid develop clearly articulated poverty reduction strategies in close consultation with civil society and their development partners.

Such strategies would:

- Aim at a better understanding of the nature and locus of poverty.
- Identify and implement public policies that have the greatest impact on poverty.
- Set clear goals for progress in poverty reduction, tracked in a participatory manner through carefully selected intermediate and outcome indicators.

Early candidates for this approach would be the heavily indebted poor countries pursuing policy and institutional reforms, most of them in Sub-Saharan Africa, the region with the farthest to go. The underlying premise of this new approach is that governments can measurably increase the efficiency of their poverty reduction efforts by improving the policy and institutional environment. Much research now shows this. As policies and institutions improve, the cost of poverty reduction falls, so that for a given volume of resources more people can be lifted out of poverty.

The same research shows that donors can double the poverty reduction efficiency of their aid by targeting poorer countries, particularly those pursuing good policies and institutional environments (see Collier and Dollar 1999). The new approach to poverty—supporting countries willing to fight poverty—raises hopes that the international development goals can be reached.

Notes

1. These estimates are based on purchasing power parities (PPPs), which take into account differences in the relative prices of goods and services between countries. The poverty line for extreme poverty was estimated as the average of the 10 lowest poverty lines of 33 countries for which poverty lines were available in 1990. That average in 1993 dollars—converted using PPPs—is $1.08 a day. In the text this poverty line is loosely referred to as $1 a day.
2. Achieving the maternal mortality goal has different implications for countries with different mortality levels. By 2005 countries with intermediate levels of mortality should aim to lower the maternal mortality ratio to less than 100 per 100,000 live births, and by 2015 to less than 60. Countries with the highest levels of mortality should aim to achieve a maternal mortality ratio of less than 125 per 100,000 live births by 2005, and less than 75 by 2015.

GOAL: to reduce income poverty by half by 2015

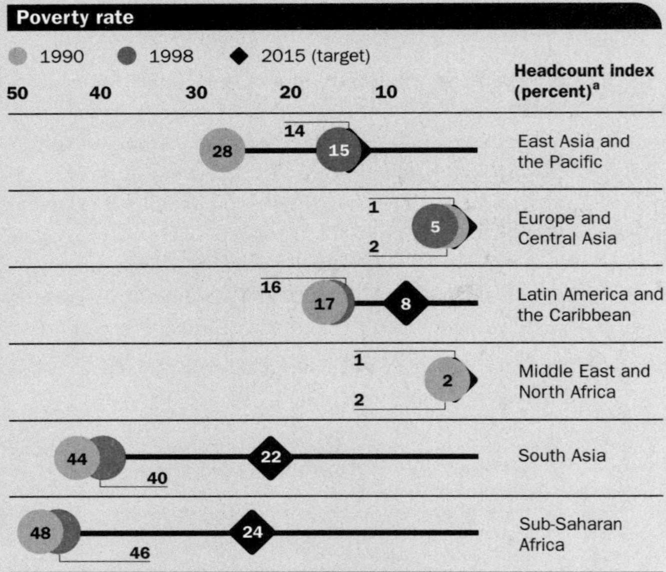

Source: World Bank staff estimates. a. People living on less than PPP$1 a day.

GOAL: to reduce infant and child mortality rates by two-thirds by 2015

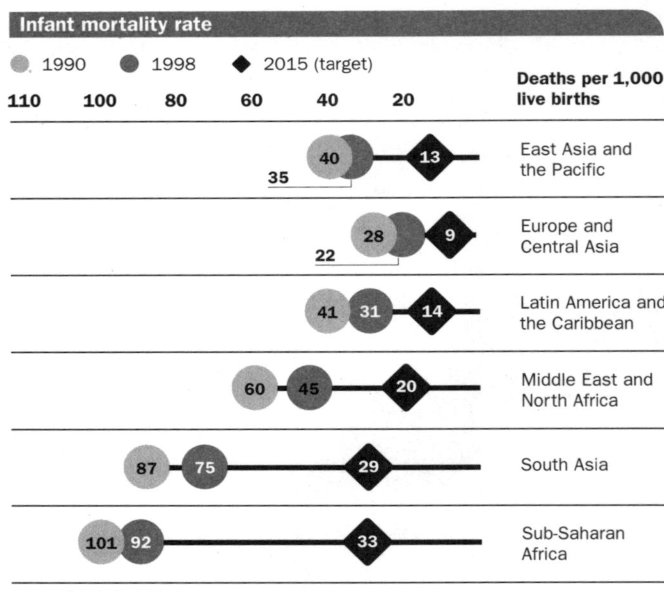

Source: World Bank staff estimates.

GOALS

GOAL: to achieve universal primary enrollment by 2015

Net primary enrollment ratio

1990 1998 2015 (target)

Percent 50 60 70 80 90 100

East Asia and the Pacific 100 97 99

Europe and Central Asia 100 96 99

Latin America and the Caribbean 88 93 100

Middle East and North Africa 79 80 100

South Asia 73 78 100

Sub-Saharan Africa 58 61 100

Source: UNESCO estimates, 1999.

GOAL: to achieve gender equality in primary and secondary education by 2005

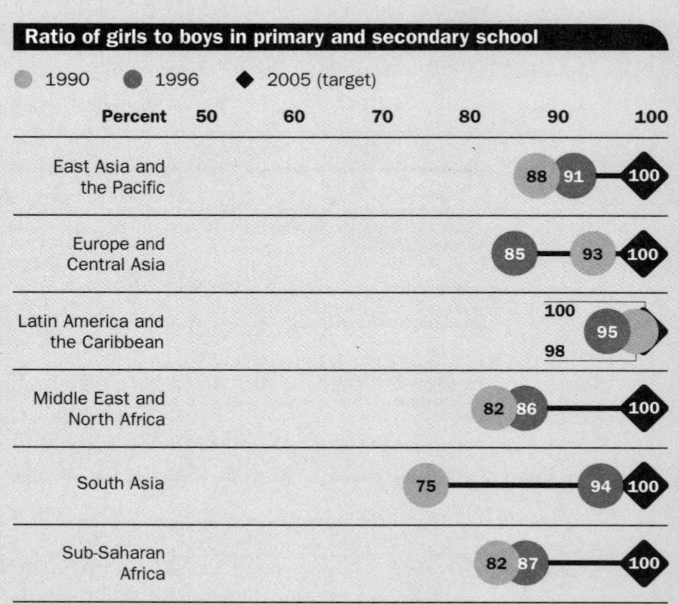

Source: UNESCO.

The challenge of meeting our goals

I believe that the greatest moral challenge we face is the fact that one in four of the people with whom we share this small and beautiful planet live in abject poverty. I also believe that we live at a time when it is possible to make massive reductions in poverty. But to do so, we must turn the development efforts of the international community from an obsession with inputs and generalized rhetoric about poverty to a clear focus on outputs and year-on-year effectiveness in reducing poverty measured against our agreed goals in each and every country.

— The Hon. Clare Short, U.K. Secretary of State for International Development, Paris, 1999

GOAL: to provide access to reproductive health services for all who need them by 2015

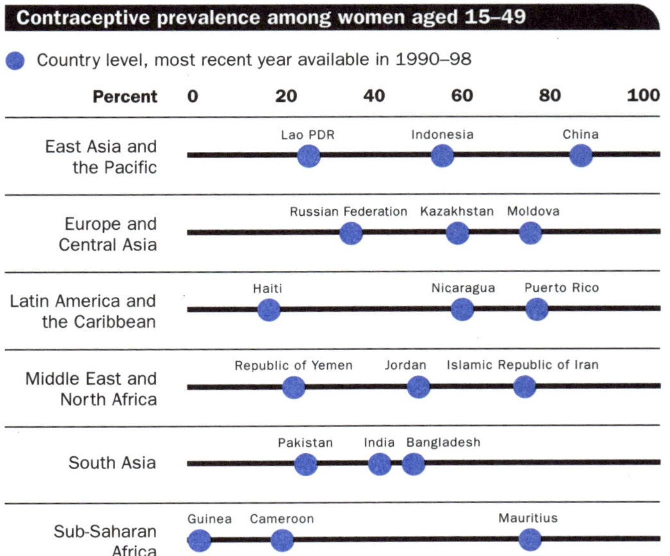

Note: Use of contraceptives is affected by many factors, including access to reproductive health services. There is no established goal. The data shown are for the lowest, median, and highest value in each region for the most recent year available in 1990–98.
Source: National estimates.

GOAL: to reduce maternal mortality ratios by three-quarters by 2015

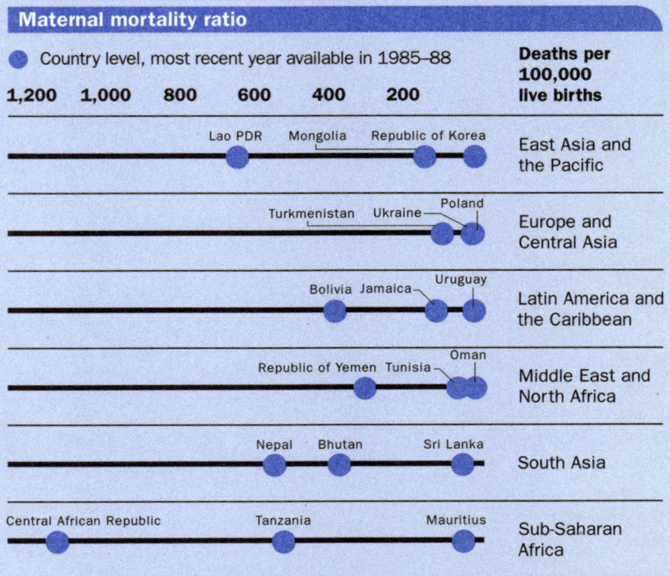

Note: The data shown are for the lowest, median, and highest value in each region for the most recent year available in 1985–1988.
Source: National estimates.

1.1 Size of the economy

	Population	Surface area	Population density	GNP			GNP per capita			PPP GNP[a]		
	millions **1998**	thousand sq. km **1998**	people per sq. km **1998**	$ billions **1998[b]**	Rank **1998**	Average annual growth % **1997–98**	$ **1998[b]**	Rank **1998**	Average annual growth % **1997–98**	$ billions **1998**	Per capita $ **1998**	Rank **1998**
Albania	3	29	122	2.7	135	7.9	810	139	6.8	10	2,864	137
Algeria	30	2,382	13	46.4	51	5.8	1,550	113	3.6	137 [c]	4,595 [c]	101
Angola	12	1,247	10	4.6	115	19.8	380	165	16.3	12 [c]	999 [c]	183
Argentina	36	2,780	13	290.3	17	3.9	8,030	55	2.6	424	11,728	53
Armenia	4	30	135	1.7	155	3.4	460	160	3.1	8	2,074	150
Australia	19	7,741	2	387.0	14	5.6	20,640	23	4.4	409	21,795	20
Austria	8	84	98	216.7	21	3.3	26,830	12	3.2	187	23,145	15
Azerbaijan	8	87	91	3.8	123	9.9	480	156	8.9	17	2,168	149
Bangladesh	126	144	965	44.2	53	5.9	350	173	4.2	177	1,407	168
Belarus	10	208	49	22.3	62	10.5	2,180	99	10.8	65	6,314	81
Belgium	10	33	311	259.0	19	3.0	25,380	15	2.8	241	23,622	13
Benin	6	113	54	2.3	141	4.7	380	165	1.9	5	857	189
Bolivia	8	1,099	7	8.0	93	5.1	1,010	134	2.7	18	2,205	146
Bosnia and Herzegovina	4	51	74	..	..	..	.. [d]	..	..	..	..	..
Botswana	2	582	3	4.8	111	3.7	3,070	87	1.8	9	5,796	86
Brazil	166	8,547	20	767.6	8	0.0	4,630	68	–1.4	1,070	6,460	80
Bulgaria	8	111	75	10.1	84	4.4	1,220	125	5.1	39	4,683	100
Burkina Faso	11	274	39	2.6	138	6.3	240	191	3.8	9 [c]	866 [c]	188
Burundi	7	28	255	0.9	170	4.7	140	202	2.6	4 [c]	561 [c]	203
Cambodia	11	181	65	2.9	132	–0.1	260	187	–2.3	14 [c]	1,246 [c]	175
Cameroon	14	475	31	8.7	89	6.7	610	152	3.8	20	1,395	170
Canada	30	9,971	3	580.9	9	2.9	19,170	26	2.0	691	22,814	17
Central African Republic	3	623	6	1.1	166	4.5	300	181	2.6	4 [c]	1,098 [c]	179
Chad	7	1,284	6	1.7	157	8.4	230	192	5.5	6 [c]	843 [c]	191
Chile	15	757	20	73.9	42	8.7	4,990	66	7.2	126	8,507	68
China	1,239	9,597 [e]	133	923.6	7	7.4	750	145	6.4	3,779	3,051	132
Hong Kong, China	7	1	6,755	158.2 [f]	24	–5.1	23,660 [f]	21	–7.8	139	20,763	23
Colombia	41	1,139	39	100.7	35	–0.6	2,470	93	–2.4	239 [c]	5,861 [c]	84
Congo, Dem. Rep.	48	2,345	21	5.4	104	4.0	110	205	0.7	35 [c]	733 [c]	195
Congo, Rep.	3	342	8	1.9	149	11.4	680	148	8.4	2	846	190
Costa Rica	4	51	69	9.8	85	4.7	2,770	89	2.9	20 [c]	5,812 [c]	85
Côte d'Ivoire	14	322	46	10.2	83	5.9	700	147	3.9	21	1,484	164
Croatia	5	57	80	20.8	64	1.8	4,620	69	2.6	30	6,698	78
Cuba	11	111	101	..	..	..	.. [g]	..	..	..	..	..
Czech Republic	10	79	133	53.0	48	–2.2	5,150	65	–2.1	126	12,197	52
Denmark	5	43	125	175.2	23	2.7	33,040	6	2.4	126	23,855	12
Dominican Republic	8	49	171	14.6	77	6.8	1,770	105	4.9	36 [c]	4,337 [c]	104
Ecuador	12	284	44	18.4	70	4.2	1,520	116	2.2	37	3,003	133
Egypt, Arab Rep.	61	1,001	62	79.2	40	6.3	1,290	121	4.5	193	3,146	129
El Salvador	6	21	292	11.2	80	3.3	1,850	103	1.1	24 [c]	4,008 [c]	114
Eritrea	4	118	38	0.8	174	–4.0	200	198	–6.7	4 [c]	984 [c]	184
Estonia	1	45	34	4.9	110	5.7	3,360	82	6.4	11	7,563	73
Ethiopia	61	1,104	61	6.2	101	–1.8	100	206	–4.2	35 [c]	566 [c]	202
Finland	5	338	17	125.1	31	6.7	24,280	19	6.5	106	20,641	24
France	59	552	107	1,465.4 [h]	4	3.2	24,210 [h]	20	2.8	1,248	21,214	22
Gabon	1	268	5	4.9	107	5.7	4,170	72	3.2	7	5,615	89
Gambia, The	1	11	122	0.4	189	5.0	340	176	2.0	2 [c]	1,428 [c]	167
Georgia	5	70	78	5.3	105	2.7	970	136	2.5	19	3,429	124
Germany	82	357	235	2,179.8	3	2.8	26,570	13	2.8	1,807	22,026	19
Ghana	18	239	81	7.3	96	4.6	390	164	1.9	32 [c]	1,735 [c]	157
Greece	11	132	82	123.4	32	3.3	11,740	46	3.1	147	13,994	49
Guatemala	11	109	100	17.8	71	5.5	1,640	111	2.8	38 [c]	3,474 [c]	122
Guinea	7	246	29	3.8	125	3.9	530	154	1.5	12	1,722	158
Guinea-Bissau	1	36	41	0.2	200	–28.9	160	201	–30.4	1 [c]	573 [c]	201
Haiti	8	28	277	3.2	131	3.2	410	162	1.1	11 [c]	1,379 [c]	171
Honduras	6	112	55	4.6	116	4.0	740	146	1.1	14 [c]	2,338 [c]	142

Size of the economy 1.1

	Population	Surface area	Population density	GNP			GNP per capita			PPP GNP[a]		
	millions	thousand sq. km	people per sq. km	$ billions	Rank	Average annual growth %	$	Rank	Average annual growth %	$ billions	Per capita $	Rank
	1998	1998	1998	1998[b]	1998	1997–98	1998[b]	1998	1997–98	1998	1998	1998
Hungary	10	93	110	45.7	52	4.2	4,510	71	4.6	99	9,832	63
India	980	3,288	330	427.4	11	6.2	440	161	4.3	2,018[c]	2,060[c]	151
Indonesia	204	1,905	112	130.6	30	–16.7	640	149	–18.0	490	2,407	141
Iran, Islamic Rep.	62	1,633	38	102.2	34	1.5	1,650	110	–0.2	317	5,121	95
Iraq	22	438	51	..	..	..	..[g]	..	..	..	..	..
Ireland	4	70	54	69.3	43	9.2	18,710	27	7.9	67	17,991	33
Israel	6	21	289	96.5	36	3.4	16,180	32	1.2	101	16,861	38
Italy	58	301	196	1,157.0	6	1.4	20,090	25	1.3	1,173	20,365	25
Jamaica	3	11	238	4.5	117	0.9	1,740	108	0.1	9	3,344	126
Japan	126	378	336	4,089.1	2	–2.7	32,350	7	–2.9	2,982	23,592	14
Jordan	5	89	51	5.3	106	3.3	1,150	128	0.5	12	2,615	139
Kazakhstan	16	2,717	6	20.9	63	–2.2	1,340	120	–1.2	67	4,317	105
Kenya	29	580	51	10.2	82	2.7	350	173	0.3	28	964	186
Korea, Dem. Rep.	23	121	192	..	..	..	..[d]	..	..	..	..	..
Korea, Rep.	46	99	470	398.8	12	–6.6	8,600	51	–7.5	616	13,286	51
Kuwait	2	18	105	..	..	..	..[i]	..	..	..	..	..
Kyrgyz Republic	5	199	24	1.8	152	4.2	380	165	2.8	11	2,247	143
Lao PDR	5	237	22	1.6	159	4.0	320	179	1.4	8	1,683	160
Latvia	2	65	39	5.9	102	3.4	2,420	95	4.3	14	5,777	87
Lebanon	4	10	412	15.0	76	3.0	3,560	80	1.4	17	4,144	111
Lesotho	2	30	68	1.2	164	–3.1	570	153	–5.3	5	2,194	148
Libya	5	1,760	3	..	..	..	..[j]	..	..	..	..	..
Lithuania	4	65	57	9.4	86	4.8	2,540	92	4.8	23	6,283	82
Macedonia, FYR	2	26	79	2.6	137	3.1	1,290	121	2.4	8	4,224	107
Madagascar	15	587	25	3.7	126	4.9	260	187	1.7	11	741	192
Malawi	11	118	112	2.2	142	1.5	210	195	–1.0	6	551	204
Malaysia	22	330	68	81.3	39	–5.8	3,670	78	–8.0	171	7,699	72
Mali	11	1,240	9	2.6	136	4.3	250	189	1.3	7	673	199
Mauritania	3	1,026	2	1.0	167	4.3	410	162	1.5	4[c]	1,500[c]	163
Mauritius	1	2	571	4.3	118	5.1	3,730	76	4.0	10	8,236	70
Mexico	96	1,958	50	368.1	15	4.7	3,840	75	3.0	714	7,450	75
Moldova	4	34	130	1.7	158	–9.5	380	165	–9.2	9	1,995	153
Mongolia	3	1,567	2	1.0	168	3.6	380	165	1.9	4	1,463	165
Morocco	28	447	62	34.4	56	7.0	1,240	124	5.3	89	3,188	128
Mozambique	17	802	22	3.5	127	11.8	210	195	9.7	13[c]	740[c]	193
Myanmar	44	677	68	..	..	..	..[d]	..	..	..	..	..
Namibia	2	824	2	3.2	129	1.2	1,940	102	–1.2	9[c]	5,280[c]	93
Nepal	23	147	160	4.9	109	2.7	210	195	0.3	27	1,181	177
Netherlands	16	41	463	389.1	13	3.3	24,780	17	2.7	350	22,325	18
New Zealand	4	271	14	55.4	46	–0.6	14,600	36	–1.5	61	16,084	41
Nicaragua	5	130	39	1.8	153	6.1	370	170	3.3	9[c]	1,896[c]	156
Niger	10	1,267	8	2.0	146	8.4	200	198	4.8	7[c]	729[c]	196
Nigeria	121	924	133	36.4	55	1.1	300	181	–1.5	89	740	194
Norway	4	324	14	152.0	25	2.3	34,310	4	1.7	116	26,196	7
Oman	2	212	11	..	..	..	..[j]	..	..	..	..	..
Pakistan	132	796	171	61.5	44	3.0	470	158	0.5	217	1,652	161
Panama	3	76	37	8.3	90	2.5	2,990	88	0.9	14	4,925	96
Papua New Guinea	5	463	10	4.1	120	2.3	890	138	0.0	10[c]	2,205[c]	147
Paraguay	5	407	13	9.2	87	–0.5	1,760	106	–3.0	23[c]	4,312[c]	106
Peru	25	1,285	19	60.5	45	–1.6	2,440	94	–3.3	104	4,180	110
Philippines	75	300	252	78.9	41	0.1	1,050	132	–2.1	280	3,725	118
Poland	39	323	127	151.3	26	4.4	3,910	74	4.4	292	7,543	74
Portugal	10	92	109	106.4	33	3.9	10,670	48	3.7	145	14,569	46
Puerto Rico	4	9	435	..	..	..	..[j]	..	..	..	..	..
Romania	23	238	98	30.6	59	–8.3	1,360	119	–8.1	125	5,572	90
Russian Federation	147	17,075	9	331.8	16	–6.6	2,260	97	–6.4	907	6,180	83

1.1 Size of the economy

	Population	Surface area	Population density	GNP			GNP per capita			PPP GNP[a]		
	millions 1998	thousand sq. km 1998	people per sq. km 1998	$ billions 1998[b]	Rank 1998	Average annual growth % 1997–98	$ 1998[b]	Rank 1998	Average annual growth % 1997–98	$ billions 1998	Per capita $ 1998	Rank 1998
Rwanda	8	26	329	1.9	150	9.9	230	192	7.1	..	..	..
Saudi Arabia	21	2,150	10	143.4	27	2.3	6,910	60	–1.0	218 [c]	10,498 [c]	60
Senegal	9	197	47	4.7	112	6.7	520	155	3.8	12	1,297	173
Sierra Leone	5	72	68	0.7	175	–0.7	140	202	–2.9	2	445	206
Singapore	3	1	5,186	95.5	37	1.5	30,170	9	–0.4	80	25,295	8
Slovak Republic	5	49	112	19.9	66	4.2	3,700	77	4.1	52	9,624	65
Slovenia	2	20	99	19.4	67	3.9	9,780	50	4.1	29	14,400	48
South Africa	41	1,221	34	136.9	28	0.5	3,310	83	–1.3	343 [c]	8,296 [c]	69
Spain	39	506	79	555.2	10	3.7	14,100	39	3.6	628	15,960	43
Sri Lanka	19	66	291	15.2	75	4.6	810	139	3.3	55	2,945	134
Sudan	28	2,506	12	8.2	91	5.0	290	183	2.7	35 [c]	1,240 [c]	176
Sweden	9	450	22	226.5	20	2.8	25,580	14	2.8	176	19,848	27
Switzerland	7	41	180	284.1	18	1.8	39,980	3	1.5	191	26,876	6
Syrian Arab Republic	15	185	83	15.5	74	0.2	1,020	133	–2.3	41	2,702	138
Tajikistan	6	143	43	2.3	140	15.2	370	170	13.3	6	1,041	181
Tanzania	32	945	36	7.2 [k]	98	6.5	220 [k]	194	3.8	16	483	205
Thailand	61	513	120	131.9	29	–7.7	2,160	100	–8.6	338	5,524	92
Togo	4	57	82	1.5	160	–1.0	330	177	–3.5	6 [c]	1,352 [c]	172
Trinidad and Tobago	1	5	251	5.8	103	6.2	4,520	70	5.6	9	7,208	76
Tunisia	9	164	60	19.2	69	5.5	2,060	101	4.1	48	5,169	94
Turkey	63	775	82	200.5	22	3.9	3,160	85	2.3	419	6,594	79
Turkmenistan	5	488	10	..	..	..	.. [d]	..	..	..	..	..
Uganda	21	241	105	6.6	99	5.7	310	180	2.8	22 [c]	1,072 [c]	180
Ukraine	50	604	87	49.2	49	–2.4	980	135	–1.6	157	3,130	131
United Arab Emirates	3	84	33	48.7	50	–5.7	17,870	28	–10.6	51	18,871	31
United Kingdom	59	245	244	1,264.3	5	2.1	21,410	22	2.0	1,200	20,314	26
United States	270	9,364	30	7,903.0	1	2.5	29,240	10	1.5	7,904	29,240	4
Uruguay	3	177	19	20.0	65	3.9	6,070	64	3.2	28	8,541	67
Uzbekistan	24	447	58	22.9	61	5.2	950	137	3.6	49	2,044	152
Venezuela, RB	23	912	26	82.1	38	–0.4	3,530	81	–2.4	133	5,706	88
Vietnam	77	332	235	26.5	60	5.8	350	173	4.3	129	1,689	159
West Bank and Gaza	3	..	..	4.3	119	7.0	1,560	112	3.0	..	..	..
Yemen, Rep.	17	528	31	4.6	114	7.3	280	185	4.3	11	658	200
Yugoslavia, FR (Serb./Mont.)	11	102	104	..	..	..	.. [g]	..	..	..	..	..
Zambia	10	753	13	3.2	128	–1.9	330	177	–4.1	7	678	198
Zimbabwe	12	391	30	7.2	97	0.5	620	150	–1.4	29	2,489	140
World	5,897 s	133,567 s	45 w	28,835 t		1.3 w	4,890 w		0.0 w	37,136 t	6,300 w	
Low income	3,536	42,815	85	1,842		3.5	520		1.8	7,678	2,170	
Excl. China & India	1,295	29,810	45	491		–4.5	370		–6.5	1,759	1,360	
Middle income	1,474	58,669	25	4,401		–0.1	2,990		–1.3	8,834	5,990	
Lower middle income	886	36,609	25	1,541		–1.2	1,740		–2.3	4,164	4,700	
Upper middle income	588	22,061	27	2,860		0.5	4,870		–0.8	4,714	8,020	
Low & middle income	5,011	101,485	50	6,243		1.0	1,250		–0.5	16,541	3,300	
East Asia & Pacific	1,817	16,384	114	1,802		–1.5	990		–2.6	5,959	3,280	
Europe & Central Asia	475	24,208	20	1,044		–0.4	2,200		–0.5	2,617	5,510	
Latin America & Carib.	502	20,462	25	1,933		2.1	3,860		0.5	3,182	6,340	
Middle East & N. Africa	286	11,023	26	581		3.7	2,030		1.6	1,324	4,630	
South Asia	1,305	5,140	273	560		5.7	430		3.7	2,531	1,940	
Sub-Saharan Africa	627	24,267	27	323		2.2	510		–0.4	902	1,440	
High income	886	32,082	29	22,592		1.4	25,480		0.9	20,745	23,420	
Europe EMU	291	2,374	126	6,542		3.0	22,350		2.8	5,985	20,440	

a. PPP is purchasing power parity; see *Definitions*. b. Calculated using the World Bank Atlas method. c. The estimate is based on regression; others are extrapolated from the latest International Comparison Programme benchmark estimates. d. Estimated to be low income ($760 or less). e. Includes Taiwan, China. f. GNP data refer to GDP. g. Estimated to be lower middle income ($761–3,030). h. GNP and GNP per capita estimates include the French overseas departments of French Guiana, Guadeloupe, Martinique, and Réunion. i. Estimated to be high income ($9,361 or more). j. Estimated to be upper middle income ($3,031–9,360). k. Data refer to mainland Tanzania only.

Size of the economy 1.1

About the data

Population, land area, and output are basic measures of the size of an economy. They also provide a broad indication of actual and potential resources. Therefore, population, land area, and output—as measured by gross national product (GNP) or gross domestic product (GDP)—are used throughout the *World Development Indicators* to normalize other indicators.

Population estimates are generally based on extrapolations from the most recent national census. See *About the data* for tables 2.1 and 2.2 for further discussion of the measurement of population and population growth.

The surface area of a country or economy includes inland bodies of water and some coastal waterways. Surface area thus differs from land area, which excludes bodies of water, and from gross area, which may include offshore territorial waters. Land area is particularly important for understanding the agricultural capacity of an economy and the effects of human activity on the environment. (See tables 3.1–3.3 for measures of land area and data on rural population density, land use, and agricultural productivity.) Recent innovations in satellite mapping techniques and computer databases have resulted in more precise measurements of land and water areas.

GNP, the broadest measure of national income, measures the total domestic and foreign value added claimed by residents. GNP comprises GDP plus net receipts of primary income from nonresident sources. The World Bank uses GNP per capita in U.S. dollars to classify countries for analytical purposes and to determine borrowing eligibility. See the *Users guide* for definitions of the income groups used in the *World Development Indicators*. See *About the data* for tables 4.1 and 4.2 for further discussion of the usefulness of national income as a measure of productivity or welfare.

When calculating GNP in U.S. dollars from GNP reported in national currencies, the World Bank follows its Atlas conversion method. This involves using a three-year average of exchange rates to smooth the effects of transitory exchange rate fluctuations. See *Statistical methods* for further discussion of the Atlas method. Note that growth rates are calculated from data in constant prices and national currency units, not from the Atlas estimates.

Because exchange rates do not always reflect international differences in relative prices, this table also shows GNP and GNP per capita estimates converted into international dollars using purchasing power parities (PPPs). PPPs provide a standard measure allowing comparison of real price levels between countries, just as conventional price indexes allow comparison of real values over time. The PPP conversion factors used here are derived from price surveys covering 118 countries conducted by the International Comparison Programme (ICP). For 62 countries data come from the most recent round of surveys, completed in 1996; the rest are from the 1993 round and have been extrapolated to the 1996 benchmark. Estimates for countries not included in the surveys are derived from statistical models using available data. See *About the data* for tables 4.11 and 4.12 for more information on the ICP and the calculation of PPPs.

All economies shown in the *World Development Indicators* are ranked by size, including those that appear in table 1.6. Ranks are shown only in table 1.1. (The *World Bank Atlas* includes a table comparing the GNP per capita rankings based on the Atlas method with those based on the PPP method for all economies with available data.) No rank is shown for economies for which numerical estimates of GNP per capita are not published. Economies with missing data are included in the ranking process at their approximate level, so that the relative order of other economies remains consistent. In 1998 Luxembourg was judged to have the highest GNP per capita in the world.

Definitions

• **Population** is based on the de facto definition of population, which counts all residents regardless of legal status or citizenship—except for refugees not permanently settled in the country of asylum, who are generally considered part of the population of their country of origin. The values shown are midyear estimates for 1998. See also table 2.1. • **Surface area** is a country's total area, including areas under inland bodies of water and some coastal waterways. • **Population density** is midyear population divided by land area in square kilometers. • **Gross national product** (GNP) is the sum of value added by all resident producers plus any taxes (less subsidies) not included in the valuation of output plus net receipts of primary income (compensation of employees and property income) from abroad. Data are in current U.S. dollars converted using the World Bank Atlas method (see *Statistical methods*). Growth is calculated from constant price GNP in national currency units. • **GNP per capita** is gross national product divided by midyear population. GNP per capita in U.S. dollars is converted using the World Bank Atlas method. Growth is calculated from constant price GNP per capita in national currency units. • **PPP GNP** is gross national product converted to international dollars using purchasing power parity rates. An international dollar has the same purchasing power over GNP as a U.S. dollar has in the United States.

Data sources

Population estimates are prepared by World Bank staff from a variety of sources (see *Data sources* for table 2.1). The data on surface and land area are from the Food and Agriculture Organization (see *Data sources* for table 3.1). GNP and GNP per capita are estimated by World Bank staff based on national accounts data collected by Bank staff during economic missions or reported by national statistical offices to other international organizations such as the Organisation for Economic Co-operation and Development. Purchasing power parity conversion factors are estimates by World Bank staff based on data collected by the International Comparison Programme.

1.2 Development progress

	Private consumption per capita average annual % growth 1980–98	distribution corrected	Net primary enrollment ratio[a] Male % of relevant age group 1980	1997	Female % of relevant age group 1980	1997	Infant mortality rate per 1,000 live births 1970	1998	Under-five mortality rate per 1,000 1970	1998	Maternal mortality ratio per 100,000 live births 1990–98[b]	Access to safe water % of population 1990–96[b]
Albania	..	..	..	..	..	..	66	25	82	31	..	76
Algeria	–2.3	–1.5	92	99	71	93	139	35	192	40	..	..
Angola	–6.5	..	87	35	80	34	178	124	301	204	..	32
Argentina	..	..	97	100	98	100	52	19	71	22	38[c]	65
Armenia	..	..	..	..	..	..	..	15	..	18	35[c]	..
Australia	1.7	1.1	100	100	100	100	18	5	20	6	..	99
Austria	2.0	1.5	100	100	100	100	26	5	33	6	..	..
Azerbaijan	..	..	..	..	..	..	..	17	..	21	37[c]	..
Bangladesh	2.1	1.5	74	80	45	70	140	73	239	96	440[d]	84
Belarus	–2.7	–2.1	..	*87*	..	*84*	..	11	..	14	22[e]	..
Belgium	1.6	1.2	100	100	100	100	21	6	29	6	..	..
Benin	–0.4	..	72	85	34	50	146	87	..	140	500[d]	50
Bolivia	0.1	0.1	85	100	74	95	153	60	243	78	390[d]	55
Bosnia and Herzegovina	..	..	..	..	..	..	59	13	..	..	10[c]	..
Botswana	3.0	..	69	78	83	83	95	62	139	105	330[e]	70
Brazil	0.7	0.3	82	100	79	94	95	33	135	40	160[d]	72
Bulgaria	–0.8	–0.5	98	97	98	99	27	14	32	15	15[e]	..
Burkina Faso	0.4	..	18	39	11	25	141	104	278	210	..	..
Burundi	–0.9	..	23	38	16	33	138	118	228	196	..	52
Cambodia	..	..	100	100	100	100	161	102	244	143	..	13
Cameroon	–1.3	..	77	64	66	59	126	77	215	150	430[d]	41
Canada	1.4	0.9	100	100	100	100	19	5	23	7	..	99
Central African Republic	–1.7	..	73	55	41	38	139	98	248	162	1,100[d]	19
Chad	..	..	38	61	15	35	171	99	252	172	830[d]	24
Chile	4.0	1.7	93	92	93	89	77	10	96	12	23[c]	85
China	7.2	4.2	89	100	80	100	69	31	120	36	65[d]	90
Hong Kong, China	4.9	..	97	90	98	93	19	3	..	..	..	..
Colombia	1.2	0.5	72	89	75	89	70	23	113	28	80[c]	78
Congo, Dem. Rep.	–4.5	..	82	69	59	48	131	90	245	141	..	27
Congo, Rep.	–0.1	..	100	81	94	76	101	90	160	143	..	47
Costa Rica	0.8	0.4	89	89	90	89	62	13	77	15	29[d]	92
Côte d'Ivoire	–2.2	–1.4	65	66	45	50	135	88	240	143	600[d]	72
Croatia	..	..	100	100	100	100	..	8	..	10	12[c]	63
Cuba	..	..	97	100	97	100	39	7	43	9	27[c]	93
Czech Republic	..	..	95	100	95	100	21	5	24	6	9[e]	..
Denmark	1.8	1.4	96	100	96	100	14	5	19	6	10[e]	..
Dominican Republic	0.0	0.0	98	89	100	94	98	40	128	..	..	71
Ecuador	–0.2	–0.1	92	100	91	100	100	32	140	37	160[d]	70
Egypt, Arab Rep.	2.0	1.4	83	100	61	91	158	49	235	59	170[d]	64
El Salvador	3.0	1.5	69	89	70	89	107	31	160	36	..	55
Eritrea	..	..	..	31	..	28	..	61	..	90	1,000[d]	7
Estonia	–1.0	–0.6	100	100	100	100	20	9	27	12	50[e]	..
Ethiopia	–0.4	..	35	44	22	27	158	107	239	173	..	27
Finland	1.4	1.1	100	100	100	100	13	4	16	5	6[e]	98
France	1.6	1.1	100	100	100	100	18	5	24	5	10[e]	100
Gabon	–2.6	..	..	..	..	..	138	86	232	132	..	67
Gambia, The	–2.3	..	70	74	36	58	185	76	319	..	..	76
Georgia	..	..	93	89	92	89	..	15	..	20	70[c]	..
Germany	..	..	100	100	100	100	23	5	26	6	8[e]	..
Ghana	0.3	0.2	..	..	..	..	112	65	186	96	..	56
Greece	1.9	..	100	100	100	100	30	6	54	8	1[e]	..
Guatemala	0.2	0.1	63	77	55	70	107	42	168	52	190[d]	67
Guinea	1.4	0.8	39	58	20	33	181	118	345	184	..	62
Guinea-Bissau	–0.3	–0.1	63	66	31	39	185	128	316	205	910[e]	53
Haiti	..	..	..	..	..	..	141	71	221	116	..	28
Honduras	–0.1	–0.1	79	86	79	89	110	36	170	46	220[e]	65

Development progress 1.2

	Private consumption per capita		Net primary enrollment ratio[a]				Infant mortality rate		Under-five mortality rate		Maternal mortality ratio	Access to safe water
	average annual % growth 1980–98	distribution corrected	Male % of relevant age group		Female % of relevant age group		per 1,000 live births		per 1,000		per 100,000 live births	% of population
			1980	1997	1980	1997	1970	1998	1970	1998	1990–98[b]	1990–96[b]
Hungary	–0.1	–0.1	94	98	95	97	36	10	39	12	15[e]	..
India	2.7	1.9	75	83	53	71	137	70	206	83	410[d]	81
Indonesia	4.6	3.0	93	100	84	99	118	43	172	52	450[d]	62
Iran, Islamic Rep.	0.5	..	83	91	61	89	131	26	208	33	37[d]	83
Iraq	..	..	100	80	94	70	102	103	127	125	..	44
Ireland	2.9	1.9	100	100	100	100	20	6	27	7	6[e]	..
Israel	3.3	2.1	..	..	..	..	25	6	27	8	5[e]	99
Italy	2.1	1.5	100	100	100	100	30	5	33	6	7[e]	..
Jamaica	1.3	0.8	97	96	99	96	48	21	62	24	..	70
Japan	2.8	..	100	100	100	100	13	4	21	5	8[e]	96
Jordan	–1.5	–0.9	73	*67*	73	*68*	60	27	..	31	41[c]	89
Kazakhstan	..	..	..	..	..	..	..	22	..	29	70[f]	..
Kenya	0.4	0.2	92	63	89	67	102	76	156	124	590[d]	53
Korea, Dem. Rep.	..	..	..	..	..	..	51	54	70	68	110[e]	..
Korea, Rep.	6.5	..	100	100	100	100	46	9	54	11	20[e]	83
Kuwait	..	..	89	66	80	64	48	12	59	13	5[e]	100
Kyrgyz Republic	..	..	100	100	100	99	..	26	..	41	65[c]	81
Lao PDR	..	..	75	77	69	69	146	96	218	..	650[c]	39
Latvia	..	..	100	100	100	100	21	15	27	19	45[e]	..
Lebanon	..	..	..	..	..	..	50	27	50	30	100[d]	100
Lesotho	–2.7	–1.2	55	63	80	74	134	93	190	144	..	52
Libya	..	..	100	100	100	100	122	23	160	27	75[d]	90
Lithuania	..	..	..	..	..	..	24	9	30	12	18[e]	..
Macedonia, FYR	..	..	..	*96*	..	*95*	..	16	..	18	11[c]	..
Madagascar	–2.2	–0.1	..	*60*	..	*62*	153	92	285	146	490[d]	29
Malawi	0.8	..	48	97	38	100	193	134	330	229	620[d]	45
Malaysia	2.9	1.5	93	100	92	100	45	8	63	12	39[c]	89
Mali	–1.0	..	26	45	15	31	204	117	391	218	580[d]	37
Mauritania	–0.5	–0.3	..	*61*	..	*53*	148	90	250	140	..	64
Mauritius	5.1	..	80	96	79	97	56	19	86	22	50[c]	98
Mexico	0.2	0.1	97	100	99	100	73	30	110	35	48[d]	83
Moldova	..	..	..	..	..	..	..	18	..	22	42[e]	56
Mongolia	..	..	100	83	100	88	102	50	150	60	150[e]	..
Morocco	1.9	1.2	76	86	48	67	128	49	187	61	230[d]	52
Mozambique	–0.9	..	37	45	32	34	171	134	281	213	..	32
Myanmar	..	..	72	100	70	99	128	78	179	118	230[d]	38
Namibia	–3.0	..	81	89	92	94	118	67	155	112	230[d]	57
Nepal	2.0	1.3	90	93	39	63	166	77	234	107	540[d]	44
Netherlands	1.6	1.1	100	100	100	100	13	5	15	7	7[e]	100
New Zealand	0.8	..	100	100	100	100	17	5	20	7	15[e]	..
Nicaragua	–2.2	–1.1	70	77	72	80	104	36	168	42	150[c]	81
Niger	–2.2	–1.4	28	30	15	19	170	118	320	250	590[d]	53
Nigeria	–4.2	–2.3	..	..	..	..	139	76	201	119	..	39
Norway	1.6	1.2	98	100	99	100	13	4	15	6	6[e]	100
Oman	..	..	54	69	31	67	119	18	200	25	19[c]	68
Pakistan	2.0	1.4	..	..	..	..	142	91	183	120	..	60
Panama	2.4	1.0	89	90	90	90	47	21	71	25	85[e]	84
Papua New Guinea	–0.6	–0.3	..	..	..	..	112	59	130	76	..	28
Paraguay	1.7	0.7	91	96	90	97	55	24	76	27	190[d]	39
Peru	–0.4	–0.2	88	94	87	93	108	40	178	47	270[d]	80
Philippines	0.8	0.5	97	100	94	100	67	32	90	40	170[d]	83
Poland	..	..	99	100	99	99	37	10	36	11	8[e]	..
Portugal	3.1	..	97	100	100	100	56	8	62	8	8[e]	82
Puerto Rico	..	..	..	..	..	..	29	10	..	..	..	97
Romania	0.4	0.3	93	100	90	100	49	21	..	25	41[e]	62
Russian Federation	..	..	92	100	92	100	..	17	..	20	50[c]	..

1.2 Development progress

	Private consumption per capita		Net primary enrollment ratio[a]				Infant mortality rate		Under-five mortality rate		Maternal mortality ratio	Access to safe water
	average annual % growth 1980–98	distribution corrected	Male % of relevant age group 1980	Male % of relevant age group 1997	Female % of relevant age group 1980	Female % of relevant age group 1997	per 1,000 live births 1970	per 1,000 live births 1998	per 1,000 1970	per 1,000 1998	per 100,000 live births 1990–98[b]	% of population 1990–96[b]
Rwanda	–1.0	–0.7	62	76	57	75	142	123	210	205	..	..
Saudi Arabia	..	..	61	62	37	58	119	20	185	26	..	93
Senegal	–0.6	–0.3	45	65	30	54	135	69	279	121	560[d]	50
Sierra Leone	–3.4	–1.3	*55*	..	*39*	..	197	169	363	283	..	34
Singapore	4.8	..	100	92	99	91	20	4	27	6	6[e]	100
Slovak Republic	..	..	..	..	..	..	25	9	29	10	9[e]	..
Slovenia	..	..	..	95	..	94	24	5	29	7	11[e]	98
South Africa	–0.1	0.0	67	100	68	100	79	51	108	83	..	70
Spain	2.2	1.5	100	100	100	100	28	5	34	7	6[e]	..
Sri Lanka	2.9	2.0	99	100	94	100	53	16	100	18	60[e]	46
Sudan	..	..	..	..	..	..	118	69	177	105	..	50
Sweden	0.7	0.5	100	100	100	100	11	4	15	5	5[e]	..
Switzerland	0.5	0.3	100	100	100	100	15	4	18	5	5[e]	100
Syrian Arab Republic	0.9	..	99	99	80	91	96	28	129	32	..	85
Tajikistan	..	..	..	..	..	..	..	23	..	33	65[c]	69
Tanzania	0.0	0.0	*68*	48	*65*	49	129	85	218	136	530[d]	49
Thailand	5.0	2.7	93	87	91	89	73	29	102	33	44[d]	89
Togo	–0.1	..	95	94	64	70	134	78	216	144	480[d]	63
Trinidad and Tobago	–1.5	..	91	100	92	100	52	16	57	18	..	82
Tunisia	1.1	0.7	93	100	72	100	121	28	201	32	70[c]	99
Turkey	2.6	..	85	100	78	98	144	38	201	42	..	..
Turkmenistan	..	..	..	..	..	..	..	33	..	44	110[c]	60
Uganda	1.9	1.1	*43*	..	*35*	..	109	101	185	170	510[d]	34
Ukraine	..	..	..	..	..	..	22	14	..	17	25[c]	55
United Arab Emirates	..	..	74	83	76	81	87	8	90	10	3[c]	98
United Kingdom	2.6	1.7	100	100	100	100	19	6	23	7	7[e]	100
United States	1.9	1.1	89	100	90	100	20	7	26	..	8[c]	..
Uruguay	2.6	..	87	94	87	95	46	16	57	19	21[c]	89
Uzbekistan	5.5	..	..	..	..	..	..	22	..	29	21[c]	57
Venezuela, RB	–0.8	–0.4	81	81	85	84	53	21	61	25	65[d]	79
Vietnam	..	..	98	100	93	100	104	34	157	42	160[d]	36
West Bank and Gaza	..	..	..	..	..	..	..	24	..	26	..	..
Yemen, Rep.	..	..	..	..	..	..	186	82	303	96	350[d]	39
Yugoslavia, FR (Serb./Mont.)	..	..	..	69	..	70	54	13	..	16	10[e]	..
Zambia	–3.6	–2.0	81	73	73	72	106	114	181	192	650[d]	43
Zimbabwe	0.4	..	77	94	68	92	96	73	138	125	400[e]	77
World	**1.3 w**		**86 w**	**92 w**	**77 w**	**88 w**	**98 w**	**54 w**	**152 w**	**75 w**		**.. w**
Low income	3.5		81	89	67	82	113	68	178	92		..
Excl. China & India	1.1		75	78	61	71	137	83	213	125		..
Middle income	2.0		89	96	85	94	87	31	130	39		..
Lower middle income	..		88	95	82	93	93	35	..	44		..
Upper middle income	2.4		90	97	88	95	80	26	113	31		..
Low & middle income	1.9		83	91	72	86	107	59	167	79		..
East Asia & Pacific	5.6		90	99	82	99	78	35	126	43		84
Europe & Central Asia	..		93	100	91	99	..	22	..	26		..
Latin America & Carib.	0.6		86	95	85	93	84	31	123	38		..
Middle East & N. Africa	..		84	91	64	84	134	45	200	55		..
South Asia	2.6		75	83	52	70	139	75	209	89		77
Sub-Saharan Africa	–1.3		*59*	..	*49*	..	137	92	222	151		..
High income	2.2		96	100	97	100	21	6	26	6		..
Europe EMU	..		100	100	100	100	25	5	29	6		..

a. UNESCO enrollment estimates and projections as assessed in 1999. b. Data are for the most recent year available. c. Official estimate. d. Estimate based on survey data. e. Estimate by the World Health Organization and Eurostat. f. Estimate by UNICEF.

Development progress 1.2

About the data

The indicators in this table are intended to measure progress toward the international development goals. The net enrollment ratio, infant and under-five mortality rates, maternal mortality ratio, and access to safe water are included in the set of 28 social and environmental indicators selected for monitoring development progress by the Organisation for Economic Co-operation and Development, the World Bank, and the United Nations in consultation with countries that provide and those that receive development assistance.

The growth of private consumption per capita is included here as an indicator of the effect of economic development on income poverty. Positive growth rates are generally associated with a reduction in poverty, but where the distribution of income or consumption is highly unequal, the poor may not share equally in the improvement. The relationship between the rate of poverty reduction and the distribution of income or consumption, as measured by an index such as the Gini index, is complicated. But Ravallion and Chen (1997) have found that the rate of poverty reduction is directly proportional to the distribution-corrected rate of growth of private consumption per capita. The distribution-corrected rate of growth is calculated as $(1 - G)r$, where G is the Gini index (0 = perfect equality, 1 = perfect inequality) and r is the rate of growth in mean private consumption. The distribution-corrected growth rate may be thought of as the rate of growth in consumption that would produce the same rate of poverty reduction as the observed growth in consumption, if consumption were evenly distributed. It is not necessarily the rate of growth experienced by the poor or any other group in the economy.

In empirical tests covering 23 developing countries, Ravallion and Chen estimated that factor of proportionality to be 4.4, implying a growth elasticity of poverty reduction of between 3.3 for a low Gini index of 0.25 and 1.8 for a high Gini index of 0.60. This implies that a country such as China—with average annual growth in private consumption per capita of 7.2 percent and a Gini index of 0.4—could reduce its poverty rate by 1.8 percentage points a year on average. China's actual experience may have been different because the distribution of income or consumption may change over time.

Estimates of the share of people living in poverty appear in table 2.7. Discussions of the other indicators can be found in *About the data* for tables 2.10 (net enrollment ratio), 2.16 (maternal mortality ratio), 2.18 (infant and under-five mortality rates), and 2.15 (access to safe water).

Definitions

• **Growth of private consumption per capita** is the average annual rate of change in private consumption divided by the midyear population. For the definition of private consumption see *Definitions* for table 4.10. • **Distribution-corrected growth of private consumption per capita** is 1 minus the Gini index multiplied by the annual rate of growth in private consumption per capita. • **Net primary enrollment ratio** is the ratio of the number of children of official school age (as defined by the education system) enrolled in school to the number of children of official school age in the population. • **Infant mortality rate** is the number of deaths of infants under one year of age during the indicated year per 1,000 live births in the same year. • **Under-five mortality rate** is the probability of a child born in the indicated year dying before reaching the age of five, if subject to current age-specific mortality rates. The probability is expressed as a rate per 1,000. • **Maternal mortality ratio** is the number of women who die during pregnancy and childbirth, per 100,000 live births. • **Access to safe water** is the percentage of the population with reasonable access to an adequate amount of safe water (including treated surface water and untreated but uncontaminated water, such as from springs, sanitary wells, and protected boreholes). In urban areas the source may be a public fountain or standpipe located not more than 200 meters away. In rural areas the definition implies that members of the household do not have to spend a disproportionate part of the day fetching water. An adequate amount of safe water is that needed to satisfy metabolic, hygienic, and domestic requirements—usually about 20 liters a person a day. The definition of safe water has changed over time.

Data sources

The indicators here and throughout the rest of the book have been compiled by World Bank staff from primary and secondary sources. More information about the indicators and their sources can be found in the *About the data, Definitions,* and *Data sources* entries that accompany each table in subsequent sections.

1.3 Gender differences

	Female population	Female advantage								
	% of total	Labor force participation ratio of female to male		Adult illiteracy rate female-male difference		Net primary enrollment ratio female-male difference		Life expectancy at birth female-male difference		Child mortality rate female-male difference
	1998	1970	1998	1970	1998	1980	1997	1970	1998	1988–98[a]
Albania	48.7	0.7	0.7	29	14	..	*3*	3	6	0
Algeria	49.4	0.3	0.4	27	22	–20	–7	2	3	..
Angola	50.6	0.9	0.9	..	..	–8	–1	3	3	..
Argentina	50.9	0.3	0.5	1	0	1	0	7	7	..
Armenia	51.4	0.9	0.9	8	2	..	..	6	7	..
Australia	50.1	0.5	0.8	..	..	0	0	7	6	..
Austria	50.9	0.6	0.7	..	..	0	0	7	6	..
Azerbaijan	51.0	0.8	0.8	..	..	..	..	8	7	..
Bangladesh	49.4	0.7	0.7	24	23	–29	–11	–2	0	10
Belarus	53.0	1.0	1.0	3	0	..	..	8	12	..
Belgium	51.0	0.4	0.7	..	..	0	0	7	6	..
Benin	50.7	0.9	0.9	10	31	–38	–34	2	4	1
Bolivia	50.3	0.5	0.6	25	14	–10	–5	4	3	0
Bosnia and Herzegovina	50.4	0.6	0.6	..	..	..	..	4	6	..
Botswana	51.0	1.2	0.8	–2	–5	14	5	4	2	–2
Brazil	50.6	0.3	0.5	7	0	–4	–6	4	8	1
Bulgaria	51.2	0.8	0.9	7	1	0	3	5	7	..
Burkina Faso	50.6	1.0	0.9	10	19	–7	–14	4	2	3
Burundi	51.0	1.0	1.0	27	17	–8	–5	3	3	13
Cambodia	51.6	1.0	1.1	25	38	0	0	3	3	..
Cameroon	50.3	0.6	0.6	26	13	–11	–5	3	3	6
Canada	50.4	0.5	0.8	..	..	0	0	7	6	..
Central African Republic	51.4	..	..	20	26	–32	–17	5	4	1
Chad	50.5	0.7	0.8	11	18	–23	–25	3	3	–7
Chile	50.5	0.3	0.5	2	0	1	–2	6	6	–1
China	48.4	0.7	0.8	31	16	–9	0	1	3	1
Hong Kong, China	49.9	0.5	0.6	27	7	1	4	6	6	..
Colombia	50.6	0.3	0.6	3	0	2	0	4	6	0
Congo, Dem. Rep.	50.5	0.8	0.8	24	24	–23	–21	3	3	..
Congo, Rep.	51.1	0.7	0.8	28	14	–6	–5	5	4	..
Costa Rica	49.3	0.2	0.4	1	0	1	1	4	5	..
Côte d'Ivoire	49.1	0.5	0.5	18	17	–20	–16	3	1	–13
Croatia	51.6	0.6	0.8	12	2	0	0	..	9	..
Cuba	49.9	0.3	0.6	0	0	0	0	3	4	..
Czech Republic	51.3	0.8	0.9	..	..	0	0	..	7	..
Denmark	50.4	0.6	0.9	..	..	0	0	5	5	..
Dominican Republic	49.2	0.3	0.4	5	0	2	5	4	4	0
Ecuador	49.8	0.2	0.4	10	4	0	0	3	5	–3
Egypt, Arab Rep.	49.1	0.3	0.4	29	24	–22	–9	3	3	6
El Salvador	50.9	0.3	0.6	11	6	0	0	4	6	3
Eritrea	50.4	0.9	0.9	29	27	..	–3	3	3	–11
Estonia	53.2	1.0	1.0	..	..	0	0	9	11	..
Ethiopia	49.8	0.7	0.7	13	12	–13	–17	3	2	..
Finland	51.2	0.8	0.9	..	..	0	0	8	7	..
France	51.3	0.6	0.8	..	..	0	0	8	8	..
Gabon	50.6	0.8	0.8	..	..	..	..	3	3	..
Gambia, The	50.6	0.8	0.8	6	14	–34	–15	3	4	–4
Georgia	52.3	0.9	0.9	..	..	–1	–1	..	8	..
Germany	51.1	0.6	0.7	..	..	0	0	6	6	..
Ghana	50.3	1.0	1.0	26	19	..	..	3	3	–1
Greece	50.8	0.3	0.6	16	3	0	0	4	5	..
Guatemala	49.6	0.2	0.4	16	15	–8	–7	2	6	2
Guinea	49.7	0.9	0.9	..	..	–19	–25	1	1	–10
Guinea-Bissau	50.8	0.7	0.7	18	40	–32	–27	2	3	..
Haiti	50.8	0.9	0.8	8	5	..	..	3	5	–1
Honduras	49.6	0.3	0.4	6	0	1	2	4	5	..

Gender differences 1.3

	Female population	Female advantage								
	% of total	Labor force participation ratio of female to male		Adult illiteracy rate female-male difference		Net primary enrollment ratio female-male difference		Life expectancy at birth female-male difference		Child mortality rate female-male difference
	1998	**1970**	**1998**	**1970**	**1998**	**1980**	**1997**	**1970**	**1998**	**1988–98[a]**
Hungary	52.1	0.7	0.8	1	0	1	–2	6	9	..
India	48.4	0.5	0.5	28	24	–22	–12	–2	2	13
Indonesia	50.1	0.4	0.7	25	11	–10	–1	2	4	1
Iran, Islamic Rep.	49.8	0.2	0.4	23	14	–22	–2	–1	2	..
Iraq	49.1	0.2	0.2	25	21	–6	–10	2	2	..
Ireland	50.1	0.4	0.5	..	..	0	0	5	5	..
Israel	50.3	0.4	0.7	10	4	..	..	3	4	..
Italy	51.4	0.4	0.6	3	1	0	0	6	7	..
Jamaica	50.4	0.8	0.9	–7	–8	2	0	3	4	..
Japan	51.0	0.6	0.7	..	..	0	0	5	7	..
Jordan	48.2	0.2	0.3	38	12	–1	*1*	..	3	3
Kazakhstan	51.5	0.9	0.9	..	..	..	..	..	11	–5
Kenya	49.9	0.8	0.9	30	14	–4	3	4	2	2
Korea, Dem. Rep.	49.8	0.8	0.8	..	..	..	..	4	4	..
Korea, Rep.	49.6	0.5	0.7	14	3	0	0	4	7	..
Kuwait	47.5	0.1	0.5	20	5	–9	–2	4	6	..
Kyrgyz Republic	51.0	0.9	0.9	..	..	0	0	..	8	1
Lao PDR	50.5	..	..	24	32	–7	–7	3	3	..
Latvia	54.0	1.0	1.0	0	0	0	0	9	11	..
Lebanon	50.9	0.2	0.4	25	12	..	..	4	4	..
Lesotho	50.8	0.7	0.6	–26	–22	25	11	4	2	..
Libya	48.1	0.2	0.3	43	24	0	0	3	4	–1
Lithuania	52.8	1.0	0.9	1	0	..	..	8	10	..
Macedonia, FYR	50.0	0.4	0.7	..	..	..	*–2*	..	4	..
Madagascar	50.2	0.8	0.8	21	14	..	*2*	3	3	–7
Malawi	50.6	1.0	1.0	39	29	–10	2	1	0	–12
Malaysia	49.3	0.4	0.6	24	9	–1	0	3	5	0
Mali	50.7	0.9	0.9	7	15	–11	–14	3	4	2
Mauritania	50.4	0.9	0.8	19	21	..	*–8*	3	3	..
Mauritius	50.1	0.2	0.5	19	7	–1	0	4	8	..
Mexico	50.5	0.2	0.5	10	4	3	0	5	6	2
Moldova	52.2	1.1	0.9	10	2	..	..	..	7	..
Mongolia	49.8	0.8	0.9	28	21	0	5	3	3	..
Morocco	50.0	0.5	0.5	24	26	–28	–19	3	4	–2
Mozambique	51.5	1.0	0.9	21	31	–6	–11	3	3	–2
Myanmar	50.2	0.8	0.8	27	9	–2	–1	3	3	..
Namibia	50.2	0.7	0.7	13	2	12	5	3	2	4
Nepal	49.4	0.6	0.7	25	35	–51	–31	–1	0	..
Netherlands	50.5	0.3	0.7	..	..	0	0	6	6	..
New Zealand	50.8	0.4	0.8	..	..	0	0	6	5	..
Nicaragua	50.3	0.3	0.5	2	–3	2	3	3	5	–1
Niger	50.6	0.8	0.8	9	15	–13	–12	3	4	18
Nigeria	50.7	0.6	0.6	20	18	..	..	3	3	84
Norway	50.2	0.4	0.9	..	..	1	0	6	6	..
Oman	46.7	0.1	0.2	27	21	–23	–2	2	3	..
Pakistan	48.2	0.3	0.4	23	29	..	..	0	2	15
Panama	49.5	0.3	0.5	2	1	1	1	3	5	..
Papua New Guinea	48.5	0.7	0.7	22	16	..	..	0	2	–7
Paraguay	49.6	0.4	0.4	11	3	–2	1	4	5	2
Peru	50.3	0.3	0.4	22	10	–1	–1	3	5	1
Philippines	49.6	0.5	0.6	4	1	–3	0	3	4	–2
Poland	51.3	0.8	0.9	1	0	0	0	7	8	..
Portugal	52.1	0.3	0.8	12	5	3	0	7	7	..
Puerto Rico	51.8	0.4	0.6	2	0	..	..	6	9	..
Romania	50.9	0.8	0.8	7	2	–3	0	4	8	–2
Russian Federation	53.3	1.0	1.0	2	0	0	0	..	12	–1

1.3 Gender differences

	Female population	Female advantage								
	% of total	Labor force participation ratio of female to male		Adult illiteracy rate female-male difference		Net primary enrollment ratio female-male difference		Life expectancy at birth female-male difference		Child mortality rate female-male difference
	1998	**1970**	**1998**	**1970**	**1998**	**1980**	**1997**	**1970**	**1998**	**1988–98[a]**
Rwanda	50.6	1.0	1.0	24	15	–5	..	3	2	–14
Saudi Arabia	44.7	0.1	0.2	35	18	–24	–4	3	4	..
Senegal	50.1	0.7	0.7	17	20	–14	–12	5	4	–2
Sierra Leone	50.9	0.6	0.6	..	..	..	..	3	3	..
Singapore	49.7	0.3	0.6	26	8	–1	–2	5	4	..
Slovak Republic	51.2	0.7	0.9	..	..	..	..	..	8	..
Slovenia	51.4	0.6	0.9	0	0	..	*0*	7	8	..
South Africa	51.9	0.5	0.6	4	2	2	0	6	5	..
Spain	51.1	0.3	0.6	7	2	0	0	5	7	..
Sri Lanka	49.1	0.3	0.6	17	6	–5	0	2	4	–1
Sudan	49.8	0.4	0.4	31	25	..	..	3	3	1
Sweden	50.5	0.6	0.9	..	..	0	0	5	5	..
Switzerland	50.4	0.5	0.7	..	..	0	0	6	6	..
Syrian Arab Republic	49.4	0.3	0.4	40	29	–19	–8	3	5	..
Tajikistan	50.2	0.8	0.8	9	1	..	..	5	6	..
Tanzania	50.5	1.0	1.0	35	19	..	1	3	2	–7
Thailand	50.0	0.9	0.9	15	4	–1	2	4	5	0
Togo	50.4	0.6	0.7	28	34	–31	–24	3	2	15
Trinidad and Tobago	50.2	0.4	0.5	12	4	1	0	5	5	–1
Tunisia	49.5	0.3	0.5	26	22	–21	0	1	4	0
Turkey	49.5	0.6	0.6	33	18	–7	–2	4	5	2
Turkmenistan	50.5	0.8	0.8	..	..	..	..	7	7	..
Uganda	50.2	0.9	0.9	30	22	..	..	2	–1	–10
Ukraine	53.5	1.0	0.9	1	0	..	..	8	11	..
United Arab Emirates	33.6	0.0	0.2	23	–4	3	–1	4	3	..
United Kingdom	50.9	0.6	0.8	..	..	0	0	6	5	..
United States	50.7	0.6	0.8	..	..	1	0	8	6	..
Uruguay	51.5	0.4	0.7	–1	–1	–1	1	7	8	..
Uzbekistan	50.4	0.9	0.9	19	9	..	..	..	6	–6
Venezuela, RB	49.7	0.3	0.5	7	1	4	2	5	6	..
Vietnam	51.1	0.9	1.0	19	5	–5	0	3	5	..
West Bank and Gaza	49.2	..	..	..	..	..	..	..	3	..
Yemen, Rep.	48.9	0.4	0.4	25	43	..	..	1	1	3
Yugoslavia, FR (Serb./Mont.)	50.2	0.6	0.7	..	..	..	..	4	5	..
Zambia	50.4	0.8	0.8	32	15	–8	–1	3	0	–3
Zimbabwe	50.4	0.8	0.8	17	9	–9	–2	3	3	0
World	**49.6 w**	**0.6 w**	**0.7 w**	**21 w**	**14 w**	**–9 w**	**–4 w**	**3 w**	**4 w**	**..**
Low income	49.0	0.6	0.7	28	19	–14	–6	1	3	..
Excl. China & India	50.0	0.6	0.7	22	18	–14	–8	2	3	..
Middle income	50.5	0.6	0.6	10	6	–4	–2	4	6	..
Lower middle income	50.8	0.7	0.7	9	7	–6	–2	4	6	..
Upper middle income	50.2	0.4	0.6	11	4	–2	–2	5	7	..
Low & middle income	49.4	0.6	0.7	22	15	–11	–5	2	4	..
East Asia & Pacific	48.9	0.7	0.8	28	14	–8	0	2	4	..
Europe & Central Asia	51.9	0.9	0.9	6	4	–1	0	6	9	..
Latin America & Carib.	50.4	0.3	0.5	7	2	–1	–2	4	6	..
Middle East & N. Africa	49.0	0.3	0.4	27	22	–20	–7	2	3	..
South Asia	48.5	0.5	0.5	27	24	–23	–12	–1	1	..
Sub-Saharan Africa	50.5	0.7	0.7	20	17	–11	–9	3	3	..
High income	50.7	0.5	0.8	..	..	0	0	6	6	..
Europe EMU	51.2	0.5	0.7	..	..	0	..	6	7	..

a. Data are for the most recent year available.

Gender differences 1.3

About the data

This table contrasts male and female outcomes for selected social indicators: labor force participation, adult illiteracy, net primary school enrollment, life expectancy at birth, and child mortality. A labor force participation ratio of 1.0 indicates gender equality in labor force participation in the formal sector, while a lower ratio shows that women's participation is lower than men's. For net primary enrollment, a positive value means that the enrollment ratio for girls is higher than that for boys, and a negative number that girls are falling behind. Conversely, for adult illiteracy and child mortality, a positive value indicates female disadvantage. A positive value for life expectancy represents female advantage.

Differences in outcome are the consequence of differences in the opportunities and resources available to men and women. Such disparities exist throughout the world, but they are most prevalent in poor developing countries. Inequalities in the allocation of such resources as education, health care, and nutrition matter because of the strong association of these resources with well-being, productivity, and growth. This pattern of inequality begins at an early age, with boys routinely receiving a larger share of education and health spending than girls do, for example. Girls in many developing countries are allowed less education by their families than boys are—a disparity reflected in lower female primary school enrollment and higher female illiteracy. As a result women have fewer employment opportunities, especially in the formal sector. Women who do work outside the home often also bear a disproportionate share of the responsibility for household chores and child-rearing.

Life expectancy has increased for both men and women in all regions, but female morbidity and mortality rates sometimes exceed male rates, particularly during early childhood and the reproductive years. In high-income countries women tend to outlive men by four to eight years on average, while in low-income countries the difference is narrower—about two to three years. The female disadvantage is best reflected in differences in child mortality rates in some countries. Child mortality captures the effect of preferences for boys because adequate nutrition and medical interventions are particularly important for the age group 1–5. Because of the natural female biological advantage, when female child mortality is as high as or higher than male child mortality, there is good reason to believe that girls are discriminated against.

For more information on the underlying indicators see *About the data* for tables 2.1 (population), 2.3 (labor force), 2.10 (net primary enrollment), 2.12 (illiteracy), and 2.18 (child mortality and life expectancy at birth). For other gender-related indicators see tables 1.2 (maternal mortality), 2.1 (women per 100 men aged 65 and older), 2.4 and 2.5 (employment and unemployment), 2.12 (education outcomes), 2.13 (pupils and teachers), 2.16 (reproductive health), 2.17 (prevalence of anemia and smoking), and 2.18 (adult mortality).

Definitions

• **Female population** is the percentage of the population that is female. • **Labor force** comprises people who meet the International Labour Organization definition of the economically active population: all people who supply labor for the production of goods and services during a specified period. It includes both the employed and the unemployed. While national practices vary in the treatment of such groups as the armed forces and seasonal or part-time workers, in general the labor force includes the armed forces, the unemployed, and first-time job-seekers, but excludes homemakers and other unpaid caregivers and workers in the informal sector. • **Adult illiteracy rate** is the percentage of adults aged 15 and above who cannot, with understanding, read and write a short, simple statement about their everyday life. • **Net primary enrollment ratio** is the ratio of the number of children of official school age (as defined by the education system) enrolled in school to the number of children of official school age in the population. • **Life expectancy at birth** is the number of years a newborn would live if prevailing patterns of mortality at the time of its birth were to stay the same throughout its life. • **Child mortality rate** is the probability of dying between the ages of one and five, if subject to current age-specific mortality rates.

Data sources

The calculations of gender ratios and differences were carried out by World Bank staff. For the sources of the underlying indicators see *Data sources* for the tables referred to in *About the data.*

1.4 Trends in long-term economic development

	Gross national product		Population		Value added			Private consumption	Gross domestic fixed investment	Exports of goods and services
	average annual % growth		average annual % growth		average annual % growth			average annual % growth	average annual % growth	average annual % growth
	Total 1965–98	Per capita 1965–98	Total 1965–98	Labor force 1965–98	Agriculture 1965–98	Industry 1965–98	Services 1965–98	1965–98	1965–98	1965–98
Albania	..	..	1.8	2.2	3.0	–5.3	–1.1	..	..	..
Algeria	3.9	1.0	2.8	3.3	4.8	2.8	4.1	4.7	2.2	2.6
Angola	..	..	2.5	2.1	..	..	..	..	–1.3	4.3
Argentina	1.9	0.4	1.5	1.5	1.6	1.1	2.6	2.4	1.0	5.2
Armenia	..	..	1.6	2.3	..	..	..	..	..	..
Australia	3.2	1.7	1.5	2.1	1.8	2.2	3.5	3.4	2.6	5.7
Austria	2.9	2.6	0.3	0.5	0.8	2.0	2.6	2.9	2.9	6.2
Azerbaijan	..	..	1.7	2.1	..	..	..	..	..	..
Bangladesh	3.9	1.4	2.3	2.3	2.1	4.1	4.7	3.7	3.7	7.6
Belarus	..	..	0.5	0.6	..	..	..	..	..	..
Belgium	2.5	2.3	0.2	0.5	1.9	2.0	2.2	2.7	1.8	4.7
Benin	3.0	0.1	2.8	2.3	4.0	4.0	2.4	2.6	..	3.3
Bolivia	..	..	2.3	2.4	..	..	..	2.4	2.1	3.0
Bosnia and Herzegovina	..	..	0.2	0.6	..	..	..	..	..	..
Botswana	11.4	7.7	3.2	2.9	3.3	13.4	11.0	..	..	..
Brazil	4.3	2.2	2.0	2.9	3.4	4.5	4.9	4.4	1.7	8.3
Bulgaria	–0.7	–0.3	0.0	–0.1	–2.5	–1.3	1.7	–1.2	–5.0	–11.8
Burkina Faso	3.3	0.9	2.3	1.7	2.6	2.5	5.5	3.0	5.9	3.3
Burundi	3.2	0.9	2.2	2.0	2.6	3.7	3.7	3.2	–2.7	2.6
Cambodia	..	..	1.9	1.9	..	..	..	..	..	..
Cameroon	4.1	1.3	2.7	2.3	3.3	6.4	3.6	3.6	0.1	6.0
Canada	3.1	1.8	1.3	2.3	..	..	..	3.2	4.1	5.9
Central African Republic	1.1	–1.2	2.2	..	1.6	2.1	0.3	2.0	2.4	3.0
Chad	1.8	–0.6	2.4	2.2	1.7	1.7	2.3	2.6	..	1.6
Chile	3.6	1.9	1.7	2.3	3.5	3.2	4.9	3.3	4.8	8.3
China	8.6	6.8	1.7	2.1	4.1	10.9	9.3	7.4	9.9	13.5
Hong Kong, China	7.4[a]	5.5[a]	1.8	2.6	..	..	..	7.9	7.7	11.8
Colombia	4.2	2.0	2.2	3.2	2.7	4.5	5.0	4.1	4.6	5.7
Congo, Dem. Rep.	–0.8	–3.8	3.1	2.7	2.0	–3.0	–2.2	0.1	–0.5	2.4
Congo, Rep.	4.3	1.4	2.8	2.6	2.8	7.3	4.3	3.9	..	6.5
Costa Rica	4.0	1.2	2.7	3.5	3.2	4.7	4.1	3.2	4.8	7.0
Côte d'Ivoire	2.8	–0.8	3.5	3.3	2.2	6.1	2.9	2.6	0.2	5.2
Croatia	..	..	0.1	0.1	..	..	..	..	..	..
Cuba	..	..	1.1	2.1	..	..	..	..	..	..
Czech Republic	..	..	0.2	0.4	..	..	..	..	..	..
Denmark	2.2	1.9	0.3	0.9	2.3	1.9	2.6	1.7	0.9	4.5
Dominican Republic	4.7	2.3	2.3	3.2	3.0	5.7	5.1	4.2	6.0	6.2
Ecuador	4.6	1.8	2.6	3.0	3.5	6.1	4.6	4.2	3.1	7.2
Egypt, Arab Rep.	5.9	3.5	2.2	2.4	2.8	6.6	7.9	5.2	5.9	5.5
El Salvador	1.5	–0.4	2.1	2.8	0.6	0.7	2.2	1.9	2.6	1.3
Eritrea	..	..	2.7	2.5	..	..	..	..	..	..
Estonia	..	..	0.4	0.5	..	..	..	..	..	..
Ethiopia	2.2	–0.5	2.7	2.4	1.9	0.4	3.5	2.3	3.9	1.2
Finland	2.8	2.4	0.4	0.6	0.2	3.0	3.4	2.8	1.1	4.9
France	2.6	2.1	0.6	0.7	1.7	0.9	2.6	2.8	1.9	5.6
Gabon	3.4	0.4	2.6	2.0	–0.4	2.6	2.4	3.5	–2.5	5.6
Gambia, The	3.9	0.4	3.3	3.2	1.8	4.1	4.2	1.6	9.4	3.2
Georgia	–0.6	–1.2	0.6	0.8	..	..	..	..	..	..
Germany	..	..	0.2	0.4	..	..	..	..	..	..
Ghana	1.9	–0.8	2.6	2.6	1.3	0.8	3.2	1.5	0.6	–0.5
Greece	3.1	2.4	0.6	0.8	1.3	3.2	4.0	3.4	1.3	7.4
Guatemala	3.4	0.7	2.6	2.8	2.8	3.6	3.5	3.3	2.5	2.4
Guinea	..	..	2.1	1.8	..	..	..	..	..	..
Guinea-Bissau	2.7	–0.1	2.4	2.1	1.5	2.3	6.0	1.1	..	3.0
Haiti	1.1	–0.8	1.9	1.2	0.2	1.3	1.6	1.8	8.6	4.3
Honduras	3.8	0.6	3.1	3.3	2.6	4.4	4.4	3.7	4.0	2.6

Trends in long-term economic development 1.4

	Gross national product		Population		Value added			Private consumption	Gross domestic fixed investment	Exports of goods and services
	average annual % growth		average annual % growth		average annual % growth			average annual % growth	average annual % growth	average annual % growth
	Total 1965–98	Per capita 1965–98	Total 1965–98	Labor force 1965–98	Agriculture 1965–98	Industry 1965–98	Services 1965–98	1965–98	1965–98	1965–98
Hungary	2.2	2.2	0.0	–0.2	–1.8	–1.1	0.7	1.0	2.2	4.4
India	4.9	2.7	2.1	2.0	2.9	5.5	5.8	4.4	5.5	7.1
Indonesia	6.8	4.7	2.0	2.7	3.8	8.9	7.7	7.2	8.5	5.7
Iran, Islamic Rep.	1.6	–1.2	2.8	2.6	4.5	0.1	1.7	3.6	–0.5	–1.1
Iraq	–0.3	..	3.1	2.8	..	..	..	..	..	..
Ireland	3.8	3.0	0.8	0.9	..	..	..	3.1	3.1	8.7
Israel	5.0	2.4	2.6	3.1	..	..	..	5.6	2.8	7.1
Italy	2.7	2.5	0.3	0.6	0.9	2.1	2.8	3.3	1.5	5.5
Jamaica	0.8	–0.4	1.2	1.9	0.9	0.1	1.9	1.3	–0.1	1.9
Japan	4.3	3.5	0.7	1.0	–0.2	4.4	4.7	4.1	4.7	7.6
Jordan	3.9	–0.4	4.2	4.3	6.7	5.7	3.9	4.6	4.9	8.3
Kazakhstan	..	..	0.8	1.3	..	..	..	..	..	..
Kenya	4.8	1.3	3.3	3.4	3.4	5.5	5.4	4.1	1.8	3.0
Korea, Dem. Rep.	..	..	2.0	2.7	..	..	..	..	..	..
Korea, Rep.	8.1	6.6	1.5	2.6	2.2	11.0	7.7	7.4	11.9	15.8
Kuwait	1.1	–3.0	4.2	4.3	9.8	–4.2	6.3	7.8	8.5	–3.0
Kyrgyz Republic	..	..	1.8	2.0	..	..	..	..	..	..
Lao PDR	..	..	2.2	..	..	..	..	..	..	..
Latvia	1.7	1.4	0.2	0.3	15.8	–0.9	10.9	..	..	..
Lebanon	..	..	1.9	2.4	..	..	..	..	..	..
Lesotho	5.6	3.1	2.3	2.0	–0.8	12.7	5.7	3.4	11.4	6.0
Libya	1.2	..	3.6	3.3	10.3	–1.2	11.4	12.1	..	–1.2
Lithuania	..	..	0.7	0.8	..	..	..	..	..	..
Macedonia, FYR	..	..	..	..	..	..	..	..	..	..
Madagascar	0.8	–1.8	2.6	2.4	1.5	–0.1	0.4	0.3	1.1	–0.6
Malawi	3.7	0.5	3.0	2.7	3.0	3.6	3.9	3.1	–3.6	3.7
Malaysia	6.8	4.1	2.6	3.1	3.5	8.5	7.0	6.0	9.8	9.8
Mali	2.4	–0.1	2.4	2.2	3.3	3.4	2.4	2.5	2.1	6.8
Mauritania	2.4	–0.1	2.5	2.2	1.3	2.6	3.1	2.7	..	2.2
Mauritius	5.2	3.8	1.3	2.4	–0.2	7.5	6.5	5.0	4.3	5.8
Mexico	3.9	1.5	2.4	3.3	2.1	4.1	4.2	3.7	3.6	10.0
Moldova	..	..	0.8	0.7	..	..	..	..	..	..
Mongolia	1.9	–0.6	2.6	2.7	0.9	0.5	2.1	..	..	..
Morocco	4.1	1.8	2.2	2.6	2.4	4.0	5.3	4.7	4.2	3.7
Mozambique	2.2	0.5	2.1	1.9	..	..	..	0.8	5.6	6.0
Myanmar	3.3	..	1.8	2.0	3.3	4.3	3.4	2.8	5.4	3.8
Namibia	3.4	0.7	2.6	2.2	3.3	1.0	2.5	–0.4	2.2	2.6
Nepal	3.7	1.1	2.4	2.0	2.3	8.0	4.6	3.9	6.2	8.8
Netherlands	2.6	1.9	0.7	1.5	4.1	1.3	2.5	2.6	1.4	5.0
New Zealand	1.7	0.7	1.1	1.9	3.5	1.2	2.0	1.6	2.1	4.3
Nicaragua	–0.4	–3.3	3.0	3.6	0.0	–0.1	–0.2	–0.8	0.6	0.8
Niger	0.6	–2.5	3.1	2.8	0.1	5.0	0.2	1.4	–5.5	–0.7
Nigeria	3.0	0.0	2.9	2.7	1.5	4.0	4.8	2.4	0.2	2.5
Norway	3.5	3.0	0.5	1.3	1.5	3.9	2.6	2.7	1.9	5.3
Oman	9.7	5.1	3.9	3.8	..	..	..	..	..	..
Pakistan	5.6	2.7	2.8	2.9	4.1	6.7	6.2	5.1	4.4	6.4
Panama	3.0	0.7	2.3	2.9	2.1	2.5	2.5	4.4	4.3	–0.1
Papua New Guinea	2.8	0.5	2.3	2.1	2.7	5.9	2.4	2.8	1.7	7.4
Paraguay	5.3	2.3	2.8	3.0	4.4	5.8	5.4	5.8	7.0	8.8
Peru	2.1	–0.3	2.3	2.9	1.7	2.2	2.1	2.0	2.6	2.0
Philippines	3.5	0.9	2.6	2.9	2.3	3.5	4.0	3.7	4.4	6.5
Poland	2.3	1.8	0.6	0.6	..	..	..	..	3.5	10.7
Portugal	3.6	3.2	0.3	1.0	..	..	..	3.4	3.1	5.5
Puerto Rico	2.9	1.6	1.2	2.0	1.7	4.3	3.3	2.9	0.4	4.4
Romania	–0.1	–0.4	0.5	0.0	..	..	..	..	..	..
Russian Federation	..	..	0.4	0.7	..	..	..	..	..	..

1.4 Trends in long-term economic development

	Gross national product		Population		Value added			Private consumption	Gross domestic fixed investment	Exports of goods and services
	average annual % growth		average annual % growth		average annual % growth			average annual % growth	average annual % growth	average annual % growth
	Total 1965–98	Per capita 1965–98	Total 1965–98	Labor force 1965–98	Agriculture 1965–98	Industry 1965–98	Services 1965–98	1965–98	1965–98	1965–98
Rwanda	2.7	0.0	2.8	2.8	2.3	2.5	4.3	3.3	6.4	2.9
Saudi Arabia	*5.4*	0.5	4.4	4.9	*7.4*	*3.2*	*6.9*	..	..	..
Senegal	*2.4*	–0.4	2.8	2.6	1.1	3.7	2.4	2.4	3.1	1.6
Sierra Leone	0.5	–1.6	2.1	1.7	3.2	*–0.8*	*0.6*	*–1.2*	..	*–3.7*
Singapore	8.4	6.4	1.9	3.1	–1.4	8.5	8.5	6.6	9.6	..
Slovak Republic	..	..	0.6	1.3	..	..	..	..	..	..
Slovenia	..	..	0.6	0.8	..	..	..	..	..	..
South Africa	2.4	0.1	2.2	2.4	2.0	1.9	3.1	3.2	1.6	1.7
Spain	3.0	2.3	0.6	1.1	..	..	..	*2.9*	*2.8*	*7.3*
Sri Lanka	4.6	3.0	1.6	2.2	2.7	5.1	5.2	4.1	7.6	*4.4*
Sudan	2.5	–0.2	2.5	2.6	3.0	*3.7*	*3.5*	*4.0*	..	*–2.1*
Sweden	1.7	1.4	0.4	1.0	*0.5*	*1.4*	*2.4*	*1.4*	*0.9*	*4.5*
Switzerland	1.6	1.2	0.6	1.0	..	..	..	*1.7*	*1.9*	*3.7*
Syrian Arab Republic	5.3	2.0	3.2	3.3	*4.4*	*8.4*	*6.3*	*4.6*	*0.6*	*6.3*
Tajikistan	..	..	2.7	2.7	..	..	..	..	..	..
Tanzania	..	..	3.0	2.9	..	..	..	..	..	..
Thailand	7.3	5.0	2.1	2.6	4.0	9.5	7.3	6.1	*9.0*	11.3
Togo	2.4	–0.6	3.1	2.7	3.5	2.9	1.4	3.2	*–0.9*	3.4
Trinidad and Tobago	3.7	2.6	1.1	2.0	*–2.0*	*0.1*	*2.4*	3.3	..	4.0
Tunisia	5.1	2.7	2.1	2.8	3.9	6.0	5.0	5.7	4.4	6.8
Turkey	*4.3*	2.1	2.2	2.1	*1.3*	*5.6*	*5.0*	..	..	..
Turkmenistan	..	..	2.8	3.1	..	..	..	..	..	..
Uganda	..	..	2.9	2.6	..	..	..	..	..	..
Ukraine	..	..	0.3	0.3	..	..	..	..	..	..
United Arab Emirates	*3.7*	–3.6	9.5	10.5	*11.5*	*1.2*	*6.4*	..	..	..
United Kingdom	2.1	1.9	0.3	0.5	..	..	..	*2.5*	*1.8*	*4.1*
United States	2.6	1.6	1.0	1.6	..	..	..	*3.0*	*2.4*	*5.7*
Uruguay	1.8	1.2	0.6	1.0	1.5	1.2	2.4	1.7	2.0	5.9
Uzbekistan	..	..	2.6	2.9	..	..	..	..	..	..
Venezuela, RB	*2.0*	–0.8	2.8	3.7	2.7	1.6	2.7	*2.4*	1.2	*2.0*
Vietnam	..	..	2.1	2.1	..	..	..	..	..	..
West Bank and Gaza	..	..	..	..	..	..	..	..	..	..
Yemen, Rep.	..	..	3.2	2.8	..	..	..	..	..	..
Yugoslavia, FR (Serb./Mont.)	..	..	0.7	0.9	..	..	..	..	..	..
Zambia	1.1	–2.0	3.0	2.7	0.8	0.0	2.2	0.6	*–5.3*	–0.8
Zimbabwe	3.5	0.5	2.9	2.9	*2.1*	*1.3*	*4.5*	4.1	*2.6*	*6.7*
World	**3.2 w**	**1.4 w**	**1.7 w**	**2.0 w**	**2.3 w**	**.. w**	**.. w**	**3.4 w**	**3.2 w**	**5.7 w**
Low income	5.9	3.7	2.1	2.2	3.3	7.8	6.5	5.3	7.0	7.0
Excl. China & India	4.3	1.7	2.5	2.5	2.8	5.7	5.1	4.2	4.0	4.3
Middle income	3.7	1.9	1.7	1.9	2.3	2.9	3.9	..	2.6	6.1
Lower middle income	..	..	1.6	1.7	..	..	..	..	..	..
Upper middle income	4.2	2.2	1.9	2.3	2.4	3.6	4.2	..	3.6	8.4
Low & middle income	4.2	2.2	2.0	2.1	2.9	4.3	4.6	4.1	3.7	5.6
East Asia & Pacific	7.5	5.7	1.8	2.2	3.6	9.9	7.9	6.7	9.8	10.5
Europe & Central Asia	..	..	0.8	0.9	..	..	..	..	..	..
Latin America & Carib.	3.5	1.3	2.1	2.8	2.6	3.2	3.9	3.5	1.8	5.9
Middle East & N. Africa	3.1	0.2	2.8	2.8	4.2	1.3	4.1	..	..	..
South Asia	4.9	2.7	2.2	2.1	2.9	5.5	5.7	4.5	5.2	7.2
Sub-Saharan Africa	2.6	–0.3	2.7	2.5	1.9	2.5	3.1	2.7	0.0	2.5
High income	3.0	2.3	0.7	1.1	..	..	..	3.2	3.0	5.7
Europe EMU	..	..	0.4	0.7	..	..	..	..	..	5.4

a. Data refer to GDP.

Trends in long-term economic development 1.4

About the data

The long-term trends shown in this table provide a view of the relative rates of change of key social and economic indicators over the period 1965–98. In viewing these growth rates, it may be helpful to keep in mind that a quantity growing at 2.3 percent a year will double in 30 years, while a quantity growing at 7 percent a year will double in 10 years. But like all averages, the rates reflect the general tendency and may disguise considerable year-to-year variation, especially for economic indicators.

Average annual growth rates of gross national product, value added, private consumption, gross domestic fixed investment, and exports of goods and services are calculated from data in 1995 constant prices using the least-squares method. See *Statistical methods* for more information on the calculation of growth rates. All the indicators shown here appear elsewhere in the *World Development Indicators*. For more information about them see *About the data* for tables 1.1 (GNP and GNP per capita), 2.1 (population), 2.3 (labor force), 4.2 (value added by industrial origin), 4.9 (exports of goods and services), and 4.10 (private consumption and gross domestic investment).

Definitions

• **Gross national product** (GNP) is the sum of value added by all resident producers plus any taxes (less subsidies) not included in the valuation of output plus net receipts of primary income (compensation of employees and property income) from abroad. • **GNP per capita** is gross national product divided by midyear population. • **Average annual growth of total population** and **labor force** is calculated using the exponential endpoint method. • **Labor force** comprises all people who meet the International Labour Organization's definition of the economically active population. • **Value added** is the net output of a sector after adding up all outputs and subtracting intermediate inputs. It is calculated without making deductions for depreciation of fabricated assets or depletion and degradation of natural resources. The industrial origin of value added is determined by the International Standard Industrial Classification (ISIC) revision 3. • **Agriculture** corresponds to ISIC major divisions 1–5. • **Industry** comprises ISIC divisions 10–45. • **Services** correspond to ISIC divisions 50–99. • **Private consumption** is the market value of all goods and services, including durable products, purchased or received as income in kind by households and nonprofit institutions. It excludes purchases of dwellings but includes imputed rent for owner-occupied dwellings. • **Gross domestic fixed investment** consists of outlays on additions to the fixed assets of the economy. • **Exports of goods and services** are the value of all goods and market services provided to the rest of the world.

Data sources

The indicators here and throughout the rest of the book have been compiled by World Bank staff from primary and secondary sources. More information about the indicators and their sources can be found in the *About the data, Definitions,* and *Data sources* entries that accompany each table in subsequent sections.

1.5 Long-term structural change

	Agriculture value added		Labor force in agriculture		Urban population		Trade		Central government revenue		Money and quasi money	
	% of GDP		% of total labor force		% of total population		% of GDP		% of GDP		% of GDP	
	1970	1998	1970	1990	1970	1998	1970	1998	1970	1998	1970	1998
Albania	..	54	66	55	32	40	..	42	..	19	..	48
Algeria	11	12	47	26	40	59	51	47	..	*32*	51	43
Angola	..	12	78	75	15	33	..	93	..	..	..	17
Argentina	10	6	16	12	78	89	10	23	..	*14*	21	27
Armenia	..	33	27	18	59	69	..	71	..	..	..	9
Australia	6	*3*	8	6	85	85	29	*42*	21	24	44	64
Austria	..	*1*	15	8	65	65	60	*85*	28	*37*	..	..
Azerbaijan	..	20	35	31	50	57	..	83	..	19	..	12
Bangladesh	42	22	81	65	8	23	17	33	..	..	..	29
Belarus	..	13	35	20	44	71	..	130	..	31	..	21
Belgium	3	*1*	5	3	94	97	100	*141*	35	*44*	..	..
Benin	36	39	81	64	17	41	50	55	..	..	10	21
Bolivia	..	15	55	47	41	61	62	49	..	17	16	45
Bosnia and Herzegovina	..	..	50	11	27	42	..	..	..	..	..	..
Botswana	28	4	82	46	8	49	71	69	*17*	*44*	..	24
Brazil	12	8	45	23	56	80	14	18	..	..	17	30
Bulgaria	..	19	35	13	52	69	..	91	..	34	..	28
Burkina Faso	35	33	92	92	6	17	23	44	..	..	8	23
Burundi	71	54	94	92	2	8	22	28	..	*14*	9	*19*
Cambodia	..	51	79	74	12	15	14	78	..	..	..	11
Cameroon	31	42	85	70	20	47	51	51	..	..	14	14
Canada	5	..	8	3	76	77	43	*80*	*19*	..	36	64
Central African Republic	35	53	89	80	30	40	74	41	..	..	15	17
Chad	40	40	92	83	12	23	38	51	*8*	..	7	11
Chile	7	7	24	19	75	85	29	56	*29*	22	12	42
China	35	18	78	72	17	31	4	39	..	*6*	..	124
Hong Kong, China	..	*0*	4	1	88	100	181	250	..	..	..	187
Colombia	29	13	41	27	57	73	31	34	*9*	12	15	21
Congo, Dem. Rep.	15	*58*	75	68	30	30	35	*46*	*11*	*5*	8	..
Congo, Rep.	18	12	66	49	33	61	92	135	22	*30*	17	16
Costa Rica	23	15	43	26	40	47	63	100	*15*	*26*	19	39
Côte d'Ivoire	32	26	76	60	27	45	65	82	..	21	25	26
Croatia	..	9	50	16	40	57	..	89	..	45	..	39
Cuba	..	..	30	18	60	75	..	..	..	..	..	..
Czech Republic	..	4	17	11	52	75	..	121	..	33	..	66
Denmark	6	..	11	6	80	85	60	*69*	34	..	44	58
Dominican Republic	23	12	48	25	40	64	42	70	*18*	*17*	18	28
Ecuador	24	13	51	33	40	63	33	62	..	..	20	33
Egypt, Arab Rep.	29	17	52	40	42	45	33	40	..	*26*	34	75
El Salvador	40	12	57	36	39	46	49	59	*11*	..	20	44
Eritrea	..	*9*	86	80	11	18	..	110	..	..	..	..
Estonia	..	6	18	14	65	69	..	169	..	32	..	28
Ethiopia	..	50	91	86	9	17	..	43	..	..	..	40
Finland	12	*4*	20	8	50	66	53	*71*	*26*	*32*	..	..
France	..	*2*	14	5	71	75	31	*49*	*33*	*42*	..	..
Gabon	19	7	79	52	31	79	88	91	..	..	15	17
Gambia, The	34	27	87	82	15	31	79	113	*16*	..	17	28
Georgia	..	26	37	26	48	60	..	42	..	6	..	5
Germany	..	*1*	9	4	80	87	..	*52*	..	31	..	..
Ghana	47	10	60	59	29	37	44	63	*15*	..	18	17
Greece	15	..	42	23	53	60	23	*40*	*22*	*23*	34	45
Guatemala	27	23	62	52	36	39	36	46	*9*	..	17	21
Guinea	..	22	92	87	14	31	..	45	..	10	..	*9*
Guinea-Bissau	50	62	89	85	15	23	34	50	..	..	..	*13*
Haiti	..	30	74	68	20	34	31	41	..	..	12	28
Honduras	32	20	65	41	29	51	62	98	12	..	19	35

Long-term structural change 1.5

	Agriculture value added % of GDP 1970	1998	Labor force in agriculture % of total labor force 1970	1990	Urban population % of total population 1970	1998	Trade % of GDP 1970	1998	Central government revenue % of GDP 1970	1998	Money and quasi money % of GDP 1970	1998
Hungary	..	*6*	25	15	49	64	63	102	..	36	..	..
India	45	29	71	64	20	28	8	25	..	12	20	44
Indonesia	45	20	66	55	17	39	28	98	*13*	17	8	49
Iran, Islamic Rep.	..	*25*	44	39	42	61	..	28	..	27	..	39
Iraq	..	..	47	16	56	71	..	..	..	..	22	..
Ireland	..	..	26	14	52	59	79	*142*	30	*33*	..	..
Israel	..	..	10	4	84	91	79	75	*33*	43	47	84
Italy	8	*3*	19	9	64	67	33	*50*	..	41	..	..
Jamaica	7	8	33	25	42	55	71	112	..	..	30	49
Japan	6	*2*	20	7	71	79	20	*21*	11	..	69	119
Jordan	12	3	28	15	51	73	..	120	..	*27*	54	101
Kazakhstan	..	9	27	22	50	56	..	66	..	..	..	9
Kenya	33	26	86	80	10	31	60	57	*17*	*27*	27	40
Korea, Dem. Rep.	..	..	55	38	54	60	..	..	..	..	..	..
Korea, Rep.	26	5	49	18	41	80	37	85	15	*20*	29	51
Kuwait	0	..	2	1	78	97	84	92	*42*	..	36	99
Kyrgyz Republic	..	46	36	32	37	34	..	87	..	..	..	13
Lao PDR	..	53	81	78	10	22	..	9	..	..	..	15
Latvia	..	5	19	16	62	69	..	109	..	32	..	25
Lebanon	..	12	20	7	59	89	..	62	..	17	..	143
Lesotho	35	11	43	40	9	26	65	158	*20*	49	..	36
Libya	2	..	29	11	45	87	89	..	..	..	20	..
Lithuania	..	10	31	18	50	68	..	106	..	27	..	18
Macedonia, FYR	..	11	50	22	47	61	..	98	..	..	..	14
Madagascar	24	31	84	78	14	28	41	50	*14*	*9*	17	19
Malawi	44	36	91	87	6	22	63	74	*16*	..	18	15
Malaysia	29	13	54	27	34	56	80	207	*20*	*23*	31	96
Mali	66	47	93	86	14	29	31	58	..	..	13	22
Mauritania	29	25	84	55	14	55	57	95	..	..	8	15
Mauritius	16	9	34	17	42	41	85	130	..	21	35	75
Mexico	12	5	44	28	59	74	17	64	*10*	*15*	15	26
Moldova	..	29	54	33	32	46	..	122	..	..	..	21
Mongolia	..	33	48	32	45	62	..	105	..	20	..	19
Morocco	20	17	58	45	35	55	38	44	19	..	28	70
Mozambique	..	34	86	83	6	38	..	42	..	..	..	20
Myanmar	38	53	78	73	23	27	14	2	..	*8*	24	24
Namibia	..	10	64	49	19	30	..	126	..	..	..	40
Nepal	67	40	94	83	4	11	13	58	*5*	11	11	41
Netherlands	..	..	7	5	86	89	89	*105*	..	*46*	..	..
New Zealand	*12*	..	12	10	81	86	48	*57*	28	34	20	91
Nicaragua	25	34	50	28	47	55	56	111	12	..	14	59
Niger	65	41	93	90	9	20	29	40	..	..	5	7
Nigeria	41	32	71	43	20	42	20	55	*10*	..	9	13
Norway	..	*2*	12	6	65	75	74	*75*	*32*	*43*	49	53
Oman	16	..	57	45	11	81	93	..	38	25	..	36
Pakistan	37	26	59	52	25	36	22	36	..	16	41	44
Panama	..	8	42	26	48	56	..	77	..	*25*	22	74
Papua New Guinea	37	24	86	79	10	17	72	138	..	..	..	35
Paraguay	32	25	53	39	37	55	31	94	*11*	..	17	28
Peru	19	7	48	36	57	72	34	29	14	16	18	26
Philippines	30	17	58	46	33	57	43	116	*13*	*19*	23	58
Poland	..	*5*	39	27	52	65	..	*56*	..	36	..	36
Portugal	..	..	32	18	26	61	50	*72*	..	*36*	..	..
Puerto Rico	3	..	14	4	58	74	107	..	..	..	..	..
Romania	..	16	49	24	42	56	..	60	..	*26*	..	23
Russian Federation	..	7	19	14	63	77	..	58	..	..	..	20

1.5 Long-term structural change

	Agriculture value added		Labor force in agriculture		Urban population		Trade		Central government revenue		Money and quasi money	
	% of GDP		% of total labor force		% of total population		% of GDP		% of GDP		% of GDP	
	1970	1998	1970	1990	1970	1998	1970	1998	1970	1998	1970	1998
Rwanda	66	47	94	92	3	6	27	28	..	..	11	14
Saudi Arabia	4	7	64	19	49	85	89	67	..	..	13	57
Senegal	24	17	83	77	33	46	56	71	16	..	14	22
Sierra Leone	30	44	76	67	18	35	48	53	..	*11*	13	13
Singapore	2	0	3	0	100	100	232	287	21	*24*	62	101
Slovak Republic	..	4	17	12	41	57	..	139	..	..	..	64
Slovenia	..	4	50	6	37	50	..	115	..	..	..	42
South Africa	7	4	31	14	48	53	46	50	*21*	26	58	53
Spain	..	*3*	26	12	66	77	27	*56*	18	*30*	..	..
Sri Lanka	28	21	55	48	22	23	54	78	20	17	22	30
Sudan	44	39	77	69	16	34	33	..	*17*	..	17	8
Sweden	..	..	..	..	81	83	48	*81*	29	40	..	..
Switzerland	..	..	8	6	55	68	64	*75*	14	*24*	100	144
Syrian Arab Republic	20	..	50	33	43	54	39	69	*25*	*24*	34	34
Tajikistan	..	6	46	41	37	28	..	..	..	..	..	..
Tanzania	..	46[a]	90	84	7	31	..	43[a]	..	..	..	19
Thailand	26	11	80	64	13	21	34	101	*12*	16	27	99
Togo	34	42	74	66	13	32	88	74	..	..	17	22
Trinidad and Tobago	5	2	19	11	63	73	84	98	..	..	27	47
Tunisia	17	12	42	28	45	64	47	88	*23*	*30*	32	47
Turkey	40	18	71	53	38	73	10	53	14	*22*	20	30
Turkmenistan	..	25	38	37	48	45	..	..	..	..	..	..
Uganda	54	45	90	85	8	14	44	30	*14*	..	17	11
Ukraine	..	14	31	20	55	68	..	83	..	..	..	13
United Arab Emirates	..	..	9	8	57	85	..	..	..	3	..	56
United Kingdom	3	*2*	3	2	89	89	45	*58*	37	38	..	..
United States	3	*2*	4	3	74	77	11	*26*	*18*	22	63	61
Uruguay	18	8	19	14	82	91	29	44	*24*	32	20	41
Uzbekistan	..	31	44	35	37	38	..	45	..	..	..	..
Venezuela, RB	6	5	26	12	72	86	38	40	17	17	19	18
Vietnam	..	26	77	71	18	20	..	*95*	..	18	..	*20*
West Bank and Gaza	..	7	..	..	..	..	..	90	..	..	..	..
Yemen, Rep.	..	18	70	61	13	24	..	88	..	41	..	43
Yugoslavia, FR (Serb./Mont.)	..	..	50	30	39	52	..	..	..	..	..	..
Zambia	11	17	79	75	30	39	90	68	*22*	..	25	16
Zimbabwe	17	19	77	68	17	34	..	94	..	*29*	..	24
World	9 w	*4* w	55 w	49 w	37 w	46 w	28 w	*45* w	*18* w	*27* w		
Low income	39	23	75	68	18	30	12	46	..	*10*		
Excl. China & India	41	26	76	65	17	31	30	74	..	*18*		
Middle income	17	9	40	28	49	65	30	56	*9*	..		
Lower middle income	..	11	39	30	46	58	..	65	..	..		
Upper middle income	16	8	42	25	54	77	27	52	5	..		
Low & middle income	24	13	66	57	28	41	25	53	..	..		
East Asia & Pacific	33	15	76	68	19	34	24	75	..	*14*		
Europe & Central Asia	..	12	33	23	52	66	..	71	..	..		
Latin America & Carib.	13	8	41	25	57	75	20	32	1	..		
Middle East & N. Africa	13	*14*	50	35	41	57	..	53	..	..		
South Asia	43	28	71	63	19	28	12	29	..	12		
Sub-Saharan Africa	21	17	78	68	19	33	47	59	*18*	..		
High income	5	*2*	11	5	73	77	29	*44*	*19*	*30*		
Europe EMU	..	*2*	15	7	71	78	..	*61*	..	*39*		

a. The data for GDP and its components refer to mainland Tanzania only.

Long-term structural change 1.5

About the data

Over a period of 25 years or longer cumulative processes of change reshape an economy and the social order built on that economy. This table highlights some of the notable trends at work for much of the past century: the shift of production from agriculture to manufacturing and services; the reduction of the agricultural labor force and the growth of urban centers; the expansion of trade; the increasing size of the central government in most countries—and the reversal of this trend in some; and the monetization of economies that have achieved stable macroeconomic management. All the indicators shown here appear elsewhere in the *World Development Indicators*. For more information about them see tables 2.4 (labor force employed in agriculture), 3.10 (urban population), 4.2 (agriculture value added), 4.13 (central government revenue), 4.16 (money and quasi money), and 6.1 (trade).

Definitions

• **Agriculture value added** is the sum of outputs of the agricultural sector (International Standard Industrial Classification major divisions 1–5) less the cost of intermediate inputs, measured as a share of gross domestic product (GDP). • **Labor force in agriculture** is the percentage of the total labor force recorded as working in agriculture, hunting, forestry, and fishing (ISIC major divisions 1–5). • **Urban population** is the share of the total population living in areas defined as urban in each country. • **Trade** is the sum of exports and imports of goods and services, measured as a share of GDP. • **Central government revenue** includes all revenue to the central government from taxes and nonrepayable receipts (other than grants), measured as a share of GDP. • **Money and quasi money** comprise the sum of currency outside banks, demand deposits other than those of the central government, and the time, savings, and foreign currency deposits of resident sectors other than the central government. This measure of the money supply is commonly called M2.

Data sources

The indicators here and throughout the rest of the book have been compiled by World Bank staff from primary and secondary sources. More information about the indicators and their sources can be found in the *About the data, Definitions,* and *Data sources* entries that accompany each table in subsequent sections.

1.6 Key indicators for other economies

	Population	Surface area	Population density	Gross national product						Life expectancy at birth	Adult illiteracy rate	Carbon dioxide emissions
						Per capita						
	thousands	thousand sq. km	people per sq. km	$ millions	Average annual growth %	$	Average annual growth %	PPP $ millions	PPP per capita $	years	% of people 15 and above	thousand metric tons
	1998	1998	1998	1998[a]	1997–98	1998[a]	1997–98	1998[b]	1998[b]	1998	1998	1996
Afghanistan	25,051	652.1	38	..	..	..[c]	..	..	..	46	65	1,176
American Samoa	63	0.2	315	..	..	..[d]	..	..	..	..	..	282
Andorra	65	0.5	144	..	..	..[e]	..	..	..	..	..	..
Antigua and Barbuda	67	0.4	152	565	3.7	8,450	2.9	594	8,890	75	..	322
Aruba	94	0.2	495	..	..	..[e]	..	..	..	..	..	1,517
Bahamas, The	294	13.9	29	..	3.0	..[e]	1.2	4,113	13,990	74	5	1,707
Bahrain	643	0.7	932	4,909	2.1	7,640	–1.5	7,430	11,556	73	14	10,578
Barbados	266	0.4	618	..	4.4	..[d]	4.1	..	..	76	..	835
Belize	239	23.0	10	635	3.0	2,660	–0.9	1,042	4,367	75	..	355
Bermuda	63	0.1	1,260	..	..	..[e]	..	1,458	23,302	..	..	462
Bhutan	759	47.0	16	354	5.5	470	2.4	1,092[f]	1,438[f]	61	..	260
Brunei	315	5.8	60	..	..	..[e]	..	7,836[f]	24,886[f]	76	9	5,071
Cape Verde	416	4.0	103	499	5.2	1,200	2.2	1,327[f]	3,192[f]	68	27	121
Cayman Islands	36	0.3	138	..	..	..[e]	..	..	..	..	..	282
Channel Islands	149	0.3	479	..	..	..[e]	..	..	..	79	..	..
Comoros	531	2.2	238	197	0.0	370	–2.5	743[f]	1,400[f]	60	42	55
Cyprus	753	9.3	82	8,983	5.0	11,920	4.1	13,258[f]	17,599[f]	78	3	5,379
Djibouti	636	23.2	27	..	..	..[g]	..	..	..	50	..	366
Dominica	73	0.8	97	230	4.1	3,150	4.1	349	4,777	76	..	81
Equatorial Guinea	431	28.1	15	478	34.7	1,110	31.2	..	..	50	19	143
Faeroe Islands	44	1.4	31	..	..	..[e]	..	..	..	..	..	630
Fiji	790	18.3	43	1,748	–4.2	2,210	–5.2	3,236	4,094	73	8	762
French Polynesia	227	4.0	62	..	..	..[e]	..	4,608[f]	20,586[f]	72	..	561
Greenland	56	341.7	0	..	..	..[e]	..	..	..	68	..	509
Grenada	96	0.3	283	313	5.3	3,250	4.5	535	5,557	72	..	161
Guam	149	0.6	271	..	..	..[e]	..	..	..	77	..	4,078
Guyana	849	215.0	4	661	0.8	780	0.1	2,665[f]	3,139[f]	64	2	953
Iceland	274	103.0	3	7,626	5.9	27,830	5.1	6,788	24,774	79	..	2,195
Isle of Man	76	0.6	129	..	..	..[d]	..	..	..	..	..	..

About the data

This table shows data for 58 economies—small economies with populations between 30,000 and 1 million, smaller economies if they are members of the World Bank, and larger economies for which data are not regularly reported. Where data on GNP per capita are not available, the estimated range is given. In this year's edition this table excludes France's overseas departments—French Guiana, Guadeloupe, Martinique, and Réunion. The national accounts (GNP and other economic measures) of France now include these French overseas departments.

Definitions

• **Population** is based on the de facto definition of population, which counts all residents regardless of legal status or citizenship—except for refugees not permanently settled in the country of asylum, who are generally considered part of the population of their country of origin. The values shown are midyear estimates for 1998. See also table 2.1. • **Surface area** is a country's total area, including areas under inland bodies of water and some coastal waterways. • **Population density** is midyear population divided by land area in square kilometers. • **Gross national product** (GNP) is the sum of value added by all resident producers plus any taxes (less subsidies) not included in the valuation of output plus net receipts of primary income (compensation of employees and property

Key indicators for other economies 1.6

	Population	Surface area	Population density	Gross national product						Life expectancy at birth	Adult illiteracy rate	Carbon dioxide emissions
						Per capita						
					Average annual growth		Average annual growth	PPP	PPP per capita		% of people 15 and above	
	thousands	thousand sq. km	people per sq. km	$ millions	%	$	%	$ millions	$	years		thousand metric tons
	1998	1998	1998	1998[a]	1997–98	1998[a]	1997–98	1998[b]	1998[b]	1998	1998	1996
Kiribati	86	0.7	118	101	15.3	1,170	11.8	334[f]	3,880[f]	61	..	22
Liberia	2,962	111.4	31	..	..	..[c]	..	..	..	47	49	326
Liechtenstein	32	0.2	200	..	..	..[e]	..	..	..	..	..	..
Luxembourg	427	2.6	165	19,239	5.1	45,100	3.9	15,658	36,703	77	..	8,281
Macao, China	459	0.0	22,950	..	..	..[e]	..	..	..	78	..	1,407
Maldives	263	0.3	875	296	7.1	1,130	4.4	902[f]	3,436[f]	67	4	297
Malta	377	0.3	1,178	3,807	4.1	10,100	3.5	8,634[f]	22,901[f]	77	9	1,751
Marshall Islands	62	0.2	342	96	–4.3	1,540	–7.4	..	..	..	..	..
Mayotte	128	0.4	341	..	..	..[d]	..	..	..	..	..	..
Micronesia, Fed. Sts.	113	0.7	162	204	–3.1	1,800	–5.0	..	..	67	..	..
Monaco	32	0.0	16,410	..	..	..[e]	..	..	..	..	..	..
Netherlands Antilles	213	0.8	266	..	..	..[e]	..	..	..	76	4	6,430
New Caledonia	207	18.6	11	..	..	..[e]	..	..	..	73	..	1,751
Northern Mariana Islands	68	0.5	143	..	..	..[e]	..	..	..	..	..	..
Palau	19	0.5	40	..	..	..[d]	..	..	..	71	..	245
Qatar	742	11.0	67	..	..	..[e]	..	..	..	74	20	29,121
Samoa	169	2.8	60	181	1.3	1,070	0.9	652[f]	3,854[f]	69	..	132
São Tomé and Principe	142	1.0	148	38	1.4	270	–0.9	183[f]	1,289[f]	64	..	77
Seychelles	79	0.5	175	505	–1.7	6,420	–3.0	801[f]	10,185[f]	72	..	169
Solomon Islands	416	28.9	15	315	–7.0	760	–9.8	793[f]	1,904[f]	71	..	161
Somalia	9,076	637.7	14	..	..	..[c]	..	..	..	48	..	15
St. Kitts and Nevis	41	0.4	113	253	3.6	6,190	3.6	400	9,790	70	..	103
St. Lucia	152	0.6	249	556	3.0	3,660	1.4	744	4,897	72	..	191
St. Vincent and the Grenadines	113	0.4	290	290	5.2	2,560	4.4	508	4,484	73	..	125
Suriname	412	163.3	3	684	2.8	1,660	2.5	..	..	70	..	2,099
Swaziland	989	17.4	57	1,384	1.8	1,400	–1.3	4,147	4,195	56	22	341
Tonga	99	0.8	137	173	–1.5	1,750	–2.3	413[f]	4,187[f]	71	..	117
Vanuatu	183	12.2	15	231	2.1	1,260	–0.9	530[f]	2,892[f]	65	..	62
Virgin Islands (U.S.)	118	0.3	348	..	..	..[e]	..	..	..	77	..	12,912

a. Calculated using the World Bank Atlas method. b. PPP is purchasing power parity. See *Definitions*. c. Estimated to be low income ($760 or less). d. Estimated to be upper middle income ($3,031–9,360). e. Estimated to be high income ($9,361 or more). f. The estimate is based on regression; others are extrapolated from the latest International Comparison Programme benchmark estimates. g. Estimated to be lower middle income ($761–3,030).

income) from abroad. Data are in current U.S. dollars converted using the World Bank Atlas method (see *Statistical methods*). Growth is calculated from constant price GNP in national currency units. • **GNP per capita** is gross national product divided by midyear population. GNP per capita in U.S. dollars is converted using the World Bank Atlas method. Growth is calculated from constant price GNP per capita in national currency units. • **PPP GNP** is gross national product converted to international dollars using purchasing power parity rates. An international dollar has the same purchasing power over GNP as a U.S. dollar has in the United States. • **Life expectancy at birth** is the number of years a newborn infant would live if prevailing patterns of mortality at the time of its birth were to stay the same throughout its life. • **Adult illiteracy rate** is the percentage of adults aged 15 and above who cannot, with understanding, read and write a short, simple statement about their everyday life. • **Carbon dioxide emissions** are those stemming from the burning of fossil fuels and the manufacture of cement. They include carbon dioxide produced during consumption of solid, liquid, and gas fuels and gas flaring.

Data sources

The indicators here and throughout the rest of the book have been compiled by World Bank staff from primary and secondary sources. More information about the indicators and their sources can be found in the *About the data*, *Definitions*, and *Data sources* entries that accompany each table in subsequent sections.

The next billion people: who? where?

No social phenomenon has attracted more attention in the past half century than the "population explosion"—that surge from about 2.5 billion people in 1950 to more than 6 billion in 1999, making the 20th century one of unprecedented population growth. As the number of people grew, the interval for adding another billion people became shorter and shorter, with the increase from 5 billion to 6 billion occurring in only 12 years (figure 2a).

According to recent projections,[1] the 7 billion mark will be exceeded in 2014—the first time since reaching one billion that adding the next billion people is expected to take longer than for the previous billion (box 2a). More than half of the next billion will come from South Asia (310 million) and Sub-Saharan Africa (240 million). East Asia and the Pacific will add about 220 million, and the remaining 230 million will be divided mostly between the Middle East and North Africa and Latin America and the Caribbean. Europe and Central Asia will add 9 million people—just 1 percent—and the world's high-income countries will add 30 million (figure 2b).

Why the differences? Because of different rates of population growth and different base populations. Regions with the same growth rate will add more people when the rate is applied to a larger base. For example, Sub-Saharan Africa is growing at a much faster rate than South Asia, but South Asia will claim a larger share of the next billion people because of its larger population base.

The next billion people will also be born into less favorable economic circumstances. The majority—just under 600 million—are projected to be in low-income countries (as defined in 1999). Middle-income countries will add 375 million people, most of them in the lower-middle-income group. Today's high-income countries will add a scant 30 million, or 3 percent of the total, in the next 15 years (figure 2c).

And the next billion people will be predominantly urban, concentrated in cities and areas of current population settlement, particularly environmentally stressed seacoasts and river valleys. During these 15 years the urban population will increase from about 47 percent of the total to 54 percent, a net gain of 925 million, mostly due to migration from rural to urban areas and to the urbanization of rural areas.

Population's momentum in developing countries

The population growth rate is a key demographic characteristic of a country, but the composition of the population by age can have more important consequences. The age structure determines not only the allocation of resources

Box 2a

Projecting the future

By far the most common methodology for projecting future populations is the cohort component method, used in the projections by the World Bank and by many other international organizations and national statistical agencies.

The cohort component method involves first compiling information on the characteristics of a country's population in the starting, or base, year for the projection. The necessary pieces of information consist of estimates of the population by age and sex in the projection's base year—and estimates of fertility, mortality, and net migration by age and sex for the base year or the period immediately preceding it.

The sources for these base year estimates vary. For population, they are usually recent censuses or estimates from national statistical offices based on registration data. For vital rates, vital registration systems are the preferred source, but demographic surveys are frequently the only source available.

In many developing countries no recent census is available, and current estimates may be extrapolations by the country, United Nations agencies, or others. The lack or poor quality of base year data is an important source of error in projections, which often becomes magnified as the projections extend into the future.

Few countries collect reliable data on net migration, as movements in, and especially out of, countries often are not monitored. Data from censuses, in countries that receive more migrants as well as in countries from which more migrants depart, are often used to obtain a picture of migratory movements.

The cohort component method for projecting national populations is based on assumptions on future trends in the three components of population growth:

- Fertility—the distribution over age at which women bear children.
- Mortality—the distribution over age at which people die.
- Migration—the number of people who move from one country to another.

In the World Bank's projections these future trends in vital rates and migration are derived from recent country-specific trends, in combination with a set of assumptions and demographic models.

For example, future fertility in countries with declining family size is assumed to follow a pattern in the near future similar to that in the recent past. The result: countries that had a fast fertility decline over the past 10 years are projected to maintain a faster than average decline. A similar assumption is made for changes in mortality: countries in which health conditions have been improving rapidly are assumed to have continued mortality decline in the near future. Models—such as model life tables and model fertility and migration schedules—are used to supplement and adjust empirical data.

Future patterns of vital rates and migration thus play a major role in projections, and misspecified patterns are an important source of error. The projections in the tables here use assumptions based on an analysis of observed past patterns, in which it was determined that preceding trends are the best predictor for following trends in vital rates.

Only two added variables are included in the projection of future trends in vital rates: urbanization and female enrollment in secondary education, both of which are fairly stable in the short term. Other variables, such as income, are subject to rapid changes and are therefore unsuitable for use in predicting changes in vital rates.

Complications in determining future trends in the components arise from the fact that not all future patterns reflect the past. In countries with high HIV prevalence, as in some Sub-Saharan countries, mortality trends are not likely to resemble past trends, but are more likely to turn upward as mortality from AIDS becomes more frequent. Projections for countries with measurable levels of HIV infection have been modified by separate projections of the impact of AIDS on mortality. In the most severely affected countries this has resulted in substantial declines in life expectancy and other mortality measures. Migration trends are particularly difficult to predict, as recent migration flows often reflect short-term causes of population movements, such as political violence, economic differences, or natural disasters.

Once estimates of a population's current size and composition have been made—and a method to estimate future levels of fertility, mortality, and migration has been established—the cohort component projection is carried out by applying age- and sex-specific estimates of the components to the age and sex distribution of the base population. The results consist of future estimates of population by age and sex, which in turn can be used as a base to which subsequent component estimates are applied.

Figure 2a

The interval for adding another billion in world population has become shorter and shorter

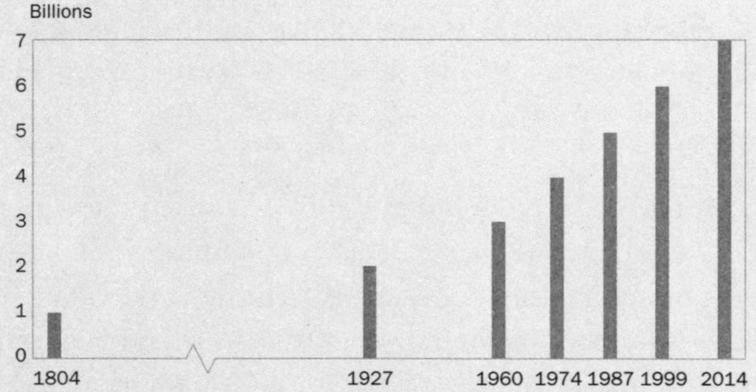

Source: World Bank staff estimates.

Figure 2b

Where the next billion will come from

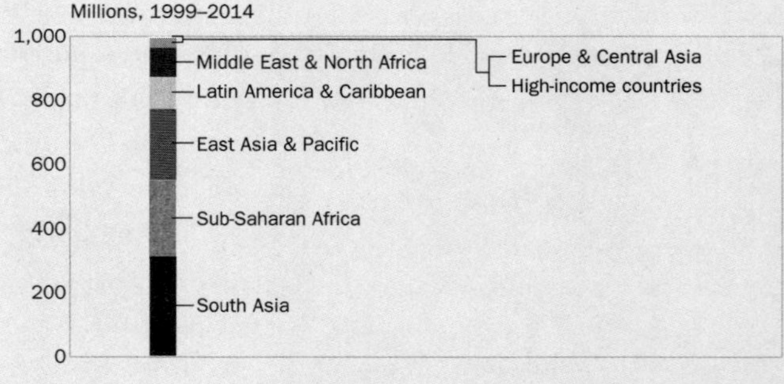

Source: World Bank staff estimates.

Figure 2c

Most of the next billion will be born in low-income countries

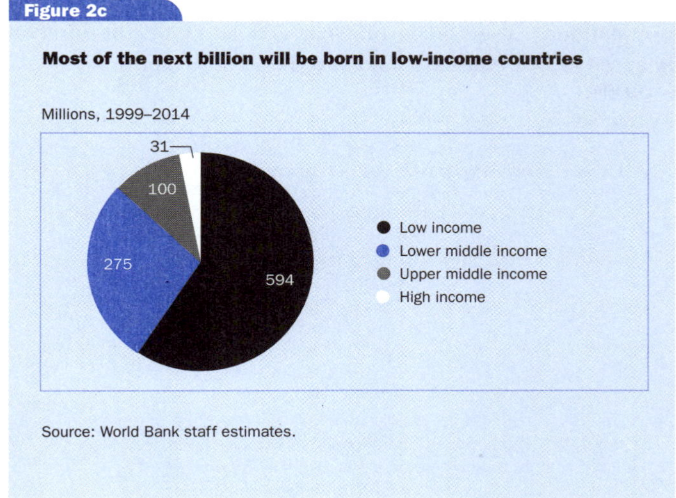

Source: World Bank staff estimates.

Figure 2d

Rapid growth in the working-age population in low-income countries will add to population momentum

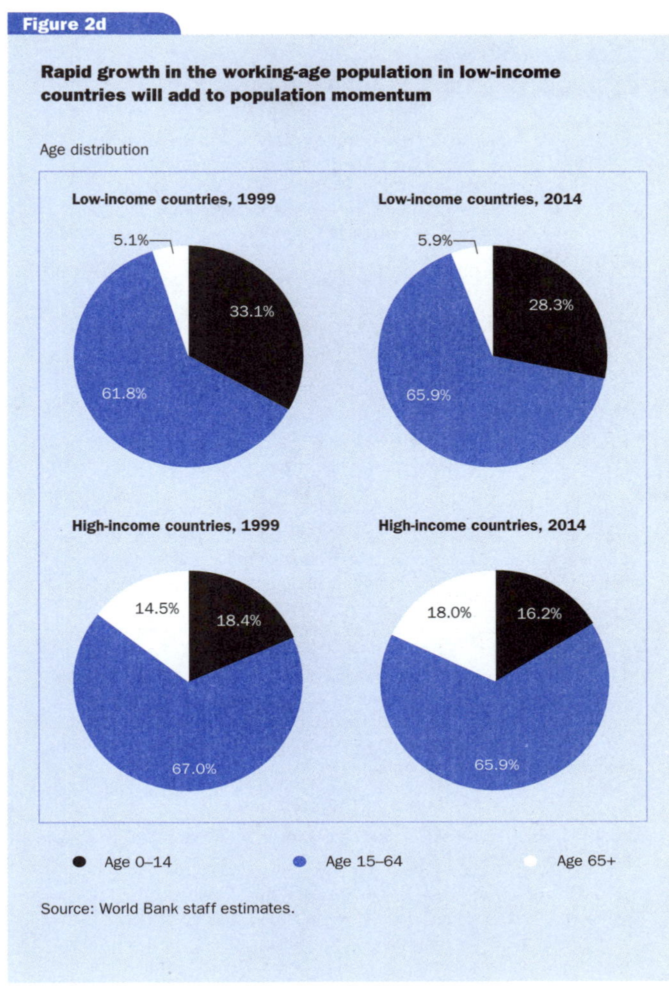

Source: World Bank staff estimates.

to education, health, and social security, but also birth and death rates. In 1999 a third of the people in the poorest countries were in the young-age dependent group (under 15 years old), but only a small fraction were aged 65 or older (figure 2d). By contrast, the high-income countries have a much smaller percentage under 15 (about 18 percent in 1999), but much greater old-age dependency.

By 2014 young-age dependency is expected to decline to 28 percent in the low-income countries as a result of projected fertility declines, and only a small increase is expected in the percentage at older ages. As a result the proportion of people of working age will increase to 66 percent. The rapid increase in the number of young working-age people will contribute to "population momentum." Although fertility rates will decline, the number of births will remain high because the number of couples entering reproductive ages is outpacing the decline in fertility rates. Such population momentum is becoming more important in South Asia. Bangladesh and India can expect to grow by 30–40 percent even as they reach replacement-level fertility, expected in the next 10–15 years.

A demographic bonus?

Why are these changes in age structure important? Because when fertility declines, young-age dependency ratios quickly follow suit. The ratio of working-age people to dependents rises as the young population increases more slowly than the working-age population. This happened first in East Asian countries, followed by Latin America and South Asia.

The long period of economic growth in East Asia occurred as young-age dependency dropped rapidly, but before the rise in old-age dependency, providing a demographic window of opportunity. Bloom and Williamson (1998) estimate that a third of the per capita GNP growth in some East Asian countries is due to this "demographic bonus." Pressures on education systems were reduced, allowing greater coverage and improvements in quality. These shifts brought transitory rises in savings rates—which, with increases in productive employment, gave an added boost to the East Asian economies.

But this demographic bonus does not come automatically. It requires a combination of policies that strengthen human capital development and allow the labor force to absorb new entrants. The declining dependency projected for low-income countries thus provides an opportunity as well as a challenge.

New demands for services

Countries that experienced earlier fertility declines, such as those in Europe, face rapid aging of their populations. In 2014 the proportion aged 65 or older in high-income countries will reach 18 percent. These shifts change the demands on health care systems and other social services, many of which may be unsustainable when the full effects of the new age structure are felt. To the extent that better management of chronic conditions increases life expectancy at older ages, resources for old-age support and health care may have to increase beyond current expectations.

Although developing countries have more time before their populations reach a mature age structure, the population aging will be faster than in Europe because of the rapid increase in the availability of technologies for reducing fertility. For countries now moving through these transitions, the required reforms in the financing and delivery of social services need to be enacted well in advance of the time when larger beneficiary populations will be using them. The timing of these reforms is critical.

Box 2b

Population and development

The 1994 International Conference on Population and Development (ICPD) held in Cairo adopted a program of action calling for new approaches to address the relationships between population and sustainable development. Human development issues—women's reproductive health, gender equality, adolescence—are at the core of the agreed action plan.

The conference endorsed an approach to population that deemphasizes demographic targets and instead stresses individuals' reproductive health rights, such as access to family planning, safe pregnancy and delivery, and prevention and treatment of sexually transmitted diseases. Sustainable population growth is seen as best achieved through individual reproductive choices freely made by women and men. The ICPD action plan led to the formulation of several indicators and targets that are now core international development goals, such as maternal mortality ratios (to be reduced by 75 percent by 2015), or that inform other goals, such as access to reproductive health. This second group includes universal access to safe and effective contraceptive methods, by 2015; a 50 percent reduction in the number of people who want to space or limit births but are not using family planning, by 2005; and an increase in the presence of skilled attendants to 90 percent of all births, by 2015.

In 1999, five years after the Cairo conference, the United Nations reviewed progress by countries in implementing the action program, at an "ICPD + 5" intergovernmental meeting. Among the achievements noted at ICPD + 5 was the widespread acceptance of viewing population as more than a demographic concept: population has become recognized as part of the development agenda, with governments and nongovernmental organizations jointly implementing reproductive health programs. Nevertheless, some parts of the action plan were seen as lagging, among them the capacity for data collection and analysis. Inadequate capacity in many countries is making it difficult to monitor ICPD goals for improving reproductive health.

Population growth, poverty, and human development

Most of the increase in the global population over the past five decades has occurred in developing countries, and future increases are projected to occur in the poorest of them, mainly in South Asia and Sub-Saharan Africa. Has this rapid population growth been good or bad for the economic prospects of these countries?

The links between population growth and poverty are complex. Evidence suggests that high fertility is as much a symptom of poverty as a cause. The poor continue to experience unacceptably poor reproductive health, including unwanted fertility, malnutrition, and high child and maternal mortality rates (box 2b). While poverty affects all, many of the burdens of poverty weigh more heavily on girls and women. In most parts of the developing world fewer girls than boys enroll, stay, and learn in school—with negative implications for future reductions in fertility and child mortality.

Some of the factors that affect fertility, and thus population growth, can be addressed by ensuring that programs in health and education are more focused, taking into account the different situations and needs of women and men. Since investment in health and education is the most widely accepted way of improving the asset base of the poor, gender-sensitive investment in human capital now not only will improve the environment in which future populations will be born, but may also lengthen the interval between the six billionth child and the seven billionth.

Note

1. For summary statistics see tables 2.1 and 2.2. The full set of demographic projections by country is available on the *World Development Indicators* CD-ROM.

2.1 Population

	Total population			Average annual population growth rate		Age dependency ratio		Population aged 65 and above		Women aged 65 and above	
	millions			%		dependents as proportion of working-age population		% of total		per 100 men	
	1980	1998	2015	1980–98	1998–2015	1980	1998	1998	2015	1998	2015
Albania	2.7	3.3	3.9	1.2	1.0	0.7	0.6	6.5	8.6	128	123
Algeria	18.7	29.9	39.8	2.6	1.7	1.0	0.7	3.8	4.7	115	117
Angola	7.0	12.0	19.4	3.0	2.8	0.9	1.0	2.9	2.5	124	123
Argentina	28.1	36.1	42.8	1.4	1.0	0.6	0.6	9.5	10.6	144	142
Armenia	3.1	3.8	4.1	1.1	0.4	0.6	0.5	8.4	10.9	150	157
Australia	14.7	18.8	21.5	1.4	0.8	0.5	0.5	11.8	15.2	129	120
Austria	7.6	8.1	8.0	0.4	–0.1	0.6	0.5	14.9	19.2	166	136
Azerbaijan	6.2	7.9	9.3	1.4	0.9	0.7	0.6	6.4	7.3	159	158
Bangladesh	86.7	125.6	161.8	2.1	1.5	1.0	0.8	3.3	4.0	81	94
Belarus	9.6	10.2	9.4	0.3	–0.5	0.5	0.5	13.0	13.4	202	181
Belgium	9.8	10.2	10.2	0.2	0.0	0.5	0.5	16.2	19.5	147	133
Benin	3.5	5.9	9.1	3.0	2.5	1.0	1.0	2.9	2.6	102	118
Bolivia	5.4	7.9	10.9	2.2	1.9	0.9	0.8	3.9	4.6	123	128
Bosnia and Herzegovina	4.1	3.8	4.3	–0.5	0.8	0.5	0.4	8.1	12.9	147	146
Botswana	0.9	1.6	1.8	3.0	0.9	1.0	0.8	2.3	1.7	173	146
Brazil	121.7	165.9	200.0	1.7	1.1	0.7	0.5	4.9	6.5	130	142
Bulgaria	8.9	8.3	7.3	–0.4	–0.7	0.5	0.5	15.5	18.9	134	148
Burkina Faso	7.0	10.7	15.9	2.4	2.3	1.0	1.0	2.8	2.2	110	143
Burundi	4.1	6.5	9.2	2.6	2.0	0.9	0.9	2.6	1.9	155	153
Cambodia	6.8	11.5	14.8	2.9	1.5	0.7	0.8	3.0	3.8	179	159
Cameroon	8.7	14.3	20.3	2.8	2.1	0.9	0.9	3.5	3.4	120	119
Canada	24.6	30.3	33.7	1.2	0.6	0.5	0.5	12.3	15.9	134	126
Central African Republic	2.3	3.5	4.6	2.3	1.6	0.8	0.9	3.6	2.6	138	139
Chad	4.5	7.3	11.6	2.7	2.7	0.8	1.2	3.1	2.2	89	150
Chile	11.1	14.8	17.7	1.6	1.1	0.6	0.6	6.9	9.7	143	136
China	981.2	1,238.6	1,388.5	1.3	0.7	0.7	0.5	6.7	8.9	105	104
Hong Kong, China	5.0	6.7	7.9	1.6	1.0	0.5	0.4	10.0	12.8	125	113
Colombia	28.4	40.8	51.4	2.0	1.4	0.8	0.6	4.5	5.7	130	138
Congo, Dem. Rep.	27.0	48.2	79.1	3.2	2.9	1.0	1.0	2.7	2.6	134	125
Congo, Rep.	1.7	2.8	4.3	2.8	2.6	0.9	1.0	3.1	2.4	131	140
Costa Rica	2.3	3.5	4.4	2.4	1.3	0.7	0.6	5.0	7.7	115	118
Côte d'Ivoire	8.2	14.5	19.1	3.2	1.6	1.0	0.9	2.7	2.3	93	86
Croatia	4.6	4.5	4.3	–0.1	–0.3	0.5	0.5	14.1	18.1	168	156
Cuba	9.7	11.1	11.6	0.7	0.3	0.7	0.4	9.2	14.0	110	120
Czech Republic	10.2	10.3	9.9	0.0	–0.2	0.6	0.4	13.5	18.6	160	141
Denmark	5.1	5.3	5.3	0.2	0.0	0.5	0.5	14.7	19.0	140	122
Dominican Republic	5.7	8.3	10.4	2.1	1.3	0.8	0.6	4.3	5.9	106	113
Ecuador	8.0	12.2	15.6	2.4	1.5	0.9	0.6	4.4	5.7	119	124
Egypt, Arab Rep.	40.9	61.4	78.7	2.3	1.5	0.8	0.7	4.4	5.5	120	115
El Salvador	4.6	6.1	8.0	1.5	1.6	0.9	0.7	4.7	5.1	131	135
Eritrea	2.4	3.9	5.7	2.7	2.3	..	0.9	2.7	2.8	130	121
Estonia	1.5	1.4	1.3	–0.1	–0.5	0.5	0.5	13.6	16.7	210	200
Ethiopia	37.7	61.3	87.6	2.7	2.1	0.9	1.0	2.7	2.0	127	105
Finland	4.8	5.2	5.3	0.4	0.1	0.5	0.5	14.5	20.2	165	138
France	53.9	58.8	61.1	0.5	0.2	0.6	0.5	15.5	18.1	150	139
Gabon	0.7	1.2	1.7	3.0	2.2	0.7	0.8	5.7	4.9	123	118
Gambia, The	0.6	1.2	1.8	3.6	2.2	0.8	0.8	3.0	3.4	121	118
Georgia	5.1	5.4	5.3	0.4	–0.1	0.5	0.5	12.2	14.7	170	172
Germany	78.3	82.0	78.7	0.3	–0.2	0.5	0.5	15.7	20.3	167	133
Ghana	10.7	18.5	26.8	3.0	2.2	0.9	0.9	3.1	3.5	120	119
Greece	9.6	10.5	10.3	0.5	–0.1	0.6	0.5	16.9	21.0	127	132
Guatemala	6.8	10.8	15.5	2.6	2.1	1.0	0.9	3.4	3.4	110	126
Guinea	4.5	7.1	10.0	2.6	2.0	0.9	0.9	2.6	2.7	110	105
Guinea-Bissau	0.8	1.2	1.6	2.1	1.8	0.8	0.9	4.0	3.5	124	120
Haiti	5.4	7.6	10.0	2.0	1.6	0.9	0.8	3.6	3.6	126	142
Honduras	3.6	6.2	8.8	3.0	2.1	1.0	0.8	3.2	3.6	118	121

Population 2.1

	Total population			Average annual population growth rate		Age dependency ratio		Population aged 65 and above		Women aged 65 and above	
		millions		%		dependents as proportion of working-age population		% of total		per 100 men	
	1980	1998	2015	1980–98	1998–2015	1980	1998	1998	2015	1998	2015
Hungary	10.7	10.1	9.4	–0.3	–0.4	0.5	0.5	14.3	17.1	166	166
India	687.3	979.7	1,224.4	2.0	1.3	0.7	0.6	4.7	5.7	107	107
Indonesia	148.3	203.7	250.5	1.8	1.2	0.8	0.6	4.5	6.0	117	123
Iran, Islamic Rep.	39.1	61.9	82.1	2.6	1.7	0.9	0.7	4.6	5.0	105	107
Iraq	13.0	22.3	31.3	3.0	2.0	0.9	0.8	3.1	4.2	114	111
Ireland	3.4	3.7	4.1	0.5	0.6	0.7	0.5	11.4	13.5	134	125
Israel	3.9	6.0	7.6	2.4	1.4	0.7	0.6	9.3	10.7	133	129
Italy	56.4	57.6	54.4	0.1	–0.3	0.5	0.5	17.0	22.5	145	142
Jamaica	2.1	2.6	3.0	1.0	0.9	0.9	0.6	6.4	7.3	126	120
Japan	116.8	126.4	124.4	0.4	–0.1	0.5	0.5	16.0	24.7	139	130
Jordan	2.2	4.6	6.7	4.1	2.3	1.1	0.8	2.9	4.1	79	101
Kazakhstan	14.9	15.6	16.3	0.3	0.3	0.6	0.5	7.1	8.1	197	173
Kenya	16.6	29.3	39.1	3.1	1.7	1.1	0.9	2.8	2.1	117	107
Korea, Dem. Rep.	17.7	23.2	26.2	1.5	0.7	0.8	0.5	4.9	7.2	189	126
Korea, Rep.	38.1	46.4	51.1	1.1	0.6	0.6	0.4	6.3	10.8	162	138
Kuwait	1.4	1.9	2.9	1.7	2.5	0.7	0.6	1.9	4.8	85	97
Kyrgyz Republic	3.6	4.7	5.6	1.4	1.1	0.8	0.7	5.9	5.5	170	159
Lao PDR	3.2	5.0	7.2	2.4	2.2	0.8	0.9	3.6	3.3	113	131
Latvia	2.5	2.4	2.1	–0.2	–0.8	0.5	0.5	14.0	17.8	218	197
Lebanon	3.0	4.2	5.2	1.9	1.2	0.8	0.6	5.7	5.9	117	132
Lesotho	1.3	2.1	2.7	2.4	1.6	0.9	0.8	4.1	4.7	132	123
Libya	3.0	5.3	7.4	3.1	2.0	1.0	0.7	3.0	5.0	90	95
Lithuania	3.4	3.7	3.6	0.5	–0.1	0.5	0.5	12.8	15.7	194	195
Macedonia, FYR	1.9	2.0	2.2	0.3	0.4	0.6	0.5	9.5	12.7	121	131
Madagascar	8.9	14.6	22.9	2.8	2.7	0.9	0.9	3.0	3.5	124	117
Malawi	6.2	10.5	15.3	3.0	2.2	1.0	1.0	2.5	2.5	118	103
Malaysia	13.8	22.2	29.2	2.7	1.6	0.8	0.6	4.0	6.0	118	119
Mali	6.6	10.6	16.7	2.6	2.7	1.0	1.0	3.3	2.7	134	135
Mauritania	1.6	2.5	3.7	2.7	2.3	0.9	0.9	3.1	3.3	136	122
Mauritius	1.0	1.2	1.3	1.0	0.9	0.6	0.5	6.1	8.7	133	139
Mexico	67.6	95.8	120.8	1.9	1.4	1.0	0.6	4.4	6.0	126	134
Moldova	4.0	4.3	4.2	0.4	–0.2	0.5	0.5	9.6	10.6	167	163
Mongolia	1.7	2.6	3.3	2.4	1.5	0.9	0.7	3.9	4.4	128	116
Morocco	19.4	27.8	35.3	2.0	1.4	0.9	0.6	4.3	5.2	116	134
Mozambique	12.1	16.9	23.8	1.9	2.0	0.9	0.9	3.9	3.2	84	132
Myanmar	33.8	44.5	53.8	1.5	1.1	0.8	0.5	4.7	5.3	118	125
Namibia	1.0	1.7	2.2	2.7	1.7	0.9	0.8	3.7	3.3	120	109
Nepal	14.5	22.9	32.5	2.5	2.1	0.8	0.8	3.6	3.9	98	108
Netherlands	14.2	15.7	16.3	0.6	0.2	0.5	0.5	13.5	17.9	144	124
New Zealand	3.1	3.8	4.1	1.1	0.5	0.6	0.5	11.6	14.8	130	126
Nicaragua	2.9	4.8	6.9	2.8	2.2	1.0	0.9	3.0	3.5	126	126
Niger	5.6	10.1	17.0	3.3	3.0	1.0	1.0	2.4	2.1	130	130
Nigeria	71.1	120.8	184.7	2.9	2.5	1.0	0.9	2.5	2.8	135	126
Norway	4.1	4.4	4.7	0.4	0.3	0.6	0.5	15.6	18.1	136	124
Oman	1.1	2.3	3.3	4.1	2.2	0.9	0.9	2.6	4.6	102	75
Pakistan	82.7	131.6	194.6	2.6	2.3	0.9	0.8	3.2	3.8	97	103
Panama	2.0	2.8	3.4	1.9	1.2	0.8	0.6	5.4	7.4	106	117
Papua New Guinea	3.1	4.6	6.2	2.2	1.8	0.8	0.7	3.1	3.9	105	113
Paraguay	3.1	5.2	7.3	2.9	1.9	0.9	0.8	3.4	4.1	140	122
Peru	17.3	24.8	31.8	2.0	1.5	0.8	0.6	4.5	5.6	120	125
Philippines	48.3	75.2	100.0	2.5	1.7	0.8	0.7	3.6	5.1	119	117
Poland	35.6	38.7	38.9	0.5	0.0	0.5	0.5	11.6	14.4	165	157
Portugal	9.8	10.0	9.8	0.1	–0.1	0.6	0.5	16.1	16.8	161	155
Puerto Rico	3.2	3.9	4.4	1.0	0.7	0.7	0.5	10.0	13.0	135	167
Romania	22.2	22.5	21.3	0.1	–0.3	0.6	0.5	12.5	14.5	138	149
Russian Federation	139.0	146.9	137.6	0.3	–0.4	0.5	0.5	12.2	13.4	223	190

2.1 Population

	Total population			Average annual population growth rate		Age dependency ratio		Population aged 65 and above		Women aged 65 and above	
	millions			%		dependents as proportion of working-age population		% of total		per 100 men	
	1980	1998	2015	1980–98	1998–2015	1980	1998	1998	2015	1998	2015
Rwanda	5.2	8.1	11.8	2.5	2.2	1.0	0.9	2.0	1.9	137	116
Saudi Arabia	9.4	20.7	33.7	4.4	2.9	0.9	0.8	2.8	4.4	97	71
Senegal	5.5	9.0	13.3	2.7	2.3	0.9	0.9	2.6	2.6	123	122
Sierra Leone	3.2	4.9	6.7	2.3	1.9	0.9	0.9	2.6	2.8	134	134
Singapore	2.3	3.2	3.7	1.8	1.0	0.5	0.4	6.6	11.4	122	114
Slovak Republic	5.0	5.4	5.5	0.4	0.1	0.6	0.5	11.1	13.4	159	158
Slovenia	1.9	2.0	1.9	0.2	–0.2	0.5	0.4	13.1	18.2	179	146
South Africa	27.6	41.4	49.4	2.3	1.0	0.7	0.6	4.8	4.7	164	124
Spain	37.4	39.4	38.1	0.3	–0.2	0.6	0.5	16.3	18.8	140	142
Sri Lanka	14.7	18.8	22.6	1.3	1.1	0.7	0.5	6.3	9.2	103	126
Sudan	18.7	28.3	40.6	2.3	2.1	0.9	0.7	3.1	3.4	119	118
Sweden	8.3	8.9	8.6	0.4	–0.1	0.6	0.6	17.2	22.0	135	124
Switzerland	6.3	7.1	7.0	0.7	–0.1	0.5	0.5	14.9	20.8	147	130
Syrian Arab Republic	8.7	15.3	21.8	3.1	2.1	1.1	0.8	3.0	3.5	111	128
Tajikistan	4.0	6.1	7.9	2.4	1.5	0.9	0.8	4.4	4.1	141	128
Tanzania	18.6	32.1	44.8	3.0	2.0	1.0	0.9	2.4	2.0	123	112
Thailand	46.7	61.2	71.0	1.5	0.9	0.8	0.5	5.3	7.9	130	130
Togo	2.6	4.5	6.3	3.0	2.0	0.9	1.0	3.0	2.5	124	120
Trinidad and Tobago	1.1	1.3	1.5	1.0	0.7	0.7	0.5	6.2	8.5	118	121
Tunisia	6.4	9.3	11.5	2.1	1.2	0.8	0.6	5.6	6.5	97	117
Turkey	44.5	63.5	77.9	2.0	1.2	0.8	0.5	5.5	6.9	119	122
Turkmenistan	2.9	4.7	6.0	2.8	1.5	0.8	0.7	4.2	4.3	157	142
Uganda	12.8	20.9	30.7	2.7	2.3	1.0	1.0	2.1	1.3	115	96
Ukraine	50.0	50.3	44.0	0.0	–0.8	0.5	0.5	13.9	14.9	205	184
United Arab Emirates	1.0	2.7	3.7	5.3	1.9	0.4	0.4	2.1	8.3	48	28
United Kingdom	56.3	59.1	59.2	0.3	0.0	0.6	0.5	15.8	18.9	138	125
United States	227.2	270.3	304.9	1.0	0.7	0.5	0.5	12.3	15.1	142	132
Uruguay	2.9	3.3	3.6	0.7	0.6	0.6	0.6	12.5	12.8	148	161
Uzbekistan	16.0	24.1	30.3	2.3	1.4	0.9	0.8	4.4	4.6	152	139
Venezuela, RB	15.1	23.2	30.2	2.4	1.5	0.8	0.6	4.3	6.3	122	123
Vietnam	53.7	76.5	94.4	2.0	1.2	0.9	0.7	4.9	4.9	142	146
West Bank and Gaza	..	2.7	5.0	..	3.5	..	1.0	3.5	2.8	126	140
Yemen, Rep.	8.5	16.6	26.6	3.7	2.8	1.1	1.1	3.0	2.4	91	105
Yugoslavia, FR (Serb./Mont.)	9.8	10.6	10.7	0.5	0.0	0.5	0.5	12.9	14.6	129	130
Zambia	5.7	9.7	13.0	2.9	1.7	1.1	0.9	2.2	1.9	97	94
Zimbabwe	7.0	11.7	14.1	2.8	1.1	1.0	0.8	2.8	2.3	117	108
World	**4,430.2 s**	**5,896.6 s**	**7,112.9 s**	**1.6 w**	**1.1 w**	**0.7 w**	**0.6 w**	**6.8 w**	**7.9 w**	**128 w**	**122 w**
Low income	2,526.6	3,536.4	4,436.2	1.9	1.3	0.8	0.6	5.0	5.9	109	108
Excl. China & India	840.4	1,295.0	1,797.1	2.4	1.9	0.9	0.8	3.4	3.7	116	118
Middle income	1,114.4	1,474.4	1,748.3	1.6	1.0	0.7	0.6	6.6	7.7	151	141
Lower middle income	677.4	886.5	1,039.8	1.5	0.9	0.7	0.6	7.0	7.6	158	144
Upper middle income	437.1	587.9	708.5	1.6	1.1	0.7	0.6	6.1	7.9	139	136
Low & middle income	3,641.0	5,010.8	6,184.5	1.8	1.2	0.8	0.6	5.5	6.4	122	118
East Asia & Pacific	1,397.8	1,817.1	2,098.6	1.5	0.8	0.7	0.5	6.1	8.0	110	109
Europe & Central Asia	425.8	474.6	482.8	0.6	0.1	0.6	0.5	10.6	11.7	181	165
Latin America & Carib.	360.3	501.7	623.3	1.8	1.3	0.8	0.6	5.2	6.6	129	136
Middle East & N. Africa	174.0	285.7	390.2	2.8	1.8	0.9	0.7	4.0	4.7	110	110
South Asia	902.6	1,304.6	1,676.2	2.0	1.5	0.8	0.7	4.4	5.2	104	106
Sub-Saharan Africa	380.5	627.1	913.5	2.8	2.2	0.9	0.9	2.9	2.7	126	120
High income	789.1	885.8	928.4	0.6	0.3	0.5	0.5	14.1	18.0	143	131
Europe EMU	275.9	291.1	286.5	0.3	–0.1	0.5	0.5	15.8	19.6	152	138

Population 2.1

About the data

Knowing the size, growth rate, and age distribution of a country's population is important for evaluating the welfare of the country's citizens, assessing the productive capacity of its economy, and estimating the quantity of goods and services that will be needed to meet its future needs. Thus governments, businesses, and anyone interested in analyzing economic performance must have accurate population estimates.

Population estimates are usually based on national population censuses, but the frequency and quality of these vary by country. Most countries conduct a complete enumeration no more than once a decade. Precensus and postcensus estimates are interpolations or extrapolations based on demographic models. Errors and undercounting occur even in high-income countries; in developing countries such errors may be substantial because of limits on the transport, communications, and other resources required to conduct a full census. Moreover, the international comparability of population indicators is limited by differences in the concepts, definitions, data collection procedures, and estimation methods used by national statistical agencies and other organizations that collect population data.

Of the 148 economies listed in the table, 125 (about 85 percent) conducted a census between 1989 and 1999. The currentness of a census, along with the availability of complementary data from surveys or registration systems, is one of many objective ways to judge the quality of demographic data. In some European countries registration systems offer complete information on population in the absence of a census. See *Primary data documentation* for the most recent census or survey year and for registration completeness.

Current population estimates for developing countries that lack recent census-based data, and pre- and postcensus estimates for countries with census data, are provided by national statistical offices, the United Nations Population Division, or other agencies. The standard estimation method requires fertility, mortality, and net migration data, which are often collected from sample surveys, some of which may be small or limited in coverage. These estimates are the product of demographic modeling and so are also susceptible to biases and errors because of shortcomings of the model as well as the data. Population projections are made using the cohort component method (see box 2a in the introduction to this section).

The quality and reliability of official demographic data are also affected by the public trust in the government, the government's commitment to full and accurate enumeration, the confidentiality and protection against misuse accorded to census data, and the independence of census agencies from undue political influence.

Figure 2.1

The rate of population growth is slowing faster than absolute growth is

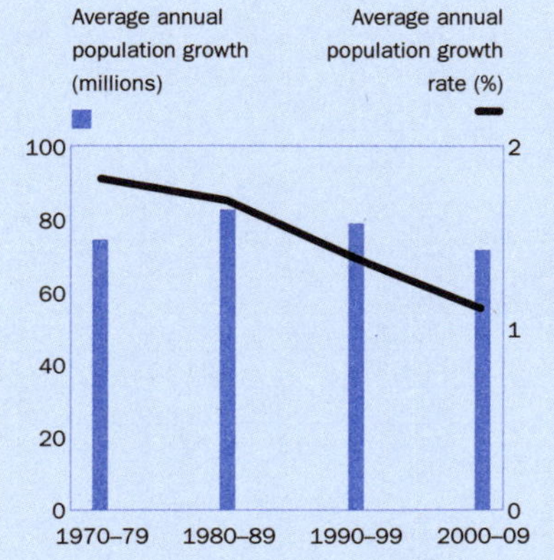

Source: World Bank staff estimates.

The global population growth rate has declined rapidly since the 1970s, but the number of people added each year started to decline—gradually—only in the early 1990s. In the first decade of the 21st century the world's population is projected to grow 1.1 percent a year, adding 70 million people annually.

Definitions

• **Total population** of an economy includes all residents regardless of legal status or citizenship—except for refugees not permanently settled in the country of asylum, who are generally considered part of the population of their country of origin. The indicators shown are midyear estimates for 1980 and 1998 and projections for 2015. • **Average annual population growth rate** is the exponential change for the period indicated. See *Statistical methods* for more information. • **Age dependency ratio** is the ratio of dependents—people younger than 15 and older than 64—to the working-age population—those aged 15–64. • **Population aged 65 and above** is the percentage of the total population that is 65 or older. • **Women aged 65 and above** is the ratio of women to men in that age group.

Data sources

The World Bank's population estimates are produced by its Human Development Network and Development Data Group in consultation with its operational staff and resident missions. Important inputs to the World Bank's demographic work come from the following sources: census reports and other statistical publications from country statistical offices; demographic and health surveys conducted by national agencies, Macro International, and the U.S. Centers for Disease Control and Prevention; United Nations Statistics Division, *Population and Vital Statistics Report* (quarterly); United Nations Population Division, *World Population Prospects: The 1998 Revision;* Eurostat, *Demographic Statistics* (various years); South Pacific Commission, *Pacific Island Populations Data Sheet 1999;* Centro Latinoamericano de Demografía, *Boletín Demográfico* (various years); and U.S. Bureau of the Census, International Database.

2.2 Population dynamics

	Crude death rate per 1,000 people		Crude birth rate per 1,000 people		Projected population by 2030	Population momentum	Average annual population growth rates					
							Age 0–14 %		Age 15–64 %		Age 65+ %	
	1980	1998	1980	1998	millions	1998	1980–98	1998–2015	1980–98	1998–2015	1980–98	1998–2015
Albania	6	7	29	18	4	1.4	0.3	–0.7	1.6	1.4	2.5	2.6
Algeria	12	6	42	26	48	1.6	1.4	–0.2	3.6	2.5	2.4	3.0
Angola	23	19	50	48	27	1.5	3.3	2.6	2.7	3.1	2.8	2.1
Argentina	9	8	24	19	48	1.4	1.0	0.0	1.5	1.3	2.3	1.6
Armenia	6	6	23	11	4	1.2	0.2	–2.1	1.3	0.9	3.0	1.9
Australia	7	7	15	13	23	1.2	0.3	–0.2	1.5	0.8	2.5	2.3
Austria	12	10	12	10	8	1.0	–0.6	–1.6	0.7	–0.1	0.2	1.4
Azerbaijan	7	6	25	16	10	1.3	0.7	–0.6	1.7	1.5	2.3	1.7
Bangladesh	18	10	44	28	190	1.6	1.3	–0.2	2.7	2.4	1.8	2.7
Belarus	10	13	16	9	9	1.0	–0.5	–2.1	0.4	–0.1	1.4	–0.3
Belgium	12	10	13	11	10	1.0	–0.6	–1.0	0.3	0.0	0.9	1.1
Benin	19	13	49	41	12	1.5	3.2	1.6	3.0	3.2	1.1	1.9
Bolivia	15	9	39	32	13	1.5	1.8	0.5	2.4	2.6	2.8	2.8
Bosnia and Herzegovina	7	7	19	13	4	1.1	–1.9	–0.5	–0.1	0.7	1.2	3.5
Botswana	10	16	45	33	2	1.2	2.3	–0.4	3.6	1.8	3.9	–0.7
Brazil	9	7	31	20	224	1.4	0.4	0.0	2.4	1.4	2.6	2.8
Bulgaria	11	14	15	8	7	0.9	–1.9	–2.4	–0.2	–0.6	1.1	0.5
Burkina Faso	20	19	47	44	22	1.3	2.4	1.8	2.4	2.8	2.4	0.9
Burundi	18	20	46	42	12	1.3	2.7	1.2	2.5	2.7	0.9	0.3
Cambodia	27	12	40	33	17	1.4	3.2	–0.2	2.7	2.4	3.2	2.8
Cameroon	16	12	45	38	26	1.4	2.8	1.1	2.8	2.8	2.6	1.9
Canada	7	7	15	12	34	1.1	0.3	–0.6	1.2	0.6	2.7	2.1
Central African Republic	19	19	43	37	6	1.3	2.4	1.0	2.2	2.1	1.8	–0.5
Chad	22	16	44	45	16	1.5	3.8	2.0	1.8	3.5	1.9	0.7
Chile	7	5	23	18	20	1.4	0.7	–0.5	1.9	1.4	2.8	3.1
China	6	8	18	16	1,477	1.2	–0.5	–0.8	2.0	1.0	3.2	2.3
Hong Kong, China	5	5	17	8	8	1.1	–0.2	–0.4	1.8	1.1	4.0	2.4
Colombia	7	6	31	24	60	1.5	0.9	–0.2	2.6	2.0	2.9	2.8
Congo, Dem. Rep.	16	15	48	46	114	1.5	3.4	2.5	3.1	3.3	3.0	2.6
Congo, Rep.	16	16	45	43	6	1.4	3.0	2.2	2.8	3.0	2.3	1.1
Costa Rica	4	4	31	22	5	1.6	1.5	–0.7	2.8	1.9	4.3	3.9
Côte d'Ivoire	17	17	51	37	23	1.3	2.8	0.8	3.4	2.3	3.6	0.7
Croatia	..	12	..	11	4	0.9	–1.1	–1.4	0.0	–0.3	0.9	1.2
Cuba	6	7	14	13	12	1.1	–1.4	–1.6	1.5	0.4	1.9	2.7
Czech Republic	13	11	15	9	9	1.0	–1.6	–2.0	0.5	–0.3	0.1	1.7
Denmark	11	11	11	13	5	1.0	–0.6	–0.6	0.4	–0.2	0.3	1.6
Dominican Republic	7	5	33	25	12	1.5	0.9	–0.4	2.7	2.0	3.8	3.2
Ecuador	9	6	36	24	18	1.5	1.2	–0.3	3.1	2.2	2.9	2.9
Egypt, Arab Rep.	13	7	39	24	92	1.5	1.7	–0.2	2.6	2.2	2.8	2.7
El Salvador	11	6	36	27	10	1.6	0.4	0.3	2.3	2.3	3.6	2.1
Eritrea	..	12	..	40	7	1.4	..	1.7	..	2.8	..	2.5
Estonia	12	13	15	9	1	0.9	–1.0	–2.3	0.1	–0.4	0.3	0.7
Ethiopia	22	20	48	45	114	1.3	2.9	1.7	2.5	2.5	2.1	0.4
Finland	9	10	13	11	5	0.8	–0.1	–0.8	0.3	–0.1	1.5	2.1
France	10	9	15	13	62	1.0	–0.4	–0.5	0.6	0.2	1.1	1.1
Gabon	19	16	33	36	2	1.3	3.8	2.1	2.5	2.3	2.4	1.2
Gambia, The	24	13	48	42	2	1.4	3.5	1.7	3.6	2.5	3.6	3.1
Georgia	9	7	18	9	5	1.1	–0.5	–2.6	0.4	0.3	2.0	1.0
Germany	12	10	11	10	74	0.9	–0.6	–1.6	0.5	–0.4	0.3	1.3
Ghana	14	9	45	35	33	1.6	2.8	1.1	3.1	2.9	3.5	2.9
Greece	9	10	15	9	10	1.0	–1.5	–1.1	0.7	–0.3	1.9	1.1
Guatemala	11	7	43	33	19	1.6	2.3	0.7	2.7	3.1	3.4	2.1
Guinea	24	17	46	41	12	1.4	2.5	1.1	2.6	2.7	2.6	2.1
Guinea-Bissau	26	21	44	41	2	1.3	2.6	1.4	1.7	2.3	2.1	1.0
Haiti	15	13	37	31	12	1.4	1.9	0.3	2.1	2.4	0.9	1.7
Honduras	10	5	43	33	11	1.7	2.5	0.5	3.5	3.1	3.9	2.8

Population dynamics 2.2

	Crude death rate per 1,000 people		Crude birth rate per 1,000 people		Projected population by 2030	Population momentum	Average annual population growth rates					
							Age 0–14 %		Age 15–64 %		Age 65+ %	
	1980	1998	1980	1998	millions	1998	1980–98	1998–2015	1980–98	1998–2015	1980–98	1998–2015
Hungary	14	14	14	10	9	0.9	–1.6	–1.6	0.0	–0.4	0.0	0.6
India	13	9	34	27	1,398	1.4	1.3	0.0	2.3	1.9	2.8	2.4
Indonesia	12	8	34	23	285	1.4	0.3	–0.2	2.5	1.7	3.4	2.9
Iran, Islamic Rep.	11	5	44	22	98	1.7	1.4	0.0	3.2	2.5	4.3	2.2
Iraq	9	10	41	32	38	1.6	2.4	0.5	3.5	2.8	3.8	3.8
Ireland	10	9	22	15	4	1.3	–1.2	–0.2	1.1	0.7	0.8	1.6
Israel	7	6	24	22	9	1.5	1.6	0.2	2.7	1.8	2.8	2.3
Italy	10	10	11	9	50	0.9	–2.2	–1.6	0.4	–0.6	1.5	1.3
Jamaica	7	6	28	23	3	1.5	–0.2	–0.8	1.9	1.5	0.7	1.6
Japan	6	7	14	10	117	0.7	–2.0	–0.9	0.5	–0.7	3.6	2.5
Jordan	..	4	..	31	8	1.7	2.9	1.0	5.1	2.9	3.7	4.4
Kazakhstan	8	10	24	14	17	1.2	–0.5	–0.8	0.5	0.6	1.1	1.1
Kenya	13	12	51	35	47	1.4	2.5	0.4	3.8	2.6	2.1	0.0
Korea, Dem. Rep.	6	9	21	20	29	1.2	–0.6	–0.8	2.5	1.1	3.4	2.9
Korea, Rep.	6	6	22	14	53	1.2	–1.3	–0.9	1.9	0.6	3.9	3.8
Kuwait	4	2	37	23	3	1.7	1.0	0.4	2.1	3.2	3.7	8.1
Kyrgyz Republic	9	7	30	22	7	1.5	1.2	–0.9	1.6	2.0	1.5	0.7
Lao PDR	20	13	45	38	9	1.5	2.6	1.3	2.2	2.8	3.8	1.7
Latvia	13	14	15	8	2	0.9	–0.7	–3.0	–0.2	–0.6	0.2	0.6
Lebanon	9	6	30	21	6	1.5	0.8	–0.5	2.5	2.0	2.3	1.3
Lesotho	15	13	40	35	3	1.4	2.1	0.4	2.6	2.3	2.1	2.4
Libya	12	4	46	29	9	1.7	2.1	0.5	3.8	2.6	4.7	4.9
Lithuania	10	11	16	10	4	1.0	–0.4	–1.8	0.6	0.0	1.2	1.1
Macedonia, FYR	7	8	21	15	2	1.2	–0.8	–0.8	0.6	0.6	2.1	2.1
Madagascar	16	11	47	41	30	1.7	2.9	1.8	2.8	3.3	1.2	3.6
Malawi	23	23	55	47	20	1.3	2.8	1.6	3.1	2.7	3.5	2.1
Malaysia	6	5	31	25	34	1.5	2.0	0.0	3.0	2.2	3.2	4.0
Mali	22	16	49	47	23	1.6	2.7	2.2	2.5	3.2	4.0	1.6
Mauritania	19	13	43	40	5	1.5	2.7	1.4	2.7	2.9	3.0	2.5
Mauritius	6	7	24	17	1	1.3	–0.8	–0.1	1.6	1.1	3.8	2.9
Mexico	7	5	34	28	141	1.6	0.4	–0.2	3.0	1.9	2.8	3.1
Moldova	10	9	20	10	4	1.1	–0.1	–1.6	0.4	0.2	1.6	0.4
Mongolia	11	7	38	21	4	1.6	1.5	–0.5	3.0	2.3	4.1	2.2
Morocco	12	7	38	25	41	1.5	0.6	0.0	2.9	2.0	2.3	2.6
Mozambique	20	20	46	41	30	1.4	2.0	1.2	1.7	2.7	3.1	0.8
Myanmar	14	10	36	26	59	1.3	–0.1	0.8	2.4	1.2	2.4	1.9
Namibia	14	13	41	35	3	1.3	2.5	0.9	2.8	2.4	2.6	1.0
Nepal	17	11	43	34	40	1.5	2.4	1.1	2.6	2.7	3.5	2.6
Netherlands	8	9	13	12	16	1.0	–0.5	–0.9	0.7	0.1	1.5	1.9
New Zealand	9	7	16	15	4	1.2	0.2	–0.5	1.3	0.5	1.9	1.9
Nicaragua	11	5	46	31	9	1.7	2.2	0.5	3.2	3.2	3.7	3.1
Niger	23	18	51	52	24	1.5	3.5	2.8	3.1	3.3	3.2	2.2
Nigeria	18	12	50	40	252	1.5	2.7	2.0	3.1	2.9	2.7	3.2
Norway	10	10	12	13	5	0.9	–0.3	–0.6	0.6	0.3	0.7	1.2
Oman	10	3	45	29	4	1.8	4.0	0.3	4.2	3.2	4.1	5.6
Pakistan	15	8	47	35	244	1.7	2.3	1.1	2.8	3.0	3.1	3.3
Panama	6	5	30	22	4	1.5	0.7	–0.5	2.6	1.8	2.9	3.1
Papua New Guinea	14	10	36	32	7	1.4	1.7	0.8	2.5	2.3	6.0	3.3
Paraguay	8	5	37	30	9	1.6	2.6	0.2	3.2	2.8	1.4	3.0
Peru	10	6	35	25	37	1.5	1.0	0.1	2.6	2.0	3.2	2.8
Philippines	9	6	35	28	119	1.6	1.8	0.1	2.8	2.3	3.8	3.8
Poland	10	10	20	10	38	1.1	–0.4	–1.6	0.6	0.2	1.2	1.3
Portugal	10	11	16	12	10	1.0	–2.1	–0.9	0.4	0.1	2.5	0.2
Puerto Rico	6	7	23	15	5	1.3	–0.4	–0.3	1.5	0.9	2.3	2.2
Romania	10	12	18	11	20	1.0	–1.8	–1.8	0.5	–0.1	1.2	0.6
Russian Federation	11	14	16	9	129	0.9	–0.3	–1.9	0.3	–0.1	1.3	0.2

2.2 Population dynamics

	Crude death rate per 1,000 people		Crude birth rate per 1,000 people		Projected population by 2030 millions	Population momentum	Average annual population growth rates Age 0–14 %		Age 15–64 %		Age 65+ %	
	1980	**1998**	**1980**	**1998**		**1998**	**1980–98**	**1998–2015**	**1980–98**	**1998–2015**	**1980–98**	**1998–2015**
Rwanda	19	21	51	46	15	1.3	2.1	1.7	3.0	2.6	1.6	2.0
Saudi Arabia	9	4	43	34	46	1.6	4.0	2.3	4.7	3.1	4.4	5.5
Senegal	18	13	46	39	17	1.4	2.7	1.6	2.8	2.8	2.3	2.2
Sierra Leone	29	25	49	45	9	1.4	2.6	1.1	2.0	2.5	1.2	2.4
Singapore	5	5	17	13	4	1.0	0.8	–1.0	2.0	1.1	3.6	4.2
Slovak Republic	10	10	19	11	5	1.1	–0.8	–1.4	0.8	0.3	0.8	1.2
Slovenia	10	9	15	9	2	0.9	–1.6	–1.7	0.6	–0.3	1.0	1.7
South Africa	12	9	36	25	56	1.3	1.3	0.0	2.7	1.5	4.2	1.0
Spain	8	9	15	9	36	1.0	–2.8	–1.0	0.8	–0.2	2.6	0.7
Sri Lanka	6	6	28	18	25	1.4	0.0	0.2	1.9	1.2	3.4	3.4
Sudan	17	11	45	33	50	1.4	1.6	1.8	2.8	2.3	3.1	2.6
Sweden	11	11	12	10	8	0.8	0.1	–1.9	0.3	–0.1	0.7	1.3
Switzerland	9	9	12	11	7	0.9	–0.1	–1.7	0.8	–0.2	1.0	1.9
Syrian Arab Republic	9	5	46	29	27	1.7	2.4	0.3	3.8	3.1	2.8	3.0
Tajikistan	8	5	37	21	10	1.6	2.1	–0.8	2.7	2.8	2.2	1.1
Tanzania	15	16	47	41	56	1.3	2.8	1.2	3.2	2.6	3.3	0.8
Thailand	8	7	28	17	77	1.3	–0.8	–0.3	2.6	1.1	3.8	3.2
Togo	16	16	45	40	8	1.4	3.1	1.1	2.8	2.8	2.6	0.9
Trinidad and Tobago	7	6	29	15	2	1.3	–0.3	–0.9	1.5	1.1	1.6	2.6
Tunisia	9	6	35	18	13	1.5	0.7	–0.5	2.8	1.9	4.4	2.1
Turkey	10	6	32	21	88	1.4	0.4	0.1	2.8	1.5	2.8	2.6
Turkmenistan	8	6	34	20	7	1.5	2.3	–0.6	3.2	2.5	2.7	1.6
Uganda	18	20	49	47	41	1.3	2.8	1.7	2.6	2.9	1.8	–0.4
Ukraine	11	15	15	9	40	0.9	–0.7	–2.2	0.1	–0.5	0.9	–0.4
United Arab Emirates	5	3	30	17	4	1.2	5.2	0.2	5.3	1.9	8.1	9.9
United Kingdom	12	11	13	12	59	1.1	–0.3	–1.0	0.4	0.0	0.5	1.0
United States	9	9	16	14	327	1.2	0.8	–0.1	0.9	0.7	1.5	1.9
Uruguay	10	9	19	17	4	1.2	0.2	–0.2	0.7	0.8	1.7	0.7
Uzbekistan	8	6	34	23	36	1.6	1.9	–1.1	2.6	2.6	1.5	1.6
Venezuela, RB	6	4	33	25	36	1.6	1.5	–0.2	2.9	2.2	3.9	3.8
Vietnam	8	6	36	21	110	1.5	0.8	–0.8	2.7	2.1	2.1	1.1
West Bank and Gaza	..	5	..	42	7	1.9	..	2.7	..	4.3	..	2.2
Yemen, Rep.	19	12	53	40	36	1.6	3.5	2.0	3.9	3.5	4.6	1.3
Yugoslavia, FR (Serb./Mont.)	9	10	18	11	11	1.0	–0.3	–0.8	0.5	0.2	2.0	0.8
Zambia	15	19	50	42	16	1.3	2.5	0.7	3.3	2.5	2.4	0.8
Zimbabwe	12	13	43	31	16	1.3	2.1	–0.5	3.5	2.1	3.1	0.1
World	**10 w**	**9 w**	**27 w**	**22 w**	**8,043 s**	**1.3 w**	**0.8 w**	**0.1 w**	**2.0 w**	**1.4 w**	**2.3 w**	**2.0 w**
Low income	11	9	31	26	5,149	1.4	1.0	0.3	2.3	1.8	3.0	2.3
Excl. China & India	16	12	43	34	2,246	1.5	2.0	1.1	2.7	2.5	2.7	2.3
Middle income	9	8	28	20	1,957	1.4	0.7	–0.2	2.0	1.4	2.1	1.9
Lower middle income	10	9	28	20	1,158	1.3	0.8	–0.4	1.8	1.4	2.0	1.5
Upper middle income	8	7	28	21	798	1.4	0.5	–0.1	2.2	1.4	2.3	2.6
Low & middle income	11	9	30	24	7,106	1.4	0.9	0.1	2.2	1.7	2.7	2.2
East Asia & Pacific	7	7	22	18	2,284	1.3	–0.2	–0.6	2.1	1.2	3.2	2.5
Europe & Central Asia	10	11	19	12	489	1.1	–0.1	–1.3	0.8	0.4	1.3	0.7
Latin America & Carib.	8	6	31	23	715	1.5	0.7	–0.1	2.5	1.8	2.7	2.7
Middle East & N. Africa	12	7	41	27	475	1.6	1.9	0.4	3.3	2.5	3.4	2.8
South Asia	14	9	37	28	1,951	1.5	1.5	0.2	2.4	2.1	2.8	2.5
Sub-Saharan Africa	18	15	47	40	1,191	1.4	2.7	1.6	2.9	2.7	2.8	1.8
High income	9	9	14	12	937	1.0	–0.2	–0.6	0.9	0.2	1.7	1.7
Europe EMU	10	10	13	10	276	1.0	–1.2	–1.1	0.6	–0.2	1.2	1.2

Population dynamics 2.2

About the data

The vital rates shown in the table are based on data derived from birth and death registration systems, censuses, and sample surveys conducted by national statistical offices, United Nations agencies, and other organizations. The estimates for 1998 for many countries are based on extrapolations of levels and trends measured in earlier years.

Vital registers are the preferred source of these data, but in many developing countries systems for registering births and deaths do not exist or are incomplete because of deficiencies in geographic coverage or coverage of events. Many developing countries carry out specialized household surveys that estimate vital rates by asking respondents about births and deaths in the recent past. Estimates derived in this way are subject to sampling errors due to inaccurate recall by the respondents.

The United Nations Statistics Division monitors the completeness of vital registration systems. It compiles quarterly reports of the latest birth and death rates, as well as an indication of their completeness, in the *Population and Vital Statistics Report*. The share of countries with at least 90 percent complete vital registration increased from 45 percent in 1988 to 54 percent in 1999. Still, some of the most populous developing countries—China, India, Indonesia, Brazil, Pakistan, Nigeria, Bangladesh—do not have complete vital registration systems. Fewer than 25 percent of vital events worldwide are thought to be recorded.

International migration is the only other factor besides birth and death rates that directly determines a country's population growth. In the industrial world about 40 percent of annual population growth in 1990–95 was due to migration, while in the developing world migration reduced the population growth rate by about 3 percent. Estimating international migration is difficult. At any time many people are located outside their home country as tourists, workers, or refugees or for other reasons. Standards relating to the duration and purpose of international moves that qualify as migration vary, and accurate estimates require information on flows into and out of countries that is difficult to collect.

Over the next several decades the population of low- and middle-income countries will continue to grow. The rate of growth will decline, but the absolute increases will be large—and accompanied by substantial shifts in the age structure. Even when fertility reaches the replacement level of about two children per couple, the number of births will remain high—and population growth will not stop for several decades. This phenomenon, called population momentum, is a facet of the youthful age structures typical of developing country populations. It occurs because large cohorts born in previous years move through the reproductive ages, generating more births than are offset by deaths in the smaller, older cohorts.

The growth rate of the total population (see table 2.1) conceals the fact that different age groups may grow at very different rates. In many developing countries the population under 15 was earlier growing rapidly, but is now starting to shrink. Previously high fertility rates and declining mortality are now reflected in rapid growth of the working-age population.

Figure 2.2

Growth in the working-age and elderly populations has accelerated in developing countries

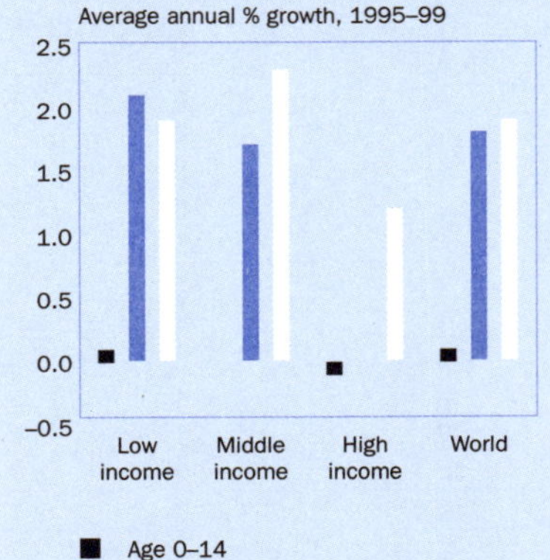

Age 0–14
Age 15–64
Age 65+

Source: World Bank staff estimates.

Population dynamics are reflected in the growth rates of different age groups. Changes in the size of the youth population (age 0–14), once the driving force behind total population growth, are no longer an important factor. Lower birth rates combined with an increasing number of women of childbearing age indicate that the size of the youth population will remain almost constant in the near future. In contrast, the working-age (15–64) and elderly populations are both increasing rapidly in many low- and middle-income countries, while in high-income countries only the elderly population is growing.

Definitions

• **Crude death rate** and **crude birth rate** are the number of deaths and the number of live births occurring during the year, per 1,000 population estimated at midyear. Subtracting the crude death rate from the crude birth rate provides the rate of natural increase, which is equal to the population growth rate in the absence of net migration. • **Projected population by 2030** is the total number of people expected to be alive in 2030, based on a cohort component projection in which assumed future patterns in fertility, mortality, and international migration are applied to the current age structure. • **Population momentum** is the ratio of the population when zero growth has been achieved to the population in year *t* (in this case 2000), given the assumption that fertility remains at replacement level from year *t* onward. • **Average annual population growth rates** are calculated using the exponential endpoint method (see *Statistical methods* for more information).

Data sources

The World Bank's population estimates are produced by its Human Development Network and Development Data Group in consultation with its operational staff and resident missions. Important inputs to the World Bank's demographic work come from many sources: census reports and other statistical publications from country statistical offices; demographic and health surveys conducted by national sources, Macro International, and the U.S. Centers for Disease Control and Prevention; United Nations Statistics Division, *Population and Vital Statistics Report* (quarterly); United Nations Population Division, *World Population Prospects: The 1998 Revision;* Eurostat, *Demographic Statistics* (various years); South Pacific Commission, *Pacific Island Populations Data Sheet 1999;* Centro Latinoamericano de Demografía, *Boletín Demográfico* (various years); and U.S. Bureau of the Census, International Database.

2.3 Labor force structure

	Population aged 15–64		Labor force								
	millions		Total millions			Average annual growth rate %		Female % of labor force		Children 10–14 % of age group	
	1980	1998	1980	1998	2010	1980–98	1998–2010	1980	1998	1980	1998
Albania	2	2	1	2	2	1.7	1.6	38.8	41.1	4	1
Algeria	9	18	5	10	15	3.9	3.4	21.4	26.4	7	1
Angola	4	6	3	6	8	2.6	3.1	47.0	46.3	30	26
Argentina	17	23	11	14	18	1.7	2.0	27.6	32.3	8	3
Armenia	2	2	1	2	2	1.4	1.4	47.9	48.4	0	0
Australia	10	13	7	10	11	1.9	0.9	36.8	43.3	0	0
Austria	5	5	3	4	4	0.6	0.0	40.5	40.3	0	0
Azerbaijan	4	5	3	3	4	1.4	2.0	47.5	44.2	0	0
Bangladesh	44	71	41	64	83	2.5	2.2	42.3	42.3	35	29
Belarus	6	7	5	5	5	0.2	0.0	49.9	48.8	0	0
Belgium	6	7	4	4	4	0.3	0.1	33.9	40.6	0	0
Benin	2	3	2	3	4	2.6	2.9	47.0	48.3	30	27
Bolivia	3	4	2	3	4	2.5	2.6	33.3	37.6	19	13
Bosnia and Herzegovina	3	3	2	2	2	0.5	1.1	32.8	38.1	1	..
Botswana	0	1	0	1	1	3.0	1.3	50.1	45.5	26	15
Brazil	70	108	47	76	90	2.6	1.3	28.4	35.4	19	15
Bulgaria	6	6	5	4	4	–0.5	–0.7	45.3	48.2	0	0
Burkina Faso	3	5	4	5	7	1.9	2.0	47.6	46.6	71	47
Burundi	2	3	2	4	5	2.5	2.4	50.2	48.9	50	49
Cambodia	4	6	4	6	8	2.7	2.2	55.4	51.9	27	24
Cameroon	5	7	4	6	8	2.7	2.3	36.8	37.8	34	24
Canada	17	21	12	16	18	1.6	0.6	39.5	45.4	0	0
Central African Republic	1	2	..	..	..	..	..	..	..	..	..
Chad	2	3	2	3	5	2.5	2.9	43.4	44.6	42	37
Chile	7	10	4	6	8	2.5	2.1	26.3	32.9	0	0
China	586	837	540	743	822	1.8	0.8	43.2	45.2	30	9
Hong Kong, China	3	5	2	3	4	1.9	1.4	34.3	36.9	6	0
Colombia	16	25	9	18	23	3.5	2.2	26.2	38.2	12	6
Congo, Dem. Rep.	14	24	12	20	29	3.0	2.9	44.5	43.5	33	29
Congo, Rep.	1	1	1	1	2	2.7	2.8	42.4	43.4	27	26
Costa Rica	1	2	1	1	2	3.2	1.7	20.8	30.5	10	5
Côte d'Ivoire	4	8	3	6	7	3.2	2.0	32.2	33.1	28	19
Croatia	3	3	2	2	2	–0.1	–0.2	40.2	43.9	0	0
Cuba	6	8	4	5	6	2.2	0.6	31.4	38.9	0	0
Czech Republic	6	7	5	6	6	0.4	–0.4	47.1	47.4	0	0
Denmark	3	4	3	3	3	0.5	–0.5	44.0	46.4	0	0
Dominican Republic	3	5	2	4	5	2.9	2.3	24.7	30.1	25	14
Ecuador	4	7	3	5	6	3.3	2.8	20.1	27.4	9	5
Egypt, Arab Rep.	23	37	14	23	32	2.6	2.8	26.5	29.7	18	10
El Salvador	2	4	2	3	4	2.7	2.9	26.5	35.5	17	14
Eritrea	..	2	1	2	3	2.6	2.7	47.4	47.4	44	39
Estonia	1	1	1	1	1	–0.1	–0.1	50.6	49.0	0	0
Ethiopia	20	31	17	26	34	2.4	2.1	42.3	40.9	46	42
Finland	3	3	2	3	2	0.5	–0.5	46.5	47.9	0	0
France	34	39	24	26	27	0.6	0.3	40.1	44.8	0	0
Gabon	0	1	0	1	1	2.3	2.0	45.0	44.5	29	16
Gambia, The	0	1	0	1	1	3.6	2.3	44.8	45.0	44	35
Georgia	3	4	3	3	3	0.3	0.2	49.3	46.6	0	0
Germany	52	56	38	41	40	0.5	–0.2	40.1	42.1	0	0
Ghana	6	10	5	9	12	3.0	2.7	51.0	50.6	16	13
Greece	6	7	4	5	5	1.0	0.2	27.9	37.4	5	0
Guatemala	3	6	2	4	6	2.9	3.4	22.4	27.8	19	15
Guinea	2	4	2	3	4	2.2	2.2	47.1	47.2	41	32
Guinea-Bissau	0	1	0	1	1	1.8	1.9	39.9	40.4	43	37
Haiti	3	4	3	3	4	1.6	1.6	44.6	43.0	33	24
Honduras	2	3	1	2	3	3.5	3.5	25.2	31.0	14	8

Labor force structure 2.3

	Population aged 15–64		Labor force								
	millions		Total millions			Average annual growth rate %		Female % of labor force		Children 10–14 % of age group	
	1980	1998	1980	1998	2010	1980–98	1998–2010	1980	1998	1980	1998
Hungary	7	7	5	5	5	–0.3	–0.6	43.3	44.6	0	0
India	394	595	302	431	546	2.0	2.0	33.7	32.1	21	13
Indonesia	83	130	58	98	124	2.9	2.0	35.2	40.4	13	9
Iran, Islamic Rep.	20	36	12	19	28	2.6	3.4	20.4	25.9	14	3
Iraq	7	12	4	6	9	3.0	2.9	17.3	19.0	11	3
Ireland	2	2	1	2	2	1.0	1.4	28.1	33.9	1	0
Israel	2	4	1	3	3	3.2	2.3	33.7	40.6	0	0
Italy	36	39	23	25	25	0.6	–0.3	32.9	38.2	2	0
Jamaica	1	2	1	1	2	1.9	1.3	46.3	46.2	0	0
Japan	79	87	57	68	66	1.0	–0.3	37.9	41.2	0	0
Jordan	1	3	1	1	2	5.2	3.6	14.7	23.3	4	0
Kazakhstan	9	10	7	7	8	0.4	0.8	47.6	46.8	0	0
Kenya	8	15	8	15	20	3.6	2.3	46.0	46.1	45	40
Korea, Dem. Rep.	10	16	8	12	13	2.5	0.6	44.8	43.4	3	0
Korea, Rep.	24	33	16	23	27	2.2	1.1	38.7	41.0	0	0
Kuwait	1	1	0	1	1	2.1	4.4	13.1	31.2	0	0
Kyrgyz Republic	2	3	2	2	3	1.4	1.9	47.5	47.0	0	0
Lao PDR	2	3	..	..	..	..	..	..	..	31	26
Latvia	2	2	1	1	1	–0.4	–0.3	50.8	50.3	0	0
Lebanon	2	3	1	1	2	3.0	2.6	22.6	29.0	5	0
Lesotho	1	1	1	1	1	2.2	2.1	37.9	36.8	28	21
Libya	2	3	1	2	2	2.7	2.4	18.6	22.1	9	0
Lithuania	2	2	2	2	2	0.3	0.2	49.7	48.0	0	0
Macedonia, FYR	1	1	1	1	1	0.7	0.7	36.1	41.3	1	0
Madagascar	5	8	4	7	10	2.5	3.1	45.2	44.7	40	35
Malawi	3	5	3	5	7	2.7	2.2	50.6	48.8	45	33
Malaysia	8	14	5	9	13	3.1	2.7	33.7	37.5	8	3
Mali	3	5	3	5	7	2.4	2.7	46.7	46.3	61	52
Mauritania	1	1	1	1	2	2.5	2.6	45.0	43.8	30	23
Mauritius	1	1	0	0	1	2.0	1.1	25.7	32.2	5	2
Mexico	35	59	22	38	51	3.0	2.4	26.9	32.6	9	6
Moldova	3	3	2	2	2	0.2	0.1	50.3	48.6	3	0
Mongolia	1	2	1	1	2	2.8	2.3	45.7	46.9	4	2
Morocco	10	17	7	11	15	2.4	2.5	33.5	34.7	21	3
Mozambique	6	9	7	9	11	1.6	2.2	49.0	48.4	39	33
Myanmar	19	29	17	24	28	1.7	1.6	43.7	43.4	28	24
Namibia	1	1	0	1	1	2.4	2.0	40.1	40.8	34	19
Nepal	8	13	7	11	14	2.3	2.6	38.8	40.5	56	43
Netherlands	9	11	6	7	7	1.5	–0.1	31.5	40.2	0	0
New Zealand	2	2	1	2	2	2.1	0.5	34.3	44.6	0	0
Nicaragua	1	3	1	2	3	3.7	3.3	27.6	35.1	19	13
Niger	3	5	3	5	7	3.0	3.3	44.6	44.3	48	44
Nigeria	36	64	29	48	67	2.8	2.7	36.2	36.3	29	25
Norway	3	3	2	2	2	0.9	0.2	40.5	46.1	0	0
Oman	1	1	0	1	1	3.5	2.6	6.2	15.7	6	0
Pakistan	44	72	29	49	72	2.9	3.3	22.7	27.7	23	16
Panama	1	2	1	1	1	3.0	1.9	29.9	34.7	6	3
Papua New Guinea	2	3	2	2	3	2.2	2.1	41.7	42.0	28	18
Paraguay	2	3	1	2	3	2.9	2.8	26.7	29.6	15	7
Peru	9	15	5	9	13	3.0	2.8	23.9	30.6	4	2
Philippines	27	44	19	32	42	2.9	2.4	35.0	37.6	14	6
Poland	23	26	19	20	20	0.4	0.2	45.3	46.2	0	0
Portugal	6	7	5	5	5	0.5	0.1	38.7	43.8	8	1
Puerto Rico	2	3	1	1	2	1.8	1.4	31.8	36.6	0	0
Romania	14	15	11	11	11	–0.2	0.1	45.8	44.5	0	0
Russian Federation	95	101	76	78	79	0.1	0.1	49.4	48.9	0	0

2.3 Labor force structure

	Population aged 15–64 millions		Labor force Total millions			Average annual growth rate %		Female % of labor force		Children 10–14 % of age group	
	1980	1998	1980	1998	2010	1980–98	1998–2010	1980	1998	1980	1998
Rwanda	3	4	3	4	6	2.8	2.6	49.1	48.9	43	41
Saudi Arabia	5	12	3	7	10	4.9	3.2	7.6	14.8	5	0
Senegal	3	5	3	4	5	2.6	2.4	42.2	42.6	43	29
Sierra Leone	2	3	1	2	2	2.0	2.2	35.5	36.6	19	15
Singapore	2	2	1	2	2	2.3	0.7	34.6	39.0	2	0
Slovak Republic	3	4	2	3	3	0.9	0.4	45.3	47.8	0	0
Slovenia	1	1	1	1	1	0.2	–0.1	45.8	46.5	0	0
South Africa	16	26	10	16	19	2.4	1.5	35.1	37.6	1	0
Spain	23	27	14	17	17	1.3	0.1	28.3	36.7	0	0
Sri Lanka	9	12	5	8	10	2.2	1.7	26.9	36.2	4	2
Sudan	10	16	7	11	15	2.6	2.8	26.9	29.0	33	28
Sweden	5	6	4	5	5	0.7	–0.3	43.8	47.9	0	0
Switzerland	4	5	3	4	4	1.3	0.0	36.7	40.2	0	0
Syrian Arab Republic	4	8	2	5	7	3.7	3.7	23.5	26.5	14	4
Tajikistan	2	3	2	2	3	2.3	3.0	46.9	44.3	0	0
Tanzania	9	17	9	16	21	3.0	2.2	49.8	49.2	43	38
Thailand	26	42	24	37	42	2.3	1.2	47.4	46.3	25	14
Togo	1	2	1	2	2	2.6	2.4	39.3	40.0	36	28
Trinidad and Tobago	1	1	0	1	1	1.6	1.6	31.4	33.7	1	0
Tunisia	3	6	2	4	5	2.9	2.2	28.9	31.2	6	0
Turkey	25	41	19	30	37	2.6	1.8	35.5	37.0	21	9
Turkmenistan	2	3	1	2	3	3.0	2.4	47.0	45.7	0	0
Uganda	6	10	7	10	13	2.4	2.3	47.9	47.6	49	44
Ukraine	33	34	27	25	24	–0.3	–0.3	50.2	48.7	0	0
United Arab Emirates	1	2	1	1	2	4.9	1.8	5.1	14.1	0	0
United Kingdom	36	38	27	30	30	0.5	0.0	38.9	43.7	0	0
United States	151	178	109	138	153	1.3	0.9	41.0	45.7	0	0
Uruguay	2	2	1	1	2	1.3	0.9	30.8	41.3	4	1
Uzbekistan	9	14	6	10	13	2.6	2.3	48.0	46.6	0	0
Venezuela, RB	8	14	5	9	13	3.3	2.6	26.7	34.1	4	0
Vietnam	28	46	26	39	48	2.3	1.7	48.1	49.1	22	7
West Bank and Gaza	..	1	..	..	..	..	..	..	..	..	..
Yemen, Rep.	4	8	2	5	8	4.2	3.1	32.5	28.0	26	19
Yugoslavia, FR (Serb./Mont.)	6	7	4	5	5	0.7	0.2	38.7	42.7	0	0
Zambia	3	5	2	4	5	2.9	2.4	45.4	45.0	19	16
Zimbabwe	3	6	3	5	7	3.0	1.6	44.4	44.5	37	28
World	2,595 s	3,701 s	2,035 s	2,846 s	3,384 s	1.9 w	1.4 w	39.1 w	40.5 w	20 w	12 w
Low income	1,433	2,172	1,214	1,771	2,156	2.1	1.6	40.0	40.6	27	17
Excl. China & India	442	723	364	584	775	2.6	2.4	40.2	41.2	29	24
Middle income	657	936	464	646	780	1.8	1.6	37.5	38.6	10	5
Lower middle income	403	558	291	386	465	1.6	1.6	40.2	40.1	9	4
Upper middle income	254	378	173	260	315	2.3	1.6	32.9	36.3	11	7
Low & middle income	2,090	3,107	1,679	2,416	2,936	2.0	1.6	39.3	40.1	23	13
East Asia & Pacific	820	1,206	719	1,026	1,172	2.0	1.1	42.6	44.5	26	9
Europe & Central Asia	274	315	214	236	251	0.5	0.5	46.7	46.1	3	1
Latin America & Carib.	201	313	130	212	269	2.7	2.0	27.8	34.4	13	9
Middle East & N. Africa	91	166	54	94	135	3.1	3.0	23.8	26.9	14	5
South Asia	508	777	392	573	740	2.1	2.1	33.8	33.1	23	16
Sub-Saharan Africa	195	330	170	275	369	2.7	2.5	42.3	42.2	35	30
High income	505	594	357	430	447	1.0	0.3	38.4	42.9	0	0
Europe EMU	178	197	119	135	134	0.7	0.0	36.7	41.1	1	0

Labor force structure 2.3

About the data

The labor force is the supply of labor available for the production of goods and services in an economy. It includes people who are currently employed and people who are unemployed but seeking work, as well as first-time job-seekers. Not everyone who works is included, however. Unpaid workers, family workers, and students are among those usually omitted, and in some countries members of the military are not counted. The size of the labor force tends to vary during the year as seasonal workers enter and leave it.

Data on the labor force are compiled by the International Labour Organization (ILO) from census or labor force surveys. For international comparisons, the most comprehensive source is labor force surveys. Despite the ILO's efforts to encourage the use of international standards, labor force data are not fully comparable because of differences among countries, and sometimes within countries, in their scope and coverage. In some countries data on the labor force refer to people above a specific age, while in others there is no specific age provision. The reference period of the census or survey is another important source of differences: in some countries data refer to a person's status on the day of the census or survey or during a specific period before the inquiry date, while in others the data are recorded without reference to any period. In developing countries, where the household is often the basic unit of production and all members contribute to output, but some at low intensity or irregular intervals, the estimated labor force may be significantly smaller than the numbers actually working (ILO, *Yearbook of Labour Statistics 1997*).

The labor force estimates in the table were calculated by World Bank staff by applying labor force activity rates from the ILO database to World Bank population estimates to create a series consistent with these population estimates. This procedure sometimes results in estimates of labor force size that differ slightly from those published in the ILO's *Yearbook of Labour Statistics*. The population aged 15–64 is often used to provide a rough estimate of the potential labor force. But in many developing countries children under 15 work full or part time. And in some high-income countries many workers postpone retirement past age 65. As a result labor force participation rates calculated in this way may systematically over- or underestimate actual rates.

In general, estimates of women in the labor force are lower than those of men and are not comparable internationally, reflecting the fact that for women, demographic, social, legal, and cultural trends and norms determine whether their activities are regarded as economic. In many countries large numbers of women work on farms or in other family enterprises without pay, while others work in or near their homes, mixing work and personal activities during the day. Countries differ in the criteria used to determine the extent to which such workers are to be counted as part of the labor force.

Reliable estimates of child labor are hard to obtain. In many countries child labor is officially presumed not to exist and so is not included in surveys or in official data. Underreporting also occurs because data exclude children engaged in agricultural or household activities with their families. Most child workers are in Asia. But the share of children working is highest in Africa, where, on average, one in three children aged 10–14 is engaged in some form of economic activity, mostly in agriculture (Fallon and Tzannatos 1998). Available statistics suggest that more boys than girls work. But the number of girls working is often underestimated because surveys exclude those working as unregistered domestic help or doing full-time household work to enable their parents to work outside the home.

Definitions

• **Population aged 15–64** is the number of people who could potentially be economically active. • **Total labor force** comprises people who meet the ILO definition of the economically active population: all people who supply labor for the production of goods and services during a specified period. It includes both the employed and the unemployed. While national practices vary in the treatment of such groups as the armed forces and seasonal or part-time workers, in general the labor force includes the armed forces, the unemployed, and first-time job-seekers, but excludes homemakers and other unpaid caregivers and workers in the informal sector. • **Average annual growth rate of the labor force** is calculated using the exponential endpoint method (see *Statistical methods* for more information). • **Females as a percentage of the labor force** show the extent to which women are active in the labor force. • **Children 10–14 in the labor force** are the share of that age group active in the labor force.

Data sources

Population estimates are from the World Bank's population database. Labor force activity rates are from the ILO database Estimates and Projections of the Economically Active Population, 1950–2010. The ILO publishes estimates of the economically active population in its *Yearbook of Labour Statistics*.

Table 2.3a

The gap between men's and women's labor force participation is narrowing

Labor force participation rate (%)

	1980		1997	
	Male	Female	Male	Female
Colombia	78.4	22.4	78.4	52.0
Egypt, Arab Rep.	72.4	7.4	73.4	21.6
France	70.7	44.4	62.3	47.2
Indonesia	84.7	44.3	82.3	52.8
Pakistan	87.2	7.0	82.3	12.7
Senegal	88.0	61.3	85.7	61.2

Source: International Labour Organization, Key Indicators of the Labour Market.

In almost all countries for which data are available, women are less likely than men to participate in the labor force. But the rates at which women do participate vary widely. Female labor force participation tends to be lowest in the Middle East and North Africa—and highest in Sub-Saharan Africa and the transition economies of Europe and Central Asia.

Where women's labor force participation is low, there are often cultural reasons. In the Middle East and North Africa strict gender segregation, stemming from religious strictures and concerns about marriageability, discourage schooling and work outside the home for girls and women. Where women's participation is high, as in several Sub-Saharan African countries, it often reflects their large role in agricultural work.

In many countries the gap between men's and women's participation narrowed in 1980–97, reflecting women's rising education levels, the expanding employment in services (occupations typically dominated by women), and changing norms and laws relating to women's economic role.

2.4 Employment by economic activity

	Agriculture				Industry				Services			
	Male % of male labor force		Female % of female labor force		Male % of male labor force		Female % of female labor force		Male % of male labor force		Female % of female labor force	
	1980	1992–97[a]	1980	1992–97[a]	1980	1992–97[a]	1980	1992–97[a]	1980	1992–97[a]	1980	1992–97[a]
Albania	54	22	62	27	28	45	17	45	18	34	21	28
Algeria	27	..	69	..	33	..	6	..	40	..	25	..
Angola	67	..	87	..	13	..	1	..	20	..	11	..
Argentina	17	2	3	0	40	33	18	12	44	65	79	88
Armenia	21	..	21	..	48	..	38	..	31	..	41	..
Australia	8	6	4	4	39	31	16	11	53	63	80	85
Austria	..	6	..	8	..	42	..	14	..	52	..	78
Azerbaijan	28	..	42	..	36	..	20	..	36	..	38	..
Bangladesh	67	54	81	78	5	11	14	8	29	34	5	11
Belarus	29	..	23	..	44	..	33	..	28	..	44	..
Belgium	..	3	..	2	..	41	..	16	..	56	..	81
Benin	66	..	69	..	10	..	4	..	24	..	27	..
Bolivia	52	2	28	2	21	40	19	16	27	58	53	82
Bosnia and Herzegovina	26	..	38	..	45	..	24	..	30	..	39	..
Botswana	6	3	3	2	41	38	8	18	53	60	89	80
Brazil	*34*	28	*20*	23	*30*	26	*13*	9	*36*	45	*67*	68
Bulgaria	..	..	..	..	..	..	..	..	..	..	..	..
Burkina Faso	92	..	93	..	3	..	2	..	5	..	5	..
Burundi	88	..	98	..	4	..	1	..	9	..	1	..
Cambodia	70	71	80	79	7	6	7	3	23	23	14	18
Cameroon	65	..	87	..	11	..	2	..	24	..	11	..
Canada	7	5	3	2	38	32	16	12	58	63	84	86
Central African Republic	79	..	90	..	5	..	1	..	15	..	9	..
Chad	82	..	95	..	6	..	0	..	12	..	4	..
Chile	22	19	3	4	27	34	16	14	51	47	81	81
China	..	..	..	..	..	..	..	..	..	..	..	..
Hong Kong, China	2	0	1	0	47	31	56	15	52	69	43	85
Colombia	2	1	1	0	39	32	26	21	59	66	74	76
Congo, Dem. Rep.	62	..	84	..	18	..	4	..	20	..	12	..
Congo, Rep.	42	..	81	..	20	..	2	..	38	..	17	..
Costa Rica	34	27	6	6	25	26	20	17	40	46	74	76
Côte d'Ivoire	60	..	75	..	10	..	5	..	30	..	20	..
Croatia	..	7	..	3	..	50	..	34	..	43	..	63
Cuba	30	..	10	..	32	..	22	..	39	..	68	..
Czech Republic	13	7	11	4	57	50	39	29	30	43	50	66
Denmark	*11*	5	*4*	2	*41*	36	*16*	15	*48*	58	*80*	83
Dominican Republic	40	..	11	..	26	..	16	..	34	..	73	..
Ecuador	44	10	22	2	21	27	15	16	34	64	63	83
Egypt, Arab Rep.	46	32	10	43	21	25	14	9	34	43	76	48
El Salvador	51	38	10	7	21	25	21	21	28	37	69	72
Eritrea	79	..	88	..	7	..	2	..	14	..	11	..
Estonia	19	16	12	8	50	39	36	27	31	44	52	65
Ethiopia	90	89	89	88	2	2	2	2	8	9	10	11
Finland	15	9	12	5	45	39	23	14	39	52	63	81
France	9	6	7	4	44	37	22	15	47	57	71	81
Gabon	59	..	74	..	18	..	6	..	24	..	21	..
Gambia, The	78	..	93	..	10	..	3	..	13	..	5	..
Georgia	31	..	34	..	33	..	21	..	37	..	45	..
Germany	..	3	..	3	..	46	..	19	..	51	..	79
Ghana	66	..	57	..	12	..	14	..	22	..	29	..
Greece	..	18	..	23	..	28	..	13	..	54	..	64
Guatemala	64	..	17	..	17	..	27	..	19	..	56	..
Guinea	86	..	97	..	2	..	1	..	12	..	3	..
Guinea-Bissau	81	..	98	..	3	..	0	..	17	..	3	..
Haiti	*81*	..	*53*	..	*8*	..	*8*	..	*11*	..	*39*	..
Honduras	63	53	40	7	17	19	9	27	20	28	51	66

Employment by economic activity 2.4

	Agriculture				Industry				Services			
	Male % of male labor force		Female % of female labor force		Male % of male labor force		Female % of female labor force		Male % of male labor force		Female % of female labor force	
	1980	1992–97[a]	1980	1992–97[a]	1980	1992–97[a]	1980	1992–97[a]	1980	1992–97[a]	1980	1992–97[a]
Hungary	24	11	19	5	45	40	36	25	31	50	45	71
India	63	..	83	..	15	..	9	..	22	..	8	..
Indonesia	57	41	53	42	13	21	13	16	29	39	32	42
Iran, Islamic Rep.	36	..	50	..	28	..	17	..	35	..	33	..
Iraq	21	..	62	..	24	..	11	..	55	..	28	..
Ireland	..	15	..	3	..	34	..	15	..	49	..	79
Israel	8	3	4	1	39	38	16	14	52	58	80	84
Italy	13	7	16	7	43	38	28	22	44	55	56	72
Jamaica	47	31	23	11	20	27	8	12	33	42	69	77
Japan	9	5	13	6	40	39	28	24	51	55	58	69
Jordan	..	6	..	4	24	27	7	10	76	66	93	87
Kazakhstan	28	..	20	..	38	..	25	..	34	..	55	..
Kenya	23	19	25	20	24	23	9	9	53	58	65	71
Korea, Dem. Rep.	39	..	52	..	37	..	20	..	24	..	28	..
Korea, Rep.	31	10	39	13	32	38	24	21	37	52	37	66
Kuwait	2	..	0	..	36	..	3	..	62	..	97	..
Kyrgyz Republic	35	48	33	49	34	12	23	7	32	31	44	38
Lao PDR	77	..	82	..	7	..	4	..	16	..	13	..
Latvia	18	23	14	18	49	33	35	20	32	44	50	62
Lebanon	13	..	20	..	29	..	21	..	58	..	59	..
Lesotho	26	..	64	..	52	..	5	..	22	..	31	..
Libya	16	..	63	..	29	..	3	..	55	..	34	..
Lithuania	26	23	29	18	47	35	30	21	27	42	41	61
Macedonia, FYR	30	10	47	6	38	53	23	41	32	32	30	51
Madagascar	73	..	93	..	9	..	2	..	19	..	5	..
Malawi	78	50	96	73	10	25	1	7	12	25	3	20
Malaysia	34	19	43	14	26	36	21	30	40	46	36	56
Mali	86	..	92	..	2	..	1	..	12	..	7	..
Mauritania	65	..	79	..	11	..	2	..	24	..	19	..
Mauritius	29	15	30	13	19	39	40	43	47	46	31	45
Mexico	..	30	..	13	..	24	..	19	..	46	..	68
Moldova	49	..	38	..	32	..	21	..	19	..	41	..
Mongolia	43	..	36	..	21	..	21	..	36	..	43	..
Morocco	48	4	72	3	23	33	14	46	29	63	14	51
Mozambique	72	..	97	..	14	..	1	..	14	..	2	..
Myanmar	..	..	..	..	..	..	..	..	..	..	..	..
Namibia	52	..	42	..	22	..	10	..	27	..	47	..
Nepal	91	..	98	..	1	..	0	..	8	..	2	..
Netherlands	..	4	..	3	..	32	..	10	..	62	..	85
New Zealand	..	11	..	6	..	33	..	13	..	56	..	81
Nicaragua	..	..	..	..	..	..	..	..	..	..	..	..
Niger	7	8	6	5	69	51	29	24	25	41	66	71
Nigeria	52	..	57	..	10	..	5	..	38	..	38	..
Norway	10	7	6	3	40	35	14	10	50	59	80	87
Oman	52	..	24	..	21	..	33	..	27	..	43	..
Pakistan	..	44	..	67	..	20	..	11	..	36	..	22
Panama	*37*	29	*6*	3	*21*	21	*12*	11	*39*	50	*81*	86
Papua New Guinea	76	..	92	..	8	..	2	..	16	..	6	..
Paraguay	58	6	9	1	20	37	22	13	22	57	70	87
Peru	45	10	25	5	20	27	14	12	35	63	61	83
Philippines	60	48	37	28	16	19	15	13	25	33	48	59
Poland	..	21	..	20	..	41	..	21	..	38	..	59
Portugal	22	12	35	16	44	40	25	21	34	48	40	64
Puerto Rico	8	5	1	0	24	26	29	15	67	70	70	84
Romania	..	35	..	43	..	36	..	24	..	29	..	33
Russian Federation	19	..	13	..	50	..	37	..	31	..	50	..

2.4 Employment by economic activity

	Agriculture				Industry				Services			
	Male % of male labor force		Female % of female labor force		Male % of male labor force		Female % of female labor force		Male % of male labor force		Female % of female labor force	
	1980	1992–97[a]	1980	1992–97[a]	1980	1992–97[a]	1980	1992–97[a]	1980	1992–97[a]	1980	1992–97[a]
Rwanda	88	..	98	..	5	..	1	..	7	..	1	..
Saudi Arabia	45	..	25	..	17	..	5	..	39	..	70	..
Senegal	74	..	90	..	9	..	..	..	17	..	8	..
Sierra Leone	63	..	82	..	20	..	4	..	17	..	14	..
Singapore	2	0	..	0	33	34	40	25	65	66	59	75
Slovak Republic	15	11	13	6	38	49	34	28	48	41	54	67
Slovenia	14	12	17	13	49	49	37	31	38	38	46	57
South Africa	18	..	16	..	45	..	16	..	37	..	68	..
Spain	20	10	18	6	42	39	21	14	39	52	60	80
Sri Lanka	*44*	33	*51*	40	*19*	22	*18*	24	*30*	41	*28*	34
Sudan	66	..	88	..	9	..	4	..	24	..	8	..
Sweden	8	4	3	1	45	39	16	12	47	57	81	87
Switzerland	8	5	5	4	47	35	23	15	46	59	72	82
Syrian Arab Republic	..	23	..	54	..	28	..	8	..	49	..	38
Tajikistan	36	..	54	..	29	..	16	..	35	..	30	..
Tanzania	80	..	92	..	7	..	2	..	13	..	7	..
Thailand	68	49	74	52	13	22	8	17	20	29	18	32
Togo	70	..	67	..	12	..	7	..	19	..	26	..
Trinidad and Tobago	11	14	9	5	44	33	21	13	45	54	70	82
Tunisia	33	22	53	20	30	32	32	40	37	44	16	38
Turkey	45	30	88	65	22	29	5	13	33	41	8	21
Turkmenistan	33	..	46	..	32	..	16	..	36	..	38	..
Uganda	84	..	91	..	6	..	2	..	10	..	8	..
Ukraine	26	..	24	..	46	..	33	..	28	..	44	..
United Arab Emirates	5	..	0	..	40	..	7	..	55	..	93	..
United Kingdom	4	3	1	1	48	38	23	13	49	59	76	86
United States	5	4	2	2	40	34	19	13	55	63	80	85
Uruguay	..	7	..	2	..	34	..	17	..	59	..	82
Uzbekistan	35	..	46	..	34	..	19	..	32	..	36	..
Venezuela, RB	20	19	2	2	31	28	18	14	49	53	79	84
Vietnam	71	70	75	71	16	12	10	9	13	18	15	20
West Bank and Gaza	..	..	..	..	..	..	..	..	..	..	..	..
Yemen, Rep.	60	..	98	..	19	..	1	..	21	..	1	..
Yugoslavia, FR (Serb./Mont.)	..	..	49	..	..	..	19	..	..	..	32	..
Zambia	69	..	85	..	13	..	3	..	19	..	13	..
Zimbabwe	29	23	50	38	31	32	8	10	40	46	42	52
World	.. w	.. w	.. w	.. w	.. w	.. w	.. w	.. w	.. w	.. w	.. w	.. w
Low income	..	..	..	..	..	..	..	..	..	..	..	..
Excl. China & India	64	..	73	..	12	..	8	..	24	..	19	..
Middle income	33	..	31	..	33	..	25	..	34	..	45	..
Lower middle income	34	..	29	..	34	..	26	..	32	..	45	..
Upper middle income	..	24	..	22	..	30	..	15	..	46	..	62
Low & middle income	..	..	..	..	..	..	..	..	..	..	..	..
East Asia & Pacific	..	..	..	..	..	..	..	..	..	..	..	..
Europe & Central Asia	26	..	26	..	43	..	31	..	31	..	43	..
Latin America & Carib.	..	22	..	13	..	28	..	13	..	50	..	74
Middle East & N. Africa	39	..	47	..	25	..	14	..	37	..	40	..
South Asia	64	..	83	..	14	..	10	..	23	..	8	..
Sub-Saharan Africa	62	..	74	..	14	..	5	..	24	..	22	..
High income	8	5	7	3	41	37	22	16	51	58	71	81
Europe EMU	..	6	..	5	..	41	..	18	..	53	..	77

a. Data are for the most recent year available.

Employment by economic activity 2.4

About the data

The International Labour Organization (ILO) classifies economic activity on the basis of the International Standard Industrial Classification (ISIC) of All Economic Activities. Because this classification is based on where work is performed (industry) rather than on the type of work performed (occupation), all of an enterprise's employees are classified under the same industry, regardless of their trade or occupation. The categories should add up to 100 percent. Where they do not, the differences arise because of people who are not classifiable by economic activity.

Data on employment are drawn from labor force surveys, establishment censuses and surveys, administrative records of social insurance schemes, and official national estimates. The concept of employment generally refers to people above a certain age who worked, or who held a job, during a reference period. Employment data include both full-time and part-time workers. There are, however, many differences in how countries define and measure employment status, particularly for part-time workers, students, members of the armed forces, and household, or contributing family, workers. Where data are obtained from establishment surveys, they cover only employees; thus self-employed and contributing family workers are excluded. In such cases the employment share of the agricultural sector is underreported. Countries also take very different approaches to the treatment of unemployed people. In most countries unemployed people with previous job experience are classified according to their last job. But in some countries the unemployed and people seeking their first job are not classifiable by economic activity. Because of these differences, the size and distribution of employment by economic activity may not be fully comparable across countries (ILO, *Yearbook of Labour Statistics 1996,* p. 64).

The ILO's *Yearbook of Labour Statistics* reports data by major divisions of the ISIC revision 2 or ISIC revision 3. In this table the reported divisions or categories are aggregated into three broad groups: agriculture, industry, and services. An increasing number of countries report economic activity according to the ISIC. Where data are supplied according to national classifications, however, industry definitions and descriptions may differ. In addition, classification into broad groups may obscure fundamental differences in countries' industrial patterns.

The distribution of economic activity by gender reveals some interesting patterns. Agriculture accounts for the largest share of female employment in much of Africa and Asia. Services account for much of the increase in women's labor force participation in North Africa, Latin America and the Caribbean, and high-income economies. Worldwide, women are underrepresented in industry.

Segregating one sex in a narrow range of occupations significantly reduces economic efficiency by reducing labor market flexibility and the economy's ability to adapt to change. This segregation is particularly harmful for women, who have a much narrower range of labor market choices and lower levels of pay than men. But it is also detrimental to men when job losses are concentrated in industries dominated by men and job growth is centered in service occupations, where women often dominate, as has been the recent experience in many countries.

There are several explanations for the rising importance of service jobs for women. Many service jobs—such as nursing and social and clerical work—are considered "feminine" because of a perceived similarity with women's traditional roles. Women often do not receive the training needed to take advantage of changing employment opportunities. And the greater availability of part-time work in service industries may lure more women, although it is not clear whether this is a cause or an effect (United Nations Statistics Division 1991).

Figure 2.4

The informal sector is a vital source of employment

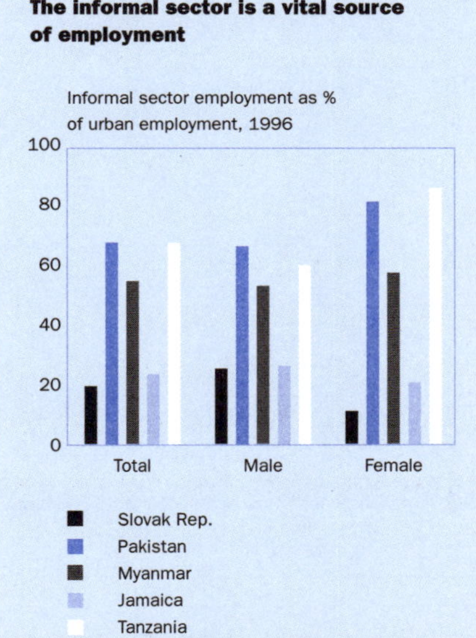

Note: Data for Pakistan refer to 1992 and those for Tanzania to 1995.

Source: International Labour Organization, Key Indicators of the Labour Market.

Informal sector employment is an essential survival strategy in countries lacking social safety nets such as unemployment insurance or where pensions and wages—especially in the public sector—are low. The informal sector is a vital part of the economy and of the labor market in many developing countries, especially in Asia and Sub-Saharan Africa.

Definitions

• **Agriculture** includes hunting, forestry, and fishing, corresponding to major division 1 (ISIC revision 2) or tabulation categories A and B (ISIC revision 3). • **Industry** includes mining and quarrying (including oil production), manufacturing, electricity, gas and water, and construction, corresponding to major divisions 2–5 (ISIC revision 2) or tabulation categories C–F (ISIC revision 3). • **Services** include wholesale and retail trade and restaurants and hotels; transport, storage, and communications; financing, insurance, real estate, and business services; and community, social, and personal services—corresponding to major divisions 6–9 (ISIC revision 2) or tabulation categories G–P (ISIC revision 3).

Data sources

The employment data are from the ILO database Key Indicators of the Labour Market (1999 issue).

2.5 Unemployment

	Unemployment						Long-term unemployment			Unemployment by level of educational attainment		
	Male % of male labor force		Female % of female labor force		Total % of total labor force		% of total unemployment			% of total unemployment		
							Male	Female	Total	Primary	Secondary	Tertiary
	1980–82[a]	1994–97[a]	1980–82[a]	1994–97[a]	1980–82[a]	1994–97[a]	1994–97[a]	1994–97[a]	1994–97[a]	1994–97[a]	1994–97[a]	1994–97[a]
Albania	..	..	..	..	5.6	..	..	..	..	..	..	..
Algeria	..	26.9	..	24.0	..	26.4	..	..	..	55.9	32.1	4.6
Angola	..	..	..	..	..	..	..	..	..	..	..	..
Argentina	..	15.4	..	17.6	2.3	16.3	..	..	..	55.7	28.7	4.8
Armenia	..	..	..	..	..	..	..	..	..	..	..	..
Australia	5.0	8.6	7.4	8.1	5.9	8.4	33.1	27.5	30.8	55.1	30.5	11.3
Austria	1.6	5.3	2.3	5.2	1.9	5.3	28.9	28.4	28.7	37.2	57.8	5.0
Azerbaijan	..	..	..	..	..	1.3	..	..	..	2.1	50.7	47.2
Bangladesh	..	2.7	..	2.3	..	..	..	..	..	47.4	28.4	..
Belarus	..	2.2	..	3.3	..	2.7	..	..	..	..	63.6	26.9
Belgium	..	7.1	..	11.5	..	9.0	59.4	61.5	60.5	..	..	..
Benin	..	..	..	..	..	..	..	..	..	..	..	..
Bolivia	..	3.7	..	4.5	..	4.2	..	..	..	24.0	42.1	28.9
Bosnia and Herzegovina	..	..	..	..	..	..	..	..	..	..	..	..
Botswana	..	19.4	..	23.9	..	21.5	..	..	..	..	..	..
Brazil	2.8	5.7	2.8	8.8	2.8	6.9	..	..	..	..	..	..
Bulgaria	..	14.2	..	14.1	..	13.7	59.4	61.7	60.4	..	52.7	7.3
Burkina Faso	..	..	..	..	..	..	..	..	..	..	..	..
Burundi	..	..	..	..	..	..	..	..	..	..	..	..
Cambodia	..	..	..	..	..	..	..	..	..	..	..	..
Cameroon	..	..	..	..	..	..	..	..	..	..	..	..
Canada	6.9	9.2	8.4	9.2	7.5	9.2	14.5	10.2	12.5	33.9	30.5	35.6
Central African Republic	..	..	..	..	..	..	..	..	..	54.3	3.7	2.0
Chad	..	..	..	..	..	..	..	..	..	..	..	..
Chile	10.6	4.7	10.0	6.6	10.4	5.3	53.2	72.5	59.7	30.5	53.3	12.4
China	..	..	..	..	4.9	3.0	..	..	..	..	..	..
Hong Kong, China	..	2.3	..	2.0	..	2.2	..	..	..	..	..	..
Colombia	..	9.8	..	15.1	..	12.1	..	..	..	21.1	58.5	18.7
Congo, Dem. Rep.	..	..	..	..	..	..	..	..	..	..	..	..
Congo, Rep.	..	..	..	..	..	..	..	..	..	..	..	..
Costa Rica	5.3	4.9	7.8	7.5	5.9	5.7	..	..	..	69.8	16.0	..
Côte d'Ivoire	..	..	..	..	..	..	..	..	..	..	..	..
Croatia	3.4	14.0	8.2	20.1	5.3	16.8	..	..	..	..	..	..
Cuba	..	..	..	..	..	..	..	..	..	..	..	..
Czech Republic	..	3.8	..	5.8	..	4.7	31.3	29.9	30.5	33.3	63.7	3.1
Denmark	6.5	4.5	7.6	6.4	7.0	5.4	26.3	27.9	27.2	35.0	46.7	16.8
Dominican Republic	..	9.5	..	28.6	..	15.9	..	..	..	50.4	31.1	9.6
Ecuador	..	7.0	..	12.7	..	9.2	..	..	..	..	..	..
Egypt, Arab Rep.	3.9	7.6	19.2	24.1	5.2	11.3	..	..	..	..	..	..
El Salvador	..	9.5	..	5.3	12.9	8.0	..	..	..	53.9	18.8	8.3
Eritrea	..	..	..	..	..	..	..	..	..	..	..	..
Estonia	..	10.7	..	9.2	..	10.0	..	..	..	22.0	45.7	32.9
Ethiopia	..	..	..	..	..	..	..	..	..	27.5	38.3	3.3
Finland	4.5	13.8	4.7	15.1	4.6	14.4	33.9	28.9	31.4	40.0	50.2	10.0
France	4.1	10.8	9.1	14.2	6.1	12.3	39.1	43.3	41.2	..	..	..
Gabon	..	..	..	..	..	..	..	..	..	..	..	..
Gambia, The	..	..	..	..	..	..	..	..	..	..	..	..
Georgia	..	..	..	..	..	..	..	..	..	..	..	..
Germany	..	8.9	..	10.9	..	9.8	44.5	51.7	47.8	23.1	59.4	13.6
Ghana	..	..	..	..	..	..	..	..	..	..	..	..
Greece	3.3	6.2	5.7	14.8	2.4	9.6	45.8	62.2	55.7	35.2	40.5	23.2
Guatemala	..	..	..	..	..	..	..	..	..	..	..	..
Guinea	..	..	..	..	..	..	..	..	..	..	..	..
Guinea-Bissau	..	..	..	..	..	..	..	..	..	..	..	..
Haiti	..	..	..	..	..	..	..	..	..	..	..	..
Honduras	..	3.2	..	3.2	..	3.2	..	..	..	..	..	..

Unemployment 2.5

	Unemployment						Long-term unemployment			Unemployment by level of educational attainment		
	Male % of male labor force		Female % of female labor force		Total % of total labor force		% of total unemployment			% of total unemployment		
							Male	Female	Total	Primary	Secondary	Tertiary
	1980–82[a]	1994–97[a]	1980–82[a]	1994–97[a]	1980–82[a]	1994–97[a]	1994–97[a]	1994–97[a]	1994–97[a]	1994–97[a]	1994–97[a]	1994–97[a]
Hungary	..	9.5	..	7.7	..	8.7	52.6	49.2	51.3	41.1	56.1	2.8
India	..	..	..	..	..	..	..	..	..	..	38.1	27.3
Indonesia	..	3.3	..	5.1	..	4.0	..	..	..	..	..	..
Iran, Islamic Rep.	..	..	..	..	..	..	..	..	..	..	..	..
Iraq	..	..	..	..	..	..	..	..	..	..	..	..
Ireland	11.4	10.3	8.2	10.3	10.5	10.3	63.3	46.9	57.0	63.4	25.5	10.8
Israel	4.1	6.8	6.0	8.8	4.8	7.7	..	..	..	23.6	44.3	31.2
Italy	4.8	9.7	13.2	16.9	7.6	12.5	66.5	66.2	66.3	60.2	31.7	6.4
Jamaica	16.3	9.9	39.6	23.0	27.3	16.0	18.3	29.3	25.6	..	..	..
Japan	2.0	3.4	2.0	3.4	2.0	3.4	28.8	11.8	21.8	22.8	53.6	23.7
Jordan	..	..	..	..	..	..	..	..	..	50.2	14.8	32.4
Kazakhstan	..	..	..	..	..	4.1	..	..	..	..	..	..
Kenya	..	..	..	..	..	..	..	..	..	..	..	..
Korea, Dem. Rep.	..	..	..	..	..	..	..	..	..	..	..	..
Korea, Rep.	..	2.8	..	2.3	..	2.6	3.5	0.9	2.5	14.0	55.4	23.4
Kuwait	..	..	..	..	..	..	..	..	..	..	..	..
Kyrgyz Republic	..	..	..	..	..	..	..	..	..	34.4	54.5	11.1
Lao PDR	..	..	..	..	..	..	..	..	..	..	..	..
Latvia	..	14.3	..	14.6	..	14.4	63.1	63.0	63.0	..	72.2	7.9
Lebanon	..	..	..	..	..	..	..	..	..	..	..	..
Lesotho	..	..	..	..	..	..	..	..	..	..	..	..
Libya	..	..	..	..	..	..	..	..	..	..	..	..
Lithuania	..	6.6	..	6.9	..	6.7	..	..	..	37.5	37.8	24.7
Macedonia, FYR	15.6	35.0	32.8	44.5	22.0	38.8	..	..	..	..	..	..
Madagascar	..	..	..	..	..	..	..	..	..	..	37.4	4.1
Malawi	..	..	..	..	..	..	..	..	..	..	..	..
Malaysia	..	..	..	..	..	2.5	..	..	..	..	..	..
Mali	..	..	..	..	..	..	..	..	..	..	..	..
Mauritania	..	..	..	..	..	..	..	..	..	..	..	..
Mauritius	..	7.8	..	13.9	..	9.8	..	..	..	35.4	63.8	..
Mexico	..	2.9	..	4.7	..	3.5	2.1	2.6	2.3	16.3	40.9	17.0
Moldova	..	..	..	..	..	1.0	..	..	..	..	..	..
Mongolia	..	..	..	..	..	..	..	..	..	..	..	..
Morocco	..	15.8	..	23.0	..	17.8	..	..	..	..	..	..
Mozambique	..	..	..	..	..	..	..	..	..	..	..	..
Myanmar	..	..	..	..	..	..	..	..	..	..	..	..
Namibia	..	..	..	..	..	..	..	..	..	..	..	..
Nepal	..	..	..	..	..	..	..	..	..	..	..	..
Netherlands	4.3	4.4	5.2	7.0	4.6	5.5	49.9	48.5	49.1	30.1	33.6	15.5
New Zealand	..	6.6	..	6.7	..	6.7	22.2	16.1	19.5	..	..	..
Nicaragua	..	12.6	..	14.8	..	..	..	..	..	..	..	..
Niger	..	..	..	..	..	..	..	..	..	..	..	..
Nigeria	..	..	..	..	..	..	..	..	..	..	..	..
Norway	1.2	4.0	2.1	4.3	1.7	4.1	13.0	7.7	10.6	25.8	55.9	15.1
Oman	..	..	..	..	..	..	..	..	..	..	..	..
Pakistan	3.0	4.1	7.5	13.7	3.6	5.4	..	..	..	25.0	13.9	9.8
Panama	..	11.3	..	20.0	..	14.3	..	..	..	43.3	35.8	20.1
Papua New Guinea	..	..	..	..	..	..	..	..	..	..	..	..
Paraguay	3.8	7.8	4.8	8.6	4.1	8.2	..	..	..	..	..	..
Peru	..	6.8	..	8.9	..	7.7	..	..	..	15.4	57.1	25.7
Philippines	3.2	7.5	7.5	8.5	4.8	7.4	..	..	..	..	..	..
Poland	..	9.5	..	13.2	..	11.2	33.5	41.9	38.0	23.9	71.5	4.6
Portugal	3.7	6.6	12.2	8.5	7.0	7.5	53.4	57.7	55.6	73.6	15.9	5.8
Puerto Rico	19.5	14.4	12.3	12.1	17.1	13.5	..	..	..	..	..	..
Romania	..	5.7	..	6.4	..	6.0	44.1	50.1	47.0	23.9	69.0	5.9
Russian Federation	..	9.6	..	9.0	..	11.3	29.5	36.8	32.8	19.4	72.3	8.3

2.5 Unemployment

	Unemployment						Long-term unemployment			Unemployment by level of educational attainment		
	Male % of male labor force		Female % of female labor force		Total % of total labor force		% of total unemployment			% of total unemployment		
							Male	Female	Total	Primary	Secondary	Tertiary
	1980–82[a]	1994–97[a]	1980–82[a]	1994–97[a]	1980–82[a]	1994–97[a]	1994–97[a]	1994–97[a]	1994–97[a]	1994–97[a]	1994–97[a]	1994–97[a]
Rwanda	..	..	..	..	..	..	..	..	..	..	..	..
Saudi Arabia	..	..	..	..	..	..	..	..	..	..	..	..
Senegal	..	..	..	..	..	..	..	..	..	..	..	..
Sierra Leone	..	..	..	..	..	..	..	..	..	..	..	..
Singapore	..	2.4	..	2.4	..	2.4	..	..	..	26.8	27.3	29.7
Slovak Republic	..	10.8	..	12.5	..	11.6	49.2	52.5	50.3	..	67.5	3.3
Slovenia	..	7.0	..	7.3	..	7.1	61.1	50.0	55.1	31.9	60.9	4.3
South Africa	..	..	..	..	..	5.1	..	..	..	..	..	..
Spain	10.4	15.8	12.8	28.3	11.1	20.6	49.9	60.4	55.5	55.9	17.8	18.8
Sri Lanka	..	8.0	..	17.6	..	11.3	..	..	..	..	..	..
Sudan	..	..	..	..	..	..	..	..	..	..	..	..
Sweden	1.7	8.3	2.3	7.5	2.0	7.9	31.8	26.9	29.6	31.0	53.2	9.1
Switzerland	0.2	4.3	0.3	3.9	0.2	4.1	25.5	32.8	28.5	..	..	..
Syrian Arab Republic	..	..	3.8	..	3.9	..	..	..	..	..	..	..
Tajikistan	..	2.4	..	2.9	..	2.7	..	..	..	10.6	83.2	6.3
Tanzania	..	..	..	..	..	..	..	..	..	..	..	..
Thailand	1.0	0.9	0.7	0.9	0.8	0.9	..	..	..	63.3	11.3	20.5
Togo	..	..	..	..	..	..	..	..	..	..	..	..
Trinidad and Tobago	8.0	13.2	14.0	21.0	10.0	16.2	24.0	39.9	31.7	40.5	57.5	1.3
Tunisia	..	..	..	..	..	..	..	..	..	..	26.1	1.7
Turkey	9.0	6.0	23.0	7.4	10.9	6.4	38.1	49.0	41.6	..	..	..
Turkmenistan	..	..	..	..	..	..	..	..	..	..	..	..
Uganda	..	..	..	..	..	..	..	..	..	..	..	..
Ukraine	..	9.5	..	8.4	..	8.9	..	..	..	5.6	27.6	66.9
United Arab Emirates	..	..	..	..	..	..	..	..	..	..	..	..
United Kingdom	..	8.1	..	5.8	..	7.1	44.9	27.8	38.6	..	43.6	10.3
United States	6.9	4.9	7.4	5.0	7.1	4.9	9.4	8.0	8.7	..	37.2	39.2
Uruguay	..	8.0	..	13.2	..	10.2	..	..	..	..	..	..
Uzbekistan	..	0.3	..	0.5	..	0.4	..	..	..	..	..	..
Venezuela, RB	..	9.0	..	12.8	5.9	10.3	..	..	..	60.0	22.6	13.1
Vietnam	..	..	..	..	..	..	..	..	..	..	..	..
West Bank and Gaza	..	..	..	..	..	..	..	..	..	..	..	..
Yemen, Rep.	..	..	..	..	..	..	..	..	..	..	..	..
Yugoslavia, FR (Serb./Mont.)	..	..	..	..	..	..	..	..	..	..	..	..
Zambia	..	..	..	..	..	..	..	..	..	..	..	..
Zimbabwe	..	..	..	..	..	..	..	..	..	41.1	52.7	0.1

a. Data are for the most recent year available.

Unemployment 2.5

About the data

Unemployment and total employment in a country are the broadest indicators of economic activity as reflected by the labor market. The International Labour Organization (ILO) defines the unemployed as members of the economically active population who are without work but available for and seeking work, including people who have lost their jobs and those who have voluntarily left work. Some unemployment is unavoidable in all economies. At any time some workers are temporarily unemployed—between jobs as employers look for the right workers and workers search for better jobs. Such unemployment, often called frictional unemployment, results from the normal operation of labor markets.

Changes in unemployment over time may reflect changes in the demand for and supply of labor, but they may also reflect changes in reporting practices. Ironically, low unemployment rates can often disguise substantial poverty in a country, while high unemployment rates can occur in countries with a high level of economic development and low incidence of poverty. In countries without unemployment or welfare benefits, people eke out a living in the informal sector. In countries with well-developed safety nets, workers can afford to wait for suitable or desirable jobs. But high and sustained unemployment indicates serious inefficiencies in the allocation of resources.

The ILO definition of unemployment notwithstanding, reference periods, criteria for seeking work, and the treatment of people temporarily laid off and those seeking work for the first time vary across countries. In many developing countries it is especially difficult to measure employment and unemployment in agriculture. The timing of a survey, for example, can maximize the seasonal effects of agricultural unemployment. And informal sector employment is difficult to quantify in the absence of regulation for registering and tracking informal activities.

Data on unemployment are drawn from labor force sample surveys and general household sample surveys, social insurance statistics, employment office statistics, and official estimates, which are usually based on combined information drawn from one or more of the above sources. Labor force surveys generally yield the most comprehensive data because they include groups—particularly people seeking work for the first time—not covered in other unemployment statistics. These surveys generally use a definition of unemployment that follows the international recommendations more closely than that used by other sources and therefore generate statistics that are more comparable internationally.

By contrast, the quality and completeness of data obtained from employment offices and social insurance programs vary widely. Where employment offices work closely with social insurance schemes, and registration with such offices is a prerequisite for receipt of unemployment benefits, the two sets of unemployment estimates tend to be comparable. Where registration is voluntary, and where employment offices function only in more populous areas, employment office statistics do not give a reliable indication of unemployment. Most commonly excluded from both these sources are discouraged workers who have given up their job search because they believe that no employment opportunities exist or do not register as unemployed after their benefits have been exhausted. Thus measured unemployment may be higher in economies that offer more or longer unemployment benefits.

Long-term unemployment is measured in terms of duration, that is, the length of time that an unemployed person has been without work and looking for a job. The underlying assumption is that shorter periods of joblessness are of less concern, especially when the unemployed are covered by unemployment benefits or similar forms of welfare support. The length of time a person has been unemployed is difficult to measure, because the ability to recall the length of that time diminishes as the period of joblessness extends. Women's long-term unemployment is likely to be lower in countries where women constitute a large share of the unpaid family workforce. Such women have more access than men to nonmarket work and are more likely to drop out of the labor force and not be counted as unemployed.

Economies for which unemployment data are not consistently available or were deemed unreliable have been omitted from the table.

Definitions

• **Unemployment** refers to the share of the labor force without work but available for and seeking employment. Definitions of labor force and unemployment differ by country (see *About the data*). • **Long-term unemployment** refers to the number of people with continuous periods of unemployment extending for a year or longer, expressed as a percentage of total unemployment. • **Unemployment by level of educational attainment** shows the unemployed by level of educational attainment, as a percentage of total unemployed. The levels of educational attainment accord with the United Nations Educational, Cultural, and Scientific Organization's (UNESCO) International Standard Classification of Education.

Data sources

The unemployment data are from the ILO database Key Indicators of the Labour Market (1999 issue).

Table 2.5a

Unemployment rate by level of educational attainment

%

		Less than primary	Primary	Secondary	Tertiary
Austria	1997	..	37.2	57.8	5.0
Canada	1997	..	33.9	30.5	35.6
Japan	1997	..	22.8	53.6	23.7
Jordan	1996	2.5	50.2	14.8	32.4
Peru	1997	1.8	15.4	57.1	25.7
Poland	1997	..	23.9	71.5	4.6
Russian Federation	1996	..	19.4	72.3	8.3
Thailand	1997	4.7	63.3	11.3	20.5
Venezuela, RB	1996	4.1	60.0	22.6	13.1
Zimbabwe	1997	6.0	41.1	52.7	0.1

.. Not available.
Source: International Labour Organization, Key Indicators of the Labour Market.

The distribution of unemployed workers across education levels varies among countries, largely reflecting economic conditions and labor market institutions. Information about this distribution can aid both employment and education policy.

Knowing the education and skill levels of the unemployed can help in improving training programs for the jobless or designing job creation programs. And data on unemployment at different education levels can help in developing education and training strategies that improve education outcomes for workers.

2.6 Wages and productivity

	Average hours worked per week		Minimum wage		Agricultural wage		Labor cost per worker in manufacturing		Value added per worker in manufacturing	
			$ per year		$ per year		$ per year		$ per year	
	1980–84	1995–99[a]	1980–84	1995–99[a]	1980–84	1995–99[a]	1980–84	1995–99[a]	1980–84	1995–99[a]
Albania	..	..	..	..	..	..	..	..	..	..
Algeria	..	..	..	*1,340*	..	..	6,242	..	11,306	..
Angola	..	..	..	..	..	..	..	..	..	..
Argentina	41	*40*	..	2,400	..	..	6,768	*7,338*	33,694	*37,480*
Armenia	..	..	..	..	..	..	..	..	..	..
Australia	37	*39*	..	*12,712*	11,212	*15,124*	14,749	26,087	27,801	*57,857*
Austria	33	*32*	..	[b]	..	..	11,949	*28,342*	20,956	*53,061*
Azerbaijan	..	..	..	..	..	..	..	..	..	..
Bangladesh	..	*52*	..	*492*	192	*360*	556	*671*	1,820	*1,711*
Belarus	..	..	..	..	1,641	410	2,233	754	..	..
Belgium	..	*38*	7,661	15,882	6,399	..	12,805	*24,132*	25,579	*58,678*
Benin	..	..	..	..	..	..	..	..	..	..
Bolivia	..	*46*	..	529	..	..	4,432	*2,343*	21,519	*26,282*
Bosnia and Herzegovina	..	..	..	..	..	..	..	..	..	..
Botswana	45	..	894	961	650	*1,223*	3,250	*2,884*	7,791	..
Brazil	..	..	1,690	1,308	..	..	10,080	*14,134*	43,232	*61,595*
Bulgaria	..	..	..	*573*	..	*1,372*	2,485	*1,179*	..	..
Burkina Faso	..	..	695	585	..	..	3,282	..	15,886	..
Burundi	..	..	..	..	..	..	..	..	..	..
Cambodia	..	..	..	..	..	..	..	..	..	..
Cameroon	..	..	..	..	..	..	..	..	..	..
Canada	38	*38*	4,974	7,897	20,429	*30,625*	17,710	*28,424*	36,903	*60,712*
Central African Republic	..	..	..	..	..	..	..	..	..	..
Chad	..	..	..	..	..	..	..	..	..	..
Chile	43	45	663	1,781	..	..	6,234	*5,822*	32,805	*32,977*
China	..	..	..	..	349	*325*	472	729	3,061	*2,885*
Hong Kong, China	48	*46*	..	..	..	..	4,127	13,539	7,886	*19,533*
Colombia	..	..	..	*1,128*	..	..	2,988	*2,507*	15,096	*17,061*
Congo, Dem. Rep.	..	..	..	..	..	..	..	..	..	..
Congo, Rep.	..	..	..	..	..	..	..	..	..	..
Costa Rica	..	*47*	1,042	*1,638*	982	*1,697*	2,433	*2,829*	7,185	*7,184*
Côte d'Ivoire	..	..	1,246	871	..	..	5,132	*9,995*	16,158	..
Croatia	..	..	..	..	..	..	..	..	..	..
Cuba	..	..	..	..	..	..	..	..	..	..
Czech Republic	43	*40*	..	..	2,277	*1,885*	2,306	*1,876*	5,782	*5,094*
Denmark	..	*37*	9,170	19,933	..	..	16,169	*29,235*	27,919	*49,273*
Dominican Republic	44	44	..	*1,439*	..	..	2,191	*1,806*	8,603	..
Ecuador	..	..	1,637	*492*	..	..	5,065	*3,738*	12,197	*9,747*
Egypt, Arab Rep.	58	..	343	*415*	..	..	2,210	*1,863*	3,691	*5,976*
El Salvador	..	..	..	*790*	..	..	3,654	..	14,423	..
Eritrea	..	..	..	..	..	..	..	..	..	..
Estonia	..	..	..	..	..	..	..	..	..	..
Ethiopia	..	..	..	..	..	..	..	*1,596*	..	*7,094*
Finland	..	*38*	..	[b]	..	..	11,522	*26,615*	25,945	*55,037*
France	40	*39*	6,053	*12,072*	..	..	18,488	..	26,751	*61,019*
Gabon	..	..	..	..	..	..	..	..	..	..
Gambia, The	..	..	..	..	..	..	..	..	..	..
Georgia	..	..	..	..	..	..	..	..	..	..
Germany	41	*40*	..	[b]	..	..	15,708	*33,226*	34,945	*79,616*
Ghana	..	..	..	..	1,470	..	2,306	..	12,130	..
Greece	..	*41*	..	*5,246*	..	..	6,461	15,899	14,561	*30,429*
Guatemala	..	..	..	*459*	..	..	2,605	*1,802*	11,144	*9,235*
Guinea	40	..	..	..	..	..	..	..	..	..
Guinea-Bissau	48	..	..	..	..	..	..	..	..	..
Haiti	..	..	..	..	..	..	..	..	..	..
Honduras	..	*44*	..	..	1,623	..	2,949	*2,658*	7,458	*7,427*

Wages and productivity 2.6

	Average hours worked per week		Minimum wage $ per year		Agricultural wage $ per year		Labor cost per worker in manufacturing $ per year		Value added per worker in manufacturing $ per year	
	1980–84	1995–99[a]	1980–84	1995–99[a]	1980–84	1995–99[a]	1980–84	1995–99[a]	1980–84	1995–99[a]
Hungary	35	33	..	1,132	1,186	1,766	1,410	2,777	4,307	6,106
India	46	..	..	408	205	245	1,035	1,192	2,108	3,118
Indonesia	..	..	..	241	..	..	898	1,008	3,807	5,139
Iran, Islamic Rep.	..	..	..	..	..	..	9,737	..	17,679	..
Iraq	..	..	..	..	..	..	4,624	13,288	13,599	34,316
Ireland	41	41	..	..	..	..	10,190	25,414	26,510	86,036
Israel	36	36	..	5,861	4,582	7,906	13,541	26,635	23,459	35,526
Italy	..	32	..	[b]	..	..	15,895	35,138	..	..
Jamaica	..	39	782	692	..	..	5,218	3,655	12,056	11,091
Japan	47	47	3,920	12,265	..	..	12,306	31,687	34,456	92,582
Jordan	..	50	[b]	[b]	..	..	4,643	2,082	16,337	11,906
Kazakhstan	..	..	..	..	..	..	..	..	..	..
Kenya	41	39	..	..	508	568	104	94	234	228
Korea, Dem. Rep.	..	..	..	..	..	..	..	..	..	..
Korea, Rep.	52	48	..	3,903	..	..	3,153	10,743	11,617	40,916
Kuwait	..	..	..	8,244	..	..	10,281	..	30,341	..
Kyrgyz Republic	..	..	..	89	1,695	168	2,287	687	..	..
Lao PDR	..	..	..	..	..	..	..	..	..	..
Latvia	..	..	..	..	..	..	..	366	..	..
Lebanon	..	..	..	..	..	..	..	..	..	..
Lesotho	..	45	..	..	..	..	1,442	..	6,047	..
Libya	..	..	..	..	..	..	8,648	..	21,119	..
Lithuania	..	..	..	..	..	..	..	..	..	..
Macedonia, FYR	..	..	..	..	..	..	..	..	..	..
Madagascar	..	40	..	..	..	..	1,575	..	3,542	..
Malawi	..	..	..	..	..	..	..	..	..	..
Malaysia	..	..	..	[b]	..	..	2,519	3,429	8,454	12,661
Mali	..	..	321	459	..	..	2,983	..	10,477	..
Mauritania	..	..	..	..	..	..	..	..	..	..
Mauritius	..	..	..	..	..	..	1,465	1,973	2,969	4,217
Mexico	43	45	1,343	768	1,031	908	3,772	7,607	17,448	25,931
Moldova	..	..	..	..	..	..	..	..	..	..
Mongolia	..	..	..	..	..	..	..	..	..	..
Morocco	..	..	..	1,672	..	..	2,583	3,391	6,328	9,089
Mozambique	..	..	..	..	..	..	..	..	..	..
Myanmar	..	..	..	..	..	..	..	..	..	..
Namibia	..	..	..	..	..	..	..	..	..	..
Nepal	..	..	..	..	..	..	371	..	1,523	..
Netherlands	40	39	9,074	15,170	..	..	18,891	39,865	27,491	56,801
New Zealand	39	39	3,309	9,091	..	..	10,605	23,767	16,835	32,723
Nicaragua	..	44	..	..	..	..	..	..	..	..
Niger	40	..	..	..	..	..	4,074	..	22,477	..
Nigeria	..	..	..	300	..	..	4,812	..	20,000	..
Norway	35	35	..	[b]	..	..	14,935	38,415	24,905	51,510
Oman	..	..	..	..	..	..	..	3,099	..	61,422
Pakistan	48	..	..	600	..	..	1,264	..	6,214	..
Panama	..	..	..	..	..	..	4,768	6,351	15,327	17,320
Papua New Guinea	44	..	..	..	..	..	4,825	..	13,563	..
Paraguay	36	39	..	..	1,606	1,210	2,509	3,241	..	14,873
Peru	48	..	..	..	..	944	2,988	..	15,962	..
Philippines	47	43	915	1,472	382	..	1,240	2,450	5,266	10,781
Poland	36	33	320	1,584	1,726	1,301	1,682	1,714	6,242	7,637
Portugal	39	40	1,606	4,086	..	..	3,115	7,577	7,161	17,273
Puerto Rico	..	..	..	..	..	..	..	..	..	..
Romania	..	40	..	..	1,669	1,864	1,739	1,190	..	3,482
Russian Federation	..	..	863	297	2,417	659	2,524	1,528	..	..

2.6 Wages and productivity

	Average hours worked per week		Minimum wage $ per year		Agricultural wage $ per year		Labor cost per worker in manufacturing $ per year		Value added per worker in manufacturing $ per year	
	1980–84	1995–99[a]	1980–84	1995–99[a]	1980–84	1995–99[a]	1980–84	1995–99[a]	1980–84	1995–99[a]
Rwanda	..	..	..	..	..	..	1,871	..	9,835	..
Saudi Arabia	..	..	..	..	..	..	9,814	..	..	..
Senegal	..	..	993	848	..	..	2,828	*7,754*	6,415	..
Sierra Leone	44	..	..	..	..	..	1,624	..	7,807	..
Singapore	..	*46*	..	..	..	*4,856*	5,576	21,534	16,442	*40,674*
Slovak Republic	..	..	..	..	..	..	..	..	..	..
Slovenia	..	..	..	..	..	..	..	*9,632*	..	*12,536*
South Africa	..	*42*	..	b	..	..	6,261	*8,475*	12,705	*16,612*
Spain	38	*37*	3,058	5,778	..	..	8,276	*19,329*	18,936	*47,016*
Sri Lanka	50	*53*	..	..	198	*264*	447	*604*	2,057	*3,405*
Sudan	..	..	..	..	..	..	..	..	..	..
Sweden	36	*37*	..	..	9,576	*27,098*	13,038	29,043	32,308	*56,675*
Switzerland	44	*42*	..	b		..		..	..	*61,848*
Syrian Arab Republic	..	..	..	..	..	..	2,844	*4,338*	9,607	*9,918*
Tajikistan	..	..	..	..	..	..	..	..	..	..
Tanzania	..	..	..	..	..	..	1,123	..	3,339	..
Thailand	48	..	..	*1,083*	..	..	2,305	*2,705*	11,072	*19,946*
Togo	..	..	..	..	..	..	..	..	..	..
Trinidad and Tobago	..	*40*	..	*2,974*	..	..	..	..	14,008	..
Tunisia	..	..	1,381	*1,525*	668	*968*	3,344	*3,599*	7,111	..
Turkey	..	*48*	594	1,254	1,015	*2,896*	3,582	*7,958*	13,994	*32,961*
Turkmenistan	..	..	..	..	..	..	..	..	..	..
Uganda	43	..	..	..	..	..	253	..	..	..
Ukraine	..	..	..	..	..	..	..	..	..	..
United Arab Emirates	..	..	..	..	..	..	6,968	..	20,344	..
United Kingdom	42	*40*	..	b	..	..	11,406	*23,843*	24,716	*55,060*
United States	40	*41*	6,006	8,056	..	..	19,103	*28,907*	47,276	*81,353*
Uruguay	48	*42*	1,262	1,027	1,289	..	4,128	*3,738*	13,722	*16,028*
Uzbekistan	..	..	..	..	..	..	..	..	..	..
Venezuela, RB	41	..	1,869	*1,463*	..	..	11,188	*4,667*	37,063	*24,867*
Vietnam	..	47	..	134	..	442	..	711	..	..
West Bank and Gaza	..	..	..	..	..	..	..	..	..	..
Yemen, Rep.	..	..	..	..	..	..	4,492	1,291	17,935	5,782
Yugoslavia, FR (Serb./Mont.)	..	..	..	..	..	..	..	..	..	..
Zambia	..	*45*	..	..	..	..	3,183	*4,292*	11,753	*16,615*
Zimbabwe	..	..	..	..	1,065	..	4,097	*3,422*	9,625	*11,944*

a. Figures in italics refer to 1990–94. b. Country has sectoral minimum wages but no minimum wage policy.

Wages and productivity 2.6

About the data

Much of the available data on labor markets are collected through national reporting systems that depend on plant-level surveys. Even when these data are compiled and reported by international agencies such as the International Labour Organization or the United Nations Industrial Development Organization, differences in definitions, coverage, and units of account limit their comparability across countries. The indicators in this table are the result of a research project at the World Bank that has compiled results from more than 300 national and international sources in an effort to provide a set of uniform and representative labor market indicators. Nevertheless, many differences in reporting practices persist, some of which are described below.

Analyses of labor force participation, employment, and underemployment often rely on the number of hours of work per week. The indicator reported in the table is the time spent at the workplace working, preparing for work, or waiting for work to be supplied or for a machine to be fixed. It also includes the time spent at the workplace when no work is being performed but for which payment is made under a guaranteed work contract or time spent on short periods of rest. Hours paid for but not spent at the place of work, such as paid annual and sick leave, paid holidays, paid meal breaks, and time spent in commuting between home and workplace, are not included, however. When this information is not available, the table reports the number of hours paid for, comprising the hours actually worked plus the hours paid for but not spent in the workplace. Data on hours worked are influenced by differences in methods of compilation and coverage as well as by national practices relating to the number of days worked and overtime, making comparisons across countries difficult.

Wages refer to remuneration in cash and in kind paid to employees at regular intervals.They exclude employers' contributions to social security and pension schemes as well as other benefits received by employees under these schemes. In some countries the national minimum wage represents a "floor," with higher minimum wages for particular occupations and skills set through collective bargaining. In those countries the agreements reached by employers associations and trade unions are extended by the government to all firms in a specific sector, or at least to large firms. In general, changes in the national minimum wage are associated with parallel changes in the minimum wages set through collective bargaining.

In many developing countries agricultural workers are hired on a casual or daily basis and lack any social security benefits. International comparisons of agricultural wages are subject to greater reservations than those of wages in other activities. The nature of the work carried out by different categories of agricultural workers and the length of the workday and workweek vary considerably from one country to another. Seasonal fluctuations in agricultural wages are more important in some countries than in others. And the methods followed in different countries for estimating the monetary value of payments in kind are not uniform.

Labor cost per worker in manufacturing is sometimes used as a measure of international competitiveness. The indicator reported in the table is the ratio of total compensation to the number of workers in the manufacturing sector. Compensation includes direct wages, salaries, and other remuneration paid directly by employers plus all contributions by employers to social security programs on behalf of their employees. But there are unavoidable differences in concepts and reference periods and in reporting practices. Remuneration for time not worked, bonuses and gratuities, and housing and family allowances should be considered part of the compensation costs, along with severance and termination pay. These indirect labor costs can vary substantially from country to country, depending on the labor laws and collective bargaining agreements in force. Figures are converted into U.S. dollars using the average exchange rate for each year.

International competitiveness also depends on productivity. Value added per worker in manufacturing is a frequently cited measure of productivity. The indicator reported in the table is the ratio of total value added in manufacturing to the number of employees engaged in that sector. Total value added is estimated as the difference between the value of industrial output and the value of materials and supplies for production (including fuel and purchased electricity) and cost of industrial services received. Figures are converted into U.S. dollars using the average exchange rate for each year.

Observations on labor costs and value added per worker are from plant-level surveys covering relatively large establishments, usually employing 10 or more workers and mostly in the formal sector. In high-income countries the coverage of these surveys tends to be quite good. In developing countries there is often a substantial bias toward very large establishments in the formal sector. As a result figures may not be strictly comparable across countries.

The data in the table are period averages and refer to workers of both sexes.

Definitions

• **Average hours worked per week** refer to all workers (male and female) in nonagricultural activities or, if unavailable, in manufacturing. The data correspond to hours actually worked, to hours paid for, or to statutory hours of work in a normal workweek. • **Minimum wage** corresponds to the most general regime for nonagricultural activities. When rates vary across sectors, only that for manufacturing (or commerce, if the manufacturing wage is unavailable) is reported. • **Agricultural wage** is based on daily wages in agriculture. • **Labor cost per worker in manufacturing** is obtained by dividing the total payroll by the number of employees, or the number of people engaged, in manufacturing establishments. • **Value added per worker in manufacturing** is obtained by dividing the value added of manufacturing establishments by the number of employees, or the number of people engaged, in those establishments.

Data sources

The data in the table are drawn from Martin Rama and Raquel Artecona's "Database of Labor Market Indicators across Countries" (1999).

2.7 Poverty

	National poverty line								International poverty line				
	Survey year	Population below the poverty line Rural %	Population below the poverty line Urban %	Population below the poverty line National %	Survey year	Population below the poverty line Rural %	Population below the poverty line Urban %	Population below the poverty line National %	Survey year	Population below $1 a day %	Poverty gap at $1 a day %	Population below $2 a day %	Poverty gap at $2 a day %
Albania		..	..	..		..	..	..		..	..	..	..
Algeria	1988	16.6	7.3	12.2	1995	30.3	14.7	22.6	1995	<2	<0.5	15.1	3.6
Angola		..	..	..		..	..	..		..	..	..	..
Argentina	1991	..	..	25.5	1993	..	..	17.6		..	..	..	..
Armenia		..	..	..		..	..	..		..	..	..	..
Australia		..	..	..		..	..	..		..	..	..	..
Austria		..	..	..		..	..	..		..	..	..	..
Azerbaijan	1995	..	..	68.1		..	..	..		..	..	..	..
Bangladesh	1991–92	46.0	23.3	42.7	1995–96	39.8	14.3	35.6	1996	29.1	5.9	77.8	31.8
Belarus	1995	..	..	22.5		..	..	..	1998	<2	<0.5	<2	0.1
Belgium		..	..	..		..	..	..		..	..	..	..
Benin	1995	..	..	33.0		..	..	..		..	..	..	..
Bolivia	1993	..	29.3	..	1995	79.1	..	..	1990	11.3	2.2	38.6	13.5
Bosnia and Herzegovina		..	..	..		..	..	..		..	..	..	..
Botswana		..	..	..		..	..	..	1985–86	33.3	12.5	61.4	30.7
Brazil	1990	32.6	13.1	17.4		..	..	..	1997	5.1	1.3	17.4	6.3
Bulgaria		..	..	..		..	..	..	1995	<2	<0.5	7.8	1.6
Burkina Faso		..	..	..		..	..	..	1994	61.2	25.5	85.8	50.9
Burundi	1990	..	..	36.2		..	..	..		..	..	..	..
Cambodia	1993–94	43.1	24.8	39.0	1997	40.1	21.1	36.1		..	..	..	..
Cameroon	1984	32.4	44.4	40.0		..	..	..		..	..	..	..
Canada		..	..	..		..	..	..		..	..	..	..
Central African Republic		..	..	..		..	..	..	1993	66.6	38.1	84.0	58.4
Chad	1995–96	67.0	63.0	64.0		..	..	..		..	..	..	..
Chile	1992	..	..	21.6	1994	..	..	20.5	1994	4.2	0.7	20.3	5.9
China	1996	7.9	<2	6.0	1998	4.6	<2	4.6	1998	18.5	4.2	53.7	21.0
Hong Kong, China		..	..	..		..	..	..		..	..	..	..
Colombia	1991	29.0	7.8	16.9	1992	*31.2*	8.0	17.7	1996	11.0	3.2	28.7	11.6
Congo, Dem. Rep.		..	..	..		..	..	..		..	..	..	..
Congo, Rep.		..	..	..		..	..	..		..	..	..	..
Costa Rica		..	..	..		..	..	..	1996	9.6	3.2	26.3	10.1
Côte d'Ivoire		..	..	..		..	..	..	1995	12.3	2.4	49.4	16.8
Croatia		..	..	..		..	..	..		..	..	..	..
Cuba		..	..	..		..	..	..		..	..	..	..
Czech Republic		..	..	..		..	..	..	1993	<2	<0.5	<2	<0.5
Denmark		..	..	..		..	..	..		..	..	..	..
Dominican Republic	1989	27.4	23.3	24.5	1992	29.8	10.9	20.6	1996	3.2	0.7	16.0	5.0
Ecuador	1994	47.0	25.0	35.0		..	..	..	1995	20.2	5.8	52.3	21.2
Egypt, Arab Rep.	1995–96	23.3	22.5	22.9		..	..	..	1995	3.1	0.3	52.7	11.4
El Salvador	1992	55.7	43.1	48.3		..	..	..	1996	25.3	10.4	51.9	24.7
Eritrea		..	..	..		..	..	..		..	..	..	..
Estonia	1995	14.7	6.8	8.9		..	..	..	1995	4.9	1.2	17.7	6.0
Ethiopia		..	..	..		..	..	..	1995	31.3	8.0	76.4	32.9
Finland		..	..	..		..	..	..		..	..	..	..
France		..	..	..		..	..	..		..	..	..	..
Gabon		..	..	..		..	..	..		..	..	..	..
Gambia, The	1992	..	..	64.0		..	..	..	1992	53.7	23.3	84.0	47.5
Georgia	1997	9.9	12.1	11.1		..	..	..		..	..	..	..
Germany		..	..	..		..	..	..		..	..	..	..
Ghana	1992	34.3	26.7	31.4		..	..	..		..	..	..	..
Greece		..	..	..		..	..	..		..	..	..	..
Guatemala	1989	71.9	33.7	57.9		..	..	..	1989	39.8	19.8	64.3	36.6
Guinea	1994	..	..	40.0		..	..	..		..	..	..	..
Guinea-Bissau		..	..	..		..	..	..		..	..	..	..
Haiti	1987	..	..	65.0	1995	66.0	..	..		..	..	..	..
Honduras	1992	46.0	56.0	50.0	1993	51.0	57.0	53.0	1996	40.5	17.5	68.8	36.9

Poverty 2.7

	National poverty line								International poverty line				
		Population below the poverty line				Population below the poverty line							
	Survey year	Rural %	Urban %	National %	Survey year	Rural %	Urban %	National %	Survey year	Population below $1 a day %	Poverty gap at $1 a day %	Population below $2 a day %	Poverty gap at $2 a day %
Hungary	1989	..	..	1.6	1993	..	..	8.6	1993	<2	<0.5	4.0	0.9
India	1992	43.5	33.7	40.9	1994	36.7	30.5	35.0	1997	44.2	12.0	86.2	41.4
Indonesia	1996	12.3	9.7	11.3	1998	22.0	17.8	20.3	1999	15.2	2.5	66.1	22.6
Iran, Islamic Rep.		..	..	..		..	..	..		..	..	..	..
Iraq		..	..	..		..	..	..		..	..	..	..
Ireland		..	..	..		..	..	..		..	..	..	..
Israel		..	..	..		..	..	..		..	..	..	..
Italy		..	..	..		..	..	..		..	..	..	..
Jamaica	1992	..	..	34.2		..	..	..	1996	3.2	0.7	25.2	6.9
Japan		..	..	..		..	..	..		..	..	..	..
Jordan	1991	..	..	15.0	1997	..	..	11.7	1997	<2	<0.5	7.4	1.4
Kazakhstan	1996	39.0	30.0	34.6		..	..	..	1996	1.5	0.3	15.3	3.9
Kenya	1992	46.4	29.3	42.0		..	..	..	1994	26.5	9.0	62.3	27.5
Korea, Dem. Rep.		..	..	..		..	..	..		..	..	..	..
Korea, Rep.		..	..	..		..	..	..	1993	<2	<0.5	<2	<0.5
Kuwait		..	..	..		..	..	..		..	..	..	..
Kyrgyz Republic	1993	48.1	28.7	40.0	1997	64.5	28.5	51.0		..	..	..	..
Lao PDR	1993	53.0	24.0	46.1		..	..	..		..	..	..	..
Latvia		..	..	..		..	..	..	1998	<2	<0.5	8.3	2.0
Lebanon		..	..	..		..	..	..		..	..	..	..
Lesotho	1993	53.9	27.8	49.2		..	..	..	1993	43.1	20.3	65.7	38.1
Libya		..	..	..		..	..	..		..	..	..	..
Lithuania		..	..	..		..	..	..	1996	<2	<0.5	7.8	2.0
Macedonia, FYR		..	..	..		..	..	..		..	..	..	..
Madagascar	1993–94	77.0	47.0	70.0		..	..	..	1993	60.2	24.5	88.8	51.3
Malawi	1990–91	..	..	54.0		..	..	..		..	..	..	..
Malaysia	1989	..	..	15.5		..	..	..		..	..	..	..
Mali		..	..	..		..	..	..	1994	72.8	37.4	90.6	60.5
Mauritania	1989–90	..	..	57.0		..	..	..	1995	3.8	1.0	22.1	6.6
Mauritius	1992	..	..	10.6		..	..	..		..	..	..	..
Mexico	1988	..	..	10.1		..	..	..	1995	17.9	6.1	42.5	18.1
Moldova	1997	26.7	..	23.3		..	..	..	1992	7.3	1.3	31.9	10.2
Mongolia	1995	33.1	38.5	36.3		..	..	..	1995	13.9	3.1	50.0	17.5
Morocco	1990–91	18.0	7.6	13.1	1998–99	27.2	12.0	19.0	1990–91	<2	<0.5	7.5	1.3
Mozambique		..	..	..		..	..	..	1996	37.9	12.0	78.4	36.8
Myanmar		..	..	..		..	..	..		..	..	..	..
Namibia		..	..	..		..	..	..	1993	34.9	14.0	55.8	30.4
Nepal	1995–96	44.0	23.0	42.0		..	..	..	1995	37.7	9.7	82.5	37.5
Netherlands		..	..	..		..	..	..		..	..	..	..
New Zealand		..	..	..		..	..	..		..	..	..	..
Nicaragua	1993	76.1	31.9	50.3		..	..	..	1993	3.0	0.5	18.1	5.4
Niger	1989–93	66.0	52.0	63.0		..	..	..	1995	61.4	33.9	85.3	54.8
Nigeria	1985	49.5	31.7	43.0	1992–93	36.4	30.4	34.1	1997	70.2	34.9	90.8	59.0
Norway		..	..	..		..	..	..		..	..	..	..
Oman		..	..	..		..	..	..		..	..	..	..
Pakistan	1991	36.9	28.0	34.0		..	..	..	1996	31.0	6.2	84.7	35.0
Panama	1997	64.9	15.3	37.3		..	..	..	1997	10.3	3.2	25.1	10.2
Papua New Guinea		..	..	..		..	..	..		..	..	..	..
Paraguay	1991	28.5	19.7	21.8		..	..	..	1995	19.4	8.3	38.5	18.8
Peru	1994	67.0	46.1	53.5	1997	64.7	40.4	49.0	1996	15.5	5.4	41.4	17.1
Philippines	1994	53.1	28.0	40.6	1997	51.2	22.5	40.6		..	..	..	..
Poland	1993	..	..	23.8		..	..	..	1993	5.4	4.3	10.5	6.0
Portugal		..	..	..		..	..	..	1994	<2	<0.5	<2	<0.5
Puerto Rico		..	..	..		..	..	..		..	..	..	..
Romania	1994	27.9	20.4	21.5		..	..	..	1994	2.8	0.8	27.5	6.9
Russian Federation	1994	..	..	30.9		..	..	..	1998	7.1	1.4	25.1	8.7

2.7 Poverty

	National poverty line								International poverty line				
		Population below the poverty line				Population below the poverty line							
	Survey year	Rural %	Urban %	National %	Survey year	Rural %	Urban %	National %	Survey year	Population below $1 a day %	Poverty gap at $1 a day %	Population below $2 a day %	Poverty gap at $2 a day %
Rwanda	1993	..	..	51.2		..	..	..	1983–85	35.7	7.7	84.6	36.7
Saudi Arabia		..	..	..		..	..	..		..	..	..	..
Senegal		..	..	..		..	..	..	1995	26.3	7.0	67.8	28.2
Sierra Leone	1989	76.0	53.0	68.0		..	..	..	1989	57.0	39.5	74.5	51.8
Singapore		..	..	..		..	..	..		..	..	..	..
Slovak Republic		..	..	..		..	..	..	1992	<2	<0.5	<2	<0.5
Slovenia		..	..	..		..	..	..	1993	<2	<0.5	<2	<0.5
South Africa		..	..	..		..	..	..	1993	11.5	1.8	35.8	13.4
Spain		..	..	..		..	..	..		..	..	..	..
Sri Lanka	1985–86	45.5	26.8	40.6	1990–91	38.1	28.4	35.3	1995	6.6	1.0	45.4	13.5
Sudan		..	..	..		..	..	..		..	..	..	..
Sweden		..	..	..		..	..	..		..	..	..	..
Switzerland		..	..	..		..	..	..		..	..	..	..
Syrian Arab Republic		..	..	..		..	..	..		..	..	..	..
Tajikistan		..	..	..		..	..	..		..	..	..	..
Tanzania	1991	..	..	51.1		..	..	..	1993	19.9	4.8	59.7	23.0
Thailand	1990	..	..	18.0	1992	15.5	10.2	13.1	1998	<2	<0.5	28.2	7.1
Togo	1987–89	..	..	32.3		..	..	..		..	..	..	..
Trinidad and Tobago	1992	20.0	24.0	21.0		..	..	..	1992	12.4	3.5	39.0	14.6
Tunisia	1985	29.2	12.0	19.9	1990	21.6	8.9	14.1	1990	<2	<0.5	11.6	2.9
Turkey		..	..	..		..	..	..	1994	2.4	0.5	18.0	5.0
Turkmenistan		..	..	..		..	..	..	1993	20.9	5.7	59.0	23.3
Uganda	1993	..	..	55.0		..	..	..	1992	36.7	11.4	77.2	35.8
Ukraine	1995	..	..	31.7		..	..	..	1996	<2	<0.5	23.7	4.4
United Arab Emirates		..	..	..		..	..	..		..	..	..	..
United Kingdom		..	..	..		..	..	..		..	..	..	..
United States		..	..	..		..	..	..		..	..	..	..
Uruguay		..	..	..		..	..	..	1989	<2	<0.5	6.6	1.9
Uzbekistan		..	..	..		..	..	..	1993	3.3	0.5	26.5	7.3
Venezuela, RB	1989	..	..	31.3		..	..	..	1996	14.7	5.6	36.4	15.7
Vietnam	1993	57.2	25.9	50.9		..	..	..		..	..	..	..
West Bank and Gaza		..	..	..		..	..	..		..	..	..	..
Yemen, Rep.	1992	19.2	18.6	19.1		..	..	..	1998	5.1	0.9	35.5	10.1
Yugoslavia, FR (Serb./Mont.)		..	..	..		..	..	..		..	..	..	..
Zambia	1991	88.0	46.0	68.0	1993	..	..	86.0	1996	72.6	37.7	91.7	61.2
Zimbabwe	1990–91	31.0	10.0	25.5		..	..	..	1990–91	36.0	9.6	64.2	29.4

Poverty 2.7

About the data

International comparisons of poverty data entail both conceptual and practical problems. Different countries have different definitions of poverty, and consistent comparisons between countries can be difficult. Local poverty lines tend to have higher purchasing power in rich countries, where more generous standards are used than in poor countries.

Is it reasonable to treat two people with the same standard of living—in terms of their command over commodities—differently because one happens to live in a better-off country? Can we hold the real value of the poverty line constant between countries, just as we do when making comparisons over time?

Poverty measures based on an international poverty line attempt to do this. The commonly used $1 a day standard, measured in 1985 international prices and adjusted to local currency using purchasing power parities (PPPs), was chosen for the World Bank's *World Development Report 1990: Poverty* because it is typical of the poverty lines in low-income countries. PPP exchange rates, such as those from the Penn World Tables or the World Bank, are used because they take into account the local prices of goods and services not traded internationally. But PPP rates were designed not for making international poverty comparisons but for comparing aggregates from national accounts. As a result there is no certainty that an international poverty line measures the same degree of need or deprivation across countries.

Past editions of the *World Development Indicators* used PPPs from the Penn World Tables. Because the Penn World Tables updated to 1993 are not yet available, this year's edition uses 1993 consumption PPP estimates produced by the World Bank. The international poverty line, set at $1 a day in 1985 PPP terms, has been recalculated in 1993 PPP terms at about $1.08 a day.

Problems also exist in comparing poverty measures within countries. For example, the cost of living is typically higher in urban than in rural areas. (Food staples, for example, tend to be more expensive in urban areas.) So the urban monetary poverty line should be higher than the rural poverty line. But it is not always clear that the difference between urban and rural poverty lines found in practice properly reflects the difference in the cost of living. For some countries the urban poverty line in common use has a higher real value—meaning that it allows poor people to buy more commodities for consumption—than does the rural poverty line. Sometimes the difference has been so large as to imply that the incidence of poverty is greater in urban than in rural areas, even though the reverse is found when adjustments are made only for differences in the cost of living. As with international comparisons, when the real value of the poverty line varies, it is not clear how meaningful such urban-rural comparisons are.

The problems of making poverty comparisons do not end there. Further issues arise in measuring household living standards. The choice between income and consumption as a welfare indicator is one issue. Income is generally more difficult to measure accurately, and consumption accords better with the idea of the standard of living than does income, which can vary over time even if the standard of living does not. But consumption data are not always available, and when they are not there is little choice but to use income. There are still other problems. Household survey questionnaires can differ widely, for example, in the number of distinct categories of consumer goods they identify. Survey quality varies, and even similar surveys may not be strictly comparable.

Comparisons across countries at different levels of development also pose a potential problem, because of differences in the relative importance of consumption of nonmarket goods. The local market value of all consumption in kind (including consumption from own production, particularly important in underdeveloped rural economies) should be included in the measure of total consumption expenditure. Similarly, the imputed profit from production of nonmarket goods should be included in income. This is not always done, though such omissions were a far bigger problem in surveys before the 1980s. Most survey data now include valuations for consumption or income from own production. Nonetheless, valuation methods vary—for example, some surveys use the price at the nearest market, while others use the average farm gate selling price.

The international poverty measures shown here are based on the most recent consumption PPP estimates in 1993 prices from the World Bank. Any revisions in the PPP of a country to incorporate better price indexes can produce dramatically different poverty lines in local currency.

Whenever possible, consumption has been used as the welfare indicator for deciding who is poor. When only household income is available, average income has been adjusted to accord with either a survey-based estimate of mean consumption (when available) or an estimate based on consumption data from national accounts. This procedure adjusts only the mean, however; nothing can be done to correct for the difference in Lorenz (income distribution) curves between consumption and income.

Empirical Lorenz curves were weighted by household size, so they are based on percentiles of population, not households. In all cases the measures of poverty have been calculated from primary data sources (tabulations or household data) rather than existing estimates. Estimation from tabulations requires an interpolation method; the method chosen was Lorenz curves with flexible functional forms, which have proved reliable in past work.

Definitions

• **Survey year** is the year in which the underlying data were collected. • **Rural poverty rate** is the percentage of the rural population living below the national rural poverty line. • **Urban poverty rate** is the percentage of the urban population living below the national urban poverty line. • **National poverty rate** is the percentage of the population living below the national poverty line. National estimates are based on population-weighted subgroup estimates from household surveys. • **Population below $1 a day** and **$2 a day** are the percentages of the population living on less than $1.08 a day and $2.15 a day at 1993 international prices (equivalent to $1 and $2 in 1985 prices, adjusted for purchasing power parity using rates from the Penn World Tables). Poverty rates are comparable across countries, but as a result of revisions in PPP exchange rates, they cannot be compared with poverty rates reported in previous editions for individual countries. • **Poverty gap** is the mean shortfall below the poverty line (counting the nonpoor as having zero shortfall), expressed as a percentage of the poverty line. This measure reflects the depth of poverty as well as its incidence.

Data sources

Poverty measures are prepared by the World Bank's Development Research Group. National poverty lines are based on the Bank's country poverty assessments. International poverty lines are based on nationally representative primary household surveys conducted by national statistical offices or by private agencies under government or international agency supervision and obtained from government statistical offices and World Bank country departments. The World Bank has prepared an annual review of poverty work in the Bank since 1993. The most recent is *Poverty Reduction and the World Bank: Progress in Fiscal 1999* (forthcoming a).

2.8 Distribution of income or consumption

	Survey year	Gini index	Percentage share of income or consumption						
			Lowest 10%	Lowest 20%	Second 20%	Third 20%	Fourth 20%	Highest 20%	Highest 10%
Albania		..	..	..	..	..	..	..	..
Algeria	1995[a,b]	35.3	2.8	7.0	11.6	16.1	22.7	42.6	26.8
Angola		..	..	..	..	..	..	..	..
Argentina		..	..	..	..	..	..	..	..
Armenia		..	..	..	..	..	..	..	..
Australia	1994[c,d]	35.2	2.0	5.9	12.0	17.2	23.6	41.3	25.4
Austria	1987[c,d]	23.1	4.4	10.4	14.8	18.5	22.9	33.3	19.3
Azerbaijan		..	..	..	..	..	..	..	..
Bangladesh	1995–96[a,b]	33.6	3.9	8.7	12.0	15.7	20.8	42.8	28.6
Belarus	1998[a,b]	21.7	5.1	11.4	15.2	18.2	21.9	33.3	20.0
Belgium	1992[c,d]	25.0	3.7	9.5	14.6	18.4	23.0	34.5	20.2
Benin		..	..	..	..	..	..	..	..
Bolivia	1990[c,d]	42.0	2.3	5.6	9.7	14.5	22.0	48.2	31.7
Bosnia and Herzegovina		..	..	..	..	..	..	..	..
Botswana		..	..	..	..	..	..	..	..
Brazil	1996[c,d]	60.0	0.9	2.5	5.5	10.0	18.3	63.8	47.6
Bulgaria	1995[a,b]	28.3	3.4	8.5	13.8	17.9	22.7	37.0	22.5
Burkina Faso	1994[a,b]	48.2	2.2	5.5	8.7	12.0	18.7	55.0	39.5
Burundi	1992[a,b]	33.3	3.4	7.9	12.1	16.3	22.1	41.6	26.6
Cambodia	1997[a,b]	40.4	2.9	6.9	10.7	14.7	20.1	47.6	33.8
Cameroon		..	..	..	..	..	..	..	..
Canada	1994[c,d]	31.5	2.8	7.5	12.9	17.2	23.0	39.3	23.8
Central African Republic	1993[a,b]	61.3	0.7	2.0	4.9	9.6	18.5	65.0	47.7
Chad		..	..	..	..	..	..	..	..
Chile	1994[c,d]	56.5	1.4	3.5	6.6	10.9	18.1	61.0	46.1
China	1998[c,d]	40.3	2.4	5.9	10.2	15.1	22.2	46.6	30.4
Hong Kong, China		..	..	..	..	..	..	..	..
Colombia	1996[c,d]	57.1	1.1	3.0	6.6	11.1	18.4	60.9	46.1
Congo, Dem. Rep.		..	..	..	..	..	..	..	..
Congo, Rep.		..	..	..	..	..	..	..	..
Costa Rica	1996[c,d]	47.0	1.3	4.0	8.8	13.7	21.7	51.8	34.7
Côte d'Ivoire	1995[a,b]	36.7	3.1	7.1	11.2	15.6	21.9	44.3	28.8
Croatia	1998[a,b]	26.8	4.0	9.3	13.8	17.8	22.9	36.2	21.6
Cuba		..	..	..	..	..	..	..	..
Czech Republic	1996[c,d]	25.4	4.3	10.3	14.5	17.7	21.7	35.9	22.4
Denmark	1992[c,d]	24.7	3.6	9.6	14.9	18.3	22.7	34.5	20.5
Dominican Republic	1996[c,d]	48.7	1.7	4.3	8.3	13.1	20.6	53.7	37.8
Ecuador	1995[a,b]	43.7	2.2	5.4	9.4	14.2	21.3	49.7	33.8
Egypt, Arab Rep.	1995[a,b]	28.9	4.4	9.8	13.2	16.6	21.4	39.0	25.0
El Salvador	1996[c,d]	52.3	1.2	3.4	7.5	12.5	20.2	56.5	40.5
Eritrea		..	..	..	..	..	..	..	..
Estonia	1995[c,d]	35.4	2.2	6.2	12.0	17.0	23.1	41.8	26.2
Ethiopia	1995[a,b]	40.0	3.0	7.1	10.9	14.5	19.8	47.7	33.7
Finland	1991[c,d]	25.6	4.2	10.0	14.2	17.6	22.3	35.8	21.6
France	1995[c,d]	32.7	2.8	7.2	12.6	17.2	22.8	40.2	25.1
Gabon		..	..	..	..	..	..	..	..
Gambia, The	1992[a,b]	47.8	1.5	4.4	9.0	13.5	20.4	52.8	37.6
Georgia		..	..	..	..	..	..	..	..
Germany	1994[c,d]	30.0	3.3	8.2	13.2	17.5	22.7	38.5	23.7
Ghana	1997[a,b]	32.7	3.6	8.4	12.2	15.8	21.9	41.7	26.1
Greece	1993[c,d]	32.7	3.0	7.5	12.4	16.9	22.8	40.3	25.3
Guatemala	1989[c,d]	59.6	0.6	2.1	5.8	10.5	18.6	63.0	46.6
Guinea	1994[a,b]	40.3	2.6	6.4	10.4	14.8	21.2	47.2	32.0
Guinea-Bissau	1991[a,b]	56.2	0.5	2.1	6.5	12.0	20.6	58.9	42.4
Guyana	1993[a,b]	40.2	2.4	6.3	10.7	15.0	21.2	46.9	32.0
Haiti		..	..	..	..	..	..	..	..
Honduras	1996[c,d]	53.7	1.2	3.4	7.1	11.7	19.7	58.0	42.1

Distribution of income or consumption 2.8

	Survey year	Gini index	Percentage share of income or consumption						
			Lowest 10%	Lowest 20%	Second 20%	Third 20%	Fourth 20%	Highest 20%	Highest 10%
Hungary	1996[c,d]	30.8	3.9	8.8	12.5	16.6	22.3	39.9	24.8
India	1997[a,b]	37.8	3.5	8.1	11.6	15.0	19.3	46.1	33.5
Indonesia	1996[c,d]	36.5	3.6	8.0	11.3	15.1	20.8	44.9	30.3
Iran, Islamic Rep.		..	..	..	..	..	..	..	..
Iraq		..	..	..	..	..	..	..	..
Ireland	1987[c,d]	35.9	2.5	6.7	11.6	16.4	22.4	42.9	27.4
Israel	1992[c,d]	35.5	2.8	6.9	11.4	16.3	22.9	42.5	26.9
Italy	1995[c,d]	27.3	3.5	8.7	14.0	18.1	22.9	36.3	21.8
Jamaica	1996[a,b]	36.4	2.9	7.0	11.5	15.8	21.8	43.9	28.9
Japan	1993[c,d]	24.9	4.8	10.6	14.2	17.6	22.0	35.7	21.7
Jordan	1997[a,b]	36.4	3.3	7.6	11.4	15.5	21.1	44.4	29.8
Kazakhstan	1996[a,b]	35.4	2.7	6.7	11.5	16.4	23.1	42.3	26.3
Kenya	1994[a,b]	44.5	1.8	5.0	9.7	14.2	20.9	50.2	34.9
Korea, Dem. Rep.		..	..	..	..	..	..	..	..
Korea, Rep.	1993[a,b]	31.6	2.9	7.5	12.9	17.4	22.9	39.3	24.3
Kuwait		..	..	..	..	..	..	..	..
Kyrgyz Republic	1997[c,d]	40.5	2.7	6.3	10.2	14.7	21.4	47.4	31.7
Lao PDR	1992[a,b]	30.4	4.2	9.6	12.9	16.3	21.0	40.2	26.4
Latvia	1998[c,d]	32.4	2.9	7.6	12.9	17.1	22.1	40.3	25.9
Lebanon		..	..	..	..	..	..	..	..
Lesotho	1986–87[a,b]	56.0	0.9	2.8	6.5	11.2	19.4	60.1	43.4
Libya		..	..	..	..	..	..	..	..
Lithuania	1996[a,b]	32.4	3.1	7.8	12.6	16.8	22.4	40.3	25.6
Luxembourg	1994[c,d]	26.9	4.0	9.4	13.8	17.7	22.6	36.5	22.0
Macedonia, FYR		..	..	..	..	..	..	..	..
Madagascar	1993[a,b]	46.0	1.9	5.1	9.4	13.3	20.1	52.1	36.7
Malawi		..	..	..	..	..	..	..	..
Malaysia	1995[c,d]	48.5	1.8	4.5	8.3	13.0	20.4	53.8	37.9
Mali	1994[a,b]	50.5	1.8	4.6	8.0	11.9	19.3	56.2	40.4
Mauritania	1995[a,b]	38.9	2.3	6.2	10.8	15.4	22.0	45.6	29.9
Mauritius		..	..	..	..	..	..	..	..
Mexico	1995[c,d]	53.7	1.4	3.6	7.2	11.8	19.2	58.2	42.8
Moldova	1992[c,d]	34.4	2.7	6.9	11.9	16.7	23.1	41.5	25.8
Mongolia	1995[a,b]	33.2	2.9	7.3	12.2	16.6	23.0	40.9	24.5
Morocco	1998–99[a,b]	39.5	2.6	6.5	10.6	14.8	21.3	46.6	30.9
Mozambique	1996–97[a,b]	39.6	2.5	6.5	10.8	15.1	21.1	46.5	31.7
Myanmar		..	..	..	..	..	..	..	..
Namibia		..	..	..	..	..	..	..	..
Nepal	1995–96[a,b]	36.7	3.2	7.6	11.5	15.1	21.0	44.8	29.8
Netherlands	1994[c,d]	32.6	2.8	7.3	12.7	17.2	22.8	40.1	25.1
New Zealand	1991[c,d]	43.9	0.3	2.7	10.0	16.3	24.1	46.9	29.8
Nicaragua	1993[a,b]	50.3	1.6	4.2	8.0	12.6	20.0	55.2	39.8
Niger	1995[a,b]	50.5	0.8	2.6	7.1	13.9	23.1	53.3	35.4
Nigeria	1996–97[a,b]	50.6	1.6	4.4	8.2	12.5	19.3	55.7	40.8
Norway	1995[c,d]	25.8	4.1	9.7	14.3	17.9	22.2	35.8	21.8
Oman		..	..	..	..	..	..	..	..
Pakistan	1996–97[a,b]	31.2	4.1	9.5	12.9	16.0	20.5	41.1	27.6
Panama	1997[a,b]	48.5	1.2	3.6	8.1	13.6	21.9	52.8	35.7
Papua New Guinea	1996[a,b]	50.9	1.7	4.5	7.9	11.9	19.2	56.5	40.5
Paraguay	1995[c,d]	59.1	0.7	2.3	5.9	10.7	18.7	62.4	46.6
Peru	1996[c,d]	46.2	1.6	4.4	9.1	14.1	21.3	51.2	35.4
Philippines	1997[a,b]	46.2	2.3	5.4	8.8	13.2	20.3	52.3	36.6
Poland	1996[c,d]	32.9	3.0	7.7	12.6	16.7	22.1	40.9	26.3
Portugal	1994–95[c,d]	35.6	3.1	7.3	11.6	15.9	21.8	43.4	28.4
Puerto Rico		..	..	..	..	..	..	..	..
Romania	1994[c,d]	28.2	3.7	8.9	13.6	17.6	22.6	37.3	22.7
Russian Federation	1998[a,b]	48.7	1.7	4.4	8.6	13.3	20.1	53.7	38.7

2.8 Distribution of income or consumption

	Survey year	Gini index	Percentage share of income or consumption						
			Lowest 10%	Lowest 20%	Second 20%	Third 20%	Fourth 20%	Highest 20%	Highest 10%
Rwanda	1983–85[a,b]	28.9	4.2	9.7	13.2	16.5	21.6	39.1	24.2
Saudi Arabia		..	..	..	..	..	..	..	..
Senegal	1995[a,b]	41.3	2.6	6.4	10.3	14.5	20.6	48.2	33.5
Sierra Leone	1989[a,b]	62.9	0.5	1.1	2.0	9.8	23.7	63.4	43.6
Singapore		..	..	..	..	..	..	..	..
Slovak Republic	1992[c,d]	19.5	5.1	11.9	15.8	18.8	22.2	31.4	18.2
Slovenia	1995[c,d]	26.8	3.2	8.4	14.3	18.5	23.4	35.4	20.7
South Africa	1993–94[a,b]	59.3	1.1	2.9	5.5	9.2	17.7	64.8	45.9
Spain	1990[c,d]	32.5	2.8	7.5	12.6	17.0	22.6	40.3	25.2
Sri Lanka	1995[a,b]	34.4	3.5	8.0	11.8	15.8	21.5	42.8	28.0
St.Lucia	1995[c,d]	42.6	2.0	5.2	9.9	14.8	21.8	48.3	32.5
Sudan		..	..	..	..	..	..	..	..
Swaziland	1994[c,d]	60.9	1.0	2.7	5.8	10.0	17.1	64.4	50.2
Sweden	1992[c,d]	25.0	3.7	9.6	14.5	18.1	23.2	34.5	20.1
Switzerland	1992[c,d]	33.1	2.6	6.9	12.7	17.3	22.9	40.3	25.2
Syrian Arab Republic		..	..	..	..	..	..	..	..
Tajikistan		..	..	..	..	..	..	..	..
Tanzania	1993[a,b]	38.2	2.8	6.8	11.0	15.1	21.6	45.5	30.1
Thailand	1998[a,b]	41.4	2.8	6.4	9.8	14.2	21.2	48.4	32.4
Togo		..	..	..	..	..	..	..	..
Trinidad and Tobago	1992[c,d]	40.3	2.1	5.5	10.3	15.5	22.7	45.9	29.9
Tunisia	1990[a,b]	40.2	2.3	5.9	10.4	15.3	22.1	46.3	30.7
Turkey	1994[a,b]	41.5	2.3	5.8	10.2	14.8	21.6	47.7	32.3
Turkmenistan	1998[a,b]	40.8	2.6	6.1	10.2	14.7	21.5	47.5	31.7
Uganda	1992–93[a,b]	39.2	2.6	6.6	10.9	15.2	21.3	46.1	31.2
Ukraine	1996[a,b]	32.5	3.9	8.6	12.0	16.2	22.0	41.2	26.4
United Arab Emirates		..	..	..	..	..	..	..	..
United Kingdom	1991[c,d]	36.1	2.6	6.6	11.5	16.3	22.7	43.0	27.3
United States	1997[c,d]	40.8	1.8	5.2	10.5	15.6	22.4	46.4	30.5
Uruguay	1989[c,d]	42.3	2.1	5.4	10.0	14.8	21.5	48.3	32.7
Uzbekistan	1993[c,d]	33.3	3.1	7.4	12.0	16.7	23.0	40.9	25.2
Venezuela, RB	1996[c,d]	48.8	1.3	3.7	8.4	13.6	21.2	53.1	37.0
Vietnam	1998[a,b]	36.1	3.6	8.0	11.4	15.2	20.9	44.5	29.9
West Bank and Gaza		..	..	..	..	..	..	..	..
Yemen, Rep.	1992[a,b]	39.5	2.3	6.1	10.9	15.3	21.6	46.1	30.8
Yugoslavia, FR (Serb./Mont.)		..	..	..	..	..	..	..	..
Zambia	1996[a,b]	49.8	1.6	4.2	8.2	12.8	20.1	54.8	39.2
Zimbabwe	1990–91[a,b]	56.8	1.8	4.0	6.3	10.0	17.4	62.3	46.9

a. Refers to expenditure shares by percentiles of population. b. Ranked by per capita expenditure. c. Refers to income shares by percentiles of population. d. Ranked by per capita income.

Distribution of income or consumption 2.8

About the data

Inequality in the distribution of income is reflected in the percentage shares of either income or consumption accruing to segments of the population ranked by income or consumption levels. The segments ranked lowest by personal income receive the smallest share of total income. The Gini index provides a convenient summary measure of the degree of inequality.

Data on personal or household income or consumption come from nationally representative household surveys. The data in the table refer to different years between 1985 and 1999. Footnotes to the survey year indicate whether the rankings are based on per capita income or consumption. Each distribution (including for high-income economies) is based on percentiles of population—rather than of households—with households ranked by income or expenditure per person.

Where the original data from the household survey were available, they have been used to directly calculate the income (or consumption) shares by quintile. Otherwise, shares have been estimated from the best available grouped data.

The distribution indicators have been adjusted for household size, providing a more consistent measure of per capita income or consumption. No adjustment has been made for spatial differences in cost of living within countries, because the data needed for such calculations are generally unavailable. For further details on the estimation method for low- and middle-income economies see Ravallion and Chen (1996).

Because the underlying household surveys differ in method and in the type of data collected, the distribution indicators are not strictly comparable across countries. These problems are diminishing as survey methods improve and become more standardized, but achieving strict comparability is still impossible (see *About the data* for table 2.7).

The following sources of noncomparability should be noted. First, the surveys can differ in many respects, including whether they use income or consumption expenditure as the living standard indicator. The distribution of income is typically more unequal than the distribution of consumption. In addition, the definitions of income used usually differ among surveys. Consumption is usually a much better welfare indicator, particularly in developing countries. Second, household units differ in size (number of members) and in extent of income sharing among members. And individuals differ in age and consumption needs. Differences between countries in these respects may bias comparisons of distribution.

World Bank staff have made an effort to ensure that the data are as comparable as possible. Whenever possible, consumption has been used rather than income. The income distribution and Gini indexes for high-income countries are calculated directly from the Luxembourg Income Study database, using an estimation method consistent with that applied for developing countries.

Definitions

• **Survey year** is the year in which the underlying data were collected. • **Gini index** measures the extent to which the distribution of income (or, in some cases, consumption expenditures) among individuals or households within an economy deviates from a perfectly equal distribution. A Lorenz curve plots the cumulative percentages of total income received against the cumulative number of recipients, starting with the poorest individual or household. The Gini index measures the area between the Lorenz curve and a hypothetical line of absolute equality, expressed as a percentage of the maximum area under the line. Thus a Gini index of zero represents perfect equality, while an index of 100 implies perfect inequality. • **Percentage share of income or consumption** is the share that accrues to subgroups of population indicated by deciles or quintiles. Percentage shares by quintile may not sum to 100 because of rounding.

Data sources

Data on distribution are compiled by the World Bank's Development Research Group using primary household survey data obtained from government statistical agencies and World Bank country departments. Data for high-income economies are from the Luxembourg Income Study database.

2.9 Education inputs

	Public expenditure on education		Expenditure per student						Expenditure on teachers' compensation		Primary pupil-teacher ratio	Duration of primary education
	% of GNP		Primary % of GNP per capita		Secondary % of GNP per capita		Tertiary % of GNP per capita		% of total current education expenditure		pupils per teacher	years
	1980	1997	1980	1997	1980	1997	1980	1997	1980	1997	1997	1997
Albania	..	*3.1*	..	*9.4*	..	..	..	..	..	..	*18*	8
Algeria	7.8	*5.1*	8.9	*26.1*[a]	23.9	..	..	..	63.6	*74.2*[b]	*27*	9
Angola	..	..	..	..	..	..	..	..	*62.2*	..	..	8
Argentina	2.7	*3.5*	6.5[c]	*8.3*	..	..	29.3	*19.9*	..	*84.1*	17	10[d]
Armenia	..	*2.0*	..	..	..	..	..	*25.8*	..	..	*19*	11
Australia	5.5	*5.4*	..	*16.7*	44.5	*16.8*	51.1	*29.7*	..	*54.2*	*18*	10[d]
Austria	5.5	*5.4*	15.7	*21.7*	..	*24.7*	37.4	*35.3*	53.0[e]	*61.7*	*12*	9[d]
Azerbaijan	..	3.0	..	*17.9*	..	..	..	*15.3*	..	..	*20*	11
Bangladesh	1.1	*2.2*	3.6[c]	..	*10.4*	..	34.9	..	33.5[f]	..	..	5
Belarus	..	*5.9*	..	*12.8*[c]	..	..	..	*18.7*	..	..	*20*	9[d]
Belgium	6.0	*3.1*	17.4[c]	..	*33.8*	*13.4*	51.0	*17.5*	73.0[f]	*73.6*	..	12
Benin	..	*3.2*	..	*11.8*	..	..	..	*249.0*	..	..	*52*	6
Bolivia	4.4	*4.9*	13.7[c]	..	15.2	..	..	..	75.7	*48.5*	..	8
Bosnia and Herzegovina	..	..	..	..	..	..	..	..	..	..	..	..
Botswana	6.0	8.6	*12.5*	..	..	..	*611.7*	..	*54.9*	..	*25*	..
Brazil	3.6	*5.1*	8.7[c]	..	11.0	..	58.7	..	..	..	*23*	8
Bulgaria	4.5	*3.2*	17.5	*30.8*	..	..	51.3	*17.4*	..	..	*17*	8[d]
Burkina Faso	2.2	*1.5*	23.1[c]	*21.2*	*87.5*	..	2,957.4	*590.6*	61.0	*67.8*	*50*	7
Burundi	*3.4*	*4.0*	*24.2*	*23.0*	*222.2*	..	*1,479.8*	..	*74.3*	..	*50*	6
Cambodia	..	*2.9*	..	..	..	..	..	..	..	..	46	6
Cameroon	3.8	..	*11.0*	..	..	..	*401.2*	..	*65.4*	..	..	6[d]
Canada	6.9	*6.9*	..	..	*48.3*[g]	*50.1*	38.7	*39.8*	55.4	*62.0*	*16*	10[d]
Central African Republic	..	1.5	22.1[c]	..	..	..	936.1	..	..	..	..	6
Chad	..	*1.7*	..	*6.3*	..	..	..	..	..	*64.4*	*67*	6
Chile	4.6	3.6	9.6	*11.1*	*16.8*	*11.8*	112.0	21.1	76.8	..	*30*	8
China	2.5	*2.3*	3.8	*6.6*	..	..	246.2	*66.2*	..	..	*24*	9[d]
Hong Kong, China	2.4	*2.9*	6.7[c]	*7.8*	8.2	*12.6*	*4.2*	..	73.0	..	*24*	9[d]
Colombia	1.9	*4.1*	5.3	*10.3*[c]	..	*11.7*	43.8	*35.4*	*93.4*	*81.9*	*25*	5
Congo, Dem. Rep.	2.6	..	..	..	..	..	747.9	..	..	..	*45*	..
Congo, Rep.	7.0	*6.1*	10.1[c]	*15.4*	..	..	369.4	..	70.8	..	*70*	10
Costa Rica	7.8	*5.4*	13.0	*13.6*[c]	25.7	*23.2*	75.8	..	50.2	..	29	10[d]
Côte d'Ivoire	7.2	5.0	22.6[c]	*16.9*[c]	..	..	375.7	*210.1*	..	..	*41*	6
Croatia	..	*5.3*	..	..	..	..	..	..	..	..	*19*	8
Cuba	7.2	*6.7*	10.4	*16.3*	..	..	28.5	*98.1*	38.8	..	*12*	9
Czech Republic	..	*5.1*	..	*15.2*	..	*21.9*	..	*34.9*	..	*44.4*	*19*	9
Denmark	6.7	*8.1*	37.2[c]	*24.3*	11.2	*34.5*	50.0	*49.6*	49.3	*43.1*	*10*	9
Dominican Republic	2.2	2.3	3.1[c]	*3.3*	..	*4.4*	..	*9.7*	62.2	..	..	10
Ecuador	5.6	*3.5*	5.6[c]	*7.6*[c]	..	..	24.2	..	77.4	..	*25*	10
Egypt, Arab Rep.	*5.7*	*4.8*	..	..	..	*25.9*[g]	57.8	..	..	..	*23*	8
El Salvador	3.9	2.5	12.5[c]	*7.1*	..	*5.5*	141.6	*7.7*	..	..	*33*	9
Eritrea	..	*1.8*	..	*9.2*	..	*9.9*	..	..	..	..	*44*	7
Estonia	..	*7.2*	..	..	..	*45.4*	..	*38.4*	..	..	*17*	9
Ethiopia	3.1	*4.0*	*17.6*	*26.7*	..	..	*1,119.5*	*868.9*	*68.3*	..	*43*	6
Finland	5.3	*7.5*	20.7[c]	23.0	..	*27.5*	37.3	*45.6*	52.6	*47.7*	*18*	9
France	5.0	*6.0*	12.0	*15.8*	20.2	*26.9*	29.3	*28.2*	68.1	..	*19*	10
Gabon	2.7	*2.9*	..	..	..	..	..	..	56.7	..	*51*	10
Gambia, The	3.2	*4.9*	18.6	*13.7*	..	..	..	*269.1*	..	..	*30*	..
Georgia	..	*5.2*	..	..	..	*25.0*	..	*25.5*	..	..	*18*	9
Germany	..	*4.8*	..	..	..	*30.8*[g]	..	*37.8*	..	..	*17*	12
Ghana	3.1	*4.2*	3.7[c]	..	..	..	*26.7*	..	60.0	..	..	8[d]
Greece	*2.0*	*3.1*	*7.0*	*17.5*[c]	*9.5*	*15.1*	*30.1*	*22.3*	*84.8*	..	*14*	9[d]
Guatemala	1.8	*1.7*	*4.8*	*6.2*	*10.4*	..	..	*31.1*	..	*62.8*[f]	*35*	6
Guinea	..	1.9	..	*7.9*[c]	..	..	..	*444.7*	..	..	*49*	6
Guinea-Bissau	..	..	20.9	..	69.8	..	..	..	73.5	..	..	6
Haiti	1.5	..	5.9[c]	..	..	..	130.0	..	66.9	..	..	6[d]
Honduras	3.2	*3.6*	10.7[c]	*9.0*	..	..	77.4	*68.7*	71.1	*67.8*	*35*	6

Education inputs 2.9

	Public expenditure on education		Expenditure per student						Expenditure on teachers' compensation		Primary pupil-teacher ratio	Duration of primary education
	% of GNP		Primary % of GNP per capita		Secondary % of GNP per capita		Tertiary % of GNP per capita		% of total current education expenditure		pupils per teacher	years
	1980	1997	1980	1997	1980	1997	1980	1997	1980	1997	1997	1997
Hungary	4.7	4.6	14.0	20.6	..	20.2	85.3	47.0	45.2	..	11	10
India	3.0	3.2	10.5 [c]	11.4	..	..	88.2	99.8	..	..	64	8
Indonesia	1.7	1.4	..	..	..	6.6	..	12.9	..	..	22	9
Iran, Islamic Rep.	7.5	4.0	16.2	8.2	..	11.0	67.6	7.6	..	47.4	31	5
Iraq	3.0	..	7.0 [c]	..	6.5	..	87.5	..	..	..	20	6
Ireland	6.3	6.0	11.6	14.1	24.3	21.9	60.0	36.3	67.6	73.6	22	9 [d]
Israel	8.2	7.6	16.0	20.6	..	..	75.2	37.1	51.1	..	..	11
Italy	..	4.9	..	22.4	..	..	..	21.2	..	67.3	11	8
Jamaica	7.0	7.4	13.9	..	22.0	..	202.9	..	65.6 [e,f]	54.5	..	6
Japan	5.8	3.6	14.8	19.3	16.6	19.0	21.0	13.9	49.8	..	19	9 [d]
Jordan	6.6	6.8	..	..	24.5 [g]	112.4 [g]	59.9	81.0	70.4	70.4	21	9
Kazakhstan	..	4.4	..	..	..	..	..	21.9	..	..	..	11
Kenya	6.8	6.5	15.7 [c]	..	..	..	928.2	..	..	..	30	8
Korea, Dem. Rep.	..	..	..	..	..	..	..	..	..	..	..	10
Korea, Rep.	3.7	3.7	10.6 [c]	18.8	9.3	12.9	16.1	6.0	69.2	..	31	9
Kuwait	2.4	5.0	14.8	39.6	..	5.5	37.5	87.9	46.5	..	14	8 [d]
Kyrgyz Republic	..	5.3	..	..	..	..	..	48.8	..	..	20	10
Lao PDR	..	2.1	..	6.4	..	13.8	..	60.6	..	67.2	30	5
Latvia	3.3	6.3	..	..	..	37.1	19.1	32.9	..	40.5	13	..
Lebanon	..	2.5	..	18.5 [a]	..	..	..	22.3	..	..	..	9
Lesotho	5.1	8.4	8.6	13.8	72.5	53.7	1,003.6	779.3	60.9	57.6	47	7
Libya	3.4	..	..	..	..	..	58.2	..	..	..	..	9
Lithuania	..	5.4	..	..	..	28.5	..	42.1	..	..	16	9
Macedonia, FYR	..	5.1	..	20.2	..	27.3	..	69.5	..	..	19	8
Madagascar	4.4	1.9	9.1 [c]	..	..	..	402.5	..	81.8	..	37	6
Malawi	3.4	5.4	7.6	8.8	..	..	1,839.9	1,593.7	43.4	..	59	8
Malaysia	6.0	4.9	12.0 [c]	11.1	..	..	148.9	57.3	57.5 [e]	58.6	20	.. [d]
Mali	3.7	2.2	31.7	13.8	..	..	3,631.4	382.7	51.0	..	80	9 [d]
Mauritania	..	5.1	30.4	11.1	..	..	..	205.9	..	..	50	6
Mauritius	5.3	4.6	15.8 [c]	9.8	..	..	343.6	69.5	31.4	..	24	7
Mexico	4.7	4.9	4.4	11.8	..	17.9	26.4	46.8	..	..	28	6
Moldova	3.4	10.6	..	..	..	..	..	63.2	..	..	23	11 [d]
Mongolia	..	5.7	..	..	..	46.1 [h]	..	37.7	..	..	31	8
Morocco	6.1	5.0	15.5 [c]	14.3 [c]	54.9	..	155.3	69.5	..	78.0	28	6
Mozambique	3.1	..	..	..	..	..	..	..	..	..	58	7 [d]
Myanmar	1.7	1.2	..	..	..	..	..	19.0	..	..	..	5
Namibia	1.5	9.1	..	21.0	..	34.1	..	101.7	..	..	..	10 [d]
Nepal	1.8	3.2	14.6 [i]	..	..	..	271.9	115.3	..	..	..	5
Netherlands	7.7	5.1	13.8	..	23.3	21.2	73.3	47.3	70.8	..	..	13 [d]
New Zealand	5.8	7.3	15.1	17.9	13.7	23.8	59.9	45.7	82.7	..	18	10 [d]
Nicaragua	3.4	3.9	8.2	11.4	15.5	..	25.8	..	69.7	..	38	6
Niger	3.2	2.3	26.2	32.1 [c]	..	82.5	1,538.5	..	68.2	..	41	8
Nigeria	6.4	0.7	4.7	..	..	..	529.6	..	..	..	37	6
Norway	6.5	7.4	27.2 [c]	31.2	14.9	18.8	38.2	45.3	..	..	..	9
Oman	2.1	4.5	..	13.1	..	..	..	26.7	60.3	..	26	..
Pakistan	2.1	2.7	9.2 [c]	..	..	..	..	..	..	..	..	..
Panama	4.9	5.1	12.3 [c]	..	11.5	..	29.8	40.2	65.3 [e]	51.2	..	6
Papua New Guinea	..	..	..	..	..	..	..	..	..	..	38	.. [d]
Paraguay	1.5	4.0	..	10.9	..	12.0	..	90.9	..	..	21	6
Peru	3.1	2.9	7.2	..	11.3	6.8	5.2	15.4	59.4	40.1	28	6
Philippines	1.7	3.4	5.8 [c]	9.2	4.3	7.6	13.8	14.8	..	..	35	6
Poland	..	7.5	8.1	17.1	14.8	..	47.3	40.7	..	..	15	8
Portugal	3.8	5.8	13.5 [c]	..	..	20.2	36.3	24.5	..	..	..	9
Puerto Rico	..	..	..	..	..	..	..	..	..	..	..	10
Romania	3.3	3.6	..	20.1	..	8.8	..	31.8	..	..	20	8
Russian Federation	3.5	3.5	..	..	..	..	..	..	..	..	..	9 [d]

2.9 Education inputs

	Public expenditure on education		Expenditure per student						Expenditure on teachers' compensation		Primary pupil-teacher ratio	Duration of primary education
	% of GNP		Primary % of GNP per capita		Secondary % of GNP per capita		Tertiary % of GNP per capita		% of total current education expenditure		pupils per teacher	years
	1980	1997	1980	1997	1980	1997	1980	1997	1980	1997	1997	1997
Rwanda	2.7	..	11.1	..	..	..	901.7	..	74.8	..	..	6
Saudi Arabia	4.1	7.5	18.9 [a]	33.8 [a]	..	..	109.2	60.0	..	..	13	..
Senegal	..	3.7	24.9 [c]	11.3 [c]	..	..	447.5	..	..	..	56	6 [d]
Sierra Leone	3.5	..	..	..	..	..	..	..	..	..	..	..
Singapore	2.8	3.0	6.8 [c]	7.8 [c]	..	..	40.6	28.0	47.5	..	22	.. [d]
Slovak Republic	..	5.0	..	23.6	..	..	..	30.8	..	37.9	19	9
Slovenia	..	5.7	..	20.4	..	..	..	37.5	..	62.2	14	8
South Africa	..	7.9	..	25.1	..	..	..	..	..	64.5	36	9
Spain	2.3	5.0	..	17.4	..	..	..	17.8	..	..	17	10
Sri Lanka	2.7	3.4	..	..	..	..	65.6	85.0	..	..	28	9
Sudan	4.3	0.9	24.1 [c]	4.9	..	..	528.1	..	..	..	29	8
Sweden	9.0	8.3	43.0	284.6	15.8	34.1	35.0	72.4	46.3	..	1	9 [d]
Switzerland	4.7	5.4	..	19.2	29.9	29.0	58.5	45.4	61.0	59.9	..	9 [d]
Syrian Arab Republic	4.6	3.1	8.0 [c]	8.2 [c]	15.1	16.5	74.7	..	85.9	..	23	6
Tajikistan	..	2.2	..	..	..	..	..	..	..	..	24	9
Tanzania	..	..	..	..	..	..	..	..	..	..	37	7
Thailand	3.4	4.8	8.8	12.5	..	..	60.1	26.7	80.3	56.8	..	6
Togo	5.6	4.5	8.3	7.7	..	..	891.5	333.8	68.4	74.2	51	6
Trinidad and Tobago	4.0	3.6	9.2 [c]	10.8	20.4	..	59.4	..	73.2	..	25	7
Tunisia	5.4	7.7	11.8 [c]	15.2 [c]	37.7	..	194.6	79.1	81.3	77.0	24	9
Turkey	2.2	2.2	6.4 [c]	13.3	..	9.2	95.0	51.1	..	..	28	8 [d]
Turkmenistan	..	..	..	..	..	..	..	..	..	..	..	..
Uganda	1.3	2.6	4.3	..	..	..	1,034.8	..	..	69.9 [b]	35	..
Ukraine	5.6	7.3	21.2	..	..	..	20.2	22.7	..	..	..	9 [d]
United Arab Emirates	1.3	1.8	..	..	..	..	..	..	..	32.4	16	6
United Kingdom	5.6	5.3	..	..	22.1	20.5	79.8	40.7	52.1	..	..	11
United States	6.7	5.4	27.1 [c]	18.5	..	23.8	48.2	24.6	..	..	16	10 [d]
Uruguay	2.3	3.3	11.1	9.3 [c]	..	..	28.1	24.2	56.9 [e]	41.5	20	6
Uzbekistan	..	7.7	..	..	..	..	..	..	..	..	21	..
Venezuela, RB	4.4	5.2	5.7	2.1	23.1	4.8	71.1	..	60.7	21.4	21	10
Vietnam	..	3.0	..	..	..	..	..	87.8	..	66.0	..	5
West Bank and Gaza	..	..	..	..	..	..	..	..	..	..	..	..
Yemen, Rep.	..	7.0	..	..	..	..	..	..	..	..	..	9
Yugoslavia, FR (Serb./Mont.)	..	..	..	..	..	..	..	..	..	..	..	8
Zambia	4.5	2.2	10.6	5.0	..	..	605.4	356.2	52.6 [e]	..	39	7
Zimbabwe	5.3	..	19.4	19.4	..	..	324.8	340.3	75.2	91.1 [b]	39	8
World	**3.9 m**	**4.8 m**	**11.1 m**	**.. m**	**.. m**	**.. m**	**60.0 m**	**.. m**	**..**	**..**	**33 w**	**9 m**
Low income	3.2	3.2	..	..	..	..	..	..	..	..	39	7
Excl. China & India	3.3	3.2	..	..	..	..	..	..	..	..	..	7
Middle income	4.0	4.9	9.4	..	..	..	58.7	..	..	..	..	9
Lower middle income	4.2	4.9	..	..	..	..	..	..	..	..	..	8
Upper middle income	4.0	5.0	9.4	..	..	..	58.7	39.8	..	..	24	9
Low & middle income	3.5	4.1	..	..	..	..	..	..	..	..	36	8
East Asia & Pacific	2.5	2.9	..	..	..	..	..	41.7	..	..	24	8
Europe & Central Asia	..	5.1	..	..	..	..	..	39.8	..	..	..	9
Latin America & Carib.	3.8	3.6	8.9	..	..	..	51.3	..	..	..	24	9
Middle East & N. Africa	5.0	5.2	..	15.2	..	..	81.1	..	..	..	26	9
South Asia	2.0	3.1	10.5	..	..	..	88.2	85.0	..	..	63	6
Sub-Saharan Africa	3.8	4.1	13.6	..	..	..	790.7	..	..	..	41	7
High income	5.6	5.4	15.1	19.9	22.5	22.2	44.4	37.5	..	..	17	10
Europe EMU	5.4	5.3	13.8	21.7	..	25.8	37.4	35.8	..	..	15	9

a. Includes expenditure on preprimary and secondary. b. Excludes expenditure on tertiary. c. Includes expenditure on preprimary. d. The education system allows other alternatives. e. Includes administration other than personnel. f. Refers only to ministry of education expenditure. g. Includes expenditure on preprimary and primary. h. Includes expenditure on primary. i. Includes expenditure on secondary.

Education inputs 2.9

About the data

Data on education are compiled by the United Nations Educational, Scientific, and Cultural Organization (UNESCO) from official responses to surveys and from reports provided by education authorities in each country. Such data are used for monitoring, policymaking, and resource allocation. For a variety of reasons education statistics generally fail to provide a complete and accurate picture of a country's education system and should be interpreted with caution. Statistics often are out of date by two to three years. The information collected focuses more on inputs than on outcomes. And coverage, definitions, and data collection methods vary across countries and over time within countries. (For further discussion of the reliability of education data see Behrman and Rosenzweig 1994.)

The data on education spending in the table refer solely to public spending—that is, government spending on public education plus subsidies for private education. The data generally exclude foreign aid for education. They also may exclude spending by religious schools, which play a significant role in many developing countries. Data for some countries and for some years refer to spending by the ministry of education at the center only (excluding education expenditures by other ministries and departments, local authorities, and so on).

Many developing countries have sought to supplement public funds for education. Some countries have adopted tuition fees to recover part of the cost of providing education services or to encourage development of private schools. Charging fees raises difficult questions relating to equity, efficiency, access, and taxation, however, and some governments have used scholarships, vouchers, and other methods of public finance to counter this criticism. Data for a few countries include private spending, although national practices vary with respect to whether parents or schools pay for books, uniforms, and other supplies. For greater detail see the country- and indicator-specific notes in the source cited below.

The percentage of GNP devoted to education can be interpreted as reflecting a country's effort in education. Often it bears a weak relationship to measures of output of the education system, as reflected in educational attainment. The pattern suggests wide variations across countries in the efficiency with which the government's resources are translated into education outcomes.

Well-trained and motivated teachers are a critical input to education, but they come at a cost. Typically, two-thirds of education spending goes to teachers' compensation (gross salaries and other benefits). Teachers are defined here as including both full- and part-time teaching staff and teachers assigned to nonteaching duties, but country reporting varies. Comparisons should thus be made with caution.

The comparability of pupil-teacher ratios is affected by the definition of teachers, by whether teachers are assigned nonteaching duties, and by differences in class size by grade and in the number of hours taught. Moreover, the underlying enrollment levels are subject to a variety of reporting errors. (See *About the data* for table 2.10 for further discussion of enrollment data.) While the pupil-teacher ratio is often used to compare the quality of schooling across countries, it is often only weakly related to the value added of schooling systems (Behrman and Rosenzweig 1994).

Years of compulsory education show the level of development of the country's education system and education policy. The actual length of compulsory education is influenced by the length of the school day and school year.

Figure 2.9

Households account for much of the spending on education

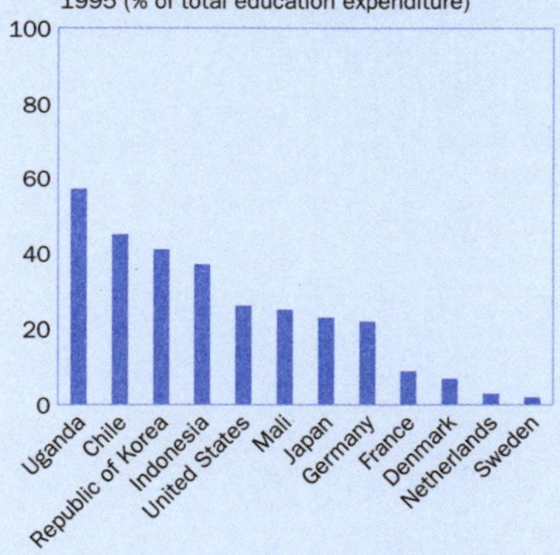

Note: Data for Uganda refer to 1990, data for Indonesia to 1991, data for Japan, the Republic of Korea, and the United States to 1994, and data for Chile to 1996.
Source: World Bank, EDSTATS.

Private spending on education is sizable in many countries, averaging 25 percent of all education expenditures in developing countries and 12 percent in high-income countries. Globally, households contribute close to 20 percent of education expenditures.

Definitions

• **Public expenditure on education** is the percentage of GNP accounted for by public spending on public education plus subsidies to private education at the primary, secondary, and tertiary levels. • **Expenditure per student** is the public current spending on education divided by the total number of students by level, as a percentage of GNP per capita. • **Expenditure on teachers' compensation** is the public expenditure on teachers' gross salaries and other benefits as a percentage of the total public current spending on education. • **Primary pupil-teacher ratio** is the number of pupils enrolled in primary school divided by the number of primary school teachers (regardless of their teaching assignment). • **Duration of compulsory education** is the number of years of compulsory school attendance a child must complete, within a stipulated age range.

Data sources

International data on education are compiled by UNESCO's Institute for Statistics in cooperation with national commissions and national statistical services. The data in the table were compiled using a UNESCO electronic database corresponding to tables in UNESCO's *Statistical Yearbook 1999.*

2.10 Participation in education

	Gross enrollment ratio							Net enrollment ratio[a]			
	Preprimary % of relevant age group	Primary % of relevant age group		Secondary % of relevant age group		Tertiary % of relevant age group		Primary % of relevant age group		Secondary % of relevant age group	
	1997	**1980**	**1997**	**1980**	**1997**	**1980**	**1997**	**1980**	**1997**	**1980**	**1997**
Albania	*39*	113	*107*	67	*38*	5	*11*	..	..	..	..
Algeria	*2*	95	*108*	33	*63*	6	*13*	82	96	43	69
Angola	*62*	175	..	21	..	0	*1*	83	35	81	31
Argentina	*54*	106	111	56	73	22	*42*	97	100	59	77
Armenia	*26*	..	*87*	..	*90*	..	12	..	..	..	..
Australia	80	112	101	71	153 [b]	25	80	100	100	81	96
Austria	*80*	99	*100*	93	*103*	22	*48*	100	100	91	97
Azerbaijan	*19*	115	*106*	95	*77*	24	*18*	..	..	..	..
Bangladesh	*75*	61	..	18	..	3	*6*	60	75	18	22
Belarus	*82*	104	*98*	98	93	39	*44*	..	*85*	..	..
Belgium	*121*	104	*103*	91	*146* [b]	26	*57*	100	100	96	100
Benin	*3*	67	*78*	16	18	1	*3*	53	68	25	28
Bolivia	*42*	87	..	37	..	16	*24*	79	97	34	40
Bosnia and Herzegovina	..	..	..	..	..	..	..	..	..	..	..
Botswana	..	91	*108*	19	*65*	1	6	76	80	40	89
Brazil	58	98	125	34	62	11	*15*	80	97	46	66
Bulgaria	*63*	98	*99*	85	*77*	16	*41*	98	98	75	78
Burkina Faso	*2*	18	*40*	3	..	0	*1*	15	32	5	13
Burundi	*1*	26	*51*	3	*7*	1	*1*	20	36	8	17
Cambodia	5	139	113	..	24	2	1	100	100	15	39
Cameroon	*11*	98	*85*	18	*27*	2	*4*	71	62	40	40
Canada	*64*	99	*102*	88	*105*	57	*90*	100	100	84	95
Central African Republic	*6*	71	..	14	..	1	*1*	57	46	27	19
Chad	*1*	..	*58*	..	*10*	0	*1*	26	48	13	18
Chile	*98*	109	*101*	53	*75*	12	31	93	90	70	85
China	28	113	123	46	70	2	6	84	100	63	70
Hong Kong, China	*85*	107	*94*	64	*73*	10	*28*	98	91	67	69
Colombia	*33*	112	*113*	39	*67*	9	*17*	73	89	60	76
Congo, Dem. Rep.	*1*	92	*72*	24	*26*	1	*2*	71	58	44	37
Congo, Rep.	*2*	141	*114*	74	*53*	5	*8*	97	78	98	84
Costa Rica	74	105	104	48	48	21	*33*	89	89	39	*40*
Côte d'Ivoire	*3*	75	*71*	19	25	3	*5*	55	58	39	34
Croatia	*40*	..	*87*	77	*82*	19	*28*	100	100	80	72
Cuba	*88*	106	*106*	81	*81*	17	*12*	97	100	80	70
Czech Republic	*91*	96	*104*	99	*99*	18	*24*	95	100	93	100
Denmark	*83*	96	*102*	105	*121*	28	*45*	96	100	89	95
Dominican Republic	33	118	*94*	42	54	10	*23*	99	91	50	79
Ecuador	*56*	118	*127*	53	*50*	35	*26*	92	100	66	51
Egypt, Arab Rep.	*9*	73	101	51	78	16	*23*	72	95	43	75
El Salvador	40	75	97	24	37	13	*18*	70	89	23	36
Eritrea	*4*	..	*53*	..	*20*	..	1	..	29	..	38
Estonia	75	103	*94*	127	*104*	25	45	100	100	100	86
Ethiopia	*1*	37	*43*	9	*12*	0	*1*	28	35	19	25
Finland	*45*	96	*99*	100	*118*	32	*74*	100	100	87	95
France	*83*	111	*105*	85	*111*	25	*51*	100	100	94	99
Gabon	..	174	*162*	34	*56*	4	*8*	..	..	..	..
Gambia, The	28	53	*77*	11	*25*	..	2	53	66	10	33
Georgia	34	93	*88*	109	*77*	30	41	93	89	97	76
Germany	*89*	..	*104*	..	*104*	27	*47*	100	100	82	95
Ghana	*36*	79	*79*	41	..	2	*1*	..	..	..	..
Greece	*64*	103	*93*	81	*95*	17	*47*	100	100	75	91
Guatemala	35	71	88	19	26	8	*8*	59	74	28	35
Guinea	4	36	54	17	14	5	*1*	30	46	20	15
Guinea-Bissau	*1*	68	*62*	6	..	..	..	47	52	29	24
Haiti	*37*	77	..	14	..	1	*1*	..	..	..	..
Honduras	*15*	98	*111*	30	..	8	*11*	79	88	44	36

Participation in education 2.10

	Gross enrollment ratio								Net enrollment ratio[a]			
	Preprimary % of relevant age group	Primary % of relevant age group		Secondary % of relevant age group		Tertiary % of relevant age group		Primary % of relevant age group		Secondary % of relevant age group	
	1997	1980	1997	1980	1997	1980	1997	1980	1997	1980	1997
Hungary	112	96	103	70	98	14	25	95	98	71	97
India	5	83	100	30	49	5	7	65	77	41	60
Indonesia	19	107	113	29	56	4	11	89	99	42	56
Iran, Islamic Rep.	11	87	98	42	77	..	18	72	90	50	81
Iraq	7	113	85	57	42	9	11	97	75	66	43
Ireland	114	100	105	90	118	18	41	100	100	90	100
Israel	70	95	98	73	88	29	44	..	..	..	..
Italy	95	100	101	72	95	27	47	100	100	70	95
Jamaica	83	103	100	67	..	7	8	98	96	71	70
Japan	49	101	101	93	103	31	43	100	100	93	100
Jordan	..	82	71	59	57	13	19	73	68	53	41
Kazakhstan	30	85	98	93	87	34	32	..	..	..	..
Kenya	36	115	85	20	24	1	2	91	65	55	61
Korea, Dem. Rep.	..	..	..	..	..	..	..	..	..	..	..
Korea, Rep.	88	110	94	78	102	15	68	100	100	76	100
Kuwait	63	102	77	80	65	11	19	85	65	81	63
Kyrgyz Republic	8	116	104	110	79	16	12	100	100	100	78
Lao PDR	8	114	112	21	29	0	3	72	73	53	63
Latvia	47	102	96	99	84	24	33	100	100	90	81
Lebanon	75	111	111	59	81	30	27	..	76	..	..
Lesotho	..	104	108	18	31	1	2	67	69	69	73
Libya	5	125	..	76	..	8	20	100	100	83	100
Lithuania	40	79	98	114	86	35	31	..	..	..	81
Macedonia, FYR	26	100	99	61	63	28	20	..	95	..	56
Madagascar	4	130	92	..	16	3	2	..	61	..	..
Malawi	..	60	134	5	17	1	1	43	99	39	73
Malaysia	42	93	101	48	64	4	11	92	100	48	64
Mali	2	26	49	8	13	1	1	20	38	10	18
Mauritania	1	37	79	11	16	1	4	..	57	..	..
Mauritius	104	93	106	50	65	1	6	79	97	56	68
Mexico	73	120	114	49	64	14	16	98	100	67	66
Moldova	45	83	97	78	81	30	27	..	..	..	..
Mongolia	27	107	88	92	56	22	19	100	85	89	56
Morocco	98	83	86	26	39	6	11	62	77	36	38
Mozambique	..	99	60	5	7	0	1	35	40	40	22
Myanmar	..	91	121	22	30	5	6	71	99	38	54
Namibia	9	..	131	..	62	..	9	86	91	67	81
Nepal	1	86	113	22	42	3	5	66	78	26	55
Netherlands	100	100	108	93	132 [b]	29	47	100	100	93	100
New Zealand	76	111	101	83	113	27	63	100	100	85	93
Nicaragua	23	94	102	41	55	12	12	71	79	51	51
Niger	1	25	29	5	7	0	1	22	24	7	9
Nigeria	..	109	98	18	33	3	4	..	..	..	..
Norway	103	100	100	94	119	26	62	99	100	84	98
Oman	5	51	76	12	67	..	8	43	68	20	67
Pakistan	16	40	..	14	..	2	4	..	..	..	..
Panama	76	107	106	61	69	21	32	89	90	65	71
Papua New Guinea	1	59	80	12	14	2	3	..	..	..	..
Paraguay	61	106	111	27	47	9	10	91	96	37	61
Peru	40	114	123	59	73	17	26	87	94	80	84
Philippines	11	112	117	64	78	24	35	95	100	72	78
Poland	48	100	96	77	98	18	24	99	99	73	87
Portugal	59	123	128	37	111 [b]	11	38	99	100	45	90
Puerto Rico	..	..	..	..	..	42	42	..	..	..	..
Romania	53	104	104	94	78	12	23	91	100	100	76
Russian Federation	74	102	107	96	..	46	41	92	100	98	88

2.10 Participation in education

	Gross enrollment ratio							Net enrollment ratio[a]			
	Preprimary % of relevant age group	Primary % of relevant age group		Secondary % of relevant age group		Tertiary % of relevant age group		Primary % of relevant age group		Secondary % of relevant age group	
	1997	1980	1997	1980	1997	1980	1997	1980	1997	1980	1997
Rwanda	2	63	..	3	..	0	1	59	..	..	..
Saudi Arabia	8	61	76	30	61	7	16	49	60	37	59
Senegal	2	46	71	11	16	3	3	37	60	19	20
Sierra Leone	2	52	..	14	..	1	2	..	..	..	..
Singapore	19	108	94	60	74	8	39	100	91	66	76
Slovak Republic	76	..	102	..	94	18	22	..	..	..	..
Slovenia	61	98	98	..	92	20	36	..	95	..	..
South Africa	35	90	133	..	95	5	17	68	100	62	95
Spain	72	109	107	87	120	23	53	100	100	79	92
Sri Lanka	60	103	109	55	75	3	5	96	100	59	76
Sudan	24	50	51	16	21	2	4	..	..	..	..
Sweden	73	97	107	88	140[b]	31	50	100	100	83	100
Switzerland	95	84	97	94	100	18	34	100	100	80	84
Syrian Arab Republic	7	100	101	46	43	17	15	90	95	48	42
Tajikistan	10	..	95	..	78	24	20	..	..	..	..
Tanzania	0	93	67	3	6	0	1	68	48	..	..
Thailand	62	99	89	29	59	15	21	92	88	25	48
Togo	3	118	120	33	27	2	4	79	82	65	58
Trinidad and Tobago	12	99	99	69	74	4	8	92	100	73	72
Tunisia	11	102	118	27	64	5	14	83	100	40	74
Turkey	8	96	107	35	58	5	21	81	100	42	58
Turkmenistan	37	..	..	..	..	23	20	..	..	..	..
Uganda	..	50	74	5	12	1	2	..	..	..	..
Ukraine	61	102	..	94	..	42	42	..	..	..	..
United Arab Emirates	57	89	89	52	80	3	12	75	82	63	78
United Kingdom	30	103	116	84	129[b]	19	52	100	100	88	92
United States	70	99	102	91	97	56	81	90	100	94	96
Uruguay	45	107	109	62	85	17	30	87	94	70	84
Uzbekistan	50	81	78	106	94	29	36	..	..	..	..
Venezuela, RB	44	93	91	21	40	21	25	83	83	24	49
Vietnam	40	109	114	42	57	2	7	96	100	47	55
West Bank and Gaza	..	..	..	..	..	..	..	..	..	..	..
Yemen, Rep.	1	..	70	..	34	4	4	..	..	..	..
Yugoslavia, FR (Serb./Mont.)	32	..	69	..	62	18	22	..	..	..	..
Zambia	1	90	89	16	27	2	3	77	72	35	42
Zimbabwe	..	85	112	8	50	1	7	72	93	20	59
World	**35 w**	**97 w**	**106 w**	**49 w**	**64 w**	**13 w**	**19 w**	**81 w**	**90 w**	**60 w**	**68 w**
Low income	20	94	107	34	56	3	6	74	86	49	59
Excl. China & India	22	81	90	22	32	3	5	68	75	34	41
Middle income	48	100	106	60	66	20	25	87	95	62	72
Lower middle income	42	98	103	67	67	24	27	85	94	66	73
Upper middle income	56	103	109	50	65	13	23	89	96	57	71
Low & middle income	28	96	107	42	59	8	12	78	88	53	63
East Asia & Pacific	30	111	119	44	69	4	8	86	99	59	67
Europe & Central Asia	53	99	100	86	..	30	32	92	100	84	81
Latin America & Carib.	56	105	113	42	60	14	20	85	94	55	66
Middle East & N. Africa	18	87	95	42	64	11	16	74	87	46	66
South Asia	14	77	100	27	49	5	6	64	77	38	55
Sub-Saharan Africa	12	81	78	15	27	2	2	..	..	..	..
High income	70	102	103	87	106	35	59	97	100	87	96
Europe EMU	87	106	104	81	108	25	49	100	100	82	96

a. UNESCO enrollment estimates and projections as assessed in 1999. b. Includes training for the unemployed.

Participation in education 2.10

About the data

School enrollment data are reported to the United Nations Educational, Scientific, and Cultural Organization (UNESCO) by national education authorities. Enrollment ratios are a useful measure of participation in education, but they may also have significant limitations. Enrollment ratios are based on data collected during annual school surveys, which are typically conducted at the beginning of the school year and therefore do not reflect actual rates of attendance or dropouts during the school year. And school administrators may report exaggerated enrollments, especially if there is a financial incentive to do so. Often the number of teachers paid by the government is related to the number of pupils enrolled. Behrman and Rosenzweig (1994), comparing official school enrollment data for Malaysia in 1988 with gross school attendance rates from a household survey, found that the official statistics systematically overstated enrollment.

Overage or underage enrollments frequently occur, particularly when parents prefer, for cultural or economic reasons, to have children start school at other than the official age. Children's age at enrollment may be inaccurately estimated or misstated, especially in communities where registration of births is not strictly enforced. Parents who want to enroll their underage children in primary school may do so by overstating the age of the children. And in some education systems ages for children repeating a grade may be deliberately or inadvertently underreported.

As an international indicator, the gross primary enrollment ratio has been used to indicate broad levels of participation as well as school capacity. It has an inherent weakness: the length of primary education differs significantly across countries. A short duration tends to increase the ratio and a long duration to decrease it (in part because there are more dropouts among older children).

Other problems affecting cross-country comparisons of enrollment data stem from errors in estimates of school-age populations. Age-gender structures from censuses or vital registration systems, the primary sources of data on school-age populations, are commonly subject to underenumeration (especially of young children) aimed at circumventing laws or regulations; errors are also introduced when parents round up children's ages. While census data are often adjusted for age bias, adjustments are rarely made for inadequate vital registration systems. Compounding these problems, pre- and postcensus estimates of school-age children are interpolations or projections based on models that may miss important demographic events (see the discussion of demographic data in *About the data* for table 2.1).

In using enrollment data, it is also important to consider repetition rates, which are quite high in some developing countries, leading to a substantial number of overage children enrolled in each grade and raising the gross enrollment ratio. A common error that may also distort enrollment ratios is the lack of distinction between new entrants and repeaters, which, other things equal, leads to underreporting of repeaters and overestimation of dropouts. Thus gross enrollment ratios provide an indication of the capacity of each level of the education system, but a high ratio does not necessarily indicate a successful education system. The net enrollment ratio excludes overage students in an attempt to capture more accurately the system's coverage and internal efficiency. It does not solve the problem completely, however, because some children fall outside the official school age simply because of late or early entry rather than because of grade repetition. The difference between gross and net enrollment ratios shows the incidence of overage and underage enrollments.

Figure 2.10

Millions of the world's children still are not in school

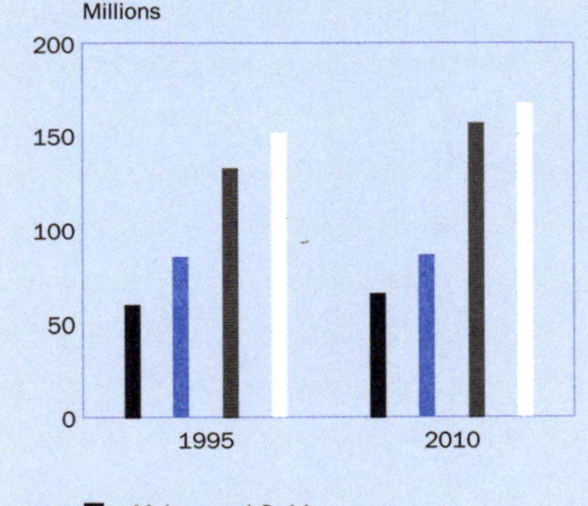

Source: UNESCO 1998.

Education for All 2000 efforts over the past decade have boosted enrollment, especially at the primary level. Yet millions of primary- and secondary-school-age children remain out of school, and their numbers are projected to grow.

Where access remains a problem, especially for the poor and disadvantaged, several strategies to increase access are being successfully implemented, including multiple shifts, multigrade classrooms, and nontraditional schooling.

But to encourage girls' attendance, strategies will need to go beyond increasing supply. Measures will be needed that lower barriers to their enrollment—by providing incentives, improving the relevance of education, and establishing supportive national policies.

Definitions

• **Gross enrollment ratio** is the ratio of total enrollment, regardless of age, to the population of the age group that officially corresponds to the level of education shown. • **Net enrollment ratio** is the ratio of the number of children of official school age (as defined by the national education system) who are enrolled in school to the population of the corresponding official school age. Based on the International Standard Classification of Education (ISCED), • **Preprimary** education refers to the initial stage of organized instruction, designed primarily to introduce very young children to a school-type environment. • **Primary** education provides children with basic reading, writing, and mathematics skills along with an elementary understanding of such subjects as history, geography, natural science, social science, art, and music. • **Secondary** education completes the provision of basic education that began at the primary level, and aims at laying the foundations for lifelong learning and human development, by offering more subject- or skill-oriented instruction using more specialized teachers. • **Tertiary** education, whether or not leading to an advanced research qualification, normally requires, as a minimum condition of admission, the successful completion of education at the secondary level.

Data sources

The gross enrollment ratios are from UNESCO's *Statistical Yearbook 1999,* and the net enrollment ratios are the results of UNESCO's 1999 enrollment estimates and projections.

2.11 Education efficiency

	Percentage of cohort reaching grade 5				Repeaters				Children out of school			
	Male		Female		Primary % of total enrollment		Secondary % of total enrollment		Primary thousands		Secondary thousands	
	1980	1996	1980	1996	1980	1997	1980	1997	1980	1997	1980	1997
Albania	..	81	..	83	..	5.3	..	..	..	..	..	..
Algeria	90	94	85	95	11.7	10.5	8.5	19.6	608	176	1,765	1,319
Angola	..	..	..	..	29.2	..	..	..	124	931	178	1,367
Argentina	..	..	..	..	..	5.3	..	..	98	5	972	776
Armenia	..	..	..	..	..	0.2	..	..	..	..	..	..
Australia	..	..	..	..	..	..	..	..	..	..	..	..
Austria	..	..	..	..	..	..	..	..	..	..	..	..
Azerbaijan	..	..	..	..	..	0.4	..	..	..	..	..	..
Bangladesh	18	..	26	..	17.8	..	..	..	5,464	3,896	12,524	18,130
Belarus	..	..	..	..	0.3	0.9	..	..	..	..	..	..
Belgium	..	..	..	..	19.4	..	..	..	..	..	..	..
Benin	59	64	62	57	19.6	25.1	..	..	269	330	427	686
Bolivia	..	..	..	..	..	..	..	..	233	40	309	402
Bosnia and Herzegovina	..	..	..	..	..	..	..	..	..	..	..	..
Botswana	80	87	84	93	2.9	3.3	..	2.8	46	60	67	21
Brazil	..	..	..	..	20.2	18.4	7.3	10.8	4,514	784	4,560	3,552
Bulgaria	..	93	..	90	1.7	3.4	0.1	2.0	23	9	93	211
Burkina Faso	77	74	74	77	17.1	16.0	14.3	..	985	1,271	971	1,499
Burundi	100	..	96	..	30.2	..	4.3	..	535	699	615	807
Cambodia	..	51	..	46	..	26.3	..	..	1	2	876	789
Cameroon	70	..	70	..	30.0	..	13.7	..	406	882	771	1,347
Canada	..	..	..	..	..	..	..	..	..	..	..	..
Central African Republic	63	..	50	..	35.1	..	..	..	151	304	242	440
Chad	..	62	..	53	..	32.0	..	18.4	510	635	582	903
Chile	94	100	97	100	..	5.4	..	4.3	145	217	312	148
China	..	93	..	94	..	1.6	..	..	20,399	114	53,306	36,421
Hong Kong, China	98	..	99	..	3.6	1.1	6.5	3.9	12	43	243	209
Colombia	36	70	39	76	13.2	7.2	..	..	992	471	1,781	1,180
Congo, Dem. Rep.	56	..	59	..	18.8	..	..	..	1,326	3,520	2,010	4,113
Congo, Rep.	81	40	83	78	25.7	33.2	..	..	9	101	5	68
Costa Rica	77	86	82	89	7.9	10.1	7.5	9.6	33	42	122	177
Côte d'Ivoire	86	77	79	71	19.6	24.2	..	..	610	1,022	733	1,614
Croatia	..	98	..	98	..	0.5	..	0.3	0	0	51	140
Cuba	..	..	..	..	5.7	3.1	..	..	38	1	283	272
Czech Republic	..	..	..	..	..	1.2	..	0.7	..	..	..	..
Denmark	99	100	99	99	..	..	..	..	..	..	..	..
Dominican Republic	..	..	..	..	18.0	..	..	..	12	127	427	143
Ecuador	..	84	..	86	9.7	3.5	..	..	111	2	383	782
Egypt, Arab Rep.	92	..	88	..	7.9	6.5	..	..	1,785	378	3,291	2,297
El Salvador	46	76	48	77	8.8	4.3	..	0.9	340	133	232	263
Eritrea	..	73	..	67	..	20.5	..	15.0	..	333	..	287
Estonia	..	96	..	97	..	2.8	..	3.4	0	0	0	15
Ethiopia	50	51	51	50	12.2	7.8	..	..	4,085	6,264	3,762	5,667
Finland	..	100	..	100	..	0.4	..	..	..	..	..	..
France	..	..	..	..	..	..	9.3	8.1	..	..	..	..
Gabon	57	58	56	61	34.8	34.9	..	..	..	..	..	..
Gambia, The	74	78	71	83	12.4	12.7	2.1	..	42	59	76	93
Georgia	..	..	..	..	..	0.4	..	0.5	25	36	21	138
Germany	..	..	..	..	..	1.7	..	2.2	..	..	..	..
Ghana	..	..	..	..	2.1	..	..	..	..	..	..	..
Greece	99	..	98	..	1.1	..	3.9	..	..	..	..	..
Guatemala	..	52	..	47	15.0	15.3	2.5	..	462	460	666	976
Guinea	59	85	41	68	21.9	27.9	..	..	498	675	463	985
Guinea-Bissau	..	..	..	..	28.9	..	14.5	..	58	84	56	91
Haiti	33	..	34	..	15.5	..	..	..	517	1,085	433	776
Honduras	..	..	..	..	16.2	12.0	..	..	129	122	238	451

Education efficiency 2.11

	Percentage of cohort reaching grade 5				Repeaters				Children out of school			
	Male		Female		Primary % of total enrollment		Secondary % of total enrollment		Primary thousands		Secondary thousands	
	1980	**1996**	**1980**	**1996**	**1980**	**1997**	**1980**	**1997**	**1980**	**1997**	**1980**	**1997**
Hungary	96	..	97	..	2.1	..	..	..	..	..	..	..
India	..	62	..	55	..	3.7	..	..	31,412	25,434	64,986	57,216
Indonesia	..	88	..	88	8.3	5.8	..	0.7	2,718	192	11,399	11,211
Iran, Islamic Rep.	..	92	..	89	..	5.9	..	..	1,536	927	3,271	2,237
Iraq	77	..	64	..	23.2	..	..	..	70	891	624	1,696
Ireland	..	99	..	100	..	1.7	..	2.2	..	..	..	..
Israel	..	..	..	..	..	..	..	..	..	..	..	..
Italy	99	98	99	99	1.2	0.4	..	..	..	..	..	..
Jamaica	91	..	91	..	3.9	..	2.1	..	8	14	109	108
Japan	100	100	100	100	..	..	..	..	..	..	..	..
Jordan	100	..	98	..	3.2	1.3	4.4	..	..	..	..	..
Kazakhstan	..	..	..	..	..	0.6	..	..	..	..	..	..
Kenya	60	..	62	..	12.9	..	..	..	320	2,350	983	1,125
Korea, Dem. Rep.	..	..	..	..	..	..	..	..	..	..	..	..
Korea, Rep.	94	98	94	99	..	..	0.0	..	..	..	..	..
Kuwait	..	..	..	..	6.2	3.4	7.0	5.4	22	64	42	128
Kyrgyz Republic	..	..	..	..	..	0.4	..	..	0	2	1	155
Lao PDR	..	57	..	54	..	23.4	..	5.5	118	196	205	252
Latvia	..	..	..	..	..	2.5	..	1.3	0	0	28	56
Lebanon	..	..	..	..	..	13.4	..	..	..	..	..	..
Lesotho	50	72	68	87	20.7	20.1	..	..	78	111	44	61
Libya	..	..	..	..	9.2	..	12.7	..	1	1	67	0
Lithuania	..	..	..	..	..	1.3	..	1.2	..	..	..	..
Macedonia, FYR	..	95	..	95	..	0.5	..	0.2	..	..	..	..
Madagascar	..	49	..	33	..	33.8	..	..	..	..	..	..
Malawi	48	..	40	..	17.4	15.1	..	..	767	34	327	250
Malaysia	97	98	97	100	..	..	..	..	166	9	1,188	1,090
Mali	48	92	42	70	29.6	16.2	..	..	899	1,094	833	1,224
Mauritania	..	61	..	68	14.0	15.8	..	..	..	..	..	..
Mauritius	94	98	94	99	..	4.5	..	..	29	4	72	46
Mexico	..	85	..	86	9.8	6.9	..	2.1	..	..	..	..
Moldova	..	..	..	..	..	1.2	..	..	..	..	..	..
Mongolia	..	..	..	..	1.1	0.7	..	0.2	0	40	30	159
Morocco	79	76	78	74	29.5	12.3	14.9	..	991	853	1,966	2,302
Mozambique	..	52	..	39	28.7	25.7	..	27.1	866	1,520	1,189	2,189
Myanmar	..	..	..	..	..	..	..	..	1,338	34	2,992	2,662
Namibia	..	76	..	82	..	11.7	..	11.2	25	25	35	34
Nepal	..	..	..	..	..	..	..	..	430	669	1,760	1,244
Netherlands	94	..	98	..	2.5	..	6.6	..	..	..	..	..
New Zealand	97	..	97	..	3.5	..	2.7	0.8	..	..	..	..
Nicaragua	40	52	47	57	16.9	12.6	..	..	146	164	167	283
Niger	74	72	72	74	14.3	13.0	6.6	20.4	709	1,243	779	1,335
Nigeria	..	..	..	..	..	..	..	..	..	..	..	..
Norway	100	100	100	100	..	..	..	..	..	..	..	..
Oman	96	96	87	96	12.4	9.2	..	..	103	133	116	108
Pakistan	..	..	..	..	..	..	..	..	..	..	..	..
Panama	74	..	79	..	12.7	..	10.3	..	34	36	97	94
Papua New Guinea	..	..	..	..	..	..	..	..	..	..	..	..
Paraguay	59	77	58	80	13.6	9.1	..	3.0	47	30	274	272
Peru	78	..	74	..	18.8	15.2	10.1	9.0	354	212	411	437
Philippines	68	..	73	..	2.4	..	..	..	352	10	1,301	1,427
Poland	..	..	..	..	2.2	1.3	0.4	..	..	..	..	..
Portugal	..	..	..	..	19.5	..	..	..	..	..	..	..
Puerto Rico	..	..	..	..	..	..	..	..	..	..	..	..
Romania	..	..	..	..	..	2.8	..	1.4	273	1	1	677
Russian Federation	..	..	..	..	..	1.9	..	..	459	6	246	2,086

2.11 Education efficiency

	Percentage of cohort reaching grade 5				Repeaters				Children out of school			
	Male		Female		Primary % of total enrollment		Secondary % of total enrollment		Primary thousands		Secondary thousands	
	1980	1996	1980	1996	1980	1997	1980	1997	1980	1997	1980	1997
Rwanda	69	..	74	..	5.7	..	..	..	..	..	..	..
Saudi Arabia	82	*87*	86	*92*	15.7	*7.6*	14.8	9.2	770	1,222	749	1,077
Senegal	89	89	82	85	15.6	13.3	..	..	568	583	685	1,092
Sierra Leone	..	..	..	..	*14.8*	..	..	..	..	..	..	..
Singapore	*100*	..	*100*	..	6.6	..	..	..	1	26	106	73
Slovak Republic	..	..	..	..	..	*2.1*	..	..	..	..	..	..
Slovenia	..	..	..	..	..	*1.1*	..	..	..	..	..	..
South Africa	..	*72*	..	*79*	..	..	..	..	1,574	6	1,184	209
Spain	95	..	94	..	6.4	..	8.8	..	..	..	..	..
Sri Lanka	*92*	..	*91*	..	10.4	*2.3*	..	..	74	2	943	735
Sudan	68	..	71	..	..	..	..	..	..	..	..	..
Sweden	98	*97*	99	*97*	..	..	..	..	..	..	..	..
Switzerland	..	..	..	..	2.0	*1.6*	2.9	..	..	..	..	..
Syrian Arab Republic	93	*93*	88	*94*	8.1	*7.3*	13.9	..	155	141	679	1,358
Tajikistan	..	..	..	..	..	*0.5*	..	..	..	..	..	..
Tanzania	89	*78*	90	84	*1.2*	2.1	..	..	..	..	..	..
Thailand	..	..	..	..	8.3	..	..	..	608	798	5,010	3,631
Togo	59	*79*	45	*60*	35.5	*24.2*	..	..	89	132	142	283
Trinidad and Tobago	85	*97*	87	*97*	*3.9*	*5.6*	..	..	14	0	35	41
Tunisia	89	*90*	84	*92*	20.6	*16.1*	7.4	..	180	1	647	371
Turkey	..	*93*	..	*96*	..	*4.9*	..	..	..	..	..	..
Turkmenistan	..	..	..	..	..	..	..	..	..	..	..	..
Uganda	*82*	..	73	..	*10.3*	..	..	..	..	..	..	..
Ukraine	..	..	..	..	*0.3*	..	..	..	..	..	..	..
United Arab Emirates	100	*98*	100	*98*	9.0	*4.2*	..	*7.8*	25	52	23	54
United Kingdom	..	..	..	..	..	..	..	..	..	..	..	..
United States	..	..	..	..	..	..	..	..	..	..	..	..
Uruguay	..	*97*	..	*99*	14.9	*9.5*	..	..	41	18	87	51
Uzbekistan	..	..	..	..	..	*0.2*	..	..	..	..	..	..
Venezuela, RB	..	*86*	..	*92*	10.7	*10.3*	6.6	*4.7*	571	829	794	496
Vietnam	..	..	..	..	..	..	..	..	329	9	5,039	5,399
West Bank and Gaza	..	..	..	..	..	..	..	..	..	..	..	..
Yemen, Rep.	..	..	..	..	..	..	..	..	..	..	..	..
Yugoslavia, FR (Serb./Mont.)	..	..	..	..	..	*1.0*	..	..	..	..	..	..
Zambia	88	..	82	..	1.9	*2.8*	..	..	265	489	412	611
Zimbabwe	*82*	*78*	*76*	*79*	..	..	..	..	405	154	777	654
World	.. w	.. w	.. w	.. w	.. w	.. w	.. w	.. w	98,003 t	67,720 t	208,077 t	200,088 t
Low income	..	..	..	..	..	*4.8*	..	..	79,944	58,289	172,200	165,899
Excl. China & India	..	..	..	..	..	..	..	..	28,133	32,741	53,908	72,261
Middle income	..	..	..	..	..	..	..	..	17,988	9,218	35,442	33,683
Lower middle income	..	..	..	..	..	..	..	..	11,446	5,898	26,260	26,014
Upper middle income	..	..	..	..	..	*11.7*	..	..	6,542	3,320	9,182	7,669
Low & middle income	..	..	..	..	..	*6.2*	..	..	97,932	67,508	207,641	199,582
East Asia & Pacific	..	*93*	..	*93*	..	*2.8*	..	..	26,037	1,413	81,374	63,075
Europe & Central Asia	..	..	..	..	..	*2.4*	..	..	782	55	441	3,479
Latin America & Carib.	..	..	..	..	15.3	*12.9*	..	..	8,846	4,800	12,731	11,714
Middle East & N. Africa	*88*	..	*84*	..	*12.2*	*8.1*	..	..	6,241	4,791	13,216	12,852
South Asia	..	*62*	..	*55*	..	*3.7*	..	..	39,725	31,457	81,356	79,216
Sub-Saharan Africa	..	..	..	..	..	..	..	..	16,300	24,991	18,523	29,247
High income	..	..	..	..	..	..	..	..	71	213	435	506
Europe EMU	..	..	..	..	..	..	..	..	..	..	..	..

Education efficiency 2.11

About the data

Indicators of students' progress through school, estimated by the United Nations Educational, Scientific, and Cultural Organization (UNESCO), provide a measure of an education system's success in maintaining a flow of students from one grade to the next and thus in imparting a particular level of education. Although school attendance is mandatory in most countries, at least through the primary level, students drop out of school for a variety of reasons, including discouragement over poor performance, the cost of schooling, and the opportunity cost of time spent in school. In addition, students' progress to higher grades may be limited by the availability of teachers, classrooms, and educational materials.

The rate of progression—sometimes called the rate of persistence or survival—is estimated as the proportion of a single-year cohort of students that eventually reaches a particular grade of school. It measures the holding power and internal efficiency of an education system. Progression rates approaching 100 percent indicate a high level of retention and a low level of dropout.

Because tracking data for individual students generally are not available, aggregate student flows from one grade to the next are estimated using data on enrollment and repetition by grade for two consecutive years. This procedure, called the reconstructed cohort method (Fredricksen 1993), makes three simplifying assumptions: dropouts never return to school; promotion, repetition, and dropout rates remain constant over the entire period in which the cohort is enrolled in school; and the same rates apply to all pupils enrolled in a given grade, regardless of whether they previously repeated a grade. Given these assumptions, cross-country comparisons should be made with caution, because other flows—caused by new entrants, reentrants, grade skipping, migration, or school transfers during the school year—are not considered.

The percentage of the cohort reaching grade 5, rather than some other grade, is shown because it is generally agreed that children who reach grade 5 should have acquired the basic literacy and numeracy skills that would enable them to continue learning. This indicator provides no information on learning outcomes, however, and only indirectly reflects the quality of schooling. Assessing learning outcomes requires setting standards and measuring the attainment of those standards. In general, national assessments are concerned with the performance not of individual students, but of all or part of the education system.

The repetition rate is often used to indicate the internal efficiency of the education system. Repeaters not only increase the cost of education for the family and for the school system, but also use up limited school resources. Countries have different policies on repetition and promotion of students; in some cases the number of repeaters is controlled because of limited capacity.

Children out of school include dropouts and children who never enrolled. The large backlog of children out of school creates pressure for the education system to encourage children to enroll, and to provide classrooms, teachers, and educational materials to accommodate them, a task made difficult in many developing countries by limited education budgets.

Definitions

• **Percentage of cohort reaching grade 5** is the share of children enrolled in the first grade of primary school who eventually reach grade 5. The estimate is based on the reconstructed cohort method (see *About the data*). • **Repeaters** are the total number of students enrolled in the same grade as in the previous year, as a percentage of all students enrolled in that grade. • **Children out of school** are the number of school-age children not enrolled in school.

Data sources

The data in the table were compiled by UNESCO and published in its *World Education Report 1998* and *Statistical Yearbook 1999.*

2.12 Education outcomes

	Adult illiteracy rate				Youth illiteracy rate				Expected years of schooling			
	Male % aged 15 and over		Female % aged 15 and over		Male % aged 15–24		Female % aged 15–24		Males		Females	
	1980	**1998**	**1980**	**1998**	**1980**	**1998**	**1980**	**1998**	**1980**	**1997**	**1980**	**1997**
Albania	21	9	46	24	6	2	15	3	..	..	..	..
Algeria	46	24	76	46	24	8	54	18	10	*12*	7	*10*
Angola	..	..	..	..	..	..	..	..	8	*9*	7	*7*
Argentina	5	3	6	3	3	2	3	1	..	..	..	..
Armenia	2	1	6	3	1	0	1	0	..	..	..	..
Australia	..	..	..	..	..	..	..	..	12	*17*	12	*17*
Austria	..	..	..	..	..	..	..	..	11	*15*	11	*14*
Azerbaijan	..	..	..	..	..	..	..	..	..	..	..	..
Bangladesh	59	49	83	71	52	40	74	61	*5*	..	*3*	..
Belarus	0	0	2	1	0	0	0	0	..	..	..	..
Belgium	..	..	..	..	..	..	..	..	14	*17*	13	*17*
Benin	73	46	90	77	54	25	83	65	..	..	..	..
Bolivia	20	9	42	22	7	2	20	7	..	..	..	..
Bosnia and Herzegovina	..	..	..	..	..	..	..	..	..	..	..	..
Botswana	44	27	41	22	32	17	25	8	7	*12*	8	*12*
Brazil	23	16	27	16	14	10	12	6	..	..	..	..
Bulgaria	3	1	7	2	1	0	1	1	11	12	11	12
Burkina Faso	82	68	96	87	73	56	92	79	2	*3*	1	*2*
Burundi	57	45	83	63	48	37	71	42	3	*5*	2	*4*
Cambodia	61	43	92	80	47	26	86	61	..	..	..	..
Cameroon	41	20	65	33	18	7	33	8	8	..	6	..
Canada	..	..	..	..	..	..	..	..	15	*17*	15	*17*
Central African Republic	64	43	89	68	44	26	76	45	..	..	..	..
Chad	75	51	91	69	58	29	80	45	..	..	..	..
Chile	8	4	9	5	3	2	3	1	..	*13*	..	*13*
China	22	9	48	25	4	1	16	5	..	..	..	..
Hong Kong, China	6	4	24	11	3	1	4	0	12	*12*	11	*12*
Colombia	15	9	17	9	8	4	7	3	..	..	..	..
Congo, Dem. Rep.	52	29	79	53	31	12	62	28	..	*7*	..	*4*
Congo, Rep.	37	14	62	29	12	2	27	4	..	..	..	..
Costa Rica	8	5	9	5	4	2	3	2	10	..	10	..
Côte d'Ivoire	66	47	87	64	51	32	76	44	..	..	..	..
Croatia	2	1	9	3	0	0	1	0	..	11	..	12
Cuba	7	4	8	4	2	0	2	0	..	..	..	..
Czech Republic	..	..	..	..	..	..	..	..	..	*13*	..	*13*
Denmark	..	..	..	..	..	..	..	..	14	*15*	13	*15*
Dominican Republic	25	17	27	17	18	10	17	9	..	*11*	..	*11*
Ecuador	15	8	22	11	6	3	9	4	..	..	..	..
Egypt, Arab Rep.	47	35	75	58	36	24	61	40	..	*12*	..	*10*
El Salvador	29	19	39	25	19	12	24	13	..	*10*	..	*10*
Eritrea	51	34	82	62	37	21	69	41	..	*5*	..	*4*
Estonia	..	..	..	..	..	..	..	..	..	*12*	..	*13*
Ethiopia	72	58	89	70	59	47	78	50	..	..	..	..
Finland	..	..	..	..	..	..	..	..	..	*15*	..	*17*
France	..	..	..	..	..	..	..	..	..	*15*	..	*16*
Gabon	..	..	..	..	..	..	..	..	..	..	..	..
Gambia, The	79	58	88	73	64	37	79	54	..	*6*	..	*4*
Georgia	..	..	..	..	..	..	..	..	..	*11*	..	*11*
Germany	..	..	..	..	..	..	..	..	..	*16*	..	*16*
Ghana	43	22	70	40	21	7	46	14	..	..	..	..
Greece	4	2	14	5	1	0	1	0	*13*	*14*	*12*	*14*
Guatemala	39	25	55	40	26	15	43	28	..	..	..	..
Guinea	..	..	..	..	..	..	..	..	..	..	..	..
Guinea-Bissau	67	43	93	83	44	21	87	70	..	..	..	..
Haiti	66	50	73	54	53	38	57	38	..	..	..	..
Honduras	37	27	40	27	27	19	27	16	..	..	..	..

Education outcomes 2.12

	Adult illiteracy rate				Youth illiteracy rate				Expected years of schooling			
	Male % aged 15 and over		Female % aged 15 and over		Male % aged 15–24		Female % aged 15–24		Males		Females	
	1980	1998	1980	1998	1980	1998	1980	1998	1980	1997	1980	1997
Hungary	1	1	2	1	0	0	1	0	..	*13*	..	*13*
India	45	33	74	57	33	22	58	37	..	..	..	..
Indonesia	21	9	40	20	7	2	15	4	..	10	..	10
Iran, Islamic Rep.	38	18	61	33	16	4	35	10	..	*12*	..	*11*
Iraq	53	36	78	57	39	23	64	36	12	..	9	..
Ireland	..	..	..	..	..	..	..	..	11	*14*	12	*14*
Israel	5	2	13	6	1	0	3	1	..	..	..	..
Italy	3	1	5	2	0	0	0	0	..	..	..	..
Jamaica	28	18	20	10	17	10	8	3	..	*11*	..	*11*
Japan	..	..	..	..	..	..	..	..	14	..	13	..
Jordan	18	6	46	17	4	1	14	1	12	..	12	..
Kazakhstan	..	..	..	..	..	..	..	..	..	..	..	..
Kenya	30	12	57	27	13	5	32	7	..	..	..	..
Korea, Dem. Rep.	..	..	..	..	..	..	..	..	..	..	..	..
Korea, Rep.	3	1	11	4	0	0	0	0	12	*15*	11	*14*
Kuwait	26	17	39	22	17	9	22	8	*12*	*9*	*12*	*9*
Kyrgyz Republic	..	..	..	..	..	..	..	..	..	..	..	..
Lao PDR	59	38	90	70	40	19	79	46	..	..	..	..
Latvia	0	0	0	0	0	0	0	0	..	*12*	..	*13*
Lebanon	17	9	37	21	7	3	18	8	..	..	..	..
Lesotho	42	29	17	7	30	18	5	2	7	*9*	10	*10*
Libya	29	10	70	35	5	0	39	8	13	..	11	..
Lithuania	1	0	2	1	0	0	0	0	..	..	..	..
Macedonia, FYR	..	..	..	..	..	..	..	..	..	*11*	..	*11*
Madagascar	43	28	61	42	29	18	45	25	..	..	..	..
Malawi	36	27	73	56	29	20	60	41	..	..	..	..
Malaysia	20	9	37	18	7	3	12	3	..	..	..	..
Mali	81	54	92	69	66	31	82	44	..	..	..	..
Mauritania	59	48	79	69	51	40	72	60	..	..	..	..
Mauritius	19	13	33	20	11	7	15	6	..	..	..	..
Mexico	14	7	22	11	6	3	10	4	..	..	..	..
Moldova	2	1	8	2	0	0	0	0	..	..	..	..
Mongolia	44	28	72	49	30	16	54	28	..	*7*	..	*9*
Morocco	58	40	85	66	43	25	72	45	8	..	5	..
Mozambique	62	42	89	73	43	26	80	57	5	*4*	4	*3*
Myanmar	15	11	34	21	11	9	19	10	..	..	..	..
Namibia	29	18	38	20	18	11	20	7	..	..	..	..
Nepal	62	43	93	78	48	26	86	61	..	..	..	..
Netherlands	..	..	..	..	..	..	..	..	13	*16*	13	*16*
New Zealand	..	..	..	..	..	..	..	..	14	*16*	13	*17*
Nicaragua	39	34	39	31	35	30	32	24	..	*9*	..	*9*
Niger	87	78	97	93	82	69	95	88	..	*3*	..	*2*
Nigeria	55	30	78	48	32	12	58	19	..	..	..	..
Norway	..	..	..	..	..	..	..	..	13	*15*	13	*16*
Oman	49	22	84	43	18	1	65	6	5	*9*	2	*9*
Pakistan	59	42	86	71	48	25	78	53	..	..	..	..
Panama	14	8	16	9	6	3	8	4	11	..	12	..
Papua New Guinea	41	29	61	45	30	20	47	30	..	..	..	..
Paraguay	11	6	18	9	6	3	7	3	..	*10*	..	*10*
Peru	12	6	29	16	4	2	13	5	11	..	10	..
Philippines	10	5	12	5	5	2	5	1	11	..	11	..
Poland	1	0	1	0	0	0	0	0	12	13	12	13
Portugal	13	6	23	11	2	0	2	0	..	14	..	15
Puerto Rico	11	7	12	7	6	3	4	2	..	..	..	..
Romania	2	1	7	3	1	1	1	0	..	*12*	..	*12*
Russian Federation	1	0	2	1	0	0	0	0	..	..	..	..

2.12 Education outcomes

	Adult illiteracy rate				Youth illiteracy rate				Expected years of schooling			
	Male % aged 15 and over		Female % aged 15 and over		Male % aged 15–24		Female % aged 15–24		Males		Females	
	1980	**1998**	**1980**	**1998**	**1980**	**1998**	**1980**	**1998**	**1980**	**1997**	**1980**	**1997**
Rwanda	48	29	71	43	32	16	51	21	..	..	..	..
Saudi Arabia	33	17	67	36	15	5	40	11	7	*10*	5	*9*
Senegal	70	55	88	74	59	42	79	60	..	..	..	..
Sierra Leone	..	..	..	..	..	..	..	..	..	..	..	..
Singapore	9	4	26	12	2	1	3	0	..	..	..	..
Slovak Republic	..	..	..	..	..	..	..	..	..	..	..	..
Slovenia	1	0	1	0	0	0	0	0	..	..	..	..
South Africa	22	15	25	16	15	9	15	9	..	14	..	14
Spain	3	2	8	4	1	0	1	0	13	..	13	..
Sri Lanka	9	6	21	12	6	3	9	4	..	..	..	..
Sudan	49	32	81	57	34	18	65	32	..	..	..	..
Sweden	..	..	..	..	..	..	..	..	*12*	*14*	*13*	*15*
Switzerland	..	..	..	..	..	..	..	..	13	*15*	12	*14*
Syrian Arab Republic	28	13	66	42	13	5	47	23	11	*10*	8	*9*
Tajikistan	2	1	7	1	0	0	0	0	..	..	..	..
Tanzania	33	17	66	36	18	7	43	13	*10*	..	*7*	..
Thailand	8	3	17	7	3	1	4	2	..	..	..	..
Togo	48	28	81	62	29	14	68	44	..	..	..	..
Trinidad and Tobago	7	5	16	8	4	2	7	3	11	..	11	..
Tunisia	42	21	69	42	14	3	42	13	10	..	7	..
Turkey	17	7	46	25	4	2	20	7	..	11	..	9
Turkmenistan	..	..	..	..	..	..	..	..	..	..	..	..
Uganda	39	24	69	46	27	15	53	30	..	..	..	..
Ukraine	0	0	1	1	0	0	0	0	..	..	..	..
United Arab Emirates	33	27	42	23	26	15	22	6	8	*10*	*7*	*11*
United Kingdom	..	..	..	..	..	..	..	..	13	*16*	13	*17*
United States	..	..	..	..	..	..	..	..	14	*16*	15	*16*
Uruguay	6	3	5	2	2	1	1	1	..	..	..	..
Uzbekistan	17	7	33	17	6	2	14	5	..	..	..	..
Venezuela, RB	14	7	18	9	6	3	6	2	..	*10*	..	*11*
Vietnam	7	5	19	9	4	3	7	3	..	..	..	..
West Bank and Gaza	..	..	..	..	..	..	..	..	..	..	..	..
Yemen, Rep.	62	34	95	77	45	18	89	58	..	..	..	..
Yugoslavia, FR (Serb./Mont.)	..	..	..	..	..	..	..	..	..	..	..	..
Zambia	29	16	53	31	18	10	35	16	..	*8*	..	*7*
Zimbabwe	22	8	38	17	8	2	20	5	..	..	..	..
World	**28 w**	**18 w**	**46 w**	**32 w**	**17 w**	**11 w**	**30 w**	**19 w**				
Low income	35	22	60	41	21	14	39	24				
Excl. China & India	43	29	65	46	31	18	49	30				
Middle income	15	10	22	15	9	5	14	8				
Lower middle income	15	11	22	17	10	6	17	10				
Upper middle income	14	9	21	13	7	4	10	4				
Low & middle income	29	18	48	33	17	11	31	19				
East Asia & Pacific	20	9	43	22	5	2	15	5				
Europe & Central Asia	3	2	8	5	1	1	4	2				
Latin America & Carib.	18	11	23	13	10	7	11	6				
Middle East & N. Africa	44	26	72	48	27	13	53	25				
South Asia	48	35	75	59	36	24	62	42				
Sub-Saharan Africa	51	32	72	49	34	19	56	28				
High income	..	..	..	..	..	..	..	..				
Europe EMU	..	..	..	..	..	..	..	..				

Education outcomes 2.12

About the data

Many governments have recently collected and published statistics that indicate how their education systems are working and developing—statistics on student enrollments and on such efficiency indicators as pupil-teacher ratios, repetition rates, and cohort progression through school. But despite an obvious interest in what education achieves, few systems in high-income or developing countries have until recently systematically collected information on outcomes of education.

Basic student outcomes include achievements in reading and mathematics judged against established standards. In many countries national learning assessments are enabling ministries of education to monitor progress in these outcomes. Internationally, the United Nations Educational, Scientific, and Cultural Organization (UNESCO) has established literacy as an outcome indicator based on an internationally agreed definition. The illiteracy rate is defined as the percentage of people who cannot, with understanding, read and write a short, simple statement about their everyday life. In practice, illiteracy is difficult to measure. To estimate illiteracy using such a definition requires census or survey measurements under controlled conditions. Many countries estimate the number of illiterate people from self-reported data, or by taking people with no schooling as illiterate.

Literacy statistics for most countries cover the population aged 15 and above, by five-year age groups, but some include younger ages or are confined to age ranges that tend to inflate literacy rates. As an alternative, UNESCO has proposed a narrower age range of 15–24, which better captures the ability of participants in the formal education system. The youth illiteracy rate reported in the table measures the accumulated outcomes of primary education over the previous 10 years or so by indicating the proportion of people who have passed through the primary education system (or never entered it) without acquiring basic literacy and numeracy skills. Reasons for this may include difficulties in attending school or dropping out before reaching grade 5 (see *About the data* for table 2.11) and thereby failing to achieve basic learning competencies.

The indicator expected years of schooling is an estimate of the total years of schooling that an average child at the age of school entry will receive, including years spent on repetition, given the current patterns of enrollment across cycles of education. It may also be interpreted as an indicator of the total education resources, measured in school years, that a child will acquire over his or her "lifetime" in school—or as an indicator of an education system's overall level of development.

Because the calculation of this indicator assumes that the probability of a child's being enrolled in school at any future age is equal to the current enrollment ratio for that age, it does not account for changes and trends in future enrollment ratios. The expected number of years and the expected number of grades completed are not necessarily consistent, because the first includes years spent in repetition. Comparability across countries and over time may be affected by differences in the length of the school year or changes in policies on automatic promotions and grade repetition.

Definitions

• **Adult illiteracy rate** is the percentage of people aged 15 and over who cannot, with understanding, read and write a short, simple statement about their everyday life. • **Youth illiteracy rate** is the illiteracy rate among people aged 15–24. • **Expected years of schooling** are the average number of years of formal schooling that a child is expected to receive, including university education and years spent in repetition. They are the sum of the underlying age-specific enrollment ratios for primary, secondary, and tertiary education.

Data sources

The data shown in the table were compiled by UNESCO and published in its *World Education Report 1998* and *Statistical Yearbook 1999.* The data on illiteracy are based on the results of UNESCO's 1999 literacy estimates and projections.

2.13 Gender and education

	Female teachers				Female pupils				Girls out of school			
	Primary % of total		Secondary % of total		Primary % of total		Secondary % of total		Primary % of total out of school		Secondary % of total out of school	
	1980	1996	1980	1996	1980	1996	1980	1996	1980	1997	1980	1997
Albania	50	*60*	35	*51*	47	*48*	..	..	..	..	..	..
Algeria	37	45	..	45	42	46	39	48	77	90	58	56
Angola	..	..	..	..	*47*	..	*33*	..	62	50	88	52
Argentina	*92*	*89*	..	*66*	49	49	..	..	37	49	47	43
Armenia	..	*97*	..	..	..	..	..	..	..	..	..	..
Australia	*70*	76	45	..	49	49	50	49	..	..	..	..
Austria	75	84	49	56	49	49	..	48	..	..	..	..
Azerbaijan	..	80	..	..	..	48	..	..	..	..	..	..
Bangladesh	8	..	7	..	37	..	*19*	..	67	60	53	52
Belarus	..	..	..	..	..	48	..	..	..	..	..	..
Belgium	59	..	..	..	49	..	*50*	*50*	..	..	..	..
Benin	23	24	..	..	32	*36*	..	..	70	76	60	57
Bolivia	48	..	..	..	47	..	43	..	62	98	54	52
Bosnia and Herzegovina	..	..	..	..	..	..	..	..	..	..	..	..
Botswana	72	77	37	*43*	55	50	55	*52*	36	44	46	39
Brazil	85	..	53	..	..	..	54	..	55	98	49	48
Bulgaria	72	89	53	72	49	48	48	*50*	46	19	50	53
Burkina Faso	20	*24*	..	..	37	*39*	*34*	..	52	55	51	52
Burundi	47	*50*	*20*	..	39	*45*	*37*	..	52	52	52	52
Cambodia	..	36	..	*27*	..	45	..	..	50	49	54	56
Cameroon	20	*32*	*20*	..	45	..	35	..	60	53	56	54
Canada	*66*	*67*	*44*	*67*	49	*48*	*49*	*49*	..	..	..	..
Central African Republic	25	..	16	..	37	..	..	..	70	58	59	55
Chad	..	8	..	4	..	34	..	..	58	62	54	55
Chile	..	72	..	*52*	49	49	*52*	51	48	55	50	42
China	37	47	25	36	..	47	..	..	63	48	63	56
Hong Kong, China	73	*76*	49	*50*	48	*49*	49	*49*	41	38	47	43
Colombia	79	77	42	48	50	49	..	*53*	47	49	48	45
Congo, Dem. Rep.	..	*22*	..	..	42	*41*	..	*38*	70	62	62	57
Congo, Rep.	25	*36*	..	*16*	48	*48*	..	..	95	56	97	82
Costa Rica	*79*	78	*54*	59	49	49	53	..	46	44	47	48
Côte d'Ivoire	15	*21*	..	..	40	42	..	..	61	59	60	58
Croatia	*73*	89	..	64	..	49	..	*51*	49	49	43	48
Cuba	75	81	46	57	48	48	..	..	47	49	53	44
Czech Republic	..	*93*	..	*61*	..	*48*	..	*50*	..	..	..	..
Denmark	..	*58*	..	*52*	49	*49*	49	*49*	..	..	..	..
Dominican Republic	..	..	..	*49*	..	*49*	..	*57*	4	36	49	41
Ecuador	65	67	*38*	..	49	49	..	..	50	49	51	49
Egypt, Arab Rep.	*47*	49	31	39	40	45	..	45	68	99	57	58
El Salvador	65	..	27	..	49	49	..	*52*	49	49	50	49
Eritrea	..	36	..	14	..	45	..	42	..	51	..	53
Estonia	..	*89*	..	*80*	..	*48*	..	*52*	49	49	48	45
Ethiopia	22	28	..	*10*	35	36	..	..	53	57	53	55
Finland	..	69	..	..	49	49	..	52	..	..	..	..
France	68	79	*55*	59	48	..	*52*	49	..	..	..	..
Gabon	27	*39*	24	*18*	49	*50*	..	..	..	..	..	..
Gambia, The	32	*29*	25	*17*	35	*44*	*30*	..	68	61	53	56
Georgia	89	95	54	71	..	48	..	49	53	50	99	50
Germany	..	81	..	49	..	*49*	..	48	..	..	..	..
Ghana	42	*34*	21	..	44	..	..	..	..	..	..	..
Greece	48	57	49	56	48	48	*46*	49	..	..	..	..
Guatemala	*62*	..	*36*	..	45	46	..	..	54	56	52	51
Guinea	14	25	*10*	..	33	*37*	..	..	56	61	54	54
Guinea-Bissau	24	..	21	..	32	..	20	..	66	64	60	56
Haiti	49	..	..	..	46	..	..	..	50	49	54	50
Honduras	74	..	48	..	50	*50*	..	..	48	45	49	48

Gender and education 2.13

	Female teachers				Female pupils				Girls out of school			
	Primary % of total		Secondary % of total		Primary % of total		Secondary % of total		Primary % of total out of school		Secondary % of total out of school	
	1980	1996	1980	1996	1980	1996	1980	1996	1980	1997	1980	1997
Hungary	80	*92*	..	*66*	49	*48*	..	*50*	..	..	..	..
India	26	33	..	..	39	*43*	..	..	63	61	58	62
Indonesia	*33*	*52*	..	*39*	46	48	..	*45*	71	93	56	52
Iran, Islamic Rep.	*57*	55	*30*	44	*40*	47	..	46	68	53	61	63
Iraq	48	*71*	40	*56*	46	*45*	32	..	98	59	74	56
Ireland	74	78	*50*	55	49	49	52	51	..	..	..	..
Israel	..	..	57	..	*49*	..	..	..	..	..	..	..
Italy	87	*94*	58	*64*	49	48	..	..	..	..	..	..
Jamaica	87	90	..	..	50	..	53	..	27	48	45	46
Japan	57	62	26	*33*	49	*49*	49	..	..	..	..	..
Jordan	59	61	43	48	48	*49*	45	*50*	..	..	..	..
Kazakhstan	..	..	..	..	..	49	..	..	..	..	..	..
Kenya	*31*	*40*	..	..	47	*49*	..	..	59	47	57	54
Korea, Dem. Rep.	..	..	..	..	..	..	..	..	..	..	..	..
Korea, Rep.	37	61	26	39	49	48	45	48	..	..	..	..
Kuwait	56	63	50	55	48	49	*46*	49	63	51	53	49
Kyrgyz Republic	88	*83*	..	*67*	..	*49*	..	..	50	65	50	47
Lao PDR	30	42	..	*38*	45	44	..	39	55	56	58	64
Latvia	..	95	..	79	..	48	..	51	49	50	51	50
Lebanon	..	..	..	..	..	..	..	..	..	..	..	..
Lesotho	75	79	..	53	59	52	60	59	31	41	29	36
Libya	47	..	24	..	47	..	40	..	49	49	80	49
Lithuania	97	91	..	77	..	48	..	*50*	..	..	..	..
Macedonia, FYR	..	54	..	51	..	48	..	48	..	..	..	..
Madagascar	..	*51*	..	..	49	*49*	..	..	..	..	..	..
Malawi	32	*39*	..	..	41	*47*	..	..	55	10	66	83
Malaysia	44	60	45	60	49	*49*	..	..	52	16	52	43
Mali	20	23	..	..	36	*39*	..	..	54	56	53	53
Mauritania	9	*20*	..	*8*	35	47	..	..	..	..	..	..
Mauritius	43	51	..	45	49	49	..	..	51	48	50	46
Mexico	..	..	..	..	49	48	..	..	..	..	..	..
Moldova	96	97	..	73	..	49	..	..	..	..	..	..
Mongolia	87	90	..	66	*50*	51	..	57	49	41	33	41
Morocco	30	38	*26*	32	37	42	38	..	67	69	58	54
Mozambique	22	*23*	*22*	*17*	*43*	*42*	*28*	*39*	52	54	58	54
Myanmar	*54*	*67*	..	*73*	..	..	..	..	51	94	52	51
Namibia	..	..	..	..	..	50	..	..	28	35	44	41
Nepal	10	..	9	..	28	..	..	..	85	83	57	63
Netherlands	46	60	..	29	49	..	48	48	..	..	..	..
New Zealand	*66*	82	..	57	49	49	49	50	..	..	..	..
Nicaragua	78	*84*	..	..	51	*50*	53	..	48	46	46	48
Niger	30	32	21	21	35	38	29	35	54	54	52	52
Nigeria	34	*46*	29	*36*	*43*	*44*	..	..	..	..	..	..
Norway	*56*	..	..	..	49	*49*	50	48	..	..	..	..
Oman	34	*50*	*27*	48	34	48	24	..	60	51	56	52
Pakistan	32	..	30	..	33	..	..	..	..	..	..	..
Panama	80	..	53	..	48	..	52	..	48	47	48	48
Papua New Guinea	27	*36*	*32*	..	*42*	*45*	..	..	..	..	..	..
Paraguay	..	..	..	..	48	48	..	51	53	40	51	51
Peru	60	*58*	*46*	*39*	48	*49*	*46*	*48*	51	53	64	58
Philippines	80	..	..	..	49	..	53	..	66	49	45	48
Poland	..	..	..	..	..	*48*	50	*49*	..	..	..	..
Portugal	..	..	59	..	48	..	..	*51*	..	..	..	..
Puerto Rico	..	..	..	..	..	..	..	..	..	..	..	..
Romania	70	85	43	63	..	49	..	49	56	49	49	48
Russian Federation	98	..	..	..	..	*49*	..	..	50	49	33	37

2.13 Gender and education

	Female teachers				Female pupils				Girls out of school			
	Primary % of total		Secondary % of total		Primary % of total		Secondary % of total		Primary % of total out of school		Secondary % of total out of school	
	1980	1996	1980	1996	1980	1996	1980	1996	1980	1997	1980	1997
Rwanda	38	..	16	..	48	..	..	..	..	..	..	..
Saudi Arabia	39	52	34	50	39	48	38	*46*	61	51	53	56
Senegal	24	*26*	..	..	40	45	..	..	55	57	53	52
Sierra Leone	*22*	..	..	..	..	..	..	..	..	..	..	..
Singapore	66	*77*	..	..	48	*48*	..	..	71	53	49	50
Slovak Republic	..	91	..	70	..	49	..	..	..	..	..	..
Slovenia	..	92	..	70	..	49	..	..	..	..	..	..
South Africa	..	*74*	..	..	..	*49*	..	*54*	49	50	51	31
Spain	67	*66*	40	*52*	49	48	50	..	..	..	..	..
Sri Lanka	..	96	..	*62*	48	48	..	..	81	49	47	42
Sudan	31	62	..	45	40	45	..	..	..	..	..	..
Sweden	..	73	..	59	49	490	*52*	52	..	..	..	..
Switzerland	..	*69*	..	..	49	*49*	46	*47*	..	..	..	..
Syrian Arab Republic	54	65	*22*	44	43	47	37	46	97	88	59	52
Tajikistan	..	54	..	..	..	49	..	..	..	..	..	..
Tanzania	37	44	*28*	26	47	49	..	..	..	..	..	..
Thailand	..	..	..	..	48	..	..	..	53	44	50	50
Togo	21	14	..	*12*	39	*41*	..	..	87	84	85	72
Trinidad and Tobago	66	74	..	..	50	49	*50*	..	46	49	51	48
Tunisia	29	49	29	*34*	42	47	37	..	78	49	57	53
Turkey	41	*44*	*35*	41	45	*47*	..	40	..	..	..	..
Turkmenistan	..	..	..	..	..	..	..	..	..	..	..	..
Uganda	30	*32*	..	..	*43*	*46*	..	..	..	..	..	..
Ukraine	97	..	..	..	..	..	..	..	..	..	..	..
United Arab Emirates	54	70	*46*	*54*	48	48	..	50	45	51	55	44
United Kingdom	*78*	81	..	55	..	..	50	52	..	..	..	..
United States	..	*86*	..	*56*	49	*49*	..	*49*	..	..	..	..
Uruguay	..	..	..	..	48	49	..	..	50	45	49	34
Uzbekistan	78	*82*	..	..	..	*49*	..	..	..	..	..	..
Venezuela, RB	*83*	75	..	..	*51*	50	*57*	58	43	46	47	44
Vietnam	65	*77*	..	..	47	..	..	..	74	49	51	50
West Bank and Gaza	..	..	..	..	..	..	..	..	..	..	..	..
Yemen, Rep.	..	17	..	..	..	..	..	..	..	..	..	..
Yugoslavia, FR (Serb./Mont.)	..	..	..	..	..	49	..	..	..	..	..	..
Zambia	40	*43*	..	..	47	*48*	..	..	60	51	60	56
Zimbabwe	*38*	44	..	36	*48*	49	..	..	58	57	52	54
World	**44 w**	***51* w**	**.. w**	**.. w**	**.. w**	***46* w**	**.. w**	**.. w**	**61 w**	**58 w**	**56 w**	**55 w**
Low income	32	41	..	..	..	*45*	..	..	63	57	59	57
Excl. China & India	..	..	..	..	43	..	..	..	65	67	55	54
Middle income	..	..	..	..	..	..	..	..	56	61	49	48
Lower middle income	..	..	..	..	..	..	..	..	58	56	48	48
Upper middle income	..	..	..	..	..	..	..	..	..	..	..	..
Low & middle income	42	*44*	..	..	..	*46*	..	..	61	58	57	55
East Asia & Pacific	40	48	25	37	..	48	..	..	63	54	60	54
Europe & Central Asia	84	..	..	..	..	*48*	..	..	..	..	..	..
Latin America & Carib.	..	..	..	..	..	..	..	..	49	70	50	47
Middle East & N. Africa	*46*	48	*32*	42	42	46	..	..	73	72	60	57
South Asia	24	34	..	..	38	*43*	..	..	64	62	57	60
Sub-Saharan Africa	30	*38*	..	..	*44*	*45*	..	..	..	..	..	..
High income	..	*78*	..	*55*	49	*49*	..	*49*	..	..	..	..
Europe EMU	72	*80*	..	*54*	49	*48*	..	*49*	..	..	..	..

Gender and education 2.13

About the data

Data on female enrollment suffer from the same problems affecting data on general enrollment discussed in *About the data* for table 2.10. But female enrollment as a share of total enrollment is a relatively simple indicator raising no serious problems of cross-country comparability.

Because gender disparities in enrollment are not correlated with overall standard of living—as measured by GNP per capita, for example—countries can achieve gender parity in primary and secondary schooling if public policies and education strategies address constraints that inhibit girls' attendance. Providing segregated schools and separate sanitation facilities, recruiting female teachers, and reducing the direct and opportunity costs of educating girls are among the strategies that have worked in some countries. But disparities remain, and female enrollment ratios tend to be positively correlated with other indicators of development, such as maternal and child health, and negatively with total fertility rates (UNRISD 1977).

Girls' enrollments have caught up with boys' in most high-income, Latin American and Caribbean, and Eastern European countries. But they lag behind in South Asia and the Middle East. And regional aggregates mask large disparities between countries. In Africa, for example, Mauritius and South Africa have achieved nearly universal primary enrollment, but many other countries still have primary enrollment ratios for girls that are less than 50 percent (see table 1.2). In low-income and lower-middle-income countries dropout rates at the primary level are higher for girls than for boys, indicating that the gap in actual enrollment in these countries is wider than is reflected by enrollment ratios. One reason for this in many of these countries is early childbearing, which is clearly incompatible with schooling. Many girls, especially in South Asia, still remain outside the formal education system. And girls who attend school tend to be directed away from science, mathematics, and other technical subjects in high demand in the labor market, and toward vocations considered "feminine," such as nursing, teaching, and clerical work.

Limited employment opportunities and lower market returns for women discourage parents of girls from investing in education. Consequently, female participation in the labor market is limited, with many women concentrated in the informal sector and those in the modern sector relegated to the low end of the hierarchy. Ensuring that the market is competitive, making labor laws gender-neutral, and strengthening the machinery that enforces labor laws can improve women's employment prospects. Traditionally, teaching has been one of the first professions open to women, and the number of female teachers is a revealing indicator of employment opportunities for women in the modern sector. In addition, female teachers are important role models for girls, particularly where female education is not encouraged or men are forbidden to teach girls. Over the past decade the share of female primary school teachers has increased everywhere. But data on teachers may not reflect the functions they perform. Schools may employ teachers in many capacities outside the classroom, and the responsibilities assigned to male and female teachers may differ systematically.

Definitions

• **Female teachers as a percentage of total teachers** include full-time and part-time teachers. • **Female pupils as a percentage of total pupils** include enrollments in public and private schools. • **Girls out of school as a percentage of all children out of school** are the number of girls not enrolled in school as a share of all children not enrolled.

Data sources

The estimates in this table were compiled using the United Nations Educational, Scientific, and Cultural Organization's (UNESCO) electronic database on institutions, teachers, and pupils and UNESCO's *World Education Report 1998*.

Table 2.13a

Male and female unemployment rate by education level, 1994–97

%

	Primary		Secondary		Tertiary	
	Male	Female	Male	Female	Male	Female
Bangladesh	46.0	50.2	32.2	20.8	..	..
Colombia	26.3	16.7	53.6	62.6	18.5	18.9
India	37.1[a]	26.0[a]	37.3	40.9	25.6	33.1
Jordan	60.9	16.8	14.8	14.7	21.2	67.5
Poland	26.5	21.7	69.7	72.9	3.7	5.4
Russian Federation	23.3	14.6	69.6	75.6	7.1	9.8

.. Not available.
a. Less than primary education.
Source: International Labour Organization, Key Indicators of the Labour Market.

Among those with only a primary education, men are more likely than women to be unemployed. But among those with secondary and higher education, women are more likely to be unemployed.

The explanation for this pattern? Women with only a primary education are more likely to leave the labor force—or to never enter it—than women with a higher education. More educated women generally have more labor market opportunities, and it is also more costly for them to withdraw from the labor force.

2.14 Health expenditure, services, and use

	Health expenditure			Health expenditure per capita		Physicians		Hospital beds		Inpatient admission rate	Average length of stay	Outpatient visits per capita
	Public % of GDP 1990–98[a]	Private % of GDP 1990–98[a]	Total % of GDP 1990–98[a,b]	PPP $ 1990–98[a]	$ 1990–98[a]	per 1,000 people 1980	per 1,000 people 1990–98[a]	per 1,000 people 1980	per 1,000 people 1990–98[a]	% of population 1990–98[a]	days 1990–98[a]	1990–98[a]
Albania	2.7	7.8	10.5	282	73	..	1.4	..	3.2	..	13	2
Algeria	3.3	1.3	4.6	217	68	..	0.8	..	2.1	..	..	..
Angola	3.9	..	..	..	..	..	0.0 [c]	..	1.3	..	..	..
Argentina	4.0	5.6	9.6	1,147	792	..	2.7	..	3.3	..	..	..
Armenia	3.1	4.2	7.8	147	27	3.5	3.0	8.4	7.6	8	15	3
Australia	5.5	2.8	8.4	1,866	1,842	1.8	2.5	..	8.5	17	16	7
Austria	6.0	2.2	8.3	1,896	2,108	*2.3*	2.8	11.2	9.2	25	11	6
Azerbaijan	1.2	5.9	7.2	146	36	3.4	3.8	9.7	9.7	6	18	1
Bangladesh	1.6	2.0	3.5	45	12	0.1	0.2	0.2	0.3	..	..	..
Belarus	4.9	1.1	6.0	303	82	3.4	4.3	12.5	12.2	26	18	11
Belgium	6.8	0.9	7.6	1,759	1,812	2.5	3.4	*9.4*	7.2	20	11	8
Benin	1.6	0.4	2.0	19	8	0.1	0.1	1.5	0.2	..	..	..
Bolivia	1.1	1.6	2.6	60	28	*0.5*	1.3	..	1.7	..	..	..
Bosnia and Herzegovina	..	..	..	..	..	..	0.5	..	1.8	..	15	..
Botswana	2.7	1.6	4.3	310	133	0.1	0.2	2.4	1.6	..	..	..
Brazil	3.4	4.0	7.3	503	359	*0.8*	1.3	..	3.1	0 [d]	..	2
Bulgaria	3.2	0.8	4.0	193	59	2.5	3.5	11.1	10.6	18	14	5
Burkina Faso	1.2	2.7	3.9	34	9	0.0 [c]	0.0 [c]	..	1.4	2	3	0 [d]
Burundi	0.6	3.0	3.6	21	5	..	0.1	..	0.7	..	..	..
Cambodia	0.6	6.3	6.9	87	17	..	0.1	..	2.1	..	..	..
Cameroon	1.0	4.0	5.0	83	31	..	0.1	..	2.6	..	..	..
Canada	6.4	2.8	9.2	2,158	1,855	*1.8*	2.1	..	4.2	13	12	7
Central African Republic	1.9	0.9	2.8	31	..	0.0 [c]	0.1	1.6	0.9	..	..	..
Chad	2.4	0.6	3.1	26	7	..	0.0 [c]	..	0.7	..	..	..
Chile	2.4	1.5	3.9	344	201	..	1.1	3.4	2.7	..	..	..
China	2.0	2.6	4.5	142	33	0.9	2.0	2.0	2.9	4	13	..
Hong Kong, China	2.1	2.8	5.0	1,121	1,134	0.8	1.3	9.1	..	2	..	1
Colombia	4.9	2.4	9.4	594	256	..	1.1	1.6	1.5	..	..	..
Congo, Dem. Rep.	1.2	1.3	2.5	..	..	..	0.1	..	1.4	..	..	..
Congo, Rep.	1.8	3.2	5.0	62	42	*0.1*	0.3	..	3.4	..	..	..
Costa Rica	6.9	2.1	9.0	542	268	..	1.4	3.3	1.9	..	..	..
Côte d'Ivoire	1.4	2.6	3.7	66	27	..	0.1	..	0.8	..	..	..
Croatia	8.1	1.6	9.6	643	431	..	2.0	..	5.9	12	..	..
Cuba	8.2	..	..	..	..	*1.4*	5.3	..	5.1	..	..	..
Czech Republic	6.4	0.6	7.0	865	384	..	2.9	..	9.2	22	12	15
Denmark	6.7	1.3	8.0	1,931	2,576	*2.4*	2.9	..	4.7	20	7	5
Dominican Republic	1.6	3.6	5.2	234	97	..	2.2	..	1.5	..	..	..
Ecuador	2.5	2.4	4.9	146	74	..	1.7	1.9	1.6	..	..	..
Egypt, Arab Rep.	1.8	2.0	3.8	124	48	1.1	2.1	2.0	2.0	3	6	4
El Salvador	2.6	4.4	7.0	282	136	0.3	1.0	..	1.6	..	..	..
Eritrea	2.9	0.9	2.0	15	..	..	0.0 [c]	..	..	..	..	..
Estonia	5.1	1.4	6.4	492	230	4.2	3.1	12.4	7.4	18	9	5
Ethiopia	1.7	2.4	4.1	24	4	0.0 [c]	0.0 [c]	0.3	0.2	..	..	..
Finland	5.7	1.8	7.4	1,520	1,736	1.9	2.8	15.5	9.2	26	12	4
France	7.1	2.5	9.6	2,026	2,287	*2.2*	2.9	..	8.7	23	11	6
Gabon	0.6	..	..	..	..	*0.5*	0.2	..	3.2	..	..	..
Gambia, The	1.4	1.7	3.1	46	11	..	0.0 [c]	..	0.6	..	..	..
Georgia	0.7	4.0	4.7	156	46	4.8	3.8	10.7	4.8	5	13	2
Germany	8.3	2.5	10.7	2,364	2,727	2.2	3.4	..	9.6	21	14	6
Ghana	1.8	2.9	4.7	82	19	..	..	..	1.5	..	..	..
Greece	5.3	3.6	8.9	1,226	1,016	2.4	3.9	6.2	5.0	15	8	..
Guatemala	1.5	0.9	2.4	83	41	..	0.9	..	1.0	..	..	..
Guinea	1.2	1.0	2.2	43	13	*0.0* [c]	0.2	..	0.6	..	..	..
Guinea-Bissau	1.1	..	..	..	..	0.1	0.2	1.8	1.5	..	..	..
Haiti	1.3	2.1	3.4	47	17	*0.1*	0.2	0.7	0.7	..	..	..
Honduras	2.7	5.6	8.3	202	72	*0.3*	0.8	1.3	1.1	..	..	..

Health expenditure, services, and use 2.14

	Health expenditure			Health expenditure per capita		Physicians		Hospital beds		Inpatient admission rate	Average length of stay	Outpatient visits per capita
	Public % of GDP 1990–98[a]	Private % of GDP 1990–98[a]	Total % of GDP 1990–98[a,b]	PPP $ 1990–98[a]	$ 1990–98[a]	per 1,000 people 1980	per 1,000 people 1990–98[a]	per 1,000 people 1980	per 1,000 people 1990–98[a]	% of population 1990–98[a]	days 1990–98[a]	1990–98[a]
Hungary	4.1	2.0	6.4	638	290	2.5	3.4	9.1	9.1	24	11	15
India	0.6	4.1	5.2	73	18	0.4	0.4	0.8	0.8	..	..	..
Indonesia	0.6	0.7	1.3	38	6	0.1	0.2	..	0.7	..	..	..
Iran, Islamic Rep.	1.7	2.5	4.3	216	93	0.3	0.9	1.5	1.6	..	..	..
Iraq	..	..	..	..	..	0.6	0.6	1.9	1.5	..	..	..
Ireland	4.9	1.5	6.3	1,293	1,333	1.3	2.1	9.7	3.7	16	7	..
Israel	7.0	3.4	10.4	1,801	1,701	2.5	4.6	5.1	6.0	..	..	..
Italy	5.3	2.3	7.6	1,539	1,511	1.3	5.5	..	6.5	16	10	..
Jamaica	2.3	2.4	4.7	158	116	0.4	1.3	..	2.1	..	..	..
Japan	5.9	1.4	7.1	1,757	2,379	1.4	1.8	11.3	16.2	9	44	16
Jordan	3.7	4.2	7.9	215	123	0.8	1.7	1.3	1.8	11	3	3
Kazakhstan	2.1	2.5	4.8	217	68	3.2	3.5	13.2	8.5	15	16	1
Kenya	2.2	1.0	1.0	10	3	0.1	0.0 [c]	..	1.6	..	..	..
Korea, Dem. Rep.	..	..	..	..	..	2.5	..	..	..	..	..	..
Korea, Rep.	2.5	3.0	5.6	824	578	0.6	1.1	1.7	4.6	6	13	10
Kuwait	2.9	0.4	3.3	..	551	1.7	1.9	4.1	2.8	..	..	..
Kyrgyz Republic	2.7	0.4	3.1	71	11	2.9	3.1	12.0	9.5	21	15	1
Lao PDR	1.2	1.3	2.6	34	6	..	0.2	..	2.6	..	..	..
Latvia	4.0	2.4	6.4	366	168	4.1	3.4	13.7	10.3	21	14	4
Lebanon	3.0	7.0	10.0	594	361	1.7	2.8	..	2.7	14	4	..
Lesotho	3.7	2.4	..	..	..	..	0.1	..	..	..	..	..
Libya	..	..	..	..	..	1.3	1.3	4.8	4.3	..	..	..
Lithuania	7.2	1.0	8.3	533	240	3.9	3.9	12.1	9.6	24	12	7
Macedonia, FYR	7.8	0.8	7.5	..	171	..	2.3	..	5.2	10	15	3
Madagascar	1.1	1.0	2.1	..	5	0.1	0.3	..	0.9	..	..	..
Malawi	2.8	0.4	3.3	20	5	0.0 [c]	0.0 [c]	..	1.3	..	..	2
Malaysia	1.3	1.0	2.4	180	78	0.3	0.5	2.3	2.0	..	..	..
Mali	2.0	1.8	3.8	28	10	0.0 [c]	0.1	..	0.2	1	7	0 [d]
Mauritania	1.8	4.1	5.2	68	28	..	0.1	..	0.7	..	..	..
Mauritius	1.9	1.6	3.5	361	120	0.5	0.9	3.1	3.1	0 [d]	..	4
Mexico	2.8	1.9	4.7	369	201	0.9	1.2	..	1.2	6	4	2
Moldova	4.8	1.9	6.7	145	30	3.1	3.6	12.0	12.1	19	18	8
Mongolia	4.3	0.4	4.7	68	23	9.9	2.6	11.2	11.5	..	..	..
Morocco	1.3	2.7	4.0	140	49	0.1	0.5	1.2	1.0	3	3	..
Mozambique	2.1	..	..	..	..	0.0 [c]	..	1.1	0.9	..	..	..
Myanmar	0.2	0.8	1.0	..	58	0.2	0.3	0.9	0.6	..	..	..
Namibia	3.8	3.6	7.4	399	150	..	0.2	..	..	..	..	..
Nepal	1.3	4.2	5.5	58	11	0.0 [c]	0.0 [c]	0.2	0.2	..	..	..
Netherlands	6.1	2.3	8.5	1,874	1,988	2.1	2.6	12.5	11.3	11	33	5
New Zealand	5.9	1.7	7.6	1,357	1,310	1.6	2.1	..	6.1	14	7	..
Nicaragua	4.4	5.3	9.7	209	43	0.4	0.8	..	1.5	..	..	..
Niger	1.3	..	..	..	..	..	0.0 [c]	..	0.1	28	5	0 [d]
Nigeria	0.2	0.5	0.7	6	9	0.1	0.2	0.9	1.7	..	..	..
Norway	6.2	1.3	7.5	1,996	2,616	1.9	2.5	15.0	15.0	15	10	4
Oman	2.1	..	..	..	..	0.5	1.3	1.6	2.2	9	4	4
Pakistan	0.9	3.0	3.9	65	18	0.3	0.6	0.6	0.7	..	..	3
Panama	6.0	1.7	7.6	402	253	1.0	1.7	..	2.2	..	..	..
Papua New Guinea	2.6	0.6	..	77	34	0.1	0.1	5.5	4.0	..	..	..
Paraguay	2.6	4.8	7.4	348	122	0.6	1.1	..	1.3	..	..	..
Peru	2.2	3.4	5.6	240	141	0.7	0.9	..	1.5	1	6	2
Philippines	1.7	0.1	3.7	124	32	0.1	0.1	1.7	1.1	..	..	..
Poland	4.2	1.7	5.9	449	242	1.8	2.3	5.6	5.4	14	11	5
Portugal	4.7	3.2	7.9	1,142	803	2.0	3.0	..	4.1	11	10	3
Puerto Rico	..	6.5	..	..	..	..	1.8	..	3.3	..	..	..
Romania	2.9	1.8	4.2	192	65	1.5	1.8	8.8	7.6	18	10	4
Russian Federation	4.5	1.2	5.7	404	130	4.0	4.6	13.0	12.1	22	17	8

2.14 Health expenditure, services, and use

	Health expenditure			Health expenditure per capita		Physicians		Hospital beds		Inpatient admission rate	Average length of stay	Outpatient visits per capita
	Public % of GDP 1990–98[a]	Private % of GDP 1990–98[a]	Total % of GDP 1990–98[a,b]	PPP $ 1990–98[a]	$ 1990–98[a]	per 1,000 people 1980	per 1,000 people 1990–98[a]	per 1,000 people 1980	per 1,000 people 1990–98[a]	% of population 1990–98[a]	days 1990–98[a]	1990–98[a]
Rwanda	2.1	..	..	..	..	0.0 [c]	0.0 [c]	1.5	1.7	..	..	..
Saudi Arabia	6.4	1.6	8.0	844	584	*0.5*	1.7	*1.5*	2.3	11	11	1
Senegal	2.6	2.1	4.7	66	23	*0.1*	0.1	..	0.4	22	10	1
Sierra Leone	1.7	6.2	7.9	39	14	0.1	..	1.2		..	..	..
Singapore	1.1	2.0	3.2	744	841	0.9	1.4	4.2	3.6	12	..	..
Slovak Republic	5.2	1.6	6.8	655	255	..	3.0	..	7.5	20	11	12
Slovenia	6.8	1.0	7.8	1,115	768	..	2.1	7.0	5.7	16	11	..
South Africa	3.2	3.5	7.1	571	246	..	0.6	..		..	..	..
Spain	5.6	1.8	7.4	1,182	1,001	*2.8*	4.2	..	3.9	10	11	..
Sri Lanka	1.4	1.2	2.6	72	22	0.1	0.2	2.9	2.7	..	..	..
Sudan	..	1.9	..	..	..	0.1	0.1	0.9	1.1	..	..	..
Sweden	7.2	1.4	8.6	1,773	2,220	2.2	3.1	14.8	5.6	18	8	3
Switzerland	7.1	3.0	10.0	2,573	3,616	..	3.2	..	20.8	15	..	11
Syrian Arab Republic	..	..	..	..	..	0.4	1.4	1.1	1.5	..	..	..
Tajikistan	6.6	0.1	5.9	67	8	2.4	2.1	10.0	8.8	16	15	..
Tanzania	1.3	..	..	..	..	..	0.0 [c]	1.4	0.9	..	..	..
Thailand	1.7	4.5	6.2	329	112	0.1	0.4	1.5	2.0	..	..	1
Togo	1.1	2.1	3.2	46	11	0.1	0.1	..	1.5	..	..	..
Trinidad and Tobago	2.8	1.6	4.3	334	215	0.7	0.8	..	5.1	..	..	..
Tunisia	3.0	2.9	5.9	320	118	0.3	0.7	2.1	1.7	8	..	..
Turkey	2.9	2.9	5.8	377	177	0.6	1.1	2.2	2.5	6	6	1
Turkmenistan	3.5	..	..	..	..	2.9	0.2	10.6	11.5	17	15	..
Uganda	1.8	2.9	4.7	50	14	*0.0* [c]	0.0 [c]	*1.5*	0.9	..	..	..
Ukraine	4.1	1.4	5.4	179	54	3.7	4.5	12.5	11.8	20	17	10
United Arab Emirates	4.5	0.4	2.4	446	396	1.1	1.8	2.8	2.6	11	5	..
United Kingdom	5.9	1.0	6.8	1,391	1,480	*1.6*	1.6	9.3	4.5	23	10	6
United States	6.5	7.5	13.9	4,121	4,080	1.8	2.6	5.9	4.0	12	8	6
Uruguay	1.9	6.5	8.4	719	529	*2.0*	3.7	..	4.4	..	..	..
Uzbekistan	3.3	..	..	..	..	2.9	3.3	11.5	8.3	19	14	..
Venezuela, RB	3.0	4.5	7.5	426	205	0.8	2.4	0.3	1.5	..	..	..
Vietnam	0.4	3.9	4.3	..	16	0.2	0.4	3.5	3.8	7	8	3
West Bank and Gaza	4.9	3.7	8.6	..	81	..	0.5	..	1.2	9	3	4
Yemen, Rep.	2.1	3.0	5.0	38	18	*0.1*	0.2	..	0.7	..	..	..
Yugoslavia, FR (Serb./Mont.)	..	..	..	..	..	..	2.0	..	5.3	8	12	2
Zambia	2.3	1.8	4.1	33	14	0.1	0.1	*3.5*	..	..	..	..
Zimbabwe	3.1	3.3	6.4	191	31	0.2	0.1	3.1	0.5	..	..	..
World	**2.5 w**	**2.9 w**	**5.5 w**	**561 w**	**483 w**	**1.0 w**	**1.5 w**	**3.4 w**	**3.3 w**	**9 w**	**13 w**	**6 w**
Low income	1.3	2.8	4.2	93	23	0.6	1.0	1.5	1.8	5	13	3
Excl. China & India	1.2	2.0	3.1	46	14	..	0.3	..	1.3	10	9	3
Middle income	3.1	2.6	5.7	384	199	*1.6*	1.8	..	4.3	10	11	5
Lower middle income	3.0	2.2	5.3	275	102	2.2	2.0	7.2	5.1	15	13	6
Upper middle income	3.3	3.0	6.3	535	335	*0.9*	1.5	..	3.2	6	8	4
Low & middle income	1.9	2.7	4.6	182	75	0.9	1.2	2.7	2.5	7	12	4
East Asia & Pacific	1.7	2.4	4.1	154	47	0.8	1.5	2.0	2.6	4	13	4
Europe & Central Asia	4.0	1.8	5.8	355	138	3.0	3.3	10.4	8.9	17	14	6
Latin America & Carib.	3.3	3.3	6.6	461	284	*0.8*	1.5	..	2.3	2	4	2
Middle East & N. Africa	2.4	2.3	4.8	237	117	*0.7*	1.2	1.7	1.7	5	6	3
South Asia	0.8	3.7	4.8	69	17	0.3	0.4	0.7	0.7	..	..	3
Sub-Saharan Africa	1.5	1.8	3.2	84	33	..	0.1	..	1.1	12	6	1
High income	6.2	3.7	9.8	2,505	2,585	*1.9*	2.8	..	7.4	15	16	8
Europe EMU	6.6	2.3	8.9	1,842	1,974	*2.1*	3.7	..	7.8	18	13	6

a. Data are for the most recent year available. b. Data may not sum to totals because of rounding and because of differences in the year for which the most recent data are available. c. Less than 0.05. d. Less than 0.5.

Health expenditure, services, and use 2.14

About the data

National health accounts track resource inputs to the health sector, including both public and private expenditures. In contrast with high-income countries, few developing countries have health accounts that are methodologically consistent with national accounting approaches. The difficulties in creating national health accounts go beyond data collection. Before beginning to establish a national health accounting system, a country needs to define the boundaries of the health care system and a taxonomy of health care delivery institutions. The accounting system should be comprehensive and standardized, providing not only accurate bookkeeping but also critical information on the equity and efficiency of health financing to inform health policymaking and health system reform.

The absence of consistent national health accounting systems in most developing countries makes cross-country comparisons of health spending difficult. Records of private out-of-pocket expenditures are often lacking. And compiling estimates of public health expenditures is complicated in countries where state or provincial and local governments are involved in health care financing and delivery because the data on public spending often are not aggregated. The data in the table are the product of an effort to collect all available information on health expenditures from national and local government budgets, national accounts, household surveys, insurance publications, international donors, and existing tabulations.

Health service indicators (physicians and hospital beds per 1,000 people) and health utilization indicators (inpatient admission rates, average length of stay, and outpatient visits) come from a variety of sources (see *Data sources*). Data are lacking for many countries, and for others comparability is limited by differences in definitions. In estimates of health personnel, for example, some countries incorrectly include retired physicians (because deletions are made only periodically) or those working outside the health sector. There is no universally accepted definition of hospital beds. Moreover, figures on physicians and hospital beds are indicators of availability, not of quality or use. They do not show how well trained the physicians are or how well equipped the hospitals or medical centers are. And physicians and hospital beds tend to be concentrated in urban areas, so these indicators give only a partial view of health services available to the entire population.

Average length of stay in hospitals is an indicator of the efficiency of resource use. Longer stays may reflect a waste of resources if patients are kept in hospitals beyond the time medically required, inflating demand for hospital beds and increasing hospital costs. Aside from differences in cases and financing methods, cross-country variations in average length of stay may result from differences in the role of hospitals. Many developing countries do not have separate extended care facilities, so hospitals become the source of both long-term and acute care. Other factors may also explain the variations. Data for some countries may not include all public and private hospitals. Admission rates may be overstated in some countries if outpatient surgeries are counted as hospital admissions. And in many countries outpatient visits, especially emergency visits, may result in double counting if a patient receives treatment in more than one department.

Table 2.14a

Health expenditure by aggregation method, 1990–98

% of GDP

	Unweighted average	Weighted by population	Weighted by GDP
World	5.6	5.5	9.2
Low income	4.0	4.2	4.2
Middle income	5.8	5.7	5.9
High income	6.8	9.8	9.4

Source: World Bank staff estimates.

Health expenditures for the world and for country income groups will vary—often substantially—depending on how they are aggregated. A population-weighted average of global health expenditures, which gives relatively large weights to such countries as China, India, and Indonesia—all of which spend little on health—is far smaller than a GDP-weighted average, which gives the greatest weights to the largest economies.

Which aggregation method to use depends on the purpose. To show the percentage of global GDP spent on health, country data need to be weighted by GDP. To show the average percentage of GDP spent per country taking account of differences in population size, country data would need to be weighted by population. Unweighted averages would show the average percentage of GDP spent on health irrespective of the size of populations or economies.

Definitions

• **Public health expenditure** consists of recurrent and capital spending from government (central and local) budgets, external borrowings and grants (including donations from international agencies and nongovernmental organizations), and social (or compulsory) health insurance funds. • **Private health expenditure** includes direct household (out-of-pocket) spending, private insurance, charitable donations, and direct service payments by private corporations. • **Total health expenditure** is the sum of public and private health expenditure. It covers the provision of health services (preventive and curative), family planning activities, nutrition activities, and emergency aid designated for health but does not include provision of water and sanitation. • **Physicians** are defined as graduates of any faculty or school of medicine who are working in the country in any medical field (practice, teaching, research). • **Hospital beds** include inpatient beds available in public, private, general, and specialized hospitals and rehabilitation centers. In most cases beds for both acute and chronic care are included. • **Inpatient admission rate** is the percentage of the population admitted to hospitals during a year. • **Average length of stay** is the average duration of inpatient hospital admissions. • **Outpatient visits per capita** are the number of visits to health care facilities per capita, including repeat visits.

Data sources

Estimates of health expenditure come from the World Health Organization's (WHO) *World Health Report 2000* and from the Organisation for Economic Co-operation and Development for its member countries, supplemented by World Bank country and sector studies, including the Human Development Network's *Sector Strategy: Health, Nutrition, and Population* (World Bank 1997f). Data were also drawn from World Bank public expenditure reviews, the International Monetary Fund's Government Finance Statistics database, and other studies. The data on private expenditure are largely from household surveys and World Bank poverty assessments and sector studies. The data on physicians, hospital beds, and utilization of health services are from the WHO and OECD, supplemented by country data.

2.15 Disease prevention: coverage and quality

	Access to safe water		Access to sanitation		Tetanus vaccinations	Child immunization		Access to essential drugs	Tuberculosis treatment success rate	DOTS detection rate
	% of population		% of population		% of pregnant women	% of children under 12 months		% of population	% of cases	% of cases
						Measles	DPT			
	1982–85[a]	1990–96[a]	1982–85[a]	1990–96[a]	1996–97	1995–98[a]	1995–98[a]	1997	1990–97[a]	1995–97[a]
Albania	92	76	..	58	65	95	99	60	..	..
Algeria	..	..	..	..	52	74	79	95	86	97
Angola	28	32	18	16	24	78	41	20	..	70
Argentina	55	65	69	75	..	98	85	70	..	4
Armenia	..	..	..	..	..	92	87	40	77	49
Australia	99	99	99	86	..	87	86	100	..	..
Austria	99	..	..	100	..	90	90	100	..	..
Azerbaijan	..	..	..	36	..	99	95	86	7	..
Bangladesh	40	84	4	35	86	97	98	65	72	19
Belarus	..	..	..	..	..	98	97	70	..	..
Belgium	98	..	..	100	..	64	62	..	..	..
Benin	14	50	10	20	66	82	78		72	35
Bolivia	53	55	36	41	27	98	82	70	62	80
Bosnia and Herzegovina	..	..	..	41	..	85	79	..	..	..
Botswana	..	70	36	55	54	79	76	90	70	80
Brazil	75	72	24	67	30	99	79	40	..	..
Bulgaria	85	..	..	99	..	93	94	..	..	..
Burkina Faso	35	..	9	18	54	68	70	60	29	16
Burundi	23	52	..	51	9	50	63	20	45	25
Cambodia	..	13	..	..	31	68	70	30	94	50
Cameroon	36	41	36	40	49	43	44	..	..	..
Canada	100	99	85	95	..	..	..	100	..	..
Central African Republic	..	19	19	46	37	46	53	50	37	65
Chad	..	24	14	21	27	30	24	46	47	15
Chile	86	85	67	..	..	92	91	..	80	80
China	..	90	..	21	13	96	96	85	96	23
Hong Kong, China	..	..	..	..	..	82	88	..	..	..
Colombia	..	78	68	83	..	89	81	..	..	..
Congo, Dem. Rep.	..	27	..	9	..	20	18	..	80	46
Congo, Rep.	..	47	..	9	30	18	23	61	69	70
Costa Rica	..	92	95	97	..	99	91	100	..	..
Côte d'Ivoire	20	72	17	54	44	68	70	80	56	55
Croatia	..	63	67	61	..	93	92	100	..	..
Cuba	82	93	..	88	70	99	99	100	92	87
Czech Republic	100	..	..	..	..	96	98	..	66	53
Denmark	100	..	..	100	..	84	90	..	..	..
Dominican Republic	49	71	66	78	77	80	80	77	..	..
Ecuador	58	70	57	64	3	75	76	40	40	1
Egypt, Arab Rep.	90	64	..	11	61	92	94	..	81	10
El Salvador	51	55	62	68	..	97	97	80	..	45
Eritrea	..	7	..	..	34	53	60	57	..	3
Estonia	..	..	..	..	..	88	85	100	..	..
Ethiopia	..	27	..	8	30	52	63	..	72	24
Finland	95	98	100	100	..	98	100	98	..	..
France	98	100	..	96	83	83	97	..	..	..
Gabon	..	67	50	76	4	57	41	30	..	..
Gambia, The	45	76	..	37	96	91	96	90	80	75
Georgia	..	..	..	..		95	92	30	58	29
Germany	..	..	..	..	80	75	45	100	..	..
Ghana	..	56	26	42	..	59	60	..	51	33
Greece	85	..	..	96	..	90	85	100	..	..
Guatemala	58	67	54	67	38	74	78	50	81	52
Guinea	20	62	12	14	..	56	53	93	75	52
Guinea-Bissau	31	53	..	20	46	51	63	..	..	..
Haiti	..	28	19	24	38	32	34	30	..	2
Honduras	50	65	32	65	..	89	94	40	..	..

Disease prevention: coverage and quality 2.15

	Access to safe water		Access to sanitation		Tetanus vaccinations	Child immunization		Access to essential drugs	Tuberculosis treatment success rate	DOTS detection rate
	% of population		% of population		% of pregnant women	% of children under 12 months		% of population	% of cases	% of cases
						Measles	DPT			
	1982–85[a]	1990–96[a]	1982–85[a]	1990–96[a]	1996–97	1995–98[a]	1995–98[a]	1997	1990–97[a]	1995–97[a]
Hungary	87	..	..	94	..	100	100	100	..	..
India	54	81	8	16	80	81	90	35	79	1
Indonesia	39	62	30	51	53	92	91	80	81	7
Iran, Islamic Rep.	71	83	65	67	75	96	100	85	87	7
Iraq	74	44	..	36	45	98	92	85	..	..
Ireland	97	..	..	100	..	..	..	..	..	..
Israel	100	99	..	100	..	94	92	..	..	100
Italy	99	..	..	100	..	75	60	..	82	9
Jamaica	96	70	91	74	52	88	90	95	72	81
Japan	99	96	99	100	..	94	100	100	..	..
Jordan	89	89	91	95	22	95	93	100	..	..
Kazakhstan	..	..	..	..	..	97	96	..	..	..
Kenya	27	53	44	77	51	32	36	35	77	55
Korea, Dem. Rep.	..	..	100	..	5	100	100	..	..	..
Korea, Rep.	83	83	100	100	..	85	80	..	71	56
Kuwait	100	100	100	100	8	95	96	..	..	..
Kyrgyz Republic	..	81	..	..	..	98	98	..	88	4
Lao PDR	..	39	..	24	32	67	60	..	55	32
Latvia	..	..	..	..	..	97	75	90	64	69
Lebanon	92	100	75	100	..	89	92	..	89	56
Lesotho	18	52	12	6	..	53	57	80	71	65
Libya	90	90	70	86	..	92	96	100	..	..
Lithuania	..	..	..	..	..	96	90	..	..	..
Macedonia, FYR	..	..	..	..	91	98	97	..	..	..
Madagascar	31	29	..	15	30	68	73	65	55	60
Malawi	32	45	60	53	81	87	95	..	68	50
Malaysia	71	89	75	94	71	83	91	70	69	70
Mali	..	37	21	31	62	56	52	60	65	17
Mauritania	37	64	..	32	63	20	28	100	96	40
Mauritius	99	98	97	100	78	85	89	..	..	..
Mexico	82	83	57	66	70	97	83	92	75	15
Moldova	..	56	..	50	..	99	97	25	..	..
Mongolia	..	..	..	..	..	98	92	60	78	30
Morocco	32	52	50	40	33	92	95	..	88	94
Mozambique	9	32	10	21	41	70	61	50	54	57
Myanmar	27	38	24	41	78	88	90	60	79	25
Namibia	..	57	..	34	70	57	63	80	54	74
Nepal	24	44	1	6	65	85	78	20	85	11
Netherlands	100	100	..	100	..	96	95	100	81	45
New Zealand	100	..	88	..	..	114	86	100	..	..
Nicaragua	50	81	27	31	42	94	94	46	79	90
Niger	37	53	9	15	19	42	28	..	57	21
Nigeria	36	39	..	36	29	69	45	10	32	10
Norway	99	100	..	100	..	..	..	100	80	90
Oman	58	68	39	85	96	98	99	90	87	83
Pakistan	38	60	16	30	58	74	74	65	70	2
Panama	82	84	81	90	..	92	95	80	..	..
Papua New Guinea	..	28	..	22	11	40	45	90	60	4
Paraguay	23	39	49	32	32	61	82	..	51	55
Peru	53	80	48	44	57	94	98	60	89	95
Philippines	65	83	57	77	38	83	83	95	82	3
Poland	82	..	..	100	..	..	..	..	..	..
Portugal	66	82	..	100	..	99	95	100	74	67
Puerto Rico	..	97	..	..	..	..	..	..	68	81
Romania	71	62	..	44	..	97	97	85	..	..
Russian Federation	..	..	..	..	..	95	87	..	62	1

2.15 Disease prevention: coverage and quality

	Access to safe water		Access to sanitation		Tetanus vaccinations	Child immunization		Access to essential drugs	Tuberculosis treatment success rate	DOTS detection rate
	% of population		% of population		% of pregnant women	% of children under 12 months		% of population	% of cases	% of cases
	1982–85[a]	1990–96[a]	1982–85[a]	1990–96[a]	1996–97	Measles 1995–98[a]	DPT 1995–98[a]	1997	1990–97[a]	1995–97[a]
Rwanda	..	..	..	..	43	66	77	60	61	45
Saudi Arabia	91	93	86	86	66	92	92	..	..	..
Senegal	44	50	..	58	34	65	65	..	41	62
Sierra Leone	24	34	13	11	42	28	26	..	74	37
Singapore	100	100	85	100	..	89	93	100	86	28
Slovak Republic	..	..	46	51	..	98	98	100	73	34
Slovenia	..	98	80	98	..	82	91	100	87	60
South Africa	..	70	..	46	26	76	73	80	69	6
Spain	99	..	..	100	..	..	..	100	..	..
Sri Lanka	37	46	..	52	78	94	97	95	80	71
Sudan	..	50	5	22	55	92	79	15	..	1
Sweden	100	..	..	100	..	96	99	..	..	..
Switzerland	100	100	..	100	..	..	..	100	..	..
Syrian Arab Republic	71	85	45	56	53	93	95	80	92	5
Tajikistan	..	69	..	62	..	95	95	..	..	..
Tanzania	52	49	..	86	27	69	74	..	76	55
Thailand	66	89	47	96	88	92	96	95	78	5
Togo	35	63	14	26	41	38	33	70	60	15
Trinidad and Tobago	98	82	..	96	..	88	90	..	..	..
Tunisia	89	99	52	96	80	92	96	51	..	..
Turkey	69	..	..	94	32	76	79	..	..	..
Turkmenistan	..	60	..	60	..	100	98	..	..	..
Uganda	16	34	13	57	38	60	58	70	33	65
Ukraine	..	55	..	49	..	97	96	..	..	..
United Arab Emirates	100	98	86	95	..	95	92	..	..	..
United Kingdom	100	100	..	100	..	95	95	..	..	..
United States	..	..	98	..	..	89	94	..	71	86
Uruguay	83	89	59	61	..	80	88	..	80	95
Uzbekistan	..	57	..	18	..	88	96	..	..	..
Venezuela, RB	84	79	45	58	..	68	60	90	80	75
Vietnam	..	36	..	21	92	96	95	85	90	77
West Bank and Gaza	..	..	..	..	..	96	96	..	..	..
Yemen, Rep.	..	39	..	19	26	51	57	50	76	30
Yugoslavia, FR (Serb./Mont.)	..	..	..	..	..	91	94	80	..	..
Zambia	48	43	47	23	..	69	70	..	..	..
Zimbabwe	52	77	26	66	58	73	78	70	..	..
World	.. w	.. w	.. w	.. w		83 w	83 w			
Low income	..	..	..	24		80	82			
Excl. China & India	..	..	..	..		71	68			
Middle income	..	..	..	..		90	86			
Lower middle income	..	..	..	..		89	89			
Upper middle income	77	..	51	..		92	82			
Low & middle income	..	..	..	29		83	83			
East Asia & Pacific	..	84	..	29		93	93			
Europe & Central Asia	..	..	..	..		91	89			
Latin America & Carib.	72	..	46	..		93	82			
Middle East & N. Africa	68	..	..	..		88	90			
South Asia	52	77	7	16		81	87			
Sub-Saharan Africa	..	..	..	..		58	53			
High income	..	..	..	..		..	..			
Europe EMU	97	..	..	99		75	69			

a. Data are for the most recent year available.

Disease prevention: coverage and quality 2.15

About the data

The indicators in the table are based on data provided to the World Health Organization (WHO) by member states as part of their efforts to monitor and evaluate progress in implementing national health-for-all strategies. Because reliable, observation-based statistical data for these indicators do not exist in some developing countries, the data are estimated.

People's health is influenced by the environment in which they live. Lack of clean water and basic sanitation is the main reason diseases transmitted by feces are so common in developing countries. Drinking water contaminated by feces deposited near homes and an inadequate supply of water cause diseases accounting for 10 percent of the disease burden in developing countries (World Bank 1993c). The data on access to safe water measure the share of the population served by improved sources of water. An improved source can be any form of collection or piping used to make water regularly available. The reported data are based on surveys and estimates provided by governments. The underlying definitions vary from country to country and among locations within countries. They have also changed over time. Moreover, water quality generally is not tested during the surveys on which these data are based. Similar reservations apply to the data on access to sanitation.

Neonatal tetanus is an important cause of infant mortality in some developing countries and can be prevented through immunization of the mother during pregnancy. Recommended doses for full protection are generally two tetanus shots during the first pregnancy and one booster shot during each subsequent pregnancy, with five doses considered adequate for lifetime protection. Information on tetanus shots during pregnancy is collected through surveys in which pregnant respondents are asked to show antenatal cards on which tetanus shots have been recorded. Because not all women have antenatal cards, respondents are also asked about their receipt of these injections. Poor recall may result in a downward bias in estimates of the share of births protected. But in settings where receiving injections is common, respondents may erroneously report having received tetanus toxoid.

Governments in developing countries usually finance immunization against measles and diphtheria, pertussis (whooping cough), and tetanus (DPT) as part of the basic public health package, though they often rely on personnel with limited training to provide the vaccines. According to the World Bank's *World Development Report 1993: Investing in Health,* these diseases accounted for about 10 percent of the disease burden among children under five in 1990, compared with an expected 23 percent at 1970 levels of vaccination. In many developing countries, however, data recording practices make immunization coverage difficult to measure (WHO 1996).

Essential drugs are pharmaceutical products included by the WHO on a periodically updated list of safe and effective treatments for both communicable and noncommunicable diseases. They are cost-effective elements of a health system that can treat many common diseases and conditions, including, among many others, anemia, hypertension, tuberculosis, and malaria.

Data on the success rate of tuberculosis treatment are provided for countries that have implemented the recommended control strategy: directly observed treatment, short-course (DOTS). Countries that have not adopted DOTS or have only recently done so are omitted because of lack of data or poor comparability or reliability of reported results. The treatment success rate for tuberculosis provides a useful indicator of the quality of health services. A low rate or no success suggests that infectious patients may not be receiving adequate treatment. An essential complement to the tuberculosis treatment success rate is the DOTS detection rate, which indicates whether there is adequate coverage by the recommended case detection and treatment strategy. A country with a high treatment success rate may still face big challenges if its DOTS detection rate remains low.

Figure 2.15

Poor children are much less likely to be fully immunized

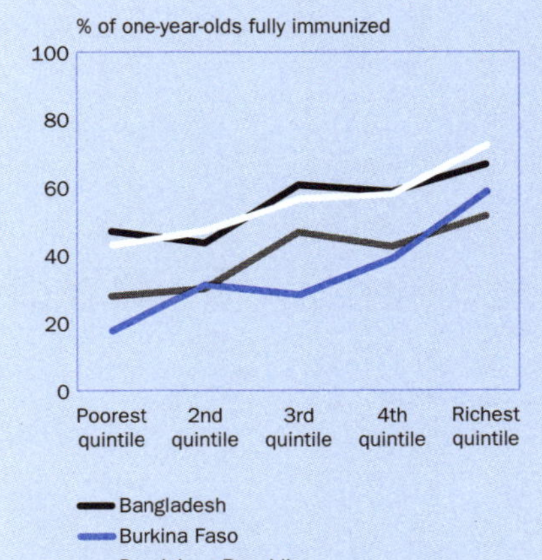

Note: Households are grouped into quintiles by assets.
Source: Analysis of demographic and health surveys conducted by the World Bank and Macro International.

Children in poor households are significantly less likely to be immunized against such diseases as measles, polio, and diphtheria, pertussis (whooping cough), and tetanus (DPT) than those in wealthier households.

Definitions

• **Percentage of population with access to safe water** is the share of the population with reasonable access to an adequate amount of safe water (including treated surface water and untreated but uncontaminated water, such as from springs, sanitary wells, and protected boreholes). In urban areas the source may be a public fountain or standpipe located not more than 200 meters away from the dwelling. In rural areas the definition implies that members of the household do not have to spend a disproportionate part of the day fetching water. An adequate amount of safe water is that needed to satisfy metabolic, hygienic, and domestic requirements—usually about 20 liters a person a day. The definition of safe water has changed over time. • **Percentage of population with access to sanitation** is the share of the population with at least adequate excreta disposal facilities that can effectively prevent human, animal, and insect contact with excreta. Suitable facilities range from simple but protected pit latrines to flush toilets with a sewerage connection. To be effective, all facilities must be correctly constructed and properly maintained. • **Pregnant women receiving tetanus vaccinations** are the percentage of pregnant women who receive two tetanus toxoid injections during their first pregnancy and one booster shot during each subsequent pregnancy. • **Child immunization** is the rate of vaccination coverage of children under one year of age for four diseases—measles and diphtheria, pertussis (or whooping cough), and tetanus (DPT). A child is considered adequately immunized against measles after receiving one dose of vaccine, and against DPT after receiving two or three doses of vaccine, depending on the immunization scheme. • **Percentage of population with access to essential drugs** is the share of the population for which a minimum of 20 of the most essential drugs are continuously available and affordable at public or private health facilities or drug outlets within one hour's walk. • **Tuberculosis treatment success rate** refers to the percentage of new, registered smear-positive (infectious) cases that were cured or in which a full-course treatment was completed. • **DOTS detection rate** is the percentage of estimated new infectious tuberculosis cases detected under the directly observed treatment, short-course (DOTS) case detection and treatment strategy.

Data sources

The table was produced using information provided to the WHO by countries, the WHO's *EPI Information System: Global Summary, September 1998,* its Essential Drugs and Medicine Policy, and its *Global Tuberculosis Control Report 1999* and the United Nations Children's Fund's (UNICEF) *State of the World's Children 2000.*

2.16 Reproductive health

	Total fertility rate births per woman		Adolescent fertility rate births per 1,000 women aged 15–19	Women at risk of unintended pregnancy % of married women aged 15–49	Contraceptive prevalence rate % of women aged 15–49	Births attended by skilled health staff % of total		Maternal mortality ratio per 100,000 live births
	1980	1998	1998	1990–98[a]	1990–98[a]	1982	1996–98[a]	1990–98[a]
Albania	3.6	2.5	12	..	..	..	99	..
Algeria	6.7	3.5	21	..	51	..	77	..
Angola	6.9	6.7	217	..	..	34	17	..
Argentina	3.3	2.6	64	..	..	..	97	38[b]
Armenia	2.3	1.3	46	..	..	..	95	35[b]
Australia	1.9	1.8	30	..	..	99	100	..
Austria	1.6	1.3	22	..	..	..	100	..
Azerbaijan	3.2	2.0	23	..	..	..	99	37[b]
Bangladesh	6.1	3.1	140	16	49	2	8	440[c]
Belarus	2.0	1.3	21	..	..	..	..	22[d]
Belgium	1.7	1.6	11	..	..	..	100	..
Benin	7.0	5.7	111	21	16	34	60	500[c]
Bolivia	5.5	4.1	78	24	49	..	46	390[c]
Bosnia and Herzegovina	2.1	1.6	33	..	..	..	..	10[b]
Botswana	6.1	4.2	76	..	..	..	77	330[d]
Brazil	3.9	2.3	72	7	77	98	92	160[c]
Bulgaria	2.0	1.1	44	..	..	..	99	15[d]
Burkina Faso	7.5	6.7	145	33	12	12	42	..
Burundi	6.8	6.2	54	..	..	..	24	..
Cambodia	4.7	4.5	14	..	..	..	31	..
Cameroon	6.4	5.0	137	22	19	..	55	430[c]
Canada	1.7	1.6	24	..	..	..	100	..
Central African Republic	5.8	4.8	130	16	14	..	46	1,100[c]
Chad	6.9	6.4	188	9	4	24	15	830[c]
Chile	2.8	2.2	47	..	..	92	99	23[b]
China	2.5	1.9	15	..	85	..	..	65[c]
Hong Kong, China	2.0	1.1	7	..	..	89	100	..
Colombia	3.9	2.7	86	8	72	..	85	80[b]
Congo, Dem. Rep.	6.6	6.3	214	..	..	..	45	..
Congo, Rep.	6.3	6.0	140	..	..	..	50	..
Costa Rica	3.6	2.6	82	..	..	93	97	29[c]
Côte d'Ivoire	7.4	5.0	130	43	11	..	45	600[c]
Croatia	..	1.5	19	..	..	..	..	12[b]
Cuba	2.0	1.5	65	..	..	..	99	27[b]
Czech Republic	2.1	1.2	23	..	69	..	100	9[d]
Denmark	1.5	1.8	9	..	..	..	100	10[d]
Dominican Republic	4.2	2.9	12	13	64	..	96	..
Ecuador	5.0	2.9	68	..	57	62	64	160[c]
Egypt, Arab Rep.	5.1	3.2	50	16	48	..	46	170[c]
El Salvador	4.9	3.3	107	..	60	..	87	..
Eritrea	..	5.7	118	28	8	..	21	1,000[c]
Estonia	2.0	1.2	36	..	..	..	100	50[d]
Ethiopia	6.6	6.4	154	..	4	..	8	..
Finland	1.6	1.8	11	..	..	..	100	6[d]
France	1.9	1.8	9	..	71	..	99	10[d]
Gabon	4.5	5.1	164	..	..	..	80	..
Gambia, The	6.5	5.6	170	..	..	41	44	..
Georgia	2.3	1.3	35	..	..	..	100	70[b]
Germany	1.4	1.4	14	..	..	..	99	8[d]
Ghana	6.5	4.8	104	33	20	..	44	..
Greece	2.2	1.3	17	..	..	..	97	1[d]
Guatemala	6.3	4.4	106	24	32	..	29	190[c]
Guinea	6.1	5.4	186	25	2	..	31	..
Guinea-Bissau	5.8	5.6	187	..	..	..	25	910[d]
Haiti	5.9	4.3	68	48	18	34	21	..
Honduras	6.5	4.2	111	..	50	..	47	220[d]

Reproductive health 2.16

	Total fertility rate		Adolescent fertility rate	Women at risk of unintended pregnancy	Contraceptive prevalence rate	Births attended by skilled health staff		Maternal mortality ratio
	births per woman		births per 1,000 women aged 15–19	% of married women aged 15–49	% of women aged 15–49	% of total		per 100,000 live births
	1980	1998	1998	1990–98[a]	1990–98[a]	1982	1996–98[a]	1990–98[a]
Hungary	1.9	1.3	28	..	73	99	96	15[d]
India	5.0	3.2	115	20	41	23	35	410[c]
Indonesia	4.3	2.7	59	11	57	27	36	450[c]
Iran, Islamic Rep.	6.7	2.7	49	..	73	..	74	37[c]
Iraq	6.4	4.6	39	..	..	..	54	..
Ireland	3.2	1.9	14	..	60	..	100	6[d]
Israel	3.2	2.7	19	..	..	..	99	5[d]
Italy	1.6	1.2	8	..	..	..	100	7[d]
Jamaica	3.7	2.6	100	..	65	86	92	..
Japan	1.8	1.4	3	..	..	..	100	8[d]
Jordan	6.8	4.1	41	22	50	..	97	41[b]
Kazakhstan	2.9	2.0	46	11	59	..	..	70[e]
Kenya	7.8	4.6	109	36	39	..	45	590[c]
Korea, Dem. Rep.	2.8	2.0	2	..	..	..	100	110[d]
Korea, Rep.	2.6	1.6	4	..	..	70	98	20[d]
Kuwait	5.3	2.8	33	..	..	98	98	5[d]
Kyrgyz Republic	4.1	2.8	34	12	60	..	98	65[b]
Lao PDR	6.7	5.5	42	..	25	..	30	650[b]
Latvia	2.0	1.1	32	..	..	..	100	45[d]
Lebanon	4.0	2.4	25	..	..	..	89	100[c]
Lesotho	5.5	4.6	83	..	23	..	50	..
Libya	7.3	3.7	54	..	45	68	94	75[c]
Lithuania	2.0	1.4	35	..	..	..	100	18[d]
Macedonia, FYR	2.5	1.8	38	..	..	..	95	11[b]
Madagascar	6.6	5.7	171	26	19	..	57	490[c]
Malawi	7.6	6.4	152	36	22	..	55	620[c]
Malaysia	4.2	3.1	25	..	..	88	98	39[b]
Mali	7.1	6.5	178	26	7	14	24	580[c]
Mauritania	6.3	5.4	132	..	..	..	40	..
Mauritius	2.7	2.0	38	..	75	..	97	50[b]
Mexico	4.7	2.8	69	..	65	..	68	48[c]
Moldova	2.4	1.7	50	..	74	..	..	42[d]
Mongolia	5.3	2.5	46	..	..	..	99	150[d]
Morocco	5.4	3.0	48	16	59	20	31	230[c]
Mozambique	6.5	5.2	161	7	6	29	44	..
Myanmar	4.9	3.1	19	..	..	..	57	230[c]
Namibia	5.9	4.8	103	22	29	..	68	230[c]
Nepal	6.1	4.4	118	28	29	..	9	540[c]
Netherlands	1.6	1.6	4	..	75	100	100	7[d]
New Zealand	2.0	1.9	52	..	..	..	..	15[d]
Nicaragua	6.3	3.7	133	..	60	..	65	150[b]
Niger	7.4	7.3	213	19	8	26	15	590[c]
Nigeria	6.9	5.3	115	22	6	..	31	..
Norway	1.7	1.8	16	..	..	100	100	6[d]
Oman	9.0	4.6	63	..	..	..	91	19[b]
Pakistan	7.0	4.9	102	32	24	..	18	..
Panama	3.7	2.6	80	..	..	80	84	85[d]
Papua New Guinea	5.8	4.2	67	29	26	..	53	..
Paraguay	5.2	3.9	73	15	59	..	61	190[c]
Peru	4.5	3.1	66	12	64	30	56	270[c]
Philippines	4.8	3.6	44	26	47	..	53	170[c]
Poland	2.3	1.4	23	..	..	..	98	8[d]
Portugal	2.2	1.5	21	..	..	..	..	8[d]
Puerto Rico	2.6	1.9	68	..	78	..	90	..
Romania	2.4	1.3	41	..	57	..	99	41[d]
Russian Federation	1.9	1.2	46	..	34	..	99	50[b]

2.16 Reproductive health

	Total fertility rate births per woman		Adolescent fertility rate births per 1,000 women aged 15–19	Women at risk of unintended pregnancy % of married women aged 15–49	Contraceptive prevalence rate % of women aged 15–49	Births attended by skilled health staff % of total		Maternal mortality ratio per 100,000 live births
	1980	1998	1998	1990–98[a]	1990–98[a]	1982	1996–98[a]	1990–98[a]
Rwanda	8.3	6.1	55	37	21	20	26	..
Saudi Arabia	7.3	5.7	112	..	..	..	90	..
Senegal	6.8	5.5	114	33	13	..	47	560[c]
Sierra Leone	6.5	6.0	199	..	..	..	25	..
Singapore	1.7	1.5	10	..	..	100	100	6[d]
Slovak Republic	2.3	1.4	33	..	..	..	100	9[d]
Slovenia	2.1	1.2	16	..	..	..	100	11[d]
South Africa	4.6	2.8	42	..	69	..	82	..
Spain	2.2	1.2	8	..	..	..	96	6[d]
Sri Lanka	3.5	2.1	21	..	..	85	..	60[d]
Sudan	6.5	4.6	54	25	10	23	69	..
Sweden	1.7	1.5	10	..	..	..	99	5[d]
Switzerland	1.5	1.5	4	..	..	..	99	5[d]
Syrian Arab Republic	7.4	3.9	43	..	40	43	67	..
Tajikistan	5.6	3.4	29	..	..	..	92	65[b]
Tanzania	6.7	5.4	123	24	18	..	38	530[c]
Thailand	3.5	1.9	71	..	72	40	78	44[c]
Togo	6.8	5.1	110	..	24	..	50	480[c]
Trinidad and Tobago	3.3	1.8	42	..	..	..	98	..
Tunisia	5.2	2.2	13	..	60	50	81	70[b]
Turkey	4.3	2.4	43	11	..	70	76	..
Turkmenistan	4.9	2.9	17	..	..	..	96	110[b]
Uganda	7.2	6.5	193	29	15	..	38	510[c]
Ukraine	2.0	1.3	34	..	..	..	..	25[b]
United Arab Emirates	5.4	3.4	57	..	..	94	86	3[b]
United Kingdom	1.9	1.7	28	..	..	..	100	7[d]
United States	1.8	2.0	51	..	76	100	99	8[b]
Uruguay	2.7	2.4	69	..	..	..	96	21[b]
Uzbekistan	4.8	2.8	48	..	56	..	98	21[b]
Venezuela, RB	4.2	2.9	96	..	..	82	97	65[c]
Vietnam	5.0	2.3	34	..	75	100	79	160[c]
West Bank and Gaza	..	5.9	98	..	42	..	..	..
Yemen, Rep.	7.9	6.3	103	..	21	..	43	350[c]
Yugoslavia, FR (Serb./Mont.)	2.3	1.7	34	..	..	..	99	10[d]
Zambia	7.0	5.5	141	27	26	..	47	650[c]
Zimbabwe	6.4	3.7	87	15	48	49	69	400[d]
World	**3.7 w**	**2.7 w**	**69 w**		**49 w**	**.. w**	**52 w**	
Low income	4.3	3.1	84		24	..	35	
Excl. China & India	6.0	4.3	108		24	..	34	
Middle income	3.7	2.5	53		53	..	77	
Lower middle income	3.7	2.5	50		53	..	69	
Upper middle income	3.7	2.4	58		65	87	86	
Low & middle income	4.1	2.9	74		48	..	47	
East Asia & Pacific	3.0	2.1	26		52	..	..	
Europe & Central Asia	2.5	1.6	39		67	..	92	
Latin America & Carib.	4.1	2.7	74		59	85	78	
Middle East & N. Africa	6.2	3.5	51		55	..	62	
South Asia	5.3	3.4	116		49	21	29	
Sub-Saharan Africa	6.6	5.4	132		21	..	38	
High income	1.8	1.7	25		75	..	99	
Europe EMU	1.8	1.4	11		75	..	99	

a. Data are for most recent year available. b. Official estimate. c. Estimate based on survey data. d. Estimate by the World Health Organization and Eurostat. e. Estimate by UNICEF.

Reproductive health 2.16

About the data

Reproductive health is a state of physical and mental well-being in relation to the reproductive system and its functions and processes. Means of achieving reproductive health include education and services during pregnancy and childbirth, provision of safe and effective contraception, and prevention and treatment of sexually transmitted diseases. Health conditions related to sex and reproduction have been estimated to account for 25 percent of the global disease burden in adult women (Murray and Lopez 1998). Reproductive health services will need to expand rapidly over the next two decades, when the number of women and men of reproductive age is projected to increase by more than 300 million.

Total and adolescent fertility rates are based on data on registered live births from vital registration systems or, in the absence of such systems, from censuses or sample surveys. As long as the surveys are fairly recent, the estimated rates are generally considered reliable measures of fertility in the recent past. In cases where no empirical information on age-specific fertility rates is available, a model is used to estimate the share of births to adolescents. For countries without vital registration systems, fertility rates for 1998 are generally based on extrapolations from trends observed in censuses or surveys from earlier years.

An increasing number of couples in the developing world want to limit or postpone childbearing but are not using effective contraceptive methods. These couples face the risk of unintended pregnancy, shown in the table as the percentage of married women of reproductive age who do not want to become pregnant but are not using contraception (Bulatao 1998). Information on this indicator is collected through surveys and excludes women not exposed to the risk of pregnancy because of postpartum anovulation, menopause, or infertility. Common reasons for not using contraception are lack of knowledge about contraceptive methods and concerns about their possible health side-effects.

Contraceptive prevalence reflects all methods—ineffective traditional methods as well as highly effective modern methods. Contraceptive prevalence rates are obtained mainly from demographic and health surveys and contraceptive prevalence surveys (see *Primary data documentation* for the most recent survey year). Unmarried women are often excluded from such surveys, which may bias the estimates.

The share of births attended by skilled health staff is an indicator of a health system's ability to provide adequate care for pregnant women. Good antenatal and postnatal care improves maternal health and reduces maternal and infant mortality. But data may not reflect such improvements because health information systems are often weak, maternal deaths are underreported, and rates of maternal mortality are difficult to measure.

Household surveys such as the demographic and health surveys attempt to measure maternal mortality by asking respondents about survivorship of sisters. The main disadvantage of this method is that the estimates of maternal mortality that it produces pertain to 12 years or so before the survey, making them unsuitable for monitoring recent changes or observing the impact of interventions. In addition, measurement of maternal mortality is subject to many types of errors. Even in high-income countries with vital registration systems, misclassification of maternal deaths has been found to lead to serious underestimation. The data in the table are official estimates based on national surveys or derived from official community and hospital records. Some reflect only births in hospitals and other medical institutions. In some cases smaller private and rural hospitals are excluded, and sometimes even primitive local facilities are included. Thus the coverage is not always comprehensive, and cross-country comparisons should be made with extreme caution.

Definitions

• **Total fertility rate** is the number of children that would be born to a woman if she were to live to the end of her childbearing years and bear children in accordance with current age-specific fertility rates. • **Adolescent fertility rate** is the number of births per 1,000 women aged 15–19. • **Women at risk of unintended pregnancy** are fertile, married women of reproductive age who do not want to become pregnant and are not using contraception. • **Contraceptive prevalence rate** is the percentage of women who are practicing, or whose sexual partners are practicing, any form of contraception. It is usually measured for married women aged 15–49 only. • **Births attended by skilled health staff** are the percentage of deliveries attended by personnel trained to give the necessary supervision, care, and advice to women during pregnancy, labor, and the postpartum period, to conduct deliveries on their own, and to care for newborns. • **Maternal mortality ratio** is the number of women who die during pregnancy and childbirth, per 100,000 live births.

Data sources

The data on reproductive health come from demographic and health surveys, the World Health Organization's *Coverage of Maternity Care* (1997a), and national statistical offices.

Table 2.16a

Total fertility and access to reproductive health care among the poorest and richest, various years, 1990s

	Total fertility rate births per woman			Antenatal care received % of pregnant women			Births attended by skilled staff % of deliveries		
	Poorest quintile	Richest quintile	Average	Poorest quintile	Richest quintile	Average	Poorest quintile	Richest quintile	Average
Bolivia	7.4	2.1	4.2	39	95	65	20	98	57
Cameroon	6.2	4.8	5.8	53	99	79	32	95	64
Guatemala	8.0	2.4	5.1	35	90	53	9	92	35
India	4.1	2.1	3.4	25	89	49	12	79	34
Indonesia	3.3	2.0	2.8	74	99	89	21	89	49
Morocco	6.7	2.3	4.0	8	74	32	5	78	31
Vietnam	3.1	1.6	2.3	50	92	71	49	99	77

Note: Households are grouped into quintiles by assets.
Source: Analysis of demographic and health surveys conducted by the World Bank and Macro International.

In all regions reproductive health continues to be worst among the poor. Women in the poorest households have much higher fertility rates than those in the wealthiest—and far fewer births in the presence of skilled health professionals, contributing to higher maternal mortality ratios. Indicators of reproductive health by income level can help focus interventions where they are needed most.

2.17 Health: risk factors and future challenges

	Prevalence of anemia	Low-birthweight babies	Prevalence of child malnutrition		Consumption of iodized salt	Prevalence of smoking		Cigarette consumption	Tuberculosis		Prevalence of HIV	
			Weight for age	Height for age					Incidence			
	% of pregnant women 1985–99[a]	% of births 1992–98[a]	% of children under 5 1992–98[a]	% of children under 5 1992–98[a]	% of households 1992–98[a]	Males % of adults 1985–98[a]	Females % of adults 1985–98[a]	per smoker per year 1988–98[a]	per 100,000 people 1997	Prevalence thousands of cases 1997	% of adults 1997	People infected (all ages) 1997
Albania	..	7	8	15	..	50	8	..	28	2	0.01	<100
Algeria	42	9	13	18	92	..	..	..	44	14	0.07	..
Angola	29	..	..	..	10	..	..	..	238	56	2.12	110,000
Argentina	26	7	2	5	90	40	23	2,771	56	30	0.69	120,000
Armenia	..	..	3	12	..	..	..	..	44	2	0.01	<100
Australia	..	6	0	0	..	29	21	4,951	8	2	0.14	11,000
Austria	..	6	..	..	..	42	27	3,041	19	2	0.18	7,500
Azerbaijan	36	6	10	22	..	..	..	..	58	7	0.01	<100
Bangladesh	53	50	56	55	78	60	15	351	246	620	0.03	21,000
Belarus	..	5	..	..	37	..	..	..	65	10	0.17	9,000
Belgium	..	6	..	..	..	31	19	5,300	16	2	0.14	7,500
Benin	41	..	29	25	79	..	..	..	220	21	2.06	54,000
Bolivia	54	10	8	27	90	50	21	..	253	27	0.07	2,600
Bosnia and Herzegovina	..	..	..	..	..	..	..	..	81	5	0.04	..
Botswana	..	8	..	..	27	..	..	..	503	9	25.10	190,000
Brazil	33	..	6	11	95	40	25	..	78	194	0.63	580,000
Bulgaria	..	7	..	..	..	49	17	3,058	43	6	0.01	..
Burkina Faso	24	21	33	33	23	..	..	..	155	19	7.17	370,000
Burundi	68	16	..	..	80	..	..	..	252	16	8.30	260,000
Cambodia	..	18	..	..	7	70	10	912	539	101	2.40	130,000
Cameroon	44	13	22	29	82	..	..	..	133	35	4.89	320,000
Canada	..	6	..	..	..	31	29	3,081	7	2	0.33	44,000
Central African Republic	67	15	23	28	65	..	..	..	237	9	10.77	180,000
Chad	37	..	39	40	55	..	..	..	205	22	2.72	87,000
Chile	13	7	1	2	97	38	25	1,718	29	5	0.20	16,000
China	52	6	16	31	83	..	..	..	113	2,721	0.06	400,000
Hong Kong, China	..	5	..	..	..	29	3	2,679	95	6	0.08	3,100
Colombia	24	9	8	15	92	35	19	1,684	55	31	0.36	72,000
Congo, Dem. Rep.	..	..	34	45	90	..	..	..	263	188	4.35	950,000
Congo, Rep.	..	16	..	45	..	..	..	..	277	11	7.78	100,000
Costa Rica	27	7	5	6	89	35	20	..	18	1	0.55	10,000
Côte d'Ivoire	34	14	24	24	..	..	..	..	290	48	10.06	700,000
Croatia	..	8	1	1	70	..	..	..	64	5	0.01	..
Cuba	47	8	..	..	45	49	25	2,566	18	2	0.02	1,400
Czech Republic	23	6	1	2	..	43	31	3,187	20	2	0.04	2,000
Denmark	..	5	..	..	..	37	37	2,532	11	1	0.12	3,100
Dominican Republic	..	11	6	11	13	66	14	1,303	114	14	1.89	83,000
Ecuador	17	13	..	..	97	..	..	..	165	32	0.28	18,000
Egypt, Arab Rep.	24	12	12	25	0	..	..	..	36	35	0.03	..
El Salvador	14	9	11	23	91	38	12	..	74	7	0.58	18,000
Eritrea	..	..	44	38	80	..	..	..	227	15	3.17	..
Estonia	..	..	..	..	..	52	24	1,819	52	1	0.01	<100
Ethiopia	42	16	48	64	0	..	..	..	251	213	9.31	2,600,000
Finland	..	5	..	..	..	27	19	2,906	13	1	0.02	500
France	..	6	..	..	..	40	27	3,088	19	11	0.37	110,000
Gabon	..	10	..	..	..	..	..	..	174	4	4.25	23,000
Gambia, The	80	..	26	30	0	..	..	..	211	4	2.24	13,000
Georgia	..	..	..	..	..	..	..	..	67	5	0.01	<100
Germany	..	..	..	..	..	37	22	3,927	15	12	0.08	35,000
Ghana	64	17	27	26	10	..	..	..	214	67	2.38	210,000
Greece	..	9	..	..	..	46	28	4,877	29	3	0.14	7,500
Guatemala	45	14	27	50	64	38	18	646	85	13	0.52	27,000
Guinea	..	13	..	..	37	..	..	..	171	22	2.09	74,000
Guinea-Bissau	74	20	..	..	..	..	..	..	181	4	2.25	12,000
Haiti	64	15	28	32	10	..	..	..	385	36	5.17	190,000
Honduras	14	9	25	39	85	36	11	1,978	96	9	1.46	43,000

Health: risk factors and future challenges 2.17

	Prevalence of anemia	Low-birthweight babies	Prevalence of child malnutrition		Consumption of iodized salt	Prevalence of smoking		Cigarette consumption	Tuberculosis		Prevalence of HIV	
	% of pregnant women	% of births	Weight for age % of children under 5	Height for age % of children under 5	% of households	Males % of adults	Females % of adults	per smoker per year	Incidence per 100,000 people	Prevalence thousands of cases	% of adults	People infected (all ages)
	1985–99[a]	1992–98[a]	1992–98[a]	1992–98[a]	1992–98[a]	1985–98[a]	1985–98[a]	1988–98[a]	1997	1997	1997	1997
Hungary	..	9	..	..	..	40	27	4,949	47	7	0.04	2,000
India	88	33		53	52	70	..	..	187	4,854	0.82	4,100,000
Indonesia	64	11	34	42	62	..	..	..	285	1,606	0.05	52,000
Iran, Islamic Rep.	17	10	16	19	94	..	..	..	55	62	0.01	..
Iraq	18	24	12	22	10	40	5	5,751	160	56	0.01	..
Ireland	..	4	..	..	..	29	28	4,013	21	1	0.09	1,700
Israel	..	8	..	..	..	45	30	3,331	7	0	0.07	..
Italy	..	7	..	..	..	38	26	3,101	10	5	0.31	90,000
Jamaica	40	10	10	10	100	43	13	1,446	8	0	0.99	14,000
Japan	..	6	..	..	..	59	15	4,126	29	48	0.01	6,800
Jordan	50	2	5	8	95	..	..	..	11	1	0.02	..
Kazakhstan	27	9	8	16	53	..	..	..	104	27	0.03	2,500
Kenya	35	16	23	34	100	..	..	..	297	106	11.64	1,600,000
Korea, Dem. Rep.	71	..	32	15	5	..	..	..	178	91	0.01	..
Korea, Rep.	..	4	..	..	..	68	..	..	142	90	0.01	3,100
Kuwait	40	6	2	3	..	52	12	1,403	81	3	0.12	..
Kyrgyz Republic	..	6	11	25	27	..	..	..	99	7	0.01	<100
Lao PDR	62	18	40	47	93	62	8	949	167	17	0.04	1,100
Latvia	..	4	..	..	..	67	12	..	82	2	0.01	<100
Lebanon	49	19	3	12	92	..	..	..	26	1	0.09	..
Lesotho	7	11	16	44	73	38	1	..	407	13	8.35	85,000
Libya	..	5	5	15	90	..	..	..	19	2	0.05	..
Lithuania	..	4	..	..	..	52	10	2,509	80	5	0.01	<100
Macedonia, FYR	..	8	..	..	100	..	..	..	47	2	0.01	<100
Madagascar	..	15	40	48	73	..	..	..	205	58	0.12	8,600
Malawi	55	20	30	48	58	..	..	..	404	33	14.92	710,000
Malaysia	56	8	20	..	..	..	..	..	112	30	0.62	68,000
Mali	58	17	27	49	9	..	..	..	292	58	1.67	89,000
Mauritania	24	9	23	44	3	..	..	..	226	13	0.52	6,100
Mauritius	29	..	15	10	0	47	4	..	66	1	0.08	..
Mexico	41	8	..	..	99	38	14	1,940	41	60	0.35	180,000
Moldova	20	7	..	..	..	..	..	..	73	5	0.11	2,500
Mongolia	45	10	9	15	68	40	7	..	205	9	0.01	<100
Morocco	45	4	10	24	..	40	9	2,022	122	28	0.03	..
Mozambique	58	20	26	36	62	..	..	..	255	66	14.17	1,200,000
Myanmar	58	16	43	45	65	58	2	..	171	163	1.79	440,000
Namibia	16	..	26	29	59	..	..	..	527	12	19.94	150,000
Nepal	65	23	57	53	93	69	13	750	211	99	0.24	26,000
Netherlands	..	4	..	..	..	36	29	3,169	10	1	0.17	14,000
New Zealand	..	6	..	..	..	24	22	2,927	5	0	0.07	1,300
Nicaragua	36	15	12	25	86	..	..	..	95	5	0.19	4,100
Niger	41	15	50	41	64	..	..	..	148	32	1.45	65,000
Nigeria	55	16	39	38	98	24	7	1,131	214	442	4.12	2,300,000
Norway	..	5	..	..	..	36	36	..	6	0	0.06	1,300
Oman	54	8	23	23	65	..	..	..	13	0	0.11	..
Pakistan	37	25	38	36	19	27	4	2,354	181	583	0.09	64,000
Panama	..	8	6	10	92	..	..	..	57	2	0.61	9,000
Papua New Guinea	16	23	30	..	..	46	28	..	250	30	0.19	4,500
Paraguay	44	9	..	..	79	24	6	..	73	5	0.13	3,200
Peru	53	11	8	26	93	41	13	..	265	70	0.56	72,000
Philippines	48	11	30	33	15	..	..	..	310	481	0.06	24,000
Poland	..	9	..	..	..	51	29	4,544	44	26	0.06	12,000
Portugal	..	5	..	..	..	38	15	..	55	4	0.69	35,000
Puerto Rico	..	..	..	..	..	..	..	..	10	0	..	..
Romania	31	8	6	8	..	68	32	2,162	121	42	0.01	5,000
Russian Federation	30	..	3	13	30	67	30	2,256	106	241	0.05	40,000

2.17 Health: risk factors and future challenges

	Prevalence of anemia	Low-birthweight babies	Prevalence of child malnutrition		Consumption of iodized salt	Prevalence of smoking		Cigarette consumption	Tuberculosis		Prevalence of HIV	
			Weight for age	Height for age								
	% of pregnant women 1985–99[a]	% of births 1992–98[a]	% of children under 5 1992–98[a]	% of children under 5 1992–98[a]	% of households 1992–98[a]	Males % of adults 1985–98[a]	Females % of adults 1985–98[a]	per smoker per year 1988–98[a]	Incidence per 100,000 people 1997	Prevalence thousands of cases 1997	% of adults 1997	People infected (all ages) 1997
Rwanda	..	17	29	49	95	..	..	..	276	17	12.75	370,000
Saudi Arabia	..	..	..	..	..	53	..	3,800	46	14	0.01	..
Senegal	26	..	22	23	9	..	..	..	223	33	1.77	75,000
Sierra Leone	31	..	..	..	75	..	..	..	315	23	3.17	68,000
Singapore	..	..	..	..	..	32	3	4,250	48	2	0.15	3,100
Slovak Republic	..	6	..	..	..	43	26	2,973	35	2	0.01	<100
Slovenia	..	6	..	..	..	35	23	..	30	1	0.01	<100
South Africa	37	..	9	23	40	52	17	2,276	394	266	12.91	2,900,000
Spain	..	1	..	..	..	48	25	3,384	61	23	0.57	120,000
Sri Lanka	39	18	38	24	47	55	1	786	48	14	0.07	6,900
Sudan	36	15	34	34	0	..	..	..	180	112	0.99	..
Sweden	..	5	..	..	..	22	24	2,641	5	0	0.07	3,000
Switzerland	..	5	..	..	..	36	26	4,618	11	1	0.32	12,000
Syrian Arab Republic	..	7	13	21	40	..	..	..	75	17	0.01	..
Tajikistan	50	8	..	..	20	..	..	..	87	9	0.01	<100
Tanzania	59	14	31	43	74	..	..	..	307	124	9.42	1,400,000
Thailand	57	7	..	..	50	49	4	2,140	142	180	2.23	780,000
Togo	48	20	25	22	73	65	14	..	353	19	8.52	170,000
Trinidad and Tobago	53	10	..	..	..	..	..	..	11	0	0.94	6,800
Tunisia	38	16	9	23	98	..	..	..	40	6	0.04	..
Turkey	74	8	10	21	18	63	24	2,319	41	42	0.01	..
Turkmenistan	..	5	..	..	0	27	1	..	74	5	0.01	<100
Uganda	30	..	26	38	69	..	..	..	312	94	9.51	930,000
Ukraine	..	8	..	..	4	57	22	2,471	61	49	0.43	110,000
United Arab Emirates	..	8	7	..	..	..	..	..	21	1	0.18	..
United Kingdom	..	6	..	..	..	28	26	3,706	18	11	0.09	25,000
United States	..	8	1	2	..	28	23	4,938	7	15	0.76	820,000
Uruguay	20	8	4	10	..	41	27	..	31	1	0.33	5,200
Uzbekistan	..	6	19	31	0	..	..	..	81	29	0.01	<100
Venezuela, RB	29	9	5	15	65	29	12	1,699	42	11	0.69	..
Vietnam	52	17	40	36	65	73	4	730	189	221	0.22	88,000
West Bank and Gaza	..	..	..	..	..	..	..	..	26	1	..	..
Yemen, Rep.	..	19	46	52	39	..	..	..	111	31	0.01	..
Yugoslavia, FR (Serb./Mont.)	..	..	2	7	70	..	..	..	51	8	0.10	..
Zambia	34	13	24	42	78	..	..	..	576	61	19.07	770,000
Zimbabwe	..	14	16	21	80	36	15	..	543	74	25.84	1,500,000
World	55 w	17 w	30 w	36 w	.. w	.. w	.. w		136 w	16,146 t	0.95 w	
Low income	62	21	36	42	66	..	..		180		1.22	
Excl. China & India	51	6	37	42	68	..	..		241		2.98	
Middle income	37	8	12	19	58	50	21		101		0.71	
Lower middle income	35	9	14	22	59	..	..		126		0.92	
Upper middle income	40	8	7	12	46	46	22		64		0.41	
Low & middle income	55	18	31	37	82	..	..		157		1.06	
East Asia & Pacific	54	6	22	33	66	..	..		151		0.20	
Europe & Central Asia	39	7	8	18	72	60	27		75		0.08	
Latin America & Carib.	34	8	8	16	23	39	20		81		0.59	
Middle East & N. Africa	29	10	15	24	88	..	..		67		0.03	
South Asia	79	33	51	50	50	..	..		193		0.66	
Sub-Saharan Africa	45	..	33	40	64	..	..		267		7.28	
High income	..	7	..	..	60	37	23		18		0.36	
Europe EMU	..	5	..	..	..	39	24		22		0.28	

a. Data are for the most recent year available.

Health: risk factors and future challenges 2.17

About the data

The limited availability of data on health status is a major constraint in assessing the health situation in developing countries. Surveillance data are lacking for a number of major public health concerns. Estimates of prevalence and incidence are available for some diseases but are often unreliable and incomplete. National health authorities differ widely in their capacity and willingness to collect or report information. Even when intentions are good, reporting is based on definitions that may vary widely across countries or over time. To compensate for the paucity of data and ensure reasonable reliability and international comparability, the World Health Organization (WHO) prepares estimates in accordance with epidemiological and statistical standards.

Adequate quantities of micronutrients (vitamins and minerals) are essential for healthy growth and development. Studies indicate that more people are deficient in iron (anemic) than any other micronutrient, and most are women of reproductive age. Anemia during pregnancy can harm both the mother and the fetus, causing loss of the baby, premature birth, or low birthweight. Estimates of the prevalence of anemia among pregnant women are generally drawn from clinical data, which suffer from two weaknesses: the sample is based on those who seek care and is therefore not random, and private clinics or hospitals may not be part of the reporting network.

Low birthweight, which is associated with maternal malnutrition, raises the risk of infant mortality and stunts growth in infancy and childhood. Estimates of low-birthweight infants are drawn mostly from hospital records. But many births in developing countries take place at home, and these births are seldom recorded. A hospital birth may indicate higher income and therefore better nutrition, or it could indicate a higher-risk birth, possibly skewing the data on birthweights downward. The data should therefore be treated with caution.

Estimates of child malnutrition, based on both weight for age (underweight) and height for age (stunting), are from national survey data. The proportion of children underweight is the most common indicator of malnutrition. Being underweight, even mildly, increases the risk of death and inhibits cognitive development in children. Moreover, it perpetuates the problem from one generation to the next, as malnourished women are more likely to have low-birthweight babies. Height for age reflects linear growth achieved pre- and postnatally, and a deficit indicates long-term, cumulative effects of inadequacies of health, diet, or care. It is often argued that stunting is a proxy for multifaceted deprivation.

Iodine deficiency is the single most important cause of preventable mental retardation, and it contributes significantly to the risk of stillbirth and miscarriage. Iodized salt is the best source of iodine, and a global campaign to iodize edible salt is significantly reducing the risks (UNICEF, *The State of the World's Children 1999*).

Data on smoking are obtained through surveys. Because they give a one-time estimate of the prevalence of smoking with no information on intensity or duration, they should be interpreted with caution.

Tuberculosis is the major cause of death from a single infectious agent among adults in developing countries (WHO 1999a). In industrial countries tuberculosis has reemerged largely as a result of cases among immigrants. The estimates of tuberculosis incidence in the table are based on a new approach in which reported cases are adjusted using the ratio of case notifications to the estimated share of cases detected by panels of 80 epidemiologists convened by the WHO.

Adult HIV prevalence rates reflect the rate of HIV infection for each country's population. Estimates of HIV prevalence among adults and of the total number of people currently infected are based on plausible extrapolations from surveys of smaller, nonrepresentative groups.

Figure 2.17

Developing countries will see a rapidly growing health impact from smoking

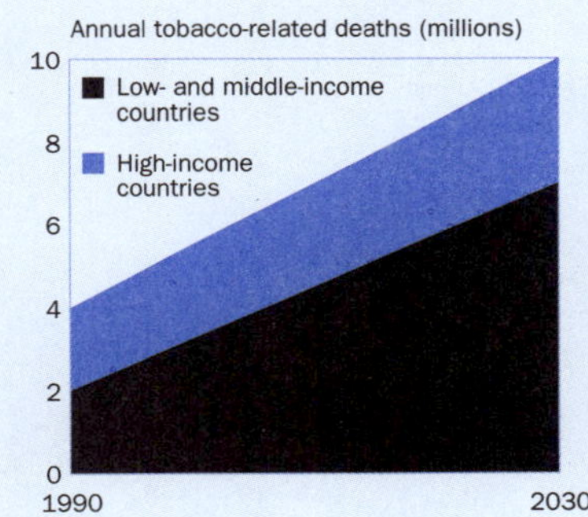

Source: WHO 1999b.

By the mid-1990s one in three adults were smokers (1.1 billion worldwide). The prevalence of smoking has been declining in high-income countries, but it has been increasing in many low- and middle-income countries.

Tobacco use causes heart and other vascular diseases and cancers of the lung and other organs. Given the long delay between starting to smoke and developing a fatal disease, the health impact in developing countries will increase rapidly in the next few decades.

Definitions

• **Prevalence of anemia,** or iron deficiency, refers to the percentage of pregnant women with hemoglobin levels less than 11 grams per deciliter. • **Low-birthweight babies** are newborns weighing less than 2,500 grams, with the measurement taken within the first hours of life, before significant postnatal weight loss has occurred. • **Prevalence of child malnutrition** is the percentage of children under five whose weight for age and height for age are less than minus two standard deviations from the median for the international reference population aged 0–59 months. For children up to two years of age, height is measured by recumbent length. For older children, height is measured by stature while standing. The reference population, adopted by the WHO in 1983, is based on children from the United States, who are assumed to be well nourished. • **Consumption of iodized salt** refers to the percentage of households that use edible salt fortified with iodine. • **Prevalence of smoking** is the percentage of men and women over 15 who smoke cigarettes. • **Cigarette consumption** shows the number of cigarettes consumed per smoker in a year. • **Incidence of tuberculosis** is the estimated number of new tuberculosis cases (pulmonary, smear positive, extrapulmonary). • **Prevalence of tuberculosis** refers to the number of people suffering from tuberculosis in 1997. • **Prevalence of HIV** refers to the percentage of people aged 15–49 who are infected with HIV. • **People infected with HIV** include all estimated cases, regardless of age.

Data sources

The data presented here are drawn from a variety of sources, including the United Nations Administrative Committee on Coordination, Subcommittee on Nutrition's *Update on the Nutrition Situation;* the WHO's *World Health Statistics Annual, Global Tuberculosis Control Report 1999,* and *Tobacco or Health: A Global Status Report, 1997;* UNICEF's *State of the World's Children 1999;* the WHO and UNICEF's *Low Birth Weight: A Tabulation of Available Information* (1992); and UNAIDS and the WHO's *Report on the Global HIV/AIDS Epidemic* (1998).

2.18 Mortality

	Life expectancy at birth		Infant mortality rate		Under-five mortality rate		Child mortality rate		Adult mortality rate		Survival to age 65	
	years		per 1,000 live births		per 1,000		Male per 1,000	Female per 1,000	Male per 1,000	Female per 1,000	Male % of cohort	Female % of cohort
	1980	1998	1980	1998	1980	1998	1988–98[a]	1988–98[a]	1998	1998	1997	1997
Albania	69	72	47	25	57	31	15	15	171	95	72	83
Algeria	59	71	98	35	139	40	..	..	158	123	72	79
Angola	41	47	154	124	261	204	..	..	416	358	36	42
Argentina	70	73	35	19	38	22	..	..	163	79	73	86
Armenia	73	74	26	15	..	18	..	..	162	79	74	86
Australia	74	79	11	5	13	6	..	..	110	56	83	91
Austria	73	78	14	5	17	6	..	..	122	60	81	90
Azerbaijan	68	71	30	17	..	21	..	..	209	99	68	83
Bangladesh	48	59	132	73	211	96	37	47	283	306	54	54
Belarus	71	68	16	11	..	14	..	..	332	116	55	81
Belgium	73	78	12	6	15	6	..	..	130	60	80	90
Benin	48	53	116	87	214	140	89	90	367	308	44	51
Bolivia	52	62	118	60	170	78	26	26	265	215	57	64
Bosnia and Herzegovina	70	73	31	13	..	..	..	..	165	93	74	85
Botswana	58	46	71	62	94	105	18	16	617	576	25	29
Brazil	63	67	70	33	80	40	8	9	279	139	59	76
Bulgaria	71	71	20	14	25	15	..	..	222	107	67	82
Burkina Faso	44	44	121	104	..	210	107	110	547	522	28	31
Burundi	47	42	122	118	193	196	101	114	554	496	26	31
Cambodia	39	54	201	102	330	143	..	..	357	309	45	51
Cameroon	50	54	103	77	173	150	69	75	336	303	47	51
Canada	75	79	10	5	13	7	..	..	106	52	83	91
Central African Republic	46	44	117	98	..	162	63	64	576	488	26	34
Chad	42	48	123	99	235	172	106	99	454	388	36	42
Chile	69	75	32	10	35	12	3	2	142	73	77	87
China	..	70	42	31	65	36	10	11	171	135	71	77
Hong Kong, China	74	79	11	3	..	..	..	..	109	56	83	91
Colombia	66	70	41	23	58	28	7	7	211	115	67	80
Congo, Dem. Rep.	49	51	112	90	210	141	..	..	422	367	39	45
Congo, Rep.	50	48	89	90	125	143	..	..	503	408	32	42
Costa Rica	73	77	19	13	29	15	..	..	115	69	81	88
Côte d'Ivoire	49	46	108	88	170	143	71	58	526	513	31	32
Croatia	70	73	21	8	23	10	..	..	216	87	68	86
Cuba	74	76	20	7	22	9	..	..	124	79	80	87
Czech Republic	70	75	16	5	19	6	..	..	177	84	73	87
Denmark	74	76	8	5	10	..	..	..	138	78	78	87
Dominican Republic	64	71	76	40	92	47	13	13	153	96	73	81
Ecuador	63	70	74	32	101	37	12	9	182	105	70	81
Egypt, Arab Rep.	56	67	120	49	175	59	22	28	195	171	66	71
El Salvador	57	69	84	31	120	36	17	20	207	119	67	79
Eritrea	44	51	..	61	..	90	89	78	511	447	34	41
Estonia	69	70	17	9	25	12	..	..	300	95	59	84
Ethiopia	42	43	155	107	213	173	..	..	562	529	26	29
Finland	73	77	8	4	9	5	..	..	139	60	78	90
France	74	78	10	5	13	5	..	..	127	51	80	92
Gabon	48	53	116	86	194	132	..	..	384	342	43	48
Gambia, The	40	53	159	76	216	..	83	79	408	344	42	49
Georgia	71	73	25	15	..	20	..	..	194	82	70	86
Germany	73	77	12	5	16	6	..	..	132	66	79	89
Ghana	53	60	94	65	157	96	63	62	282	230	55	62
Greece	74	78	18	6	23	8	..	..	114	61	82	90
Guatemala	57	64	84	42	..	52	22	24	297	195	56	69
Guinea	40	47	185	118	299	184	122	112	404	404	38	39
Guinea-Bissau	39	44	169	128	290	205	..	..	471	419	31	36
Haiti	51	54	123	71	200	116	59	58	432	339	40	50
Honduras	60	69	70	36	103	46	..	..	196	121	68	78

Mortality 2.18

	Life expectancy at birth		Infant mortality rate		Under-five mortality rate		Child mortality rate		Adult mortality rate		Survival to age 65	
	years		per 1,000 live births		per 1,000		Male per 1,000	Female per 1,000	Male per 1,000	Female per 1,000	Male % of cohort	Female % of cohort
	1980	1998	1980	1998	1980	1998	1988–98[a]	1988–98[a]	1998	1998	1997	1997
Hungary	70	71	23	10	26	12	..	..	255	105	64	83
India	54	63	115	70	177	83	29	42	215	204	62	65
Indonesia	55	65	90	43	125	52	19	20	237	186	62	70
Iran, Islamic Rep.	60	71	87	26	126	33	..	..	161	150	72	76
Iraq	62	59	80	103	95	125	..	..	197	171	59	63
Ireland	73	76	11	6	14	7	..	..	135	73	79	88
Israel	73	78	16	6	19	8	..	..	110	68	83	89
Italy	74	78	15	5	17	6	..	..	117	53	81	91
Jamaica	71	75	33	21	39	24	..	..	140	86	77	86
Japan	76	81	8	4	11	5	..	..	98	45	85	93
Jordan	..	71	41	27	..	31	4	7	158	119	73	80
Kazakhstan	67	65	33	22	..	29	10	5	382	167	49	74
Kenya	55	51	75	76	115	124	36	38	442	418	39	42
Korea, Dem. Rep.	67	63	32	54	43	68	..	..	267	200	58	67
Korea, Rep.	67	73	26	9	27	11	..	..	204	94	69	85
Kuwait	71	77	27	12	35	13	..	..	125	65	80	89
Kyrgyz Republic	65	67	43	26	..	41	10	11	303	140	57	77
Lao PDR	45	54	127	96	200	..	..	..	376	320	43	50
Latvia	69	70	20	15	26	19	..	..	301	102	58	83
Lebanon	65	70	48	27	..	30	..	..	176	132	71	78
Lesotho	53	55	119	93	168	144	..	..	320	286	48	54
Libya	60	70	70	23	80	27	6	5	185	129	70	79
Lithuania	71	72	20	9	24	12	..	..	264	87	63	86
Macedonia, FYR	..	73	54	16	69	18	..	..	162	104	74	83
Madagascar	51	58	119	92	216	146	75	68	273	231	53	59
Malawi	44	42	169	134	265	229	126	114	464	483	31	31
Malaysia	67	72	30	8	42	12	4	4	186	113	71	82
Mali	42	50	184	117	..	218	136	138	404	325	39	47
Mauritania	47	54	120	90	175	140	..	..	345	294	46	52
Mauritius	66	71	32	19	40	22	..	..	202	96	69	84
Mexico	67	72	51	30	74	35	15	17	165	84	72	84
Moldova	66	67	35	18	..	22	..	..	315	176	57	74
Mongolia	58	66	82	50	..	60	..	..	201	165	65	71
Morocco	58	67	99	49	152	61	21	19	203	147	65	74
Mozambique	44	45	145	134	..	213	84	82	408	364	36	40
Myanmar	52	60	109	78	134	118	..	..	270	223	55	62
Namibia	53	54	90	67	114	112	30	34	383	364	45	48
Nepal	48	58	132	77	180	107	..	..	273	309	54	53
Netherlands	76	78	9	5	11	7	..	..	121	62	81	90
New Zealand	73	77	13	5	16	7	..	..	120	65	81	89
Nicaragua	59	68	84	36	143	42	12	11	208	139	66	76
Niger	42	46	135	118	317	250	184	202	453	352	34	43
Nigeria	46	53	99	76	196	119	118	202	401	339	43	50
Norway	76	78	8	4	11	6	..	..	112	58	82	91
Oman	60	73	41	18	95	25	..	..	141	106	76	82
Pakistan	55	62	127	91	161	120	22	37	172	152	64	68
Panama	70	74	32	21	36	25	..	..	139	82	77	85
Papua New Guinea	51	58	78	59	..	76	28	21	348	331	49	53
Paraguay	67	70	50	24	61	27	10	12	203	129	68	79
Peru	60	69	81	40	126	47	19	20	199	123	67	78
Philippines	61	69	52	32	81	40	21	19	197	149	68	75
Poland	70	73	26	10	..	11	..	..	208	85	69	86
Portugal	71	75	24	8	31	8	..	..	151	71	76	88
Puerto Rico	74	76	19	10	..	..	..	..	156	61	75	89
Romania	69	69	29	21	36	25	7	5	256	122	62	80
Russian Federation	67	67	22	17	..	20	3	2	364	128	52	79

2.18 Mortality

	Life expectancy at birth		Infant mortality rate		Under-five mortality rate		Child mortality rate		Adult mortality rate		Survival to age 65	
	years		per 1,000 live births		per 1,000		Male per 1,000	Female per 1,000	Male per 1,000	Female per 1,000	Male % of cohort	Female % of cohort
	1980	1998	1980	1998	1980	1998	1988–98[a]	1988–98[a]	1998	1998	1997	1997
Rwanda	46	41	128	123	..	205	87	73	578	527	24	28
Saudi Arabia	61	72	65	20	85	26	..	..	165	138	73	78
Senegal	45	52	117	69	..	121	76	74	456	385	38	46
Sierra Leone	35	37	190	169	336	283	..	..	544	483	23	28
Singapore	71	77	12	4	13	6	..	..	131	75	80	88
Slovak Republic	70	73	21	9	23	10	..	..	207	90	69	85
Slovenia	70	75	15	5	18	7	..	..	169	75	74	88
South Africa	57	63	67	51	91	83	..	..	282	194	57	68
Spain	76	78	12	5	16	7	..	..	124	56	81	91
Sri Lanka	68	73	34	16	48	18	10	9	153	97	75	84
Sudan	48	55	94	69	145	105	62	63	378	333	46	51
Sweden	76	79	7	4	9	5	..	..	104	54	84	91
Switzerland	76	79	9	4	11	5	..	..	106	50	83	92
Syrian Arab Republic	62	69	56	28	73	32	..	..	203	138	67	77
Tajikistan	66	69	58	23	..	33	..	..	233	142	64	77
Tanzania	50	47	108	85	176	136	59	52	521	482	31	35
Thailand	64	72	49	29	58	33	11	11	206	116	67	79
Togo	49	49	100	78	188	144	75	90	488	444	34	39
Trinidad and Tobago	68	73	35	16	40	18	4	3	161	101	74	83
Tunisia	62	72	69	28	100	32	19	19	166	142	72	77
Turkey	61	69	109	38	133	42	12	14	186	122	68	78
Turkmenistan	64	66	54	33	..	44	..	..	282	159	58	74
Uganda	48	42	116	101	180	170	82	72	579	615	25	23
Ukraine	69	67	17	14	..	17	..	..	351	135	53	79
United Arab Emirates	68	75	55	8	..	10	..	..	127	92	80	85
United Kingdom	74	77	12	6	14	7	..	..	122	66	81	89
United States	74	77	13	7	15	..	..	..	133	68	79	89
Uruguay	70	74	37	16	42	19	..	..	171	76	73	87
Uzbekistan	67	69	47	22	..	29	15	9	229	126	65	79
Venezuela, RB	68	73	36	21	42	25	..	..	157	89	74	84
Vietnam	63	68	57	34	105	42	..	..	225	153	65	75
West Bank and Gaza	..	71	..	24	..	26	10	7	167	109	72	81
Yemen, Rep.	49	56	141	82	198	96	33	36	335	333	48	50
Yugoslavia, FR (Serb./Mont.)	70	72	33	13	..	16	..	..	178	107	72	82
Zambia	50	43	90	114	149	192	96	93	521	545	29	28
Zimbabwe	55	51	80	73	108	125	26	26	470	417	37	43
World	**61 w**	**67 w**	**80 w**	**54 w**	**123 w**	**75 w**	**32 w**	**41 w**	**216 w**	**163 w**	**69 w**	**78 w**
Low income	..	63	97	68	150	92	37	48	235	208	64	69
Excl. China & India	51	57	114	83	177	125	62	78	329	292	52	58
Middle income	65	69	60	31	89	39	..	..	230	126	63	80
Lower middle income	64	68	62	35	..	44	15	15	244	137	61	78
Upper middle income	66	71	57	26	72	31	..	..	210	110	68	82
Low & middle income	58	65	87	59	135	79	32	41	234	183	64	73
East Asia & Pacific	..	69	55	35	82	43	12	13	188	145	69	76
Europe & Central Asia	68	69	41	22	..	26	..	..	283	120	59	80
Latin America & Carib.	65	70	61	31	78	38	13	14	216	116	67	81
Middle East & N. Africa	59	68	95	45	136	55	..	..	187	159	68	73
South Asia	54	62	119	75	180	89	29	42	220	213	62	65
Sub-Saharan Africa	48	50	115	92	188	151	92	114	432	383	40	46
High income	74	78	12	6	15	6	..	..	123	61	81	90
Europe EMU	74	78	12	5	16	6	..	..	127	59	80	90

a. Data are for the most recent year available.

Mortality 2.18

About the data

Mortality rates for different age groups—infants, children, or adults—and overall indicators of mortality—life expectancy at birth or survival to a given age—are important indicators of the health status in a country. Because data on the incidence or prevalence of diseases (morbidity data) frequently are unavailable, mortality rates are often used to identify vulnerable populations. And they are among the indicators most frequently used to compare levels of socioeconomic development across countries.

The main sources of mortality data are vital registration systems and direct or indirect estimates based on sample surveys or censuses. A complete vital registration system—that is, a system covering at least 90 percent of the population—is the best source of age-specific mortality data. But such systems are fairly uncommon in developing countries. Thus estimates must be obtained from sample surveys or derived by applying indirect estimation techniques to registration, census, or survey data. Survey data are subject to recall error, and surveys estimating infant deaths require large samples, because households in which a birth or an infant death has occurred during a given year cannot ordinarily be preselected for sampling. Indirect estimates rely on estimated actuarial ("life") tables that may be inappropriate for the population concerned. Because life expectancy at birth is constructed using infant mortality data and life tables, similar reliability issues arise for this indicator.

Life expectancy at birth and age-specific mortality rates for 1998 are generally estimates based on vital registration or the most recent census or survey available (see *Primary data documentation*). Extrapolations based on outdated surveys may not be reliable for monitoring changes in health status or for comparative analytical work.

Infant and child mortality rates are higher for boys than for girls in countries in which parental gender preferences are absent. Child mortality captures the effect of gender discrimination better than does infant mortality, as malnutrition and medical interventions are more important in this age group. Where female child mortality is higher, as in some countries in South Asia, it is likely that girls have unequal access to resources.

Adult mortality rates have increased in many countries in Sub-Saharan Africa as well as in Eastern Europe and the countries of the former Soviet Union. In Sub-Saharan Africa the increase stems from AIDS-related mortality and affects both men and women. In Europe and Central Asia the causes are more diverse and affect men more. They include a high prevalence of smoking, a high-fat diet, excessive alcohol use, and stressful conditions related to the economic transition.

The percentage of a cohort surviving to age 65 combines child and adult mortality rates. Like life expectancy, it is a synthetic measure that is based on current age-specific mortality rates and used in the construction of life tables. It shows that in countries where mortality is high, a certain share of the current birth cohort will live well beyond the life expectancy at birth, while in low-mortality countries close to 90 percent will reach at least age 65.

Figure 2.18

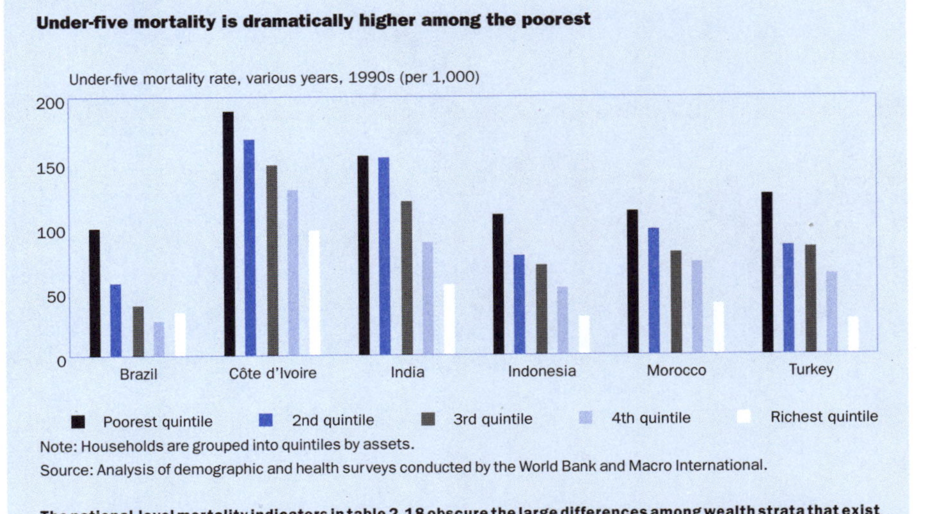

Note: Households are grouped into quintiles by assets.
Source: Analysis of demographic and health surveys conducted by the World Bank and Macro International.

The national-level mortality indicators in table 2.18 obscure the large differences among wealth strata that exist in most countries. The under-five mortality rate in the poorest quintile is often at least twice that in the wealthiest.

Definitions

• **Life expectancy at birth** is the number of years a newborn infant would live if prevailing patterns of mortality at the time of its birth were to stay the same throughout its life. • **Infant mortality rate** is the number of infants who die before reaching one year of age, per 1,000 live births in a given year. • **Under-five mortality rate** is the probability that a newborn baby will die before reaching age five, if subject to current age-specific mortality rates. • **Child mortality rate** is the probability of dying between the ages of one and five, if subject to current age-specific mortality rates. • **Adult mortality rate** is the probability of dying between the ages of 15 and 60—that is, the probability of a 15-year-old dying before reaching age 60, if subject to current age-specific mortality rates between ages 15 and 60. • **Survival to age 65** refers to the percentage of a cohort of newborn infants who would survive to age 65, if subject to current age-specific mortality rates.

Data sources

The data in the table are from the United Nations Statistics Division's *Population and Vital Statistics Report;* demographic and health surveys from national sources and Macro International; and UNICEF's *State of the World's Children 2000.*

ENVIRONMENT

Rural and urban development can bring relief to more than 1.2 billion poor. But only with more attention to the links between development and the environment, including the environment's impact on health and the productive capacity of natural resources, can development be sustainable.

More people are using more natural resources than ever, and demand will only increase. Food supply needs to double in the next 35 years to satisfy the growth of populations and economies. This will happen, to a large extent, at the expense of forests, wetlands, and biodiversity. More than a fifth of the world's tropical forests have been cleared since 1960, and at least 484 animal species and 654 plant species have become extinct since 1600 (Watson and others 1998).

Water stress and water scarcity affect almost half a billion people; in 25 years that number will rise to 3 billion. Without efficient management, existing freshwater supply cannot meet the needs of growing populations in many countries. Millions of people die every year from contaminated water—almost all of them in low- and middle-income countries. And the irony is that the poor pay more than the rich for potable water (World Bank 1999d).

To balance demand for growth and the use of resources and to monitor their environmental impact, we need information on how the environment is changing and how its degradation affects the poor—in both rural and urban areas. But lack of meaningful data with meaningful breakdowns constrains the efforts to address the consequences of rural and urban development.

Rural development should preserve the environment

Poverty is overwhelmingly rural, with about 70 percent of the poorest people in developing countries in rural areas. Although the number and proportion of poor people in cities are expected to grow rapidly in the next decades, the majority of the poor will continue to live in the countryside. Reducing poverty and ending hunger thus requires more attention to the rural economy and rural development.

Environmental problems affect the poor for several reasons. Dirty water and dirty air are major causes of diarrhea and respiratory infections, the two biggest killers of poor children. And standing water and accumulated solid waste promote the transmission of malaria and dengue fever.

Poor people are often more vulnerable to environmental changes because they use natural resources directly and because they have fewer alternative

Figure 3a

The world has shifted toward cleaner energy . . .

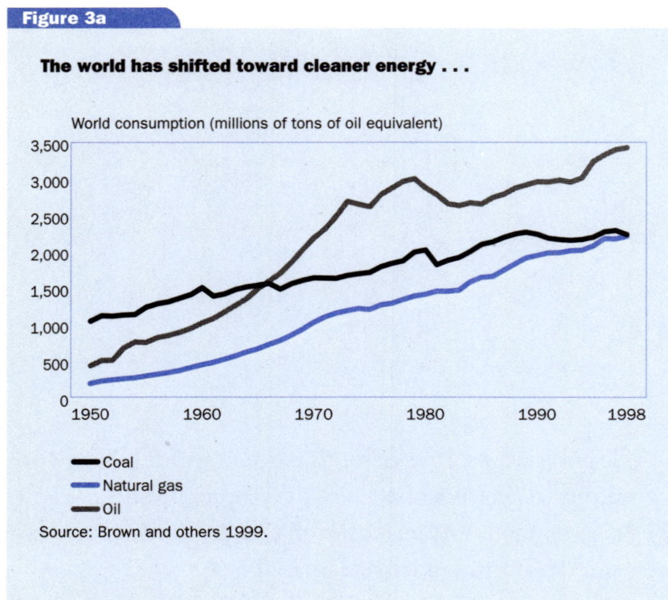

Source: Brown and others 1999.

Figure 3b

. . . and the trend is expected to continue

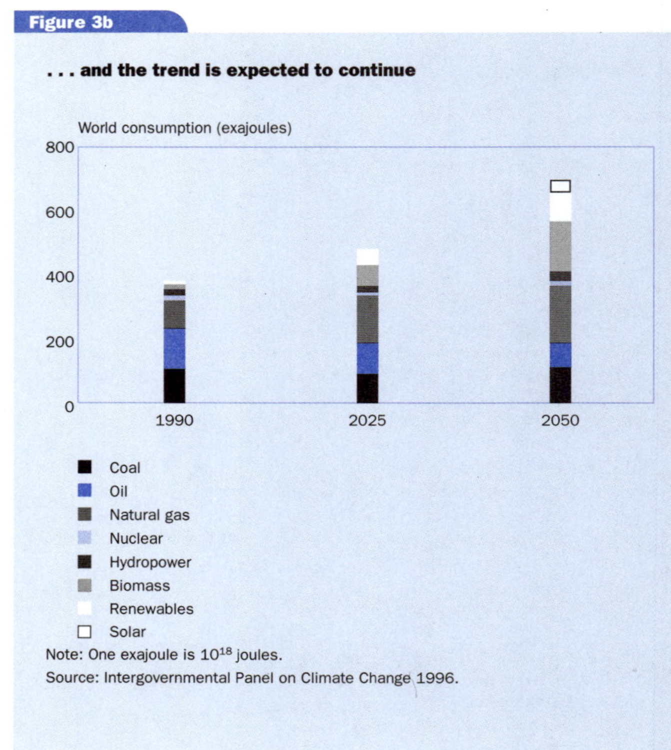

Note: One exajoule is 10^{18} joules.
Source: Intergovernmental Panel on Climate Change 1996.

ways to earn income, fewer alternative places to live, and fewer mechanisms for coping with shocks. And the rural poor are vulnerable because they often live on marginal land and in unstable housing—places most susceptible to natural disasters and extreme weather.

Agricultural production—now keeping pace with population growth in developing countries—contributes to environmental degradation and suffers from it. Unsustainable farming methods—such as the excessive use of pesticides and fertilizer—reduce biodiversity, degrade soil, and pollute water. In some parts of the world poor farming techniques are the leading cause of deforestation, as farmers continually seek to expand their landholdings and improve their economic condition.

Environmental damage can also harm agriculture. The destruction of watersheds dries up sources of irrigation, while pollution destroys fisheries and reduces crop yields. These lead to increased use of marginal land, reducing production and perpetuating poverty for those whose livelihood depends on agriculture.

Urban development brings pollution and congestion in its wake, affecting the poor most of all

More than 2.7 billion people (almost half the world's population) live in urban areas, a number projected to reach 5.1 billion by 2030, with 98 percent of the increase taking place in developing countries. With increasing inequality between the north and the south, growing urbanization will have far-reaching consequences. Already close to 30 percent of the developing world's urban population lives below the poverty line.

The ability of cities to reap the benefits of economic growth and sustainable development will depend largely on their success in improving the quality of life—and the quality of the environment—for this growing number of urban poor. Traffic congestion in urban areas affects health, economic productivity, and quality of life. In Bangkok about half a billion dollars a year could be saved just by making peak hour traffic move 10 percent faster. The costs to health are even higher: the annual price of dust and lead pollution in Bangkok, Jakarta, and Kuala Lumpur has been estimated at $5 billion, or about 10 percent of city income (World Bank 1996a).

Just as the rural poor suffer more from pollution than their wealthy neighbors, so the urban poor bear the brunt of urban pollution. In Indonesia researchers found that factories in municipalities in the bottom quartile of income and education have organic pollution 15 times as intense as plants in communities in the top quartile. Rio de Janeiro and São Paulo also show that pollution-intensive industry dominates in poorer municipalities (World Bank 1999b).

In China the density of suspended particulate pollution rises as wages fall. Why this tragic association between poverty and pollution? Industrial production in richer areas is cleaner because citizen feedback is strong and regulation tight. Industrial facilities in areas with unskilled workers generally operate at lower efficiency and create more waste. Another cause of the disparity is the poor's lack of access to cleaner sources of energy.

No country has developed much beyond a subsistence economy without ensuring access to energy services for a large segment of its population. At the same time, providing energy services—especially through combustion of fossil fuels and biomass—can harm the environment. And this harms the poor, who must rely on inefficient and polluting sources of energy for lack of better alternatives (tables 3.7, 3.8, and 3.9). In cities, burning coal and other dirty fuels for household heating and small-scale commercial and industrial activity causes smog and acid rain. And in rural areas, burning traditional fuels in ill-designed stoves or hearths causes indoor air pollution, which damages the health of women and children.

The World Energy Council (1995) forecasts that energy use will grow 1.4 percent a year until 2020, 2.6 percent a year in devel-

Box 3a

Monitoring progress in rural development

As economies develop and incomes rise, people use a smaller share of their income for food and raw materials, and the share of agricultural and other natural resource–based activities in the economy declines. Although not the only economic activity in rural areas, agriculture is the backbone of all but the most advanced economies. Its relative decline is the primary reason for the decline in the rural population share and the high incidence of rural poverty in most countries.

Rural development is the outcome of all productive activities in rural areas—agricultural and nonagricultural. It improves the livelihood and well-being of rural people. To understand the link between rural development and rural well-being, a comprehensive view reflecting both the process of rural development and the progress toward rural well-being must be articulated. The World Bank is developing a framework for monitoring progress in rural development and rural well-being that focuses on three key development goals: an improved rural economy, a sustainable natural resource base, and sound institutions and governance.

Progress toward each goal will be monitored using a set of indicators, with poverty reduction a proxy for rural well-being. Poverty must be tackled not only by increasing incomes but also by enhancing equity and improving access to basic services. The framework emphasizes the following tasks:

- Reduce the proportion of the rural population with incomes below the poverty level.
- Improve social and physical well-being.
- Foster human development.
- Foster gender equity.
- Enhance food security.

The work on this monitoring framework has brought to the fore the immense problems in the availability, quality, and reliability of rural data in most developing countries.

Box 3b

International goal for environmental sustainability and regeneration

The international community has set a goal of implementing national strategies for sustainable development by 2005 to reverse the loss of environmental resources globally and nationally by 2015. To monitor progress toward this goal, a joint OECD–United Nations–World Bank working group has suggested the following set of indicators:

- Existence of a national strategy for sustainable development.
- Population with access to safe water.
- Land area protected.
- GDP per unit of energy use.
- Per capita carbon dioxide emissions.
- Forest area.

oping countries. This growth has major environmental implications, particularly for the level of pollution and for future emissions of greenhouse gases and their likely impact on climate change. Fortunately, the recent shift toward cleaner energy sources is expected to continue (figures 3a and 3b). But even in scenarios with fairly optimistic assumptions about the growth of hydropower and other forms of renewable energy, carbon emissions from burning fossil fuels are predicted to double by 2050.

Strike a balance between growth and resource use by measuring and monitoring

Successful rural and urban development requires close monitoring of the impact of policy. Monitoring requires meaningful data broken down along rural and urban lines, reflecting the different characteristics of rural and urban development. But today's coverage of rural and environmental indicators is sparse.

Another problem: many environmental indicators have little meaning at the national level. Some national activities have transnational consequences, and some environmental issues are highly localized and location specific. So in many cases global, regional, or rural and city indicators are more meaningful than national aggregates (tables 3.11 and 3.13). Moreover, even on a national level many relevant indicators cannot be compiled because adequate or comparable data are lacking. And many do not capture depletion of natural resources—a serious constraint on measuring the state of the environment and designing sound policies.

Another policy-relevant issue is how to present national accounts and thus economic growth. Because the standard national account estimates do not reflect environmental depletion and degradation, they often send false policy signals to nations aiming for environmentally sustainable development. "Green GNP," which integrates environmental depletion and degradation, is one indicator gaining currency. While a greener measure of GNP would have some policy use, a related measure—genuine savings (table 3.15)—gets directly to the question of whether a country is on a sustainable path, making the data more useful for policymakers. The genuine savings measure links environment and economy by accounting for depletion and degradation of natural resources.

To examine the links between growth, environment, and poverty and the role of rural development in reducing poverty and improving rural well-being, new approaches to monitoring rural development, resource use, and environmental sustainability are being developed (boxes 3a and 3b). World Bank publications contribute to this work. *Rural Development: From Vision to Action*—a broad strategy to develop rural economies—identifies four goals that a country can use to assess its rural development (World Bank 1997e). *Fuel for Thought: Environmental Strategy for the Energy Sector* attempts to improve understanding of the nexus of energy and the environment (World Bank 1999a). And a new environmental strategy emphasizes understanding the contribution of environmental activities to poverty reduction.

3.1 Rural environment and land use

	Rural population			Rural population density	Land area	Land use					
	% of total		average annual % growth	people per sq. km of arable land	thousand sq. km	Arable land % of land area		Permanent cropland % of land area		Other % of land area	
	1980	**1998**	**1980–98**	**1997**	**1997**	**1980**	**1997**	**1980**	**1997**	**1980**	**1997**
Albania	66	60	0.6	344	27	21.4	21.1	4.3	4.6	74.4	74.4
Algeria	57	41	0.8	163	2,382	2.9	3.2	0.3	0.2	96.8	96.6
Angola	79	67	2.1	263	1,247	2.3	2.4	0.4	0.4	97.3	97.2
Argentina	17	11	–1.2	16	2,737	9.1	9.1	0.8	0.8	90.1	90.1
Armenia	34	31	0.6	236	28	..	17.5	..	2.3	..	80.2
Australia	14	15	1.8	5	7,682	5.7	6.9	0.0	0.0	94.2	93.1
Austria	35	35	0.6	205	83	18.6	16.9	1.2	1.0	80.2	82.1
Azerbaijan	47	43	1.0	205	87	..	19.3	..	3.0	..	77.7
Bangladesh	86	77	1.5	1,204	130	68.3	60.8	2.0	2.5	29.6	36.7
Belarus	44	29	–1.7	49	207	..	29.8	..	0.7	..	69.5
Belgium	5	3	–2.5	..	33 [a]	23.2 [a]	23.4 [a]	0.4 [a]	0.5 [a]	76.4 [a]	76.1 [a]
Benin	73	59	1.9	240	111	12.2	13.1	0.8	1.4	87.0	85.6
Bolivia	55	39	0.3	163	1,084	1.7	1.7	0.2	0.2	98.1	98.1
Bosnia and Herzegovina	65	58	–1.5	425	51	..	9.8	..	2.9	..	87.3
Botswana	85	51	–0.1	229	567	0.7	0.6	0.0	0.0	99.3	99.4
Brazil	34	20	–1.3	63	8,457	4.6	6.3	1.2	1.4	94.2	92.3
Bulgaria	39	31	–1.7	60	111	34.6	39.0	3.2	1.8	62.2	59.2
Burkina Faso	92	83	1.9	257	274	10.0	12.4	0.1	0.2	89.8	87.4
Burundi	96	92	2.4	766	26	35.8	30.0	10.1	12.9	54.0	57.2
Cambodia	88	85	2.9	259	177	11.3	21.0	0.4	0.6	88.3	78.4
Cameroon	69	53	1.3	125	465	12.7	12.8	2.2	2.6	85.1	84.6
Canada	24	23	1.0	15	9,221	4.9	4.9	0.0	0.0	95.0	95.0
Central African Republic	65	60	1.9	106	623	3.0	3.1	0.1	0.1	96.9	96.8
Chad	81	77	2.4	169	1,259	2.5	2.6	0.0	0.0	97.5	97.4
Chile	19	15	0.4	111	749	5.1	2.6	0.3	0.4	94.6	96.9
China[b]	80	69	0.5	685	9,326	10.4	13.3	0.4	1.2	89.3	85.5
Hong Kong, China	9	0	*–37.2*	0	1	7.0	5.1	*1.0*	1.0	*92.0*	93.9
Colombia	36	27	0.4	568	1,039	3.6	1.9	1.4	2.4	95.0	95.7
Congo, Dem. Rep.	71	70	3.2	493	2,267	2.9	3.0	0.4	0.5	96.6	96.5
Congo, Rep.	59	39	0.5	773	342	0.4	0.4	0.1	0.1	99.5	99.5
Costa Rica	57	53	2.0	813	51	5.5	4.4	4.4	5.5	90.1	90.1
Côte d'Ivoire	65	55	2.3	267	318	6.1	9.3	7.2	13.8	86.6	76.9
Croatia	50	43	–0.9	150	56	..	23.6	..	2.2	..	74.2
Cuba	32	25	–0.6	75	110	23.9	33.7	6.4	6.8	69.7	59.5
Czech Republic	25	25	0.1	85	77	..	40.0	..	3.1	..	56.9
Denmark	16	15	–0.4	33	42	62.3	55.7	0.3	0.2	37.4	44.1
Dominican Republic	50	36	0.3	293	48	22.1	21.1	7.2	9.9	70.6	69.0
Ecuador	53	37	0.3	286	277	5.6	5.7	3.3	5.2	91.1	89.2
Egypt, Arab Rep.	56	55	2.2	1,177	995	2.3	2.8	0.2	0.5	97.5	96.7
El Salvador	58	54	1.1	570	21	26.9	27.3	11.7	12.1	61.4	60.6
Eritrea	87	82	2.5	794	101	..	3.9	..	0.0	..	96.1
Estonia	30	31	0.0	40	42	..	26.7	..	0.4	..	73.0
Ethiopia	90	83	2.3	508	1,000	..	9.9	..	0.6	..	89.5
Finland	40	34	–0.6	83	305	7.8	7.0	..	0.0	..	93.0
France	27	25	0.1	80	550	31.8	33.3	2.5	2.1	65.7	64.6
Gabon	50	21	–2.0	78	258	1.1	1.3	0.6	0.7	98.2	98.1
Gambia, The	80	69	2.9	421	10	15.5	19.5	0.4	0.5	84.1	80.0
Georgia	48	40	–0.6	283	70	..	11.2	..	4.1	..	84.7
Germany	17	13	–1.3	91	349	34.4	33.9	1.4	0.7	64.1	65.5
Ghana	69	63	2.6	398	228	8.4	12.5	7.5	7.5	84.2	80.0
Greece	42	40	0.3	150	129	22.5	21.9	7.9	8.5	69.6	69.6
Guatemala	63	61	2.4	471	108	11.7	12.5	4.4	5.0	83.9	82.4
Guinea	81	69	1.8	542	246	2.9	3.6	1.8	2.4	95.4	94.0
Guinea-Bissau	83	77	1.7	294	28	9.1	10.7	1.1	1.8	89.9	87.6
Haiti	76	66	1.1	885	28	19.8	20.3	12.5	12.7	67.7	67.0
Honduras	65	49	1.5	178	112	13.9	15.1	1.8	3.1	84.3	81.7

Rural environment and land use 3.1

	Rural population			Rural population density	Land area	Land use					
	% of total		average annual % growth	people per sq. km of arable land	thousand sq. km	Arable land % of land area		Permanent cropland % of land area		Other % of land area	
	1980	1998	1980–98	1997	1997	1980	1997	1980	1997	1980	1997
Hungary	43	36	–1.3	77	92	54.4	52.2	3.3	2.5	42.2	45.3
India	77	72	1.6	431	2,973	54.8	54.5	1.8	2.7	43.4	42.9
Indonesia	78	61	0.4	696	1,812	9.9	9.9	4.4	7.2	85.6	82.9
Iran, Islamic Rep.	50	39	1.2	137	1,622	8.0	10.9	0.5	1.0	91.5	88.0
Iraq	35	29	1.9	134	437	12.0	11.9	0.4	0.8	87.6	87.3
Ireland	45	41	–0.1	114	69	16.1	19.5	0.0	0.0	83.9	80.5
Israel	11	9	1.3	151	21	15.8	17.0	4.3	4.2	80.0	78.8
Italy	33	33	0.1	231	294	32.2	28.2	10.0	9.0	57.7	62.8
Jamaica	53	45	0.1	666	11	12.5	16.1	9.7	9.2	77.8	74.7
Japan	24	21	–0.2	696	377	11.4	10.4	1.6	1.0	87.0	88.6
Jordan	40	27	2.1	478	89	3.4	2.9	0.4	1.5	96.2	95.6
Kazakhstan	46	44	0.1	23	2,671	..	11.2	..	0.1	..	88.7
Kenya	84	69	2.1	498	569	6.7	7.0	0.8	0.9	92.5	92.1
Korea, Dem. Rep.	43	40	1.2	545	120	13.4	14.1	2.4	2.5	84.2	83.4
Korea, Rep.	43	20	–3.5	542	99	20.9	17.5	1.4	2.0	77.8	80.5
Kuwait	10	3	–6.7	832	18	0.1	0.3	..	0.1	..	99.6
Kyrgyz Republic	62	66	1.8	226	192	..	7.0	..	0.4	..	92.6
Lao PDR	87	78	1.9	474	231	2.9	3.5	0.1	0.2	97.0	96.3
Latvia	32	31	–0.3	42	62	..	29.0	..	0.5	..	70.5
Lebanon	26	11	–2.9	268	10	20.5	17.6	8.9	12.5	70.6	69.9
Lesotho	87	74	1.5	461	30	9.6	10.7	..	..	..	..
Libya	31	13	–1.7	39	1,760	1.0	1.0	0.2	0.2	98.8	98.8
Lithuania	39	32	–0.6	40	65	..	45.5	..	0.9	..	53.6
Macedonia, FYR	47	39	–0.8	129	25	..	23.9	..	1.9	..	74.1
Madagascar	82	72	2.0	399	582	4.3	4.4	0.9	0.9	94.8	94.7
Malawi	91	78	2.2	512	94	13.3	16.8	0.9	1.3	85.8	81.8
Malaysia	58	44	1.2	534	329	3.0	5.5	11.6	17.6	85.4	76.9
Mali	82	71	1.9	161	1,220	1.6	3.8	0.0	0.0	98.3	96.2
Mauritania	73	45	0.0	233	1,025	0.2	0.5	0.0	0.0	99.8	99.5
Mauritius	58	59	1.1	679	2	49.3	49.3	3.4	3.0	47.3	47.8
Mexico	34	26	0.5	98	1,909	12.1	13.2	0.8	1.1	87.1	85.7
Moldova	60	54	–0.2	130	33	..	54.1	..	12.1	..	33.8
Mongolia	48	38	1.2	73	1,567	0.8	0.8	..	0.0	..	99.2
Morocco	59	46	0.6	145	446	16.6	19.6	1.1	1.9	82.3	78.5
Mozambique	87	62	–0.2	359	784	3.6	3.8	0.3	0.3	96.1	95.9
Myanmar	76	73	1.3	338	658	14.6	14.5	0.7	0.9	84.8	84.6
Namibia	77	70	2.2	140	823	0.8	1.0	0.0	0.0	99.2	99.0
Nepal	94	89	2.3	686	143	16.0	20.3	0.2	0.5	83.8	79.2
Netherlands	12	11	0.2	188	34	23.3	26.5	0.9	1.0	75.8	72.4
New Zealand	17	14	0.2	35	268	9.3	5.8	3.7	6.4	86.9	87.8
Nicaragua	50	45	2.1	85	121	9.5	20.2	1.5	2.4	89.1	77.4
Niger	87	80	2.9	159	1,267	2.8	3.9	0.0	0.0	97.2	96.1
Nigeria	73	58	1.6	245	911	30.6	31.0	2.8	2.8	66.6	66.3
Norway	30	25	–0.4	125	307	2.7	2.9	..	..	..	..
Oman	69	19	–3.0	2,967	212	0.1	0.1	0.1	0.2	99.8	99.7
Pakistan	72	64	2.0	395	771	25.9	27.3	0.4	0.7	73.7	72.0
Panama	50	44	1.3	242	74	5.8	6.7	1.6	2.1	92.5	91.2
Papua New Guinea	87	83	2.0	6,260	453	0.0	0.1	1.1	1.3	98.9	98.5
Paraguay	58	45	1.5	107	397	4.1	5.5	0.3	0.2	95.6	94.2
Peru	35	28	0.7	187	1,280	2.5	2.9	0.3	0.4	97.2	96.7
Philippines	63	43	0.4	634	298	14.5	17.2	14.8	14.8	70.8	68.1
Poland	42	35	–0.5	98	304	48.0	46.2	1.1	1.2	50.9	52.6
Portugal	71	39	–3.3	187	92	26.5	23.5	7.8	8.2	65.7	68.3
Puerto Rico	33	26	–0.4	3,008	9	5.6	3.7	5.6	5.1	88.7	91.2
Romania	51	44	–0.9	108	230	42.7	40.4	2.9	2.6	54.4	57.0
Russian Federation	30	23	–1.2	27	16,889	..	7.5	..	0.1	..	92.4

3.1 Rural environment and land use

	Rural population			Rural population density	Land area	Land use					
	% of total		average annual % growth	people per sq. km of arable land	thousand sq. km	Arable land % of land area		Permanent cropland % of land area		Other % of land area	
	1980	1998	1980–98	1997	1997	1980	1997	1980	1997	1980	1997
Rwanda	95	94	1.9	874	25	30.8	34.5	10.3	12.2	58.9	53.4
Saudi Arabia	34	15	–0.1	87	2,150	0.9	1.7	0.0	0.1	99.1	98.2
Senegal	64	54	1.7	216	193	12.2	11.6	0.0	0.2	87.8	88.2
Sierra Leone	76	65	1.4	639	72	6.3	6.8	0.7	0.8	93.0	92.4
Singapore	0	0	..	0	1	3.3	1.6	9.8	..	86.9	..
Slovak Republic	48	43	–0.3	156	48	..	30.7	..	2.6	..	66.6
Slovenia	52	50	0.0	428	20	..	11.5	..	2.7	..	85.8
South Africa	52	47	1.7	121	1,221	10.2	12.6	0.7	0.8	89.1	86.7
Spain	27	23	–0.7	63	499	31.1	28.7	9.9	9.7	59.0	61.6
Sri Lanka	78	77	1.2	1,652	65	13.2	13.4	15.9	15.8	70.9	70.8
Sudan	80	66	1.1	111	2,376	5.2	7.0	0.0	0.1	94.8	92.9
Sweden	17	17	0.4	53	412	7.2	6.8	..	..	..	..
Switzerland	43	32	–1.1	545	40	9.9	10.6	0.5	0.6	89.6	88.8
Syrian Arab Republic	53	46	2.4	146	184	28.5	26.0	2.5	4.1	69.1	70.0
Tajikistan	66	73	3.2	574	141	..	5.4	..	0.9	..	93.7
Tanzania	85	70	2.0	714	884	2.5	3.5	1.0	1.0	96.5	95.5
Thailand	83	79	1.3	281	511	32.3	33.4	3.5	6.6	64.2	60.0
Togo	77	68	2.4	143	54	36.8	38.1	6.6	6.6	56.6	55.3
Trinidad and Tobago	37	27	–0.9	466	5	13.6	14.6	9.0	9.2	77.4	76.2
Tunisia	49	36	0.4	116	155	20.5	18.7	9.7	12.9	69.7	68.5
Turkey	56	27	–2.1	67	770	32.9	34.5	4.1	3.4	63.0	62.1
Turkmenistan	53	55	3.3	158	470	..	3.5	..	0.1	..	96.4
Uganda	91	86	2.6	349	200	20.4	25.3	8.0	8.8	71.6	65.9
Ukraine	38	32	–0.7	50	579	..	57.1	..	1.7	..	41.2
United Arab Emirates	29	15	1.7	991	84	0.2	0.5	0.1	0.5	99.7	99.0
United Kingdom	11	11	0.0	99	242	28.7	26.4	0.3	0.2	71.1	73.4
United States	26	23	0.3	35	9,159	20.6	19.3	0.2	0.2	79.2	80.5
Uruguay	15	9	–1.9	25	175	8.0	7.2	0.3	0.3	91.7	92.5
Uzbekistan	59	62	2.7	329	414	..	10.8	..	0.9	..	88.3
Venezuela, RB	21	14	0.1	120	882	3.2	3.0	0.9	1.0	95.9	96.0
Vietnam	81	80	2.1	1,071	325	18.2	17.4	1.9	4.7	79.8	77.9
West Bank and Gaza	..	..	..	..	..	..	..	..	..	..	..
Yemen, Rep.	81	76	3.7	850	528	2.6	2.7	0.2	0.2	97.2	97.1
Yugoslavia, FR (Serb./Mont.)	54	48	–0.2	138	102	..	36.3	..	3.4	..	60.2
Zambia	60	61	3.0	109	743	6.9	7.1	0.0	0.0	93.1	92.9
Zimbabwe	78	66	2.0	249	387	6.4	8.0	0.3	0.3	93.4	91.7
World	**60 w**	**54 w**	**1.0 w**	**519 w**	**130,181 s**	**10.1 w**	**10.6 w**	**0.9 w**	**1.0 w**	**88.9 w**	**88.4 w**
Low income	78	70	1.2	573	41,383	11.5	12.4	0.9	1.4	87.7	86.2
Excl. China & India	78	69	1.7	576	28,963	7.0	7.8	1.0	1.3	92.0	90.9
Middle income	44	35	0.2	378	57,873	7.1	8.7	1.2	1.0	91.7	90.3
Lower middle income	49	42	0.7	449	36,096	7.5	9.2	1.3	0.8	91.2	90.0
Upper middle income	37	23	–0.9	188	21,777	6.9	7.9	1.1	1.3	92.0	90.8
Low & middle income	68	59	1.0	539	99,257	9.4	10.3	1.0	1.2	89.5	88.6
East Asia & Pacific	78	66	0.6	688	15,968	10.0	12.0	1.5	2.6	88.5	85.4
Europe & Central Asia	41	34	–0.5	123	23,844	38.6	11.9	3.1	0.4	58.3	87.7
Latin America & Carib.	35	25	0.1	253	20,064	5.8	6.7	1.1	1.3	93.1	92.0
Middle East & N. Africa	52	43	1.5	522	10,995	4.4	5.2	0.4	0.7	95.1	94.1
South Asia	78	72	1.7	531	4,781	42.5	42.4	1.5	2.1	56.1	55.5
Sub-Saharan Africa	77	67	2.0	378	23,605	5.4	6.4	0.7	0.9	93.9	92.7
High income	25	23	–0.2	190	30,925	12.0	11.7	0.5	0.5	87.5	87.8
Europe EMU	26	22	–0.5	139	2,307	27.6	26.7	4.7	4.3	67.7	69.0

a. Includes Luxembourg. b. Includes Taiwan, China.

Rural environment and land use 3.1

About the data

Indicators of rural development are sparse, as few indicators are disaggregated by a rural-urban breakdown (for some of these indicators see tables 2.7, 3.5, and 3.10). This table shows indicators of rural population and land use. Rural population is approximated as the midyear nonurban population.

The data in the table show that land use patterns are changing. They also indicate major differences in resource endowments and uses among countries. True comparability is limited, however, by variations in definitions, statistical methods, and the quality of data collection. For example, countries use different definitions of rural population and land use. The Food and Agriculture Organization (FAO), the primary compiler of these data, occasionally adjusts its definitions of land use categories and sometimes revises earlier data. (In 1985, for example, the FAO began to exclude from cropland land used for shifting cultivation but currently lying fallow.) And following FAO practice, this year's edition of the *World Development Indicators,* like last year's, breaks down the category *cropland,* used in previous editions, into *arable land* and *permanent cropland.* Because the data reflect changes in data reporting procedures as well as actual changes in land use, apparent trends should be interpreted with caution.

Satellite images show land use that differs from that given by ground-based measures in both area under cultivation and type of land use. Furthermore, land use data in countries such as India are based on reporting systems that were geared to the collection of tax revenue. Because taxes on land are no longer a major source of government revenue, the quality and coverage of land use data (except for cropland) have declined. Data on forest area, aggregated in the category *other,* may be particularly unreliable because of differences in definitions and irregular surveys (see *About the data* for table 3.4).

Figure 3.1a

Rural areas hold a shrinking share of the population everywhere . . .

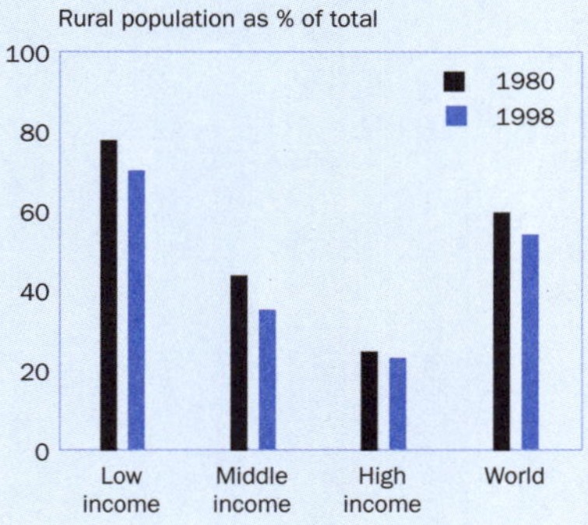

Rural population as % of total

100
80
60
40
20
0
1980
1998
Low income
Middle income
High income
World

Source: Table 3.1.

Figure 3.1b

. . . but in low-income countries rural dwellers continue to grow in number

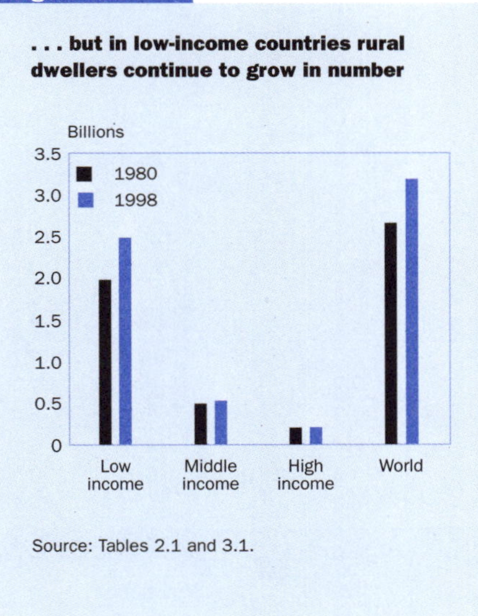

Source: Tables 2.1 and 3.1.

Definitions

• **Rural population** is calculated as the difference between the total population and the urban population (see *Definitions* for tables 2.1 and 3.10). • **Rural population density** is the rural population divided by the arable land area. • **Land area** is a country's total area, excluding area under inland water bodies, national claims to continental shelf, and exclusive economic zones. In most cases the definition of inland water bodies includes major rivers and lakes. (See table 1.1 for the total surface area of countries.) • **Land use** is broken into three categories. • **Arable land** includes land defined by the FAO as land under temporary crops (double-cropped areas are counted once), temporary meadows for mowing or for pasture, land under market or kitchen gardens, and land temporarily fallow. Land abandoned as a result of shifting cultivation is excluded. • **Permanent cropland** is land cultivated with crops that occupy the land for long periods and need not be replanted after each harvest, such as cocoa, coffee, and rubber. This category includes land under flowering shrubs, fruit trees, nut trees, and vines, but excludes land under trees grown for wood or timber. • **Other land** includes forest and woodland as well as logged-over areas to be forested in the near future. Also included are uncultivated land, grassland not used for pasture, wetlands, wastelands, and built-up areas—residential, recreational, and industrial lands and areas covered by roads and other fabricated infrastructure.

Data sources

The data on urban population shares used to estimate rural population come from the United Nations Population Division's *World Urbanization Prospects: The 1998 Revision.* The total population figures are World Bank estimates. The data on land area and land use are from the FAO's electronic files and are published in its *Production Yearbook.* The FAO gathers these data from national agencies through annual questionnaires and by analyzing the results of national agricultural censuses.

3.2 Agricultural inputs

	Arable land		Irrigated land		Land under cereal production		Fertilizer consumption		Agricultural machinery			
	hectares per capita		% of cropland		thousand hectares		hundreds of grams per hectare of arable land		Tractors per 1,000 agricultural workers		Tractors per 100 hectares of arable land	
	1979–81	1995–97	1979–81	1995–97	1979–81	1996–98	1979–81	1995–97	1979–81	1995–97	1979–81	1995–97
Albania	0.22	0.18	53.0	48.4	367	225	1,556	133	15	11	173	147
Algeria	0.37	0.26	3.4	6.9	2,968	2,785	277	80	27	41	68	122
Angola	0.41	0.26	2.2	2.1	705	837	49	16	4	3	35	34
Argentina	0.89	0.71	5.8	6.3	11,099	10,455	46	295	132	190	73	112
Armenia	..	0.13	..	51.5	..	190	..	155	..	68	..	291
Australia	2.97	2.79	3.5	5.1	15,986	16,356	269	406	751	700	75	64
Austria	0.20	0.17	0.2	0.3	1,062	838	2,615	1,688	945	1,567	2,084	2,507
Azerbaijan	..	0.21	..	74.9	..	618	..	178	..	33	..	181
Bangladesh	0.10	0.06	17.1	43.4	10,823	10,983	459	1,453	0	0	5	6
Belarus	..	0.60	..	1.8	..	2,412	..	1,101	..	124	..	175
Belgium[a]	..	..	1.7	3.8	426	323	5,323	4,150	917	1,156	1,416	1,491
Benin	0.39	0.25	0.3	0.8	525	754	12	240	0	0	1	1
Bolivia	0.35	0.23	6.6	4.1	559	750	23	54	4	4	21	28
Bosnia and Herzegovina	..	0.14	..	0.3	..	194	..	140	..	257	..	580
Botswana	0.44	0.23	0.5	0.3	153	167	32	91	9	20	54	173
Brazil	0.32	0.33	3.3	4.8	20,612	18,116	915	927	31	57	139	137
Bulgaria	0.43	0.51	28.3	18.0	2,110	1,869	2,334	441	66	63	161	62
Burkina Faso	0.39	0.33	0.4	0.7	2,026	3,014	26	90	0	0	0	6
Burundi	0.22	0.12	0.7	1.3	203	209	11	45	0	0	1	2
Cambodia	0.29	0.33	5.8	7.1	1,241	1,959	68	23	0	0	6	3
Cameroon	0.68	0.43	0.2	0.3	1,021	1,036	56	55	0	0	1	1
Canada	1.86	1.53	1.3	1.6	19,561	19,360	416	587	824	1,642	144	163
Central African Republic	0.81	0.57	..	..	194	148	5	2	0	0	1	1
Chad	0.70	0.46	0.2	0.6	907	1,758	9	33	0	0	1	1
Chile	0.34	0.14	31.1	54.3	820	633	338	2,082	43	49	86	124
China	0.10	0.10	45.1	37.7	94,647	92,911	1,494	2,882	2	1	76	55
Hong Kong, China	0.00	0.00	*37.5*	30.2	0	0	..	..	0	0	10	7
Colombia	0.13	0.05	7.7	23.7	1,361	1,208	812	2,783	8	6	77	114
Congo, Dem. Rep.	0.25	0.15	0.1	0.1	1,115	2,088	12	10	0	0	3	4
Congo, Rep.	0.08	0.05	0.6	0.5	19	5	28	238	2	1	55	52
Costa Rica	0.12	0.07	12.1	24.7	136	71	2,650	7,021	22	22	210	246
Côte d'Ivoire	0.24	0.21	1.0	1.0	1,008	1,605	261	280	1	1	16	13
Croatia	..	0.29	..	0.2	..	644	..	1,656	..	14	..	28
Cuba	0.27	0.34	22.9	20.3	224	254	2,024	593	78	95	259	207
Czech Republic	..	0.30	..	0.7	..	1,636	..	1,082	..	164	..	276
Denmark	0.52	0.44	14.5	20.5	1,818	1,525	2,453	1,890	973	1,116	708	626
Dominican Republic	0.19	0.13	11.7	17.2	149	142	572	922	3	4	20	17
Ecuador	0.20	0.13	19.4	8.1	419	1,059	471	814	6	7	40	57
Egypt, Arab Rep.	0.06	0.05	100.0	99.8	2,007	2,581	2,864	3,899	4	11	158	319
El Salvador	0.12	0.10	13.7	14.5	422	426	1,376	1,450	5	5	59	54
Eritrea	..	0.10	..	7.0	..	313	..	109	..	0	..	19
Estonia	..	0.77	..	0.3	..	323	..	244	..	495	..	443
Ethiopia	..	0.17	..	1.8	..	7,181	..	150	..	0	..	3
Finland	0.50	0.42	..	3.0	1,190	1,106	2,022	1,483	721	1,147	824	923
France	0.32	0.31	4.6	8.5	9,804	9,095	3,260	2,742	737	1,236	836	717
Gabon	0.42	0.29	0.9	1.4	6	18	20	8	5	7	43	46
Gambia, The	0.26	0.16	0.6	1.0	54	103	136	51	0	0	3	3
Georgia	..	0.14	..	43.3	..	384	..	458	..	29	..	214
Germany	0.15	0.14	3.7	3.9	7,692	6,921	4,249	2,394	624	991	1,340	1,027
Ghana	0.18	0.16	0.2	0.2	902	1,292	104	57	1	1	18	15
Greece	0.30	0.27	24.2	34.5	1,600	1,307	1,927	1,777	120	277	485	808
Guatemala	0.19	0.13	5.0	6.6	716	613	726	1,394	3	2	32	32
Guinea	0.16	0.13	7.9	6.4	708	719	16	45	0	0	3	8
Guinea-Bissau	0.32	0.27	6.0	4.9	142	128	24	10	0	0	1	1
Haiti	0.10	0.08	7.9	9.9	416	455	62	143	0	0	3	4
Honduras	0.44	0.29	4.1	3.6	421	507	163	598	5	7	21	29

Agricultural inputs 3.2

	Arable land		Irrigated land		Land under cereal production		Fertilizer consumption		Agricultural machinery			
	hectares per capita		% of cropland		thousand hectares		hundreds of grams per hectare of arable land		Tractors per 1,000 agricultural workers		Tractors per 100 hectares of arable land	
	1979–81	1995–97	1979–81	1995–97	1979–81	1996–98	1979–81	1995–97	1979–81	1995–97	1979–81	1995–97
Hungary	0.47	0.47	3.6	4.2	2,878	2,874	2,906	871	59	156	111	64
India	0.24	0.17	22.8	32.4	104,349	100,697	345	912	2	6	24	85
Indonesia	0.12	0.09	16.2	15.5	11,825	15,085	645	1,480	0	1	5	34
Iran, Islamic Rep.	0.36	0.29	35.5	37.7	8,062	8,662	430	614	17	40	57	134
Iraq	0.40	0.24	32.1	63.6	2,159	3,023	172	631	23	74	44	67
Ireland	0.33	0.37	..	..	425	296	5,373	5,228	606	978	1,289	1,259
Israel	0.08	0.06	49.3	45.5	129	84	2,384	3,260	294	322	809	731
Italy	0.17	0.14	19.3	24.9	5,082	4,165	2,295	2,264	370	913	1,117	1,814
Jamaica	0.06	0.07	13.4	12.0	4	3	1,208	1,383	9	11	156	173
Japan	0.04	0.03	62.6	62.8	2,724	2,155	4,687	3,989	209	637	3,091	5,463
Jordan	0.14	0.06	11.0	19.5	158	98	404	802	48	34	153	188
Kazakhstan	..	1.93	..	7.2	..	14,734	..	41	..	91	..	49
Kenya	0.23	0.14	0.9	1.5	1,692	1,860	160	310	1	1	17	35
Korea, Dem. Rep.	0.09	0.07	58.9	73.0	1,625	1,408	4,688	699	13	19	275	441
Korea, Rep.	0.05	0.04	59.6	60.6	1,689	1,159	3,920	5,274	1	41	14	605
Kuwait	0.00	0.00	..	75.4	0	1	4,500	1,778	3	14	220	200
Kyrgyz Republic	..	0.29	..	77.3	..	632	..	227	..	39	..	260
Lao PDR	0.21	0.17	15.4	18.6	751	631	40	56	0	0	8	11
Latvia	..	0.70	..	1.1	..	466	..	302	..	312	..	311
Lebanon	0.07	0.04	28.3	36.0	34	38	1,663	2,971	28	100	141	217
Lesotho	0.22	0.16	..	..	203	192	150	182	6	6	47	63
Libya	0.58	0.35	10.7	22.2	538	225	357	388	101	288	134	187
Lithuania	..	0.79	..	0.3	..	1,134	..	383	..	263	..	242
Macedonia, FYR	..	0.31	..	8.7	..	225	..	722	..	381	..	889
Madagascar	0.28	0.18	21.5	35.0	1,309	1,367	31	50	1	1	11	14
Malawi	0.20	0.16	1.3	1.6	1,155	1,403	246	333	0	0	10	9
Malaysia	0.07	0.09	6.7	4.5	729	700	4,273	6,125	4	23	77	238
Mali	0.31	0.45	2.9	2.1	1,346	2,237	61	81	0	1	5	6
Mauritania	0.14	0.20	22.8	9.7	125	227	85	87	1	1	13	7
Mauritius	0.10	0.09	15.0	17.0	0	0	2,547	3,593	4	6	33	37
Mexico	0.34	0.27	20.3	22.8	9,356	11,072	570	597	16	20	54	68
Moldova	..	0.41	..	14.1	..	919	..	659	..	85	..	279
Mongolia	0.71	0.52	..	6.4	559	317	83	15	32	21	82	54
Morocco	0.38	0.32	15.2	13.1	4,414	5,600	273	315	7	10	35	48
Mozambique	0.24	0.18	2.1	3.4	1,077	1,851	109	25	1	1	20	19
Myanmar	0.28	0.22	10.4	15.4	5,133	6,095	111	183	1	0	9	8
Namibia	0.64	0.51	0.6	0.9	195	322	..	..	10	11	39	39
Nepal	0.16	0.13	22.5	38.2	2,251	3,258	98	350	0	0	10	15
Netherlands	0.06	0.06	58.5	61.0	225	199	8,620	5,854	561	631	2,238	2,061
New Zealand	0.80	0.42	5.2	8.7	193	166	1,965	4,392	619	437	367	485
Nicaragua	0.39	0.53	6.0	3.2	266	396	392	160	6	7	19	11
Niger	0.62	0.52	0.7	1.3	3,872	6,505	10	19	0	0	0	0
Nigeria	0.39	0.25	0.7	0.7	6,048	18,166	59	56	1	2	3	4
Norway	0.20	0.22	..	..	311	333	3,146	2,172	824	1,276	1,603	1,486
Oman	0.01	0.01	92.7	98.4	2	3	840	4,792	1	1	76	94
Pakistan	0.24	0.17	72.7	80.8	10,693	12,420	525	1,201	5	13	50	145
Panama	0.22	0.19	5.0	4.9	166	118	692	704	27	20	122	100
Papua New Guinea	0.01	0.01	..	..	2	2	3,827	2,167	1	1	699	190
Paraguay	0.52	0.44	3.4	2.9	304	629	44	136	14	25	45	75
Peru	0.19	0.15	32.8	42.0	732	945	381	452	5	3	37	20
Philippines	0.09	0.07	14.0	16.3	6,790	6,220	765	1,354	1	1	24	22
Poland	0.41	0.36	0.7	0.7	7,875	8,821	2,393	1,107	112	281	425	927
Portugal	0.25	0.22	20.1	21.8	1,099	629	1,113	1,158	72	208	351	697
Puerto Rico	0.02	0.01	39.0	51.3	1	0	..	..	..	..	..	..
Romania	0.44	0.41	21.9	31.3	6,340	5,985	1,448	402	39	84	150	176
Russian Federation	..	0.85	..	4.0	..	51,313	..	140	..	106	..	88

3.2 Agricultural inputs

	Arable land		Irrigated land		Land under cereal production		Fertilizer consumption		Agricultural machinery			
	hectares per capita		% of cropland		thousand hectares		hundreds of grams per hectare of arable land		Tractors per 1,000 agricultural workers		Tractors per 100 hectares of arable land	
	1979–81	1995–97	1979–81	1995–97	1979–81	1996–98	1979–81	1995–97	1979–81	1995–97	1979–81	1995–97
Rwanda	0.15	0.12	0.4	0.3	239	165	3	4	0	0	1	1
Saudi Arabia	0.20	0.19	28.9	42.3	388	585	228	835	2	12	10	26
Senegal	0.42	0.26	2.6	3.1	1,216	1,176	104	91	0	0	2	2
Sierra Leone	0.14	0.10	4.1	5.3	434	376	58	62	0	0	6	11
Singapore	0.00	0.00	..	..	..	..	22,333	32,473	3	18	220	650
Slovak Republic	..	0.28	..	12.5	..	865	..	777	..	92	..	188
Slovenia	..	0.12	..	0.7	..	98	..	3,116	..	3,082	..	3,840
South Africa	0.45	0.38	8.4	7.9	6,760	5,448	874	520	94	68	140	87
Spain	0.42	0.38	14.8	18.1	7,391	6,754	1,012	1,354	200	546	335	535
Sri Lanka	0.06	0.05	28.3	30.7	864	762	1,800	2,393	4	2	276	355
Sudan	0.66	0.61	14.4	11.7	4,447	9,010	51	45	2	2	8	8
Sweden	0.36	0.32	..	..	1,505	1,254	1,654	1,084	715	958	623	592
Switzerland	0.06	0.06	6.2	5.8	172	189	4,623	2,785	494	627	2,428	2,832
Syrian Arab Republic	0.60	0.32	9.6	20.5	2,642	3,294	250	746	29	66	54	186
Tajikistan	..	0.13	..	79.7	..	308	..	805	..	38	..	366
Tanzania	0.12	0.10	3.8	3.8	2,835	3,183	143	120	1	1	45	24
Thailand	0.35	0.28	16.4	23.9	10,625	11,157	177	889	1	7	11	87
Togo	0.76	0.48	0.3	0.3	416	776	13	77	0	0	1	2
Trinidad and Tobago	0.06	0.06	17.8	18.0	4	5	1,064	1,216	50	52	337	353
Tunisia	0.51	0.32	4.9	7.6	1,416	1,452	212	316	30	39	79	123
Turkey	0.57	0.43	9.6	14.7	13,499	14,001	529	684	38	58	169	322
Turkmenistan	..	0.35	..	..	..	662	..	854	..	82	..	347
Uganda	0.32	0.25	0.1	0.1	752	1,339	2	2	0	1	6	9
Ukraine	..	0.65	..	7.4	..	12,521	..	268	..	89	..	119
United Arab Emirates	0.01	0.02	..	87.6	0	1	2,250	7,808	6	4	106	80
United Kingdom	0.12	0.11	2.0	1.7	3,930	3,431	3,185	3,600	726	883	742	832
United States	0.83	0.66	10.8	12.0	72,630	63,366	1,092	1,141	1,230	1,484	253	273
Uruguay	0.48	0.39	5.4	10.7	614	639	564	923	171	173	236	262
Uzbekistan	..	0.19	..	88.3	..	1,662	..	1,158	..	59	..	376
Venezuela, RB	0.19	0.12	3.6	5.7	814	744	711	1,116	50	59	133	183
Vietnam	0.11	0.07	24.1	31.0	5,963	7,799	302	2,566	1	4	38	178
West Bank and Gaza	..	..	..	..	..	..	..	..	..	..	..	..
Yemen, Rep.	0.16	0.09	19.9	31.3	865	732	93	77	3	2	33	41
Yugoslavia, FR (Serb./Mont.)	..	0.35	..	1.6	..	2,337	..	477	..	353	..	..
Zambia	0.89	0.56	0.4	0.9	595	729	145	103	3	2	9	11
Zimbabwe	0.36	0.27	3.1	4.7	1,633	1,964	609	536	7	7	66	81
World	**0.24 w**	**0.24 w**	**17.8 w**	**19.2 w**	**583,798 s**	**703,133 s**	**866 w**	**971 w**	**18 w**	**20 w**	**172 w**	**187 w**
Low income	0.18	0.15	25.6	29.7	294,763	336,301	550	1,175	2	3	20	59
Excl. China & India	0.23	0.18	16.2	20.0	94,142	141,284	206	430	1	3	..	..
Middle income	0.24	0.35	15.5	14.1	134,447	227,139	796	558	23	49	100	124
Lower middle income	0.18	0.38	22.3	14.9	63,168	153,297	679	396	17	32	69	90
Upper middle income	0.34	0.30	10.3	12.4	71,278	73,842	886	874	37	75	144	208
Low & middle income	0.20	0.21	21.9	21.9	429,210	563,440	640	869	4	8	62	100
East Asia & Pacific	0.11	0.11	37.0	36.3	141,594	145,454	1,162	2,329	2	2	55	61
Europe & Central Asia	0.16	0.59	11.6	10.4	33,069	127,954	1,467	344	..	101	223	172
Latin America & Carib.	0.32	0.27	11.6	13.5	49,788	49,463	587	741	25	35	95	110
Middle East & N. Africa	0.29	0.21	25.8	35.5	25,653	29,076	422	661	12	25	61	119
South Asia	0.23	0.16	28.7	39.7	132,128	130,930	360	926	2	5	26	85
Sub-Saharan Africa	0.32	0.25	4.0	4.2	46,978	80,562	160	132	3	2	23	18
High income	0.46	0.41	9.8	11.2	154,588	139,693	1,307	1,264	520	906	383	437
Europe EMU	0.23	0.21	12.6	15.8	33,970	30,003	2,705	2,247	451	841	888	955

a. Includes Luxembourg.

Agricultural inputs 3.2

About the data

Agricultural activities provide developing countries with food and revenue, but they also can degrade natural resources. Poor farming practices can cause soil erosion and loss of fertility. Efforts to increase productivity through the use of chemical fertilizers, pesticides, and intensive irrigation have environmental costs and health impacts. Excessive use of chemical fertilizers can alter the chemistry of soil. Pesticide poisoning is common in developing countries. And salinization of irrigated land diminishes soil fertility. Thus inappropriate use of inputs for agricultural production has far-reaching effects.

This table provides indicators of major inputs to agricultural production: land, fertilizers, and agricultural machinery. There is no single correct mix of inputs: appropriate levels and application rates vary by country and over time, depending on the type of crops, the climate and soils, and the production process used. The data shown here and in table 3.3 are collected by the Food and Agriculture Organization (FAO) through annual questionnaires. The FAO tries to impose standard definitions and reporting methods, but exact consistency across countries and over time is not possible. Data on agricultural employment in particular should be used with caution. In many countries much agricultural employment is informal and unrecorded, including substantial work performed by women and children.

Fertilizer consumption measures the quantity of plant nutrients in the form of nitrogen, potassium, and phosphorous compounds available for direct application. Consumption is calculated as production plus imports minus exports. Traditional nutrients—animal and plant manures—are not included. Because some chemical compounds used for fertilizers have other industrial applications, the consumption data may overstate the quantity available for crops.

To smooth annual fluctuations in agricultural activity, the indicators in the table have been averaged over three years.

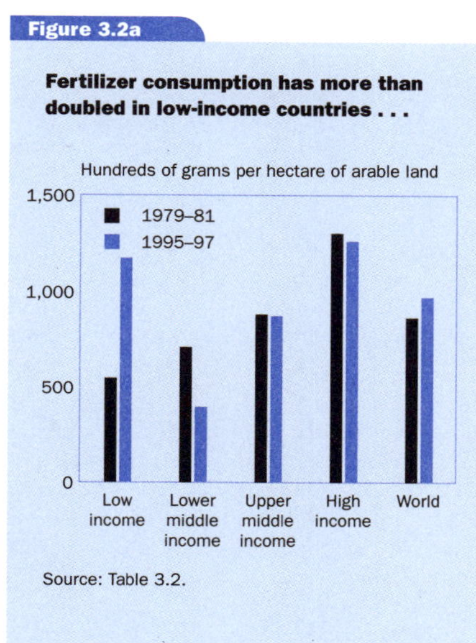

Figure 3.2a

Fertilizer consumption has more than doubled in low-income countries . . .

Source: Table 3.2.

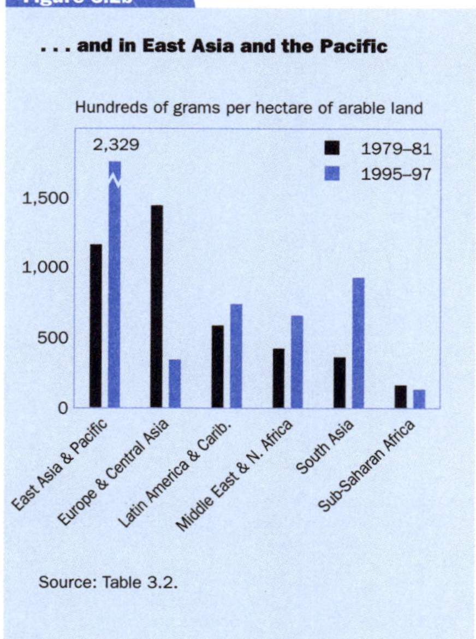

Figure 3.2b

. . . and in East Asia and the Pacific

Source: Table 3.2.

Definitions

• **Arable land** includes land defined by the FAO as land under temporary crops (double-cropped areas are counted once), temporary meadows for mowing or for pasture, land under market or kitchen gardens, and land temporarily fallow. Land abandoned as a result of shifting cultivation is excluded. • **Irrigated land** refers to areas purposely provided with water, including land irrigated by controlled flooding. Cropland refers to arable land and land used for permanent crops (see table 3.1). • **Land under cereal production** refers to harvested areas, although some countries report only sown or cultivated area. • **Fertilizer consumption** measures the quantity of plant nutrients used per unit of arable land. Fertilizer products cover nitrogenous, potash, and phosphate fertilizers (including ground rock phosphate). The time reference for fertilizer consumption is the crop year (July through June). • **Agricultural machinery** refers to wheel and crawler tractors (excluding garden tractors) in use in agriculture at the end of the calendar year specified or during the first quarter of the following year.

Data sources

The data in the table are from electronic files that the FAO makes available to the World Bank. Data on arable land, irrigated land, and land under cereal production are published in the FAO's *Production Yearbook*.

3.3 Agricultural output and productivity

	Crop production index 1989–91 = 100		Food production index 1989–91 = 100		Livestock production index 1989–91 = 100		Cereal yield kilograms per hectare		Agricultural productivity Agriculture value added per worker 1995 $	
	1979–81	**1996–98**	**1979–81**	**1996–98**	**1979–81**	**1996–98**	**1979–81**	**1996–98**	**1979–81**	**1996–98**
Albania	..	..	..	..	..	..	2,500	2,597	1,223	1,847
Algeria	77.5	128.9	67.6	129.4	55.0	119.0	656	988	1,411	1,943
Angola	102.0	141.1	91.9	130.0	87.8	113.8	526	642	..	123
Argentina	83.9	143.8	92.0	125.9	100.8	103.4	2,183	3,284	10,539	13,715
Armenia	..	110.8	..	76.8	..	58.3	..	1,772	..	4,828
Australia	79.9	150.7	91.3	130.4	85.5	106.5	1,321	1,993	20,880	*30,904*
Austria	92.8	98.5	92.2	102.3	94.5	104.7	4,131	5,673	9,761	*16,070*
Azerbaijan	..	45.8	..	60.6	..	66.3	..	1,647	..	776
Bangladesh	80.0	106.9	79.2	110.8	81.3	135.9	1,938	2,716	175	227
Belarus	..	98.2	..	65.9	..	63.8	..	2,204	..	3,509
Belgium[a]	84.9	131.2	88.5	113.0	88.8	113.7	4,861	7,728	..	..
Benin	54.2	167.5	63.5	140.6	68.9	118.1	698	1,096	311	534
Bolivia	71.2	145.7	70.9	134.1	75.5	122.3	1,183	1,603	..	..
Bosnia and Herzegovina	..	..	..	..	..	..	..	2,348	..	..
Botswana	86.3	87.5	87.2	98.7	87.5	100.2	203	255	639	676
Brazil	75.3	116.3	69.5	125.7	67.9	133.9	1,496	2,480	2,047	4,081
Bulgaria	107.7	64.4	105.5	67.8	96.3	61.0	3,853	2,657	2,754	5,135
Burkina Faso	58.6	132.0	62.1	127.8	59.9	136.4	575	820	134	161
Burundi	79.9	93.6	80.3	95.8	86.6	93.9	1,081	1,337	177	141
Cambodia	55.2	128.9	48.9	130.6	27.3	136.7	1,025	1,784	..	408
Cameroon	91.0	119.2	83.0	120.2	61.1	115.2	849	1,172	834	1,015
Canada	77.7	118.9	79.8	117.7	88.4	121.6	2,173	2,738	..	..
Central African Republic	102.8	128.2	79.7	127.9	48.9	126.3	529	927	396	462
Chad	67.1	154.6	90.8	139.1	120.4	111.4	587	647	155	217
Chile	70.7	121.6	71.5	129.6	75.8	140.3	2,124	4,608	3,174	5,039
China	67.1	135.8	60.9	153.5	45.3	185.6	3,027	4,821	161	307
Hong Kong, China	133.6	74.6	97.4	25.9	188.7	*19.7*	1,712	..	..	..
Colombia	84.3	96.0	76.0	109.7	72.6	116.0	2,452	2,798	2,370	2,693
Congo, Dem. Rep.	72.5	93.9	71.7	95.9	77.3	104.0	807	781	270	285
Congo, Rep.	83.1	109.9	81.1	112.1	80.7	118.3	838	707	385	492
Costa Rica	70.6	128.7	73.0	128.6	77.2	119.5	2,498	3,387	3,160	4,409
Côte d'Ivoire	73.8	124.7	70.8	128.5	74.7	120.0	867	1,102	1,074	1,028
Croatia	..	86.3	..	59.4	..	42.5	..	4,733	..	8,521
Cuba	84.3	62.1	89.9	63.8	96.0	62.1	2,458	1,973	..	..
Czech Republic	..	86.4	..	79.7	..	75.3	..	4,141	..	..
Denmark	65.2	94.4	83.2	103.0	95.0	112.6	4,040	6,130	21,321	..
Dominican Republic	96.5	97.0	85.2	105.4	68.8	123.4	3,024	3,841	1,839	2,599
Ecuador	78.2	134.1	77.4	143.6	73.0	151.3	1,633	1,743	1,206	1,795
Egypt, Arab Rep.	75.5	132.6	68.0	139.7	65.8	150.3	4,053	6,595	721	1,189
El Salvador	120.4	103.3	90.8	111.3	88.8	120.4	1,702	1,930	1,925	1,679
Eritrea	..	141.3	..	114.6	..	96.3	..	580	..	..
Estonia	..	69.1	..	47.0	..	41.8	..	1,931	..	3,519
Ethiopia	..	130.9	..	123.7	..	110.4	..	1,206	..	..
Finland	76.3	89.6	93.5	90.7	107.1	92.5	2,511	3,103	16,995	*28,231*
France	87.4	109.2	93.8	105.4	97.8	105.6	4,700	7,126	14,956	36,889
Gabon	76.3	111.7	79.0	108.7	86.4	112.0	1,718	1,742	1,814	1,839
Gambia, The	79.5	79.4	82.8	84.9	94.4	111.4	1,284	1,048	325	203
Georgia	..	61.7	..	85.2	..	91.9	..	1,692	..	2,120
Germany	89.4	108.6	91.2	92.3	98.7	85.2	4,166	6,366	..	22,452
Ghana	67.0	151.7	68.7	144.1	79.7	104.5	807	1,342	354	286
Greece	86.8	103.6	91.2	99.0	99.9	98.2	3,090	3,535	8,804	..
Guatemala	89.6	115.2	69.7	124.1	76.0	124.5	1,578	1,882	2,143	2,075
Guinea	89.7	135.6	96.3	137.4	116.4	134.9	958	1,294	..	271
Guinea-Bissau	64.8	116.6	68.3	117.1	78.4	117.4	711	1,410	221	315
Haiti	103.4	87.5	101.3	94.4	100.2	121.2	1,009	969	578	396
Honduras	90.4	120.0	88.2	113.0	80.8	121.7	1,170	1,528	694	1,018

Agricultural output and productivity 3.3

	Crop production index		Food production index		Livestock production index		Cereal yield		Agricultural productivity	
	1989–91 = 100		1989–91 = 100		1989–91 = 100		kilograms per hectare		Agriculture value added per worker 1995 $	
	1979–81	**1996–98**	**1979–81**	**1996–98**	**1979–81**	**1996–98**	**1979–81**	**1996–98**	**1979–81**	**1996–98**
Hungary	93.4	81.0	90.8	76.3	94.1	70.6	4,519	4,275	3,389	4,770
India	70.9	118.9	68.1	119.9	62.2	126.7	1,324	2,200	275	406
Indonesia	66.2	116.8	62.8	120.4	47.2	139.0	2,837	3,915	610	749
Iran, Islamic Rep.	56.7	144.9	61.1	144.7	68.1	139.5	1,108	1,956	2,570	4,089
Iraq	74.7	110.0	77.9	98.7	81.3	69.0	832	848	..	..
Ireland	93.9	109.0	83.3	106.2	83.3	105.6	4,733	6,721	..	..
Israel	98.2	104.8	85.4	107.0	78.2	118.3	1,840	1,869	..	..
Italy	106.1	100.4	101.4	101.2	93.0	103.6	3,548	4,920	9,993	20,031
Jamaica	98.6	127.3	86.0	120.1	73.9	110.0	1,667	1,228	894	1,291
Japan	107.9	92.6	94.0	95.2	85.1	95.6	5,252	6,017	15,655	30,272
Jordan	54.6	150.3	57.3	152.5	51.2	166.8	521	933	1,176	1,431
Kazakhstan	..	52.7	..	57.2	..	49.5	..	668	..	1,450
Kenya	74.8	110.0	67.7	104.9	60.2	102.9	1,364	1,535	262	228
Korea, Dem. Rep.	..	..	..	..	..	..	3,694	2,280	..	..
Korea, Rep.	87.8	105.9	77.6	122.2	52.6	155.2	4,986	6,450	3,745	11,760
Kuwait	37.1	142.4	93.2	161.2	108.8	168.0	3,124	5,879	..	..
Kyrgyz Republic	..	104.1	..	102.0	..	74.7	..	2,544	..	3,144
Lao PDR	73.7	113.7	70.8	126.7	58.0	164.1	1,402	2,643	..	546
Latvia	..	79.2	..	48.1	..	37.4	..	2,115	..	3,191
Lebanon	52.0	136.7	59.2	138.2	100.5	140.5	1,307	2,456	..	27,409
Lesotho	95.1	122.2	90.0	111.1	87.7	106.0	977	1,011	505	393
Libya	77.9	121.9	81.6	130.1	68.4	128.9	430	820	..	..
Lithuania	..	100.8	..	69.2	..	55.0	..	2,474	..	3,228
Macedonia, FYR	..	103.6	..	97.0	..	89.7	..	2,812	..	1,826
Madagascar	82.9	104.5	84.4	108.7	89.6	106.3	1,664	1,961	197	186
Malawi	84.1	115.7	91.1	109.7	78.2	113.8	1,161	1,224	100	136
Malaysia	74.7	108.9	55.4	125.2	41.4	146.2	2,828	3,065	3,275	6,061
Mali	57.4	128.6	77.9	114.5	94.5	116.9	804	984	224	263
Mauritania	62.1	133.0	86.5	104.7	89.4	100.8	384	810	299	449
Mauritius	92.5	101.3	89.0	111.0	63.8	137.0	2,536	5,030	3,087	5,630
Mexico	82.4	116.8	83.8	120.2	83.5	123.3	2,164	2,610	1,482	1,704
Moldova	..	68.3	..	53.2	..	41.3	..	2,861	..	1,474
Mongolia	44.6	32.1	88.1	88.5	93.2	93.8	573	687	*932*	1,151
Morocco	54.8	107.8	55.9	107.2	59.8	102.9	811	1,215	1,146	1,836
Mozambique	109.6	141.5	100.1	130.9	85.7	96.8	603	827	..	127
Myanmar	89.0	140.3	87.7	138.1	86.2	129.6	2,521	2,944	..	..
Namibia	80.6	107.8	107.4	123.5	115.9	125.9	377	315	876	1,190
Nepal	62.7	116.6	65.9	117.2	77.3	117.1	1,615	1,951	162	189
Netherlands	79.8	111.5	86.5	99.0	88.3	96.5	5,696	7,480	21,663	..
New Zealand	74.4	142.6	90.7	124.6	95.5	115.8	4,089	5,575	..	..
Nicaragua	122.8	116.7	117.0	122.7	139.7	119.0	1,475	1,611	1,620	1,821
Niger	95.1	134.1	101.4	127.8	109.8	116.6	440	354	222	195
Nigeria	52.3	142.4	57.9	142.5	82.5	135.2	1,269	1,197	414	624
Norway	91.2	94.6	92.1	100.9	95.2	105.2	3,634	4,051	17,044	32,600
Oman	60.4	113.3	62.5	111.1	61.6	99.9	982	2,167	..	..
Pakistan	65.6	116.2	66.4	136.2	59.5	145.5	1,608	2,064	392	623
Panama	97.1	81.7	85.6	99.6	71.3	125.4	1,524	2,164	2,122	2,512
Papua New Guinea	86.5	104.6	86.2	107.8	85.0	130.0	2,087	3,840	717	799
Paraguay	58.4	104.6	60.6	120.0	62.1	114.6	1,511	2,207	2,618	3,448
Peru	82.1	142.2	77.3	140.5	78.0	131.3	1,946	2,726	1,348	1,663
Philippines	87.7	113.8	86.0	125.8	73.3	160.4	1,611	2,437	1,348	1,352
Poland	84.6	89.1	87.9	88.2	98.0	84.0	2,345	2,937	..	1,752
Portugal	84.5	86.9	71.9	97.0	71.8	113.7	1,102	2,456	..	..
Puerto Rico	131.2	64.3	99.7	82.0	90.3	87.6	8,925	4,000	..	..
Romania	114.1	98.5	112.8	95.9	110.0	87.3	2,854	2,867	..	3,193
Russian Federation	..	75.6	..	64.4	..	54.8	..	1,302	..	2,476

3.3 Agricultural output and productivity

	Crop production index		Food production index		Livestock production index		Cereal yield		Agricultural productivity	
									Agriculture value added per worker	
	1989–91 = 100		1989–91 = 100		1989–91 = 100		kilograms per hectare		1995 $	
	1979–81	**1996–98**	**1979–81**	**1996–98**	**1979–81**	**1996–98**	**1979–81**	**1996–98**	**1979–81**	**1996–98**
Rwanda	88.9	75.5	89.7	79.1	81.0	95.1	1,134	1,218	316	212
Saudi Arabia	27.2	90.7	26.7	78.8	32.8	129.3	820	3,880	2,167	10,742
Senegal	77.6	88.7	74.2	100.4	65.1	134.3	690	719	341	320
Sierra Leone	80.3	99.2	84.5	99.5	84.1	108.1	1,249	1,223	368	411
Singapore	595.0	50.6	154.3	31.8	173.7	34.1	..	..	13,937	42,851
Slovak Republic	..	..	..	74.7	..	..	..	4,209	..	3,379
Slovenia	..	105.5	..	100.3	..	101.7	..	5,435	..	26,521
South Africa	95.0	104.6	92.6	100.8	89.7	90.9	2,105	2,261	2,819	3,884
Spain	83.0	108.7	82.1	110.1	84.2	116.2	1,986	3,173	..	*13,499*
Sri Lanka	99.3	108.2	98.3	109.1	93.2	131.8	2,462	3,103	648	726
Sudan	131.1	174.8	105.4	156.0	89.3	140.8	645	569	..	..
Sweden	92.0	96.9	100.1	100.8	103.8	103.3	3,595	4,687	..	..
Switzerland	95.5	99.9	95.8	95.8	98.8	93.8	4,883	6,709	..	..
Syrian Arab Republic	100.4	162.1	94.2	148.7	72.2	120.2	1,156	1,586	..	..
Tajikistan	..	64.5	..	59.0	..	41.5	..	1,682	..	396
Tanzania	82.2	96.8	76.9	100.0	69.3	113.9	1,063	1,288	..	174
Thailand	79.0	111.8	80.4	112.6	65.4	130.1	1,911	2,466	630	924
Togo	70.4	140.0	77.0	135.9	51.9	125.4	729	876	345	539
Trinidad and Tobago	119.9	96.9	101.9	99.9	84.3	96.7	3,167	3,292	2,887	2,102
Tunisia	68.5	116.4	67.6	121.4	63.7	129.6	828	1,241	1,743	2,959
Turkey	76.6	113.7	75.8	111.3	80.4	107.3	1,869	2,196	1,852	1,851
Turkmenistan	..	56.7	..	101.7	..	113.8	..	1,292	..	..
Uganda	67.5	110.6	70.4	107.1	84.8	115.7	1,555	1,280	..	345
Ukraine	..	63.8	..	52.3	..	50.9	..	2,211	..	2,544
United Arab Emirates	38.9	232.3	49.2	222.7	46.0	158.5	2,224	1,360	..	..
United Kingdom	80.1	104.2	92.0	99.7	98.1	97.1	4,792	6,891	..	..
United States	98.9	119.1	94.5	117.9	88.8	115.1	4,151	5,380	..	39,523
Uruguay	86.6	148.0	86.9	130.8	85.5	119.6	1,644	3,257	6,821	9,826
Uzbekistan	..	83.6	..	109.8	..	108.7	..	2,292	..	2,128
Venezuela, RB	76.5	109.0	80.3	114.4	84.9	112.4	1,904	2,959	4,041	5,036
Vietnam	66.7	143.7	63.8	140.5	52.9	145.8	2,049	3,754	..	..
West Bank and Gaza	..	..	..	..	..	..	..	..	..	..
Yemen, Rep.	82.3	116.2	75.0	120.7	68.9	129.0	1,038	902	..	302
Yugoslavia, FR (Serb./Mont.)	..	93.3	..	102.4	..	112.9	..	3,799	..	..
Zambia	65.7	95.5	74.0	104.5	86.2	116.3	1,676	1,584	328	209
Zimbabwe	77.9	118.7	81.9	101.9	84.5	99.2	1,359	1,283	307	347
World	**79.5 w**	**125.1 w**	**75.7 w**	**130.3 w**	**80.7 w**	**134.1 w**	**1,600 w**	**2,022 w**	**.. w**	**.. w**
Low income	73.3	121.0	68.7	138.7	71.9	135.5	1,097	1,267	..	348
Excl. China & India	..	..	73.8	127.1	..	..	1,069	1,251	..	..
Middle income	74.4	134.7	80.2	123.1	69.4	168.5	1,789	2,358	..	..
Lower middle income	71.7	144.8	..	126.1	57.8	208.2	1,724	2,084	..	..
Upper middle income	80.8	111.4	78.5	119.9	84.3	117.5	1,884	2,892	..	..
Low & middle income	74.1	130.3	71.7	134.7	70.0	160.7	1,419	1,828	..	*568*
East Asia & Pacific	69.6	132.1	67.0	152.1	49.6	185.8	2,116	2,729	..	..
Europe & Central Asia	..	192.7	..	..	..	263.3	2,677	2,383	..	2,186
Latin America & Carib.	82.1	118.5	80.5	123.9	82.2	121.6	1,842	2,453	..	..
Middle East & N. Africa	68.5	126.8	70.1	137.9	65.0	125.0	925	1,412	..	..
South Asia	72.5	117.4	70.4	122.1	63.9	131.1	1,510	2,099	265	*356*
Sub-Saharan Africa	77.1	114.1	78.8	124.3	92.6	121.8	895	1,143	418	379
High income	92.7	112.5	93.1	107.4	91.5	107.4	3,170	4,051	..	..
Europe EMU	90.1	105.0	91.9	100.9	95.0	100.2	4,035	5,673	..	..

a. Includes Luxembourg.

Agricultural output and productivity 3.3

About the data

The agricultural production indexes in the table are prepared by the Food and Agriculture Organization (FAO). The FAO obtains data from official and semiofficial reports of crop yields, area under production, and livestock numbers. If data are not available, the FAO makes estimates. The indexes are calculated using the Laspeyres formula: production quantities of each commodity are weighted by average international commodity prices in the base period and summed for each year. Because the FAO's indexes are based on the concept of agriculture as a single enterprise, estimates of the amounts retained for seed and feed are subtracted from the production data to avoid double counting. The resulting aggregate represents production available for any use except as seed and feed. The FAO's indexes may differ from other sources because of differences in coverage, weights, concepts, time periods, calculation methods, and use of international prices.

To ease cross-country comparisons, the FAO uses international commodity prices to value production. These prices, expressed in international dollars (equivalent in purchasing power to the U.S. dollar), are derived using a Geary-Khamis formula applied to agricultural outputs (see Inter-Secretariat Working Group on National Accounts 1993, sections 16.93–96). This method assigns a single price to each commodity so that, for example, one metric ton of wheat has the same price regardless of where it was produced. The use of international prices eliminates fluctuations in the value of output due to transitory movements of nominal exchange rates unrelated to the purchasing power of the domestic currency. Unlike the International Comparison Programme (ICP), the FAO calculates international prices only for agricultural products. Substantial differences may arise between the implicit exchange rate derived by the ICP and that of the FAO. (For further discussion of the FAO's methods see FAO 1986. For a discussion of the ICP see *About the data* for tables 4.11 and 4.12.)

Data on cereal yields may be affected by a variety of reporting and timing differences. The FAO allocates production data to the calendar year in which the bulk of the harvest took place. But most of a crop harvested near the end of a year will be used in the following year. In general, cereal crops harvested for hay or harvested green for food, feed, or silage and those used for grazing are excluded. But millet and sorghum, which are grown as feed for livestock and poultry in Europe and North America, are used as food in Africa, Asia, and countries of the former Soviet Union.

Agricultural productivity is measured by value added per unit of input. (See *About the data* for tables 4.1 and 4.2 for further discussion of the calculation of value added in national accounts.) Agricultural value added includes that from forestry and fishing. Thus interpretations of land productivity should be made with caution.

To smooth annual fluctuations in agricultural activity, the indicators in the table have been averaged over three years.

Figure 3.3a

The world's food production has outpaced its population growth . . .

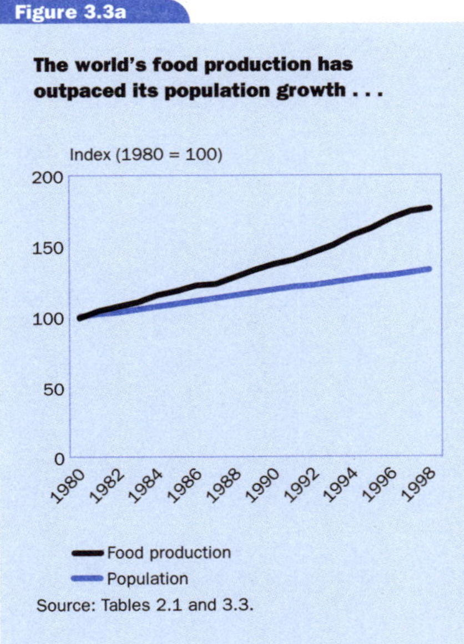

Source: Tables 2.1 and 3.3.

Figure 3.3b

. . . except in Sub-Saharan Africa, where food production has barely kept up with population growth

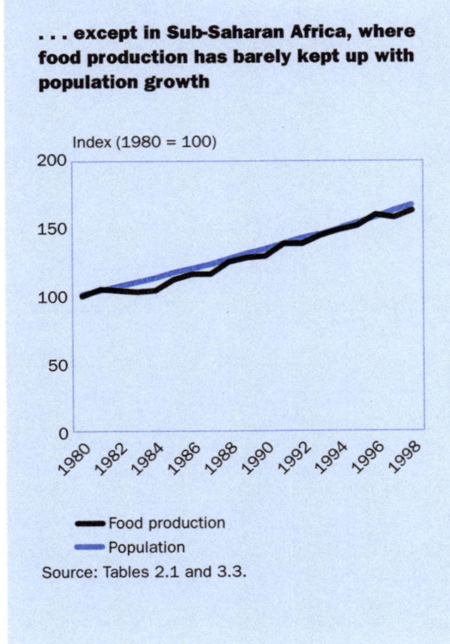

Source: Tables 2.1 and 3.3.

Definitions

• **Crop production index** shows agricultural production for each period relative to the base period 1989–91. It includes all crops except fodder crops. The regional and income group aggregates for the FAO's production indexes are calculated from the underlying values in international dollars, normalized to the base period 1989–91. The data in this table are three-year averages. However, missing observations have not been estimated or imputed. • **Food production index** covers food crops that are considered edible and that contain nutrients. Coffee and tea are excluded because, although edible, they have no nutritive value. • **Livestock production index** includes meat and milk from all sources, dairy products such as cheese, and eggs, honey, raw silk, wool, and hides and skins. • **Cereal yield**, measured in kilograms per hectare of harvested land, includes wheat, rice, maize, barley, oats, rye, millet, sorghum, buckwheat, and mixed grains. Production data on cereals refer to crops harvested for dry grain only. Cereal crops harvested for hay or harvested green for food, feed, or silage and those used for grazing are excluded. • **Agricultural productivity** refers to the ratio of agricultural value added, measured in constant 1995 U.S. dollars, to the number of workers in agriculture.

Data sources

The agricultural production indexes are prepared by the FAO and published annually in its *Production Yearbook*. The FAO makes these data and the data on cereal yields and agricultural employment available to the World Bank in electronic files that may contain more recent information than the published versions. For sources of agricultural value added see table 4.2.

3.4 Deforestation and biodiversity

	Forest area		Average annual deforestation		Mammals		Birds		Higher plants[a]		Nationally protected areas	
	thousand sq. km 1995	% of total land area 1995[b]	sq. km 1990–95	% change 1990–95	Species 1996[b]	Threatened species 1996[b]	Species 1996[b]	Threatened species 1996[b]	Species 1997[b]	Threatened species 1997[b]	thousand sq. km 1996[b]	% of total land area 1996[b]
Albania	10	38.2	0	0.0	68	2	230	7	3,031	79	0.8	2.9
Algeria	19	0.8	234	1.2	92	15	192	8	3,164	141	58.9	2.5
Angola	222	17.8	2,370	1.0	276	17	765	13	5,185	30	81.8	6.6
Argentina	339	12.4	894	0.3	320	27	897	41	9,372	247	46.6	1.7
Armenia	3	11.8	–84	–2.7	..	4	..	5	..	31	2.1	7.4
Australia	409	5.3	–170	0.0	252	58	649	45	15,638	2,245	563.9	7.3
Austria	39	46.9	0	0.0	83	7	213	5	3,100	23	23.4	28.3
Azerbaijan	10	11.4	0	0.0	..	11	..	8	..	28	4.8	5.5
Bangladesh	10	7.8	88	0.8	109	18	295	30	5,000	24	1.0	0.8
Belarus	74	35.5	–688	–1.0	..	4	221	4	..	1	8.6	4.1
Belgium	..	..	..	..	58	6	180	3	1,550	2	0.8	..
Benin	46	41.8	596	1.2	188	9	307	1	2,201	4	7.8	7.1
Bolivia	483	44.6	5,814	1.2	316	24	*1,274*	27	17,367	227	156.0	14.4
Bosnia and Herzegovina	27	53.1	0	0.0	..	10	..	2	..	64	0.2	0.4
Botswana	139	24.6	708	0.5	164	5	386	7	2,151	7	105.0	18.5
Brazil	5,511	65.2	25,544	0.5	394	71	1,492	103	56,215	1,358	355.5	4.2
Bulgaria	32	29.3	–6	0.0	81	13	240	12	3,572	106	4.9	4.4
Burkina Faso	43	15.6	320	0.7	147	6	335	1	1,100	0	28.6	10.5
Burundi	3	12.3	14	0.4	107	5	451	6	2,500	1	1.4	5.5
Cambodia	98	55.7	1,638	1.6	123	23	307	18	..	5	28.6	16.2
Cameroon	196	42.1	1,292	0.6	297	32	690	14	8,260	89	21.0	4.5
Canada	2,446	26.5	–1,764	–0.1	193	7	426	5	3,270	278	921.0	10.0
Central African Republic	299	48.0	1,282	0.4	209	11	537	2	3,602	1	51.1	8.2
Chad	110	8.8	942	0.8	134	14	370	3	1,600	12	114.9	9.1
Chile	79	10.5	292	0.4	91	16	296	18	5,284	329	141.3	18.9
China	1,333	14.3	866	0.1	394	75	1,100	90	32,200	312	598.1	6.4
Hong Kong, China	..	..	..	..	24	0	76	14	1,984	9	0.4	40.4
Colombia	530	51.0	2,622	0.5	359	35	1,695	64	51,220	712	93.6	9.0
Congo, Dem. Rep.	..	..	..	..	415	38	929	26	11,007	78	101.9	4.5
Congo, Rep.	195	57.2	416	0.2	200	10	449	3	6,000	3	15.4	4.5
Costa Rica	12	24.4	414	3.0	205	14	600	13	12,119	527	7.0	13.7
Côte d'Ivoire	55	17.2	308	0.6	230	16	535	12	3,660	94	19.9	6.3
Croatia	18	32.6	0	0.0	..	10	224	4	..	6	3.7	6.6
Cuba	18	16.8	236	1.2	31	9	137	13	6,522	888	19.1	17.4
Czech Republic	26	34.0	–2	0.0	..	7	199	6	..	81	12.2	15.8
Denmark	4	9.8	0	0.0	43	3	196	2	1,450	2	13.7	32.3
Dominican Republic	16	32.7	264	1.6	20	4	136	11	5,657	136	12.2	25.2
Ecuador	111	40.2	1,890	1.6	302	28	1,388	53	19,362	824	119.3	43.1
Egypt, Arab Rep.	0	0.0	0	0.0	98	15	153	11	2,076	82	7.9	0.8
El Salvador	1	5.1	38	3.3	135	2	251	0	2,911	42	0.1	0.5
Eritrea	3	2.8	0	0.0	112	6	319	3	..	0	5.0	5.0
Estonia	20	47.6	–196	–1.0	65	4	213	2	..	2	5.1	12.1
Ethiopia	136	13.6	624	0.5	255	35	626	20	6,603	163	55.2	5.5
Finland	200	65.8	166	0.1	60	4	248	4	1,102	6	18.2	6.0
France	150	27.3	–1,608	–1.1	93	13	269	7	4,630	195	58.8	10.7
Gabon	179	69.3	910	0.5	190	12	466	4	6,651	91	7.2	2.8
Gambia, The	1	9.1	8	0.9	108	4	280	1	974	1	0.2	2.0
Georgia	30	42.9	0	0.0	..	10	..	5	..	29	1.9	2.7
Germany	107	30.7	0	0.0	76	8	239	5	2,682	14	94.2	27.0
Ghana	90	39.7	1,172	1.3	222	13	529	10	3,725	103	11.0	4.8
Greece	65	50.5	–1,408	–2.3	95	13	251	10	4,992	571	3.1	2.4
Guatemala	38	35.4	824	2.0	250	8	458	4	8,681	355	18.2	16.8
Guinea	64	25.9	748	1.1	190	11	409	12	3,000	39	1.6	0.7
Guinea-Bissau	23	82.1	104	0.4	108	4	243	1	1,000	0	0.0	0.0
Haiti	0	0.8	8	3.4	3	4	75	11	5,242	100	0.1	0.4
Honduras	41	36.8	1,022	2.3	173	7	422	4	5,680	96	11.1	9.9

Deforestation and biodiversity 3.4

	Forest area		Average annual deforestation		Mammals		Birds		Higher plants[a]		Nationally protected areas	
	thousand sq. km 1995	% of total land area 1995[b]	sq. km 1990–95	% change 1990–95	Species 1996[b]	Threatened species 1996[b]	Species 1996[b]	Threatened species 1996[b]	Species 1997[b]	Threatened species 1997[b]	thousand sq. km 1996[b]	% of total land area 1996[b]
Hungary	17	18.6	–88	–0.5	72	8	205	10	2,214	30	6.3	6.8
India	650	21.9	–72	0.0	316	75	923	73	16,000	1,236	142.9	4.8
Indonesia	1,098	60.6	10,844	1.0	436	128	1,519	104	29,375	264	192.3	10.6
Iran, Islamic Rep.	15	1.0	284	1.7	140	20	323	14	8,000	2	83.0	5.1
Iraq	1	0.2	0	0.0	81	7	172	12	..	2	0.0	0.0
Ireland	6	8.3	–140	–2.7	25	2	142	1	950	1	0.6	0.9
Israel	1	4.9	0	0.0	92	13	180	8	2,317	32	3.1	15.0
Italy	65	22.1	–58	–0.1	90	10	234	7	5,599	311	21.5	7.3
Jamaica	2	16.2	158	7.2	24	4	113	7	3,308	744	0.0	0.0
Japan	251	66.8	132	0.1	132	29	250	33	5,565	707	25.5	6.8
Jordan	0	0.5	12	2.5	71	7	141	4	2,100	9	3.0	3.4
Kazakhstan	105	3.9	–1,928	–1.9	..	15	..	15	..	71	73.4	2.7
Kenya	13	2.3	34	0.3	359	43	844	24	6,506	240	35.0	6.1
Korea, Dem. Rep.	62	51.2	0	0.0	..	7	115	19	2,898	4	3.1	2.6
Korea, Rep.	76	77.2	130	0.2	49	6	112	19	2,898	66	6.8	6.9
Kuwait	0	0.3	0	0.0	21	1	20	3	234	0	0.3	1.7
Kyrgyz Republic	7	3.8	0	0.0	..	6	..	5	..	34	6.9	3.6
Lao PDR	..	..	..	..	172	30	487	27	..	2	0.0	0.0
Latvia	29	46.4	–250	–0.9	83	4	217	6	1,153	0	7.8	12.6
Lebanon	1	5.1	52	7.8	54	5	154	5	3,000	5	0.0	0.0
Lesotho	0	0.2	0	0.0	33	2	58	5	1,591	21	0.1	0.3
Libya	4	0.2	0	0.0	76	11	91	2	1,825	57	1.7	0.1
Lithuania	20	30.5	–112	–0.6	68	5	202	4	..	1	6.5	10.0
Macedonia, FYR	10	38.9	2	0.0	..	10	..	3	..	0	1.8	7.1
Madagascar	151	26.0	1,300	0.8	105	46	202	28	9,505	306	11.2	1.9
Malawi	33	35.5	546	1.6	195	7	521	9	3,765	61	10.6	11.3
Malaysia	155	47.1	4,002	2.4	286	42	501	34	15,500	490	14.8	4.5
Mali	116	9.5	1,138	1.0	137	13	397	6	1,741	15	45.3	3.7
Mauritania	6	0.5	0	0.0	61	14	273	3	1,100	3	17.5	1.7
Mauritius	0	5.9	0	0.0	4	4	27	10	750	294	0.1	4.9
Mexico	554	29.0	5,080	0.9	450	64	769	36	26,071	1,593	71.0	3.7
Moldova	4	10.8	0	0.0	68	2	177	7	..	5	0.4	1.2
Mongolia	94	6.0	0	0.0	134	12	*390*	14	2,272	0	161.3	10.3
Morocco	38	8.6	118	0.3	105	18	210	11	3,675	186	3.2	0.7
Mozambique	169	21.5	1,162	0.7	179	13	498	14	5,692	89	47.8	6.1
Myanmar	272	41.3	3,874	1.4	251	31	867	44	7,000	32	1.7	0.3
Namibia	124	15.0	420	0.3	154	11	469	8	3,174	75	106.2	12.9
Nepal	48	33.7	548	1.1	167	28	611	27	6,973	20	11.1	7.8
Netherlands	3	9.8	0	0.0	55	6	191	3	1,221	1	2.4	7.1
New Zealand	79	29.4	–434	–0.6	10	3	150	44	2,382	211	63.3	23.6
Nicaragua	56	45.8	1,508	2.5	200	4	482	3	7,590	98	9.0	7.4
Niger	26	2.0	0	0.0	131	11	299	2	1,170	0	96.9	7.6
Nigeria	138	15.1	1,214	0.9	274	26	681	9	4,715	37	30.2	3.3
Norway	81	26.3	–180	–0.2	54	4	243	3	1,715	12	93.7	30.5
Oman	0	0.0	0	..	56	9	107	5	1,204	30	34.3	16.1
Pakistan	17	2.3	550	2.9	151	13	375	25	4,950	14	37.2	4.8
Panama	28	37.6	636	2.1	218	17	732	10	9,915	1,302	14.2	19.1
Papua New Guinea	369	81.6	1,332	0.4	214	57	644	31	11,544	92	0.1	0.0
Paraguay	115	29.0	3,266	2.6	305	10	556	26	7,851	129	14.0	3.5
Peru	676	52.8	2,168	0.3	344	46	1,538	64	18,245	906	34.6	2.7
Philippines	68	22.7	2,624	3.5	153	49	395	86	8,931	360	14.5	4.9
Poland	87	28.7	–120	–0.1	84	10	227	6	2,450	27	29.1	9.6
Portugal	29	31.4	–240	–0.9	63	13	207	7	5,050	269	5.9	6.4
Puerto Rico	3	31.0	24	0.9	16	3	105	11	2,493	223	0.1	1.1
Romania	62	27.1	12	0.0	84	16	247	11	3,400	99	10.7	4.6
Russian Federation	7,635	45.2	0	0.0	269	31	628	38	..	214	516.7	3.1

3.4 Deforestation and biodiversity

	Forest area		Average annual deforestation		Mammals		Birds		Higher plants[a]		Nationally protected areas	
	thousand sq. km 1995	% of total land area 1995[b]	sq. km 1990–95	% change 1990–95	Species 1996[b]	Threatened species 1996[b]	Species 1996[b]	Threatened species 1996[b]	Species 1997[b]	Threatened species 1997[b]	thousand sq. km 1996[b]	% of total land area 1996[b]
Rwanda	3	10.1	4	0.2	151	9	513	6	2,288	0	3.6	14.6
Saudi Arabia	2	0.1	18	0.8	77	9	155	11	2,028	7	49.6	2.3
Senegal	74	38.3	496	0.7	155	13	384	6	2,086	31	21.8	11.3
Sierra Leone	13	18.3	426	3.0	147	9	466	12	2,090	29	0.8	1.1
Singapore	0	6.6	0	0.0	45	6	118	9	2,168	29	0.0	0.0
Slovak Republic	20	41.4	–24	–0.1	..	8	209	4	..	65	10.5	21.8
Slovenia	11	53.5	0	0.0	69	10	207	3	..	13	1.1	5.5
South Africa	85	7.0	150	0.2	247	33	596	16	23,420	2,215	65.8	5.4
Spain	84	16.8	0	0.0	82	19	278	10	5,050	985	42.2	8.4
Sri Lanka	18	27.8	202	1.1	88	14	250	11	3,314	455	8.6	13.3
Sudan	416	17.5	3,526	0.8	267	21	680	9	3,137	10	86.4	3.6
Sweden	244	59.3	24	0.0	60	5	249	4	1,750	13	36.2	8.8
Switzerland	11	28.6	0	0.0	75	6	193	4	3,030	30	7.1	18.0
Syrian Arab Republic	2	1.2	52	2.2	63	4	204	7	3,000	8	0.0	0.0
Tajikistan	4	2.9	0	0.0	..	5	..	9	..	50	5.9	4.2
Tanzania	325	36.8	3,226	1.0	316	33	822	30	10,008	436	138.2	15.6
Thailand	116	22.8	3,294	2.6	265	34	616	45	11,625	385	70.7	13.8
Togo	12	22.9	186	1.4	196	8	391	1	2,201	4	4.3	7.9
Trinidad and Tobago	2	31.4	26	1.5	100	1	260	3	2,259	21	0.2	3.9
Tunisia	6	3.6	30	0.5	78	11	173	6	2,196	24	0.4	0.3
Turkey	89	11.5	0	0.0	116	15	302	14	8,650	1,876	10.7	1.4
Turkmenistan	38	8.0	0	0.0	..	11	..	12	..	17	19.8	4.2
Uganda	61	30.6	592	0.9	338	18	830	10	5,406	15	19.1	9.6
Ukraine	92	15.9	–54	–0.1	..	15	263	10	..	52	9.0	1.6
United Arab Emirates	1	0.7	0	0.0	25	3	67	4	..	0	0.0	0.0
United Kingdom	24	9.9	–128	–0.5	50	4	230	2	1,623	18	50.6	20.9
United States	2,125	23.2	–5,886	–0.3	428	35	650	50	19,473	4,669	1,226.7	13.4
Uruguay	8	4.7	4	0.0	81	5	237	11	2,278	15	0.5	0.3
Uzbekistan	91	22.0	–2,260	–2.7	..	7	..	11	..	41	8.2	2.0
Venezuela, RB	440	49.9	5,034	1.1	305	24	1,181	22	21,073	426	319.8	36.3
Vietnam	91	28.0	1,352	1.4	213	38	535	47	10,500	341	9.9	3.0
West Bank and Gaza	..	..	..	..	..	..	..	..	..	..	..	..
Yemen, Rep.	0	0.0	0	0.0	66	5	143	13	..	149	0.0	0.0
Yugoslavia, FR (Serb./Mont.)	18	..	..	..	..	..	..	..	..	..	..	..
Zambia	314	42.2	2,644	0.8	229	11	605	10	4,747	12	63.6	8.6
Zimbabwe	87	22.5	500	0.6	270	9	532	9	4,440	100	30.7	7.9
World	32,712 s	25.1 w	101,724 s	0.3 w	..	..	..	..	..	..	8,543.5 s	6.6 w
Low income	7,379	17.8	49,332	0.7	..	..	..	..	..	..	2,442.5	5.9
Excl. China & India	5,334	18.4	48,538	0.9	..	..	..	..	..	..	1,698.4	5.9
Middle income	18,898	32.7	64,086	0.3	..	..	..	..	..	..	2,806.8	4.9
Lower middle income	11,101	30.8	21,162	0.2	..	..	..	..	..	..	1,560.5	4.3
Upper middle income	7,797	35.8	42,924	0.5	..	..	..	..	..	..	1,246.3	5.7
Low & middle income	26,277	26.5	113,418	0.4	..	..	..	..	..	..	5,249.3	5.3
East Asia & Pacific	3,832	24.0	29,956	0.8	..	..	..	..	..	..	1,102.2	6.9
Europe & Central Asia	8,579	36.1	–5,798	–0.1	..	..	..	..	..	..	768.0	3.2
Latin America & Carib.	9,064	45.2	57,766	0.6	..	..	..	..	..	..	1,456.3	7.3
Middle East & N. Africa	89	0.8	800	0.9	..	..	..	..	..	..	242.1	2.2
South Asia	744	15.6	1,316	0.2	..	..	..	..	..	..	213.0	4.5
Sub-Saharan Africa	3,969	16.8	29,378	0.7	..	..	..	..	..	..	1,467.7	6.2
High income	6,436	20.8	–11,694	–0.2	..	..	..	..	..	..	3,294.2	10.8
Europe EMU	683	29.6	–1,880	–0.3	..	..	..	..	..	..	268.4	11.7

a. Flowering plants only. b. Data may refer to earlier years. They are the most recent reported by the World Conservation Monitoring Centre in 1997.

Deforestation and biodiversity 3.4

About the data

The estimates of forest area are from the Food and Agriculture Organization's (FAO) *State of the World's Forests 1999*, which provides information on forest cover as of 1995 and a revised estimate of forest cover in 1990. Forest cover data for developing countries are based on country assessments that were prepared at different times and that, for reporting purposes, had to be adapted to the standard reference years of 1990 and 1995. This adjustment was made with a deforestation model designed to correlate forest cover change over time with ancillary variables, including population change and density, initial forest cover, and the ecological zone of the forest area under consideration. Although the same model was used to estimate forest cover for the 1990 forest assessment, the inputs to *State of the World's Forests 1999* had more recent and accurate information on boundaries of ecological zones and, for some countries, new national forest cover assessments. For the calculation of forest cover for 1995 and the recalculation of the 1990 estimates, new forest inventory information was used for Bolivia, Brazil, Cambodia, Côte d'Ivoire, Guinea-Bissau, Mexico, Papua New Guinea, the Philippines, and Sierra Leone. New information on global totals raised estimates of forest cover. For high-income countries, the United Nations Economic Commission for Europe and the FAO use a detailed questionnaire to survey the forest cover in each country.

No breakdown of forest cover between natural forest and plantation is shown in the table because of space limitations. (This breakdown is provided by the FAO only for developing countries.) For this reason the deforestation data in the table may underestimate the rate at which natural forest is disappearing in some countries.

Deforestation is a major cause of loss of biodiversity, and habitat conservation is vital for stemming this loss. Conservation efforts traditionally have focused on protected areas, which have grown substantially in recent decades. Measures of species richness are one of the most straightforward ways to indicate the importance of an area for biodiversity. The number of small plants and animals is usually estimated by sampling of plots. It is also important to know which aspects are under the most immediate threat. This, however, requires a large amount of data and time-consuming analysis. For this reason global analyses of the status of threatened species have been carried out for few groups of organisms. Only for birds has the status of all species been assessed. An estimated 45 percent of mammal species remain to be assessed. For plants the World Conservation Union's (IUCN) *1997 IUCN Red List of Threatened Plants* provides the first-ever comprehensive listing of threatened species on a global scale, the result of more than 20 years' work by botanists from around the world. Nearly 34,000 plant species, 12.5 percent of the total, are threatened with extinction.

The table shows information on protected areas, numbers of certain species, and numbers of those species under threat. The World Conservation Monitoring Centre (WCMC) compiles these data from a variety of sources. Because of differences in definitions and reporting practices, cross-country comparability is limited. Compounding these problems, available data cover different periods.

Nationally protected areas are areas of at least 1,000 hectares that fall into one of five management categories defined by the WCMC:

- Scientific reserves and strict nature reserves with limited public access.
- National parks of national or international significance (not materially affected by human activity).
- Natural monuments and natural landscapes with unique aspects.
- Managed nature reserves and wildlife sanctuaries.
- Protected landscapes and seascapes (which may include cultural landscapes).

Designating land as a protected area does not necessarily mean that protection is in force, however. For small countries that may only have protected areas smaller than 1,000 hectares, this size limit in the definition will result in an underestimate of the extent and number of protected areas.

Threatened species are defined according to the IUCN's classification categories: endangered (in danger of extinction and unlikely to survive if causal factors continue operating), vulnerable (likely to move into the endangered category in the near future if causal factors continue operating), rare (not endangered or vulnerable, but at risk), indeterminate (known to be endangered, vulnerable, or rare but not enough information is available to say which), out of danger (formerly included in one of the above categories but now considered relatively secure because appropriate conservation measures are in effect), and insufficiently known (suspected but not definitely known to belong to one of the above categories).

Figures on species are not necessarily comparable across countries because taxonomic concepts and coverage vary. And while the number of birds and mammals is fairly well known, it is difficult to make an accurate count of plants. Although the data in the table should be interpreted with caution, especially for numbers of threatened species (where our knowledge is very incomplete), they do identify countries that are major sources of global biodiversity and show national commitments to habitat protection.

Definitions

• **Forest area** is land under natural or planted stands of trees, whether productive or not (see *About the data*). • **Average annual deforestation** refers to the permanent conversion of natural forest area to other uses, including shifting cultivation, permanent agriculture, ranching, settlements, and infrastructure development. Deforested areas do not include areas logged but intended for regeneration or areas degraded by fuelwood gathering, acid precipitation, or forest fires. Negative numbers indicate an increase in forest area. • **Mammals** exclude whales and porpoises. • **Birds** are listed for countries included within their breeding or wintering ranges. • **Higher plants** refer to native vascular plant species. • **Threatened species** are the number of species classified by the IUCN as endangered, vulnerable, rare, indeterminate, out of danger, or insufficiently known. • **Nationally protected areas** are totally or partially protected areas of at least 1,000 hectares that are designated as national parks, natural monuments, nature reserves or wildlife sanctuaries, protected landscapes and seascapes, or scientific reserves with limited public access. The data do not include sites protected under local or provincial law. Total land area is used to calculate the percentage of total area protected (see table 3.1).

Data sources

The forestry data are from the FAO's *State of the World's Forests 1999*. The data on species are from the WCMC's *Biodiversity Data Sourcebook* (1994) and the IUCN's *1996 IUCN Red List of Threatened Animals* and *1997 IUCN Red List of Threatened Plants*. The data on protected areas are from the WCMC's Protected Areas Data Unit.

3.5 Freshwater

	Freshwater resources	Annual freshwater withdrawals					Access to safe water			
							Urban % of population		Rural % of population	
	cubic meters per capita **1998**	billion cu. m[a]	% of total resources[a]	% for agriculture[b]	% for industry[b]	% for domestic[b]	**1982–85**[c]	**1990–96**[c]	**1982–85**[c]	**1990–96**[c]
Albania	12,758[d]	1.4	3.3[d]	71	0	29	*100*	97	*88*	70
Algeria	478[d]	4.5	31.5[d]	60[e]	15[e]	*25*[e]	..	..	..	..
Angola	15,783	0.5	0.3	76[e]	10[e]	*14*[e]	*80*	69	*15*	15
Argentina	27,865[d]	28.6	2.8[d]	75	9	*16*	*63*	71	*17*	24
Armenia	2,767[d]	2.9	27.9[d]	66	4	30	..	..	..	..
Australia	18,772	15.1	4.3	33	2	65	..	..	..	..
Austria	10,399[d]	2.2	2.7[d]	9	60	31	100	..	98	..
Azerbaijan	3,831[d]	16.5	54.6[d]	70	25	5	..	..	..	..
Bangladesh	9,636[d]	14.6	1.2[d]	86	2	*12*	*29*	47	*43*	85
Belarus	5,665[d]	2.7	4.7[d]	35	43	22	..	..	..	..
Belgium	1,228[d]	9.0	72.2[d]	4	85	*11*	100	..	91	..
Benin	4,337[d]	0.2	0.6[d]	67[e]	10[e]	*23*[e]	*45*	41	*9*	53
Bolivia	38,625	1.4	0.4	48	20	*32*	81	..	27	..
Bosnia and Herzegovina	*9,952*	..	..	..	..	..	..	..	..	..
Botswana	9,413[d]	0.1	0.7[d]	48[e]	20[e]	*32*[e]	..	100	..	53
Brazil	42,459[d]	54.9	0.5[d]	61	18	*21*	..	..	52	..
Bulgaria	24,663[d]	13.9	6.8[d]	22	76	3	95	..	67	..
Burkina Faso	1,671	0.4	2.2	81[e]	0[e]	*19*[e]	50	..	26	..
Burundi	561	0.1	2.8	64[e]	0[e]	*36*[e]	33	..	22	..
Cambodia	41,407	0.5	0.1	94	1	5	..	20	..	12
Cameroon	18,737	0.4	0.1	35[e]	19[e]	*46*[e]	*46*	71	*30*	24
Canada	92,142	45.1	1.6	9	80	11	100	..	100	..
Central African Republic	41,250	0.1	0.0	73[e]	6[e]	*21*[e]	..	..	..	..
Chad	5,904[d]	0.2	0.4[d]	82[e]	2[e]	16[e]	*27*	48	*30*	17
Chile	32,007	21.4	3.6	84	11	*5*	97	..	22	..
China	2,285	525.5	18.6	77	18	5	..	93	..	89
Hong Kong, China	..	..	..	..	..	..	..	..	..	..
Colombia	26,722	8.9	0.5	37	4	*59*	..	88	..	48
Congo, Dem. Rep.	21,134	0.4	0.0	23[e]	16[e]	*61*[e]	43	..	5	..
Congo, Rep.	298,963[d]	0.0	0.0[d]	11[e]	27[e]	62[e]	*42*	50	*7*	8
Costa Rica	27,425	5.8	1.4	80	7	*13*	..	..	..	..
Côte d'Ivoire	5,362	0.7	0.9	67[e]	11[e]	*22*[e]	*30*	59	*10*	81
Croatia	15,863	0.1	0.1	..	50	*50*	..	75	..	41
Cuba	3,120	5.2	23.5	51	0	49	..	96	..	85
Czech Republic	1,554	2.5	15.8	2	57	41	100	..	100	..
Denmark	2,460[d]	0.9	9.2[d]	43	27	30	100	..	99	..
Dominican Republic	2,467	8.3	14.9	89	1	*11*	*72*	74	*24*	67
Ecuador	26,305	17.0	1.8	82	6	*12*	*83*	82	*33*	55
Egypt, Arab Rep.	949[d]	55.1	94.5[d]	86[e]	8[e]	*6*[e]	*93*	82	*61*	50
El Salvador	3,197	0.7	5.3	46	20	*34*	*76*	78	*47*	37
Eritrea	2,269	..	..	..	..	..	..	..	..	..
Estonia	8,829	0.2	1.3[d]	5	39	56	..	..	..	..
Ethiopia	1,795	2.2	2.0	86[e]	3[e]	11[e]	..	90	..	20
Finland	21,347	2.4	2.2[d]	3	85	12	*98*	100	*86*	85
France	3,246[d]	40.6	21.3[d]	12	73	15	*100*	100	*95*	100
Gabon	138,942	0.1	0.0	6[e]	22[e]	72[e]	*75*	80	*34*	30
Gambia, The	6,579[d]	0.0	0.4[d]	91[e]	2[e]	7[e]	100	..	33	..
Georgia	11,632[d]	3.5	5.5[d]	59	20	21	..	..	..	..
Germany	2,169[d]	46.3	26.0[d]	0	86	*14*	..	..	..	..
Ghana	2,882[d]	0.3[f]	0.6[d]	52[e]	13[e]	*35*[e]	*57*	70	*40*	49
Greece	6,562[d]	7.0	10.2[d]	81	3	16	91	..	73	..
Guatemala	11,030	1.2	0.6	74	17	*9*	*89*	97	*39*	48
Guinea	31,910	0.7	0.3	87[e]	3[e]	*10*[e]	..	61	2	62
Guinea-Bissau	23,249[d]	0.0	0.1[d]	36[e]	4[e]	*60*[e]	*21*	38	*37*	57
Haiti	1,468	1.0	0.4	94	1	5	..	37	..	23
Honduras	9,258	1.5	2.7	91	5	4	*51*	81	*49*	53

Freshwater 3.5

	Freshwater resources	Annual freshwater withdrawals					Access to safe water			
							Urban % of population		Rural % of population	
	cubic meters per capita 1998	billion cu. m[a]	% of total resources[a]	% for agriculture[b]	% for industry[b]	% for domestic[b]	1982–85[c]	1990–96[c]	1982–85[c]	1990–96[c]
Hungary	11,865[d]	6.3	5.2[d]	36	55	9	92	..	81	..
India	1,947[d]	500.0	26.2[d]	92	3	5	80	85	47	79
Indonesia	12,625	74.3	0.7	93	1	6	60	78	32	54
Iran, Islamic Rep.	1,339	70.0	85.8	92	2	6	90	..	52	..
Iraq	3,451	42.8	56.8	92	5	3	92	..	22	..
Ireland	14,035[d]	1.2	2.3[d]	10	74	16	100	..	92	..
Israel	184[d]	1.7	155.5[d]	64[e]	7[e]	29[e]	100	100	100	95
Italy	2,909[d]	57.5	34.4[d]	45	37	18	100	..	96	..
Jamaica	3,250	0.9	3.9	77	7	15	99	92	93	48
Japan	3,402	91.4	21.3	64	17	19	..	..	..	..
Jordan	198[d]	1.0	51.1[d]	75	3	22	100	..	65	..
Kazakhstan	7,029[d]	33.7	30.7[d]	81	17	2	..	..	..	..
Kenya	1,031[d]	2.1	6.8[d]	76[e]	4[e]	20[e]	61	67	21	49
Korea, Dem. Rep.	3,327	14.2	18.4	73	16	11	..	..	..	..
Korea, Rep.	1,501	23.7	34.0	63	11	26	..	93	..	77
Kuwait	0	0.5	2,700.0	60	2	37	100	100	100	100
Kyrgyz Republic	2,509	10.1	94.9	94	3	3	..	93	..	42
Lao PDR	56,638	1.0	0.4	82	10	8	..	40	..	39
Latvia	14,455[d]	0.3	0.8[d]	13	32	55	..	92	..	..
Lebanon	1,140	1.3	26.9	68	4	28	95	100	85	100
Lesotho	2,527	0.1	1.0	56[e]	22[e]	22[e]	37	..	14	64
Libya	151	3.9	486.3	87[e]	4[e]	9[e]	92	90	75	91
Lithuania	6,724[d]	0.3	1.0[d]	3	16	81	..	..	..	..
Macedonia, FYR	3,483	..	..	..	..	..	100	..	98	..
Madagascar	23,094	19.7	5.8	99[e]	0[e]	1[e]	81	83	17	10
Malawi	1,775[d]	0.9	5.0[d]	86[e]	3[e]	10[e]	70	52	27	44
Malaysia	21,046	12.7	2.1	76	13	11	..	100	..	86
Mali	9,438	1.4	1.4	97[e]	1[e]	2[e]	..	36	..	38
Mauritania	4,508[d]	16.3	143.0[d]	92	2	6	80	87	16	41
Mauritius	1,897	0.4[f]	16.4	77[e]	7[e]	16[e]	100	..	98	..
Mexico	4,779	77.8	17.0	78	5	17	95	91	50	62
Moldova	2,722	3.0	25.3[d]	26	65	9	..	98	..	18
Mongolia	9,677	0.4	2.2	53	27	20	..	..	..	..
Morocco	1,080	11.1	36.8	92[e]	3[e]	5[e]	63	98	2	14
Mozambique	12,746[d]	0.6	0.3[d]	89	2[e]	9[e]	82	17	2	40
Myanmar	23,515	4.0	0.4	90	3	7	36	36	21	39
Namibia	27,373[d]	0.3	0.5[d]	68[e]	3[e]	29[e]	..	..	..	..
Nepal	9,199	29.0	13.8	99	0	1	78	..	20	..
Netherlands	5,797[d]	7.8	8.6	34	61	5	100	100	99	100
New Zealand	532	2.0	100.0	44	10	46	100	..	100	..
Nicaragua	37,467	1.3	0.5	84	2	14	77	81	13	27
Niger	3,204[d]	0.5	1.5[d]	82[e]	2[e]	16[e]	48	46	34	55
Nigeria	2,318[d]	4.0	1.4[d]	54[e]	15[e]	31[e]	60	63	30	26
Norway	88,673[d]	2.0	0.5[d]	8	72	20	100	100	95	100
Oman	439	1.2	123.2	94	2	5	90	98	55	56
Pakistan	1,938[d]	155.6	61.0[d]	97	2	2	77	77	22	52
Panama	52,961	1.6	0.9	70	2	28	100	99	64	73
Papua New Guinea	177,940	0.1	0.0	49	22	29	54	84	10	17
Paraguay	61,750	0.4	0.1[d]	78	7	15	49	70	8	6
Peru	1,641	19.0	15.3	86	7	7	73	74	17	24
Philippines	4,393	55.4	9.1	88	4	8	..	91	..	81
Poland	1,629[d]	12.1	19.2[d]	11	76	13	89	..	73	..
Portugal	7,223[d]	7.3	10.1[d]	48	37	15	97	..	50	..
Puerto Rico	..	..	..	..	..	..	..	..	..	..
Romania	9,222[d]	26.0	12.5[d]	59	33	8	91	69	50	..
Russian Federation	30,619[d]	77.1	1.7[d]	20	62	19	..	..	..	..

3.5 Freshwater

	Freshwater resources	Annual freshwater withdrawals					Access to safe water			
							Urban % of population		Rural % of population	
	cubic meters per capita 1998	billion cu. m[a]	% of total resources[a]	% for agriculture[b]	% for industry[b]	% for domestic[b]	1982–85[c]	1990–96[c]	1982–85[c]	1990–96[c]
Rwanda	798	0.8	12.2	94[e]	1[e]	5[e]	55	..	*60*	44
Saudi Arabia	116	17.0	708.3	90	1	9	*92*	..	*87*	..
Senegal	4,359[d]	1.5	3.8[d]	92[e]	3[e]	5[e]	*63*	82	*27*	28
Sierra Leone	32,957	0.4	0.2	89[e]	4[e]	*7*[e]	*58*	58	*8*	21
Singapore	193	0.2	31.7	4	51	*45*	*100*	100	..	..
Slovak Republic	15,396	1.4	1.7	..	..	..	..	..	..	..
Slovenia	*9,334*	0.5	2.7	..	50	50	..	100	..	97
South Africa	1,208[d]	13.3	26.6[d]	72[e]	11[e]	17[e]	..	..	..	..
Spain	2,847[d]	35.5	31.7[d]	62	26	12	100	..	95	..
Sri Lanka	2,329	9.8	14.6	96	2	*2*	76	..	26	..
Sudan	5,433	17.8	11.6	94[e]	1[e]	*5*[e]	*49*	66	*45*	45
Sweden	20,109[d]	2.7	1.5[d]	9	55	36	100	..	98	..
Switzerland	7,458[d]	2.6	4.9[d]	0	58	*42*	*100*	100	*100*	100
Syrian Arab Republic	2,926	14.4	32.2	94	2	*4*	*77*	92	*65*	78
Tajikistan	13,017[d]	11.9	14.9[d]	92	4	4	..	86	..	32
Tanzania	2,770[d]	1.2	1.3[d]	89[e]	2[e]	*9*[e]	*85*	65	*47*	45
Thailand	6,698[d]	33.1	8.1[d]	91	4	*5*	..	94	..	88
Togo	2,692[d]	0.1	0.8[d]	25[e]	13[e]	62[e]	68	..	26	..
Trinidad and Tobago	3,991	0.2	2.9	35	38	*27*	*100*	83	93	80
Tunisia	439[d]	2.8	69.0[d]	86[e]	2[e]	*13*[e]	98	..	79	..
Turkey	3,209[d]	35.5	17.4[d]	73[e]	11[e]	*16*[e]	73	..	65	..
Turkmenistan	9,644[d]	23.8	52.3[d]	98	1	1	..	80	..	5
Uganda	3,158[d]	0.2	0.3[d]	60	8	*32*	*45*	47	*12*	32
Ukraine	2,776[d]	26.0[f]	18.6[d]	30	52	18	..	77	..	12
United Arab Emirates	73	2.1	1,055.0	67	9	*24*	*100*	98	*100*	98
United Kingdom	2,489	9.3	6.4	3	77	20	*100*	100	*100*	100
United States	9,168[d]	447.7	18.1[d]	27[e]	65[e]	8[e]	..	..	..	..
Uruguay	37,971[d]	4.2	0.5[d]	91	3	*6*	*95*	99	27	..
Uzbekistan	5,476[d]	58.1	63.4[d]	94	2	4	..	72	..	46
Venezuela, RB	57,821[d]	4.1	0.3[d]	46	10	*44*	88	..	65	..
Vietnam	11,647	54.3	6.1	86	10	*4*	..	53	..	32
West Bank and Gaza	..	..	..	..	..	..	..	..	..	..
Yemen, Rep.	254	2.9	71.5	92	1	7	..	74	..	14
Yugoslavia, FR (Serb./Mont.)	..	..	..	..	..	..	..	..	..	..
Zambia	12,001[d]	1.7	1.5[d]	77[e]	7[e]	16[e]	*70*	64	*32*	27
Zimbabwe	1,711[d]	1.2	6.1	79[e]	7[e]	*14*[e]	*100*	99	*10*	64
World	**8,354 w**	..	..	**70 w**	**22 w**	**8 w**	.. w	.. w	.. w	.. w
Low income	4,330	..	..	87	8	*5*	..	..	..	..
Excl. China & India	9,187	..	..	92	4	4	..	..	..	..
Middle income	15,145	..	..	74	13	12	..	..	..	..
Lower middle income	*11,805*	..	..	75	15	*10*	..	..	..	..
Upper middle income	..	..	..	73	10	17	..	..	58	..
Low & middle income	*8,113*	..	..	82	10	7	..	..	..	..
East Asia & Pacific	..	..	..	80	14	6	..	89	..	82
Europe & Central Asia	14,339	..	..	63	26	*11*	..	..	..	..
Latin America & Carib.	27,393	..	..	74	9	*18*	..	..	44	..
Middle East & N. Africa	1,044	..	..	89	4	*6*	*82*	..	*42*	..
South Asia	4,088	..	..	93	2	4	*76*	83	*46*	75
Sub-Saharan Africa	*8,441*	..	..	87	4	9	61	..	26	..
High income	..	..	..	30	59	11	..	..	..	..
Europe EMU	3,771	..	..	21	63	16	100	..	90	..

a. Data refer to any year from 1980 to 1998, unless otherwise noted. b. Unless otherwise noted, sectoral withdrawal shares are estimated for 1987. c. Data refer to the most recent year available in the period. d. Total water resources include river flows from other countries. e. Data refer to years other than 1987 (see *Primary data documentation*). f. Data refer to estimates for years before 1980 (see *Primary data documentation*).

Freshwater 3.5

About the data

The data on freshwater resources are based on estimates of runoff into rivers and recharge of groundwater. These estimates are based on different sources and refer to different years, so cross-country comparisons should be made with caution. Because they are collected intermittently, the data may hide significant variations in total renewable water resources from one year to the next. The data also fail to distinguish between seasonal and geographic variations in water availability within countries. Data for small countries and countries in arid and semiarid zones are less reliable than those for larger countries and countries with higher rainfall. Finally, caution is also needed in comparing data on annual freshwater withdrawals, which are subject to variations in collection and estimation methods.

This year's edition of the *World Development Indicators* and last year's define freshwater resources as including river flows arising outside the country. The data in these editions therefore are not comparable with those published in previous years, which exclude external sources. Because the definition includes river flows entering a country but does not deduct river flows out of countries, it double counts the availability of water from international river ways. This can be important in water-short countries, notably in the Middle East.

Access to safe water measures the share of the population served by improved sources of water. An improved source can be any form of collection or piping used to make water regularly available. While information on access to safe water is widely used, it is extremely subjective, and such terms as *safe* and *adequate amount* may have very different meanings in different countries despite official World Health Organization (WHO) definitions (see *Definitions* for table 2.15). Even in high-income countries treated water may not always be safe to drink. While access to safe water is equated with connection to a public supply system, this does not take account of variations in the quality and cost (broadly defined) of the service once connected. Thus cross-country comparisons must be made cautiously. Changes over time within countries may result from changes in definitions or measurements.

Figure 3.5

Agriculture accounted for most freshwater withdrawals in developing economies in the past two decades . . .

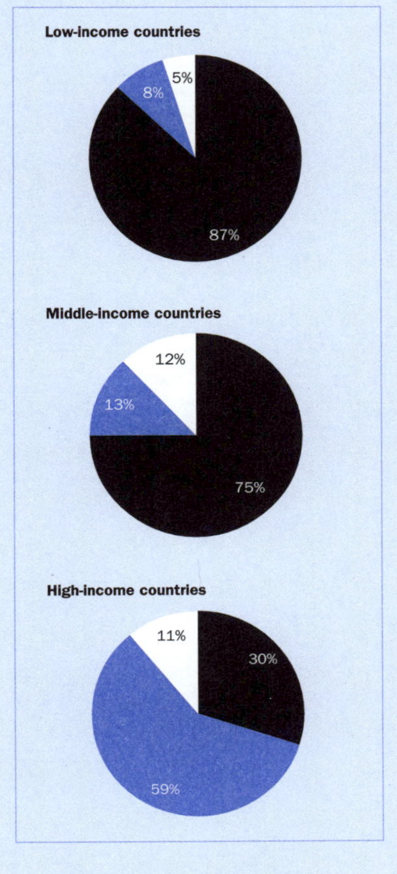

. . . and for most of the growth in withdrawals in the past century

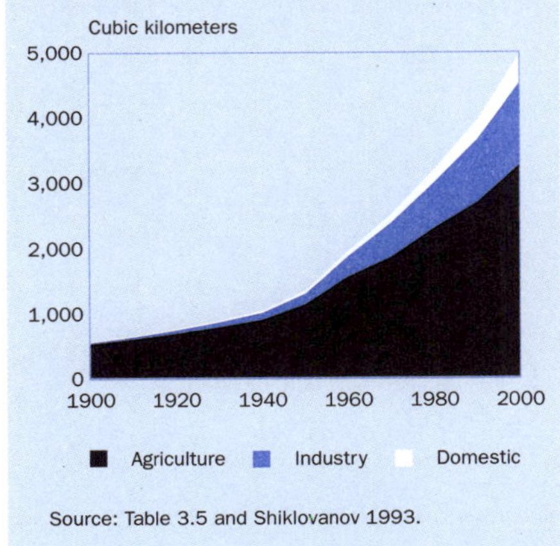

Source: Table 3.5 and Shiklovanov 1993.

Definitions

• **Freshwater resources** refer to total renewable resources, which include flows of rivers and groundwater from rainfall in the country, and river flows from other countries. Freshwater resources per capita are calculated using the World Bank's population estimates (see table 2.1). • **Annual freshwater withdrawals** refer to total water withdrawal, not counting evaporation losses from storage basins. Withdrawals also include water from desalination plants in countries where they are a significant source. Withdrawal data are for single years between 1980 and 1998 unless otherwise indicated. Withdrawals can exceed 100 percent of total renewable resources where extraction from nonrenewable aquifers or desalination plants is considerable or where there is significant water reuse. Withdrawals for agriculture and industry are total withdrawals for irrigation and livestock production and for direct industrial use (including withdrawals for cooling thermoelectric plants). Withdrawals for domestic uses include drinking water, municipal use or supply, and use for public services, commercial establishments, and homes. For most countries sectoral withdrawal data are estimated for 1987. • **Access to safe water** refers to the percentage of people with reasonable access to an adequate amount of safe water in a dwelling or within a convenient distance of their dwelling (see *About the data*).

Data sources

The data on freshwater resources and withdrawals are compiled by the World Resources Institute from various sources and published in *World Resources 1998–99* and *World Resources 2000–01* (produced in collaboration with the United Nations Environment Programme, United Nations Development Programme, and World Bank). The data on access to safe water come from the WHO.

3.6 Water pollution

	Emissions of organic water pollutants				Industry shares of emissions of organic water pollutants							
	kilograms per day		kilograms per day per worker		Primary metals %	Paper and pulp %	Chemicals %	Food and beverages %	Stone, ceramics, and glass %	Textiles %	Wood %	Other %
	1980	1997[a]	1980	1997[a]	1997[a]	1997[a]	1997[a]	1997[a]	1997[a]	1997[a]	1997[a]	1997[a]
Albania	..	5,844	..	0.24	22.9	1.5	6.2	62.0	0.4	4.7	0.7	1.5
Algeria	60,290	102,969	0.19	0.25	44.6	..	3.8	40.8	0.4	8.0	2.5	..
Angola	..	1,472	..	0.20	7.6	3.0	9.1	65.9	0.3	5.5	4.4	4.1
Argentina	244,711	186,844	0.18	0.21	6.3	12.6	8.1	59.4	0.2	7.4	1.5	4.6
Armenia	..	12,858	..	0.23	..	..	0.0	66.5	..	33.5	..	..
Australia	204,333	173,269	0.18	0.19	12.4	22.8	6.7	43.5	0.2	5.3	2.8	6.3
Austria	108,416	78,040	0.16	0.14	13.1	19.5	9.1	36.1	0.3	6.7	4.3	10.9
Azerbaijan	..	45,025	..	0.17	11.6	2.5	12.0	49.0	0.2	18.1	1.0	5.6
Bangladesh	66,713	186,852	0.16	0.16	2.8	6.8	3.5	34.2	0.1	50.9	0.6	1.1
Belarus	..	..	..	..	..	..	..	..	..	..	..	..
Belgium	136,452	113,460	0.16	0.16	14.4	17.7	11.6	36.8	0.2	8.8	2.0	8.4
Benin	1,646	..	0.28	..	..	..	..	..	..	..	..	..
Bolivia	9,343	10,251	0.22	0.23	4.7	13.8	6.5	61.8	0.3	9.0	2.6	1.2
Bosnia and Herzegovina	..	8,903	..	0.18	20.5	13.1	6.6	33.3	0.2	17.6	5.8	2.8
Botswana	1,307	4,386	0.24	0.18	0.0	11.5	2.8	67.5	0.0	12.5	2.1	3.7
Brazil	866,790	690,876	0.16	0.19	19.0	12.6	9.3	41.6	0.2	10.9	1.6	4.8
Bulgaria	152,125	88,729	0.13	0.15	14.6	8.6	11.0	38.8	0.3	15.2	2.1	9.3
Burkina Faso	2,385	..	0.29	..	..	..	..	..	..	..	..	..
Burundi	769	1,644	0.22	0.24	0.0	8.3	4.7	67.8	0.1	16.7	1.6	0.8
Cambodia	..	12,078	..	0.16	0.0	3.4	3.3	59.2	0.6	24.7	5.8	3.1
Cameroon	14,569	12,796	0.29	0.24	3.0	5.7	20.8	63.4	0.0	2.9	3.8	0.3
Canada	330,241	295,525	0.18	0.17	9.6	29.8	9.1	34.0	0.1	5.8	3.9	7.6
Central African Republic	861	..	..	..	..	..	..	..	..	..	..	..
Chad	..	..	..	..	..	..	..	..	..	..	..	..
Chile	44,371	77,111	0.21	0.23	7.2	11.8	8.6	59.6	0.1	7.2	2.6	2.9
China	3,377,105	7,396,000	0.14	0.14	20.6	11.9	14.2	28.9	0.4	14.1	1.0	8.9
Hong Kong, China	102,002	51,577	0.11	0.15	1.4	37.2	3.9	20.5	0.1	29.0	0.2	7.6
Colombia	96,055	111,139	0.19	0.20	3.6	15.2	10.6	51.3	0.2	14.8	0.9	3.3
Congo, Dem. Rep.	..	..	..	..	..	..	..	..	..	..	..	..
Congo, Rep.	1,039	..	0.21	..	..	..	..	..	..	..	..	..
Costa Rica	..	32,301	..	0.22	1.2	10.2	6.6	62.3	0.1	15.8	1.5	2.3
Côte d'Ivoire	15,414	..	0.23	..	..	..	..	..	..	..	..	..
Croatia	..	50,014	..	0.16	4.7	14.2	8.9	45.8	0.2	16.2	3.6	6.4
Cuba	120,703	172,973	0.24	0.25	5.0	4.6	2.3	78.4	0.3	6.1	0.7	2.7
Czech Republic	..	162,615	..	0.14	24.6	9.2	6.8	32.7	0.4	12.3	2.4	11.7
Denmark	65,465	91,815	0.17	0.18	2.1	28.9	7.7	46.6	0.2	3.5	2.9	8.3
Dominican Republic	54,935	..	0.38	..	..	..	..	..	..	..	..	..
Ecuador	25,297	28,969	0.23	0.25	2.4	13.2	7.5	66.1	0.2	7.2	1.7	1.6
Egypt, Arab Rep.	169,146	216,060	0.19	0.19	12.4	5.3	9.5	50.1	0.3	18.2	0.6	3.7
El Salvador	9,390	16,385	0.24	0.18	1.0	10.6	8.6	46.5	0.1	30.9	0.5	1.7
Eritrea	16,754	22,175	..	..	1.4	8.9	4.4	58.5	0.1	24.8	1.4	0.5
Estonia	..	..	..	..	..	..	..	..	..	..	..	..
Ethiopia	..	19,390	0.22	0.22	2.0	11.3	3.4	56.6	0.2	24.2	1.7	0.6
Finland	92,275	64,253	0.17	0.18	9.1	39.8	7.0	30.0	0.1	2.6	3.5	7.9
France	729,776	585,382	0.14	0.15	11.6	21.2	10.8	37.7	0.2	6.1	1.8	10.8
Gabon	2,661	1,886	0.15	0.26	0.0	6.0	4.9	79.7	0.1	1.2	6.9	1.2
Gambia, The	549	832	0.30	0.34	0.0	15.3	1.9	77.8	0.1	2.6	1.9	0.4
Georgia	..	..	..	..	..	..	..	..	..	..	..	..
Germany	..	811,315	..	0.12	12.7	16.8	15.5	30.6	0.3	4.8	2.2	17.2
Ghana	15,868	14,449	0.20	0.17	9.8	16.9	10.5	39.5	0.2	9.1	12.4	1.7
Greece	65,304	58,229	0.17	0.19	6.1	12.1	8.6	53.3	0.3	14.7	1.5	3.5
Guatemala	20,856	19,052	0.25	0.28	5.3	8.0	6.2	71.4	0.1	6.9	1.1	1.0
Guinea	..	..	..	..	..	..	..	..	..	..	..	..
Guinea-Bissau	..	..	..	..	..	..	..	..	..	..	..	..
Haiti	4,734	..	0.19	..	..	..	..	..	..	..	..	..
Honduras	13,067	34,036	0.23	0.20	1.1	7.8	3.9	55.5	0.1	26.8	4.0	0.8

Water pollution 3.6

	Emissions of organic water pollutants				Industry shares of emissions of organic water pollutants							
	kilograms per day		kilograms per day per worker		Primary metals %	Paper and pulp %	Chemicals %	Food and beverages %	Stone, ceramics, and glass %	Textiles %	Wood %	Other %
	1980	1997[a]	1980	1997[a]	1997[a]	1997[a]	1997[a]	1997[a]	1997[a]	1997[a]	1997[a]	1997[a]
Hungary	201,888	139,453	0.15	0.18	10.7	10.2	8.3	50.3	0.2	11.6	1.8	6.9
India	1,422,564	1,664,150	0.21	0.19	15.5	7.5	8.2	51.5	0.2	11.6	0.3	5.2
Indonesia	214,010	*727,496*	0.22	*0.17*	2.4	*8.9*	8.6	*50.2*	0.2	*21.7*	5.3	*2.8*
Iran, Islamic Rep.	72,334	*101,900*	0.15	*0.17*	20.6	*8.0*	8.0	*39.7*	0.5	*17.3*	0.7	*5.4*
Iraq	32,986	*19,617*	0.19	*0.16*	8.8	*14.1*	15.1	*39.4*	0.7	*16.7*	0.3	*4.8*
Ireland	43,544	*33,994*	0.19	*0.16*	1.8	*17.2*	10.6	*52.2*	0.2	*6.8*	1.8	*9.4*
Israel	39,113	*54,251*	0.15	*0.16*	3.7	*19.7*	9.4	*43.9*	0.2	*12.1*	1.8	*9.3*
Italy	442,712	*359,578*	0.13	*0.13*	12.1	*16.0*	11.8	*28.7*	0.3	*16.1*	2.5	*12.6*
Jamaica	11,123	*17,507*	0.25	*0.29*	6.9	*7.2*	3.8	*70.8*	0.1	*9.8*	1.3	..
Japan	1,456,016	1,468,545	0.14	0.14	8.6	21.9	8.9	38.9	0.2	6.8	1.9	12.8
Jordan	4,146	*15,225*	0.17	*0.18*	3.9	*15.6*	14.4	*50.6*	0.6	*8.3*	3.4	*3.2*
Kazakhstan	..	..	..	..	..	..	..	..	..	..	..	..
Kenya	26,834	*48,354*	0.19	*0.24*	4.1	*11.7*	5.6	*65.2*	0.1	*8.7*	1.9	*2.7*
Korea, Dem. Rep.	..	..	..	..	..	..	..	..	..	..	..	..
Korea, Rep.	281,900	*340,035*	0.14	*0.12*	11.8	*17.5*	11.7	*26.3*	0.3	*16.6*	1.6	*14.3*
Kuwait	6,921	*8,761*	0.16	*0.15*	3.1	*4.4*	13.8	*50.9*	0.5	*17.0*	3.9	*6.4*
Kyrgyz Republic	..	*20,700*	..	*0.16*	13.7	*0.2*	0.9	*54.8*	0.4	*21.0*	1.0	*8.0*
Lao PDR	..	..	..	..	..	..	..	..	..	..	..	..
Latvia	..	*27,357*	..	*0.18*	2.8	*11.8*	4.5	*58.2*	0.1	*11.0*	5.9	*5.7*
Lebanon	14,586	..	0.20	..	..	..	..	..	..	..	..	..
Lesotho	*993*	*2,550*	*0.24*	*0.16*	0.8	*2.2*	*0.9*	*41.0*	*0.1*	54.8	*0.2*	*0.1*
Libya	3,532	..	0.21	..	..	..	..	..	..	..	..	..
Lithuania	..	*48,621*	..	*0.15*	1.3	*8.4*	3.9	*55.4*	0.4	*19.2*	4.2	*7.4*
Macedonia, FYR	..	*23,490*	..	*0.18*	11.7	*9.6*	6.2	*45.0*	0.1	*20.9*	1.7	*4.9*
Madagascar	9,131	..	0.23	..	..	..	..	..	..	..	..	..
Malawi	12,224	*9,055*	0.32	*0.26*	0.0	*12.6*	5.1	*67.7*	0.1	*11.6*	1.7	1.1
Malaysia	77,215	*166,960*	0.15	*0.11*	7.3	*13.1*	15.2	*32.0*	0.3	*8.5*	8.5	*14.9*
Mali	..	..	..	..	..	..	..	..	..	..	..	..
Mauritania	..	..	..	..	..	..	..	..	..	..	..	..
Mauritius	9,224	*17,424*	0.21	*0.16*	1.2	*5.2*	2.2	*38.4*	0.1	51.1	0.8	*1.1*
Mexico	130,993	*142,921*	0.22	*0.19*	9.9	*9.4*	13.2	*54.5*	0.2	*6.6*	0.4	*5.8*
Moldova	..	*34,234*	..	*0.29*	0.2	*4.0*	1.4	*81.7*	0.2	*10.8*	1.3	*0.5*
Mongolia	9,254	*7,939*	0.19	*0.18*	1.8	*4.3*	0.9	*64.2*	0.3	*24.6*	4.9	..
Morocco	26,598	*84,601*	0.15	*0.18*	0.8	*7.7*	7.3	*54.1*	0.3	*26.4*	0.9	*2.5*
Mozambique	..	*9,217*	..	*0.25*	3.1	*7.9*	4.1	*71.1*	0.1	*8.2*	4.4	*1.2*
Myanmar	..	*4,479*	..	*0.09*	11.4	*6.8*	29.6	*18.5*	1.5	*3.9*	27.1	*1.2*
Namibia	..	*7,350*	..	*0.35*	0.0	*5.0*	1.6	*90.4*	0.1	*1.2*	0.9	*0.8*
Nepal	*18,692*	*26,550*	0.25	*0.14*	*1.5*	*8.1*	*3.9*	*43.3*	*1.2*	*39.3*	*1.7*	*1.0*
Netherlands	165,416	*126,892*	0.18	*0.18*	7.6	*26.0*	11.7	*42.7*	0.2	*2.4*	1.2	*8.2*
New Zealand	59,012	*47,321*	0.21	*0.22*	5.0	*19.9*	5.2	*56.6*	0.1	*6.3*	3.0	*3.9*
Nicaragua	9,647	..	0.28	..	..	..	..	..	..	..	..	..
Niger	372	..	0.19	..	..	..	..	..	..	..	..	..
Nigeria	72,082	*57,224*	0.17	*0.23*	12.1	*9.3*	10.4	*57.0*	0.2	*7.3*	2.2	*1.6*
Norway	67,897	*49,494*	0.19	*0.20*	10.1	*31.0*	5.2	*42.4*	0.1	*1.6*	2.6	*6.9*
Oman	..	*236*	..	*0.15*	2.5	*6.0*	13.6	*55.2*	0.5	*10.9*	4.2	*7.0*
Pakistan	75,125	*114,726*	0.17	*0.18*	14.1	*5.8*	7.3	*39.5*	0.2	*30.1*	0.3	*2.7*
Panama	8,121	*11,396*	0.26	*0.28*	1.0	*10.5*	4.8	*74.3*	0.1	*7.4*	1.2	*0.7*
Papua New Guinea	4,365	*5,729*	0.22	*0.25*	0.6	*7.3*	1.7	*80.1*	0.1	*1.1*	6.2	2.9
Paraguay	..	*3,250*	..	*0.28*	2.3	*9.9*	6.0	*73.6*	0.3	*6.7*	0.3	*0.9*
Peru	50,367	*51,828*	0.18	*0.21*	9.6	*12.0*	8.4	*53.0*	0.2	*12.3*	1.6	*2.9*
Philippines	182,052	178,239	0.19	0.18	5.2	9.8	7.3	54.5	0.2	16.4	2.0	4.6
Poland	580,869	385,331	0.14	0.16	15.5	4.9	6.7	48.7	0.3	13.4	2.0	8.5
Portugal	105,441	137,362	0.15	0.14	3.5	14.2	5.1	38.9	0.4	26.7	4.8	6.5
Puerto Rico	24,034	*18,202*	0.16	*0.14*	0.9	*9.7*	16.9	*41.4*	0.1	*21.9*	1.1	*8.0*
Romania	343,145	*333,168*	0.12	*0.14*	17.1	*6.7*	9.0	*34.3*	0.3	*18.5*	4.8	*9.4*
Russian Federation	..	*1,615,346*	..	*0.15*	18.2	*6.8*	9.2	*44.7*	0.4	*8.0*	2.6	*10.0*

3.6 Water pollution

	Emissions of organic water pollutants				Industry shares of emissions of organic water pollutants							
	kilograms per day		kilograms per day per worker		Primary metals %	Paper and pulp %	Chemicals %	Food and beverages %	Stone, ceramics, and glass %	Textiles %	Wood %	Other %
	1980	1997[a]	1980	1997[a]	1997[a]	1997[a]	1997[a]	1997[a]	1997[a]	1997[a]	1997[a]	1997[a]
Rwanda	..	..	..	..	..	..	..	..	..	..	..	..
Saudi Arabia	18,181	24,436	0.12	0.14	4.4	15.9	21.1	45.1	1.0	3.8	2.0	6.8
Senegal	9,865	10,223	0.31	0.33	0.0	7.4	7.4	81.6	0.0	3.0	0.1	0.6
Sierra Leone	1,612	4,170	0.24	0.32	..	9.6	3.0	82.3	0.1	2.0	2.2	0.8
Singapore	28,558	34,267	0.10	0.09	2.4	27.9	14.2	18.7	0.1	6.2	1.5	29.0
Slovak Republic	..	64,293	..	0.14	15.5	13.8	9.6	34.9	0.3	14.0	1.6	10.3
Slovenia	..	40,148	..	0.16	29.2	16.8	8.3	24.2	0.2	13.2	2.2	5.9
South Africa	237,599	241,756	0.17	0.17	11.6	16.4	9.7	41.8	0.2	10.8	3.3	6.2
Spain	376,253	335,240	0.16	0.16	7.3	17.7	8.8	46.3	0.3	8.6	3.4	7.6
Sri Lanka	30,086	55,665	0.18	0.17	1.2	8.9	7.2	42.2	0.2	38.3	0.7	1.3
Sudan	..	..	..	..	..	..	..	..	..	..	..	..
Sweden	130,439	91,981	0.15	0.16	10.9	37.0	7.6	27.8	0.1	1.6	3.3	11.7
Switzerland	..	123,752	..	0.17	24.9	23.6	10.4	25.0	0.2	3.2	4.2	8.7
Syrian Arab Republic	36,262	21,421	0.19	0.22	2.9	1.5	8.4	68.3	0.4	17.2	0.3	1.1
Tajikistan	..	..	..	..	..	..	..	..	..	..	..	..
Tanzania	21,084	32,508	0.21	0.26	4.7	10.8	5.0	65.2	0.1	11.8	1.4	1.2
Thailand	213,271	355,819	0.22	0.16	6.1	5.3	5.3	42.2	0.2	35.4	1.5	3.9
Togo	963	..	0.27	..	10.4	38.7	5.8	41.8	0.2	2.1	0.8	..
Trinidad and Tobago	7,835	11,787	0.18	0.28	4.4	10.9	6.7	72.6	0.1	2.9	1.3	1.2
Tunisia	20,294	45,806	0.16	0.16	6.4	7.9	6.0	40.4	0.4	34.0	1.7	3.2
Turkey	160,173	177,161	0.20	0.17	12.7	7.6	7.3	43.8	0.3	22.5	0.9	4.9
Turkmenistan	..	..	..	..	..	..	..	..	..	..	..	..
Uganda	..	16,728	..	0.30	1.6	5.2	1.0	81.6	0.1	8.0	1.5	1.0
Ukraine	..	539,490	..	0.16	20.5	3.7	7.5	50.7	0.4	6.7	1.6	8.9
United Arab Emirates	4,524	..	0.15	..	..	..	..	..	..	..	..	..
United Kingdom	964,510	642,362	0.15	0.15	7.4	26.3	10.6	35.7	0.2	7.5	2.0	10.4
United States	2,742,993	2,584,818	0.14	0.15	8.8	32.8	10.1	27.3	0.2	7.3	2.7	10.9
Uruguay	34,270	27,727	0.21	0.25	1.5	11.4	5.6	67.7	0.1	11.1	0.8	1.9
Uzbekistan	..	..	..	..	..	..	..	..	..	..	..	..
Venezuela, RB	84,797	92,026	0.20	0.21	14.1	11.5	9.9	51.8	0.2	7.3	1.7	3.4
Vietnam	..	..	..	..	..	..	..	..	..	..	..	..
West Bank and Gaza	..	..	..	..	..	..	..	..	..	..	..	..
Yemen, Rep.	..	7,823	..	0.25	0.0	9.1	12.9	71.1	0.3	4.9	1.0	0.9
Yugoslavia, FR (Serb./Mont.)	..	123,247	..	0.16	9.7	12.6	7.6	43.4	0.3	16.1	2.1	8.1
Zambia	13,605	11,433	0.23	0.22	3.4	10.8	7.3	63.6	0.2	9.3	3.0	2.4
Zimbabwe	32,681	33,223	0.20	0.19	14.0	11.4	5.6	47.3	0.2	14.9	3.4	3.2

Note: Industry shares may not sum to 100 percent because data may be from different years.
a. Data refer to most recent year between 1993 and 1997.

Water pollution 3.6

About the data

Emissions of organic pollutants from industrial activities are a major cause of degradation of water quality. Water quality and pollution levels are generally measured in terms of concentration, or load—the rate of occurrence of a substance in an aqueous solution. Polluting substances include organic matter, metals, minerals, sediment, bacteria, and toxic chemicals. This table focuses on organic water pollution resulting from industrial activities. Because water pollution tends to be sensitive to local conditions, the national-level data in the table may not reflect the quality of water in specific locations.

The data in the table come from an international study of industrial emissions that may be the first to include data from developing countries (Hettige, Mani, and Wheeler 1998). Unlike estimates from earlier studies based on engineering or economic models, these estimates are based on actual measurements of plant-level water pollution. The focus is on organic water pollution measured in terms of biochemical oxygen demand (BOD) because the data for this indicator are the most plentiful and reliable for cross-country comparisons of emissions. BOD measures the strength of an organic waste in terms of the amount of oxygen consumed in breaking it down. A sewage overload in natural waters exhausts the water's dissolved oxygen content. Wastewater treatment, by contrast, reduces BOD.

Data on water pollution are more readily available than other emissions data because most industrial pollution control programs start by regulating emissions of organic water pollutants. Such data are fairly reliable because sampling techniques for measuring water pollution are more widely understood and much less expensive than those for air pollution.

In their study Hettige, Mani, and Wheeler (1998) used plant- and sector-level information on emissions and employment from 13 national environmental protection agencies and sector-level information on output and employment from the United Nations Industrial Development Organization (UNIDO). Their econometric analysis found that the ratio of BOD to employment in each industrial sector is about the same across countries. This finding allowed the authors to estimate BOD loads across countries and over time. The estimated BOD intensities per unit of employment were multiplied by sectoral employment numbers from UNIDO's industry database for 1980–97. The sectoral emissions estimates were then totaled to get daily BOD emissions in kilograms per day for each country and year.

Figure 3.6

As per capita income rises, pollution intensity falls

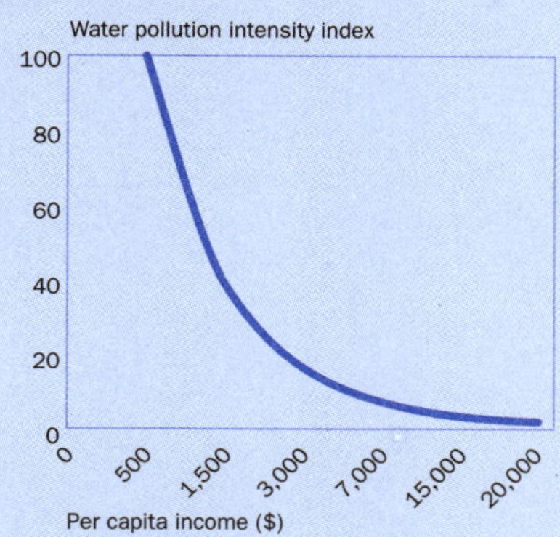

Note: The water pollution intensity index measures the organic pollutant per unit of industrial output.
Source: Hettige, Mani, and Wheeler 1998.

A recent World Bank study shows a continuous relationship between per capita income and the intensity of organic water pollution. For each 1 percent increase in per capita income, there is a 1 percent decline in pollution intensity. The fastest decline occurs before countries reach middle-income status.

Definitions

- **Emissions of organic water pollutants** are measured in terms of biochemical oxygen demand, which refers to the amount of oxygen that bacteria in water will consume in breaking down waste. This is a standard water treatment test for the presence of organic pollutants. Emissions per worker are total emissions divided by the number of industrial workers. • **Industry shares of emissions of organic water pollutants** refer to emissions from manufacturing activities as defined by two-digit divisions of the International Standard Industrial Classification (ISIC) revision 2: primary metals (ISIC division 37), paper and pulp (34), chemicals (35), food and beverages (31), stone, ceramics, and glass (36), textiles (32), wood (33), and other (38 and 39).

Data sources

Indicators for 1980–93 were drawn from a 1998 study by Hemamala Hettige, Muthukumara Mani, and David Wheeler, "Industrial Pollution in Economic Development: Kuznets Revisited" (available on the World Wide Web at www.worldbank.org/nipr). These indicators were then updated through 1997 by the World Bank's Development Research Group using the same methodology as the initial study. Sectoral employment numbers are from UNIDO's industry database.

3.7 Energy production and use

	Commercial energy production		Commercial energy use			Commercial energy use per capita			Net energy imports[a]	
	thousand metric tons of oil equivalent		thousand metric tons of oil equivalent		average annual % growth	kg of oil equivalent		average annual % growth	% of commercial energy use	
	1980	1997	1980	1997	1980–97	1980	1997	1980–97	1980	1997
Albania	3,428	912	3,049	1,048	–6.7	1,142	317	–8	–12	13
Algeria	67,061	125,576	12,410	26,497	3.6	665	904	0.9	–440	–374
Angola	11,301	41,430	4,538	6,848	2.4	647	587	–0.6	–149	–505
Argentina	38,813	80,134	41,868	61,710	2.3	1,490	1,730	0.9	7	–30
Armenia	1,263	537	1,070	1,804	–4.9	346	476	*–6.0*	–18	70
Australia	86,096	199,167	70,372	101,626	2.3	4,790	5,484	0.9	–22	–96
Austria	7,655	8,007	23,450	27,761	1.4	3,105	3,439	0.9	67	71
Azerbaijan	14,821	14,027	15,001	11,987	–4.9	2,433	1,529	*–6.3*	1	–17
Bangladesh	13,204	21,894	14,900	24,327	3.1	172	197	0.9	11	10
Belarus	2,566	3,275	2,385	25,142	6.3	247	2,449	*5.9*	–8	87
Belgium	7,986	13,153	46,100	57,125	1.7	4,682	5,611	1.5	83	77
Benin	1,212	1,897	1,363	2,182	2.5	393	377	–0.6	11	13
Bolivia	4,241	5,953	2,287	4,254	2.6	427	548	0.4	–85	–40
Bosnia and Herzegovina	..	626	..	1,750	..	..	479	..	..	64
Botswana	..	..	..	..	..	..	..	..	..	..
Brazil	62,069	120,236	108,999	172,030	2.9	896	1,051	1.1	43	30
Bulgaria	7,737	9,981	28,673	20,616	–2.5	3,236	2,480	–2.1	73	52
Burkina Faso	..	..	..	..	..	..	..	..	..	..
Burundi	..	..	..	..	..	..	..	..	..	..
Cambodia	..	..	..	..	..	..	..	..	..	..
Cameroon	5,824	11,250	3,687	5,756	2.3	426	413	–0.5	–58	–95
Canada	207,417	362,701	193,000	237,983	1.6	7,848	7,930	0.4	–7	–52
Central African Republic	..	..	..	..	..	..	..	..	..	..
Chad	..	..	..	..	..	..	..	..	..	..
Chile	5,664	8,168	9,525	23,012	5.7	854	1,574	4.0	41	65
China	608,664	1,097,210	598,628	1,113,050	4.0	610	907	2.6	–2	1
Hong Kong, China	39	48	5,518	14,121	5.9	1,095	2,172	4.6	99	100
Colombia	18,212	67,524	19,127	30,481	3.0	672	761	0.9	5	–122
Congo, Dem. Rep.	8,697	14,364	8,706	14,539	3.1	322	311	–0.2	0	1
Congo, Rep.	3,970	13,540	845	1,242	2.1	506	459	–0.8	–370	–990
Costa Rica	767	1,157	1,527	2,663	4.0	669	769	1.5	50	57
Côte d'Ivoire	2,419	4,908	3,662	5,597	2.8	447	394	–0.5	34	12
Croatia	..	4,011	..	7,650	..	..	1,687	..	..	48
Cuba	3,891	7,255	14,570	14,273	–1.1	1,501	1,291	–1.9	73	49
Czech Republic	42,913	31,539	47,029	40,576	–1.4	4,596	3,938	–1.5	9	22
Denmark	896	20,274	19,734	21,107	0.9	3,852	3,994	0.8	95	4
Dominican Republic	1,332	1,423	3,464	5,453	2.4	608	673	0.2	62	74
Ecuador	11,756	22,792	5,191	8,513	2.7	652	713	0.3	–126	–168
Egypt, Arab Rep.	34,168	57,997	15,970	39,581	4.9	391	656	2.5	–114	–47
El Salvador	1,913	2,649	2,537	4,095	2.7	553	691	1.1	25	35
Eritrea	..	..	..	..	..	..	..	..	..	..
Estonia	6,951	3,788	6,275	5,556	–1.1	4,240	3,811	*–0.9*	–11	32
Ethiopia	10,588	16,316	11,157	17,131	2.7	296	287	–0.1	5	5
Finland	6,912	15,059	25,413	33,075	1.6	5,317	6,435	1.2	73	54
France	46,829	127,843	190,111	247,534	2.1	3,528	4,224	1.5	75	48
Gabon	9,441	19,786	1,493	1,635	–0.7	2,161	1,419	–3.7	–532	–1,110
Gambia, The	..	..	..	..	..	..	..	..	..	..
Georgia	1,504	694	4,474	2,295	–6.2	882	423	*–6.5*	66	70
Germany	185,684	139,734	360,441	347,272	–0.1	4,603	4,231	–0.5	48	60
Ghana	3,305	5,843	4,071	6,896	3.6	379	383	0.5	19	15
Greece	3,696	9,645	15,960	25,556	3.1	1,655	2,435	2.6	77	62
Guatemala	2,503	4,433	3,754	5,633	2.8	550	536	0.2	33	21
Guinea	..	..	..	..	..	..	..	..	..	..
Guinea-Bissau	..	..	..	..	..	..	..	..	..	..
Haiti	1,877	1,298	2,099	1,779	–0.7	392	237	–2.6	11	27
Honduras	1,316	2,003	1,878	3,182	3.0	526	532	–0.1	30	37

Energy production and use 3.7

	Commercial energy production		Commercial energy use			Commercial energy use per capita			Net energy imports[a]	
	thousand metric tons of oil equivalent		thousand metric tons of oil equivalent		average annual % growth	kg of oil equivalent		average annual % growth	% of commercial energy use	
	1980	1997	1980	1997	1980–97	1980	1997	1980–97	1980	1997
Hungary	14,857	12,747	28,870	25,311	–1.1	2,696	2,492	–0.8	49	50
India	221,887	404,503	242,024	461,032	3.9	352	479	1.9	8	12
Indonesia	128,403	221,549	59,561	138,779	5.4	402	693	3.5	–116	–60
Iran, Islamic Rep.	84,001	224,935	38,918	108,289	7.0	995	1,777	4.2	–116	–108
Iraq	136,643	62,088	12,030	27,091	4.1	925	1,240	0.9	–1,036	–129
Ireland	1,894	2,871	8,485	12,491	2.4	2,495	3,412	2.1	78	77
Israel	153	601	8,609	17,591	5.1	2,220	3,014	2.6	98	97
Italy	19,644	29,311	138,629	163,315	1.4	2,456	2,839	1.3	86	82
Jamaica	224	595	2,378	3,963	3.7	1,115	1,552	2.6	91	85
Japan	43,247	106,978	346,491	514,898	2.8	2,967	4,084	2.4	88	79
Jordan	1	193	1,714	4,795	5.1	786	1,081	0.6	100	96
Kazakhstan	76,799	64,784	76,799	38,418	–5.3	5,163	2,439	*–5.6*	0	–69
Kenya	7,891	11,651	9,791	14,138	2.2	589	494	–1.1	19	18
Korea, Dem. Rep.	..	..	..	..	..	..	..	..	..	..
Korea, Rep.	9,644	24,037	41,238	176,351	9.8	1,082	3,834	8.6	77	86
Kuwait	94,085	116,087	9,564	16,165	1.5	6,956	8,936	1.2	–884	–618
Kyrgyz Republic	2,190	1,408	1,717	2,793	4.9	473	603	*3.5*	–28	50
Lao PDR	..	..	..	..	..	..	..	..	..	..
Latvia	261	1,636	566	4,460	20.9	222	1,806	21.1	54	63
Lebanon	178	207	2,483	5,244	4.2	827	1,265	2.2	93	96
Lesotho	..	..	..	..	..	..	..	..	..	..
Libya	96,662	78,942	7,173	15,090	4.2	2,357	2,909	1.1	–1,248	–423
Lithuania	534	3,970	11,701	8,806	–3.6	3,428	2,376	*–4.1*	95	55
Macedonia, FYR	..	..	..	..	..	..	..	..	..	..
Madagascar	..	..	..	..	..	..	..	..	..	..
Malawi	..	..	..	..	..	..	..	..	..	..
Malaysia	16,644	73,979	11,128	48,473	9.1	809	2,237	6.2	–50	–53
Mali	..	..	..	..	..	..	..	..	..	..
Mauritania	..	..	..	..	..	..	..	..	..	..
Mauritius	..	..	..	..	..	..	..	..	..	..
Mexico	149,359	223,132	98,898	141,520	2.1	1,464	1,501	0.1	–51	–58
Moldova	35	98	..	4,436	..	..	1,029	..	..	98
Mongolia	..	..	..	..	..	..	..	..	..	..
Morocco	877	1,067	4,778	9,275	4.3	247	340	2.2	82	88
Mozambique	7,417	6,994	8,079	7,664	–0.4	668	461	–2.0	8	9
Myanmar	9,513	12,249	9,430	13,009	1.7	279	296	0.2	–1	6
Namibia	..	..	..	..	..	..	..	..	..	..
Nepal	4,504	6,559	4,663	7,160	2.7	322	321	0.1	3	8
Netherlands	71,830	65,298	65,000	74,910	1.5	4,594	4,800	0.9	–11	13
New Zealand	5,488	14,158	9,251	16,679	3.8	2,972	4,435	2.6	41	15
Nicaragua	910	1,529	1,558	2,573	2.7	533	551	–0.1	42	41
Niger	..	..	..	..	..	..	..	..	..	..
Nigeria	148,479	191,034	52,846	88,652	2.9	743	753	–0.1	–181	–115
Norway	55,743	212,653	18,819	24,226	1.7	4,600	5,501	1.3	–196	–778
Oman	15,090	51,620	996	6,775	13.0	905	3,003	8.3	–1,415	–662
Pakistan	20,998	42,048	25,479	56,818	4.9	308	442	2.3	18	26
Panama	529	808	1,865	2,328	1.7	956	856	–0.3	72	65
Papua New Guinea	..	..	..	..	..	..	..	..	..	..
Paraguay	1,605	6,960	2,094	4,191	4.5	672	824	1.4	23	–66
Peru	14,655	12,225	11,700	15,127	1.1	675	621	–0.9	–25	19
Philippines	10,670	16,616	21,212	38,251	3.7	439	520	1.1	50	57
Poland	122,420	100,935	124,806	105,155	–1.4	3,508	2,721	–1.8	2	4
Portugal	1,481	2,317	10,291	20,400	4.4	1,054	2,051	4.4	86	89
Puerto Rico	..	..	..	..	..	..	..	..	..	..
Romania	52,587	31,013	64,694	44,135	–2.7	2,914	1,957	–2.8	19	30
Russian Federation	748,647	927,341	763,707	591,982	–3.6	5,494	4,019	*–3.9*	2	–57

3.7 Energy production and use

	Commercial energy production		Commercial energy use			Commercial energy use per capita			Net energy imports[a]	
	thousand metric tons of oil equivalent		thousand metric tons of oil equivalent		average annual % growth	kg of oil equivalent		average annual % growth	% of commercial energy use	
	1980	**1997**	**1980**	**1997**	**1980–97**	**1980**	**1997**	**1980–97**	**1980**	**1997**
Rwanda	..	..	..	..	..	..	..	..	..	..
Saudi Arabia	533,071	487,095	35,357	98,449	5.2	3,773	4,906	0.6	–1,408	–395
Senegal	1,046	1,654	1,921	2,770	2.2	347	315	–0.6	46	40
Sierra Leone	..	..	..	..	..	..	..	..	..	..
Singapore	..	61	6,062	26,878	10.1	2,656	8,661	8.1	..	100
Slovak Republic	3,416	4,688	20,810	17,216	–1.4	4,175	3,198	–1.8	84	73
Slovenia	1,623	2,870	4,313	6,380	1.4	2,269	3,213	1.1	62	55
South Africa	73,169	142,139	65,417	107,220	2.2	2,372	2,636	–0.1	–12	–33
Spain	15,781	31,358	68,583	107,328	3.1	1,834	2,729	2.8	77	71
Sri Lanka	3,209	4,345	4,493	7,159	2.3	305	386	0.9	29	39
Sudan	7,089	9,881	8,406	11,480	1.7	450	414	–0.5	16	14
Sweden	16,133	33,067	40,984	51,934	1.3	4,932	5,869	0.9	61	36
Switzerland	7,030	10,993	20,861	26,218	1.5	3,301	3,699	0.8	66	58
Syrian Arab Republic	9,502	32,794	5,348	14,642	5.4	614	983	2.2	–78	–124
Tajikistan	1,986	1,253	1,650	3,384	5.9	416	562	*3.4*	–20	63
Tanzania	9,502	13,529	10,280	14,258	2.0	553	455	–1.1	8	5
Thailand	11,182	46,166	22,740	79,963	8.8	487	1,319	7.1	51	42
Togo	..	..	..	..	..	..	..	..	..	..
Trinidad and Tobago	13,141	13,579	3,873	8,196	4.3	3,579	6,414	3.4	–239	–66
Tunisia	6,966	6,655	3,900	6,805	3.6	611	738	1.3	–79	2
Turkey	17,190	27,556	31,314	71,273	4.9	704	1,140	2.9	45	61
Turkmenistan	8,034	18,739	7,948	12,181	–5.5	2,778	2,615	*–8.4*	–1	–54
Uganda	..	..	..	..	..	..	..	..	..	..
Ukraine	109,708	81,175	97,893	150,059	0.6	1,956	2,960	*0.5*	–12	46
United Arab Emirates	93,915	153,555	8,576	30,874	7.0	8,222	11,967	1.5	–995	–397
United Kingdom	197,864	268,985	201,299	227,977	1.1	3,574	3,863	0.8	2	–18
United States	1,553,260	1,683,810	1,811,650	2,162,190	1.4	7,973	8,076	0.4	14	22
Uruguay	763	1,086	2,636	2,883	1.1	905	883	0.5	71	62
Uzbekistan	4,615	49,054	4,821	42,553	8.2	302	1,798	*5.8*	4	–15
Venezuela, RB	133,269	203,979	35,361	57,530	2.3	2,343	2,526	–0.2	–277	–255
Vietnam	18,052	43,525	19,347	39,306	3.5	360	521	1.4	7	–11
West Bank and Gaza	..	..	..	..	..	..	..	..	..	..
Yemen, Rep.	60	19,105	1,424	3,355	4.8	167	208	0.7	96	–469
Yugoslavia, FR (Serb./Mont.)	..	..	..	..	..	..	..	..	..	..
Zambia	4,198	5,556	4,551	5,987	1.3	793	634	–1.7	8	7
Zimbabwe	5,711	8,152	6,488	9,926	3.0	926	866	0.0	12	18
World	**6,889,350 t**	**9,579,862 t**	**6,922,832 t**	**9,431,190 t**	**2.8 w**	**1,625 w**	**1,692 w**	**0.9 w**	**.. w**	**.. w**
Low income	1,296,366	2,267,533	1,148,189	2,116,021	3.9	480	646	2.0	–14	*–9*
Excl. China & India	465,815	765,820	307,537	541,939	3.7	425	500	1.1	..	..
Middle income	2,804,139	3,607,537	2,001,642	2,601,928	4.7	1,854	1,830	1.8	–35	*–33*
Lower middle income	1,506,934	2,027,998	1,336,321	1,499,478	6.9	2,045	1,765	*–2.4*	–13	*–20*
Upper middle income	1,297,205	1,579,539	665,321	1,102,450	3.0	1,560	1,926	1.2	–98	*–65*
Low & middle income	4,100,505	5,875,070	3,149,831	4,717,949	4.3	907	1,005	2.0	–32	*–28*
East Asia & Pacific	812,772	1,535,331	783,284	1,647,182	4.8	574	942	3.2	..	..
Europe & Central Asia	1,244,462	1,395,787	1,344,673	1,240,586	6.4	3,316	2,689	*–3.1*	7	*–13*
Latin America & Carib.	468,809	788,918	377,189	575,389	2.5	1,063	1,181	0.6	–24	*–35*
Middle East & N. Africa	989,401	1,155,761	145,825	374,375	5.4	839	1,353	2.5	–577	*–225*
South Asia	263,802	479,349	291,559	556,496	4.0	329	443	1.8	10	*15*
Sub-Saharan Africa	321,259	519,924	207,301	323,921	2.4	719	695	–0.5	..	..
High income	2,788,845	3,704,792	3,773,001	4,713,241	1.7	4,794	5,369	1.0	27	24
Europe EMU	365,725	434,996	940,146	1,094,605	1.2	3,408	3,767	0.9	61	59

a. A negative value indicates that a country is a net exporter.

Energy production and use 3.7

About the data

In developing countries growth in commercial energy use is closely related to growth in the modern sectors—industry, motorized transport, and urban areas—but commercial energy use also reflects climatic, geographic, and economic factors (such as the relative price of energy). Commercial energy use has been growing rapidly in low- and middle-income countries, but high-income countries still use almost seven times as much on a per capita basis. Because commercial energy is widely traded, it is necessary to distinguish between its production and its use. Net energy imports show the extent to which an economy's use exceeds its domestic production. High-income countries are net energy importers; middle-income countries have been their main suppliers.

Energy data are compiled by the International Energy Agency (IEA) and the United Nations Statistics Division (UNSD). IEA data for non-OECD countries are based on national energy data adjusted to conform with annual questionnaires completed by OECD member governments. UNSD data are primarily from responses to questionnaires sent to national governments, supplemented by official national statistical publications and by data from intergovernmental organizations. When official data are not available, the UNSD prepares estimates based on the professional and commercial literature. This variety of sources affects the cross-country comparability of data.

Commercial energy use refers to the use of domestic primary energy before transformation to other end-use fuels (such as electricity and refined petroleum products). It includes energy from combustible renewables and waste, which comprises solid biomass and animal products, gas and liquid from biomass, industrial waste, and municipal waste. Biomass is defined as any plant matter used directly as fuel or converted into fuel, heat, or electricity. (The data series published in *World Development Indicators 1998* and earlier editions did not include energy from combustible renewables and waste.) All forms of commercial energy—primary energy and primary electricity—are converted into oil equivalents. To convert nuclear electricity into oil equivalents, a notional thermal efficiency of 33 percent is assumed; for hydroelectric power 100 percent efficiency is assumed.

Figure 3.7a

Access to energy is uneven

Per capita energy use
(thousands of kilograms of oil equivalent)

6
5
4
3
2
1
0
1980
1997
Low income
Lower middle
Upper middle
High income
World

Source: Table 3.7.

People in high-income economies use more than eight times as much commercial energy as do people in low-income economies.

Figure 3.7b

Wealthy countries consume a disproportionate share of the world's energy

Commercial energy use, 1997

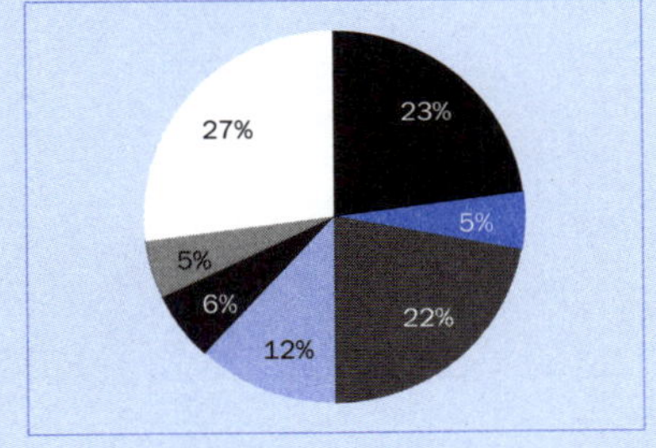

United States
Japan
Other high-income countries
China
Russian Federation
India
Rest of world

Source: Table 3.7.

The United States, Japan, and other high-income countries, with 15 percent of the world's population, consume half of the world's commercial energy.

Definitions

• **Commercial energy production** refers to commercial forms of primary energy—petroleum (crude oil, natural gas liquids, and oil from nonconventional sources), natural gas, and solid fuels (coal, lignite, and other derived fuels)—and primary electricity, all converted into oil equivalents (see *About the data*). • **Commercial energy use** refers to apparent consumption, which is equal to indigenous production plus imports and stock changes, minus exports and fuels supplied to ships and aircraft engaged in international transport (see *About the data*). • **Net energy imports** are calculated as energy use less production, both measured in oil equivalents. A negative value indicates that the country is a net exporter.

Data sources

The data on commercial energy production and use are primarily from IEA electronic files and from the United Nations Statistics Division's *Energy Statistics Yearbook*. The IEA data are published in its annual publications, *Energy Statistics and Balances of Non-OECD Countries, Energy Statistics of OECD Countries,* and *Energy Balances of OECD Countries*.

3.8 Energy efficiency and emissions

	GDP per unit of energy use		Traditional fuel use		Carbon dioxide emissions					
	PPP $ per kg oil equivalent		% of total energy use		Total million metric tons		Per capita metric tons		kg per PPP $ of GDP	
	1980	1997	1980	1996	1980	1996	1980	1996	1980	1996
Albania	..	8.5	13.1	9.3	4.8	1.9	1.8	0.6	..	0.2
Algeria	4.7	5.3	1.9	1.5	66.2	94.3	3.5	3.3	1.1	0.7
Angola	..	2.6	64.9	69.3	5.3	5.1	0.8	0.5	..	0.3
Argentina	4.3	6.9	5.9	3.5	107.5	129.9	3.8	3.7	0.6	0.3
Armenia	..	4.3	..	0.0	..	3.7	..	1.0	..	0.5
Australia	2.0	4.0	3.8	3.7	202.8	306.6	13.8	16.7	1.4	0.8
Austria	3.2	6.7	1.2	3.1	52.2	59.3	6.9	7.4	0.7	0.3
Azerbaijan	..	1.3	..	0.0	..	30.0	..	3.9	..	2.0
Bangladesh	2.9	6.8	81.3	43.3	7.6	23.0	0.1	0.2	0.2	0.1
Belarus	..	2.4	..	0.8	..	61.7	..	6.0	..	1.1
Belgium	2.2	4.1	0.2	0.3	127.2	106.0	12.9	10.4	1.3	0.5
Benin	1.2	2.3	85.4	87.5	0.5	0.7	0.1	0.1	0.3	0.1
Bolivia	..	4.1	19.3	13.4	4.5	10.1	0.8	1.3	..	0.6
Bosnia and Herzegovina	..	..	..	12.7	..	3.1	..	0.9	..	..
Botswana	..	..	35.7	..	1.0	2.1	1.1	1.4	0.7	0.2
Brazil	4.4	6.5	35.5	29.2	183.4	273.4	1.5	1.7	0.4	0.3
Bulgaria	0.8	1.9	0.5	1.2	75.3	55.3	8.5	6.6	3.1	1.3
Burkina Faso	..	..	91.3	87.4	0.4	1.0	0.1	0.1	0.1	0.1
Burundi	..	..	97.0	92.4	0.1	0.2	0.0	0.0	0.1	0.1
Cambodia	..	..	100.0	89.3	0.3	0.5	0.0	0.0	..	0.0
Cameroon	2.3	3.6	51.7	68.8	3.9	3.5	0.4	0.3	0.5	0.2
Canada	1.4	3.0	0.4	0.5	420.9	409.4	17.1	13.8	1.5	0.6
Central African Republic	..	..	88.9	91.4	0.1	0.2	0.0	0.1	0.1	0.1
Chad	..	..	95.9	97.6	0.2	0.1	0.0	0.0	0.1	0.0
Chile	3.0	5.7	12.3	12.7	27.9	48.8	2.5	3.4	1.0	0.4
China	0.7	3.3	8.4	5.6	1,476.8	3,363.5	1.5	2.8	3.6	1.0
Hong Kong, China	5.8	10.6	0.9	0.7	16.3	23.1	3.2	3.7	0.5	0.2
Colombia	4.9	8.2	15.9	22.9	39.8	65.3	1.4	1.7	0.4	0.3
Congo, Dem. Rep.	3.7	2.7	73.9	90.8	3.5	2.3	0.1	0.1	0.1	0.1
Congo, Rep.	1.1	2.2	77.8	52.1	0.4	5.0	0.2	1.9	0.4	1.8
Costa Rica	4.7	7.7	26.3	12.6	2.5	4.7	1.1	1.4	0.3	0.2
Côte d'Ivoire	2.7	4.0	52.8	55.3	4.6	13.1	0.6	0.9	0.5	0.6
Croatia	..	4.0	..	3.4	..	17.5	..	3.9	..	0.6
Cuba	..	..	27.9	26.0	31.0	31.2	3.2	2.8	..	..
Czech Republic	..	3.3	0.6	0.4	..	126.7	..	12.3	..	0.9
Denmark	2.5	6.0	0.4	2.3	62.9	56.6	12.3	10.7	1.3	0.5
Dominican Republic	3.3	6.6	27.5	15.1	6.4	12.9	1.1	1.6	0.6	0.4
Ecuador	2.8	4.6	26.7	14.3	13.4	24.5	1.7	2.1	0.9	0.6
Egypt, Arab Rep.	2.8	4.7	4.7	3.5	45.2	97.9	1.1	1.7	1.0	0.6
El Salvador	4.0	5.9	52.9	36.5	2.1	4.0	0.5	0.7	0.2	0.2
Eritrea	..	..	..	..	..	..	..	..	..	..
Estonia	..	2.0	..	2.8	..	16.4	..	11.2	..	1.6
Ethiopia	*1.3*	2.1	89.6	93.0	1.8	3.4	0.0	0.1	0.1	0.1
Finland	1.6	3.2	4.3	5.1	54.9	59.2	11.5	11.5	1.3	0.6
France	2.7	5.0	1.3	1.0	482.7	361.8	9.0	6.2	0.9	0.3
Gabon	2.0	4.5	30.8	32.6	4.9	3.7	7.1	3.3	1.6	0.5
Gambia, The	..	..	72.7	78.6	0.2	0.2	0.2	0.2	0.3	0.1
Georgia	7.0	7.9	..	1.4	..	3.0	..	0.5	..	0.2
Germany	..	5.2	0.3	0.3	..	861.2	..	10.5	..	0.5
Ghana	2.7	4.5	43.7	78.1	2.4	4.0	0.2	0.2	0.2	0.1
Greece	4.0	5.7	3.0	1.2	51.7	80.6	5.4	7.7	0.8	0.6
Guatemala	3.9	6.5	54.6	58.6	4.5	6.8	0.7	0.7	0.3	0.2
Guinea	..	..	71.4	72.4	0.9	1.1	0.2	0.2	..	0.1
Guinea-Bissau	..	..	80.0	57.1	0.1	0.2	0.2	0.2	0.5	0.2
Haiti	3.4	5.9	80.7	80.5	0.8	1.1	0.1	0.1	0.1	0.1
Honduras	2.7	4.7	55.3	50.0	2.1	4.0	0.6	0.7	0.4	0.3

Energy efficiency and emissions 3.8

	GDP per unit of energy use		Traditional fuel use		Carbon dioxide emissions					
	PPP $ per kg oil equivalent		% of total energy use		Total million metric tons		Per capita metric tons		kg per PPP $ of GDP	
	1980	1997	1980	1996	1980	1996	1980	1996	1980	1996
Hungary	1.9	4.0	2.0	1.5	82.5	59.5	7.7	5.8	1.5	0.6
India	1.8	4.2	31.5	21.2	347.3	997.4	0.5	1.1	0.8	0.5
Indonesia	2.0	4.5	51.5	28.7	94.6	245.1	0.6	1.2	0.8	0.4
Iran, Islamic Rep.	2.7	3.0	0.4	0.9	116.1	266.7	3.0	4.4	1.1	0.9
Iraq	..	..	0.3	0.1	44.0	91.4	3.4	4.3	..	..
Ireland	2.2	6.0	0.0	0.2	25.2	34.9	7.4	9.6	1.4	0.5
Israel	3.3	5.8	0.0	0.0	21.1	52.3	5.4	9.2	0.7	0.5
Italy	3.7	7.3	0.8	0.8	371.9	403.2	6.6	7.0	0.7	0.3
Jamaica	1.7	2.2	5.0	6.3	8.4	10.1	4.0	4.0	2.1	1.1
Japan	3.0	6.0	0.1	0.4	920.4	1,167.7	7.9	9.3	0.9	0.4
Jordan	2.3	3.3	0.0	0.0	..	..	..	..	..	..
Kazakhstan	..	1.8	..	0.1	..	173.8	..	10.9	..	2.5
Kenya	1.0	2.0	76.8	78.9	6.2	6.8	0.4	0.2	0.6	0.2
Korea, Dem. Rep.	..	..	3.1	1.5	124.9	254.3	7.1	11.3	..	..
Korea, Rep.	2.5	3.9	4.0	0.7	125.2	408.1	3.3	9.0	1.2	0.6
Kuwait	..	..	0.0	0.0	..	..	..	..	..	..
Kyrgyz Republic	..	3.8	..	0.0	..	6.1	..	1.3	..	0.6
Lao PDR	..	..	72.3	86.5	0.2	0.3	0.1	0.1	..	0.0
Latvia	18.3	3.1	..	24.1	..	9.3	..	3.7	..	0.7
Lebanon	..	3.3	2.4	2.8	6.2	14.2	2.1	3.5	..	0.9
Lesotho	..	..	..	..	..	..	..	..	..	..
Libya	..	..	2.3	0.9	26.9	40.6	8.8	8.0	..	..
Lithuania	..	2.6	..	5.9	..	13.8	..	3.7	..	0.6
Macedonia, FYR	..	..	..	5.2	..	12.7	..	6.4	..	1.5
Madagascar	..	..	78.4	85.6	1.6	1.2	0.2	0.1	0.3	0.1
Malawi	..	..	90.6	89.7	0.7	0.7	0.1	0.1	0.3	0.1
Malaysia	3.2	4.0	15.7	6.0	28.0	119.1	2.0	5.6	0.8	0.6
Mali	..	..	86.7	88.6	0.4	0.5	0.1	0.0	0.1	0.1
Mauritania	..	..	0.0	0.0	0.6	2.9	0.4	1.2	0.4	0.8
Mauritius	..	..	59.1	32.4	0.6	1.7	0.6	1.5	0.3	0.2
Mexico	2.9	5.1	5.0	5.6	251.6	348.1	3.7	3.8	0.9	0.5
Moldova	..	2.1	..	0.5	..	12.1	..	2.8	..	1.3
Mongolia	..	..	14.4	3.8	6.8	8.9	4.1	3.6	*3.8*	2.4
Morocco	6.4	9.5	5.2	4.8	15.9	27.9	0.8	1.0	0.5	0.3
Mozambique	0.6	1.6	43.7	91.4	3.2	1.0	0.3	0.1	0.6	0.1
Myanmar	..	..	69.3	63.9	4.8	7.3	0.1	0.2	..	..
Namibia	..	..	..	..	..	..	..	..	..	..
Nepal	1.5	3.7	94.2	90.9	0.5	1.6	0.0	0.1	0.1	0.1
Netherlands	2.1	4.6	0.0	0.1	152.6	155.2	10.8	10.0	1.1	0.5
New Zealand	2.9	4.0	0.2	0.0	17.6	29.8	5.6	8.0	0.6	0.4
Nicaragua	3.0	3.9	49.2	43.4	2.0	2.9	0.7	0.6	0.4	0.3
Niger	..	..	79.5	80.0	0.6	1.1	0.1	0.1	0.2	0.2
Nigeria	0.7	1.1	66.8	69.0	68.1	83.3	1.0	0.7	1.9	0.9
Norway	2.2	4.8	0.4	10.1	90.4	67.0	22.1	15.3	2.2	0.6
Oman	..	..	0.0	..	5.9	15.1	5.3	7.0	..	..
Pakistan	2.0	3.9	24.4	17.3	31.6	94.3	0.4	0.8	0.6	0.4
Panama	2.8	6.1	26.6	18.6	3.5	6.7	1.8	2.5	0.7	0.5
Papua New Guinea	..	..	65.4	62.5	1.8	2.4	0.6	0.5	0.5	0.2
Paraguay	4.0	5.5	62.0	47.5	1.5	3.7	0.5	0.7	0.2	0.2
Peru	4.0	7.3	15.2	27.2	23.6	26.2	1.4	1.1	0.5	0.3
Philippines	5.1	7.2	37.0	31.7	36.5	63.2	0.8	0.9	0.3	0.2
Poland	1.0	2.7	0.4	0.4	456.2	356.8	12.8	9.2	3.7	1.3
Portugal	5.1	7.1	1.2	0.9	27.1	47.9	2.8	4.8	0.5	0.3
Puerto Rico	..	..	*0.0*	..	14.0	15.8	4.4	4.2	..	..
Romania	1.4	3.2	1.3	4.7	191.8	119.3	8.6	5.3	2.1	0.8
Russian Federation	..	1.7	..	1.1	..	1,579.5	..	10.7	..	1.5

3.8 Energy efficiency and emissions

	GDP per unit of energy use		Traditional fuel use		Carbon dioxide emissions					
	PPP $ per kg oil equivalent		% of total energy use		Total million metric tons		Per capita metric tons		kg per PPP $ of GDP	
	1980	1997	1980	1996	1980	1996	1980	1996	1980	1996
Rwanda	..	..	89.8	88.3	0.3	0.5	0.1	0.1	..	..
Saudi Arabia	2.8	2.1	0.0	0.0	130.7	267.8	14.0	13.8	1.3	1.3
Senegal	2.1	4.1	50.8	56.3	2.8	3.1	0.5	0.4	0.7	0.3
Sierra Leone	..	..	90.0	84.2	0.6	0.4	0.2	0.1	0.3	0.2
Singapore	2.1	2.9	0.4	0.0	30.1	65.8	13.2	21.6	2.4	0.9
Slovak Republic	..	3.0	..	0.6	..	39.6	..	7.4	..	0.8
Slovenia	..	4.4	..	0.9	..	13.0	..	6.5	..	0.5
South Africa	2.5	3.3	4.9	..	211.3	292.7	7.7	7.3	1.3	0.8
Spain	3.5	5.9	0.4	0.7	200.0	232.5	5.3	5.9	0.8	0.4
Sri Lanka	3.3	7.6	53.5	48.0	3.4	7.1	0.2	0.4	0.2	0.1
Sudan	1.5	3.3	86.9	76.5	3.3	3.5	0.2	0.1	0.3	0.1
Sweden	2.0	3.5	7.7	16.2	71.4	54.1	8.6	6.1	0.9	0.3
Switzerland	4.0	6.9	0.9	1.6	40.9	44.2	6.5	6.3	0.5	0.2
Syrian Arab Republic	2.9	3.0	0.0	0.0	19.3	44.3	2.2	3.1	1.3	1.0
Tajikistan	..	1.6	..	..	..	5.8	..	1.0	..	1.0
Tanzania	..	1.0	92.0	91.4	1.9	2.4	0.1	0.1	..	0.2
Thailand	2.9	4.7	40.3	30.0	40.0	205.4	0.9	3.4	0.6	0.5
Togo	..	..	35.7	71.0	0.6	0.8	0.2	0.2	0.2	0.1
Trinidad and Tobago	1.4	1.2	1.4	0.8	16.7	22.2	15.4	17.5	3.1	2.4
Tunisia	3.7	7.2	16.1	12.7	9.4	16.2	1.5	1.8	0.6	0.3
Turkey	3.3	5.7	20.5	3.4	76.3	178.3	1.7	2.9	0.7	0.5
Turkmenistan	..	1.0	..	..	..	34.2	..	7.4	..	2.4
Uganda	..	..	93.6	90.6	0.6	1.0	0.1	0.1	*0.1*	0.0
Ukraine	..	1.1	..	0.4	..	397.3	..	7.8	..	2.3
United Arab Emirates	2.9	1.7	*0.0*	..	36.3	81.8	34.8	33.3	1.5	1.6
United Kingdom	2.4	5.3	0.0	0.9	583.8	557.0	10.4	9.5	1.2	0.5
United States	1.6	3.6	1.3	3.6	4,575.4	5,301.0	20.1	20.0	1.6	0.7
Uruguay	4.9	9.7	11.1	26.0	5.8	5.6	2.0	1.7	0.4	0.2
Uzbekistan	..	1.1	..	0.0	..	95.0	..	4.1	..	2.0
Venezuela, RB	1.7	2.4	0.9	0.8	89.6	144.5	5.9	6.5	1.5	1.1
Vietnam	..	3.2	49.1	40.5	16.8	37.6	0.3	0.5	..	0.3
West Bank and Gaza	..	..	..	..	..	..	..	..	..	..
Yemen, Rep.	..	3.5	*0.0*	2.0	..	..	..	..	..	..
Yugoslavia, FR (Serb./Mont.)	..	..	1.6	2.0	..	..	..	..	..	..
Zambia	0.8	1.2	37.4	73.1	3.5	2.4	0.6	0.3	1.0	0.3
Zimbabwe	1.6	3.1	27.6	23.4	9.6	18.4	1.4	1.6	1.0	0.6
World	.. w	.. w	7.4 w	7.2 w	13,640.7 t	22,653.9 t	3.4 w	4.0 w	1.2 w	0.6 w
Low income	..	..	26.3	19.5	2,251.0	5,306.2	0.9	1.6	1.6	0.7
Excl. China & India	..	..	59.9	48.1	302.0	690.9	0.4	0.6	0.6	0.4
Middle income	..	..	*11.5*	6.0	2,679.6	6,617.1	3.2	4.7	1.0	0.7
Lower middle income	..	..	*12.3*	5.5	1,025.2	3,940.6	2.5	4.6	1.0	0.9
Upper middle income	..	..	9.4	6.7	1,654.4	2,676.6	4.0	4.7	1.0	0.6
Low & middle income	..	..	18.6	12.2	4,930.6	11,923.3	1.5	2.5	1.2	0.7
East Asia & Pacific	..	..	15.0	10.0	1,958.5	4,717.5	1.4	2.7	2.1	0.8
Europe & Central Asia	..	2.2	*3.1*	1.2	886.9	3,412.7	..	7.4	2.2	1.3
Latin America & Carib.	..	..	18.2	16.3	848.5	1,209.1	2.4	2.5	0.6	0.4
Middle East & N. Africa	..	3.3	1.6	1.2	493.9	987.2	3.0	3.9	1.1	0.8
South Asia	..	..	34.8	23.0	392.4	1,125.1	0.4	0.9	0.7	0.5
Sub-Saharan Africa	..	..	47.3	73.3	350.4	471.7	0.9	0.8	1.0	0.5
High income	..	..	1.0	2.4	8,710.2	10,730.6	12.3	12.3	1.2	0.5
Europe EMU	2.9	5.5	0.7	0.8	1,504.4	2,329.5	7.6	8.0	0.9	0.4

Energy efficiency and emissions 3.8

About the data

The ratio of GDP to energy use provides a measure of energy efficiency. In estimating this ratio, previous editions of the *World Development Indicators* used GDP in 1995 U.S. dollars. This year's edition adopts GDP converted to international dollars using purchasing power parity (PPP) rates to produce comparable and consistent estimates of real GDP across countries relative to physical inputs to GDP—that is, units of energy use. Differences in this ratio over time and across countries reflect in part structural changes in the economy, changes in the energy efficiency of particular sectors of the economy, and differences in fuel mixes.

The data on traditional fuel are from the United Nations Statistics Division's *Energy Statistics Yearbook.* This series differs from those published in previous editions of the *World Development Indicators,* which came from other sources.

Carbon dioxide (CO_2) emissions, largely a by-product of energy production and use (see table 3.7), account for the largest share of greenhouse gases, which are associated with global warming. Anthropogenic CO_2 emissions result primarily from fossil fuel combustion and cement manufacturing. In combustion, different fossil fuels release different amounts of CO_2 for the same level of energy use. Burning oil releases about 50 percent more CO_2 than burning natural gas, and burning coal releases about twice as much. During cement manufacturing about half a metric ton of CO_2 is released for each ton of cement produced.

The Carbon Dioxide Information Analysis Center (CDIAC), sponsored by the U.S. Department of Energy, calculates annual anthropogenic emissions of CO_2. These calculations are derived from data on fossil fuel consumption, based on the World Energy Data Set maintained by the United Nations Statistics Division, and from data on world cement manufacturing, based on the Cement Manufacturing Data Set maintained by the U.S. Bureau of Mines. Emissions of CO_2 are often calculated and reported in terms of their content of elemental carbon. For this table these values were converted to the actual mass of CO_2 by multiplying the carbon mass by 3.664 (the ratio of the mass of carbon to that of CO_2).

Although the estimates of global CO_2 emissions are probably within 10 percent of actual emissions (as calculated from global average fuel chemistry and use), country estimates may have larger error bounds. Trends estimated from a consistent time series tend to be more accurate than individual values. Each year the CDIAC recalculates the entire time series from 1950 to the present, incorporating its most recent findings and the latest corrections to its database. Estimates do not include fuels supplied to ships and aircraft engaged in international transport because of the difficulty of apportioning these fuels among the countries benefiting from that transport.

Figure 3.8a

Carbon dioxide emissions vary widely across countries

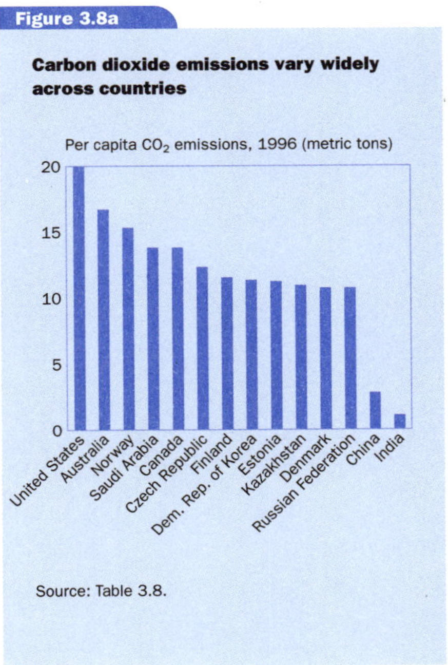

Source: Table 3.8.

Figure 3.8b

High-income countries account for most of the world's carbon dioxide emissions

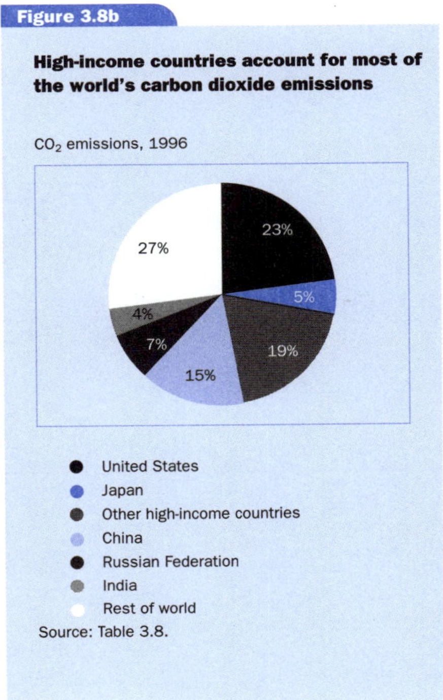

Source: Table 3.8.

Definitions

• **GDP per unit of energy use** is the PPP GDP per kilogram of oil equivalent of commercial energy use. PPP GDP is gross domestic product converted to international dollars using purchasing power parity rates. An international dollar has the same purchasing power over GDP as a U.S. dollar has in the United States. • **Traditional fuel use** includes estimates of the consumption of fuelwood, charcoal, bagasse, and animal and vegetable wastes. Total energy use comprises commercial energy use (see table 3.7) and traditional fuel use. • **Carbon dioxide emissions** are those stemming from the burning of fossil fuels and the manufacture of cement. They include carbon dioxide produced during consumption of solid, liquid, and gas fuels and gas flaring.

Data sources

The underlying data on commercial energy production and use are from International Energy Agency electronic files. The data on traditional fuel are from the United Nations Statistics Division's *Energy Statistics Yearbook*. The data on CO_2 emissions are from the Carbon Dioxide Information Analysis Center, Environmental Sciences Division, Oak Ridge National Laboratory, in the U.S. state of Tennessee.

3.9 Sources of electricity

	Electricity production		Sources of electricity[a]									
	billion kwh		Hydropower %		Coal %		Oil %		Gas %		Nuclear power %	
	1980	1997	1980	1997	1980	1997	1980	1997	1980	1997	1980	1997
Albania	3.7	5.6	79.4	96.3	..	..	20.6	3.7	..	..	..	..
Algeria	7.1	21.7	3.6	0.3	..	..	12.2	3.6	84.1	96.1	..	..
Angola	0.7	1.1	88.1	90.7	..	..	11.9	9.3	..	..	..	..
Argentina	39.7	71.9	38.1	39.1	2.5	1.0	31.9	3.6	21.0	44.9	5.9	11.0
Armenia	13.0	6.0	12.0	23.1	..	..	54.8	2.1	..	48.2	33.2	26.6
Australia	95.2	182.6	13.6	9.2	73.3	80.1	5.4	1.3	7.3	7.6	..	..
Austria	41.6	55.5	69.1	64.8	7.0	11.8	14.0	5.0	9.2	15.5	..	..
Azerbaijan	15.0	16.8	7.3	9.0	..	..	92.7	72.8	..	18.1	..	..
Bangladesh	2.4	11.9	24.8	6.1	..	..	26.6	9.4	48.6	84.5	..	..
Belarus	34.1	26.1	0.1	0.1	..	..	99.9	14.8	..	85.1	..	..
Belgium	53.1	78.1	0.5	0.4	29.4	20.9	34.7	1.8	11.2	14.8	23.6	60.7
Benin	0.0	0.1	..	..	..	..	100.0	100.0	..	..	..	..
Bolivia	1.6	3.4	68.2	67.2	..	..	10.3	5.8	18.4	25.7	..	..
Bosnia and Herzegovina	..	2.2	..	64.5	..	35.5	..	..	..	..	..	..
Botswana	..	..	..	..	..	..	..	..	..	..	..	..
Brazil	139.4	307.3	92.5	90.8	2.0	1.8	3.8	3.2	..	0.4	..	1.0
Bulgaria	34.8	41.6	10.7	4.1	49.2	44.3	22.5	3.1	..	5.9	17.7	42.7
Burkina Faso	..	..	..	..	..	..	..	..	..	..	..	..
Burundi	..	..	..	..	..	..	..	..	..	..	..	..
Cambodia	..	..	..	..	..	..	..	..	..	..	..	..
Cameroon	1.5	3.1	93.9	98.8	..	..	6.1	1.2	..	..	..	..
Canada	373.3	575.0	67.3	61.1	16.0	17.4	3.7	2.4	2.5	4.1	10.2	14.4
Central African Republic	..	..	..	..	..	..	..	..	..	..	..	..
Chad	..	..	..	..	..	..	..	..	..	..	..	..
Chile	11.8	34.0	62.5	55.7	14.9	33.8	19.1	7.7	1.2	2.1	..	..
China	313.3	1,163.4	18.6	16.8	57.0	74.2	24.2	7.2	0.2	0.6	..	1.2
Hong Kong, China	12.6	28.9	..	..	..	98.9	..	1.1	..	..	..	..
Colombia	20.6	46.1	70.0	71.1	9.7	7.9	2.1	0.5	17.6	19.8	..	..
Congo, Dem. Rep.	4.4	6.0	95.5	97.8	..	..	4.5	2.2	..	..	..	..
Congo, Rep.	0.2	0.4	62.2	98.6	..	..	35.9	0.7	1.9	0.7	..	..
Costa Rica	2.2	5.6	95.2	85.9	..	..	4.8	3.1	..	..	..	..
Côte d'Ivoire	1.7	3.2	77.6	62.9	..	..	22.4	37.1	..	..	..	..
Croatia	..	9.7	..	54.7	..	5.3	..	27.9	..	12.1	..	..
Cuba	9.9	14.1	1.0	0.7	..	..	89.6	88.7	..	0.1	..	..
Czech Republic	52.7	64.2	4.6	2.6	84.8	74.0	9.6	1.0	1.1	1.4	..	19.5
Denmark	26.8	44.3	0.1	0.0	81.8	64.9	18.0	12.2	..	15.4	..	..
Dominican Republic	3.3	7.3	18.8	18.2	..	4.4	78.8	77.0	..	..	..	..
Ecuador	3.4	9.6	25.9	70.6	..	..	74.1	29.4	..	..	..	..
Egypt, Arab Rep.	18.9	57.7	51.8	20.8	..	..	27.7	35.2	20.5	44.0	..	..
El Salvador	1.5	3.6	63.7	32.8	..	..	2.7	46.8	..	..	..	..
Eritrea	..	..	..	..	..	..	..	..	..	..	..	..
Estonia	18.9	9.2	..	0.0	..	95.3	100.0	1.9	..	2.6	..	..
Ethiopia	0.7	1.3	70.2	87.3	..	..	27.6	4.9	..	..	..	..
Finland	40.7	69.2	25.1	17.7	42.6	28.3	10.8	2.0	4.2	10.0	17.2	30.2
France	256.9	498.9	26.9	12.5	27.2	5.2	18.9	1.5	2.7	1.0	23.8	79.3
Gabon	0.5	1.0	49.1	73.5	..	..	50.9	16.0	..	10.5	..	..
Gambia, The	..	..	..	..	..	..	..	..	..	..	..	..
Georgia	14.7	7.2	43.8	84.3	..	..	56.2	0.1	..	15.6	..	..
Germany	466.3	548.0	4.1	3.2	62.9	53.4	5.7	1.3	14.2	9.2	11.9	31.1
Ghana	5.3	6.2	99.2	99.9	..	..	0.8	0.1	..	..	..	..
Greece	22.7	43.3	15.0	9.0	44.8	70.7	40.1	19.2	..	0.8	..	..
Guatemala	1.8	4.9	12.9	76.8	..	..	70.3	18.7	..	..	..	..
Guinea	..	..	..	..	..	..	..	..	..	..	..	..
Guinea-Bissau	..	..	..	..	..	..	..	..	..	..	..	..
Haiti	0.3	0.6	70.1	32.0	..	..	26.1	64.8	..	..	..	..
Honduras	0.9	3.3	86.7	98.5	..	..	13.3	1.5	..	..	..	..

Sources of electricity 3.9

	Electricity production		Sources of electricity[a]									
	billion kwh		Hydropower %		Coal %		Oil %		Gas %		Nuclear power %	
	1980	1997	1980	1997	1980	1997	1980	1997	1980	1997	1980	1997
Hungary	23.9	35.4	0.5	0.6	53.5	29.8	12.6	15.3	33.5	14.8	..	39.5
India	119.3	463.4	39.0	16.1	49.9	73.1	7.7	2.6	0.8	6.0	2.5	2.2
Indonesia	8.4	74.8	16.0	8.0	..	30.7	84.0	30.0	..	27.8	..	..
Iran, Islamic Rep.	22.4	95.8	25.1	7.7	..	..	50.1	33.9	24.8	58.4	..	..
Iraq	11.4	29.6	6.1	2.0	..	..	93.9	98.0	..	..	..	..
Ireland	10.6	19.7	7.9	3.4	16.4	44.9	60.4	17.6	15.2	33.4	..	..
Israel	12.5	35.1	..	0.2	*17.9*	70.7	100.0	29.1	..	..	..	..
Italy	183.5	246.5	24.7	16.9	9.9	10.0	57.0	46.0	5.0	24.9	1.2	..
Jamaica	1.5	6.3	8.3	1.9	..	..	87.9	92.9	..	..	..	..
Japan	572.5	1,029.5	15.4	8.7	9.6	19.1	46.2	18.2	14.2	20.5	14.4	31.0
Jordan	1.1	6.3	..	0.4	..	..	100.0	87.2	..	12.5	..	..
Kazakhstan	61.5	52.0	9.3	12.5	..	72.0	90.7	7.3	..	8.2	..	..
Kenya	1.5	4.2	71.1	82.4	..	..	28.9	8.4	..	..	..	..
Korea, Dem. Rep.	..	..	..	..	..	..	..	..	..	..	..	..
Korea, Rep.	37.2	244.0	5.3	1.2	6.7	37.4	78.7	16.8	..	13.0	9.3	31.6
Kuwait	9.4	27.1	..	..	..	..	37.2	26.0	62.8	74.0	..	..
Kyrgyz Republic	9.2	12.6	53.1	89.1	..	6.6	46.9	4.3	..	..	..	..
Lao PDR	..	..	..	..	..	..	..	..	..	..	..	..
Latvia	4.7	4.5	64.9	65.6	..	2.3	35.1	5.3	..	26.8	..	..
Lebanon	2.8	8.5	30.9	10.6	..	..	69.1	89.4	..	..	..	..
Lesotho	..	..	..	..	..	..	..	..	..	..	..	..
Libya	4.8	18.2	..	..	..	..	100.0	100.0	..	..	..	..
Lithuania	11.7	14.4	4.0	2.1	..	..	96.0	10.9	..	3.5	..	83.6
Macedonia, FYR	..	..	..	..	..	..	..	..	..	..	..	..
Madagascar	..	..	..	..	..	..	..	..	..	..	..	..
Malawi	..	..	..	..	..	..	..	..	..	..	..	..
Malaysia	10.0	57.9	13.9	5.7	..	5.3	84.7	10.2	1.3	78.8	..	..
Mali	..	..	..	..	..	..	..	..	..	..	..	..
Mauritania	..	..	..	..	..	..	..	..	..	..	..	..
Mauritius	..	..	..	..	..	..	..	..	..	..	..	..
Mexico	67.0	175.0	25.2	15.1	*0.0*	10.0	57.9	54.3	15.5	11.5	..	6.0
Moldova	15.4	5.3	2.6	7.2	..	9.3	97.4	4.0	..	79.5	..	..
Mongolia	..	..	..	..	..	..	..	..	..	..	..	..
Morocco	5.2	13.1	28.9	15.7	19.5	45.0	51.6	39.3	..	..	..	..
Mozambique	0.5	1.0	65.2	78.7	17.5	..	17.3	21.1	..	0.2	..	..
Myanmar	1.5	4.2	53.5	39.4	2.0	..	31.3	12.2	13.2	48.5	..	..
Namibia	..	..	..	..	..	..	..	..	..	..	..	..
Nepal	0.2	1.2	82.3	90.5	..	..	17.7	9.5	..	..	..	..
Netherlands	64.8	86.7	..	0.1	13.7	30.0	38.4	4.2	39.8	58.3	6.5	2.8
New Zealand	22.6	36.8	83.6	63.2	1.9	5.5	0.2	*0.0*	7.5	23.7	..	..
Nicaragua	1.1	1.9	51.3	21.3	..	..	45.3	65.4	..	..	..	..
Niger	..	..	..	..	..	..	..	..	..	..	..	..
Nigeria	7.1	15.2	39.0	36.8	0.4	..	45.1	25.8	15.5	37.3	..	..
Norway	83.8	110.5	99.8	99.4	0.0	0.2	0.1	..	..	0.2	..	..
Oman	0.8	7.3	..	..	..	..	21.5	16.5	78.5	83.5	..	..
Pakistan	15.0	59.1	58.2	35.3	0.2	0.6	1.1	38.5	40.5	24.9	0.0	0.6
Panama	2.0	4.2	49.4	66.6	..	..	48.4	32.6	..	..	..	..
Papua New Guinea	..	..	..	..	..	..	..	..	..	..	..	..
Paraguay	0.8	50.6	80.0	99.7	..	..	13.4	0.1	..	..	..	..
Peru	10.0	18.0	69.8	73.6	..	..	27.4	20.7	1.7	1.8	..	..
Philippines	18.0	39.8	19.6	15.3	1.0	18.5	67.9	48.0	..	0.0	..	..
Poland	120.9	140.9	1.9	1.4	94.7	96.7	2.9	1.4	0.1	0.2	..	..
Portugal	15.2	34.1	52.7	38.4	2.3	38.2	42.9	19.8	..	0.3	..	..
Puerto Rico	..	..	..	..	..	..	..	..	..	..	..	..
Romania	67.5	57.1	18.7	30.6	31.4	30.2	9.6	12.0	38.2	17.6	..	9.4
Russian Federation	804.9	833.1	16.1	18.8	..	16.8	77.2	5.3	..	45.3	6.7	13.1

3.9 Sources of electricity

	Electricity production		Sources of electricity[a]									
	billion kwh		Hydropower %		Coal %		Oil %		Gas %		Nuclear power %	
	1980	1997	1980	1997	1980	1997	1980	1997	1980	1997	1980	1997
Rwanda	..	..	..	..	..	..	..	..	..	..	..	..
Saudi Arabia	20.5	103.8	..	..	..	..	58.5	57.5	41.5	42.5	..	..
Senegal	0.6	1.3	..	..	..	..	100.0	93.9	..	6.1	..	..
Sierra Leone	..	..	..	..	..	..	..	..	..	..	..	..
Singapore	7.0	26.9	..	..	..	..	100.0	80.9	..	16.5	..	..
Slovak Republic	20.0	24.3	11.3	17.0	37.9	24.0	17.9	5.0	10.2	9.6	22.7	44.4
Slovenia	8.0	13.2	42.3	23.5	51.6	35.8	3.9	2.6	2.2	..	*3.4*	38.1
South Africa	99.0	207.7	1.0	1.0	99.0	92.9	..	..	..	..	..	6.1
Spain	109.2	185.8	27.1	18.6	30.0	34.3	35.2	7.2	2.7	8.8	4.7	29.8
Sri Lanka	1.7	5.1	88.7	67.0	..	..	11.3	33.0	..	..	..	..
Sudan	0.8	2.0	70.0	53.0	..	..	30.0	47.0	..	..	..	..
Sweden	96.3	149.4	61.1	46.2	0.2	1.9	10.4	2.1	..	0.5	27.5	46.8
Switzerland	48.2	61.6	68.1	55.3	0.1	*0.0*	1.0	0.3	0.6	1.4	29.8	41.2
Syrian Arab Republic	4.0	18.0	64.7	55.9	..	..	31.9	26.3	3.4	17.7	..	..
Tajikistan	13.6	14.0	93.4	98.8	..	..	6.6	..	..	1.3	..	..
Tanzania	0.8	1.9	86.4	74.9	..	..	13.6	25.1	..	..	..	..
Thailand	14.4	93.3	8.8	7.7	9.8	20.3	81.4	23.4	*9.9*	46.3	..	..
Togo	..	..	..	..	..	..	..	..	..	..	..	..
Trinidad and Tobago	2.0	5.0	..	..	..	..	2.3	..	96.5	99.3	..	..
Tunisia	2.9	8.0	0.8	0.6	..	..	64.5	15.7	34.7	83.7	..	..
Turkey	23.3	103.3	48.8	38.5	25.6	32.8	25.1	6.9	..	21.4	..	..
Turkmenistan	6.7	9.4	0.1	0.1	..	..	99.9	..	..	99.9	..	..
Uganda	..	..	..	..	..	..	..	..	..	..	..	..
Ukraine	236.0	177.8	5.7	5.5	..	27.6	88.3	4.3	..	17.9	6.0	44.7
United Arab Emirates	6.3	20.6	..	..	..	..	44.8	16.2	55.2	83.8	..	..
United Kingdom	284.1	343.9	1.4	1.2	73.2	34.8	11.7	2.3	0.7	31.3	13.0	28.5
United States	2,427.3	3,670.6	11.5	9.0	51.2	53.8	10.8	2.9	15.3	13.8	11.0	18.2
Uruguay	4.6	7.1	76.3	90.7	..	..	23.5	8.7	..	..	..	..
Uzbekistan	33.9	46.1	14.6	12.5	..	4.1	85.4	11.9	..	71.5	..	..
Venezuela, RB	36.9	74.9	39.6	76.3	..	..	14.5	2.7	45.9	21.0	..	..
Vietnam	3.6	19.2	41.8	84.5	39.9	..	18.3	10.7	*0.4*	4.8	..	..
West Bank and Gaza	..	..	..	..	..	..	..	..	..	..	..	..
Yemen, Rep.	0.5	2.4	..	..	..	..	100.0	100.0	..	..	..	..
Yugoslavia, FR (Serb./Mont.)	..	..	..	..	..	..	..	..	..	..	..	..
Zambia	9.5	8.0	98.8	99.5	0.7	0.5	0.5	0.0	..	..	..	..
Zimbabwe	4.5	7.3	88.3	24.4	11.7	75.6	..	..	..	..	..	..
World	**8,192.7 s**	**1,3872.6 s**	**20.4 w**	**18.2 w**	**33.1 w**	**38.4 w**	**28.5 w**	**9.1 w**	**8.8 w**	**15.5 w**	**8.7 w**	**17.3 w**
Low income	579.1	1,931.8	29.7	20.3	41.5	63.8	25.8	8.8	1.8	5.6	1.3	1.4
Excl. China & India	146.6	305.0	46.0	39.5	1.5	9.9	43.7	24.5	5.8	24.3	3.0	0.6
Middle income	2,211.2	3,545.2	20.3	24.3	15.1	24.4	55.5	14.6	4.8	25.1	3.8	10.5
Lower middle income	1,570.0	2,033.1	15.2	18.8	9.0	24.3	67.8	12.3	3.0	32.0	4.7	11.6
Upper middle income	641.1	1,512.2	32.8	31.7	30.2	24.7	25.4	17.7	9.3	15.9	1.6	9.0
Low & middle income	2,790.3	5,477.1	22.3	22.9	20.6	38.3	49.3	12.6	4.2	18.2	3.3	7.3
East Asia & Pacific	406.4	1,696.6	17.2	14.1	45.3	59.3	35.9	11.6	0.3	8.9	0.9	5.4
Europe & Central Asia	1,640.1	1,718.7	13.5	17.2	13.6	29.6	65.4	6.2	2.2	31.2	5.1	15.3
Latin America & Carib.	362.0	854.8	59.9	63.1	2.1	4.6	24.1	17.5	11.5	10.0	0.6	2.5
Middle East & N. Africa	104.0	395.1	20.5	8.4	1.0	1.5	52.2	47.6	26.3	42.5	..	..
South Asia	138.5	540.8	41.5	18.7	43.0	62.7	7.4	7.0	5.9	9.7	2.2	1.9
Sub-Saharan Africa	139.3	271.1	24.0	16.5	70.8	73.3	4.4	3.3	0.8	2.2	..	4.7
High income	5,402.4	8,395.6	19.5	15.1	39.6	38.4	17.7	6.9	11.3	13.8	11.5	23.8
Europe EMU	1,242.9	1,822.8	17.0	12.0	37.2	27.3	22.9	8.8	10.0	11.9	11.9	38.0

a. Shares may not sum to 100 percent because other sources of generated electricity (such as geothermal, solar, and wind) are not shown.

Sources of electricity 3.9

About the data

Use of energy in general, and access to electricity in particular, are important in improving people's standard of living. But electricity generation also can damage the environment. Whether such damage occurs depends largely on how electricity is generated. For example, burning coal releases twice as much carbon dioxide—a major contributor to global warming—as does burning an equivalent amount of natural gas (see *About the data* for table 3.8). Nuclear energy does not generate carbon dioxide emissions, but it produces other dangerous waste products. The table provides information on electricity production by source. Shares may not sum to 100 percent because some sources of generated electricity (such as geothermal, solar, and wind) are not shown.

The International Energy Agency (IEA) compiles data on energy inputs used to generate electricity. IEA data for non-OECD countries are based on national energy data adjusted to conform with annual questionnaires completed by OECD member governments. In addition, estimates are sometimes made to complete major aggregates from which key data are missing, and adjustments are made to compensate for differences in definitions. The IEA makes these estimates in consultation with national statistical offices, oil companies, electricity utilities, and national energy experts.

The IEA occasionally revises its time series to reflect political changes. Since 1990, for example, it has constructed energy statistics for countries of the former Soviet Union. In addition, energy statistics for other countries have undergone continuous changes in coverage or methodology as more detailed energy accounts have become available in recent years. Breaks in series are therefore unavoidable.

Figure 3.9

The world's electricity sources are shifting—but coal still dominates

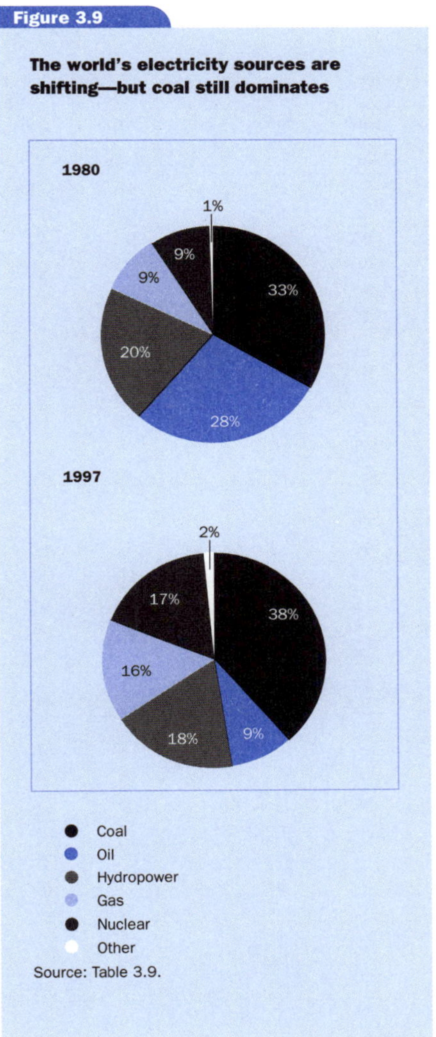

Source: Table 3.9.

Definitions

• **Electricity production** is measured at the terminals of all alternator sets in a station. In addition to hydropower, coal, oil, gas, and nuclear power generation, it covers generation by geothermal, solar, wind, and tide and wave energy, as well as that from combustible renewables and waste. Production includes the output of electricity plants designed to produce electricity only as well as that of combined heat and power plants. • **Sources of electricity** refer to the inputs used to generate electricity: hydropower, coal, oil, gas, and nuclear power. Hydropower refers to electricity produced by hydroelectric power plants, oil refers to crude oil and petroleum products, gas refers to natural gas but excludes natural gas liquids, and nuclear power refers to electricity produced by nuclear power plants.

Data sources

The data on electricity production are from the IEA's electronic files and its annual publications, *Energy Statistics and Balances of Non-OECD Countries, Energy Statistics of OECD Countries,* and *Energy Balances of OECD Countries.*

3.10 Urbanization

	Urban population				Population in urban agglomerations of more than one million			Population in largest city		Access to sanitation			
										Urban		Rural	
	millions		% of total population		% of total population			% of urban population		% of population		% of population	
	1980	1998	1980	1998	1980	1995	2015	1980	1995	1982–85[a]	1990–96[a]	1982–85[a]	1990–96[a]
Albania	0.9	1.4	34	40	0	0	0	..	..	..	97	..	10
Algeria	8.1	17.6	44	59	11	13	16	25	23	95	..	70	..
Angola	1.5	4.0	21	33	13	20	29	63	61	*27*	34	16	8
Argentina	23.3	32.3	83	89	35	39	36	43	38	*76*	80	35	42
Armenia	2.0	2.6	66	69	34	35	41	51	50	..	..	..	..
Australia	12.6	15.9	86	85	47	58	57	26	23	..	..	..	..
Austria	4.9	5.2	65	65	27	26	27	42	40	..	100	..	100
Azerbaijan	3.3	4.5	53	57	26	24	27	48	43	..	67	..	..
Bangladesh	12.5	29.4	14	23	5	9	15	26	33	*21*	77	2	30
Belarus	5.4	7.2	57	71	14	17	20	24	25	..	..	..	..
Belgium	9.4	9.9	95	97	12	11	11	13	11	..	100	..	100
Benin	0.9	2.4	27	41	0	0	0	..	..	*45*	54	4	6
Bolivia	2.4	4.9	46	61	14	17	20	30	28	*51*	77	22	39
Bosnia and Herzegovina	1.5	1.6	36	42	..	..	..	..	..	..	71	..	12
Botswana	0.1	0.8	15	49	0	0	0	..	..	*79*	91	13	41
Brazil	80.5	132.9	66	80	27	33	34	16	13	*33*	74	2	43
Bulgaria	5.4	5.7	61	69	12	16	19	20	21	..	100	..	96
Burkina Faso	0.6	1.9	9	17	0	0	0	44	52	*38*	78	5	11
Burundi	0.2	0.6	4	8	0	0	0	..	..	..	60	..	50
Cambodia	0.8	1.7	12	15	..	..	..	..	..	..	..	..	..
Cameroon	2.7	6.8	31	47	6	10	15	19	22	..	73	..	21
Canada	18.6	23.3	76	77	29	36	35	16	19	..	..	..	..
Central African Republic	0.8	1.4	35	40	0	0	0	..	..	*36*	..	9	..
Chad	0.8	1.7	19	23	0	0	0	40	55	..	74	..	7
Chile	9.1	12.6	81	85	33	36	35	41	41	*79*	82	21	..
China	192.3	385.7	20	31	8	11	14	6	4	..	58	..	7
Hong Kong, China	4.6	6.7	92	100	91	95	74	100	95	..	..	..	..
Colombia	18.2	29.8	64	73	21	27	27	20	22	*96*	76	13	33
Congo, Dem. Rep.	7.8	14.3	29	30	..	..	..	28	34	*8*	23	..	4
Congo, Rep.	0.7	1.7	41	61	0	0	0	67	67	..	15	..	4
Costa Rica	1.0	1.7	43	47	0	0	0	61	59	*100*	100	88	95
Côte d'Ivoire	2.8	6.5	35	45	15	21	35	44	48	*13*	59	20	51
Croatia	2.3	2.6	50	57	0	0	0	28	38	*72*	71	27	26
Cuba	6.6	8.3	68	75	20	20	22	29	27	..	71	..	51
Czech Republic	7.6	7.7	75	75	12	12	13	15	16	..	..	..	..
Denmark	4.3	4.5	84	85	27	25	25	32	30	..	100	..	100
Dominican Republic	2.9	5.3	51	64	25	33	36	50	65	*72*	76	59	83
Ecuador	3.7	7.7	47	63	14	26	31	30	26	*79*	87	34	34
Egypt, Arab Rep.	17.9	27.6	44	45	23	23	25	38	38	..	20	..	5
El Salvador	1.9	2.8	42	46	0	0	0	39	48	*89*	78	35	59
Eritrea	0.3	0.7	14	18	..	..	..	..	..	..	12	..	..
Estonia	1.0	1.0	70	69	0	0	0	..	..	..	..	..	..
Ethiopia	4.0	10.2	11	17	3	4	7	30	28	..	..	..	..
Finland	2.9	3.4	60	66	0	0	0	22	32	*100*	100	100	100
France	39.5	44.3	73	75	21	21	20	23	22	..	100	..	90
Gabon	0.3	0.9	50	79	0	0	0	..	..	..	79	..	67
Gambia, The	0.1	0.4	20	31	0	0	0	..	..	..	83	..	23
Georgia	2.6	3.3	52	60	22	25	31	42	42	..	..	..	..
Germany	64.7	71.5	83	87	38	41	43	10	9	..	..	..	..
Ghana	3.4	6.9	31	37	9	10	14	30	27	*47*	53	17	36
Greece	5.6	6.3	58	60	31	35	38	54	50	..	100	..	94
Guatemala	2.6	4.2	37	39	0	0	0	29	57	*73*	91	42	50
Guinea	0.9	2.2	19	31	12	23	39	65	81	*54*	..	1	10
Guinea-Bissau	0.1	0.3	17	23	0	0	0	..	..	*21*	32	13	17
Haiti	1.3	2.6	24	34	13	18	26	55	63	*42*	42	14	16
Honduras	1.2	3.1	35	51	0	0	0	33	37	*22*	81	38	53

Urbanization 3.10

	Urban population				Population in urban agglomerations of more than one million			Population in largest city		Access to sanitation			
										Urban		Rural	
	millions		% of total population		% of total population			% of urban population		% of population		% of population	
	1980	1998	1980	1998	1980	1995	2015	1980	1995	1982–85[a]	1990–96[a]	1982–85[a]	1990–96[a]
Hungary	6.1	6.4	57	64	19	20	22	34	31	..	100	..	85
India	158.8	272.0	23	28	6	10	12	5	6	*25*	46	1	2
Indonesia	32.9	79.0	22	39	7	13	16	18	12	*30*	73	30	40
Iran, Islamic Rep.	19.4	37.5	50	61	13	22	25	26	20	*90*	89	30	37
Iraq	8.5	15.8	66	71	26	22	23	39	28	30	..	..	..
Ireland	1.9	2.2	55	59	0	0	0	48	44	..	100	..	100
Israel	3.4	5.4	89	91	37	35	31	41	39	..	100	..	99
Italy	37.6	38.5	67	67	26	20	21	14	11	..	100	..	100
Jamaica	1.0	1.4	47	55	0	0	0	..	..	*92*	89	90	59
Japan	89.0	99.3	76	79	34	37	40	25	28	..	..	..	..
Jordan	1.3	3.3	60	73	29	28	35	49	39	91	..	61	..
Kazakhstan	8.0	8.8	54	56	6	8	10	12	14	..	..	..	..
Kenya	2.7	9.2	16	31	5	8	14	32	23	*75*	69	39	81
Korea, Dem. Rep.	10.1	13.8	57	60	10	11	13	18	19	*100*	..	100	..
Korea, Rep.	21.7	37.3	57	80	37	52	55	2	2	*100*	100	100	100
Kuwait	1.2	1.8	90	97	60	69	55	67	71	*100*	100	100	100
Kyrgyz Republic	1.4	1.6	38	34	0	0	0	..	..	*78*	87	..	31
Lao PDR	0.4	1.1	13	22	0	0	0	..	..	..	70	..	13
Latvia	1.7	1.7	68	69	0	0	0	49	53	..	90	..	..
Lebanon	2.2	3.7	74	89	..	..	..	55	52	*94*	100	18	100
Lesotho	0.2	0.5	13	26	0	0	0	..	..	*22*	..	11	7
Libya	2.1	4.6	69	87	38	66	81	38	40	..	90	..	75
Lithuania	2.1	2.5	61	68	0	0	0	..	..	..	..	..	..
Macedonia, FYR	1.0	1.2	54	61	0	0	0	..	..	*62*	68	9	13
Madagascar	1.6	4.1	18	28	0	0	0	29	25	*8*	50	..	3
Malawi	0.6	2.3	9	22	0	0	0	..	..	*88*	70	56	51
Malaysia	5.8	12.4	42	56	7	6	7	16	11	..	100	..	89
Mali	1.2	3.0	19	29	0	0	0	40	35	*90*	58	5	21
Mauritania	0.4	1.4	27	55	0	0	0	..	..	..	44	..	19
Mauritius	0.4	0.5	42	41	0	0	0	..	..	*100*	100	95	100
Mexico	44.8	70.9	66	74	27	28	26	31	25	*77*	81	15	26
Moldova	1.6	2.0	40	46	0	0	0	..	..	..	96	..	9
Mongolia	0.9	1.6	52	62	0	0	0	..	..	..	..	..	..
Morocco	8.0	15.1	41	55	11	18	22	26	23	*85*	69	13	18
Mozambique	1.6	6.4	13	38	6	14	24	47	41	*51*	53	..	12
Myanmar	8.1	12.0	24	27	7	9	14	27	35	*34*	42	15	40
Namibia	0.2	0.5	23	30	0	0	0	..	..	..	77	..	12
Nepal	0.9	2.6	7	11	0	0	0	..	..	*5*	34	0	3
Netherlands	12.5	14.0	88	89	7	14	14	8	8	..	100	..	100
New Zealand	2.6	3.2	83	86	0	0	0	30	30	..	..	..	..
Nicaragua	1.5	2.7	50	55	22	27	32	43	47	*35*	34	16	27
Niger	0.7	2.0	13	20	0	0	0	..	..	*20*	71	3	4
Nigeria	19.1	51.0	27	42	6	11	15	23	23	*30*	61	..	21
Norway	2.9	3.3	71	75	0	0	0	..	..	..	100	..	100
Oman	0.3	1.9	32	81	0	0	0	..	..	*60*	98	25	72
Pakistan	23.2	47.3	28	36	11	19	25	22	23	*48*	53	4	19
Panama	1.0	1.5	50	56	0	0	0	62	67	*99*	99	61	81
Papua New Guinea	0.4	0.8	13	17	0	0	0	..	..	*51*	82	3	11
Paraguay	1.3	2.8	42	55	0	0	0	52	43	*66*	..	40	..
Peru	11.2	17.9	65	72	26	32	33	39	40	*67*	62	13	10
Philippines	18.1	42.7	38	57	12	13	15	33	24	..	88	..	64
Poland	20.7	25.1	58	65	18	18	20	16	14	..	100	..	100
Portugal	2.9	6.1	29	61	13	19	24	46	33	..	100	..	100
Puerto Rico	2.1	2.9	67	74	34	30	29	51	48	..	..	..	..
Romania	10.9	12.5	49	56	9	9	10	18	17	..	81	..	3
Russian Federation	97.0	113.1	70	77	16	19	20	8	8	..	..	..	..

3.10 Urbanization

	Urban population				Population in urban agglomerations of more than one million			Population in largest city		Access to sanitation			
	millions		% of total population		% of total population			% of urban population		Urban % of population		Rural % of population	
	1980	1998	1980	1998	1980	1995	2015	1980	1995	1982–85[a]	1990–96[a]	1982–85[a]	1990–96[a]
Rwanda	0.2	0.5	5	6	0	0	0	..	..	60	..	60	..
Saudi Arabia	6.2	17.5	66	85	19	21	23	16	17	100	100	33	55
Senegal	2.0	4.2	36	46	18	24	31	48	47	..	83	..	40
Sierra Leone	0.8	1.7	24	35	0	0	0	..	..	30	17	6	8
Singapore	2.3	3.2	100	100	100	100	86	100	100	85	100	..	..
Slovak Republic	2.6	3.1	52	57	0	0	0	..	..	..	..	..	..
Slovenia	0.9	1.0	48	50	0	0	0	..	..	90	100	80	95
South Africa	13.3	21.9	48	53	11	20	23	12	11	..	79	..	12
Spain	27.2	30.4	73	77	20	18	18	16	14	..	100	..	100
Sri Lanka	3.2	4.3	22	23	0	0	0	..	..	..	33	..	58
Sudan	3.7	9.7	20	34	6	9	14	31	27	20	79	1	4
Sweden	6.9	7.4	83	83	17	17	19	20	21	..	100	..	100
Switzerland	3.6	4.8	57	68	0	0	0	20	19	..	100	..	100
Syrian Arab Republic	4.1	8.2	47	54	28	28	36	34	28	58	77	33	35
Tajikistan	1.4	1.7	34	28	0	0	0	..	..	..	83	..	14
Tanzania	2.7	9.8	15	31	5	6	9	30	22	93	97	40	83
Thailand	7.9	12.8	17	21	10	11	15	59	55	50	98	44	95
Togo	0.6	1.4	23	32	0	0	0	..	..	34	57	8	13
Trinidad and Tobago	0.7	0.9	63	73	0	0	0	..	..	..	97	..	92
Tunisia	3.3	6.0	52	64	17	23	27	35	31	64	100	29	85
Turkey	19.5	46.2	44	73	17	24	25	23	19	..	99	..	90
Turkmenistan	1.3	2.1	47	45	0	0	0	..	..	..	70	..	5
Uganda	1.1	2.8	9	14	0	0	0	42	40	40	75	10	55
Ukraine	30.9	34.1	62	68	14	16	19	7	8	..	70	..	8
United Arab Emirates	0.7	2.3	72	85	0	0	0	31	41	93	..	22	..
United Kingdom	50.0	52.8	89	89	25	23	23	15	15	..	100	..	100
United States	167.5	207.5	74	77	36	39	39	9	8	..	..	..	..
Uruguay	2.5	3.0	85	91	42	41	40	49	46	59	56	59	..
Uzbekistan	6.5	9.0	41	38	11	10	12	28	26	..	46	..	5
Venezuela, RB	12.0	20.1	79	86	16	27	28	21	16	57	64	5	30
Vietnam	10.3	15.0	19	20	5	7	9	27	25	..	43	..	15
West Bank and Gaza	..	..	..	..	..	..	..	..	..	..	..	..	..
Yemen, Rep.	1.6	4.0	19	24	0	0	0	..	..	..	40	..	14
Yugoslavia, FR (Serb./Mont.)	4.5	5.5	46	52	11	13	16	24	22	..	..	..	..
Zambia	2.3	3.8	40	39	9	15	23	23	37	56	40	41	..
Zimbabwe	1.6	4.0	22	34	0	13	..	39	40	100	99	5	48
World	**1,760.2 s**	**2,717.5 s**	**40 w**	**46 w**	**14 w**	**16 w**	**18 w**	**18 w**	**17 w**	**.. w**	**.. w**	**.. w**	**.. w**
Low income	543.3	1,077.2	22	30	7	10	13	13	13	..	56	..	10
Excl. China & India	182.1	405.7	22	31	6	10	14	27	27	..	..	..	..
Middle income	622.2	961.5	56	65	18	22	24	22	21	..	..	..	..
Lower middle income	346.5	511.3	51	58	14	17	20	21	22	..	..	..	..
Upper middle income	275.8	450.2	63	77	24	29	29	23	19	62	..	25	..
Low & middle income	1,165.5	2,038.8	32	41	10	14	16	18	17	..	..	..	..
East Asia & Pacific	310.2	616.7	22	34	9	12	15	12	9	..	61	..	13
Europe & Central Asia	249.3	314.1	59	66	14	16	18	15	15	..	..	..	..
Latin America & Carib.	233.8	373.9	65	75	24	28	28	27	25	60	..	18	..
Middle East & N. Africa	83.5	164.0	48	57	17	21	24	31	27	..	..	..	..
South Asia	201.2	360.9	22	28	6	10	13	9	11	28	46	1	2
Sub-Saharan Africa	87.5	209.1	23	33	5	8	12	28	29	..	..	..	..
High income	594.7	678.8	75	77	30	32	33	17	17	..	..	..	..
Europe EMU	203.7	225.8	74	78	25	25	25	16	15	..	100	..	97

a. Data are for the most recent year available in the period.

Urbanization 3.10

About the data

The population of a city or metropolitan area depends on the boundaries chosen. For example, in 1990 Beijing, China, contained 2.3 million people in 87 square kilometers of "inner city" and 5.4 million people in 158 square kilometers of "core city." The population of "inner city and inner suburban districts" was 6.3 million, and that of "inner city, inner and outer suburban districts, and inner and outer counties" was 10.8 million. (For most countries, the last definition is used.)

Estimates of the world's urban population would change significantly if China, India, and a few other populous nations were to change their definition of urban centers. According to China's State Statistical Bureau, by the end of 1996 urban residents accounted for about 43 percent of China's population, while in 1994 only 20 percent of the population was considered urban. Besides the continuous migration of people from rural to urban areas, one of the main reasons for this shift was the rapid growth in the hundreds of towns reclassified as cities in recent years. Because the estimates in the table are based on national definitions of what constitutes a city or metropolitan area, cross-country comparisons should be made with caution.

To estimate urban populations, the United Nations' ratios of urban to total population were applied to the World Bank's estimates of total population (see table 2.1). The resulting urban population estimates were used to calculate the population in the largest city as a percentage of the urban population.

Access to sanitation services in urban areas is defined as the percentage of the urban population served by connections to public sewers or household systems such as pit privies, pour-flush latrines, septic tanks, communal toilets, and similar facilities. Access to sanitation in rural areas is included to allow comparison of rural and urban access. The rural population with access is defined as those with adequate means of disposal, such as pit privies, pour-flush latrines, and the like. These definitions and definitions of urban areas vary, however, so comparisons between countries can be misleading (see *Definitions* for table 2.15).

Figure 3.10

The world's largest cities continue to boom

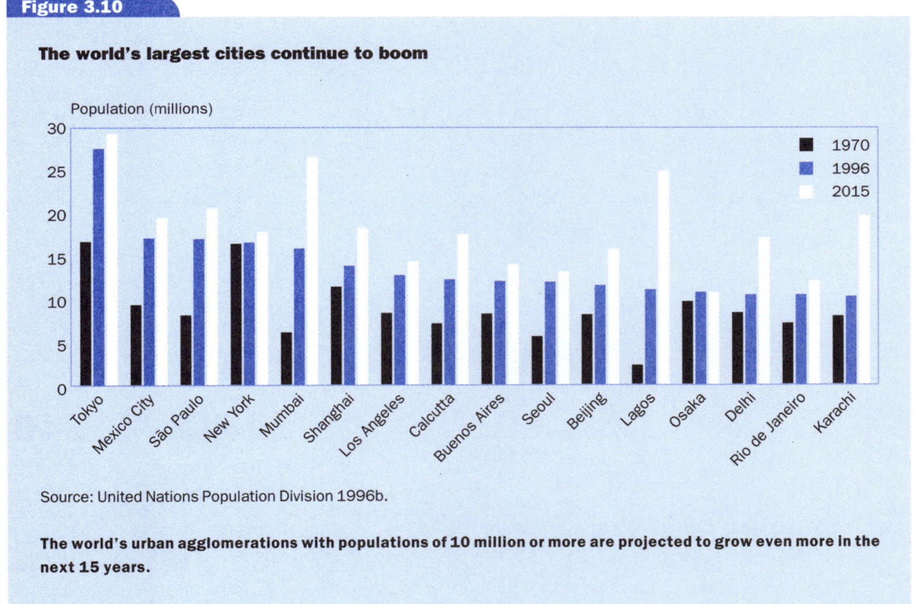

Source: United Nations Population Division 1996b.

The world's urban agglomerations with populations of 10 million or more are projected to grow even more in the next 15 years.

Definitions

• **Urban population** is the midyear population of areas defined as urban in each country and reported to the United Nations (see *About the data*). • **Population in urban agglomerations of more than one million** is the percentage of a country's population living in metropolitan areas that in 1990 had a population of more than one million people. • **Population in largest city** is the percentage of a country's urban population living in that country's largest metropolitan area. • **Access to sanitation** is the percentage of the urban or rural population served by connections to public sewers or household systems such as pit privies, pour-flush latrines, septic tanks, communal toilets, and similar facilities.

Data sources

The data on urban population come from the United Nations Population Division's *World Urbanization Prospects: The 1998 Revision,* and the data on population in urban agglomerations and in the largest city are from the United Nations Population Division's *World Urbanization Prospects: The 1996 Revision.* The total population figures are World Bank estimates. The data on access to sanitation in urban and rural areas are from the World Health Organization.

3.11 Urban environment

	City	Urban area	Urban population	Average household income	Income differential	House price to income ratio	Crowding	Work trips by public transportation	Travel time to work	Households with access to services		
					average income in fifth quintile to first quintile		Average floor space per person			Sewerage connection	Regular waste collection	Access to potable water
		sq. km	thousands	$			sq. m	%	minutes	%	%	%
		1993	**1993**	**1993**	**1993**	**1993**	**1993**	**1993**	**1993**	**1993**	**1993**	**1993**
Angola	Luanda	..	1,400	..	..	..	40.7	..	..	13	50	38
Armenia	Yerevan	215	1,223	1,407	28.4	39.0	13.0	98	52	93	81	98
Australia	Melbourne	1,148	3,023	30,216	12.0	3.6	55.0	16	25	99	100	100
Azerbaijan	Baku	2,300	..	977	8.7	13.0	12.9	80	57	79	..	100
Bangladesh	Dhaka	1,194	7,500	478	6.9	5.0	2.7	..	..	44	50	..
	Tangail	32	155	228	6.9	8.0	1.2	..	15	..	..	51
Benin	Cotonou	88	559	2,745	6.0	1.6	5.9	..	60	1	25	60
	Porto Novo	50	183	1,479	6.1	3.4	5.5	..	40	1	25	76
Bolivia	Santa Cruz de la Sierra	165	742	3,786	7.6	2.6	..	60	25	22	100	87
	La Paz	51	726	3,787	11.7	1.2	..	51	35	58	92	90
	El Alto	58	442	1,786	7.2	1.4	..	..	25	20	95	86
	Cochabamba	68	425	4,035	8.3	2.6	..	46	17	47	95	71
Botswana	Gaborone	..	473	..	..	7.2	12.5	42	20	33	98	100
Brazil	Rio de Janeiro	1,255	5,554	12,087	20.3	2.5	18.9	67	51	87	88	98
	Recife	..	1,503	815	28.7	2.2	15.5	70	40	38	95	95
	Curitiba	..	1,352	1,091	16.1	5.7	21.0	72	30	75	95	97
	Brasília	..	199	12,087	20.3	3.0	17.3	..	49	74	95	89
Bulgaria	Sofia	..	1,294	..	..	5.8	16.7	75	35	98	95	100
Burkina Faso	Ouagadougou	170	716	2,622	3.3	8.5	12.2	..	22	..	40	75
	Bobo-Dioulasso	67	284	2,379	9.1	10.2	12.0	..	15	..	30	81
Burundi	Bujumbura	100	278	1,823	17.0	1.9	5.8	..	30	29	41	93
Cameroon	Douala	144	1,094	..	..	4.6	10.0	11	45	3	60	83
	Yaoundé	..	923	677	..	3.9	12.6	6	50	3	44	85
Canada	Toronto	..	4,236	49,791	9.5	3.9	41.1	30	23	100	100	100
Central African Rep.	Bangui	163	471	..	..	6.2	11.2	..	45	1	25	45
Chile	Santiago	..	4,820	8,043	16.6	2.4	14.4	54	36	92	95	98
China	Hefei	..	3,809	2,080	13.8	..	11.0	..	..	57	..	100
	Quingdao	..	2,121	1,165	1.8	..	11.1	..	..	11	..	100
	Shanghai	..	..	..	..	..	9.9	..	47	58	..	100
	Foshan	32	385	3,354	3.2	..	16.3	..	..	100	..	100
	Zhangjiagang	..	178	8,468	..	..	14.3	..	..	91	..	100
Colombia	Bogotá	482	5,314	7,120	14.7	3.1	8.8	75	39	99	94	97
Congo, Dem. Rep.	Kinshasa	591	4,566	2,241	6.7	..	..	61	120	3	0	70
Côte d'Ivoire	Abidjan	369	2,462	2,827	7.9	7.2	7.2	49	90	45	70	62
	Bouake	..	439	1,820	9.5	5.6	7.4	10	35	..	35	28
Croatia	Zagreb	..	868	4,354	5.9	11	22.1	52	26	80	100	90
Cuba	Havana	..	2,176	..	..	2.1	16.0	58	42	85	100	85
	Camaguey	155	296	..	..	..	18.7	6	30	46	93	71
	Cienfuegos	44	131	..	..	1.5	19.2	..	30	70	97	100
	Pinar del Rio	28	129	..	..	3.7	21.0	..	80	48	100	93
Czech Republic	Prague	496	1,214	..	..	11.9	26.0	67	57	94	100	100
Denmark	Copenhagen	2,863	1,326	29,320	14.0	3.1	44.0	27	22	100	100	100
Djibouti	Djibouti	..	..	6,856	12.0	3.7	13.1	19	22	15	65	69
Ecuador	Guayaquil	178	1,773	5,406	12.1	2.0	15.6	50	45	55	70	85
	Quito	178	1,615	..	..	2.4	8.6	0	..	93	89	..
Egypt, Arab Rep.	Cairo	420	14,524	1,658	6.1	4.9	13.0	58	60	91	65	98
	Gharbeya	..	383	1,656	6.1	3.9	13.3	32	30	91	45	99
	Assiout	10	322	1,721	6.7	3.1	14.0	29	25	30	25	93
El Salvador	San Salvador	163	1,343	4,320	12.7	2.7	6.6	..	..	80	46	91
	Santa Ana	18	142	2,998	10.6	3.2	8.1	..	..	57	90	82
	San Miguel	..	132	3,420	13.2	4.3	9.7	..	..	46	99	56
Estonia	Tallin	185	468	..	..	3.6	21.3	..	27	95	99	100
Ethiopia	Addis Ababa	..	8,044	..	..	..	..	..	62	..	54	77
France	Paris	2,586	9,319	20,899	14.7	4.3	30.0	40	35	98	100	100
	Lyon	..	1,262	..	..	..	..	..	..	90	100	100
	Marseilles	351	800	14,640	5.2	..	..	..	25	99	99	100

Urban environment 3.11

	City	Urban area	Urban population	Average household income	Income differential	House price to income ratio	Crowding	Work trips by public transportation	Travel time to work	Households with access to services		
					average income in fifth quintile to first quintile		Average floor space per person			Sewerage connection	Regular waste collection	Access to potable water
		sq. km	thousands	$			sq. m	%	minutes	%	%	%
		1993	1993	1993	1993	1993	1993	1993	1993	1993	1993	1993
	Strasbourg	78	388	15,942	9.7	..	..	..	15	98	100	100
Gabon	Libreville	..	362	5,726	..	..	12.3	38	..	..	40	100
Gambia, The	Banjul	..	479	230	8.1	4.8	11.5	60	40	13	35	74
Georgia	Tbilisi	204	1,295	..	..	..	16.2	98	70	100	52	100
Germany	Cologne	405	1,006	..	..	..	34.0	17	..	99	100	100
	Duisburg	233	536	..	..	7.9	32.1	21	..	100	100	100
	Leipzig	151	481	..	..	..	33.0	33	..	95	100	100
	Wiesbaden	204	266	..	..	..	37.0	23	..	100	100	100
	Erfurt	268	213	..	..	5.1	29.1	32	..	95	100	100
Ghana	Accra	411	1,718	403	..	8.0	6.2	47	45	12	60	86
	Kumasi	..	758	822	2.9	17.8	5.8	55	20	12	11	57
	Tamale	22	193	682	1.9	17.4	5.2	45	18	6	5	38
Greece	Athens	..	1,464	..	..	3.1	29.0	34	53	95	90	100
Guatemala	Guatemala City	..	1,327	2,760	76.7	9.0	8.0	53	40	..	53	64
Guinea	Conakry	..	1,308	..	..	6.4	6.5	26	55	17	50	75
Hungary	Budapest	..	320	5,621	9.2	7.7	29.4	66	40	90	100	100
India	Hubli-Dharbad	..	..	1,114	7.1	3.6	6.2	37	22	37	89	89
	Mumbai	..	12,810	1,504	6.7	3.5	3.5	79	33	51	90	96
	Delhi	624	8,957	1,196	11.4	7.0	6.9	53	44	40	77	92
	Chennai	612	5,651	1,184	8.0	7.0	6.2	42	22	37	90	60
	Bangalore	..	4,472	1,224	6.5	10.8	9.5	46	18	35	96	81
	Lucknow	..	1,804	992	7.5	4.6	5.5	1	23	30	74	88
	Varanasi	104	1,078	928	7.8	5.1	4.5	21	22	41	88	85
	Mysore	..	701	1,236	6.4	7.5	11.8	13	20	60	60	90
	Bhiwandi	26	572	..	..	0.3	2.4	8	15	15	40	86
	Gulbarga	..	330	1,028	7.6	3.5	6.1	8	11	14	74	90
	Tumkur	..	194	809	6.1	4.9	7.4	21	8	..	50	86
Indonesia	Banjarmasin	..	..	1,474	4.4	4.0	6.4	12	37	..	70	94
	Surabaya	..	..	1,970	8.1	8.6	11.5	23	23	..	87	99
	Jakarta	..	13,048	2,460	6.6	9.9	15.0	38	82	..	84	93
	Bandung	..	1,819	1,625	5.8	12	13.1	..	29	27	97	86
	Medan	..	1,810	1,674	4.5	5.5	13.9	44	30	19	19	94
	Semarang	..	1,076	1,351	6.0	5.4	12.0	14	25	..	69	88
Iran, Islamic Rep.	Tehran	..	..	..	..	11.0	22.6	36	..	..	100	..
Jordan	Amman	..	..	12,813	13.9	6.5	15.4	14	31	79	100	100
Kazakhstan	Almaty	..	1,173	..	..	7.2	14.5	43	35	88	83	100
Kenya	Mombasa	234	382	..	..	1.9	5.9	31	27	2	40	95
	Nairobi	..	1,598	..	..	12.5	11.3	68	48	35	47	93
Kyrgyz Republic	Bishkek	..	703	..	..	..	..	60	35	65	89	100
Latvia	Riga	..	1,026	..	..	..	19.4	57	27	97	85	100
Liberia	Monrovia	..	697	..	..	24.0	14.0	75	60	1	0	20
Lithuania	Vilnius	..	670	..	..	5.4	16.2	49	25	94	95	100
Madagascar	Antananarivo	..	932	..	..	18.7	6.4	30	..	17	..	95
Malawi	Blantyre	..	403	..	..	8.3	8.3	39	44	8	20	80
	Lilongwe	..	220	..	..	4.2	6.6	5	31	12	..	80
	Mzuzu	..	115	..	..	5.2	6.5	10	35	..	16	60
Mali	Bamako	267	..	..	..	3.7	3.2	12	40	2	95	53
Mauritania	Nouakchott	72	576	1,481	8.9	6.4	10.0	45	50	4	15	68
Moldova	Chisinau	131	662	1,055	9.7	13.0	15.0	48	25	86	83	100
Mongolia	Ulaanbaatar	3,542	..	317	3.2	37.7	9.2	85	29	51	..	49
Morocco	Rabat	..	1,345	7,514	8.1	6.8	10.0	..	..	95	90	100
Mozambique	Maputo	..	..	414	4.9	..	12.0	13	..	23	37	73
Namibia	Windhoek	69	142	11,618	15.2	6.0	43.0	..	20	75	93	98
Netherlands	Amsterdam	202	724	21,687	5.2	3.5	38.3	22	22	100	100	100
New Zealand	Auckland	..	942	25,900	8.1	4.4	40.0	6	..	98	..	..
Niger	Niamey	224	505	1,369	13.2	7.3	7.7	17	27	..	25	77

3.11 Urban environment

	City	Urban area	Urban population	Average house-hold income	Income differential average income in fifth quintile to first quintile	House price to income ratio	Crowding Average floor space per person	Work trips by public trans-portation	Travel time to work	Households with access to services Sewerage connection	Regular waste collection	Access to potable water
		sq. km 1993	thousands 1993	$ 1993	1993	1993	sq. m 1993	% 1993	minutes 1993	% 1993	% 1993	% 1993
Nigeria	Onitsha	9	..	623	18.5	..	12.0	53	33	..	38	95
	Lagos	959	5,968	492	18.2	10.0	5.5	54	85	2	8	75
	Ibadan	2,937	1,941	415	50.0	6.8	9.0	40	40	..	40	70
	Kano	123	1,510	340	6.9	3.2	2.8	56	..	25	38	16
Pakistan	Lahore	..	5,150	3,298	7.7	16.0	1.2	16	25	74	50	90
Paraguay	Asunción	67	949	5,496	8.8	5.3	4.7	31	60	10	79	58
Peru	Lima	..	6,232	1,109	..	9.2	25.7	65	35	69	57	87
	Trujillo	45	509	..	..	3.8	15.2	74	30	71	48	98
Philippines	Manila	..	9,286	5,318	8.4	..	34.1	40	120	80	85	94
Poland	Warsaw	..	2,219	3,021	3.1	5.4	18.2	..	34	91	97	100
Romania	Bucharest	..	2,350	..	..	6.8	12.9	65	78	90	86	98
Russian Federation	Kostroma	..	..	2,357	5.1	5.1	17.8	65	21	91	90	100
	Moscow	..	9,269	4,040	7.6	17.0	19.7	85	62	100	100	100
	Nizhny Novgorod	..	..	2,459	4.6	6.4	17.1	78	35	95	100	100
	Novgorod	..	..	2,865	5.9	7.3	16.3	44	30	96	99	100
	Ryazan	..	..	2,348	6.9	8.9	16.2	88	25	92	99	100
Rwanda	Kigali	47	275	2,279	11.6	..	..	32	..	..	..	48
Senegal	Dakar	..	1,801	3,008	17.0	3.0	8.1	53	45	25	75	92
	Kaoloack	..	187	1,488	20.9	..	..	13	27	3	..	56
	Ziguinchor	..	155	1,150	22.0	..	..	27	20	2	..	30
	Mbour	..	101	2,192	15.9	..	..	20	31	2	..	79
Sierra Leone	Freetown	82	395	370	11.4	..	10.0	84	..	1	..	53
Slovak Republic	Bratislava	2,144	651	3,984	5.1	5.6	22.3	72	34	96	100	100
Slovenia	Ljubljana	275	316	11,729	6.1	..	..	1	22	99	99	100
	Maribor	738	185	9,314	6.2	..	..	41	28	58	90	100
Sri Lanka	Colombo	..	2,190	436	3.4	..	18.7	74	35	60	94	98
Sudan	Khartoum	249	826	..	..	..	21.9	63	42	3	12	55
Sweden	Stockholm	309	1,545	30,840	4.5	4.6	40.0	37	35	100	100	100
Tanzania	Arusha	..	..	564	4.1	5.0	5.0	61	30	16	..	60
	Dar es Salaam	..	..	564	4.1	5.0	4.5	48	30	6	25	60
	Mwanza	94	..	..	..	5.0	4.0	24	30	8	15	74
Togo	Lomé	288	802	..	..	3.5	12.0	30	30	..	37	..
Tunisia	Tunis	..	1,684	4,032	6.0	5.2	12.0	..	45	73	61	96
Uganda	Kampala	202	840	..	..	2.3	4.0	45	23	9	20	87
United Arab Emirates	Dubai	604	594	26,564	22.8	..	..	..	18	60	100	100
United Kingdom	Hertfordshire	1,604	1,000	28,270	10.9	6.0	34.8	7	27	100	100	100
	Glasgow	..	618	7,329	1.8	4.5	..	39	..	99	..	99
	Bedfordshire	..	539	32,080	10.9	3.0	34.6	10	..	93	98	98
	Cardiff	137	306	..	..	2.9	17.5	13	..	100	100	100
United States	New York	..	16,332	39,256	14.8	6.3	..	51	37	99	..	100
	Des Moines	..	..	31,732	8.6	1.8	..	..	16	99	..	100
	Atlanta	..	..	32,966	22.4	3.1	..	..	24	98	..	100
Vietnam	Hanoi	47	..	32,966	3.4	10.4	5.8	..	..	40	45	100
Yemen	Sana'a	..	..	183	..	17.0	4.0	..	15	12	51	60
Yugoslavia, FR	Belgrade	765	1,318	..	..	16.0	19.4	..	35	71	86	99
(Serb./Mont.)	Novi Sad	290	232	..	..	30.0	21.8	60	21	93	95	100
	Nis	150	214	..	..	17.4	19.7	61	25	84	87	92
Zambia	Lusaka	..	..	867	14.0	6.5	6.9	65	20	36	..	60
Zimbabwe	Harare	..	..	754	5.0	9.8	8.0	48	56	93	100	97

Urban environment 3.11

About the data

Despite the importance of cities and urban agglomerations as home to almost half the world's people, the data on many aspects of urban life are sparse. Compiling comparable data has been difficult, and the available indicators have been scattered among international agencies with different mandates. Even within cities it is difficult to assemble an integrated data set. Urban areas are often spread across many jurisdictions, with no single agency responsible for collecting and reporting data for the entire area. Adding to the difficulties of data collection are gaps and overlaps in the data collection and reporting responsibilities of different administrative units. Creating a comprehensive, comparable international data set is further complicated by differences in the definition of an urban area and by uneven data quality.

The United Nations Global Plan of Action calls for monitoring the changing role of the world's cities and human settlements. The international agency with a mandate to assemble information on urban areas is the United Nations Centre for Human Settlements (UNCHS, or Habitat). Its Urban Indicators Programme is intended to provide data for monitoring and evaluating the performance of urban areas and for developing government policies and strategies. These data are collected through questionnaires completed by city officials in more than a hundred countries. The table shows selected indicators for 150 cities from the UNCHS data set, which covers 237 cities and 43 indicators. A few more indicators are included on the *World Development Indicators* CD-ROM.

The UNCHS selection of 237 cities does not reflect population weights or the economic importance of cities and is therefore biased toward smaller cities. Moreover, it is based on demand for participation in the Urban Indicators Programme. As a result the database excludes a large number of major cities. The table reflects this bias, as well as the criterion of data availability for the indicators shown in the table.

The data should be used with care. Because different data collection methods and definitions may have been used, comparisons can be misleading. And because data are available only for 1993, no conclusions can be drawn about any improvement or worsening of conditions. The definitions used here for urban population and access to potable water are not necessarily consistent with those for tables 3.5 and 3.10 (see *Definitions*).

Table 3.11a

Population of the world's 10 largest metropolitan areas in 1000, 1800, 1900, and 2000

Millions

1000		1800		1900		2000	
City	**Population**	**City**	**Population**	**City**	**Population**	**City**	**Population**
Cordova	0.45	Peking	1.10	London	6.5	Tokyo	28.0
Kaifeng	0.40	London	0.86	New York	4.2	Mexico City	18.1
Constantinople	0.30	Canton	0.80	Paris	3.3	Mumbai	18.0
Angkor	0.20	Edo (Tokyo)	0.69	Berlin	2.7	São Paulo	17.7
Kyoto	0.18	Constantinople	0.57	Chicago	1.7	New York	16.6
Cairo	0.14	Paris	0.55	Vienna	1.7	Shanghai	14.2
Baghdad	0.13	Naples	0.43	Tokyo	1.5	Lagos	13.5
Nishapur	0.13	Hangchow	0.39	St. Petersburg	1.4	Los Angeles	13.1
Hasa	0.11	Osaka	0.38	Manchester	1.4	Seoul	12.9
Anhilvada	0.10	Kyoto	0.38	Philadelphia	1.4	Beijing	12.4

Source: O'Meara 1999 and United Nations Population Division 1996.

Definitions

• **Urban area** refers to the city proper along with the suburban fringe and any built-up, thickly settled areas lying outside, but adjacent to, the city boundaries. • **Urban population** refers to the population of the urban agglomeration, a contiguous inhabited territory without regard to administrative boundaries. • **Average household income** is the average of the household income in all five quintiles. Household income is based on survey data. It is the total income of all household members from all sources, including wages, pensions or benefits, business earnings, rents, and the value of any business or subsistence products consumed (for example, foodstuffs). • **Income differential** is the ratio of average household income in the highest quintile to that in the lowest quintile. • **House price to income ratio** is the average house price divided by the average household income. • **Crowding** is measured by floor area per person, the median usable living space per person in square meters. • **Work trips by public transportation** are the percentage of trips to work made by bus or minibus, tram, or train. Buses or minibuses refer to road vehicles other than cars taking passengers on a fare-paying basis. Other means of transport commonly used in developing countries, such as taxi, ferry, rickshaw, or animal, are not included. • **Travel time to work** is the average time in minutes, for all modes, for a one-way trip to work. Train and bus times include average walking and waiting times, and car times include parking and walking to the workplace. • **Households with sewerage connection** are the percentage of households with a connection to sewerage. • **Households with regular waste collection** are the percentage of households with regular household or "dumpster" group collection, but not household transport of garbage to a local dump. • **Households with access to potable water** are the percentage of households having access to safe or potable drinking water within 200 meters of the dwelling. Potable water is water that is free from contamination and safe to drink without further treatment.

Data sources

The data in the table are from the Global Urban Indicators database of the UNCHS's Urban Indicators Programme.

3.12 Traffic and congestion

	Motor vehicles				Passenger cars		Two-wheelers		Road traffic		Traffic accidents	
	per 1,000 people		per kilometer of road		per 1,000 people		per 1,000 people		million vehicle kilometers		people injured or killed per 1,000 vehicles	
	1980	1998	1980	1998	1980	1998	1980	1998	1980	1998	1980	1998
Albania	..	40	..	8	..	27	..	1	..	..	..	5
Algeria	..	52	..	15	30	25	1	..	..	..	..	..
Angola	..	20	..	3	..	18	..	..	..	..	..	..
Argentina	155	176	20	29	..	137	..	1	..	..	..	..
Armenia	..	2	..	1	..	0	..	2	..	..	..	347
Australia	502	605	..	12	401	488	24	16	204	..	5	..
Austria	330	521	23	13	297	481	76	74	35,430	..	27	13
Azerbaijan	..	47	..	15	..	36	..	1	..	..	..	8
Bangladesh	..	1	..	1	..	1	..	1	..	..	..	66
Belarus	..	112	..	20	..	..	..	54	..	5,650	..	8
Belgium	349	485	28	33	..	435	..	23	45,779	..	25	14
Benin	..	8	..	7	..	7	..	44	..	..	..	74
Bolivia	19	52	3	7	..	32	..	9	795	1,730	41	..
Bosnia and Herzegovina	..	26	..	5	..	23	..	..	..	..	..	25
Botswana	27	45	3	4	9	15	1	..	..	..	50	94
Brazil	85	77	7	6	75	..	3	..	..	..	3	..
Bulgaria	..	252	..	56	92	220	..	62	665	..	..	4
Burkina Faso	..	5	..	5	..	4	..	10	..	..	..	..
Burundi	..	..	..	..	..	..	..	..	..	..	..	..
Cambodia	..	6	..	2	..	5	..	41	..	1,407	..	31
Cameroon	8	12	4	5	..	7	..	..	..	..	112	..
Canada	548	560	..	19	417	455	19	11	205,515	..	..	13
Central African Republic	8	1	1	0	..	0	..	0	..	1,250	..	138
Chad	..	8	..	1	..	3	..	1	..	..	..	..
Chile	61	110	8	20	45	71	4	2	7,540	..	38	33
China	2	8	2	7	..	3	..	8	2,032	..	12	..
Hong Kong, China	54	77	234	279	41	56	5	5	4,407	10,685	77	37
Colombia	..	40	..	13	11	21	17	..	2,480	..	..	..
Congo, Dem. Rep.	..	..	..	..	..	..	..	..	..	..	..	..
Congo, Rep.	..	20	..	4	..	14	..	..	..	..	..	..
Costa Rica	..	130	..	13	20	85	..	15	..	..	..	29
Côte d'Ivoire	24	28	..	9	..	18	..	..	..	..	..	..
Croatia	..	..	..	..	..	..	..	..	..	..	..	..
Cuba	..	32	..	6	..	16	..	16	..	..	..	28
Czech Republic	..	402	..	32	..	358	..	106	..	43,753	..	9
Denmark	322	413	24	3	271	355	..	11	26,300	44,053	10	4
Dominican Republic	36	45	11	30	20	27	12	..	..	..	18	..
Ecuador	..	45	..	15	28	41	..	2	..	..	..	16
Egypt, Arab Rep.	..	30	..	28	8	23	..	7	..	..	..	..
El Salvador	..	61	..	36	16	30	..	5	..	4,244	..	26
Eritrea	..	2	..	2	..	2	..	..	..	..	..	..
Estonia	..	372	..	11	..	312	..	4	..	..	..	4
Ethiopia	2	2	1	4	1	1	0	0	2	..	38	..
Finland	288	448	18	30	256	392	36	33	26,750	44,800	7	4
France	402	530	27	35	355	442	97	..	298,000	491,300	16	6
Gabon	..	29	..	5	..	17	..	..	..	..	..	..
Gambia, The	..	17	..	7	11	8	1	..	..	..	..	..
Georgia	..	87	..	23	..	80	..	5	..	..	..	5
Germany	399	522	51	69	297	506	38	36	..	583,100	..	12
Ghana	..	7	..	4	..	5	..	..	..	..	..	..
Greece	134	328	35	28	91	238	12	203	..	..	23	10
Guatemala	..	17	..	15	..	9	..	..	..	..	..	..
Guinea	..	5	..	1	..	2	..	..	..	..	..	..
Guinea-Bissau	..	10	..	3	..	6	..	..	..	..	..	..
Haiti	..	7	..	13	..	4	..	..	..	..	..	..
Honduras	..	37	..	13	..	..	..	..	..	..	..	..

Traffic and congestion 3.12

	Motor vehicles per 1,000 people		Motor vehicles per kilometer of road		Passenger cars per 1,000 people		Two-wheelers per 1,000 people		Road traffic million vehicle kilometers		Traffic accidents people injured or killed per 1,000 vehicles	
	1980	1998	1980	1998	1980	1998	1980	1998	1980	1998	1980	1998
Hungary	108	268	13	16	95	229	..	14	..	..	22	10
India	2	*7*	1	*3*	..	*5*	..	*24*	..	..	..	*61*
Indonesia	8	*22*	8	*11*	..	*12*	..	*59*	..	..	59	*1*
Iran, Islamic Rep.	..	*36*	..	*15*	..	*26*	..	*43*	..	..	..	*14*
Iraq	..	*56*	..	*23*	..	*39*	..	..	..	..	..	*5*
Ireland	236	*314*	9	*12*	216	*279*	8	*6*	14,917	28,390	11	*12*
Israel	123	264	114	100	107	215	..	13	10,442	33,456	38	31
Italy	334	*591*	65	*108*	303	*539*	114	*66*	226,569	..	12	8
Jamaica	..	*48*	..	*7*	..	*40*	..	..	..	..	..	..
Japan	323	560	34	*61*	203	394	102	115	389,052	744,380	16	14
Jordan	56	*66*	25	*44*	41	*48*	2	*0*	623	2,154	63	*54*
Kazakhstan	..	82	..	11	..	62	..	13	..	..	..	*10*
Kenya	8	*14*	3	*6*	7	*11*	1	*1*	..	..	74	..
Korea, Dem. Rep.	..	..	..	..	..	..	..	..	..	..	..	..
Korea, Rep.	14	226	11	120	7	163	6	56	8,728	67,266	212	33
Kuwait	390	*462*	..	*156*	..	*359*	..	..	12,189	..	7	..
Kyrgyz Republic	..	*32*	..	*8*	..	*32*	..	*1*	..	..	..	..
Lao PDR	..	*4*	..	*1*	..	*3*	..	*49*	..	..	..	..
Latvia	..	237	..	10	..	198	..	8	..	..	..	10
Lebanon	..	..	..	*205*	..	..	..	*15*	..	..	..	*3*
Lesotho	10	*17*	3	*8*	3	*6*	0	..	..	..	85	..
Libya	..	*209*	..	*948*	..	*154*	..	*0*	..	..	..	*8*
Lithuania	..	293	..	15	..	265	..	5	..	..	..	8
Macedonia, FYR	..	*156*	..	*35*	..	*142*	..	*1*	..	4,247	..	*12*
Madagascar	..	*5*	3	*2*	..	*4*	..	..	1	..	..	*9*
Malawi	5	*5*	3	*2*	2	*2*	2	..	..	..	..	*89*
Malaysia	..	*172*	..	*37*	52	*145*	101	212	..	..	..	13
Mali	..	*5*	..	*3*	..	*3*	..	..	..	*3*	..	..
Mauritania	..	*12*	..	*4*	..	*8*	..	..	..	..	..	..
Mauritius	44	92	23	57	27	71	27	94	46	..	..	35
Mexico	..	144	..	*41*	60	97	..	3	..	..	..	..
Moldova	..	*65*	..	*19*	..	*46*	..	*25*	..	910	..	*15*
Mongolia	..	30	..	2	..	16	..	*10*	..	1,889	..	25
Morocco	..	*48*	..	*21*	..	*38*	..	*1*	18	..	..	*46*
Mozambique	..	*1*	..	*0*	..	*0*	..	..	..	..	..	..
Myanmar	..	*1*	..	*2*	..	*1*	..	..	..	..	..	..
Namibia	..	*82*	..	*2*	..	*46*	..	*1*	..	2,317	..	*5*
Nepal	..	..	..	..	..	..	..	..	..	..	..	..
Netherlands	343	421	..	57	322	391	61	67	70,825	109,030	12	3
New Zealand	492	*579*	17	*22*	420	470	43	*13*	16,545	..	11	..
Nicaragua	..	*34*	..	*8*	*8*	18	..	*5*	..	150	..	*29*
Niger	6	*5*	..	5	5	4	..	..	..	240	63	..
Nigeria	4	*26*	3	*14*	3	9	4	*4*	..	..	123	*10*
Norway	342	498	17	24	302	402	36	52	..	30,974	8	6
Oman	..	*152*	..	*9*	..	103	..	*2*	..	..	..	*23*
Pakistan	2	8	5	4	2	5	3	14	..	31,950	71	*18*
Panama	..	*102*	..	*25*	..	79	..	*3*	..	..	..	*39*
Papua New Guinea	..	*27*	..	*6*	..	7	..	..	..	..	..	..
Paraguay	..	*24*	..	*4*	..	14	..	..	..	..	..	..
Peru	..	42	..	13	..	26	..	..	..	..	..	*32*
Philippines	..	31	..	11	*6*	10	*4*	14	..	9,548	..	*6*
Poland	86	273	10	28	67	230	..	40	44,597	153,060	..	8
Portugal	145	*347*	26	*0*	..	309	..	*77*	..	89,130	31	*20*
Puerto Rico	..	*280*	..	*74*	..	229	..	..	..	..	..	..
Romania	..	*135*	..	*20*	..	116	..	*15*	..	35,675	..	*3*
Russian Federation	..	*154*	..	*44*	..	120	..	..	..	..	..	*10*

3.12 Traffic and congestion

	Motor vehicles				Passenger cars		Two-wheelers		Road traffic		Traffic accidents	
	per 1,000 people		per kilometer of road		per 1,000 people		per 1,000 people		million vehicle kilometers		people injured or killed per 1,000 vehicles	
	1980	1998	1980	1998	1980	1998	1980	1998	1980	1998	1980	1998
Rwanda	2	3	2	2	1	1	1	..	..	..	..	..
Saudi Arabia	163	166	26	18	67	98	..	0	..	..	..	10
Senegal	19	14	8	8	..	10	..	0	..	..	56	86
Sierra Leone	..	6	..	3	..	5	..	2	..	529	..	30
Singapore	..	168	..	168	71	108	55	42	..	..	..	14
Slovak Republic	..	253	..	77	..	222	..	19	..	9,593	..	10
Slovenia	..	440	..	44	..	403	..	5	..	7,482	..	9
South Africa	133	..	18	17	85	85	7	7	52,939	..	25	..
Spain	239	467	120	54	202	385	33	34	70,489	178,495	13	7
Sri Lanka	..	34	..	7	8	15	6	40	..	15,630	..	26
Sudan	..	10	..	28	..	9	..	..	..	..	..	..
Sweden	370	468	24	20	347	428	2	29	35,000	66,806	7	5
Switzerland	383	516	38	51	356	477	128	103	..	50,110	14	8
Syrian Arab Republic	..	27	..	10	..	9	..	..	..	..	..	24
Tajikistan	..	2	..	1	..	0	..	..	..	..	..	..
Tanzania	3	5	1	2	2	1	1	..	..	..	..	..
Thailand	13	103	13	97	9	27	19	171	16,824	99,900	29	..
Togo	..	27	1	15	..	19	..	14	..	..	..	..
Trinidad and Tobago	..	108	..	18	..	90	..	..	..	..	..	..
Tunisia	38	64	10	25	20	30	2	..	..	..	45	..
Turkey	23	81	4	10	..	64	..	15	14,785	49,869	26	23
Turkmenistan	..	..	..	..	..	..	..	..	..	..	..	..
Uganda	1	4	1	..	1	2	0	2	479	..	..	130
Ukraine	..	94	..	27	..	..	..	52	..	59,150	..	11
United Arab Emirates	..	14	..	52	..	11	..	..	..	..	..	..
United Kingdom	303	439	50	67	268	375	24	12	245,900	404,500	19	13
United States	..	767	25	33	536	483	30	14	2,418,619	..	..	16
Uruguay	..	169	..	63	..	154	..	110	..	..	..	5
Uzbekistan	..	..	..	..	..	..	..	..	..	..	..	..
Venezuela, RB	112	..	27	23	91	69	41	..	56,900	..	32	3
Vietnam	..	..	..	..	..	..	..	45	..	..	..	..
West Bank and Gaza	..	..	..	..	..	..	..	..	..	..	..	..
Yemen, Rep.	..	32	..	8	8	14	3	..	1,251	11,476	..	15
Yugoslavia, FR (Serb./Mont.)	118	188	23	42	..	173	..	4	..	..	59	11
Zambia	..	23	..	6	..	15	..	..	..	..	..	..
Zimbabwe	..	31	..	19	..	28	..	32	..	..	..	54
World	72 w	116 w	..	..	.. w	91 w	..	..	..	..	..	..
Low income	3	9	..	..	..	5	..	..	..	..	..	..
Excl. China & India	6	13	..	..	..	7	..	..	..	..	..	..
Middle income	..	104	..	..	..	79	..	..	..	..	..	..
Lower middle income	..	78	..	..	..	55	..	..	..	..	..	..
Upper middle income	77	173	..	..	62	140	..	..	..	..	..	..
Low & middle income	14	38	..	..	..	25	..	..	..	..	..	..
East Asia & Pacific	3	21	..	..	..	11	..	..	..	..	..	..
Europe & Central Asia	..	157	..	..	..	138	..	..	..	..	..	..
Latin America & Carib.	93	89	..	..	62	67	..	..	..	..	..	..
Middle East & N. Africa	..	65	..	..	..	45	..	..	..	..	..	..
South Asia	2	6	..	..	..	4	..	..	..	..	..	..
Sub-Saharan Africa	21	21	..	..	14	13	..	..	..	..	..	..
High income	321	585	..	..	355	429	..	..	..	..	..	..
Europe EMU	345	511	..	..	296	453	..	..	..	..	..	..

Traffic and congestion 3.12

About the data

Traffic congestion in urban areas constrains economic productivity, damages people's health, and degrades the quality of their lives. The particulate air pollution—the dust and soot in exhaust—emitted by motor vehicles is proving to be far more damaging to human health than was once believed. (See table 3.13 for information on suspended particulates and other air pollutants.)

In recent years ownership of passenger cars has increased, and the expansion of economic activity has led to the transport by road of more goods and services over greater distances (see table 5.9). These developments have increased demand for roads and vehicles, adding to urban congestion, air pollution, health hazards, traffic accidents, and injuries.

Congestion, the most visible cost of expanding vehicle ownership, is reflected in the indicators in the table. Other relevant indicators—such as average vehicle speed in major cities or the cost of traffic congestion, which exact a heavy toll on economic productivity—are not included here because data are incomplete or difficult to compare.

The data in the table are compiled by the International Road Federation (IRF) through questionnaires sent to national organizations. The IRF uses a hierarchy of sources to gather as much information as possible. The primary sources are national road associations. When such an association is lacking or does not respond, other agencies are contacted, including road directorates, ministries of transport or public works, and central statistical offices. As a result the compiled data are of uneven quality. The coverage of each indicator may differ across countries because of differences in definitions. Comparability also is limited when time-series data are reported. Moreover, the data do not capture the quality or age of vehicles or the condition or width of roads. Thus comparisons over time and between countries should be made with caution.

Figure 3.12

Growth in passenger cars accelerates

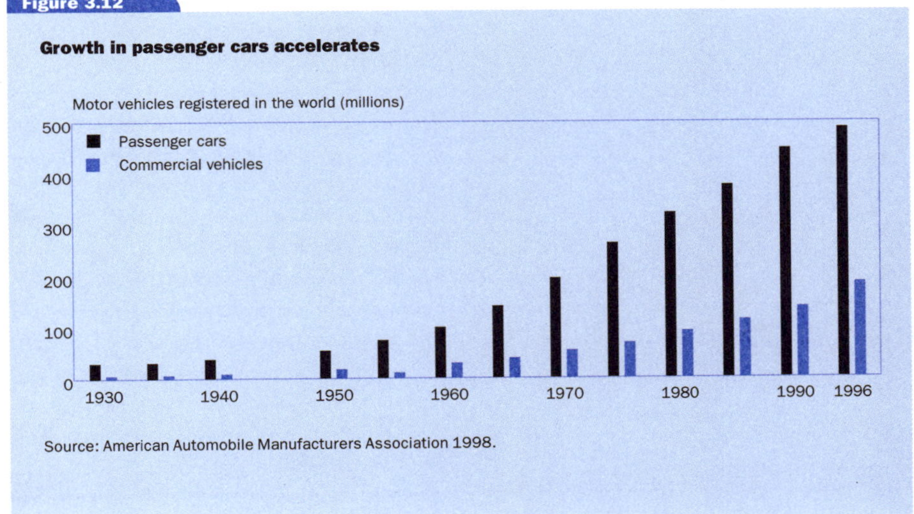

Source: American Automobile Manufacturers Association 1998.

Definitions

• **Motor vehicles** include cars, buses, and freight vehicles but not two-wheelers. Population figures refer to the midyear population in the year for which data are available. Roads refer to motorways, highways, main or national roads, or secondary or regional roads. A motorway is a road specially designed and built for motor traffic that separates the traffic flowing in opposite directions. • **Passenger cars** refer to road motor vehicles, other than two-wheelers, intended for the carriage of passengers and designed to seat no more than nine people (including the driver). • **Two-wheelers** refer to mopeds and motorcycles. • **Road traffic** is the number of vehicles multiplied by the average distances they travel. • **Traffic accidents** refer to accident-related injuries reported to the authorities and to deaths resulting from accidents that occur within 30 days of the accident.

Data sources

The data in the table are from the IRF's electronic files and its annual *World Road Statistics*.

Table 3.12a

The top 10 vehicle-owning countries, 1998

	Vehicles per 1,000 people
United States	767
Australia	605
Italy	591
New Zealand	579
Canada	560
Japan	560
France	530
Germany	522
Austria	521
Switzerland	516
World	116
Low-income countries	9
Middle-income countries	104
High-income countries	585

Source: Table 3.12.

3.13 Air pollution

	City	City population	Total suspended particulates	Sulfur dioxide	Nitrogen dioxide
		thousands 1995	micrograms per cubic meter 1995[a]	micrograms per cubic meter 1995[a]	micrograms per cubic meter 1995[a]
Argentina	Córdoba City	1,294	97	..	97
Australia	Sydney	3,590	54	28	..
	Melbourne	3,094	35	0	30
	Perth	1,220	45	5	19
Austria	Vienna	2,060	47	14	42
Belgium	Brussels	1,122	78	20	48
Brazil	São Paulo	16,533	86	43	83
	Rio de Janeiro	10,181	139	129	..
Bulgaria	Sofia	1,188	195	39	122
Canada	Toronto	4,319	36	17	43
	Montreal	3,320	34	10	42
	Vancouver	1,823	29	14	37
Chile	Santiago	4,891	..	29	81
China	Shanghai	13,584	246	53	73
	Beijing	11,299	377	90	122
	Tianjin	9,415	306	82	50
	Shenyang	5,116	374	99	73
	Chengdu	4,323	366	77	74
	Wuhan	4,247	211	40	43
	Guangzhu	4,056	295	57	136
	Zibo	3,779	453	198	43
	Liupanshui	3,615	408	102	..
	Chongquing	3,525	320	340	70
	Harbin	3,303	359	23	30
	Quingdao	3,138	..	190	64
	Dalian	3,132	185	61	100
	Jinan	3,019	472	132	45
	Changchun	2,523	381	21	64
	Taiyuan	2,502	568	211	55
	Pinxiang	2,040	276	75	..
	Zhengzhou	1,999	474	63	95
	Kunming	1,942	253	19	33
	Guiyang	1,792	330	424	53
	Lanzhou	1,747	732	102	104
	Anshan	1,648	305	115	88
	Nanchang	1,646	279	69	29
	Urumqi	1,643	515	60	70
Colombia	Bogotá	6,079	120	..	..
Croatia	Zagreb	981	71	31	..
Cuba	Havana	2,241	..	1	5
Czech Republic	Prague	1,225	59	32	23
Denmark	Copenhagen	1,326	61	7	54
Ecuador	Guayaquil	1,831	127	15	..
	Quito	1,298	175	31	..
Egypt, Arab Rep.	Cairo	9,690	..	69	..
Finland	Helsinki	1,059	40	4	35
France	Paris	9,523	14	14	57
Germany	Frankfurt	3,606	36	11	45
	Berlin	3,317	50	18	26
	Munich	2,238	45	8	53
Ghana	Accra	1,673	137	..	..
Greece	Athens	3,093	178	34	64
Hungary	Budapest	2,017	63	39	51
Iceland	Reykjavik	100	24	5	42
India	Mumbai	15,138	240	33	39
	Calcutta	11,923	375	49	34

About the data

In many towns and cities exposure to air pollution is the main environmental threat to human health. Winter smog—made up of soot, dust, and sulfur dioxide—has long been associated with temporary spikes in the number of deaths. Long-term exposure to high levels of soot and small particles in the air also contributes to a wide range of chronic respiratory diseases and exacerbates heart disease and other conditions. Particulate pollution, on its own or in combination with sulfur dioxide, leads to an enormous burden of ill health, causing at least 500,000 premature deaths and 4–5 million new cases of chronic bronchitis each year (World Bank 1992).

Emissions of sulfur dioxide and nitrogen oxides lead to the deposition of acid rain and other acidic compounds over long distances—often more than 1,000 kilometers from their source. Acid deposition changes the chemical balance of soils and can lead to the leaching of trace minerals and nutrients critical to trees and plants. The links between forest damage and acid deposition are complex. Direct exposure to high levels of sulfur dioxide or acid deposition can cause defoliation and dieback.

Where coal is the primary fuel for power plants, steel mills, industrial boilers, and domestic heating, the result is usually high levels of urban air pollution—especially particulates and sometimes sulfur dioxide—and, if the sulfur content of the coal is high, widespread acid deposition. Where coal is not an important primary fuel or is used by plants with effective dust control, the worst emissions of air pollutants stem from the combustion of petroleum products.

The data on air pollution are based on reports from urban monitoring sites. Annual means (measured in micrograms per cubic meter) are average concentrations observed at these sites. Coverage is not comprehensive because not all cities have monitoring systems. For example, data are reported for just 5 cities in Africa but for more than 87 cities in China. Pollutant concentrations are sensitive to local conditions, and even in the same city different monitoring sites may register different concentrations. Thus these data should be considered only a general indication of air quality in each city, and cross-country comparisons should be made with caution. World Health Organization (WHO) annual mean guidelines for air quality standards are 90 micrograms per cubic meter for total suspended particulates, and 50 for sulfur dioxide and nitrogen dioxide.

Air pollution 3.13

	City	City population	Total suspended particulates	Sulfur dioxide	Nitrogen dioxide
		thousands 1995	micrograms per cubic meter 1995[a]	micrograms per cubic meter 1995[a]	micrograms per cubic meter 1995[a]
	Delhi	9,948	415	24	41
	Chennai	6,002	130	15	17
	Hyderabad	5,477	152	12	17
	Bangalore	4,799	123	..	..
	Ahmedabad	3,711	299	30	21
	Pune	2,955	208		
	Kanpur	2,227	459	15	14
	Lucknow	2,078	463	26	25
	Nagpur	1,851	185	6	13
Indonesia	Jakarta	8,621	271	..	..
Iran, Islamic Rep.	Tehran	6,836	248	209	..
Ireland	Dublin	911	..	20	..
Italy	Milan	4,251	77	31	248
	Rome	2,931	73	..	..
	Torino	1,294	151	..	..
Japan	Tokyo	26,959	49	18	68
	Osaka	10,609	43	19	63
	Yokohama	3,178	..	100	13
Kenya	Nairobi	1,810	69	..	..
Korea, Rep.	Seoul	11,609	84	44	60
	Pusan	4,082	94	60	51
	Taegu	2,432	72	81	62
Malaysia	Kuala Lumpur	1,238	85	24	..
Mexico	Mexico City	16,562	279	74	130
Netherlands	Amsterdam	1,108	40	10	58
New Zealand	Auckland	945	26	3	20
Norway	Oslo	477	15	8	43
Philippines	Manila	9,286	200	33	..
Poland	Warsaw	2,219	..	16	32
	Lodz	1,063	..	21	43
Portugal	Lisbon	1,863	61	8	52
Romania	Bucharest	2,100	82	10	71
Russian Federation	Moscow	9,269	100	109	..
	Omsk	1,199	100	9	30
Singapore	Singapore	2,848	..	20	30
Slovak Republic	Bratislava	651	62	21	27
South Africa	Cape Town	2,671	..	21	72
	Johannesburg	1,849	..	19	31
	Durban	1,149	..	31	..
Spain	Madrid	4,072	42	11	25
	Barcelona	2,819	117	11	43
Sweden	Stockholm	1,545	9	5	29
Switzerland	Zurich	897	31	11	39
Thailand	Bangkok	6,547	223	11	23
Turkey	Istanbul	7,911	..	120	..
	Ankara	2,826	57	55	46
Ukraine	Kiev	2,809	100	14	51
United Kingdom	London	7,640	..	25	77
	Manchester	2,434	..	26	49
	Birmingham	2,271	..	9	45
United States	New York	16,332	..	26	79
	Los Angeles	12,410	..	9	74
	Chicago	6,844	..	14	57
Venezuela, RB	Caracas	3,007	53	33	57

a. Data are for the most recent year available in 1990–95. Most are for 1995.

Definitions

• **City population** is the number of residents of the city as defined by national authorities and reported to the United Nations. • **Total suspended particulates** refer to smoke, soot, dust, and liquid droplets from combustion that are in the air. Particulate levels indicate the quality of the air people are breathing and the state of a country's technology and pollution controls. • **Sulfur dioxide** (SO_2) is an air pollutant produced when fossil fuels containing sulfur are burned. It contributes to acid rain and can damage human health, particularly that of the young and the elderly. • **Nitrogen dioxide** (NO_2) is a poisonous, pungent gas formed when nitric oxide combines with hydrocarbons and sunlight, producing a photochemical reaction. These conditions occur in both natural and anthropogenic activities. NO_2 is emitted by bacteria, nitrogenous fertilizers, aerobic decomposition of organic matter in oceans and soils, combustion of fuels and biomass, and motor vehicles and industrial activities.

Data sources

The data in the table are from the WHO's Healthy Cities Air Management Information System and the World Resources Institute, which relies on various national sources as well as, among others, the United Nations Environment Programme and WHO's *Urban Air Pollution in Megacities of the World*, the Organisation for Economic Co-operation and Development's *OECD Environmental Data: Compendium 1997*, the U.S. Environmental Protection Agency's *National Air Quality and Emissions Trends Report 1995* and AIRS Executive International database, and the *China Environmental Yearbook 1997*.

3.14 Government commitment

	Environmental strategy or action plan	Country environmental profile	Biodiversity assessment, strategy, or action plan	Participation in treaties[a]				
				Climate change	Ozone layer	CFC control	Law of the Sea[b]	Biological diversity
Albania	1993	..	..	1995	2000	2000	..	1994
Algeria	..	..	..	1994	1993	1993	1996	1995
Angola	..	..	..	..	..	..	1994	1998
Argentina	1992	..	..	1994	1990	1990	1996	1995
Armenia	..	..	..	1994	2000	2000	..	1993
Australia	1992	..	1994	1994	1987	1989	1995	1993
Austria	..	..	..	1994	1987	1989	1995	1994
Azerbaijan	..	..	..	1995	1996	1996	..	..
Bangladesh	1991	1989	1990	1994	1990	1990	..	1994
Belarus	..	..	..	..	1986	1989	..	1993
Belgium	..	..	..	1996	1989	1989	..	1997
Benin	1993	..	..	1994	1993	1993	..	1994
Bolivia	1994	1986	1988	1995	1995	1995	1995	1995
Bosnia and Herzegovina	..	..	..	..	1992	1992	1994	..
Botswana	1990	1986	1991	1994	1992	1992	1994	1996
Brazil	..	..	1988	1994	1990	1990	1994	1994
Bulgaria	..	..	1994	1995	1991	1991	1996	1996
Burkina Faso	1993	1994	..	1994	1989	1989	..	1993
Burundi	1994	1981	1989	1997	1997	1997	..	1997
Cambodia	1997	..	..	1996	..	..	..	1995
Cameroon	..	1989	1989	1995	1989	1989	1994	1995
Canada	1990	..	1994	1994	1986	1988	..	1993
Central African Republic	..	..	..	1995	1993	1993	..	1995
Chad	1990	1982	..	1994	1989	1994	..	1994
Chile	..	1987	1993	1995	1990	1990	..	1994
China	1994	..	1994	1994	1989	1991	1996	1993
Hong Kong, China	..	..	..	..	..	..	..	..
Colombia	..	1990	1988	1995	1990	1994	..	1995
Congo, Dem. Rep.	..	1986	1990	1995	1995	1995	1994	1995
Congo, Rep.	..	..	1990	1997	1995	1995	..	1996
Costa Rica	1990	1987	1992	1994	1991	1991	1994	1994
Côte d'Ivoire	1994	..	1991	1995	1993	1993	1994	1995
Croatia	..	..	..	1996	1992	1992	1994	1997
Cuba	..	..	..	1994	1992	1992	1994	1994
Czech Republic	1991	..	..	1994	1993	1993	1996	1994
Denmark	1994	..	..	1994	1988	1989	..	1994
Dominican Republic	..	1984	1995	1999	1993	1993	..	1996
Ecuador	1993	1987	1995	1994	1990	1990	..	1993
Egypt, Arab Rep.	1992	1992	1988	1995	1988	1988	1994	1994
El Salvador	1994	1985	1988	1996	1993	1993	..	1994
Eritrea	1995	..	..	1995	..	..	..	1996
Estonia	..	..	..	1994	1997	1997	..	1994
Ethiopia	1994	..	1991	1994	1995	1995	..	1994
Finland	1995	..	..	1994	1986	1989	1996	1994
France	1990	..	..	1994	1988	1989	1996	1994
Gabon	..	..	1990	1998	1994	1994	..	1997
Gambia, The	1992	1981	1989	1994	1990	1990	1994	1994
Georgia	..	..	..	1994	1996	1996	1996	1994
Germany	..	..	..	1994	1988	1989	1994	1994
Ghana	1992	1985	1988	1995	1989	1989	1994	1994
Greece	..	..	..	1994	1989	1989	1995	1994
Guatemala	1994	1984	1988	1996	1987	1990	..	1995
Guinea	1994	1983	1988	1994	1992	1992	1994	1993
Guinea-Bissau	1993	..	1991	1996	..	..	1994	1996
Haiti	..	1985	..	1996	..	..	1996	1996
Honduras	1993	1989	..	1996	1994	1994	1994	1995

Table 3.14a

Status of national environmental action plans

Completed

Albania	Georgia	Mongolia
Azerbaijan	Ghana	Montserrat
Bangladesh	Grenada	Mozambique
Belarus	Guinea	Namibia
Benin	Guinea-Bissau	Nepal
Bhutan	Guyana	Nicaragua
Bolivia	Haiti	Niger
Botswana	Honduras	Nigeria
Bulgaria	Hungary	Pakistan
Burkina Faso	India	Papua New Guinea
Burundi	Indonesia	Philippines
Cambodia	Kenya	Poland
Cameroon	Lao PDR	Romania
Cape Verde	Latvia	Rwanda
China	Lebanon	São Tomé and Principe
Comoros	Lesotho	Senegal
Congo, Dem. Rep.	Lithuania	Seychelles
Congo, Rep.	Macedonia, FYR	Sierra Leone
Costa Rica	Madagascar	Sri Lanka
Côte d'Ivoire	Malawi	St. Kitts and Nevis
El Salvador	Maldives	Swaziland
Eritrea	Mali	Tanzania
Estonia	Mauritania	Togo
Ethiopia	Mauritius	Uganda
Gabon	Mexico	Ukraine
Gambia, The	Moldova	Zambia

Being prepared

Armenia	Equatorial Guinea	South Africa
Central African Rep.	Kazakhstan	Uzbekistan
Djibouti	Korea, Rep.	Vietnam
Dominican Rep.	Malaysia	Zimbabwe
Ecuador	Paraguay	

Note: Status is as of September 1999.
Source: World Resources Institute, International Institute for Environment and Development, and IUCN, *1996 World Directory of Country Environmental Studies;* World Bank data; World Bank 1998b.

Government commitment 3.14

	Environmental strategy or action plan	Country environmental profile	Biodiversity assessment, strategy, or action plan	Participation in treaties[a]				
				Climate change	Ozone layer	CFC control	Law of the Sea[b]	Biological diversity
Hungary	1995	..	..	1994	1988	1989	..	1994
India	1993	1989	1994	1994	1991	1992	1995	1994
Indonesia	1992	1994	1993	1994	1992	1992	1994	1994
Iran, Islamic Rep.	..	..	..	1996	1991	1991	..	1996
Iraq	..	..	..	..	..	..	1994	..
Ireland	..	..	..	1994	1988	1989	..	1996
Israel	..	..	..	1994	1992	1992	..	1995
Italy	..	..	..	1994	1988	1989	1995	1994
Jamaica	1994	1987	..	1995	1993	1993	1994	1995
Japan	..	..	..	1994	1988	1988	1996	1993
Jordan	1991	1979	..	1994	1989	1989	1995	1994
Kazakhstan	..	..	..	1995	1998	1998	..	1994
Kenya	1994	1989	1992	1994	1989	1989	1994	1994
Korea, Dem. Rep.	..	..	..	1995	1995	1995	..	1995
Korea, Rep.	..	..	..	1994	1992	1992	1996	1995
Kuwait	..	..	..	1995	1993	1993	1994	..
Kyrgyz Republic	..	..	..	..	..	..	..	1996
Lao PDR	1995	..	..	1995	1998	1998	..	1996
Latvia	..	..	..	1995	1995	1995	..	1996
Lebanon	..	..	..	1995	1993	1993	1995	1995
Lesotho	1989	1982	..	1995	1994	1994	..	1995
Libya	..	..	..	..	1990	1990	..	..
Lithuania	..	..	..	1995	1995	1995	..	1996
Macedonia, FYR	..	..	..	1998	1994	1994	1994	..
Madagascar	1988	..	1991	1996	1997	1997	..	1996
Malawi	1994	1982	..	1994	1991	1991	..	1994
Malaysia	1991	1979	1988	1994	1989	1989	1997	1994
Mali	..	1991	1989	1995	1995	1995	1994	1995
Mauritania	1988	1984	..	1994	1994	1994	1996	1996
Mauritius	1990	..	..	1994	1992	1992	1994	1993
Mexico	..	..	1988	1994	1987	1988	1994	1993
Moldova	..	..	..	1995	1997	1997	..	1996
Mongolia	1995	..	..	1994	1996	1996	..	1993
Morocco	..	1980	1988	1996	1996	1996	..	1995
Mozambique	1994	..	..	1995	1994	1994	..	1995
Myanmar	..	1982	1989	1995	1994	1994	1996	1995
Namibia	1992	..	..	1995	1993	1993	1994	1997
Nepal	1993	1983	..	1994	1994	1994	..	1994
Netherlands	1994	..	..	1994	1988	1989	1996	1994
New Zealand	1994	..	..	1994	1987	1988	1996	1993
Nicaragua	1994	1981	..	1996	1993	1993	..	1996
Niger	..	1985	1991	1995	1993	1993	..	1995
Nigeria	1990	..	1992	1994	1989	1989	1994	1994
Norway	..	..	1994	1994	1986	1988	1996	1993
Oman	..	1981	..	1995	1999	1999	1994	1995
Pakistan	1994	1994	1991	1994	1993	1993	..	1994
Panama	1990	1980	..	1995	1989	1989	1996	1995
Papua New Guinea	1992	1994	1993	1994	1993	1993	..	1993
Paraguay	..	1985	..	1994	1993	1993	1994	1994
Peru	..	1988	1988	1994	1989	1993	..	1993
Philippines	1989	1992	1989	1994	1991	1991	1994	1994
Poland	1993	..	1991	1994	1990	1990	..	1996
Portugal	1995	..	..	1994	1989	1989	..	1994
Puerto Rico	..	..	..	..	..	..	..	..
Romania	..	..	..	1994	1993	1993	1997	1994
Russian Federation	..	..	1994	1995	1986	1989	..	1995

Table 3.14b

States that have signed the Convention on Climate Change

Antigua and Barbuda[a]	Guatemala[a]	Paraguay[a]
	Honduras	Peru
Argentina	Indonesia	Philippines
Australia	Ireland	Poland
Austria	Israel	Portugal
Bahamas, The[a]	Italy	Romania
Belgium	Jamaica[a]	Russian Federation
Bolivia[a]	Japan	Samoa
Brazil	Kazakhstan	Seychelles
Bulgaria	Korea, Rep.	Slovak Republic
Canada	Latvia	Slovenia
Chile	Liechtenstein	Solomon Islands
China	Lithuania	Spain
Cook Islands	Luxembourg	St. Lucia
Costa Rica	Malaysia	St. Vincent and the Grenadines
Croatia	Maldives[a]	
Cuba	Mali	Sweden
Cyprus[a]	Malta	Switzerland
Czech Republic	Marshall Islands	Thailand
Denmark	Mexico	Trinidad and Tobago[a]
Ecuador	Micronesia[a]	Turkmenistan[a]
Egypt, Arab Rep.	Monaco	Tuvalu[a]
El Salvador[a]	Netherlands	Ukraine
Estonia	New Zealand	United Kingdom
Fiji[a]	Nicaragua[a]	United States
Finland	Niger	Uruguay
France	Niue[a]	Uzbekistan[a]
Georgia[a]	Norway	Vietnam
Germany	Panama[a]	Zambia
Greece	Papua New Guinea	

Note: Status is as of November 1999.

a. Ratification or accession signed.

Source: Secretariat of the United Nations Framework Convention on Climate Change.

3.14 Government commitment

	Environmental strategy or action plan	Country environmental profile	Biodiversity assessment, strategy, or action plan	Participation in treaties[a]				
				Climate change	Ozone layer	CFC control	Law of the Sea[b]	Biological diversity
Rwanda	1991	1987	..	1998	..	..	..	1996
Saudi Arabia	..	..	..	1995	1993	1993	..	..
Senegal	1984	1990	1991	1995	1993	1993	1994	1995
Sierra Leone	1994	..	..	1995	..	..	1995	1995
Singapore	1993	1988	1995	1997	1989	1989	1994	1996
Slovak Republic	..	..	..	1994	1993	1993	1996	1994
Slovenia	..	..	..	1996	1992	1992	1994	1996
South Africa	1993	..	..	1997	1990	1990	1994	1996
Spain	..	..	..	1994	1988	1989	..	1994
Sri Lanka	1994	1983	1991	1994	1990	1990	1994	1994
Sudan	..	1989	..	1994	1993	1993	1994	1996
Sweden	..	..	..	1994	1987	1988	1996	1994
Switzerland	..	..	..	1994	1988	1989	..	1995
Syrian Arab Republic	..	1981	..	1996	1990	1990	..	1996
Tajikistan	..	..	..	1998	1996	1998	..	1997
Tanzania	1994	1989	1988	1996	1993	1993	1994	1996
Thailand	..	1992	..	1995	1989	1989	..	..
Togo	1991	..	..	1995	1991	1991	1994	1996
Trinidad and Tobago	..	..	..	1994	1989	1989	1994	1996
Tunisia	1994	1980	1988	1994	1989	1989	1994	1993
Turkey	..	1982	..	..	1991	1991	..	1997
Turkmenistan	..	..	..	1995	1994	1994	..	1996
Uganda	1994	1982	1988	1994	1988	1988	1994	1993
Ukraine	..	..	..	1997	1986	1988	..	1995
United Arab Emirates	..	..	..	1996	1990	1990	..	..
United Kingdom	1995	..	1994	1994	1987	1989	..	1994
United States	1995	..	1995	1994	1986	1988	..	1993
Uruguay	..	..	..	1994	1989	1991	1994	1994
Uzbekistan	..	..	..	1994	1993	1993	..	1995
Venezuela, RB	..	..	..	1995	1988	1989	..	1994
Vietnam	..	..	1993	1995	1994	1994	1994	1995
West Bank and Gaza	..	..	..	..	..	..	..	..
Yemen, Rep.	..	1990	1992	1996	1996	1996	1994	1996
Yugoslavia, FR (Serb./Mont.)	..	..	..	1997	1990	1991	..	
Zambia	1994	1988	..	1994	1990	1990	1994	1993
Zimbabwe	1987	1982	..	1994	1993	1993	1994	1995

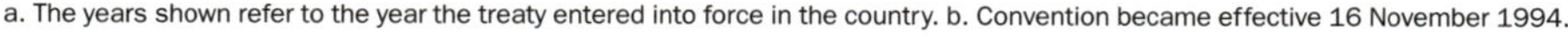

a. The years shown refer to the year the treaty entered into force in the country. b. Convention became effective 16 November 1994.

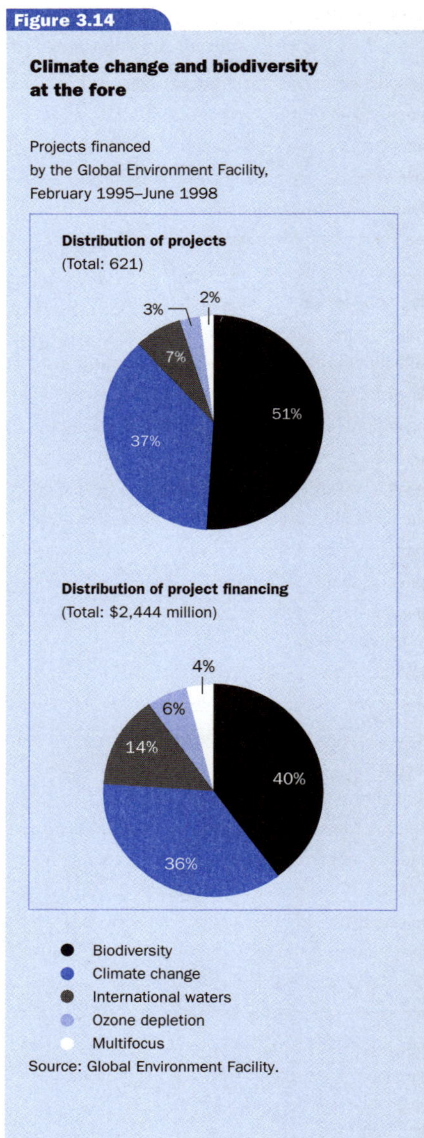

Source: Global Environment Facility.

Government commitment 3.14

About the data

National environmental strategies and participation in international treaties on environmental issues provide some evidence of government commitment to sound environmental management. But the signing of these treaties does not always imply ratification. Nor does it guarantee that governments will comply with treaty obligations.

In many countries efforts to halt environmental degradation have failed, primarily because governments have neglected to make this issue a priority, a reflection of competing claims on scarce resources. To address this problem, many countries are preparing national environmental strategies—some focusing narrowly on environmental issues, others integrating environmental, economic, and social concerns. Among such initiatives are conservation strategies and environmental action plans. Some countries have also prepared country environmental profiles and biological diversity strategies and profiles.

National conservation strategies—promoted by the World Conservation Union (IUCN)—provide a comprehensive, cross-sectoral analysis of conservation and resource management issues to help integrate environmental concerns with the development process. Such strategies discuss current and future needs, institutional capabilities, prevailing technical conditions, and the status of natural resources in a country.

National environmental action plans (NEAPs), supported by the World Bank and other development agencies, describe a country's main environmental concerns, identify the principal causes of environmental problems, and formulate policies and actions to deal with them (table 3.14a). The NEAP is a continuing process in which governments develop comprehensive environmental policies, recommend specific actions, and outline the investment strategies, legislation, and institutional arrangements required to implement them.

Country environmental profiles identify how national economic and other activities can stay within the constraints imposed by the need to conserve natural resources. Some profiles consider issues of equity, justice, and fairness. Biodiversity profiles—prepared by the World Conservation Monitoring Centre and the IUCN—provide basic background on species diversity, protected areas, major ecosystems and habitat types, and legislative and administrative support. In an effort to establish a scientific baseline for measuring progress in biodiversity conservation, the United Nations Environment Programme (UNEP) coordinates global biodiversity assessments.

To address global issues, many governments have also signed international treaties and agreements launched in the wake of the 1972 United Nations Conference on Human Environment in Stockholm and the 1992 United Nations Conference on Environment and Development (the Earth Summit) in Rio de Janeiro:

- The Framework Convention on Climate Change aims to stabilize atmospheric concentrations of greenhouse gases at levels that will prevent human activities from interfering dangerously with the global climate.
- The Vienna Convention for the Protection of the Ozone Layer aims to protect human health and the environment by promoting research on the effects of changes in the ozone layer and on alternative substances (such as substitutes for chlorofluorocarbons) and technologies, monitoring the ozone layer, and taking measures to control the activities that produce adverse effects.
- The Montreal Protocol for CFC Control requires that countries help protect the earth from excessive ultraviolet radiation by cutting chlorofluorocarbon consumption by 20 percent over their 1986 level by 1994 and by 50 percent over their 1986 level by 1999, with allowances for increases in consumption by developing countries.
- The United Nations Convention on the Law of the Sea, which became effective in November 1994, establishes a comprehensive legal regime for seas and oceans, establishes rules for environmental standards and enforcement provisions, and develops international rules and national legislation to prevent and control marine pollution.
- The Convention on Biological Diversity promotes conservation of biodiversity among nations through scientific and technological cooperation, access to financial and genetic resources, and transfer of ecologically sound technologies.

To help developing countries comply with their obligations under these agreements, the Global Environment Facility (GEF) was created to focus on global improvement in biodiversity, climate change, international waters, and ozone layer depletion. The UNEP, United Nations Development Programme (UNDP), and World Bank manage the GEF according to the policies of its governing body of country representatives. The World Bank is responsible for the GEF Trust Fund and is chair of the GEF.

Definitions

• **Environmental strategies and action plans** provide a comprehensive, cross-sectoral analysis of conservation and resource management issues to help integrate environmental concerns with the development process. They include national conservation strategies, national environmental action plans, national environmental management strategies, and national sustainable development strategies. The years shown refer to the year in which a strategy or action plan was adopted. • **Country environmental profiles** identify how national economic and other activities can stay within the constraints imposed by the need to conserve natural resources. The years shown refer to the year in which a profile was completed. • **Biodiversity assessments, strategies, and action plans** include biodiversity profiles (see *About the data*). • **Participation in treaties** covers five international treaties (see *About the data*). • **Climate change** refers to the Framework Convention on Climate Change (signed in New York in 1992). • **Ozone layer** refers to the Vienna Convention for the Protection of the Ozone Layer (signed in 1985). • **CFC control** refers to the Montreal Protocol for CFC Control (formally, the Protocol on Substances That Deplete the Ozone Layer, signed in 1987). • **Law of the Sea** refers to the United Nations Convention on the Law of the Sea (signed in Montego Bay, Jamaica, in 1982). • **Biological diversity** refers to the Convention on Biological Diversity (signed at the Earth Summit in Rio de Janeiro in 1992). The years shown refer to the year in which a treaty entered into force in a country.

Data sources

The data are from the Secretariat of the United Nations Framework Convention on Climate Change; the Ozone Secretariat of UNEP; the World Resources Institute, UNEP, and UNDP's *World Resources 1994–95;* the World Resources Institute, International Institute for Environment and Development, and IUCN's *1996 World Directory of Country Environmental Studies;* and the World Bank's *1998 Catalog: Operational Documents as of July 31, 1998.*

3.15 Toward a measure of genuine savings

	Gross domestic savings[a]	Consumption of fixed capital	Net domestic savings	Education expenditure	Energy depletion	Mineral depletion	Net forest depletion	Carbon dioxide damage	Genuine domestic savings
	% of GDP 1998	% of GDP 1998	% of GDP 1998	% of GDP 1998	% of GDP 1998	% of GDP 1998	% of GDP 1998	% of GDP 1998	% of GDP 1998
Albania	–6.7	8.5	–15.1	2.9	0.7	0.0	0.0	0.4	–13.4
Algeria	27.2	9.1	18.1	4.3	15.6	0.1	0.0	1.1	5.6
Angola	30.4	8.0	22.4	2.4	13.8	0.0	0.0	0.5	10.4
Argentina	17.4	11.1	6.3	3.3	4.5	0.1	0.0	0.3	4.8
Armenia	–14.2	8.3	–22.5	2.7	0.0	0.0	0.0	1.2	–21.0
Australia	23.4	14.1	9.3	5.3	0.4	1.4	0.0	0.5	12.2
Austria	28.5	12.4	16.1	5.2	0.0	0.0	0.0	0.2	21.1
Azerbaijan	4.8	14.1	–9.2	3.0	17.8	0.0	0.0	5.5	–29.5
Bangladesh	17.1	6.2	10.9	1.8	0.2	0.0	2.1	0.3	10.0
Belarus	20.1	9.5	10.6	5.5	0.0	0.0	0.0	1.8	14.4
Belgium	..	10.0	..	3.1	0.0	0.0	0.0	0.2	..
Benin	8.3	7.5	0.8	2.7	0.0	0.0	0.6	0.2	2.7
Bolivia	10.8	8.7	2.1	5.4	1.4	0.8	0.0	0.7	4.7
Bosnia and Herzegovina	..	..	..	..	0.0	0.0	0.0	..	..
Botswana	21.8	14.3	7.5	7.4	0.0	0.2	0.0	0.3	14.5
Brazil	18.6	10.4	8.2	5.0	0.5	0.6	0.0	0.2	11.9
Bulgaria	13.7	9.1	4.6	3.0	0.2	0.5	0.0	2.4	4.6
Burkina Faso	12.4	6.9	5.5	1.4	0.0	0.0	4.3	0.2	2.3
Burundi	–2.5	6.3	–8.8	3.0	0.0	0.0	8.9	0.1	–14.8
Cambodia	5.5	7.0	–1.5	1.8	0.0	0.0	0.0	0.1	0.2
Cameroon	19.9	8.0	11.9	2.8	3.9	0.0	0.0	0.4	10.4
Canada	22.2	12.1	10.1	6.3	2.6	0.2	0.0	0.4	13.2
Central African Republic	4.4	7.2	–2.8	1.6	0.0	0.0	0.0	0.1	–1.3
Chad	2.6	6.9	–4.3	2.0	0.0	0.0	0.0	0.0	–2.3
Chile	25.2	10.4	14.8	2.8	0.0	3.6	0.0	0.4	13.6
China	42.6	8.1	34.5	2.0	1.5	0.3	0.4	2.3	32.0
Hong Kong, China	30.5	12.4	18.1	2.8	0.0	0.0	0.0	0.1	20.8
Colombia	13.9	9.7	4.3	3.1	2.8	0.1	0.0	0.4	4.1
Congo, Dem. Rep.	..	6.3	..	0.8	0.0	0.2	0.0	0.2	..
Congo, Rep.	26.4	8.2	18.2	5.5	17.1	0.0	0.0	1.2	5.4
Costa Rica	26.8	9.9	17.0	4.9	0.0	0.0	1.0	0.3	20.6
Côte d'Ivoire	24.5	8.3	16.3	4.3	0.0	0.0	0.5	0.7	19.4
Croatia	14.2	10.3	3.9	..	0.3	0.0	0.0	0.5	..
Cuba	..	..	..	..	0.0	0.0	0.0	..	..
Czech Republic	28.5	10.6	17.9	4.7	0.1	0.0	0.0	1.3	21.2
Denmark	24.4	14.2	10.2	7.6	0.0	0.0	0.0	0.2	17.6
Dominican Republic	16.9	5.9	11.0	1.7	0.0	0.2	0.0	0.5	11.9
Ecuador	19.3	9.1	10.2	3.2	6.8	0.0	0.0	0.7	5.9
Egypt, Arab Rep.	15.8	8.9	6.8	4.6	0.6	0.1	0.1	0.7	10.0
El Salvador	4.0	9.3	–5.3	2.2	0.0	0.0	1.1	0.2	–4.5
Eritrea	–29.0	6.5	–35.5	1.6	0.0	0.0	0.0	..	–33.9
Estonia	19.7	10.1	9.6	6.2	1.0	0.0	0.0	2.1	12.8
Ethiopia	6.3	5.9	0.4	2.7	0.0	0.0	11.4	0.3	–8.7
Finland	28.7	15.9	12.8	7.1	0.0	0.0	0.0	0.3	19.6
France	21.8	12.3	9.4	5.5	0.0	0.0	0.0	0.1	14.8
Gabon	43.2	10.4	32.8	1.9	8.9	0.0	0.0	0.4	25.4
Gambia, The	7.4	7.3	0.1	3.4	0.0	0.0	9.3	0.3	–6.1
Georgia	–6.1	7.9	–14.0	4.1	0.0	0.0	0.0	0.6	–10.5
Germany	24.2	12.4	11.8	4.3	0.0	0.0	0.0	0.2	15.8
Ghana	13.2	7.5	5.7	3.0	0.0	0.9	6.1	0.3	1.4
Greece	..	6.5	..	2.3	0.1	0.0	0.0	0.4	..
Guatemala	7.7	9.2	–1.6	1.5	0.4	0.0	1.6	0.2	–2.3
Guinea	19.4	7.8	11.6	1.8	0.0	4.5	0.0	0.2	8.7
Guinea-Bissau	–8.9	6.5	–15.5	2.5	0.0	0.0	0.0	0.5	–13.5
Haiti	–6.9	1.9	–8.8	1.6	0.0	0.0	5.2	0.1	–12.6
Honduras	23.4	6.0	17.4	3.3	0.0	0.2	0.0	0.4	20.1

Toward a measure of genuine savings 3.15

	Gross domestic savings[a] % of GDP 1998	Consumption of fixed capital % of GDP 1998	Net domestic savings % of GDP 1998	Education expenditure % of GDP 1998	Energy depletion % of GDP 1998	Mineral depletion % of GDP 1998	Net forest depletion % of GDP 1998	Carbon dioxide damage % of GDP 1998	Genuine domestic savings % of GDP 1998
Hungary	28.4	10.3	18.1	4.1	0.2	0.0	0.0	0.7	21.3
India	20.9	9.0	11.8	3.3	1.5	0.4	1.6	1.4	10.3
Indonesia	24.1	7.7	16.4	0.6	7.0	1.6	1.2	1.3	5.9
Iran, Islamic Rep.	14.5	8.8	5.7	3.3	15.4	0.2	0.0	1.4	–7.9
Iraq	..	..	..	..	0.0	0.0	0.0	..	..
Ireland	..	9.0	..	4.6	0.0	0.0	0.0	0.3	..
Israel	9.2	14.8	–5.7	6.1	0.0	0.0	0.0	0.3	0.1
Italy	21.7	12.1	9.6	4.6	0.0	0.0	0.0	0.2	13.9
Jamaica	18.4	9.1	9.2	6.7	0.0	2.3	0.0	0.8	12.8
Japan	31.5	16.0	15.6	4.7	0.0	0.0	0.0	0.2	20.1
Jordan	3.8	9.2	–5.3	4.4	0.0	0.9	0.0	..	–1.8
Kazakhstan	12.8	8.9	3.9	4.5	11.2	0.0	0.0	5.0	–7.8
Kenya	6.7	7.5	–0.7	6.0	0.0	0.0	7.6	0.3	–2.7
Korea, Dem. Rep.	..	..	..	..	0.0	0.0	0.0	..	..
Korea, Rep.	33.8	10.9	22.9	3.6	0.0	0.0	0.0	0.7	25.9
Kuwait	12.7	11.6	1.0	5.4	37.6	0.0	0.0	..	–31.2
Kyrgyz Republic	2.2	7.4	–5.2	5.3	0.1	0.0	0.0	2.7	–2.7
Lao PDR	23.7	7.0	16.8	2.1	0.0	0.1	0.0	0.2	18.5
Latvia	9.8	9.7	0.1	6.3	0.0	0.0	0.0	1.0	5.4
Lebanon	–12.8	10.2	–23.1	1.6	0.0	0.0	0.1	0.5	–22.0
Lesotho	–42.7	7.5	–50.1	7.7	0.0	0.0	2.1	..	–44.5
Libya	..	..	..	..	0.0	0.0	0.0	..	..
Lithuania	12.3	9.8	2.4	5.2	0.0	0.0	0.0	0.8	6.8
Macedonia, FYR	7.1	8.8	–1.7	..	0.0	0.0	0.0	2.7	..
Madagascar	5.3	7.0	–1.6	1.7	0.0	0.0	0.0	0.2	–0.2
Malawi	0.4	6.4	–6.1	4.0	0.0	0.0	5.9	0.3	–8.2
Malaysia	48.5	10.0	38.5	4.0	3.0	0.1	1.7	0.9	36.8
Mali	10.1	7.0	3.1	2.2	0.0	0.0	0.0	0.1	5.2
Mauritania	8.0	7.5	0.5	3.5	0.0	20.7	0.0	1.9	–18.5
Mauritius	24.0	10.1	13.9	3.1	0.0	0.0	0.0	0.2	16.8
Mexico	22.4	10.2	12.2	4.3	3.5	0.1	0.0	0.5	12.4
Moldova	–2.8	7.4	–10.2	8.7	0.0	0.0	0.0	3.6	–5.2
Mongolia	20.0	7.5	12.5	..	0.0	6.3	0.0	5.0	..
Morocco	14.7	8.9	5.8	4.9	0.0	0.4	0.0	0.5	9.7
Mozambique	1.7	6.9	–5.2	3.5	0.0	0.0	2.4	0.2	–4.3
Myanmar	..	2.5	..	..	0.0	0.0	0.0	..	..
Namibia	18.8	13.9	4.9	8.6	0.0	0.3	0.0	..	13.2
Nepal	10.5	4.4	6.1	2.1	0.0	0.0	9.8	0.2	–1.8
Netherlands	27.8	12.3	15.4	5.1	0.0	0.0	0.0	0.2	20.3
New Zealand	19.5	9.3	10.2	6.4	0.4	0.1	0.0	0.3	15.9
Nicaragua	1.1	7.5	–6.5	2.2	0.0	0.1	0.0	0.8	–5.2
Niger	3.3	6.7	–3.4	3.0	0.0	0.0	4.2	0.3	–4.9
Nigeria	11.8	7.3	4.5	0.7	16.2	0.0	1.8	1.3	–14.2
Norway	33.2	16.1	17.1	6.8	0.6	0.0	0.0	0.3	23.1
Oman	..	10.6	..	3.4	20.7	0.0	0.0	..	..
Pakistan	12.7	7.4	5.3	2.3	1.5	0.0	1.3	0.8	4.0
Panama	23.5	6.8	16.7	4.3	0.0	0.0	0.0	0.4	20.5
Papua New Guinea	28.3	8.8	19.5	..	4.3	8.6	0.0	0.4	..
Paraguay	16.6	9.2	7.4	3.5	0.0	0.0	0.0	0.2	10.6
Peru	19.5	9.7	9.9	2.5	0.1	0.9	0.0	0.3	11.1
Philippines	16.3	8.4	7.9	2.0	0.0	0.1	1.6	0.5	7.6
Poland	21.3	10.2	11.0	5.5	0.3	0.2	0.0	1.4	14.6
Portugal	14.5	4.3	10.2	5.0	0.0	0.0	0.0	0.3	15.0
Puerto Rico	..	6.9	..	..	0.0	0.0	0.0	..	..
Romania	9.2	9.2	0.0	3.3	1.3	0.0	0.0	1.5	0.4
Russian Federation	21.2	9.3	11.9	3.9	16.0	0.0	0.0	3.0	–3.3

3.15 Toward a measure of genuine savings

	Gross domestic savings[a] % of GDP 1998	Consumption of fixed capital % of GDP 1998	Net domestic savings % of GDP 1998	Education expenditure % of GDP 1998	Energy depletion % of GDP 1998	Mineral depletion % of GDP 1998	Net forest depletion % of GDP 1998	Carbon dioxide damage % of GDP 1998	Genuine domestic savings % of GDP 1998
Rwanda	–1.8	7.0	–8.8	3.3	0.0	0.0	4.7	0.2	–10.4
Saudi Arabia	26.2	10.7	15.5	5.5	30.8	0.0	0.0	1.2	–11.0
Senegal	14.9	7.8	7.1	3.4	0.0	0.2	0.0	0.4	9.9
Sierra Leone	–1.3	6.7	–8.0	1.0	0.0	0.1	3.1	0.3	–10.6
Singapore	51.3	12.5	38.9	2.4	0.0	0.0	0.0	0.5	40.7
Slovak Republic	28.2	10.2	18.1	4.3	0.0	0.0	0.0	1.2	21.1
Slovenia	23.7	16.6	7.2	5.2	0.0	0.0	0.0	0.4	12.0
South Africa	16.9	12.0	4.8	6.8	1.0	1.0	0.4	1.3	7.9
Spain	23.5	11.7	11.8	4.5	0.0	0.0	0.0	0.2	16.0
Sri Lanka	18.9	5.0	13.9	2.6	0.0	0.0	1.5	0.2	14.8
Sudan	..	7.4	..	..	0.0	0.0	0.0	0.2	..
Sweden	24.5	12.4	12.0	7.2	0.0	0.1	0.0	0.1	19.0
Switzerland	26.3	13.0	13.3	5.0	0.0	0.0	0.0	0.1	18.2
Syrian Arab Republic	..	3.5	..	2.5	14.2	0.1	0.0	1.5	..
Tajikistan	..	7.3	..	2.0	0.0	0.0	0.0	1.4	..
Tanzania	8.4	6.9	1.5	3.4	0.0	0.0	0.2	0.2	4.5
Thailand	41.8	9.3	32.5	3.2	0.2	0.0	0.9	0.8	33.7
Togo	7.5	7.3	0.2	4.2	0.0	1.0	4.7	0.3	–1.6
Trinidad and Tobago	7.1	10.4	–3.4	3.3	3.7	0.0	0.0	1.9	–5.7
Tunisia	24.3	9.5	14.9	5.5	0.9	0.5	0.4	0.5	18.0
Turkey	21.1	6.5	14.7	3.2	0.2	0.1	0.0	0.6	17.1
Turkmenistan	..	8.4	..	..	32.2	0.0	0.0	7.1	..
Uganda	5.7	7.3	–1.6	2.2	0.0	0.0	2.3	0.1	–1.8
Ukraine	17.7	8.4	9.3	6.0	4.2	0.0	0.0	4.5	6.6
United Arab Emirates	..	12.1	..	1.8	16.6	0.0	0.0	0.9	..
United Kingdom	16.3	12.3	4.0	4.7	0.2	0.0	0.0	0.2	8.2
United States	17.4	12.6	4.8	4.6	0.6	0.0	0.0	0.4	8.4
Uruguay	15.3	10.7	4.5	3.0	0.0	0.0	0.3	0.2	7.1
Uzbekistan	19.0	8.4	10.6	7.7	12.6	0.0	0.0	2.9	2.9
Venezuela, RB	19.6	6.8	12.7	4.9	11.9	0.3	0.0	1.0	4.4
Vietnam	21.3	7.3	13.9	2.2	2.2	0.1	2.7	0.8	10.3
West Bank and Gaza	–14.9	8.9	–23.8	..	0.0	0.0	0.0	..	..
Yemen, Rep.	2.4	7.0	–4.7	5.2	26.8	0.0	0.0	..	–26.3
Yugoslavia, FR (Serb./Mont.)	..	..	..	..	0.0	0.0	0.0	..	..
Zambia	5.3	7.3	–2.0	1.9	0.0	3.0	0.0	0.4	–3.6
Zimbabwe	15.4	7.9	7.5	7.5	0.0	0.6	0.3	1.8	12.3
World	22.7 w	12.2 w	10.4 w	4.5 w	1.1 w	0.1 w	0.1 w	0.5 w	13.3 w
Low income	31.1	8.1	23.0	2.3	2.2	0.4	1.1	1.8	20.0
Excl. China & India	..	..	..	..	..	..	..	..	..
Middle income	21.5	9.8	11.7	4.2	4.2	0.3	0.1	0.9	10.6
Lower middle income	19.1	9.3	9.8	4.1	6.0	0.2	0.2	1.5	5.9
Upper middle income	22.7	10.1	12.6	4.3	3.2	0.3	0.0	0.6	12.9
Low & middle income	24.5	9.3	15.1	3.6	3.6	0.3	0.4	1.1	13.5
East Asia & Pacific	38.6	8.8	29.8	2.4	1.4	0.3	0.6	1.7	28.3
Europe & Central Asia	20.3	9.0	11.3	4.3	5.5	0.1	..	1.9	8.3
Latin America & Carib.	19.0	10.1	8.9	4.2	2.4	0.5	0.0	0.4	9.8
Middle East & N. Africa	18.2	9.5	8.8	4.4	14.6	0.1	0.0	1.0	–2.2
South Asia	19.5	8.5	11.0	3.1	1.3	0.3	1.7	1.2	9.6
Sub-Saharan Africa	14.9	9.5	5.3	4.5	3.1	0.6	1.3	0.9	3.7
High income	22.3	13.0	9.1	4.8	0.4	0.0	0.0	0.3	13.3
Europe EMU	23.4	12.1	11.2	4.7	0.0	0.0	..	0.2	15.8

a. The cutoff date for these data is 14 January 2000; later revisions are not captured in this table.

Toward a measure of genuine savings 3.15

About the data

Genuine domestic savings are derived from standard national accounting measures of gross domestic savings by making four types of adjustments. First, estimates of capital consumption of produced assets are deducted to obtain net domestic savings. Then current expenditures on education are added to net domestic savings as an approximate value of investments in human capital (in standard national accounting these expenditures are treated as consumption). Next, estimates of the depletion of a variety of natural resources are deducted to reflect the decline in asset values associated with their extraction and harvest. Finally, a deduction is made for damage from carbon dioxide emissions.

There are important gaps in the accounting of natural resource depletion and costs of pollution. On the resource side, key estimates that are missing include the value of fossil water extracted from aquifers, depletion and degradation of soils, and net depletion of fish stocks. The most important pollutants affecting human health and economic assets are also excluded, because no internationally comparable data are widely available on damage from particulate emissions, ground-level ozone, or acid rain.

Estimates of resource depletion are based on the calculation of unit resource rents. An economic rent represents an excess return to a given factor of production—that is, in this case, the returns from resource depletion are higher than the normal rate of return on capital. Because natural resources are fixed in extent (at least for a given state of technology), resource rents will persist over time; in contrast, for produced goods and services competitive forces will expand supply until economic profits are driven to zero. For each type of resource and each country, unit resource rents are derived by taking the difference between world prices and the average unit extraction or harvest costs (including a "normal" return on capital). Unit rents are then multiplied by the physical quantity extracted or harvested in order to arrive at a depletion figure. This figure is one of a range of depletion estimates that are possible, depending on the assumptions made about future quantities, prices, and costs, and there is reason to believe that it is at the high end of the range. Some of the largest depletion estimates in the table should therefore be viewed with caution.

A positive depletion figure for forest resources implies that the harvest rate exceeds the rate of natural growth, and a negative figure that growth exceeds harvest. In principle, there should be an addition to savings in countries where growth exceeds harvest, but there is good reason to believe that most of this net growth is in forested areas that cannot be exploited economically at present. The average world prices used to estimate unit rents on timber are probably too high for countries with low-grade timber resources, so caution is required in viewing some of the net forest depletion estimates, especially for Sub-Saharan Africa. In addition, because the depletion estimates reflect only timber values, they ignore all the external benefits associated with standing forests.

Pollution damage is calculated as the marginal social cost associated with a unit of pollution multiplied by the increase in the stock of pollutant in the receiving medium. For carbon dioxide the unit damage figure represents the present value of damage to economic assets and decline in human welfare over the time the unit of pollution remains in the atmosphere.

Definitions

• **Gross domestic savings** are calculated as the difference between GDP and public and private consumption. • **Consumption of fixed capital** represents the replacement value of capital used up in the process of production. • **Net domestic savings** are equal to gross domestic savings less the value of consumption of fixed capital. • **Education expenditure** refers to the current operating expenditures in education, including wages and salaries and excluding capital investments in buildings and equipment. • **Energy depletion** is equal to the product of unit resource rents and the physical quantities of energy extracted. It covers crude oil, natural gas, and coal. • **Mineral depletion** is equal to the product of unit resource rents and the physical quantities of minerals extracted. It refers to bauxite, copper, iron, lead, nickel, phosphate, tin, gold, and silver. • **Net forest depletion** is calculated as the product of unit resource rents and the excess of roundwood harvest over natural growth. • **Carbon dioxide damage** is estimated to be $20 per ton of carbon (the unit damage) times the number of tons of carbon emitted. • **Genuine domestic savings** are equal to net domestic savings, plus education expenditure and minus energy depletion, mineral depletion, net forest depletion, and carbon dioxide damage.

Data sources

Gross domestic savings are derived from the World Bank's national accounts data files described in the Economy section. Consumption of fixed capital is from the United Nations Statistics Division's *National Accounts Statistics: Main Aggregates and Detailed Tables, 1997,* extrapolated to 1998. The education expenditure data are from the United Nations Statistics Division's *Statistical Yearbook,* extrapolated to 1998. The wide range of data sources and estimation methods used to arrive at resource depletion estimates are described in a World Bank working paper, "Estimating National Wealth" (Kunte and others 1998). The unit damage figure for carbon dioxide emissions is from Fankhauser (1995).

ECONOMY

Economic growth alone will not eliminate poverty in the world. But if it is equitable growth that reaches the poor, it can create the opportunities and resources to reduce poverty. Similarly, development assistance, no matter how well intended, cannot guarantee that economies will grow. To be effective, it must be used wisely.

Over the past three decades some countries have made great progress. Botswana, China, and the Republic of Korea, along with other nations of Southeast Asia, have maintained growth in per capita incomes of more than 8 percent a year, with big reductions in poverty. Some of them recently sustained setbacks because of the financial crisis that began in 1997. But all show signs of rebounding under good economic management.

At the other end of the scale are a large group of countries that have seen their prospects worsen. Slow growth and rising populations have lowered their per capita incomes. And the financing offered to them in the hopes of stimulating new growth has become a burden of unmanageable debt. Which are the heavily indebted poor countries? How did they get that way? And what can be done to help them?

Profiling the heavily indebted poor countries

The poor countries classified today as heavily indebted (HIPCs) were richer than other low-income countries in 1980. Their per capita incomes then fell from $400 to $300, a loss of 25 percent. Meanwhile, those of the others doubled—from $290 to $580 (figure 4a).

HIPCs have always had worse social indicators than other developing countries, and this may have slowed their GDP growth. Because their rates of illiteracy, infant mortality, and fertility have been going down, the social gap between them and other low-income countries has widened only slightly since 1980 (figures 4b, 4c, and 4d). But with the income gap widening so dramatically, it is clear that their problems go well beyond inadequate social investments—to poor policies and poor institutions.

Infrastructure is poorer in HIPCs—and, again, the gap with the others has been widening. Their proportion of paved roads fell from 15 percent to 12 percent in 1990–96, while for the others it rose from 30 percent to 42 percent (figure 4e). Both groups had just 3 telephone mainlines per 1,000 people in 1980, but by 1998 the others had 41—the HIPCs only 9 (figure 4f).

Figure 4a

HIPCs have seen their incomes decline—while those of other poor countries have risen

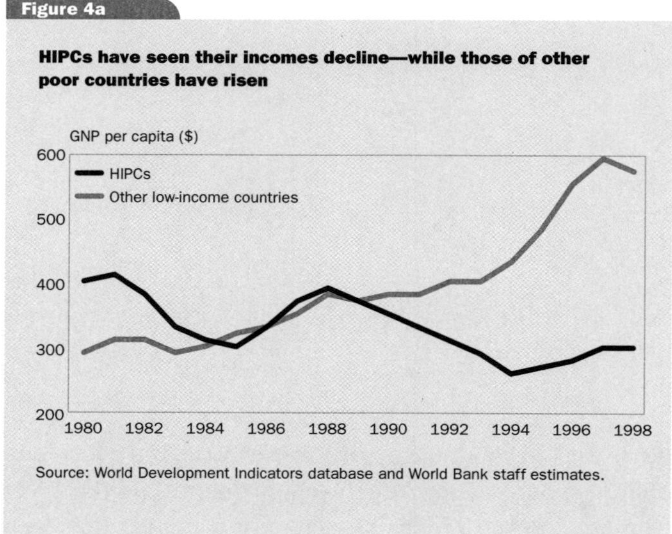

Source: World Development Indicators database and World Bank staff estimates.

Figure 4b

HIPCs have made less progress in reducing illiteracy . . .

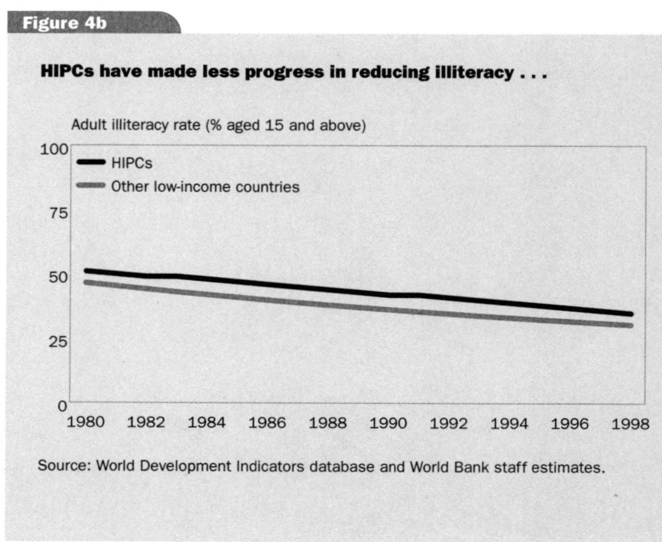

Source: World Development Indicators database and World Bank staff estimates.

Figure 4c

. . . in lowering infant mortality . . .

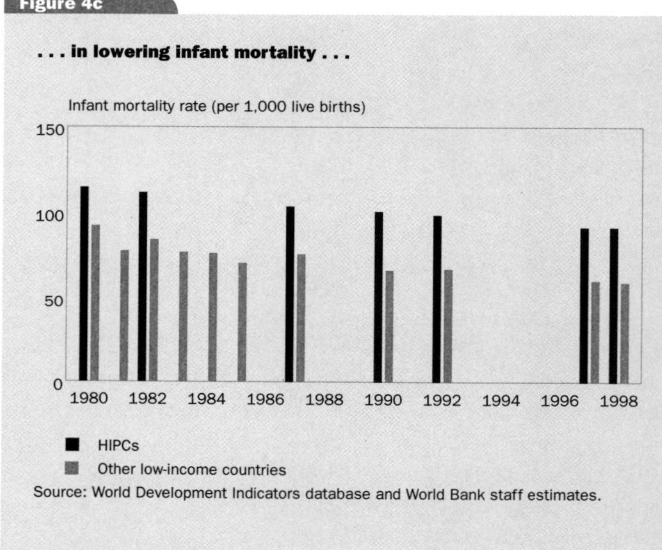

Source: World Development Indicators database and World Bank staff estimates.

Figure 4d

. . . and in slowing fertility

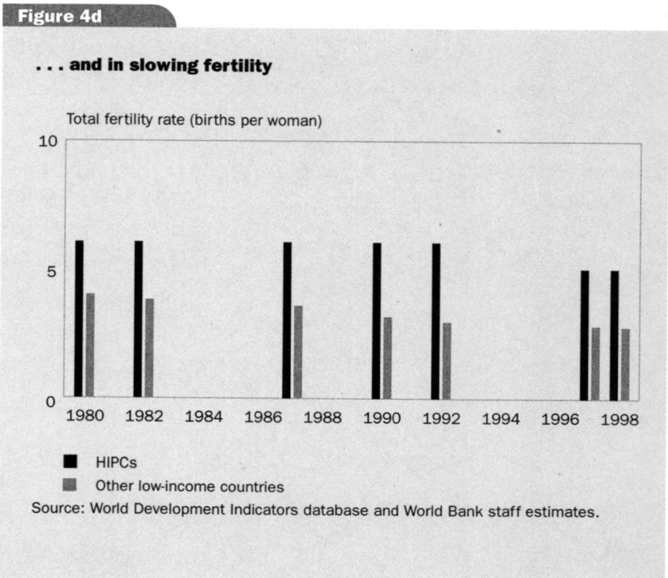

Source: World Development Indicators database and World Bank staff estimates.

Other low-income countries have diversified into industry and services. The HIPCs—despite attempts at import-substituting industrialization—have not. The share of agriculture in the economy has fallen from 31 percent to 22 percent in other low-income countries, but remained stuck in HIPCs at 33–38 percent (figure 4g).

HIPCs are not closed economies. Their export-to-GDP ratio has consistently been higher than that of other low-income countries (figure 4h). So a high export ratio is not enough to indicate good policies. Structural weaknesses must be addressed for the HIPCs to achieve sustainable growth.

HIPCs obtained much more aid per capita than the others. But since they didn't use the money efficiently, that aid simply translated into higher debt per capita (figures 4i and 4j). Recent studies have overturned the traditional notion that more aid means more investment and thus faster growth (World Bank 1998a). Indeed, there is little correlation between investment and growth—or between aid and growth. It all depends on how well a country uses development funds. Aid helps growth in countries with good policies and institutions, but can lead to unsustainable debt where these are lacking.

Why do indebted countries take on more debt?

The net present value of HIPC debt has kept rising—despite two decades of debt relief and the replacement of nonconcessional loans with highly concessional loans. Easterly (1999) explores the hypothesis that governments that have a very high discount rate take on excessive debt: they want to spend now with no regard for the future. What fuels such profligacy? Political instability, ethnic conflict, or interest groups seizing what they can while in power.

Easterly's results suggest that such countries, if given debt relief, will accumulate more debt until they go bust again. If loan conditions seek to check the deficits in their budgets or current accounts, bad governments will reduce investments or run down old assets to continue financing unproductive spending. For such

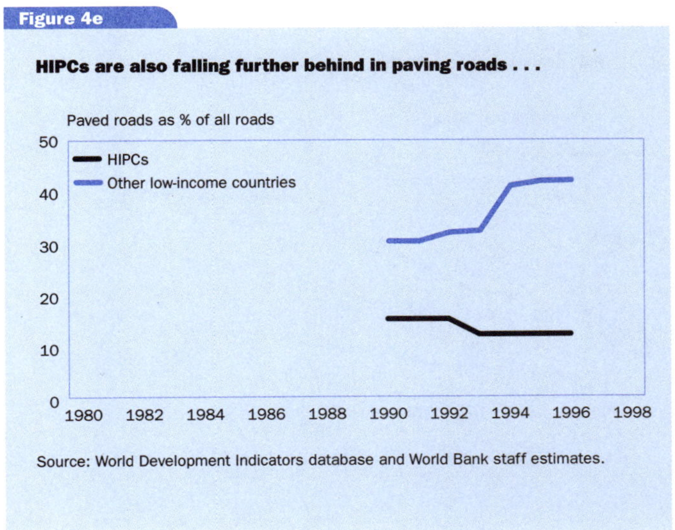

Figure 4e

HIPCs are also falling further behind in paving roads . . .

Source: World Development Indicators database and World Bank staff estimates.

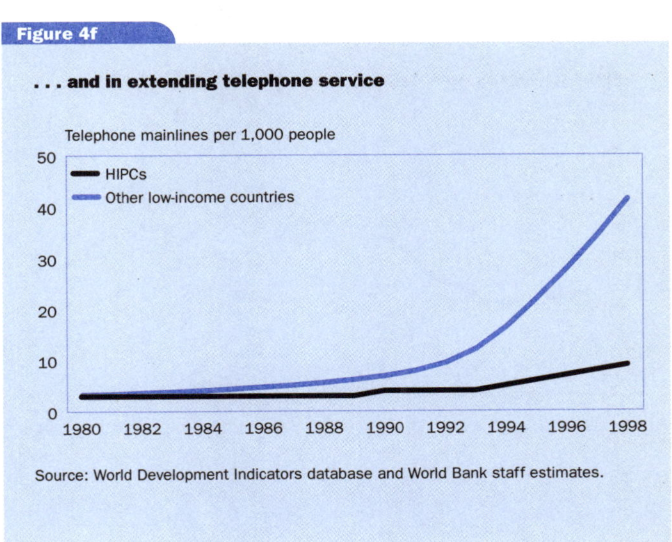

Figure 4f

. . . and in extending telephone service

Source: World Development Indicators database and World Bank staff estimates.

countries debt relief leads not to prudence, but to more borrowing—and policies get worse.

Contrary to conventional wisdom, debt relief in such circumstances does not finance fresh human and physical capital or reduce unsustainable debt over time. The route out of this downward spiral is a broad-based commitment to policies and public actions that promote growth and benefit the poor.

The new HIPC Initiative

To reduce the debt of countries with good policies, donors launched the Heavily Indebted Poor Countries Initiative in 1996. Sustainable debt was defined originally as a stock of debt with a net present value of 200–250 percent of annual exports. And for extremely open economies, it was defined as a debt-to–government revenue ratio of 280 percent. Following widespread criticism that this did not go far enough, these parameters were lowered in 1999 to a debt-to-export ratio of 150 percent and a debt-to-revenue ratio of 250 percent. That boosted the number of potential beneficiaries from 29 countries to 41 and the net present value of potential debt reduction from $12.5 billion to $27 billion.

The HIPC Initiative represents the first time that the World Bank and International Monetary Fund (IMF) have forgiven debt. (The Bank's writeoff could pass $5 billion.) And relief from other donors goes well beyond the terms of three earlier debt relief packages, known as the Toronto terms, the Trinidad terms, and the Naples terms. The most important new feature of the HIPC Initiative is that it seeks to integrate debt relief with an enhanced poverty reduction framework (box 4a).

The Bank and IMF have consulted extensively with nongovernmental organizations (NGOs) on the enhanced poverty reduction framework. Many of them are concerned that debt service in many HIPCs exceeds spending on health and education. Some suggest that immediate, unconditional debt relief is required

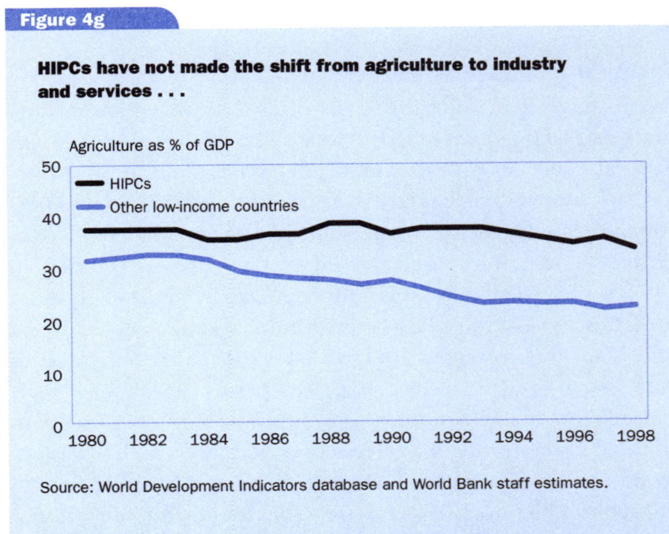

Figure 4g

HIPCs have not made the shift from agriculture to industry and services . . .

Source: World Development Indicators database and World Bank staff estimates.

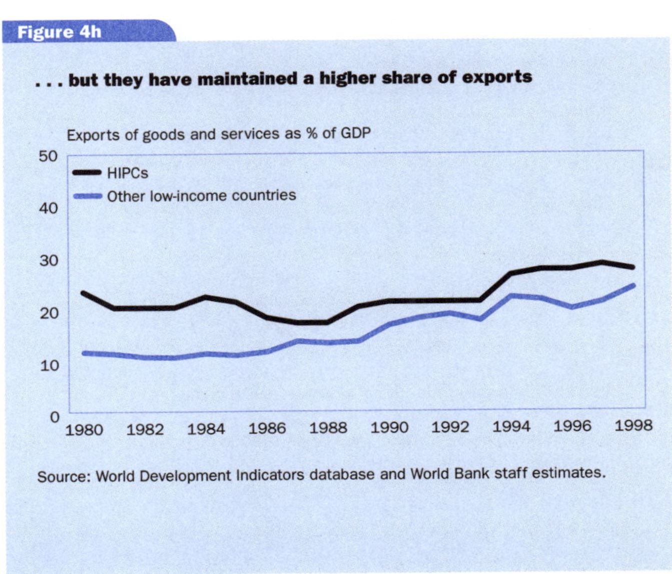

Figure 4h

. . . but they have maintained a higher share of exports

Source: World Development Indicators database and World Bank staff estimates.

Figure 4i

HIPCs' higher aid per capita . . .

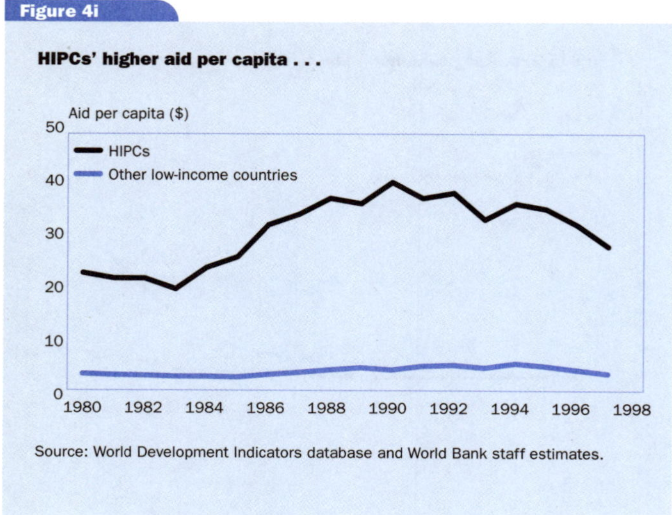

Source: World Development Indicators database and World Bank staff estimates.

Figure 4j

. . . has translated into higher debt per capita

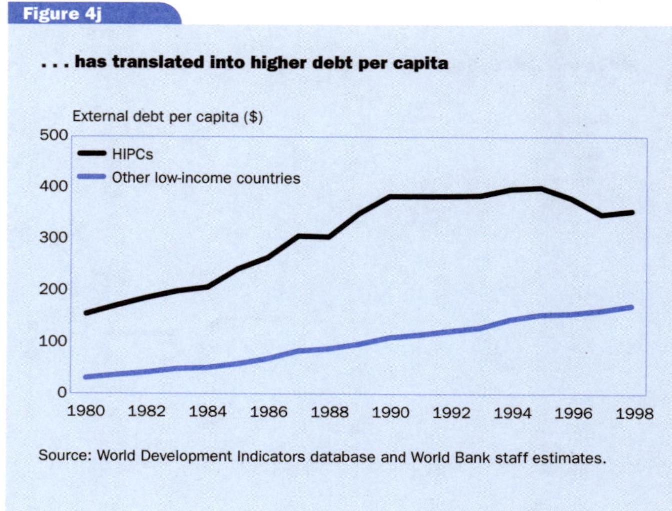

Source: World Development Indicators database and World Bank staff estimates.

to meet the need for additional social spending. But this argument is incomplete and sometimes false.

Fresh aid to HIPCs now exceeds their actual debt service, leaving them with net inflows per person among the highest in the world (table 6.10). In 1998 net aid amounted to $117 per person in Nicaragua, $82 in Guinea-Bissau, $68 in Mauritania, and $61 in Mozambique. By contrast, it was only $10 in Bangladesh and $2 in India, which are also poor but manage their economies better and get no debt relief. Mozambique had debt service due of $361 million in 1998, three times its social spending of $120 million. But in practice it paid creditors only $105 million, less than its social spending. And fresh aid inflows, net of debt service, were $450 million.

Relief under the HIPC Initiative is tied to firm evidence of the country's ownership and implementation of a reform program. Qualifying countries reach a decision point after displaying a track record of good policies for three years. At that decision point donors assess the prospects of the country and decide how much debt forgiveness is needed to reduce its debt to sustainable levels. Under the first set of conditions three more years of good policies were then needed to reach the completion point, when the debt is actually written down.

Donors decided in 1999 not to stick rigidly to a three-year requirement, and instead have a floating completion point reached when a country fulfills a set of reform commitments.

So far Bolivia, Burkina Faso, Côte d'Ivoire, Guyana, Mali, Mozambique, and Uganda have qualified for debt relief—of $3.4 billion. Benin and Senegal have been considered ineligible because their debt has been judged sustainable without recourse to extraordinary measures. Preliminary reviews have been completed for Ethiopia, Guinea-Bissau, Mauritania, Nicaragua, and Tanzania.

Box 4a

An enhanced framework for poverty reduction

- Country ownership of the poverty reduction strategy is paramount. Donors can help in designing programs, but the country must be in the driver's seat.
- Each country should be encouraged to produce a poverty reduction strategy paper illuminating the nature and causes of poverty in that country.
- This analysis should then be followed by implementation of country-owned plans to reduce poverty.
- Macroeconomic, structural, and social policies must be consistent with actions to reduce poverty.
- Countries should set medium- and long-term goals for poverty reduction. But setting goals in terms of inputs—say, education spending—is not good enough, because teacher absenteeism and other inefficiencies can make this a poor indicator of progress. Outcomes should be used instead—such as literacy rates or female enrollment.
- The poor must gain more access to social services and infrastructure. Groups that are socially, politically, and economically marginalized must participate more fully in development.
- The participation of civil society groups is essential—and not just in helping to design new schemes. They can also select and monitor indicators of progress, showing whether new spending is having its intended effect. Closer to the ground, they can give a more accurate picture of enrollments, the availability of textbooks, and the attendance of girls and minority groups—vital for spotting flaws and finding remedies.

Prospects—improving

Some trends are positive. Exchange rate overvaluation and the black market premium in HIPCs have fallen. In the past three years with data available, their debt ratios fell and per capita incomes rose. Perhaps the new donor and recipient attitudes enshrined in the HIPC Initiative are producing better results. And the enhanced poverty reduction framework should accelerate these positive trends.

It is encouraging that Sub-Saharan Africa, with the lion's share of HIPCs, also has two of the fastest-growing economies—Botswana and Mauritius. A recent study showed that while Sub-Saharan Africa's overall GDP growth averaged 3.8 percent a year in 1995–97, it was 4.4 percent in countries enjoying social stability, 5.1 percent in those also enjoying macroeconomic stability, and 5.5 percent in those that also had policies encouraging efficient resource allocation (Bhattasali 1998). HIPCs that learn from this will not remain heavily indebted—or poor—for long.

Table 4a **Recent economic performance**

	Gross domestic product		Exports of goods and services		Imports of goods and services		GDP deflator		Current account balance		Gross international reserves	
	average annual % growth		average annual % growth		average annual % growth		% growth		% of GDP		$ millions	months of import coverage
	1998	**1999**	**1998**	**1999**	**1998**	**1999**	**1998**	**1999**	**1998**	**1999**	**1999**	**1999**
Algeria	5.1	3.5	3.5	6.1	5.8	0.7	–4.2	8.7	..	0.8	..	..
Argentina	3.9	–3.5	9.2	–7.7	8.4	–12.5	–2.0	–2.0	–4.9	–4.1	22,109	5.9
Armenia	7.2	5.5	–0.1	–2.0	–4.4	–10.0	11.2	1.1	–20.5	–14.5	297	3.9
Azerbaijan	10.0	–0.9	–7.8	18.2	16.9	–8.6	–8.3	5.5	–34.8	–29.3	–2	0.0
Bangladesh	5.1	4.3	14.3	7.1	0.6	8.7	5.3	7.0	–0.6	–1.9	1,772	2.3
Bolivia	4.7	2.5	2.7	–1.2	10.1	–15.0	7.7	2.7	–7.8	–6.3	1,081	6.0
Brazil	0.2	0.8	0.2	–6.5	8.9	–17.4	3.6	4.3	–4.3	–4.4	36,342	9.0
Bulgaria	3.5	1.5	–15.6	–8.5	–2.8	–3.7	22.2	0.5	–3.1	–5.7	3,251	6.4
Cameroon	5.0	4.4	4.7	6.5	8.3	1.9	1.1	–1.2	–2.7	–4.5	11	0.0
Chile	3.4	–1.0	5.9	5.4	2.1	–3.8	5.1	4.0	–5.3	–2.7	15,013	7.7
China	7.8	7.2	7.3	8.2	3.0	18.4	–1.1	–2.6	3.1	0.8	152,853	8.3
Colombia	0.6	–4.5	8.7	7.4	0.3	–23.6	17.5	11.0	–5.7	–1.5	8,215	6.3
Congo, Rep.	3.5	–1.1	6.9	88.3	–9.0	49.1	–16.9	22.3	..	–1.6	..	..
Costa Rica	6.2	8.0	13.1	23.0	18.3	12.6	12.3	9.1	–4.4	–4.2	963	1.3
Côte d'Ivoire	5.4	5.5	0.9	2.4	4.5	2.4	3.0	2.7	–1.9	–4.2	..	..
Croatia	2.5	–1.5	6.9	–6.8	–4.6	–9.6	9.0	5.6	–7.1	–6.7	2,997	..
Dominican Republic	7.3	7.3	4.4	13.1	17.1	8.9	4.9	5.8	–2.1	–4.3	725	1.1
Ecuador	0.6	–7.3	–2.5	–2.6	3.8	–37.0	25.8	63.0	–11.8	7.0	1,790	3.4
Egypt, Arab Rep.	5.6	5.9	–7.7	30.9	1.1	24.0	3.6	7.5	–3.3	–2.7	..	..
El Salvador	3.2	2.0	1.8	4.9	5.6	8.5	2.6	1.0	–0.7	–2.1	1,969	4.9
Estonia	4.0	–1.0	12.1	1.2	11.1	–0.8	9.4	3.3	–9.2	–7.2	894	2.2
Ghana	4.6	5.5	14.4	3.0	8.3	3.3	17.6	8.6	–4.7	–5.8	..	..
Guatemala	5.1	3.6	6.0	0.2	23.0	2.3	6.8	6.5	–5.5	–5.7	1,161	2.6
Honduras	3.0	–3.0	1.8	–5.0	6.0	14.4	13.6	8.9	–2.9	–13.9	1,023	3.6
Hungary	5.1	4.0	16.0	12.5	22.2	11.1	14.2	7.6	–4.8	–4.1	9,502	3.7
India	6.1	6.1	4.2	8.1	12.0	5.5	8.9	5.5	–1.2	–1.4	35,226	6.0
Indonesia	–13.2	0.1	11.2	–32.5	–5.3	–45.3	73.1	18.3	4.2	3.1	29,887	6.3
Iran, Islamic Rep.	1.7	2.0	–2.5	9.3	2.3	7.2	15.9	9.9	–1.7	–2.0	4,500	..
Jamaica	0.1	0.4	–3.2	0.2	–2.3	–2.4	5.0	4.7	–4.0	–5.3	714	2.0
Jordan	2.2	1.2	4.9	3.3	4.6	6.9	3.7	1.8	0.1	0.8	1,903	3.9
Kazakhstan	–1.9	0.0	10.1	–6.5	–2.5	–16.3	4.9	8.3	–5.5	–1.7	1,790	3.1
Kenya	1.8	1.6	–5.8	4.9	–4.2	1.0	10.6	5.0	–3.1	–3.6	833	2.7
Latvia	3.6	0.3	6.6	–7.0	16.9	–4.0	11.3	3.0	–11.1	–8.2	1,111	3.5
Lithuania	5.1	–3.4	–2.9	–12.8	1.8	–11.5	6.6	0.8	–12.1	–10.2	1,365	2.8

continues on page 180

Table 4b **Key macroeconomic indicators**

	Nominal exchange rate			Real effective exchange rate		Money and quasi money		Gross domestic credit		Real interest rate		Short-term debt[a]
	local currency units per $	% change		1995 = 100		average annual % growth		average annual % growth		%	%	% of exports
	1999	**1998**	**1999**	**1998**	**1999**	**1998**	**1999**	**1998**	**1999**	**1998**	**1999**	**1998**
Algeria	69.3	3.3	14.8	115.1	109.1	18.9	..	9.3	..	..	..	1.5
Argentina	1.0	0.0	0.0	..	..	10.5	5.6	8.7	1.1	12.9	9.4	83.5
Armenia	523.8	5.5	0.3	111.5	112.8	38.2	..	62.4	–100.0	33.5	..	9.5
Azerbaijan	4,361.0	0.1	12.7	..	..	–17.4	7.5	5.2	–12.5	..	..	0.1
Bangladesh	51.0	6.7	5.2	..	..	11.4	15.9	13.0	14.4	8.3	7.5	2.0
Bolivia	6.0	5.2	6.1	114.9	117.8	12.9	7.1	29.4	7.2	29.4	29.5	81.4
Brazil	1.8	8.3	48.0	..	..	10.0	4.3	28.7	8.1	..	..	38.9
Bulgaria	1.9	–5.7	16.2	122.7	124.6	10.1	12.7	–17.7	–2.2	–7.3	6.3	7.8
Cameroon	653.0	–6.1	16.1	103.8	109.9	7.8	16.2	9.3	5.9	20.6	19.6	58.5
Chile	530.1	7.7	11.9	111.1	98.5	9.6	11.8	11.8	9.1	14.3	8.5	38.6
China	8.3	0.0	0.0	112.4	105.2	14.9	..	20.0	..	7.5	..	13.1
Colombia	1,873.8	16.5	24.3	112.5	90.4	20.9	13.9	29.2	8.0	21.0	20.8	41.9
Congo, Rep.	653.0	–6.1	16.1	..	..	–12.8	–1.9	11.4	–6.3	46.8	29.0	66.4
Costa Rica	298.2	11.1	9.9	104.9	102.8	26.3	25.0	35.6	6.4	9.1	14.7	9.6
Côte d'Ivoire	653.0	–6.1	16.1	105.6	105.1	7.1	..	6.1	..	..	..	29.8
Croatia	7.6	–0.9	22.4	105.3	101.1	13.0	–1.8	19.1	0.4	6.2	..	12.5
Dominican Republic	16.0	9.9	1.6	105.4	102.7	16.6	..	17.4	..	19.8	..	9.6
Ecuador	20,243.0	54.1	196.6	107.7	81.5	43.3	..	66.3	..	18.9	25.9	38.3
Egypt, Arab Rep.	3.4	0.0	0.5	..	..	10.8	7.9	19.0	17.4	9.1	7.1	22.3
El Salvador	8.8	0.0	0.0	..	..	10.5	0.5	1.8	1.6	12.1	12.6	20.3
Estonia	15.6	–6.5	16.0	..	..	6.6	24.7	22.7	10.5	6.6	4.5	7.2
Ghana	3,448.3	2.3	48.3	125.2	135.9	26.1	24.6	23.4	52.1	..	..	35.1
Guatemala	7.8	10.9	14.2	..	..	19.4	12.5	10.5	17.8	9.2	13.8	34.5
Honduras	14.5	5.4	5.0	..	..	23.2	24.2	24.3	2.6	15.0	21.0	19.7
Hungary	252.5	7.6	15.3	105.8	110.6	..	..	..	..	..	..	17.8
India	43.5	8.1	2.4	..	..	18.2	10.7	15.7	9.1	4.3	6.1	7.4
Indonesia	7,085.0	72.6	–11.7	..	..	63.5	16.6	53.7	24.9	–23.6	12.6	35.0
Iran, Islamic Rep.	1,752.3	–0.2	0.1	206.1	256.3	20.4	..	31.4	..	..	..	41.9
Jamaica	41.3	2.0	11.4	..	..	7.7	16.0	34.6	..	28.3	..	15.0
Jordan	0.7	0.0	0.0	..	..	6.3	..	14.2	..	..	..	10.8
Kazakhstan	138.2	10.9	64.9	..	..	–14.1	43.8	40.5	40.5	..	..	6.6
Kenya	72.9	–1.2	17.8	..	..	2.3	1.0	9.0	13.0	17.1	..	29.7
Latvia	0.6	–3.6	2.5	..	..	6.8	5.6	33.4	9.7	2.7	..	6.0
Lithuania	4.0	0.0	0.0	..	..	14.5	7.8	12.2	18.4	5.3	..	7.2

continues on page 181

Table 4a **Recent economic performance**

	Gross domestic product		Exports of goods and services		Imports of goods and services		GDP deflator		Current account balance		Gross international reserves	
	average annual % growth		average annual % growth		average annual % growth		% growth		% of GDP		$ millions	months of import coverage
	1998	**1999**	**1998**	**1999**	**1998**	**1999**	**1998**	**1999**	**1998**	**1999**	**1999**	**1999**
Macedonia, FYR	3.3	2.5	18.2	2.0	16.7	–8.0	1.0	–1.0	–11.6	–2.8	473	2.9
Malawi	3.1	4.2	3.8	–0.2	–8.0	–2.6	23.2	45.8	..	–16.3	..	..
Malaysia	–7.5	4.9	–0.2	6.3	–19.4	5.0	9.1	2.0	..	13.8	30,506	4.1
Mauritius	5.6	5.3	10.1	3.5	3.6	2.3	5.6	5.1	0.8	1.0	726	3.0
Mexico	4.8	3.4	9.7	11.8	14.2	11.1	14.0	15.9	–4.1	–2.8	31,829	2.3
Moldova	–8.6	–5.0	3.3	–22.4	–10.2	–36.6	8.0	37.3	–20.7	–6.4	249	3.7
Morocco	6.5	0.2	3.3	3.5	20.7	1.1	0.7	1.0	–0.4	–1.4	..	..
Nicaragua	4.0	6.3	–6.4	7.7	7.9	12.9	12.9	13.9	–29.9	–33.9	576	3.6
Nigeria	1.8	0.8	–8.3	..	7.8	..	10.5	..	–10.3	..	..	..
Pakistan	3.3	3.1	3.7	–1.2	–11.3	–8.2	7.8	6.3	–2.7	–2.6	2,228	2.0
Panama	4.1	3.5	–10.8	5.7	8.4	8.7	1.4	1.5	–13.3	–13.7	845	1.6
Papua New Guinea	2.5	3.9	10.4	3.7	13.4	4.2	10.3	14.6	1.3	–1.5	170	0.8
Paraguay	–0.4	–0.8	3.6	–27.3	–4.9	–26.9	13.8	6.9	–3.1	–1.5	1,030	3.6
Peru	0.3	2.3	3.3	19.9	0.1	–13.2	5.5	3.2	–6.0	–3.6	9,480	10.1
Philippines	–0.5	2.9	–10.4	8.4	–11.4	13.6	10.5	7.5	2.0	1.4	15,633	3.9
Poland	4.8	3.8	..	–6.4	..	–7.0	12.0	7.6	–4.4	–6.7	29,085	7.2
Romania	–7.5	–4.5	2.5	–0.4	5.2	–14.9	46.6	60.0	–7.6	–5.4	2,625	2.6
Russian Federation	–4.6	2.0	–0.9	0.8	–14.7	–21.4	11.6	64.3	0.4	9.2	12,500	2.2
Slovak Republic	4.4	1.5	10.8	6.0	10.4	–3.5	5.1	10.0	–10.4	–5.9	2,535	2.2
South Africa	0.5	1.0	2.3	0.3	2.1	3.4	7.9	7.5	–1.5	–0.7	9,857	3.3
Sri Lanka	4.7	4.0	1.0	5.1	11.5	0.5	8.8	8.0	–1.8	–3.9	1,850	..
Sudan	5.0	4.0	..	..	..	..	28.9	..	–19.3	..	..	..
Swaziland	2.0	2.0	3.0	3.3	–26.3	–0.1	8.5	9.5	–0.6	–5.2	379	2.7
Thailand	–9.4	3.3	–0.8	24.5	–23.8	30.8	8.7	2.2	12.8	8.8	30,235	7.3
Trinidad and Tobago	4.1	4.2	4.7	4.7	5.2	5.5	6.7	5.2	–10.1	–12.3	760	2.3
Tunisia	5.0	6.2	3.7	5.1	4.2	6.9	3.5	3.6	–3.4	–3.6	..	..
Turkey	2.8	–4.0	10.5	..	2.2	..	74.2	..	0.9	..	35,192	..
Uganda	5.6	7.8	–14.9	33.0	3.1	0.9	10.7	3.0	–10.4	–11.7	732	4.6
Ukraine	–1.7	–0.5	–13.0	–5.5	–14.0	–20.8	13.2	25.0	–3.0	–1.4	1,237	..
Uruguay	4.5	–2.0	1.6	–4.0	9.0	–12.2	10.7	7.2	–1.9	–2.6	2,357	6.9
Uzbekistan	4.4	2.0	–17.5	–7.6	–24.5	–3.2	33.2	30.0	–0.3	–2.3	865	3.0
Venezuela, RB	–0.7	–7.2	2.6	–11.1	7.9	–21.0	21.2	27.6	–2.7	5.5	15,164	7.8
Zambia	–2.0	1.3	–7.5	–0.8	–8.2	3.8	23.2	25.6	..	–18.2	..	..
Zimbabwe	2.5	1.2	25.2	2.7	10.1	–14.7	29.8	59.4	..	0.7	..	..

Note: Data for 1999 are the latest preliminary estimates and may differ from those in earlier World Bank publications.
Source: World Bank staff estimates.

Table 4b **Key macroeconomic indicators**

	Nominal exchange rate			Real effective exchange rate		Money and quasi money		Gross domestic credit		Real interest rate		Short-term debt[a]
	local currency units per $	% change		1995 = 100		average annual % growth		average annual % growth		%	%	% of exports
	1999	1998	1999	1998	1999	1998	1999	1998	1999	1998	1999	1998
Macedonia, FYR	60.3	–6.5	16.4	72.3	73.5	13.0	..	–33.1	..	19.8	..	10.2
Malawi	46.4	106.7	5.8	111.2	114.8	60.0	..	–3.3	..	11.8	..	5.6
Malaysia	3.8	–2.4	0.0	80.9	81.9	–1.4	..	–2.7	..	1.4	3.7	12.0
Mauritius	25.5	11.3	2.8	..	..	11.2	15.2	21.5	9.2	13.6	15.2	20.7
Mexico	9.5	22.0	–3.6	..	..	19.7	16.6	10.5	3.9	12.9	15.5	19.6
Moldova	11.6	78.6	39.3	106.9	102.5	–8.3	42.9	29.2	17.8	21.1	..	4.6
Morocco	10.1	–4.7	9.0	105.1	106.4	6.0	9.6	8.5	2.0	..	..	1.0
Nicaragua	12.3	12.0	10.0	103.6	102.0	30.5	..	20.0	..	7.7	..	71.8
Nigeria	97.0	0.0	343.2	155.7	75.7	21.2	..	55.7	..	..	..	55.9
Pakistan	51.6	4.4	12.5	98.1	89.8	7.9	6.0	8.3	..	..	..	19.0
Panama	1.0	0.0	0.0	..	..	13.0	..	27.5	..	9.3	..	7.7
Papua New Guinea	2.8	19.7	34.9	92.4	82.4	2.5	..	17.1	..	6.7	..	7.4
Paraguay	3,420.0	16.9	19.4	99.4	93.7	9.0	..	–4.0	..	14.2	22.1	16.1
Peru	3.5	15.8	11.1	..	..	17.3	15.9	33.9	18.5	23.9	25.8	85.4
Philippines	40.3	–2.3	3.2	88.8	93.1	8.5	11.3	–1.8	..	5.7	..	16.5
Poland	4.1	–0.4	18.4	117.7	109.5	25.2	22.9	22.1	23.2	11.1	..	13.3
Romania	16.2	36.5	75.6	..	..	48.9	51.2	71.3	22.4	..	..	11.7
Russian Federation	27.0	246.5	30.8	114.2	82.6	37.5	64.5	68.2	37.0	27.1	–1.2	20.8
Slovak Republic	42.5	6.1	16.4	102.3	104.5	4.9	..	3.1	..	15.3	..	14.7
South Africa	6.2	20.4	5.0	89.4	83.1	13.7	..	17.4	..	12.9	7.9	31.9
Sri Lanka	72.1	10.6	6.4	..	..	9.6	..	12.7	..	–2.6	..	6.3
Sudan	2,568.0	38.1	31.0	..	..	29.9	24.2	24.2	..	..	..	1,015.7
Swaziland	6.2	20.4	5.0	..	..	12.9	21.8	–268.9	33.4	11.5	8.0	2.6
Thailand	37.5	–22.3	2.3	..	..	9.7	5.5	–1.3	–0.3	5.2	6.0	34.0
Trinidad and Tobago	6.3	4.7	–4.9	106.0	108.4	14.5	4.3	3.8	6.1	10.0	10.7	18.9
Tunisia	1.2	–4.1	11.7	100.5	100.9	5.4	19.2	7.9	16.1	..	..	11.2
Turkey	541,400.0	52.9	72.2	..	..	89.7	..	92.4	..	..	..	43.7
Uganda	1,506.0	19.5	13.2	94.6	87.4	21.7	..	32.5	..	9.1	..	20.0
Ukraine	5.2	80.5	52.2	130.3	117.6	22.3	41.7	58.0	28.2	36.5	..	2.7
Uruguay	11.6	7.7	7.4	108.8	111.1	19.3	..	19.2	..	42.6	45.9	41.6
Uzbekistan	..	..	..	..	..	..	..	..	..	..	..	4.5
Venezuela, RB	648.3	11.9	14.8	135.5	151.7	6.5	..	20.5	..	20.7	..	11.2
Zambia	2,632.2	62.5	14.5	114.5	116.4	25.6	25.7	71.1	34.2	7.0	25.6	28.8
Zimbabwe	38.1	100.8	2.1	..	..	11.3	58.3	41.1	8.3	9.5	51.9	29.9

Note: Data for 1999 are preliminary and may not cover the entire year.

a. More recent data on short-term debt are available on a website maintained by the Bank for International Settlements, the International Monetary Fund, the Organisation for Economic Co-operation and Development, and the World Bank: www.oecd.org/dac/debt.

Source: International Monetary Fund, *International Financial Statistics;* World Bank, Debtor Reporting System.

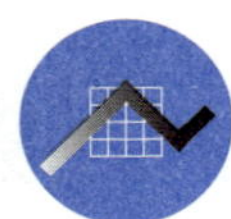

4.1 Growth of output

	Gross domestic product		Agriculture		Industry		Manufacturing		Services	
	average annual % growth		average annual % growth		average annual % growth		average annual % growth		average annual % growth	
	1980–90	1990–98	1980–90	1990–98	1980–90	1990–98	1980–90	1990–98	1980–90	1990–98
Albania	1.5	2.3	1.9	6.2	2.1	–4.6	..	..	–0.4	5.0
Algeria	2.7	1.2	4.6	2.9	2.3	–1.0	3.3	–9.0	3.6	3.6
Angola	3.4	0.1	*0.5*	–4.1	*6.4*	3.7	*–11.1*	–2.7	*1.8*	–4.2
Argentina	–0.7	5.6	0.7	3.4	–1.3	5.4	–0.8	4.3	0.0	5.4
Armenia	..	–4.7	..	–0.3	..	–9.0	..	–9.8	..	–6.2
Australia	3.4	3.8	3.3	*1.1*	2.9	*2.5*	1.9	*2.2*	3.7	*4.4*
Austria	2.2	1.9	1.1	*–0.7*	1.9	*1.3*	2.7	*0.8*	2.5	*2.1*
Azerbaijan	..	–11.5	..	*–1.4*	..	*5.8*	..	*–6.1*	..	*–0.5*
Bangladesh	4.3	4.7	2.7	2.2	4.9	5.1	3.1	7.7	5.2	5.8
Belarus	..	–4.3	..	–5.4	..	–5.6	..	–4.4	..	–2.4
Belgium	1.9	1.6	2.0	*1.7*	2.2	*1.1*	2.7	*1.0*	1.8	*1.6*
Benin	2.5	4.6	5.1	5.3	3.4	3.9	5.1	5.6	0.7	4.3
Bolivia	–0.2	4.2	..	..	..	..	..	..	..	..
Bosnia and Herzegovina	..	..	..	..	..	..	..	..	..	..
Botswana	10.3	4.3	3.3	–0.2	10.2	2.7	8.7	3.5	11.7	6.4
Brazil	2.7	3.2	2.8	3.1	2.0	3.2	1.6	2.5	3.3	3.2
Bulgaria	3.4	–3.1	–2.1	–0.7	5.2	–4.9	..	..	4.5	–2.0
Burkina Faso	3.6	3.5	3.1	3.4	3.8	3.5	2.0	3.1	4.6	3.0
Burundi	4.4	–3.3	3.1	–2.3	4.5	–7.8	5.7	–9.3	5.6	–2.9
Cambodia	..	5.1	..	2.1	..	9.6	..	8.2	..	6.9
Cameroon	3.4	0.6	2.2	5.0	5.9	–3.3	5.0	–1.0	2.1	0.0
Canada	3.3	2.2	*1.2*	*1.1*	*3.1*	*2.2*	*3.7*	*3.3*	*3.6*	*1.9*
Central African Republic	1.4	1.5	1.6	3.5	1.4	0.2	5.0	–0.7	1.0	–1.3
Chad	6.1	2.2	2.3	5.4	8.1	1.7	..	..	6.7	0.5
Chile	4.2	7.9	5.9	1.2	3.5	6.7	3.4	5.7	4.4	9.4
China	10.1	11.2	5.9	4.4	11.1	15.4	10.4	14.7	13.5	9.4
Hong Kong, China	6.9	4.4	..	..	..	..	..	..	..	..
Colombia	3.6	3.9	2.9	–3.0	5.0	3.1	3.5	–1.1	3.1	6.7
Congo, Dem. Rep.	1.6	–5.1	2.5	2.9	0.9	*–11.7*	1.6	*–13.4*	1.3	*–15.2*
Congo, Rep.	3.3	0.9	3.4	1.6	5.2	0.2	6.8	–2.5	2.1	1.4
Costa Rica	3.0	3.9	3.1	2.7	2.8	3.8	3.0	3.9	3.1	4.3
Côte d'Ivoire	0.7	3.5	0.3	2.4	4.4	5.2	3.0	3.7	–0.3	3.4
Croatia	..	–0.4	..	–3.3	..	–4.8	..	–6.2	..	3.0
Cuba	..	..	..	..	..	..	..	..	..	..
Czech Republic	*1.7*	0.9	..	2.6	..	–0.1	..	..	..	1.1
Denmark	2.3	2.9	3.1	*1.7*	2.9	*1.9*	1.4	*1.3*	2.6	*1.4*
Dominican Republic	3.1	5.5	0.4	3.6	3.6	6.1	2.9	4.1	3.5	5.6
Ecuador	2.0	2.9	4.4	2.7	1.2	3.6	0.0	3.0	1.7	2.5
Egypt, Arab Rep.	5.4	4.2	2.7	3.0	5.2	4.4	..	5.3	6.6	4.1
El Salvador	0.2	5.2	–1.1	0.9	0.1	5.5	–0.2	5.5	0.7	6.2
Eritrea	..	*5.2*	..	..	..	..	..	..	..	..
Estonia	2.2	–2.2	..	–4.2	..	–6.1	..	*0.4*	..	0.7
Ethiopia	*1.1*	4.8	*0.2*	2.6	*0.4*	6.0	*–0.9*	6.6	*3.1*	6.4
Finland	3.3	2.0	–0.2	*0.2*	3.3	*2.1*	3.4	*4.9*	4.1	*–0.1*
France	2.3	1.5	2.0	*0.5*	1.1	*0.6*	0.8	*1.2*	3.0	*1.7*
Gabon	0.9	3.3	1.2	–2.3	1.5	2.7	1.8	0.9	0.1	4.8
Gambia, The	3.6	2.4	0.9	0.4	4.7	0.3	7.8	0.8	2.7	4.1
Georgia	0.4	–12.8	..	*5.5*	..	*5.6*	..	*0.7*	..	*17.2*
Germany[a]	2.2	*1.5*	1.7	*0.5*	1.2	..	..	*–0.5*	2.9	*2.5*
Ghana	3.0	4.2	1.0	3.1	3.3	4.7	3.9	3.2	5.7	5.2
Greece	1.8	1.7	–0.1	*2.0*	1.3	*–0.5*	0.5	*–1.1*	2.7	*1.8*
Guatemala	0.8	4.2	1.2	2.8	–0.2	4.3	0.0	2.8	0.9	4.8
Guinea	..	4.2	..	4.4	..	4.5	..	3.6	..	3.2
Guinea-Bissau	4.0	1.1	4.7	4.0	2.2	–1.4	..	0.1	3.5	–1.4
Haiti	–0.2	–1.7	–0.1	–4.3	–1.7	–1.0	–1.7	–14.8	0.5	0.0
Honduras	2.7	3.6	2.7	2.8	3.3	3.9	3.7	4.1	2.5	4.0

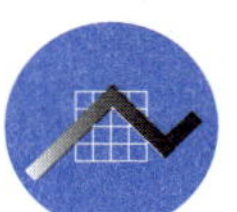

Growth of output 4.1

	Gross domestic product		Agriculture		Industry		Manufacturing		Services	
	average annual % growth		average annual % growth		average annual % growth		average annual % growth		average annual % growth	
	1980–90	1990–98	1980–90	1990–98	1980–90	1990–98	1980–90	1990–98	1980–90	1990–98
Hungary	1.3	0.5	1.7	–3.2	0.2	2.4	..	*6.5*	2.1	0.6
India	5.8	6.1	3.1	3.8	7.0	6.7	7.4	8.0	6.9	7.7
Indonesia	6.1	5.8	3.4	2.6	6.9	7.8	12.6	8.8	7.0	5.4
Iran, Islamic Rep.	1.7	3.6	4.5	3.8	3.3	*3.7*	4.5	4.9	–1.0	*5.8*
Iraq	–6.8	..	..	..	..	..	..	..	..	..
Ireland	3.2	7.7	..	..	..	..	..	..	..	..
Israel	3.5	5.4	..	..	..	..	..	..	..	..
Italy	2.4	1.2	0.1	*1.1*	2.0	*0.9*	2.9	*1.4*	2.8	*1.2*
Jamaica	2.0	0.2	0.6	3.0	2.4	–0.4	2.7	–1.8	1.8	0.3
Japan	4.0	1.5	1.3	*–1.3*	4.2	*1.1*	4.8	*1.4*	3.9	*2.3*
Jordan	2.5	5.4	6.8	–3.1	1.7	7.1	0.5	6.5	2.0	5.5
Kazakhstan	..	–6.9	..	*–13.4*	..	*–10.1*	..	..	..	*2.2*
Kenya	4.2	2.2	3.3	1.3	3.9	1.9	4.9	2.5	4.9	3.6
Korea, Dem. Rep.	..	..	..	..	..	..	..	..	..	..
Korea, Rep.	9.4	6.1	2.8	2.7	12.0	6.4	13.0	6.9	8.9	6.2
Kuwait	*1.3*	..	*14.7*	..	*1.0*	..	*2.3*	..	*2.1*	..
Kyrgyz Republic	..	–7.3	..	–1.2	..	*–12.0*	..	*–3.9*	..	*–7.2*
Lao PDR	..	6.6	3.5	4.6	*6.1*	11.8	*8.9*	12.6	*3.3*	6.5
Latvia	3.5	–6.3	13.9	–8.9	7.5	–12.8	10.3	–11.7	9.0	1.3
Lebanon	..	7.7	..	*3.2*	..	*2.1*	..	*2.1*	..	*2.6*
Lesotho	4.4	7.2	2.2	6.0	7.1	9.2	13.7	*9.4*	4.6	6.2
Libya	*–5.7*	..	..	..	..	..	..	..	..	..
Lithuania	..	–5.0	..	–1.5	..	–9.9	..	–12.4	..	–0.4
Macedonia, FYR	..	*1.7*	..	3.1	..	–2.1	..	..	..	0.8
Madagascar	1.1	1.3	2.5	1.5	0.9	1.5	*2.1*	*0.6*	0.3	1.5
Malawi	2.5	3.8	2.0	8.9	2.9	1.3	3.6	0.5	3.6	0.4
Malaysia	5.3	7.4	3.8	1.3	7.2	9.4	8.9	10.8	4.2	7.6
Mali	0.8	3.7	3.3	3.3	4.3	7.6	6.8	4.6	1.9	2.2
Mauritania	0.0	4.2	1.7	4.8	4.9	3.4	*–2.1*	–1.7	0.4	4.3
Mauritius	6.2	5.2	2.9	0.7	10.3	5.4	11.1	5.5	5.5	6.4
Mexico	1.1	2.5	0.8	1.4	1.1	3.1	1.5	3.6	1.1	2.4
Moldova	3.0	–12.6	..	–6.3	..	–12.8	..	..	..	*–17.2*
Mongolia	*5.4*	0.2	*1.4*	2.9	*6.6*	–1.8	..	..	*5.9*	0.8
Morocco	4.2	2.2	6.7	0.0	3.0	3.1	4.1	2.6	4.2	2.5
Mozambique	–0.1	5.7	*6.6*	4.8	*–4.5*	8.5	..	*16.8*	*9.1*	5.2
Myanmar	0.6	6.3	0.5	4.9	0.5	10.1	–0.2	6.7	0.8	6.6
Namibia	0.9	3.5	1.8	2.9	–1.2	3.3	3.7	3.6	1.5	3.6
Nepal	4.6	5.0	4.0	2.3	8.7	7.6	9.3	10.2	3.9	6.4
Netherlands	2.3	2.6	3.4	*3.7*	1.6	*1.2*	2.3	*1.7*	2.6	*2.3*
New Zealand	1.7	3.1	3.8	*2.6*	1.1	*3.5*	0.5	*3.7*	1.8	*3.4*
Nicaragua	–1.9	2.8	–2.2	5.3	–2.3	3.1	–3.2	1.3	–1.5	1.1
Niger	–0.1	2.1	1.7	3.1	–1.7	1.6	*–2.7*	1.9	–0.7	1.5
Nigeria	1.6	2.6	3.3	2.9	–1.1	1.4	0.7	1.9	3.7	3.4
Norway	2.8	3.9	–0.2	*4.1*	3.3	*5.5*	0.2	*2.3*	2.7	*3.2*
Oman	8.4	*5.9*	7.9	..	10.3	..	20.6	..	5.9	..
Pakistan	6.3	4.2	4.3	4.5	7.3	5.1	7.7	5.0	6.8	4.7
Panama	0.5	4.4	2.5	2.0	–1.3	6.2	0.4	4.2	0.5	4.3
Papua New Guinea	1.9	4.7	1.8	3.0	1.9	7.9	0.1	5.8	2.0	3.4
Paraguay	2.5	2.8	3.6	2.8	0.3	3.1	4.0	0.9	3.1	2.5
Peru	–0.3	5.7	2.7	5.5	–0.9	6.9	–1.5	8.0	–0.7	4.8
Philippines	1.0	3.3	1.0	1.5	–0.9	3.6	0.2	3.1	2.8	3.9
Poland	2.2	4.6	*–0.4*	–0.5	*0.3*	6.4	..	..	..	..
Portugal	3.1	2.3	..	*–0.4*	..	*0.7*	..	*0.2*	..	*2.2*
Puerto Rico	4.0	..	1.8	..	3.6	..	1.5	..	4.6	..
Romania	0.5	–0.7	..	0.0	..	–0.8	..	..	..	–0.5
Russian Federation	..	–7.0	..	*–6.9*	..	*–11.1*	..	..	..	*–2.6*

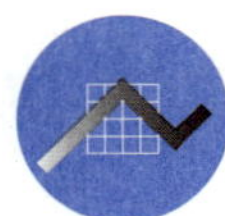

4.1 Growth of output

	Gross domestic product		Agriculture		Industry		Manufacturing		Services	
	average annual % growth		average annual % growth		average annual % growth		average annual % growth		average annual % growth	
	1980–90	**1990–98**	**1980–90**	**1990–98**	**1980–90**	**1990–98**	**1980–90**	**1990–98**	**1980–90**	**1990–98**
Rwanda	2.2	–3.2	0.5	–5.1	2.5	–0.6	2.6	4.6	5.5	–2.9
Saudi Arabia	0.0	1.6	13.4	*0.7*	–2.3	*1.5*	7.5	*2.7*	1.3	*2.0*
Senegal	3.1	2.9	2.8	1.4	4.3	4.0	4.6	2.4	2.8	3.0
Sierra Leone	0.3	–4.7	3.1	1.5	1.7	*–4.7*	..	*5.0*	–2.8	*–2.7*
Singapore	6.7	8.5	–6.2	1.4	5.3	8.4	6.6	6.7	7.6	8.6
Slovak Republic	*2.0*	1.5	1.6	–0.2	*2.0*	–4.9	..	..	*0.8*	8.0
Slovenia	..	2.0	..	*–0.1*	..	*2.0*	..	*3.7*	..	*3.8*
South Africa	1.0	1.9	2.9	0.8	0.7	1.0	1.1	1.1	2.4	2.4
Spain	3.0	1.9	..	*–2.5*	..	*–0.4*	..	*–0.7*	..	..
Sri Lanka	4.0	5.3	2.2	1.5	4.6	7.4	6.3	8.5	4.7	5.6
Sudan	0.4	8.0	–0.6	15.3	2.5	*5.4*	3.4	*2.4*	1.7	*3.0*
Sweden	2.3	1.2	1.5	*–1.9*	2.8	*–0.7*	2.6	*0.8*	2.6	*–0.1*
Switzerland	2.0	0.4	..	..	..	..	..	..	..	..
Syrian Arab Republic	1.5	5.9	–0.6	..	6.6	..	..	..	0.1	..
Tajikistan	..	–9.8	..	*–12.2*	..	*–17.2*	..	..	..	*–10.7*
Tanzania[b]	..	3.0	..	3.6	..	1.9	..	1.8	..	2.4
Thailand	7.6	5.7	3.9	2.6	9.8	6.9	9.5	7.7	7.3	5.4
Togo	1.7	2.3	5.6	4.5	1.1	2.6	1.7	2.1	–0.3	0.2
Trinidad and Tobago	–0.8	1.6	–5.8	1.8	–5.5	1.5	–10.1	1.9	–2.9	3.2
Tunisia	3.3	4.4	2.8	1.4	3.1	4.4	3.7	5.4	3.5	5.3
Turkey	5.4	4.2	1.3	1.4	7.8	5.0	7.9	5.9	4.4	4.3
Turkmenistan	..	–8.7	..	..	..	..	..	..	..	..
Uganda	*2.9*	7.3	*2.1*	3.6	*5.0*	12.8	*3.7*	14.2	*2.8*	8.3
Ukraine	..	–11.9	..	–5.8	..	–15.5	..	–15.5	..	–13.7
United Arab Emirates	–2.1	2.9	9.6	..	–4.2	..	3.1	..	3.6	..
United Kingdom	3.2	2.2	..	..	..	..	..	..	..	..
United States	3.0	3.2	..	*2.5*	..	*4.9*	..	*6.0*	..	*2.3*
Uruguay	0.4	4.0	0.0	4.4	–0.2	1.4	0.4	0.3	0.8	5.2
Uzbekistan	..	–2.0	..	–1.0	..	–5.1	..	..	..	–1.1
Venezuela, RB	1.1	2.2	3.0	1.1	1.6	3.5	4.3	1.5	0.5	0.9
Vietnam	*4.6*	8.4	*4.3*	4.9	..	13.0	..	..	..	8.6
West Bank and Gaza	..	*0.0*	..	*–15.4*	..	*11.7*	..	*9.8*	..	*–1.4*
Yemen, Rep.	..	3.8	..	4.3	..	6.4	..	1.6	..	1.0
Yugoslavia, FR (Serb./Mont.)	..	..	..	..	..	..	..	..	..	..
Zambia	1.0	1.0	3.6	–4.9	0.8	–4.7	4.1	–14.5	–0.4	8.9
Zimbabwe	3.6	2.3	3.1	3.9	3.2	–1.2	2.8	–1.7	3.1	3.6
World	**3.2 w**	**2.5 w**	**2.7 w**	**1.7 w**	**.. w**	**3.0 w**	**.. w**	**3.3 w**	**.. w**	**2.3 w**
Low income	6.5	7.4	4.1	3.7	7.8	10.8	9.2	11.8	7.9	7.0
Excl. China & India	4.1	3.7	3.0	2.7	4.6	5.1	8.0	6.3	4.9	4.2
Middle income	2.6	2.2	2.7	0.8	2.6	1.5	3.3	3.7	2.9	2.7
Lower middle income	2.3	–0.8	..	–0.5	..	–3.1	..	..	..	0.4
Upper middle income	2.8	3.9	2.5	2.0	2.6	4.4	3.4	4.4	2.9	4.0
Low & middle income	3.3	3.5	3.4	2.2	3.8	4.0	4.7	6.4	3.8	3.7
East Asia & Pacific	8.0	7.9	4.4	3.5	9.4	10.5	10.2	10.9	8.7	7.0
Europe & Central Asia	2.4	–2.9	..	–3.1	..	*–4.8*	..	..	..	*–1.4*
Latin America & Carib.	1.7	3.6	2.1	2.2	1.2	3.8	1.2	3.1	1.8	3.7
Middle East & N. Africa	2.0	3.0	5.5	2.5	0.6	*2.1*	..	3.1	2.1	*3.5*
South Asia	5.7	5.7	3.2	3.7	6.8	6.4	7.0	7.6	6.6	7.0
Sub-Saharan Africa	1.6	2.3	2.5	2.4	1.2	1.3	1.7	1.2	2.5	2.5
High income	3.1	2.3	..	*0.8*	..	*2.6*	..	*2.5*	..	*2.0*
Europe EMU	..	*1.8*	..	*0.7*	..	..	..	*0.7*	..	*0.9*

a. Data prior to 1990 refer to the Federal Republic of Germany before unification. b. Data cover mainland Tanzania only.

Growth of output 4.1

About the data

An economy's growth is measured by the change in the volume of its output or in the real incomes of persons resident in the economy. The 1993 United Nations System of National Accounts (SNA) offers three plausible indicators from which to calculate growth: the volume of gross domestic product, real gross domestic income, and real gross national income. The volume of GDP is the sum of value added, measured at constant prices, by households, government, and the enterprises operating in the economy. This year's edition of the *World Development Indicators* continues to follow the practice of past editions, measuring the growth of the economy by the change in GDP measured at constant prices.

The contribution of each industry to the growth in the economy's output is measured by the growth in value added by the industry. In principle, value added in constant prices can be estimated by measuring the quantity of goods and services produced in a period, valuing them at an agreed set of base year prices, and subtracting the cost of inputs, also in constant prices. This double deflation method, recommended by the SNA, requires detailed information on the structure of prices of inputs and outputs. In many industries, however, value added is extrapolated from the base year using single volume indexes of outputs or, more rarely, inputs. In others, particularly service industries, constant price output is imputed from labor inputs, such as real wages or the number of employees. The output of government and other nonmarket services is calculated in the same way. In the absence of well-defined measures of output, measuring the growth of services remains difficult. Moreover, technical progress can lead to improvements in production and in the quality of goods and services, which if not properly accounted for can distort measures of value added and thus of growth. When inputs are used to estimate output, as is the case for nonmarket services, unmeasured technical progress leads to underestimates of the volume of output. Similarly, unmeasured changes in the quality of goods produced lead to underestimates of the value of production. The result can be underestimates of growth and productivity change and overestimates of inflation.

Informal economic activities pose a particular measurement problem, especially in developing countries, where much economic activity may go unrecorded. Obtaining a complete picture of the economy requires estimating household outputs produced for local sale and home use, barter exchanges, and illicit or deliberately unreported activity. How consistent and complete such estimates will be depends on the skill and methods of the compiling statisticians and the resources available to them.

Rebasing national accounts

When countries rebase their national accounts, they update price indexes to reflect the relative importance of inputs and outputs in total output and generate volume indexes to reflect relative price levels. The new base year should represent normal operation of the economy—that is, it should be a year without major shocks or distortions—but the choice of base year is often arbitrary. Some developing countries have not rebased their national accounts for many years. Using an old base year can be misleading because implicit price and volume weights become progressively less relevant and useful.

For most countries that are not members of the Organisation for Economic Co-operation and Development (OECD), the World Bank collects constant price national accounts series in the national currency in the country's original base year. To obtain comparable series of constant price data, it rescales GDP (and value added) by industrial origin to a common reference year, currently 1995. This process gives rise to a discrepancy between the rescaled GDP and the sum of the rescaled components. Because allocating the discrepancy would give rise to distortions in the growth rates, the discrepancy is left unallocated. As a result the weighted average of the sector growth rates of the components generally will not equal the GDP growth rate. Data for OECD countries are from the OECD database. In some cases they may already be referenced or adjusted to conform to OECD reporting practices and may therefore differ from data in national statistical publications.

Growth rates of GDP and its components are calculated using constant price data in the local currency. Regional and income group growth rates are calculated after converting local currencies to constant price U.S. dollars using an exchange rate in the common reference year. The growth rates in the table are annual average compound growth rates. Methods of computing growth rates and the alternative conversion factor are described in *Statistical methods.*

Changes in the System of National Accounts

Most countries continue to use the definitions of the United Nations System of National Accounts, series F, no. 2, version 3, referred to as the 1968 SNA. Version 4 of the SNA was completed in 1993. Until new economic surveys can be implemented, most countries will continue to follow the 1968 SNA. Countries that use the 1993 SNA are identified in *Primary data documentation.* A few low-income countries still use concepts from older SNA guidelines, including valuations such as factor cost, in describing major economic aggregates.

Definitions

• **Gross domestic product** at purchaser prices is the sum of the gross value added by all resident producers in the economy plus any taxes and minus any subsidies not included in the value of the products. It is calculated without making deductions for depreciation of fabricated assets or for depletion and degradation of natural resources. Value added is the net output of an industry after adding up all outputs and subtracting intermediate inputs. The industrial origin of value added is determined by the International Standard Industrial Classification (ISIC) revision 3. • **Agriculture** corresponds to ISIC divisions 1–5 and includes forestry and fishing. • **Industry** comprises value added in mining, manufacturing (also reported as a separate subgroup), construction, electricity, water, and gas (ISIC divisions 10–45). • **Manufacturing** refers to industries belonging to divisions 15–37. • **Services** correspond to ISIC divisions 50–99.

Data sources

The national accounts data for most developing countries are collected from national statistical organizations and central banks by visiting and resident World Bank missions. The data for high-income economies come from OECD data files. The World Bank rescales constant price data to a common reference year. The complete national accounts time series is available on the *World Development Indicators 2000* CD-ROM. For information on the OECD national accounts series see the OECD's *Main Economic Indicators* (monthly). The United Nations Statistics Division publishes detailed national accounts for United Nations member countries in *National Accounts Statistics: Main Aggregates and Detailed Tables;* updates are published in the *Monthly Bulletin of Statistics.*

4.2 Structure of output

	Gross domestic product		Agriculture value added		Industry value added		Manufacturing value added		Services value added	
	$ millions		% of GDP		% of GDP		% of GDP		% of GDP	
	1980	1998	1980	1998	1980	1998	1980	1998	1980	1998
Albania	..	3,047	34	54	45	25	..	..	21	21
Algeria	42,345	47,347	10	12	54	47	9	11	36	41
Angola	..	7,472	..	12	..	51	..	6	..	36
Argentina	76,962	298,131	6	6	41	29	29	19	52	66
Armenia	..	1,900	..	33	..	32	..	22	..	35
Australia	160,109	361,722	5	*3*	36	*26*	19	*14*	*58*	*71*
Austria	78,539	211,858	4	*1*	36	*30*	25	*20*	*60*	*68*
Azerbaijan	..	3,926	..	20	..	39	..	22	..	41
Bangladesh	17,430	42,702	38	22	24	28	18	18	38	50
Belarus	..	22,555	..	13	..	46	..	39	..	40
Belgium	119,979	248,184	2	*1*	34	*28*	21	*18*	64	*71*
Benin	1,405	2,306	35	39	12	14	8	8	52	48
Bolivia	2,750	8,586	..	15	..	29	..	17	..	56
Bosnia and Herzegovina	..	..	..	..	..	..	..	..	..	..
Botswana	1,130	4,876	11	4	45	46	5	5	44	50
Brazil	235,025	778,209	11	8	44	29	33	23	45	63
Bulgaria	20,040	12,258	14	19	54	26	..	17	32	56
Burkina Faso	1,709	2,581	33	33	22	27	16	21	45	39
Burundi	920	885	62	54	13	16	7	8	25	29
Cambodia	..	2,871	..	51	..	15	..	6	..	35
Cameroon	6,741	8,701	31	42	26	22	10	11	43	36
Canada	266,003	580,623	4	..	38	..	19	..	58	..
Central African Republic	797	1,057	40	53	20	19	7	9	40	29
Chad	1,033	1,694	45	40	9	14	..	13	46	46
Chile	27,572	78,738	7	7	37	30	21	15	55	62
China	201,687	959,030	30	18	49	49	41	37	21	33
Hong Kong, China	28,496	166,440	1	*0*	32	*15*	24	*7*	67	*85*
Colombia	38,900	102,896	22	13	26	25	18	13	51	61
Congo, Dem. Rep.	14,922	6,964	25	*58*	33	*17*	14	..	42	*25*
Congo, Rep.	1,706	1,961	12	12	47	50	7	8	42	39
Costa Rica	4,831	10,479	18	15	27	24	19	19	55	61
Côte d'Ivoire	10,175	11,005	26	26	20	23	13	19	54	51
Croatia	..	21,752	..	9	..	32	..	21	..	59
Cuba	..	..	..	..	..	..	..	..	..	..
Czech Republic	29,123	56,379	7	4	63	39	..	..	30	57
Denmark	67,791	174,870	5	..	29	..	20	..	66	..
Dominican Republic	6,631	15,853	20	12	28	33	15	17	52	56
Ecuador	11,733	18,360	12	13	38	35	18	24	50	52
Egypt, Arab Rep.	22,912	82,710	18	17	37	32	12	26	45	50
El Salvador	3,574	11,870	38	12	22	28	16	22	40	60
Eritrea	..	650	..	*9*	..	*30*	..	*16*	..	*61*
Estonia	..	5,202	..	6	..	27	..	15	..	67
Ethiopia	*5,179*	6,544	*56*	50	*12*	7	*8*	..	*32*	44
Finland	51,306	123,502	10	*4*	40	*34*	28	*25*	51	*62*
France	664,596	1,426,967	4	*2*	34	*26*	24	*19*	62	*72*
Gabon	4,279	5,518	7	7	60	60	5	5	33	32
Gambia, The	241	416	31	27	15	14	6	6	54	59
Georgia	..	5,129	24	26	36	16	28	16	40	58
Germany	..	2,134,205	..	*1*	..	..	..	*24*	..	*44*
Ghana	4,445	7,501	58	10	12	7	8	2	30	83
Greece	48,613	120,724	14	..	25	..	16	..	61	..
Guatemala	7,879	18,942	25	23	22	20	17	14	53	57
Guinea	..	3,598	..	22	..	35	..	4	..	42
Guinea-Bissau	111	206	44	62	20	13	..	9	36	25
Haiti	1,462	3,871	..	30	..	20	..	7	..	50
Honduras	2,566	5,371	24	20	24	31	15	18	52	49

Structure of output 4.2

	Gross domestic product		Agriculture value added		Industry value added		Manufacturing value added		Services value added	
	$ millions		% of GDP		% of GDP		% of GDP		% of GDP	
	1980	1998	1980	1998	1980	1998	1980	1998	1980	1998
Hungary	22,164	47,807	19	*6*	47	*34*	..	*25*	34	*60*
India	186,392	430,024	38	29	24	25	16	16	38	46
Indonesia	78,013	94,156	24	20	42	45	13	25	34	35
Iran, Islamic Rep.	92,664	113,140	18	*25*	32	*37*	9	*15*	50	*38*
Iraq	47,562	..	..	..	..	..	..	..	..	..
Ireland	20,080	81,949	..	..	..	..	..	..	..	..
Israel	21,781	100,525	..	..	..	..	..	..	..	..
Italy	449,913	1,171,865	6	*3*	39	*31*	28	*20*	55	*67*
Jamaica	2,652	6,418	8	8	38	34	17	15	54	58
Japan	1,059,254	3,782,964	4	*2*	42	*37*	29	*24*	54	*61*
Jordan	3,962	7,393	8	3	28	26	13	14	64	71
Kazakhstan	..	21,979	..	9	..	31	..	..	..	60
Kenya	7,265	11,579	33	26	21	16	13	11	47	58
Korea, Dem. Rep.	..	..	..	..	..	..	..	..	..	..
Korea, Rep.	62,543	320,748	14	5	40	43	28	31	46	52
Kuwait	28,639	25,171	0	..	75	..	6	..	25	..
Kyrgyz Republic	..	1,704	..	46	..	24	..	18	..	30
Lao PDR	..	1,261	..	53	..	22	..	17	..	25
Latvia	..	6,396	12	5	51	29	46	20	37	66
Lebanon	..	17,229	..	12	..	27	..	17	..	61
Lesotho	368	792	24	11	29	42	7	*17*	47	47
Libya	35,545	..	2	..	76	..	2	..	22	..
Lithuania	..	10,736	..	10	..	33	..	19	..	57
Macedonia, FYR	..	2,492	..	11	..	28	..	..	..	60
Madagascar	4,042	3,749	30	31	16	14	..	*11*	54	56
Malawi	1,238	1,688	44	36	23	18	14	14	34	46
Malaysia	24,488	72,489	22	13	38	44	21	29	40	43
Mali	1,787	2,695	48	47	13	17	7	4	38	36
Mauritania	814	989	30	25	26	30	..	9	44	46
Mauritius	1,132	4,199	12	9	26	33	15	25	62	58
Mexico	223,510	393,508	8	5	31	27	21	20	61	68
Moldova	..	1,615	..	29	..	31	..	23	..	40
Mongolia	..	1,042	*15*	33	*33*	28	..	..	*52*	40
Morocco	18,821	35,546	18	17	31	32	17	17	51	51
Mozambique	3,526	3,893	37	34	34	21	..	11	28	45
Myanmar	..	..	47	53	13	9	10	6	41	38
Namibia	2,262	3,092	11	10	55	34	9	14	34	56
Nepal	1,946	4,783	62	40	12	22	4	10	26	37
Netherlands	171,861	381,819	3	..	32	..	18	..	64	..
New Zealand	22,395	52,845	11	..	31	..	22	..	58	..
Nicaragua	2,144	2,007	23	34	31	22	26	15	45	44
Niger	2,509	2,048	43	41	23	17	4	6	34	42
Nigeria	64,202	41,353	21	32	46	41	8	*5*	34	27
Norway	63,419	145,892	4	*2*	35	*32*	15	*11*	61	*66*
Oman	5,982	14,962	3	..	69	..	1	..	28	..
Pakistan	23,690	63,369	30	26	25	25	16	17	46	49
Panama	3,810	9,144	10	8	21	18	12	9	69	74
Papua New Guinea	2,548	3,746	33	24	27	42	10	9	40	33
Paraguay	4,579	8,608	29	25	27	26	16	15	44	49
Peru	20,661	62,745	10	7	42	37	20	23	48	56
Philippines	32,500	65,107	25	17	39	32	26	22	36	51
Poland	56,789	158,574	..	*5*	..	32	..	19	..	*62*
Portugal	28,730	106,697	..	..	..	..	..	..	..	..
Puerto Rico	14,436	..	3	..	39	..	37	..	58	..
Romania	..	38,158	..	16	..	40	..	30	..	43
Russian Federation	..	276,611	..	7	..	35	..	..	..	57

4.2 Structure of output

	Gross domestic product		Agriculture value added		Industry value added		Manufacturing value added		Services value added	
	$ millions		% of GDP		% of GDP		% of GDP		% of GDP	
	1980	1998	1980	1998	1980	1998	1980	1998	1980	1998
Rwanda	1,163	2,024	50	47	23	21	17	13	27	31
Saudi Arabia	156,487	128,892	1	7	81	48	5	10	18	45
Senegal	2,987	4,682	19	17	15	24	11	16	66	59
Sierra Leone	1,199	647	33	44	21	24	5	6	47	32
Singapore	11,718	84,379	1	0	38	35	29	23	61	65
Slovak Republic	..	20,362	..	4	..	32	..	23	..	64
Slovenia	..	19,524	..	4	..	39	..	28	..	57
South Africa	80,544	133,461	6	4	48	32	22	19	46	64
Spain	213,308	553,230	..	*3*	..	..	..	*18*	..	*25*
Sri Lanka	4,024	15,707	28	21	30	28	18	17	43	51
Sudan	7,617	10,366	33	39	14	18	7	9	53	43
Sweden	125,557	226,492	4	..	34	..	23	..	63	..
Switzerland	107,474	263,630	..	..	..	..	..	..	..	..
Syrian Arab Republic	13,062	17,412	20	..	23	..	..	..	56	..
Tajikistan	..	2,164	..	6	..	30	..	..	..	65
Tanzania[a]	..	8,016	..	46	..	15	..	7	..	39
Thailand	32,354	111,327	23	11	29	41	22	32	48	48
Togo	1,136	1,510	27	42	25	21	8	9	48	37
Trinidad and Tobago	6,236	6,382	2	2	60	48	9	10	38	51
Tunisia	8,743	19,956	14	12	31	28	12	18	55	59
Turkey	68,790	198,844	26	18	22	25	14	16	51	57
Turkmenistan	..	2,367	..	25	..	42	..	29	..	34
Uganda	1,245	6,775	72	45	4	18	4	9	23	38
Ukraine	..	43,615	..	14	..	34	..	29	..	51
United Arab Emirates	29,625	47,234	1	..	77	..	4	..	22	..
United Kingdom	537,383	1,357,197	2	*2*	43	*31*	27	*21*	55	*67*
United States	2,709,000	8,230,397	3	*2*	33	*26*	22	*18*	64	*72*
Uruguay	10,132	20,578	14	8	34	27	26	18	53	64
Uzbekistan	..	20,384	..	31	..	27	..	13	..	42
Venezuela, RB	69,377	95,023	5	5	46	34	16	15	49	61
Vietnam	..	27,184	..	26	..	33	..	..	..	42
West Bank and Gaza	..	3,589	..	7	..	26	..	15	..	67
Yemen, Rep.	..	4,318	..	18	..	49	..	11	..	34
Yugoslavia, FR (Serb./Mont.)	..	..	..	..	..	..	..	..	..	..
Zambia	3,884	3,352	14	17	41	26	18	11	44	56
Zimbabwe	6,679	6,338	16	19	29	24	22	17	55	56
World	10,960,147 t	28,736,978 t	7 w	*4* w	38 w	*32* w	25 w	*21* w	55 w	*62* w
Low income	811,234	1,880,673	31	23	38	39	27	27	30	38
Excl. China & India	451,833	463,829	29	26	32	33	13	19	39	41
Middle income	2,322,822	4,312,567	12	9	42	33	24	22	46	58
Lower middle income	..	1,477,327	15	11	41	34	..	*22*	44	54
Upper middle income	1,164,279	2,838,231	11	8	42	32	26	22	47	60
Low & middle income	3,137,067	6,193,861	18	13	41	35	25	23	42	52
East Asia & Pacific	503,584	1,693,340	24	15	42	45	30	32	33	41
Europe & Central Asia	..	1,003,000	..	12	..	33	..	..	..	55
Latin America & Carib.	787,863	2,028,359	10	8	40	29	28	21	50	64
Middle East & N. Africa	409,860	583,374	10	*14*	53	*43*	9	*14*	37	*43*
South Asia	237,289	565,131	37	28	24	25	16	16	39	47
Sub-Saharan Africa	271,814	333,865	18	17	38	29	16	15	44	54
High income	7,936,135	22,543,577	3	*2*	37	*30*	25	*21*	59	*65*
Europe EMU	..	6,457,663	..	*2*	..	..	..	*21*	..	*58*

a. Data cover mainland Tanzania only.

Structure of output 4.2

About the data

A country's gross domestic product represents the sum of value added by all producers in that country. Value added is the value of gross output of producers less the value of intermediate goods and services consumed in production, excluding the consumption of fixed capital in the production process. Since 1968 the United Nations System of National Accounts has called for estimates of value added to be valued at either basic prices (excluding net taxes on products) or producer prices (including net taxes on products paid by the producers, but excluding sales or value added taxes). Both valuations exclude transport charges that are invoiced separately by the producers. Some countries, however, report such data at purchaser prices—the prices at which final sales are made (including transport charges)—which may affect estimates of the distribution of output. Total GDP as shown in the table and elsewhere in this book is measured at purchaser prices. Value added by industry is normally measured at basic prices. When value added is measured at producer prices, this is noted in *Primary data documentation.*

While GDP estimated by the production approach is generally more reliable than estimates compiled from the income or expenditure side, different countries use different definitions, methods, and reporting standards. World Bank staff review the quality of national accounts data and sometimes make adjustments to increase consistency with international guidelines. Nevertheless, significant discrepancies remain between international standards and actual practice. Many statistical offices, especially those in developing countries, face severe limits in the resources, time, training, and budgets required to produce reliable and comprehensive series of national accounts.

Data problems in measuring output

Among the difficulties faced by compilers of national accounts is the extent of unreported economic activity in the informal or secondary economy. In developing countries a large share of agricultural output is either not exchanged (because it is consumed within the household) or not exchanged for money.

Agricultural production often must be estimated indirectly, using a combination of methods involving estimates of inputs, yields, and area under cultivation. This approach sometimes leads to crude approximations that can differ from the true values over time and across crops for reasons other than climatic conditions or farming techniques. Similarly, agricultural inputs, which cannot easily be allocated to specific outputs, are frequently "netted out" using equally crude and ad hoc approximations. For further discussion of the measurement of agricultural production see *About the data* for table 3.3.

Industrial output ideally should be measured through regular censuses and surveys of firms. But in most developing countries such surveys are infrequent, so survey results must be extrapolated using an appropriate indicator. The choice of sampling unit, which may be the enterprise (where responses may be based on financial records) or the establishment (where production units may be recorded separately), also affects the quality of the data. Moreover, much industrial production is organized in unincorporated or owner-operated ventures that are not captured by surveys aimed at the formal sector. Even in large industries, where regular surveys are more likely, evasion of excise and other taxes lowers the estimates of value added. Such problems become more acute as countries move from state control of industry to private enterprise, because new firms enter business and growing numbers of established firms fail to report. In accordance with the System of National Accounts, output should include all such unreported activity as well as the value of illegal activities and other unrecorded, informal, or small-scale operations. Data on these activities need to be collected using techniques other than conventional surveys.

In industries dominated by large organizations and enterprises, such as public utilities, data on output, employment, and wages are usually readily available and reasonably reliable. But in the service industry the many self-employed workers and one-person businesses are sometimes difficult to locate, and their owners have little incentive to respond to surveys, let alone report their full earnings. Compounding these problems are the many forms of economic activity that go unrecorded, including the work that women and children do for little or no pay. For further discussion of the problems of using national accounts data see Srinivasan (1994) and Heston (1994).

Dollar conversion

To produce national accounts aggregates that are internationally comparable, the value of output must be converted to a common currency. The World Bank conventionally uses the U.S. dollar and applies the average official exchange rate reported by the International Monetary Fund for the year shown. An alternative conversion factor is applied if the official exchange rate is judged to diverge by an exceptionally large margin from the rate effectively applied to transactions in foreign currencies and traded products.

Definitions

• **Gross domestic product** at purchaser prices is the sum of the gross value added by all resident institutional units engaged in production plus indirect taxes and minus any subsidies not included in the value of their products. It is calculated without making deductions for depreciation of fabricated assets or for depletion and degradation of natural resources. The residency of an institution is determined on the basis of economic interest in the territory for more than a year. • **Value added** is the net output of an industry after adding up all outputs and subtracting intermediate inputs. The origin of value added is determined by the International Standard Industrial Classification (ISIC) revision 3. • **Agriculture** corresponds to ISIC divisions 1–5 and includes forestry and fishing. • **Industry** comprises value added in mining, manufacturing (also reported as a separate subgroup), construction, electricity, water, and gas (ISIC divisions 10–45). • **Manufacturing** refers to industries belonging to divisions 15–37. • **Services** correspond to ISIC divisions 50–99.

Data sources

The national accounts indicators for most developing countries are collected from national statistical organizations and central banks by visiting and resident World Bank missions. The data for high-income economies come from Organisation for Economic Co-operation and Development (OECD) data files; see the OECD's *Main Economic Indicators* (monthly). The United Nations Statistics Division publishes detailed national accounts for United Nations member countries in *National Accounts Statistics: Main Aggregates and Detailed Tables;* updates are published in the *Monthly Bulletin of Statistics.*

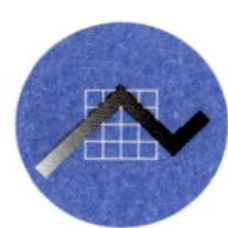

4.3 Structure of manufacturing

	Value added in manufacturing		Food, beverages, and tobacco		Textiles and clothing		Machinery and transport equipment		Chemicals		Other manufacturing[a]	
	$ millions		% of total		% of total		% of total		% of total		% of total	
	1980	1997	1980	1997	1980	1997	1980	1997	1980	1997	1980	1997
Albania	..	..	..	..	..	..	..	..	..	..	..	..
Algeria	3,257	4,088	27	*19*	18	*11*	10	*0*	3	*0*	43	*70*
Angola	..	330	..	..	..	..	..	..	..	..	..	..
Argentina	22,685	53,382	19	..	13	..	19	..	9	..	41	..
Armenia	..	368	..	..	..	..	..	..	..	..	..	..
Australia	30,722	*56,576*	17	16	7	10	21	19	7	7	46	49
Austria	19,263	*45,387*	16	19	10	15	25	16	7	8	42	42
Azerbaijan	..	948	..	..	..	..	..	..	..	..	..	..
Bangladesh	3,101	7,106	24	29	43	47	4	..	16	9	14	15
Belarus	..	6,598	..	..	..	..	..	..	..	..	..	..
Belgium	25,773	44,567	17	18	8	15	24	24	11	7	40	37
Benin	112	180	59	..	14	..	..	..	6	..	21	..
Bolivia	..	1,354	28	*35*	11	*5*	4	*1*	3	*3*	54	*55*
Bosnia and Herzegovina	..	..	..	..	..	..	..	..	..	..	..	..
Botswana	60	242	..	..	..	..	..	..	..	..	..	..
Brazil	71,098	160,432	..	..	..	..	..	..	..	..	..	..
Bulgaria	..	1,685	..	*20*	..	*10*	..	*5*	..	..	..	*65*
Burkina Faso	261	456	59	62	19	14	3	..	1	2	17	22
Burundi	63	84	78	..	11	..	0	..	3	..	8	..
Cambodia	..	178	..	..	..	..	..	..	..	..	..	..
Cameroon	593	936	56	*43*	9	*11*	4	*1*	3	*4*	29	*41*
Canada	46,128	..	14	14	7	5	23	30	8	10	48	42
Central African Republic	54	87	49	..	22	..	8	..	11	..	10	..
Chad	..	190	..	..	..	..	..	..	..	..	..	..
Chile	5,911	11,319	27	28	9	6	6	5	8	12	51	50
China	81,836	343,120	10	*15*	18	*12*	22	*25*	11	*12*	38	*36*
Hong Kong, China	6,392	10,612	5	*10*	42	*27*	18	*27*	2	*2*	34	*33*
Colombia	6,933	14,266	30	*30*	16	*11*	9	*8*	10	*17*	35	*35*
Congo, Dem. Rep.	2,144	..	..	..	..	..	..	..	..	..	..	..
Congo, Rep.	128	141	*35*	..	*16*	..	*5*	..	..	..	*44*	..
Costa Rica	899	1,832	46	53	10	13	8	3	7	7	28	24
Côte d'Ivoire	1,304	1,868	35	32	15	18	10	15	..	..	40	35
Croatia	..	3,736	..	..	..	..	..	..	..	..	..	..
Cuba	..	..	55	..	7	..	1	..	..	..	37	..
Czech Republic	..	..	..	..	..	..	..	..	..	..	..	..
Denmark	11,411	*29,628*	24	20	5	3	25	26	10	14	37	36
Dominican Republic	1,015	2,560	66	..	6	..	1	..	6	..	21	..
Ecuador	2,072	4,221	34	*26*	13	*6*	7	*4*	9	*7*	38	*56*
Egypt, Arab Rep.	2,678	17,803	19	18	30	39	11	10	9	13	31	20
El Salvador	589	2,350	37	36	22	37	4	2	11	9	27	16
Eritrea	..	91	..	..	..	..	..	..	..	..	..	..
Estonia	..	695	..	..	..	..	..	..	..	..	..	..
Ethiopia	*381*	..	..	*52*	..	*18*	..	*2*	..	*4*	..	*23*
Finland	13,019	*28,129*	..	..	..	..	..	..	..	..	..	..
France	160,811	268,930	13	13	8	12	30	23	8	7	41	45
Gabon	195	235	24	24	4	2	9	*1*	4	1	58	73
Gambia, The	12	22	35	..	2	..	..	..	3	..	60	..
Georgia	..	801	..	..	..	..	..	..	..	..	..	..
Germany	..	493,058	..	..	..	..	..	..	..	..	..	..
Ghana	347	185	37	*36*	11	*5*	2	*2*	5	*10*	46	*48*
Greece	6,968	*10,719*	18	26	23	13	14	13	8	12	37	36
Guatemala	1,312	2,445	39	..	10	..	5	..	17	..	28	..
Guinea	..	162	..	..	..	..	..	..	..	..	..	..
Guinea-Bissau	..	30	..	..	..	..	..	..	..	..	..	..
Haiti	..	..	..	*46*	..	*19*	..	..	..	..	..	*34*
Honduras	344	733	*51*	60	*9*	8	*2*	0	*5*	7	*34*	26

Structure of manufacturing 4.3

	Value added in manufacturing		Food, beverages, and tobacco		Textiles and clothing		Machinery and transport equipment		Chemicals		Other manufacturing[a]	
	$ millions		% of total		% of total		% of total		% of total		% of total	
	1980	1997	1980	1997	1980	1997	1980	1997	1980	1997	1980	1997
Hungary	..	9,698	11	20	11	7	28	24	11	9	38	40
India	27,061	64,552	9	12	21	14	25	25	14	17	30	32
Indonesia	10,133	57,805	32	19	14	19	13	18	11	9	30	35
Iran, Islamic Rep.	8,567	13,022	15	33	19	24	12	14	5	4	49	25
Iraq	..	..	..	29	..	16	..	6	..	2	..	48
Ireland	..	..	29	*23*	8	*2*	17	*34*	14	*22*	32	*18*
Israel	..	..	12	17	12	15	26	18	8	7	42	42
Italy	126,012	229,610	9	..	12	..	29	..	11	..	39	..
Jamaica	441	673	47	*48*	6	*7*	..	..	..	..	47	*46*
Japan	309,747	1,020,540	9	10	7	4	33	40	9	10	43	37
Jordan	447	835	23	*32*	7	*6*	1	*4*	7	*16*	62	*42*
Kazakhstan	..	..	..	..	..	..	..	..	..	..	..	..
Kenya	796	883	34	*48*	12	*7*	15	*10*	9	*8*	30	*27*
Korea, Dem. Rep.	..	..	..	..	..	..	..	..	..	..	..	..
Korea, Rep.	17,416	137,674	17	26	19	20	17	9	10	10	36	35
Kuwait	1,581	2,913	7	*6*	5	*4*	4	*3*	7	*5*	76	*81*
Kyrgyz Republic	..	292	..	..	..	..	..	..	..	..	..	..
Lao PDR	..	271	..	..	..	..	..	..	..	..	..	..
Latvia	..	1,093	..	*39*	..	*12*	..	*15*	..	*6*	..	*29*
Lebanon	..	2,319	..	..	..	..	..	..	..	..	..	..
Lesotho	21	141	73	..	7	..	..	..	4	..	16	..
Libya	682	..	31	43	10	12	..	2	16	7	43	36
Lithuania	..	1,760	..	..	..	..	..	..	..	..	..	..
Macedonia, FYR	..	..	..	*32*	..	*18*	..	*15*	..	*11*	..	*24*
Madagascar	..	365	*34*	..	*45*	..	*3*	..	*6*	..	*13*	..
Malawi	152	311	58	..	12	..	4	..	5	..	20	..
Malaysia	5,054	28,489	24	*10*	7	*5*	20	*39*	5	*9*	43	*38*
Mali	105	92	..	..	..	..	..	..	..	..	..	..
Mauritania	..	97	..	..	..	..	..	..	..	..	..	..
Mauritius	147	888	36	*31*	30	*46*	6	*2*	6	*4*	23	*17*
Mexico	45,939	69,728	..	*25*	..	*3*	..	*22*	..	*20*	..	*30*
Moldova	..	353	..	..	..	..	..	..	..	..	..	..
Mongolia	..	..	..	*23*	..	*63*	..	*0*	..	*1*	..	*12*
Morocco	3,167	5,900	..	..	..	..	..	..	..	..	..	..
Mozambique	..	357	..	..	..	..	..	..	..	..	..	..
Myanmar	..	..	..	..	..	..	..	..	..	..	..	..
Namibia	187	402	..	..	..	..	..	..	..	..	..	..
Nepal	78	435	..	*35*	..	*34*	..	*3*	..	*6*	..	*23*
Netherlands	30,866	*70,407*	19	*24*	4	*2*	27	*25*	11	*14*	38	*34*
New Zealand	4,950	..	26	26	11	12	17	15	6	5	40	42
Nicaragua	550	298	53	52	8	18	1	0	10	25	28	4
Niger	94	122	30	*23*	25	*1*	2	..	16	..	28	*76*
Nigeria	5,195	1,839	*21*	..	*13*	..	*13*	..	*13*	..	*39*	..
Norway	9,196	17,055	15	16	4	9	27	22	7	8	48	45
Oman	39	..	..	..	..	..	..	..	..	..	..	..
Pakistan	3,389	9,813	32	29	22	43	9	6	12	12	25	10
Panama	408	756	49	48	10	7	2	2	6	3	34	39
Papua New Guinea	242	452	40	..	1	..	16	..	3	..	41	..
Paraguay	733	1,408	38	56	12	16	1	1	3	5	46	21
Peru	4,176	14,613	25	..	13	..	13	..	10	..	40	..
Philippines	8,354	18,333	30	33	13	9	12	15	14	13	31	29
Poland	..	28,153	12	28	17	7	32	22	8	7	31	35
Portugal	..	*26,510*	13	14	22	17	16	15	7	5	42	49
Puerto Rico	5,306	..	..	*15*	..	*5*	..	*12*	..	*50*	..	*18*
Romania	..	9,791	..	..	..	..	..	..	..	..	..	..
Russian Federation	..	..	..	*17*	..	*4*	..	*20*	..	*9*	..	*51*

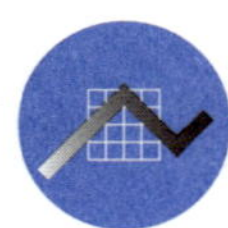

4.3 Structure of manufacturing

	Value added in manufacturing		Food, beverages, and tobacco		Textiles and clothing		Machinery and transport equipment		Chemicals		Other manufacturing[a]	
	$ millions		% of total		% of total		% of total		% of total		% of total	
	1980	1997	1980	1997	1980	1997	1980	1997	1980	1997	1980	1997
Rwanda	178	230	..	..	..	..	..	..	..	..	..	..
Saudi Arabia	7,740	13,511	..	..	..	..	..	..	..	..	..	..
Senegal	316	671	50	*44*	19	*3*	4	*2*	8	*30*	20	*20*
Sierra Leone	54	54	*51*	..	*5*	..	..	..	..	..	*44*	..
Singapore	3,415	21,995	5	3	5	1	44	60	5	9	41	26
Slovak Republic	..	4,597	..	..	..	..	..	..	..	..	..	..
Slovenia	..	4,423	..	*13*	..	*12*	..	*15*	..	*11*	..	*50*
South Africa	16,381	26,880	12	*16*	9	*7*	21	*19*	9	*10*	48	*48*
Spain	..	*103,623*	..	..	..	..	..	..	..	..	..	..
Sri Lanka	668	2,235	32	27	14	23	6	18	6	19	42	13
Sudan	517	891	..	37	..	36	..	..	..	3	..	24
Sweden	26,293	..	10	8	3	1	33	37	7	11	47	43
Switzerland	..	..	..	*10*	..	*3*	..	*30*	..	..	..	*57*
Syrian Arab Republic	..	..	*29*	35	*26*	43	..	2	..	1	*45*	19
Tajikistan	..	..	..	..	..	..	..	..	..	..	..	..
Tanzania[b]	..	458	23	42	33	29	8	9	6	7	30	12
Thailand	6,960	46,502	*55*	55	*8*	5	*9*	8	*7*	8	*21*	24
Togo	89	126	47	34	13	28	..	..	8	6	32	31
Trinidad and Tobago	557	440	22	19	4	3	9	4	4	1	61	73
Tunisia	1,030	3,479	18	29	19	15	7	4	15	20	42	32
Turkey	9,333	30,971	18	13	15	16	14	21	10	12	42	38
Turkmenistan	..	825	..	..	..	..	..	..	..	..	..	..
Uganda	53	488	..	*31*	..	*23*	..	..	..	*4*	..	*42*
Ukraine	..	13,167	..	..	..	..	..	..	..	..	..	..
United Arab Emirates	1,130	..	*12*	..	*2*	..	*2*	..	*7*	..	*77*	..
United Kingdom	125,830	*213,752*	13	14	6	5	33	30	10	12	38	39
United States	589,100	1,392,500	11	11	6	4	34	37	10	11	40	37
Uruguay	2,627	3,613	28	*44*	17	*14*	10	*5*	7	*11*	38	*26*
Uzbekistan	..	2,613	..	..	..	..	..	..	..	..	..	..
Venezuela, RB	11,112	14,252	19	*28*	7	*5*	9	*10*	8	*12*	57	*45*
Vietnam	..	..	..	..	..	..	..	..	..	..	..	..
West Bank and Gaza	..	518	..	..	..	..	..	..	..	..	..	..
Yemen, Rep.	..	592	..	..	..	..	..	..	..	..	..	..
Yugoslavia, FR (Serb./Mont.)	..	..	..	*29*	..	*9*	..	*16*	..	*11*	..	*34*
Zambia	718	466	44	36	13	13	9	10	9	4	25	37
Zimbabwe	1,384	1,293	23	31	17	15	8	8	9	9	42	36
World	**2,421,714 t**	**5,877,746 t**										
Low income	154,170	516,601										
Excl. China & India	46,667	103,992										
Middle income	..	974,235										
Lower middle income	..	..										
Upper middle income	..	607,753										
Low & middle income	509,900	1,498,231										
East Asia & Pacific	137,607	644,796										
Europe & Central Asia	..	..										
Latin America & Carib.	..	383,146										
Middle East & N. Africa	29,396	73,382										
South Asia	34,841	85,513										
Sub-Saharan Africa	33,005	43,553										
High income	1,901,096	4,382,970										
Europe EMU	..	1,289,559										

a. Includes unallocated data. b. Data cover mainland Tanzania only.

Structure of manufacturing 4.3

About the data

The data on the distribution of manufacturing value added by industry are provided by the United Nations Industrial Development Organization (UNIDO). UNIDO obtains data on manufacturing value added from a variety of national and international sources, including the United Nations Statistics Division, the World Bank, the Organisation for Economic Co-operation and Development, and the International Monetary Fund. To improve comparability over time and across countries, UNIDO supplements these data with information from industrial censuses, statistics supplied by national and international organizations, unpublished data that it collects in the field, and estimates by the UNIDO Secretariat. Nevertheless, coverage may be less than complete, particularly for the informal sector. To the extent that direct information on inputs and outputs is not available, estimates may be used that may result in errors in industry totals. Moreover, countries use different reference periods (calendar or fiscal year) and valuation methods (basic, producer, or purchaser prices) to estimate value added. (See also *About the data* for table 4.2.)

The data on manufacturing value added in U.S. dollars are from the World Bank's national accounts files. These figures may differ from those used by UNIDO to calculate the shares of value added by industry. Thus estimates of value added in a particular industry group calculated by applying the shares to total value added will not match those from UNIDO sources.

The classification of manufacturing industries in the table accords with the United Nations International Standard Industrial Classification (ISIC) revision 2. First published in 1948, the ISIC has its roots in the work of the League of Nations Committee of Statistical Experts. The committee's efforts, interrupted by the second world war, were taken up by the United Nations Statistical Commission, which at its first session appointed a committee on industrial classification. The ISIC has been revised at approximately 20-year intervals. The last revision, ISIC revision 3, was completed in 1989. Revision 2 is still widely used for compiling cross-country data, however, and concordances matching ISIC categories to national systems of classification and to related systems such as the Standard International Trade Classification (SITC) are readily available.

In establishing a classification system, compilers must define both the types of activities to be described and the organizational units whose activities are to be reported. There are many possibilities, and the choices made affect how the resulting statistics can be interpreted and how useful they are in analyzing economic behavior. The ISIC emphasizes commonalities in the production process and is explicitly not intended to measure outputs (for which there is a newly developed Central Product Classification); nevertheless, the ISIC views an activity as defined by " . . . a process resulting in a homogeneous set of products" (United Nations 1990b [ISIC, series M, no. 4, rev. 3], p. 9). Typically, firms use a multitude of processes to produce a final product. For example, an automobile manufacturer engages in forging, welding, and painting as well as advertising, accounting, and many other service activities. In some cases the processes may be carried out by different technical units within the larger enterprise, but collecting data at such a detailed level is not practical. Nor would it be useful to record production data at the very highest level of a large, multiplant, multiproduct firm. The ISIC has therefore adopted as the definition of an establishment "an enterprise or part of an enterprise which independently engages in one, or predominantly one, kind of economic activity at or from one location . . . for which data are available . . ." (United Nations 1990b, p. 25). By design, this definition matches the reporting unit required for the production accounts of the United Nations System of National Accounts.

Figure 4.3

Manufacturing growth slowed in East Asia

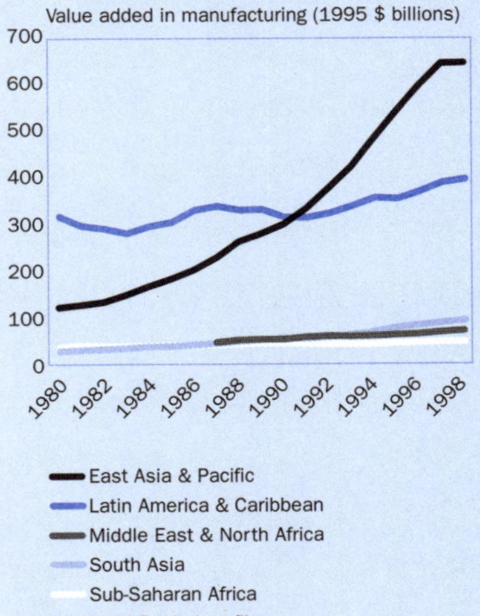

Source: World Bank data files.

As a financial crisis swept through East Asia, growth in manufacturing almost came to a halt in the region—for the first time in two decades.

Definitions

• **Value added in manufacturing** is the sum of gross output less the value of intermediate inputs used in production for industries classified in ISIC major division 3. • **Food, beverages, and tobacco** comprise ISIC division 31. • **Textiles and clothing** comprise ISIC division 32. • **Machinery and transport equipment** comprise ISIC groups 382–84. • **Chemicals** comprise ISIC groups 351 and 352. • **Other manufacturing** includes wood and related products (ISIC division 33), paper and related products (ISIC division 34), petroleum and related products (ISIC groups 353–56), basic metals and mineral products (ISIC divisions 36 and 37), fabricated metal products and professional goods (ISIC groups 381 and 385), and other industries (ISIC group 390). When data for textiles and clothing, machinery and transport equipment, or chemicals are shown as not available, they are included in other manufacturing.

Data sources

The data on value added in manufacturing in U.S. dollars are from the World Bank's national accounts files. The data used to calculate shares of value added by industry are provided to the World Bank in electronic files by UNIDO. The most recent published source is UNIDO's *International Yearbook of Industrial Statistics 1999*. The ISIC system is described in the United Nations' *International Standard Industrial Classification of all Economic Activities, Third Revision* (1990b). The discussion of the ISIC draws on Jacob Ryten's paper "Fifty Years of ISIC: Historical Origins and Future Perspectives" (1998).

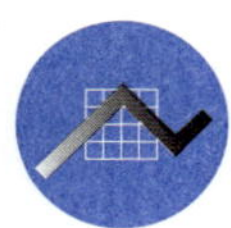

4.4 Growth of merchandise trade

	Export volume		Import volume		Export value		Import value		Net barter terms of trade	
	average annual % growth		average annual % growth		average annual % growth		average annual % growth		1995 = 100	
	1980–90	1990–97	1980–90	1990–97	1980–90	1990–97	1980–90	1990–97	1990	1997
Albania	..	..	..	..	..	..	..	..	..	..
Algeria	4.0	2.4	–4.8	0.6	–3.9	0.2	–2.9	0.7	127	119
Angola	6.0	5.0	–0.3	–0.7	6.4	1.7	1.0	–1.6	145	100
Argentina	5.0	9.6	–6.9	25.1	2.1	13.4	–6.5	27.7	94	109
Armenia[a]	..	..	..	..	..	–18.2	..	–7.4	..	..
Australia[a]	6.4	7.9	6.0	8.7	6.6	7.1	6.4	8.1	117	103
Austria[a]	6.6	..	5.7	..	10.2	6.2	8.7	5.0	..	..
Azerbaijan	..	..	..	..	..	..	..	..	..	..
Bangladesh	7.6	12.9	1.8	9.1	7.6	13.2	3.7	11.8	115	103
Belarus	..	..	..	..	..	..	..	..	..	..
Belgium[b]	4.5	6.2	4.0	5.4	7.8	6.3	6.4	4.5	100	99
Benin	3.7	31.6	–10.6	9.7	10.8	33.4	–4.9	14.7	116	86
Bolivia	3.1	2.8	–1.1	10.2	–1.9	5.8	–0.3	13.1	116	115
Bosnia and Herzegovina	..	..	..	..	..	..	..	..	..	..
Botswana	*10.0*	7.2	*12.9*	–1.9	18.0	8.4	9.3	0.5	118	104
Brazil	6.3	4.5	0.7	24.9	5.1	8.2	–1.9	19.2	60	107
Bulgaria[a]	..	..	..	..	*–12.3*	6.7	*–61.0*	–28.5	100	..
Burkina Faso	–0.3	6.1	3.2	0.0	7.9	8.6	3.8	1.1	91	95
Burundi	3.5	–2.5	1.0	–3.6	2.5	–1.8	2.2	–8.7	75	122
Cambodia	..	..	..	..	..	..	..	..	..	..
Cameroon	7.3	1.6	5.1	2.5	2.4	–1.3	0.1	–0.1	99	102
Canada[a]	6.4	9.1	7.4	8.6	6.8	8.9	7.9	7.4	100	100
Central African Republic	–0.1	20.5	4.9	15.1	3.3	20.7	8.6	5.0	68	125
Chad	8.6	–6.6	10.8	–11.2	9.4	–6.7	12.6	–8.4	116	95
Chile	7.1	10.1	3.3	15.0	8.1	11.7	2.6	15.3	84	87
China†	13.8	12.1	15.7	11.3	13.0	17.1	13.8	15.7	101	106
Hong Kong, China	10.9	11.7	9.2	13.3	16.7	12.7	15.0	14.5	102	102
Colombia	7.8	4.8	–2.1	17.7	7.7	8.6	0.0	19.0	94	113
Congo, Dem. Rep.	3.8	–15.8	4.4	–18.3	3.3	–12.5	3.6	–11.4	109	83
Congo, Rep.	5.3	9.6	–2.5	9.0	0.4	7.0	–0.5	11.0	147	124
Costa Rica	3.8	12.6	5.2	15.8	4.6	18.3	4.4	15.7	71	100
Côte d'Ivoire	2.6	5.5	–1.9	6.8	1.6	6.6	–1.4	5.4	82	96
Croatia[a]	..	..	..	..	..	2.3	..	11.5	..	..
Cuba	–1.1	–14.4	–0.4	–8.4	–0.9	–11.9	1.7	–7.4	96	104
Czech Republic	..	..	..	..	..	..	..	..	..	..
Denmark	4.1	5.6	3.1	6.3	8.4	5.5	6.3	5.7	100	100
Dominican Republic	–0.9	1.6	0.7	8.4	–2.1	4.2	3.3	10.7	94	103
Ecuador	7.1	10.2	–1.8	10.1	–0.4	10.9	–1.3	14.4	141	111
Egypt, Arab Rep.	1.8	0.7	–2.7	5.1	–3.7	4.3	1.4	7.8	82	96
El Salvador	–4.6	2.2	4.6	10.9	–4.6	13.2	2.5	14.0	69	106
Eritrea	..	..	..	..	..	..	..	..	..	..
Estonia	..	..	..	..	..	..	..	..	..	..
Ethiopia[a]	*0.4*	7.7	*4.2*	1.2	–0.8	15.5	4.4	10.5	90	82
Finland[a]	2.3	9.3	4.4	4.3	7.4	8.7	6.9	4.0	102	97
France[a]	3.6	5.5	3.7	4.6	7.5	5.1	6.5	3.1	94	99
Gabon	2.5	6.3	–3.6	2.6	–3.9	5.4	1.1	3.6	135	122
Gambia, The	–1.9	–18.5	–5.3	–0.8	1.2	–17.5	2.8	0.8	102	101
Georgia	..	..	..	..	..	..	..	..	..	..
Germany[a,c]	4.5	*3.0*	4.9	*1.8*	9.2	4.4	7.1	3.8	102	*100*
Ghana	–14.7	11.7	–17.5	15.5	0.3	13.5	2.8	16.8	93	95
Greece[a]	5.0	*9.0*	6.4	*9.8*	5.8	1.6	6.6	4.7	92	*100*
Guatemala	1.8	6.2	5.2	10.6	–2.2	11.6	0.6	11.9	75	103
Guinea	..	9.3	..	0.4	3.5	6.1	9.8	1.6	135	101
Guinea-Bissau	–2.3	18.0	–1.8	4.4	3.9	15.6	3.6	8.1	143	87
Haiti	–0.3	–3.3	–4.6	11.9	–1.1	–4.5	–2.9	11.9	116	101
Honduras	4.1	2.9	1.6	10.6	1.5	9.7	0.6	13.2	81	115
† Data for Taiwan, China[a]	16.5	4.8	17.6	6.6	14.7	9.1	12.4	10.9	101	105

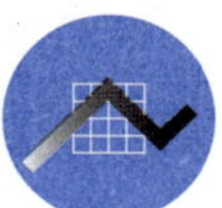

Growth of merchandise trade 4.4

	Export volume		Import volume		Export value		Import value		Net barter terms of trade	
	average annual % growth		average annual % growth		average annual % growth		average annual % growth		1995 = 100	
	1980–90	**1990–97**	**1980–90**	**1990–97**	**1980–90**	**1990–97**	**1980–90**	**1990–97**	**1990**	**1997**
Hungary[a]	3.4	*0.9*	1.3	*5.6*	1.2	6.2	0.1	11.0	100	..
India	–3.4	4.8	–2.8	5.0	7.2	11.5	4.3	10.2	79	83
Indonesia	8.6	8.0	1.9	10.0	–0.3	10.3	2.6	10.5	102	112
Iran, Islamic Rep.	10.5	0.6	–2.9	–11.7	1.1	1.6	–0.3	–8.2	169	139
Iraq	1.7	–10.9	–12.0	–16.8	–4.5	–13.0	–9.9	–14.7	120	93
Ireland[a]	9.3	13.4	4.8	9.7	12.8	13.6	7.0	10.7	107	101
Israel[a]	6.9	9.7	5.8	10.6	8.3	11.9	5.9	11.2	97	104
Italy[a]	4.3	6.7	5.3	3.1	8.7	6.5	6.9	2.4	98	104
Jamaica	1.1	4.3	3.0	9.3	0.6	4.1	2.9	10.4	105	100
Japan[a]	5.1	1.7	6.6	6.2	8.9	6.0	5.1	7.0	73	91
Jordan	1.8	5.5	–4.4	5.9	6.1	9.3	–1.9	7.9	85	99
Kazakhstan	..	..	..	..	..	..	..	..	..	..
Kenya	1.6	8.8	2.0	13.8	–1.0	11.5	1.5	9.0	72	114
Korea, Dem. Rep.	..	..	..	..	..	..	..	..	..	..
Korea, Rep.	11.5	11.7	10.9	9.7	14.9	12.3	11.8	12.4	98	78
Kuwait	–2.0	22.9	–6.3	11.6	–7.5	27.0	–4.1	10.1	91	111
Kyrgyz Republic	..	..	..	..	..	..	..	..	..	..
Lao PDR[a]	..	..	..	..	11.0	26.0	6.6	25.4	..	..
Latvia	..	..	..	..	..	..	..	..	..	..
Lebanon	–3.6	5.4	–7.4	13.4	–3.6	8.9	–5.5	16.7	104	107
Lesotho	4.1	12.4	0.4	2.5	3.3	19.2	1.7	5.8	84	94
Libya	0.4	–5.8	–6.2	–5.1	–7.0	–4.0	–4.0	–1.0	145	128
Lithuania	..	..	..	..	..	..	..	..	..	..
Macedonia, FYR[a]	..	..	..	..	..	*0.7*	..	*3.0*	..	..
Madagascar	–3.0	–4.4	–4.6	–3.3	–1.0	0.2	–2.7	–0.5	99	105
Malawi	2.4	3.5	–0.2	0.3	2.0	2.9	3.2	0.2	115	122
Malaysia	14.5	16.8	6.0	16.5	8.6	16.8	7.7	16.8	102	102
Mali	4.8	8.5	2.0	4.9	6.1	6.8	2.8	5.0	109	90
Mauritania	5.3	2.7	–1.3	8.3	7.9	4.7	0.5	8.2	93	108
Mauritius	10.3	3.9	11.2	3.0	14.4	5.5	12.8	6.0	109	100
Mexico	15.5	19.2	1.2	13.5	6.3	20.5	6.8	16.3	114	102
Moldova	..	..	..	..	..	..	..	..	..	..
Mongolia	3.2	..	0.9	..	5.0	–2.1	5.1	–5.0	..	..
Morocco	4.5	10.5	4.1	6.1	6.2	9.3	3.7	6.2	104	100
Mozambique	–9.6	9.8	–2.4	–3.3	–9.7	3.6	0.2	–2.4	141	97
Myanmar	–4.1	8.3	–6.5	21.4	–7.9	14.4	–4.5	27.0	94	96
Namibia[a]	..	..	..	..	..	*4.6*	..	*0.9*	..	..
Nepal[a]	..	..	..	..	8.1	8.1	6.9	15.1	..	..
Netherlands[a]	4.5	*6.9*	4.5	*6.3*	4.6	7.2	4.4	6.3	98	*99*
New Zealand[a]	3.5	5.5	4.3	6.4	6.2	7.5	5.4	9.0	103	97
Nicaragua	–4.8	15.4	–3.5	9.4	–5.8	16.3	–3.1	10.9	119	96
Niger	–5.1	0.0	–5.2	–2.1	–5.4	–1.6	–3.5	–1.1	120	110
Nigeria	–4.4	0.0	–21.4	–3.4	–8.4	3.4	–15.6	2.8	161	129
Norway[a]	4.1	8.2	3.4	7.3	5.3	6.1	6.2	5.4	112	112
Oman	6.7	4.6	–1.7	3.7	2.9	5.6	0.7	8.0	159	133
Pakistan	–0.3	–5.5	–5.3	–3.3	8.0	6.4	3.0	6.8	91	99
Panama	–0.5	5.8	–6.7	10.0	–0.4	11.0	–3.5	9.9	69	108
Papua New Guinea	1.3	–1.4	..	..	4.9	11.0	1.3	3.6	..	..
Paraguay	12.9	–1.1	10.4	16.4	11.6	4.6	4.3	16.9	87	118
Peru	2.7	8.7	–2.0	16.4	–1.5	12.3	1.3	18.0	93	104
Philippines	–7.5	16.2	–7.8	17.8	3.9	18.3	2.9	18.8	90	98
Poland[a]	4.8	7.9	1.5	20.3	1.4	11.0	–3.2	23.3	91	97
Portugal[a]	*11.9*	..	*15.1*	..	15.1	5.9	10.3	4.4	100	..
Puerto Rico	..	..	..	..	..	..	..	..	..	..
Romania[a]	..	..	..	..	–4.0	9.8	–3.8	7.3	..	..
Russian Federation	..	..	..	..	..	..	..	..	..	..

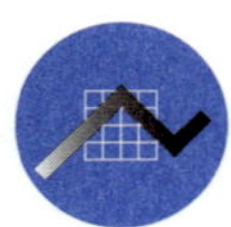

4.4 Growth of merchandise trade

	Export volume		Import volume		Export value		Import value		Net barter terms of trade	
	average annual % growth		average annual % growth		average annual % growth		average annual % growth		1995 = 100	
	1980–90	**1990–97**	**1980–90**	**1990–97**	**1980–90**	**1990–97**	**1980–90**	**1990–97**	**1990**	**1997**
Rwanda	4.7	–10.6	2.4	–2.1	1.1	–6.8	3.2	–2.7	53	105
Saudi Arabia	–6.3	4.1	–8.4	–3.4	–13.4	4.3	–6.1	0.3	169	134
Senegal	1.1	9.7	0.4	–1.6	3.5	5.4	1.4	0.8	130	87
Sierra Leone	0.0	–30.8	–5.8	–4.5	–2.4	–26.5	–8.7	–2.6	88	104
Singapore	13.6	14.7	19.2	13.4	9.9	15.3	8.2	13.5	98	100
Slovak Republic	..	..	..	..	..	..	..	..	..	..
Slovenia[a]	..	..	..	..	..	12.1	..	13.1	..	..
South Africa[a]	3.3	*7.4*	–0.8	*7.9*	0.7	4.4	–1.3	9.9	98	*105*
Spain[a]	3.0	*12.1*	8.4	*6.0*	10.8	10.5	10.6	5.2	96	100
Sri Lanka	–4.0	2.1	–6.2	4.3	5.5	13.8	2.7	12.2	83	106
Sudan	–3.0	14.4	–7.7	13.2	–2.5	10.9	–6.4	13.6	123	99
Sweden[a]	4.4	1.7	5.0	1.9	8.0	7.4	6.7	4.5	97	98
Switzerland[a]	..	..	..	..	9.4	3.4	8.8	1.8	..	..
Syrian Arab Republic	6.6	1.1	–11.7	8.1	2.4	0.8	–8.5	10.2	132	92
Tajikistan	..	..	..	..	..	..	..	..	..	..
Tanzania	–3.1	10.1	–3.8	0.6	–4.1	11.7	–2.1	1.9	103	111
Thailand	11.2	9.8	8.7	6.4	14.1	14.9	12.6	12.0	102	97
Togo	–1.1	3.3	0.7	–3.7	1.1	1.0	2.0	–3.3	128	114
Trinidad and Tobago	–11.5	1.4	–20.2	7.8	–9.9	6.0	–12.0	10.5	116	134
Tunisia	5.0	5.1	1.7	3.8	3.6	7.8	2.7	6.4	103	105
Turkey	..	11.1	..	12.1	14.2	11.2	9.4	12.9	104	106
Turkmenistan	..	..	..	..	..	..	..	..	..	..
Uganda	–3.1	23.2	–10.2	34.8	–4.6	25.8	0.6	34.5	74	68
Ukraine	..	..	..	..	..	..	..	..	..	..
United Arab Emirates	8.5	3.5	–1.3	8.4	–1.1	2.8	0.7	12.6	172	128
United Kingdom[a]	4.5	6.4	6.7	4.8	5.9	6.8	8.5	5.4	101	102
United States[a]	3.6	6.9	7.2	8.1	5.7	8.4	8.2	9.2	98	100
Uruguay	4.4	7.2	1.2	14.4	4.4	7.5	–1.2	15.2	100	96
Uzbekistan	..	..	..	..	..	..	..	..	..	..
Venezuela, RB	3.1	5.8	–3.8	2.2	–4.6	5.5	–3.2	4.4	141	111
Vietnam	..	..	..	..	..	..	..	..	..	..
West Bank and Gaza	..	..	..	..	..	..	..	..	..	..
Yemen, Rep.	..	..	..	..	..	..	..	..	..	..
Yugoslavia, FR (Serb./Mont.)	..	..	..	..	..	..	..	..	..	..
Zambia	–0.2	–2.2	–1.6	–6.7	1.4	0.2	–3.5	–3.8	119	102
Zimbabwe	3.5	9.4	4.2	9.9	2.4	7.5	0.3	7.3	100	106

a. Data are from the International Monetary Fund's International Financial Statistics database. b. Includes Luxembourg. c. Data prior to 1990 refer to the Federal Republic of Germany before unification.

Growth of merchandise trade 4.4

About the data

Data on international trade in goods are recorded in each country's balance of payments and by customs services. While the balance of payments focuses on the financial transactions that accompany trade, customs data record the direction of trade and the physical quantities and value of goods entering or leaving the customs area. Customs data may differ from those recorded in the balance of payments because of differences in valuation and the time of recording. The 1993 United Nations System of National Accounts and the fifth edition of the International Monetary Fund's (IMF) *Balance of Payments Manual* (1993) have attempted to reconcile the definitions and reporting standards for international trade statistics, but differences in sources, timing, and national practices limit comparability. Real growth rates derived from trade volume indexes and terms of trade based on unit price indexes may therefore differ from those derived from national accounts aggregates.

Trade in goods, or merchandise trade, includes all goods that add to or subtract from an economy's material resources. Currency in circulation, titles of ownership, and securities are excluded, but monetary gold is included. Trade data are collected on the basis of a country's customs area, which in most cases is the same as its geographic area. Goods provided as part of foreign aid are included, but goods destined for extraterritorial agencies (such as embassies) are not.

Collecting and tabulating trade statistics is difficult. Some developing countries lack the capacity to report timely data. As a result it is necessary to estimate their trade from the data reported by their partners. (See *About the data* for table 6.2 for further discussion of the use of partner country reports.) In some cases economic or political concerns may lead national authorities to suppress or misrepresent data on certain trade flows, such as oil, military equipment, or the exports of a dominant producer. In other cases reported trade data may be distorted by deliberate underinvoicing or overinvoicing to effect capital transfers or avoid taxes. And in some regions smuggling and black market trading result in unreported trade flows.

By international agreement customs data are reported to the United Nations Statistics Division, which maintains the Commodity Trade (COMTRADE) database. The United Nations Conference on Trade and Development (UNCTAD) compiles a variety of international trade statistics, including price and volume indexes, based on the COMTRADE data. The IMF and the World Trade Organization also compile data on trade prices and volumes. The growth rates and terms of trade for low- and middle-income economies shown in this table were calculated from index numbers compiled by UNCTAD. Volume measures for high-income economies were derived by deflating the value of trade using deflators from the IMF's *International Financial Statistics*. All indexes are rescaled to a 1995 base year. Terms of trade were computed from the same indicators.

The terms of trade measure the relative prices of a country's exports and imports. There are a number of ways to calculate terms of trade. The most common is the net barter, or commodity, terms of trade, constructed as the ratio of the export price index to the import price index. When the net barter terms of trade increase, a country's exports are becoming more valuable or its imports cheaper.

Definitions

• **Growth rates of export and import volumes** are average annual growth rates calculated for low- and middle-income economies from UNCTAD's quantum index series or from export and import data deflated by the IMF's trade price deflators. • **Growth rates of export and import values** are average annual growth rates calculated from UNCTAD's value indexes or from current values of merchandise exports and imports. • **Net barter terms of trade** are the ratio of the export price index to the corresponding import price index measured relative to the base year 1995.

Data sources

The main source of trade data for developing countries is UNCTAD's annual *Handbook of International Trade and Development Statistics*. The IMF's *International Financial Statistics* includes data on the export and import values and deflators for high-income and selected developing economies.

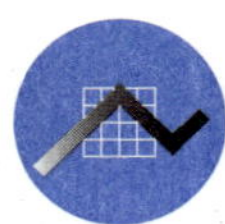

4.5 Structure of merchandise exports

	Merchandise exports $ millions		Food % of total		Agricultural raw materials % of total		Fuels % of total		Ores and metals % of total		Manufactures % of total	
	1980	1998	1980	1998	1980	1998	1980	1998	1980	1998	1980	1998
Albania	367	208	..	10	..	9	..	1	..	13	..	68
Algeria	13,652	..	1	..	0	..	98	..	0	..	0	..
Angola	..	..	..	..	..	..	..	..	..	..	..	..
Argentina	8,021	26,434	65	51	6	2	3	8	2	3	23	35
Armenia	..	229	..	*11*	..	*5*	..	*1*	..	*26*	..	*54*
Australia	21,892	55,839	34	22	11	7	11	20	17	17	22	29
Austria	17,227	62,826	4	5	8	2	2	1	4	3	83	83
Azerbaijan	..	678	..	..	..	..	..	..	..	..	..	..
Bangladesh	793	5,141	12	7	19	2	0	0	0	0	68	91
Belarus	..	7,123	..	9	..	3	..	0	..	1	..	76
Belgium[a]	57,573	153,160	..	..	..	..	..	..	..	..	..	..
Benin	164	..	62	..	25	..	4	..	1	..	3	..
Bolivia	942	1,104	8	30	3	6	24	8	62	26	3	30
Bosnia and Herzegovina	..	..	..	..	..	..	..	..	..	..	..	..
Botswana	545	2,061	..	..	..	..	..	..	..	..	..	..
Brazil	20,132	51,136	46	30	4	4	2	1	9	10	37	55
Bulgaria	8,091	4,299	..	*14*	..	*3*	..	*8*	..	*11*	..	*61*
Burkina Faso	161	..	41	..	48	..	0	..	0	..	11	..
Burundi	..	..	..	..	..	..	..	..	..	..	..	..
Cambodia	..	*705*	..	..	..	..	..	..	..	..	..	..
Cameroon	1,657	..	48	..	16	..	31	..	2	..	4	..
Canada	67,532	217,238	12	8	11	7	14	8	14	5	48	66
Central African Republic	147	..	31	..	43	..	*0*	..	0	..	26	..
Chad	71	..	4	..	81	..	0	..	0	..	15	..
Chile	4,705	14,831	15	29	10	9	1	0	64	43	9	17
China†	..	183,527	..	7	..	1	..	3	..	2	..	87
Hong Kong, China[b]	19,743	173,996	1	2	1	0	0	0	1	1	96	95
Colombia	3,986	11,363	72	32	5	5	3	30	0	1	20	32
Congo, Dem. Rep.	..	..	..	..	..	..	..	..	..	..	..	..
Congo, Rep.	911	..	1	..	2	..	90	..	0	..	7	..
Costa Rica	1,001	5,547	64	39	1	4	1	0	0	1	28	56
Côte d'Ivoire	3,013	4,575	64	..	28	..	2	..	0	..	5	..
Croatia	..	4,613	..	11	..	4	..	6	..	2	..	76
Cuba	..	..	..	..	..	..	..	..	..	..	..	..
Czech Republic	..	26,395	..	5	..	2	..	3	..	2	..	88
Denmark	11,807	47,829	33	23	5	3	3	3	2	1	55	65
Dominican Republic	962	4,981	73	11	0	0	0	0	3	0	24	8
Ecuador	2,520	4,203	33	63	1	5	63	21	0	0	3	10
Egypt, Arab Rep.	3,854	4,403	7	12	16	6	64	30	2	6	11	44
El Salvador	1,075	2,451	47	47	12	1	3	4	3	2	35	47
Eritrea	..	..	..	..	..	..	..	..	..	..	..	..
Estonia	..	2,690	..	*16*	..	*9*	..	*6*	..	*3*	..	*66*
Ethiopia	419	568	74	..	18	..	7	..	0	..	0	..
Finland	14,070	43,394	3	2	19	6	4	2	4	3	70	86
France	109,691	301,702	16	13	2	1	4	2	4	2	73	80
Gabon	*2,084*	..	..	..	..	..	88	..	12	..	..	..
Gambia, The	48	..	98	..	0	..	..	..	*3*	..	*7*	..
Georgia	..	300	..	..	..	..	..	..	..	..	..	..
Germany[c]	191,162	539,993	5	5	1	1	4	1	3	2	85	86
Ghana	1,104	1,813	78	..	4	..	0	..	17	..	1	..
Greece	4,175	..	26	..	2	..	16	..	9	..	47	..
Guatemala	1,520	2,847	53	61	16	4	1	2	5	1	24	33
Guinea	..	693	..	..	..	..	..	..	..	..	..	..
Guinea-Bissau	..	..	..	..	..	..	..	..	..	..	..	..
Haiti	216	299	31	*15*	1	*0*	0	*0*	4	*0*	63	*84*
Honduras	860	2,017	75	79	5	2	0	0	6	2	12	17
† Data for Taiwan, China	19,696	110,178	9	*3*	2	*1*	1	*1*	0	*1*	88	*93*

Structure of merchandise exports 4.5

	Merchandise exports		Food		Agricultural raw materials		Fuels		Ores and metals		Manufactures	
	$ millions		% of total		% of total		% of total		% of total		% of total	
	1980	1998	1980	1998	1980	1998	1980	1998	1980	1998	1980	1998
Hungary	..	20,747	..	11	..	1	..	2	..	2	..	82
India	8,303	34,076	28	*18*	5	*2*	0	*1*	7	*3*	59	*74*
Indonesia	..	50,371	..	11	..	5	..	19	..	4	..	45
Iran, Islamic Rep.	12,338	12,982	1	..	1	..	93	..	0	..	5	..
Iraq	..	..	..	..	..	..	..	..	..	..	..	..
Ireland	8,229	65,032	37	10	2	1	1	0	3	0	54	84
Israel	5,946	22,972	12	4	4	2	0	1	2	1	82	92
Italy	78,106	242,572	7	6	1	1	6	1	2	1	84	89
Jamaica	963	1,613	14	*24*	0	*0*	2	*0*	21	*6*	63	*70*
Japan	126,740	374,044	1	1	1	1	0	0	2	1	95	94
Jordan	575	1,802	25	..	1	..	0	..	40	..	34	..
Kazakhstan	..	5,839	..	8	..	2	..	39	..	26	..	23
Kenya	1,431	2,013	44	59	8	7	33	9	2	3	12	24
Korea, Dem. Rep.	..	..	..	..	..	..	..	..	..	..	..	..
Korea, Rep.	17,245	132,122	7	2	1	1	0	4	1	2	90	91
Kuwait	20,633	9,614	1	*0*	0	*0*	89	*85*	0	*0*	10	*14*
Kyrgyz Republic	..	535	..	*28*	..	*11*	..	*15*	..	*6*	..	*38*
Lao PDR	..	*342*	..	..	..	..	..	..	..	..	..	..
Latvia	..	2,011	..	10	..	27	..	2	..	3	..	58
Lebanon	..	..	..	..	..	..	..	..	..	..	..	..
Lesotho	58	193	..	..	..	..	..	..	..	..	..	..
Libya	21,919	..	0	..	0	..	100	..	0	..	0	..
Lithuania	..	3,962	..	14	..	4	..	19	..	2	..	61
Macedonia, FYR	..	..	..	..	..	..	..	..	..	..	..	..
Madagascar	436	538	80	*54*	4	*6*	6	*3*	4	*7*	6	*28*
Malawi	281	..	91	..	2	..	0	..	0	..	6	..
Malaysia	12,963	71,974	15	10	31	3	25	6	10	1	19	79
Mali	205	..	30	..	69	..	*0*	..	0	..	1	..
Mauritania	196	359	16	..	1	..	0	..	83	..	0	..
Mauritius	434	1,738	72	26	0	0	0	0	0	0	27	73
Mexico	18,031	117,459	12	6	2	1	67	6	6	2	12	85
Moldova	..	644	..	72	..	1	..	0	..	1	..	25
Mongolia	..	462	..	*2*	..	*28*	..	*0*	..	*60*	..	*10*
Morocco	2,450	7,144	28	*31*	3	*3*	5	*2*	41	*15*	24	*49*
Mozambique	281	248	68	*69*	7	*9*	2	*1*	5	*4*	18	*17*
Myanmar	429	1,171	40	..	33	..	9	..	10	..	7	..
Namibia	..	1,278	..	..	..	..	..	..	..	..	..	..
Nepal	102	485	21	*10*	48	*1*	..	..	0	*0*	30	*77*
Netherlands	73,230	171,271	20	17	3	3	22	6	4	2	50	70
New Zealand	5,394	12,156	48	47	26	13	1	2	4	5	20	32
Nicaragua	450	579	75	88	8	3	2	1	1	1	14	8
Niger	576	..	11	..	1	..	1	..	85	..	2	..
Nigeria	25,945	8,971	2	..	0	..	97	..	0	..	0	..
Norway	18,649	40,637	7	10	3	1	48	43	10	9	32	30
Oman	3,748	..	1	..	0	..	96	..	0	..	3	..
Pakistan	2,628	8,658	24	14	20	2	7	0	0	0	48	84
Panama	2,519	6,325	67	77	0	0	23	4	1	2	9	17
Papua New Guinea	*985*	*1,773*	*33*	..	*7*	..	*0*	..	*50*	..	*3*	..
Paraguay	400	3,824	38	*72*	50	*13*	*0*	*0*	*0*	*0*	12	*15*
Peru	3,916	5,735	16	26	4	2	21	5	43	42	17	24
Philippines	5,788	29,496	36	7	6	1	1	1	21	2	21	90
Poland	14,043	32,467	6	11	3	2	13	5	7	5	61	77
Portugal	4,668	26,016	12	7	9	3	6	1	2	1	70	87
Puerto Rico	..	..	..	..	..	..	..	..	..	..	..	..
Romania	11,024	8,302	..	5	..	4	..	5	..	5	..	81
Russian Federation	..	74,799	..	2	..	3	..	38	..	16	..	28

4.5 Structure of merchandise exports

	Merchandise exports		Food		Agricultural raw materials		Fuels		Ores and metals		Manufactures	
	$ millions		% of total		% of total		% of total		% of total		% of total	
	1980	1998	1980	1998	1980	1998	1980	1998	1980	1998	1980	1998
Rwanda	134	65	82	..	7	..	0	..	10	..	0	..
Saudi Arabia	101,574	39,772	0	*1*	0	*0*	99	*90*	0	*0*	1	*9*
Senegal	470	..	43	..	3	..	19	..	20	..	15	..
Sierra Leone	227	..	24	..	1	..	0	..	34	..	40	..
Singapore[b]	19,430	110,379	8	3	10	1	25	8	2	1	47	86
Slovak Republic	..	10,720	..	4	..	2	..	3	..	4	..	84
Slovenia	..	9,096	..	4	..	2	..	1	..	4	..	90
South Africa[d]	25,698	29,234	9	12	2	4	4	8	7	10	18	54
Spain	20,547	109,814	18	15	2	1	4	2	5	2	72	78
Sri Lanka	1,062	4,735	47	..	18	..	15	..	1	..	19	..
Sudan	689	596	47	*68*	51	*28*	1	*0*	1	*0*	1	*3*
Sweden	30,662	85,179	2	3	10	5	4	1	5	3	78	82
Switzerland	41,708	93,859	3	3	1	1	0	0	5	3	90	93
Syrian Arab Republic	2,112	3,135	4	*17*	9	*7*	79	*65*	1	*1*	7	*10*
Tajikistan	..	..	..	..	..	..	..	..	..	..	..	..
Tanzania	583	589	58	*65*	18	*23*	5	*0*	5	*0*	14	*10*
Thailand	6,449	52,747	47	*19*	11	*4*	0	*2*	14	*1*	25	*71*
Togo	476	..	21	..	2	..	26	..	40	..	11	..
Trinidad and Tobago	2,728	2,258	2	11	0	0	93	45	0	0	5	44
Tunisia	2,195	5,725	7	9	1	1	52	6	4	1	36	82
Turkey	2,910	31,220	51	17	14	1	1	1	7	2	27	77
Turkmenistan	..	..	..	..	..	..	..	..	..	..	..	..
Uganda	319	..	96	..	2	..	1	..	1	..	1	..
Ukraine	..	13,699	..	..	..	..	..	..	..	..	..	..
United Arab Emirates	..	..	..	..	..	..	..	..	..	..	..	..
United Kingdom	109,620	271,845	7	6	1	1	13	4	5	2	71	85
United States	224,250	672,207	18	8	5	2	4	2	5	2	66	82
Uruguay	1,059	2,832	39	51	22	9	0	1	1	1	38	39
Uzbekistan	..	..	..	..	..	..	..	..	..	..	..	..
Venezuela, RB	19,275	17,564	0	4	0	0	94	72	4	6	2	19
Vietnam	..	..	..	..	..	..	..	..	..	..	..	..
West Bank and Gaza	..	..	..	..	..	..	..	..	..	..	..	..
Yemen, Rep.	..	1,501	..	..	..	..	..	..	..	..	..	..
Yugoslavia, FR (Serb./Mont.)	..	..	..	..	..	..	..	..	..	..	..	..
Zambia	1,457	..	1	..	0	..	0	..	82	..	16	..
Zimbabwe	1,441	..	40	..	3	..	3	..	17	..	36	..
World	1,900,797 t	5,397,430 t	12 w	8 w	4 w	2 w	11 w	4 w	5 w	3 w	66 w	80 w
Low income	89,218	344,253	..	9	..	2	..	6	..	2	..	77
Excl. China & India	80,493	126,650	20	..	14	..	50	..	5	..	11	..
Middle income	443,065	978,169	21	12	7	3	28	12	8	6	33	65
Lower middle income	175,395	339,759	..	*13*	..	*3*	..	*23*	..	*7*	..	*46*
Upper middle income	267,670	638,410	17	12	7	2	30	7	7	4	39	74
Low & middle income	532,283	1,322,422	21	11	8	2	30	10	8	5	32	68
East Asia & Pacific	69,163	533,638	18	6	12	2	16	5	7	2	45	82
Europe & Central Asia	105,745	256,604	..	7	..	3	..	19	..	9	..	57
Latin America & Carib.	97,994	289,318	32	25	4	3	31	13	12	9	20	49
Middle East & N. Africa	167,875	108,409	3	*4*	1	*1*	87	*76*	3	*2*	6	*17*
South Asia	13,606	53,681	28	*16*	10	*2*	3	*1*	5	*2*	54	*78*
Sub-Saharan Africa	77,900	80,772	22	..	6	..	27	..	9	..	12	..
High income	1,368,514	4,075,008	11	7	4	2	7	3	4	2	73	82
Europe EMU	574,503	1,715,780	11	9	3	1	6	2	3	2	75	83

Note: Components may not sum to 100 percent due to unclassified trade.

a. Includes Luxembourg. b. Includes reexports. c. Data prior to 1990 refer to the Federal Republic of Germany before unification. d. Data on export commodity shares refer to the South African Customs Union, which comprises Botswana, Lesotho, Namibia, and South Africa.

Structure of merchandise exports 4.5

About the data

Data on merchandise trade come from customs reports of goods entering an economy or from reports of the financial transactions related to merchandise trade recorded in the balance of payments. Because of differences in timing and definitions, estimates of trade flows from customs reports are likely to differ from those based on the balance of payments. Furthermore, several international agencies process trade data, each making estimates to correct for unreported or misreported data, and this leads to other differences in the available data.

The most detailed source of data on international trade in goods is the Commodity Trade (COMTRADE) database maintained by the United Nations Statistics Division. The International Monetary Fund (IMF) also collects customs-based data on exports and imports of goods. The value of exports is recorded as the cost of the goods delivered to the frontier of the exporting country for shipment—the f.o.b. (free on board) value. Many countries report trade data in U.S. dollars. When countries report in local currency, the United Nations Statistics Division applies the average official exchange rate for the period shown.

Countries may report trade according to the general or special system of trade (see *Primary data documentation*). Under the general system exports comprise outward-moving goods that are (a) goods wholly or partly produced in the country; (b) foreign goods, neither transformed nor declared for domestic consumption in the country, that move outward from customs storage; and (c) goods previously included as imports for domestic consumption but subsequently exported without transformation. Under the special system exports comprise categories a and c. In some compilations categories b and c are classified as reexports. Because of differences in reporting practices, data on exports may not be fully comparable across economies.

The data on total exports of goods (merchandise) in this table come from the World Trade Organization (WTO). The WTO uses two main sources, national statistical offices and the IMF's *International Financial Statistics*. It supplements these with the COMTRADE database and publications or databases of regional organizations, specialized agencies, and economic groups (such as the Economic Commission for Latin America and the Caribbean, Eurostat, the Food and Agriculture Organization, the Organisation for Economic Co-operation and Development, the Commonwealth of Independent States, and the Organization of Petroleum Exporting Countries). It also consults private sources, such as country reports of the Economist Intelligence Unit and press clippings. In recent years country websites and direct contacts through email have helped significantly improve the collection of up-to-date statistics for many countries, reducing the proportion of estimated figures. The WTO database now covers most of the major traders in Africa, Asia, and Latin America, which together with the high-income countries account for nearly 90 percent of total world trade. There has also been a remarkable improvement in the availability of recent, reliable, and standardized figures for countries in Europe and Central Asia.

The shares of exports by major commodity group were estimated by World Bank staff from the COMTRADE database. The values of total exports reported here have not been fully reconciled with the estimates of exports of goods and services from the national accounts (shown in table 4.9) or those from the balance of payments (table 4.17). The classification of commodity groups is based on the Standard International Trade Classification (SITC) revision 1. Most countries now report using later revisions of the SITC or the Harmonized System. Concordance tables are used to convert data reported in one system of nomenclature to another. The conversion process may introduce some errors of classification, but conversions from later to early systems are generally reliable. Shares may not sum to 100 percent because of unclassified trade.

Definitions

• **Merchandise exports** show the f.o.b. value of goods provided to the rest of the world valued in U.S. dollars. • **Food** comprises the commodities in SITC sections 0 (food and live animals), 1 (beverages and tobacco), and 4 (animal and vegetable oils and fats) and SITC division 22 (oil seeds, oil nuts, and oil kernels). • **Agricultural raw materials** comprise SITC section 2 (crude materials except fuels) excluding divisions 22, 27 (crude fertilizers and minerals excluding coal, petroleum, and precious stones), and 28 (metalliferous ores and scrap). • **Fuels** comprise SITC section 3 (mineral fuels). • **Ores and metals** comprise the commodities in SITC divisions 27, 28, and 68 (nonferrous metals). • **Manufactures** comprise the commodities in SITC sections 5 (chemicals), 6 (basic manufactures), 7 (machinery and transport equipment), and 8 (miscellaneous manufactured goods), excluding division 68.

Data sources

The WTO publishes data on world trade in its *Annual Report*. Estimates of total exports of goods are also published in the IMF's *International Financial Statistics* and *Direction of Trade Statistics* and in the United Nations Statistics Division's *Monthly Bulletin of Statistics*. The United Nations Conference on Trade and Development (UNCTAD) publishes data on the structure of exports and imports in its *Handbook of International Trade and Development Statistics*. Tariff line records of exports and imports are compiled in the United Nations' COMTRADE database.

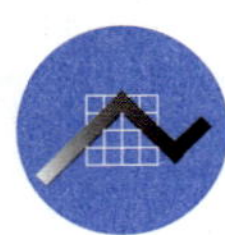

4.6 Structure of merchandise imports

	Merchandise imports		Food		Agricultural raw materials		Fuels		Ores and metals		Manufactures	
	$ millions		% of total		% of total		% of total		% of total		% of total	
	1980	**1998**	**1980**	**1998**	**1980**	**1998**	**1980**	**1998**	**1980**	**1998**	**1980**	**1998**
Albania	354	812	..	27	..	1	..	4	..	1	..	67
Algeria	9,614	..	21	..	3	..	2	..	2	..	72	..
Angola	..	..	..	..	..	..	..	..	..	..	..	..
Argentina	9,394	29,448	6	5	4	2	10	3	3	2	77	89
Armenia	..	806	..	*31*	..	*0*	..	*27*	..	*0*	..	*39*
Australia	20,521	61,232	5	5	3	1	14	5	2	1	75	87
Austria	23,716	66,480	6	6	4	2	15	4	5	3	69	84
Azerbaijan	..	1,724	..	..	..	..	..	..	..	..	..	..
Bangladesh	2,353	6,862	24	15	6	5	9	7	3	2	58	69
Belarus	..	8,482	..	11	..	2	..	0	..	3	..	57
Belgium[a]	61,432	145,599	..	..	..	..	..	..	..	..	..	..
Benin	312	..	26	..	1	..	8	..	1	..	62	..
Bolivia	574	1,759	19	8	1	1	1	5	2	1	78	86
Bosnia and Herzegovina	..	..	..	..	..	..	..	..	..	..	..	..
Botswana	603	1,983	..	..	..	..	..	..	..	..	..	..
Brazil	22,955	57,739	10	10	1	2	43	9	5	3	41	76
Bulgaria	7,445	4,757	..	*9*	..	*3*	..	*30*	..	*6*	..	*50*
Burkina Faso	368	..	20	..	2	..	13	..	1	..	64	..
Burundi	..	..	..	..	..	..	..	..	..	..	..	..
Cambodia	..	1,097	..	..	..	..	..	..	..	..	..	..
Cameroon	1,620	..	9	..	0	..	12	..	1	..	78	..
Canada	59,593	204,614	7	6	2	1	12	3	5	2	72	85
Central African Republic	185	..	21	..	1	..	2	..	2	..	75	..
Chad	55	..	23	..	2	..	2	..	1	..	72	..
Chile	5,469	17,347	15	7	2	1	18	9	2	1	60	81
China†	..	136,914	..	5	..	4	..	5	..	5	..	81
Hong Kong, China	22,467	184,941	12	5	4	1	6	2	2	2	75	89
Colombia	4,283	14,008	12	12	3	2	12	2	3	2	69	79
Congo, Dem. Rep.	..	..	..	..	..	..	..	..	..	..	..	..
Congo, Rep.	545	..	19	..	1	..	14	..	2	..	65	..
Costa Rica	1,375	5,791	9	8	2	1	15	4	2	1	68	86
Côte d'Ivoire	2,614	2,705	13	*17*	0	*2*	16	*23*	2	*1*	68	*56*
Croatia	..	8,774	..	10	..	2	..	7	..	2	..	75
Cuba	..	..	..	..	..	..	..	..	..	..	..	..
Czech Republic	..	28,989	..	6	..	2	..	6	..	4	..	82
Denmark	14,163	44,382	11	12	5	3	22	3	3	2	57	77
Dominican Republic	1,520	7,597	17	..	2	..	25	..	2	..	54	..
Ecuador	2,242	5,198	8	12	2	2	1	5	2	1	87	76
Egypt, Arab Rep.	6,814	14,617	32	21	6	5	1	5	1	3	59	59
El Salvador	897	3,718	18	16	2	3	18	10	2	1	61	68
Eritrea	..	..	..	..	..	..	..	..	..	..	..	..
Estonia	..	3,805	..	*16*	..	*2*	..	*8*	..	*2*	..	*71*
Ethiopia	650	1,042	8	..	3	..	25	..	1	..	64	..
Finland	14,752	30,902	7	7	3	3	29	7	5	5	56	77
France	123,767	275,528	10	10	4	2	27	6	5	3	54	80
Gabon	686	..	19	..	0	..	1	..	1	..	78	..
Gambia, The	138	..	26	..	1	..	9	..	0	..	61	..
Georgia	..	1,060	..	..	..	..	..	..	..	..	..	..
Germany[b]	183,221	460,951	12	9	4	2	23	6	6	4	52	73
Ghana	908	2,346	10	..	1	..	27	..	2	..	59	..
Greece	9,717	..	9	..	5	..	23	..	2	..	60	..
Guatemala	1,473	4,256	8	12	2	2	24	8	1	1	65	77
Guinea	..	572	..	..	..	..	..	..	..	..	..	..
Guinea-Bissau	..	..	..	..	..	..	..	..	..	..	..	..
Haiti	319	641	22	..	1	..	13	..	1	..	62	..
Honduras	954	2,340	10	16	1	1	16	8	1	1	72	74
† Data for Taiwan, China	19,685	99,862	8	*6*	9	*4*	25	*8*	6	*5*	50	*73*

Structure of merchandise imports 4.6

	Merchandise imports		Food		Agricultural raw materials		Fuels		Ores and metals		Manufactures	
	$ millions		% of total		% of total		% of total		% of total		% of total	
	1980	1998	1980	1998	1980	1998	1980	1998	1980	1998	1980	1998
Hungary	..	23,101	..	4	..	2	..	6	..	3	..	84
India	13,947	44,828	9	*6*	2	*4*	45	*25*	6	*6*	39	*55*
Indonesia	..	31,942	..	11	..	7	..	10	..	3	..	69
Iran, Islamic Rep.	10,888	13,608	21	..	4	..	1	..	2	..	72	..
Iraq	..	..	..	..	..	..	..	..	..	..	..	..
Ireland	10,452	41,651	12	7	3	1	15	3	2	2	66	81
Israel	9,201	26,197	11	7	3	1	26	7	4	2	57	82
Italy	94,016	206,941	13	11	7	4	28	6	6	4	45	72
Jamaica	1,038	2,710	20	*17*	1	*2*	38	*13*	2	*1*	39	*65*
Japan	124,610	251,655	12	16	9	4	50	15	10	6	19	57
Jordan	2,136	3,404	18	..	2	..	17	..	1	..	61	..
Kazakhstan	..	6,589	..	11	..	1	..	15	..	3	..	70
Kenya	2,345	3,029	8	14	1	3	34	18	1	2	56	64
Korea, Dem. Rep.	..	..	..	..	..	..	..	..	..	..	..	..
Korea, Rep.	21,859	90,495	10	6	11	4	30	20	6	7	43	61
Kuwait	6,756	7,714	15	*16*	1	*1*	1	*1*	1	*2*	81	*81*
Kyrgyz Republic	..	756	..	*21*	..	*1*	..	*29*	..	*1*	..	*48*
Lao PDR	..	507	..	..	..	..	..	..	..	..	..	..
Latvia	..	3,141	..	13	..	2	..	10	..	2	..	74
Lebanon	..	..	..	..	..	..	..	..	..	..	..	..
Lesotho	424	866	..	..	..	..	..	..	..	..	..	..
Libya	10,368	..	19	..	1	..	1	..	1	..	78	..
Lithuania	..	5,480	..	11	..	3	..	14	..	2	..	69
Macedonia, FYR	..	..	..	..	..	..	..	..	..	..	..	..
Madagascar	764	693	9	*15*	3	*1*	15	*21*	1	*0*	73	*61*
Malawi	308	..	8	..	1	..	15	..	1	..	75	..
Malaysia	10,569	54,477	12	6	2	1	15	3	4	3	67	85
Mali	308	..	19	..	0	..	35	..	0	..	45	..
Mauritania	321	319	30	..	1	..	14	..	0	..	52	..
Mauritius	516	2,018	26	16	4	3	14	6	1	1	54	73
Mexico	21,087	125,374	16	6	3	2	2	2	4	2	75	85
Moldova	..	1,043	..	8	..	2	..	31	..	1	..	57
Mongolia	..	524	..	*14*	..	*1*	..	*19*	..	*1*	..	*65*
Morocco	3,771	9,463	20	*17*	6	*5*	24	*17*	4	*4*	47	*58*
Mozambique	720	782	14	*22*	3	*2*	9	*11*	3	*1*	70	*62*
Myanmar	788	2,455	6	..	1	..	3	..	2	..	87	..
Namibia	..	1,451	..	..	..	..	..	..	..	..	..	..
Nepal	328	1,238	4	12	1	5	18	12	1	3	73	49
Netherlands	73,474	153,027	15	11	3	2	24	7	4	3	53	77
New Zealand	5,091	11,242	6	9	2	1	22	7	4	2	65	81
Nicaragua	803	1,384	15	18	1	1	20	12	1	1	63	69
Niger	677	323	14	..	0	..	26	..	3	..	55	..
Nigeria	14,728	9,211	15	..	0	..	7	..	2	..	76	..
Norway	16,753	39,070	8	7	3	2	17	3	5	4	67	83
Oman	1,780	..	15	..	1	..	11	..	0	..	66	..
Pakistan	5,570	9,834	13	21	3	5	27	16	3	2	54	55
Panama	2,806	7,696	10	12	1	0	31	9	1	1	58	78
Papua New Guinea	1,021	1,078	21	..	0	..	15	..	1	..	61	..
Paraguay	675	3,938	11	*20*	1	*0*	28	*10*	1	*1*	60	*69*
Peru	3,090	8,200	20	16	3	2	2	8	2	1	73	73
Philippines	7,727	29,524	8	9	2	1	28	7	3	2	48	80
Poland	15,819	45,303	14	8	5	2	18	6	6	3	51	80
Portugal	8,611	38,293	14	13	7	3	24	6	4	2	52	77
Puerto Rico	..	..	..	..	..	..	..	..	..	..	..	..
Romania	12,685	10,927	..	8	..	2	..	12	..	3	..	73
Russian Federation	..	57,948	..	17	..	1	..	3	..	2	..	44

4.6 Structure of merchandise imports

	Merchandise imports		Food		Agricultural raw materials		Fuels		Ores and metals		Manufactures	
	$ millions		% of total		% of total		% of total		% of total		% of total	
	1980	1998	1980	1998	1980	1998	1980	1998	1980	1998	1980	1998
Rwanda	196	263	10	..	3	..	13	..	0	..	72	..
Saudi Arabia	25,563	27,535	14	*18*	1	*1*	1	*0*	1	*4*	82	*76*
Senegal	875	..	25	..	1	..	25	..	0	..	48	..
Sierra Leone	386	..	24	..	1	..	2	..	1	..	71	..
Singapore	22,400	95,702	8	4	6	1	29	8	2	2	54	84
Slovak Republic	..	13,071	..	6	..	2	..	6	..	3	..	77
Slovenia	..	9,870	..	7	..	3	..	6	..	4	..	80
South Africa[c]	18,268	27,216	3	5	3	2	0	8	2	1	62	70
Spain	32,272	128,521	13	12	5	2	39	7	6	3	38	76
Sri Lanka	1,845	5,302	20	..	1	..	24	..	2	..	52	..
Sudan	1,127	1,732	26	*17*	1	*2*	13	*19*	1	*0*	60	*60*
Sweden	32,860	67,547	7	7	2	2	24	5	5	3	62	81
Switzerland	46,958	92,871	8	6	3	2	11	3	7	4	71	85
Syrian Arab Republic	4,010	3,307	14	*21*	3	*3*	26	*4*	2	*3*	55	*69*
Tajikistan	..	..	..	..	..	..	..	..	..	..	..	..
Tanzania	1,089	1,365	13	*17*	1	*2*	21	*14*	2	*1*	63	*66*
Thailand	8,352	36,513	5	*5*	3	*3*	30	*9*	4	*3*	51	*78*
Togo	524	..	17	..	1	..	23	..	0	..	59	..
Trinidad and Tobago	1,789	2,999	11	11	2	1	38	13	1	3	49	71
Tunisia	3,166	7,875	14	10	4	3	21	5	4	2	58	79
Turkey	7,513	45,552	4	5	2	4	48	8	3	5	43	75
Turkmenistan	..	..	..	..	..	..	..	..	..	..	..	..
Uganda	318	..	11	..	1	..	23	..	0	..	65	..
Ukraine	..	16,283	..	..	..	..	..	..	..	..	..	..
United Arab Emirates	..	..	..	..	..	..	..	..	..	..	..	..
United Kingdom	106,267	306,239	13	9	4	2	13	2	7	3	61	82
United States	249,760	917,178	8	5	3	2	33	7	5	2	50	81
Uruguay	1,668	3,594	8	11	4	3	29	6	3	1	56	79
Uzbekistan	..	..	..	..	..	..	..	..	..	..	..	..
Venezuela, RB	10,877	14,816	14	12	3	2	2	2	2	2	79	82
Vietnam	..	..	..	..	..	..	..	..	..	..	..	..
West Bank and Gaza	..	..	..	..	..	..	..	..	..	..	..	..
Yemen, Rep.	..	2,201	..	..	..	..	..	..	..	..	..	..
Yugoslavia, FR (Serb./Mont.)	..	..	..	..	..	..	..	..	..	..	..	..
Zambia	1,114	..	5	..	1	..	22	..	1	..	71	..
Zimbabwe	1,335	..	6	..	2	..	12	..	1	..	73	..
World	**1,884,105 t**	**5,304,372 t**	**11 w**	**8 w**	**4 w**	**2 w**	**25 w**	**7 w**	**5 w**	**3 w**	**54 w**	**77 w**
Low income	106,408	301,063	..	8	..	5	..	7	..	4	..	76
Excl. China & India	73,977	119,321	16	..	2	..	16	..	2	..	64	..
Middle income	359,848	972,340	11	8	4	2	21	9	4	3	57	72
Lower middle income	174,905	350,148	11	*12*	3	*2*	18	*8*	3	*2*	58	*67*
Upper middle income	184,943	622,192	11	7	5	3	23	10	4	4	57	76
Low & middle income	466,256	1,273,403	12	8	4	3	21	8	4	4	57	73
East Asia & Pacific	89,093	395,183	10	6	6	4	24	10	4	5	53	74
Europe & Central Asia	110,346	294,161	..	10	..	2	..	6	..	3	..	67
Latin America & Carib.	98,691	328,756	13	9	2	2	19	6	3	2	63	80
Middle East & N. Africa	81,230	108,232	19	*20*	3	*3*	9	*5*	2	*3*	67	*68*
South Asia	24,911	69,513	12	*10*	2	*4*	35	*22*	4	*5*	46	*56*
Sub-Saharan Africa	61,985	77,558	10	..	2	..	9	..	2	..	64	..
High income	1,417,849	4,030,969	11	8	4	2	26	6	5	3	53	78
Europe EMU	625,713	1,547,893	12	10	4	2	25	6	5	3	52	76

Note: Components may not sum to 100 percent due to unclassified trade.

a. Includes Luxembourg. b. Data prior to 1990 refer to the Federal Republic of Germany before unification. c. Data on import commodity shares refer to the South African Customs Union, which comprises Botswana, Lesotho, Namibia, and South Africa.

Structure of merchandise imports 4.6

About the data

Data on imports of goods are derived from the same sources as data on exports. In principle, world exports and imports should be identical. Similarly, exports from an economy should equal the sum of imports by the rest of the world from that economy. But differences in timing and definitions result in discrepancies in reported values at all levels. For further discussion of indicators of merchandise trade see *About the data* for tables 4.4 and 4.5.

The value of imports is generally recorded as the cost of the goods when purchased by the importer plus the cost of transport and insurance to the frontier of the importing country—the c.i.f. (cost, insurance, and freight) value. A few countries, including Australia, Canada, and the United States, collect import data on an f.o.b. (free on board) basis and adjust them for freight and insurance costs. Many countries collect and report trade data in U.S. dollars. When countries report in local currency, the United Nations Statistics Division applies the average official exchange rate for the period shown.

Countries may report trade according to the general or special system of trade (see *Primary data documentation*). Under the general system imports include goods imported for domestic consumption and imports into bonded warehouses and free trade zones. Under the special system imports comprise goods imported for domestic consumption (including transformation and repair) and withdrawals for domestic consumption from bonded warehouses and free trade zones. Goods transported through a country en route to another are excluded.

The data on total imports of goods (merchandise) in this table come from the World Trade Organization (WTO). The WTO uses two main sources, national statistical offices and the International Monetary Fund's (IMF) *International Financial Statistics*. It supplements these with the Commodity Trade (COMTRADE) database maintained by the United Nations Statistics Division and publications or databases of regional organizations, specialized agencies, and economic groups (such as the Economic Commission for Latin America and the Caribbean, Eurostat, the Food and Agriculture Organization, the Organisation for Economic Co-operation and Development, the Commonwealth of Independent States, and the Organization of Petroleum Exporting Countries). It also consults private sources, such as country reports of the Economist Intelligence Unit and press clippings. In recent years country websites and direct contacts through email have helped significantly improve the collection of up-to-date statistics for many countries, reducing the proportion of estimated figures. The WTO database now covers most of the major traders in Africa, Asia, and Latin America, which together with the high-income countries account for nearly 90 percent of total world trade. There has also been a remarkable improvement in the availability of recent, reliable, and standardized figures for countries in Europe and Central Asia.

The shares of imports by major commodity groups were estimated by World Bank staff from the COMTRADE database. The values of total imports reported here have not been fully reconciled with the estimates of imports of goods and services from the national accounts (shown in table 4.9) or those from the balance of payments (table 4.17).

The classification of commodity groups is based on the Standard International Trade Classification (SITC) revision 1. Most countries now report using later revisions of the SITC or the Harmonized System. Concordance tables are used to convert data reported in one system of nomenclature to another. The conversion process may introduce some errors of classification, but conversions from later to early systems are generally reliable. Shares may not sum to 100 percent because of unclassified trade.

Definitions

• **Merchandise imports** show the c.i.f. value of goods purchased from the rest of the world valued in U.S. dollars. • **Food** comprises the commodities in SITC sections 0 (food and live animals), 1 (beverages and tobacco), and 4 (animal and vegetable oils and fats) and SITC division 22 (oil seeds, oil nuts, and oil kernels). • **Agricultural raw materials** comprise SITC section 2 (crude materials except fuels) excluding divisions 22, 27 (crude fertilizers and minerals excluding coal, petroleum, and precious stones), and 28 (metalliferous ores and scrap). • **Fuels** comprise SITC section 3 (mineral fuels). • **Ores and metals** comprise the commodities in SITC divisions 27, 28, and 68 (nonferrous metals). • **Manufactures** comprise the commodities in SITC sections 5 (chemicals), 6 (basic manufactures), 7 (machinery and transport equipment), and 8 (miscellaneous manufactured goods), excluding division 68.

Data sources

The WTO publishes data on world trade in its *Annual Report*. Estimates of total imports of goods are also published in the IMF's *International Financial Statistics* and *Direction of Trade Statistics* and in the United Nations Statistics Division's *Monthly Bulletin of Statistics*. The United Nations Conference on Trade and Development (UNCTAD) publishes data on the structure of exports and imports in its *Handbook of International Trade and Development Statistics*. Tariff line records of exports and imports are compiled in the United Nations' COMTRADE database.

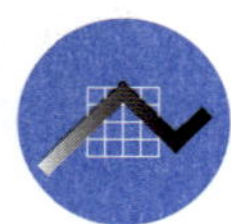

4.7 Structure of service exports

	Commercial service exports		Transport		Travel		Others	
	$ millions		% of total		% of total		% of total	
	1980	1998	1980	1998	1980	1998	1980	1998
Albania	11	83	45.5	15.7	9.1	65.1	45.5	19.3
Algeria	446	..	43.7	..	25.8	..	30.5	..
Angola	..	..	..	..	..	..	..	..
Argentina	1,427	4,507	56.4	23.8	24.1	67.1	19.5	9.1
Armenia	..	118	..	44.9	..	20.3	..	34.7
Australia	3,660	15,812	52.0	27.4	31.1	46.0	16.9	26.6
Austria	8,616	31,817	8.0	14.2	75.3	35.0	16.7	50.7
Azerbaijan	..	320	..	40.3	..	39.1	..	20.6
Bangladesh	172	252	22.7	36.5	9.3	20.6	68.0	42.9
Belarus	..	935	..	52.9	..	2.4	..	44.7
Belgium[a]	11,472	35,426	36.8	27.0	15.8	15.3	47.3	57.7
Benin	52	..	67.3	..	17.3	..	15.4	..
Bolivia	80	237	36.3	33.8	45.0	29.1	18.8	37.1
Bosnia and Herzegovina	..	..	..	..	..	..	..	..
Botswana	74	241	56.8	18.3	29.7	72.6	13.5	9.1
Brazil	1,672	7,083	48.6	26.3	7.5	18.6	43.8	55.1
Bulgaria	1,211	1,234	36.3	36.4	28.7	35.4	35.0	28.2
Burkina Faso	17	..	52.9	..	29.4	..	17.6	..
Burundi	..	..	..	..	..	..	..	..
Cambodia	..	99	..	38.4	..	44.4	..	17.2
Cameroon	348	..	55.7	..	17.8	..	26.4	..
Canada	7,115	30,281	35.7	19.6	35.8	30.9	28.5	49.5
Central African Republic	8	..	37.5	..	37.5	..	25.0	..
Chad	0	..	..	..	..	..	..	..
Chile	1,218	4,030	33.3	40.0	14.4	28.7	52.3	31.2
China	..	24,040	..	10.2	..	52.4	..	37.3
Hong Kong, China	5,763	34,171	45.8	34.8	22.8	24.4	31.4	40.8
Colombia	1,294	2,051	32.3	31.8	36.9	45.8	30.8	22.4
Congo, Dem. Rep.	..	..	..	..	..	..	..	..
Congo, Rep.	104	..	49.0	..	6.7	..	44.2	..
Costa Rica	183	1,315	26.2	15.1	46.4	68.6	27.3	16.3
Côte d'Ivoire	477	461	59.1	25.6	17.0	23.4	23.9	51.0
Croatia	..	3,964	..	14.3	..	68.9	..	16.8
Cuba	..	..	..	..	..	..	..	..
Czech Republic	..	7,366	..	18.9	..	50.8	..	30.3
Denmark	4,685	14,835	32.6	49.2	24.1	22.0	43.3	28.8
Dominican Republic	305	2,421	7.9	2.6	56.7	88.9	35.4	8.5
Ecuador	348	757	37.1	36.7	37.6	38.4	25.3	24.8
Egypt, Arab Rep.	2,321	7,832	54.0	31.8	25.5	32.8	20.4	35.4
El Salvador	122	277	20.5	15.2	10.7	30.3	68.9	54.5
Eritrea	..	..	..	..	..	..	..	..
Estonia	..	1,476	..	48.0	..	36.5	..	15.5
Ethiopia	100	348	67.0	51.7	7.0	10.6	26.0	37.6
Finland	2,676	7,154	35.8	28.9	25.6	25.6	38.6	45.5
France	42,156	84,627	25.0	24.1	19.6	35.4	55.4	40.5
Gabon	294	..	23.8	..	5.8	..	70.4	..
Gambia, The	18	..	0.0	..	100.0	..	0.0	..
Georgia	..	278	..	24.8	..	67.6	..	7.6
Germany[b]	25,764	78,903	34.2	25.7	19.4	20.8	46.4	53.4
Ghana	102	162	35.3	56.2	0.0	11.7	64.7	32.1
Greece	3,848	..	24.2	..	45.0	..	30.7	..
Guatemala	169	581	23.7	15.3	36.7	54.0	39.6	30.6
Guinea	..	66	..	74.2	..	1.5	..	24.2
Guinea-Bissau	..	..	..	..	..	..	..	..
Haiti	84	178	6.0	2.2	90.5	63.5	3.6	34.3
Honduras	73	361	41.1	20.2	34.2	45.4	24.7	34.3

Structure of service exports | 4.7

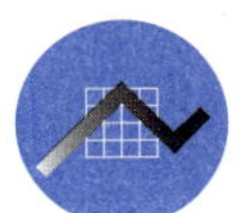

	Commercial service exports		Transport		Travel		Others	
	$ millions		% of total		% of total		% of total	
	1980	1998	1980	1998	1980	1998	1980	1998
Hungary	..	4,870	..	13.3	..	51.4	..	35.3
India	2,861	11,067	15.6	16.0	54.2	26.6	30.2	57.3
Indonesia	..	4,340	..	0.0	..	98.0	..	2.0
Iran, Islamic Rep.	731	902	4.5	46.5	4.0	1.3	91.5	52.2
Iraq	..	..	..	..	..	..	..	..
Ireland	1,315	6,586	38.4	17.9	44.0	39.4	17.6	42.7
Israel	2,707	8,980	38.3	23.3	36.2	29.6	25.5	47.1
Italy	18,823	66,621	24.4	16.0	47.6	44.7	28.0	39.3
Jamaica	375	1,727	29.9	15.1	65.3	69.3	4.8	15.6
Japan	18,760	61,795	67.9	34.4	3.4	6.1	28.7	59.5
Jordan	974	1,810	27.8	17.1	53.5	47.1	18.7	35.7
Kazakhstan	..	897	..	42.4	..	45.4	..	12.3
Kenya	511	638	42.9	48.0	46.8	45.5	10.4	6.6
Korea, Dem. Rep.	..	..	..	..	..	..	..	..
Korea, Rep.	2,402	23,843	64.3	42.8	15.4	24.9	20.3	32.3
Kuwait	1,099	1,496	64.3	80.1	34.3	13.8	1.4	6.1
Kyrgyz Republic	..	58	..	32.8	..	13.8	..	53.4
Lao PDR	..	116	..	16.4	..	81.9	..	1.7
Latvia	..	1,035	..	63.8	..	17.6	..	18.6
Lebanon	..	..	..	..	..	..	..	..
Lesotho	22	46	4.5	2.2	54.5	52.2	40.9	45.7
Libya	137	..	77.4	..	7.3	..	15.3	..
Lithuania	..	1,096	..	39.6	..	42.0	..	18.4
Macedonia, FYR	..	..	..	..	..	..	..	..
Madagascar	55	264	70.9	23.1	9.1	34.8	20.0	42.0
Malawi	32	..	50.0	..	28.1	..	21.9	..
Malaysia	1,046	10,690	45.1	22.0	30.3	22.3	24.6	55.8
Mali	39	..	46.2	..	38.5	..	15.4	..
Mauritania	25	24	60.0	4.2	28.0	83.3	12.0	12.5
Mauritius	132	968	40.9	22.4	31.8	53.8	27.3	23.8
Mexico	4,383	11,937	10.2	12.0	73.1	66.2	16.8	21.8
Moldova	..	117	..	47.9	..	26.5	..	25.6
Mongolia	..	75	..	42.7	..	46.7	..	10.7
Morocco	709	2,558	22.4	17.4	63.9	68.2	13.7	14.4
Mozambique	118	286	78.8	20.3	0.0	0.0	21.2	79.7
Myanmar	48	529	37.5	6.2	20.8	32.1	41.7	61.6
Namibia	..	315	..	0.0	..	91.4	..	8.6
Nepal	118	433	7.6	13.6	53.4	43.6	39.0	42.7
Netherlands	16,686	51,633	52.9	39.9	13.5	13.2	33.6	47.0
New Zealand	950	3,651	61.8	34.3	22.4	47.8	15.8	17.8
Nicaragua	41	151	39.0	16.6	53.7	66.2	7.3	17.2
Niger	30	..	46.7	..	20.0	..	33.3	..
Nigeria	1,127	884	80.8	12.8	6.0	5.3	13.1	81.9
Norway	8,529	13,953	75.3	61.2	8.9	15.0	15.8	23.9
Oman	9	..	100.0	..	0.0	..	0.0	..
Pakistan	576	1,416	47.6	56.9	26.2	7.3	26.2	35.7
Panama	779	1,563	54.4	56.3	22.0	24.2	23.6	19.4
Papua New Guinea	36	318	41.7	3.5	33.3	4.7	25.0	91.8
Paraguay	158	469	1.9	13.9	57.6	23.9	40.5	62.3
Peru	663	1,653	33.3	18.7	44.2	51.8	22.5	29.5
Philippines	1,214	7,465	17.0	4.3	26.4	19.0	56.7	76.7
Poland	2,018	10,890	59.2	26.4	11.9	39.4	28.9	34.2
Portugal	1,892	8,512	24.9	18.0	60.7	62.7	14.4	19.3
Puerto Rico	..	..	..	..	..	..	..	..
Romania	1,063	1,192	37.6	42.3	30.5	21.8	31.9	35.9
Russian Federation	..	12,937	..	24.5	..	50.3	..	25.2

4.7 Structure of service exports

	Commercial service exports $ millions		Transport % of total		Travel % of total		Others % of total	
	1980	1998	1980	1998	1980	1998	1980	1998
Rwanda	18	31	72.2	29.0	16.7	61.3	11.1	9.7
Saudi Arabia	5,104	4,421	15.6	12.5	26.3	22.7	58.1	64.7
Senegal	191	..	33.5	..	51.8	..	14.7	..
Sierra Leone	37	..	40.5	..	32.4	..	27.0	..
Singapore	4,774	18,243	27.4	24.4	30.0	25.2	42.6	50.4
Slovak Republic	..	2,275	..	33.7	..	21.5	..	44.9
Slovenia	..	2,045	..	26.3	..	54.6	..	19.1
South Africa	2,924	5,109	41.9	21.2	47.2	53.6	10.9	25.2
Spain	11,450	48,729	26.2	14.9	60.8	61.3	13.0	23.8
Sri Lanka	223	888	19.3	45.0	44.4	25.9	36.3	29.1
Sudan	250	14	10.8	42.9	20.8	14.3	68.4	42.9
Sweden	7,395	17,675	41.0	27.0	13.0	23.7	46.0	49.3
Switzerland	6,888	25,795	18.8	11.5	46.0	30.4	35.2	58.1
Syrian Arab Republic	252	1,551	25.0	14.2	61.9	76.7	13.1	9.0
Tajikistan	..	..	..	..	..	..	..	..
Tanzania	165	534	39.4	11.2	12.7	74.7	47.9	14.0
Thailand	1,366	13,074	21.9	20.4	63.5	47.2	14.6	32.3
Togo	61	..	45.9	..	42.6	..	11.5	..
Trinidad and Tobago	383	574	29.8	35.2	39.9	35.0	30.3	29.8
Tunisia	990	2,662	20.9	23.8	69.1	62.3	10.0	13.9
Turkey	596	23,161	44.6	13.5	54.7	31.0	0.7	55.5
Turkmenistan	..	..	..	..	..	..	..	..
Uganda	4	..	0.0	..	100.0	..	0.0	..
Ukraine	..	3,922	..	82.2	..	8.0	..	9.8
United Arab Emirates	..	..	..	..	..	..	..	..
United Kingdom	34,295	97,616	41.3	19.5	20.2	24.6	38.5	55.9
United States	38,110	239,957	37.4	19.0	27.8	34.7	34.8	46.3
Uruguay	449	1,382	19.4	24.6	66.4	50.3	14.3	25.1
Uzbekistan	..	..	..	..	..	..	..	..
Venezuela, RB	663	1,297	43.0	21.4	36.7	74.1	20.4	4.5
Vietnam	..	..	..	..	..	..	..	..
West Bank and Gaza	..	..	..	..	..	..	..	..
Yemen, Rep.	..	166	..	21.7	..	38.6	..	39.8
Yugoslavia, FR (Serb./Mont.)	..	..	..	..	..	..	..	..
Zambia	126	..	68.3	..	16.7	..	15.1	..
Zimbabwe	145	..	66.2	..	17.2	..	16.6	..
World	**363,547 t**	**1,316,688 t**	**39.2 w**	**25.3 w**	**27.0 w**	**30.3 w**	**33.9 w**	**44.7 w**
Low income	11,667	52,791	*41.6*	15.0	*33.8*	52.5	*24.6*	35.2
Excl. China & India	6,246	17,531	*31.4*	..	*36.9*	62.0	*31.9*	23.3
Middle income	53,921	215,219	39.8	27.7	32.3	38.3	28.2	34.1
Lower middle income	29,498	84,993	..	27.8	..	41.2	..	31.2
Upper middle income	24,438	130,232	45.3	27.6	27.4	36.4	27.6	36.0
Low & middle income	65,588	268,012	39.7	24.8	*32.5*	42.0	28.2	34.3
East Asia & Pacific	9,415	87,727	*43.7*	22.9	*33.4*	42.6	*22.9*	36.6
Europe & Central Asia	16,176	79,857	..	28.8	..	40.9	..	30.3
Latin America & Carib.	15,855	49,216	34.0	22.8	36.7	48.5	29.3	28.7
Middle East & N. Africa	12,099	23,387	27.7	..	26.6	..	47.1	..
South Asia	4,014	14,418	21.9	26.9	45.4	23.0	32.6	50.1
Sub-Saharan Africa	8,048	13,471	50.8	22.2	30.6	41.3	19.0	37.2
High income	297,904	1,048,583	39.1	25.4	25.9	27.1	35.0	47.5
Europe EMU	140,850	420,008	31.9	24.4	29.3	30.7	38.8	44.9

a. Includes Luxembourg. b. Data prior to 1990 refer to the Federal Republic of Germany before unification.

Structure of service exports 4.7

About the data

Balance of payments statistics, the main source of information on international trade in services, have many weaknesses. Until recently some large economies—such as the former Soviet Union—did not report data on trade in services. Disaggregation of important components may be limited, and it varies significantly across countries. There are inconsistencies in the methods used to report items. And the recording of major flows as net items is common (for example, insurance transactions are often recorded as premiums less claims). These factors contribute to a downward bias in the value of the service trade reported in the balance of payments.

Efforts are being made to improve the coverage, quality, and consistency of these data. Eurostat and the Organisation for Economic Co-operation and Development, for example, are working together to improve the collection of statistics on trade in services in member countries. In addition, the International Monetary Fund (IMF) has implemented the new classification of trade in services introduced in the fifth edition of its *Balance of Payments Manual* (1993).

Still, difficulties in capturing all the dimensions of international trade in services mean that the record is likely to remain incomplete. Cross-border intrafirm service transactions, which are usually not captured in the balance of payments, are increasing rapidly as foreign direct investment expands and electronic networks become pervasive. One example of such transactions is transnational corporations' use of mainframe computers around the clock for data processing, exploiting time zone differences between their home country and the host countries of their affiliates. Another important dimension of service trade not captured by conventional balance of payments statistics is establishment trade—sales in the host country by foreign affiliates. By contrast, cross-border intrafirm transactions in merchandise may be reported as exports or imports in the balance of payments.

The data on exports of services in table 4.7 and imports of services in table 4.8, unlike those in previous editions, include only commercial services and exclude the category "government services not included elsewhere." The data are compiled by the World Trade Organization (WTO) from balance of payments statistics provided by the IMF and from national statistics. Estimates of missing data provided by the WTO are used to compute regional and income group aggregates but are not shown in the tables. Data on total trade in goods and services from the IMF's Balance of Payments database are shown in table 4.17.

Figure 4.7

Exports of commercial services stalled in 1998

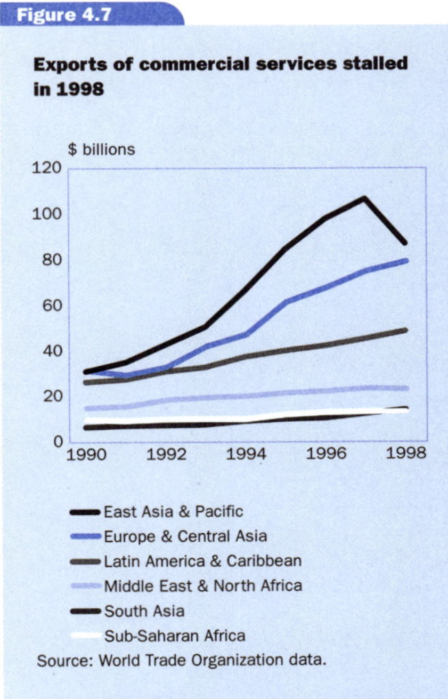

Source: World Trade Organization data.

The sharpest drop occurred in East Asia, previously the fastest-growing service exporter.

Definitions

• **Commercial service exports** are total service exports minus exports of government services not included elsewhere. International transactions in services are defined by the IMF's *Balance of Payments Manual* (1993) as the economic output of intangible commodities that may be produced, transferred, and consumed at the same time. Definitions may vary among reporting economies. • **Transport** covers all transport services (sea, air, land, internal waterway, space, and pipeline) performed by residents of one economy for those of another and involving the carriage of passengers, movement of goods (freight), rental of carriers with crew, and related support and auxiliary services. Excluded are freight insurance, which is included in insurance services; goods procured in ports by nonresident carriers and repairs of transport equipment, which are included in goods; repairs of railway facilities, harbors, and airfield facilities, which are included in construction services; and rental of carriers without crew, which is included in other services. • **Travel** covers goods and services acquired from an economy by travelers in that economy for their own use during visits of less than one year for business or personal purposes. Travel services include the goods and services consumed by travelers, such as lodging and meals and transport (within the economy visited). • **Other commercial services** include such activities as insurance and financial services, international telecommunications, and postal and courier services; computer data; news-related service transactions between residents and nonresidents; construction services; royalties and license fees; miscellaneous business, professional, and technical services; and personal, cultural, and recreational services.

Data sources

The data on exports of commercial services come from the World Trade Organization (WTO). Selected data appear in the WTO's *Annual Report*. The IMF publishes balance of payments data in its *International Financial Statistics* and *Balance of Payments Statistics Yearbook*.

4.8 Structure of service imports

	Commercial service imports $ millions		Transport % of total		Travel % of total		Others % of total	
	1980	1998	1980	1998	1980	1998	1980	1998
Albania	18	119	44.4	63.0	0.0	4.2	55.6	32.8
Algeria	2,560	..	42.0	..	13.1	..	44.9	..
Angola	..	..	..	..	..	..	..	..
Argentina	3,640	8,825	34.9	32.0	49.2	47.9	15.9	20.0
Armenia	..	175	..	62.9	..	23.4	..	13.7
Australia	6,319	16,913	49.0	35.1	29.1	31.8	21.9	33.1
Austria	5,685	30,035	13.9	10.4	55.3	31.7	30.8	57.9
Azerbaijan	..	692	..	28.0	..	24.6	..	47.4
Bangladesh	444	1,180	69.6	72.9	3.6	12.8	26.8	14.3
Belarus	..	444	..	30.0	..	27.9	..	42.1
Belgium[a]	12,388	33,938	30.7	21.5	26.6	26.1	42.7	52.5
Benin	97	..	63.9	..	8.2	..	28.9	..
Bolivia	238	423	58.0	63.8	23.1	14.2	18.9	22.0
Bosnia and Herzegovina	..	..	..	..	..	..	..	..
Botswana	191	517	48.2	42.2	29.3	24.4	22.5	33.5
Brazil	4,442	15,743	61.9	32.3	8.3	34.2	29.8	33.5
Bulgaria	549	1,103	51.4	48.2	8.6	20.0	40.1	31.6
Burkina Faso	192	..	63.0	..	16.7	..	19.8	..
Burundi	..	..	..	..	..	..	..	..
Cambodia	..	185	..	53.5	..	3.8	..	42.7
Cameroon	702	..	39.9	..	11.7	..	48.4	..
Canada	10,110	35,249	31.5	22.6	32.6	30.6	35.9	46.7
Central African Republic	129	..	51.9	..	27.1	..	20.9	..
Chad	20	..	10.0	..	70.0	..	20.0	..
Chile	1,492	4,077	55.6	53.3	13.4	23.1	31.0	23.6
China	..	28,775	..	31.5	..	32.0	..	36.5
Hong Kong, China	3,296	22,706	42.2	21.8	32.8	54.6	25.0	23.6
Colombia	1,134	3,446	46.7	37.0	21.2	32.6	32.1	30.4
Congo, Dem. Rep.	..	..	..	..	..	..	..	..
Congo, Rep.	474	..	27.4	..	6.1	..	66.5	..
Costa Rica	280	1,168	59.6	42.6	21.4	35.0	18.9	22.3
Côte d'Ivoire	1,390	1,341	42.5	42.4	17.3	17.7	40.1	40.0
Croatia	..	1,889	..	17.9	..	31.8	..	50.3
Cuba	..	..	..	..	..	..	..	..
Czech Republic	..	5,665	..	12.4	..	33.2	..	54.4
Denmark	3,486	15,496	35.1	43.4	33.1	29.6	31.8	27.0
Dominican Republic	395	1,300	40.0	60.1	42.0	19.5	18.0	20.4
Ecuador	661	1,178	38.4	52.8	34.5	20.5	27.1	26.7
Egypt, Arab Rep.	2,186	5,886	43.2	34.5	7.7	19.6	49.1	45.9
El Salvador	251	539	31.9	47.5	42.2	21.5	25.9	31.0
Eritrea	..	..	..	..	..	..	..	..
Estonia	..	814	..	50.2	..	19.0	..	30.7
Ethiopia	186	405	80.6	56.0	2.7	11.4	16.7	32.6
Finland	2,488	8,111	40.4	25.6	23.8	27.7	35.9	46.7
France	31,048	65,420	29.4	30.4	19.4	27.2	51.2	42.3
Gabon	765	..	22.7	..	12.5	..	64.8	..
Gambia, The	28	..	82.1	..	3.6	..	14.3	..
Georgia	..	335	..	23.9	..	67.5	..	8.7
Germany[b]	40,773	125,039	26.1	19.7	42.8	37.5	31.1	42.8
Ghana	186	433	57.5	61.9	17.7	5.5	24.7	32.6
Greece	1,276	..	46.4	..	24.2	..	29.4	..
Guatemala	464	759	38.8	55.2	35.3	20.7	25.9	24.1
Guinea	..	274	..	54.7	..	9.9	..	35.4
Guinea-Bissau	..	..	..	..	..	..	..	..
Haiti	129	370	62.0	88.1	31.8	10.0	6.2	1.9
Honduras	170	396	54.7	62.6	18.2	15.4	27.1	22.0

Structure of service imports 4.8

	Commercial service imports		Transport		Travel		Others	
	$ millions		% of total		% of total		% of total	
	1980	1998	1980	1998	1980	1998	1980	1998
Hungary	..	3,941	..	11.5	..	24.7	..	63.8
India	2,915	14,192	61.3	50.0	3.9	12.1	34.8	38.0
Indonesia	..	11,596	..	32.2	..	18.1	..	49.7
Iran, Islamic Rep.	5,061	2,392	45.0	54.5	33.6	6.4	21.4	39.1
Iraq	..	..	..	..	..	..	..	..
Ireland	1,569	20,005	44.6	11.1	37.1	11.8	18.3	77.0
Israel	2,221	9,626	45.8	40.9	37.1	24.7	17.1	34.4
Italy	15,699	62,887	45.3	21.7	12.2	28.0	42.5	50.4
Jamaica	356	1,233	57.6	42.9	9.3	16.1	33.1	41.0
Japan	32,100	110,705	52.6	25.6	14.3	26.0	33.1	48.3
Jordan	844	1,588	42.5	37.8	42.9	28.4	14.6	33.9
Kazakhstan	..	1,128	..	36.4	..	43.8	..	19.8
Kenya	461	603	72.0	51.2	5.0	24.4	23.0	24.4
Korea, Dem. Rep.	..	..	..	..	..	..	..	..
Korea, Rep.	3,144	23,523	64.2	38.2	11.1	12.3	24.7	49.5
Kuwait	2,634	4,243	45.2	38.3	50.8	59.3	3.9	2.4
Kyrgyz Republic	..	177	..	52.5	..	1.7	..	45.8
Lao PDR	..	92	..	41.3	..	25.0	..	33.7
Latvia	..	717	..	30.8	..	42.5	..	26.6
Lebanon	..	..	..	..	..	..	..	..
Lesotho	27	50	59.3	74.0	29.6	26.0	11.1	0.0
Libya	1,986	..	59.6	29.7	23.7	59.4	16.8	10.9
Lithuania	..	816	..	32.6	..	35.8	..	31.6
Macedonia, FYR	..	..	..	..	..	..	..	..
Madagascar	259	326	68.7	43.6	12.0	36.5	19.3	19.9
Malawi	179	..	81.6	..	5.6	..	12.8	..
Malaysia	2,865	12,353	45.7	31.9	25.3	12.9	29.0	55.1
Mali	196	..	70.9	..	10.2	..	18.9	..
Mauritania	115	130	66.1	36.9	14.8	32.3	19.1	30.8
Mauritius	168	717	67.3	36.4	13.7	27.1	19.0	36.5
Mexico	6,341	12,621	29.0	42.0	48.3	33.8	22.8	24.2
Moldova	..	178	..	43.3	..	27.5	..	29.2
Mongolia	..	142	..	57.0	..	31.7	..	11.3
Morocco	720	1,414	68.6	40.1	13.6	29.9	17.8	30.0
Mozambique	124	401	79.0	27.9	0.0	0.0	21.0	72.1
Myanmar	68	429	61.8	32.9	4.4	6.3	33.8	60.8
Namibia	..	449	..	33.4	..	19.6	..	47.0
Nepal	84	189	31.0	29.6	31.0	41.3	38.1	29.1
Netherlands	17,772	46,616	44.9	32.1	27.1	23.6	28.0	44.3
New Zealand	1,674	4,508	43.4	40.7	31.1	31.2	25.5	28.1
Nicaragua	92	264	57.6	36.7	33.7	26.5	8.7	36.7
Niger	265	..	45.3	..	6.8	..	47.9	..
Nigeria	5,285	4,054	33.7	17.4	18.7	38.7	47.6	44.0
Norway	6,948	15,211	52.5	33.9	21.3	30.0	26.2	36.1
Oman	518	..	34.2	..	6.2	..	59.7	..
Pakistan	747	2,129	77.1	76.2	11.5	9.7	11.4	14.0
Panama	564	1,129	68.1	57.9	9.9	15.6	22.0	26.5
Papua New Guinea	271	794	67.2	20.3	6.6	6.5	26.2	73.2
Paraguay	159	535	60.4	60.6	22.0	26.7	17.6	12.7
Peru	825	2,191	59.0	43.0	13.0	19.6	28.0	37.4
Philippines	1,318	10,087	56.8	19.7	8.0	19.3	35.1	61.0
Poland	2,023	6,559	59.9	25.4	12.9	11.8	27.3	62.9
Portugal	1,360	6,708	54.7	28.4	21.4	36.2	23.9	35.4
Puerto Rico	..	..	..	..	..	..	..	..
Romania	1,045	1,838	76.8	34.4	7.0	24.9	16.2	40.6
Russian Federation	..	16,127	..	15.7	..	53.8	..	30.5

4.8 Structure of service imports

	Commercial service imports		Transport		Travel		Others	
	$ millions		% of total		% of total		% of total	
	1980	1998	1980	1998	1980	1998	1980	1998
Rwanda	99	115	78.8	60.9	11.1	14.8	10.1	24.3
Saudi Arabia	14,771	8,678	35.0	29.1	16.6	13.1	48.4	57.8
Senegal	294	..	54.1	..	20.4	..	25.5	..
Sierra Leone	83	..	56.6	..	9.6	..	33.7	..
Singapore	2,890	17,884	38.5	33.4	11.5	28.2	49.9	38.4
Slovak Republic	..	2,272	..	19.5	..	20.9	..	59.6
Slovenia	..	1,520	..	26.6	..	37.8	..	35.5
South Africa	3,762	5,278	48.9	42.6	20.5	34.9	30.6	22.5
Spain	5,393	27,495	41.0	28.3	22.8	18.2	36.2	53.4
Sri Lanka	344	1,325	61.6	59.8	9.6	15.2	28.8	24.9
Sudan	315	200	38.4	80.5	18.7	14.5	42.9	5.0
Sweden	6,952	21,620	36.2	19.2	31.9	35.7	31.9	45.1
Switzerland	4,885	15,273	30.4	23.9	48.8	46.6	20.9	29.6
Syrian Arab Republic	335	1,297	41.5	48.7	52.8	44.7	5.7	6.6
Tajikistan	..	..	..	..	..	..	..	..
Tanzania	295	885	62.0	23.6	6.8	55.7	31.2	20.7
Thailand	1,608	11,874	65.9	38.8	15.2	16.5	19.0	44.7
Togo	153	..	68.6	..	15.0	..	16.3	..
Trinidad and Tobago	622	235	47.4	52.8	22.5	28.5	30.1	18.7
Tunisia	489	1,153	62.8	51.3	21.7	20.3	15.5	28.4
Turkey	466	9,441	61.6	27.6	22.3	18.6	16.1	53.9
Turkmenistan	..	..	..	..	..	..	..	..
Uganda	104	..	69.2	..	17.3	..	13.5	..
Ukraine	..	2,545	..	19.1	..	13.4	..	67.5
United Arab Emirates	..	..	..	..	..	..	..	..
United Kingdom	25,223	76,669	52.6	29.5	25.4	43.5	22.0	27.0
United States	28,890	165,827	53.2	30.3	36.0	34.9	10.7	34.8
Uruguay	434	866	34.8	48.6	46.8	30.6	18.4	20.8
Uzbekistan	..	..	..	..	..	..	..	..
Venezuela, RB	4,201	4,824	32.1	30.9	47.6	50.8	20.3	18.3
Vietnam	..	..	..	..	..	..	..	..
West Bank and Gaza	..	..	..	..	..	..	..	..
Yemen, Rep.	..	510	..	55.7	..	16.3	..	28.0
Yugoslavia, FR (Serb./Mont.)	..	..	..	..	..	..	..	..
Zambia	638	..	54.5	..	8.8	..	36.7	..
Zimbabwe	389	..	44.0	..	40.9	..	15.2	..
World	**396,454 t**	**1,304,705 t**	**44.7 w**	**28.6 w**	**27.3 w**	**31.3 w**	**28.0 w**	**40.1 w**
Low income	26,334	83,585	*61.1*	38.6	*7.7*	24.7	*31.2*	36.8
Excl. China & India	21,409	40,156	*52.5*	43.9	*13.5*	19.5	*34.0*	36.7
Middle income	90,527	219,053	53.5	33.7	19.9	24.4	26.7	41.9
Lower middle income	39,722	86,635	55.6	34.4	17.6	27.7	26.9	37.9
Upper middle income	50,782	132,428	52.3	33.2	21.1	22.2	26.5	44.6
Low & middle income	116,852	302,725	54.2	34.8	18.8	24.5	27.0	40.7
East Asia & Pacific	16,264	103,579	*54.1*	33.9	*15.6*	19.1	*30.4*	47.0
Europe & Central Asia	17,615	59,318	..	21.9	..	30.4	..	47.6
Latin America & Carib.	27,961	64,677	46.2	40.3	28.5	32.9	25.3	26.9
Middle East & N. Africa	32,147	29,886	45.8	..	20.5	..	33.7	..
South Asia	4,724	19,308	64.8	58.0	6.4	12.8	28.7	29.3
Sub-Saharan Africa	19,463	26,076	49.8	39.8	18.9	31.2	31.5	29.4
High income	279,815	1,001,849	42.5	26.7	29.2	33.3	28.3	40.0
Europe EMU	134,175	426,254	34.0	24.1	29.6	29.6	36.4	46.3

a. Includes Luxembourg. b. Data prior to 1990 refer to the Federal Republic of Germany before unification.

Structure of service imports 4.8

About the data

Trade in services differs from trade in goods because services are produced and consumed at the same time. Thus services to a traveler may be consumed in the producing country (for example, use of a hotel room) but are classified as imports of the traveler's country. In other cases services may be supplied from a remote location; for example, insurance services may be supplied from one location but consumed in another. For further discussion on the problems of measuring trade in services see *About the data* for table 4.7.

The data on exports of services in table 4.7 and imports of services in table 4.8, unlike those in previous editions, include only commercial services and exclude the category "government services not included elsewhere." The data are compiled by the World Trade Organization (WTO) from balance of payments statistics provided by the International Monetary Fund (IMF) and from national statistics. Estimates of missing data provided by the WTO are used to compute regional and income group aggregates but are not shown in the tables.

Definitions

• **Commercial service imports** are total service imports minus imports of government services not included elsewhere. International transactions in services are defined by the IMF's *Balance of Payments Manual* (1993) as the economic output of intangible commodities that may be produced, transferred, and consumed at the same time. Definitions may vary among reporting economies. • **Transport** covers all transport services (sea, air, land, internal waterway, space, and pipeline) performed by residents of one economy for those of another and involving the carriage of passengers, movement of goods (freight), rental of carriers with crew, and related support and auxiliary services. Excluded are freight insurance, which is included in insurance services; goods procured in ports by nonresident carriers and repairs of transport equipment, which are included in goods; repairs of railway facilities, harbors, and airfield facilities, which are included in construction services; and rental of carriers without crew, which is included in other services. • **Travel** covers goods and services acquired from an economy by travelers in that economy for their own use during visits of less than one year for business or personal purposes. Travel services include the goods and services consumed by travelers, such as lodging, meals, and transport (within the economy visited). • **Other commercial services** include such activities as insurance and financial services, international telecommunications, and postal and courier services; computer data; news-related service transactions between residents and nonresidents; construction services; royalties and license fees; miscellaneous business, professional, and technical services; and personal, cultural, and recreational services.

Data sources

The data on imports of commercial services come from the WTO. Selected data appear in the WTO's *Annual Report*. The IMF publishes balance of payments data in its *International Financial Statistics* and *Balance of Payments Statistics Yearbook*.

4.9 Structure of demand

	Private consumption % of GDP		General government consumption % of GDP		Gross domestic investment % of GDP		Exports of goods and services % of GDP		Imports of goods and services % of GDP		Gross domestic savings % of GDP	
	1980	1998	1980	1998	1980	1998	1980	1998	1980	1998	1980	1998
Albania	56	96	9	10	35	16	23	9	23	32	35	–7
Algeria	43	55	14	18	39	27	34	23	30	23	43	27
Angola	..	35	..	35	..	20	..	52	..	42	..	30
Argentina	76	71	.. [a]	12	25	20	5	10	6	13	24	17
Armenia	..	103	..	11	..	19	..	19	..	52	..	–14
Australia	59	*62*	18	*17*	25	*22*	16	*21*	18	*21*	24	*21*
Austria	55	*56*	18	*19*	29	*25*	36	*42*	38	*43*	27	*25*
Azerbaijan	..	84	..	11	..	39	..	25	..	59	..	5
Bangladesh	88	78	2	4	22	22	4	14	16	19	10	17
Belarus	..	60	..	19	..	26	..	62	..	68	..	20
Belgium	64	*63*	18	*14*	22	*18*	57	*73*	60	*68*	19	*22*
Benin	96	82	9	10	15	17	23	23	43	32	–5	8
Bolivia	67	75	14	14	17	20	25	20	23	29	19	11
Bosnia and Herzegovina	..	..	..	..	..	..	..	..	..	..	..	..
Botswana	46	52	20	26	37	21	50	35	52	34	34	22
Brazil	70	64	9	18	23	21	9	7	11	10	21	19
Bulgaria	55	71	6	15	34	15	36	45	31	46	39	14
Burkina Faso	95	73	10	15	17	29	10	14	33	30	–6	12
Burundi	91	89	9	13	14	9	9	8	23	20	–1	–3
Cambodia	..	86	..	9	..	15	..	34	..	44	..	5
Cameroon	69	71	10	9	21	18	28	26	27	25	22	20
Canada	53	*59*	22	*20*	23	*20*	28	*41*	26	*39*	25	*21*
Central African Republic	94	84	15	12	7	14	25	16	41	25	–9	4
Chad	*98*	88	*5*	9	*3*	15	17	19	29	32	*–4*	3
Chile	71	65	12	10	21	27	23	28	27	29	17	25
China	51	45	15	12	35	38	8	22	8	17	35	43
Hong Kong, China	60	60	6	9	35	30	90	125	91	125	34	30
Colombia	69	70	11	16	21	20	16	14	17	20	20	14
Congo, Dem. Rep.	82	*83*	8	*8*	10	8	16	*24*	16	*22*	10	*9*
Congo, Rep.	47	59	18	14	36	35	60	63	60	72	36	26
Costa Rica	66	57	18	17	27	29	26	49	37	51	16	27
Côte d'Ivoire	63	65	17	11	27	18	35	44	41	38	20	25
Croatia	..	60	..	26	..	23	..	40	..	49	..	14
Cuba	..	..	..	..	..	..	..	..	..	..	..	..
Czech Republic	..	52	..	19	31	30	..	60	..	61	..	29
Denmark	53	*51*	27	*25*	21	*21*	33	*36*	35	*33*	20	*24*
Dominican Republic	77	75	8	8	25	26	19	31	29	40	15	17
Ecuador	60	68	15	13	26	26	25	27	25	34	26	19
Egypt, Arab Rep.	69	74	16	10	28	22	31	17	43	23	15	16
El Salvador	72	87	14	9	13	17	34	23	33	36	14	4
Eritrea	..	81	..	48	..	41	..	20	..	90	..	–29
Estonia	..	58	..	23	..	29	..	80	..	89	..	20
Ethiopia	*79*	79	*14*	14	*13*	18	*11*	16	*17*	28	*7*	6
Finland	54	*53*	18	*21*	29	*17*	33	*40*	34	*31*	28	*26*
France	59	*60*	18	*19*	24	*17*	22	*27*	23	*23*	23	*21*
Gabon	26	42	13	15	28	32	65	51	32	40	61	43
Gambia, The	63	80	31	13	27	18	43	51	64	62	6	7
Georgia	56	97	13	9	29	8	..	14	..	28	31	–6
Germany	..	*58*	..	*19*	..	*21*	..	*27*	..	*25*	..	*23*
Ghana	84	77	11	10	6	23	8	27	9	36	5	13
Greece	62	*73*	12	*15*	33	*20*	16	*16*	22	*24*	27	*12*
Guatemala	79	87	8	6	16	16	22	19	25	27	13	8
Guinea	..	74	..	7	..	21	..	22	..	23	..	19
Guinea-Bissau	73	100	28	9	28	11	13	15	42	35	–1	–9
Haiti	82	100	10	7	17	11	22	11	31	29	8	–7
Honduras	70	66	13	10	25	30	36	46	44	52	17	23

Structure of demand 4.9

	Private consumption		General government consumption		Gross domestic investment		Exports of goods and services		Imports of goods and services		Gross domestic savings	
	% of GDP		% of GDP		% of GDP		% of GDP		% of GDP		% of GDP	
	1980	1998	1980	1998	1980	1998	1980	1998	1980	1998	1980	1998
Hungary	61	61	10	10	31	31	39	50	41	52	29	28
India	73	69	10	11	20	24	6	11	9	14	17	21
Indonesia	51	70	11	6	24	14	34	54	20	44	38	24
Iran, Islamic Rep.	53	65	21	20	30	16	13	13	16	15	26	15
Iraq	..	..	..	..	..	..	..	..	..	..	..	..
Ireland	67	*49*	19	*13*	27	*20*	48	*80*	61	*62*	14	*37*
Israel	53	61	40	30	22	20	44	32	59	43	7	9
Italy	61	*62*	15	*16*	27	*18*	22	*27*	25	*23*	24	*22*
Jamaica	64	60	20	22	16	31	51	49	51	62	16	18
Japan	59	*60*	10	*10*	32	*29*	14	*11*	15	*10*	31	*30*
Jordan	79	70	29	27	37	25	40	49	84	70	–8	4
Kazakhstan	..	76	..	11	..	17	..	31	..	35	..	13
Kenya	67	77	20	16	25	14	28	25	39	32	13	7
Korea, Dem. Rep.	..	..	..	..	..	..	..	..	..	..	..	..
Korea, Rep.	64	55	12	11	32	21	33	49	41	36	24	34
Kuwait	31	56	11	31	14	14	78	45	34	47	58	13
Kyrgyz Republic	..	82	..	16	..	18	..	35	..	51	..	2
Lao PDR	..	71	..	5	..	25	..	4	..	5	..	24
Latvia	59	64	8	26	26	23	..	48	..	61	33	10
Lebanon	..	98	..	15	..	28	..	11	..	51	..	–13
Lesotho	133	121	26	22	43	49	20	33	122	125	–59	–43
Libya	21	..	22	..	22	..	66	..	31	..	57	..
Lithuania	..	63	..	25	..	24	..	47	..	59	..	12
Macedonia, FYR	..	75	..	18	..	23	..	41	..	57	..	7
Madagascar	89	89	12	6	15	13	13	21	30	29	–1	5
Malawi	70	85	19	14	25	14	25	31	39	44	11	0
Malaysia	51	42	17	10	30	27	58	114	55	93	33	48
Mali	87	77	12	13	15	21	15	24	29	34	1	10
Mauritania	63	78	40	14	23	21	32	41	58	54	–3	8
Mauritius	75	65	14	11	21	24	51	65	61	65	10	24
Mexico	65	68	10	9	27	24	11	31	13	33	25	22
Moldova	..	84	..	18	..	26	..	47	..	75	..	–3
Mongolia	*44*	63	*29*	18	*63*	26	*21*	50	*57*	55	*27*	20
Morocco	69	67	18	18	24	23	15	18	26	26	13	15
Mozambique	98	89	12	9	6	20	11	12	27	30	–11	2
Myanmar	82	*89*	.. [a]	.. [a]	21	*12*	9	*1*	13	*1*	18	*11*
Namibia	47	56	17	26	29	19	76	63	68	63	37	19
Nepal	82	80	7	9	18	22	12	23	19	34	11	10
Netherlands	61	*59*	17	*14*	22	*20*	51	*56*	52	*49*	22	*27*
New Zealand	63	*63*	18	*15*	21	*21*	30	*29*	32	*28*	19	*21*
Nicaragua	83	85	20	14	17	33	24	39	43	71	–2	1
Niger	75	84	10	13	28	10	25	16	38	23	15	3
Nigeria	56	77	12	11	21	20	29	23	19	32	31	12
Norway	47	*48*	19	*20*	28	*25*	43	*41*	37	*34*	34	*32*
Oman	28	..	25	..	22	..	63	..	38	..	47	..
Pakistan	83	76	10	11	18	17	12	16	24	20	7	13
Panama	52	60	18	16	28	33	51	34	48	43	31	23
Papua New Guinea	61	51	24	21	25	30	43	68	53	70	15	28
Paraguay	76	73	6	11	32	21	15	45	29	49	18	17
Peru	57	72	11	9	29	24	22	12	19	17	32	20
Philippines	67	70	9	13	29	21	24	56	28	60	24	16
Poland	67	62	9	16	26	26	28	*26*	31	*30*	23	21
Portugal	65	*64*	13	*19*	34	*26*	25	*31*	38	*40*	21	*17*
Puerto Rico	75	..	16	..	17	..	65	..	73	..	10	..
Romania	60	76	5	15	40	18	35	26	40	34	35	9
Russian Federation	..	65	..	14	..	16	..	32	..	27	..	21

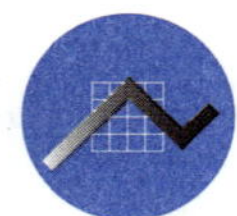

4.9 Structure of demand

	Private consumption		General government consumption		Gross domestic investment		Exports of goods and services		Imports of goods and services		Gross domestic savings	
	% of GDP		% of GDP		% of GDP		% of GDP		% of GDP		% of GDP	
	1980	1998	1980	1998	1980	1998	1980	1998	1980	1998	1980	1998
Rwanda	83	90	12	12	16	16	14	5	26	23	4	–2
Saudi Arabia	22	41	16	32	22	21	71	36	30	31	62	26
Senegal	85	75	20	10	12	20	27	33	44	38	–5	15
Sierra Leone	..	93	21	8	..	8	18	22	28	31	..	–1
Singapore	52	39	10	10	46	34	215	153	224	135	38	51
Slovak Republic	..	50	..	22	..	39	..	64	..	75	..	28
Slovenia	..	56	..	21	..	25	..	57	..	58	..	24
South Africa	54	63	14	20	23	16	35	26	27	25	31	17
Spain	66	*62*	13	*16*	23	*21*	16	*28*	18	*27*	21	*22*
Sri Lanka	80	71	9	10	34	25	32	36	55	42	11	19
Sudan	82	..	16	..	15	..	11	..	23	..	2	..
Sweden	51	*53*	29	*26*	21	*14*	29	*44*	31	*37*	19	*21*
Switzerland	62	*61*	12	*14*	29	*20*	35	*40*	38	*35*	25	*25*
Syrian Arab Republic	67	70	23	11	28	29	18	29	35	40	10	18
Tajikistan	..	..	..	..	..	..	..	..	..	..	..	..
Tanzania[b]	..	83	..	8	..	15	..	18	..	25	..	8
Thailand	65	48	12	11	29	25	24	59	30	42	23	42
Togo	54	81	22	11	28	14	51	34	56	40	23	7
Trinidad and Tobago	46	82	12	11	31	22	50	41	39	56	42	7
Tunisia	62	63	14	13	29	28	40	42	46	46	24	24
Turkey	77	66	12	13	18	25	5	25	12	28	11	21
Turkmenistan	..	..	..	..	..	..	..	..	..	..	..	..
Uganda	*89*	85	*11*	10	6	15	19	10	26	20	0	6
Ukraine	..	56	..	26	..	21	..	40	..	43	..	18
United Arab Emirates	17	..	11	..	28	..	78	..	34	..	72	..
United Kingdom	59	*64*	22	*20*	17	*16*	27	*29*	25	*29*	*19*	*15*
United States	64	*68*	17	*15*	20	*19*	10	*12*	11	*13*	*19*	*17*
Uruguay	76	71	12	14	17	16	15	22	21	22	12	15
Uzbekistan	..	59	..	22	..	19	..	22	..	22	..	19
Venezuela, RB	55	73	12	8	26	20	29	20	22	20	33	20
Vietnam	..	71	..	8	..	29	..	*44*	..	*52*	..	21
West Bank and Gaza	..	94	..	21	..	36	..	19	..	71	..	–15
Yemen, Rep.	..	76	..	22	..	22	..	34	..	54	..	2
Yugoslavia, FR (Serb./Mont.)	..	..	..	..	..	..	..	..	..	..	..	..
Zambia	55	84	26	11	23	14	41	29	45	38	19	5
Zimbabwe	68	69	19	16	17	17	23	46	27	48	14	15
World	61 w	*62* w	15 w	*15* w	25 w	*22* w	20 w	*23* w	20 w	*22* w	24 w	*23* w
Low income	60	59	12	11	28	29	12	24	13	22	28	30
Excl. China & India	65	74	11	9	22	17	25	37	24	37	23	17
Middle income	64	63	12	15	26	22	22	28	23	28	25	22
Lower middle income	..	64	..	15	..	20	..	33	..	32	..	20
Upper middle income	64	62	11	15	25	23	20	26	21	25	25	23
Low & middle income	62	62	12	14	27	24	19	27	20	26	26	24
East Asia & Pacific	56	52	13	11	32	28	22	42	23	33	30	37
Europe & Central Asia	..	64	..	16	..	22	..	35	..	36	..	20
Latin America & Carib.	68	67	10	14	24	22	12	15	14	18	22	19
Middle East & N. Africa	45	59	18	22	27	22	42	25	32	28	38	19
South Asia	76	71	9	10	21	23	8	13	13	16	15	19
Sub-Saharan Africa	61	68	15	17	22	17	32	28	31	31	23	15
High income	60	*62*	16	*15*	25	*21*	20	*22*	21	*21*	24	*22*
Europe EMU	..	*59*	..	*18*	..	*19*	..	*32*	..	*29*	..	*23*

a. General government consumption figures are not available separately; they are included in private consumption. b. Data cover mainland Tanzania only.

Structure of demand 4.9

About the data

GDP from the expenditure side is made up of private (or household) consumption expenditure, general government consumption expenditure, gross fixed capital formation (private and public investment), changes in inventories, and net exports (exports minus imports) of goods and services. Such expenditures are generally recorded in purchaser prices and so include net indirect taxes.

Because policymakers have tended to focus on fostering the growth of output, and because data on production are easier to collect than data on spending, many countries generate their primary estimate of GDP using the production approach. Moreover, many countries do not estimate all the separate components of national expenditures or, if they do, derive some of the main aggregates indirectly using GDP (output) as the control total.

Private consumption is often estimated as a residual, by subtracting from GDP all other known expenditures. The resulting aggregate may incorporate fairly large discrepancies. When household consumption is calculated separately, the household surveys on which many of the estimates are based tend to be one-year studies with limited coverage. Thus the estimates quickly become outdated and must be supplemented by price- and quantity-based statistical estimating procedures. Complicating the issue, in many developing countries the distinction between cash outlays for personal business and those for household use may be blurred. The expenditures of nonprofit institutions serving households are considered to be part of consumption. General government consumption includes expenditures on goods and services for individual consumption, as well as those on collective consumption of services. Defense expenditures, including those on capital outlays—with certain exceptions—are treated as current spending.

Gross domestic investment consists of outlays on additions to the economy's fixed assets plus net changes in the level of inventories. The new United Nations System of National Accounts (SNA) introduced in 1993 recognizes a third category of capital formation: net acquisition of valuables. Also included in gross domestic investment under the 1993 SNA guidelines are capital outlays on defense establishments that may be used by the general public, such as airfields, schools, and hospitals. These expenses were treated as consumption in the earlier version of SNA. Investment data may be estimated from direct surveys of enterprises and administrative records or based on the commodity flow method using data from trade and construction activities. While the quality of data on public fixed investment depends on the quality of government accounting systems (which tend to be weak in developing countries), measures of private fixed investment—particularly capital outlays by small, unincorporated enterprises—are usually very unreliable.

Estimates of changes in inventories are rarely complete but usually include the most important activities or commodities. In some countries these estimates are derived as a composite residual along with aggregate private consumption. According to national accounts conventions, adjustments should be made for appreciation of the value of inventory holdings due to price changes, but this is not always done. In highly inflationary economies this element can be substantial.

Data on exports and imports are compiled from customs returns and from balance of payments data obtained from central banks. Although the data on exports and imports from the payments side provide reasonably reliable records of cross-border transactions, they may not adhere strictly to the appropriate definitions of valuation and timing used in the balance of payments or, more important, correspond with the change-of-ownership criterion. This issue has assumed greater significance with the increasing globalization of international business. Neither customs nor balance of payments data capture the illegal transactions that occur in many countries. Goods carried by travelers across borders in legal but unreported shuttle trade may further distort trade statistics.

Savings are generally estimated as a residual. They represent the difference between GDP and total consumption. They also satisfy this fundamental identity: exports minus imports equal savings minus investments.

For further discussion of the problems of building and maintaining national accounts see Srinivasan (1994), Heston (1994), and Ruggles (1994). For a classic analysis of the reliability of foreign trade and national income statistics see Morgenstern (1963).

Definitions

• **Private consumption** is the market value of all goods and services, including durable products (such as cars, washing machines, and home computers), purchased or received as income in kind by households. It excludes purchases of dwellings but includes imputed rent for owner-occupied dwellings. It also includes payments and fees to governments to obtain permits and licenses. The expenditures of nonprofit institutions are also recorded as the consumption of households. In practice, private consumption may include any statistical discrepancy in the use of resources relative to the supply of resources. • **General government consumption** includes all current expenditures for purchases of goods and services (including wages and salaries). It also includes most expenditures on national defense and security, but excludes government military expenditures that are part of government capital formation. • **Gross domestic investment** consists of outlays on additions to the fixed assets of the economy plus net changes in the level of inventories. Fixed assets include land improvements (fences, ditches, drains, and so on); plant, machinery, and equipment purchases; and the construction of roads, railways, and the like, including commercial and industrial buildings, offices, schools, hospitals, and private residential dwellings. Inventories are stocks of goods held by firms to meet temporary or unexpected fluctuations in production or sales. Net acquisitions of valuables are also considered capital formation. • **Exports and imports of goods and services** represent the value of all goods and other market services provided to or received from the rest of the world. Included is the value of merchandise, freight, insurance, transport, travel, royalties, license fees, and other services, such as communication, construction, financial, information, business, personal, and government services. Labor and property income (formerly called factor services) is excluded. Transfer payments are excluded from the calculation of GDP. • **Gross domestic savings** are calculated as the difference between GDP and total consumption.

Data sources

The national accounts indicators for most developing countries are collected from national statistical organizations and central banks by visiting and resident World Bank missions. The data for high-income countries come from the Organisation for Economic Co-operation and Development (OECD) data files (see OECD, *National Accounts, 1960–1996,* volumes 1 and 2). The United Nations Statistics Division publishes detailed national accounts for United Nations member countries in *National Accounts Statistics: Main Aggregates and Detailed Tables;* updates are published in the *Monthly Bulletin of Statistics.*

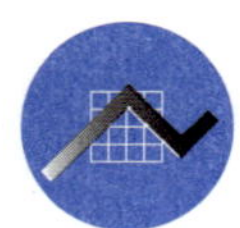

4.10 Growth of consumption and investment

	Private consumption				Private consumption per capita		General government consumption		Gross domestic investment	
	$ millions		average annual % growth		average annual % growth		average annual % growth		average annual % growth	
	1980	1998	1980–90	1990–98	1980–90	1990–98	1980–90	1990–98	1980–90	1990–98
Albania	..	2,940	..	6.1	..	5.9	..	–3.9	–0.3	22.4
Algeria	18,293	27,727	1.9	–1.4	–1.1	–3.5	4.7	3.6	–2.3	–0.7
Angola	..	2,611	*0.1*	–3.2	*–2.7*	–6.3	6.7	–0.4	–5.1	13.6
Argentina	..	210,857	..	*4.0*	..	*2.7*	..	*1.4*	–5.2	10.9
Armenia	..	1,903	..	–7.5	..	–8.2	..	–3.1	..	–29.5
Australia	94,360	*250,011*	3.0	*3.7*	1.5	*2.5*	3.5	*2.5*	2.7	*6.1*
Austria	43,264	*115,814*	2.4	*2.0*	2.2	*1.4*	1.4	*1.2*	2.2	*2.9*
Azerbaijan	..	3,304	..	*5.8*	..	*4.7*	..	*3.8*	..	*16.7*
Bangladesh	14,966	37,287	4.7	3.7	2.2	2.1	5.2	5.5	1.4	7.3
Belarus	..	12,668	..	–3.5	..	–3.4	..	–4.2	..	–10.0
Belgium	76,640	*153,409*	1.7	*1.2*	1.6	*0.9*	0.4	*1.2*	3.2	*0.3*
Benin	1,356	1,892	1.8	3.5	–1.3	0.6	0.5	3.1	–4.2	4.3
Bolivia	1,871	6,492	1.2	3.4	–0.9	0.9	–3.8	3.7	1.0	10.0
Bosnia and Herzegovina	..	..	..	..	..	..	..	..	..	..
Botswana	519	2,524	*5.9*	3.4	*2.4*	0.8	*13.6*	5.2	*13.8*	–1.0
Brazil	163,832	495,035	1.6	4.8	–0.4	3.3	7.3	–1.4	0.2	3.9
Bulgaria	11,089	8,938	2.5	–2.1	2.6	–1.5	9.1	–12.4	2.4	–3.3
Burkina Faso	1,631	1,883	2.6	3.0	0.1	0.6	6.2	2.7	8.6	4.1
Burundi	840	791	3.4	–1.8	0.5	–4.0	3.2	–3.9	6.9	–16.1
Cambodia	..	2,463	..	..	..	..	..	..	..	..
Cameroon	4,621	6,135	3.8	2.8	0.9	0.0	6.8	–1.6	–2.6	–1.3
Canada	141,521	*356,288*	3.3	*2.0*	2.1	*0.9*	2.5	*–0.3*	5.2	*2.6*
Central African Republic	747	886	1.5	0.0	–0.9	–2.1	–1.7	–16.1	10.0	–4.4
Chad	*837*	1,491	*5.3*	*1.4*	..	..	*14.5*	–3.2	..	*3.8*
Chile	19,489	50,846	2.0	8.7	0.3	7.0	0.4	3.5	6.4	13.5
China	103,442	445,974	8.8	9.2	7.2	8.0	9.8	9.6	10.8	13.4
Hong Kong, China	17,013	100,073	6.7	5.0	5.3	2.9	5.0	4.5	4.0	8.9
Colombia	25,477	69,921	2.6	3.9	0.5	1.9	4.2	7.8	1.4	11.1
Congo, Dem. Rep.	12,167	*5,038*	3.4	*–6.2*	0.0	*–9.2*	0.0	*–18.5*	–5.1	*–3.5*
Congo, Rep.	798	1,162	3.3	1.3	0.4	–1.6	2.5	–5.6	–12.6	4.1
Costa Rica	3,167	5,935	2.9	3.1	0.1	1.0	1.1	2.5	5.3	3.0
Côte d'Ivoire	6,388	7,133	1.5	1.0	–2.0	–1.8	–0.1	1.7	–9.8	17.7
Croatia	..	12,973	..	..	..	..	..	..	..	..
Cuba	..	..	..	..	..	..	..	..	..	..
Czech Republic	..	29,411	..	2.7	..	2.8	..	–1.6	*16.6*	6.3
Denmark	35,814	*86,142*	1.8	*3.4*	1.8	*3.0*	1.1	*2.4*	3.9	*4.8*
Dominican Republic	5,109	11,878	1.6	4.3	–0.6	2.4	1.9	19.9	3.5	6.7
Ecuador	6,995	13,882	1.9	2.4	–0.7	0.2	–1.4	–0.6	–3.8	4.3
Egypt, Arab Rep.	15,848	63,575	4.1	4.1	1.5	2.1	2.7	2.3	0.0	5.1
El Salvador	2,567	10,277	0.8	5.9	–0.2	3.7	0.1	3.2	2.2	8.1
Eritrea	..	526	..	..	..	..	..	..	..	..
Estonia	..	3,102	..	–1.1	..	0.0	..	4.8	..	–2.7
Ethiopia	*4,092*	5,194	*0.2*	3.1	*–2.8*	1.0	*4.5*	3.0	2.1	14.4
Finland	27,761	*63,402*	3.8	*0.4*	3.4	*–0.1*	3.4	*–0.3*	3.0	*–3.2*
France	391,263	*835,735*	2.6	*1.2*	2.1	*0.8*	2.2	*2.0*	2.8	*–1.6*
Gabon	1,119	2,312	1.5	–1.6	–1.8	–4.1	–0.6	7.3	–5.7	4.3
Gambia, The	152	332	–2.6	3.3	–6.0	–0.2	1.7	–6.1	0.0	3.2
Georgia	..	4,986	..	*6.2*	..	*6.1*	..	*23.7*	..	*81.7*
Germany	..	*1,208,283*	..	*1.3*	..	*0.9*	..	*1.6*	..	*0.5*
Ghana	3,730	5,740	2.8	3.9	–0.6	1.2	2.4	3.8	3.3	2.8
Greece	32,706	*88,059*	2.4	*1.8*	1.9	*1.3*	2.7	*0.8*	–0.8	*1.3*
Guatemala	6,217	16,438	1.2	4.4	–1.3	1.7	2.6	4.6	–1.8	4.7
Guinea	..	2,665	..	4.2	..	1.6	..	4.0	..	–1.8
Guinea-Bissau	*109*	205	0.8	4.7	–1.3	2.3	7.2	–0.1	12.9	–10.2
Haiti	1,197	*2,751*	0.9	..	..	..	–4.4	..	–0.6	1.7
Honduras	1,806	3,558	2.7	3.3	–0.5	0.3	3.3	–0.8	2.9	8.0

Growth of consumption and investment 4.10

	Private consumption				Private consumption per capita		General government consumption		Gross domestic investment	
	$ millions		average annual % growth		average annual % growth		average annual % growth		average annual % growth	
	1980	1998	1980–90	1990–98	1980–90	1990–98	1980–90	1990–98	1980–90	1990–98
Hungary	13,561	29,306	1.3	–1.3	1.7	–1.0	1.9	*1.0*	–0.9	*7.6*
India	143,021	295,060	4.6	5.8	2.5	4.0	7.7	9.2	6.5	7.3
Indonesia	40,821	66,056	5.6	7.6	3.7	5.9	4.6	0.9	6.7	4.9
Iran, Islamic Rep.	48,854	75,427	2.8	2.9	–0.6	1.2	–5.0	6.7	–2.5	1.1
Iraq	..	..	..	..	..	..	..	..	..	..
Ireland	13,585	*38,189*	2.2	*4.6*	1.9	*3.9*	–0.3	*2.7*	–0.4	*4.8*
Israel	11,493	61,627	5.3	6.5	3.5	3.4	0.5	3.1	2.2	6.8
Italy	273,819	*707,975*	3.0	*0.6*	2.9	*0.4*	2.5	*0.0*	1.9	*–1.0*
Jamaica	1,693	3,851	4.5	–0.3	3.3	–1.1	6.3	2.4	–0.1	5.3
Japan	623,284	*2,532,736*	3.7	*1.9*	3.2	*1.6*	2.4	*2.3*	5.3	*1.1*
Jordan	3,123	5,139	2.3	4.4	–1.5	0.2	2.3	6.7	–1.5	4.3
Kazakhstan	..	..	..	..	..	..	..	*–3.6*	..	*–14.6*
Kenya	4,506	7,454	4.6	2.5	1.0	–0.2	2.6	12.6	0.4	4.9
Korea, Dem. Rep.	..	..	..	..	..	..	..	..	..	..
Korea, Rep.	39,263	178,637	8.0	5.7	6.8	4.6	5.2	3.7	11.9	2.4
Kuwait	8,837	14,139	*–1.4*	..	..	..	*2.2*	..	*–4.5*	..
Kyrgyz Republic	..	1,399	..	*–4.2*	..	*–5.2*	..	*–6.6*	..	*8.6*
Lao PDR	..	897	..	..	..	..	..	..	..	..
Latvia	..	4,088	..	..	..	..	16.2	*9.6*	7.9	*–6.4*
Lebanon	..	16,930	..	7.2	..	5.3	..	7.4	..	18.4
Lesotho	492	958	2.0	–1.7	–0.5	–3.9	2.9	4.6	6.3	11.1
Libya	7,171	..	..	..	..	..	..	..	..	..
Lithuania	..	6,783	..	*–2.2*	..	*–2.0*	..	*5.2*	..	*8.8*
Macedonia, FYR	..	1,879	..	*5.5*	..	*4.7*	..	*1.3*	..	*6.7*
Madagascar	3,611	3,232	–0.6	1.8	–3.3	–1.1	0.5	–1.5	4.9	0.4
Malawi	866	1,438	1.5	7.4	–1.7	4.5	6.3	–4.6	–2.8	–8.5
Malaysia	12,378	30,094	3.7	5.0	0.9	2.4	2.7	6.2	2.6	9.5
Mali	1,555	2,077	1.8	1.7	–0.7	–1.1	4.5	9.6	3.6	–1.3
Mauritania	514	774	–0.8	4.8	–3.4	1.9	–4.6	*–2.5*	6.9	*6.8*
Mauritius	854	2,729	6.7	4.7	5.8	3.4	3.3	4.2	9.0	1.8
Mexico	145,438	268,331	1.1	1.6	–1.0	–0.2	2.4	1.3	–3.3	3.1
Moldova	..	1,363	..	*9.0*	..	*9.2*	..	*–7.0*	..	*–19.2*
Mongolia	..	578	..	..	..	..	..	..	..	..
Morocco	12,937	23,882	4.8	3.1	2.5	1.3	2.1	2.9	1.2	0.2
Mozambique	3,470	3,466	–1.7	3.1	–3.2	0.7	–2.1	–8.0	3.8	9.1
Myanmar	..	..	0.6	3.9	..	..	..	..	–4.1	14.7
Namibia	1,053	1,722	1.3	–0.1	–1.4	–2.6	3.7	2.5	–3.5	4.1
Nepal	1,600	3,839	4.5	4.4	1.8	1.9	7.2	5.9	6.0	7.4
Netherlands	104,571	*214,747*	1.7	*2.2*	1.2	*1.6*	2.1	*1.2*	3.1	*1.5*
New Zealand	13,801	*41,217*	2.1	*3.1*	1.1	*1.8*	1.5	*1.5*	2.8	*8.1*
Nicaragua	1,770	1,701	–3.6	3.4	–6.2	0.6	3.4	–5.2	–4.8	11.4
Niger	1,883	1,719	0.0	3.1	–3.2	–0.3	4.4	–0.7	–7.1	4.5
Nigeria	36,258	29,735	–2.6	1.0	–5.5	–1.9	–3.5	–2.4	–8.5	7.9
Norway	29,694	*72,914*	2.2	*3.1*	1.9	*2.6*	2.3	*2.5*	0.8	*5.1*
Oman	1,657	..	..	..	..	..	..	..	*25.5*	..
Pakistan	19,688	46,196	4.5	5.2	1.8	2.6	10.3	1.0	*6.0*	3.0
Panama	1,709	5,280	4.2	5.3	2.1	3.4	1.2	2.3	–8.9	12.9
Papua New Guinea	1,568	1,911	0.4	3.5	–1.7	1.1	–0.1	0.6	–0.9	5.8
Paraguay	3,467	6,277	3.5	2.5	0.5	–0.1	1.2	8.4	–1.1	3.6
Peru	12,006	44,924	1.0	4.7	–1.2	2.9	–1.8	5.1	–4.2	10.9
Philippines	20,910	48,449	2.6	3.7	0.0	1.4	0.6	3.4	–2.1	4.5
Poland	37,995	98,805	..	*5.0*	..	*4.8*	1.3	2.3	2.0	11.5
Portugal	19,166	*65,324*	2.5	*2.5*	2.4	*2.4*	5.0	*2.4*	3.0	*3.5*
Puerto Rico	10,756	..	3.5	..	..	..	5.1	..	6.9	..
Romania	..	29,040	..	1.3	..	1.7	..	1.6	..	–10.2
Russian Federation	..	179,608	..	*4.3*	..	*4.5*	..	*–9.4*	..	*–13.7*

4.10 Growth of consumption and investment

	Private consumption				Private consumption per capita		General government consumption		Gross domestic investment	
	$ millions		average annual % growth		average annual % growth		average annual % growth		average annual % growth	
	1980	1998	1980–90	1990–98	1980–90	1990–98	1980–90	1990–98	1980–90	1990–98
Rwanda	969	1,827	1.4	0.5	–1.6	–0.4	5.2	–6.6	4.3	–0.9
Saudi Arabia	34,538	53,244	..	..	..	..	..	..	..	..
Senegal	2,528	3,574	2.1	3.2	–0.8	0.5	3.3	–2.2	5.2	2.2
Sierra Leone	..	601	0.2	–0.9	–1.9	–3.3	0.0	–2.2	–6.7	*–10.6*
Singapore	6,030	33,841	5.8	6.6	4.1	4.5	6.6	8.8	3.1	9.6
Slovak Republic	..	10,221	*3.8*	–0.7	..	..	*4.8*	1.7	*1.1*	4.6
Slovenia	..	10,874	..	3.7	..	3.8	..	2.8	..	10.2
South Africa	43,739	84,069	2.4	2.7	–0.2	0.6	3.5	1.0	–5.3	3.4
Spain	141,274	*329,729*	2.5	*1.1*	2.2	*1.0*	5.4	*2.0*	5.7	*–0.5*
Sri Lanka	3,230	11,202	3.8	5.6	2.4	4.3	7.3	7.7	0.6	6.2
Sudan	6,241	..	0.0	..	..	..	–0.5	..	–1.8	..
Sweden	64,624	*120,882*	1.9	*0.1*	1.6	*–0.4*	1.5	*–0.2*	4.2	*–2.2*
Switzerland	66,985	*156,106*	1.6	*0.5*	1.1	*–0.3*	3.1	*0.8*	4.0	*–0.4*
Syrian Arab Republic	8,690	8,856	3.6	2.3	0.2	–0.6	–3.6	5.1	–5.3	8.3
Tajikistan	..	..	..	..	..	..	..	..	..	..
Tanzania[a]	..	6,693	..	3.0	..	0.0	..	–7.2	..	–2.3
Thailand	21,175	59,220	5.9	4.7	4.1	3.5	4.2	5.7	9.5	2.0
Togo	619	1,225	4.7	2.9	1.6	–0.2	–1.2	–1.9	2.7	12.6
Trinidad and Tobago	2,860	5,219	–1.3	–2.4	–2.5	–3.0	–1.7	1.1	–10.1	18.9
Tunisia	5,380	12,511	2.9	3.9	0.3	2.2	3.8	0.9	–1.8	2.9
Turkey	42,067	136,027	..	4.1	..	2.5	..	3.5	..	4.6
Turkmenistan	..	..	..	..	..	..	..	..	..	..
Uganda	*1,935*	5,588	*2.6*	6.8	*0.0*	3.6	*2.0*	7.5	*8.0*	10.0
Ukraine	..	24,526	..	–9.2	..	–8.8	..	–4.4	..	–24.8
United Arab Emirates	5,116	..	*4.6*	..	..	..	*–3.9*	..	*–8.7*	..
United Kingdom	320,290	*823,052*	4.1	*2.0*	3.8	*1.6*	1.1	*1.2*	6.4	*1.8*
United States	1,720,600	*5,308,500*	3.4	*3.0*	2.5	*1.9*	2.8	*0.0*	2.9	*7.0*
Uruguay	7,680	14,618	0.5	5.9	–0.1	5.2	1.8	2.5	–7.8	9.9
Uzbekistan	..	12,098	..	9.5	..	7.3	..	9.4	..	*–17.2*
Venezuela, RB	38,066	69,263	1.3	0.8	–1.2	–1.4	2.0	–1.0	–5.3	4.0
Vietnam	..	19,373	..	*10.2*	..	*8.2*	..	*12.0*	..	*25.5*
West Bank and Gaza	..	3,544	..	*4.2*	..	..	..	*8.8*	..	*7.2*
Yemen, Rep.	..	3,271	..	1.9	..	–1.8	..	3.0	..	8.8
Yugoslavia, FR (Serb./Mont.)	..	..	..	..	..	..	..	..	..	..
Zambia	2,145	2,810	1.8	0.7	–1.3	–2.0	–3.4	–16.1	–8.7	12.1
Zimbabwe	4,622	4,373	3.7	0.4	0.3	–1.9	4.7	–5.5	3.5	–2.1
World	**6,426,910 t**	***18,060,432* t**	**3.3 w**	**2.6 w**	**1.6 w**	**1.1 w**	**2.8 w**	**1.1 w**	**3.6 w**	**2.8 w**
Low income	469,483	1,097,111	5.2	6.5	3.1	4.7	6.8	6.5	7.2	10.1
Excl. China & India	224,760	341,322	3.2	4.5	0.6	2.2	3.7	0.0	2.2	4.6
Middle income	1,285,152	2,745,295	..	3.4	..	2.1	4.4	0.3	0.4	0.7
Lower middle income	..	977,346	..	2.5	..	1.3	..	0.0	..	–5.6
Upper middle income	684,466	1,770,896	..	4.0	..	2.6	5.4	0.5	0.9	5.2
Low & middle income	1,745,953	3,842,385	3.4	4.3	1.4	2.6	4.9	1.7	2.1	3.4
East Asia & Pacific	250,388	871,646	6.9	7.1	5.2	5.7	6.0	6.3	9.2	8.3
Europe & Central Asia	..	643,719	..	*2.8*	..	2.6	..	*–3.3*	..	–8.0
Latin America & Carib.	555,305	1,353,027	1.5	3.7	–0.5	2.0	5.6	–0.2	–1.6	5.6
Middle East & N. Africa	160,509	357,059	..	..	..	..	..	..	..	..
South Asia	185,246	399,452	4.6	5.5	2.4	3.5	8.1	7.7	5.5	6.9
Sub-Saharan Africa	158,427	225,625	1.5	2.1	–1.4	–0.6	2.7	0.3	–3.8	3.7
High income	4,752,819	*14,054,334*	3.3	*2.2*	2.7	1.5	2.5	*1.1*	4.0	*2.5*
Europe EMU	..	*3,740,482*	..	*1.2*	..	0.9	..	*1.3*	..	*0.4*

a. Data cover mainland Tanzania only.

Growth of consumption and investment 4.10

About the data

Measures of consumption and investment growth are subject to two kinds of inaccuracy. The first stems from the difficulty of measuring expenditures at current price levels, as described in *About the data* for table 4.9. The second arises in deflating current price data to measure growth in real terms, where results depend on the relevance and reliability of the price indexes used. Measuring price changes is more difficult for investment goods than for consumption goods because of the one-time nature of many investments and because the rate of technological progress in capital goods makes capturing change in quality difficult. (An example is computers—prices have fallen as quality has improved.) Many countries estimate investment from the supply side, identifying capital goods entering an economy directly from detailed production and international trade statistics. This means that the price indexes used in deflating production and international trade, reflecting delivered or offered prices, will determine the deflator for investment expenditures on the demand side.

The data in the table on private consumption in current U.S. dollars are converted from national currencies using official exchange rates or an alternative conversion factor as noted in *Primary data documentation.* (For a discussion of alternative conversion factors see *Statistical methods.*) These exchange rates and conversion factors differ from the purchasing power parity conversion factors used to calculate private consumption per capita in table 4.11, which provide better estimates of comparative domestic purchasing power. Growth rates of private consumption per capita, general government consumption, and gross domestic investment are estimated using constant price data. (Consumption and investment as shares of GDP are shown in table 4.9.)

To obtain government consumption in constant prices, countries may deflate current values by applying a wage (price) index or extrapolate from the change in government employment. Neither technique captures improvements in productivity or changes in the quality of government services. Deflators for private consumption are usually calculated on the basis of the consumer price index. Many countries estimate private consumption as a residual that includes statistical discrepancies accumulated from other domestic sources; thus these estimates lack detailed breakdowns of expenditures.

Because the methods used to deflate consumption and investment can vary widely among countries, comparisons between countries in a given year, perhaps even more than those over time, should be treated with caution.

Figure 4.10

Private consumption has decelerated in East Asia and the Pacific

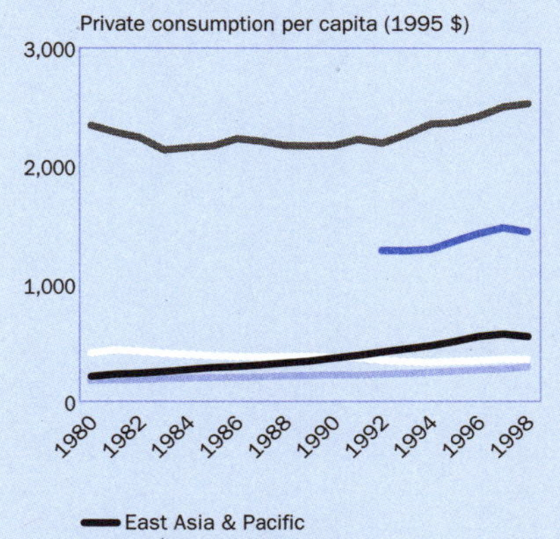

Source: World Bank data files.

In 1998 per capita private consumption (measured in constant 1995 dollars) dropped in East Asia and the Pacific, where it had grown fastest between 1980 and 1997, and in Europe and Central Asia. Sub-Saharan Africa continued its long-term decline, while all other regions posted small gains.

Definitions

• **Private consumption** is the market value of all goods and services, including durable products (such as cars, washing machines, and home computers), purchased or received as income in kind by households. It excludes purchases of dwellings but includes imputed rent for owner-occupied dwellings. It also includes payments and fees to governments to obtain permits and licenses. The expenditures of nonprofit institutions serving households are also recorded as the consumption of households. In practice, private consumption may include any statistical discrepancy in the use of resources relative to the supply of resources. • **General government consumption** includes all current expenditures for purchases of goods and services (including wages and salaries). It also includes most expenditures on national defense and security, but excludes government military expenditures that are part of government capital formation. • **Gross domestic investment** consists of outlays on additions to the fixed assets of the economy plus net changes in the level of inventories. Fixed assets include land improvements (fences, ditches, drains, and so on); plant, machinery, and equipment purchases; and the construction of roads, railways, and the like, including commercial and industrial buildings, offices, schools, hospitals, and private residential dwellings. Inventories are stocks of goods held by firms to meet temporary or unexpected fluctuations in production or sales. Net acquisitions of valuables are also considered capital formation.

Data sources

The national accounts indicators for most developing countries are collected from national statistical organizations and central banks by visiting and resident World Bank missions. Data for high-income countries come from Organisation for Economic Co-operation and Development (OECD) data files (see OECD, *National Accounts, 1960–1996,* volumes 1 and 2). The United Nations Statistics Division publishes detailed national accounts for United Nations member countries in *National Accounts Statistics: Main Aggregates and Detailed Tables;* updates are published in the *Monthly Bulletin of Statistics.*

4.11 Structure of consumption in PPP terms

	Private consumption per capita PPP 1998	Household consumption: All food % 1998	Bread and cereals % 1998	Meat % 1998	Clothing and footwear % 1998	Fuel and power % 1998	Health care % 1998	Education % 1998	Transport and communications % 1998	Other consumption % 1998
Albania	2,156	62	17	12	3	13	3	10	5	4
Antigua and Barbuda	4,603	36	10	3	3	8	3	18	9	23
Argentina	7,818	30	5	10	9	17	15	15	5	9
Armenia	1,658	52	11	4	3	18	3	15	4	5
Australia	14,890	24	3	7	5	9	2	16	9	36
Austria	13,886	20	1	5	10	11	4	9	9	38
Azerbaijan	1,674	51	25	6	5	16	9	2	4	14
Bahamas, The	10,799	32	6	9	4	5	3	8	9	41
Bahrain	3,932	32	6	4	7	8	1	6	9	37
Bangladesh	1,012	49	26	3	4	18	8	9	4	8
Belarus	4,272	36	7	8	7	15	7	10	11	14
Belgium	15,591	17	2	5	6	8	3	1	7	57
Belize	2,892	27	4	2	10	5	3	13	5	38
Benin	677	52	14	8	5	15	5	3	3	17
Bermuda	15,726	16	2	2	6	12	10	5	6	44
Bolivia	1,878	37	9	10	6	11	9	14	5	20
Botswana	2,128	24	9	5	5	12	2	7	5	45
Brazil	3,869	22	4	6	13	18	15	34	4	–6
Bulgaria	4,173	30	7	6	6	17	8	11	5	23
Cameroon	1,065	33	7	8	12	8	2	9	8	28
Canada	15,643	14	2	4	5	10	4	21	9	38
Chile	5,573	17	4	4	10	24	20	15	6	9
Congo, Rep.	662	34	4	4	2	12	3	3	11	36
Côte d'Ivoire	1,095	30	7	6	7	4	1	18	8	32
Croatia	4,925	24	3	6	4	18	4	3	6	41
Czech Republic	7,592	24	4	7	5	14	5	12	16	24
Denmark	16,385	16	1	4	6	11	3	17	5	43
Dominica	3,007	33	6	5	6	11	3	6	8	33
Ecuador	1,809	26	4	5	9	15	13	10	3	24
Egypt, Arab Rep.	2,550	44	13	11	9	7	3	17	3	17
Estonia	5,191	41	8	10	7	24	8	4	9	7
Fiji	3,039	35	7	6	5	19	2	13	4	23
Finland	12,958	17	2	4	4	10	4	15	7	43
France	14,115	22	2	6	7	9	3	8	12	40
Gabon	2,762	40	4	4	3	9	3	7	4	34
Georgia	2,732	33	10	3	4	13	2	4	8	36
Germany	15,577	14	2	4	6	7	2	10	7	53
Greece	9,873	32	2	7	11	14	5	14	8	16
Grenada	3,620	29	9	2	4	10	2	13	20	21
Guinea	1,480	29	6	6	18	5	2	9	16	21
Hong Kong, China	12,468	10	1	3	17	4	2	8	6	54
Hungary	6,591	25	3	6	5	17	6	20	12	15
Iceland	18,387	16	2	3	6	8	3	10	9	48
Indonesia	1,701	47	19	2	3	6	5	14	3	22
Iran, Islamic Rep.	3,289	20	5	4	10	32	12	8	9	10
Ireland	11,560	21	2	5	9	10	4	7	10	40
Israel	10,847	23	3	3	6	11	2	6	8	44
Italy	13,415	23	2	6	11	12	3	17	8	27
Jamaica	1,980	24	6	7	7	3	1	9	8	48
Japan	13,568	12	3	1	7	7	2	22	13	37
Jordan	2,832	32	2	9	6	17	5	8	8	23
Kazakhstan	3,500	37	14	8	10	20	9	6	6	12
Kenya	677	31	12	2	9	21	2	8	3	26
Korea, Rep.	6,695	18	4	2	3	7	5	14	6	48
Kyrgyz Republic	1,713	33	7	3	11	11	3	22	6	14
Latvia	4,324	30	6	7	5	16	6	23	11	10
Lebanon	6,135	31	3	7	13	10	7	9	7	22

Structure of consumption in PPP terms 4.11

	Private consumption per capita	Household consumption								
	PPP 1998	All food % 1998	Bread and cereals % 1998	Meat % 1998	Clothing and footwear % 1998	Fuel and power % 1998	Health care % 1998	Education % 1998	Transport and communications % 1998	Other consumption % 1998
Lithuania	4,974	33	6	8	5	13	4	27	9	8
Luxembourg	18,684	17	2	5	8	9	3	7	5	52
Macedonia, FYR	3,458	33	6	7	5	15	6	9	9	23
Madagascar	608	61	30	8	8	4	2	2	5	18
Malawi	469	50	20	11	13	7	2	6	9	13
Mali	452	53	19	9	15	7	4	5	2	15
Mauritius	4,983	21	3	4	8	13	3	13	10	32
Mexico	5,453	30	7	7	6	4	2	7	5	46
Moldova	1,572	31	8	5	5	11	3	15	12	23
Mongolia	1,085	56	17	26	14	9	8	14	1	–2
Morocco	2,062	33	7	6	11	16	5	15	6	16
Nepal	697	44	29	1	9	7	5	14	5	15
Netherlands	14,105	17	2	3	7	7	2	13	8	46
New Zealand	10,915	21	3	5	5	12	3	2	8	49
Nigeria	448	51	17	8	5	31	2	8	2	2
Norway	13,833	16	1	3	7	11	5	4	6	51
Oman	6,750	22	4	5	8	25	13	21	5	7
Pakistan	1,178	45	11	4	7	19	6	5	7	11
Panama	3,199	22	4	8	8	18	14	4	7	27
Peru	2,800	26	6	5	7	17	13	5	7	25
Philippines	2,524	37	12	5	3	11	1	14	1	32
Poland	5,532	28	4	9	4	19	6	1	8	34
Portugal	10,361	29	4	8	8	7	2	19	6	29
Qatar	7,308	22	2	6	12	11	5	13	8	29
Romania	4,472	36	7	9	7	9	3	20	9	16
Russian Federation	4,099	28	4	8	11	16	7	15	8	16
Senegal	951	46	12	6	13	13	3	15	3	7
Sierra Leone	404	47	17	3	9	9	3	13	8	12
Singapore	10,385	15	2	3	7	5	3	14	7	48
Slovak Republic	6,032	26	3	7	7	16	5	12	10	24
Slovenia	8,910	27	3	6	8	14	4	16	11	20
Spain	9,718	33	3	10	12	11	3	5	8	28
Sri Lanka	2,103	43	12	1	0	7	4	8	4	33
St. Kitts and Nevis	5,443	33	9	3	4	11	5	13	18	14
St. Lucia	3,376	40	5	10	5	11	4	17	11	11
St. Vincent and the Grenadines	2,955	27	8	3	4	8	2	13	24	22
Swaziland	1,872	25	7	7	7	9	6	13	8	32
Sweden	13,275	17	2	3	5	12	4	14	6	41
Switzerland	15,536	19	2	3	6	9	3	18	8	36
Tajikistan	660	48	20	3	7	10	0	14	5	16
Tanzania	375	67	28	8	6	5	4	12	6	0
Thailand	2,051	23	6	7	8	5	3	13	11	37
Trinidad and Tobago	5,661	20	3	3	10	23	5	13	7	22
Tunisia	3,139	28	4	4	8	8	3	12	8	34
Turkey	4,465	45	8	5	7	18	6	5	2	16
Turkmenistan	1,122	32	12	8	6	14	6	18	11	14
Ukraine	2,384	34	9	7	5	16	6	4	14	22
United Kingdom	14,804	14	2	3	7	9	3	3	6	58
United States	21,515	13	1	4	9	9	4	6	8	51
Uruguay	5,910	22	5	7	7	14	11	30	12	3
Uzbekistan	1,572	34	10	3	3	13	4	7	9	30
Venezuela, RB	3,683	30	9	7	6	17	16	13	7	12
Vietnam	1,159	49	21	10	7	15	4	18	6	2
Yemen, Rep.	768	25	11	4	5	26	3	5	5	31
Zambia	481	52	11	17	10	8	2	11	3	14
Zimbabwe	1,568	20	5	6	10	21	3	15	9	22

4.11 Structure of consumption in PPP terms

About the data

This table shows private consumption per capita in 1998 "international" dollars, calculated using purchasing power parities (PPPs), and its allocation among such components as food, clothing, and fuel and power. Cross-country comparisons of consumption expenditures must be made in a common currency. But when expenditures in different countries are converted to a single currency using official exchange rates, the comparisons do not account for the sometimes substantial differences in relative prices. Thus the results tend to undervalue real consumption in economies with relatively low prices and to overvalue consumption in countries with high prices. In addition, differences in the structure of prices distort the apparent structure of consumption. For example, services (although not always such basic provisions as private health care or education) often tend to be relatively cheaper than goods in low- and middle-income economies, so when domestic prices are used to calculate consumption patterns, services appear to be underutilized. The problem of making consistent comparisons of real consumption across countries has led to the use of PPPs to convert reported values to a common unit of account (see box 4.12).

PPPs measure the relative purchasing power of different currencies over equivalent goods and services. They are international price indexes that allow comparisons of the real value of consumption expenditures between countries in the same way that consumer price indexes allow comparisons of real values over time within countries. To calculate PPPs, data on prices and spending patterns are collected through surveys in each country. Then prices within a region, such as Africa, or a group, such as the Organisation for Economic Co-operation and Development (OECD), are compared. Finally, regions are linked by comparing regional prices, to create a globally consistent set of comparisons. The resulting PPP indexes measure the purchasing power of national currencies in "international dollars" that have the same purchasing power over GDP as the U.S. dollar has in the United States.

Because the goods and services that make up consumption are valued at uniform prices, PPP-based expenditure shares also provide a consistent view of differences in the real structure of consumption between countries. In other words, the shares shown in the table reflect the relative quantities of goods and services consumed rather than their nominal cost. Table 4.12 provides the corresponding data on the structure of prices for components of private consumption and for the other main national accounts aggregates within countries.

Private consumption refers to private (that is, household) and nonprofit (nongovernmental) consumption as defined in the United Nations System of National Accounts (SNA). Estimates of private consumption of education and health services include government as well as private outlays. The International Comparison Programme's (ICP) concept of enhanced consumption, or total consumption of the population, focuses on who consumes goods and services rather than on who pays for them. That is, it emphasizes consumption use rather than expenditure (payments). This approach, adopted in the 1993 SNA, improves international comparability because aggregate measures based on consumption are less sensitive to different national practices of financing health and education services.

Because national statistical offices tend to concentrate on the production side of national accounts, data on the detailed structure of consumption in low- and middle-income economies are generally weak. Estimates of the structure of consumption are typically obtained through household surveys. These surveys are carried out irregularly and may be targeted to specific income groups or geographic areas. In some countries surveys are limited to urban areas or even to capital cities and so do not reflect national spending patterns. Urban surveys tend to show lower-than-average shares for food and higher-than-average shares for gross rent, fuel and power, transport and communications, and other consumption. Controlled food prices and incomplete accounting of subsistence activities may also contribute to low measured shares of food consumption.

The ICP collects price data from different outlets on several hundred consumption items that are carefully reviewed to ensure comparability. ICP surveys are conducted about every five years, but because not all countries have participated in all surveys, regression methods are used to extrapolate results from earlier surveys and to provide a complete set of estimates in a given year. See Ahmad (1994) for an extensive discussion of the ICP and its methods.

Although PPPs are more useful than official exchange rates in comparing consumption patterns, caution should be used in interpreting PPP results. PPP estimates are based on price comparisons of comparable items, but not every item can be matched perfectly in quality across all countries and over time. Services are particularly difficult to compare, in part because of differences in productivity. Many services, such as government services, are not sold on the open market and so are compared using input prices (mostly wages). Because this approach ignores productivity differences, it may inflate estimates of real quantities in low-income countries.

Definitions

• **Private consumption** includes the consumption expenditures of individuals, households, and nongovernmental organizations. The ICP includes in private consumption goods and services accruing to households whether financed by individuals, governments, or nonprofit institutions. Thus as defined by the ICP private consumption includes government expenditures on education, health care, social security, and welfare services. • **Household consumption** shows the percentage shares of selected components of consumption computed from details of GDP converted using PPPs. • **All food** includes all food purchased for household consumption. • **Bread and cereals** comprise the main staple products—rice, flour, bread, and all other cereals and cereal preparations. • **Meat** includes fresh beef, veal, lamb, pork, and poultry. • **Clothing and footwear** include purchases of new and used clothing and footwear and repair services. • **Fuel and power** exclude energy used for transport (rarely reported to be more than 1 percent of total consumption in low- and middle-income economies). • **Health care** and **education** include government as well as private expenditures. • **Transport and communications** cover all personal costs of transport, telephones, and the like. • **Other consumption** covers gross rent (including repair and maintenance charges); beverages and tobacco; nondurable household goods, household services, recreational services, services (including meals) supplied by hotels and restaurants, and purchases of carryout food; and consumer durables, such as household appliances, furniture, floor coverings, recreational equipment, and watches and jewelry.

Data sources

PPP data come from the ICP, which is coordinated by the United Nations regional economic commissions and other international organizations. The World Bank collects detailed ICP benchmark data from regional sources, establishes global consistency across the regional data sets, and computes regression-based estimates for nonbenchmark countries. For detailed information on the regional sources and the compilation of benchmark data see the World Bank's *Purchasing Power of Currencies: Comparing National Incomes Using ICP Data* (1993b) and *Purchasing Power Parities: International Comparison of Volume and Price Levels* (forthcoming b).

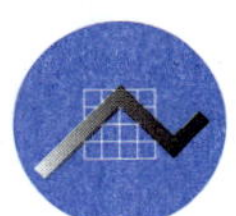

Relative prices in PPP terms 4.12

	International price level	Relative price level (price level of GDP = 100)									
		Private consumption									
	ratio of PPP rate to $ exchange rate 1998	Private consumption 1998	All food 1998	Bread and cereals 1998	Clothing and footwear 1998	Fuel and power 1998	Health care 1998	Education 1998	Transport and communi-cations 1998	Government consump-tion 1998	Gross fixed capital formation 1998
Albania	36	116	122	98	121	130	70	124	75	103	139
Antigua and Barbuda	89	111	102	100	179	141	155	129	51	68	98
Argentina	76	105	99	99	101	99	124	135	107	95	88
Armenia	28	131	167	161	190	210	66	176	36	64	156
Australia	100	105	51	77	73	103	132	75	214	185	73
Austria	128	111	54	74	70	108	160	89	263	193	69
Azerbaijan	27	125	173	142	157	23	63	117	47	67	176
Bahamas, The	87	101	89	85	102	83	128	123	110	120	86
Bahrain	72	118	98	79	92	781	111	107	115	131	158
Bangladesh	25	15	133	132	110	70	70	81	25	73	139
Barbados	53	86	158	152	146	130	154	190	130	168	180
Belarus	..	106	128	117	108	52	81	121	74	94	97
Belgium	113	101	67	85	100	129	160	92	286	220	77
Belize	69	98	97	76	78	129	92	93	86	88	128
Benin	47	101	97	96	129	112	90	121	104	78	136
Bermuda	142	109	76	94	85	82	134	92	166	192	68
Bolivia	44	96	97	102	132	95	74	80	84	78	152
Botswana	56	82	70	73	78	69	112	71	103	103	99
Brazil	73	110	101	105	89	121	147	117	96	77	102
Cameroon	47	100	108	103	122	134	63	79	99	76	115
Canada	84	103	61	67	89	87	135	88	301	254	70
Chile	60	103	122	124	98	80	122	133	121	88	106
Congo, Rep.	90	82	102	103	107	100	46	80	67	48	129
Côte d'Ivoire	52	94	112	109	113	128	90	101	81	77	164
Croatia	76	97	100	106	115	100	142	104	121	130	109
Czech Republic	45	102	79	73	111	102	68	135	122	113	104
Denmark	136	108	69	95	74	148	164	101	263	200	73
Dominica	75	105	114	123	103	142	68	119	74	71	129
Ecuador	54	106	107	107	116	86	108	88	82	72	101
Egypt, Arab Rep.	39	95	94	84	97	82	165	104	95	119	200
Estonia	50	105	76	78	86	67	81	88	70	87	117
Fiji	57	99	95	95	113	129	132	122	110	91	128
Finland	118	109	65	103	93	97	174	102	253	195	68
France	124	107	59	83	78	115	137	83	258	196	66
Gabon	82	90	98	112	100	90	134	64	79	97	192
Georgia	28	109	146	137	162	136	62	129	36	41	215
Germany	133	99	66	90	87	128	176	89	355	266	87
Greece	96	108	55	89	99	111	101	64	166	133	69
Grenada	70	102	115	103	109	143	61	158	63	70	139
Guinea	33	93	113	108	78	136	30	127	131	108	191
Hong Kong, China	110	98	86	70	86	70	118	67	294	279	88
Hungary	48	97	71	89	85	92	76	141	125	115	103
Iceland	115	100	84	116	105	71	115	99	260	216	82
Indonesia	39	95	91	86	107	73	85	83	57	54	154
Iran, Islamic Rep.	43	89	139	151	93	18	57	37	76	104	122
Ireland	91	112	57	73	72	104	136	98	221	176	72
Israel	112	112	69	106	69	90	153	85	239	192	60
Italy	97	105	65	86	75	124	137	84	234	193	72
Jamaica	67	104	132	105	134	154	73	62	86	84	99
Japan	151	109	101	126	86	134	115	72	258	211	80
Jordan	41	88	91	120	110	114	43	89	79	38	144
Kazakhstan	28	97	118	111	109	64	88	131	65	72	148
Kenya	34	99	122	121	75	147	71	162	112	85	154
Korea, Rep.	83	108	160	200	175	70	136	29	160	199	82
Kyrgyz Republic	23	124	160	167	98	104	80	164	50	64	172
Latvia	44	101	109	95	139	112	79	136	86	96	133
Lebanon	80	64	69	96	59	34	55	93	128	34	98

4.12 Relative prices in PPP terms

	International price level	Relative price level (price level of GDP = 100)									
		Private consumption									
	ratio of PPP rate to $ exchange rate 1998	Private consumption 1998	All food 1998	Bread and cereals 1998	Clothing and footwear 1998	Fuel and power 1998	Health care 1998	Education 1998	Transport and communi-cations 1998	Government consump-tion 1998	Gross fixed capital formation 1998
Lithuania	40	99	96	81	122	102	74	98	84	104	141
Luxembourg	115	108	62	82	100	99	163	75	409	290	76
Macedonia, FYR	59	99	88	104	101	110	104	92	131	125	125
Madagascar	39	106	108	105	94	177	63	119	77	49	134
Malawi	42	93	95	100	79	143	29	121	179	115	137
Mali	40	117	110	113	96	156	72	166	90	59	125
Mauritius	48	107	108	112	84	108	68	98	93	89	92
Mexico	49	98	72	88	63	72	119	94	105	104	102
Moldova	26	109	141	116	137	120	91	110	74	95	171
Mongolia	33	86	84	90	71	76	50	92	104	134	145
Morocco	41	105	129	136	66	120	86	85	97	101	96
Nepal	19	120	141	140	132	117	90	87	58	85	70
Netherlands	113	100	60	77	81	109	152	102	293	221	83
New Zealand	101	110	56	79	84	76	129	80	215	151	72
Nigeria	..	101	142	145	97	165	80	73	137	108	112
Norway	128	113	78	102	80	81	199	112	276	217	73
Oman	63	91	95	93	83	59	74	98	78	153	122
Pakistan	28	109	109	101	121	102	59	102	102	77	137
Panama	60	89	100	85	108	92	70	78	73	139	105
Peru	60	106	113	117	100	93	85	109	145	101	97
Philippines	33	97	112	113	122	244	92	106	49	113	132
Poland	52	102	81	80	123	116	122	114	121	103	98
Portugal	87	106	68	80	104	173	169	112	151	120	84
Qatar	70	92	100	118	74	67	91	81	125	148	151
Romania	25	98	108	95	83	60	79	89	77	85	164
Russian Federation	42	93	97	104	94	27	95	136	94	106	106
Senegal	44	103	111	123	89	150	73	103	97	68	143
Sierra Leone	32	110	138	139	131	160	54	37	150	97	123
Singapore	114	103	65	59	84	44	79	86	154	188	87
Slovak Republic	44	99	90	93	113	114	112	137	143	137	115
Slovenia	71	109	68	82	80	102	96	85	166	133	74
Spain	96	112	51	76	66	95	137	75	191	152	65
Sri Lanka	29	96	121	108	87	71	52	61	62	70	163
St. Kitts and Nevis	70	103	104	113	111	93	66	124	99	77	115
St. Lucia	75	102	110	134	110	121	60	77	74	85	107
St. Vincent and the Grenadines	65	105	129	118	115	180	54	123	67	62	156
Swaziland	33	119	116	118	145	132	84	84	96	80	115
Sweden	135	106	61	92	75	99	176	93	271	206	70
Switzerland	159	110	64	84	67	88	190	85	379	268	70
Syrian Arab Republic	131	58	128	198	117	56	30	86	35	29	193
Tajikistan	17	89	127	146	116	28	49	92	19	35	142
Tanzania	40	108	113	111	107	138	31	190	134	87	132
Thailand	49	136	120	104	187	90	90	104	142	140	74
Trinidad and Tobago	56	95	86	91	88	28	128	77	116	95	120
Tunisia	43	102	111	126	128	104	65	93	105	99	101
Turkey	51	102	69	83	125	134	154	91	118	109	103
Turkmenistan	10	101	151	105	183	7	91	60	47	62	107
Ukraine	27	93	113	84	109	83	75	99	71	83	165
United Kingdom	101	103	62	74	74	110	139	100	270	188	72
United States	100	101	54	83	57	72	211	74	374	243	75
Uruguay	73	104	95	106	99	99	125	110	80	90	87
Uzbekistan	..	88	118	116	83	31	64	138	48	70	313
Venezuela, RB	53	97	90	90	109	101	101	87	73	49	107
Vietnam	21	103	110	97	76	114	93	136	92	75	148
Yemen, Rep.	63	97	185	147	108	120	58	122	39	24	315
Zambia	50	110	112	117	76	133	30	151	120	59	103
Zimbabwe	30	103	112	118	96	131	53	121	110	90	100

Relative prices in PPP terms 4.12

About the data

This table presents information on the relative prices of components of GDP based on newly released data from the 1996 round of ICP surveys. Where data are not available for 1996, they have been extrapolated from the 1993 survey. The data are then updated to 1998 using similar procedures. The International Comparison Programme (ICP) collects data on prices paid for a large set of comparable items in more than 100 countries. Purchasing power parities (PPPs) computed from these data allow comparisons of prices and real GNP expenditures across countries. PPPs are used in table 1.1 to measure GNP at internationally comparable prices and in table 4.11 to evaluate the structure of consumption.

A country's international price level is the ratio of its PPP rate to its official exchange rate for U.S. dollars. PPPs can be thought of as the exchange rate of dollars for goods in the local economy, while the U.S. dollar exchange rate measures the relative cost of domestic currency in dollars. Thus the international price level is an index measuring the cost of goods in one country at the current rate of exchange relative to a numeraire country, in this case the United States. An international price level above 100 means that the general price level in the country is higher than that in the United States. For example, Japan's international price level of 151 in 1998 implies that the price of goods and services in Japan was, in general, 51 percent higher than the price of comparable goods and services in the United States. By contrast, Kenya's price level of 34 means that a bundle of goods and services purchased for $100 in the United States cost only $34 in Kenya in 1998.

The relative prices of the components of GDP shown in the table are calculated from their international prices measured relative to each country's price level of GDP. A figure above 100 indicates that the price of that component is higher than the average price level of GDP. This is not the same as saying that the component is more expensive in that country than in the United States. It indicates only that the price for that component is higher than the general price level prevailing in the country.

Relative prices for consumption items tend to be close to the overall price level of GDP. This is to be expected because consumption accounts for a large share of GDP. Relative prices for investment goods (gross fixed capital formation) in developing countries usually tend to be higher than those for other components of GDP. For example, Indonesia's relative price level of 154 for investment goods indicates a price level 54 percent higher than the overall price level. This reflects the fact that a large share of physical capital must be imported from high-income economies with higher average price levels.

Box 4.12

A question of methodology

Converting values expressed in different national currencies to a common currency and price level requires solving a difficult index number problem. The International Comparison Programme has devised several methods for doing this, but each has its drawbacks. For table 4.12 the Elteto-Koves-Szulc (EKS) formula was applied to generate purchasing power parities (PPPs) for each of the main economic aggregates in the national accounts. The EKS formula is based on a modified geometric averaging procedure applied within each expenditure category to every possible binary price ratio between all countries for each item. Implicitly, each price, whether from a rich country or a poor one, is given more or less equal weight.

The EKS formula is the preferred way of calculating individual PPPs across all countries for a single expenditure item. The problem is that the results do not add up. For example, the PPP-adjusted values for the components of private consumption do not sum to the PPP-adjusted value for total consumption.

A different procedure is needed to calculate the real shares of GNP or GDP in comparable terms. For this, compilers have adopted the Geary-Khamis method. This method uses national accounts values to weight different national prices to reflect their relative importance. Its drawback is the greater weight it gives to rich country prices, which raises poor countries' national accounts values in real terms and may give a distorted view of the expenditure shares in those countries.

To obtain the consumption shares in table 4.11, the Geary-Khamis method has been modified to attribute equal weight to all countries' prices. This modified method is similar to the Geary-Khamis method with "super country weights" adopted by the Penn World Tables to solve the same problem. Aggregates calculated with the EKS formula and the modified Geary-Khamis method generally differ by less than 5 percent.

Work is under way to develop a formula that provides consistency both between and across countries. And work continues on improving the consistency of the basic national accounts aggregates measured in nominal values, because such factors as the treatment of stocks and estimates of the net foreign balance can significantly affect the resulting PPPs for different expenditure components.

Definitions

• **International price level** is the ratio of a country's PPP rate to its official exchange rate for U.S. dollars. • **Private consumption** includes the consumption expenditures of individuals, households, and nongovernmental organizations. • **All food** includes all food purchased for household consumption. • **Bread and cereals** comprise the main staple products—rice, flour, bread, and all other cereals and cereal preparations. • **Clothing and footwear** include purchases of new and used clothing and footwear and repair services. • **Fuel and power** exclude energy used for transport (rarely reported to be more than 1 percent of total consumption in low- and middle-income economies). • **Health care** and **education** include government as well as private expenditures. • **Transport and communications** cover all personal costs of transport, telephones, and the like. • **Government consumption** includes spending on goods and services for collective consumption less spending on recreational and other related cultural services, education, health care, and housing. Expenditure on government final consumption consists of compensation of employees, consumption of intermediate goods and services, and consumption of fixed capital and indirect taxes paid less proceeds from sales of goods and services to other sectors (such as fees charged by municipalities and other government agencies, school fees, fees for medical and hospital treatment and drug sales, and sales of maps and charts). • **Gross fixed capital formation** comprises expenditures on construction, producer durables, and changes in stocks. Construction includes residential and nonresidential buildings and roads, bridges, and other civil engineering activities. Producer durables include machinery and nonelectrical equipment, electrical machinery and appliances, and transport equipment. Changes in stocks cover increases in the value of materials and supplies, works in progress, and livestock (including breeding stock and dairy cattle).

Data sources

PPP data come from the ICP, which is coordinated by the United Nations regional economic commissions and other international organizations. The World Bank collects detailed ICP benchmark data from regional sources, establishes global consistency across the regional data sets, and computes regression-based estimates for nonbenchmark countries. The data on which this table are based will appear in the World Bank's *Purchasing Power Parities: International Comparison of Volume and Price Levels* (forthcoming b).

4.13 Central government finances

	Current revenue[a] % of GDP		Total expenditure % of GDP		Overall budget deficit (including grants) % of GDP		Financing from abroad % of GDP		Domestic financing % of GDP		Debt and interest payments	
	1980	1997	1980	1997	1980	1997	1980	1997	1980	1997	Total debt % of GDP 1997	Interest % of current revenue 1997
Albania	..	15.5	..	28.5	..	–12.0	..	1.2	..	10.8	51.5	35.4
Algeria	..	*32.2*	..	*29.2*	..	*2.9*	..	*3.9*	..	*–6.9*	*64.1*	*10.4*
Angola	..	..	..	..	..	..	..	..	..	..	..	..
Argentina	15.6	13.6	18.2	15.3	–2.6	–1.5	0.0	1.5	2.6	0.0	..	14.4
Armenia	..	..	..	..	..	..	..	..	..	..	..	..
Australia	21.7	24.6	22.7	25.7	–1.5	0.4	0.2	–0.6	1.3	0.2	21.3	7.2
Austria	33.9	37.3	36.6	40.5	–3.3	–2.7	0.8	–0.1	2.5	2.7	..	10.0
Azerbaijan	..	14.9	..	19.2	..	–2.2	..	..	..	..	..	3.0
Bangladesh	8.4	..	7.4	..	1.8	..	*1.8*	..	*0.5*	..	..	..
Belarus	..	33.3	..	34.7	..	–1.6	..	0.5	..	1.2	12.7	2.0
Belgium	43.0	44.0	50.1	46.6	–8.0	–2.0	2.4	0.0	5.7	2.0	120.9	17.5
Benin	..	..	..	..	..	..	..	..	..	..	..	..
Bolivia	..	16.9	..	22.0	..	–2.3	..	2.0	..	0.3	46.3	10.0
Bosnia and Herzegovina	..	..	..	..	..	..	..	..	..	..	..	..
Botswana	29.8	*44.3*	29.8	*35.3*	–0.1	*8.4*	1.2	*0.5*	–1.1	*–8.9*	*11.0*	*1.3*
Brazil	22.6	..	20.2	..	–2.4	..	*0.0*	..	*2.4*	..	..	..
Bulgaria	..	32.1	..	33.6	..	2.1	..	0.3	..	–2.4	..	26.3
Burkina Faso	11.8	..	12.2	..	0.2	..	0.4	..	0.0	..	..	..
Burundi	13.9	13.7	21.5	24.0	–3.9	–5.5	2.0	3.1	1.9	2.4	136.4	13.2
Cambodia	..	..	..	..	..	..	..	..	..	..	..	..
Cameroon	16.4	*13.0*	15.7	*12.7*	0.5	*0.2*	0.7	*0.3*	–1.2	*–0.3*	*139.6*	*23.0*
Canada	18.5	*20.4*	21.1	*24.7*	–3.5	*–3.5*	0.6	*0.0*	2.9	*3.5*	*80.7*	*22.3*
Central African Republic	*16.5*	..	*22.0*	..	*–3.5*	..	*2.1*	..	*1.5*	..	..	..
Chad	..	..	..	..	..	..	..	..	..	..	..	..
Chile	32.0	22.7	28.0	20.7	5.4	1.9	–0.8	–0.5	–4.7	–1.4	14.2	1.9
China	..	5.8	..	8.1	..	–1.5	..	0.1	..	1.4	..	..
Hong Kong, China	..	..	..	..	..	..	..	..	..	..	..	..
Colombia	10.3	12.3	11.5	15.8	–1.5	–3.6	..	0.9	..	2.8	17.4	16.3
Congo, Dem. Rep.	9.4	5.3	12.4	10.4	–0.8	–0.8	0.3	0.0	0.5	0.8	160.4	0.2
Congo, Rep.	35.3	29.6	49.4	38.4	–5.2	–8.6	3.8	..	1.4	..	258.0	44.1
Costa Rica	17.8	*26.3*	25.0	*30.1*	–7.4	*–3.8*	1.1	*–1.1*	6.3	*4.0*	*0.0*	*22.8*
Côte d'Ivoire	22.9	22.2	31.7	25.0	–10.8	0.4	6.5	1.0	4.4	–1.4	168.0	22.8
Croatia	..	42.5	..	43.9	..	–1.3	..	2.5	..	–1.2	..	3.4
Cuba	..	..	..	..	..	..	..	..	..	..	..	..
Czech Republic	..	33.3	..	35.2	..	–1.1	..	–0.2	..	1.3	11.4	3.3
Denmark	34.7	*38.8*	38.6	*41.4*	–2.6	*–1.9*	..	..	..	..	..	*14.2*
Dominican Republic	14.2	16.9	16.9	16.7	–2.6	0.4	1.4	–1.0	1.2	0.6	..	3.1
Ecuador	12.8	..	14.2	..	–1.4	..	0.5	..	0.9	..	..	..
Egypt, Arab Rep.	44.1	26.3	50.3	30.6	–11.7	–2.0	3.6	–0.6	8.0	2.6	..	23.0
El Salvador	..	..	..	..	..	..	..	..	..	..	..	..
Eritrea	..	..	..	..	..	..	..	..	..	..	..	..
Estonia	..	33.9	..	32.0	..	2.5	..	–1.0	..	–1.5	..	1.0
Ethiopia	*16.6*	..	*19.9*	..	*–3.1*	..	*1.2*	..	*1.9*	..	..	..
Finland	27.2	32.0	28.1	35.3	–2.2	–2.5	0.8	–3.0	1.4	5.5	67.4	12.4
France	39.6	41.8	39.5	46.6	–0.1	–3.5	0.0	*0.2*	0.1	*5.1*	..	7.4
Gabon	35.5	..	36.5	..	6.1	..	0.0	..	–6.1	..	..	..
Gambia, The	23.1	..	31.7	..	–4.4	..	1.2	..	3.2	..	..	..
Georgia	..	6.7	..	9.7	..	–2.7	..	1.6	..	1.1	29.1	15.4
Germany	..	31.9	..	33.5	..	–1.4	..	2.2	..	–0.8	39.3	7.4
Ghana	6.9	..	10.9	..	–4.2	..	0.7	..	3.5	..	..	..
Greece	25.3	22.9	29.3	34.0	–4.1	–8.4	1.6	3.3	2.6	5.2	116.2	54.9
Guatemala	11.2	..	14.3	..	–3.9	..	1.5	..	2.4	..	..	..
Guinea	..	..	..	..	..	..	..	..	..	..	..	..
Guinea-Bissau	..	..	..	..	..	..	..	..	..	..	..	..
Haiti	10.6	..	17.4	..	–4.7	..	..	..	..	..	..	..
Honduras	14.6	..	..	..	..	..	..	..	..	..	..	..

Central government finances 4.13

	Current revenue[a]		Total expenditure		Overall budget deficit (including grants)		Financing from abroad		Domestic financing		Debt and interest payments	
											Total debt % of GDP	Interest % of current revenue
	% of GDP		% of GDP		% of GDP		% of GDP		% of GDP			
	1980	**1997**	**1980**	**1997**	**1980**	**1997**	**1980**	**1997**	**1980**	**1997**	**1997**	**1997**
Hungary	*53.4*	37.2	*56.2*	42.8	*–2.8*	–2.6	*2.1*	0.3	*0.7*	2.2	62.9	26.1
India	10.8	12.1	12.3	15.0	–6.0	–5.6	0.5	0.1	5.6	5.5	46.9	32.2
Indonesia	21.3	18.1	22.1	18.0	–2.3	–0.7	2.1	–0.7	0.2	1.4	*23.9*	9.5
Iran, Islamic Rep.	21.6	24.3	35.7	25.0	–13.8	–0.5	–0.6	0.1	14.4	0.4	..	0.1
Iraq	..	..	..	..	..	..	..	..	..	..	..	..
Ireland	34.7	*33.2*	45.1	*35.5*	–12.5	*–0.4*	..	..	..	..	..	*14.0*
Israel	52.2	42.3	72.8	48.1	–16.2	0.4	8.2	1.1	8.1	–1.5	113.2	13.6
Italy	31.4	45.3	41.3	48.2	–10.8	–3.1	0.2	..	10.6	..	..	20.1
Jamaica	29.0	..	41.5	..	–15.5	..	..	..	..	..	..	..
Japan	11.6	..	18.4	..	–7.0	..	..	..	6.7	..	..	..
Jordan	17.9	26.5	41.3	34.0	–9.3	–3.3	5.7	4.1	3.6	–0.8	104.3	15.3
Kazakhstan	..	..	..	..	..	..	..	..	..	..	..	..
Kenya	21.9	*27.2*	25.3	*29.0*	–4.5	*–0.9*	2.4	*–0.2*	2.1	*1.1*	..	*28.0*
Korea, Dem. Rep.	..	..	..	..	..	..	..	..	..	..	..	..
Korea, Rep.	17.7	20.0	17.3	17.4	–2.2	–1.3	0.9	1.5	1.4	–0.3	10.4	2.5
Kuwait	89.3	..	27.7	41.8	58.7	..	..	..	..	..	..	..
Kyrgyz Republic	..	..	..	..	..	..	..	..	..	..	..	..
Lao PDR	..	..	..	..	..	..	..	..	..	..	..	..
Latvia	..	31.8	..	31.4	..	0.8	..	0.9	..	–1.7	*14.4*	3.0
Lebanon	..	16.3	..	42.2	..	–25.6	..	3.2	..	22.4	102.0	92.8
Lesotho	*34.2*	51.3	*45.3*	53.3	*–7.4*	1.9	*2.6*	7.9	*4.8*	–9.8	62.2	4.0
Libya	..	..	..	..	..	..	..	..	..	..	..	..
Lithuania	..	26.4	..	27.4	..	–1.9	..	0.7	..	1.2	15.3	3.3
Macedonia, FYR	..	..	..	..	..	..	..	..	..	..	..	..
Madagascar	13.2	*8.7*	..	*17.3*	..	*–1.3*	..	*1.4*	..	*–0.1*	*119.8*	*54.1*
Malawi	19.1	..	34.6	..	–15.9	..	8.3	..	7.7	..	..	..
Malaysia	26.3	23.1	28.5	19.7	–6.0	2.9	0.6	–0.1	5.4	–1.2	..	10.2
Mali	9.9	..	19.4	..	–4.2	..	3.9	..	0.3	..	..	..
Mauritania	..	..	..	..	..	..	..	..	..	..	..	..
Mauritius	20.8	21.3	27.2	23.6	–10.3	–4.0	2.5	–0.6	7.8	4.6	36.8	12.6
Mexico	15.1	14.7	15.7	16.3	–3.0	–1.1	–0.4	–0.7	3.4	1.8	25.9	15.1
Moldova	..	..	..	..	..	..	..	..	..	..	..	..
Mongolia	..	21.3	..	23.2	..	–8.7	..	12.0	..	–3.3	65.1	11.2
Morocco	23.3	*28.5*	33.1	*33.3*	–9.7	*–4.4*	5.3	*–0.7*	4.4	*5.1*	*79.4*	*20.9*
Mozambique	..	..	..	..	..	..	..	..	..	..	..	..
Myanmar	16.0	7.7	15.8	8.9	1.2	–0.9	1.2	0.0	–2.4	0.9	..	..
Namibia	..	..	..	..	..	..	..	..	..	..	..	..
Nepal	7.8	10.4	14.3	16.8	–3.0	–3.9	1.9	2.5	1.2	1.4	59.9	13.9
Netherlands	49.4	45.7	52.9	47.6	–4.6	–1.7	0.0	0.5	4.6	1.2	58.9	9.5
New Zealand	34.2	33.7	38.3	32.0	–6.7	4.0	3.6	..	3.1	..	37.0	9.3
Nicaragua	23.3	*25.4*	30.4	*33.2*	–6.8	*–0.6*	3.6	*0.2*	3.2	*0.5*	..	*15.8*
Niger	14.6	..	18.6	..	–4.8	..	4.1	..	0.7	..	..	..
Nigeria	..	..	..	..	..	..	..	..	..	..	..	..
Norway	37.2	43.2	34.4	35.7	–1.7	0.7	–0.7	–2.2	2.4	1.4	22.0	4.2
Oman	38.2	30.8	38.5	30.7	0.4	–0.5	–3.6	–0.1	3.1	0.6	24.0	5.7
Pakistan	16.2	15.6	17.5	22.3	–5.7	–7.7	2.3	1.9	3.4	5.8	..	38.1
Panama	25.3	25.4	30.5	27.0	–5.2	0.2	5.4	1.3	–0.2	–1.5	..	13.3
Papua New Guinea	23.0	..	34.4	..	–1.9	..	2.5	..	–0.5	..	..	..
Paraguay	10.7	..	9.9	..	0.3	..	2.2	..	–2.5	..	..	..
Peru	17.1	16.0	19.5	15.7	–2.4	0.5	0.6	–0.2	1.8	–0.3	*45.9*	10.1
Philippines	14.0	19.0	13.4	19.3	–1.4	0.1	0.9	–0.3	0.5	0.2	55.8	16.9
Poland	..	36.6	..	39.0	..	–1.3	..	0.0	..	1.3	47.2	9.4
Portugal	26.0	35.8	33.1	40.8	–8.4	–2.1	1.9	2.2	6.5	–0.1	0.9	10.6
Puerto Rico	..	..	..	..	..	..	..	..	..	..	..	..
Romania	45.3	26.5	44.8	31.9	0.5	–3.9	..	0.9	..	3.0	..	13.9
Russian Federation	..	*19.5*	..	*25.4*	..	*–4.7*	..	*1.6*	..	*3.1*	..	*17.0*

4.13 Central government finances

	Current revenue[a] % of GDP 1980	Current revenue[a] % of GDP 1997	Total expenditure % of GDP 1980	Total expenditure % of GDP 1997	Overall budget deficit (including grants) % of GDP 1980	Overall budget deficit (including grants) % of GDP 1997	Financing from abroad % of GDP 1980	Financing from abroad % of GDP 1997	Domestic financing % of GDP 1980	Domestic financing % of GDP 1997	Debt and interest payments: Total debt % of GDP 1997	Debt and interest payments: Interest % of current revenue 1997
Rwanda	12.8	..	14.3	..	–1.7	..	2.6	..	–0.9	..	..	..
Saudi Arabia	..	..	..	..	..	..	..	..	..	..	..	..
Senegal	24.3	..	23.3	..	0.9	..	–2.7	..	1.8	..	..	..
Sierra Leone	15.1	10.6	26.5	17.7	–11.8	–6.0	3.5	5.1	8.3	0.9	*116.2*	21.0
Singapore	25.4	24.5	20.0	16.8	2.1	11.7	–0.2	0.0	–2.0	–11.7	75.1	2.9
Slovak Republic	..	..	..	..	..	..	..	..	..	..	..	..
Slovenia	..	..	..	..	..	..	..	..	..	..	..	..
South Africa	22.9	25.6	21.6	29.3	–2.3	–3.4	–0.2	0.6	2.5	2.8	..	22.5
Spain	24.0	*30.1*	26.5	*36.1*	–4.2	*–5.5*	0.0	*0.3*	4.2	*5.2*	*59.4*	*14.8*
Sri Lanka	20.2	18.5	41.4	25.7	–18.3	–4.5	4.5	1.1	13.8	3.4	86.1	33.5
Sudan	12.3	..	17.4	..	–2.9	..	2.5	..	0.4	..	..	..
Sweden	35.0	42.0	39.3	44.3	–8.1	–1.4	3.2	1.6	4.9	–0.2	..	13.5
Switzerland	18.6	23.7	19.2	27.9	–0.2	–1.3	..	0.0	..	1.3	26.2	3.8
Syrian Arab Republic	26.8	24.2	48.2	24.6	–9.7	–0.2	–0.2	..	9.8	..	..	..
Tajikistan	..	..	..	..	..	..	..	..	..	..	..	..
Tanzania	..	..	..	..	..	..	..	..	..	..	..	..
Thailand	14.3	18.6	18.8	19.3	–4.9	–0.9	1.1	0.2	3.7	0.7	4.7	1.8
Togo	30.3	..	30.8	..	–2.0	..	1.6	..	0.4	..	..	..
Trinidad and Tobago	43.2	*27.2*	30.9	*28.2*	7.4	*0.2*	..	*2.6*	..	*–2.8*	*51.6*	*18.3*
Tunisia	31.3	*29.6*	31.6	*32.6*	–2.8	*–3.1*	2.3	*2.8*	0.5	*0.4*	*55.3*	*13.4*
Turkey	18.1	21.9	21.3	29.9	–3.1	–8.4	0.4	*–0.9*	2.6	*9.3*	44.7	36.1
Turkmenistan	..	..	..	..	..	..	..	..	..	..	..	..
Uganda	3.2	..	6.2	..	–3.1	..	0.0	..	3.1	..	..	..
Ukraine	..	..	..	..	..	..	..	..	..	..	..	..
United Arab Emirates	0.2	3.1	12.1	10.0	2.1	0.5	0.0	0.0	–2.1	–0.5	..	0.0
United Kingdom	35.2	36.6	38.3	39.1	–4.6	–2.1	0.3	–0.2	4.3	2.3	51.2	9.8
United States	20.2	21.2	22.0	21.6	–2.8	–0.3	0.0	2.4	2.8	–2.1	48.2	15.3
Uruguay	22.3	31.7	21.8	33.1	0.0	–1.3	0.9	..	–0.9	..	..	5.0
Uzbekistan	..	..	..	..	..	..	..	..	..	..	..	..
Venezuela, RB	22.3	23.7	18.7	20.6	0.0	2.2	1.8	0.9	–1.9	–3.1	..	10.1
Vietnam	..	20.0	..	22.0	..	–0.8	..	0.1	..	0.8	..	3.0
West Bank and Gaza	..	..	..	..	..	..	..	..	..	..	..	..
Yemen, Rep.	..	38.7	..	38.6	..	–1.2	..	0.5	..	0.7	..	7.2
Yugoslavia, FR (Serb./Mont.)	..	..	..	..	..	..	..	..	..	..	..	..
Zambia	25.0	..	37.1	..	–18.5	..	8.8	..	9.7	..	..	..
Zimbabwe	19.3	29.4	27.9	35.7	–8.8	–5.0	1.8	–0.1	6.9	5.1	58.1	24.2
World	**22.2 w**	**27.0 w**	**25.3 w**	**28.7 w**	**–4.2 w**	**–1.3 w**	**.. m**	**.. m**	**2.5 m**	**.. m**	**.. m**	***12.4* m**
Low income	..	10.1	..	12.4	..	–2.6	..	..	..	..	..	..
Excl. China & India	18.0	*17.5*	19.8	*18.3*	–2.9	*–1.2*	..	..	..	..	..	..
Middle income	20.2	..	20.9	..	–3.1	..	..	0.5	..	0.6	..	10.2
Lower middle income	..	*21.5*	..	*24.0*	..	*–2.1*	..	*0.4*	..	*0.3*	..	*11.7*
Upper middle income	20.1	..	19.5	..	–2.4	..	*1.1*	0.0	*1.9*	0.0	..	10.1
Low & middle income	19.3	*17.3*	20.1	*18.9*	–3.3	*–1.7*	..	..	..	..	..	..
East Asia & Pacific	..	13.5	..	13.8	..	–1.0	1.1	0.1	0.5	0.7	..	9.5
Europe & Central Asia	..	*24.7*	..	*29.1*	..	*–3.6*	..	..	..	..	..	6.4
Latin America & Carib.	19.7	..	19.0	..	–2.2	..	0.9	..	0.9	..	..	*13.9*
Middle East & N. Africa	..	..	..	..	..	..	2.3	*3.3*	4.4	*0.1*	..	*11.2*
South Asia	11.7	12.8	13.5	16.4	–5.8	–5.8	2.1	1.5	4.5	4.5	59.9	32.9
Sub-Saharan Africa	20.9	..	22.1	..	–3.1	..	2.4	..	1.9	..	..	..
High income	22.8	29.6	26.4	31.2	–4.4	–1.2	0.3	0.0	3.0	0.7	49.7	9.6
Europe EMU	..	38.5	..	41.4	..	–2.3	0.5	0.2	4.4	1.6	58.9	10.3

a. Excluding grants.

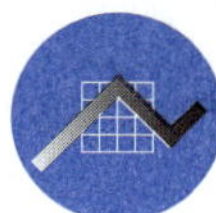

Central government finances 4.13

About the data

Tables 4.13–4.15 present an overview of the size and role of central governments relative to national economies. The International Monetary Fund's (IMF) *Manual on Government Finance Statistics* describes the government as the sector of the economy responsible for "implementation of public policy through the provision of primarily nonmarket services and the transfer of income, supported mainly by compulsory levies on other sectors" (1986, p. 3). In general, the definition of government excludes nonfinancial public enterprises and public financial institutions (such as the central bank).

Units of government meeting this definition exist at many levels, from local administrative units to the highest level of national government. Inadequate statistical coverage precludes the presentation of subnational data, however, making cross-country comparisons potentially misleading.

Central government can refer to one of two accounting concepts: consolidated or budgetary. For most countries central government finance data have been consolidated into one account, but for others only budgetary central government accounts are available. Countries reporting budgetary data are noted in *Primary data documentation*. Because budgetary accounts do not necessarily include all central government units, the picture they provide of central government activities is usually incomplete. A key issue is the failure to include the quasi-fiscal operations of the central bank. Central bank losses arising from monetary operations and subsidized financing can result in sizable quasi-fiscal deficits. Such deficits may also result from the operations of other financial intermediaries, such as public development finance institutions. Also missing from the data are governments' contingent liabilities for unfunded pension and insurance plans.

Data on government revenues and expenditures are collected by the IMF through questionnaires distributed to member governments and by the Organisation for Economic Co-operation and Development. Despite the IMF's efforts to systematize and standardize the collection of public finance data, statistics on public finance are often incomplete, untimely, and noncomparable.

Government finance statistics are reported in local currency. The indicators here are shown as percentages of GDP. Many countries report government finance data according to fiscal years; see *Primary data documentation* for the timing of these years. For further discussion of government finance statistics see *About the data* for tables 4.14 and 4.15.

Figure 4.13

Worsening fiscal balances in Asia

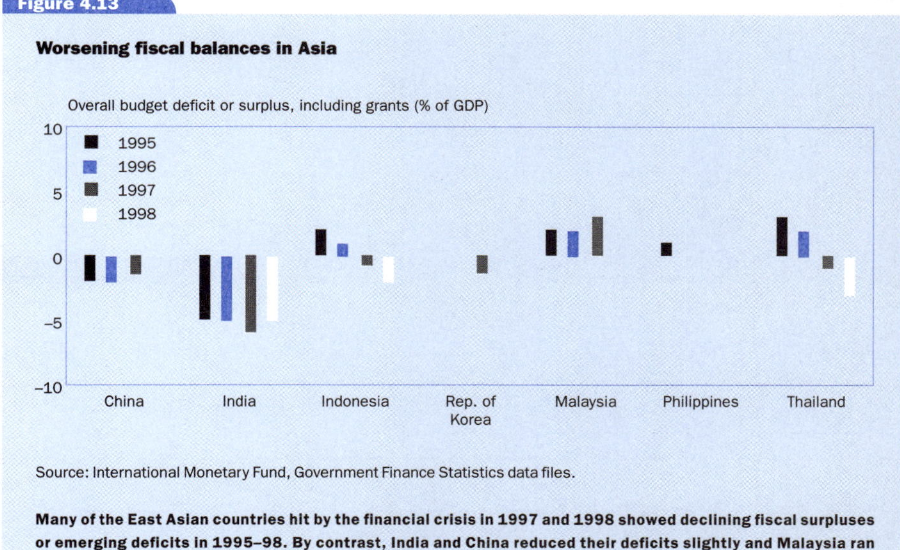

Source: International Monetary Fund, Government Finance Statistics data files.

Many of the East Asian countries hit by the financial crisis in 1997 and 1998 showed declining fiscal surpluses or emerging deficits in 1995–98. By contrast, India and China reduced their deficits slightly and Malaysia ran a surplus.

Definitions

• **Current revenue** includes all revenue from taxes and current nontax revenues (other than grants) such as fines, fees, recoveries, and income from property or sales. • **Total expenditure** includes nonrepayable current and capital expenditure. It does not include government lending or repayments to the government or government acquisition of equity for public policy purposes. • **Overall budget deficit** is current and capital revenue and official grants received, less total expenditure and lending minus repayments. • **Financing from abroad** (obtained from nonresidents) and **domestic financing** (obtained from residents) refer to the means by which a government provides financial resources to cover a budget deficit or allocates financial resources arising from a budget surplus. It includes all government liabilities—other than those for currency issues or demand, time, or savings deposits with government—or claims on others held by government and changes in government holdings of cash and deposits. Government guarantees of the debt of others are excluded. • **Debt** is the entire stock of direct, government, fixed term contractual obligations to others outstanding on a particular date. It includes domestic debt (such as debt held by monetary authorities, deposit money banks, nonfinancial public enterprises, and households) and foreign debt (such as debt to international development institutions and foreign governments). It is the gross amount of government liabilities not reduced by the amount of government claims against others. Because debt is a stock rather than a flow, it is measured as of a given date, usually the last day of the fiscal year. • **Interest** includes interest payments on government debt—including long-term bonds, long-term loans, and other debt instruments—to both domestic and foreign residents.

Data sources

The data on central government finances are from the IMF's *Government Finance Statistics Yearbook, 1999* and IMF data files. Each country's accounts are reported using the system of common definitions and classifications in the IMF's *Manual on Government Finance Statistics* (1986). See these sources for complete and authoritative explanations of concepts, definitions, and data sources.

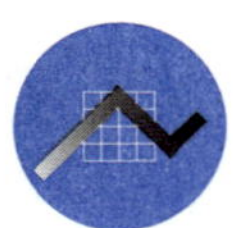

4.14 Central government expenditures

	Goods and services		Wages and salaries[a]		Interest payments		Subsidies and other current transfers		Capital expenditure	
	% of total expenditure		% of total expenditure		% of total expenditure		% of total expenditure		% of total expenditure	
	1980	1997	1980	1997	1980	1997	1980	1997	1980	1997
Albania	..	23	..	11	..	19	..	45	..	13
Algeria	..	*35*	..	*24*	..	*10*	..	*26*	..	*26*
Angola	..	..	..	..	..	..	..	..	..	..
Argentina	57	21	..	16	..	13	43	58	..	8
Armenia	..	..	..	..	..	..	..	..	..	..
Australia	22	26	..	3	7	7	65	61	7	6
Austria	26	23	11	9	5	9	60	62	9	6
Azerbaijan	..	36	..	10	..	2	..	44	..	17
Bangladesh	..	..	..	..	..	..	..	..	..	..
Belarus	..	26	..	7	..	2	..	54	..	18
Belgium	23	19	16	14	10	17	59	60	8	5
Benin	..	..	..	..	..	..	..	..	..	..
Bolivia	..	36	..	23	..	8	..	40	..	16
Bosnia and Herzegovina	..	..	..	..	..	..	..	..	..	..
Botswana	47	*48*	29	*25*	2	*2*	19	*31*	32	*19*
Brazil	20	..	16	..	8	..	64	..	8	..
Bulgaria	..	30	..	6	..	25	..	37	..	8
Burkina Faso	67	..	..	..	*3*	..	13	..	19	..
Burundi	*39*	53	*25*	30	*2*	8	*7*	11	*46*	15
Cambodia	..	..	..	..	..	..	..	..	..	..
Cameroon	55	*53*	32	*37*	1	*23*	11	*13*	33	*8*
Canada	22	*17*	10	*10*	12	*18*	65	*62*	1	*2*
Central African Republic	*67*	..	*54*	..	*1*	..	*16*	..	*6*	..
Chad	..	..	..	..	..	..	..	..	..	..
Chile	41	29	29	20	3	2	46	52	10	17
China	..	..	..	..	..	..	..	..	..	..
Hong Kong, China	..	..	..	..	..	..	..	..	..	..
Colombia	36	21	23	15	4	13	38	40	31	26
Congo, Dem. Rep.	65	94	42	54	8	0	8	1	20	5
Congo, Rep.	..	50	..	20	..	34	..	5	*45*	11
Costa Rica	53	*47*	44	*35*	9	*20*	24	*23*	21	*10*
Côte d'Ivoire	39	46	28	26	8	20	13	9	28	25
Croatia	..	48	..	23	..	3	..	38	..	10
Cuba	..	..	..	..	..	..	..	..	..	..
Czech Republic	..	14	..	8	..	3	..	74	..	9
Denmark	22	*19*	13	*11*	7	*13*	65	*64*	7	*4*
Dominican Republic	50	43	39	35	6	3	12	23	31	26
Ecuador	28	..	26	..	9	..	34	..	16	..
Egypt, Arab Rep.	39	41	19	20	8	20	32	15	21	24
El Salvador	..	..	..	..	..	..	..	..	..	..
Eritrea	..	..	..	..	..	..	..	..	..	..
Estonia	..	43	..	13	..	1	..	47	..	9
Ethiopia	86	..	36	..	3	..	4	..	15	..
Finland	22	19	11	7	2	11	66	67	11	3
France	30	24	20	16	2	7	62	65	5	4
Gabon	..	..	..	..	..	..	..	..	..	..
Gambia, The	46	..	23	..	1	..	4	..	48	..
Georgia	..	52	..	10	..	11	..	28	..	9
Germany[b]	34	32	9	8	3	7	55	58	7	4
Ghana	48	..	27	..	16	..	26	..	10	..
Greece	45	*29*	29	*24*	8	*36*	35	*22*	16	*13*
Guatemala	53	..	37	..	4	..	8	..	38	..
Guinea	..	..	..	..	..	..	..	..	..	..
Guinea-Bissau	..	..	..	..	..	..	..	..	..	..
Haiti	*82*	..	..	..	*2*	..	*5*	..	*20*	..
Honduras	..	..	..	..	..	..	..	..	..	..

Central government expenditures 4.14

	Goods and services		Wages and salaries[a]		Interest payments		Subsidies and other current transfers		Capital expenditure	
	% of total expenditure		% of total expenditure		% of total expenditure		% of total expenditure		% of total expenditure	
	1980	1997	1980	1997	1980	1997	1980	1997	1980	1997
Hungary	*20*	17	*7*	8	*3*	23	*64*	48	*13*	10
India	29	24	14	11	13	26	47	40	12	10
Indonesia	25	23	15	10	4	10	24	36	47	31
Iran, Islamic Rep.	57	57	45	44	1	0	19	14	22	29
Iraq	..	..	..	..	..	..	..	..	..	..
Ireland	19	*18*	13	*13*	14	*13*	57	*60*	10	*9*
Israel	50	33	12	14	11	12	35	48	4	7
Italy	18	17	13	15	11	19	63	58	5	5
Jamaica	..	..	..	..	..	..	..	..	..	..
Japan	13	..	..	..	13	..	54	..	19	..
Jordan	43	63	..	46	3	12	17	9	29	17
Kazakhstan	..	..	..	..	..	..	..	..	..	..
Kenya	57	*45*	27	*28*	7	*26*	13	*18*	23	*12*
Korea, Dem. Rep.	..	..	..	..	..	..	..	..	..	..
Korea, Rep.	45	27	16	13	7	3	34	49	14	22
Kuwait	45	62	22	31	..	4	23	20	32	14
Kyrgyz Republic	..	..	..	..	..	..	..	..	..	..
Lao PDR	..	..	..	..	..	..	..	..	..	..
Latvia	..	32	..	13	..	3	..	61	..	5
Lebanon	..	32	..	20	..	36	..	12	..	20
Lesotho	*50*	51	*34*	31	*10*	4	*13*	9	*27*	37
Libya	..	..	..	..	..	..	..	..	..	..
Lithuania	..	47	..	20	..	3	..	41	..	9
Macedonia, FYR	..	..	..	..	..	..	..	..	..	..
Madagascar	..	*25*	..	*18*	..	*27*	..	*8*	..	*39*
Malawi	37	..	15	..	9	..	6	..	48	..
Malaysia	38	42	28	26	10	12	19	24	35	23
Mali	46	..	33	..	1	..	11	..	9	..
Mauritania	..	..	..	..	..	..	..	..	..	..
Mauritius	42	45	32	34	14	11	28	28	17	16
Mexico	32	23	25	14	11	14	32	51	32	12
Moldova	..	..	..	..	..	..	..	..	..	..
Mongolia	..	32	..	9	..	10	..	44	..	14
Morocco	47	*49*	33	*34*	7	*18*	15	*12*	31	*22*
Mozambique	..	..	..	..	..	..	..	..	..	..
Myanmar	..	..	..	..	..	..	..	..	24	51
Namibia	..	..	..	..	..	..	..	..	..	..
Nepal	..	..	..	..	..	9	..	..	..	..
Netherlands	16	15	11	9	4	9	72	72	9	3
New Zealand	29	49	21	..	10	10	55	38	6	3
Nicaragua	60	*30*	..	*19*	8	*12*	13	*25*	19	*33*
Niger	30	..	17	..	6	..	14	..	49	..
Nigeria	..	..	..	..	..	..	..	..	..	..
Norway	20	21	9	8	7	5	67	70	6	5
Oman	71	77	13	26	3	6	5	5	21	12
Pakistan	47	52	..	..	12	27	23	8	17	12
Panama	50	53	33	37	18	13	14	27	18	7
Papua New Guinea	58	..	37	..	5	..	23	..	15	..
Paraguay	61	..	34	..	3	..	12	..	24	..
Peru	45	38	..	18	18	10	14	36	23	16
Philippines	61	*52*	27	*31*	7	17	7	18	26	*12*
Poland	..	25	..	13	..	9	..	62	..	5
Portugal	34	40	24	31	8	9	45	38	13	13
Puerto Rico	..	..	..	..	..	..	..	..	..	..
Romania	11	29	2	13	..	12	55	50	33	9
Russian Federation	..	..	..	..	..	*13*	..	..	..	..

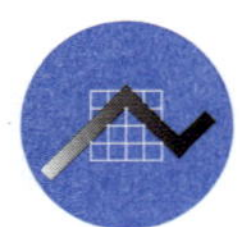

4.14 Central government expenditures

	Goods and services		Wages and salaries[a]		Interest payments		Subsidies and other current transfers		Capital expenditure	
	% of total expenditure		% of total expenditure		% of total expenditure		% of total expenditure		% of total expenditure	
	1980	1997	1980	1997	1980	1997	1980	1997	1980	1997
Rwanda	58	..	30	..	2	..	5	..	35	..
Saudi Arabia	..	..	..	..	..	..	..	..	..	..
Senegal	72	..	45	..	6	..	18	..	8	..
Sierra Leone	..	39	..	20	..	13	..	24	*20*	24
Singapore	58	58	29	29	15	4	6	8	22	30
Slovak Republic	..	..	..	..	..	..	..	..	..	..
Slovenia	..	..	..	..	..	..	..	..	..	..
South Africa	47	28	20	18	8	20	31	49	14	3
Spain	40	*16*	32	*11*	1	*12*	48	*66*	11	*5*
Sri Lanka	31	37	13	20	8	24	20	20	40	19
Sudan	46	..	12	..	6	..	28	..	23	..
Sweden	17	14	8	6	7	13	71	71	5	2
Switzerland	27	29	6	5	3	3	63	64	7	4
Syrian Arab Republic	42	..	18	..	..	..	21	..	37	37
Tajikistan	..	..	..	..	..	..	..	..	..	..
Tanzania	52	..	19	..	7	..	4	..	40	..
Thailand	55	51	21	29	8	2	14	7	23	41
Togo	*52*	..	*28*	..	*9*	..	*12*	..	*27*	..
Trinidad and Tobago	34	*51*	28	*33*	3	*18*	24	*21*	39	*10*
Tunisia	42	*38*	29	*32*	5	*12*	24	*29*	30	*21*
Turkey	47	33	32	25	3	26	23	29	28	11
Turkmenistan	..	..	..	..	..	..	..	..	..	..
Uganda	..	..	..	..	..	..	..	..	13	..
Ukraine	..	..	..	..	..	..	..	..	..	..
United Arab Emirates	80	84	..	36	0	0	12	13	8	3
United Kingdom	32	28	14	7	11	9	53	58	5	4
United States	29	22	11	8	10	15	54	60	6	3
Uruguay	47	28	30	15	2	5	43	62	8	5
Uzbekistan	..	..	..	..	..	..	..	..	..	..
Venezuela, RB	50	24	41	20	8	12	22	48	22	17
Vietnam	..	..	..	..	..	3	..	..	..	26
West Bank and Gaza	..	..	..	..	..	..	..	..	..	..
Yemen, Rep.	..	41	..	29	..	7	..	35	..	16
Yugoslavia, FR (Serb./Mont.)	..	..	..	..	..	..	..	..	..	..
Zambia	55	..	27	..	9	..	25	..	11	..
Zimbabwe	56	48	31	36	7	20	32	26	5	6
World	**45 m**	***34 m***	**.. m**	***18 m***	**7 m**	***11 m***	**24 m**	***37 m***	**18 m**	***12 m***
Low income	..	..	..	..	..	..	..	..	..	..
Excl. China & India	..	..	..	..	..	..	..	..	..	..
Middle income	47	33	..	20	6	11	23	40	23	13
Lower middle income	..	*38*	..	*20*	..	*10*	..	*26*	..	*18*
Upper middle income	46	29	28	20	5	11	28	48	20	11
Low & middle income	..	..	..	..	..	..	..	..	..	..
East Asia & Pacific	..	..	..	..	..	10	..	..	24	26
Europe & Central Asia	..	31	..	..	..	6	..	46	..	9
Latin America & Carib.	49	*30*	30	*19*	7	*11*	24	*31*	21	*16*
Middle East & N. Africa	43	*46*	..	*32*	..	*9*	19	*14*	29	20
South Asia	31	37	..	..	12	25	23	20	17	12
Sub-Saharan Africa	53	..	..	..	..	..	13	..	20	..
High income	27	26	13	9	7	9	57	60	7	4
Europe EMU	24	21	13	11	4	9	59	61	9	4

Note: Components include expenditures financed by grants in kind and other cash adjustments to total expenditure.
a. Part of goods and services. b. Data prior to 1990 refer to the Federal Republic of Germany before unification.

Central government expenditures 4.14

About the data

Government expenditures include all nonrepayable payments, whether current or capital, requited or unrequited. Total central government expenditure as presented in the International Monetary Fund's (IMF) *Government Finance Statistics Yearbook* is a more limited measure of general government consumption than that shown in the national accounts (see table 4.10) because it excludes consumption expenditures by state and local governments. At the same time, the IMF's concept of central government expenditure is broader than the national accounts definition because it includes government gross domestic investment and transfer payments.

Expenditures can be measured either by function (education, health, defense) or by economic type (wages and salaries, interest payments, purchases of goods and services). Functional data are often incomplete, and coverage varies by country because functional responsibilities stretch across levels of government for which no data are available. Defense expenditures, which are usually the central government's responsibility, are shown in table 5.7. For more information on education expenditures see table 2.9; for more on health expenditures see table 2.14.

The classification of expenditures by economic type can also be problematic. For example, the distinction between current and capital expenditure may be arbitrary, and subsidies to state-owned enterprises or banks may be disguised as capital financing. Subsidies may also be hidden in special contractual pricing for goods and services.

Expenditure shares may not sum to 100 percent because expenditures financed by grants in kind and other cash adjustments (which may be positive or negative) are not shown.

For further discussion of government finance statistics see *About the data* for tables 4.13 and 4.15.

Figure 4.14

High public interest payments strain national budgets in many developing and transition economies

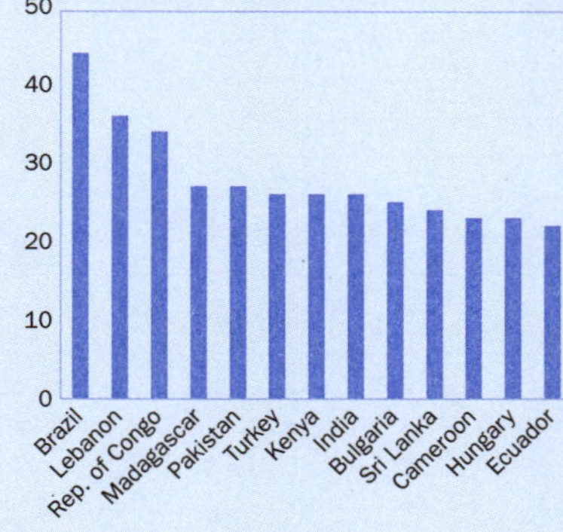

Note: The data refer to various years in 1994–97.
Source: International Monetary Fund, Government Finance Statistics data files.

Thirteen developing or transition economies had interest payments exceeding 20 percent of their national budgets in 1994–97.

Definitions

• **Total expenditure of the central government** includes both current and capital (development) expenditures and excludes lending minus repayments. • **Goods and services** include all government payments in exchange for goods and services, whether in the form of wages and salaries to employees or other purchases of goods and services. • **Wages and salaries** consist of all payments in cash, but not in kind, to employees in return for services rendered, before deduction of withholding taxes and employee contributions to social security and pension funds. • **Interest payments** are payments made to domestic sectors and to nonresidents for the use of borrowed money. (Repayment of principal is shown as a financing item, and commission charges are shown as purchases of services.) Interest payments do not include payments by government as guarantor or surety of interest on the defaulted debts of others, which are classified as government lending. • **Subsidies and other current transfers** include all unrequited, nonrepayable transfers on current account to private and public enterprises, and the cost to the public of covering the cash operating deficits on sales to the public by departmental enterprises. • **Capital expenditure** is spending to acquire fixed capital assets, land, intangible assets, government stocks, and nonmilitary, nonfinancial assets. Also included are capital grants.

Data sources

The data on central government expenditures are from the IMF's *Government Finance Statistics Yearbook, 1999* and IMF data files. Each country's accounts are reported using the system of common definitions and classifications in the IMF's *Manual on Government Finance Statistics* (1986). See these sources for complete and authoritative explanations of concepts, definitions, and data sources.

4.15 Central government revenues

	Taxes on income, profit, and capital gains		Social security taxes		Taxes on goods and services		Taxes on international trade		Other taxes		Nontax revenue	
	% of total current revenue		% of total current revenue		% of total current revenue		% of total current revenue		% of total current revenue		% of total current revenue	
	1980	**1997**	**1980**	**1997**	**1980**	**1997**	**1980**	**1997**	**1980**	**1997**	**1980**	**1997**
Albania	..	7	..	18	..	36	..	19	..	1	..	20
Algeria	..	*68*	..	*0*	..	*10*	..	*15*	..	*1*	..	*5*
Angola	..	..	..	..	..	..	..	..	..	..	..	..
Argentina	0	14	17	27	17	41	0	8	33	2	33	9
Armenia	..	..	..	..	..	..	..	..	..	..	..	..
Australia	61	68	0	0	23	21	5	2	0	2	10	7
Austria	21	24	35	38	26	25	2	0	9	6	8	7
Azerbaijan	..	20	..	23	..	41	..	8	..	2	..	5
Bangladesh	10	..	0	..	25	..	29	..	4	..	32	..
Belarus	..	10	..	30	..	41	..	8	..	7	..	4
Belgium	39	36	31	33	24	26	0	0	2	3	4	2
Benin	..	..	..	..	..	..	..	..	..	..	..	..
Bolivia	..	7	..	14	..	52	..	7	..	8	..	11
Bosnia and Herzegovina	..	..	..	..	..	..	..	..	..	..	..	..
Botswana	33	*17*	0	*0*	1	*4*	39	*12*	0	*0*	27	*67*
Brazil	11	..	25	..	32	..	7	..	4	..	21	..
Bulgaria	..	22	..	21	..	26	..	7	..	2	..	21
Burkina Faso	18	..	8	..	16	..	44	..	4	..	11	..
Burundi	19	22	1	8	25	45	40	16	8	2	6	7
Cambodia	..	..	..	..	..	..	..	..	..	..	..	..
Cameroon	22	*17*	8	*0*	18	*25*	38	*28*	5	*3*	8	*27*
Canada	53	*51*	10	*18*	17	*18*	7	*2*	0	*0*	14	*11*
Central African Republic	*16*	..	*6*	..	*21*	..	*40*	..	*8*	..	*9*	..
Chad	..	..	..	..	..	..	..	..	..	..	..	..
Chile	18	18	17	6	36	46	4	8	6	5	20	17
China	..	9	..	0	..	76	..	7	..	5	..	3
Hong Kong, China	..	..	..	..	..	..	..	..	..	..	..	..
Colombia	25	35	11	0	23	43	21	8	7	0	14	14
Congo, Dem. Rep.	30	25	2	0	12	18	38	28	5	9	12	20
Congo, Rep.	49	9	4	0	8	5	13	9	3	0	24	77
Costa Rica	14	*11*	29	*27*	30	*40*	19	*8*	2	*2*	6	*12*
Côte d'Ivoire	13	20	6	6	25	17	43	50	6	3	8	4
Croatia	..	11	..	34	..	39	..	9	..	2	..	5
Cuba	..	..	..	..	..	..	..	..	..	..	..	..
Czech Republic	..	14	..	45	..	34	..	3	..	1	..	4
Denmark	36	*39*	2	*4*	47	*41*	0	*0*	3	*3*	12	*13*
Dominican Republic	19	17	4	4	22	34	31	36	2	1	22	8
Ecuador	45	..	0	..	17	..	31	..	3	..	4	..
Egypt, Arab Rep.	16	22	9	0	15	17	17	13	8	12	35	37
El Salvador	..	..	..	..	..	..	..	..	..	..	..	..
Eritrea	..	..	..	..	..	..	..	..	..	..	..	..
Estonia	..	16	..	32	..	42	..	0	..	0	..	10
Ethiopia	21	..	0	..	24	..	36	..	4	..	15	..
Finland	29	30	10	11	49	45	2	0	3	2	8	12
France	18	20	41	42	31	29	0	0	3	4	7	6
Gabon	40	..	0	..	5	..	20	..	2	..	34	..
Gambia, The	15	..	0	..	3	..	65	..	2	..	15	..
Georgia	..	9	..	0	..	55	..	13	..	0	..	22
Germany[a]	19	14	54	49	23	20	0	0	0	0	4	16
Ghana	20	..	0	..	28	..	44	..	0	..	7	..
Greece	17	33	26	2	32	57	5	0	10	8	11	11
Guatemala	11	..	11	..	26	..	30	..	11	..	10	..
Guinea	..	..	..	..	..	..	..	..	..	..	..	..
Guinea-Bissau	..	..	..	..	..	..	..	..	..	..	..	..
Haiti	14	..	0	..	15	..	48	..	9	..	13	..
Honduras	31	..	0	..	24	..	37	..	2	..	7	..

Central government revenues 4.15

	Taxes on income, profit, and capital gains		Social security taxes		Taxes on goods and services		Taxes on international trade		Other taxes		Nontax revenue	
	% of total current revenue		% of total current revenue		% of total current revenue		% of total current revenue		% of total current revenue		% of total current revenue	
	1980	1997	1980	1997	1980	1997	1980	1997	1980	1997	1980	1997
Hungary	*19*	19	*15*	29	*38*	33	*7*	5	*5*	2	*16*	13
India	18	27	0	0	42	27	22	22	1	0	17	25
Indonesia	78	57	0	3	9	28	7	3	1	1	5	9
Iran, Islamic Rep.	4	12	7	6	4	8	12	6	5	5	68	62
Iraq	..	..	..	..	..	..	..	..	..	..	..	..
Ireland	34	*41*	13	*13*	30	*37*	9	*0*	2	*4*	11	*5*
Israel	41	36	10	14	25	32	4	0	8	4	14	14
Italy	30	33	35	33	25	24	0	0	4	3	8	6
Jamaica	34	..	4	..	49	..	3	..	6	..	4	..
Japan	71	..	0	..	21	..	2	..	5	..	5	..
Jordan	13	11	0	0	7	31	48	23	10	9	22	25
Kazakhstan	..	..	..	..	..	..	..	..	..	..	..	..
Kenya	29	*34*	0	*0*	39	*37*	19	*15*	1	*1*	13	*14*
Korea, Dem. Rep.	..	..	..	..	..	..	..	..	..	..	..	..
Korea, Rep.	22	27	1	9	46	34	15	6	3	10	12	14
Kuwait	2	..	0	..	0	..	1	..	0	..	97	..
Kyrgyz Republic	..	..	..	..	..	..	..	..	..	..	..	..
Lao PDR	..	..	..	..	..	..	..	..	..	..	..	..
Latvia	..	13	..	33	..	42	..	2	..	0	..	10
Lebanon	..	9	..	0	..	7	..	46	..	15	..	23
Lesotho	*13*	15	*0*	0	*10*	12	*61*	52	*2*	0	*14*	21
Libya	..	..	..	..	..	..	..	..	..	..	..	..
Lithuania	..	17	..	26	..	50	..	3	..	0	..	4
Macedonia, FYR	..	..	..	..	..	..	..	..	..	..	..	..
Madagascar	17	*18*	11	*0*	39	*24*	28	*53*	3	*2*	2	*2*
Malawi	34	..	0	..	31	..	22	..	0	..	13	..
Malaysia	38	36	0	1	17	26	33	13	2	5	11	18
Mali	18	..	0	..	37	..	18	..	15	..	8	..
Mauritania	..	..	..	..	..	..	..	..	..	..	..	..
Mauritius	15	13	0	5	17	29	52	30	4	6	12	17
Mexico	34	31	12	12	50	60	7	4	3	2	7	11
Moldova	..	..	..	..	..	..	..	..	..	..	..	..
Mongolia	..	26	..	19	..	28	..	5	..	1	..	20
Morocco	19	*20*	5	*7*	35	*39*	21	*15*	7	*3*	12	*16*
Mozambique	..	..	..	..	..	..	..	..	..	..	..	..
Myanmar	3	18	0	0	42	30	15	10	0	0	40	42
Namibia	..	..	..	..	..	..	..	..	..	..	..	..
Nepal	6	13	0	0	37	37	33	28	8	4	16	16
Netherlands	30	25	36	41	21	23	0	0	3	5	11	7
New Zealand	67	61	0	0	18	27	3	3	1	2	10	8
Nicaragua	8	*11*	9	*13*	37	*43*	25	*21*	8	*6*	10	*6*
Niger	24	..	4	..	18	..	36	..	3	..	15	..
Nigeria	..	..	..	..	..	..	..	..	..	..	..	..
Norway	27	21	22	21	39	36	1	1	1	1	9	21
Oman	26	23	0	0	0	1	1	2	0	2	72	71
Pakistan	14	21	0	0	34	29	34	22	0	8	18	19
Panama	21	21	21	20	17	..	10	..	4	3	27	28
Papua New Guinea	60	..	0	..	12	..	16	..	1	..	10	..
Paraguay	15	..	13	..	18	..	25	..	19	..	9	..
Peru	26	21	0	8	37	49	27	8	10	7	8	12
Philippines	21	36	0	0	42	29	24	21	2	4	11	11
Poland	..	25	..	28	..	32	..	4	..	1	..	9
Portugal	19	26	26	25	34	36	5	0	9	3	7	10
Puerto Rico	..	..	..	..	..	..	..	..	..	..	..	..
Romania	0	30	13	27	0	27	0	6	9	2	78	8
Russian Federation	..	*15*	..	*32*	..	*36*	..	*9*	..	*2*	..	*6*

4.15 Central government revenues

	Taxes on income, profit, and capital gains		Social security taxes		Taxes on goods and services		Taxes on international trade		Other taxes		Nontax revenue	
	% of total current revenue		% of total current revenue		% of total current revenue		% of total current revenue		% of total current revenue		% of total current revenue	
	1980	**1997**	**1980**	**1997**	**1980**	**1997**	**1980**	**1997**	**1980**	**1997**	**1980**	**1997**
Rwanda	18	..	4	..	19	..	42	..	2	..	14	..
Saudi Arabia	..	..	..	..	..	..	..	..	..	..	..	..
Senegal	18	..	4	..	26	..	34	..	4	..	6	..
Sierra Leone	22	17	0	0	16	33	50	46	2	0	10	3
Singapore	32	27	0	0	16	19	7	1	14	18	31	34
Slovak Republic	..	..	..	..	..	..	..	..	..	..	..	..
Slovenia	..	..	..	..	..	..	..	..	..	..	..	..
South Africa	56	55	1	2	24	35	3	0	3	3	13	6
Spain	23	*30*	48	*39*	13	*24*	4	*0*	4	*0*	8	*7*
Sri Lanka	16	13	0	0	27	53	50	16	2	4	5	14
Sudan	14	..	0	..	26	..	43	..	1	..	16	..
Sweden	18	11	33	39	29	28	1	0	4	9	14	12
Switzerland	14	13	48	53	19	23	9	1	2	3	7	7
Syrian Arab Republic	10	30	0	0	5	21	14	11	10	6	61	32
Tajikistan	..	..	..	..	..	..	..	..	..	..	..	..
Tanzania	32	..	0	..	41	..	17	..	2	..	8	..
Thailand	18	32	0	1	46	42	26	12	2	2	8	11
Togo	34	..	6	..	15	..	32	..	1	..	14	..
Trinidad and Tobago	72	*50*	1	*2*	4	*26*	7	*6*	1	*1*	16	*14*
Tunisia	15	*16*	9	*17*	24	*21*	25	*26*	4	*5*	22	*16*
Turkey	49	36	0	0	20	43	6	2	5	6	21	13
Turkmenistan	..	..	..	..	..	..	..	..	..	..	..	..
Uganda	11	..	0	..	41	..	44	..	0	..	3	..
Ukraine	..	..	..	..	..	..	..	..	..	..	..	..
United Arab Emirates	0	0	0	2	0	19	0	0	0	0	100	79
United Kingdom	38	37	16	17	28	33	0	0	6	7	13	6
United States	57	55	28	32	4	3	1	1	1	1	8	7
Uruguay	11	12	23	29	43	40	14	4	8	12	6	7
Uzbekistan	..	..	..	..	..	..	..	..	..	..	..	..
Venezuela, RB	67	39	5	2	4	30	7	7	2	0	15	27
Vietnam	..	22	..	0	..	33	..	22	..	10	..	14
West Bank and Gaza	..	..	..	..	..	..	..	..	..	..	..	..
Yemen, Rep.	..	16	..	0	..	7	..	9	..	2	..	66
Yugoslavia, FR (Serb./Mont.)	..	..	..	..	..	..	..	..	..	..	..	..
Zambia	38	..	0	..	43	..	8	..	3	..	7	..
Zimbabwe	46	43	0	0	28	24	4	20	1	2	20	10
World	**21 m**	***20 m***	**4 m**	***7 m***	**24 m**	***30 m***	**15 m**	***7 m***	**3 m**	***2 m***	**11 m**	***13 m***
Low income	20	..	0	..	26	..	34	..	3	..	11	..
Excl. China & India	20	..	0	..	25	..	34	..	3	..	11	..
Middle income	19	18	4	7	22	35	16	8	4	3	13	13
Lower middle income	17	*17*	4	*6*	23	*34*	22	*9*	6	*4*	12	*13*
Upper middle income	24	19	9	12	18	34	7	6	3	2	18	13
Low & middle income	19	*17*	1	*4*	25	*32*	24	*13*	3	*3*	13	*14*
East Asia & Pacific	22	27	0	1	42	30	16	10	2	4	11	14
Europe & Central Asia	..	17	..	28	..	40	..	5	..	1	..	9
Latin America & Carib.	19	*17*	11	*9*	24	*38*	19	*9*	6	*3*	10	*14*
Middle East & N. Africa	15	16	5	0	7	8	17	11	7	6	35	37
South Asia	14	17	0	0	34	33	33	22	2	4	17	18
Sub-Saharan Africa	22	..	1	..	25	..	35	..	3	..	10	..
High income	30	27	22	25	24	26	2	0	3	3	10	8
Europe EMU	26	26	35	36	25	25	1	0	3	3	8	7

Note: Components may not sum to 100 percent as a result of adjustments to tax revenue.
a. Data prior to 1990 refer to the Federal Republic of Germany before unification.

Central government revenues 4.15

About the data

The International Monetary Fund (IMF) classifies government transactions as receipts or payments and according to whether they are repayable or nonrepayable. If nonrepayable, they are classified as capital (meant to be used in production for more than a year) or current, and as requited (involving payment in return for a benefit or service) or unrequited. Revenues include all nonrepayable receipts (other than grants), the most important of which are taxes. Grants are unrequited, nonrepayable, noncompulsory receipts from other governments or international organizations. Transactions are generally recorded on a cash rather than an accrual basis. Measuring the accumulation of arrears on revenues or payments on an accrual basis would typically result in a higher deficit. Transactions within a level of government are not included, but transactions between levels are included. In some instances the government budget may include transfers used to finance the deficits of autonomous, extrabudgetary agencies.

The IMF's *Manual on Government Finance Statistics* (1986) describes taxes as compulsory, unrequited payments made to governments by individuals, businesses, or institutions. Taxes traditionally have been classified as either direct (those levied directly on the income or profits of individuals and corporations) or indirect (sales and excise taxes and duties levied on goods and services). This distinction may be a useful simplification, but it has no particular analytical significance.

Social security taxes do not reflect compulsory payments made by employers to provident funds or other agencies with a similar purpose. Similarly, expenditures from such funds are not reflected in government expenditure (see table 4.14). The revenue shares shown in table 4.15 may not sum to 100 percent because adjustments to tax revenues are not shown.

For further discussion of taxes and tax policies see *About the data* for table 5.5. For further discussion of government revenues and expenditures see *About the data* for tables 4.13 and 4.14.

Figure 4.15

High-income countries draw a large share of current revenue from income taxes . . .

Income taxes and social security contributions as % of current revenue, 1996–98

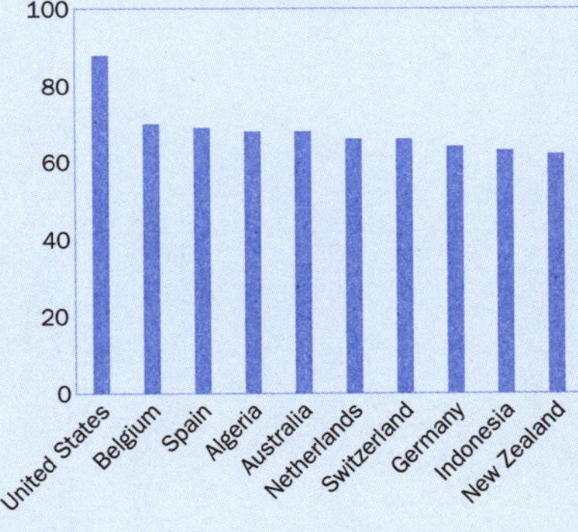

. . . while many developing countries rely on duties and excise taxes

Taxes on domestic and international trade as % of current revenue, 1996–98

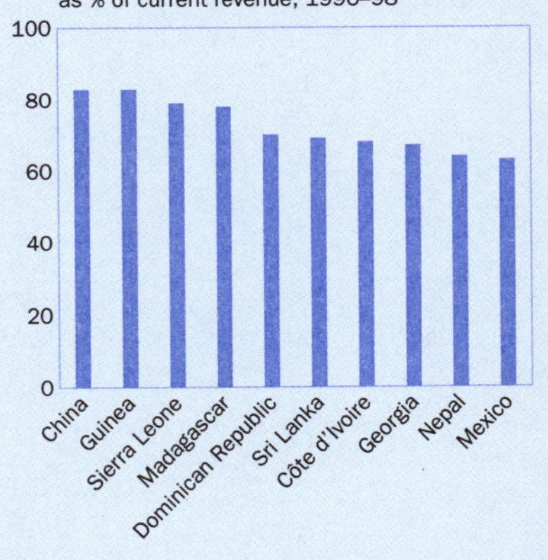

Note: The data refer to various years in 1996–98.
Source: International Monetary Fund, Government Finance Statistics data files.

Definitions

• **Taxes on income, profit, and capital gains** are levied on the actual or presumptive net income of individuals, on the profits of enterprises, and on capital gains, whether realized on land, securities, or other assets. Intragovernmental payments are eliminated in consolidation. • **Social security taxes** include employer and employee social security contributions and those of self-employed and unemployed people. • **Taxes on goods and services** include general sales and turnover or value added taxes, selective excises on goods, selective taxes on services, taxes on the use of goods or property, and profits of fiscal monopolies. • **Taxes on international trade** include import duties, export duties, profits of export or import monopolies, exchange profits, and exchange taxes. • **Other taxes** include employer payroll or labor taxes, taxes on property, and taxes not allocable to other categories. They may include negative values that are adjustments (for example, for taxes collected on behalf of state and local governments and not allocable to individual tax categories). • **Nontax revenue** includes requited, nonrepayable receipts for public purposes, such as fines, administrative fees, or entrepreneurial income from government ownership of property, and voluntary, unrequited, nonrepayable receipts other than from government sources. Proceeds of grants and borrowing, funds arising from the repayment of previous lending by governments, incurrence of liabilities, and proceeds from the sale of capital assets are not included.

Data sources

The data on central government revenues are from the IMF's *Government Finance Statistics Yearbook, 1999* and IMF data files. Each country's accounts are reported using the system of common definitions and classifications in the IMF's *Manual on Government Finance Statistics* (1986). The IMF receives additional information from the Organisation for Economic Co-operation and Development on the tax revenues of some of its members. See the IMF sources for complete and authoritative explanations of concepts, definitions, and data sources.

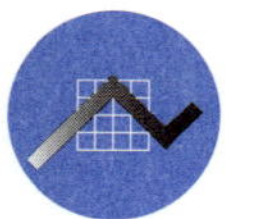

4.16 Monetary indicators and prices

	Money and quasi money annual % growth of M2		Claims on private sector annual growth as % of M2		Claims on governments and other public entities annual growth as % of M2		GDP implicit deflator average annual % growth		Consumer price index average annual % growth		Food price index average annual % growth	
	1990	1998	1990	1998	1990	1998	1980–90	1990–98	1980–90	1990–98	1980–90	1990–98
Albania	..	20.6	..	0.9	..	17.7	–0.4	51.5	..	*37.0*	..	40.4
Algeria	11.4	18.9	12.2	1.9	3.2	10.9	8.1	21.1	9.1	*24.8*	6.8	23.5
Angola	..	57.6	..	–0.1	..	69.4	*5.9*	924.3	..	*994.2*	..	*1,216.9*
Argentina	1,113.3	10.5	1,444.7	9.5	1,573.2	0.1	391.1	7.8	390.6	12.9	206.9	*15.2*
Armenia	..	38.2	..	47.9	..	8.5	..	349.1	..	*140.7*	..	..
Australia	12.8	8.4	15.3	14.0	–2.2	1.0	7.3	1.7	7.9	2.2	7.4	2.5
Austria[a]	..	..	..	..	..	..	3.3	2.5	3.2	2.6	2.6	1.8
Azerbaijan	..	–17.4	..	6.6	..	–3.1	..	322.3	..	*1,005.8*	*1.5*	339.5
Bangladesh	10.4	11.4	9.2	10.0	–0.7	3.6	9.5	3.6	..	5.4	10.4	4.3
Belarus	..	276.0	..	143.6	..	63.9	..	449.9	..	*455.3*	*2.4*	485.9
Belgium[a]	..	..	..	..	..	..	4.4	2.3	4.2	2.1	4.0	0.9
Benin	28.6	–3.1	–1.3	9.7	12.4	–8.8	1.7	10.1	..	*11.6*	..	8.2
Bolivia	52.8	12.9	40.8	25.4	8.4	5.1	327.2	9.9	322.5	10.0	322.0	10.4
Bosnia and Herzegovina	..	..	..	..	..	..	..	..	..	..	..	..
Botswana	–14.0	39.4	12.6	16.7	–52.5	–89.8	13.6	10.3	10.0	11.3	10.7	12.0
Brazil	1,289.2	10.0	1,566.4	13.6	2,815.8	14.9	284.0	347.4	285.6	333.7	238.2	327.6
Bulgaria	*53.8*	10.1	*1.9*	10.1	*47.5*	–19.7	1.8	116.9	*6.3*	138.9	..	148.6
Burkina Faso	–0.5	1.4	3.6	5.0	–1.5	–0.2	3.3	6.6	*1.0*	6.7	*–0.5*	*5.4*
Burundi	10.4	*9.4*	16.3	*4.4*	–8.1	*18.9*	4.4	11.8	7.1	16.0	6.1	*6.7*
Cambodia	..	15.7	..	1.7	..	11.7	..	32.8	..	*7.0*	..	*6.8*
Cameroon	–1.7	7.8	0.9	11.7	–1.9	–3.2	5.6	6.1	8.7	*8.6*	..	..
Canada	7.8	2.3	9.2	1.8	0.6	–1.3	4.5	1.4	5.3	1.7	4.6	1.5
Central African Republic	–3.7	–16.1	–1.6	3.2	–5.0	1.1	7.9	5.4	3.2	6.7	*2.0*	*7.8*
Chad	–2.4	–8.4	–1.3	4.3	–6.0	–4.0	1.4	8.3	*0.6*	9.5	..	9.6
Chile	23.5	9.6	21.4	12.5	9.1	0.8	20.7	9.3	20.6	10.5	20.8	10.3
China	28.9	14.9	26.5	13.6	1.5	3.7	5.9	9.7	..	11.3	..	..
Hong Kong, China	*8.5*	11.1	*7.9*	–6.2	*–1.0*	–8.4	7.7	6.4	..	7.7	6.8	6.2
Colombia	33.0	20.9	*8.7*	25.7	*1.7*	6.8	24.8	21.5	22.7	22.6	24.5	20.2
Congo, Dem. Rep.	195.4	..	18.0	..	421.6	..	62.9	1,423.1	57.1	*2,089.0*	..	..
Congo, Rep.	18.5	–12.8	5.1	2.7	–9.1	8.7	0.5	7.1	6.1	*14.8*	4.1	*10.2*
Costa Rica	27.5	26.3	7.3	25.2	5.0	6.7	23.6	17.6	23.0	16.9	23.0	14.7
Côte d'Ivoire	–2.6	7.1	–3.9	2.8	–3.0	3.6	2.8	8.7	5.4	8.5	..	..
Croatia	..	13.0	..	20.8	..	1.0	..	131.2	*304.1*	132.4	*246.3*	130.0
Cuba	..	..	..	..	..	..	..	..	..	..	..	..
Czech Republic	..	3.4	..	–2.2	..	0.6	*2.6*	13.7	..	*9.2*	..	*15.9*
Denmark	6.5	3.3	3.0	6.9	–3.1	0.2	5.6	1.6	5.5	2.0	4.8	1.9
Dominican Republic	42.5	16.6	19.1	13.3	0.6	1.1	21.6	10.6	22.4	9.6	25.2	*11.7*
Ecuador	101.6	43.3	46.7	46.2	–25.7	13.2	36.4	32.0	35.8	33.9	*43.0*	33.7
Egypt, Arab Rep.	28.7	10.8	6.3	14.1	15.2	4.9	13.7	9.7	17.4	10.5	19.0	8.3
El Salvador	32.4	10.5	8.8	12.2	13.6	–10.1	16.3	8.9	19.6	10.6	21.4	12.5
Eritrea	..	..	..	..	..	..	..	*10.1*	..	..	..	..
Estonia	*71.1*	6.6	*27.6*	9.7	–2.2	6.3	2.3	75.4	..	*30.1*	..	72.1
Ethiopia	18.5	–2.8	–1.0	3.6	21.7	4.8	*4.6*	8.0	4.0	*6.9*	3.7	6.5
Finland[a]	..	..	..	..	..	..	6.8	1.7	6.2	1.6	5.8	–1.0
France[a]	..	..	..	..	..	..	6.0	1.7	5.8	1.9	5.7	1.1
Gabon	3.3	–1.8	0.7	3.3	–19.2	25.4	1.8	7.2	5.1	*5.7*	*2.8*	*5.1*
Gambia, The	8.4	10.2	7.8	5.4	–35.4	0.6	17.9	4.4	20.0	4.6	20.4	*5.0*
Georgia	..	–1.1	..	25.4	..	27.9	1.9	709.3	..	*–1.7*	..	..
Germany[a]	..	..	..	..	..	..	..	2.2	2.2[b]	2.6	..	1.8
Ghana	13.3	26.1	4.9	18.4	3.9	17.1	42.1	28.6	39.1	30.4	33.1	*27.5*
Greece	14.3	6.7	4.6	16.3	16.3	–1.9	18.0	11.0	18.7	10.7	18.0	*11.2*
Guatemala	25.8	19.4	15.0	19.6	0.5	–14.0	14.6	11.4	14.0	11.4	14.6	11.5
Guinea	–17.4	*18.2*	*13.1*	*–0.3*	*7.3*	*–9.1*	..	6.7	..	..	..	*9.1*
Guinea-Bissau	65.3	*48.4*	57.4	*8.8*	98.1	*21.0*	57.4	41.8	..	41.9	..	..
Haiti	2.5	8.9	–0.6	4.1	2.2	2.9	7.5	23.3	5.2	24.8	4.1	*19.2*
Honduras	21.4	23.2	13.0	28.6	–10.5	–12.2	5.7	20.6	6.3	20.0	5.1	21.6

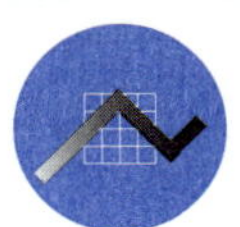

Monetary indicators and prices 4.16

	Money and quasi money		Claims on private sector		Claims on governments and other public entities		GDP implicit deflator		Consumer price index		Food price index	
	annual % growth of M2		annual growth as % of M2		annual growth as % of M2		average annual % growth		average annual % growth		average annual % growth	
	1990	1998	1990	1998	1990	1998	1980–90	1990–98	1980–90	1990–98	1980–90	1990–98
Hungary	29.2	..	22.8	..	2.3	..	8.9	22.0	9.6	22.7	9.5	22.6
India	15.1	18.2	5.9	7.6	10.5	7.3	8.0	8.9	8.6	9.7	8.4	10.3
Indonesia	44.6	63.5	66.9	36.5	–6.7	6.7	8.5	12.2	8.3	11.2	8.6	*9.6*
Iran, Islamic Rep.	18.0	20.4	14.7	9.4	5.8	21.3	14.4	28.3	18.2	28.1	16.3	29.2
Iraq	..	..	..	..	..	..	10.3	..	..	..	..	..
Ireland[a]	..	..	..	..	..	..	6.6	2.0	6.8	2.2	10.5	2.2
Israel	19.4	11.1	18.5	16.5	4.9	*–6.1*	101.1	11.0	101.7	11.1	102.4	9.1
Italy[a]	..	..	..	..	..	..	10.0	4.4	9.1	4.2	8.2	3.6
Jamaica	21.5	7.7	12.5	15.9	–15.1	8.2	18.6	29.1	15.1	29.2	16.2	32.9
Japan	8.2	4.2	9.7	0.8	1.5	2.2	1.7	0.2	1.7	1.0	1.6	0.8
Jordan	8.3	6.3	4.7	5.4	1.0	7.1	4.3	3.3	5.7	4.1	4.7	4.5
Kazakhstan	..	–14.1	..	16.1	..	9.3	..	330.7	..	*120.3*	..	*338.5*
Kenya	20.1	2.3	8.0	0.3	20.6	3.3	9.1	15.8	11.1	18.8	..	19.4
Korea, Dem. Rep.	..	..	..	..	..	..	..	..	..	..	..	..
Korea, Rep.	17.2	27.0	36.1	12.0	–1.2	6.0	6.1	6.4	4.9	5.6	5.0	5.8
Kuwait	*0.7*	–0.8	*3.3*	6.3	*–3.1*	–0.3	*–2.8*	..	2.9	2.1	1.2	*2.9*
Kyrgyz Republic	..	17.5	..	18.1	..	11.6	..	157.8	..	..	..	*84.7*
Lao PDR	7.8	113.3	3.6	60.9	–0.5	–2.0	..	16.3	..	17.2	..	..
Latvia	..	6.8	..	21.1	..	–2.3	0.0	71.1	..	*41.8*	..	*45.9*
Lebanon	55.1	16.1	27.6	9.5	18.5	10.8	..	24.0	75.5	*36.8*	..	..
Lesotho	8.4	20.6	6.8	3.6	–17.4	–3.9	13.8	7.7	13.6	*12.1*	13.2	*13.0*
Libya	20.3	*20.7*	0.9	*7.0*	8.5	*–21.7*	*0.2*	..	..	..	..	..
Lithuania	..	14.5	..	9.7	..	–3.3	..	111.5	..	*50.8*	..	*87.1*
Macedonia, FYR	..	13.0	..	–64.1	..	–8.4	..	*17.9*	..	115.5	*242.1*	*146.3*
Madagascar	4.5	6.2	23.8	0.4	–14.8	19.1	17.1	22.1	16.6	21.3	15.7	21.5
Malawi	11.1	60.0	15.8	26.9	–14.0	–25.0	14.6	33.2	16.9	33.6	16.3	*38.6*
Malaysia	10.6	–1.4	20.8	5.3	–1.2	–5.7	1.7	5.1	2.6	4.1	*1.3*	5.0
Mali	–4.9	4.0	0.1	15.7	–13.4	–1.2	4.5	9.3	..	6.3	..	..
Mauritania	11.5	4.1	20.2	9.5	1.5	–41.8	10.0	5.3	*7.1*	*6.6*	..	..
Mauritius	21.2	11.2	10.8	19.6	0.8	–0.4	9.5	6.2	6.9	7.0	*7.4*	*7.5*
Mexico	81.9	19.7	48.5	11.5	15.0	3.3	71.5	19.5	73.8	19.9	73.1	19.8
Moldova	*358.0*	–8.3	*53.3*	33.8	*322.4*	51.5	..	173.9	..	*12.3*	..	*98.6*
Mongolia	*31.6*	–1.7	*40.2*	22.4	*15.4*	4.2	*–1.6*	78.2	..	*64.8*	..	..
Morocco	21.5	6.0	*12.4*	8.1	–4.9	–0.2	7.1	3.5	7.0	4.6	6.7	6.3
Mozambique	37.2	17.7	22.0	16.5	–6.4	–16.8	38.3	41.1	..	*44.6*	..	..
Myanmar	37.7	34.2	12.8	12.5	23.9	10.7	12.2	25.9	11.5	26.8	11.9	28.2
Namibia	*30.3*	11.3	*15.4*	8.9	*–7.3*	0.7	13.9	9.5	12.6	10.2	*14.9*	9.8
Nepal	18.5	24.0	5.7	14.0	6.0	1.6	11.1	8.9	10.2	9.3	10.1	*9.6*
Netherlands[a]	..	..	..	..	..	..	1.6	2.1	2.0	2.4	1.2	1.5
New Zealand	12.5	1.8	4.1	7.9	–1.7	1.3	10.8	1.6	11.0	2.0	9.9	1.1
Nicaragua	7,677.8	30.5	4,932.9	27.3	3,222.5	17.2	422.3	45.5	535.7	*62.9*	..	..
Niger	–4.1	–18.7	–5.1	14.0	1.4	–11.2	1.9	6.8	0.7	7.2	..	..
Nigeria	32.7	21.2	7.8	15.2	27.1	25.0	16.7	38.7	21.5	40.4	21.6	37.6
Norway	5.6	5.4	5.0	10.2	–0.1	–3.2	5.6	1.8	7.4	2.1	7.8	1.5
Oman	10.0	4.8	9.6	19.3	–11.2	7.6	–3.6	*–2.9*	..	0.2	..	0.4
Pakistan	11.6	7.9	5.9	7.1	7.7	1.8	6.7	11.1	6.3	10.8	6.6	11.4
Panama	36.6	13.0	0.8	29.2	–25.7	–0.2	1.9	2.2	1.4	1.1	1.9	1.2
Papua New Guinea	4.3	2.5	1.3	9.8	7.2	5.3	5.3	7.1	5.6	8.1	4.6	*6.8*
Paraguay	52.5	9.0	33.1	–2.2	–5.6	–1.8	24.4	14.6	21.9	14.7	24.9	13.5
Peru	6,384.9	17.3	2,123.7	17.9	2,129.5	4.3	231.3	33.7	246.1	37.2	..	*41.0*
Philippines	22.5	8.5	15.7	–6.2	1.8	–0.2	14.9	8.5	13.4	8.7	14.1	7.9
Poland	160.1	25.2	20.8	15.7	–20.6	3.4	53.5	26.9	50.9	30.8	52.4	27.1
Portugal[a]	..	..	..	..	..	..	18.0	5.8	17.1	5.2	16.9	4.0
Puerto Rico	..	..	..	..	..	..	3.5	*3.7*	..	..	2.8	8.1
Romania	26.4	48.9	..	35.5	..	17.0	2.5	113.8	..	118.5	*1.8*	116.3
Russian Federation	..	37.5	..	24.0	..	74.6	..	230.9	..	*137.0*	..	*207.0*

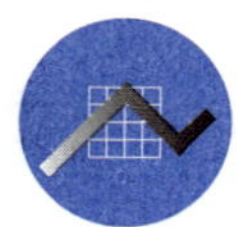

4.16 Monetary indicators and prices

	Money and quasi money		Claims on private sector		Claims on governments and other public entities		GDP implicit deflator		Consumer price index		Food price index	
	annual % growth of M2		annual growth as % of M2		annual growth as % of M2		average annual % growth		average annual % growth		average annual % growth	
	1990	1998	1990	1998	1990	1998	1980–90	1990–98	1980–90	1990–98	1980–90	1990–98
Rwanda	5.6	3.5	–10.0	10.5	26.8	–0.4	4.0	18.1	3.9	*20.0*	..	..
Saudi Arabia	4.6	3.6	–4.5	9.9	4.2	*5.8*	–4.9	1.4	–0.8	1.5	–0.4	1.5
Senegal	–4.8	8.7	–8.4	1.7	–5.3	4.8	6.5	5.6	6.2	6.6	5.3	*8.3*
Sierra Leone	74.0	11.3	4.9	1.2	228.6	26.2	64.0	32.5	72.4	32.1	..	..
Singapore	20.0	30.2	13.7	9.3	–4.9	6.0	1.9	2.1	1.6	2.1	0.9	2.0
Slovak Republic	..	4.9	..	9.0	..	–1.6	*1.8*	11.4	..	14.0	*1.6*	14.2
Slovenia	*123.0*	19.5	*96.1*	19.1	*–10.4*	1.4	..	*27.0*	..	*32.8*	*252.3*	35.3
South Africa	11.4	13.7	13.7	18.8	1.8	2.8	15.5	10.6	14.8	9.6	15.1	11.3
Spain[a]	..	..	..	..	..	..	9.3	4.2	9.0	4.2	9.3	3.3
Sri Lanka	21.1	9.6	16.2	9.4	6.8	3.5	11.0	9.7	10.9	10.7	10.9	11.3
Sudan	48.8	29.9	12.6	3.2	27.9	14.3	41.0	74.4	37.6	90.8	..	..
Sweden	..	..	..	..	..	..	7.4	2.4	7.0	2.5	8.2	–0.7
Switzerland	0.8	5.1	11.7	1.9	1.0	–2.5	3.4	1.7	2.9	2.0	3.1	0.5
Syrian Arab Republic	26.1	124.0	3.4	–0.3	11.4	*–7.6*	15.3	8.9	23.2	9.1	24.5	7.6
Tajikistan	..	..	..	..	..	..	..	300.0	..	..	..	..
Tanzania	41.9	10.8	22.6	7.9	80.6	2.6	..	24.3	31.0	24.2	30.2	24.2
Thailand	26.7	9.7	30.0	–9.9	–4.2	9.8	3.9	4.8	3.5	5.2	2.7	6.7
Togo	9.5	0.4	1.8	3.6	6.9	7.6	4.8	8.8	2.5	10.2	..	..
Trinidad and Tobago	6.2	14.5	2.7	9.0	0.9	–3.6	2.4	6.9	10.7	6.2	14.6	13.6
Tunisia	7.6	5.4	5.9	9.7	1.8	–1.1	7.4	4.8	7.4	4.8	8.3	4.8
Turkey	53.2	89.7	42.9	39.3	3.6	41.4	45.2	79.4	44.9	82.1	..	83.4
Turkmenistan	..	..	..	..	..	..	..	663.4	..	..	..	..
Uganda	60.2	21.7	..	13.1	..	3.7	*113.8*	15.3	102.5	13.0	..	*13.4*
Ukraine	..	22.3	..	45.7	..	59.8	..	440.0	..	*413.4*	..	..
United Arab Emirates	–8.2	4.2	1.3	13.2	–4.8	–1.7	0.8	2.4	..	..	..	..
United Kingdom	..	..	..	..	..	..	5.7	3.0	5.8	3.0	4.6	*2.4*
United States	4.9	10.0	1.1	13.3	0.6	1.1	4.2	1.9	4.2	2.8	3.8	3.9
Uruguay	118.5	19.3	56.2	20.9	3.3	–4.6	61.3	40.5	61.1	43.1	62.0	39.2
Uzbekistan	..	..	..	..	..	..	..	356.7	..	..	..	..
Venezuela, RB	71.2	6.5	17.0	7.9	41.8	7.2	19.3	49.2	20.9	53.6	29.7	*50.1*
Vietnam	..	*24.3*	..	*12.8*	..	*–0.1*	*210.8*	18.5	..	..	..	..
West Bank and Gaza	..	..	..	..	..	..	..	*11.0*	..	..	..	..
Yemen, Rep.	*11.3*	11.8	*1.4*	3.9	*8.3*	18.7	..	24.2	..	32.6	..	..
Yugoslavia, FR (Serb./Mont.)	..	..	..	..	..	..	..	..	..	..	..	..
Zambia	47.9	25.6	22.8	1.4	185.8	178.0	42.2	63.5	*72.5*	*80.8*	42.8	73.0
Zimbabwe	15.1	11.3	13.5	32.7	7.4	28.8	11.6	21.9	13.8	25.4	14.6	31.0

a. As members of the European Monetary Union, these countries share a single currency, the euro. b. Data prior to 1990 refer to the Federal Republic of Germany before unification.

Monetary indicators and prices 4.16

About the data

Money and the financial accounts that record the supply of money lie at the heart of a country's financial system. There are several commonly used definitions of the money supply. The narrowest, M1, encompasses currency held by the public and demand deposits with banks. M2 includes M1 plus time and savings deposits with banks that require a notice for withdrawal. M3 includes M2 as well as various money market instruments, such as certificates of deposit issued by banks, bank deposits denominated in foreign currency, and deposits with financial institutions other than banks. However defined, money is a liability of the banking system, distinguished from other bank liabilities by the special role it plays as a medium of exchange, a unit of account, and a store of value.

The banking system's assets include its net foreign assets and net domestic credit. Net domestic credit includes credit to the private sector and general government, and credit extended to the nonfinancial public sector in the form of investments in short- and long-term government securities and loans to state enterprises; liabilities to the public and private sectors in the form of deposits with the banking system are netted out. It also includes credit to banking and nonbank financial institutions.

Domestic credit is the main vehicle through which changes in the money supply are regulated, with central bank lending to the government often playing the most important role. The central bank can regulate lending to the private sector in several ways—for example, by adjusting the cost of the refinancing facilities it provides to banks, by changing market interest rates through open market operations, or by controlling the availability of credit through changes in the reserve requirements imposed on banks and ceilings on the credit provided by banks to the private sector.

Monetary accounts are derived from the balance sheets of financial institutions—the central bank, commercial banks, and nonbank financial intermediaries. Although these balance sheets are usually reliable, they are subject to errors of classification, valuation, and timing and to differences in accounting practices. For example, whether interest income is recorded on an accrual or a cash basis can make a substantial difference, as can the treatment of nonperforming assets. Valuation errors typically arise with respect to foreign exchange transactions, particularly in countries with flexible exchange rates or in those that have undergone a currency devaluation during the reporting period. The valuation of financial derivatives and the net liabilities of the banking system can also be difficult.

The quality of commercial bank reporting also may be adversely affected by delays in reports from bank branches, especially in countries where branch accounts are not computerized. Thus the data in the balance sheets of commercial banks may be based on preliminary estimates subject to constant revision. This problem is likely to be even more serious for nonbank financial intermediaries.

Controlling inflation is one of the primary goals of monetary policy and is intimately linked to the growth in money supply. Inflation is measured by the rate of increase in a price index, but actual price change can also be negative. Which index is used depends on which set of prices in the economy is being examined. The GDP deflator reflects changes in prices for total gross domestic product. It is the most general measure of the overall price level and takes into account changes in government consumption, capital formation (including inventory appreciation), international trade, and the main component, private consumption. It is usually derived implicitly as the ratio of current to constant price GDP, resulting in a Paasche index. As a general measure of inflation for use in policy, however, it is defective because of the long lags in deriving estimates and because it is often only an annual measure.

Consumer price indexes are more current and produced more frequently. They are also constructed explicitly, based on surveys of the cost of a defined basket of consumer goods and services. Consumer price indexes should be interpreted with caution. The definition of a household and the geographic (urban or rural) and income group coverage of consumer price surveys can vary widely across countries, as can the basket of goods chosen. In addition, the weights are derived from household expenditure surveys, which, for budgetary reasons, tend to be conducted infrequently in developing countries, leading to poor comparability over time. Although a useful indicator for measuring consumer price inflation within a country, the consumer price index is of less value in making comparisons across countries. Like consumer price indexes, the food price index too should be interpreted with caution because of the high variability across countries in the items covered.

The least-squares method is used to calculate the growth rates of the GDP implicit deflator, consumer price index, and food price index.

Definitions

• **Money and quasi money** comprise the sum of currency outside banks, demand deposits other than those of the central government, and the time, savings, and foreign currency deposits of resident sectors other than the central government. This definition of the money supply is frequently called M2; it corresponds to lines 34 and 35 in the International Monetary Fund's (IMF) *International Financial Statistics* (IFS). The change in money supply is measured as the difference in end-of-year totals relative to the level of M2 in the preceding year. • **Claims on private sector** (IFS line 32d) include gross credit from the financial system to individuals, enterprises, nonfinancial public entities not included under net domestic credit, and financial institutions not included elsewhere. • **Claims on governments and other public entities** (IFS line 32an + 32b + 32bx + 32c) usually comprise direct credit for specific purposes such as financing the government budget deficit, loans to state enterprises, advances against future credit authorizations, and purchases of treasury bills and bonds, net of deposits by the public sector. Public sector deposits with the banking system also include sinking funds for the service of debt and temporary deposits of government revenues. • **GDP implicit deflator** measures the average annual rate of price change in the economy as a whole for the periods shown. • **Consumer price index** reflects changes in the cost to the average consumer of acquiring a basket of goods and services that may be fixed or change at specified intervals, such as yearly. The Laspeyres formula is generally used. • **Food price index** is a subindex of the consumer price index.

Data sources

The IMF collects data on the financial systems of its member countries. The data in the table are published in its monthly *International Financial Statistics* and annual *International Financial Statistics Yearbook*. The World Bank receives data from the IMF in electronic files that may contain more recent revisions than the published sources. The GDP data are from the World Bank's national accounts files. The food price index data are from the United Nations Statistics Division's *Statistical Yearbook* and *Monthly Bulletin of Statistics*. The discussion of monetary indicators draws from an IMF publication by Marcello Caiola, *A Manual for Country Economists* (1995).

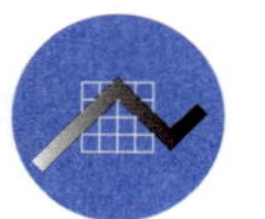

4.17 Balance of payments current account

	Goods and services				Net income		Net current transfers		Current account balance		Gross international reserves	
	Exports $ millions		Imports $ millions		$ millions		$ millions		$ millions		$ millions	
	1980	1998	1980	1998	1980	1998	1980	1998	1980	1998	1980	1998
Albania	378	295	371	941	4	77	6	504	16	–65	..	382
Algeria	14,128	10,822	12,311	9,119	–1,869	–2,316	301	..	249	..	7,064	8,452
Angola	..	3,879	..	4,546	..	–1,317	..	208	..	–1,776	..	203
Argentina	9,897	31,094	13,182	38,493	–1,512	–7,686	23	388	–4,774	–14,697	9,297	24,856
Armenia	..	360	..	988	..	60	..	177	..	–390	..	328
Australia	25,755	72,003	27,089	78,536	–2,688	–10,918	–425	–61	–4,447	–17,512	6,366	16,144
Austria	26,650	95,173	29,921	96,641	–528	–1,227	–66	–1,914	–3,865	–4,609	17,725	25,208
Azerbaijan	..	1,010	..	2,425	..	–13	..	64	..	–1,364	..	447
Bangladesh	885	5,879	2,545	8,049	14	–100	802	2,017	–844	–253	331	1,936
Belarus	..	7,957	..	8,964	..	–78	..	140	..	–945	..	339
Belgium[a]	70,498	189,973	74,259	179,857	61	6,413	–1,231	–4,419	–4,931	12,111	27,974	21,013
Benin	226	545	421	771	8	–17	151	86	–36	–157	15	261
Bolivia	1,030	1,357	833	2,201	–263	–160	60	330	–6	–673	553	1,155
Bosnia and Herzegovina	..	..	..	..	..	..	..	..	..	..	..	..
Botswana	645	2,316	818	2,506	–33	120	55	240	–151	170	344	6,025
Brazil	21,869	58,767	27,826	74,415	–7,018	–19,617	144	1,436	–12,831	–33,829	6,875	43,902
Bulgaria	9,302	5,555	7,994	5,877	–412	–284	58	230	954	–376	..	3,127
Burkina Faso	210	394	577	761	–3	–36	322	179	–49	–225	75	373
Burundi	..	72	..	172	..	–12	..	9	..	–103	105	70
Cambodia	..	815	..	1,286	..	–50	..	297	..	–224	..	324
Cameroon	1,880	2,306	1,829	2,176	–628	–469	83	105	–495	–235	206	1
Canada	74,977	248,161	70,259	240,290	–10,764	–19,618	–42	534	–6,088	–11,213	15,462	24,023
Central African Republic	201	147	327	255	3	–20	81	39	–43	–89	62	146
Chad	71	328	79	549	–4	–1	24	108	12	–113	12	120
Chile	5,968	18,953	7,052	21,583	–1,000	–1,972	113	463	–1,971	–4,139	4,128	16,014
China†	*23,637*	207,584	*18,900*	165,894	*451*	–16,644	*486*	4,279	*5,674*	29,325	10,091	152,843
Hong Kong, China	25,604	208,167	25,873	207,647	0	*904*	..	..	–269	*–5,247*	..	89,664
Colombia	5,328	13,478	5,454	17,517	–245	–2,349	165	480	–206	–5,908	6,474	8,397
Congo, Dem. Rep.	2,371	*1,446*	2,353	*1,385*	–293	*–752*	187	*33*	–88	*–658*	380	*83*
Congo, Rep.	1,021	1,254	1,025	1,235	–162	–495	–1	–20	–167	–252	93	1
Costa Rica	1,195	6,876	1,661	6,974	–212	–468	15	105	–664	–460	197	1,064
Côte d'Ivoire	3,577	5,125	4,145	4,179	–553	–710	–706	–447	–1,826	–212	46	855
Croatia	..	8,577	..	10,663	..	–165	..	708	..	–1,543	..	2,816
Cuba	..	..	..	..	..	..	..	..	..	..	..	..
Czech Republic	..	33,908	..	34,713	..	–712	..	408	..	–1,110	..	12,625
Denmark	*21,989*	62,664	*21,727*	59,878	*–1,977*	–3,673	*–161*	–1,533	*–1,875*	–2,419	4,347	15,881
Dominican Republic	1,271	7,482	1,919	8,917	–277	–887	205	1,986	–720	–336	279	507
Ecuador	2,887	5,007	2,946	6,409	–613	–1,543	30	776	–642	–2,169	1,257	1,739
Egypt, Arab Rep.	6,246	13,502	9,157	21,807	–318	1,140	2,791	4,403	–438	–2,762	2,480	18,824
El Salvador	1,214	2,741	1,170	4,266	–62	–66	52	1,507	34	–84	382	1,748
Eritrea	..	129	..	583	..	0	..	237	..	–216	..	..
Estonia	..	4,170	..	4,715	..	–81	..	148	..	–478	..	813
Ethiopia	569	1,037	782	1,815	7	–91	80	349	–126	–520	262	520
Finland	16,802	50,614	17,307	39,137	–783	–2,824	–114	–1,092	–1,403	7,561	2,451	10,271
France	153,197	387,123	155,915	342,244	2,680	4,380	–4,170	–9,097	–4,208	40,161	75,592	73,773
Gabon	2,409	2,545	1,475	1,871	–426	–590	–124	–159	384	–75	115	15
Gambia, The	66	264	179	331	–2	–6	28	29	–87	–44	6	106
Georgia	..	720	..	1,437	..	117	..	211	..	–389	..	124
Germany[b]	224,224	623,416	225,599	587,353	914	–9,204	–12,858	–30,303	–13,319	–3,443	104,702	108,265
Ghana	1,210	1,989	1,178	2,887	–83	–136	81	684	30	–350	330	457
Greece	8,122	*14,863*	11,145	*25,601*	–273	*–1,632*	1,087	*7,510*	–2,209	*–4,860*	3,607	18,501
Guatemala	1,731	3,487	1,960	5,047	–44	–184	110	705	–163	–1,039	753	1,397
Guinea	..	804	..	962	..	–81	..	121	..	–119	..	*122*
Guinea-Bissau	*17*	31	*75*	60	*–8*	–14	*–14*	*40*	*–80*	*–6*	..	*12*
Haiti	306	479	481	1,021	–14	–12	89	516	–101	–38	27	*83*
Honduras	942	2,387	1,128	2,736	–152	–176	22	367	–317	–158	159	824
† Data for Taiwan, China	21,495	126,946	22,361	124,025	48	1,454	–95	–864	–913	3,511	4,055	94,246

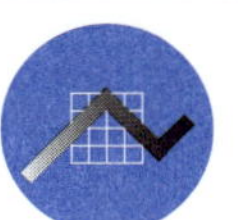

Balance of payments current account 4.17

	Goods and services				Net income		Net current transfers		Current account balance		Gross international reserves	
	Exports $ millions		Imports $ millions		$ millions		$ millions		$ millions		$ millions	
	1980	1998	1980	1998	1980	1998	1980	1998	1980	1998	1980	1998
Hungary	*9,671*	25,657	*9,152*	27,101	*–1,113*	–1,878	*63*	1,018	*–531*	–2,304	..	9,348
India	11,265	47,419	17,378	59,138	799	–3,546	2,860	10,280	–2,454	–4,984	12,010	30,647
Indonesia	*23,797*	54,850	*21,540*	43,755	*–3,073*	–8,212	*250*	1,089	*–566*	3,972	6,803	23,606
Iran, Islamic Rep.	13,069	14,297	16,111	16,189	606	–502	–2	497	–2,438	–1,897	12,783	..
Iraq	..	..	..	..	..	..	..	..	..	..	..	..
Ireland	9,610	71,749	12,044	61,713	–902	–10,718	1,204	1,488	–2,132	806	3,071	9,527
Israel	8,668	32,021	11,511	36,022	–757	–2,809	2,729	6,143	–871	–668	4,055	22,674
Italy	97,298	310,121	110,265	270,320	1,278	–12,318	1,101	–7,485	–10,587	19,998	62,428	53,880
Jamaica	1,363	3,383	1,408	3,970	–212	–304	121	635	–136	–255	105	709
Japan	146,980	436,456	156,970	363,488	770	56,570	–1,530	–8,842	–10,750	120,696	38,919	222,443
Jordan	1,181	3,636	2,417	5,200	36	–138	1,481	1,712	280	9	1,745	1,988
Kazakhstan	..	6,735	..	7,716	..	–298	..	78	..	–1,201	..	1,965
Kenya	2,007	2,851	2,846	3,695	–194	–173	157	654	–876	–363	539	783
Korea, Dem. Rep.	..	..	..	..	..	..	..	..	..	..	..	..
Korea, Rep.	19,815	156,701	25,152	114,446	–512	–5,055	536	3,352	–5,312	40,552	3,101	52,100
Kuwait	21,857	11,376	9,823	13,197	4,847	5,867	–1,580	–1,519	15,302	2,527	5,425	4,678
Kyrgyz Republic	..	602	..	877	..	–52	..	85	..	–257	..	188
Lao PDR	..	487	..	602	..	–35	..	74	..	–77	..	122
Latvia	..	3,052	..	3,902	..	53	..	85	..	–713	..	800
Lebanon	..	1,817	..	8,717	..	323	..	2,689	..	–3,888	7,025	9,210
Lesotho	90	247	475	918	266	234	175	157	56	–280	50	575
Libya	22,084	..	12,671	..	–65	..	–1,134	..	8,214	..	14,905	8,598
Lithuania	..	5,071	..	6,348	..	–255	..	235	..	–1,298	..	1,463
Macedonia, FYR	..	1,449	..	2,019	..	–45	..	327	..	–288	..	335
Madagascar	516	829	1,075	1,128	–44	–78	47	88	–556	–289	9	171
Malawi	313	563	487	1,076	–149	–98	63	..	–260	..	76	273
Malaysia	14,098	71,900	13,526	60,200	–836	*–5,074*	–2	*–1,094*	–266	*–4,792*	5,755	26,236
Mali	263	640	520	926	–17	–35	150	*126*	–124	*–178*	26	403
Mauritania	253	393	449	471	–27	–32	90	187	–133	77	146	206
Mauritius	574	2,712	690	2,748	–23	–28	22	99	–117	35	113	577
Mexico	22,622	129,523	27,601	138,441	–6,277	–13,056	834	6,014	–10,422	–15,960	4,175	31,863
Moldova	..	764	..	1,236	..	41	..	98	..	–334	..	144
Mongolia	*475*	540	*1,272*	671	*–11*	0	*0*	56	*–808*	–75	..	103
Morocco	3,233	9,970	5,207	11,358	–562	–1,101	1,130	2,345	–1,407	–144	814	4,638
Mozambique	399	534	844	1,183	22	–142	56	313	–367	–477	..	608
Myanmar	539	1,634	806	2,789	–48	38	7	515	–307	–602	409	382
Namibia	..	1,605	..	1,908	..	61	..	403	..	162	..	260
Nepal	224	1,108	365	1,646	13	13	36	103	–93	–422	272	800
Netherlands	90,380	224,087	91,622	200,646	1,535	3,411	–1,148	–6,935	–855	19,915	37,549	31,155
New Zealand	6,403	15,881	6,934	15,823	–538	–3,614	96	338	–973	–3,217	365	4,204
Nicaragua	495	761	907	1,656	–124	–151	124	446	–411	–599	75	355
Niger	617	332	956	479	–33	–24	97	–22	–276	–192	132	53
Nigeria	27,071	9,855	20,014	13,377	–1,304	–2,291	–576	1,570	5,178	–4,244	10,640	8,709
Norway	27,264	54,768	23,749	54,440	–1,922	–898	–515	–1,591	1,079	–2,161	6,746	18,947
Oman	3,757	*7,649*	2,298	*5,815*	–257	*–460*	–260	*–1,430*	942	*–57*	704	1,148
Pakistan	2,958	10,017	5,709	12,819	–281	–2,330	2,163	3,430	–869	–1,702	1,568	1,626
Panama	3,422	8,023	3,394	8,869	–397	–525	40	159	–329	–1,212	117	954
Papua New Guinea	1,029	2,091	1,322	1,872	–179	–259	184	87	–289	47	458	211
Paraguay	701	3,893	1,314	4,277	–4	61	0	58	–618	–265	783	784
Peru	4,631	7,488	3,970	10,494	–909	–1,484	147	696	–101	–3,794	2,804	9,882
Philippines	7,235	36,973	9,166	39,631	–420	3,510	447	435	–1,904	1,287	3,978	10,789
Poland	16,061	43,387	17,842	52,007	–2,357	–1,178	721	2,897	–3,417	–6,901	574	27,383
Portugal	6,674	34,621	10,136	45,323	–608	–579	3,006	4,031	–1,064	–7,250	13,863	21,606
Puerto Rico	..	..	..	..	..	..	..	..	..	..	..	..
Romania	12,087	9,519	13,730	12,798	–777	–392	0	753	–2,420	–2,918	2,511	3,795
Russian Federation	..	87,734	..	74,078	..	–12,000	..	–415	..	1,241	..	12,043

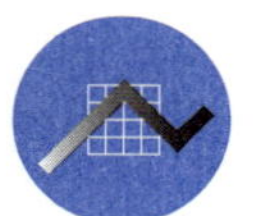

4.17 Balance of payments current account

	Goods and services				Net income		Net current transfers		Current account balance		Gross international reserves	
	Exports $ millions		Imports $ millions		$ millions		$ millions		$ millions		$ millions	
	1980	1998	1980	1998	1980	1998	1980	1998	1980	1998	1980	1998
Rwanda	165	112	319	482	2	–8	104	236	–48	–143	187	169
Saudi Arabia	106,765	44,193	55,793	44,633	526	2,641	–9,995	–15,081	41,503	–12,880	26,129	8,843
Senegal	807	1,319	1,215	1,627	–98	–37	120	264	–386	–81	25	431
Sierra Leone	275	112	471	223	–22	5	53	..	–165	..	31	44
Singapore	24,285	128,706	25,312	113,698	–429	3,783	–106	–1,177	–1,563	17,614	6,567	74,928
Slovak Republic	..	13,012	..	15,346	..	–158	..	366	..	–2,126	..	3,240
Slovenia	..	11,143	..	11,405	..	146	..	112	..	–4	..	3,639
South Africa	28,627	34,526	22,073	32,687	–3,285	–3,029	239	–746	3,508	–1,936	7,888	5,508
Spain	32,140	158,884	38,004	156,404	–1,362	–7,509	1,646	3,424	–5,580	–1,606	20,473	60,881
Sri Lanka	1,293	5,648	2,197	6,661	–26	–178	274	903	–655	–288	283	1,998
Sudan	779	612	1,698	1,968	–143	–1,146	341	507	–721	–1,996	49	91
Sweden	38,151	103,130	39,878	89,268	–1,380	–5,785	–1,224	–3,438	–4,331	4,639	6,996	15,457
Switzerland	48,595	120,542	51,843	108,277	4,186	16,018	–1,140	–3,736	–201	24,547	64,748	65,158
Syrian Arab Republic	2,477	4,930	4,531	4,788	785	–606	1,520	523	251	59	828	..
Tajikistan	..	604	..	731	..	–38	..	57	..	–107	..	..
Tanzania	748	1,144	1,384	2,353	–14	–139	129	441	–521	–907	20	599
Thailand	7,939	65,903	9,996	48,511	–229	–3,566	210	414	–2,076	14,241	3,026	29,537
Togo	550	693	691	823	–40	7	86	..	–95	..	85	118
Trinidad and Tobago	3,139	2,930	2,434	3,254	–306	–341	–42	22	357	–644	2,813	800
Tunisia	3,262	8,482	3,766	9,131	–259	–857	410	831	–353	–675	700	1,856
Turkey	3,621	54,541	8,082	55,412	–1,118	–2,985	2,171	5,727	–3,408	1,871	3,298	20,568
Turkmenistan	..	614	..	1,608	..	33	..	27	..	–934	..	..
Uganda	329	634	441	1,871	–7	–9	–2	539	–121	–706	3	725
Ukraine	..	17,621	..	18,828	..	–871	..	782	..	–1,296	..	793
United Arab Emirates	..	..	..	..	..	..	..	..	..	..	2,355	9,306
United Kingdom	146,072	371,331	134,200	385,434	–418	25,165	–4,592	–10,830	6,862	231	31,755	38,830
United States	271,800	933,906	290,730	1,098,181	29,580	–12,209	–8,500	–44,075	2,150	–220,559	171,413	146,006
Uruguay	1,526	4,225	2,144	4,507	–100	–185	9	67	–709	–400	2,401	2,587
Uzbekistan	..	3,148	..	3,182	..	–61	..	43	..	–52	..	..
Venezuela, RB	19,968	19,021	15,130	19,870	329	–1,559	–439	–154	4,728	–2,562	13,360	14,729
Vietnam	..	11,974	..	13,507	..	–689	..	951	..	–1,271	..	1,148
West Bank and Gaza	..	..	..	..	..	..	..	..	..	..	..	..
Yemen, Rep.	..	1,708	..	2,771	..	–422	..	1,256	..	–228	..	1,010
Yugoslavia, FR (Serb./Mont.)	..	..	..	..	..	..	..	..	..	..	..	..
Zambia	1,609	1,057	1,765	1,140	–205	–485	–155	..	–516	..	206	69
Zimbabwe	1,610	2,535	1,730	2,742	–61	–346	31	..	–149	..	419	310
World	2,294,081 t	6,748,117 t	2,324,205 t	6,669,967 t								
Low income	*102,167*	397,752	*128,025*	388,671								
Excl. China & India	*80,926*	141,503	*102,737*	161,302								
Middle income	509,068	1,190,620	469,691	1,208,910								
Lower middle income	196,458	425,394	207,898	441,485								
Upper middle income	312,700	765,539	267,163	767,001								
Low & middle income	635,222	1,588,398	598,946	1,597,708								
East Asia & Pacific	*105,229*	614,457	*110,191*	496,920								
Europe & Central Asia	..	340,353	..	363,065								
Latin America & Carib.	114,160	335,982	129,049	396,667								
Middle East & N. Africa	180,653	133,364	130,131	150,487								
South Asia	17,314	70,684	28,820	89,001								
Sub-Saharan Africa	89,443	90,008	83,544	104,277								
High income	1,680,420	5,159,630	1,731,756	5,072,242								
Europe EMU	727,472	2,145,761	765,073	1,979,638								

a. Includes Luxembourg. b. Data prior to 1990 refer to the Federal Republic of Germany before unification.

Balance of payments current account 4.17

About the data

The balance of payments records an economy's transactions with the rest of the world. Balance of payments accounts are divided into two groups: the current account, which records transactions in goods, services, income, and current transfers; and the capital and financial account, which records capital transfers, acquisition or disposal of nonproduced, nonfinancial assets, and transactions in financial assets and liabilities. This table presents data from the current account with the addition of gross international reserves.

The balance of payments is a double-entry accounting system that shows all flows of goods and services into and out of a country; all transfers that are the counterpart of real resources or financial claims provided to or by the rest of the world without a quid pro quo, such as donations and grants; and all changes in residents' claims on, and liabilities to, nonresidents that arise from economic transactions. All transactions are recorded twice—once as a credit and once as a debit. In principle the net balance should be zero, but in practice the accounts often do not balance. In these cases a balancing item, net errors and omissions, is included.

Discrepancies may arise in the balance of payments because there is no single source for balance of payments data and therefore no way to ensure that the data are fully consistent. Sources include customs data, monetary accounts of the banking system, external debt records, information provided by enterprises, surveys to estimate service transactions, and foreign exchange records. Differences in collection methods—such as in timing, definitions of residence and ownership, and the exchange rate used to value transactions—contribute to net errors and omissions. In addition, smuggling and other illegal or quasi-legal transactions may be unrecorded or misrecorded. For further discussion of issues relating to the recording of data on trade in goods and services see *About the data* for tables 4.4–4.8.

The concepts and definitions underlying the data here are based on the fifth edition of the International Monetary Fund's (IMF) *Balance of Payments Manual* (1993). The fifth edition redefined as capital transfers some transactions previously included in the current account, such as debt forgiveness, migrants' capital transfers, and foreign aid to acquire capital goods. Thus the current account balance now reflects more accurately net current transfer receipts in addition to transactions in goods, services (previously nonfactor services), and income (previously factor income). Many countries maintain their data collection systems according to the fourth edition. Where necessary, the IMF converts data reported in such systems to conform with the fifth edition (see *Primary data documentation*). Values are in U.S. dollars converted at market exchange rates. The data in this table come from the IMF's Balance of Payments and International Financial Statistics databases, supplemented with estimates by World Bank staff for countries whose national accounts are recorded in fiscal years (see *Primary data documentation*) and countries for which the IMF does not collect balance of payments statistics. In addition, World Bank staff make estimates of missing data for the most recent year.

Figure 4.17

On the road to recovery? Current accounts turn positive in East Asia

$ billions

Indonesia

Republic of Korea

Philippines

Thailand

Source: International Monetary Fund, Balance of Payments database; World Bank staff estimates.

After years of deficits, most East Asian economies showed a positive current account balance in 1998.

Definitions

• **Exports and imports of goods and services** comprise all transactions between residents of a country and the rest of the world involving a change in ownership of general merchandise, goods sent for processing and repairs, nonmonetary gold, and services. • **Net income** refers to receipts and payments of employee compensation to nonresident workers, and investment income (receipts and payments on direct investment, portfolio investment, and other investments, and receipts on reserve assets). Income derived from the use of intangible assets is recorded under business services. • **Net current transfers** are recorded in the balance of payments whenever an economy provides or receives goods, services, income, or financial items without a quid pro quo. All transfers not considered to be capital are current. • **Current account balance** is the sum of net exports of goods, services, net income, and net current transfers. • **Gross international reserves** comprise holdings of monetary gold, special drawing rights, reserves of IMF members held by the IMF, and holdings of foreign exchange under the control of monetary authorities. The gold component of these reserves is valued at year-end (31 December) London prices ($589.50 an ounce in 1980 and $287.80 an ounce in 1998).

Data sources

More information about the design and compilation of the balance of payments can be found in the IMF's *Balance of Payments Manual*, fifth edition (1993), *Balance of Payments Textbook* (1996a), and *Balance of Payments Compilation Guide* (1995). The balance of payments data are published in the IMF's *Balance of Payments Statistics Yearbook* and *International Financial Statistics*. The World Bank exchanges data with the IMF through electronic files that in most cases are more timely and cover a longer period than the published sources. The International Financial Statistics and Balance of Payments databases are available on CD-ROM.

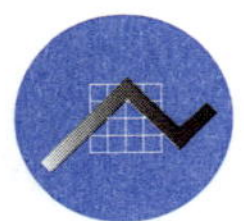

4.18 External debt

	Total external debt		Long-term debt		Public and publicly guaranteed debt				Private nonguaranteed external debt		Use of IMF credit	
					Total		IBRD loans and IDA credits					
	$ millions		$ millions		$ millions		$ millions		$ millions		$ millions	
	1980	1998	1980	1998	1980	1998	1980	1998	1980	1998	1980	1998
Albania	..	821	..	721	..	701	..	220	..	20	..	64
Algeria	19,365	30,665	17,040	28,469	17,040	28,469	253	1,676	0	0	0	2,011
Angola	..	12,173	..	10,616	..	10,616	0	179	..	0	..	0
Argentina	27,151	144,050	16,768	107,652	10,175	76,799	404	7,188	6,593	30,853	0	5,442
Armenia	..	800	..	564	..	564	..	303	..	0	..	190
Australia	..	..	..	..	..	..	..	..	..	..	..	..
Austria	..	..	..	..	..	..	..	..	..	..	..	..
Azerbaijan	..	693	..	371	..	308	..	141	..	63	..	321
Bangladesh	4,230	16,376	3,594	15,804	3,594	15,804	981	6,204	0	0	424	422
Belarus	..	1,120	..	766	..	748	..	135	..	18	..	243
Belgium	..	..	..	..	..	..	..	..	..	..	..	..
Benin	424	1,647	334	1,469	334	1,469	52	543	0	0	16	94
Bolivia	2,702	6,077	2,273	4,551	2,181	4,307	239	1,071	92	245	126	264
Bosnia and Herzegovina	..	..	..	..	..	..	..	893	..	..	..	77
Botswana	147	548	143	508	143	508	66	46	0	0	0	0
Brazil	71,520	232,004	57,981	202,054	41,375	98,959	2,035	6,298	16,605	103,095	0	4,825
Bulgaria	..	9,907	..	8,331	..	7,781	..	697	..	550	..	1,116
Burkina Faso	330	1,399	281	1,228	281	1,228	77	710	0	0	15	112
Burundi	166	1,119	118	1,079	118	1,079	37	603	0	0	36	20
Cambodia	..	2,210	..	2,102	..	2,102	0	157	..	0	0	67
Cameroon	2,588	9,829	2,251	8,274	2,073	8,096	298	1,050	178	179	59	156
Canada	..	..	..	..	..	..	..	..	..	..	..	..
Central African Republic	195	921	147	830	147	830	29	413	0	0	24	18
Chad	284	1,091	259	1,004	259	1,004	36	488	0	0	14	64
Chile	12,081	36,302	9,399	28,547	4,705	4,986	184	954	4,693	23,560	123	0
China	..	154,599	..	126,667	..	99,424	0	18,338	..	27,243	0	0
Hong Kong, China	..	..	..	..	..	..	..	..	..	..	..	..
Colombia	6,940	33,263	4,604	27,031	4,088	16,930	1,012	1,749	515	10,101	0	0
Congo, Dem. Rep.	4,770	12,929	4,071	8,949	4,071	8,949	246	1,345	0	0	373	423
Congo, Rep.	1,526	5,119	1,257	4,250	1,257	4,250	61	239	0	0	22	34
Costa Rica	2,744	3,971	2,112	3,284	1,700	3,047	183	174	412	237	57	0
Côte d'Ivoire	7,462	14,852	6,339	12,632	4,327	10,800	314	2,279	2,012	1,833	65	644
Croatia	..	8,297	..	6,878	..	4,910	..	336	..	1,969	..	234
Cuba	..	..	..	..	..	..	..	..	..	..	..	..
Czech Republic	..	25,301	..	15,365	..	12,901	..	380	..	2,465	..	0
Denmark	..	..	..	..	..	..	..	..	..	..	..	..
Dominican Republic	2,002	4,451	1,473	3,530	1,220	3,530	83	219	254	0	49	56
Ecuador	5,997	15,140	4,422	12,799	3,300	12,589	146	877	1,122	210	0	70
Egypt, Arab Rep.	19,131	31,964	14,693	27,704	14,428	27,669	728	2,114	265	34	411	0
El Salvador	911	3,633	659	2,783	499	2,443	114	305	161	340	32	0
Eritrea	..	149	..	144	..	144	..	37	..	0	..	0
Estonia	..	782	..	444	..	231	..	84	..	212	..	30
Ethiopia	824	10,352	688	9,618	688	9,618	304	1,632	0	0	79	107
Finland	..	..	..	..	..	..	..	..	..	..	..	..
France	..	..	..	..	..	..	..	..	..	..	..	..
Gabon	1,514	4,425	1,272	3,833	1,272	3,833	19	75	0	0	15	113
Gambia, The	137	477	97	451	97	451	16	173	0	0	16	10
Georgia	..	1,674	..	1,324	..	1,311	..	274	..	13	..	304
Germany	..	..	..	..	..	..	..	..	..	..	..	..
Ghana	1,398	6,884	1,162	5,833	1,152	5,570	213	2,990	10	263	105	334
Greece	..	..	..	..	..	..	..	..	..	..	..	..
Guatemala	1,180	4,565	845	3,171	563	2,989	144	203	282	182	0	0
Guinea	1,134	3,546	1,019	3,126	1,019	3,126	87	1,016	0	0	35	127
Guinea-Bissau	140	964	133	873	133	873	5	234	0	0	1	15
Haiti	302	1,048	242	980	242	980	66	493	0	0	46	38
Honduras	1,472	5,002	1,168	4,358	976	3,946	216	814	191	412	33	113

External debt 4.18

	Total external debt		Long-term debt		Public and publicly guaranteed debt				Private nonguaranteed external debt		Use of IMF credit	
					Total		IBRD loans and IDA credits					
	$ millions		$ millions		$ millions		$ millions		$ millions		$ millions	
	1980	1998	1980	1998	1980	1998	1980	1998	1980	1998	1980	1998
Hungary	9,764	28,580	6,416	23,800	6,416	15,941	0	699	0	7,859	0	0
India	20,581	98,232	18,333	93,616	17,997	85,207	5,969	26,554	336	8,409	977	288
Indonesia	20,938	150,875	18,163	121,672	15,021	66,944	1,606	11,386	3,142	54,728	0	9,090
Iran, Islamic Rep.	4,500	14,391	4,500	8,307	4,500	7,679	622	433	0	628	0	0
Iraq	..	..	..	..	..	..	..	..	..	..	..	..
Ireland	..	..	..	..	..	..	..	..	..	..	..	..
Israel	..	..	..	..	..	..	..	..	..	..	..	..
Italy	..	..	..	..	..	..	..	..	..	..	..	..
Jamaica	1,913	3,995	1,505	3,258	1,430	3,079	176	410	75	179	309	105
Japan	..	..	..	..	..	..	..	..	..	..	..	..
Jordan	1,971	8,484	1,486	7,421	1,486	7,388	102	807	0	34	0	469
Kazakhstan	..	5,714	..	4,609	..	3,040	..	899	..	1,569	..	653
Kenya	3,387	7,010	2,492	5,954	2,056	5,629	528	2,364	437	325	254	197
Korea, Dem. Rep.	..	..	..	..	..	..	..	..	..	..	..	..
Korea, Rep.	29,480	139,097	18,236	94,062	15,933	57,956	1,836	7,535	2,303	36,106	683	16,896
Kuwait	..	..	..	..	..	..	..	..	..	..	..	..
Kyrgyz Republic	..	1,148	..	944	..	909	..	328	..	35	..	175
Lao PDR	350	2,437	333	2,373	333	2,373	6	395	0	0	16	62
Latvia	..	756	..	496	..	413	..	187	..	83	..	64
Lebanon	510	6,725	216	4,765	216	3,980	27	199	0	785	0	0
Lesotho	72	692	58	661	58	661	24	241	0	0	6	24
Libya	..	..	..	..	..	..	..	..	..	..	..	..
Lithuania	..	1,950	..	1,320	..	1,216	..	174	..	104	..	253
Macedonia, FYR	..	2,392	..	2,133	..	1,944	..	289	..	189	..	102
Madagascar	1,250	4,394	920	4,107	920	4,107	152	1,318	0	0	87	58
Malawi	830	2,444	634	2,310	634	2,310	156	1,568	0	0	80	102
Malaysia	6,611	44,773	5,256	36,117	4,008	18,158	504	970	1,248	17,959	0	0
Mali	727	3,201	664	2,827	664	2,827	121	1,009	0	0	39	187
Mauritania	840	2,589	713	2,213	713	2,213	38	412	0	0	62	110
Mauritius	467	2,482	318	1,909	294	1,152	55	126	24	757	102	0
Mexico	57,365	159,959	41,202	124,073	33,902	87,996	2,063	11,514	7,300	36,077	0	8,380
Moldova	..	1,035	..	816	..	808	..	207	..	8	..	177
Mongolia	..	739	..	634	..	634	0	118	..	0	0	48
Morocco	9,258	20,687	8,024	20,571	7,874	19,325	578	3,417	150	1,246	457	0
Mozambique	..	8,208	..	7,626	..	5,651	0	1,335	..	1,975	0	207
Myanmar	1,500	5,680	1,390	5,071	1,390	5,071	146	727	0	0	106	0
Namibia	..	..	..	..	..	..	..	..	..	..	..	..
Nepal	205	2,646	156	2,591	156	2,591	76	1,131	0	0	42	24
Netherlands	..	..	..	..	..	..	..	..	..	..	..	..
New Zealand	..	..	..	..	..	..	..	..	..	..	..	..
Nicaragua	2,190	5,968	1,668	5,212	1,668	5,212	135	503	0	0	49	52
Niger	863	1,659	687	1,521	383	1,449	66	688	305	72	16	76
Nigeria	8,921	30,315	5,368	23,740	4,271	23,455	554	2,841	1,097	285	0	0
Norway	..	..	..	..	..	..	..	..	..	..	..	..
Oman	599	3,629	436	2,231	436	2,228	14	9	0	3	0	0
Pakistan	9,931	32,229	8,520	28,663	8,502	26,061	1,150	6,936	18	2,601	674	1,360
Panama	2,975	6,689	2,271	5,763	2,271	5,413	133	279	0	349	23	177
Papua New Guinea	719	2,692	624	2,490	486	1,410	110	366	139	1,080	31	46
Paraguay	954	2,304	780	1,635	630	1,593	124	196	151	43	0	0
Peru	9,386	32,397	6,828	24,094	6,218	20,803	359	2,128	610	3,290	474	905
Philippines	17,417	47,817	8,817	39,064	6,363	28,189	960	4,516	2,454	10,875	1,044	1,568
Poland	..	47,708	..	41,517	..	35,136	0	2,156	..	6,381	0	0
Portugal	..	..	..	..	..	..	..	..	..	..	..	..
Puerto Rico	..	..	..	..	..	..	..	..	..	..	..	..
Romania	9,762	9,513	7,131	7,825	7,131	6,962	806	1,442	0	863	328	539
Russian Federation	..	183,601	..	145,874	..	119,314	0	6,337	..	26,560	0	19,335

4.18 External debt

	Total external debt		Long-term debt		Public and publicly guaranteed debt				Private nonguaranteed external debt		Use of IMF credit	
					Total		IBRD loans and IDA credits					
	$ millions		$ millions		$ millions		$ millions		$ millions		$ millions	
	1980	1998	1980	1998	1980	1998	1980	1998	1980	1998	1980	1998
Rwanda	190	1,226	150	1,120	150	1,120	58	639	0	0	14	56
Saudi Arabia	..	..	..	..	..	..	..	..	..	..	..	..
Senegal	1,473	3,861	1,114	3,296	1,105	3,274	156	1,309	9	22	140	293
Sierra Leone	469	1,243	357	944	357	944	43	299	0	0	59	191
Singapore	..	..	..	..	..	..	..	..	..	..	..	..
Slovak Republic	..	9,893	..	7,722	..	4,452	0	239	..	3,270	0	190
Slovenia	..	..	..	..	..	..	..	..	..	..	..	..
South Africa	..	24,711	..	13,268	..	10,627	0	0	..	2,641	0	0
Spain	..	..	..	..	..	..	..	..	..	..	..	..
Sri Lanka	1,841	8,526	1,230	7,726	1,227	7,649	129	1,674	3	77	391	367
Sudan	5,177	16,843	4,147	9,722	3,822	9,226	236	1,232	325	496	431	772
Sweden	..	..	..	..	..	..	..	..	..	..	..	..
Switzerland	..	..	..	..	..	..	..	..	..	..	..	..
Syrian Arab Republic	3,552	22,435	2,921	16,328	2,921	16,328	257	99	0	0	0	0
Tajikistan	..	1,070	..	823	..	707	..	92	..	116	..	99
Tanzania	5,322	7,603	3,381	6,440	3,297	6,404	440	2,485	84	37	171	268
Thailand	8,297	86,172	5,646	59,410	3,943	28,113	703	2,207	1,702	31,297	348	3,239
Togo	1,049	1,448	896	1,302	896	1,302	47	620	0	0	33	95
Trinidad and Tobago	829	2,193	712	1,619	712	1,476	57	83	0	144	0	0
Tunisia	3,527	11,078	3,390	9,908	3,210	9,727	337	1,501	180	181	0	129
Turkey	19,131	102,074	15,575	74,450	15,040	49,932	1,347	3,558	535	24,518	1,054	388
Turkmenistan	..	2,266	..	1,745	..	1,731	..	9	..	14	..	0
Uganda	689	3,935	537	3,402	537	3,402	47	1,947	0	0	89	398
Ukraine	..	12,718	..	9,443	..	8,606	..	1,542	..	837	..	2,795
United Arab Emirates	..	..	..	..	..	..	..	..	..	..	..	..
United Kingdom	..	..	..	..	..	..	..	..	..	..	..	..
United States	..	..	..	..	..	..	..	..	..	..	..	..
Uruguay	1,660	7,600	1,338	5,430	1,127	5,142	72	473	211	289	0	161
Uzbekistan	..	3,162	..	2,783	..	2,485	..	177	..	298	..	233
Venezuela, RB	29,344	37,003	13,795	33,373	10,614	26,692	133	1,218	3,181	6,681	0	1,226
Vietnam	..	22,359	..	19,775	..	19,775	2	850	..	0	0	391
West Bank and Gaza	..	..	..	..	..	..	..	..	..	..	..	..
Yemen, Rep.	1,684	4,138	1,453	3,590	1,453	3,590	137	1,075	0	0	48	336
Yugoslavia, FR (Serb./Mont.)[a]	18,486	13,742	15,586	11,080	4,580	8,321	1,359	1,148	11,005	2,759	760	79
Zambia	3,244	6,865	2,211	5,348	2,124	5,320	348	1,628	87	29	447	1,188
Zimbabwe	786	4,716	696	3,541	696	3,341	3	941	0	200	0	407
World	.. s	.. s	.. s	.. s	.. s	.. s	.. s	.. s	.. s	.. s	.. s	.. s
Low income	131,253	721,592	108,649	610,973	100,419	511,587	15,451	114,421	8,230	99,386	5,310	20,516
Excl. China & India	..	..	..	..	..	..	..	..	..	..	..	..
Middle income[b]	478,150	1,814,454	342,874	1,419,370	280,534	1,017,662	18,592	85,665	62,341	401,708	6,937	73,323
Lower middle income	..	..	..	..	..	..	..	..	..	..	..	..
Upper middle income	..	..	..	..	..	..	..	..	..	..	..	..
Low & middle income[b]	609,403	2,536,046	451,524	2,030,343	380,953	1,529,249	34,043	200,086	70,571	501,094	12,246	93,839
East Asia & Pacific	94,080	667,522	66,674	517,051	55,620	337,690	5,913	47,692	11,054	179,361	2,234	31,407
Europe & Central Asia	75,394	480,539	56,196	374,244	44,656	293,468	3,512	22,943	11,540	80,775	2,143	27,661
Latin America & Carib.	257,259	786,019	187,249	640,533	144,791	424,246	8,134	37,507	42,458	216,287	1,413	21,969
Middle East & N. Africa	83,836	208,059	61,770	164,114	61,175	159,644	3,053	11,382	595	4,471	916	2,954
South Asia	38,015	163,775	33,053	154,151	32,696	143,063	8,306	42,568	357	11,088	2,508	2,461
Sub-Saharan Africa	60,820	230,132	46,580	180,250	42,014	171,137	5,125	37,994	4,567	9,112	3,033	7,388
High income												
Europe EMU												

a. Data prior to 1993 refer to the former Socialist Federal Republic of Yugoslavia. Data for 1998 are estimates and reflect borrowings by the former Socialist Federal Republic of Yugoslavia that are not yet allocated to the successor republics. b. Includes data for Gibraltar not included in other tables.

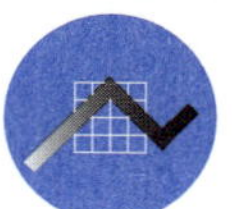

External debt 4.18

About the data

Data on the external debt of low- and middle-income economies are gathered by the World Bank through its Debtor Reporting System. World Bank staff calculate the indebtedness of developing countries using loan-by-loan reports submitted by these countries on long-term public and publicly guaranteed borrowing, along with information on short-term debt collected by the countries or collected from creditors through the reporting systems of the Bank for International Settlements and the Organisation for Economic Co-operation and Development. These data are supplemented by information on loans and credits from major multilateral banks, loan statements from official lending agencies in major creditor countries, and estimates from World Bank and International Monetary Fund (IMF) staff. In addition, some countries provide data on private nonguaranteed debt. In 1998, 34 countries reported private nonguaranteed debt to the World Bank; estimates were made for 43 additional countries known to have significant private debt.

The coverage, quality, and timeliness of debt data vary across countries. Coverage varies for both debt instruments and borrowers. With a widening spectrum of debt instruments and investors and the expansion of private nonguaranteed borrowing, comprehensive coverage of long-term external debt becomes more complex. Reporting countries differ in their capacity to monitor debt, especially private nonguaranteed debt. Even data on public and publicly guaranteed debt are affected by coverage and accuracy in reporting—again because of monitoring capacity and sometimes because of unwillingness to provide information. A key part often underreported is military debt.

Because debt data are normally reported in the currency of repayment, they have to be converted into U.S. dollars to produce summary tables. Stock figures (amount of debt outstanding) are converted using end-period exchange rates, as published in the IMF's *International Financial Statistics* (line ae). Flow figures are converted at annual average exchange rates (line rf). Projected debt service is converted using end-period exchange rates. Debt repayable in multiple currencies, goods, or services and debt with a provision for maintenance of value of the currency of repayment are shown at book value. Because flow data are converted at annual average exchange rates and stock data at year-end exchange rates, year-to-year changes in debt outstanding and disbursed are sometimes not equal to net flows (disbursements less principal repayments); similarly, changes in debt outstanding including undisbursed debt differ from commitments less repayments. Discrepancies are particularly significant when exchange rates have moved sharply during the year; cancellations and reschedulings of other liabilities into long-term public debt also contribute to the differences.

Variations in reporting rescheduled debt also affect cross-country comparability. For example, rescheduling under the auspices of the Paris Club of official creditors may be subject to lags between the completion of the general rescheduling agreement and the completion of the specific, bilateral agreements that define the terms of the rescheduled debt. Other areas of inconsistency include country treatment of arrears and of nonresident national deposits denominated in foreign currency.

Figure 4.18

World Bank and International Monetary Fund lending expanded in the regions most at risk of financial crisis in 1998

Debt outstanding and disbursed ($ billions)

IBRD loans and IDA credits

Use of IMF credit

East Asia & Pacific, Europe & Central Asia, Latin America & Caribbean, Middle East & North Africa, South Asia, Sub-Saharan Africa

1996 1997 1998

Source: World Bank data files.

Definitions

• **Total external debt** is debt owed to nonresidents repayable in foreign currency, goods, or services. It is the sum of public, publicly guaranteed, and private nonguaranteed long-term debt, use of IMF credit, and short-term debt. Short-term debt includes all debt having an original maturity of one year or less and interest in arrears on long-term debt. • **Long-term debt** is debt that has an original or extended maturity of more than one year. It has three components: public, publicly guaranteed, and private nonguaranteed debt. • **Public and publicly guaranteed debt** comprises long-term external obligations of public debtors, including the national government and political subdivisions (or an agency of either) and autonomous public bodies, and external obligations of private debtors that are guaranteed for repayment by a public entity. • **IBRD loans and IDA credits** are extended by the World Bank Group. The International Bank for Reconstruction and Development (IBRD) lends at market rates. Credits from the International Development Association (IDA) are at concessional rates. • **Private nonguaranteed debt** comprises long-term external obligations of private debtors that are not guaranteed for repayment by a public entity. • **Use of IMF credit** denotes repurchase obligations to the IMF for all uses of IMF resources (excluding those resulting from drawings on the reserve tranche). These obligations, shown for the end of the year specified, comprise purchases outstanding under the credit tranches, including enlarged access resources, and all special facilities (the buffer stock, compensatory financing, extended fund, and oil facilities), trust fund loans, and operations under the structural adjustment and enhanced structural adjustment facilities.

Data sources

The main sources of external debt information are reports to the World Bank through its Debtor Reporting System from member countries that have received IBRD loans or IDA credits. Additional information has been drawn from the files of the World Bank and the IMF. Summary tables of the external debt of developing countries are published annually in the World Bank's *Global Development Finance* and *Global Development Finance* CD-ROM.

4.19 External debt management

	Indebtedness classification[a]	Present value of debt		Total debt service				Public and publicly guaranteed debt service		Short-term debt	
		% of GNP	% of exports of goods and services	% of GNP		% of exports of goods and services		% of central government current revenue		% of total debt	
	1998	1998	1998	1980	1998	1980	1998	1980	1998	1980	1998
Albania	L	20	74	..	1.2	..	4.5	..	5.3	..	4.3
Algeria	M	66	244	9.9	11.3	27.4	42.0	..	..	12.0	0.6
Angola	S	280	292	..	33.0	..	34.4	..	..	..	12.8
Argentina	S	52	406	5.5	7.4	37.3	58.2	6.1	..	38.2	21.5
Armenia	L	30	120	..	2.2	..	8.9	..	..	..	5.7
Australia	..	..	..	..	..	..	..	..	..	..	..
Austria	..	..	..	..	..	..	..	..	..	..	..
Azerbaijan	L	14	52	..	0.6	..	2.3	..	1.4	..	0.2
Bangladesh	M	23	135	1.6	1.5	23.7	9.1	7.9	..	5.0	0.9
Belarus	L	5	13	..	0.7	..	2.0	..	..	..	9.9
Belgium-Luxembourg	..	..	..	..	..	..	..	..	..	..	..
Benin	M	46[b]	183[b]	1.4	2.7	6.3	10.6	..	..	17.3	5.1
Bolivia	S	59[b]	318[b]	..	5.6	35.0	30.2	..	23.1	11.2	20.8
Bosnia and Herzegovina	..	..	..	..	..	..	..	..	..	..	..
Botswana	L	10	15	1.4	1.7	2.1	2.7	4.1	..	2.7	7.3
Brazil	S	29	340	6.5	6.3	63.3	74.1	15.3	..	18.9	10.8
Bulgaria	S	79	160	..	10.8	..	22.1	..	19.6	..	4.6
Burkina Faso	M	32[b]	167[b]	1.3	2.1	5.9	10.7	8.4	..	10.6	4.2
Burundi	S	72	829	0.9	3.5	..	40.0	4.8	..	7.2	1.8
Cambodia	M	62	208	..	0.4	..	1.5	..	..	..	1.9
Cameroon	S	100	343	5.0	6.5	14.6	22.3	17.0	..	10.8	14.2
Canada	..	..	..	..	..	..	..	..	..	..	..
Central African Republic	S	55	394	1.3	2.9	4.9	20.9	..	..	12.6	8.0
Chad	M	38	189	0.6	2.1	8.4	10.6	..	..	4.0	2.1
Chile	M	48	183	10.2	5.9	43.1	22.3	15.2	6.3	21.2	21.4
China	L	14	63	..	2.0	..	8.6	..	..	..	18.1
Hong Kong, China	..	..	..	..	..	..	..	..	..	..	..
Colombia	M	32	218	2.8	4.5	16.0	30.7	13.2	24.8	33.7	18.7
Congo, Dem. Rep.	S	196	732	3.8	0.3	22.6	1.2	29.2	..	6.8	27.5
Congo, Rep.	S	280	372	7.1	2.5	10.6	3.3	9.5	..	16.2	16.3
Costa Rica	L	37	53	7.7	5.4	29.1	7.6	23.9	..	21.0	17.3
Côte d'Ivoire	S	124[b]	240[b]	14.5	13.5	38.7	26.1	35.6	37.5	14.2	10.6
Croatia	L	31	71	..	3.9	..	8.9	..	7.5	..	14.3
Cuba	..	..	..	..	..	..	..	..	..	..	..
Czech Republic	L	45	71	..	9.7	..	15.2	..	23.3	..	39.3
Denmark	..	..	..	..	..	..	..	..	..	..	..
Dominican Republic	L	28	46	5.9	2.5	25.3	4.2	16.1	..	24.0	19.4
Ecuador	S	78	240	9.0	9.3	33.9	28.8	37.2	..	26.3	15.0
Egypt, Arab Rep.	L	29	128	5.8	2.1	13.4	9.5	5.9	..	21.1	13.3
El Salvador	L	27	77	2.7	3.7	7.5	10.4	..	..	24.1	23.4
Eritrea	L	12	34	..	0.5	..	1.5	..	..	..	3.5
Estonia	L	13	15	..	1.7	..	2.1	..	1.7	..	39.4
Ethiopia	S	135	830	..	1.8	7.6	11.3	4.4	..	6.9	6.1
Finland	..	..	..	..	..	..	..	..	..	..	..
France	..	..	..	..	..	..	..	..	..	..	..
Gabon	S	91	174	11.2	6.3	17.7	12.0	24.0	..	15.1	10.8
Gambia, The	M	66	100	1.7	6.4	6.2	9.7	1.4	..	17.0	3.2
Georgia	M	25	141	..	1.3	..	7.6	..	19.1	..	2.8
Germany	..	..	..	..	..	..	..	..	..	..	..
Ghana	M	54[b]	196[b]	3.6	7.7	13.1	28.4	10.0	..	9.4	10.4
Greece	..	..	..	..	..	..	..	..	..	..	..
Guatemala	L	23	106	1.8	2.1	7.9	9.8	5.1	..	28.4	30.5
Guinea	S	72	307	..	4.6	..	19.5	..	34.2	7.0	8.3
Guinea-Bissau	S	363	2,253	4.4	4.1	..	25.6	..	..	3.7	7.9
Haiti	M	16	125	1.8	1.0	6.2	8.2	13.2	..	4.6	2.8
Honduras	M	62	119	8.5	9.8	21.4	18.7	26.0	..	18.5	10.6

External debt management 4.19

	Indebtedness classification[a]	Present value of debt		Total debt service				Public and publicly guaranteed debt service		Short-term debt	
		% of GNP	% of exports of goods and services	% of GNP		% of exports of goods and services		% of central government current revenue		% of total debt	
	1998	1998	1998	1980	1998	1980	1998	1980	1998	1980	1998
Hungary	M	63	107	8.8	15.9	..	27.3	..	25.3	34.3	16.7
India	M	20	143	0.8	2.8	9.3	20.6	5.6	20.2	6.2	4.4
Indonesia	M	169	252	4.1	22.2	..	33.0	10.6	49.3	13.3	13.3
Iran, Islamic Rep.	L	12	95	1.0	2.6	6.8	20.2	4.7	5.0	0.0	42.3
Iraq	..	..	..	..	..	..	..	..	..	..	..
Ireland	..	..	..	..	..	..	..	..	..	..	..
Israel	..	..	..	..	..	..	..	..	..	..	..
Italy	..	..	..	..	..	..	..	..	..	..	..
Jamaica	M	60	91	11.6	8.5	19.0	12.8	26.6	..	5.1	15.8
Japan	..	..	..	..	..	..	..	..	..	..	..
Jordan	S	136	144	5.2	15.6	11.2	16.4	25.3	..	24.6	7.0
Kazakhstan	L	25	79	..	4.1	..	13.0	..	..	..	7.9
Kenya	M	45	179	6.2	4.8	21.0	18.8	14.5	..	18.9	12.3
Korea, Dem. Rep.	..	..	..	..	..	..	..	..	..	..	..
Korea, Rep.	L	43	84	7.3	6.5	20.2	12.9	24.7	..	35.8	20.2
Kuwait	..	..	..	..	..	..	..	..	..	..	..
Kyrgyz Republic	M	50	135	..	3.5	..	9.4	..	..	..	2.5
Lao PDR	S	92	227	..	2.5	..	6.3	..	..	0.4	0.1
Latvia	L	11	22	..	1.3	..	2.5	..	1.5	..	26.0
Lebanon	M	41	237	..	3.2	..	18.7	..	8.7	57.6	29.2
Lesotho	L	46	82	0.9	4.8	1.5	8.4	..	11.7	11.1	1.1
Libya	..	..	..	..	..	..	..	..	..	..	..
Lithuania	L	17	35	..	1.6	..	3.3	..	4.0	..	19.3
Macedonia, FYR	M	87	140	..	8.1	..	13.0	..	..	..	6.6
Madagascar	S	89	383	2.6	3.4	20.1	14.7	11.5	..	19.5	5.2
Malawi	M	77[b]	241[b]	7.7	4.7	27.8	14.7	28.7	..	14.0	1.3
Malaysia	M	69	66	4.0	9.1	6.3	8.7	5.8	..	20.5	19.3
Mali	S	82[b]	335[b]	0.9	3.1	5.1	12.6	5.3	..	3.3	5.9
Mauritania	S	150	358	6.1	11.6	17.3	27.7	..	..	7.7	10.2
Mauritius	M	60	90	4.7	7.5	9.0	11.3	14.7	22.1	10.1	23.1
Mexico	L	41	111	5.0	7.7	44.4	20.8	26.9	..	28.2	17.2
Moldova	M	58	106	..	10.0	..	18.5	..	..	..	4.0
Mongolia	M	49	87	..	3.5	..	6.3	..	14.5	..	7.7
Morocco	M	54	153	7.9	8.2	33.4	23.0	27.1	..	8.4	0.6
Mozambique	S	74[b]	470[b]	..	2.8	..	18.0	..	..	..	4.6
Myanmar	S	..	279	..	..	25.4	5.3	11.9	..	0.3	10.7
Namibia	..	..	..	..	..	..	..	..	..	..	..
Nepal	L	31	119	0.4	1.8	2.9	7.0	2.6	16.7	3.4	1.2
Netherlands	..	..	..	..	..	..	..	..	..	..	..
New Zealand	..	..	..	..	..	..	..	..	..	..	..
Nicaragua	S	295[b]	534[b]	5.7	14.1	22.3	25.5	26.3	..	21.6	11.8
Niger	S	55[b]	330[b]	5.7	3.1	21.7	18.4	10.6	..	18.5	3.8
Nigeria	M	76	250	1.9	3.4	4.1	11.2	..	..	39.8	21.7
Norway	..	..	..	..	..	..	..	..	..	..	..
Oman	L	..	..	4.7	..	6.4	..	9.7	15.3	27.2	38.5
Pakistan	M	43	225	3.7	4.5	18.3	23.6	15.0	20.4	7.4	6.8
Panama	S	78	69	14.4	8.7	6.2	7.6	48.3	..	22.9	11.2
Papua New Guinea	M	69	114	6.0	5.2	13.8	8.6	10.5	..	8.9	5.8
Paraguay	L	25	52	3.1	2.5	18.6	5.3	16.0	..	18.3	29.0
Peru	S	55	388	10.9	4.0	44.5	28.3	42.7	15.3	22.2	22.8
Philippines	M	66	104	6.7	7.6	26.6	11.8	13.1	..	43.4	15.0
Poland	L	28	95	..	2.9	..	9.7	..	4.6	..	13.0
Portugal	..	..	..	..	..	..	..	..	..	..	..
Puerto Rico	..	..	..	..	..	..	..	..	..	..	..
Romania	L	26	98	..	6.1	12.6	23.5	7.4	..	23.6	12.1
Russian Federation	M	62	186	..	4.1	..	12.1	..	..	..	10.0

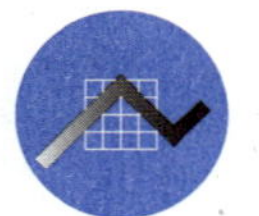

4.19 External debt management

	Indebtedness classification[a]	Present value of debt		Total debt service				Public and publicly guaranteed debt service		Short-term debt	
		% of GNP	% of exports of goods and services	% of GNP		% of exports of goods and services		% of central government current revenue		% of total debt	
	1998	1998	1998	1980	1998	1980	1998	1980	1998	1980	1998
Rwanda	S	34	556	0.7	1.0	4.1	16.9	2.8	..	13.7	4.0
Saudi Arabia	..	..	..	..	..	..	..	..	..	..	..
Senegal	M	58	195	9.0	6.9	28.7	23.2	30.1	..	14.9	7.1
Sierra Leone	S	131	735	5.6	3.2	23.8	18.2	22.7	..	11.3	8.7
Singapore	..	..	..	..	..	..	..	..	..	..	..
Slovak Republic	L	45	68	..	10.6	..	15.9	..	..	..	20.0
Slovenia	..	..	..	..	..	..	..	..	..	..	..
South Africa	L	19	67	..	3.4	..	12.2	..	7.5	..	46.3
Spain	..	..	..	..	..	..	..	..	..	..	..
Sri Lanka	L	41	92	4.5	2.9	12.0	6.6	10.3	12.5	11.9	5.1
Sudan	S	172	2,538	3.5	0.7	25.1	9.8	9.2	..	11.6	37.7
Sweden	..	..	..	..	..	..	..	..	..	..	..
Switzerland	..	..	..	..	..	..	..	..	..	..	..
Syrian Arab Republic	S	128	392	2.9	2.1	11.4	6.4	8.6	..	17.8	27.2
Tajikistan	L	40	143	..	3.8	..	13.7	..	..	..	13.8
Tanzania[c]	S	70	482	..	3.0	21.2	20.8	8.3	..	33.3	11.8
Thailand	M	76	123	5.0	11.8	18.9	19.2	9.5	12.6	27.8	27.3
Togo	M	68	142	4.8	2.7	9.0	5.7	11.0	..	11.5	3.6
Trinidad and Tobago	L	36	72	3.9	5.1	6.8	10.2	8.4	..	14.0	26.2
Tunisia	M	56	115	6.4	7.3	14.8	15.1	15.6	..	3.9	9.4
Turkey	M	49	161	2.3	6.5	28.0	21.2	8.4	..	13.1	26.7
Turkmenistan	M	83	289	..	12.0	..	42.0	..	..	..	23.0
Uganda	S	35[b]	351[b]	4.6	2.4	17.3	23.6	6.7	..	9.1	3.4
Ukraine	L	29	70	..	4.7	..	11.4	..	..	..	3.8
United Arab Emirates	..	..	..	..	..	..	..	..	..	..	..
United Kingdom	..	..	..	..	..	..	..	..	..	..	..
United States	..	..	..	..	..	..	..	..	..	..	..
Uruguay	M	37	156	3.1	5.6	18.8	23.5	8.7	14.2	19.4	26.4
Uzbekistan	L	15	93	..	2.1	..	13.2	..	..	..	4.6
Venezuela, RB	M	40	176	8.7	6.3	27.2	27.4	19.1	27.2	53.0	6.5
Vietnam	S	76	170	..	4.0	..	8.9	..	..	..	9.8
West Bank and Gaza	..	..	..	..	..	..	..	..	..	..	..
Yemen, Rep.	M	79	105	..	3.2	..	4.2	..	5.3	10.8	5.1
Yugoslavia, FR (Serb./Mont.)	..	..	..	..	..	..	..	..	..	..	..
Zambia	S	175	483	11.4	6.4	25.2	17.7	29.4	..	18.1	4.8
Zimbabwe	M	69	160	1.0	16.6	3.8	38.2	3.9	..	11.5	16.3
World				.. w	.. w	.. w	.. w			.. w	.. w
Low income				2.6	3.6	..	15.4			13.2	12.5
Excl. China & India				3.8	8.1	..	..			..	..
Middle income				5.7	6.2	14.5[d]	19.4[d]			26.8[d]	17.7[d]
Lower middle income				5.1	5.1	..	..			..	..
Upper middle income				6.0	6.7	..	..			..	..
Low & middle income				4.8	5.4	13.5[d]	18.4[d]			23.9[d]	16.2[d]
East Asia & Pacific				..	5.2	..	13.3			26.8	17.8
Europe & Central Asia				..	5.4	..	14.7			22.6	16.4
Latin America & Carib.				6.2	6.5	36.2	33.6			26.7	15.7
Middle East & N. Africa				..	4.7	5.6	14.0			25.2	19.7
South Asia				1.2	2.9	11.8	18.9			6.5	4.4
Sub-Saharan Africa				..	4.5	7.2	14.7			18.4	18.5
High income											
Europe EMU											

a. S = severely indebted, M = moderately indebted, L = less indebted. b. Data are from debt sustainability analyses undertaken as part of the Heavily Indebted Poor Countries (HIPC) Initiative. Present value estimates for these countries are for public and publicly guaranteed debt only, and export figures exclude workers' remittances. c. Data refer to mainland Tanzania only. d. Includes data for Gibraltar not included in other tables.

External debt management 4.19

About the data

The indicators in the table measure the relative burden on developing countries of servicing external debt. The present value of external debt provides a measure of future debt service obligations that can be compared with the current value of such indicators as GNP and exports of goods and services. This table shows the present value of total debt service in the most recent year (1998) both as a percentage of average GNP in 1996–98 and as a percentage of average exports in the same three-year period. The ratios compare total debt service obligations with the size of the economy and its ability to obtain foreign exchange through exports. Because workers' remittances are an important source of foreign exchange for many countries, they are included in the value of exports used to calculate debt indicators. Public and publicly guaranteed debt service is compared with the size of the central government budget. The ratios shown here may differ from those published elsewhere because estimates of exports and GNP have been revised to incorporate data available as of 1 February 2000.

The present value of external debt is calculated by discounting the debt service (interest plus amortization) due on long-term external debt over the life of existing loans. Short-term debt is included at its face value. The data on debt are in U.S. dollars converted at official exchange rates (see *About the data* for table 4.18). The discount rate applied to long-term debt is determined by the currency of repayment of the loan and is based on reference rates for commercial interest established by the Organisation for Economic Co-operation and Development. Loans from the International Bank for Reconstruction and Development (IBRD) and credits from the International Development Association (IDA) are discounted using an SDR (special drawing rights) reference rate, as are obligations to the International Monetary Fund (IMF). When the discount rate is greater than the interest rate of the loan, the present value is less than the nominal sum of future debt service obligations.

The ratios in the table are used to assess the sustainability of a country's debt service obligations, but there are no absolute rules that determine what values are too high. Empirical analysis of the experience of developing countries and their debt service performance has shown that debt service difficulties become increasingly likely when the ratio of the present value of debt to exports reaches 200 percent and the ratio of debt service to GNP exceeds 40 percent. Still, what constitutes a sustainable debt burden varies from one country to another. Countries with fast-growing economies and exports are likely to be able to sustain higher debt levels.

The World Bank classifies countries by their level of indebtedness for the purpose of developing debt management strategies. In some cases the most severely indebted countries may be eligible for debt relief under special programs such as the Heavily Indebted Poor Countries (HIPC) Initiative. Indebted countries may also apply to the Paris Club and London Club for renegotiation of obligations to public and private creditors. In 1998 countries with a present value of debt service greater than 220 percent of exports or 80 percent of GNP were classified as severely indebted (S); countries that were not severely indebted but whose present value of debt service exceeded 132 percent of exports or 48 percent of GNP were classified as moderately indebted (M); and countries that did not fall into the above two groups were classified as less indebted (L).

Definitions

• **Indebtedness** is assessed on a three-point scale: severely indebted, moderately indebted, and less indebted. • **Present value of debt** is the sum of short-term external debt plus the discounted sum of total debt service payments due on public, publicly guaranteed, and private nonguaranteed long-term external debt over the life of existing loans. • **Total debt service** is the sum of principal repayments and interest actually paid in foreign currency, goods, or services on long-term debt, interest paid on short-term debt, and repayments (repurchases and charges) to the IMF.
• **Public and publicly guaranteed debt service** is the sum of principal repayments and interest actually paid on long-term obligations of public debtors and long-term private obligations guaranteed by a public entity.
• **Short-term debt** includes all debt having an original maturity of one year or less and interest in arrears on long-term debt.

Data sources

The main sources of external debt information are reports to the World Bank through its Debtor Reporting System from member countries that have received IBRD loans or IDA credits. Additional information has been drawn from the files of the World Bank and the IMF. The data on GNP and exports of goods and services are from the World Bank's national accounts files. Summary tables of the external debt of developing countries are published annually in the World Bank's *Global Development Finance* and *Global Development Finance* CD-ROM.

STATES AND MARKETS

Poor countries—and poor people—suffer not only because they have less capital than rich countries. They also suffer because they have less scientific and technical knowledge. Without skills and information, it is difficult to combat disease, raise crop yields, improve general welfare, and get credit at fair interest rates. If countries don't narrow this "knowledge gap," they could wind up stuck with lower living standards.

All countries benefit from science and technology—in vaccines, antibiotics, and better seeds and fertilizers. But many new technologies are too expensive for widespread application in poor countries. Technological solutions to many of their problems will not come easily or quickly, so they need to be selective in how they invest in science and technology. And to reduce poverty, they need policies that take advantage of science and technology the world over—opening the door to eventually improving capacity and developing their own solutions.

Technological innovation, often fueled by government-led research and development, has been the driving force for industrial growth around the world. It has paid off handsomely in high-income countries. The evidence for the same returns in developing countries is not so clear. Even so, the best opportunities to improve living standards—including new ways of reducing poverty—will come from science and technology. The more science and technology capacity a country has, the more able it is to take advantage of emerging opportunities. Poor countries thus need to continue to find ways to make increasing science and technology capacity part of their development strategy. Building alliances with private, public, national, and international actors is essential in this, especially to overcome market failures—when private investors do not expect to recover costs and make a profit, as for vaccines for tropical diseases.

Science and technology—applied well—can reduce poverty

Science and technology—applied wisely and well—hold great promise for eradicating the worst forms of human poverty.

Improving health

The health of people in developing countries is better than ever, with life expectancy up from 60 years to 65 since 1980. But in most developing countries child mortality is still 10 times that in high-income economies. About half the deaths result from such preventable ailments as diarrhea, malnutrition, and respiratory illness. And some 3 million children die each year because they lack access to existing vaccines.

Most deaths in developing countries are preventable with improvements in low-technology health delivery systems. Oral rehydration therapy, for example, now treats half of all diarrhea cases in the world's poorest countries. But there still is an urgent need to make this therapy—a simple combination of salts, glucose, and water—more widely accessible.

Increasing farm output

Agriculture is the main source of income for around 60 percent of the labor force in developing countries, so increasing agricultural output will affect more people than advances in any other economic sector. As Collins, Frison, and Sharrock (1997) note, one of the main challenges of agricultural research is to increase food production and food security in a sustainable manner—and at the same time to improve farm income while conserving natural resources. With the global population expanding rapidly, more scientists around the world recognize that biotechnology, with the right ethical and safety standards, offers important new tools to help feed the world's 6 billion people (box 5a).

Connecting people

New communications technology offers opportunities for informing and empowering the poor—and for serving the towns, small cities, and rural areas of many developing countries. In parts of Asia and Africa rural telephone density is a fifth that in the largest cities, so small entrepreneurs and others in remote areas typically lack information about prices and market opportunities. But new access to telecommunications—telephones (especially mobile phones, which have helped to reduce the urban-rural gap in telephone density), email, and the Internet—can strengthen their voices, whether to advocate policies or to market village handicrafts.

Box 5a

What can biotechnology do?

Biotechnology uses living organisms to make and modify products, improve plants and animals, and develop microorganisms for specific uses. It mixes disciplines—genetics, molecular biology, biochemistry, embryology, and cell biology (Doyle and Persley 1996). How has biotechnology been applied?

- *Eliminating disease.* Dr. Walter Plowright received the World Food Prize in 1999 for a vaccine that eliminated rinderpest—one of the deadliest animal diseases, commonly known as cattle plague—from much of the developing world. Rinderpest control has saved farms, increased milk supplies, and boosted agricultural output and meat and hide production (World Food Prize 2000).
- *Improving crops.* Many countries are using biotechnology to improve crops and develop biofertilizers and forestry biopesticides.
- *Conserving resources.* Two research centers—the International Rice Research Institute in the Philippines and the International Water Management Institute in Sri Lanka—are leading the effort to research new water-saving techniques for cultivating rice in Asia. The techniques include wet-seeding, intermittent irrigation, land leveling, weed management, and ways to cultivate cracked soils.

Absorbing knowledge

The key to absorbing knowledge is education. Schooling at all levels is important—from basic education to technical training that helps to build a labor force that can keep up with technology's advances. Among developing countries there is a wide range in the number of trained scientists and engineers, from around 3 per million people in Senegal to more than 1,900 per million people in Croatia (table 5.12). Technical literacy is needed for successful technology transfer and to develop indigenous technological capabilities. But achieving it is far from automatic. Needed in addition is a long-term strategy for human resource development and for continually investing in a country's education system. The information technology revolution has the potential to improve the quality of life around the world, but the "digital divide"—between those connected to the Internet and those not—can be closed only by making education a top priority.

Technology is contributing to the growth of distance education and virtual universities—and helping to build cadres of professionals with internationally competitive skills. Virtual universities use satellites and the Internet to deliver courses, allowing people in scattered locations to share resources. The Virtual University of Mexico's Monterrey Institute of Technology—a consortium of collaborating universities, including 13 outside the country—delivers courses through printed texts and live and prerecorded television broadcasts, and Internet connections facilitate communication between students and faculty. In China half the 92,000 engineering and technology students who graduate each year do so through distance education. Between 1981 and 1995 China's scientists increased the number of scientific and technical articles they published in internationally recognized journals from about 1,100 a year to more than 6,000 (table 5.12).

Improving national capacity to absorb and create science and technology

Many developing countries spend less than one-hundredth of 1 percent of GNP on research and development, while others, such as the Czech Republic and Slovenia, spend more than 1 percent (table 5.12). Even with large investments in research and development there is no guarantee of progress, so governments need to evaluate programs to make sure they are effective.

For developing countries to have the resources for extensive research and development, they must acquire technical knowledge from the rest of the world and adapt it to their needs. In this, the key task of governments is to provide a policy and regulatory environment that stimulates private firms to develop technology. Governments must also enhance firm-specific and national technological capabilities in production, investment, and innovation.

National innovation systems, especially their private components, are essential for economic growth. Such systems have different characteristics in countries at different levels of development, but the common elements include:

- *A vital and self-renewing research community.* Whether in universities or in public and private laboratories, the research community must collaborate with international peers, balance basic and applied research, and train the next generation of researchers.

- *Sound public policy and selective public support for research.* Governments must implement effective policies in science education—and fund or purchase basic research in sectors where knowledge is a public good.
- *Proper incentive structures.* The government must be receptive to foreign technology—through licensing laws, legal protection of intellectual property, tax codes that promote research and development, and policies that encourage technological entrepreneurship.

Public and private partnerships to overcome market failures that hurt the poor

Despite huge advances in biotechnology, there has been little investment by the industrial world in research and development for products that help developing countries. New vaccines for tropical diseases are not developed at anywhere near the rate for vaccines demanded by rich-country markets—in part because of the science, but often because of market failure. Of the 1,233 new drugs licensed worldwide between 1975 and 1997, only 13 were for tropical diseases.

That could soon change. Developing country governments working in partnership with the private sector and with wealthy governments and international organizations show the potential for mobilizing science and technology to address the problems of the poor (box 5b). Universities, research institutes, and industry are cooperating more closely—and financing for science and technology projects is being promoted to advance knowledge and strengthen science-based industries.

Where do we go from here? Looking to the 21st century

Many types of knowledge are international public goods. No one country or private organization has the incentive to do the research to create this knowledge, and international institutions can help fill the gap. The World Bank, working within its new Comprehensive Development Framework, seeks to provide coordinated and targeted assistance. This requires:

- Conducting more dialogue with countries to get a consensus on the importance of knowledge for development.
- Identifying successful policy approaches and practices.
- Providing advice on human resource development, technology development, national innovation systems, and legal and regulatory issues in the knowledge sector.
- Lending in new and innovative ways to support knowledge-based development.

The World Bank is also exploring new mechanisms to increase the global coordination of research. It is developing partnerships with other donors to fund new global and regional research programs. It is creating new lending instruments to encourage international science and technology cooperation. And it is institutionalizing links among researchers across project and national boundaries. A new tool to promote cooperation in development is the Global Development Gateway, an initiative by international organizations, governments, businesses, universities, and nongovernmental organizations to produce the premier portal on the World Wide Web for supporting sustainable development and the alleviation of poverty.

Establishing centers of excellence

Among the new instruments for stimulating science and technology's contribution to development is the Millennium Science Initiative. A series of projects—the first in Latin America—will support research excellence and collaboration between top researchers from the developing and developed worlds. As part of the initiative, the World Bank is working with client countries to improve their systems for funding research and advanced training.

Dealing with intellectual property rights

To acquire knowledge through trade, foreign direct investment, or licensing, firms must often be encouraged to engage in a conscious, ongoing effort to learn and adapt technology. And if countries are to deal with new global rules for intellectual property rights, they must strike a compromise between preserving incentives to create knowledge and disseminating knowledge at little or no cost.

Disseminating vaccines and developing new ones

The Global Alliance for Vaccines and Immunization (GAVI)—launched on 31 January 2000 in Davos, Switzerland—brings together the World Bank, the World Health Organization, wealthy donor countries, poor recipient countries, philanthropic organizations, and the drug industry to improve access to existing vaccines and develop new ones.

Blending past and present

Technologies of the future can combine traditional and cutting-edge technology. In partnership with Nigerian collaborators, Shaman Pharmaceuticals, a California company, has begun to discover and develop new pharmaceuticals from plants with a history of local use. Some of the benefits: support for a medicinal plant reserve and new training programs on public health, botany, conservation, and ethnobotany.

Box 5b

Bridging knowledge and policy

A four-day meeting in Bonn in December 1999—on bridging knowledge and policy—brought together 28 donor agencies and more than 300 organizations in 111 developing countries to create the Global Development Network. The network will link policy-oriented think tanks in developing countries with their counterparts in industrial countries.

The World Bank believes that the network can evolve into a self-governing organization with financial support from a variety of donors. The Bank provided $10 million to help set up the regional development networks that make up the global network and will provide another $10 million in the next few years. Major bilateral donors have offered to fund an on-line network (Germany), development prizes (Japan), an evaluation exercise (Switzerland), a data initiative (Norway), and a global research project (Sweden).

5.1 Credit, investment, and expenditure

	Private investment		Foreign direct investment				Credit to private sector		Private non-guaranteed debt		Central government expenditure	
	% of gross domestic fixed investment		% of gross domestic investment		% of GDP		% of GDP		% of external debt		% of GDP	
	1980	1997	1980	1998	1980	1998	1980	1998	1980	1998	1980	1998
Albania	..	..	..	9.2	..	1.5	..	3.2	..	2.4	..	29.8
Algeria	..	..	2.1	0.0	0.8	0.0	42.2	4.6	0.0	0.0	..	*29.2*
Angola	..	..	..	23.8	..	4.8	..	3.1	..	0.0	..	..
Argentina	75.8	92.6	3.5	10.4	0.9	2.1	25.4	24.2	24.3	21.4	18.2	*15.3*
Armenia	..	..	..	64.4	..	12.2	..	8.6	..	0.0	..	..
Australia	73.5	*80.1*	4.6	*8.5*	1.2	1.7	51.9	82.9	..	..	22.7	24.5
Austria	..	..	1.1	*5.0*	0.3	2.8	74.2	*103.2*	..	..	36.6	*40.5*
Azerbaijan	..	..	..	66.5	..	26.1	..	3.3	..	9.1	..	25.1
Bangladesh	53.3	67.3	0.0	3.3	0.0	0.7	6.0	24.0	0.0	0.0	7.4	..
Belarus	..	..	..	2.5	..	0.7	..	17.1	..	1.6	..	32.2
Belgium	..	..	..	..	..	..	28.8	*77.8*	..	..	50.1	*46.6*
Benin	..	59.5	2.0	8.5	0.3	1.5	28.6	7.4	0.0	0.0	..	..
Bolivia	..	59.7	10.2	50.9	1.7	10.2	17.3	63.5	3.4	4.0	..	21.9
Bosnia and Herzegovina	..	..	..	..	..	..	..	..	..	..	..	..
Botswana	..	..	26.8	9.4	9.9	1.9	10.6	11.9	0.0	0.0	29.8	*35.3*
Brazil	71.9	80.6	3.5	19.3	0.8	4.1	42.5	34.6	23.2	44.4	20.2	..
Bulgaria	..	42.2	..	22.2	..	3.3	..	*12.6*	..	5.6	..	*48.1*
Burkina Faso	..	..	0.0	0.0	0.0	0.0	16.7	12.0	0.0	0.0	12.2	..
Burundi	..	..	0.0	1.3	0.0	0.1	9.8	17.0	0.0	0.0	21.5	*24.0*
Cambodia	..	73.9	..	28.1	..	4.2	..	6.1	..	0.0	..	..
Cameroon	..	..	9.2	3.1	1.9	0.6	29.5	8.2	6.9	1.8	15.7	*12.7*
Canada	87.4	88.5	9.4	*9.6*	2.2	2.8	68.0	91.7	..	..	21.1	*24.7*
Central African Republic	..	..	9.5	3.5	0.7	0.5	13.9	4.5	0.0	0.0	*22.0*	..
Chad	..	54.1	*0.0*	6.3	0.0	0.9	17.2	3.4	0.0	0.0	..	..
Chile	67.8	80.8	3.7	22.2	0.8	5.9	46.9	61.6	38.8	64.9	28.0	21.6
China	18.1	47.5	*0.0*	11.9	*0.0*	4.6	53.4	112.8	*0.0*	17.6	..	*8.1*
Hong Kong, China	..	..	..	..	..	..	..	169.3	..	..	..	..
Colombia	58.2	55.9	1.9	15.1	0.4	3.0	26.2	35.2	7.4	30.4	11.5	16.0
Congo, Dem. Rep.	..	..	0.0	0.1	0.0	0.0	2.7	*1.1*	0.0	0.0	12.4	*10.4*
Congo, Rep.	..	..	6.6	0.6	2.3	0.2	15.5	9.7	0.0	0.0	49.4	*38.4*
Costa Rica	61.3	73.2	4.1	18.6	1.1	5.3	27.9	24.9	15.0	6.0	25.0	*30.1*
Côte d'Ivoire	..	70.2	3.5	21.7	0.9	4.0	40.8	18.6	27.0	12.3	31.7	24.0
Croatia	..	..	..	17.3	..	4.0	..	40.9	..	23.7	..	45.6
Cuba	..	..	..	..	..	..	..	..	..	..	..	..
Czech Republic	..	..	*0.0*	15.1	*0.0*	4.5	..	59.8	..	9.7	..	35.0
Denmark	..	..	*1.0*	*8.0*	*0.2*	3.6	41.2	34.7	..	..	38.6	*41.4*
Dominican Republic	68.3	82.9	5.6	16.9	1.4	4.4	32.0	30.0	12.7	0.0	16.9	*16.7*
Ecuador	59.8	82.9	2.3	17.1	0.6	4.5	22.8	46.4	18.7	1.4	14.2	..
Egypt, Arab Rep.	*30.1*	68.6	8.7	5.8	2.4	1.3	15.2	54.0	1.4	0.1	50.3	*30.6*
El Salvador	47.4	77.3	1.2	0.6	0.2	0.1	33.6	42.5	17.6	9.4	..	..
Eritrea	..	..	..	0.0	..	0.0	..	..	..	0.0	..	..
Estonia	..	..	..	38.1	..	11.2	..	25.3	..	27.2	..	32.9
Ethiopia	..	..	0.0	0.3	*0.0*	0.1	*9.4*	22.8	0.0	0.0	*19.9*	..
Finland	..	..	0.2	*10.3*	0.1	9.7	48.5	54.6	..	..	28.1	*35.3*
France	..	..	2.0	*9.8*	0.5	2.0	104.8	*83.6*	..	..	39.5	*46.6*
Gabon	..	..	2.7	–2.8	0.7	–0.9	15.8	10.2	0.0	0.0	36.5	..
Gambia, The	..	51.1	0.0	17.0	0.0	3.1	23.9	11.5	0.0	0.0	31.7	..
Georgia	..	..	..	12.5	..	1.0	..	4.2	..	0.8	..	8.6
Germany	..	..	..	*2.3*	..	0.9	..	119.1	..	..	..	32.9
Ghana	..	..	6.2	3.3	0.4	0.7	2.2	9.4	0.7	3.8	10.9	..
Greece	51.5	..	4.2	*4.1*	1.4	*0.8*	26.0	29.8	..	..	29.3	*34.0*
Guatemala	64.0	79.8	8.9	22.2	1.4	3.6	16.2	21.0	23.9	4.0	14.3	..
Guinea	..	..	..	0.1	..	0.0	..	*4.4*	0.0	0.0	..	16.9
Guinea-Bissau	..	28.0	0.0	2.1	0.0	0.2	..	*5.7*	0.0	0.0	..	..
Haiti	..	..	5.3	2.7	0.9	0.3	14.7	14.4	0.0	0.0	17.4	..
Honduras	..	..	0.9	5.3	0.2	1.6	28.8	37.0	13.0	8.2	..	..

Credit, investment, and expenditure 5.1

	Private investment		Foreign direct investment				Credit to private sector		Private non-guaranteed debt		Central government expenditure	
	% of gross domestic fixed investment		% of gross domestic investment		% of GDP		% of GDP		% of external debt		% of GDP	
	1980	1997	1980	1998	1980	1998	1980	1998	1980	1998	1980	1998
Hungary	..	..	0.0	13.1	0.0	4.0	*48.3*	*22.3*	0.0	27.5	*56.2*	43.4
India	55.5	70.1	0.2	2.6	0.0	0.6	20.5	23.2	1.6	8.6	12.3	14.4
Indonesia	*56.5*	77.2	1.0	–2.7	0.2	–0.4	8.8	53.9	15.0	36.3	22.1	17.9
Iran, Islamic Rep.	52.4	55.5	0.0	0.1	0.0	0.0	30.2	19.3	0.0	4.4	35.7	26.7
Iraq	..	..	..	..	..	..	..	..	..	..	..	..
Ireland	..	..	5.3	*18.1*	1.4	3.6	30.2	93.9	..	..	45.1	*35.5*
Israel	..	..	1.0	9.1	0.2	1.8	70.8	81.9	..	..	72.8	49.0
Italy	..	..	0.5	*1.8*	0.1	0.2	55.9	60.2	..	..	41.3	44.6
Jamaica	..	..	6.6	18.3	1.0	5.7	21.9	32.4	3.9	4.5	41.5	..
Japan	69.8	70.9	0.1	0.3	0.0	0.1	132.7	117.8	..	..	18.4	..
Jordan	..	..	2.3	16.8	0.9	4.2	45.9	72.7	0.0	0.4	41.3	*34.0*
Kazakhstan	..	..	..	30.5	..	5.3	..	6.6	..	27.5	..	..
Kenya	54.9	56.0	4.4	0.7	1.1	0.1	29.5	30.3	12.9	4.6	25.3	*29.0*
Korea, Dem. Rep.	..	..	..	..	..	..	..	..	..	..	..	..
Korea, Rep.	75.8	*73.4*	0.0	8.1	0.0	1.7	42.2	74.2	7.8	26.0	17.3	*17.4*
Kuwait	..	..	0.0	1.6	0.0	0.2	34.0	62.6	..	..	27.7	50.9
Kyrgyz Republic	..	..	..	35.0	..	6.4	..	5.2	..	3.0	..	..
Lao PDR	..	..	..	14.7	..	3.6	..	12.8	0.0	0.0	..	..
Latvia	..	..	..	24.3	..	5.6	..	14.1	..	10.9	..	33.0
Lebanon	..	..	..	4.2	..	1.2	..	74.0	0.0	11.7	..	32.1
Lesotho	..	..	2.9	68.8	1.2	33.4	7.5	17.9	0.0	0.0	*45.3*	55.8
Libya	..	..	..	..	..	..	10.9	..	..	..	..	..
Lithuania	..	..	..	35.7	..	8.6	..	11.3	..	5.3	..	30.4
Macedonia, FYR	..	..	..	20.8	..	4.7	..	17.9	..	7.9	..	..
Madagascar	..	46.9	–0.2	3.2	0.0	0.4	19.2	9.0	0.0	0.0	..	*17.3*
Malawi	21.4	27.7	3.1	0.4	0.8	0.1	18.3	6.1	0.0	0.0	34.6	..
Malaysia	62.7	72.8	12.5	25.8	3.8	6.9	38.2	151.1	18.9	40.1	28.5	*19.7*
Mali	..	..	0.9	3.0	0.1	0.6	21.7	15.9	0.0	0.0	19.4	..
Mauritania	..	49.4	14.5	2.4	3.3	0.5	27.0	21.7	0.0	0.0	..	..
Mauritius	64.0	73.5	0.5	1.2	0.1	0.3	21.6	59.2	5.1	30.5	27.2	22.4
Mexico	56.2	81.4	3.6	10.7	1.0	2.6	19.4	19.7	12.7	22.6	15.7	*16.3*
Moldova	..	..	..	20.3	..	5.3	..	14.4	..	0.8	..	..
Mongolia	..	..	..	7.1	..	1.8	..	9.8	..	0.0	..	23.0
Morocco	53.2	67.9	2.0	4.0	0.5	0.9	16.8	50.4	1.6	6.0	33.1	*33.3*
Mozambique	..	..	*0.0*	26.8	*0.0*	5.5	..	14.2	..	24.1	..	..
Myanmar	..	..	..	..	..	..	5.5	10.0	0.0	0.0	15.8	*8.9*
Namibia	42.1	62.2	..	..	..	..	..	51.2	..	..	..	..
Nepal	..	..	0.0	1.2	0.0	0.3	8.6	29.1	0.0	0.0	14.3	17.5
Netherlands	85.2	*86.9*	6.0	*17.3*	1.3	8.7	93.6	*111.3*	..	..	52.9	*47.6*
New Zealand	69.2	86.8	3.9	*19.7*	0.8	*4.1*	21.4	112.5	..	..	38.3	33.4
Nicaragua	..	62.0	0.0	27.4	0.0	9.2	0.0	47.7	0.0	0.0	30.4	*33.2*
Niger	..	..	7.0	0.5	2.0	0.0	17.1	4.1	35.3	4.3	18.6	..
Nigeria	..	..	–5.4	12.7	–1.2	2.5	12.2	9.1	12.3	0.9	..	..
Norway	70.3	..	0.3	*9.2*	0.1	2.5	31.0	69.6	..	..	34.4	*35.7*
Oman	..	..	7.4	..	1.6	0.7	13.7	44.6	0.0	0.1	38.5	31.6
Pakistan	45.0	58.2	1.4	4.6	0.3	0.8	24.0	26.9	0.2	8.1	17.5	21.4
Panama	..	84.0	–4.4	40.2	–1.2	13.2	58.1	103.3	0.0	5.2	30.5	*27.0*
Papua New Guinea	*67.7*	79.9	11.8	9.7	3.0	2.9	17.6	23.1	19.3	40.1	34.4	..
Paraguay	82.2	67.0	2.2	14.2	0.7	3.0	18.4	27.5	15.8	1.9	9.9	..
Peru	*74.7*	84.5	0.4	12.7	0.1	3.1	12.9	25.4	6.5	10.2	19.5	16.4
Philippines	68.9	80.0	–1.1	12.8	–0.3	2.6	31.4	48.0	14.1	22.7	13.4	*19.3*
Poland	..	53.4	*0.2*	15.2	*0.0*	4.0	6.4	19.6	..	13.4	..	37.7
Portugal	..	..	1.6	*9.8*	0.5	1.7	76.0	102.8	..	..	33.1	*40.8*
Puerto Rico	..	..	..	..	..	..	..	..	..	..	..	..
Romania	..	40.1	..	30.1	..	5.3	..	12.7	0.0	9.1	44.8	*31.9*
Russian Federation	..	..	..	6.1	..	1.0	..	12.9	..	14.5	..	*25.4*

5.1 Credit, investment, and expenditure

	Private investment		Foreign direct investment				Credit to private sector		Private nonguaranteed debt		Central government expenditure	
	% of gross domestic fixed investment		% of gross domestic investment		% of GDP		% of GDP		% of external debt		% of GDP	
	1980	**1997**	**1980**	**1998**	**1980**	**1998**	**1980**	**1998**	**1980**	**1998**	**1980**	**1998**
Rwanda	..	..	8.7	2.2	1.4	0.3	5.7	8.6	0.0	0.0	14.3	..
Saudi Arabia	..	..	..	..	..	..	7.2	33.3	..	..	..	..
Senegal	..	..	4.1	4.4	0.5	0.9	42.7	16.0	0.6	0.6	23.3	..
Sierra Leone	..	..	..	9.5	–1.6	0.8	7.2	2.8	0.0	0.0	26.5	*17.7*
Singapore	..	..	22.8	25.5	10.5	8.6	71.0	109.7	..	..	20.0	*16.8*
Slovak Republic	..	..	..	7.0	..	2.8	..	45.9	..	33.1	..	..
Slovenia	..	..	..	3.4	..	0.8	..	32.9	..	..	..	..
South Africa	50.8	72.7	..	2.6	..	0.4	55.6	118.9	..	10.7	21.6	29.7
Spain	..	..	3.0	*5.1*	0.7	2.1	70.1	92.5	..	..	26.5	*36.1*
Sri Lanka	..	..	3.2	4.8	1.1	1.2	17.2	23.8	0.2	0.9	41.4	25.0
Sudan	..	..	0.0	..	0.0	3.6	13.2	2.1	6.3	2.9	17.4	..
Sweden	..	*79.7*	0.9	*32.0*	0.2	8.6	78.0	42.9	..	..	39.3	42.7
Switzerland	..	..	..	11.0	..	2.1	108.7	166.3	..	..	19.2	*27.9*
Syrian Arab Republic	..	..	0.0	1.6	0.0	0.5	5.7	8.9	0.0	0.0	48.2	*24.6*
Tajikistan	..	..	..	5.1	..	0.8	..	..	..	10.9	..	..
Tanzania	..	..	..	14.3	..	2.1	..	4.7	1.6	0.5	..	..
Thailand	68.1	65.9	2.0	24.7	0.6	6.2	41.7	156.6	20.5	36.3	18.8	18.6
Togo	..	..	13.1	0.0	3.7	0.0	27.5	18.2	0.0	0.0	30.8	..
Trinidad and Tobago	..	..	9.7	51.7	3.0	11.4	28.7	44.2	0.0	6.5	30.9	*28.2*
Tunisia	46.9	50.8	9.1	11.8	2.7	3.3	38.2	50.8	5.1	1.6	31.6	*32.6*
Turkey	60.0	77.6	0.1	1.9	0.0	0.5	13.6	*23.4*	2.8	24.0	21.3	*29.9*
Turkmenistan	..	..	..	..	..	5.5	..	*28.8*	..	0.6	..	..
Uganda	..	..	0.0	19.5	0.0	3.0	3.9	5.2	0.0	0.0	6.2	..
Ukraine	..	..	..	8.2	..	1.7	..	7.7	..	6.6	..	..
United Arab Emirates	..	..	..	..	..	..	22.9	59.1	..	..	12.1	11.0
United Kingdom	70.0	*87.0*	11.2	*18.2*	1.9	5.0	27.6	124.0	..	..	38.3	37.9
United States	86.5	85.8	3.1	7.5	0.6	2.3	80.3	137.9	..	..	22.0	21.1
Uruguay	68.3	72.0	16.5	5.0	2.9	0.8	37.2	34.6	12.7	3.8	21.8	33.3
Uzbekistan	..	..	..	5.1	..	1.0	..	..	..	9.4	..	..
Venezuela, RB	..	43.6	0.3	23.8	0.1	4.7	48.2	13.4	10.8	18.1	18.7	19.8
Vietnam	..	..	..	15.4	..	4.4	..	*10.0*	..	0.0	..	20.1
West Bank and Gaza	..	..	..	..	..	..	..	..	..	..	..	..
Yemen, Rep.	..	..	..	–22.6	..	–4.9	..	6.3	0.0	0.0	..	42.2
Yugoslavia, FR (Serb./Mont.)	..	..	..	..	..	..	..	..	59.5 [a]	20.1	..	..
Zambia	..	..	6.8	15.0	1.6	2.1	16.2	6.8	2.7	0.4	37.1	..
Zimbabwe	..	..	0.1	7.0	0.0	1.2	26.6	38.8	0.0	4.2	27.9	*35.7*
World	**73.2 w**	***76.0* w**	**2.7 w**	**7.1 w**	**0.7 w**	**2.2 w**	**68.4 w**	**103.1 w**	**.. w**	**.. w**	**25.3 w**	***28.7* w**
Low income	32.6	56.5	0.2	9.6	0.0	2.9	27.8	71.9	6.3	13.8	..	*12.4*
Excl. China & India	..	..	0.2	8.1	0.0	1.6	14.3	26.1	..	..	19.8	*18.3*
Middle income	..	74.8	2.7	13.0	0.7	2.9	28.4	40.7	13.0	22.1	20.9	..
Lower middle income	..	..	2.0	11.0	0.6	2.2	32.9	44.9	..	..	..	*24.0*
Upper middle income	65.4	77.9	3.1	14.0	0.8	3.2	26.4	38.6	..	..	19.5	..
Low & middle income	..	66.9	2.1	11.7	0.5	2.9	28.2	50.2	11.6	19.8	20.1	*18.9*
East Asia & Pacific	41.1	56.9	1.5	12.4	*0.5*	3.9	40.2	103.3	11.7	26.9	..	*13.8*
Europe & Central Asia	..	..	0.3	10.9	*0.1*	2.5	*16.9*	20.1	15.3	16.8	..	*29.1*
Latin America & Carib.	64.0	79.8	3.2	16.1	0.8	3.5	31.6	30.3	16.5	27.5	19.0	..
Middle East & N. Africa	..	..	..	3.2	..	0.7	18.7	34.3	0.7	2.1	..	..
South Asia	52.1	68.9	0.4	2.9	0.1	0.7	19.6	23.8	0.9	6.8	13.5	15.8
Sub-Saharan Africa	..	..	..	7.0	*0.7*	1.3	29.5	57.9	7.5	4.0	22.1	..
High income	79.1	*79.2*	2.9	*6.0*	0.7	2.1	80.9	118.7	..	..	26.4	*31.2*
Europe EMU	..	..	2.0	*5.5*	0.5	1.9	78.1	*90.7*	..	..	..	*41.4*

a. Data prior to 1993 refer to the former Socialist Federal Republic of Yugoslavia.

Credit, investment, and expenditure 5.1

About the data

The indicators in the table measure the relative size of states and markets in national economies. There is no ideal size for states, and size alone does not capture their full effect on markets. Large states may support prosperous and effective markets; small states may be hostile toward markets. The resources of a large state may be used to correct genuine market failures—or merely to subsidize state enterprises making goods or providing services that the private sector might have produced more efficiently. A large share of private domestic investment in total investment may reflect a highly competitive and efficient private sector—or one that is subsidized and protected.

When direct estimates are not available, private gross domestic fixed investment is estimated as the difference between total gross domestic investment and consolidated public investment. Total investment may be estimated directly from surveys of enterprises and administrative records or indirectly using the commodity flow method. Consolidated measures of public investment may omit important subnational units of government. In addition, public investment data may include financial as well as physical capital investment. As the difference between two estimated quantities, private investment may be undervalued or overvalued and subject to large errors over time. (See *About the data* for table 4.9 for further discussion on measuring domestic investment.)

The statistics on foreign direct investment are based on balance of payments data reported by the International Monetary Fund (IMF), supplemented by data on net foreign direct investment reported by the Organisation for Economic Co-operation and Development and official national sources. The data suffer from deficiencies relating to definitions, coverage, and cross-country comparability. (See *About the data* for table 6.7 for a detailed discussion of data on foreign direct investment.)

The data on domestic credit to the private sector are taken from the banking survey of the IMF's *International Financial Statistics* or, when the broader aggregate is not available, from its monetary survey. The monetary survey includes monetary authorities (the central bank) and deposit money banks. In addition to these, the banking survey includes other banking institutions, such as savings and loan institutions, finance companies, and development banks. In some cases credit to the private sector may include credit to state-owned or partially state-owned enterprises.

Because data on subnational units of government—state, provincial, and municipal—are not readily available, the size of the public sector is measured here by the size of the central government. While the central government is usually the largest economic agent in a country and typically accounts for most public sector revenues, expenditures, and deficits, in some countries—especially large ones—state, provincial, and local governments are important participants in the economy. In addition, activities attributed to the "central government" may vary depending on the accounting practice followed. In most countries central government finance data are consolidated into one overall account, but in others only budgetary central government accounts are available, which often omit the operations of state-owned enterprises (see *Primary data documentation*).

Figure 5.1

Foreign direct investment has remained resilient

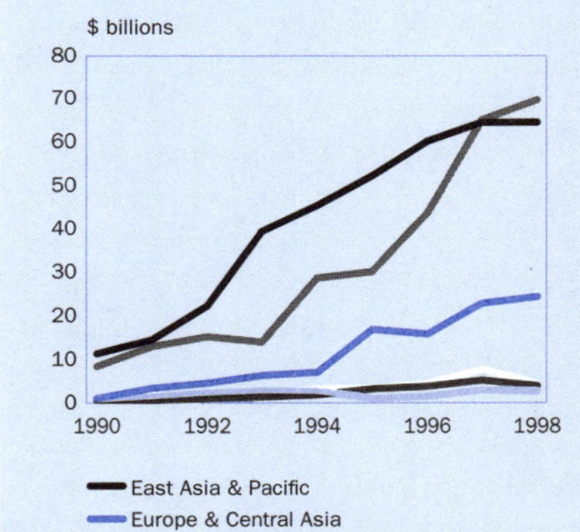

Source: World Bank, *Global Development Finance 2000* and *Global Economic Prospects and the Developing Countries 2000*.

Despite falling volumes of private capital flows, foreign direct investment has remained resilient and is likely to be the primary source of finance for developing countries for the foreseeable future. Preliminary data indicate that flows of foreign direct investment may have increased in 1999.

Definitions

• **Private investment** covers gross outlays by the private sector (including private nonprofit agencies) on additions to its fixed domestic assets. Gross domestic fixed investment includes similar outlays by the public sector. No allowance is made for the depreciation of assets. • **Foreign direct investment** is net inflows of investment to acquire a lasting management interest (10 percent or more of voting stock) in an enterprise operating in an economy other than that of the investor. It is the sum of equity capital, reinvestment of earnings, other long-term capital, and short-term capital as shown in the balance of payments. Gross domestic investment (used in the denominator) is gross domestic fixed investment plus net changes in stocks. • **Credit to private sector** refers to financial resources provided to the private sector—such as through loans, purchases of nonequity securities, and trade credits and other accounts receivable—that establish a claim for repayment. For some countries these claims include credit to public enterprises. • **Private nonguaranteed debt** consists of external obligations of private debtors that are not guaranteed for repayment by a public entity. Total external debt is the sum of public and publicly guaranteed long-term debt, private nonguaranteed long-term debt, IMF credit, and short-term debt. • **Central government expenditure** comprises the expenditures of all government offices, departments, establishments, and other bodies that are agencies or instruments of the central authority of a country. It includes both current and capital (development) expenditures.

Data sources

The data on private investment are from the International Finance Corporation's *Trends in Private Investment in Developing Countries 1999* and World Bank estimates. The data on foreign direct investment are based on estimates compiled by the IMF in the *Balance of Payments Statistics Yearbook*, supplemented by World Bank staff estimates. The data on domestic credit are from the IMF's *International Financial Statistics*, and the data on government expenditure from the IMF's *Government Finance Statistics Yearbook*. The external debt figures are from the World Bank's Debtor Reporting System as reported in *Global Development Finance 2000*.

5.2 Stock markets

	Market capitalization				Value traded		Turnover ratio		Listed domestic companies		IFC Investable index	
	$ millions		% of GDP		% of GDP		value of shares traded as % of capitalization				% change in price index	
	1990	1999	1990	1998	1990	1998	1990	1999	1990	1999	1998	1999
Albania	..	..	..	..	..	..	..	..	..	..	..	..
Algeria	..	..	..	..	..	..	..	..	..	..	..	..
Angola	..	..	..	..	..	..	..	..	..	..	..	..
Argentina	3,268	83,887	2.3	15.2	0.6	5.1	33.6	12.0	179	129	–28.5	33.4
Armenia	..	*18*	..	0.9	..	0.1	..	*5.9*	..	*82*	..	..
Australia	107,611	*874,283*	36.2	241.7	13.5	112.6	31.6	*51.9*	1,089	*1,162*	..	..
Austria	11,476	*34,106*	7.2	16.1	11.7	7.8	110.3	*47.4*	97	*96*	..	..
Azerbaijan	..	*3*	..	0.1	..	..	..	..	..	*2*	..	..
Bangladesh	321	865	1.1	2.4	0.0	1.9	1.5	2.6	134	211	–38.5 [a]	–17.5 [a]
Belarus	..	..	..	..	..	..	..	..	..	..	..	..
Belgium	65,449	*245,657*	33.4	99.0	3.3	22.3	..	*28.9*	182	*146*	..	..
Benin	..	..	..	..	..	..	..	..	..	..	..	..
Bolivia	..	*3,222*	..	37.5	..	0.4	..	*1.9*	..	*14*	..	..
Bosnia and Herzegovina	..	..	..	..	..	..	..	..	..	..	..	..
Botswana	*261*	1,052	*6.7*	14.8	*0.2*	1.4	6.1	0.7	*9*	15	9.2 [a]	45.6 [a]
Brazil	16,354	227,962	3.5	20.7	1.2	18.8	23.6	53.0	581	478	–43.0	66.9
Bulgaria	..	706	..	8.1	..	0.1	..	*2.4*	..	828	–30.1 [a]	–23.7 [a]
Burkina Faso	..	..	..	..	..	..	..	..	..	..	..	..
Burundi	..	..	..	..	..	..	..	..	..	..	..	..
Cambodia	..	..	..	..	..	..	..	..	..	..	..	..
Cameroon	..	..	..	..	..	..	..	..	..	..	..	..
Canada	241,920	*543,394*	42.2	93.6	12.4	64.1	26.7	*67.0*	1,144	*1,384*	..	..
Central African Republic	..	..	..	..	..	..	..	..	..	..	..	..
Chad	..	..	..	..	..	..	..	..	..	..	..	..
Chile	13,645	68,228	45.0	65.9	2.6	5.6	6.3	11.4	215	285	–29.8	35.8
China	*2,028*	330,703	*0.5*	24.1	*0.2*	29.7	*158.9*	134.2	*14*	950	–52.6	102.2
Hong Kong, China	83,397	*343,394*	111.5	206.3	46.3	123.7	43.1	*54.4*	284	*658*	..	..
Colombia	1,416	11,590	3.0	13.0	0.2	1.5	5.6	5.8	80	145	–46.8	–19.7
Congo, Dem. Rep.	..	..	..	..	..	..	..	..	..	..	..	..
Congo, Rep.	..	..	..	..	..	..	..	..	..	..	..	..
Costa Rica	*475*	*1,308*	*7.0*	12.5	*0.2*	*0.2*	*5.8*	..	*82*	*97*	..	..
Côte d'Ivoire	549	1,514	5.1	16.5	0.2	0.4	3.4	10.8	23	38	4.4 [a]	–12.1 [a]
Croatia	..	2,584	..	14.7	..	0.5	..	5.0	*2*	59	–33.8 [a]	–18.1 [a]
Cuba	..	..	..	..	..	..	..	..	..	..	..	..
Czech Republic	..	11,796	..	21.4	..	8.4	..	37.4	..	164	–7.3	4.2
Denmark	39,063	*98,881*	29.3	56.5	8.3	*27.6*	28.0	..	258	*242*	..	..
Dominican Republic	..	*140*	..	*0.9*	..	..	..	..	..	*6*	..	..
Ecuador	*69*	415	*0.5*	8.3	..	0.7	*0.0*	5.0	*65*	28	–36.9 [a]	–77.1 [a]
Egypt, Arab Rep.	1,765	32,838	4.1	29.5	0.3	6.1	..	31.6	573	1,033	–30.9	24.2
El Salvador	..	*1,435*	..	12.1	..	0.2	..	*1.9*	..	*80*	..	..
Eritrea	..	..	..	..	..	..	..	..	..	..	..	..
Estonia	..	1,789	..	10.0	..	18.2	..	17.6	..	25	–65.4 [a]	42.3 [a]
Ethiopia	..	..	..	..	..	..	..	..	..	..	..	..
Finland	22,721	*154,518*	16.9	125.1	2.9	48.8	..	*53.0*	73	*129*	..	..
France	314,384	*991,484*	26.3	69.5	9.8	40.1	..	*68.7*	578	*711*	..	..
Gabon	..	..	..	..	..	..	..	..	..	..	..	..
Gambia, The	..	..	..	..	..	..	..	..	..	..	..	..
Georgia	..	..	..	..	..	..	..	..	..	..	..	..
Germany	355,073	*1,093,962*	*22.9*	51.3	*22.1*	65.2	139.3	*144.9*	413	*741*	..	..
Ghana	*76*	916	*1.2*	18.5	*0.0*	0.8	*0.0*	3.3	*13*	22	17.3 [a]	–33.5 [a]
Greece	15,228	204,213	18.4	66.3	4.7	38.9	36.3	131.1	145	281	91.2	64.4
Guatemala	..	*172*	..	0.9	..	0.1	..	*9.6*	..	7	..	..
Guinea	..	..	..	..	..	..	..	..	..	..	..	..
Guinea-Bissau	..	..	..	..	..	..	..	..	..	..	..	..
Haiti	..	..	..	..	..	..	..	..	..	..	..	..
Honduras	*40*	*458*	*1.3*	8.5	*0.0*	*0.0*	0.0	..	*26*	*94*	..	..

Stock markets 5.2

	Market capitalization				Value traded		Turnover ratio		Listed domestic companies		IFC Investable index	
	$ millions		% of GDP		% of GDP		value of shares traded as % of capitalization				% change in price index	
	1990	1999	1990	1998	1990	1998	1990	1999	1990	1999	1998	1999
Hungary	*505*	16,317	*1.5*	29.3	*0.3*	33.8	*6.3*	95.8	*21*	66	–10.8	15.2
India	38,567	184,605	11.9	24.5	6.8	15.0	65.9	84.4	2,435	5,863	–23.0	81.0
Indonesia	8,081	64,087	7.1	23.5	3.5	10.3	75.8	47.0	125	277	–28.1	95.1
Iran, Islamic Rep.	*34,282*	*14,874*	..	13.1	..	1.2	*30.4*	*9.3*	*97*	*242*	..	..
Iraq	..	..	..	..	..	..	..	..	..	..	..	..
Ireland	..	*29,956*	..	36.6	..	27.0	..	*81.8*	..	*79*	..	..
Israel	3,324	63,820	6.3	39.4	10.5	11.2	95.8	29.9	216	644	–16.0	54.9
Italy	148,766	*569,731*	13.6	48.6	3.9	40.6	26.8	*104.1*	220	*320*	..	..
Jamaica	911	2,530	21.5	33.3	0.8	0.6	3.4	0.0	44	46	–21.3 [a]	1.9 [a]
Japan	2,917,679	*2,495,757*	98.2	66.0	54.0	25.1	43.8	*40.3*	2,071	*2,416*	13.4 [b]	..
Jordan	2,001	5,827	49.8	79.0	10.1	8.8	20.0	9.4	105	152	3.0	–3.6
Kazakhstan	..	*37*	..	0.2	..	..	..	..	..	*18*	..	..
Kenya	453	1,409	5.3	17.5	0.1	0.7	2.2	0.3	54	57	13.8 [a]	–27.5 [a]
Korea, Dem. Rep.	..	..	..	..	..	..	..	..	..	..	..	..
Korea, Rep.	110,594	308,534	43.8	35.7	30.1	43.0	61.3	355.8	669	725	120.7	106.5
Kuwait	..	..	..	..	..	37.1	..	..	..	*69*	..	..
Kyrgyz Republic	..	..	..	*0.3*	..	*0.0*	..	..	..	..	..	..
Lao PDR	..	..	..	..	..	..	..	..	..	..	..	..
Latvia	..	391	..	6.0	..	1.3	..	0.2	..	70	–67.4 [a]	–9.5 [a]
Lebanon	..	1,921	..	13.8	..	1.9	..	9.3	..	12	..	–18.0 [a]
Lesotho	..	..	..	..	..	..	..	..	..	..	..	..
Libya	..	..	..	..	..	..	..	..	..	..	..	..
Lithuania	..	1,138	..	10.0	..	2.1	..	48.5	..	54	–39.2 [a]	9.5 [a]
Macedonia, FYR	..	*8*	..	0.3	..	..	..	..	..	*2*	..	..
Madagascar	..	..	..	..	..	..	..	..	..	..	..	..
Malawi	..	..	..	..	..	..	..	..	..	..	..	..
Malaysia	48,611	145,445	113.6	136.0	25.4	39.8	24.6	39.8	282	757	–2.9	44.5
Mali	..	..	..	..	..	..	..	..	..	..	..	..
Mauritania	..	..	..	..	..	..	..	..	..	..	..	..
Mauritius	268	1,642	10.1	44.0	0.2	2.4	*1.9*	2.7	13	41	1.4 [a]	–6.7 [a]
Mexico	32,725	154,044	12.5	23.3	4.6	8.6	44.0	29.0	199	188	–38.9	78.5
Moldova	..	*0*	..	0.0	..	..	..	..	..	*21*	..	..
Mongolia	..	*40*	..	3.8	..	*1.6*	..	..	..	*430*	..	..
Morocco	966	13,695	3.7	44.1	0.2	3.9	..	17.6	71	55	28.7	–7.8
Mozambique	..	..	..	..	..	..	..	..	..	..	..	..
Myanmar	..	..	..	..	..	..	..	..	..	..	..	..
Namibia	*21*	691	*0.7*	13.9	..	0.4	*0.0*	0.6	*3*	14	..	5.3 [a]
Nepal	..	*267*	..	5.6	..	0.1	..	*1.7*	..	*104*	..	..
Netherlands	119,825	*603,182*	42.2	158.0	14.2	99.3	29.0	*70.7*	260	*212*	..	..
New Zealand	8,835	*89,373*	20.5	169.1	4.5	95.6	17.3	*56.2*	171	*135*	..	..
Nicaragua	..	..	..	..	..	..	..	..	..	..	..	..
Niger	..	..	..	..	..	..	..	..	..	..	..	..
Nigeria	1,372	2,940	4.8	7.0	0.0	0.4	0.9	5.1	131	194	–28.5 [a]	–10.3 [a]
Norway	26,130	*56,285*	22.6	38.6	12.1	29.2	54.4	*69.4*	112	*236*	..	..
Oman	*1,061*	4,302	*9.4*	29.4	*0.9*	13.0	12.3	*33.8*	55	140	..	7.2 [a]
Pakistan	2,850	6,965	7.1	8.5	0.6	14.4	8.7	345.2	487	765	–61.9	37.5
Panama	*226*	*3,347*	*3.4*	36.6	*0.0*	1.1	*0.9*	*3.8*	*13*	27	..	..
Papua New Guinea	..	..	..	..	..	..	..	..	..	..	..	..
Paraguay	..	*312*	..	3.6	..	0.2	..	*4.3*	..	*55*	..	..
Peru	812	13,392	2.5	18.6	0.3	4.4	*19.3*	18.6	294	242	–39.3	19.7
Philippines	*5,927*	48,105	13.4	54.2	2.7	15.3	13.6	46.5	153	226	9.2	0.9
Poland	*144*	29,577	*0.2*	12.9	*0.0*	5.6	*89.7*	45.8	*9*	221	–12.3	22.3
Portugal	9,201	*62,954*	13.3	59.0	2.4	44.6	16.9	*93.4*	181	*135*	38.4	*38.4*
Puerto Rico	..	..	..	..	..	..	..	..	..	..	..	..
Romania	..	873	..	2.7	..	1.6	..	61.5	..	5	–67.7 [a]	–36.5 [a]
Russian Federation	*244*	72,205	*0.0*	7.4	..	2.5	..	5.9	*13*	207	–84.2	284.0

5.2 Stock markets

	Market capitalization				Value traded		Turnover ratio		Listed domestic companies		IFC Investable index	
	$ millions		% of GDP		% of GDP		value of shares traded as % of capitalization				% change in price index	
	1990	1999	1990	1998	1990	1998	1990	1999	1990	1999	1998	1999
Rwanda	..	..	..	..	..	..	..	..	..	..	..	..
Saudi Arabia	*48,213*	60,440	*40.8*	33.0	*1.9*	10.6	..	28.8	*59*	73	–26.8 [a]	42.3 [a]
Senegal	..	..	..	..	..	..	..	..	..	..	..	..
Sierra Leone	..	..	..	..	..	..	..	..	..	..	..	..
Singapore	34,308	*94,469*	93.6	112.0	55.4	60.1	..	*50.5*	150	*321*	..	..
Slovak Republic	..	723	..	4.7	..	5.1	..	59.7	..	845	–56.0	–24.2
Slovenia	..	2,180	..	12.5	..	3.6	..	1.6	*24*	28	19.0 [a]	–3.7 [a]
South Africa	137,540	262,478	122.8	127.6	7.3	43.8	..	34.1	732	*668*	–30.3	56.1
Spain	111,404	*402,180*	22.6	72.7	8.3	126.4	..	*201.9*	427	*484*	..	..
Sri Lanka	917	1,584	11.4	10.9	0.5	1.8	5.8	12.9	175	239	–29.2	–6.0
Sudan	..	..	..	..	..	..	..	..	..	..	..	..
Sweden	97,929	*278,707*	42.6	123.1	7.6	89.9	14.9	*73.9*	258	*258*	..	..
Switzerland	160,044	*689,199*	70.1	261.4	*29.6*	241.8	..	*100.8*	182	*232*	..	..
Syrian Arab Republic	..	..	..	..	..	..	..	..	..	..	..	..
Tajikistan	..	..	..	..	..	..	..	..	..	..	..	..
Tanzania	..	..	..	..	..	..	..	..	..	..	..	..
Thailand	23,896	58,365	28.0	31.4	26.8	18.6	92.6	90.6	214	392	34.3	42.3
Togo	..	..	..	..	..	..	..	..	..	..	..	..
Trinidad and Tobago	696	4,367	13.7	61.5	1.1	2.8	10.0	0.9	30	27	17.5 [a]	–3.3 [a]
Tunisia	533	2,706	4.3	11.4	0.2	0.9	3.3	13.3	13	44	–6.4 [a]	16.8 [a]
Turkey	19,065	112,716	12.6	16.9	3.9	34.5	42.5	102.8	110	285	–53.1	254.5
Turkmenistan	..	..	..	..	..	..	..	..	..	..	..	..
Uganda	..	..	..	..	..	..	..	..	..	..	..	..
Ukraine	..	1,121	..	1.3	..	0.1	..	0.3	..	125	–82.3 [a]	20.2 [a]
United Arab Emirates	..	*31*	..	0.1	..	..	..	..	..	*44*	..	..
United Kingdom	848,866	*2,374,273*	87.0	174.9	28.6	86.0	33.3	*53.4*	1,701	*2,399*	15.8 [c]	14.5 [c]
United States	3,059,434	*13,451,352*	55.1	163.4	31.5	159.8	53.4	*106.2*	6,599	*8,450*	26.7 [d]	19.5 [d]
Uruguay	..	*209*	..	1.0	..	0.0	..	*1.9*	36	*19*	..	..
Uzbekistan	..	*465*	..	*1.9*	..	*0.1*	..	..	..	..	..	..
Venezuela, RB	8,361	7,471	17.2	8.0	4.6	1.6	43.0	10.2	76	87	–50.5	–12.4
Vietnam	..	..	..	..	..	..	..	..	..	..	..	..
West Bank and Gaza	..	*589*	..	16.4	..	1.9	..	*11.0*	..	*20*	..	..
Yemen, Rep.	..	..	..	..	..	..	..	..	..	..	..	..
Yugoslavia, FR (Serb./Mont.)	..	..	..	..	..	..	..	..	..	..	..	..
Zambia	..	*293*	..	8.7	..	*0.2*	..	..	..	*8*	..	..
Zimbabwe	2,395	2,514	27.3	20.7	0.6	2.6	2.9	12.0	57	70	–58.1	140.6
World	9,398,391 s	*27,458,957* s	51.2 w	97.4 w	28.4 w	81.3 w	.. w	*86.8* w	25,424 s	*47,465* s		
Low income	54,588	*375,568*	*7.5*	22.2	*3.1*	22.1	*90.8*	*99.4*	3,446	*9,089*		
Excl. China & India	16,021	*39,058*	*8.2*	13.0	*1.7*	*13.1*	..	..	1,011	*2,376*		
Middle income	430,570	*1,084,383*	*24.0*	27.0	*9.3*	15.0	..	*54.6*	4,914	*15,764*		
Lower middle income	176,701	*366,196*	*23.6*	29.2	..	9.1	..	*20.1*	2,455	*10,954*		
Upper middle income	253,869	*718,187*	18.1	26.0	8.2	17.6	*37.7*	*69.8*	2,459	*4,810*		
Low & middle income	485,158	*1,459,951*	*19.8*	25.6	*7.5*	17.1	*70.4*	*67.9*	8,360	*24,853*		
East Asia & Pacific	197,109	*536,921*	*21.3*	33.0	*13.3*	30.3	*117.2*	*124.2*	1,443	*3,702*		
Europe & Central Asia	19,065	*109,552*	*2.1*	11.8	..	12.1	..	*59.2*	110	*9,071*		
Latin America & Carib.	78,470	*402,883*	7.6	20.8	2.1	10.7	29.9	*41.8*	1,748	*2,166*		
Middle East & N. Africa	5,265	*113,928*	*27.8*	26.6	*1.5*	5.8	..	*17.9*	817	*1,619*		
South Asia	42,655	*113,612*	10.6	20.4	5.5	13.4	58.4	*64.5*	3,231	*7,178*		
Sub-Saharan Africa	142,594	*183,055*	*52.0*	80.3	*3.8*	26.3	..	*19.9*	1,011	*1,117*		
High income	8,913,233	*25,999,006*	56.0	115.7	31.7	97.5	..	*91.6*	17,064	*22,612*		
Europe EMU	1,168,755	*4,223,133*	22.1	65.4	7.4	57.6	..	*109.7*	2,485	*3,106*		

a. Data refer to the IFC Global index. b. Data refer to the Nikkei index. c. Data refer to the FT 100 index. d. Data refer to the S&P 500 index.

Stock markets 5.2

About the data

Financial market development is closely related to an economy's overall development. At low levels of economic development, commercial banks tend to dominate the financial system. As economies grow, specialized financial intermediaries and equity markets develop.

The stock market indicators presented in the table include measures of size (market capitalization and number of listed domestic companies) and liquidity (value traded as a percentage of GDP, and turnover ratio). The comparability of such indicators between countries may be limited by conceptual and statistical weaknesses such as inaccurate reporting and differences in accounting standards. The percentage change in stock market prices in U.S. dollars, from the International Finance Corporation's (IFC) Investable (IFCI) and Global (IFCG) country indexes, is an important measure of overall performance. Regulatory and institutional factors that can boost investor confidence, such as the existence of a securities and exchange commission and the quality of investor protection laws, may influence the functioning of stock markets but are not included in this table.

Stock market size can be measured in a number of ways, each of which may produce a different ranking among countries. Market capitalization shows the overall size of the stock market in U.S. dollars and as a percentage of GDP. The number of listed domestic companies is another measure of market size. Market size is positively correlated with the ability to mobilize capital and diversify risk.

Market liquidity, the ability to easily buy and sell securities, is measured by dividing the total value traded by GDP. This indicator complements the market capitalization ratio by showing whether market size is matched by trading. The turnover ratio—the value of shares traded as a percentage of market capitalization—is also a measure of liquidity as well as of transactions costs. (High turnover indicates low transactions costs.) The turnover ratio complements the ratio of value traded to GDP, because turnover is related to the size of the market and the value traded ratio to the size of the economy. A small, liquid market will have a high turnover ratio but a small value traded ratio. Liquidity is an important attribute of stock market development because, in theory, liquid markets improve the allocation of capital and enhance prospects for long-term economic growth. A more comprehensive measure of liquidity would include trading costs and the time and uncertainty in finding a counterpart in settling trades.

The International Finance Corporation has developed a series of indexes for investors interested in investing in stock markets in developing countries. At the core of the IFC family of emerging market indexes, the IFCG indexes are intended to represent the most active stocks in the markets they cover and to be the broadest possible indicator of market movements. The IFCI indexes apply the same calculation methodology as the IFCG indexes, but include only a subset of IFCG markets that IFC has determined to be "investable." The indexes are designed to measure returns on emerging market stocks that are legally and practically open to foreign portfolio investment, and they are widely used benchmarks for international portfolio management. The IFCG indexes cover 54 markets, providing regular updates on more than 2,200 stocks, and the IFCI indexes cover 30 markets and more than 1,292 stocks. See Standard & Poor's (2000) for further information on the IFCG and IFCI indexes.

Because markets included in IFC's emerging markets category vary widely in level of development, it is best to look at the entire category to identify the most significant market trends. And it is useful to remember that stock market trends may be distorted by currency conversions, especially when a currency has registered a significant devaluation.

Figure 5.2

The top 10 emerging stock markets in 1999

Source: IFC 1999a.

Market capitalization increased dramatically in some Asian markets between 1998 and 1999—almost 170 percent in the Republic of Korea and more than 40 percent in China.

Definitions

• **Market capitalization** (also known as market value) is the share price times the number of shares outstanding. • **Value traded** refers to the total value of shares traded during the period. • **Turnover ratio** is the total value of shares traded during the period divided by the average market capitalization for the period. Average market capitalization is calculated as the average of the end-of-period values for the current period and the previous period. • **Listed domestic companies** refer to the number of domestically incorporated companies listed on the country's stock exchanges at the end of the year. This indicator does not include investment companies, mutual funds, or other collective investment vehicles. • **IFC Investable index price change** is the U.S. dollar price change in the stock markets covered by the IFCI country index, supplemented by the IFCG country index.

Data sources

The data on stock markets are from IFC's *Emerging Stock Markets Factbook 1999*, with supplemental data from IFC. IFC collects data through an annual survey of the world's stock exchanges, supplemented by information provided by Reuters and IFC's network of correspondents. IFC's Emerging Market Database was acquired by Standard & Poor's in January 2000. The GDP data are from the World Bank's national accounts data files. *About the data* is based on Demirgüç-Kunt and Levine (1996b).

5.3 Portfolio investment regulation and risk

	Entry and exit regulations			Composite ICRG risk rating[a]	Institutional Investor credit rating[a]	Euromoney country credit-worthiness rating[a]	Moody's sovereign long-term debt rating[a]		Standard & Poor's sovereign long-term debt rating[a]	
	Entry 1998	Repatriation of income 1998	Repatriation of capital 1998	December 1999	September 1999	September 1999	Foreign currency January 2000	Domestic currency January 2000	Foreign currency January 2000	Domestic currency January 2000
Albania	..	..	..	64.8	12.4	18.6	..	..	..	..
Algeria	..	..	..	52.5	26.5	32.3	..	..	..	..
Angola	..	..	..	41.3	11.6	24.4	..	..	..	..
Argentina	Free	Free	Free	67.5	42.4	53.8	B1	B1	BB	BBB–
Armenia	..	..	..	58.8	..	29.6	..	..	..	..
Australia	..	..	..	81.8	75.8	88.1	Aa2	Aaa	AA+	AAA
Austria	..	..	..	83.0	89.4	91.8	Aaa	Aaa	AAA	AAA
Azerbaijan	..	..	..	54.3	..	33.4	..	..	..	..
Bangladesh	Free	Free	Free	63.3	26.8	34.9	..	..	..	..
Belarus	..	..	..	56.3	13.4	29.1	..	..	..	..
Belgium	..	..	..	78.3	84.9	89.5	Aa1	Aa1	AA+	AA+
Benin	..	..	..	..	17.2	29.7	..	..	..	..
Bolivia	..	..	..	68.5	28.4	39.8	B1	B1	BB–	BB+
Bosnia and Herzegovina	..	..	..	..	..	..	..	..	..	..
Botswana	Free	Free	Free	83.5	56.0	51.1	..	..	..	..
Brazil	Free	Free	Free	59.5	36.5	46.8	B2	B3	B+	BB–
Bulgaria	Free	Free	Free	71.0	30.3	39.3	B2	B1	B	B
Burkina Faso	..	..	..	66.8	19.1	31.4	..	..	..	..
Burundi	..	..	..	..	..	..	..	..	..	..
Cambodia	..	..	..	..	..	27.2	..	..	..	..
Cameroon	..	..	..	63.5	17.2	28.1	..	..	..	..
Canada	..	..	..	83.5	83.5	88.8	Aa2	Aa1	AA+	AAA
Central African Republic	..	..	..	..	..	25.6	..	..	..	..
Chad	..	..	..	..	..	27.2	..	..	..	..
Chile	Rel. free	Free	Delayed[b]	69.0	61.0	65.0	Baa1	A1	A–	AA
China	Special	Free	Free	74.0	56.4	55.1	A3	..	BBB	..
Hong Kong, China	..	..	..	76.8	61.3	77.1	A3	A1	A	A+
Colombia	Auth. only	Free	Free	55.0	44.1	50.8	Ba2	Baa2	BB+	BBB+
Congo, Dem. Rep.	..	..	..	40.8	11.1	20.0	..	..	..	..
Congo, Rep.	..	..	..	50.5	7.3	25.0	..	..	..	..
Costa Rica	..	..	..	76.3	40.5	45.6	Ba1	Ba1	BB	BB+
Côte d'Ivoire	Free	Free	Free	64.8	25.5	31.2	..	..	..	..
Croatia	Free	Free	Free	66.3	39.6	52.6	Baa3	Baa1	BBB–	BBB+
Cuba	..	..	..	60.0	12.1	7.4	Caa1	..	..	..
Czech Republic	Free	Free	Free	74.5	59.1	60.8	Baa1	A1	A–	AA–
Denmark	..	..	..	85.8	85.1	92.3	Aaa	Aaa	AA+	AAA
Dominican Republic	..	..	..	72.3	30.9	40.3	B1	B1	B+	..
Ecuador	Free	Free	Free	54.0	22.4	32.9	Caa3	Caa1	..	..
Egypt, Arab Rep.	Free	Free	Free	68.3	45.4	52.3	Ba1	Baa1	BBB–	A–
El Salvador	..	..	..	75.8	35.6	47.2	Baa3	Baa2	BB+	BBB+
Eritrea	..	..	..	..	..	..	..	..	..	..
Estonia	Free	Free	Free	73.5	45.9	54.3	Baa1	A1	BBB+	A–
Ethiopia	..	..	..	57.0	16.6	24.5	..	..	..	..
Finland	..	..	..	87.5	83.6	90.3	Aaa	Aaa	AA+	AA+
France	..	..	..	78.3	91.4	92.3	Aaa	Aaa	AAA	AAA
Gabon	..	..	..	69.0	22.6	33.4	..	..	..	..
Gambia, The	..	..	..	69.3	..	31.2	..	..	..	..
Georgia	..	..	..	..	10.8	25.7	..	..	..	..
Germany	..	..	..	81.3	92.0	93.4	Aaa	Aaa	AAA	AAA
Ghana	Free	Free	Free	58.3	30.7	38.8	..	..	..	..
Greece	Free	Free	Free	75.0	59.1	76.8	A2	A2	A–	A–
Guatemala	..	..	..	67.0	28.1	39.0	Ba2	Ba1	..	..
Guinea	..	..	..	61.8	16.3	25.7	..	..	..	..
Guinea-Bissau	..	..	..	43.3	..	17.4	..	..	..	..
Haiti	..	..	..	57.3	11.2	26.6	..	..	..	..
Honduras	..	..	..	62.8	19.3	33.5	B2	B2	..	..

Portfolio investment regulation and risk 5.3

	Entry and exit regulations			Composite ICRG risk rating[a]	Institutional Investor credit rating[a]	Euromoney country creditworthiness rating[a]	Moody's sovereign long-term debt rating[a]		Standard & Poor's sovereign long-term debt rating[a]	
	Entry 1998	Repatriation of income 1998	Repatriation of capital 1998	December 1999	September 1999	September 1999	Foreign currency January 2000	Domestic currency January 2000	Foreign currency January 2000	Domestic currency January 2000
Hungary	Free	Free	Free	74.5	57.3	64.3	Baa1	A1	BBB	A
India	Auth. only	Free	Free	64.3	44.2	51.8	Ba2	Ba2	BB	BBB
Indonesia	Rel. free	Restricted	Restricted	51.8	27.1	36.4	B3	B3	CCC+	B–
Iran, Islamic Rep.	..	..	..	60.8	28.0	35.7	B2	Ba2	..	..
Iraq	..	..	..	39.8	7.7	4.0	..	..	..	..
Ireland	..	..	..	86.8	83.4	90.0	Aaa	Aaa	AA+	AA+
Israel	Free	Free	Free	69.3	55.8	71.0	A3	A2	A–	AA–
Italy	..	..	..	75.5	81.3	87.1	Aa3	Aa3	AA	AA
Jamaica	Rel. free	Free	Free	71.0	28.9	41.0	Ba3	Baa3	B	B+
Japan	..	..	..	83.3	86.5	90.9	Aa1	Aa1	AAA	AAA
Jordan	Free	Free	Free	71.0	37.9	46.2	Ba3	Ba3	BB–	BBB–
Kazakhstan	..	..	..	65.0	29.7	40.3	B1	B1	B+	BB–
Kenya	Rel. free	Free	Free	58.0	24.8	35.4	..	..	..	..
Korea, Dem. Rep.	..	..	..	41.0	6.7	1.0	..	..	..	..
Korea, Rep.	Rel. free	Free	Free	79.3	56.8	64.1	Baa2	Baa1	BBB	A
Kuwait	..	..	..	74.3	58.2	70.0	Baa1	Baa1	A	A+
Kyrgyz Republic	..	..	..	..	..	32.8	..	..	..	..
Lao PDR	..	..	..	..	..	27.4	..	..	..	..
Latvia	Free	Free	Free	72.5	40.8	50.4	Baa2	A2	BBB	A–
Lebanon	..	..	..	54.8	33.6	47.3	B1	B1	BB–	BB
Lesotho	..	..	..	..	..	32.2	..	..	..	..
Libya	..	..	..	65.5	29.1	16.1	..	..	..	..
Lithuania	Free	Free	Free	70.5	38.2	48.7	Ba1	Baa1	BBB–	BBB+
Macedonia, FYR	..	..	..	..	..	23.0	..	..	..	..
Madagascar	..	..	..	64.0	..	22.3	..	..	..	..
Malawi	..	..	..	64.0	19.5	30.3	..	..	..	..
Malaysia	Rel. free	Free	Delayed[b]	74.5	51.7	57.0	Baa3	A3	BBB	A
Mali	..	..	..	67.5	15.5	31.9	..	..	..	..
Mauritania	..	..	..	..	..	27.7	..	..	..	..
Mauritius	Rel. free	Free	Free	..	53.9	62.0	Baa2	A2	..	..
Mexico	Free	Free	Free	68.8	48.2	55.7	Ba1	Baa3	BB	BBB+
Moldova	..	..	..	49.5	..	31.0	B2	Caa1	..	..
Mongolia	..	..	..	66.8	..	30.8	..	..	B	B
Morocco	Free	Free	Free	72.0	44.3	53.0	Ba1	..	BB	BBB
Mozambique	..	..	..	58.3	19.3	24.5	..	..	..	..
Myanmar	..	..	..	57.8	17.9	18.7	..	..	..	..
Namibia	..	..	..	77.8	38.0	23.3	..	..	..	..
Nepal	..	..	..	..	27.3	34.3	..	..	..	..
Netherlands	..	..	..	86.3	91.2	92.4	Aaa	Aaa	AAA	AAA
New Zealand	..	..	..	78.0	74.0	85.4	Aa2	Aaa	AA+	AAA
Nicaragua	..	..	..	52.0	12.1	25.4	B2	B2	..	..
Niger	..	..	..	59.3	..	28.0	..	..	..	..
Nigeria	Rel. free	Free	Free	57.0	17.9	31.2	..	..	..	..
Norway	..	..	..	87.3	87.7	94.1	Aaa	Aaa	AAA	AAA
Oman	..	..	..	73.0	52.0	63.3	Baa2	Baa2	BBB–	BBB
Pakistan	Free	Free	Free	56.8	19.5	30.2	Caa1	Caa1	B–	B+
Panama	Free	Free	Free	72.3	41.7	47.9	Ba1	..	BB+	BB+
Papua New Guinea	..	..	..	65.0	32.2	39.7	B1	B1	B+	BB
Paraguay	..	..	..	65.0	31.3	37.8	B2	B1	B	BB–
Peru	Free	Free	Free	66.5	37.0	44.6	Ba3	Baa3	BB	BBB–
Philippines	Special	Free	Free	71.0	45.9	54.4	Ba1	Baa3	BB+	BBB+
Poland	Free	Free	Free	74.8	57.5	62.5	Baa1	A2	BBB	A
Portugal	Free	Free	Free	80.8	78.4	82.8	Aa2	Aa2	AA	AA
Puerto Rico	..	..	..	..	..	..	..	..	..	..
Romania	Free	Free	Free	55.0	28.7	36.8	B3	Caa1	B–	B
Russian Federation	Free	Free	Free	49.8	19.3	23.0	B3	Caa2	SD	CCC

5.3 Portfolio investment regulation and risk

	Entry and exit regulations			Composite ICRG risk rating[a]	Institutional Investor credit rating[a]	Euromoney country credit-worthiness rating[a]	Moody's sovereign long-term debt rating[a]		Standard & Poor's sovereign long-term debt rating[a]	
	Entry 1998	Repatriation of income 1998	Repatriation of capital 1998	December 1999	September 1999	September 1999	Foreign currency January 2000	Domestic currency January 2000	Foreign currency January 2000	Domestic currency January 2000
Rwanda	..	..	..	..	..	20.9	..	..	..	..
Saudi Arabia[c]	Closed	Closed	Closed	68.8	54.0	66.6	Baa3	Ba1	..	..
Senegal	..	..	..	62.5	22.8	34.5	..	..	..	..
Sierra Leone	..	..	..	31.0	6.1	17.6	..	..	..	..
Singapore	..	..	..	89.3	81.9	88.5	Aa1	Aaa	AAA	AAA
Slovak Republic	..	..	..	72.0	41.6	49.0	Ba1	Baa2	BB+	BBB+
Slovenia	Closed	Restricted	Restricted	78.0	61.2	69.0	A3	Aa3	A	AA
South Africa	Free	Free	Free	69.5	45.6	53.7	Baa3	Baa1	BB+	BBB+
Spain	..	..	..	76.0	81.7	86.6	Aa2	Aa2	AA+	AA+
Sri Lanka	Rel. free	Restricted	Restricted	59.8	33.7	42.7	..	..	..	..
Sudan	..	..	..	48.5	7.1	19.0	..	..	..	..
Sweden	..	..	..	83.5	81.2	89.9	Aa1	Aaa	AA+	AAA
Switzerland	..	..	..	87.0	93.0	97.8	Aaa	Aaa	AAA	AAA
Syrian Arab Republic	..	..	..	68.3	23.8	35.0	..	..	..	..
Tajikistan	..	..	..	..	..	27.2	..	..	..	..
Tanzania	..	..	..	58.5	19.5	26.5	..	..	..	..
Thailand	Rel. free	Free	Free	74.0	48.3	56.0	Ba1	Baa1	BBB–	A–
Togo	..	..	..	60.3	17.1	29.7	..	..	..	..
Trinidad and Tobago	Rel. free	Free	Free	75.0	44.9	49.4	Ba1	Baa3	BBB–	BBB+
Tunisia	Rel. free	Free	Free	72.5	50.3	55.3	Baa3	Baa2	BBB–	A
Turkey	Free	Free	Free	52.8	38.9	48.5	B1	..	B	..
Turkmenistan	..	..	..	..	..	31.8	B2	..	..	..
Uganda	..	..	..	62.3	21.7	34.5	..	..	..	..
Ukraine	Free	Free	Free	60.0	18.7	30.7	Caa1	Caa3	..	..
United Arab Emirates	..	..	..	78.0	63.2	75.0	..	..	..	..
United Kingdom	..	..	..	84.3	90.2	91.2	Aaa	Aaa	AAA	AAA
United States	..	..	..	84.5	90.9	94.5	Aaa	Aaa	AAA	AAA
Uruguay	..	..	..	70.5	47.2	54.2	Baa3	Baa3	BBB–	BBB+
Uzbekistan	..	..	..	..	18.9	28.8	..	..	..	..
Venezuela, RB	Rel. free	Restricted	Restricted	61.0	33.8	41.3	B2	B3	B	..
Vietnam	..	..	..	64.0	28.1	36.5	B1	..	..	..
West Bank and Gaza	..	..	..	..	..	..	..	..	..	..
Yemen, Rep.	..	..	..	60.3	..	26.2	..	..	..	..
Yugoslavia, FR (Serb./Mont.)	..	..	..	43.3	8.2	14.8	..	..	..	..
Zambia	..	..	..	59.0	14.9	26.4	..	..	..	..
Zimbabwe	Rel. free	Free	Free	56.3	25.1	33.9	..	..	..	..
World				67.3 m	36.0 m	38.3 m				
Low income				58.4	18.5	28.1				
Excl. China & India				58.3	17.9	28.1				
Middle income				68.8	37.5	46.2				
Lower middle income				67.0	30.1	39.3				
Upper middle income				70.5	46.5	54.0				
Low & middle income				64.0	28.5	33.4				
East Asia & Pacific				66.8	39.0	36.5				
Europe & Central Asia				64.9	30.3	33.1				
Latin America & Carib.				67.3	34.7	43.0				
Middle East & N. Africa				68.3	35.8	46.2				
South Asia				61.5	27.0	34.6				
Sub-Saharan Africa				59.2	19.3	28.1				
High income				82.4	82.7	89.1				
Europe EMU				81.1	84.3	90.1				

Note: For explanations of the terms used to describe entry and exit regulations see *Definitions*. a. This copyrighted material is reprinted with permission from the following data providers: PRS Group, 6320 Fly Road, Suite 102, PO Box 248, East Syracuse, NY 13057; Institutional Investor, Inc., 488 Madison Avenue, New York, NY 10022; Euromoney Publications PLC, Nestor House, Playhouse Yard, London EC4V 5EX, UK; Moody's Investors Service, 99 Church Street, New York, NY 10007; Standard & Poor's Rating Services, The McGraw-Hill Companies, Inc., 1221 Avenue of the Americas, New York, NY 10020. Prior written consent from the original data providers cited must be obtained for third-party use of these data. b. After one year. c. Foreigners are barred from investing directly in the Saudi stock market, but they may invest indirectly through mutual funds.

Portfolio investment regulation and risk 5.3

About the data

As investment portfolios become increasingly global, investors as well as governments seeking to attract both foreign and domestic investment must have a good understanding of country risk. Risk, by its nature, is perceived differently by different groups. This table presents information on country risk and creditworthiness from several major international rating services and information on the regulation of entry to and exit from emerging stock markets reported by the International Finance Corporation (IFC).

Entry and exit restrictions on investments are among the mechanisms by which countries attempt to reduce the risk to their economies associated with foreign investment. Yet such restrictions may increase the risk or uncertainty perceived by investors, increasing their reluctance to participate in regulated markets. Many countries close industries considered strategic to foreign or nonresident investors. Or national law or corporate policy may limit foreign investment in a company or in certain classes of stocks. The regulations summarized in the table refer to "new money" investment by foreign institutions; other regulations may apply to capital invested through debt conversion schemes or to capital from other sources. The regulations shown here are formal ones. But even formal regulations may have very different effects in different countries because of differences in the prevailing bureaucratic culture, the speed with which applications are processed, and the extent of red tape. The effect of entry and exit regulations may also be influenced by graft and corruption, which are impossible to quantify.

Most risk ratings are numerical or alphabetical indexes. For numerical ratings, a higher number means lower risk (a good prospect). For alphabetical ratings, a letter closer to the beginning of the alphabet means lower risk. Readers should refer to the sources of the data for more details on the rating processes of the rating agencies. Risk ratings may be highly subjective, reflecting external perceptions that do not always capture the actual situation in a country. But these subjective perceptions are the reality that policymakers face in the climate they create for foreign private inflows. Countries that are not rated by credit risk rating agencies typically do not attract registered flows of private capital. The risk ratings presented here are included for their analytic usefulness and are not endorsed by the World Bank.

The PRS Group's *International Country Risk Guide* (ICRG) collects information on 22 components of risk, groups it into three major categories (political, financial, and economic), and converts it into a single numerical risk assessment ranging from 0 to 100. Ratings below 50 are considered very high risk, and those above 80 very low risk. Ratings are updated every month.

Institutional Investor country credit ratings are based on information provided by leading international banks. Responses are weighted using a formula that gives more importance to responses from banks with greater worldwide exposure and more sophisticated country analysis systems. Countries are rated on a scale of 0 to 100 (highest risk to lowest), and ratings are updated every six months.

Euromoney country creditworthiness ratings are based on nine weighted categories (covering economic performance, political risk, debt, and access to financial and capital markets) that assess country risk. The ratings, also on a scale of 0 to 100 (highest risk to lowest), are based on polls of economists and political analysts supplemented by quantitative data such as debt ratios and access to capital markets.

Moody's sovereign long-term debt ratings are opinions of the ability of entities to honor senior unsecured financial obligations and contracts denominated in foreign currency (foreign currency issuer ratings) or in their domestic currency (domestic currency issuer ratings).

Standard & Poor's ratings of sovereign long-term foreign and domestic currency debt are based on current information furnished by obligors or obtained by Standard & Poor's from other sources it considers reliable. A Standard & Poor's issuer credit rating (one form of which is a sovereign credit rating) is a current opinion of an obligor's overall financial capacity to pay its financial obligations (its creditworthiness). This opinion focuses on the obligor's capacity and willingness to meet its financial commitments as they come due. It does not apply to any specific financial obligation, as it does not take into account the nature and provisions of obligations, their standing in bankruptcy or liquidation, statutory preferences, or the legality and enforceability of obligations.

Definitions

• **Regulations on entry to emerging stock markets** are evaluated using the following terms: *free* (no significant restrictions), *relatively free* (some registration procedures required to ensure repatriation rights), *special classes* (foreigners restricted to certain classes of stocks designated for foreign investors), *authorized investors only* (only approved foreign investors may buy stocks), and *closed* (closed or access severely restricted, as for nonresident nationals only). • **Regulations on repatriation of income** (dividends, interest, and realized capital gains) and **repatriation of capital from emerging markets** are evaluated as free (repatriation done routinely) or restricted (repatriation requires registration with or permission of a government agency that may restrict the timing of exchange release). • **Composite International Country Risk Guide (ICRG) risk rating** is an overall index, ranging from 0 to 100, based on 22 components of risk. • **Institutional Investor credit rating** ranks, from 0 to 100, the chances of a country's default. • **Euromoney country creditworthiness rating** ranks, from 0 to 100, the riskiness of investing in an economy. • **Moody's sovereign foreign and domestic currency long-term debt ratings** assess the risk of lending to governments. Rating gradations from Aaa to C measure an entity's ability to meet its senior financial obligations. Issuers rated Aaa offer exceptional financial security, while issuers rated C are usually in default on their obligations and the potential recovery values are low. Numerical modifiers 1–3 are applied to classifications from Aa to B, with 1 indicating that the obligation ranks at the high end of its letter rating category. • **Standard & Poor's sovereign foreign and domestic currency long-term debt ratings** range from AAA (indicating that an obligor has extremely strong capacity to meet its financial commitments) through CC (indicating that an obligor is currently highly vulnerable). Ratings from AA to CCC may be modified by the addition of a plus (+) or minus (–) sign to show relative standing within the rating category. An obligor rated SD (selective default) has failed to pay one or more of its financial obligations when it came due.

Data sources

The data on emerging stock markets' entry and exit regulations are from IFC's *Emerging Stock Markets Factbook 1999*. The country risk and creditworthiness ratings are from several sources: the PRS Group's monthly *International Country Risk Guide;* the monthly *Institutional Investor;* the monthly *Euromoney;* Moody's Investors Service's *Sovereign, Subnational and Sovereign-Guaranteed Issuers;* and Standard & Poor's Sovereign List in *Credit Week.*

5.4 Financial depth and efficiency

	Domestic credit provided by banking sector % of GDP		Liquid liabilities % of GDP		Quasi-liquid liabilities % of GDP		Ratio of bank liquid reserves to bank assets %		Interest rate spread Lending minus deposit rate percentage points		Spread over LIBOR Lending rate minus LIBOR percentage points	
	1990	1998	1990	1998	1990	1998	1990	1998	1990	1998	1990	1998
Albania	..	47.2	..	52.0	..	33.8	..	11.0	*2.1*	*7.2*	*16.7*	*18.4*
Algeria	74.7	45.8	61.9	46.4	13.2	17.1	1.3	1.4	..	..	..	..
Angola	..	15.2	..	21.2	..	11.9	..	14.9	..	8.1	..	39.4
Argentina	32.4	32.6	11.5	28.7	7.0	21.5	7.4	2.6	..	3.1	..	5.0
Armenia	*58.7*	10.8	*79.9*	10.1	*42.9*	4.6	*13.6*	10.5	..	23.5	..	42.9
Australia	103.5	89.9	57.5	67.0	45.2	47.1	1.5	1.7	4.5	3.4	9.9	2.5
Austria	123.0	*132.1*	..	..	..	..	2.1	*2.3*	..	3.8	..	0.8
Azerbaijan	*57.2*	13.5	*33.5*	11.3	*11.6*	4.2	*4.5*	7.9	..	..	..	..
Bangladesh	24.1	32.9	23.6	30.8	17.0	22.4	12.8	9.7	4.0	5.6	7.7	8.4
Belarus	..	37.4	..	32.8	..	20.6	..	12.4	..	12.7	..	21.4
Belgium	70.9	*147.9*	..	..	..	..	0.2	*1.0*	6.9	4.2	4.7	1.7
Benin	22.4	7.1	26.7	20.9	5.9	7.2	29.3	10.7	9.0	..	7.7	..
Bolivia	30.7	66.9	24.5	47.8	18.0	39.6	18.8	4.8	18.0	26.6	33.5	33.8
Bosnia and Herzegovina	..	..	..	..	..	..	..	..	..	..	..	..
Botswana	–46.4	–78.5	22.1	27.8	13.7	20.4	11.0	7.5	1.8	4.8	–0.4	7.9
Brazil	89.8	54.6	25.3	31.2	17.3	25.1	6.7	8.4	..	..	..	..
Bulgaria	*118.5*	19.6	*71.9*	33.6	*53.6*	16.2	*10.2*	7.9	*8.9*	10.3	*42.4*	7.7
Burkina Faso	13.7	13.4	20.4	23.4	6.6	6.2	12.7	4.7	9.0	..	7.7	..
Burundi	24.5	*25.4*	18.0	*19.9*	6.3	*5.7*	2.8	4.1	..	..	4.0	..
Cambodia	..	7.8	..	11.4	..	6.4	..	29.1	..	10.5	..	12.7
Cameroon	31.2	16.8	22.6	14.2	10.1	5.0	3.4	9.5	11.0	17.0	10.2	16.4
Canada	85.8	102.1	49.0	65.0	34.5	44.2	1.6	0.6	1.3	1.6	5.7	1.0
Central African Republic	12.9	10.6	15.3	15.6	1.8	1.6	2.8	2.0	11.0	17.0	10.2	16.4
Chad	10.1	9.4	14.6	10.5	0.6	0.6	3.6	14.6	11.0	17.0	10.2	16.4
Chile	73.0	66.3	40.0	43.8	32.0	35.8	3.8	4.0	8.6	5.3	40.5	14.6
China	90.0	120.2	79.2	133.0	41.4	78.5	15.7	15.0	0.7	2.6	1.0	0.8
Hong Kong, China	156.3	146.7	*181.7*	196.6	*166.8*	184.2	0.1	0.2	3.3	2.4	1.7	3.4
Colombia	30.8	41.1	16.6	23.4	7.6	16.1	26.3	4.9	8.8	9.7	36.9	36.7
Congo, Dem. Rep.	25.3	..	12.9	..	2.1	..	..	..	..	..	..	..
Congo, Rep.	29.1	21.8	22.0	15.2	6.1	2.8	2.0	8.0	11.0	17.0	10.2	16.4
Costa Rica	29.9	44.6	42.6	43.9	29.9	28.5	68.5	30.5	11.4	9.7	24.2	16.9
Côte d'Ivoire	44.5	28.2	28.8	26.5	10.9	7.5	2.1	3.8	9.0	..	7.7	..
Croatia	..	48.4	..	41.4	..	31.5	..	6.8	*499.3*	11.1	*1,153.9*	10.2
Cuba	..	..	..	..	..	..	..	..	..	..	..	..
Czech Republic	..	64.2	..	66.7	..	44.5	..	18.0	..	4.7	..	7.2
Denmark	63.0	61.0	59.0	58.6	29.4	27.8	1.1	4.6	6.2	4.8	5.8	2.3
Dominican Republic	31.5	33.1	25.6	30.1	10.4	17.9	31.1	26.3	*15.2*	8.0	*29.3*	20.1
Ecuador	17.2	49.7	21.8	38.7	11.3	29.4	23.1	7.7	–6.0	10.2	29.2	44.0
Egypt, Arab Rep.	106.8	94.9	85.8	79.0	58.6	58.1	17.1	13.3	7.0	3.7	10.7	7.4
El Salvador	32.0	41.8	30.6	46.5	19.6	36.8	33.4	26.9	3.2	4.7	12.9	9.4
Eritrea	..	..	..	..	..	..	..	..	..	..	..	..
Estonia	*65.0*	32.3	*136.2*	28.4	*93.5*	11.0	*43.1*	17.2	..	8.6	*26.6*	11.1
Ethiopia	50.4	44.3	40.3	39.5	10.6	18.8	23.3	12.6	3.6	4.5	–2.3	4.9
Finland	84.3	58.4	..	..	..	..	4.1	4.1	4.1	*3.3*	3.3	–0.2
France	106.1	*103.1*	..	..	..	..	1.0	*0.4*	6.0	3.3	2.2	1.0
Gabon	20.0	22.5	17.8	16.4	6.6	6.3	2.0	5.7	11.0	17.0	10.2	16.4
Gambia, The	3.4	11.0	20.7	29.6	8.8	15.5	8.8	16.5	15.2	12.9	18.2	19.8
Georgia	..	11.0	..	5.1	..	1.6	..	14.1	..	29.0	..	40.4
Germany	*108.5*	146.4	..	..	..	..	3.2	1.3	4.5	6.1	3.3	3.4
Ghana	13.2	27.7	14.1	19.1	3.4	7.1	20.2	8.0	..	..	..	..
Greece	73.3	57.2	53.8	46.7	39.8	31.1	22.4	31.4	8.1	7.9	19.3	13.0
Guatemala	17.4	16.3	21.3	22.9	11.8	11.6	31.8	18.2	5.1	11.1	15.0	11.0
Guinea	*5.4*	*6.8*	0.8	*9.7*	0.8	*1.9*	6.2	*14.7*	0.2	..	12.9	..
Guinea-Bissau	42.1	*7.4*	16.5	*15.7*	4.4	*5.8*	10.8	13.2	13.1	*4.5*	37.4	*46.2*
Haiti	32.9	24.1	31.4	29.5	15.9	20.4	74.9	30.4	..	10.6	..	18.0
Honduras	40.9	28.8	31.7	39.0	16.9	26.0	6.6	22.0	8.3	12.1	8.7	25.1

Financial depth and efficiency 5.4

	Domestic credit provided by banking sector % of GDP		Liquid liabilities % of GDP		Quasi-liquid liabilities % of GDP		Ratio of bank liquid reserves to bank assets %		Interest rate spread Lending minus deposit rate percentage points		Spread over LIBOR Lending rate minus LIBOR percentage points	
	1990	1998	1990	1998	1990	1998	1990	1998	1990	1998	1990	1998
Hungary	82.6	..	43.8	..	19.0	..	28.5	..	4.1	*3.2*	20.5	*16.0*
India	50.6	45.1	42.0	48.0	27.2	33.0	14.8	12.2	..	..	8.2	8.0
Indonesia	45.5	59.2	40.1	60.3	28.8	51.1	4.5	5.3	3.3	–6.9	12.5	26.6
Iran, Islamic Rep.	62.1	46.0	55.6	43.0	29.1	22.6	66.0	54.8	..	..	..	..
Iraq	..	..	..	..	..	..	..	..	..	..	..	..
Ireland	57.3	98.7	..	..	..	..	4.8	1.8	5.0	5.8	3.0	0.6
Israel	106.2	*81.9*	70.2	88.1	63.6	88.1	11.9	13.0	12.0	5.2	18.1	10.6
Italy	90.1	93.5	..	..	..	..	12.0	1.2	7.3	4.7	5.8	2.3
Jamaica	34.8	43.9	42.2	50.4	29.1	34.6	37.4	25.9	6.6	19.1	22.2	29.1
Japan	266.8	139.4	115.1	121.6	87.3	78.4	1.5	1.3	3.4	2.1	–1.4	–3.3
Jordan	110.0	91.2	131.4	103.6	78.0	72.9	20.5	29.8	2.2	*3.2*	2.0	*6.5*
Kazakhstan	..	8.9	..	8.6	..	1.7	..	7.7	..	..	..	..
Kenya	52.9	49.5	29.7	40.8	15.6	27.3	9.9	10.8	5.1	11.1	10.4	23.9
Korea, Dem. Rep.	..	..	..	..	..	..	..	..	..	..	..	..
Korea, Rep.	57.2	78.1	38.4	57.5	29.5	49.6	6.3	1.8	0.0	2.0	1.7	9.7
Kuwait	*217.6*	116.8	*192.2*	98.5	*153.9*	83.6	*1.2*	0.9	*0.4*	2.6	*4.1*	3.3
Kyrgyz Republic	..	19.1	..	14.0	..	4.9	..	16.7	..	37.7	..	67.9
Lao PDR	5.1	16.9	7.2	20.8	3.1	16.8	3.4	20.0	*2.5*	11.5	*20.0*	23.7
Latvia	..	17.2	..	25.4	..	9.5	..	8.9	..	9.0	..	8.7
Lebanon	132.6	134.9	193.7	153.7	170.9	145.8	3.9	14.0	23.1	*6.9*	31.6	*14.5*
Lesotho	27.5	–22.4	37.4	39.9	21.0	17.7	24.1	38.3	7.4	9.3	12.1	14.5
Libya	..	..	..	..	..	..	40.8	56.8	1.5	..	–1.3	..
Lithuania	..	13.1	..	19.4	..	6.4	..	17.2	..	6.2	..	6.6
Macedonia, FYR	..	19.0	..	14.8	..	7.0	..	4.4	..	9.4	..	15.4
Madagascar	26.2	15.8	16.2	19.1	3.7	4.7	8.5	22.5	5.3	19.0	17.5	21.4
Malawi	17.8	6.4	19.5	18.0	9.7	8.5	32.8	29.0	8.9	18.6	12.7	32.1
Malaysia	77.9	159.8	66.3	95.3	44.3	74.7	5.9	8.7	1.3	2.1	–1.1	5.0
Mali	13.7	14.4	20.5	22.6	5.5	5.8	50.8	4.9	9.0	..	7.7	..
Mauritania	49.2	2.3	25.6	14.8	6.3	4.9	6.1	4.9	5.0	..	1.7	..
Mauritius	45.1	78.6	62.6	78.8	48.4	66.7	8.8	4.9	5.4	10.6	9.7	14.3
Mexico	36.6	36.1	21.7	28.3	15.3	20.2	4.2	6.4	..	14.9	..	23.1
Moldova	*62.8*	34.0	*70.3*	20.0	*35.4*	7.9	*8.3*	10.4	..	9.2	..	25.2
Mongolia	*68.5*	13.3	*52.4*	19.1	*13.8*	9.7	*2.0*	11.8	..	15.7	..	34.4
Morocco	43.0	83.8	53.9	71.7	11.3	19.1	11.3	5.1	0.5	5.7	0.7	..
Mozambique	15.6	2.5	26.5	21.2	5.2	9.0	61.5	14.3	..	..	..	..
Myanmar	32.8	29.1	27.9	27.8	7.8	9.7	271.8	25.1	2.1	4.0	–0.3	10.9
Namibia	19.5	53.9	23.4	41.9	13.7	20.4	4.4	3.1	*10.6*	7.8	17.4	15.1
Nepal	28.9	39.7	32.2	45.6	18.5	30.3	12.7	15.2	2.5	5.1	6.1	8.4
Netherlands	107.4	*131.5*	..	..	..	..	0.3	*0.2*	8.4	3.4	3.4	0.9
New Zealand	79.9	112.4	77.9	92.3	64.8	79.8	0.8	0.4	4.4	4.4	7.7	5.6
Nicaragua	..	149.4	28.6	66.8	11.7	55.5	20.2	23.1	12.5	10.9	13.7	16.0
Niger	16.2	9.3	19.8	6.6	8.3	1.7	42.9	9.2	9.0	..	7.7	..
Nigeria	23.7	14.2	22.1	14.4	8.8	5.5	11.6	13.5	5.5	*13.1*	17.0	*14.6*
Norway	67.4	62.4	59.9	54.3	27.0	14.1	0.5	1.3	4.6	0.7	5.9	2.3
Oman	16.6	44.7	28.9	37.0	19.3	28.3	6.9	4.1	1.4	1.6	1.4	4.5
Pakistan	50.9	49.3	39.1	46.1	9.4	19.4	8.9	10.5	..	..	..	..
Panama	52.7	93.6	41.1	78.8	33.0	66.5	..	..	3.6	4.1	3.7	5.2
Papua New Guinea	35.8	36.0	35.2	35.4	24.0	21.0	3.2	3.6	6.9	4.0	7.2	12.1
Paraguay	14.9	28.2	19.8	29.6	11.2	21.1	31.0	25.3	8.1	14.0	22.7	24.4
Peru	16.2	22.2	19.4	28.6	9.0	18.1	22.0	20.8	2,335.0	15.7	4,766.2	25.2
Philippines	23.2	69.8	34.1	60.8	25.4	50.1	11.7	4.4	4.6	4.7	15.8	11.2
Poland	18.8	36.4	32.8	40.1	16.6	27.1	20.6	10.7	462.5	6.3	495.9	18.9
Portugal	71.8	107.9	..	..	..	..	29.0	5.1	7.8	3.9	13.5	1.7
Puerto Rico	..	..	..	..	..	..	..	..	..	..	..	..
Romania	79.7	24.0	60.4	27.3	32.7	21.1	1.2	14.3	..	..	..	..
Russian Federation	..	41.3	..	23.4	..	10.6	..	7.8	..	24.7	..	36.2

5.4 Financial depth and efficiency

	Domestic credit provided by banking sector		Liquid liabilities		Quasi-liquid liabilities		Ratio of bank liquid reserves to bank assets		Interest rate spread		Spread over LIBOR	
	% of GDP		% of GDP		% of GDP		%		Lending minus deposit rate percentage points		Lending rate minus LIBOR percentage points	
	1990	1998	1990	1998	1990	1998	1990	1998	1990	1998	1990	1998
Rwanda	17.1	12.5	14.9	14.5	7.0	5.7	4.3	13.9	6.3	..	4.9	..
Saudi Arabia	14.4	*34.5*	47.9	58.5	21.9	29.4	5.6	3.5	..	..	..	..
Senegal	33.8	22.5	22.6	22.8	9.5	8.4	14.1	4.0	9.0	..	7.7	..
Sierra Leone	26.3	52.1	13.1	13.6	2.6	5.0	64.1	8.2	12.0	16.7	44.2	18.2
Singapore	62.2	86.4	93.1	113.9	70.1	94.6	3.7	2.5	2.7	2.8	–1.0	1.9
Slovak Republic	..	67.5	..	65.2	..	44.7	..	6.5	..	4.9	..	15.6
Slovenia	*36.8*	40.1	*34.2*	45.5	*25.8*	36.6	*2.7*	4.1	*142.0*	5.5	*818.6*	10.5
South Africa	97.8	140.0	53.8	56.9	36.4	27.9	3.3	2.6	2.1	5.3	12.7	16.2
Spain	110.8	114.6	..	..	..	..	8.7	2.6	5.4	2.1	7.7	–0.6
Sri Lanka	43.1	31.9	28.5	31.2	16.2	21.7	9.9	11.5	–6.4	–7.0	4.7	0.4
Sudan	20.4	6.8	20.1	9.6	2.9	3.5	79.5	28.1	..	..	..	..
Sweden	145.5	80.3	..	..	..	..	1.9	0.6	6.8	4.0	8.4	0.4
Switzerland	179.0	177.7	116.0	147.3	89.5	108.3	1.1	0.9	–0.9	3.4	–0.9	–1.5
Syrian Arab Republic	56.6	28.9	54.7	47.0	10.5	13.0	46.0	7.0	..	..	..	..
Tajikistan	..	..	..	..	..	..	..	..	..	..	..	..
Tanzania	39.2	13.3	22.6	20.1	7.1	9.4	5.3	13.8	..	18.9	..	21.1
Thailand	91.1	164.9	70.0	103.4	61.1	93.6	3.1	2.4	2.2	3.8	6.1	8.8
Togo	21.3	24.9	36.1	22.2	19.1	7.3	59.0	3.6	9.0	..	7.7	..
Trinidad and Tobago	58.5	53.2	44.9	50.4	32.9	38.6	13.5	16.2	6.9	9.4	4.6	11.7
Tunisia	62.5	53.2	51.5	47.8	26.7	25.8	1.6	2.8	..	..	..	..
Turkey	25.9	36.6	23.9	39.7	16.2	34.9	16.3	10.2	..	..	..	..
Turkmenistan	..	..	..	..	..	..	..	35.7	..	..	..	..
Uganda	*17.8*	7.1	7.6	12.5	1.4	4.3	17.9	15.0	7.4	9.5	30.4	15.3
Ukraine	*83.2*	24.3	*50.1*	14.8	*9.0*	4.8	*49.0*	10.4	..	32.2	..	48.9
United Arab Emirates	34.7	58.9	46.3	56.9	37.7	40.9	4.4	6.1	..	..	..	..
United Kingdom	123.0	129.5	..	..	..	..	0.5	0.4	2.2	2.7	6.4	1.6
United States	114.6	162.2	67.8	64.2	51.2	48.1	2.3	1.4	..	..	1.7	2.8
Uruguay	60.1	40.0	64.5	44.3	57.2	38.9	31.1	12.1	76.6	42.8	166.1	52.3
Uzbekistan	..	..	..	..	..	..	..	..	..	..	..	..
Venezuela, RB	37.4	18.1	32.3	19.0	20.6	9.1	21.9	32.4	7.7	11.5	27.2	40.8
Vietnam	*15.9*	*21.3*	*22.7*	*22.6*	*9.3*	*9.8*	*13.3*	*12.1*	..	*5.3*	..	*9.4*
West Bank and Gaza	..	..	..	..	..	..	..	..	..	..	..	..
Yemen, Rep.	62.0	35.7	56.3	44.9	10.7	20.4	121.2	24.2	..	..	..	..
Yugoslavia, FR (Serb./Mont.)	..	..	..	..	..	..	..	..	..	..	..	..
Zambia	67.8	63.5	21.8	17.5	10.6	10.9	33.7	12.0	9.5	18.7	26.8	26.2
Zimbabwe	41.7	64.6	23.1	25.5	11.7	6.1	12.2	11.5	2.9	13.0	3.4	36.5
World	**125.1 w**	**123.2 w**	**71.0 w**	**75.2 w**	**51.9 w**	**52.5 w**	**9.9 m**	**9.2 m**				
Low income	59.8	83.5	50.8	90.8	28.1	55.1	12.8	12.4				
Excl. China & India	37.7	36.9	30.5	35.8	15.8	22.6	12.7	12.3				
Middle income	57.6	56.1	36.5	41.4	23.1	29.8	12.6	8.5				
Lower middle income	..	63.8	..	44.0	..	27.9	19.7	9.7				
Upper middle income	54.1	52.1	29.8	40.1	19.9	30.8	8.1	7.9				
Low & middle income	58.2	64.7	40.8	56.4	24.6	37.5	12.8	10.8				
East Asia & Pacific	71.0	110.5	58.8	106.7	37.6	70.6	5.9	8.7				
Europe & Central Asia	..	37.6	..	33.0	..	22.1	..	10.4				
Latin America & Carib.	58.6	43.7	23.6	30.5	15.9	23.0	22.5	19.5				
Middle East & N. Africa	54.2	65.2	58.6	60.9	27.3	35.1	14.2	10.1				
South Asia	48.3	44.2	40.0	46.0	24.4	30.3	12.7	11.5				
Sub-Saharan Africa	56.4	70.9	34.8	36.7	19.7	17.8	11.6	10.1				
High income	140.0	140.2	81.1	..	61.0	..	1.9	1.4				
Europe EMU	98.9	*117.9*	..	..	..	..	3.7	2.2				

Financial depth and efficiency 5.4

About the data

Households and institutions save and invest independently. The financial system's role is to intermediate between them and to cycle available funds to where they are needed. Savers accumulate claims on financial institutions, which pass these funds to their final users. As an economy develops, this indirect lending by savers to investors becomes more efficient and gradually increases financial assets relative to GDP. This wealth allows increased saving and investment, facilitating and enhancing economic growth. As more specialized savings and financial institutions emerge, more financing instruments become available, spreading risks and reducing costs to liability holders. As securities markets mature, savers can invest their resources directly in financial assets issued by firms.

The ratio of domestic credit provided by the banking sector to GDP is used to measure the growth of the banking system because it reflects the extent to which savings are financial. Liquid liabilities include bank deposits of generally less than one year plus currency. Their ratio to GDP indicates the relative size of these readily available forms of money that the owners can use to buy goods and services without incurring any cost. Quasi-liquid liabilities are long-term deposits and assets—such as certificates of deposit, commercial paper, and bonds—that can be converted into currency or demand deposits, but at a cost. The ratio of bank liquid reserves to bank assets captures the banking system's liquidity. In countries whose banking system is liquid, adverse macroeconomic conditions should be less likely to lead to banking and financial crises. Data on domestic credit and liquid and quasi-liquid liabilities are cited on an end-of-year basis.

No less important than the size and structure of the financial sector is its efficiency, as indicated by the margin between the cost of mobilizing liabilities and the earnings on assets—or the interest spread. Narrowing of the interest spread reduces transactions costs, which lowers the overall cost of investment and is therefore crucial to economic growth. Interest rates reflect the responsiveness of financial institutions to competition and price incentives. The interest rate spread, also known as the intermediation margin, is a summary measure of a banking system's efficiency. To the extent that information about interest rates is inaccurate, banks do not monitor all bank managers, or the government sets deposit and lending rates, the interest rate spread may not be a reliable measure of efficiency. The spread over LIBOR reflects the differential between a country's lending rate and the London interbank offered rate (ignoring expected changes in the exchange rate). Interest rates are expressed as annual averages.

In some countries financial markets are distorted by restrictions on foreign investment, selective credit controls, and controls on deposit and lending rates. Interest rates may reflect the diversion of resources to finance the public sector deficit through statutory reserve requirements and direct borrowing from the banking system. And where state-owned banks dominate the financial sector, noncommercial considerations may unduly influence credit allocation. The indicators in the table provide quantitative assessments of each country's financial sector, but qualitative assessments of policies, laws, and regulations are needed to analyze overall financial conditions. Recent events in East Asia highlight the risks of weak financial intermediation, poor corporate governance, and deficient government policies, including procyclical macroeconomic policy responses to large capital inflows.

The accuracy of financial data depends on the quality of accounting systems, which are weak in some developing economies. Some of the indicators in the table are highly correlated, particularly the ratios of domestic credit, liquid liabilities, and quasi-liquid liabilities to GDP, because changes in liquid and quasi-liquid liabilities flow directly from changes in domestic credit. Moreover, the precise definition of the financial aggregates presented varies by country.

The indicators reported here do not capture the activities of the informal sector, which remains an important source of finance in developing economies. Personal credit or credit extended through community-based pooling of assets may be the only source of credit available to small farmers, small businesses, or home-based producers. And in financially repressed economies the rationing of formal credit forces many borrowers and lenders to turn to the informal market, which is very expensive, or to self-financing and family savings.

Definitions

• **Domestic credit provided by banking sector** includes all credit to various sectors on a gross basis, with the exception of credit to the central government, which is net. The banking sector includes monetary authorities, deposit money banks, and other banking institutions for which data are available (including institutions that do not accept transferable deposits but do incur such liabilities as time and savings deposits). Examples of other banking institutions include savings and mortgage loan institutions and building and loan associations. • **Liquid liabilities** are also known as broad money, or M3. They are the sum of currency and deposits in the central bank (M0), plus transferable deposits and electronic currency (M1), plus time and savings deposits, foreign currency transferable deposits, certificates of deposit, and securities repurchase agreements (M2), plus travelers checks, foreign currency time deposits, commercial paper, and shares of mutual funds or market funds held by residents. • **Quasi-liquid liabilities** are the M3 money supply less M1. • **Ratio of bank liquid reserves to bank assets** is the ratio of domestic currency holdings and deposits with the monetary authorities to claims on other governments, nonfinancial public enterprises, the private sector, and other banking institutions. • **Interest rate spread** is the interest rate charged by banks on loans to prime customers minus the interest rate paid by commercial or similar banks for demand, time, or savings deposits. • **Spread over LIBOR** (London interbank offered rate) is the interest rate charged by banks on short-term loans in local currency to prime customers minus LIBOR. LIBOR is the most commonly recognized international interest rate and is quoted in several currencies. The average three-month LIBOR on U.S. dollar deposits is used here.

Data sources

The data on credit, liabilities, bank reserves, and interest rates are collected from central banks and finance ministries and reported in the print and electronic versions of the International Monetary Fund's *International Financial Statistics*.

5.5 Tax policies

	Tax revenue	Taxes on income, profits, and capital gains		Domestic taxes on goods and services		Export duties		Import duties		Highest marginal tax rate[a]		
										Individual		Corporate
	% of GDP	% of total taxes		% of value added in industry and services		% of exports		% of imports		rate %	on income over $	rate %
	1998	1980	1998	1980	1998	1980	1998	1980	1998	1999	1999	1999
Albania	14.8	..	9.4	..	16.9	..	0.0	..	10.8	..	..	..
Algeria	*30.7*	..	*71.6*	..	*4.1*	..	..	..	..	..	..	..
Angola	..	..	..	..	..	..	..	..	..	..	..	..
Argentina	*12.4*	..	*14.9*	2.8	*6.3*	0.0	*0.5*	0.0	*9.2*	35	200,000	35
Armenia	..	..	..	..	..	..	..	..	..	..	..	..
Australia	22.7	67.6	72.8	5.4	*5.4*	0.5	0.0	8.5	3.7	47	30,579	36
Austria	*34.8*	22.8	*25.7*	9.1	*9.5*	0.2	*0.0*	1.6	*0.4*	50	59,590	34
Azerbaijan	18.2	..	22.2	..	9.2	..	0.0	..	4.2	40	3,704	30
Bangladesh	..	14.8	..	3.4	..	3.9	..	16.4	..	..	..	..
Belarus	28.7	..	11.1	..	16.8	..	*0.0*	..	*3.9*	..	..	..
Belgium	*43.3*	40.2	*36.8*	10.6	*11.6*	0.0	*0.0*	0.0	*0.0*	55	69,993	39
Benin	..	..	..	..	..	2.2	..	..	..	..	..	..
Bolivia	15.1	..	8.7	..	10.2	..	0.0	..	5.7	13	..	25
Bosnia and Herzegovina	..	..	..	..	..	..	..	..	..	..	..	..
Botswana	*14.7*	45.5	*51.3*	0.2	*1.7*	0.1	*0.0*	21.8	*18.4*	30	17,960	15
Brazil	..	13.6	..	9.0	..	0.0	..	16.5	..	28	17,881	15
Bulgaria	27.0	..	19.0	..	14.4	..	0.0	..	5.3	40	9,403	27
Burkina Faso	..	20.1	..	2.9	..	3.6	..	20.7	..	..	..	..
Burundi	*12.7*	20.4	*24.1*	10.1	*14.5*	..	*2.3*	..	*18.9*	..	..	..
Cambodia	..	..	..	..	..	..	..	..	..	20	39,915	20
Cameroon	..	23.7	..	4.7	..	7.1	..	21.3	..	60	13,321	39
Canada	..	60.8	..	3.5	..	1.1	..	4.6	..	29	38,604	38
Central African Republic	..	*17.7*	..	*6.0*	..	*9.2*	..	*23.9*	..	..	..	..
Chad	..	..	..	..	..	..	..	..	..	..	..	..
Chile	18.4	22.0	22.2	12.4	11.0	0.0	..	7.0	..	45	6,526	15
China	*5.7*	..	*9.6*	..	*5.4*	..	*0.0*	..	*2.8*	45	12,079	30
Hong Kong, China	..	..	..	..	..	..	..	..	..	17	13,583	16
Colombia	10.1	28.9	41.2	3.0	5.5	7.2	0.0	12.3	8.2	35	32,221	35
Congo, Dem. Rep.	*4.3*	34.5	*31.0*	1.6	*2.3*	10.7	..	18.3	..	50	13,167	..
Congo, Rep.	*6.7*	63.8	*37.9*	3.1	*1.5*	0.1	*0.0*	14.0	*7.5*	50	14,210	45
Costa Rica	*23.1*	14.6	*12.1*	6.6	*12.4*	6.6	*0.5*	7.0	*4.2*	25	14,185	30
Côte d'Ivoire	20.8	14.0	21.3	7.6	4.9	8.0	5.9	28.9	26.1	10	4,263	35
Croatia	43.3	..	12.3	..	27.8	..	0.0	..	7.6	35	5,556	..
Cuba	..	..	..	..	..	..	..	..	..	..	..	..
Czech Republic	31.6	..	15.2	..	11.4	..	0.0	..	1.5	40	36,979	35
Denmark	..	40.6	..	20.3	..	*0.0*	..	*0.1*	..	59	..	32
Dominican Republic	*15.5*	24.8	*18.0*	3.8	*6.6*	6.2	*0.0*	15.0	*12.9*	25	14,309	25
Ecuador	..	46.6	..	2.5	..	3.0	..	16.3	..	0	..	0
Egypt, Arab Rep.	*16.6*	24.8	*34.4*	8.5	*5.9*	0.0	*0.0*	26.3	*17.8*	32	14,706	40
El Salvador	..	..	..	..	..	..	..	..	..	30	22,857	25
Eritrea	..	..	..	..	..	..	..	..	..	..	..	..
Estonia	29.9	..	21.3	..	15.3	..	0.0	..	0.0	26	..	26
Ethiopia	..	24.7	..	*9.2*	..	35.1	..	16.4	..	..	..	..
Finland	*28.1*	30.9	*33.8*	16.5	*16.8*	0.0	*0.0*	1.9	*0.0*	38	61,164	28
France	*39.2*	19.1	*20.9*	12.8	*12.2*	0.0	*0.0*	0.1	*0.0*	..	..	33
Gabon	..	60.2	..	1.8	..	1.7	..	38.3	..	55	2,290	40
Gambia, The	..	18.1	..	1.2	..	12.5	..	21.8	..	..	..	..
Georgia	4.6	..	18.1	..	4.1	..	0.0	..	3.6	..	..	..
Germany	26.5	19.4	*17.0*	..	..	0.0	*0.0*	0.0	*0.0*	53	66,690	30
Ghana	..	22.0	..	4.6	..	30.5	..	14.5	..	35	7,102	35
Greece	*20.6*	19.5	*36.6*	10.2	..	0.0	*0.0*	6.3	*0.1*	45	56,271	35
Guatemala	..	12.4	..	3.9	..	9.9	..	7.6	..	25	26,740	28
Guinea	10.0	..	10.5	..	0.8	..	0.1	..	25.9	..	..	..
Guinea-Bissau	..	..	..	..	..	..	..	..	..	..	..	..
Haiti	..	15.9	..	..	..	10.2	..	12.3	..	..	..	..
Honduras	..	32.9	..	5.1	..	7.5	..	7.8	..	30	75,758	15

Tax policies 5.5

	Tax revenue	Taxes on income, profits, and capital gains		Domestic taxes on goods and services		Export duties		Import duties		Highest marginal tax rate[a]		
	% of GDP	% of total taxes		% of value added in industry and services		% of exports		% of imports		Individual rate %	Individual on income over $	Corporate rate %
	1998	1980	1998	1980	1998	1980	1998	1980	1998	1999	1999	1999
Hungary	31.4	*22.1*	21.6	*28.2*	*15.1*	*0.1*	0.0	*7.5*	2.7	40	4,566	18
India	8.6	21.9	31.0	8.1	5.1	1.8	0.1	26.4	24.2	30	3,538	35
Indonesia	15.6	82.0	65.9	2.4	5.2	*0.9*	0.9	*5.1*	0.7	30	6,623	30
Iran, Islamic Rep.	11.2	12.2	28.5	1.0	*1.9*	0.0	0.0	20.9	27.0	54	174,171	54
Iraq	..	..	..	..	..	..	..	..	..	..	..	..
Ireland	*31.6*	38.6	*42.9*	..	..	0.0	*0.0*	6.2	*0.0*	46	14,799	32
Israel	36.4	47.3	42.4	..	..	0.0	0.0	4.5	0.7	50	57,789	36
Italy	38.6	32.1	32.4	8.2	*11.1*	0.0	0.0	0.1	0.0	46	81,665	37
Jamaica	..	35.1	..	15.6	..	0.0	..	2.3	..	25	2,712	33
Japan	..	74.7	..	2.5	..	0.0	..	2.3	..	50	259,291	35
Jordan	*19.8*	17.0	*15.3*	1.6	*10.0*	0.0	*0.0*	21.2	*10.8*	..	..	..
Kazakhstan	..	..	..	..	..	..	..	..	..	30	..	30
Kenya	*23.5*	33.3	*38.9*	14.8	*16.9*	1.3	*0.0*	11.8	*14.3*	33	382	33
Korea, Dem. Rep.	..	..	..	..	..	..	..	..	..	..	..	..
Korea, Rep.	*17.3*	25.5	*31.0*	9.5	7.1	0.0	*0.0*	7.6	*4.3*	40	66,236	28
Kuwait	1.5	63.6	24.6	0.2	..	0.0	0.0	3.0	3.5	0	..	0
Kyrgyz Republic	..	..	..	..	..	..	..	..	..	..	..	30
Lao PDR	..	..	..	..	..	..	..	..	..	40	1,064	..
Latvia	28.0	..	14.6	..	15.8	..	0.0	..	1.1	25	..	25
Lebanon	12.7	..	12.1	..	1.9	..	..	..	15.9	..	..	..
Lesotho	38.7	*15.6*	23.2	*5.4*	8.0	6.2	..	21.6	..	..	..	..
Libya	..	..	..	..	..	..	..	..	..	..	..	..
Lithuania	25.4	..	14.7	..	16.7	..	0.0	..	1.1	33	..	29
Macedonia, FYR	..	..	..	..	..	..	..	..	..	..	..	..
Madagascar	*8.5*	17.1	*18.8*	8.4	*3.3*	3.0	*0.9*	17.6	*28.6*	..	..	..
Malawi	..	38.9	..	11.7	..	0.0	..	16.8	..	38	948	38
Malaysia	*18.9*	41.9	*44.4*	5.7	*6.9*	9.1	*0.5*	9.0	*3.4*	30	39,474	28
Mali	..	20.5	..	7.8	..	3.0	..	8.0	..	..	..	..
Mauritania	..	..	..	..	..	..	..	..	..	..	..	..
Mauritius	17.7	17.3	14.2	4.8	8.0	8.6	0.0	16.2	12.7	30	2,220	15
Mexico	*13.0*	36.9	*34.9*	8.3	*9.2*	0.5	*0.0*	9.3	*2.1*	40	200,000	35
Moldova	..	..	..	..	..	..	..	..	..	..	..	..
Mongolia	13.5	..	16.1	..	9.7	..	0.2	..	0.2	..	..	..
Morocco	..	22.0	..	9.9	..	2.2	..	22.3	..	44	6,445	35
Mozambique	..	..	..	..	..	..	..	..	..	20	792	35
Myanmar	*4.5*	4.9	*31.3*	12.7	*5.6*	0.0	*0.0*	19.3	*59.9*	30	..	30
Namibia	..	..	..	..	..	..	..	..	..	40	16,129	40
Nepal	8.8	6.6	17.6	8.0	6.9	5.4	0.7	16.0	8.7	..	..	..
Netherlands	*42.7*	33.1	*26.6*	10.6	..	0.0	*0.0*	0.0	*0.0*	60	56,075	35
New Zealand	32.1	75.0	66.4	6.9	..	0.1	0.0	4.4	4.0	33	18,134	33
Nicaragua	..	8.9	..	0.0	..	3.9	..	8.1	..	30	18,083	30
Niger	..	28.1	..	4.6	..	2.6	..	17.0	..	..	..	..
Nigeria	..	..	..	..	..	..	..	..	..	25	1,395	28
Norway	*34.1*	30.3	*26.9*	15.2	*15.7*	0.1	*0.0*	0.8	*0.9*	28	6,835	28
Oman	6.4	92.4	63.7	0.2	..	0.0	*0.0*	1.4	*2.5*	0	..	12
Pakistan	12.6	16.8	28.6	8.6	6.2	2.0	0.0	25.8	16.2	..	..	..
Panama	*18.4*	29.0	*28.7*	5.2	..	0.5	*0.1*	3.0	..	30	200,000	30
Papua New Guinea	..	67.5	..	4.2	..	1.4	..	8.0	..	47	48,251	25
Paraguay	..	16.6	..	2.7	..	0.5	..	8.4	..	0	..	30
Peru	13.7	28.1	23.2	7.1	8.3	10.9	0.0	17.1	11.3	30	47,985	30
Philippines	*17.0*	23.6	*39.8*	7.8	*6.8*	1.0	*0.0*	13.4	*8.8*	33	12,773	33
Poland	32.7	..	27.6	..	*12.4*	..	0.0	..	3.9	40	15,192	34
Portugal	*32.1*	20.9	*29.5*	..	..	0.0	*0.0*	4.4	*0.0*	40	36,478	34
Puerto Rico	..	..	..	..	..	..	..	..	..	33	50,000	20
Romania	*24.4*	0.0	*32.8*	..	*9.6*	0.0	*0.0*	0.0	*5.1*	45	4,080	38
Russian Federation	..	..	..	..	..	..	..	..	..	35	6,036	35

5.5 Tax policies

	Tax revenue	Taxes on income, profits, and capital gains		Domestic taxes on goods and services		Export duties		Import duties		Highest marginal tax rate[a]		
										Individual		Corporate
	% of GDP	% of total taxes		% of value added in industry and services		% of exports		% of imports		rate %	on income over $	rate %
	1998	1980	1998	1980	1998	1980	1998	1980	1998	1999	1999	1999
Rwanda	..	20.7	..	5.3	..	21.3	..	17.7	..	..	..	..
Saudi Arabia	..	..	..	..	..	..	..	..	..	0	..	45
Senegal	..	21.4	..	7.8	..	2.8	..	26.9	..	50	22,469	35
Sierra Leone	*10.2*	25.0	*17.6*	4.1	*7.2*	10.1	..	17.2	..	..	..	..
Singapore	*16.1*	47.0	*41.7*	4.1	*4.7*	0.0	*0.0*	0.9	*0.2*	28	240,964	26
Slovak Republic	..	..	..	..	..	..	..	..	..	42	29,258	40
Slovenia	..	..	..	..	..	..	..	..	..	..	..	..
South Africa	24.6	64.1	59.5	6.2	10.2	0.1	0.0	3.0	0.3	45	20,391	30
Spain	*28.1*	25.2	*32.3*	..	..	0.0	*0.0*	6.0	*0.0*	40	77,139	35
Sri Lanka	14.5	16.4	13.9	8.0	12.7	22.0	0.0	9.6	8.2	35	4,405	35
Sudan	..	17.2	..	5.2	..	3.4	..	31.1	..	..	..	..
Sweden	35.8	21.1	16.6	11.7	..	0.0	0.0	1.5	0.1	31	27,198	28
Switzerland	*22.0*	15.1	*14.2*	..	..	0.0	*0.0*	4.0	*0.7*	..	..	45
Syrian Arab Republic	*16.4*	24.7	*44.5*	1.8	..	1.7	*9.1*	11.6	*35.6*	..	..	..
Tajikistan	..	..	..	..	..	..	..	..	..	..	..	..
Tanzania	..	35.2	..	..	..	9.7	..	9.2	..	35	12,335	30
Thailand	14.5	19.3	32.1	8.6	8.9	4.4	0.1	11.1	4.4	37	108,430	30
Togo	..	38.6	..	6.4	..	3.3	..	15.2	..	..	..	..
Trinidad and Tobago	..	85.7	..	1.6	..	0.0	..	9.8	..	35	7,937	35
Tunisia	*24.8*	19.2	*18.8*	8.7	*7.2*	1.1	*0.2*	20.6	*19.9*	..	..	..
Turkey	*19.1*	61.8	*41.2*	5.1	*12.5*	0.0	*0.0*	8.9	*2.0*	40	159,898	30
Turkmenistan	..	..	..	..	..	..	..	..	..	..	..	..
Uganda	..	11.8	..	4.6	..	55.7	..	15.8	..	30	3,578	30
Ukraine	..	..	..	..	..	..	..	..	..	40	5,953	30
United Arab Emirates	0.7	..	0.0	0.0	..	..	..	..	..	0	..	20
United Kingdom	36.4	43.4	41.1	11.5	*13.7*	0.0	0.0	0.1	0.0	40	46,589	31
United States	20.5	61.6	60.4	0.9	*0.7*	0.0	0.0	3.0	2.0	40	283,150	35
Uruguay	30.0	11.5	13.6	11.1	13.9	0.0	0.0	19.3	6.4	..	..	30
Uzbekistan	..	..	..	..	..	..	..	..	..	45	2,400	33
Venezuela, RB	12.8	79.4	30.9	1.0	7.2	0.0	0.0	9.6	12.6	34	78,500	34
Vietnam	15.8	..	23.3	..	8.1	..	*0.0*	..	*11.4*	50	5,695	32
West Bank and Gaza	..	..	..	..	..	..	..	..	..	..	..	..
Yemen, Rep.	15.2	..	48.7	..	3.8	..	0.0	..	10.2	..	..	..
Yugoslavia, FR (Serb./Mont.)	..	..	..	..	..	..	..	..	..	..	..	..
Zambia	..	41.1	..	12.5	..	0.0	..	7.2	..	30	742	35
Zimbabwe	*26.4*	57.9	*48.2*	6.7	*9.9*	0.0	..	4.3	..	50	20,455	35

a. These data are from PricewaterhouseCoopers's *Individual Taxes: Worldwide Summaries 1999-2000* and *Corporate Taxes: Worldwide Summaries 1999-2000*, copyright 1999 by PricewaterhouseCoopers by permission of John Wiley & Sons, Inc.

Tax policies 5.5

About the data

Taxes are compulsory, unrequited payments made to governments by individuals, businesses, or institutions. They are considered unrequited because governments provide nothing specifically in return for them, although taxes typically are used to provide goods or services to individuals or communities on a collective basis. The sources of the revenue received by governments and the relative contributions of these sources are determined by policy choices about where and how to impose taxes and by changes in the structure of the economy. Tax policy may reflect concerns about distributional effects, economic efficiency (including corrections for externalities), and the practical problems of administering a tax system. There is no ideal level of taxation. But taxes influence incentives and thus the behavior of economic actors and the country's competitiveness.

The level of taxation is typically measured by tax revenue as a share of GDP. Comparing levels of taxation across countries provides a quick overview of the fiscal obligations and incentives facing the private sector. In this table tax data measured in local currencies are normalized by scaling variables in the same units to ease cross-country comparisons. The table refers only to central government data, which may considerably understate the total tax burden, particularly in countries where provincial and municipal governments are large or have considerable tax authority.

Low ratios of tax collections to GDP may reflect weak administration and large-scale tax avoidance or evasion. They may also reflect the presence of a sizable parallel economy with unrecorded and undisclosed incomes. Tax collection ratios tend to rise with income, with higher-income countries relying on taxes to finance a much broader range of social services and social security than lower-income countries are able to provide.

As countries develop, they typically expand their capacity to tax residents directly, and indirect taxes become less important as a source of revenue. Thus the share of taxes on income, profits, and capital gains is one measure of a tax system's level of development. In the early stages of development governments tend to rely on indirect taxes because the administrative costs of collecting them are relatively low. The two main indirect taxes are international trade taxes (including customs revenues) and domestic taxes on goods and services. The table shows these domestic taxes as a percentage of value added in industry and services. Agriculture and mining are excluded from the denominator because indirect taxes on goods originating from these sectors are usually negligible. What is missing here is a measure of the uniformity of these taxes across industries and along the value added chain of production. Without such data no clear inferences can be drawn about how neutral a tax system is between subsectors. "Surplus" revenues raised by some governments by charging higher prices for goods produced under monopoly by state-owned enterprises are not counted as tax revenues. Similarly, losses from charging below-market prices for products are rarely identified as subsidies.

Export and import duties are shown separately because their burdens on the economy (and thus growth) are likely to be high. Export duties, typically levied on primary (particularly agricultural) products, often take the place of direct taxes on income and profits, but they reduce the incentive to export and encourage a shift to other products. High import duties penalize consumers, create protective barriers—which promote higher-priced output and inefficient production—and implicitly tax exports. By contrast, lower trade taxes enhance openness—to foreign competition, knowledge, technologies, and resources—energizing development in many ways. The economies growing fastest over the past 15 years have not relied on tax revenues from imports. Seeing this pattern, many developing countries have lowered tariffs over the past decade, and this trend is expected to continue. In some countries, such as members of the European Union, most customs duties are collected by a supranational authority; these revenues are not reported in the individual countries' accounts.

The tax revenues collected by governments are the outcomes of systems that are often complex, containing many exceptions, exemptions, penalties, and other inducements that affect tax incidence and thus influence the decisions of workers, managers, and entrepreneurs. A potentially important influence on both domestic and international investors is a tax system's progressivity, as reflected in the highest marginal tax rate on individual and corporate income. Figures for individual marginal tax rates generally refer to employment income. For some countries the highest marginal tax rate is also the basic or flat rate, and other surtaxes, deductions, and the like may apply.

Definitions

• **Tax revenue** comprises compulsory, unrequited, nonrepayable receipts collected by central governments for public purposes. It includes interest collected on tax arrears and penalties collected on nonpayment or late payment of taxes and is shown net of refunds and other corrective transactions. • **Taxes on income, profits, and capital gains** include taxes levied by central governments on the actual or presumptive net income of individuals and profits of enterprises. Also included are taxes on capital gains, whether realized or not, on the sale of land, securities, and other assets. Social security contributions based on gross pay, payroll, or number of employees are not included, but social security contributions based on personal income after deductions and personal exemptions are included. • **Domestic taxes on goods and services** include all taxes and duties levied by central governments on the production, extraction, sale, transfer, leasing, or delivery of goods and rendering of services, or on the use of goods or permission to use goods or perform activities. These include general sales taxes, turnover or value added taxes, excise taxes, and motor vehicle taxes. • **Export duties** include all levies collected on goods at the point of export. Rebates on exported goods—that is, repayments of previously paid general consumption taxes, excise taxes, or import duties—should be deducted from the gross receipts of the appropriate taxes, not from export duty receipts. • **Import duties** comprise all levies collected on goods at the point of entry into the country. They include levies for revenue purposes or import protection, whether on a specific or ad valorem basis, as long as they are restricted to imported products. • **Highest marginal tax rate** is the highest rate shown on the schedule of tax rates applied to the taxable income of individuals and corporations. Also presented are the income levels above which the highest marginal tax rates for individuals apply.

Data sources

The definitions used here are from the International Monetary Fund's (IMF) *Manual on Government Finance Statistics* (1986). The data on tax revenues are from print and electronic editions of the IMF's *Government Finance Statistics Yearbook*. The data on individual and corporate tax rates are from PricewaterhouseCoopers's *Individual Taxes: Worldwide Summaries* (1999b) and *Corporate Taxes: Worldwide Summaries* (1999a).

5.6 Relative prices and exchange rates

	Exchange rate arrangements		Official exchange rate	Ratio of official to parallel exchange rate	Real effective exchange rate	Purchasing power parity conversion factor		Interest rate			Food prices in PPP terms	
			local currency units to $		1995 = 100	local currency units to international $		Deposit %	Lending %	Real %	U.S. price = 100 Bread and cereals	Meat
	Classification 1998	Structure 1998	1998	1998	1998	1990	1998	1998	1998	1998	1998	1998
Albania	IF	U	150.6	0.9	..	1.9	49.2	*16.8*	*24.0*	*8.2*	42	92
Algeria	MF	U	58.7	0.4	115.1	4.9	19.4	..	..	..	..	..
Angola	P	U	392,823.5	0.7	..	0.0	134,824.4	36.9	45.0	–9.9		
Argentina	CB	U	1.0	1.0	..	0.3	0.7	7.6	10.6	12.9	92	136
Armenia	IF	U	504.9	..	111.5	0.0	121.9	24.9	48.5	33.5	55	106
Australia	IF	U	1.6	1.0	96.9	1.4	1.4	4.7	8.0	7.4	94	73
Austria	Euro	U	12.4	1.0	94.6	12.9	14.0	2.7	6.4	5.3	114	163
Azerbaijan	MF	U	3,869.0	..	..	0.1	926.1	..	..	..	47	108
Bangladesh	P	U	46.9	0.9	..	9.4	11.3	8.4	14.0	8.3	41	54
Belarus	MF	M	*25,964.1*	..	..	0.1	10,237.2	14.3	27.0	–27.1	..	..
Belgium	Euro	U	36.3	1.0	93.4	35.5	38.0	3.0	7.3	6.3	116	161
Benin	FF	U	590.0	..	..	157.0	263.8	3.5	..	..	55	89
Bolivia	P	U	5.5	1.0	114.9	1.3	2.6	12.8	39.4	29.4	54	87
Bosnia and Herzegovina	CB	U	..	..	..	..	..	..	..	..	..	..
Botswana	P	D	4.2	1.0	..	1.1	2.2	8.7	13.5	5.2	49	65
Brazil	IF	U	1.2	1.0	..	0.0	0.8	28.0	..	..	93	138
Bulgaria	CB	U	1,760.4	1.0	122.7	1.0	543.4	3.0	13.3	–7.3	180	391
Burkina Faso	FF	U	590.0	..	..	125.6	163.1	3.5	..	..	..	..
Burundi	P	U	447.8	0.8	111.8	50.0	106.3	..	..	..	..	..
Cambodia	MF	D	3,744.4	0.9	..	68.0	743.8	7.8	18.3	1.2	..	..
Cameroon	FF	U	590.0	..	103.8	187.8	248.5	5.0	22.0	20.6	58	86
Canada	IF	U	1.5	1.0	98.6	1.2	1.2	5.0	6.6	7.2	68	78
Central African Republic	FF	U	590.0	1.0	96.4	129.9	160.2	5.0	22.0	19.9	..	..
Chad	FF	U	590.0	..	..	109.7	160.2	5.0	22.0	17.2	..	..
Chile	P	D	460.3	0.9	111.1	146.7	269.7	14.9	20.2	14.3	91	147
China	P	U	8.3	1.0	112.4	1.2	2.1	3.8	6.4	7.5	93	175
Hong Kong, China	CB	U	7.7	1.0	..	6.4	9.3	6.6	9.0	7.8	..	..
Colombia	P	U	1,426.0	0.9	112.5	119.7	599.0	32.6	42.2	21.0	..	..
Congo, Dem. Rep.	IF	U	..	..	126.8	0.0	22,675.9	..	..	..	..	..
Congo, Rep.	FF	U	590.0	..	..	340.9	417.9	5.0	22.0	46.8	112	164
Costa Rica	P	U	257.2	1.0	104.9	37.9	127.7	12.8	22.5	9.1	..	..
Côte d'Ivoire	FF	U	590.0	..	105.6	180.2	280.3	3.5	..	..	68	102
Croatia	P	U	6.4	0.7	105.3	0.0	4.6	4.6	15.8	6.2	98	173
Cuba	..	..	..	..	..	..	..	..	..	..	..	..
Czech Republic	MF	U	32.3	1.0	116.3	4.9	14.3	8.1	12.8	1.7	40	78
Denmark	P	U	6.7	1.0	98.3	8.9	9.1	3.1	7.9	6.4	156	210
Dominican Republic	MF	D	15.3	1.0	105.4	2.7	6.4	17.6	25.6	19.8	..	..
Ecuador	IF	U	5,446.6	0.9	107.7	304.7	2,734.7	39.4	49.5	18.9	69	131
Egypt, Arab Rep.	P	M	3.4	1.0	..	0.8	1.5	9.4	13.0	9.1	40	74
El Salvador	P	U	8.8	0.9	..	2.5	4.3	10.3	15.0	12.1	..	..
Eritrea	IF	U	..	..	..	..	1.5	..	..	..	..	..
Estonia	CB	U	14.1	0.8	..	0.1	6.6	8.1	16.7	6.6	47	80
Ethiopia	MF	U	7.1	1.0	..	0.7	1.3	6.0	10.5	0.7	..	..
Finland	Euro	U	5.3	1.0	93.1	6.0	6.1	2.0	5.3	3.9	147	156
France	Euro	U	5.9	1.0	96.0	6.6	6.8	3.2	6.6	6.3	125	157
Gabon	FF	U	590.0	..	100.7	315.7	373.7	5.0	22.0	33.5	111	148
Gambia, The	IF	U	10.6	1.0	102.0	2.0	2.5	12.5	25.4	23.2	..	..
Georgia	IF	U	1.4	..	135.7	0.0	0.4	17.0	46.0	41.2	46	101
Germany	Euro	U	1.8	1.0	92.5	..	2.1	2.9	9.0	8.1	145	187
Ghana	IF	U	2,314.1	1.0	125.2	92.7	542.0	32.0	..	..	..	..
Greece	P	U	295.5	1.0	102.5	117.1	243.3	10.7	18.6	12.7	104	102
Guatemala	IF	U	6.4	1.0	..	1.4	3.2	5.4	16.6	9.2	..	..
Guinea	IF	U	1,236.8	1.0	..	228.5	370.6	..	..	..	44	71
Guinea-Bissau	FF	U	590.0	..	..	12.0	169.7	*4.6*	*51.8*	*2.1*	..	..
Haiti	IF	U	16.8	0.7	..	1.4	6.2	13.1	23.6	9.7	..	..
Honduras	P	D	13.4	1.0	..	1.3	4.8	18.6	30.7	15.0	..	..

Relative prices and exchange rates 5.6

	Exchange rate arrangements		Official exchange rate	Ratio of official to parallel exchange rate	Real effective exchange rate	Purchasing power parity conversion factor		Interest rate			Food prices in PPP terms	
			local currency units to $		1995 = 100	local currency units to international $		Deposit %	Lending %	Real %	U.S. price = 100 Bread and cereals	Meat
	Classification 1998	Structure 1998	1998	1998	1998	1990	1998	1998	1998	1998	1998	1998
Hungary	P	U	214.4	1.0	105.8	22.4	99.0	*18.5*	*21.8*	*2.8*	52	73
India	IF	U	41.3	1.0	..	4.9	8.9	..	13.5	4.3	..	..
Indonesia	IF	D	10,013.6	0.9	..	636.7	1,745.9	39.1	32.2	–23.6	41	94
Iran, Islamic Rep.	P	M	1,751.9	0.4	206.1	177.4	1,040.3	..	..	..	79	151
Iraq	P	U	0.3	0.0	..	..	..	..	..	..	..	..
Ireland	Euro	U	0.7	1.0	97.0	0.7	0.7	0.4	6.2	3.7	80	103
Israel	P	U	3.8	1.0	109.9	1.7	3.6	11.0	16.2	10.2	143	184
Italy	Euro	U	1,736.2	1.0	113.2	1,359.6	1,716.3	3.2	7.9	4.9	101	135
Jamaica	MF	U	36.5	0.9	..	4.0	26.5	15.6	34.7	28.3	86	175
Japan	IF	U	130.9	1.0	78.9	182.6	168.4	0.3	2.3	2.0	231	398
Jordan	P	U	0.7	1.0	..	0.4	0.3	*9.1*	*12.3*	*8.3*	60	85
Kazakhstan	MF	U	78.3	*0.9*	..	0.0	25.2	..	..	..	38	57
Kenya	MF	U	60.4	0.9	..	8.9	24.4	18.4	29.5	17.1	50	77
Korea, Dem. Rep.	..	..	..	..	..	..	..	..	..	..	..	..
Korea, Rep.	IF	U	1,401.4	*1.0*	..	485.2	718.3	13.3	15.3	9.5	201	319
Kuwait	P	U	0.3	1.0	..	..	..	6.3	8.9	..	..	..
Kyrgyz Republic	MF	U	20.8	..	..	0.0	3.3	35.8	73.4	55.6	47	79
Lao PDR	MF	D	3,298.3	0.9	..	133.1	482.2	17.8	29.3	–29.7	..	..
Latvia	P	U	0.6	0.9	..	0.0	0.3	5.3	14.3	2.7	51	99
Lebanon	P	U	1,516.1	1.0	..	270.5	1,434.0	13.6	*20.3*	*10.9*	93	106
Lesotho	P	U	5.5	1.0	85.2	0.9	1.3	10.7	20.1	15.8	..	..
Libya	P	U	0.4	0.2	..	..	..	..	..	..	..	..
Lithuania	CB	U	4.0	0.9	..	*0.0*	1.8	6.0	12.2	5.3	39	82
Macedonia, FYR	P	U	54.5	0.8	72.3	..	22.6	11.7	21.0	19.8	74	110
Madagascar	IF	U	5,441.4	1.0	..	505.1	1,849.4	8.0	27.0	16.8	49	67
Malawi	MF	U	31.1	0.9	111.2	1.2	9.5	19.1	37.7	11.8	51	67
Malaysia	P	U	3.9	1.0	80.9	1.2	1.6	8.5	10.6	1.4	..	..
Mali	FF	U	590.0	..	..	137.5	220.7	3.5	..	..	55	80
Mauritania	MF	U	188.5	1.0	..	35.5	47.5	..	..	..	..	..
Mauritius	IF	U	24.0	1.0	..	6.8	9.9	9.3	19.9	13.6	65	113
Mexico	IF	U	9.1	1.0	..	1.4	5.1	13.8	28.7	12.9	52	63
Moldova	IF	U	5.4	..	106.9	..	1.0	21.7	30.8	21.1	37	75
Mongolia	IF	U	840.8	1.0	..	2.8	220.0	24.3	40.0	25.6	36	40
Morocco	P	U	9.6	1.0	105.1	3.2	3.7	..	..	..	68	133
Mozambique	IF	U	11,874.6	0.9	..	309.9	3,478.9	..	..	..	..	..
Myanmar	P	D	6.3	..	..	..	..	12.5	16.5	–13.0	..	..
Namibia	P	U	5.5	1.0	..	1.1	2.0	12.9	20.7	8.3	..	..
Nepal	P	U	66.0	0.9	..	6.4	11.2	8.9	14.0	10.4	33	68
Netherlands	Euro	U	2.0	1.0	94.5	2.0	2.2	3.1	6.5	3.5	106	176
New Zealand	IF	U	1.9	1.0	94.4	1.5	1.5	6.8	11.2	9.8	97	95
Nicaragua	P	U	10.6	1.0	103.6	0.1	2.2	10.8	21.6	7.7	..	..
Niger	FF	U	590.0	..	..	121.5	161.1	3.5	..	..	..	..
Nigeria	MF	U	21.9	0.2	155.7	3.9	37.9	*7.3*	*20.4*	*8.9*	249	351
Norway	MF	U	7.5	1.0	98.2	9.3	9.4	7.2	7.9	8.5	159	235
Oman	P	U	0.4	1.0	..	..	..	8.5	10.1	..	70	98
Pakistan	MF	M	44.5	0.9	98.1	6.0	12.1	..	..	..	34	60
Panama	Other	U	1.0	..	..	0.6	0.6	6.8	10.8	9.3	62	126
Papua New Guinea	IF	U	2.1	0.6	92.4	0.5	0.7	13.7	17.7	6.7	..	..
Paraguay	MF	U	2,755.7	0.9	99.4	395.9	1,060.1	15.9	30.0	14.2	..	..
Peru	IF	U	2.9	1.0	..	0.1	1.7	15.1	30.8	23.9	85	158
Philippines	IF	U	40.9	1.0	88.8	5.6	10.0	12.1	16.8	5.7	46	89
Poland	P	U	3.5	1.0	117.7	0.3	1.9	18.2	24.5	11.1	50	73
Portugal	Euro	U	180.1	1.0	99.3	91.5	131.1	3.4	7.2	3.0	85	116
Puerto Rico	..	..	..	..	..	..	..	..	..	..	..	..
Romania	MF	U	8,875.6	0.9	..	6.1	2,664.8	..	..	..	29	61
Russian Federation	MF	M	9.7	0.7	114.2	0.0	2.8	17.0	41.8	27.1	52	77

5.6 Relative prices and exchange rates

	Exchange rate arrangements		Official exchange rate	Ratio of official to parallel exchange rate	Real effective exchange rate	Purchasing power parity conversion factor		Interest rate			Food prices in PPP terms	
			local currency units to $		1995 = 100	local currency units to international $		Deposit %	Lending %	Real %	U.S. price = 100 Bread and cereals	Meat
	Classification 1998	Structure 1998	1998	1998	1998	1990	1998	1998	1998	1998	1998	1998
Rwanda	IF	U	312.3	0.5	..	..	..	8.5	..	..	..	..
Saudi Arabia	P	U	3.7	1.0	111.3	2.5	2.3	6.2	..	..	..	..
Senegal	FF	U	590.0	..	..	184.9	233.9	3.5	..	..	65	113
Sierra Leone	IF	U	1,563.6	0.8	99.5	44.9	464.5	7.1	23.8	–2.5	54	72
Singapore	MF	U	1.7	1.0	101.8	1.8	1.8	4.6	7.4	9.1	81	141
Slovak Republic	MF	U	35.2	0.9	102.3	6.1	13.7	16.3	21.2	15.3	49	84
Slovenia	MF	U	166.1	0.9	..	..	114.5	10.5	16.1	8.1	71	117
South Africa	IF	U	5.5	1.0	89.4	1.0	2.1	16.5	21.8	12.9	..	..
Spain	Euro	U	149.4	1.0	97.4	103.8	129.5	2.9	5.0	2.7	89	91
Sri Lanka	P	U	64.6	1.0	..	9.4	18.1	13.0	6.0	–2.6	39	68
Sudan	IF	U	2,008.0	..	..	7.4	543.6	..	..	..	..	..
Sweden	IF	U	7.9	1.0	100.1	9.1	9.9	1.9	5.9	5.3	151	179
Switzerland	IF	U	1.4	1.0	91.1	2.0	2.1	0.7	4.1	3.0	162	274
Syrian Arab Republic	P	M	11.2	0.2	..	9.3	18.8	..	..	..	314	298
Tajikistan	MF	U	776.6	..	..	0.0	161.0	..	..	..	30	40
Tanzania	IF	U	664.7	0.9	..	65.7	331.4	7.8	26.7	8.0	54	74
Thailand	IF	U	41.4	1.0	..	10.3	13.8	10.6	14.4	5.2	61	105
Togo	FF	U	590.0	..	109.4	91.7	145.6	3.5	..	..	..	..
Trinidad and Tobago	IF	U	6.3	1.0	106.0	3.0	4.2	8.0	17.3	10.0	62	106
Tunisia	P	U	1.1	1.0	100.5	0.3	0.4	..	..	..	66	115
Turkey	P	U	260,724.3	..	..	1,501.8	126,696.2	80.1	..	..	52	87
Turkmenistan	P	U	5,277.0	..	..	0.0	935.3	..	..	..	13	32
Uganda	IF	U	1,240.3	0.9	94.6	117.2	347.1	11.4	20.9	9.1	..	..
Ukraine	P	U	2.4	0.9	130.3	0.0	0.6	22.3	54.5	36.5	27	68
United Arab Emirates	P	U	3.7	..	..	3.4	3.6	..	..	..	..	..
United Kingdom	IF	U	0.6	1.0	128.1	0.6	0.7	4.5	7.2	4.6	90	128
United States	IF	U	1.0	..	120.0	1.0	1.0	..	8.4	7.3	100	100
Uruguay	P	U	10.5	1.0	108.8	0.5	7.7	15.1	57.9	42.6	94	113
Uzbekistan	MF	M	..	..	..	..	27.5	..	..	..	..	..
Venezuela, RB	P	U	547.6	1.0	135.5	23.3	385.4	34.8	46.4	20.7	58	95
Vietnam	MF	U	*11,359.4*	*1.0*	..	*481.7*	2,797.4	*9.9*	*15.2*	*2.7*	25	54
West Bank and Gaza	..	..	..	..	..	..	..	..	..	..	..	..
Yemen, Rep.	IF	U	135.9	1.0	..	15.7	61.5	..	..	..	111	208
Yugoslavia, FR (Serb./Mont.)	..	..	..	..	..	..	..	..	..	..	..	..
Zambia	IF	M	1,862.1	0.8	114.5	19.8	897.5	13.1	31.8	7.0	71	95
Zimbabwe	IF	U	23.7	..	..	0.9	4.3	29.1	42.1	9.5	42	56

Note: Exchange rate arrangements are given for the end of the year in 1998. Exchange rate classifications include independent floating (IF), managed floating (MF), pegged (P), currency board (CB), and several exchange arrangements (euro means that the euro is used, FF that the currency is pegged to the French franc, and other that the currency of another country is used as legal tender). Exchange rate structures include dual exchange rates (D), multiple exchange rates (M), and unitary rate (U).

Relative prices and exchange rates 5.6

About the data

In a market-based economy the choices households, producers, and governments make about the allocation of resources are influenced by relative prices, including the real exchange rate, real wages, real interest rates, and commodity prices. Relative prices also reflect, to a large extent, the choices of these agents. Thus relative prices convey vital information about the interaction of economic agents in an economy and with the rest of the world.

The exchange rate is the price of one currency in terms of another. Official exchange rates and exchange rate arrangements are established by governments (other exchange rates fully recognized by governments include market rates, which are determined largely by legal market forces, and, for countries maintaining multiple exchange arrangements, principal rates, secondary rates, and tertiary rates). Parallel, or black market, exchange rates reflect unofficial rates negotiated by traders and are by nature difficult to measure. Parallel exchange rate markets often account for only a small share of transactions and so may be both thin and volatile. But in countries with weak policies and financial systems they often represent the "going" rate. The parallel rates used here are collected by Currency Data & Intelligence from a variety of sources, some within the country and some outside but doing business with entities based in the country.

Real effective exchange rates are derived by deflating a trade-weighted average of the nominal exchange rates that apply between trading partners. For most industrial countries the weights are based on trade in manufactured goods with other industrial countries during 1989–91, and an index of relative, normalized unit labor costs is used as the deflator. (Normalization smooths a time series by removing short-term fluctuations while retaining changes of a large amplitude over the longer economic cycle.) For other countries, prior to 1990, the weights take into account trade in manufactured and primary products during 1980–82; from January 1990 onward weights are based on trade in manufactured and primary products during 1988–90, and an index of relative changes in consumer prices is used as the deflator. An increase in the real effective exchange rate represents an appreciation of the local currency. Because of conceptual and data limitations, changes in real effective exchange rates should be interpreted with caution.

The official or market exchange rate is often used to compare prices in different currencies, but because market imperfections are extensive and exchange rates reflect at best the relative prices of tradable goods, the volume of goods and services that a U.S. dollar buys in the United States may not correspond to what a U.S. dollar converted to another country's currency at the official exchange rate would buy in that country. The alternative approach is to convert national currency estimates of GNP to a common currency by using conversion factors that reflect equivalent purchasing power. Purchasing power parity (PPP) conversion factors are based on price and expenditure surveys conducted by the International Comparison Programme (ICP) and represent the conversion factors applied to equalize price levels across countries. See *About the data* for tables 4.11 and 4.12 for further discussion of the PPP conversion factor.

Many interest rates coexist in an economy, reflecting competitive conditions, the terms governing loans and deposits, and differences in the position and status of creditors and debtors. In some economies interest rates are set by regulation or administrative fiat. In economies with imperfect markets or where reported nominal rates are not indicative of effective rates, it may be difficult to obtain data on interest rates that reflect actual market transactions. Deposit and lending rates are collected by the International Monetary Fund (IMF) as representative interest rates offered by banks to resident customers. The terms and conditions attached to these rates differ by country, however, limiting their comparability. Real interest rates are calculated by adjusting nominal rates by an estimate of the inflation rate in the economy. A negative real interest rate indicates a loss in the purchasing power of the principal. The real interest rates in the table are calculated as $(i - P)/(1 + P)$, where i is the nominal interest rate and P is the inflation rate (as measured by the GDP deflator).

The table also shows price levels for bread and cereals (including barley, maize, rice, wheat, and others) and for meat (including beef, pork, fish, and poultry) in PPP terms. These price levels are expressed relative to the corresponding price level in the United States. They are the ratio of the PPP of the good to the relevant exchange rate, usually the U.S. dollar. A price level of more than 100 indicates that the item is more expensive in the country than in the United States.

Definitions

• **Exchange rate arrangement** describes the arrangement that an IMF member country has furnished to the IMF under article IV, section 2(a) of the IMF's Articles of Agreement. *Exchange rate classification* indicates how the exchange rate is determined in the main market when there is more than one market: floating (managed or independent), pegged (conventional, within horizontal bands, crawling peg, or crawling band), currency board (implicit legislative commitment to exchange domestic currency for a specified foreign currency at a fixed exchange rate), and exchange arrangement (country is adopting the euro, currency is pegged to the French franc, or another country's currency is used as legal tender). *Exchange rate structure* shows whether countries have unitary, dual, or multiple exchange rates. • **Official exchange rate** refers to the exchange rate determined by country authorities or to the rate determined in the legally sanctioned exchange market. It is calculated as an annual average based on monthly averages (local currency units relative to the U.S. dollar). • **Ratio of official to parallel exchange rate** measures the premium people must pay, relative to the official exchange rate, to exchange the domestic currency for U.S. dollars in the black market. • **Real effective exchange rate** is the nominal effective exchange rate (a measure of the value of a currency against a weighted average of several foreign currencies) divided by a price deflator or index of costs. • **Purchasing power parity conversion factor** is the number of units of a country's currency required to buy the same amount of goods and services in the domestic market as a U.S. dollar would buy in the United States. • **Deposit interest rate** is the rate paid by commercial or similar banks for demand, time, or savings deposits. • **Lending interest rate** is the rate charged by banks on loans to prime customers. • **Real interest rate** is the lending interest rate adjusted for inflation as measured by the GDP deflator. • **Food prices in PPP terms** are the prices in each country for bread and cereals and for meat relative to the U.S. price level for those goods.

Data sources

The information on exchange rate arrangements is from the IMF's *Exchange Arrangements and Exchange Restrictions Annual Report, 1999.* The official and real effective exchange rates and deposit and lending rates are from the IMF's *International Financial Statistics.* The estimates of parallel market exchange rates are from Currency Data & Intelligence's *Global Currency Report.* The PPP conversion factors and food prices are from the ICP and World Bank staff estimates. The real interest rates are calculated using World Bank data on the GDP deflator.

5.7 Defense expenditures and trade in arms

	Military expenditures				Armed forces personnel				Arms trade			
	% of GNP		% of central government expenditure		Total thousands		% of labor force		Exports % of total exports		Imports % of total imports	
	1992	**1997**	**1992**	**1997**	**1992**	**1997**	**1992**	**1997**	**1992**	**1997**	**1992**	**1997**
Albania	4.7	1.4	10.1	4.9	65	52	4.2	3.2	0.0	0.0	0.0	1.3
Algeria	1.8	3.9	5.9	12.0	126	124	1.7	1.3	0.0	0.0	0.1	5.6
Angola	24.2	20.5	*24.6*	36.3	128	95	2.8	1.8	0.0	0.0	1.5	3.5
Argentina	1.9	1.2	16.0	6.3	65	65	0.5	0.5	0.0	0.0	0.3	0.2
Armenia	*3.5*	3.5	..	..	20	60	1.1	3.2	0.0	2.1	0.0	0.0
Australia	2.5	2.2	9.2	8.6	68	65	0.8	0.7	0.1	0.0	2.1	1.4
Austria	1.0	0.9	2.4	1.9	52	48	1.4	1.3	0.2	0.0	0.1	0.3
Azerbaijan	2.9	1.9	*9.0*	10.8	43	75	1.4	2.2	0.0	1.3	0.0	0.0
Bangladesh	1.3	1.4	11.2	10.7	107	110	0.2	0.2	0.0	0.0	1.0	0.7
Belarus	1.9	1.7	4.9	4.8	102	65	1.9	1.2	0.0	6.7	0.0	0.0
Belgium	1.8	1.5	3.7	3.2	79	46	1.9	1.1	0.3	0.1	0.2	0.2
Benin	1.3	1.3	6.3	6.8	7	8	0.3	0.3	0.0	0.0	0.0	0.0
Bolivia	2.2	1.9	10.4	6.7	32	33	1.2	1.1	0.0	0.0	0.9	1.6
Bosnia and Herzegovina	*16.5*	5.9	..	14.1	60	40	3.2	2.4	0.0	0.0	0.0	6.5
Botswana	4.4	5.1	10.3	13.4	7	8	1.2	1.2	0.0	0.0	1.1	0.9
Brazil	1.1	1.8	3.5	*3.9*	296	296	0.4	0.4	0.5	0.1	0.9	0.7
Bulgaria	3.3	3.0	7.9	9.2	99	80	2.3	1.9	3.1	2.4	0.0	0.2
Burkina Faso	2.4	2.8	11.5	12.3	9	9	0.2	0.2	0.0	0.0	1.1	0.0
Burundi	2.7	6.1	7.8	25.8	13	35	0.4	1.0	0.0	0.0	0.0	16.5
Cambodia	4.9	4.1	..	25.8	135	60	2.7	1.0	0.0	0.0	0.0	0.9
Cameroon	1.6	3.0	8.2	17.7	12	13	0.2	0.2	0.0	0.0	0.0	0.7
Canada	2.0	1.3	7.5	..	82	61	0.5	0.4	0.7	0.3	0.6	0.2
Central African Republic	2.0	3.9	8.3	27.7	4	5	..	..	0.0	0.0	0.0	0.0
Chad	4.0	2.7	17.3	12.6	38	35	1.3	1.0	0.0	0.0	4.1	2.1
Chile	2.5	3.9	11.7	17.8	92	102	1.7	1.7	0.0	0.0	1.0	0.3
China	2.8	2.2	19.8	17.6	3,160	2,600	0.5	0.4	1.3	0.6	1.6	0.4
Hong Kong, China	..	..	..	..	..	..	..	..	..	..	..	..
Colombia	2.4	3.7	14.7	19.9	139	149	0.9	0.9	0.0	0.0	1.7	0.8
Congo, Dem. Rep.	3.0	5.0	16.1	41.4	45	*50*	0.3	*0.3*	0.0	0.0	0.0	2.4
Congo, Rep.	5.7	4.1	13.5	12.3	10	10	1.0	0.9	0.0	0.0	0.0	1.1
Costa Rica	1.4	0.6	7.5	3.1	8	10	0.7	0.7	0.0	0.0	0.2	0.1
Côte d'Ivoire	1.5	1.1	4.3	4.0	15	15	0.3	0.3	0.0	0.0	0.0	0.0
Croatia	7.7	6.3	19.2	20.1	103	58	4.6	2.7	0.0	0.0	0.0	0.1
Cuba	*2.4*	2.3	..	..	175	55	3.5	1.0	0.0	0.0	4.5	0.0
Czech Republic	*2.7*	1.9	*6.9*	5.8	*107*	55	*1.9*	1.0	*1.6*	0.4	*0.0*	0.5
Denmark	2.0	1.7	4.8	3.9	28	29	1.0	1.0	0.0	0.0	0.5	0.5
Dominican Republic	0.9	1.1	6.8	7.3	22	22	0.7	0.6	0.0	0.0	0.2	0.1
Ecuador	3.5	4.0	25.4	20.3	57	58	1.5	1.3	0.0	0.0	1.2	3.2
Egypt, Arab Rep.	3.7	2.8	8.5	11.0	424	430	2.2	1.9	0.7	0.1	19.4	12.1
El Salvador	2.1	0.9	13.4	6.7	49	15	2.4	0.6	0.0	0.0	4.1	0.3
Eritrea	..	7.8	..	18.1	*55*	55	*3.2*	2.9	*0.0*	0.0	*0.0*	0.0
Estonia	0.5	1.5	2.2	4.5	3	7	0.4	0.9	0.0	0.0	1.2	0.2
Ethiopia	3.7	1.9	17.9	7.9	120	100	0.5	0.4	0.0	0.0	0.0	0.0
Finland	2.2	1.7	4.3	*4.3*	33	35	1.3	1.3	0.0	0.1	2.1	1.2
France	3.4	3.0	7.6	6.4	522	475	2.1	1.8	0.9	2.0	0.2	0.1
Gabon	3.1	2.0	10.1	7.0	7	10	1.4	1.8	0.0	0.0	0.0	0.0
Gambia, The	3.6	3.7	19.7	15.0	1	1	0.2	0.2	0.0	0.0	2.1	11.9
Georgia	2.4	1.4	..	9.6	*25*	11	*0.9*	0.4	0.0	0.0	0.0	1.1
Germany	2.1	1.6	6.3	4.7	442	335	1.1	0.8	0.3	0.1	0.6	0.2
Ghana	0.8	0.7	4.6	2.4	7	7	0.1	0.1	0.0	0.0	0.0	0.0
Greece	4.4	4.6	13.5	13.8	208	206	4.8	4.6	0.2	0.3	3.9	3.1
Guatemala	1.5	*1.4*	14.0	*15.0*	44	30	1.4	0.8	0.0	0.0	0.2	0.1
Guinea	1.4	1.5	7.0	8.0	15	12	0.5	0.4	0.0	0.0	0.0	3.7
Guinea-Bissau	3.2	3.2	7.6	13.0	11	7	2.3	1.3	0.0	0.0	0.0	0.0
Haiti	1.5	..	14.7	..	8	0	0.3	0.0	0.0	0.0	0.0	0.8
Honduras	1.4	*1.3*	5.5	*5.6*	17	10	0.9	0.5	0.0	0.0	2.9	0.5

Defense expenditures and trade in arms 5.7

	Military expenditures				Armed forces personnel				Arms trade			
	% of GNP		% of central government expenditure		Total thousands		% of labor force		Exports % of total exports		Imports % of total imports	
	1992	1997	1992	1997	1992	1997	1992	1997	1992	1997	1992	1997
Hungary	2.1	1.9	3.8	4.3	78	50	1.6	1.0	0.4	0.0	0.0	0.5
India	2.5	2.8	12.4	14.3	1,260	1,260	0.3	0.3	0.0	0.3	2.9	1.0
Indonesia	1.4	2.3	7.2	13.1	283	280	0.3	0.3	0.1	0.0	0.4	1.0
Iran, Islamic Rep.	3.0	3.0	14.9	11.6	528	575	3.2	3.1	0.1	0.1	3.3	5.8
Iraq	9.7	4.9	..	..	407	400	8.2	6.8	0.0	0.0	0.0	0.0
Ireland	1.4	1.2	3.8	3.3	13	17	1.0	1.1	0.0	0.0	0.1	0.1
Israel	11.7	9.7	23.3	20.9	181	185	8.8	7.5	4.8	1.6	7.9	3.6
Italy	2.1	2.0	3.9	4.1	471	419	1.9	1.7	0.3	0.3	0.2	0.2
Jamaica	1.0	0.9	*3.0*	2.4	3	3	0.2	0.2	0.0	0.0	0.6	0.2
Japan	1.0	1.0	6.3	6.6	242	250	0.4	0.4	0.0	0.0	0.9	0.8
Jordan	8.8	9.0	*27.3*	25.0	100	102	9.9	7.9	0.0	0.0	1.2	3.2
Kazakhstan	2.9	1.3	*14.2*	4.4	*15*	34	*0.2*	0.4	0.0	0.0	0.0	3.3
Kenya	3.0	2.1	9.9	7.2	24	24	0.2	0.2	0.0	0.0	1.2	1.2
Korea, Dem. Rep.	25.0	27.5	28.5	..	1,200	1,100	10.9	9.1	13.1	8.1	7.9	2.1
Korea, Rep.	3.7	3.4	19.8	14.6	750	670	3.7	2.9	0.1	0.0	1.5	0.8
Kuwait	77.0	7.5	96.3	26.8	12	28	2.1	4.1	0.2	0.0	13.8	24.3
Kyrgyz Republic	*0.7*	1.6	7.1	..	12	14	0.6	0.7	0.0	0.0	0.0	0.0
Lao PDR	9.8	3.4	*23.6*	17.5	37	50	..	..	0.0	0.0	2.3	1.4
Latvia	1.6	0.9	2.5	..	5	5	0.4	0.4	0.0	0.0	0.0	0.0
Lebanon	4.0	3.0	18.5	8.4	37	57	3.1	4.0	0.0	0.0	0.0	0.5
Lesotho	3.6	2.5	10.5	6.1	2	2	0.3	0.2	0.0	0.0	0.0	0.0
Libya	7.6	*6.1*	*16.4*	*19.7*	85	70	6.3	4.7	0.1	0.0	1.7	0.1
Lithuania	*0.7*	0.8	*2.5*	2.8	10	12	0.5	0.6	0.0	0.0	0.0	0.1
Macedonia, FYR	*2.2*	2.5	..	10.2	10	15	1.2	1.6	*0.0*	0.0	*0.0*	0.0
Madagascar	1.1	1.5	5.4	8.5	21	21	0.4	0.3	0.0	0.0	0.0	0.0
Malawi	1.1	1.0	3.9	2.9	10	8	0.2	0.2	0.0	0.0	0.0	0.0
Malaysia	3.2	2.2	10.3	9.9	128	110	1.7	1.3	0.0	0.0	0.6	0.9
Mali	2.3	1.7	9.4	7.2	12	10	0.3	0.2	0.0	0.0	0.0	1.5
Mauritania	3.5	2.3	13.3	9.8	16	11	1.6	1.0	0.0	0.0	0.0	0.0
Mauritius	0.4	0.3	1.5	1.2	1	1	0.2	0.2	0.0	0.0	0.3	0.4
Mexico	0.5	1.1	3.7	6.2	175	250	0.5	0.7	0.0	0.0	0.5	0.1
Moldova	*0.5*	1.0	*1.5*	1.9	9	11	0.4	0.5	0.0	7.9	0.8	0.0
Mongolia	2.6	1.9	9.3	5.1	21	20	1.9	1.6	0.0	0.0	0.0	0.0
Morocco	4.5	4.3	14.3	12.9	195	195	2.1	1.8	0.0	0.0	1.4	1.9
Mozambique	7.6	2.8	17.0	9.2	50	14	0.6	0.2	0.0	0.0	0.6	0.0
Myanmar	8.3	*7.6*	74.3	*75.5*	286	322	1.3	1.4	0.0	0.0	23.0	13.6
Namibia	2.2	2.7	5.6	7.3	8	8	1.4	1.2	0.0	0.0	0.0	0.3
Nepal	1.0	0.8	6.0	5.1	35	35	0.4	0.3	0.0	0.0	0.0	0.0
Netherlands	2.5	1.9	6.9	6.4	90	57	1.3	0.8	0.1	0.3	0.4	0.3
New Zealand	1.6	1.3	4.0	3.9	11	10	0.6	0.5	0.0	0.0	1.2	0.7
Nicaragua	3.1	1.5	8.1	4.5	15	14	1.0	0.8	13.5	0.0	0.6	0.0
Niger	1.3	1.1	7.9	6.9	5	5	0.1	0.1	0.0	0.0	0.0	1.4
Nigeria	2.6	1.4	15.6	12.3	76	76	0.2	0.2	0.0	0.0	2.0	0.7
Norway	3.1	2.1	6.4	4.8	36	33	1.6	1.4	0.1	0.0	1.7	0.7
Oman	20.5	26.1	40.2	36.4	35	38	6.6	6.2	0.0	0.0	0.3	3.2
Pakistan	7.4	5.7	27.9	24.2	580	610	1.4	1.3	0.4	0.0	6.7	5.2
Panama	1.3	1.4	5.7	4.8	11	12	1.1	1.1	2.0	0.0	0.5	0.3
Papua New Guinea	1.5	1.3	4.2	4.1	4	5	0.2	0.2	0.0	0.0	4.0	0.0
Paraguay	1.8	1.3	13.2	10.5	16	16	1.0	0.9	0.0	0.0	0.7	0.1
Peru	1.8	2.1	11.1	13.4	112	115	1.4	1.3	0.0	0.0	1.4	3.0
Philippines	1.9	1.5	10.2	7.9	107	105	0.4	0.3	0.0	0.0	1.6	0.3
Poland	2.3	2.3	8.8	5.6	270	230	1.4	1.2	0.2	0.2	0.0	0.4
Portugal	2.7	2.4	6.4	5.9	80	72	1.7	1.4	0.1	0.0	0.6	0.3
Puerto Rico	..	..	..	..	..	..	..	..	..	..	..	..
Romania	3.3	2.4	7.9	6.9	172	200	1.6	1.9	0.5	0.1	0.6	2.2
Russian Federation	8.0	5.8	28.0	30.9	1,900	1,300	2.5	1.7	5.9	2.6	0.0	0.0

5.7 Defense expenditures and trade in arms

	Military expenditures				Armed forces personnel				Arms trade			
	% of GNP		% of central government expenditure		Total thousands		% of labor force		Exports % of total exports		Imports % of total imports	
	1992	**1997**	**1992**	**1997**	**1992**	**1997**	**1992**	**1997**	**1992**	**1997**	**1992**	**1997**
Rwanda	4.4	4.4	21.7	22.2	30	40	0.8	1.0	0.0	0.0	0.0	6.7
Saudi Arabia	26.8	14.5	72.5	35.8	172	180	3.1	2.7	0.0	0.0	25.2	40.4
Senegal	2.8	1.6	13.5	8.5	18	14	0.5	0.4	0.0	0.0	1.0	0.0
Sierra Leone	3.2	5.9	17.7	33.0	8	5	0.5	0.3	0.0	0.0	6.8	0.0
Singapore	5.2	5.7	27.2	19.4	56	55	3.9	3.5	0.0	0.1	0.4	0.3
Slovak Republic	*2.2*	2.1	*5.1*	8.0	*33*	44	*1.2*	1.5	*0.7*	0.5	*3.5*	0.1
Slovenia	2.3	5.2	*4.0*	12.5	15	10	1.5	1.0	0.0	0.0	0.0	0.2
South Africa	3.2	1.8	9.8	5.6	75	75	0.5	0.5	0.4	1.2	1.3	0.1
Spain	1.6	1.5	6.4	6.0	198	107	1.2	0.6	0.3	0.5	0.4	0.4
Sri Lanka	3.8	5.1	13.6	21.2	110	110	1.5	1.4	0.0	0.0	0.3	1.5
Sudan	*7.8*	4.6	*60.0*	53.8	82	105	0.9	1.0	0.0	0.0	13.4	1.3
Sweden	2.6	2.5	5.3	5.4	70	60	1.5	1.3	1.5	1.1	0.3	0.5
Switzerland	1.8	1.4	7.2	*5.8*	31	39	0.9	1.0	1.2	0.1	0.7	0.4
Syrian Arab Republic	9.7	5.6	39.0	*26.2*	408	320	10.9	6.9	0.6	0.0	11.2	1.7
Tajikistan	0.3	1.7	0.7	10.6	3	10	0.1	0.4	0.0	0.0	0.0	0.0
Tanzania	2.2	1.3	10.0	10.7	46	35	0.3	0.2	0.0	0.0	0.3	1.5
Thailand	2.6	2.3	16.6	12.1	283	288	0.9	0.8	0.0	0.0	1.2	1.5
Togo	2.9	2.0	13.2	11.6	8	12	0.5	0.7	0.0	0.0	0.0	1.3
Trinidad and Tobago	1.5	1.5	*4.8*	5.4	2	2	0.4	0.4	0.0	0.0	0.0	0.2
Tunisia	2.4	2.0	7.1	5.3	35	35	1.1	1.0	0.0	0.0	0.3	0.3
Turkey	3.8	4.0	18.8	14.7	704	820	2.8	2.8	0.1	0.0	6.6	3.3
Turkmenistan	..	4.6	..	15.6	28	21	1.7	1.1	1.4	0.0	0.0	0.0
Uganda	2.4	4.2	11.7	23.9	70	50	0.8	0.5	0.0	0.0	2.3	2.3
Ukraine	1.9	3.7	..	8.4	438	450	1.7	1.8	0.0	3.5	0.0	0.0
United Arab Emirates	5.7	6.9	49.5	46.5	55	60	5.3	4.7	0.0	0.1	4.2	4.7
United Kingdom	3.8	2.7	9.3	7.1	293	218	1.0	0.7	3.3	2.3	1.3	0.7
United States	4.8	3.3	21.1	16.3	1,920	1,530	1.5	1.1	5.6	4.6	0.3	0.2
Uruguay	2.3	1.4	8.0	4.4	25	25	1.8	1.7	0.0	0.0	0.5	0.3
Uzbekistan	2.7	*2.5*	6.0	*6.1*	40	65	0.5	0.7	0.0	1.7	0.0	0.1
Venezuela, RB	2.6	2.2	11.9	9.8	75	75	1.0	0.8	0.0	0.0	0.9	1.8
Vietnam	3.4	2.8	14.5	11.1	857	650	2.4	1.7	0.4	0.0	0.4	1.1
West Bank and Gaza	..	..	..	..	..	..	..	..	..	..	..	..
Yemen, Rep.	9.4	8.1	29.8	17.4	64	69	1.5	1.3	0.0	0.0	0.2	5.5
Yugoslavia, FR (Serb./Mont.)	..	4.9	..	..	137	115	2.8	2.3	0.0	1.6	0.0	0.4
Zambia	3.3	1.1	9.3	3.9	16	21	0.5	0.5	0.0	0.0	0.0	0.0
Zimbabwe	3.8	3.8	10.1	11.9	48	40	1.0	0.8	0.3	0.0	4.1	0.5
World	**3.2 w**	**2.5 w**	**13.0 w**	**11.0 w**	**24,539 t**	**22,157 t**	**0.9 w**	**0.8 w**	**1.2 w**	**1.0 w**	**1.1 w**	**1.0 w**
Low income	2.8	2.5	15.8	16.4	9,210	8,290	0.6	0.5	0.6	0.4	1.8	1.0
Excl. China & India	3.0	2.8	13.1	15.7	3,590	3,330	0.7	0.6	0.2	0.1	1.7	1.6
Middle income	3.8	2.8	18.7	14.7	9,656	8,988	1.7	1.4	0.7	0.4	2.8	2.0
Lower middle income	3.7	2.6	17.4	15.7	6,528	5,744	1.9	1.5	1.7	1.1	2.0	1.3
Upper middle income	3.9	2.9	19.6	13.8	3,128	3,244	1.4	1.3	0.1	0.0	3.4	2.3
Low & middle income	3.6	2.7	18.0	15.2	18,866	17,278	0.9	0.7	0.7	0.4	2.6	1.8
East Asia & Pacific	2.9	2.5	17.2	15.1	7,256	6,264	0.8	0.6	0.4	0.2	1.3	0.8
Europe & Central Asia	4.2	..	19.2	16.8	4,311	3,899	2.1	1.7	2.9	1.4	1.4	0.8
Latin America & Carib.	1.4	1.8	5.9	*6.5*	1,443	1,362	0.8	0.7	0.2	0.0	0.7	0.5
Middle East & N. Africa	14.5	7.0	48.6	22.4	2,631	2,612	3.3	2.8	0.1	0.0	11.3	14.5
South Asia	3.1	3.1	14.9	15.6	2,142	2,133	0.4	0.4	0.1	0.2	3.3	1.6
Sub-Saharan Africa	3.1	2.3	10.5	9.8	1,083	1,008	0.5	0.4	0.2	0.5	1.3	0.5
High income	3.1	2.4	12.1	10.1	5,673	4,879	1.3	1.1	1.4	1.2	0.7	0.7
Europe EMU	2.3	2.0	5.9	5.1	1,981	1,612	1.5	1.2	0.4	0.5	0.4	0.2

Note: Data for some countries are based on partial or uncertain data or rough estimates; see U.S. Department of State 1999.

Defense expenditures and trade in arms 5.7

About the data

Although national defense is an important function of government and security from external threats contributes to economic development, high levels of defense spending burden the economy and may impede growth. Comparisons of defense spending between countries should take into account the many factors that influence perceptions of vulnerability and risk, including historical and cultural traditions, the length of borders that need defending, the quality of relations with neighbors, and the role of the armed forces in the body politic.

Data on defense spending from governments are often incomplete and unreliable. Even in countries where parliaments vigilantly review government budgets and spending, defense spending and trade in arms often do not receive close scrutiny. For a detailed critique of the quality of such data see Ball (1984) and Happe and Wakeman-Linn (1994).

The International Monetary Fund's (IMF) *Government Finance Statistics Yearbook* is the primary source of data on defense spending. It uses a consistent definition of defense spending based on the United Nations' classification of the functions of government and the North Atlantic Treaty Organization (NATO) definition. The IMF checks data on defense spending for broad consistency with other macroeconomic data reported to it but is not always able to verify the accuracy and completeness of such data. Moreover, country coverage is affected by delays or failure to report data. Thus most researchers supplement the IMF's data with assessments by other organizations. However, these organizations rely heavily on reporting by governments, on confidential intelligence estimates of varying quality, on sources that they do not or cannot reveal, and on one another's publications. The data in this table are from the U.S. Department of State's Bureau of Arms Control.

Definitions of military spending differ depending on whether they include civil defense, reserves and auxiliary forces, police and paramilitary forces, dual-purpose forces such as military and civilian police, military grants in kind, pensions for military personnel, and social security contributions paid by one part of government to another. Official government data may omit parts of military spending, disguise financing through extrabudgetary accounts or unrecorded use of foreign exchange receipts, or fail to include military assistance or secret military equipment imports. Current spending is more likely to be reported than capital spending. In some cases a more accurate estimate of military spending can be obtained by adding the value of estimated arms imports and nominal military expenditures. This method may understate or overstate spending in a particular year, however, because payments for arms may not coincide with deliveries.

The data on armed forces refer to active duty military personnel, including paramilitary forces. These data exclude civilians in the defense establishment and so are not consistent with the data on military spending on personnel. Moreover, because they exclude payments to personnel not on active duty, they underestimate the share of the labor force that works for the defense establishment. Because governments rarely report the size of their armed forces, such data typically come from intelligence sources. The Bureau of Arms Control attributes its data to unspecified U.S. government sources.

The Standard International Trade Classification does not clearly distinguish trade in military goods. For this and other reasons, customs-based data on trade in arms are of little use, so most compilers rely on trade publications, confidential government information on third-country trade, and other sources. The construction of defense production facilities and the licensing fees paid for the production of arms are included in trade data when they are specified in military transfer agreements. Grants in kind are usually included as well. Definitional issues include treatment of dual-use equipment such as aircraft, use of military establishments such as schools and hospitals by civilians, and purchases by non-government buyers. Bureau of Arms Control data do not include arms supplied to subnational groups. Valuation problems arise when data are reported in volume terms and the purchase price must be estimated. Differences between sources may reflect reporting lags or differences in the period covered. Most compilers revise their time-series data regularly, so estimates for the same year may not be consistent between publication dates.

The data on U.S. arms exports have been substantially revised upward in this year's edition of the *World Development Indicators,* based on data from the most recent edition of the Bureau of Arms Control's *World Military Expenditures and Arms Transfers* (U.S. Department of State 1999). Revisions were made in commercial arms sales made directly by U.S. firms to foreign importers under authorization of the U.S. Department of State in accordance with U.S. regulations on international traffic in arms. Under the previous methodology the commercial arms component was represented by preliminary data on the deliveries made under approved export licenses. But because of weaknesses in data reporting, the extent to which authorized exports matched actual exports was uncertain. The new methodology assumes that deliveries constitute 50 percent of total authorizations by country. These deliveries are then distributed in a fixed pattern over the years of the license.

Definitions

• **Military expenditures** for NATO countries are based on the NATO definition, which covers military-related expenditures of the defense ministry (including recruiting, training, construction, and the purchase of military supplies and equipment) and other ministries. Civilian-type expenditures of the defense ministry are excluded. Military assistance is included in the expenditures of the donor country, and purchases of military equipment on credit are included at the time the debt is incurred, not at the time of payment. Data for other countries generally cover expenditures of the ministry of defense (excluded are expenditures on public order and safety, which are classified separately).
• **Armed forces personnel** refer to active duty military personnel, including paramilitary forces if those forces resemble regular units in their organization, equipment, training, or mission. • **Arms trade** is exports and imports of military equipment usually referred to as "conventional," including weapons of war, parts thereof, ammunition, support equipment, and other commodities designed for military use. See *About the data* for more details.

Data sources

The data on military expenditures, armed forces, and arms trade are from the Bureau of Arms Control's *World Military Expenditures and Arms Transfers 1998* (U.S. Department of State 1999).

5.8 State-owned enterprises

	Economic activity		Investment		Credit		Net financial flows from government		Overall balance before transfers		Employment		Proceeds from privatization
	% of GDP		% of gross domestic investment		% of gross domestic credit		% of GDP		% of GDP		% of total		$ millions
	1985–90	1990–97	1985–90	1990–97	1985–90	1990–97	1985–90	1990–97	1985–90	1990–97	1985–90	1990–97	1990–98
Albania	..	..	..	..	..	..	..	..	..	..	..	..	28.5
Algeria	..	..	..	..	..	33.5	..	..	..	..	7.2[a]	..	9.3
Angola	..	..	..	..	..	..	..	..	..	..	..	..	6.2
Argentina	2.7	1.3	9.4	3.1	..	..	..	..	–0.6	–0.1	2.7	..	28,431.5
Armenia	..	..	..	..	..	..	..	..	..	..	..	..	212.1
Australia	..	..	15.0[b]	12.0[b]	..	..	..	..	..	..	..	..	..
Austria	..	..	..	..	..	..	..	..	..	..	..	..	..
Azerbaijan	..	..	..	..	..	59.3	..	..	..	..	..	..	15.8
Bangladesh[c]	2.3	2.5	16.8	11.9	18.5	14.7	..	–0.5	–2.9	–2.6	..	..	59.6
Belarus	..	..	..	..	..	..	..	..	..	..	..	..	10.8
Belgium	2.8[a]	..	7.8	..	..	..	..	..	..	..	..	..	..
Benin	..	..	21.8	..	..	..	..	..	..	..	..	..	39.0
Bolivia	13.4[a]	11.4	21.1	18.0	6.4	9.9	–7.3[a]	–6.9	7.6[a]	6.2	2.3[a]	..	894.1
Bosnia and Herzegovina	..	..	..	..	..	..	..	..	..	..	..	..	..
Botswana	5.6[a]	5.5[a]	16.2[a]	12.4[a]	9.8	7.3	–0.3[a]	–0.3[a]	–2.5[a]	–2.7[a]	6.3[a]	5.8[a]	..
Brazil	7.7	7.4	13.1	8.2	18.4	7.7	–0.6[b]	–2.2	0.9[b]	3.1	..	..	66,727.9
Bulgaria	..	..	..	..	..	49.1	..	..	..	..	..	..	1,446.7
Burkina Faso	..	..	..	..	..	..	..	..	..	..	..	..	6.3
Burundi	7.3	..	41.1	..	19.3	16.4	2.7	..	..	..	32.1[b,d]	..	4.2
Cambodia	..	..	..	..	..	..	..	..	..	..	..	..	..
Cameroon	18.0	5.4	..	6.8	..	9.8	1.3	–0.6	..	1.0	..	..	113.1
Canada	..	..	..	..	..	..	..	..	..	..	..	..	..
Central African Republic	4.1	..	..	..	..	10.8	..	..	–3.1	..	..	..	..
Chad	..	..	..	..	..	23.7	..	..	..	..	..	..	..
Chile	14.4	8.3	15.5	6.7	1.8	1.9	–8.6[e]	–4.9[e]	8.8[e]	4.9[e]	..	..	1,085.2
China[f]	..	..	37.0	27.6	..	..	..	..	..	..	7.7	6.8	17,467.0
Hong Kong, China	..	..	..	..	..	..	..	..	..	..	..	..	..
Colombia	7.0	..	13.5	..	5.0	3.2	–0.6	..	0.8	..	..	..	5,979.5
Congo, Dem. Rep.	..	..	18.8	..	0.8	1.6	..	..	..	..	..	..	..
Congo, Rep.	15.1[a]	..	..	..	..	10.2	..	..	..	..	..	..	..
Costa Rica	8.1	..	8.5	11.5	30.5	20.0	–1.9	..	1.9	..	..	..	50.8
Côte d'Ivoire	..	..	21.4[b]	..	..	..	..	..	..	..	..	..	570.1
Croatia	..	..	..	..	..	..	..	..	..	..	..	..	468.3
Cuba	..	..	..	..	..	..	..	..	..	..	..	..	706.0
Czech Republic	..	..	..	..	..	..	..	..	..	..	..	..	4,458.1
Denmark	..	..	..	..	..	..	..	..	..	..	..	..	..
Dominican Republic	..	..	11.6[b]	..	15.6	12.9	..	..	..	..	..	..	..
Ecuador	10.2	..	12.7	13.9	0.0	0.4	0.1	..	–1.1	..	..	..	169.3
Egypt, Arab Rep.	..	..	65.5	..	21.5	19.7	–0.7	..	–2.6	..	13.8	..	2,048.9
El Salvador	1.8[a]	..	7.1	..	4.2	1.4	0.1[a]	..	–0.3[a]	..	..	..	902.1
Eritrea	..	..	..	..	..	..	..	..	..	..	..	..	2.0
Estonia	..	..	..	..	..	33.1	..	..	..	..	..	..	510.3
Ethiopia	..	..	..	..	..	..	..	..	..	..	..	..	172.0
Finland	..	..	..	..	..	..	..	..	..	..	..	..	..
France	11.2	..	..	..	..	..	..	..	..	..	..	..	..
Gabon	..	..	..	..	..	4.1	..	..	..	..	25.1	..	..
Gambia, The	3.8	..	..	..	..	..	2.9[a]	..	..	..	..	..	..
Georgia	..	..	..	..	..	..	..	..	..	..	..	..	..
Germany	..	..	..	..	..	..	..	..	..	..	..	..	..
Ghana	8.5	..	18.5	..	12.4	10.1	0.4[a]	..	0.1	..	34.3[d]	..	885.4
Greece	11.5	..	20.2	..	..	..	..	..	..	..	..	..	..
Guatemala	1.9	2.0	6.7	4.8	0.2	0.1	0.2[a]	0.1	0.1	0.5	..	..	1,250.0
Guinea	..	..	..	..	..	0.9	..	..	..	..	..	..	45.0
Guinea-Bissau	..	..	..	..	..	..	..	..	..	..	..	..	0.5
Haiti	..	..	11.3	..	7.7	5.9	..	..	..	..	..	..	..
Honduras	5.5	..	15.1	..	..	..	0.0	..	–0.9	..	..	..	74.1

State-owned enterprises 5.8

	Economic activity		Investment		Credit		Net financial flows from government		Overall balance before transfers		Employment		Proceeds from privati-zation
	% of GDP		% of gross domestic investment		% of gross domestic credit		% of GDP		% of GDP		% of total		$ millions
	1985–90	1990–97	1985–90	1990–97	1985–90	1990–97	1985–90	1990–97	1985–90	1990–97	1985–90	1990–97	1990–98
Hungary	..	..	..	..	..	..	..	..	..	..	..	..	12,634.8
India	13.4	13.4	35.4	32.4	..	..	–0.3[g]	–0.9[g]	–2.5[g]	–1.2[g]	8.5[g]	8.1[g]	7,125.3
Indonesia	14.5	..	8.9	15.7	..	3.6	1.3	..	–0.5	–2.6	0.9	1.2	5,284.9
Iran, Islamic Rep.	..	..	..	..	..	..	..	..	..	..	..	..	..
Iraq	..	..	..	..	..	..	..	..	..	..	..	..	..
Ireland	..	..	..	..	..	..	..	..	..	..	..	..	..
Israel	..	..	..	..	..	..	..	..	..	..	..	..	..
Italy	..	..	12.9	..	..	..	..	..	..	..	..	..	..
Jamaica	..	..	23.6	..	3.1	2.1	..	..	–1.4	..	..	..	385.5
Japan	..	..	5.8	6.5	3.0	2.4	..	..	..	..	..	..	..
Jordan	..	..	..	..	9.9	8.3	..	..	..	..	..	..	63.8
Kazakhstan	..	..	..	..	..	..	..	..	..	..	..	..	6,375.9
Kenya	11.6	..	24.6	..	5.6	4.5	0.2	..	..	..	7.9	7.7	256.7
Korea, Dem. Rep.	..	..	..	..	..	..	..	..	..	..	..	..	..
Korea, Rep.	10.3	..	14.3	..	..	..	–0.2	..	0.7	..	1.9	..	..
Kuwait	..	..	..	..	..	..	..	..	..	..	..	..	..
Kyrgyz Republic	..	..	..	..	..	..	..	..	..	..	..	..	139.5
Lao PDR	..	..	..	..	..	42.5	..	..	..	..	..	..	32.0
Latvia	..	..	..	..	..	..	..	..	..	..	..	..	490.9
Lebanon	..	..	..	..	..	..	..	..	..	..	..	..	..
Lesotho	..	..	..	..	..	..	..	..	..	..	..	..	..
Libya	..	..	..	..	..	..	..	..	..	..	..	..	..
Lithuania	..	..	..	..	..	..	..	..	..	..	..	..	1,482.3
Macedonia, FYR	..	..	..	..	..	..	..	..	..	..	..	..	621.3
Madagascar	..	..	..	..	..	..	..	..	..	..	..	..	..
Malawi	4.3[a]	..	9.2	..	13.9	10.9	0.8[a]	..	–1.2[a]	..	..	..	13.9
Malaysia[h]	..	..	..	25.7	..	0.0	..	..	..	–1.2	..	..	10,029.6
Mali	..	..	..	..	..	..	..	..	..	..	..	..	21.9
Mauritania	..	..	19.3	..	..	0.1	..	..	..	..	..	..	1.1
Mauritius	1.9	..	..	..	..	..	–0.3	..	..	..	..	..	..
Mexico[i]	6.7	4.9	14.4	10.3	1.6	0.7	–2.4	–3.1	2.4	3.0	3.5	2.1	28,302.0
Moldova	..	..	..	..	..	36.8	..	..	..	..	..	..	1.6
Mongolia	..	..	..	..	..	43.5	..	..	..	..	..	..	..
Morocco	16.8[b]	..	19.3	..	..	..	0.0[a]	..	..	..	..	..	1,938.9
Mozambique	..	..	..	..	8.9	7.5	..	..	..	..	..	..	138.2
Myanmar	..	..	37.1[b]	..	116.8	33.0	..	..	..	..	..	..	..
Namibia	..	..	11.9	..	..	1.3	2.5[a]	..	–1.0	..	..	..	..
Nepal	..	..	50.0	..	8.5	4.8	..	..	..	..	..	..	15.1
Netherlands	..	..	..	..	..	..	..	..	..	..	..	..	..
New Zealand	..	..	..	..	..	..	..	..	..	..	..	..	..
Nicaragua	..	..	..	..	33.1	30.4	..	..	..	..	..	..	130.3
Niger	5.1	..	..	..	..	..	..	..	–0.1	..	..	..	..
Nigeria	..	..	..	..	..	0.8	..	..	..	..	..	..	730.2
Norway	..	..	25.8[b]	..	2.3	1.5	..	..	..	..	..	..	..
Oman	..	..	..	..	1.2	1.0	..	..	..	..	..	..	60.1
Pakistan	..	..	28.8	28.2	..	..	..	..	..	..	..	..	1,992.3
Panama	7.6	7.3	9.7	4.6	..	..	–0.8	–2.0	2.1	3.4	..	..	1,125.6
Papua New Guinea	..	..	7.8	..	..	..	..	..	..	..	..	..	223.6
Paraguay	4.8	4.6	11.2	5.5	16.1	13.5	0.2	–0.4	–2.0	1.1	..	..	42.0
Peru	6.4	5.1	10.7	4.5	..	..	–3.0	–3.2	1.5	2.9	2.5	..	7,848.4
Philippines	2.3	2.2	8.4	9.9	9.0	6.0	..	..	–2.2	–3.7	0.8	..	3,730.0
Poland	..	..	..	..	78.2	49.3	..	..	..	..	..	..	8,281.6
Portugal	15.1	..	16.6	..	..	..	..	..	..	..	..	..	..
Puerto Rico	..	..	..	..	..	..	..	..	..	..	..	..	..
Romania	..	63.0[j]	..	72.9[j]	..	70.4	..	..	..	..	..	..	1,772.7
Russian Federation	..	..	..	..	..	..	..	..	..	..	..	..	1,910.6

5.8 State-owned enterprises

	Economic activity		Investment		Credit		Net financial flows from government		Overall balance before transfers		Employment		Proceeds from privatization
	% of GDP		% of gross domestic investment		% of gross domestic credit		% of GDP		% of GDP		% of total		$ millions
	1985–90	1990–97	1985–90	1990–97	1985–90	1990–97	1985–90	1990–97	1985–90	1990–97	1985–90	1990–97	1990–98
Rwanda	..	..	..	..	..	..	0.4	..	1.0	..	..	..	..
Saudi Arabia	..	..	..	..	..	14.7	..	..	..	..	..	..	..
Senegal	6.9	..	28.2	..	..	..	4.5	..	–1.0	..	20.4 [d]	..	341.7
Sierra Leone	..	..	..	..	0.4	0.2	0.1 [b]	..	..	..	..	..	1.6
Singapore	..	..	..	..	..	..	..	..	..	..	..	..	..
Slovak Republic	..	..	..	..	..	..	..	..	..	..	..	..	1,979.4
Slovenia	..	..	..	..	..	..	..	..	..	..	..	..	521.1
South Africa	14.9	..	16.5	..	..	..	..	..	..	..	..	..	2,729.2
Spain	..	..	..	..	..	..	..	..	..	..	..	..	..
Sri Lanka	..	..	26.8	..	..	..	2.8	1.4	..	..	..	12.4	803.9
Sudan	..	..	..	..	18.4	10.0	..	..	..	..	..	..	..
Sweden	..	..	10.3	8.7	..	..	..	..	..	..	..	..	..
Switzerland	..	..	..	..	..	..	..	..	..	..	..	..	..
Syrian Arab Republic	..	..	..	..	..	..	..	..	..	..	..	..	..
Tajikistan	..	..	..	..	..	..	..	..	..	..	..	..	..
Tanzania	9.0	8.6	46.0	22.9	..	..	..	..	–7.4	..	21.4	..	251.6
Thailand	..	..	11.5	10.0	1.7	1.9	–0.3	–0.4	..	..	1.0 [b]	..	1,642.0
Togo	..	..	10.7	..	..	..	1.6	..	..	..	..	..	38.1
Trinidad and Tobago	9.1 [a]	..	16.4	..	10.8	8.7	0.0	..	0.7 [a]	..	..	..	276.2
Tunisia	..	..	31.0	..	..	..	7.6	..	..	..	..	..	514.6
Turkey	6.5	5.0	27.1	13.8	6.4	6.0	1.6	0.8	–3.2	–5.5	3.7	2.9	4,616.4
Turkmenistan	..	..	..	..	..	..	..	..	..	..	..	..	..
Uganda	..	..	..	..	..	..	..	..	..	..	..	..	166.3
Ukraine	..	..	..	..	..	55.9	..	..	..	..	..	..	31.5
United Arab Emirates	..	..	..	..	..	..	..	..	..	..	..	..	..
United Kingdom	3.6	2.8	6.4 [b]	4.6	..	..	..	..	..	..	..	..	..
United States	..	..	3.9	4.0	..	..	..	..	..	..	..	..	..
Uruguay	5.0	..	14.2	..	9.5	12.0	–3.2	..	3.3	..	..	..	17.0
Uzbekistan	..	..	..	..	..	..	..	..	..	..	..	..	212.0
Venezuela, RB	22.3	..	50.9	..	0.7	3.3	–11.1	..	9.3	..	..	..	6,026.5
Vietnam	..	..	..	..	..	44.4	..	..	..	..	..	..	7.6
West Bank and Gaza	..	..	..	..	..	..	..	..	..	..	..	..	..
Yemen, Rep.	..	..	..	..	..	3.0	..	..	..	..	..	..	..
Yugoslavia, FR (Serb./Mont.)	..	..	..	..	..	..	..	..	..	..	..	..	921.7
Zambia	32.2	..	..	..	10.7	6.1	..	..	..	..	..	..	826.0
Zimbabwe	8.6	9.2	..	..	33.8	15.8	..	..	..	..	..	..	197.3

Note: Data are averages for the period shown except for proceeds from privatization, for which the data refer to the total for the period.

a. Selected major state-owned enterprises only. b. Includes financial state-owned enterprises. c. Data for 1985–90 refer to the 10 largest state-owned enterprises. Data for 1990–97 refer to 210 enterprises. d. As a percentage of formal sector employment. e. Nonoperating revenue before 1989 is split between current transfers and grants. All nonoperating revenue from 1989 onward is classified as current transfers. f. Data refer to industrial state-owned enterprises. g. Data refer to central public enterprises only. h. Data prior to 1991 have not been shown because of lack of consistency. i. Data on economic activity and employment refer to nonfinancial enterprises in both the controlled and the noncontrolled sectors. Data on investment through 1986 refer to nonfinancial enterprises in both the controlled and the noncontrolled sectors. Data from 1987 onward include financial enterprises in the noncontrolled sector. Data on overall balances before transfers and net financial flows from government refer only to nonfinancial enterprises in the controlled sector. j. Data refer to state-owned and majority state-owned enterprises.

State-owned enterprises 5.8

About the data

State-owned enterprises are government-owned or -controlled economic entities that generate most of their revenue by selling goods and services. This definition encompasses commercial enterprises directly operated by a government department and those in which the government holds a majority of shares directly or indirectly through other state enterprises. It also includes enterprises in which the state holds a minority of shares if the distribution of the remaining shares leaves the government with effective control. It excludes public sector activity—such as education, health services, and road construction and maintenance—that is financed in other ways, usually from the government's general revenue. Because financial enterprises are of a different nature, they have generally been excluded from the data on state enterprises.

The definition of a state enterprise varies among countries and within countries over time. In exceptional cases governments include noncommercial activities, such as agricultural research institutes, in their data on state enterprises. But more often they omit activities that clearly are state enterprises. The most common omissions occur when governments use a narrow definition of state enterprises—for example, by excluding those with a particular legal form (such as departmental enterprises), those owned by local governments (typically utilities), or those considered unimportant in terms of size or need for fiscal resources. Accordingly, data on state enterprises tend to underestimate their relative importance in the economy.

Although attempts have been made to correct for differences in definitions and coverage across countries, inconsistencies remain. These cases are detailed in the country notes in the World Bank's *Bureaucrats in Business* (1995a). The state enterprises covered in the table are limited to central or federal government enterprises because data on enterprises owned by local governments are extremely limited. Another weakness in the data is that many state enterprises do not follow generally accepted accounting principles, so accounting rules can vary by country and enterprise. In many cases small state enterprises are not audited by internationally accredited accounting firms, so there may be no independent check on their record keeping and reporting.

To aid in assessing the importance of government ownership, the table includes three measures of the economic size of state enterprises: share in economic activity, share in investment, and share in employment. Indicators that measure the performance of state enterprises and their effect on the macroeconomy and growth include credit, net financial flows from government, and overall balance before transfers. These indicators do not, however, allow analysis of the relative efficiency of state enterprises and private firms because not enough data are available on ownership by economic sector. The data in the table are period averages for 1985–90 and 1990–97. Updating of data has necessitated revisions to data for earlier years to ensure consistency over the time series.

Data on proceeds from privatization are included in the table because privatization—the transfer of productive assets from the public to the private sector—has been one of the defining economic changes of the past two decades. Direct sales are the most common method of privatization, accounting for more than half of privatization revenues in 1998. Direct sales enable governments to attract strategic investors who can transfer capital, technology, and managerial know-how to newly privatized enterprises. Share issues in domestic and international capital markets are the second most common method, accounting for most of the remaining sales.

Large sales proceeds do not necessarily imply major changes in the control of stock of state-owned enterprises. For example, selling equity may not change effective control. It may only generate revenue, with no gains in efficiency. A preliminary analysis suggests that the increase in proceeds from privatization in recent years is due to a larger number of countries privatizing a few firms rather than to a radical restructuring of ownership in many countries (Haggarty and Shirley 1997).

The data on privatization proceeds are from various sources, including reports from official privatization agencies and World Bank estimates, supplemented by such publications as the *Financial Times, Privatization International, Institutional Investor, International Financing Review, Latin Finance, Project Finance,* the *Middle East Economic Digest,* and *Euromoney.* All data are in U.S. dollars. Estimates of privatization proceeds include data on the largest transactions, but in some cases total privatization revenues may be underreported because of lack of data.

Definitions

• **Economic activity** is the value added by state enterprises, estimated as their sales revenue minus the cost of their intermediate inputs, or as the sum of their operating surplus (balance) and wage payments. • **Investment** refers to fixed capital formation by state enterprises. • **Credit** is credit extended to state enterprises by domestic financial institutions. • **Net financial flows from government** are calculated as the difference between total financial flows from the government to state enterprises (including government loans, equity, and subsidies) and total flows from state enterprises to the government (including dividends and taxes). Taxes paid by state enterprises are treated as a transfer of financial resources to the government. • **Overall balance before transfers** is the sum of net operating and net nonoperating revenues minus net capital expenditure. Net operating revenues (or operating surplus or balance) refer to gross operating profits, or operating revenues, minus the costs of intermediate inputs, wages, factor rentals, and depreciation. • **Employment** for many countries refers to the share of full-time state enterprise employees in total employment, but for some it refers to employment only in selected state enterprises, including financial ones, and for others it refers to employment as a share of total formal sector employment. Thus the data on state enterprise employment are not directly comparable. • **Proceeds from privatization** include all sales of public assets to private entities through public offers, direct sales, management and employee buyouts, concessions or licensing agreements, and joint ventures.

Data sources

The data on state enterprises were collected from World Bank member country central banks, finance ministries, enterprises, and World Bank and International Monetary Fund reports. These data were then collated into a database for the World Bank Policy Research Report *Bureaucrats in Business: The Economics and Politics of Government Ownership* (1995a). Updates to this database have been made for several economies. The data on privatization are from the World Bank's Privatization Database and are available on the *Global Development Finance 2000* CD-ROM. The data on credit are from the International Monetary Fund's *International Financial Statistics.*

5.9 Transport infrastructure

	Roads			Railways			Air		
	Paved roads % 1998	Normalized road index 1998	Goods hauled million ton-km 1998	Passenger-km per PPP $ million of GDP 1998	Goods transported ton-km per PPP $ million of GDP 1998	Diesel locomotives available % 1995–98	Aircraft departures thousands 1998	Passengers carried thousands 1998	Air freight million ton-km 1998
Albania	*30.0*	53	1,830	9,611	2,029	..	1	21	0
Algeria	*68.9*	182	..	*13,564*	..	..	44	3,382	19
Angola	*25.0*	..	..	..	..	..	7	553	38
Argentina	29.5	88	..	..	..	..	145	8,447	246
Armenia	*100.0*	171	213	6,612	53,150	30	5	365	10
Australia	*38.7*	113	..	..	..	..	378	30,186	1,904
Austria	100.0	130	*15,700*	*52,099*	*79,889*	89	128	5,872	269
Azerbaijan	92.3	..	706	..	..	..	10	669	93
Bangladesh	*9.5*	71	..	*24,687*	*5,148*	81	12	1,153	141
Belarus	95.6	150	9,747	205,057	469,369	93	6	226	4
Belgium	80.7	90	*36,000*	29,898	32,071	86	213	8,748	473
Benin	*20.0*	81	..	..	..	..	2	91	14
Bolivia	*5.5*	62	..	..	..	..	32	2,116	43
Bosnia and Herzegovina	*52.3*	..	..	..	..	..	1	50	0
Botswana	*23.5*	260	..	..	..	..	5	124	0
Brazil	*9.3*	127	..	..	*31,663*	..	610	28,091	1,714
Bulgaria	92.0	95	307	119,375	154,935	80	15	828	30
Burkina Faso	*16.0*	90	..	..	..	..	2	102	14
Burundi	..	..	..	..	..	..	1	12	0
Cambodia	*7.5*	..	*1,200*	..	*78,146*	..	..	..	..
Cameroon	*12.5*	77	..	*13,282*	*37,719*	68	7	278	31
Canada	*35.3*	68	*72,240*	*1,979*	*440,137*	83	318	24,653	1,806
Central African Republic	2.7	47	*60*	..	..	..	2	91	14
Chad	*0.8*	13	..	..	..	..	2	98	14
Chile	*13.8*	57	..	*6,398*	*7,959*	65	119	5,150	1,308
China	..	..	..	91,741	304,775	82	511	53,234	3,037
Hong Kong, China	*100.0*	..	..	..	..	..	235	12,254	4,185
Colombia	*12.0*	42	..	*62*	*1,945*	..	235	9,290	801
Congo, Dem. Rep.	..	..	..	*695*	..	15	..	..	..
Congo, Rep.	*9.7*	125	..	*93,827*	..	35	10	241	14
Costa Rica	21.0	247	*3,070*	..	..	50	37	1,170	96
Côte d'Ivoire	*9.7*	84	..	*6,125*	*19,827*	53	4	162	14
Croatia	..	..	..	30,318	60,241	63	17	828	2
Cuba	*49.0*	..	..	..	..	53	20	1,138	73
Czech Republic	100.0	..	33,912	55,011	143,684	86	30	1,601	25
Denmark	100.0	96	*14,700*	41,923	12,268	..	115	5,947	201
Dominican Republic	*49.4*	124	..	..	..	..	1	34	0
Ecuador	16.8	123	*3,753*	..	..	..	27	1,919	59
Egypt, Arab Rep.	*78.1*	176	*31,500*	*306,406*	*20,062*	..	40	3,895	255
El Salvador	*19.8*	54	..	..	..	..	19	1,694	15
Eritrea	*21.8*	..	..	..	..	..	..	..	..
Estonia	22.1	111	3,791	21,190	519,698	80	11	297	1
Ethiopia	*15.0*	42	..	..	..	..	27	790	127
Finland	64.0	68	*25,400*	31,436	92,017	88	119	6,771	276
France	100.0	135	*237,200*	51,844	43,309	93	692	42,232	4,752
Gabon	*8.2*	41	..	*11,575*	*67,137*	89	10	467	35
Gambia, The	*35.4*	252	..	..	..	..	..	..	..
Georgia	*93.5*	..	*98*	*30,492*	*146,315*	34	2	110	1
Germany	*99.1*	..	*301,800*	..	..	92	673	49,280	6,242
Ghana	*24.1*	119	..	..	..	..	4	210	30
Greece	*91.8*	111	*96,200*	12,386	2,196	..	91	6,403	113
Guatemala	*27.6*	62	..	..	..	..	7	506	40
Guinea	*16.5*	154	..	..	..	..	1	36	1
Guinea-Bissau	*10.3*	..	..	..	..	..	1	20	0
Haiti	*24.3*	..	..	..	..	..	..	..	..
Honduras	*20.3*	120	..	..	..	..	..	..	..

Transport infrastructure 5.9

	Roads			Railways			Air		
	Paved roads % 1998	Normalized road index 1998	Goods hauled million ton-km 1998	Passenger-km per PPP $ million of GDP 1998	Goods transported ton-km per PPP $ million of GDP 1998	Diesel locomotives available % 1995–98	Aircraft departures thousands 1998	Passengers carried thousands 1998	Air freight million ton-km 1998
Hungary	43.4	127	..	64,345	74,713	64	28	1,749	37
India	*45.7*	..	..	*188,510*	*137,082*	90	196	16,521	531
Indonesia	*46.3*	235	..	29,795	9,125	83	197	12,614	696
Iran, Islamic Rep.	*50.0*	..	..	*19,626*	*46,269*	47	80	9,200	103
Iraq	*86.0*	..	..	..	..	..	..	..	..
Ireland	*94.1*	216	*5,500*	19,839	4,875	82	123	10,401	130
Israel	100.0	97	..	*3,411*	*9,605*	92	50	3,699	1,117
Italy	*100.0*	115	*207,200*	39,886	18,885	79	338	27,463	1,476
Jamaica	*70.7*	..	..	..	..	..	13	1,454	24
Japan	*74.9*	74	*306,263*	*79,919*	*7,854*	88	637	101,701	7,514
Jordan	*100.0*	122	..	..	*40,974*	90	15	1,187	219
Kazakhstan	86.5	145	4,637	*180,227*	*1,498,375*	..	10	566	15
Kenya	*13.9*	141	..	*12,585*	*41,917*	..	20	1,138	54
Korea, Dem. Rep.	*6.4*	..	..	..	..	..	1	64	2
Korea, Rep.	74.5	135	*74,504*	48,617	20,362	88	208	27,109	7,290
Kuwait	*80.6*	..	..	..	..	..	19	2,241	322
Kyrgyz Republic	*91.1*	..	*350*	..	..	..	15	620	6
Lao PDR	*13.8*	122	..	..	..	..	4	124	1
Latvia	38.6	176	4,108	*110,948*	*788,435*	88	10	229	1
Lebanon	*95.0*	..	..	..	..	..	10	716	108
Lesotho	*17.9*	118	..	..	..	..	2	28	0
Libya	*57.1*	..	..	..	..	..	6	571	0
Lithuania	91.0	274	5,611	30,001	346,800	88	10	259	3
Macedonia, FYR	*63.8*	52	*1,210*	17,428	47,137	45	8	489	0
Madagascar	*11.6*	140	..	..	..	..	18	601	31
Malawi	*19.0*	202	..	*3,095*	*11,185*	..	4	158	4
Malaysia	*75.1*	..	..	8,314	*7,339*	65	174	13,654	1,376
Mali	*12.1*	71	..	*29,433*	*34,053*	..	2	91	14
Mauritania	*11.3*	44	..	..	..	..	5	250	14
Mauritius	96.0	190	..	..	..	..	11	848	167
Mexico	*29.7*	102	*154,083*	2,580	62,102	68	292	17,717	278
Moldova	*87.3*	128	*780*	..	..	..	3	118	0
Mongolia	3.4	..	123	*242,287*	*653,947*	..	5	240	1
Morocco	52.3	142	*2,086*	*17,268*	*49,613*	75	40	3,012	58
Mozambique	*18.7*	112	*110*	..	..	..	5	201	6
Myanmar	*12.2*	..	..	..	..	..	15	333	1
Namibia	*8.3*	167	..	*5,887*	*129,941*	89	8	214	32
Nepal	*41.5*	70	..	..	..	..	29	754	18
Netherlands	90.0	62	*45,000*	*42,090*	*9,938*	88	188	18,676	3,833
New Zealand	*58.1*	94	..	..	*51,977*	..	236	8,655	826
Nicaragua	*10.1*	60	..	..	..	..	1	51	8
Niger	*7.9*	26	..	..	..	..	2	91	14
Nigeria	*30.9*	274	..	*26,710*	*4,834*	18	8	313	8
Norway	74.5	100	*11,838*	..	..	..	305	14,292	203
Oman	*30.0*	..	..	..	..	..	16	1,849	105
Pakistan	57.0	415	90,268	*87,755*	*26,278*	..	69	5,414	402
Panama	28.1	115	..	..	..	..	22	860	22
Papua New Guinea	*3.5*	26	..	..	..	..	30	1,110	15
Paraguay	*9.5*	..	..	..	..	..	4	222	0
Peru	12.9	43	..	*1,432*	*4,757*	..	45	2,775	9
Philippines	19.8	83	..	976	4	..	62	6,732	363
Poland	65.6	118	69,543	87,112	209,664	55	38	2,213	104
Portugal	..	70	*13,500*	31,403	13,975	88	98	7,023	248
Puerto Rico	*100.0*	..	..	..	..	..	..	..	..
Romania	67.6	82	15,785	105,645	146,252	78	15	908	12
Russian Federation	..	..	..	*151,547*	*1,042,132*	..	281	15,224	737

5.9 Transport infrastructure

	Roads			Railways			Air		
	Paved roads % 1998	Normalized road index 1998	Goods hauled million ton-km 1998	Passenger-km per PPP $ million of GDP 1998	Goods transported ton-km per PPP $ million of GDP 1998	Diesel locomotives available % 1995–98	Aircraft departures thousands 1998	Passengers carried thousands 1998	Air freight million ton-km 1998
Rwanda	*9.1*	116	..	..	..	..	..	..	..
Saudi Arabia	*30.1*	82	..	*1,007*	*3,843*	80	101	11,816	934
Senegal	*29.3*	125	..	*6,223*	*35,183*	79	4	121	14
Sierra Leone	*8.0*	97	..	..	..	..	0	0	0
Singapore	97.3	..	..	..	..	..	62	13,331	4,714
Slovak Republic	99.0	..	4,750	59,138	224,788	87	5	107	0
Slovenia	90.6	95	325	22,804	92,945	..	10	460	3
South Africa	11.8	101	..	*28,670*	*283,262*	96	93	6,480	301
Spain	*99.0*	97	*16,500*	27,378	17,569	87	388	31,594	767
Sri Lanka	95.0	131	*30*	*64,743*	*2,035*	..	9	1,213	157
Sudan	*36.3*	..	..	*4,511*	*41,113*	42	4	499	6
Sweden	77.5	121	*33,100*	38,261	*99,690*	..	223	11,878	294
Switzerland	..	..	13,250	..	..	..	250	14,299	1,962
Syrian Arab Republic	*23.1*	..	..	*5,374*	*26,484*	100	9	685	14
Tajikistan	*82.7*	..	..	..	..	..	3	592	3
Tanzania	*4.2*	77	..	*71,671*	*71,671*	66	6	220	4
Thailand	*97.5*	205	..	33,653	8,835	72	94	15,015	1,522
Togo	*31.6*	152	..	..	..	..	2	91	14
Trinidad and Tobago	*51.1*	275	..	..	..	..	13	804	18
Tunisia	*78.9*	173	..	*20,214*	*42,976*	71	20	1,859	20
Turkey	28.0	43	152,210	15,146	20,310	74	104	9,949	260
Turkmenistan	*81.2*	..	..	..	..	..	9	521	2
Uganda	..	..	..	..	4,990	..	1	100	1
Ukraine	96.5	132	18,266	310,851	987,824	87	30	1,066	27
United Arab Emirates	100.0	7	..	..	..	..	41	5,264	900
United Kingdom	100.0	59	*152,500*	..	..	..	802	61,940	4,663
United States	*58.8*	98	*1,534,430*	*1,050*	213,751	..	7,824	588,171	25,756
Uruguay	*90.0*	151	..	*7,941*	*6,290*	..	10	557	12
Uzbekistan	*87.3*	..	..	44,314	317,391	..	12	1,560	7
Venezuela, RB	*33.6*	136	..	0	*354*	65	67	3,737	63
Vietnam	*25.1*	..	..	21,841	11,367	95	30	2,304	96
West Bank and Gaza	..	..	..	..	..	..	..	..	..
Yemen, Rep.	*8.1*	..	..	..	..	..	7	765	12
Yugoslavia, FR (Serb./Mont.)	59.3	..	*1,244*	..	..	..	..	..	..
Zambia	..	235	..	*28,868*	*57,858*	62	1	49	1
Zimbabwe	*47.4*	120	..	*16,784*	*140,231*	70	18	789	140
World	*43.1* m	114 m					19,654 s	1,466,848 s	
Low income	*18.3*	120					1,302	104,083	
Excl. China & India	*18.3*	119					594	34,264	
Middle income	*50.6*	124					3,677	241,704	
Lower middle income	*50.7*	124					1,244	84,422	
Upper middle income	*43.1*	118					2,433	157,283	
Low & middle income	*29.5*	121					4,979	345,787	
East Asia & Pacific	*17.4*	..					1,450	133,490	
Europe & Central Asia	86.5	127					676	41,143	
Latin America & Carib.	*26.0*	115					1,797	89,378	
Middle East & N. Africa	*50.2*	..					401	40,144	
South Asia	57.0	131					323	25,390	
Sub-Saharan Africa	*15.0*	118					332	16,242	
High income	93.9	97					14,674	1,121,061	
Europe EMU	90.0	97					2,984	208,761	

Transport infrastructure 5.9

About the data

Transport infrastructure—highways, railways, ports and waterways, and airports and air traffic control systems—and the services that flow from it are crucial to the activities of households, producers, and governments. Because performance indicators vary significantly by transport mode and by focus (whether physical infrastructure or the services flowing from that infrastructure), highly specialized and carefully specified indicators are required. The table provides selected indicators of the size and extent of roads, railways, and air transport systems and the volume of freight and passengers carried.

Data for most transport sectors are not internationally comparable. Unlike for demographic statistics, national income accounts, and international trade data, the collection of infrastructure data has not been "internationalized." Data on roads are collected by the International Road Federation (IRF), and data on air transport by the International Civil Aviation Organization. National road associations are the primary source of IRF data; in countries where such an association is lacking or does not respond, other agencies are contacted, such as road directorates, ministries of transport or public works, or central statistical offices. As a result the compiled data are of uneven quality.

Even when data are available, they are often of limited value because of incompatible definitions, inappropriate geographical units of observation, lack of timeliness, and variations in the nature of the terrain. Data on passengers carried, for example, may be distorted because of "ticketless" travel or breaks in journeys; in such cases the statistics may report the number of passenger-kilometers for two passengers rather than one. Measurement problems are compounded because the mix of transported commodities changes over time, and in some cases shorter-haul traffic has been excluded from intercity traffic. Finally, the quality of transport service (reliability, transit time, and condition of goods delivered) is rarely measured but may be as important as quantity in assessing an economy's transport system. Serious efforts are needed to create international databases whose comparability and accuracy can be gradually improved.

Some form of normalization is required to measure the relative size of an indicator over time or across countries. The table presents normalized indicators for railway passengers and goods transported by rail as well as the normalized road index. While the rail traffic indicators are normalized by a single indicator—the size of the economy—the normalized road index uses a multidimensional regression function to estimate a country's "normal," or expected, stock of roads (Armington and Dikhanov 1996). This index is an attempt to assess the adequacy of the stock of paved roads in a country at a given level of development. Normalizing variables include population, population density, per capita income, urbanization, and regional characteristics. The value of the normalized road index shows whether a country's stock of paved roads exceeds or falls short of the average for countries with similar characteristics. There are many reasons that the stock of paved roads may be considerably smaller or larger than the expected stock. The region-specific dummy variables may not adequately capture such country-level variables as variations in terrain (steep mountains, deserts), differing definitions of urban and rural and dispersion of the population, and differing modes of transport (for example, travel by waterway may substitute for road travel).

Figure 5.9

Air traffic is concentrated in high-income economies

Domestic and international aircraft departures in top five high-income countries, 1998 (thousands)

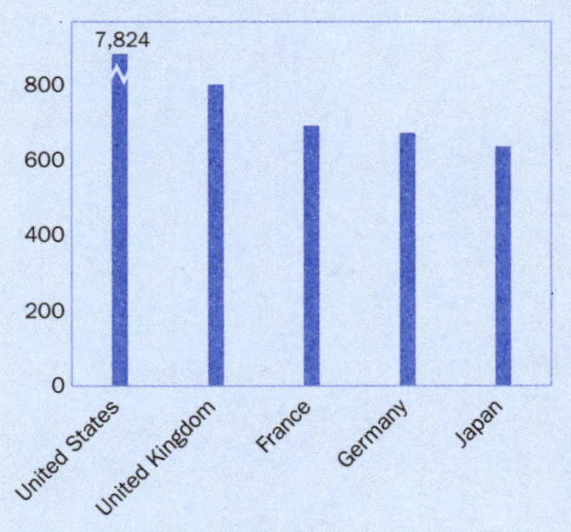

Source: Table 5.9.

High-income economies account for about 75 percent of aircraft departures. Among developing economies, Brazil, China, Colombia, Mexico, and Russia lead, with about 40 percent of this group's air traffic.

Definitions

• **Paved roads** are those surfaced with crushed stone (macadam) and hydrocarbon binder or bituminized agents, with concrete, or with cobblestones, as a percentage of all the country's roads, measured in length. • **Normalized road index** is the total length of paved roads in a country compared with the expected length, where the expectation is conditioned on population, population density, per capita income, urbanization, and region-specific dummy variables. A value of 100 is "normal." If the index is more than 100, the country's stock of paved roads exceeds the average for a country at that level of development. • **Goods hauled by road** are the volume of goods transported by road vehicles, measured in millions of metric tons times kilometers traveled. • **Railway passengers** refer to the total number of passengers transported times kilometers traveled per million dollars of GDP measured in purchasing power parity (PPP) terms (see *About the data* for tables 4.11 and 4.12 for discussion of PPP). • **Goods transported by rail** are the tonnage of goods transported times kilometers traveled per million dollars of GDP measured in purchasing power parity (PPP) terms. • **Diesel locomotives available** are those in service as a percentage of all diesel locomotives. • **Aircraft departures** are the number of domestic and international takeoffs of aircraft. • **Air passengers carried** include both domestic and international aircraft passengers. • **Air freight** is the sum of the metric tons of freight, express, and diplomatic bags carried on each flight stage (the operation of an aircraft from takeoff to its next landing) multiplied by the stage distance.

Data sources

The data on roads are from the International Road Federation's *World Road Statistics* and from Eurostat (europa.eu.int/eurostat.html). The normalized road index is based on World Bank staff estimates. The railway data are from a database maintained by the World Bank's Transportation, Water, and Urban Development Department, Transport Division. The air transport data are from the International Civil Aviation Organization's *Civil Aviation Statistics of the World*.

5.10 Power and communications

	Electric power			Telephone mainlines[a]							International telecommunications[a]	
	Consumption per capita kwh 1997	Production average annual % growth 1980–97	Transmission and distribution losses % of output 1997	per 1,000 people 1998	In largest city per 1,000 people 1998	Waiting list thousands 1998	Waiting time years 1998	per employee 1998	Revenue per line $ 1998	Cost of local call $ per 3 minutes 1998	Outgoing traffic minutes per subscriber 1998	Cost of call to U.S. $ per 3 minutes 1998
Albania	851	1.4	53	31	176	70.0	2.9	26	505	0.02	425	4.37
Algeria	566	6.4	15	53	*55*	730.0	5.2	88	157	0.02	76	4.70
Angola	64	2.5	28	6	17	..	..	35	1,625	0.14	385	5.13
Argentina	1,634	3.5	17	203	247	58.2	0.1	345	903	0.10	45	*7.37*
Armenia	1,141	*–7.1*	21	157	206	110.0	..	66	86	0.12	102	..
Australia	8,307	4.0	6	512	495	0.0	0.0	132	1,351	0.16	125	2.36
Austria	6,051	1.9	6	491	*519*	0.0	0.0	199	1,031	0.19	313	1.60
Azerbaijan	1,631	*–0.7*	23	89	184	146.3	>10.0	54	118	0.13	94	12.49
Bangladesh	76	10.1	15	3	21	144.9	4.8	19	683	0.04	111	..
Belarus	2,607	*–2.1*	15	241	340	487.5	2.8	93	38	0.00	71	*5.00*
Belgium	7,055	2.8	5	500	*501*	..	*0.0*	233	974	0.17	*270*	2.00
Benin	43	7.0	76	7	*36*	*3.4*	1.0	30	1,189	*0.12*	296	7.16
Bolivia	391	4.8	11	*69*	*96*	..	..	*290*	*391*	..	*45*	..
Bosnia and Herzegovina	476	*–21.6*	23	91	445	*70.0*	*4.0*	190	431	0.03	285	3.69
Botswana	..	..	..	65	*180*	*11.8*	*1.0*	60	897	*0.03*	*432*	4.77
Brazil	1,743	4.5	17	121	*165*	*2,400.0*	..	236	*882*	0.09	27	2.76
Bulgaria	3,203	0.0	14	329	*378*	416.0	7.0	104	111	0.00	31	..
Burkina Faso	..	..	..	4	32	..	..	33	1,277	0.10	212	11.49
Burundi	..	..	..	3	62	10.0	>10.0	29	627	0.03	*140*	9.25
Cambodia	..	..	..	2	*10*	..	*2.8*	32	940	*0.09*	309	..
Cameroon	181	3.0	20	*5*	*30*	*45.0*	7.9	*41*	*1,000*	*0.06*	*335*	3.39
Canada	15,829	2.5	4	634	..	0.0	0.0	213	881	..	*230*	*1.16*
Central African Republic	..	..	..	3	*15*	*0.3*	*0.4*	24	1,292	*0.20*	431	8.37
Chad	..	..	..	1	7	0.6	0.5	23	1,452	0.17	376	*14.07*
Chile	2,011	6.6	9	205	281	58.3	0.2	323	778	0.12	85	2.86
China	714	8.6	8	70	294	*812.0*	*0.1*	197	235	*0.01*	20	*6.66*
Hong Kong, China	4,959	5.6	14	558	558	0.0	0.0	104	1,761	0.00	504	2.63
Colombia	885	4.8	22	173	322	1,594.0	1.9	180	*693*	0.02	32	1.75
Congo, Dem. Rep.	120	2.1	3	*0*	*5*	*6.0*	..	*17*	..	..	*36*	..
Congo, Rep.	197	6.6	1	8	..	..	*0.8*	*23*	*2,200*	..	..	..
Costa Rica	1,353	5.1	8	172	*478*	40.8	0.7	147	411	*0.03*	116	3.37
Côte d'Ivoire	181	2.3	16	12	47	33.1	1.8	46	1,434	0.11	337	7.86
Croatia	2,429	*0.5*	19	348	*324*	*72.0*	0.8	143	474	*0.03*	176	*5.66*
Cuba	1,044	1.1	17	35	75	..	..	23	1,356	0.00	75	7.35
Czech Republic	4,817	0.8	8	364	670	141.0	0.3	153	539	0.07	91	3.28
Denmark	6,027	4.2	5	660	..	0.0	0.0	202	1,076	0.13	167	1.77
Dominican Republic	620	4.9	28	93	*129*	..	..	200	..	..	*201*	..
Ecuador	611	6.2	23	78	234	..	*0.8*	140	444	0.01	76	3.73
Egypt, Arab Rep.	803	6.6	12	60	..	..	*3.9*	73	266	..	32	5.84
El Salvador	537	6.0	13	80	*198*	..	*4.0*	112	432	0.06	135	..
Eritrea	..	..	..	7	37	18.4	8.6	32	922	0.03	119	*8.24*
Estonia	3,466	*–5.8*	16	343	381	59.0	2.0	136	432	0.07	151	3.41
Ethiopia	21	4.3	1	3	42	230.2	>10.0	26	542	0.03	72	7.37
Finland	13,689	3.4	4	554	*677*	0.0	0.0	147	1,274	*0.12*	142	1.75
France	6,060	4.2	6	570	..	0.0	0.0	201	806	0.13	100	1.14
Gabon	752	2.9	10	*33*	*89*	*10.0*	*5.1*	*48*	*2,002*	*0.15*	*494*	..
Gambia, The	..	..	..	21	78	24.0	>10.0	29	681	0.32	*216*	*6.18*
Georgia	1,142	*–5.6*	16	115	206	133.8	5.4	69	60	..	73	..
Germany	5,626	0.9	4	567	572	0.0	0.0	212	1,075	0.12	101	1.43
Ghana	276	3.7	0	8	54	*28.3*	*1.5*	40	1,015	0.09	*208*	..
Greece	3,493	4.3	9	522	728	31.3	0.3	252	624	0.04	124	*2.59*
Guatemala	404	6.6	13	*41*	*103*	..	*1.6*	*82*	*586*	*0.03*	*113*	..
Guinea	..	..	..	5	16	1.3	0.2	44	*1,678*	*0.10*	422	9.04
Guinea-Bissau	..	..	..	7	109	3.0	>10.0	34	*1,920*	*0.14*	33	..
Haiti	42	2.0	43	*8*	*17*	*100.0*	>10.0	*21*	*1,457*	*0.00*	*205*	*7.07*
Honduras	411	7.6	24	38	96	689.0	>10.0	56	739	0.06	195	4.86

Power and communications 5.10

	Electric power			Telephone mainlines[a]							International telecommunications[a]	
	Consumption per capita kwh **1997**	Production average annual % growth **1980–97**	Transmission and distribution losses % of output **1997**	per 1,000 people **1998**	In largest city per 1,000 people **1998**	Waiting list thousands **1998**	Waiting time years **1998**	per employee **1998**	Revenue per line $ **1998**	Cost of local call $ per 3 minutes **1998**	Outgoing traffic minutes per subscriber **1998**	Cost of call to U.S. $ per 3 minutes **1998**
Hungary	2,840	2.4	13	336	*412*	80.3	0.2	257	*448*	0.13	70	1.68
India	363	8.6	18	22	*104*	*2,705.7*	*1.0*	50	*284*	*0.02*	20	5.45
Indonesia	329	13.5	12	27	225	..	..	*131*	*509*	*0.03*	58	3.28
Iran, Islamic Rep.	1,163	8.8	22	112	*286*	1,185.0	1.6	154	*203*	0.01	24	7.71
Iraq	1,353	5.4	..	31	75	..	..	..	..	..	..	..
Ireland	4,559	4.0	8	435	..	..	..	133	1,278	0.17	*463*	1.54
Israel	5,069	6.2	9	471	*398*	*22.0*	*0.1*	164	1,409	0.07	*128*	*3.43*
Italy	4,315	2.1	7	451	*498*	*32.0*	*0.1*	282	1,002	0.10	104	1.95
Jamaica	2,170	9.1	11	*166*	..	*183.1*	*3.8*	*102*	*1,020*	*0.06*	*183*	*5.19*
Japan	7,241	3.9	4	503	*933*	0.0	*0.0*	370	1,322	0.08	28	3.44
Jordan	1,196	10.2	10	86	232	73.7	1.1	91	*707*	0.04	239	..
Kazakhstan	2,595	*–1.6*	15	104	224	293.7	..	47	169	*0.00*	113	2.68
Kenya	127	6.0	17	*9*	*71*	*93.9*	*5.6*	*20*	*1,145*	*0.05*	*107*	*11.17*
Korea, Dem. Rep.	..	..	..	47	..	..	..	..	..	..	..	..
Korea, Rep.	4,847	12.1	4	433	*521*	0.0	0.0	331	533	0.03	30	1.50
Kuwait	12,886	5.1	..	236	46	37.5	2.5	49	807	0.00	405	5.41
Kyrgyz Republic	1,372	*1.8*	34	76	241	49.8	*>10.0*	53	76	..	84	15.48
Lao PDR	..	..	..	6	..	8.3	2.1	26	766	..	301	4.00
Latvia	1,758	–1.0	29	302	399	39.9	3.3	152	244	0.08	75	3.00
Lebanon	1,930	4.0	13	194	96	..	..	124	*580*	0.07	113	4.45
Lesotho	..	..	..	10	58	20.0	>10.0	32	688	0.03	*1,593*	..
Libya	3,505	7.9	..	84	94	..	..	*32*	*619*	*0.02*	*93*	..
Lithuania	1,818	*–1.9*	11	300	401	74.5	1.3	118	201	0.05	46	5.49
Macedonia, FYR	..	..	..	*199*	*235*	*40.0*	*1.7*	*117*	*245*	*0.01*	*127*	4.13
Madagascar	..	..	..	3	7	16.9	5.0	16	1,107	0.09	197	11.16
Malawi	..	..	..	3	*62*	*30.9*	*>10.0*	16	897	*0.03*	341	*12.45*
Malaysia	2,352	10.9	9	198	*300*	*160.0*	*0.4*	162	569	0.02	*172*	3.82
Mali	..	..	..	3	18	..	..	20	2,193	0.14	444	*17.59*
Mauritania	..	..	..	6	16	2.9	1.6	32	1,986	0.10	427	..
Mauritius	..	..	..	214	306	25.0	0.8	133	515	0.04	113	4.60
Mexico	1,459	5.5	14	104	135	*6.1*	0.0	155	895	0.13	132	2.59
Moldova	1,217	*–7.5*	27	150	298	167.1	5.5	85	50	0.02	81	3.53
Mongolia	..	..	..	*37*	*88*	*46.9*	*7.7*	*17*	*254*	*0.01*	*34*	5.65
Morocco	423	5.1	4	54	115	17.9	0.2	107	511	0.08	119	4.50
Mozambique	47	2.5	31	4	*24*	19.7	4.2	33	867	*0.04*	251	..
Myanmar	57	6.7	35	5	28	85.8	3.6	30	2,288	*0.16*	83	*26.86*
Namibia	..	..	..	69	317	7.1	0.6	63	721	0.05	543	..
Nepal	39	11.1	28	8	..	*215.3*	5.8	43	339	0.02	95	..
Netherlands	5,736	2.1	4	593	..	0.0	0.0	287	1,046	*0.09*	*173*	0.82
New Zealand	8,380	2.8	11	479	..	0.0	0.0	239	984	0.00	235	0.95
Nicaragua	286	4.3	26	31	*57*	*29.3*	*2.1*	51	*562*	*0.10*	*266*	..
Niger	..	..	..	2	*18*	*1.4*	*1.1*	12	1,315	*0.15*	322	..
Nigeria	84	4.7	32	4	11	42.0	>10.0	35	*3,904*	..	*113*	..
Norway	23,499	1.4	8	660	809	0.0	0.0	128	1,373	*0.10*	*176*	1.05
Oman	2,613	13.0	17	92	*165*	*3.9*	*0.2*	105	1,448	*0.07*	425	..
Pakistan	333	8.9	24	19	61	298.0	1.4	47	356	0.03	30	..
Panama	1,152	3.7	22	151	*250*	*28.8*	*1.4*	*99*	*765*	*0.00*	119	4.36
Papua New Guinea	..	..	..	*11*	*200*	..	*0.1*	*23*	*2,429*	*0.13*	*572*	..
Paraguay	759	33.1	2	55	*129*	20.1	0.5	47	775	*0.06*	131	..
Peru	607	3.0	16	67	*132*	48.0	0.3	292	*926*	*0.09*	52	*5.76*
Philippines	432	4.1	17	37	*92*	*900.2*	*2.8*	*132*	*584*	..	106	4.96
Poland	2,451	0.8	12	228	199	1,801.0	1.8	121	333	0.07	68	3.65
Portugal	3,206	5.7	10	413	*701*	10.0	0.1	192	*896*	0.09	114	1.88
Puerto Rico	..	..	..	*351*	*437*	*57.0*	*0.9*	*168*	*920*	*0.13*	*723*	..
Romania	1,704	–1.6	12	162	357	966.0	4.3	75	185	0.09	36	4.29
Russian Federation	3,981	*–0.5*	10	197	465	7,120.0	5.3	65	127	..	36	6.12

5.10 Power and communications

	Electric power			Telephone mainlines[a]							International telecommunications[a]	
	Consumption per capita kwh 1997	Production average annual % growth 1980–97	Transmission and distribution losses % of output 1997	per 1,000 people 1998	In largest city per 1,000 people 1998	Waiting list thousands 1998	Waiting time years 1998	per employee 1998	Revenue per line $ 1998	Cost of local call $ per 3 minutes 1998	Outgoing traffic minutes per subscriber 1998	Cost of call to U.S. $ per 3 minutes 1998
Rwanda	..	..	..	2	40	3.5	2.7	42	818	0.04	421	..
Saudi Arabia	4,085	9.0	8	143	253	927.4	2.4	130	1,156	0.02	324	*6.41*
Senegal	107	3.8	17	16	47	24.1	1.3	103	1,095	0.13	225	4.48
Sierra Leone	..	..	..	4	18	25.0	>10.0	18	*130*	0.04	*230*	..
Singapore	7,944	8.3	4	562	562	0.0	0.0	202	1,418	0.03	695	1.79
Slovak Republic	4,243	1.5	9	286	636	174.6	1.2	104	304	0.12	100	3.97
Slovenia	4,955	1.6	5	375	*661*	9.2	0.2	*229*	*434*	*0.03*	*157*	*5.56*
South Africa	3,800	3.8	8	115	*415*	*116.2*	*0.4*	84	1,177	0.07	*79*	..
Spain	3,899	3.1	9	414	483	3.3	0.0	267	679	0.10	111	1.88
Sri Lanka	227	6.5	17	28	*271*	*283.8*	*6.3*	49	4,104	*0.03*	75	4.49
Sudan	48	5.7	31	6	33	340.0	>10.0	65	634	0.02	114	7.79
Sweden	14,042	2.4	7	674	*844*	0.0	0.0	*186*	*806*	*0.13*	*169*	1.40
Switzerland	6,885	1.2	6	675	*966*	0.0	0.0	219	1,502	0.14	396	1.55
Syrian Arab Republic	776	8.2	..	95	140	2,904.0	>10.0	74	929	0.05	70	26.71
Tajikistan	2,177	*0.4*	12	37	150	49.1	..	45	36	0.00	45	8.16
Tanzania	54	6.4	14	4	28	37.3	3.6	26	925	0.09	917	13.30
Thailand	1,360	12.5	9	84	361	556.3	1.1	144	322	0.07	58	3.58
Togo	..	..	..	7	28	13.2	4.1	36	1,516	0.10	242	11.44
Trinidad and Tobago	3,368	4.2	8	206	215	7.4	0.4	93	805	0.04	251	3.29
Tunisia	709	6.1	11	81	90	80.7	1.0	117	467	0.06	150	*6.47*
Turkey	1,275	9.5	18	254	398	463.7	0.4	233	201	0.08	38	3.31
Turkmenistan	934	*0.6*	11	82	155	66.9	5.9	47	80	..	43	..
Uganda	..	..	..	3	37	9.0	1.5	29	590	0.18	112	*8.60*
Ukraine	2,449	*–2.5*	16	191	418	2,729.4	5.9	75	128	0.01	*52*	..
United Arab Emirates	7,973	6.5	..	389	374	0.7	0.0	113	1,509	0.00	956	3.77
United Kingdom	5,241	1.4	7	557	..	0.0	0.0	212	1,127	0.20	177	1.18
United States	11,822	2.9	6	661	..	0.0	0.0	175	1,376	0.09	136	..
Uruguay	1,710	1.6	19	250	347	0.0	0.0	142	844	0.18	97	5.21
Uzbekistan	1,645	*0.7*	9	65	231	69.8	..	53	*80*	..	*42*	..
Venezuela, RB	2,488	4.6	21	117	*329*	*392.0*	*2.5*	206	830	*0.06*	62	*5.25*
Vietnam	203	10.4	18	26	90	..	..	*20*	*521*	*0.10*	*32*	..
West Bank and Gaza	..	..	..	..	..	..	5.4	..	..	0.04	..	*0.61*
Yemen, Rep.	93	9.9	26	*13*	*74*	*78.6*	*5.0*	*52*	*303*	*0.02*	*116*	..
Yugoslavia, FR (Serb./Mont.)	..	..	..	218	455	123.0	1.2	153	394	0.02	95	12.08
Zambia	563	–2.1	11	9	23	8.0	>10.0	23	1,321	0.06	174	2.60
Zimbabwe	919	4.7	13	*17*	*75*	*109.0*	*4.2*	*33*	*641*	*0.03*	*278*	2.81
World	**2,053 w**	**4.2 w**	**8 w**	**146 w**	***213* w**	***36,924.8* s**	**1.3 m**	***195* m**	***752* w**	**0.07 m**	**113 m**	**3.77 m**
Low income	448	8.4	12	37	*131*	*6,736.0*	5.5	*121*	*290*	*0.07*	195	..
Excl. China & India	222	7.8	18	14	*77*	*2,779.6*	5.5	*74*	*541*	0.09	197	..
Middle income	1,928	6.6	12	145	*269*	*28,900.2*	1.2	*158*	*522*	0.05	85	4.05
Lower middle income	1,737	8.5	12	115	*286*	*19,845.3*	1.9	*102*	*355*	0.04	75	4.49
Upper middle income	2,211	5.2	13	189	*245*	*7,701.4*	0.4	*206*	*663*	0.07	98	3.41
Low & middle income	896	7.1	12	69	*171*	*36,746.4*	2.4	*145*	*439*	0.06	108	4.49
East Asia & Pacific	771	9.3	8	70	280	*1,901.5*	*1.1*	*173*	*378*	*0.03*	71	3.82
Europe & Central Asia	2,692	8.3	12	200	380	15,832.4	2.8	*111*	*219*	0.07	78	3.97
Latin America & Carib.	1,402	5.0	16	123	*175*	*4,141.2*	*1.1*	*203*	*843*	*0.09*	91	*5.25*
Middle East & N. Africa	1,158	7.7	13	81	*142*	..	2.0	*103*	*463*	0.04	116	..
South Asia	324	8.6	18	19	*96*	*3,292.4*	4.8	*42*	*378*	0.03	75	..
Sub-Saharan Africa	446	3.5	10	14	29	*1,440.0*	4.2	*68*	*962*	0.09	296	..
High income	8,238	2.9	6	567	..	101.4	0.0	*241*	*1,035*	0.10	142	1.76
Europe EMU	5,344	2.4	6	514	*508*	13.3	0.0	*225*	*899*	0.13	111	1.67

a. The data are from the International Telecommunication Union's (ITU) *World Telecommunication Development Report 1999*. Please cite the ITU for third-party use of these data.

Power and communications 5.10

About the data

An economy's production of electricity is a basic indicator of its size and level of development. Although a few countries export electric power, most production is for domestic consumption. Expanding the supply of electricity to meet the growing demand of increasingly urbanized and industrialized economies without incurring unacceptable social, economic, and environmental costs is one of the great challenges facing developing countries.

Data on electric power production and consumption are collected from national energy agencies by the International Energy Agency (IEA) and adjusted by the IEA to meet international definitions. Adjustments are made, for example, to account for self-production by establishments that, in addition to their main activities, generate electricity wholly or partly for their own use. In some countries self-production by households and small entrepreneurs is substantial because of remoteness or unreliable public power sources, and in these cases it may not be adequately reflected in these adjustments. Electricity consumption is equivalent to production less power plants' own use and transmission, distribution, and transformation losses. It includes consumption by auxiliary stations, losses in transformers that are considered integral parts of those stations, and electricity produced by pumping installations. It covers electricity generated by primary sources of energy—coal, oil, gas, nuclear, hydro, geothermal, wind, tide and wave, and combustible renewables—where data are available. Neither production nor consumption data capture the reliability of supplies, including frequency of outages, breakdowns, and load factors.

Over the past decade privatization and liberalization have spurred dramatic growth in telecommunications in many countries. The table presents some common performance indicators for telecommunications, including measures of supply and demand, service quality, productivity, economic and financial performance, and tariffs. The quality of data varies among reporting countries as a result of differences in regulatory obligations for the provision of data.

Demand for telecommunications is often measured by the sum of telephone mainlines and registered applicants for new connections. (A mainline is normally identified by a unique number that is the one billed.) In some countries the list of registered applicants does not reflect real current pending demand, which is often hidden or suppressed, reflecting an extremely short supply that has discouraged potential applicants from applying for telephone service. And in some cases waiting lists may overstate demand because applicants have placed their names on the list several times to improve their chances. Waiting time is calculated by dividing the number of applicants on the waiting list by the average number of mainlines added each year over the past three years. The number of mainlines no longer reflects a telephone system's full capacity because mobile telephones—whose use has been expanding rapidly in most countries, rich and poor—provide an alternative point of access. (See table 5.11 for data on mobile phones.)

The table includes two measures of efficiency in telecommunications: mainlines per employee and revenue per mainline. Caution should be used in interpreting the estimates of mainlines per employee because firms often subcontract part of their work. The cross-country comparability of revenue per mainline may also be limited because, for example, some countries do not require telecommunications providers to submit financial information; the data usually do not include revenues from cellular and mobile phones or radio, paging, and data services; and there are definitional and accounting differences between countries.

Figure 5.10

Mobile phones are connecting the world

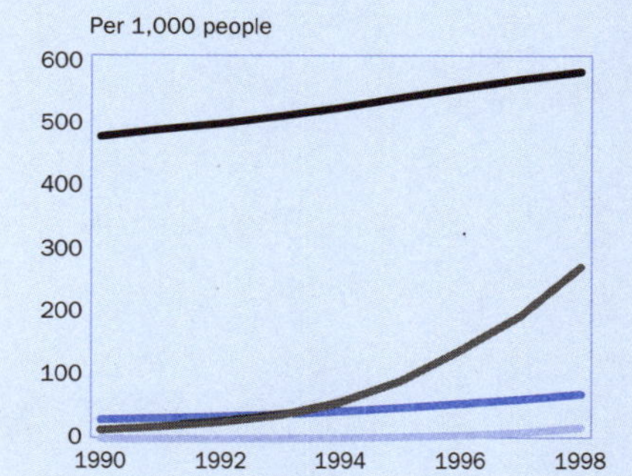

Fixed lines, high-income countries
Mobile phones, high-income countries
Fixed lines, low- and middle-income countries
Mobile phones, low- and middle-income countries

Source: Tables 5.10 and 5.11 based on International Telecommunication Union data.

More people have access to fixed line phones than to mobile phones. But mobile phones are spreading rapidly. In high-income economies there were 20 times as many in 1998 as there were in 1990—and in low- and middle-income economies an astonishing 160 times as many.

Definitions

• **Electric power consumption** measures the production of power plants and combined heat and power plants less transmission, distribution, and transformation losses and own use by heat and power plants. • **Electric power production** refers to gross production in kilowatt-hours by private companies, cooperative organizations, local and regional authorities, government organizations, and self-producers. Electric power production growth is average annual growth in power production. • **Electric power transmission and distribution losses** are losses in transmission between sources of supply and points of distribution and in distribution to consumers, including pilferage. • **Telephone mainlines** are telephone lines connecting a customer's equipment to the public switched telephone network. Data are presented for the entire country and for the largest city. • **Waiting list** shows the number of applications for a connection to a mainline that have been held up by a lack of technical capacity. • **Waiting time** is the approximate number of years applicants must wait for a telephone line. • **Mainlines per employee** are calculated by dividing the number of mainlines by the number of telecommunications staff (with part-time staff converted to full-time equivalents) employed by telecommunications enterprises providing public telecommunications services. • **Revenue per line** is the revenue received per mainline by firms for providing telecommunications services. • **Cost of local call** is the cost of a three-minute call within the same exchange area using the subscriber's equipment (that is, not from a public phone). • **Outgoing traffic** is the telephone traffic, measured in minutes per subscriber, that originates in the country and has a destination outside the country. • **Cost of international call to U.S.** is the cost of a three-minute peak rate call from the country to the United States.

Data sources

The data on electricity consumption, production growth, and losses are from the IEA's *Energy Statistics and Balances of Non-OECD Countries 1996–97*, the IEA's *Energy Statistics of OECD Countries 1996–97*, and the United Nations Statistics Division's *Energy Statistics Yearbook*. The telecommunications data are from the International Telecommunication Union's (ITU) *World Telecommunication Development Report 1999*, except for the data on telephone traffic, which are from *Direction of Traffic*, published by TeleGeography and the ITU.

5.11 The information age

	Daily newspapers	Radios	Television[a]		Mobile phones[a]	Fax machines[a]	Personal computers[a]	Internet hosts[b]
	per 1,000 people 1996	per 1,000 people 1997	Sets per 1,000 people 1998	Cable subscribers per 1,000 people 1998	per 1,000 people 1998	per 1,000 people 1998	per 1,000 people 1998	per 10,000 people July 1999
Albania	36	217	109	0.0	1	3.6	..	0.24
Algeria	38	241	105	0.0	1	0.2	4.2	0.01
Angola	11	54	14	..	1	..	0.8	0.00
Argentina	123	681	289	163.1	78	2.0	44.3	27.85
Armenia	23	224	218	0.4	2	0.1	4.2	1.85
Australia	293	1,376	639	43.6	286	48.6	411.6	477.85
Austria	296	753	516	139.1	282	..	233.4	252.01
Azerbaijan	27	23	254	0.1	8	..	..	0.23
Bangladesh	9	50	6	..	1	..	..	0.00
Belarus	174	296	314	..	1	1.9	..	0.77
Belgium	160	793	510	367.3	173	18.7	286.0	266.90
Benin	2	108	10	..	1	0.2	0.9	0.04
Bolivia	55	675	116	..	27	..	7.5	0.47
Bosnia and Herzegovina	152	248	41	..	7	..	..	1.38
Botswana	27	156	20	..	15	2.3	25.5	6.00
Brazil	40	444	316	16.3	47	3.1	30.1	18.45
Bulgaria	257	543	398	28.8	15	..	..	11.89
Burkina Faso	1	33	9	..	0	..	0.7	0.19
Burundi	3	71	4	..	0	0.7	..	0.00
Cambodia	2	127	123	..	6	0.3	0.9	0.12
Cameroon	7	163	32	..	0	..	..	0.00
Canada	159	1,077	715	263.8	176	33.3	330.0	422.97
Central African Republic	2	83	5	..	0	0.1	..	0.00
Chad	0	242	1	0.0	0	0.0	..	0.00
Chile	98	354	232	44.8	65	2.7	48.2	21.45
China	..	333	272	40.0	19	1.6	8.9	0.50
Hong Kong, China	792	684	431	61.8	475	54.3	254.2	142.77
Colombia	46	581	217	16.7	49	4.8	27.9	7.51
Congo, Dem. Rep.	3	375	135	..	0	..	..	0.00
Congo, Rep.	8	124	12	..	1	..	..	0.00
Costa Rica	94	271	387	13.8	28	2.3	39.1	10.41
Côte d'Ivoire	17	164	70	0.0	6	..	3.6	0.25
Croatia	115	336	272	..	41	11.2	111.6	25.94
Cuba	118	353	239	0.0	0	..	..	0.06
Czech Republic	254	803	447	77.1	94	10.4	97.3	85.58
Denmark	309	1,141	585	248.4	364	..	377.4	540.30
Dominican Republic	52	178	95	15.5	31	0.3	..	7.63
Ecuador	70	419	293	11.7	25	..	18.5	1.42
Egypt, Arab Rep.	40	324	122	..	1	0.5	9.1	0.28
El Salvador	48	464	675	..	18	..	..	1.17
Eritrea	..	91	14	..	0	0.4	..	0.01
Estonia	174	693	480	15.1	170	..	34.4	174.65
Ethiopia	1	195	5	..	0	0.0	..	0.01
Finland	455	1,496	640	175.7	572	38.5	349.2	1,116.78
France	218	937	601	27.5	188	47.4	207.8	110.64
Gabon	29	183	55	..	8	0.4	8.6	0.02
Gambia, The	2	168	3	..	4	1.0	2.6	0.02
Georgia	..	555	473	2.8	11	..	..	1.59
Germany	311	948	580	214.5	170	73.1	304.7	173.96
Ghana	14	238	99	..	1	..	1.6	0.06
Greece	153	477	466	1.2	194	3.8	51.9	59.57
Guatemala	33	79	126	28.5	10	..	8.3	1.26
Guinea	..	47	41	0.0	3	0.4	2.6	0.00
Guinea-Bissau	5	44	..	..	0	0.4	..	0.13
Haiti	3	55	5	..	0	..	..	0.00
Honduras	55	386	90	..	5	..	7.6	0.19

The information age 5.11

	Daily newspapers	Radios	Television[a]		Mobile phones[a]	Fax machines[a]	Personal computers[a]	Internet hosts[b]
	per 1,000 people 1996	per 1,000 people 1997	Sets per 1,000 people 1998	Cable subscribers per 1,000 people 1998	per 1,000 people 1998	per 1,000 people 1998	per 1,000 people 1998	per 10,000 people July 1999
Hungary	186	689	437	146.5	105	17.7	58.9	93.13
India	..	121	69	18.8	1	0.2	2.7	0.18
Indonesia	24	156	136	..	5	0.9	8.2	0.76
Iran, Islamic Rep.	28	265	157	0.0	6	..	31.9	0.05
Iraq	19	229	83	..	0	..	..	0.00
Ireland	150	699	403	171.1	257	27.4	271.7	156.68
Israel	290	520	318	184.0	359	24.9	217.2	187.41
Italy	104	878	486	2.8	355	31.3	173.4	68.28
Jamaica	62	480	182	73.1	22	..	39.4	1.04
Japan	578	955	707	114.8	374	126.8	237.2	163.75
Jordan	58	287	52	0.1	12	8.6	8.7	1.17
Kazakhstan	..	384	231	..	2	0.1	..	1.42
Kenya	9	104	21	..	0	..	2.5	0.19
Korea, Dem. Rep.	199	147	53	..	0	..	..	..
Korea, Rep.	393	1,033	346	138.3	302	..	156.8	55.53
Kuwait	374	660	491	..	138	27.6	104.9	23.76
Kyrgyz Republic	15	112	45	..	0	..	..	4.13
Lao PDR	4	143	4	..	1	..	1.1	0.00
Latvia	247	710	492	58.0	68	..	..	50.86
Lebanon	107	906	352	1.4	157	..	39.2	7.02
Lesotho	8	49	25	..	5	..	..	0.08
Libya	14	233	126	0.0	3	..	..	0.00
Lithuania	93	513	459	67.5	72	1.7	54.0	30.45
Macedonia, FYR	21	200	250	..	15	1.5	..	4.40
Madagascar	5	192	21	..	1	..	1.3	0.12
Malawi	3	249	2	..	1	0.1	..	0.00
Malaysia	158	420	166	5.2	99	6.9	58.6	23.53
Mali	1	54	12	0.0	0	..	0.7	0.01
Mauritania	0	151	91	..	0	1.7	5.5	0.00
Mauritius	75	368	226	..	53	24.5	87.1	4.56
Mexico	97	325	261	15.7	35	3.0	47.0	23.02
Moldova	60	740	297	17.6	2	0.2	6.4	2.42
Mongolia	27	151	63	10.8	1	2.7	5.4	0.04
Morocco	26	241	160	..	4	0.7	2.5	0.28
Mozambique	3	40	5	..	0	..	1.6	0.09
Myanmar	10	95	7	..	0	0.1	..	0.00
Namibia	19	144	37	..	12	..	18.6	11.73
Nepal	11	38	6	0.2	0	..	..	0.07
Netherlands	306	978	543	378.3	213	38.4	317.6	403.49
New Zealand	216	990	508	1.3	203	..	282.1	476.18
Nicaragua	30	285	190	40.2	4	..	7.8	2.21
Niger	0	69	27	..	0	..	0.2	0.03
Nigeria	24	223	66	..	0	..	5.7	0.00
Norway	588	915	579	160.1	474	50.0	373.4	754.15
Oman	29	598	595	0.0	43	2.7	21.0	2.87
Pakistan	23	98	88	0.1	1	1.9	3.9	0.22
Panama	62	299	187	..	29	..	27.1	2.97
Papua New Guinea	15	97	24	..	1	..	..	0.49
Paraguay	43	182	101	..	41	..	9.6	2.43
Peru	84	273	144	14.1	30	..	18.1	3.09
Philippines	79	159	108	8.2	22	..	15.1	1.29
Poland	113	523	413	83.3	50	..	43.9	40.86
Portugal	75	304	542	59.8	309	7.0	81.3	59.40
Puerto Rico	126	753	271	..	152	..	..	3.01
Romania	300	319	233	119.2	29	..	10.2	9.01
Russian Federation	105	418	420	78.5	5	0.4	40.6	13.06

5.11 The information age

	Daily newspapers	Radios	Television[a]		Mobile phones[a]	Fax machines[a]	Personal computers[a]	Internet hosts[b]
	per 1,000 people 1996	per 1,000 people 1997	Sets per 1,000 people 1998	Cable subscribers per 1,000 people 1998	per 1,000 people 1998	per 1,000 people 1998	per 1,000 people 1998	per 10,000 people July 1999
Rwanda	*0*	102	*0*	..	1	0.1	..	0.00
Saudi Arabia	57	321	*262*	..	31	..	49.6	1.17
Senegal	5	142	*41*	..	2	..	*11.4*	0.28
Sierra Leone	4	253	13	0.0	0	0.5	..	0.14
Singapore	360	822	348	49.5	346	31.6	458.4	322.30
Slovak Republic	185	580	*402*	*105.1*	87	10.0	65.1	38.79
Slovenia	199	406	356	150.5	84	*9.8*	250.9	99.34
South Africa	32	317	*125*	..	56	*3.5*	47.4	33.36
Spain	100	333	*506*	*11.8*	179	*17.8*	144.8	76.75
Sri Lanka	29	209	*92*	*0.0*	9	..	*4.1*	0.52
Sudan	27	271	87	0.0	0	0.6	1.9	0.00
Sweden	445	932	*531*	221.4	464	*50.9*	361.4	581.47
Switzerland	337	1,000	*535*	*352.7*	235	*29.2*	421.8	371.37
Syrian Arab Republic	20	278	*70*	..	0	1.4	*1.7*	0.00
Tajikistan	20	142	*285*	..	0	0.3	..	0.24
Tanzania	4	279	*21*	*0.0*	1	..	*1.6*	0.05
Thailand	63	232	*236*	10.1	32	*2.5*	21.6	4.49
Togo	4	218	18	..	2	4.1	6.8	0.17
Trinidad and Tobago	123	534	*334*	..	20	3.9	46.8	28.20
Tunisia	31	223	198	..	4	*3.4*	14.7	0.06
Turkey	111	180	*286*	9.2	53	*1.7*	23.2	8.06
Turkmenistan	..	276	201	..	1	..	..	0.56
Uganda	2	128	*27*	..	1	*0.1*	*1.5*	0.06
Ukraine	54	884	*490*	*15.7*	2	*0.0*	13.8	4.56
United Arab Emirates	156	345	*294*	..	210	*21.0*	106.2	39.44
United Kingdom	329	1,436	645	45.9	252	*33.9*	263.0	270.60
United States	215	2,146	*847*	244.3	256	*78.4*	458.6	1,508.77
Uruguay	293	607	*241*	..	60	..	91.2	38.34
Uzbekistan	3	465	*275*	..	1	..	..	0.05
Venezuela, RB	206	468	185	25.8	87	*3.0*	43.0	3.98
Vietnam	4	107	*47*	..	2	*0.3*	6.4	0.00
West Bank and Gaza	..	..	..	..	..	..	..	..
Yemen, Rep.	15	64	*29*	..	1	..	*1.2*	0.02
Yugoslavia, FR (Serb./Mont.)	107	297	*259*	..	23	1.9	18.8	7.65
Zambia	12	121	137	..	1	0.1	..	0.48
Zimbabwe	19	93	*30*	..	4	..	*9.0*	1.19
World	**.. w**	**418 w**	***247* w**	***55.8* w**	**55 w**	***12.7* w**	**70.6 w**	**94.47 w**
Low income	..	206	*138*	*27.7*	8	*0.9*	6.2	0.31
Excl. China & India	13	148	*60*	..	2	..	..	0.22
Middle income	74	401	*255*	*36.3*	39	*1.9*	37.4	13.40
Lower middle income	59	354	*227*	..	15	..	24.9	5.89
Upper middle income	96	471	*297*	*44.8*	75	*3.5*	50.3	24.65
Low & middle income	..	263	*172*	*29.5*	17	*1.3*	15.6	4.16
East Asia & Pacific	..	302	*228*	*39.7*	25	*1.6*	14.1	2.39
Europe & Central Asia	102	442	*353*	*60.5*	23	*1.6*	34.6	15.47
Latin America & Carib.	71	420	*255*	*28.3*	45	*3.1*	34.0	14.78
Middle East & N. Africa	33	274	*135*	..	8	..	*9.9*	0.37
South Asia	..	112	*61*	*16.3*	1	*0.3*	2.9	0.17
Sub-Saharan Africa	12	198	*52*	..	5	..	*7.5*	2.32
High income	286	1,286	*662*	184.0	265	*72.3*	311.2	607.55
Europe EMU	209	824	*541*	*110.3*	230	*47.9*	228.9	157.53

a. Data are from the International Telecommunication Union's (ITU) *World Telecommunication Development Report 1999*. Please cite the ITU for third-party use of these data. b. Data are from the Internet Software Consortium (http://www.isc.org).

The information age 5.11

About the data

The table includes indicators that measure the penetration of the information economy—newspapers, radios, television sets, mobile phones, fax machines, personal computers, and Internet hosts. Other important indicators of information and communications technology—such as the use of teleconferencing or the use of the Internet in organizing conferences, distance education, and commercial transactions—are not collected systematically and so are not reported here. All these indicators fail to capture important elements of the information disseminated, such as its quality.

The data on the number of daily newspapers in circulation and radio receivers in use are from statistical surveys carried out by the United Nations Educational, Scientific, and Cultural Organization (UNESCO). In some countries definitions, classifications, and methods of enumeration do not entirely conform to UNESCO standards. For example, newspaper circulation data should refer to the number of copies distributed, but in some cases the figures reported are the number of copies printed. In addition, many countries impose radio and television license fees to help pay for public broadcasting, discouraging radio and television owners from declaring ownership. Because of these and other data collection problems, estimates of the number of newspapers and radios vary widely in reliability and should be interpreted with caution.

The data presented for other electronic communications and information technology are from the International Telecommunication Union (ITU) and the Internet Software Consortium (formerly Network Wizards). Data on television sets and cable television subscribers are supplied to the ITU through annual questionnaires sent to national broadcasting authorities and industry associations. Some countries require that television sets be registered. To the extent that households do not register their televisions or do not register all of their televisions, the number of licensed sets may understate the true number.

Because of different regulatory requirements for the provision of data, complete measurement of the telecommunications sector is not possible. Telecommunications data are compiled through annual questionnaires sent to telecommunications authorities and operating companies. The data are supplemented by annual reports and statistical yearbooks of telecommunications ministries, regulators, operators, and industry associations. In some cases estimates are derived from ITU documents or other references.

The data on fax machines exclude fax modems attached to computers. Some operators report only the equipment they sell, lease, or register, so the actual number is almost certainly much higher.

The estimates of the number of personal computers are derived from an annual questionnaire, supplemented by other sources. In many countries mainframe computers are used extensively, and thousands of users can be connected to a single mainframe computer; thus the number of personal computers understates the total use of computers.

Internet hosts are computers connected directly to the worldwide network, each allowing many computer users to access the Internet. Hosts are assigned to countries on the basis of the host's country code, though this does not necessarily indicate that the host is physically located in that country. All hosts lacking a country code identification are assigned to the United States. The Internet Software Consortium changed the methods used in its Internet domain survey beginning in July 1998. The new survey is believed to be more reliable and to avoid the undercounting that occurs when organizations restrict download access to their domain data. Nevertheless, some measurement problems remain, so the number of Internet hosts shown for each country should be considered an approximation.

Figure 5.11

The information technology revolution has not reached all shores

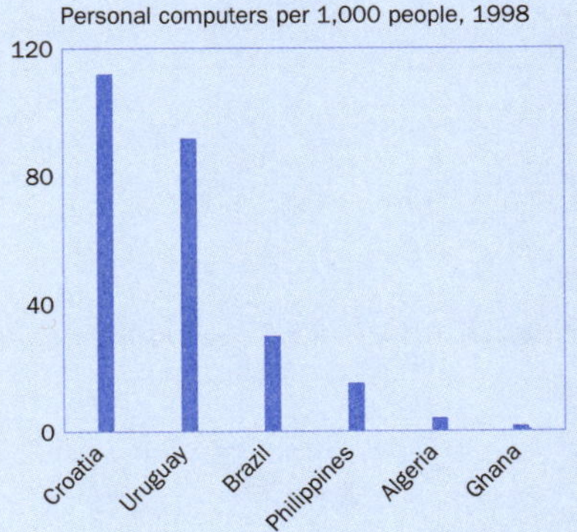

Source: Table 5.11 based on International Telecommunication Union data.

Developing economies have about 16 personal computers per 1,000 people on average. In some, access to computers is similar to that in high-income economies. But in many, access remains extremely limited.

Definitions

• **Daily newspapers** are the number of newspapers published at least four times a week, per 1,000 people. • **Radios** are the estimated number of radio receivers in use for broadcasts to the general public, per 1,000 people. • **Television sets** are the estimated number of television sets in use, per 1,000 people. • **Cable television subscribers** are households that subscribe to a multichannel television service delivered by a fixed line connection. Some countries also report subscribers to pay television using wireless technology or those cabled to community antenna systems. • **Mobile phones** refer to users of portable telephones subscribing to an automatic public mobile telephone service using cellular technology that provides access to the public switched telephone network, per 1,000 people. • **Fax machines** are the estimated number of facsimile machines connected to the public switched telephone network, per 1,000 people. • **Personal computers** are the estimated number of self-contained computers designed to be used by a single individual, per 1,000 people. • **Internet hosts** are the number of computers with active Internet Protocol (IP) addresses connected to the Internet, per 10,000 people. All hosts without a country code identification are assumed to be located in the United States.

Data sources

The data on newspapers and radios are compiled by UNESCO, mainly from official replies by member states to UNESCO questionnaires and special surveys, but also from official reports and publications, supplemented by information from national and international sources. The data on television sets, cable television subscribers, mobile phones, fax machines, and personal computers are from the annual questionnaire sent to member countries by the ITU. These data are reported in the ITU's *World Telecommunication Development Report 1999* and Telecommunications Indicators database. The data on radios are also reported in these sources. The text also draws on ITU sources. The data on Internet hosts are from the Internet Software Consortium (http://www.isc.org).

5.12 Science and technology

	Scientists and engineers in R&D	Technicians in R&D	Science and engineering students	Scientific and technical journal articles	Expenditures for R&D	High-technology exports		Royalty and license fees		Patent applications filed[a]	
	per million people 1987–97[b]	per million people 1987–97[b]	% of total tertiary students 1987–97[b]	1995	% of GNP 1987–97[b]	$ millions 1998	% of manufactured exports 1998	Receipts $ millions 1998	Payments $ millions 1998	Residents 1997	Non-residents 1997
Albania	..	..	19	..	..	1	1	..	..	..	26,005
Algeria	..	..	58	..	..	*5*	*1*	..	..	34	206
Angola	..	..	24	..	..	..	..	*17*	*0*	..	..
Argentina	660	147	28	1,581	0.38	491	5	8	422	824	5,035
Armenia	1,485	177	29	..	..	*6*	*5*	..	..	63	25,059
Australia	3,357	797	24	9,747	1.80	1,564	11	275	1,010	8,937	39,274
Austria	1,627	812	33	2,807	1.53	5,877	12	99	811	2,681	108,543
Azerbaijan	2,791	188	37	..	0.21	..	..	..	..	..	24,308
Bangladesh	52	33	47	..	0.03	3	0	*0*	5	*70*	*156*
Belarus	2,248	266	48	..	1.07	204	4	1	1	755	25,280
Belgium	2,272	2,201	41	3,996	1.60	11,115	8	645	1,099	1,687	84,958
Benin	176	54	18	..	0.00	..	..	..	*0*	..	..
Bolivia	172	154	30	..	0.50	*15*	*8*	*0*	5	*17*	*106*
Bosnia and Herzegovina	..	..	..	5	..	..	..	..	..	..	23,197
Botswana	..	..	37	..	..	..	..	0	9	1	92
Brazil	168	59	27	2,760	0.81	2,554	9	142	1,075	36	31,947
Bulgaria	1,747	967	27	779	0.57	*111*	*4*	..	..	400	27,600
Burkina Faso	17	16	18	..	0.19	..	..	..	..	..	..
Burundi	33	32	20	..	0.31	..	..	*0*	*0*	*1*	*4*
Cambodia	..	..	13	..	..	..	..	..	..	..	..
Cameroon	..	..	45	..	..	*2*	*2*	..	..	..	..
Canada	2,719	1,070	16	17,359	1.66	21,736	15	574	2,073	4,192	50,254
Central African Republic	56	32	30	..	..	*0*	*0*	..	..	..	..
Chad	..	..	14	..	..	..	..	..	..	..	..
Chile	445	233	42	700	0.68	92	4	91	56	*189*	*1,771*
China	454	200	43	6,200	0.66	23,308	15	63	420	12,786	48,596
Hong Kong, China	..	..	36	1,091	..	4,751	21	..	..	26	2,359
Colombia	..	..	28	..	..	303	9	1	54	*87*	*1,172*
Congo, Dem. Rep.	..	..	..	..	..	..	..	..	..	*2*	*27*
Congo, Rep.	..	..	48	..	..	..	..	*0*	*0*	..	..
Costa Rica	532	..	20	..	0.21	*221*	13	2	22	..	..
Côte d'Ivoire	..	..	31	..	..	..	..	*0*	*16*	..	..
Croatia	1,916	714	30	434	1.03	266	8	..	..	273	439
Cuba	1,612	1,121	16	..	0.84	..	..	..	..	109	23,162
Czech Republic	1,222	693	28	1,577	1.20	1,981	8	57	113	601	29,976
Denmark	3,259	2,644	25	3,513	1.95	5,479	18	..	..	2,658	106,403
Dominican Republic	..	..	35	..	..	*2*	*1*	*0*	25	..	..
Ecuador	146	42	27	..	0.02	20	4	*0*	68	8	302
Egypt, Arab Rep.	459	341	12	1,136	0.22	2	0	56	392	*504*	*706*
El Salvador	20	356	59	..	..	45	8	0	7	*3*	*64*
Eritrea	..	..	30	..	..	..	..	..	..	..	..
Estonia	2,017	391	27	..	0.57	*173*	*9*	1	7	18	26,626
Ethiopia	..	..	26	..	..	..	..	0	0	4[c]	..
Finland	2,799	1,996	39	3,246	2.78	8,124	22	106	411	4,061	105,376
France	2,659	2,873	37	23,811	2.25	54,183	23	2,336	2,717	18,669	93,962
Gabon	234	22	29	..	..	*17*	..	..	..	..	..
Gambia, The	..	..	..	..	..	..	..	..	..	..	200
Georgia	..	..	39	..	..	..	..	..	..	265	26,561
Germany	2,831	1,472	47	30,654	2.41	63,698	14	3,252	4,893	62,052	113,543
Ghana	..	..	32	..	..	..	..	..	0	..	34,103
Greece	773	314	26	1,639	0.47	422	7	*0*	*58*	53	82,390
Guatemala	104	112	..	..	0.16	60	7	..	..	4	131
Guinea	..	..	34	..	..	..	..	..	..	..	..
Guinea-Bissau	..	..	0	..	..	..	..	..	..	..	25
Haiti	..	..	..	..	..	*2*	*4*	..	..	*3*	*6*
Honduras	..	..	24	..	..	2	1	*0*	5	*10*	*126*

Science and technology 5.12

	Scientists and engineers in R&D	Technicians in R&D	Science and engineering students	Scientific and technical journal articles	Expenditures for R&D	High-technology exports		Royalty and license fees		Patent applications filed[a]	
	per million people 1987–97[b]	per million people 1987–97[b]	% of total tertiary students 1987–97[b]	1995	% of GNP 1987–97[b]	$ millions 1998	% of manufactured exports 1998	Receipts $ millions 1998	Payments $ millions 1998	Residents 1997	Non-residents 1997
Hungary	1,099	510	32	1,469	0.68	3,891	21	46	215	774	29,331
India	149	108	25	7,851	0.73	*1,314*	*5*	19	201	10,155 [c]	..
Indonesia	182	..	39	..	0.07	2,120	10	..	..	..	4,517
Iran, Islamic Rep.	560	166	39	..	0.48	..	..	0	0	418 [c]	..
Iraq	..	..	41	..	..	..	..	..	..	*68*	*18*
Ireland	2,319	506	31	900	1.61	23,944	45	177	6,236	946	82,484
Israel	..	..	49	4,322	2.35	4,249	20	218	210	1,796	28,548
Italy	1,318	798	30	14,117	2.21	17,066	8	477	1,155	2,574	88,836
Jamaica	..	..	64	..	..	*1*	*0*	7	30	..	..
Japan	4,909	827	21	39,498	2.80	94,777	26	7,388	8,947	351,487	66,487
Jordan	94	10	26	..	0.26	..	..	..	..	..	..
Kazakhstan	..	..	20	..	0.32	103	9	..	..	1,171	24,998
Kenya	..	..	19	253	..	20	4	2	40	25	49,935
Korea, Dem. Rep.	..	..	..	..	..	..	..	..	..	..	25,467
Korea, Rep.	2,193	318	32	2,964	2.82	30,582	27	260	2,369	92,798	37,184
Kuwait	230	71	29	..	0.16	*9*	*0*	..	..	..	..
Kyrgyz Republic	584	50	14	..	0.20	*31*	*16*	..	..	152	24,951
Lao PDR	..	..	20	..	..	..	..	..	..	..	..
Latvia	1,049	351	23	..	0.43	42	4	2	7	163	26,860
Lebanon	..	..	30	..	..	..	..	..	..	..	..
Lesotho	..	..	19	..	..	..	..	20	1	..	49,483
Libya	..	493	..	..	..	..	..	..	..	*12*	*23*
Lithuania	2,028	631	31	..	0.70	71	3	0	6	125	26,673
Macedonia, FYR	1,335	546	47	..	..	*11*	*1*	1	2	66	26,087
Madagascar	12	37	25	..	0.18	*1*	*1*	1	10	..	26,174
Malawi	..	..	27	..	..	..	..	..	..	2	49,932
Malaysia	93	32	27	..	0.24	31,419	54	*0*	*0*	179	6,272
Mali	..	..	12	..	..	..	..	..	..	..	..
Mauritania	..	..	41	..	..	..	..	0	0	..	..
Mauritius	361	158	14	..	0.40	15	1	0	0	3	12
Mexico	214	74	32	1,408	0.33	19,266	19	139	454	429	35,503
Moldova	330	1,641	52	..	0.90	11	7	0	0	295	25,030
Mongolia	910	176	24	..	..	*0*	*1*	..	..	186	26,197
Morocco	..	..	41	..	..	*9*	*0*	7	171	*90*	*237*
Mozambique	..	..	42	..	..	*2*	*6*	..	..	..	..
Myanmar	..	..	56	..	..	..	..	..	..	..	..
Namibia	..	..	4	..	..	..	..	6	3	..	..
Nepal	..	..	13	..	..	..	..	0	0	..	..
Netherlands	2,219	1,358	39	9,239	2.08	35,377	30	2,432	2,964	5,227	85,402
New Zealand	1,663	809	20	1,830	1.04	471	..	44	267	1,735	33,402
Nicaragua	204	85	33	..	..	2	4	..	..	..	..
Niger	..	..	32	..	..	..	..	..	..	..	..
Nigeria	15	76	42	342	0.09	..	..	*0*	*0*	..	..
Norway	3,664	1,842	26	2,180	1.58	1,889	16	90	341	1,518	30,489
Oman	..	..	13	..	..	66	*5*	..	..	..	..
Pakistan	72	13	32	..	0.92	*9*	0	*2*	*20*	*16*	*782*
Panama	..	..	29	..	..	*0*	0	..	18	*31*	*142*
Papua New Guinea	..	..	10	..	..	..	..	..	..	..	..
Paraguay	..	..	20	..	..	*4*	*2*	185	1	..	..
Peru	233	10	34	..	..	35	3	8	80	48	756
Philippines	157	22	14	..	0.22	18,907	71	0	70	125	3,440
Poland	1,358	1,377	28	3,895	0.77	684	3	22	195	2,401	30,137
Portugal	1,182	167	36	764	0.62	812	4	41	290	92	106,595
Puerto Rico	..	..	..	..	..	..	..	..	..	..	..
Romania	1,387	581	21	..	0.72	117	2	3	21	1,709	27,346
Russian Federation	3,587	600	50	17,180	0.88	2,449	12	28	2	15,277	32,943

	Scientists and engineers in R&D	Technicians in R&D	Science and engineering students	Scientific and technical journal articles	Expenditures for R&D	High-technology exports		Royalty and license fees		Patent applications filed[a]	
	per million people	per million people	% of total tertiary students		% of GNP	$ millions	% of manufactured exports	Receipts $ millions	Payments $ millions	Residents	Non-residents
	1987–97[b]	1987–97[b]	1987–97[b]	1995	1987–97[b]	1998	1998	1998	1998	1997	1997
Rwanda	35	8	28	..	0.04	..	..	0	1	..	..
Saudi Arabia	..	..	17	..	..	*39*	*1*	0	0	57	1,001
Senegal	3	4	21	..	0.01	..	..	*0*	*2*	..	..
Sierra Leone	..	..	17	..	..	..	..	..	..	..	9,506
Singapore	2,318	301	..	891	1.13	54,783	59	..	..	8,188	29,467
Slovak Republic	1,866	792	40	854	1.05	289	3	14	55	234	27,973
Slovenia	2,251	1,027	26	339	1.46	357	4	7	39	285	27,162
South Africa	1,031	315	29	1,744	0.70	923	9	72	165	..	..
Spain	1,305	343	31	8,811	0.90	5,635	7	243	1,866	2,856	110,911
Sri Lanka	191	47	34	..	..	..	..	..	..	81	26,322
Sudan	..	..	16	..	..	*0*	*0*	0	0	..	49,920
Sweden	3,826	3,166	38	7,190	3.76	13,725	20	1,114	939	7,893	107,107
Switzerland	3,006	1,374	34	5,896	2.60	12,030	16	..	..	5,814	107,038
Syrian Arab Republic	30	25	23	..	0.20	..	..	..	..	..	..
Tajikistan	666	..	17	..	..	..	..	..	..	23	24,742
Tanzania	..	..	37	..	..	*0*	*0*	1	5	..	..
Thailand	103	39	18	..	0.13	*12,599*	*31*	7	514	238	5,205
Togo	98	63	35	..	0.48	..	..	..	..	..	..
Trinidad and Tobago	..	..	58	..	..	13	1	0	0	17	26,322
Tunisia	125	57	33	..	0.30	104	2	11	3	*46*	*128*
Turkey	291	..	45	1,359	0.45	445	2	..	..	233	27,985
Turkmenistan	..	..	..	..	..	..	..	..	..	52	24,584
Uganda	21	14	17	..	0.57	..	..	*0*	*0*	..	49,760
Ukraine	2,171	575	42	2,489	..	..	..	..	..	4,692	28,036
United Arab Emirates	..	..	24	..	..	..	..	..	..	..	..
United Kingdom	2,448	1,017	34	32,980	1.95	64,461	28	6,724	6,123	26,591	121,618
United States	3,676	..	19	142,792	2.63	170,681	33	36,808	11,292	125,808	110,884
Uruguay	..	..	32	..	..	22	2	*0*	6	32	370
Uzbekistan	1,763	314	..	..	..	..	..	..	..	817	26,490
Venezuela, RB	209	32	26	..	0.49	79	3	0	0	201	2,323
Vietnam	..	..	..	..	..	..	..	..	..	30	27,410
West Bank and Gaza	..	..	..	..	..	..	..	..	..	..	..
Yemen, Rep.	..	..	5	..	..	..	..	..	..	..	..
Yugoslavia, FR (Serb./Mont.)	1,099	515	47	442	..	..	..	..	..	522	16,499
Zambia	..	..	16	..	..	..	..	..	..	..	96
Zimbabwe	..	..	24	..	..	*13*	*2*	..	..	3	21,966
World	.. w	.. w	35 w	436,951 s	2.18 w	820,617 s	22 w	64,334 s	61,114 s	798,003 s	3,602,785 s
Low income	257	..	35	14,646	0.57	25,475	13	106	688	23,772	648,006
Excl. China & India	..	..	..	595	..	2,167	..	24	67	831	573,943
Middle income	..	..	36	42,776	0.92	116,876	20	1,177	6,703	126,138	817,452
Lower middle income	..	..	37	23,775	..	24,762	17	395	1,688	27,027	449,771
Upper middle income	607	..	34	19,001	1.08	92,114	20	781	5,015	99,111	367,681
Low & middle income	..	..	35	57,422	0.81	142,351	18	1,283	7,391	149,910	1,465,458
East Asia & Pacific	492	192	42	9,164	1.32	106,336	28	330	3,374	106,342	184,288
Europe & Central Asia	2,533	..	44	30,483	0.77	10,553	9	176	623	31,081	685,716
Latin America & Carib.	..	..	30	6,449	0.58	24,385	12	583	2,350	1,708	175,004
Middle East & N. Africa	..	..	29	1,136	..	107	1	73	566	509	1,207
South Asia	137	98	24	7,851	0.66	12	4	19	206	10,236	26,322
Sub-Saharan Africa	..	..	29	2,339	..	958	..	102	273	38	392,921
High income	3,166	..	25	379,529	2.36	678,267	33	63,051	53,723	648,093	2,137,327
Europe EMU	2,126	1,510	38	98,365	2.16	225,832	15	9,808	22,443	101,037	1,086,902

a. Other patent applications filed in 1997 include those filed under the auspices of the African Intellectual Property Organization (31 by residents, 26,057 by nonresidents), African Regional Industrial Property Organization (7 by residents, 25,724 by nonresidents), European Patent Office (44,604 by residents, 53,339 by nonresidents), and Eurasian Patent Organization (258 by residents, 26,207 by nonresidents). The original information was provided by the World Intellectual Property Organization (WIPO). The International Bureau of WIPO assumes no liability or responsibility with regard to the transformation of these data. b. Data are for the latest year available; see *Primary data documentation* for most recent year available. c. Total for residents and nonresidents.

Science and technology 5.12

About the data

Science is advancing rapidly in virtually all fields, particularly biotechnology, and playing a growing economic role: countries unable to access, generate, and apply relevant scientific knowledge will fall even further behind. And there is greater appreciation of the need for high-quality scientific input into public policy issues such as regional and global environmental concerns.

Science and technology cover a range of issues too complex and too broad to be quantified by any single set of indicators, but those in the table shed light on countries' "technological base"—the availability of skilled human resources (students enrolled in science and engineering, and scientists, engineers, and technicians employed in research and development, or R&D), the number of scientific and technical articles published, the competitive edge countries enjoy in high-technology exports, sales and purchases of technology through royalties and licenses, and the number of patent applications filed. Two of the indicators are new—science and engineering students and scientific and technical journal articles—and an updated methodology is used to calculate high-technology exports.

The United Nations Educational, Scientific, and Cultural Organization (UNESCO) collects data on scientific and technical workers and R&D expenditures from member states, mainly through questionnaires and special surveys as well as from official reports and publications, supplemented by information from other national and international sources. UNESCO reports either the stock of scientists, engineers, and technicians or the number of economically active persons (people engaged in or actively seeking work in any branch of the economy on a given date) qualified to be scientists, engineers, or technicians. Stock data generally come from censuses and are less timely than measures of the economically active population. UNESCO supplements these data with estimates of the number of qualified scientists and engineers by counting the number of people who have completed education at ISCED (International Standard Classification of Education) levels 6 and 7; qualified technicians are estimated using the number of people who have completed education at ISCED level 5. The data on scientists, engineers, and technicians, normally calculated in terms of full-time-equivalent staff, cannot take into account the considerable variations in quality of training and education. Similarly, R&D expenditures are no guarantee of progress; governments need to pay close attention to the practices that make them effective.

The data on science and engineering students refer to those enrolled at the tertiary level, which normally requires as a minimum condition of admission the successful completion of education at the secondary level. These data are reported to UNESCO by national education authorities. (See *About the data* for table 2.10 for further details on UNESCO education surveys.)

The revised methodology used in this year's edition for determining a country's high-technology exports was developed by the Organisation for Economic Co-operation and Development in collaboration with Eurostat. Termed the "product approach" to distinguish it from a "sectoral approach," the method is based on the calculation of R&D intensity (R&D expenditure divided by total sales) for groups of products from six countries (Germany, Italy, Japan, the Netherlands, Sweden, and the United States). Because industrial sectors characterized by a few high-technology products may also produce many low-technology products, the product approach is more appropriate for analyzing international trade than is the sectoral approach. To construct a list of high-technology manufactured products (services are excluded), the R&D intensity was calculated for products classified at the three-digit level of the Standard International Trade Classification revision 3. The final list was determined at the four- and five-digit level. At this level, since no R&D data were available, final selection was based on patent data and expert opinion. This methodology takes only R&D intensity into account. Other characteristics of high technology are also important, such as know-how, scientific and technical personnel, and technology embodied in patents; considering these characteristics would result in a different list. (See Hatzichronoglou 1997 for further details.)

The counts of scientific and technical journal articles include those published in a stable set of about 4,800 journals selected by the Institute of Scientific Information as the base of its Science Citation Index in 1981 and published by the National Science Foundation. (See *Definitions* for the fields covered.) The Institute of Scientific Information's database covers the core set of scientific journals, but may exclude some of regional or local importance. It may also reflect some bias toward English-language journals.

Most countries have adopted systems that protect patentable inventions. Under most patent legislation, to be protected by law (patentable), an idea must be new in the sense that it has not already been published or publicly used; it must be nonobvious (involve an inventive step) in the sense that it would not have occurred to any specialist in the industrial field, had such a specialist been asked to find a solution to the problem; and it must be capable of industrial application in the sense that it can be industrially manufactured or used. Information on patent applications filed is shown separately for residents and nonresidents of the country. The World Intellectual Property Organization estimates that at the end of 1996 about 3.8 million patents were in force in the world.

Definitions

• **Scientists and engineers in R&D** are people trained at the tertiary level to work in any field of science who are engaged in professional R&D activity. • **Technicians in R&D** are people engaged in professional R&D activity who have received vocational or technical training in any branch of knowledge or technology. Most of these jobs require three years beyond the first stage of secondary education. • **Science and engineering students** include students at the tertiary level in the following fields: engineering, natural science, mathematics and computers, and social and behavioral science. • **Scientific and technical journal articles** refer to the number of scientific and engineering articles published in the following fields: physics, biology, chemistry, mathematics, clinical medicine, biomedical research, engineering and technology, and earth and space sciences. • **Expenditures for R&D** are current and capital expenditures on creative, systematic activity that increases the stock of knowledge. Included are fundamental and applied research and experimental development work leading to new devices, products, or processes. • **High-technology exports** are products with high R&D intensity. They include high-technology products such as in aerospace, computers, pharmaceuticals, scientific instruments, and electrical machinery. • **Royalty and license fees** are payments and receipts between residents and nonresidents for the authorized use of intangible, nonproduced, nonfinancial assets and proprietary rights (such as patents, copyrights, trademarks, industrial processes, and franchises) and for the use, through licensing agreements, of produced originals of prototypes (such as manuscripts and films). • **Patents** are documents, issued by a government office, that describe an invention and create a legal situation in which the patented invention can normally be exploited (made, used, sold, imported) only by, or with the authorization of, the patentee. The protection of inventions is generally limited to 20 years from the filing date of the application for the grant of a patent.

Data sources

The data on technical personnel, science and engineering students, and R&D expenditures are from UNESCO's *Statistical Yearbook*. The data on scientific and technical journal articles are from the National Science Foundation's *Science and Engineering Indicators 1998*. The information on high-technology exports is from the United Nations' Commodity Trade (COMTRADE) database. The data on royalty and license fees are from the International Monetary Fund's *Balance of Payments Statistics Yearbook*, and the data on patents from the World Intellectual Property Organization's *Industrial Property Statistics*.

GLOBAL LINKS

Trade, investment, foreign aid, migration, and tourism are all evidence of the many ties between nations that have come to be termed "globalization." This section documents the flow of goods, resources, and people through the global economy. But the forces of globalization appear throughout the book: population growth and changing patterns of employment (section 2), the pressure that economic and demographic change has placed on the world's resources (section 3), the expansion of service industries and the growing trade in services (section 4), and the growth of telecommunications and the spread of new technologies (section 5).

In the past year the preparation for another round of negotiations on global trade rules became the focus of an international debate on the effects of globalization. What is at stake, and why has trade come to be seen as the cause of both the goods and the ills of globalization? Can global trade rules be revised to improve lives in poor nations as well as rich? Can this be accomplished while protecting the environment?

The rapid growth of world trade in the past five decades owes much to cuts in trade barriers through eight rounds of negotiations under the General Agreement on Tariffs and Trade, now the World Trade Organization (WTO). A ministerial meeting of the WTO in Seattle last November was expected to launch a new Millennium Round. It failed for many reasons, but three stand out. First, the United States and the European Union could not agree on liberalizing agricultural trade. Second, developing countries feared that industrial countries would force labor and environmental standards onto the agenda. Third, procedural problems arose from the fact that WTO membership is up from fewer than 80 in the 1980s to 135 today, and the developing countries are no longer willing to accept the traditional "green room" procedure, in which a small group of key countries negotiate a package while others have only limited opportunities to revise it.

A development round

After Seattle a new agenda is needed to relaunch the Millennium Round. This, finally, should be the "development round," in which the world's poor win large gains. At least three key issues should be on the agenda—agriculture, services, and industrial tariffs. Also needing to be addressed are the concerns of developing countries about Uruguay Round commitments and the interactions between trade and environmental rules. Labor standards, it has been agreed, are primarily the responsibility of the International Labour Organization.

Agriculture

In developing countries in the past decade 62 percent of the female workforce—and 54 percent of the male—were in agriculture (figure 6a). So making agriculture more dynamic is essential to reduce poverty, especially in poor countries that depend on agricultural exports. But trade barriers and subsidies in rich countries reduce incomes in developing countries by $20 billion a year, four times the global grant aid of $5.4 billion. Such protectionism is part of the reason that world trade in agriculture grew only 1.8 percent a year in 1985–94, less than a third of the 5.8 percent for manufactured goods. The share of manufactures in developing country exports to the high-income OECD countries has increased from 40 to 66 percent since 1990, while agricultural exports dropped from 19 to 14 percent (figure 6b; Binswanger and Lutz 2000).

Resistance to change is substantial in both poor and rich countries. OECD countries suffer welfare losses of almost $63 billion a year from agricultural protection, but farmers there are sufficiently well organized to gain at the expense of consumers. The Uruguay Round sought to liberalize agriculture, yet the average rate of agricultural protection in the European Union actually increased—from 32 percent in 1997 to 37 percent in 1998. Agricultural tariff reforms in OECD countries could increase incomes by $6 per person in Sub-Saharan Africa and $30 in Latin America (Binswanger and Lutz 2000).

Some developing countries are food importers, and worry that liberalization will increase world food prices. But projections suggest that the increase will be no more than 4–6 percent (Valdes and Zietz 1995). Real food prices are falling. And technical assistance to developing countries can help to increase agricultural productivity and thus the incomes of the poor.

Services

Negotiations to liberalize services have so far focused on areas of OECD interest, notably telecommunications and financial services. Developing countries have much to gain by integrating themselves into the fast-growing global communications network (tables 5.10 and 5.11), which can greatly aid efficiency, export competitiveness, and the spread of knowledge. But the East Asian crisis shows that opening financial services can lead to disaster if the ground has not been carefully prepared. Where financial systems are weak and poorly supervised, where corporate governance is of questionable quality, opening to international financial flows can lead to booms and busts. So financial liberalization needs to be approached cautiously and sequenced properly (Stiglitz 1999).

The new development round must pay attention to four service areas of special interest to developing countries:

- *Movement of professionals.* Visa requirements and other curbs prevent poor countries from sending more professionals to perform services in OECD countries (table 6.13). These curbs need to be reduced in the next round. Although 54 countries have committed themselves in negotiations to providing transparent, nondiscretionary criteria for the entry of foreign service providers, only 3 have actually done so (Michalopoulos 1999).
- *Construction.* Many poor countries have a comparative advantage in construction, but they can harness it only if they are allowed to move workers to sites in rich countries for the duration of a construction contract.
- *Maritime services.* Cheap maritime skills will enable many developing countries to gain a larger share of global and coastal shipping services, if these are opened.
- *Teleworking.* Modern communications and the Internet have made possible the shift of many clerical and professional services to low-wage countries. GE Capital, for example, has hired 5,000 people in India to support its global operations. The shift of jobs could give rise to protectionist pres-

Figure 6a

Agriculture employs the majority of workers in developing countries

% employed in agriculture, various years, 1990–97

Female labor force
Male labor force

100
80
60
40
20
0

Low-income countries
Middle-income countries
Low- and middle-income countries
High-income countries

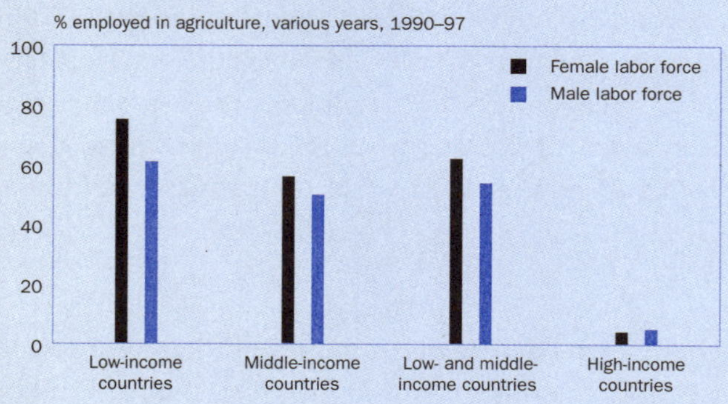

Source: World Bank, *World Development Indicators 1999.*

Figure 6b

Developing countries are exporting more and more manufactures to high-income OECD countries

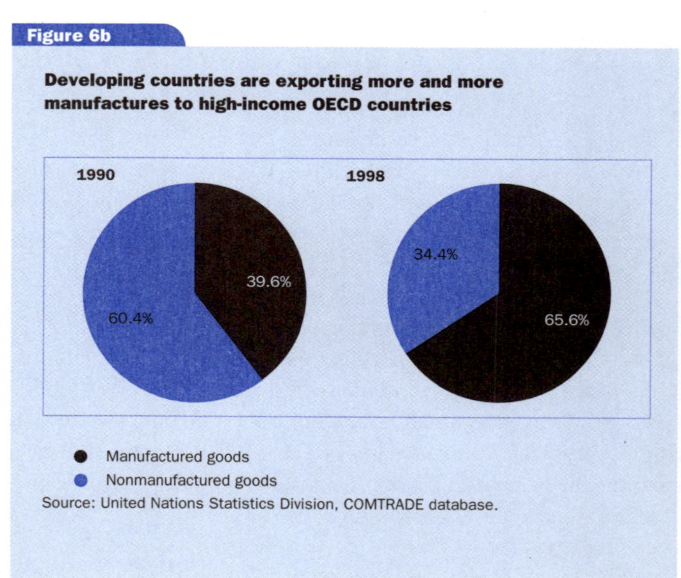

Source: United Nations Statistics Division, COMTRADE database.

sures, so the Millennium Round needs to ensure that services delivered electronically are not subject to tariff and nontariff barriers.

Industrial tariffs

The Uruguay Round reduced the trade-weighted import duty on manufactures in rich countries to 3.4 percent (table 6.6). But duties on labor-intensive goods are disproportionately high, so the average rate actually paid by developing countries is four times the average paid by high-income countries. Peak tariffs exceed 12 percent in a wide range of goods of interest to developing countries.

The share of manufactures in exports of developing countries—up from 16 percent in 1964 to 68 percent in 1998 (table 4.5)—is expected to approach 80 percent by 2005 (Hertel and Martin 1999). The boom owes much to lower protection in developing countries, which spurred south-south trade—now 39 percent of manufactured exports of developing countries and projected to rise to 45 percent by 2005.

That is why reducing tariffs on industrial products should be part of the WTO's agenda. Hertel and Martin (1999) estimate that a 40 percent cut in industrial tariffs would increase world trade in manufactures by $380 billion, and south-south trade by 11 percent. The largest welfare gains would accrue to countries with high tariffs today, notably China and India.

Antidumping

Antidumping rules should in theory be concerned only with predatory pricing, but this is not so under current WTO rules. They are being used as protectionist devices—and need reform as soon as possible. One study estimates that there is no predatory intent—and no government intervention required—in more than 90 percent of antidumping suits (Willig 1998). An earlier study says that by the WTO's criteria for dumping, 18 of the top 20 Fortune 500 firms in the United States are dumping their output in the domestic market (Thurow 1985).

Labor standards

Governments in some high-income countries want the future agenda to consider trade sanctions against countries that do not meet core labor standards. Developing countries fear this could degenerate into pure protectionism and shut out developing country workers. Their critics claim that low labor standards lead to "social dumping" by developing countries—and enable multinationals to impose low wages on poor countries desperate for exports.

But empirical evidence shows no link between low labor standards and either exports or foreign direct investment (OECD 1996; Rodrik 1996). Indeed, the OECD study shows that handmade carpets from developing countries are exported at much higher prices than machine-made ones from Belgium and the Netherlands: no social dumping is in evidence. In developing countries workers in firms with high export ratios typically receive much higher wages on average than those in firms that export little or nothing (Aggarwal 1995).

The use of trade sanctions for perceived violations of labor standards would raise troubling issues. Quantifying social dumping margins for the purpose of imposing sanctions is simply not feasible. Because suppressing workers' rights typically reduces competitiveness, the most likely effect of social dumping sanctions would be to create additional barriers to exports produced by workers in poor countries (Martin and Maskus 1999). Advocates of high labor standards claim that their aim is not to deny developing countries the comparative advantage of their poverty—lower wages. But developing countries believe that labor standards, once introduced in the WTO, will become the thin end of the wedge for protectionism.

Child labor, widespread in many developing countries, is concentrated overwhelmingly in agriculture, not in export industries, and it signals poverty, not exploitation. Children's labor force participation drops rapidly as GNP per capita rises (figure 6c; table 2.3; San Martin 1996). So the best way to reduce child labor is to raise incomes and schooling opportunities.

This will not be accomplished by trade sanctions. In Bangladesh and Pakistan western boycotts led to children losing jobs making soccer balls and garments. But contrary to the boycott's aims, parents sent their children not to school but to industries with worse working conditions. Unless better school facilities are available and policies are targeted specifically at the problem, children and their families will not be better off.

Environment and trade

Fears that polluting industries will migrate from rich countries to poor to take advantage of low environmental standards have proved largely unfounded. Rich countries are net exporters of goods produced by the six most polluting industries, and developing countries are net importers (figure 6d). Trade liberalization in 1986–95 did not change this pattern: high-income countries became even bigger net exporters (their export-import ratio rose from 1.02 to 1.32). The ratio fell in middle-income countries. In the same period it rose in low-income countries, but only to

Figure 6c

Children work less as incomes rise

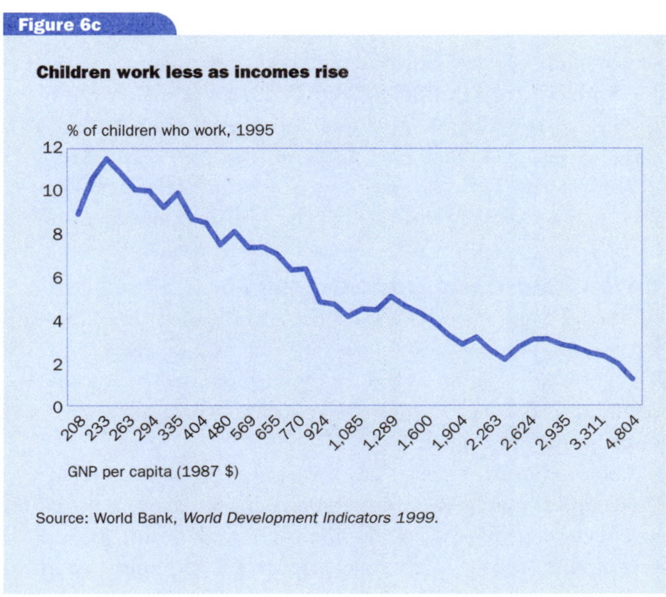

Source: World Bank, *World Development Indicators 1999*.

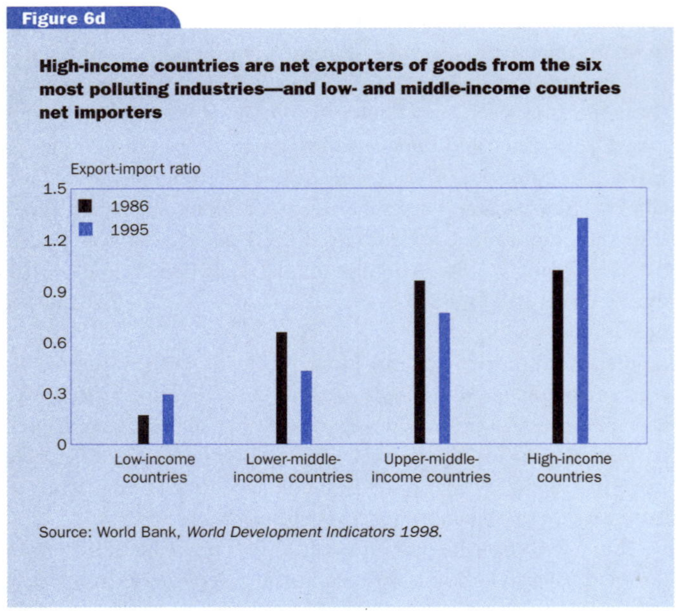

0.29, still the lowest among all income groups.

Political economy

WTO rules require consensus on most issues, and this would seem to give substantial power to smaller developing countries. In practice, however, a country's influence at the WTO depends heavily on its ability to contribute to debates, and OECD countries have enjoyed the major say.

Developing countries complain that developed ones are trying to expand the WTO beyond trade to other issues. Developing countries also fear that new issues will mean obligations without compensation: they fear that trade sanctions on labor and environmental grounds will hit them alone. Sanctions are not proposed against rich countries that emit greenhouse gases—only against poor countries whose fishermen say they cannot afford turtle excluders. This threatens to change the WTO's character from a forum for exchanging mutual concessions to a one-way street—and so raises political hackles.

The Montreal Protocol, Kyoto Protocol, and Convention on Biological Diversity suggest that forums other than the WTO can also deal with many environmental issues. As in the Montreal Protocol, solutions can include compensation for poor countries, a way of making the next WTO round a development round.

Beyond the World Trade Organization

Reducing trade barriers is important but not enough. Developing countries must establish better institutional structures for trade. These include systems to reduce corruption, speed up trade documentation, improve trade-related infrastructure, and gain access to insurance and credit.

Many countries need technical assistance to meet global standards and Uruguay Round commitments on customs valuation, intellectual property, and agriculture. And having refused to accept the green room procedure at Seattle, developing countries now need help in establishing better research capacity to formulate negotiating positions for the Millennium Round. Today 19 of 42 African WTO members have no representative at WTO headquarters in Geneva, while OECD countries have on average seven representatives each (World Bank 1999d).

Developing countries must also create better economic environments to enable entrepreneurs and farmers to take advantage of open markets. And they must construct safety nets for the people dislocated by liberalization, for the WTO mainly helps those that help themselves.

6.1 Integration with the global economy

	Trade in goods				Growth in real trade less growth in real GDP	Gross private capital flows		Gross foreign direct investment	
	% of PPP GDP		% of goods GDP		percentage points	% of PPP GDP		% of PPP GDP	
	1988	1998	1988	1998	1988–98	1988	1998	1988	1998
Albania	*9.0*	10.9	44.0	42.4	15.8	*4.3*	1.9	*0.0*	0.5
Algeria	13.2	16.4	38.3	79.1	–1.0	0.7	..	0.0	..
Angola	22.4	33.0	87.5	151.3	7.5	0.8	*3.9*	0.8	*0.9*
Argentina	5.3	12.9	23.3	48.4	9.0	1.6	6.2	0.4	1.9
Armenia	*2.8*	13.2	..	..	–12.6	..	5.5	..	2.7
Australia	24.9	27.8	78.4	*110.5*	4.7	14.8	12.0	6.5	3.3
Austria	51.0	69.1	128.2	*152.7*	3.1	9.1	25.7	0.6	4.7
Azerbaijan	2.5	14.0	..	..	..	..	..	..	..
Bangladesh	4.2	7.0	29.9	56.1	7.2	0.3	0.8	0.0	0.2
Belarus	4.4	24.1	13.2	109.6	–6.7	..	1.3	..	0.2
Belgium	101.0	126.1	309.6	*366.3*	2.6	..	..	..	..
Benin	16.5	19.1	67.3	81.8	–2.6	4.1	*5.7*	0.3	*0.8*
Bolivia	10.2	15.9	*72.4*	*71.7*	2.9	2.1	7.3	0.6	4.9
Bosnia and Herzegovina	..	..	..	..	..	..	..	..	..
Botswana	47.7	42.4	127.3	*178.6*	–3.6	1.4	4.6	0.8	1.1
Brazil	5.8	9.9	32.9	30.4	6.5	1.9	9.3	0.4	3.2
Bulgaria	36.6	22.8	115.1	133.6	–13.4	4.3	2.9	0.0	1.0
Burkina Faso	12.0	7.7	52.2	*50.2*	–2.3	0.3	..	0.1	..
Burundi	7.9	4.9	36.1	29.5	0.1	0.5	*0.6*	0.0	*0.0*
Cambodia	6.2	12.5	51.6	96.0	..	..	1.5	..	0.9
Cameroon	16.0	14.6	44.4	54.2	0.1	5.7	..	0.7	..
Canada	42.7	59.0	104.7	..	5.2	10.0	13.3	2.8	6.3
Central African Republic	10.2	9.2	36.3	46.1	2.6	1.8	..	0.3	..
Chad	8.8	7.2	48.2	47.4	–3.2	1.9	..	0.4	..
Chile	21.9	24.7	91.1	83.5	4.2	6.8	13.9	1.8	5.7
China	6.3	8.3	40.8	49.8	3.5	0.6	2.3	0.3	1.3
Hong Kong, China	149.8	258.5	713.7	*1,121.7*	6.9	..	..	..	..
Colombia	5.5	10.4	36.0	53.8	6.5	0.7	3.3	0.1	1.5
Congo, Dem. Rep.	6.8	13.7	74.1	*121.3*	–5.3	..	..	..	..
Congo, Rep.	63.1	90.2	141.0	207.4	3.0	22.8	*8.3*	0.4	*0.0*
Costa Rica	19.9	53.7	134.4	274.1	5.0	2.2	4.4	1.0	2.7
Côte d'Ivoire	29.0	31.4	79.5	135.9	1.1	3.1	2.4	0.3	1.9
Croatia	..	44.1	..	115.8	..	..	8.7	..	3.2
Cuba	..	..	..	..	..	..	..	..	..
Czech Republic	..	43.5	..	..	11.0	..	7.2	..	2.0
Denmark	59.3	71.8	114.0	..	2.0	24.8	16.2	1.4	8.3
Dominican Republic	11.3	33.1	112.9	178.5	0.7	1.1	2.8	0.5	1.8
Ecuador	14.7	25.7	75.3	125.9	1.9	2.2	4.5	0.6	2.3
Egypt, Arab Rep.	11.1	10.2	68.8	43.4	–0.7	2.5	3.8	1.1	0.6
El Salvador	11.5	25.2	81.2	129.7	7.0	0.5	5.1	0.2	3.6
Eritrea	..	..	..	..	8.2	..	..	..	..
Estonia	5.5	58.3	*20.4*	306.8	..	..	13.4	..	6.0
Ethiopia	5.9	4.6	26.6	..	–0.8	0.0	0.2	0.0	0.0
Finland	54.0	69.2	85.9	*127.1*	3.7	16.9	62.6	3.9	35.5
France	36.5	46.3	92.6	*116.6*	2.8	10.4	22.8	2.5	5.5
Gabon	44.6	51.2	93.1	*112.1*	0.1	11.8	..	3.2	..
Gambia, The	16.6	18.2	173.4	158.9	–1.0	0.5	*1.5*	0.2	*0.7*
Georgia	1.0	7.5	..	*36.1*	..	..	..	..	..
Germany	..	55.0	..	*67.3*	2.4	..	36.7	..	5.8
Ghana	10.0	13.0	54.5	320.8	3.6	0.1	0.6	0.0	0.2
Greece	16.9	18.8	46.5	..	2.1	1.6	*7.9*	0.9	*0.7*
Guatemala	11.1	18.8	..	..	3.7	3.1	10.3	1.5	5.3
Guinea	13.8	10.0	74.6	59.3	–1.8	1.4	0.9	0.2	0.1
Guinea-Bissau	12.4	15.2	61.1	70.4	–2.1	6.9	0.4	0.0	..
Haiti	4.6	8.9	*43.2*	..	8.4	0.4	1.5	0.1	0.1
Honduras	19.6	29.1	88.9	140.7	–0.7	1.3	2.5	0.5	0.6

Integration with the global economy 6.1

	Trade in goods				Growth in real trade less growth in real GDP	Gross private capital flows		Gross foreign direct investment	
	% of PPP GDP		% of goods GDP		percentage points	% of PPP GDP		% of PPP GDP	
	1988	1998	1988	1998	1988–98	1988	1998	1988	1998
Hungary	20.5	42.4	104.7	*185.5*	5.1	0.3	7.7	0.0	2.3
India	3.3	3.9	18.2	*33.6*	4.5	0.2	0.9	0.0	0.1
Indonesia	12.1	15.2	62.8	134.9	3.2	0.6	4.4	0.2	0.9
Iran, Islamic Rep.	12.1	8.4	36.1	*73.9*	–4.2	0.4	1.1	0.0	0.0
Iraq	..	..	..	..	..	..	..	..	..
Ireland	96.5	134.0	189.8	..	3.3	16.6	111.9	0.3	5.1
Israel	42.1	47.7	..	..	2.1	14.3	9.1	0.5	2.3
Italy	28.3	37.9	77.7	*110.2*	4.2	6.0	25.0	1.3	1.3
Jamaica	32.3	49.5	141.7	195.3	0.9	2.5	12.9	0.4	5.2
Japan	20.4	21.3	37.8	*49.5*	3.5	7.4	20.7	1.7	1.0
Jordan	41.7	34.1	143.2	175.9	4.9	6.0	2.1	0.3	2.0
Kazakhstan	5.6	18.2	..	126.4	6.8	..	3.6	..	1.7
Kenya	14.5	17.6	58.5	86.5	3.9	0.9	3.3	0.2	0.0
Korea, Dem. Rep.	..	..	..	..	..	..	..	..	..
Korea, Rep.	34.8	35.6	112.5	146.7	5.3	3.3	13.2	0.5	1.6
Kuwait	..	..	144.6	..	..	..	..	..	..
Kyrgyz Republic	3.6	11.9	*30.3*	*103.6*	..	..	2.6	..	1.0
Lao PDR	5.6	9.8	*48.7*	90.0	..	1.1	0.9	0.1	0.5
Latvia	5.5	36.7	*16.2*	188.4	7.1	..	8.9	..	3.1
Lebanon	..	..	..	..	5.2	..	..	..	..
Lesotho	38.2	31.6	215.2	*214.7*	–3.8	3.2	8.2	1.3	7.9
Libya	..	..	..	..	..	..	..	..	..
Lithuania	9.9	39.6	33.1	170.0	..	..	8.1	..	3.9
Macedonia, FYR	..	..	..	..	..	..	4.6	..	1.4
Madagascar	7.2	11.2	36.3	..	2.2	0.5	0.4	0.0	0.2
Malawi	14.9	23.3	53.4	133.9	0.8	0.7	..	0.0	..
Malaysia	45.7	70.1	192.1	307.6	6.3	4.2	*7.6*	0.9	*2.6*
Mali	14.7	15.1	52.3	58.3	1.4	1.7	*1.7*	0.2	*0.6*
Mauritania	31.7	17.2	108.5	115.9	–3.8	3.4	10.3	0.1	0.0
Mauritius	43.7	39.0	190.6	181.5	0.3	4.0	3.5	0.5	0.3
Mexico	12.6	32.9	71.5	153.9	9.4	3.0	3.4	0.6	1.4
Moldova	..	20.2	..	157.2	19.9	..	4.0	..	0.9
Mongolia	69.2	24.8	..	156.8	..	32.7	4.0	0.0	0.5
Morocco	12.9	18.1	71.1	96.1	2.6	1.6	1.1	0.1	0.4
Mozambique	11.1	7.8	52.2	52.5	–1.7	0.1	2.3	0.1	1.6
Myanmar	..	..	..	..	..	..	..	..	..
Namibia	33.2	31.7	134.9	*176.1*	–1.1	*7.6*	4.5	*2.1*	1.4
Nepal	5.9	6.5	35.7	..	8.0	0.5	0.1	0.0	0.0
Netherlands	86.2	93.2	222.1	..	1.9	25.1	56.7	5.2	21.0
New Zealand	32.5	35.7	98.5	..	3.2	8.6	*9.4*	4.6	*5.2*
Nicaragua	14.0	19.1	70.7	175.8	6.0	0.4	4.3	0.0	1.8
Niger	16.1	8.5	73.6	53.4	–0.8	1.6	..	0.2	..
Nigeria	20.7	18.9	68.3	60.2	1.5	4.1	4.1	0.7	1.1
Norway	61.9	68.3	115.5	*126.1*	1.8	16.6	34.5	1.7	7.7
Oman	..	..	129.3	..	..	..	..	..	..
Pakistan	9.3	8.2	54.8	53.4	0.1	0.7	*1.6*	0.2	*0.3*
Panama	60.9	96.6	387.4	644.5	–1.1	396.7	*44.6*	9.0	8.7
Papua New Guinea	42.0	26.3	123.5	114.1	2.0	4.2	25.1	2.7	1.1
Paraguay	12.8	34.7	58.8	176.5	9.2	0.9	3.1	0.1	1.1
Peru	7.5	13.1	74.4	50.6	4.6	1.0	3.7	0.1	1.8
Philippines	8.8	22.1	69.2	186.9	6.8	1.3	3.6	0.5	0.7
Poland	13.0	26.4	59.0	*99.0*	13.9	1.5	5.9	0.0	2.5
Portugal	28.3	43.9	119.6	..	4.3	6.8	25.9	1.0	3.2
Puerto Rico	..	..	..	..	..	..	..	..	..
Romania	12.1	15.1	64.0	83.8	4.7	2.4	3.0	0.0	1.6
Russian Federation	*5.9*	14.0	*21.0*	101.4	6.6	..	1.9	..	0.4

6.1 Integration with the global economy

	Trade in goods				Growth in real trade less growth in real GDP	Gross private capital flows		Gross foreign direct investment	
	% of PPP GDP		% of goods GDP		percentage points	% of PPP GDP		% of PPP GDP	
	1988	1998	1988	1998	1988–98	1988	1998	1988	1998
Rwanda	..	..	25.6	22.9	4.9	..	..	..	..
Saudi Arabia	31.3	31.9	113.6	..	..	9.3	9.1	0.2	2.2
Senegal	20.6	17.3	82.0	105.2	–1.4	3.2	*3.5*	0.4	*1.6*
Sierra Leone	8.8	10.0	26.8	49.9	12.5	2.6	..	0.8	..
Singapore	263.8	269.1	839.5	690.8	..	32.6	57.6	12.2	13.5
Slovak Republic	..	45.5	..	324.5	9.1	..	6.8	..	1.7
Slovenia	..	66.9	..	191.1	–0.5	..	4.7	..	0.6
South Africa	14.7	16.1	82.7	102.3	4.5	0.8	7.1	0.1	0.6
Spain	22.8	37.3	72.2	*44.1*	6.0	4.9	26.0	1.9	5.1
Sri Lanka	11.5	17.9	88.0	118.8	2.9	2.1	1.8	0.2	0.4
Sudan	6.5	5.9	..	..	..	0.7	1.1	0.0	0.9
Sweden	65.7	83.5	125.0	..	3.7	18.7	88.6	6.4	23.0
Switzerland	92.4	103.0	..	..	1.4	34.2	71.9	7.7	13.6
Syrian Arab Republic	11.4	14.6	62.4	..	–0.9	0.6	5.2	0.0	0.2
Tajikistan	2.1	24.7	9.9	205.8	..	..	..	..	..
Tanzania	14.2	12.7	39.8	38.2	0.2	0.0	2.1	0.0	1.1
Thailand	20.0	26.7	107.5	153.2	4.2	2.8	5.9	0.7	2.1
Togo	20.5	14.6	123.5	93.5	–4.4	2.0	..	0.3	..
Trinidad and Tobago	36.0	54.7	139.0	*193.5*	2.0	5.6	8.7	1.3	7.6
Tunisia	21.0	27.0	137.6	166.7	0.7	2.6	4.1	0.2	1.3
Turkey	10.9	18.8	51.3	79.0	6.4	1.6	4.5	0.2	0.3
Turkmenistan	6.7	*15.0*	*46.6*	101.4	..	..	*3.8*	..	*0.9*
Uganda	7.7	7.1	17.8	35.8	1.7	0.3	*1.0*	0.0	*0.8*
Ukraine	5.8	18.7	39.5	126.3	7.8	..	2.8	..	0.5
United Arab Emirates	73.5	114.3	153.5	..	..	..	..	..	..
United Kingdom	36.4	48.1	88.3	*81.4*	2.8	26.5	47.2	7.7	18.5
United States	14.5	19.9	53.8	*78.9*	5.3	6.9	10.3	2.0	4.6
Uruguay	13.9	22.7	69.1	97.1	6.5	6.7	8.6	0.3	0.6
Uzbekistan	..	15.4	..	57.6	..	..	..	..	..
Venezuela, RB	23.4	24.0	79.2	*81.2*	3.0	4.2	13.3	0.2	3.7
Vietnam	*5.1*	13.1	12.3	..	20.4	..	..	..	..
West Bank and Gaza	..	..	..	..	..	..	..	..	..
Yemen, Rep.	*36.3*	31.0	*105.6*	140.2	0.1	*6.9*	4.1	*1.7*	1.8
Yugoslavia, FR (Serb./Mont.)	..	..	..	..	..	..	..	..	..
Zambia	33.6	37.3	75.9	141.6	–0.7	14.4	..	1.7	..
Zimbabwe	13.8	15.5	66.6	147.5	7.7	0.7	..	0.2	..
World	21.2 w	28.3 w	71.9 w	*92.1* w	..	6.9 w	14.5 w	1.7 w	3.8 w
Low income	6.8	8.3	38.6	62.5	..	0.7	2.0	0.2	0.9
Excl. China & India	..	..	..	..	..	..	..	..	..
Middle income	13.2	22.1	66.6	98.9	..	3.0	6.4	0.4	1.6
Lower middle income	11.4	17.2	63.6	106.8	..	1.6	3.5	0.3	1.0
Upper middle income	14.5	26.4	68.3	94.5	..	3.9	8.8	0.5	2.2
Low & middle income	10.7	15.7	57.8	88.8	..	2.0	4.4	0.3	1.3
East Asia & Pacific	13.3	15.5	74.8	98.1	..	1.3	4.0	0.4	1.3
Europe & Central Asia	9.0	21.1	48.7	106.4	..	..	3.8	..	1.0
Latin America & Carib.	9.4	19.1	52.3	74.5	..	3.7	7.1	0.5	2.5
Middle East & N. Africa	17.6	17.4	70.3	*80.5*	..	3.1	7.3	0.3	0.9
South Asia	4.2	4.8	24.2	*40.5*	..	0.3	0.9	0.0	0.1
Sub-Saharan Africa	15.4	16.8	73.2	99.5	..	1.7	4.9	0.3	0.7
High income	28.3	38.3	75.2	*95.1*	..	9.9	22.3	2.6	5.7
Europe EMU	41.0	54.4	111.1	*106.4*	..	9.4	32.2	2.1	6.1

Integration with the global economy 6.1

About the data

The growing importance of trade in the world's economy is one indication of the increasing global economic integration. Another is the increased size and importance of private capital flows to developing countries that have liberalized their financial markets. This table presents standardized measures of the size of trade and capital flows relative to gross domestic product. For three of the indicators GDP measured in purchasing power parity (PPP) terms has been used in the denominator to adjust for differences in domestic prices. (No adjustment has been made to the numerators because goods and capital exchanged on international markets are assumed to be valued at international prices.)

The numerators are based on gross flows that capture the two-way flow of goods and capital. In conventional balance of payments accounting exports are recorded as a credit and imports as a debit. And in the financial account inward investment is a credit and outward investment a debit. Thus net flows, the sum of credits and debits, represent a balance in which many transactions are canceled out. Gross flows are a better measure of integration because they show the total value of financial transactions during a given period.

The growth of services has affected the historical record. Compared with the levels achieved at the end of the 19th century, trade in goods appears to have declined in importance relative to GDP, especially in economies with growing service sectors. Measuring merchandise trade relative to GDP after deducting value added by services thus provides a better measure of its relative size than does comparing it with total GDP, although this neglects the growing service component of most goods output.

Trade in services, traditionally called invisibles, is becoming an important element of global integration. The difference between the growth of real trade in goods and services and the growth of GDP helps to identify economies with dynamic trade regimes.

The investment indicators in the table were constructed from data recorded at the most detailed level available. Higher-level aggregates tend to be affected by the netting out of credits and debits and so produce a smaller total. The comparability of these indicators between countries and over time is affected by the accuracy and completeness of balance of payments records and by their level of detail.

Figure 6.1

The importance of trade continues to grow

Source: World Trade Organization.

World trade in goods increased from 21.2 to 28.3 percent of PPP GDP between 1988 and 1998. A few well-integrated trading nations—Singapore, Hong Kong (China), and Belgium—remained in the top spots, but there were many more gainers than losers.

Definitions

• **Trade in goods as a share of PPP GDP** is the sum of merchandise exports and imports measured in current U.S. dollars divided by the value of GDP converted to international dollars using purchasing power parity rates. • **Trade in goods as a share of goods GDP** is the sum of merchandise exports and imports divided by the value of GDP after subtracting value added in services, all in current U.S. dollars. • **Growth in real trade less growth in real GDP** is the difference between annual growth in trade of goods and services and annual growth in GDP. Growth rates are calculated using constant price series taken from national accounts and are expressed as a percentage. • **Gross private capital flows** are the sum of the absolute values of direct, portfolio, and other investment inflows and outflows recorded in the balance of payments financial account, excluding changes in the assets and liabilities of monetary authorities and general government. The indicator is calculated as a ratio to GDP converted to international dollars using purchasing power parity rates. • **Gross foreign direct investment** is the sum of the absolute values of inflows and outflows of foreign direct investment recorded in the balance of payments financial account. It includes equity capital, reinvestment of earnings, other long-term capital, and short-term capital. This indicator differs from the standard measure of foreign direct investment, which captures only inward investment (see table 6.7). The indicator is calculated as a ratio to GDP converted to international dollars using purchasing power parity rates.

Data sources

The data on merchandise trade are from the World Trade Organization. The data on GDP in PPP terms come from the World Bank's International Comparison Programme database. The data on real trade and GDP growth come from the World Bank's national accounts files. Gross private capital flows and foreign direct investment were calculated using the International Monetary Fund's Balance of Payments database.

6.2 Direction and growth of merchandise trade

High-income importers

Direction of trade % of world trade, 1998	European Union	Japan	United States	Other industrial	All industrial	Other high income	All high income
Source of exports							
High-income economies	32.0	2.8	11.0	7.6	53.4	5.2	58.5
Industrial economies	30.6	2.1	9.1	7.3	49.1	4.0	53.1
European Union	24.7	0.6	3.2	3.4	32.0	1.4	33.4
Japan	1.3		2.2	0.4	3.9	1.3	5.1
United States	2.8	1.1		3.3	7.1	1.1	8.1
Other industrial economies	1.8	0.4	3.7	0.3	6.2	0.3	6.5
Other high-income economies	1.4	0.7	1.9	0.3	4.3	1.1	5.4
Low- and middle-income economies	6.1	1.9	5.6	0.9	14.4	2.6	17.0
East Asia & Pacific	1.6	1.4	2.0	0.5	5.5	2.2	7.6
Europe & Central Asia	2.3	0.1	0.2	0.1	2.7	0.1	2.8
Latin America & Caribbean	0.7	0.1	2.7	0.1	3.7	0.1	3.7
Middle East & N. Africa	0.7	0.2	0.2	0.0	1.1	0.1	1.2
South Asia	0.3	0.0	0.2	0.0	0.6	0.1	0.7
Sub-Saharan Africa	0.5	0.1	0.2	0.0	0.8	0.1	0.9
World	38.0	4.7	16.6	8.5	67.8	7.8	75.6

Low- and middle-income importers

Direction of trade % of world trade, 1998	East Asia & Pacific	Europe & Central Asia	Latin America & Caribbean	Middle East & N. Africa	South Asia	Sub-Saharan Africa	All low & middle income	World
Source of exports								
High-income economies	5.8	3.8	4.4	1.7	0.7	0.9	17.3	75.8
Industrial economies	3.6	3.7	4.2	1.6	0.5	0.8	14.4	67.5
European Union	1.0	3.2	1.1	1.0	0.2	0.6	7.2	40.5
Japan	1.3	0.1	0.4	0.2	0.1	0.1	2.0	7.1
United States	1.0	0.2	2.6	0.3	0.1	0.1	4.3	12.5
Other industrial economies	0.4	0.1	0.1	0.1	0.1	0.0	0.9	7.3
Other high-income economies	2.2	0.1	0.2	0.1	0.2	0.1	2.9	8.3
Low- and middle-income economies	2.1	2.0	1.5	0.6	0.5	0.5	7.1	24.2
East Asia & Pacific	1.4	0.3	0.3	0.2	0.2	0.1	2.5	11.1
Europe & Central Asia	0.1	1.5	0.1	0.1	0.0	0.0	1.9	4.7
Latin America & Caribbean	0.1	0.1	1.1	0.1	0.0	0.0	1.4	5.1
Middle East & N. Africa	0.3	0.1	0.0	0.1	0.1	0.0	0.7	1.9
South Asia	0.1	0.0	0.0	0.0	0.1	0.0	0.2	1.0
Sub-Saharan Africa	0.1	0.0	0.0	0.0	0.0	0.2	0.4	1.3
World	7.9	5.8	5.9	2.3	1.1	1.4	24.4	100.0

Direction and growth of merchandise trade 6.2

High-income importers

Nominal growth of trade annual % growth, 1988–98	European Union	Japan	United States	Other industrial	All industrial	Other high income	All high income
Source of exports							
High-income economies	5.9	4.0	6.3	7.4	6.0	8.3	6.2
Industrial economies	5.8	3.7	6.1	7.4	6.0	7.4	6.1
European Union	6.0	5.0	6.8	8.0	6.2	9.1	6.3
Japan	3.2		2.9	0.8	2.8	6.3	3.5
United States	6.5	4.4		7.9	6.8	7.5	6.9
Other industrial economies	4.0	0.5	8.1	6.8	6.0	5.3	6.0
Other high-income economies	8.6	5.0	7.0	6.8	7.0	12.5	8.0
Low- and middle-income economies	8.2	5.5	11.6	9.9	9.0	10.5	9.2
East Asia & Pacific	13.1	7.1	11.2	13.9	10.7	11.6	10.9
Europe & Central Asia	10.4	–1.6	14.0	10.0	10.2	13.5	10.3
Latin America & Caribbean	4.5	1.6	14.0	7.3	10.4	6.2	10.2
Middle East & N. Africa	2.6	4.5	1.1	0.2	2.5	0.1	2.2
South Asia	10.3	1.6	12.9	9.1	10.0	13.1	10.5
Sub-Saharan Africa	3.6	1.3	4.3	2.1	3.5	12.3	3.9
World	6.2	4.6	7.8	7.6	6.6	9.0	6.8

Low- and middle-income importers

Nominal growth of trade annual % growth, 1988–98	East Asia & Pacific	Europe & Central Asia	Latin America & Caribbean	Middle East & N. Africa	South Asia	Sub-Saharan Africa	All low & middle income	World
Source of exports								
High-income economies	8.8	12.3	11.4	3.9	4.0	2.8	8.7	6.7
Industrial economies	7.2	12.2	11.3	4.0	2.3	2.7	8.3	6.5
European Union	8.7	14.1	10.6	3.7	2.6	2.6	8.9	6.7
Japan	5.7	0.0	8.6	2.1	0.2	–0.6	4.9	3.9
United States	8.8	6.8	12.5	5.6	1.8	6.0	10.1	7.9
Other industrial economies	5.2	2.8	5.6	5.0	5.5	3.2	4.7	5.8
Other high-income economies	12.0	19.0	13.9	2.7	10.2	3.3	11.2	9.0
Low- and middle-income economies	15.3	6.0	14.1	2.8	10.2	10.2	9.7	9.4
East Asia & Pacific	19.0	11.8	23.2	7.0	12.7	10.0	15.8	11.9
Europe & Central Asia	3.8	6.8	14.1	–1.1	–2.2	4.7	5.7	8.2
Latin America & Caribbean	5.8	0.8	13.9	5.0	9.8	5.9	10.9	10.4
Middle East & N. Africa	16.5	–2.9	–3.2	0.5	8.8	10.2	5.1	3.1
South Asia	13.3	–3.1	28.6	7.3	13.7	15.9	8.4	9.9
Sub-Saharan Africa	11.9	3.6	11.0	11.5	25.0	11.6	11.6	5.8
World	10.1	9.7	12.0	3.6	6.1	4.7	9.0	7.3

6.2 Direction and growth of merchandise trade

About the data

This table provides estimates of the flow of trade in goods between groups of economies. Most high-income countries and about 22 developing countries report their trade data to the International Monetary Fund (IMF) each month. Together these countries account for about 80 percent of world exports. Trade by less timely reporters and by countries that do not report is estimated using reports of partner countries. Because the largest exporting and importing countries are reliable reporters, a large portion of the missing trade flows can be estimated from partner reports. Even so, a small amount of trade between developing countries, particularly in Africa, is not captured in partner data. Estimates of intra-European trade have been significantly affected by changes in reporting methods following the creation of a customs union.

Most countries report their trade data in national currencies, which are converted using the IMF's published exchange rate series rf (official rate, period average) or rh (market rate, period average). Because imports are reported at c.i.f. (cost, insurance, and freight) valuations and exports at f.o.b. (free on board) valuations, the IMF divides partner country reports of import values by 1.10 to estimate equivalent export values. This approximation is more or less accurate, depending on the set of partners and the items traded. Other factors affecting the accuracy of trade data include lags in reporting, recording differences across countries, and whether the country reports trade according to the general or special system of trade. (See *About the data* for tables 4.5 and 4.6 for further discussion of the measurement of exports and imports.)

The regional trade flows shown in this table were calculated from current price values. Growth rates therefore include the effects of changes in both volumes and prices.

Definitions

• **Merchandise trade** includes all trade in goods. Trade in services is excluded. • **Regional groupings** are based on World Bank definitions and may differ from those used by other organizations. • **European Union** comprises Austria, Belgium, Denmark, Finland, France, Germany, Greece, Ireland, Italy, Luxembourg, the Netherlands, Portugal, Spain, Sweden, and the United Kingdom. • **Other industrial economies** include Australia, Canada, Iceland, New Zealand, Norway, and Switzerland. • **Other high-income economies** include Cyprus, Hong Kong (China), Israel, Kuwait, Malta, Qatar, Singapore, Taiwan (China), and the United Arab Emirates. Some small high-income economies such as Aruba, the Bahamas, and Bermuda have been included in the Latin America and Caribbean group.

Data sources

Intercountry trade flows are published in the IMF's *Direction of Trade Statistics Yearbook* and *Direction of Trade Statistics Quarterly;* the data in the table were calculated using the IMF's Direction of Trade database.

Figure 6.2

Developing economies make their own market

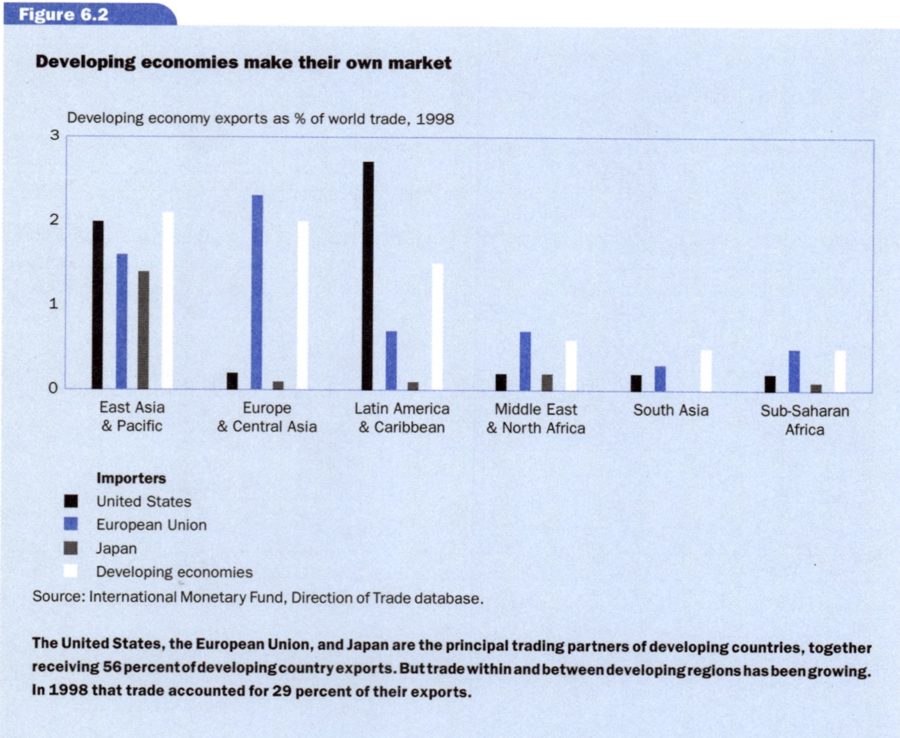

Source: International Monetary Fund, Direction of Trade database.

The United States, the European Union, and Japan are the principal trading partners of developing countries, together receiving 56 percent of developing country exports. But trade within and between developing regions has been growing. In 1998 that trade accounted for 29 percent of their exports.

OECD trade with low- and middle-income economies 6.3

Exports to low- and middle-income economies	High-income OECD countries		European Union		Japan		United States	
	1990	1998	1990	1998	1990	1998	1990	1998
$ billions								
Food	32.4	54.9	16.0	27.1	0.3	0.5	10.2	18.7
Cereals	13.2	13.4	4.1	4.6	0.1	0.2	5.5	6.2
Agricultural raw materials	8.6	13.0	3.1	4.3	0.6	1.0	3.5	5.0
Ores and nonferrous metals	7.0	11.9	2.8	5.0	0.5	1.4	2.1	3.1
Fuels	6.5	11.7	2.5	5.2	0.3	0.6	2.6	3.9
Crude petroleum	0.3	0.6	0.0	0.3	..	0.0	0.0	0.1
Petroleum products	4.6	7.2	2.4	3.4	0.2	0.5	1.7	2.9
Manufactured goods	274.9	571.0	144.1	296.0	52.9	86.7	64.2	168.7
Chemical products	40.4	73.6	22.8	41.5	3.6	6.2	10.4	20.5
Mach. & transport equip.	157.9	339.2	77.4	161.9	34.9	60.7	39.3	107.5
Other	76.6	158.2	44.0	92.5	14.5	19.8	14.5	40.7
Miscellaneous goods	10.3	24.6	3.5	13.7	0.5	1.8	4.3	8.3
Total	**339.7**	**693.7**	**172.0**	**354.7**	**55.1**	**92.0**	**86.9**	**207.7**
% of total exports								
Food	9.5	7.9	9.3	7.6	0.6	0.6	11.7	9.0
Cereals	3.9	1.9	2.4	1.3	0.1	0.2	6.3	3.0
Agricultural raw materials	2.5	1.9	1.8	1.2	1.0	1.1	4.1	2.4
Ores and nonferrous metals	2.1	1.7	1.6	1.4	0.9	1.5	2.4	1.5
Fuels	1.9	1.7	1.5	1.5	0.5	0.6	3.0	1.9
Crude petroleum	0.1	0.1	0.0	0.1	..	0.0	0.0	0.0
Petroleum products	1.3	1.0	1.4	0.9	0.4	0.6	2.0	1.4
Manufactured goods	80.9	82.3	83.8	83.4	96.1	94.2	73.9	81.3
Chemical products	11.9	10.6	13.2	11.7	6.4	6.8	12.0	9.9
Mach. & transport equip.	46.5	48.9	45.0	45.6	63.4	66.0	45.2	51.8
Other	22.5	22.8	25.6	26.1	26.3	21.5	16.6	19.6
Miscellaneous goods	3.0	3.5	2.0	3.9	0.9	2.0	5.0	4.0
Total	**100.0**	**100.0**	**100.0**	**100.0**	**100.0**	**100.0**	**100.0**	**100.0**

6.3 OECD trade with low- and middle-income economies

Imports from low- and middle-income economies	High-income OECD countries 1990	High-income OECD countries 1998	European Union 1990	European Union 1998	Japan 1990	Japan 1998	United States 1990	United States 1998
$ billions								
Food	63.1	92.9	34.9	46.9	9.4	16.8	15.4	23.9
Cereals	1.3	2.3	0.5	0.9	0.5	0.6	0.2	0.6
Agricultural raw materials	17.4	21.8	9.9	13.0	4.7	3.6	2.3	4.4
Ores and nonferrous metals	29.9	42.2	15.0	21.0	8.9	9.0	5.1	9.4
Fuels	144.0	111.8	58.6	47.9	33.1	20.3	48.7	38.8
Crude petroleum	107.5	79.7	46.6	32.8	20.8	11.7	37.3	31.0
Petroleum products	23.2	14.0	6.2	5.2	5.4	1.6	10.8	6.9
Manufactured goods	170.3	540.7	76.1	205.7	15.4	51.7	66.6	251.0
Chemical products	13.4	28.2	7.7	14.4	1.7	3.1	2.7	8.2
Mach. and transport. equip.	45.2	208.9	14.6	68.0	2.0	17.1	24.8	111.7
Other	111.7	303.6	53.8	123.3	11.7	31.5	39.1	131.1
Miscellaneous goods	5.2	13.2	2.0	4.2	0.5	1.2	2.5	7.7
Total	**429.9**	**823.6**	**196.5**	**339.5**	**71.9**	**102.5**	**140.6**	**335.2**
% of total imports								
Food	14.7	11.3	17.8	13.8	13.1	16.4	10.9	7.1
Cereals	0.3	0.3	0.3	0.3	0.7	0.6	0.1	0.2
Agricultural raw materials	4.0	2.7	5.0	3.8	6.6	3.5	1.6	1.3
Ores and nonferrous metals	7.0	5.1	7.6	6.2	12.3	8.8	3.6	2.8
Fuels	33.5	13.6	29.8	14.1	46.0	19.8	34.7	11.6
Crude petroleum	25.0	9.7	23.7	9.7	28.9	11.4	26.5	9.2
Petroleum products	5.4	1.7	3.2	1.5	7.5	1.5	7.7	2.1
Manufactured goods	39.6	65.6	38.7	60.6	21.5	50.4	47.4	74.9
Chemical products	3.1	3.4	3.9	4.2	2.4	3.1	2.0	2.5
Mach. and transport. equip.	10.5	25.4	7.4	20.0	2.7	16.7	17.7	33.3
Other	26.0	36.9	27.4	36.3	16.3	30.7	27.8	39.1
Miscellaneous goods	1.2	1.6	1.0	1.2	0.6	1.1	1.8	2.3
Total	**100.0**	**100.0**	**100.0**	**100.0**	**100.0**	**100.0**	**100.0**	**100.0**

OECD trade with low- and middle-income economies 6.3

About the data

Trade flows between high-income members of the Organisation for Economic Co-operation and Development (OECD) and low- and middle-income economies reflect the changing mix of exports to and imports from developing economies. While food and primary commodities have continued to fall as a share of OECD imports, the share of manufactured goods supplied by developing countries has grown. At the same time developing countries have increased their imports of manufactured goods from high-income countries—particularly capital-intensive goods such as machinery and transport equipment. Although trade between developing countries has grown substantially over the past decade (see table 6.5), high-income OECD countries remain the developing world's most important partners.

The aggregate flows in the table were compiled from intercountry flows recorded in the United Nations Statistics Division's Commodity Trade (COMTRADE) database. Partner country reports by high-income OECD countries were used for both exports and imports. Exports are recorded free on board (f.o.b.); imports include insurance and freight charges (c.i.f.). Because of differences in sources of data, timing, and treatment of missing data, the data in this table may not be fully comparable with those used to calculate the direction of trade statistics in table 6.2 or the aggregate flows shown in tables 4.4–4.6.

For further discussion of merchandise trade statistics see *About the data* for tables 4.4–4.6 and 6.2.

Figure 6.3

High-income economies' imports of manufactures from low- and middle-income economies have surged

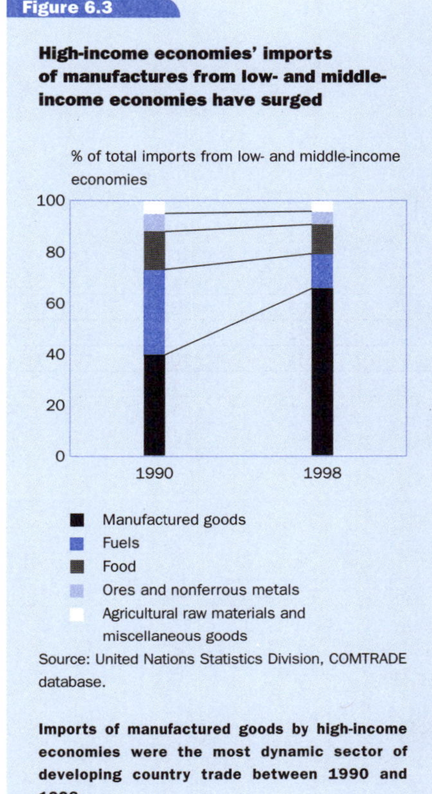

Source: United Nations Statistics Division, COMTRADE database.

Imports of manufactured goods by high-income economies were the most dynamic sector of developing country trade between 1990 and 1998.

Definitions

The product groups in the table are defined in accordance with the Standard International Trade Classification (SITC) revision 1: food (0, 1, 22, and 4) and cereals (04); agricultural raw materials (2 excluding 22, 27, and 28); ores and nonferrous metals (27, 28, and 68); fuels (3), crude petroleum (331), and petroleum products (332); manufactured goods (5–8 excluding 68), chemical products (5), machinery and transport equipment (7), and other manufactured goods (6 and 8 excluding 68); and miscellaneous goods (9). • **Exports** are all merchandise exports by high-income OECD countries to low- and middle-income economies as recorded in the United Nations Statistics Division's COMTRADE database. • **Imports** are all merchandise imports by high-income OECD countries from low- and middle-income economies as recorded in the United Nations Statistics Division's COMTRADE database. • **High-income OECD countries** in 1998 were Australia, Austria, Belgium, Canada, Denmark, Finland, France, Germany, Greece, Iceland, Ireland, Italy, Japan, Luxembourg, the Netherlands, New Zealand, Norway, Portugal, Spain, Sweden, Switzerland, the United Kingdom, and the United States. • **European Union** comprises Austria, Belgium, Denmark, Finland, France, Germany, Greece, Ireland, Italy, Luxembourg, the Netherlands, Portugal, Spain, Sweden, and the United Kingdom.

Data sources

COMTRADE data are available in machine-readable form from the United Nations Statistics Division. Although not as comprehensive as the underlying COMTRADE records, detailed statistics on international trade are published annually in the United Nations Conference on Trade and Development's (UNCTAD) *Handbook of International Trade and Development Statistics* and the United Nations Statistics Division's *International Trade Statistics Yearbook*.

6.4 Primary commodity prices

	1960	1965	1970	1975	1980	1985	1990	1995	1997	1998	1999
World Bank commodity price index (1990 = 100)											
Nonfuel commodities	187	187	175	166	174	133	100	102	109	95	85
Agriculture	208	193	182	179	192	146	100	110	119	103	90
Beverages	234	213	227	180	252	239	100	127	158	135	104
Food	184	197	186	223	193	126	100	98	107	101	85
Raw materials	220	174	145	121	145	103	100	113	105	84	85
Fertilizers	180	179	121	350	179	130	100	87	110	117	110
Metals and minerals	137	173	161	117	131	101	100	85	83	72	71
Petroleum	34	29	21	101	224	173	100	63	77	55	76
Steel products[a]	..	..	124	115	110	89	100	90	82	72	66
MUV G-5 index	21	22	25	45	72	69	100	119	108	104	104
Commodity prices (1990 $)											
Agricultural raw materials											
Cotton (cents/kg)	314	290	252	257	284	192	182	179	161	139	113
Logs, Cameroon ($/cu. m)[a]	168	183	171	280	349	253	344	285	263	275	260
Logs, Malaysian ($/cu. m)	154	162	172	149	272	177	177	214	220	156	181
Rubber (cents/kg)	377	234	162	124	198	111	86	133	94	69	61
Sawnwood, Malaysian ($/cu. m)	721	726	699	494	550	448	533	621	612	465	580
Tobacco ($/mt)	8,391	5,858	4,287	4,075	3,161	3,807	3,392	2,214	3,256	3,222	2,922
Beverages (cents/kg)											
Cocoa	285	169	269	276	362	329	127	120	149	161	110
Coffee, robustas	270	323	369	298	450	386	118	232	160	175	144
Coffee, Arabica	446	464	457	319	481	471	197	280	385	286	221
Tea, avg., 3 auctions	497	463	333	253	230	255	206	125	190	196	178
Energy											
Coal, Australian ($/mt)	..	..	..	..	55	49	40	33	32	28	25
Coal, U.S. ($/mt)	..	..	..	..	60	68	42	33	34	33	32
Natural gas, Europe ($/mmbtu)	..	..	..	2	5	5	3	2	3	2	2
Natural gas, U.S. ($/mmbtu)	1	1	1	1	2	4	2	1	2	2	2
Petroleum ($/bbl)	8	7	5	23	51	40	23	14	18	13	17

About the data

Primary commodities are raw or partially processed materials that will be transformed into finished goods. They are often the most significant exports of developing countries, and revenues obtained from them have an important effect on living standards. Price data for primary commodities are collected from a variety of sources, including international study groups, trade journals, newspaper and wire service reports, government market surveys, and commodity exchange spot and near-term forward prices. This table is based on frequently updated price reports. When possible, the prices received by exporters are used; if export prices are unavailable, the prices paid by importers are used. Annual price series are generally simple averages based on higher-frequency data. The constant price series in the table are deflated using the manufactures unit value (MUV) index for the G-5 countries (see below).

The commodity price indexes are calculated as Laspeyres index numbers in which the fixed weights are the 1987–89 export values for low- and middle-income economies, rebased to 1990. Each index represents a fixed basket of primary commodity exports. The nonfuel commodity price index contains 37 price series for 31 nonfuel commodities. Separate indexes are compiled for petroleum and steel products, which are not included in the nonfuel commodity price index.

The MUV index is a composite index of prices for manufactured exports from the five major (G-5) industrial countries (France, Germany, Japan, the United Kingdom, and the United States) to low- and middle-income economies, valued in U.S. dollars. The index covers products in Standard International Trade Classification (SITC) groups 5–8. To construct the MUV G-5 index, unit value indexes for each country are combined using weights determined by each country's export share.

Primary commodity prices 6.4

	1960	1965	1970	1975	1980	1985	1990	1995	1997	1998	1999
Fertilizers ($/mt)											
Phosphate rock	65	60	44	148	65	49	41	29	38	41	42
TSP	..	..	169	448	250	177	132	126	159	166	149
Food											
Fats and oils ($/mt)											
Coconut oil	1,507	1,610	1,583	871	936	860	337	562	606	631	712
Groundnut oil	1,576	1,499	1,508	1,898	1,193	1,319	964	831	932	873	761
Palm oil	1,102	1,262	1,036	961	810	730	290	527	504	644	421
Soybeans	444	542	466	487	411	327	247	217	273	233	195
Soybean meal	377	435	410	343	364	229	200	165	254	163	147
Soybean oil	1,082	1,250	1,141	1,246	830	834	447	524	521	601	413
Grains ($/mt)											
Grain sorghum	182	219	206	248	179	150	104	100	101	94	81
Maize	209	255	233	265	174	164	109	104	108	98	87
Rice	519	550	503	755	570	287	271	269	280	292	240
Wheat	280	275	219	330	240	198	136	148	147	121	108
Other food											
Bananas ($/mt)	692	735	659	546	526	554	541	373	477	470	360
Beef (cents/kg)	356	408	520	294	383	314	256	160	171	166	178
Oranges ($/mt)	928	755	669	504	543	581	531	446	423	425	416
Sugar, EU domestic (cents/kg)	59	58	45	75	68	51	58	58	58	57	57
Sugar, U.S. domestic (cents/kg)	61	63	66	110	92	65	51	43	45	47	45
Sugar, world (cents/kg)	33	22	33	100	88	13	28	25	23	19	13
Metals and minerals											
Aluminum ($/mt)	2,430	2,194	2,215	1,763	2,022	1,517	1,639	1,515	1,476	1,303	1,314
Copper ($/mt)	3,271	5,972	5,629	2,737	3,031	2,066	2,662	2,463	2,101	1,588	1,519
Iron ore (cents/DMTU)	55	47	39	38	39	39	31	23	28	30	27
Lead (cents/kg)	96	147	121	92	126	57	81	53	58	51	49
Nickel ($/mt)	7,881	8,032	11,339	10,111	9,054	7,142	8,864	6,903	6,392	4,443	5,805
Tin (cents/kg)	1,061	1,801	1,464	1,521	2,330	1,682	609	521	521	532	522
Zinc (cents/kg)	119	144	118	164	106	114	151	87	121	98	104

a. Series not included in the nonfuel index.

Definitions

• **Nonfuel commodities price index** covers the 31 nonfuel primary commodities that make up the agriculture, fertilizer, and metals and minerals indexes. • **Agriculture,** in addition to food, beverages, and agricultural raw materials, includes sugar, bananas, beef, and oranges. • **Beverages** include cocoa, coffee, and tea. • **Food** includes rice, wheat, maize, sorghum, soybeans, soybean oil, soybean meal, palm oil, coconut oil, and groundnut oil. • **Agricultural raw materials** include timber (logs and sawnwood), cotton, natural rubber, and tobacco. • **Fertilizers** include phosphate rock and triple superphosphate (TSP). • **Metals and minerals** include aluminum, copper, iron ore, lead, nickel, tin, and zinc. • **Petroleum price index** refers to the average spot price of Brent, Dubai, and West Texas Intermediate crude oil, equally weighted. • **Steel products price index** is the composite price index for eight steel products based on quotations f.o.b. (free on board) Japan excluding shipments to China and the United States, weighted by product shares of apparent combined consumption (volume of deliveries) for Germany, Japan, and the United States. • **MUV G-5 index** is the manufactures unit value index for G-5 country exports to developing countries. • **Commodity prices**—for definitions and sources see the World Bank's quarterly *Global Commodity Markets*.

Data sources

The commodity price data are compiled by the World Bank's Development Prospects Group. More information can be obtained from the World Bank's quarterly *Global Commodity Markets*. The MUV G-5 index is constructed by the Development Prospects Group. Monthly updates of commodity prices are available on the World Wide Web at www.worldbank.org/prospects.

6.5 Regional trade blocs

Exports within bloc

$ millions	1970	1980	1985	1990	1995	1996	1997	1998
High-income and low- and middle-income economies								
APEC	57,612	357,697	494,464	901,590	1,689,780	1,754,745	1,869,563	1,736,868
European Union	76,451	456,857	419,134	981,260	1,259,699	1,273,431	1,042,610	1,076,512
NAFTA	22,078	102,218	143,191	226,273	394,472	437,804	496,423	521,649
Latin America and the Caribbean								
Andean Group	97	1,161	768	1,312	4,751	4,806	5,102	5,075
CACM	287	1,174	544	671	1,499	1,676	1,835	2,059
CARICOM	52	577	415	449	305	909	978	1,015
LAIA	1,263	10,981	7,139	12,331	34,513	38,532	44,725	42,941
MERCOSUR	451	3,424	1,953	4,127	14,199	17,075	20,772	20,352
OECS	..	4	10	30	38	32	35	34
Africa								
CEMAC	22	75	84	139	120	164	161	179
CEPGL	3	2	9	7	8	9	6	8
COMESA	412	616	466	963	1,184	1,582	1,486	1,516
ECCAS	37	89	131	163	156	212	211	239
ECOWAS	86	692	1,026	1,533	2,015	2,338	2,358	2,461
MRU	1	7	4	0	2	5	7	8
SADC	76	96	294	930	3,744	4,137	4,163	4,540
UEMOA	52	460	397	614	548	649	680	719
Middle East and Asia								
ASEAN	1,360	12,238	13,423	27,196	77,910	82,543	83,735	67,756
Bangkok Agreement	132	1,464	1,953	4,476	12,070	13,128	13,639	13,243
ECO	31	392	2,447	1,243	4,746	4,773	4,943	4,836
GCC	117	4,632	3,101	6,906	6,529	6,370	5,915	4,248
SAARC	99	664	641	863	2,024	2,147	2,007	2,858
UMA	60	109	274	958	1,124	1,142	916	740

Regional trade blocs 6.5

Exports within bloc

% of total exports	1970	1980	1985	1990	1995	1996	1997	1998
High-income and low- and middle-income economies								
APEC	57.9	57.9	67.7	68.5	72.0	72.1	71.8	69.7
European Union	59.5	60.8	59.2	65.9	62.4	61.4	53.8	55.2
NAFTA	36.0	33.6	43.9	41.4	46.2	47.6	49.1	51.7
Latin America and the Caribbean								
Andean Group	1.8	3.8	3.2	4.1	12.1	10.7	10.3	11.9
CACM	26.0	24.4	14.4	15.4	17.0	18.9	15.5	14.5
CARICOM	4.2	5.3	6.4	8.1	4.7	13.3	13.5	17.1
LAIA	9.9	13.7	8.3	10.9	16.8	16.6	17.2	16.7
MERCOSUR	9.4	11.6	5.5	8.9	20.3	22.7	24.8	25.1
OECS	..	9.2	6.5	8.2	11.7	9.1	9.7	10.6
Africa								
CEMAC	4.8	1.6	1.9	2.3	2.2	2.3	2.1	2.6
CEPGL	0.4	0.1	0.8	0.5	0.5	0.5	0.4	0.6
COMESA	9.1	6.1	4.7	6.6	6.6	7.9	7.6	7.7
ECCAS	2.2	1.4	1.7	1.4	1.5	1.6	1.6	2.0
ECOWAS	2.9	10.1	5.2	7.8	9.3	8.8	9.0	10.8
MRU	0.2	0.8	0.4	0.0	0.1	0.2	0.4	0.4
SADC	1.4	0.3	1.4	2.8	10.1	10.3	10.0	10.2
UEMOA	6.5	9.6	8.7	12.9	9.8	9.6	11.5	11.1
Middle East and Asia								
ASEAN	22.3	17.2	18.6	18.9	24.3	24.2	23.7	20.4
Bangkok Agreement	2.7	3.7	3.7	3.8	5.1	5.3	5.2	5.1
ECO	2.2	6.3	9.9	3.2	8.0	7.1	7.6	8.3
GCC	4.6	3.0	4.9	8.0	6.6	5.6	4.6	4.5
SAARC	3.2	5.2	4.8	3.2	4.4	4.3	4.0	5.3
UMA	1.4	0.3	1.0	2.9	3.7	3.4	2.6	2.6

6.5 Regional trade blocs

Total exports by bloc

% of world exports	1970	1980	1985	1990	1995	1996	1997	1998
High-income and low- and middle-income economies								
APEC	35.3	33.7	38.9	38.9	46.3	46.1	46.2	45.3
European Union	45.6	41.0	37.8	44.1	39.8	39.3	34.4	35.5
NAFTA	21.7	16.6	17.4	16.2	16.8	17.4	18.0	18.4
Latin America and the Caribbean								
Andean Group	1.9	1.7	1.3	0.9	0.8	0.9	0.9	0.8
CACM	0.4	0.3	0.2	0.1	0.2	0.2	0.2	0.3
CARICOM	0.4	0.6	0.3	0.2	0.1	0.1	0.1	0.1
LAIA	4.5	4.4	4.6	3.4	4.1	4.4	4.6	4.7
MERCOSUR	1.7	1.6	1.9	1.4	1.4	1.4	1.5	1.5
OECS	..	0.0	0.0	0.0	0.0	0.0	0.0	0.0
Africa								
CEMAC	0.2	0.3	0.2	0.2	0.1	0.1	0.1	0.1
CEPGL	0.3	0.1	0.1	0.0	0.0	0.0	0.0	0.0
COMESA	1.6	0.6	0.5	0.4	0.4	0.4	0.3	0.4
ECCAS	0.6	0.3	0.4	0.3	0.2	0.3	0.2	0.2
ECOWAS	1.1	0.4	1.0	0.6	0.4	0.5	0.5	0.4
MRU	0.1	0.0	0.1	0.1	0.0	0.0	0.0	0.0
SADC	1.9	1.5	1.1	1.0	0.7	0.8	0.7	0.8
UEMOA	0.3	0.3	0.2	0.1	0.1	0.1	0.1	0.1
Middle East and Asia								
ASEAN	2.2	3.9	3.9	4.3	6.3	6.5	6.3	6.1
Bangkok Agreement	1.8	2.2	2.8	3.5	4.7	4.7	4.6	4.8
ECO	0.5	0.3	1.3	1.1	1.2	1.3	1.2	1.1
GCC	0.9	8.5	3.4	2.6	2.0	2.2	2.3	1.7
SAARC	1.1	0.7	0.7	0.8	0.9	0.9	0.9	1.0
UMA	1.5	2.3	1.5	1.0	0.6	0.6	0.6	0.5

Regional trade blocs 6.5

About the data

Trade blocs are groups of countries that have established special preferential arrangements governing trade between members. Although in some cases the preferences—such as lower tariff duties or exemptions from quantitative restrictions—may be no greater than those available to other trading partners, the general purpose of such arrangements is to encourage exports by bloc members to one another—sometimes called intratrade. The table shows the value of merchandise intratrade for important regional trade blocs (service exports are excluded) as well as the size of intratrade relative to each bloc's total exports of goods and the share of the bloc's total exports in world exports.

The data on country exports are drawn from the International Monetary Fund's (IMF) Direction of Trade database and should be broadly consistent with those from other sources, such as the United Nations Statistics Division's Commodity Trade (COMTRADE) database. However, trade flows between many developing countries, particularly in Africa, are not well recorded. Thus the value of intratrade for certain groups may be understated. Data on trade between developing and high-income countries are generally complete.

Membership in the trade blocs shown is based on the most recent information available from the International Trade Centre, a joint project of the World Trade Organization and the United Nations Conference on Trade and Development (UNCTAD). Although bloc exports have been calculated back to 1970 on the basis of current membership, most of the blocs came into existence in later years and their membership may have changed over time. For this reason, and because systems of preferences also change over time, intratrade in earlier years may not have been affected by the same preferences as in recent years. Differences from previously published estimates may be due to changes in bloc membership or to revisions in the underlying data.

Definitions

• **Exports within bloc** are the sum of exports by members of a trade bloc to other members of the bloc. They are shown both in U.S. dollars and as a percentage of total exports by the bloc. • **Total exports by bloc as a share of world exports** are the ratio of the bloc's total exports (within the bloc and to the rest of the world) to total exports by all economies in the world. • **Regional bloc memberships: Asia Pacific Economic Cooperation (APEC),** Australia, Brunei Darussalam, Canada, Chile, China, Hong Kong (China), Indonesia, Japan, the Republic of Korea, Malaysia, Mexico, New Zealand, Papua New Guinea, Peru, the Philippines, the Russian Federation, Singapore, Taiwan (China), Thailand, the United States, and Vietnam; **European Union,** Austria, Belgium, Denmark, Finland, France, Germany, Greece, Ireland, Italy, Luxembourg, the Netherlands, Portugal, Spain, Sweden, and the United Kingdom; **North American Free Trade Association (NAFTA),** Canada, Mexico, and the United States; **Andean Group,** Bolivia, Colombia, Ecuador, Peru, and República Bolivariana de Venezuela; **Central American Common Market (CACM),** Costa Rica, El Salvador, Guatemala, Honduras, and Nicaragua; **Caribbean Community (CARICOM),** Antigua and Barbuda, the Bahamas, Barbados, Belize, Dominica, Grenada, Guyana, Jamaica, Montserrat, St. Kitts and Nevis, St. Lucia, St. Vincent and the Grenadines, Suriname, and Trinidad and Tobago; **Latin American Integration Association (LAIA),** Argentina, Bolivia, Brazil, Chile, Colombia, Ecuador, Mexico, Paraguay, Peru, Uruguay, and República Bolivariana de Venezuela; **Southern Common Market (MERCOSUR),** Argentina, Brazil, Paraguay, and Uruguay; **Organization of Eastern Caribbean States (OECS),** Antigua and Barbuda, Dominica, Grenada, Montserrat, St. Kitts and Nevis, St. Lucia, and St. Vincent and the Grenadines; **Economic and Monetary Community of Central Africa (CEMAC),** Cameroon, the Central African Republic, Chad, the Republic of Congo, Equatorial Guinea, Gabon, and São Tomé and Principe; **Economic Community of the Great Lakes Countries (CEPGL),** Burundi, the Democratic Republic of the Congo, and Rwanda; **Common Market for Eastern and Southern Africa (COMESA),** Angola, Burundi, Comoros, the Democratic Republic of the Congo, Djibouti, the Arab Republic of Egypt, Eritrea, Ethiopia, Kenya, Madagascar, Malawi, Mauritius, Namibia, Rwanda, Seychelles, Sudan, Swaziland, Uganda, Tanzania, Zambia, and Zimbabwe; **Economic Community of Central African States (ECCAS),** Angola, Burundi, Cameroon, the Central African Republic, Chad, the Democratic Republic of the Congo, the Republic of Congo, Equatorial Guinea, Gabon, Rwanda, and São Tomé and Principe; **Economic Community of West African States (ECOWAS),** Benin, Burkina Faso, Cape Verde, Côte d'Ivoire, the Gambia, Ghana, Guinea, Guinea-Bissau, Liberia, Mali, Mauritania, Niger, Nigeria, Senegal, Sierra Leone, and Togo; **Mano River Union (MRU),** Guinea, Liberia, and Sierra Leone; **Southern African Development Community (SADC),** Angola, Botswana, Lesotho, Malawi, Mauritius, Mozambique, Namibia, Swaziland, South Africa, Tanzania, Zambia, and Zimbabwe; **West African Economic and Monetary Union (UEMOA),** Benin, Burkina Faso, Côte d'Ivoire, Guinea-Bissau, Mali, Niger, Senegal, and Togo; **Association of South-East Asian Nations (ASEAN),** Brunei Darussalam, Indonesia, the Lao People's Democratic Republic, Malaysia, Myanmar, the Philippines, Singapore, Thailand, and Vietnam; **Bangkok Agreement (First Agreement on Trade Negotiation among Developing Member Countries of the Economic and Social Commission for Asia and the Pacific),** Bangladesh, India, the Republic of Korea, the Lao People's Democratic Republic, the Philippines, Sri Lanka, and Thailand; **Economic Cooperation Organization (ECO),** Afghanistan, Azerbaijan, the Islamic Republic of Iran, Kazakhstan, the Kyrgyz Republic, Pakistan, Tajikistan, Turkey, Turkmenistan, and Uzbekistan; **Gulf Cooperation Council (GCC),** Bahrain, Kuwait, Oman, Qatar, Saudi Arabia, and the United Arab Emirates; **South Asian Association for Regional Cooperation (SAARC),** Bangladesh, Bhutan, India, Maldives, Nepal, Pakistan, and Sri Lanka; and **Arab Maghreb Union (UMA),** Algeria, Libya, Mauritania, Morocco, and Tunisia.

Data sources

Data on merchandise trade flows are published in the IMF's *Direction of Trade Statistics Yearbook* and *Direction of Trade Statistics Quarterly;* the data in the table were calculated using the IMF's Direction of Trade database. UNCTAD publishes data on intratrade in its *Handbook of International Trade and Development Statistics.* Information on trade bloc memberships comes from the International Trade Centre's website at www.intracen.org/infobase/tguide/welcome.htm.

6.6 Tariff barriers

	Year	All products Mean tariff %	All products Standard deviation of tariff rates %	All products Weighted mean tariff %	Primary products Mean tariff %	Primary products Standard deviation of tariff rates %	Primary products Weighted mean tariff %	Manufactured products Mean tariff %	Manufactured products Standard deviation of tariff rates %	Manufactured products Weighted mean tariff %
Algeria	1998	24.2	16.7	17.2	21.8	18.1	14.7	24.9	16.2	17.7
Argentina	1993	10.9	5.0	11.3	6.0	2.9	3.7	12.1	4.7	13.7
	1995	10.5	7.6	10.5	8.5	5.3	5.6	10.9	7.9	12.1
	1997	11.3	6.8	11.3	8.4	5.3	5.6	11.9	6.9	12.7
	1998	13.5	6.9	12.9	11.1	5.7	7.4	14.0	7.0	14.1
Australia	1993	9.8	11.9	7.7	2.5	4.8	1.3	11.7	12.4	9.7
	1997	5.7	8.2	3.9	1.2	2.2	0.7	6.8	8.7	4.6
	1998	5.3	7.4	3.7	1.2	2.2	0.7	6.4	7.8	4.4
	1999	5.0	6.7	3.5	1.2	2.2	0.7	6.0	7.1	4.2
Bangladesh	1999	22.1	14.6	19.0	21.1	13.1	21.0	22.4	15.0	18.5
Belarus	1996	12.3	10.4	13.5	10.3	7.9	7.8	13.2	11.2	15.4
	1997	12.6	8.4	13.7	11.0	6.7	8.4	13.3	8.9	15.0
Bolivia	1993	9.8	1.0	9.8	10.0	0.2	10.0	9.7	1.1	9.7
	1998	9.7	1.2	9.7	10.0	0.2	10.0	9.6	1.4	9.7
Brazil	1994	11.9	8.2	14.6	8.2	7.1	7.2	12.8	8.2	17.0
	1997	11.9	7.7	14.6	8.6	5.7	7.1	12.6	7.8	16.4
	1998	14.6	7.3	16.6	11.3	5.9	9.1	15.2	7.4	18.3
Canada	1993	8.7	7.0	6.8	4.7	5.8	2.7	9.7	6.9	8.0
	1995	10.1	24.2	7.2	14.2	49.3	5.5	8.9	6.6	7.7
	1996	9.1	27.2	5.6	16.5	55.7	7.8	7.0	6.6	5.2
	1997	5.9	8.0	4.4	4.0	12.2	3.0	6.4	6.3	4.7
	1998	7.5	26.5	3.8	16.1	54.9	6.7	5.1	6.1	3.2
	1999	7.1	25.7	3.6	15.6	54.1	6.4	4.9	6.0	2.9
Central African Republic	1995	18.6	9.6	17.1	20.6	9.7	16.2	17.9	9.5	17.4
Chile	1998	11.0	0.7	10.9	11.0	0.0	11.0	10.9	0.8	10.9
China	1993	39.9	29.9	38.4	33.3	24.7	20.9	41.8	31.0	44.0
	1994	36.3	27.9	35.5	32.1	24.3	19.6	37.6	28.8	40.6
	1996	23.6	17.4	22.6	25.4	22.1	20.0	23.1	15.8	23.2
	1997	17.6	13.0	18.2	17.9	18.1	20.0	17.5	11.0	17.8
	1998	17.5	13.0	18.7	17.9	18.6	20.0	17.4	10.8	18.5
Colombia	1994	11.8	6.3	12.0	12.1	6.0	10.6	11.7	6.4	12.4
	1995	13.3	4.9	12.7	12.7	5.9	10.7	13.5	4.6	13.4
	1998	11.7	6.2	10.6	12.4	6.1	11.0	11.4	6.3	10.5
Costa Rica	1999	7.2	13.8	4.3	12.2	24.8	7.6	5.7	7.3	3.5
Cuba	1997	10.7	6.9	9.7	7.6	7.3	4.9	11.6	6.5	11.5
Czech Republic	1999	6.8	11.0	5.8	10.4	18.8	5.8	5.4	4.2	5.8
Dominican Republic	1997	14.5	9.2	13.6	15.3	10.2	10.8	14.2	8.9	14.5
Ecuador	1993	9.3	6.0	8.5	9.4	5.8	7.6	9.2	6.1	8.8
	1995	12.3	5.6	11.9	12.2	6.2	10.4	12.4	5.4	12.4
	1998	11.3	6.4	10.4	11.8	6.5	10.2	11.2	6.3	10.4
El Salvador	1995	10.2	7.6	8.5	11.5	6.4	8.8	9.8	8.0	8.4
	1998	5.7	7.9	4.3	10.0	8.4	6.5	4.4	7.3	3.8
Estonia	1995	0.1	1.2	0.4	0.1	1.1	0.0	0.1	1.2	0.5
European Union	1994	7.7	6.3	6.6	10.3	10.6	4.9	6.9	3.8	7.0
	1996	6.7	5.8	4.9	10.3	8.8	3.8	5.5	3.7	5.1
	1998	6.0	5.6	3.5	9.4	8.1	3.4	4.8	3.9	3.5
	1999	5.6	5.9	3.2	9.8	8.1	3.3	4.1	3.9	3.2
Georgia	1999	10.6	2.8	8.6	11.9	1.0	11.8	10.2	3.1	7.8
Guatemala	1998	8.4	9.5	5.7	8.6	7.3	8.3	8.3	10.1	5.1
Honduras	1999	7.8	8.0	5.7	9.3	8.5	10.2	7.3	7.7	4.7
Hungary	1996	15.2	18.2	10.7	30.6	27.4	14.4	9.2	6.1	9.8
	1997	14.3	17.0	10.2	28.8	25.6	13.7	8.7	5.9	9.4
India	1997	30.0	14.0	27.7	25.7	22.6	22.6	31.3	9.8	29.5
	1999	32.9	12.7	27.6	28.8	21.7	25.9	34.2	8.0	28.0
Indonesia	1993	19.4	16.1	21.7	16.7	12.3	10.0	20.3	17.0	25.4
	1996	13.0	16.7	13.8	12.3	19.6	9.3	13.2	15.7	14.9
	1999	11.9	16.6	13.2	11.9	20.4	8.7	11.8	15.3	14.3

Tariff barriers 6.6

	Year	All products			Primary products			Manufactured products		
		Mean tariff %	Standard deviation of tariff rates %	Weighted mean tariff %	Mean tariff %	Standard deviation of tariff rates %	Weighted mean tariff %	Mean tariff %	Standard deviation of tariff rates %	Weighted mean tariff %
Jamaica	1999	19.0	11.1	19.2	23.2	15.4	19.8	16.8	7.0	19.0
Japan	1998	5.7	7.7	2.0	8.9	10.5	4.5	4.5	5.9	1.5
	1999	6.6	9.3	2.5	9.8	11.3	4.5	5.5	8.2	2.0
Kazakhstan	1996	9.4	10.9	7.1	9.9	8.7	7.1	9.2	11.7	7.1
Korea, Rep.	1996	11.1	26.1	9.5	21.0	47.2	17.0	8.2	13.5	7.8
	1999	9.4	7.6	7.4	13.9	13.6	9.0	7.8	2.4	7.0
Latvia	1996	4.5	7.9	2.5	8.5	11.0	3.0	2.9	5.3	2.3
	1997	5.9	10.7	2.5	11.5	16.2	4.3	3.5	5.7	2.0
Lebanon	1999	9.8	9.2	10.5	9.2	11.5	8.3	10.0	8.3	11.0
Libya	1996	21.5	31.8	30.5	18.0	26.4	22.0	22.3	32.9	33.0
Lithuania	1995	4.5	9.0	2.5	8.7	13.0	3.6	2.8	5.9	2.1
	1997	4.6	9.3	1.9	9.1	13.3	4.1	2.7	5.8	1.4
Malawi	1994	30.8	15.5	27.1	24.6	15.6	14.8	32.8	15.0	32.2
	1997	25.3	11.6	23.5	21.2	12.6	13.6	26.5	11.0	26.7
Malaysia	1993	14.3	14.1	11.1	10.9	12.7	6.0	15.3	14.3	12.6
	1996	8.7	14.4	8.1	2.4	6.5	2.7	11.8	16.1	9.3
	1997	9.1	19.6	9.4	4.1	22.2	9.8	12.0	17.2	9.4
Malta	1997	7.6	5.8	8.2	6.7	8.5	5.9	8.1	3.7	8.8
Mauritius	1997	29.1	26.2	31.9	19.7	19.1	19.1	31.7	27.3	36.0
Mexico	1995	12.6	5.4	11.8	12.3	6.0	10.8	12.6	5.3	12.2
	1998	13.3	13.5	12.5	16.8	29.0	14.6	12.6	7.8	12.0
Moldova	1996	6.7	9.4	4.0	11.2	11.9	4.3	4.9	7.5	3.8
Mozambique	1997	15.6	14.3	14.1	16.9	15.1	12.0	15.3	14.0	14.8
Nepal	1998	16.3	15.5	18.6	9.2	13.6	8.2	18.3	15.4	21.0
	1999	12.4	11.3	15.7	8.4	10.0	6.6	13.5	11.5	17.8
New Zealand	1993	8.5	10.3	7.7	4.3	6.0	2.1	9.7	11.0	9.4
	1996	6.1	7.8	4.7	3.1	4.3	1.6	7.0	8.4	5.4
	1997	5.3	7.0	4.1	2.6	3.8	1.4	6.1	7.5	4.7
	1998	4.5	6.0	3.5	2.0	3.3	1.1	5.2	6.4	4.0
	1999	3.8	5.1	2.9	1.7	2.8	0.9	4.4	5.4	3.4
Nicaragua	1998	5.9	7.3	4.0	8.3	10.1	5.9	5.2	5.9	3.6
	1999	10.9	7.5	8.5	13.6	10.3	11.3	10.1	6.1	7.8
Norway	1996	6.0	15.2	4.3	4.9	30.5	1.5	6.2	8.3	4.9
	1998	4.1	16.5	2.2	5.1	29.9	1.4	3.9	11.5	2.4
Panama	1998	9.2	5.9	8.0	11.4	6.9	9.3	8.5	5.4	7.7
Papua New Guinea	1997	20.5	19.2	18.4	30.5	22.9	23.9	17.6	16.9	17.2
Paraguay	1994	8.0	7.7	8.1	7.9	7.4	5.3	8.1	7.8	8.9
	1995	9.3	6.9	9.0	8.2	5.2	5.2	9.5	7.2	10.3
	1996	9.3	7.1	8.3	8.9	6.3	6.2	9.4	7.3	8.8
	1998	9.5	6.5	8.7	8.6	5.6	5.9	9.7	6.6	9.3
Peru	1993	17.6	4.4	17.1	17.3	4.2	16.3	17.7	4.4	17.3
	1998	13.2	2.9	12.6	13.7	3.3	13.0	13.1	2.7	12.5
Philippines	1993	22.5	14.1	20.2	23.9	15.3	17.9	22.1	13.7	21.0
	1994	21.6	13.3	19.5	22.3	14.0	16.8	21.5	13.1	20.4
	1995	20.0	11.0	18.4	21.6	12.8	16.8	19.5	10.4	18.9
	1998	11.2	11.4	9.3	14.4	17.8	10.2	10.3	8.3	9.1
	1999	10.2	9.7	8.7	13.1	14.7	9.4	9.3	7.3	8.5
Poland	1995	11.6	7.6	9.0	11.5	9.6	5.3	11.7	6.9	10.1
	1996	18.7	28.1	14.9	29.2	47.4	18.0	14.1	8.7	14.2
Romania	1999	19.4	18.1	13.5	26.7	28.9	13.7	16.4	9.1	13.5
Russian Federation	1993	7.3	9.8	9.7	3.8	12.2	5.7	8.7	8.2	10.9
	1994	11.5	12.4	14.0	8.0	8.4	5.1	12.9	13.4	16.8
	1996	10.9	8.3	11.3	10.3	7.5	7.8	11.1	8.5	12.1
	1997	12.6	8.4	13.8	10.9	6.6	8.4	13.4	8.9	15.1
Saudi Arabia	1999	12.2	4.0	12.1	12.3	6.7	12.7	12.2	2.8	11.9
Slovenia	1999	10.6	7.4	9.7	10.6	11.7	4.8	10.5	5.1	10.8
South Africa[a]	1993	19.7	21.9	14.3	9.4	11.7	5.2	21.2	22.6	16.9

6.6 Tariff barriers

	Year	All products: Mean tariff %	All products: Standard deviation of tariff rates %	All products: Weighted mean tariff %	Primary products: Mean tariff %	Primary products: Standard deviation of tariff rates %	Primary products: Weighted mean tariff %	Manufactured products: Mean tariff %	Manufactured products: Standard deviation of tariff rates %	Manufactured products: Weighted mean tariff %
	1997	8.7	10.9	6.6	8.0	11.3	4.4	8.9	10.8	7.1
	1999	7.2	10.0	5.2	6.6	10.5	3.8	7.3	9.9	5.5
Sri Lanka	1993	24.2	18.1	23.0	26.8	21.9	25.3	23.5	16.8	22.3
	1997	20.0	15.4	20.7	23.8	23.0	23.6	19.1	12.6	19.8
Taiwan, China	1996	9.7	11.0	7.2	17.2	16.8	10.0	6.7	5.4	6.5
Tanzania	1997	21.8	13.9	23.6	30.6	10.9	22.7	19.9	13.7	23.7
	1998	22.1	13.9	23.7	30.0	11.8	22.7	20.3	13.7	24.0
Thailand	1993	45.6	25.0	41.5	40.3	19.4	33.9	47.2	26.2	43.7
Trinidad and Tobago	1999	19.3	11.4	20.4	23.2	15.5	20.1	17.3	7.7	20.5
Tunisia	1998	29.9	12.8	23.4	31.0	11.7	23.2	29.6	13.0	23.5
Turkey	1997	13.5	25.4	7.4	34.1	42.2	14.8	6.0	4.6	5.7
Ukraine	1997	10.0	10.9	6.9	15.7	12.2	6.4	7.5	9.2	7.1
United States	1995	5.9	7.0	4.1	5.5	10.9	2.7	6.0	5.8	4.4
	1997	6.6	14.9	3.2	9.2	28.3	2.9	5.7	6.2	3.3
	1998	5.2	11.8	2.8	6.4	25.1	3.2	4.9	5.5	2.7
	1999	4.8	11.6	2.5	6.1	24.7	3.1	4.5	5.5	2.4
Uruguay	1995	9.3	7.1	8.9	8.4	5.4	5.3	9.5	7.4	10.1
	1996	9.5	7.3	8.0	8.6	5.6	5.6	9.7	7.6	8.6
	1997	10.0	6.9	8.3	8.8	5.3	5.5	10.3	7.3	9.0
	1998	12.2	7.9	10.0	11.4	5.5	7.2	12.4	8.4	10.7
Venezuela, RB	1995	13.4	4.8	12.8	12.8	5.8	10.9	13.5	4.5	13.4
	1997	11.9	6.1	10.9	12.4	6.1	10.9	11.8	6.1	10.9
	1998	12.0	6.1	10.9	12.5	6.1	10.9	11.9	6.1	10.9
Vietnam	1999	16.3	18.7	15.0	18.2	20.6	17.4	15.8	18.2	14.5
Zambia	1997	13.6	9.3	14.3	15.9	8.7	12.6	13.0	9.4	14.7
Zimbabwe	1997	24.0	23.1	21.7	21.9	20.1	17.1	24.7	23.9	22.8
	1998	22.2	17.8	20.0	22.0	20.1	17.7	22.3	17.1	20.5

a. Data refer to the South African Customs Union, which comprises Botswana, Lesotho, Namibia, and South Africa.

Tariff barriers 6.6

About the data

Economies regulate their imports through a combination of tariff and nontariff measures. The most common form of tariff is an ad valorem duty, but tariffs may also be levied on a specific, or per unit, basis. Tariffs may be used to raise fiscal revenues or to protect domestic industries from foreign competition—or both. Nontariff barriers, which limit the quantity of imports of a particular good, take many forms. Some common ones are licensing schemes, quotas, prohibitions, export restraint arrangements, and health and quarantine measures. Nontariff barriers are generally considered more detrimental to economic efficiency than tariffs because efficient foreign producers cannot undercut the barriers by reducing their costs and thus their prices. A high percentage of products subject to nontariff barriers indicates a protectionist trade regime, but the frequency of nontariff barriers does not measure their restrictiveness. Moreover, a wide range of domestic policies and regulations (such as health regulations) may act as nontariff barriers. Because of the difficulty of combining nontariff barriers into an aggregate indicator, they are not included in this table.

The table shows both simple average tariffs and average tariffs weighted by world imports. Simple averages are a better indicator of tariff protection than averages weighted by the country's own import values, which are biased downward, especially when tariffs are set so high as to discourage trade. Weights based on world imports provide an alternative measure of a country's tariff barriers that reflects average world trading patterns.

Mean tariffs are calculated as the average ad valorem duty across all tariff lines. Specific duties—duties not expressed as a proportion of the declared value—are not included. Countries typically maintain a hierarchy of trade preferences applicable to specific trading partners. The rates used in calculating the indicators here are the applied most-favored-nation duties. Applied rates are less than or equal to the bound rates that countries have agreed to in World Trade Organization negotiations, but they may exceed the rates applied to partners in preferential trade agreements such as the North American Free Trade Agreement. (See table 6.5 for the membership of regional trade blocs and data on their exports.)

Some countries set fairly uniform tariff rates across all imports. Others are more selective, setting high tariffs to protect favored domestic industries and low tariffs on goods that have few domestic suppliers or that are necessary inputs for domestic industry. The standard deviation of tariffs is a measure of the dispersion of tariff rates around their mean value. Highly dispersed rates are evidence of discriminatory tariffs that may distort production and consumption decisions. But this tells only part of the story. The effective rate of protection—the degree to which the value added in an industry is protected— may exceed the nominal rate if the tariff system systematically differentiates among imports of raw materials, intermediate products, and finished goods.

The indicators in this table were calculated from data supplied by the United Nations Conference on Trade and Development (UNCTAD). Data are classified using the Harmonized System of trade codes at the six- or eight-digit level. Tariff line data were matched to Standard International Trade Classification (SITC) revision 2 codes to define the commodity groups and global import weights. Import weights were calculated for 1995 using the United Nations Statistics Division's Commodity Trade (COMTRADE) database. Data are shown only for the countries and years for which complete data are available and, to conserve space, observations were dropped when there was no change in the average tariff rate in successive years.

Definitions

• **Primary products** are commodities classified in SITC revision 2 sections 0–4 plus division 68 (nonferrous metals). • **Manufactured products** are commodities classified in SITC revision 2 sections 5–9, excluding division 68. • **Mean tariff** is the unweighted average of the applied rates for all products subject to tariffs. • **Standard deviation of tariff rates** measures the average dispersion of tariff rates around the simple mean. • **Weighted mean tariff** is the average of applied rates weighted by product shares in 1995 world imports.

Data sources

Mean tariff rates and their standard deviations were calculated by World Bank staff using data from the UNCTAD Trade Analysis Information System. Data on global imports come from the United Nations Statistics Division's COMTRADE database.

6.7 Global financial flows

	Net private capital flows		Foreign direct investment		Portfolio investment flows				Bank and trade-related lending	
					Bonds		Equity			
	$ millions		$ millions		$ millions		$ millions		$ millions	
	1990	1998	1990	1998	1990	1998	1990	1998	1990	1998
Albania	31	42	0	45	0	0	0	0	31	–3
Algeria	–424	–1,321	0	5	–16	0	0	2	–409	–1,328
Angola	235	40	–335	360	0	0	0	0	570	–320
Argentina	–203	18,899	1,836	6,150	–857	9,037	13	50	–1,196	3,662
Armenia	0	232	0	232	0	0	0	0	0	0
Australia	..	..	7,465	6,165	..	..	..	..	..	..
Austria	..	..	653	6,034	..	..	..	..	..	..
Azerbaijan	..	1,081	..	1,023	..	0	..	0	..	58
Bangladesh	70	288	3	308	0	0	0	3	67	–23
Belarus	..	122	..	149	..	0	..	0	..	–27
Belgium	..	..	..	..	..	..	..	..	..	..
Benin	1	34	1	34	0	0	0	0	0	0
Bolivia	3	860	27	872	0	0	0	0	–24	–12
Bosnia and Herzegovina	..	..	..	..	..	..	..	..	..	..
Botswana	77	91	95	95	0	0	0	0	–19	–4
Brazil	562	54,385	989	31,913	129	1,409	0	542	–556	20,521
Bulgaria	–42	498	4	401	65	–57	0	66	–111	88
Burkina Faso	0	0	0	0	0	0	0	0	0	0
Burundi	–5	2	1	1	0	0	0	0	–6	1
Cambodia	0	118	0	121	0	0	0	0	0	–3
Cameroon	–125	1	–113	50	0	0	0	0	–12	–49
Canada	..	..	7,581	16,514	..	..	..	..	..	..
Central African Republic	0	5	1	5	0	0	0	0	–1	0
Chad	–1	16	0	16	0	0	0	0	–1	0
Chile	2,098	9,252	590	4,638	–7	702	320	87	1,194	3,825
China	8,107	42,676	3,487	43,751	–48	1,587	0	1,273	4,668	–3,936
Hong Kong, China	..	..	..	..	..	..	..	..	..	..
Colombia	345	3,629	500	3,038	–4	1,752	0	26	–151	–1,187
Congo, Dem. Rep.	–24	1	–12	1	0	0	0	0	–12	0
Congo, Rep.	–100	4	0	4	0	0	0	0	–100	0
Costa Rica	23	800	163	559	–42	184	0	0	–99	57
Côte d'Ivoire	57	181	48	435	–1	–23	0	6	10	–237
Croatia	..	1,666	..	873	..	89	..	205	..	499
Cuba	..	..	..	..	..	..	..	..	..	..
Czech Republic	876	3,331	207	2,554	0	837	0	129	669	–188
Denmark	..	..	1,132	6,373	..	..	..	..	..	..
Dominican Republic	130	771	133	691	0	–4	0	74	–3	10
Ecuador	183	584	126	831	0	–10	0	0	57	–238
Egypt, Arab Rep.	698	1,385	734	1,076	–1	0	0	494	–35	–186
El Salvador	8	242	2	12	0	0	0	0	6	230
Eritrea	..	0	..	0	..	0	..	0	..	0
Estonia	..	714	..	581	..	17	..	53	..	63
Ethiopia	–45	6	12	4	0	0	0	0	–57	2
Finland	..	..	812	12,029	..	..	..	..	..	..
France	..	..	13,183	27,998	..	..	..	..	..	..
Gabon	103	–57	74	–50	0	0	0	0	29	–7
Gambia, The	–8	13	0	13	0	0	0	0	–8	0
Georgia	..	57	..	50	..	0	..	0	..	7
Germany	..	..	2,532	18,712	..	..	..	..	..	..
Ghana	–5	42	15	56	0	0	0	15	–20	–29
Greece	..	..	1,005	..	..	..	..	..	..	..
Guatemala	44	621	48	673	–11	–31	0	0	7	–21
Guinea	–1	–9	18	1	0	0	0	0	–19	–10
Guinea-Bissau	2	1	2	1	0	0	0	0	0	0
Haiti	8	11	8	11	0	0	0	0	0	0
Honduras	77	193	44	84	0	–32	0	0	33	141

Global financial flows 6.7

	Net private capital flows		Foreign direct investment		Portfolio investment flows				Bank and trade-related lending	
					Bonds		Equity			
	$ millions		$ millions		$ millions		$ millions		$ millions	
	1990	1998	1990	1998	1990	1998	1990	1998	1990	1998
Hungary	–308	4,683	0	1,936	921	688	150	259	–1,379	1,800
India	1,872	6,151	162	2,635	147	4,120	105	342	1,458	–946
Indonesia	3,235	–3,759	1,093	–356	26	–141	312	250	1,804	–3,512
Iran, Islamic Rep.	–392	588	–362	24	0	0	0	0	–30	564
Iraq	..	..	..	..	..	..	..	..	..	..
Ireland	..	..	627	2,920	..	..	..	..	..	..
Israel	..	..	129	1,850	..	..	..	..	..	..
Italy	..	..	6,411	2,635	..	..	..	..	..	..
Jamaica	92	586	138	369	0	250	0	0	–46	–33
Japan	..	..	1,777	3,268	..	..	..	..	..	..
Jordan	254	207	38	310	0	–10	0	11	216	–104
Kazakhstan	..	1,983	..	1,158	..	100	..	0	..	725
Kenya	122	–57	57	11	0	0	0	4	65	–72
Korea, Dem. Rep.	..	..	..	..	..	..	..	..	..	..
Korea, Rep.	1,056	7,644	788	5,415	168	1,220	518	4,096	–418	–3,087
Kuwait	..	..	..	59	..	..	..	..	..	..
Kyrgyz Republic	..	108	..	109	..	0	..	0	..	–2
Lao PDR	6	46	6	46	0	0	0	0	0	0
Latvia	..	366	..	357	..	0	..	4	..	5
Lebanon	12	1,740	6	200	0	1,350	0	147	6	43
Lesotho	17	281	17	265	0	0	0	0	0	16
Libya	..	..	..	..	..	..	..	..	..	..
Lithuania	..	982	..	926	..	0	..	0	..	57
Macedonia, FYR	..	190	..	118	..	0	..	0	..	72
Madagascar	7	15	22	16	0	0	0	0	–15	–1
Malawi	2	24	0	1	0	0	0	24	2	–1
Malaysia	769	8,295	2,333	5,000	–1,239	–314	293	592	–617	3,017
Mali	–8	17	–7	17	0	0	0	0	–1	0
Mauritania	6	3	7	5	0	0	0	0	–1	–2
Mauritius	86	–79	41	12	0	0	0	8	45	–99
Mexico	8,253	23,188	2,634	10,238	661	2,428	563	730	4,396	9,792
Moldova	..	62	..	85	..	0	..	0	..	–23
Mongolia	..	7	..	19	..	0	..	0	..	–12
Morocco	341	965	165	322	0	0	0	174	176	470
Mozambique	35	209	9	213	0	0	0	0	26	–4
Myanmar	153	153	161	70	0	0	0	0	–8	83
Namibia	..	..	..	..	..	..	..	..	..	..
Nepal	–8	–1	6	12	0	0	0	0	–14	–13
Netherlands	..	..	12,352	33,346	..	..	..	..	..	..
New Zealand	..	..	1,735	..	..	..	..	..	..	..
Nicaragua	21	171	0	184	0	0	0	0	21	–13
Niger	9	–23	–1	1	0	0	0	0	10	–24
Nigeria	467	1,028	588	1,051	0	0	0	2	–121	–25
Norway	..	..	1,003	3,597	..	..	..	..	..	..
Oman	–259	–214	141	106	0	0	0	10	–400	–330
Pakistan	182	806	244	500	0	0	0	0	–63	306
Panama	127	1,459	132	1,206	–2	218	0	0	–4	34
Papua New Guinea	204	230	155	110	0	0	0	0	49	120
Paraguay	67	236	76	256	0	0	0	0	–9	–20
Peru	59	2,724	41	1,930	0	0	0	174	18	620
Philippines	639	2,587	530	1,713	395	151	0	454	–286	269
Poland	71	9,653	89	6,365	0	1,202	0	969	–18	1,117
Portugal	..	..	2,610	1,783	..	..	..	..	..	..
Puerto Rico	..	..	..	..	..	..	..	..	..	..
Romania	4	1,826	0	2,031	0	0	0	42	4	–247
Russian Federation	5,562	19,346	0	2,764	310	11,538	0	296	5,252	4,748

6.7 Global financial flows

	Net private capital flows		Foreign direct investment		Portfolio investment flows				Bank and trade-related lending	
					Bonds		Equity			
	$ millions		$ millions		$ millions		$ millions		$ millions	
	1990	1998	1990	1998	1990	1998	1990	1998	1990	1998
Rwanda	6	7	8	7	0	0	0	0	–2	0
Saudi Arabia	..	..	..	..	..	..	..	..	..	..
Senegal	42	24	57	40	0	0	0	0	–15	–16
Sierra Leone	36	5	32	5	0	0	0	0	4	0
Singapore	..	..	5,575	7,218	..	..	..	..	..	..
Slovak Republic	278	1,480	0	562	0	–570	0	0	278	1,488
Slovenia	..	..	..	165	..	..	..	..	..	..
South Africa	..	783	..	550	..	303	..	619	..	–689
Spain	..	..	13,984	11,392	..	..	..	..	..	..
Sri Lanka	54	325	43	193	0	65	0	6	11	61
Sudan	0	371	0	371	0	0	0	0	0	0
Sweden	..	..	1,982	19,413	..	..	..	..	..	..
Switzerland	..	..	4,961	5,488	..	..	..	..	..	..
Syrian Arab Republic	18	76	71	80	0	0	0	0	–53	–4
Tajikistan	..	–3	..	18	..	0	..	0	..	–21
Tanzania	4	157	0	172	0	0	0	0	4	–16
Thailand	4,399	7,825	2,444	6,941	–87	–632	449	2,341	1,593	–826
Togo	0	0	0	0	0	0	0	0	0	0
Trinidad and Tobago	–69	761	109	730	–52	0	0	0	–126	31
Tunisia	–122	694	76	650	–60	0	0	40	–138	4
Turkey	1,782	1,641	684	940	597	–535	35	880	466	357
Turkmenistan	..	473	..	130	..	0	..	0	..	343
Uganda	16	198	0	200	0	0	0	0	16	–2
Ukraine	..	2,087	..	743	..	1,076	..	0	..	267
United Arab Emirates	..	..	..	..	..	..	..	..	..	..
United Kingdom	..	..	32,518	67,481	..	..	..	..	..	..
United States	..	..	48,954	193,373	..	..	..	..	..	..
Uruguay	–192	496	0	164	–16	336	0	0	–176	–5
Uzbekistan	..	592	..	200	..	0	..	0	..	392
Venezuela, RB	–126	6,866	451	4,435	345	1,408	0	64	–922	959
Vietnam	16	832	16	1,200	0	0	0	0	0	–368
West Bank and Gaza	..	..	..	..	..	..	..	..	..	..
Yemen, Rep.	30	–210	–131	–210	0	0	0	0	161	0
Yugoslavia, FR (Serb./Mont.)	..	0	..	0	..	0	..	0	..	0
Zambia	194	40	203	72	0	0	0	0	–9	–32
Zimbabwe	85	–217	–12	76	–30	–30	0	3	127	–266
World	.. s	.. s	198,382 s	619,258 s	.. s	.. s	.. s	.. s	.. s	.. s
Low income	14,831	52,365	5,732	53,517	95	5,482	417	1,921	8,588	–8,556
Excl. China & India	..	..	..	..	..	..	..	..	..	..
Middle income	27,775	215,336	18,398	117,425	1,083	34,175	2,340	13,646	5,953	50,090
Lower middle income	..	..	..	..	..	..	..	..	..	..
Upper middle income	..	..	..	..	..	..	..	..	..	..
Low & middle income	42,606	267,700	24,130	170,942	1,178	39,658	2,757	15,567	14,541	41,534
East Asia & Pacific	18,720	67,249	11,135	64,162	–784	1,870	1,571	9,007	6,798	–7,790
Europe & Central Asia	7,649	53,342	1,051	24,350	1,893	14,385	185	2,904	4,520	11,704
Latin America & Carib.	12,411	126,854	8,188	69,323	101	17,627	896	1,748	3,226	38,156
Middle East & N. Africa	369	9,223	2,458	5,054	–148	1,340	0	878	–1,941	1,950
South Asia	2,174	7,580	464	3,659	147	4,185	105	351	1,458	–615
Sub-Saharan Africa	1,283	3,452	834	4,394	–31	250	0	679	480	–1,872
High income	..	..	169,252	448,316	..	..	..	..	..	..
Europe EMU	..	..	53,165	116,849	..	..	..	..	..	..

Global financial flows 6.7

About the data

The data on foreign direct investment are based on balance of payments data reported by the International Monetary Fund (IMF), supplemented by data on net foreign direct investment reported by the Organisation for Economic Co-operation and Development (OECD) and official national sources. The internationally accepted definition of foreign direct investment is that provided in the fifth edition of the IMF's *Balance of Payments Manual* (1993).

Under this definition foreign direct investment has three components: equity investment, reinvested earnings, and short- and long-term intercompany loans between parent firms and foreign affiliates. However, many countries fail to report reinvested earnings, and the definition of long-term loans differs among countries. Foreign direct investment, as distinguished from other kinds of international investment, is made to establish a lasting interest in or effective management control over an enterprise in another country. As a guideline, the IMF suggests that investments should account for at least 10 percent of voting stock to be counted as foreign direct investment. In practice many countries set a higher threshold.

The OECD has also published a definition, in consultation with the IMF, Eurostat, and the United Nations. Because of the multiplicity of sources and differences in definitions and reporting methods, there may be more than one estimate of foreign direct investment for a country and data may not be comparable across countries.

Foreign direct investment data do not give a complete picture of international investment in an economy. Balance of payments data on foreign direct investment do not include capital raised locally, which has become an important source of financing for investment projects in some developing countries. In addition, foreign direct investment data capture only cross-border investment flows involving equity participation and thus omit non-equity cross-border transactions such as intrafirm flows of goods and services. For a detailed discussion of the data issues see the World Bank's *World Debt Tables 1993–94* (volume 1, chapter 3).

Portfolio flow data are compiled from several official and market sources, including Euromoney databases and publications, Micropal, Lipper Analytical Services, published reports of private investment houses, central banks, national securities and exchange commissions, national stock exchanges, and the World Bank's Debtor Reporting System.

Gross statistics on international bond and equity issues are produced by aggregating individual transactions reported by market sources. Transactions of public and publicly guaranteed bonds are reported through the Debtor Reporting System by World Bank member economies that have received either International Bank for Reconstruction and Development loans or International Development Association credits. Information on private nonguaranteed bonds is collected from market sources, because official national sources reporting to the Debtor Reporting System are not asked to report the breakdown between private nonguaranteed bonds and private nonguaranteed loans. Information on transactions by nonresidents in local equity markets is gathered from national authorities, investment positions of mutual funds, and market sources.

The volume of portfolio investment reported by the World Bank generally differs from that reported by other sources because of differences in the classification of economies, in the sources, and in the method used to adjust and disaggregate reported information. Differences in reporting arise particularly for foreign investments in local equity markets because clarity, adequate disaggregation, and comprehensive and periodic reporting are lacking in many developing economies. By contrast, capital flows through international debt and equity instruments are well recorded, and for these the differences in reporting lie primarily in the classification of economies, the exchange rates used, whether particular tranches of the transactions are included, and the treatment of certain offshore issuances.

Definitions

• **Net private capital flows** consist of private debt and nondebt flows. Private debt flows include commercial bank lending, bonds, and other private credits; nondebt private flows are foreign direct investment and portfolio equity investment. • **Foreign direct investment** is net inflows of investment to acquire a lasting management interest (10 percent or more of voting stock) in an enterprise operating in an economy other than that of the investor. It is the sum of equity capital, reinvestment of earnings, other long-term capital, and short-term capital, as shown in the balance of payments. • **Portfolio investment flows** are net and include non-debt-creating portfolio equity flows (the sum of country funds, depository receipts, and direct purchases of shares by foreign investors) and portfolio debt flows (bond issues purchased by foreign investors). • **Bank and trade-related lending** covers commercial bank lending and other private credits.

Data sources

The data in this table are compiled from a variety of public and private sources, including the World Bank's Debtor Reporting System, the IMF's International Financial Statistics and Balance of Payments databases, and other sources mentioned in *About the data*. These data are also published in the World Bank's *Global Development Finance 2000*.

6.8 Net financial flows from Development Assistance Committee members

Net flows to part I countries	Official development assistance: Total	Official development assistance: Bilateral grants	Official development assistance: Bilateral loans	Official development assistance: Contributions to multilateral institutions	Other official flows	Private flows: Total	Private flows: Foreign direct investment	Private flows: Bilateral portfolio investment	Private flows: Multilateral portfolio investment	Private flows: Private export credits	Net grants by NGOs	Total net flows
$ millions, 1998												
Australia	960	752	0	209	146	..	..	..	..	..	111	1,217
Austria	456	274	18	164	81	306	215	0	0	91	46	889
Belgium	883	546	–10	346	79	6,727	1,011	6,172	0	–457	36	7,725
Canada	1,691	1,232	–26	484	1,896	5,469	5,656	–313	0	127	155	9,211
Denmark	1,704	1,026	–12	690	127	–60	–60	0	0	0	35	1,806
Finland	396	217	–8	187	56	1,219	26	1,151	0	42	5	1,676
France	5,742	4,540	–355	1,557	–191	2,851	6,188	–2,895	0	–442	..	8,402
Germany	5,581	3,315	176	2,090	–321	15,695	5,486	6,773	1,343	2,094	972	21,926
Ireland	199	124	0	75	..	90	..	..	..	..	45	333
Italy	2,278	624	73	1,581	–209	11,061	1,813	7,832	0	1,416	40	13,171
Japan	10,640	4,901	3,652	2,087	10,804	–3,744	5,850	–2,400	–4,556	–2,638	203	17,902
Luxembourg	112	77	0	35	..	..	..	..	..	..	6	118
Netherlands	3,042	2,323	–190	909	253	9,300	7,673	787	760	81	158	12,752
New Zealand	130	98	0	32	..	11	11	0	0	0	12	154
Norway	1,321	944	6	371	0	535	391	0	0	144	126	1,983
Portugal	259	156	20	82	417	1,333	1,333	0	0	0	7	2,015
Spain	1,376	666	171	538	35	10,297	10,370	0	0	–72	133	11,841
Sweden	1,573	1,045	–5	532	13	1,221	1,221	0	0	0	40	2,847
Switzerland	898	632	0	265	35	3,583	3,583	..	..	..	167	4,683
United Kingdom	3,864	2,328	–196	1,732	–54	7,919	9,286	–1,313	0	–55	408	12,136
United States	8,786	6,574	–585	2,798	618	36,112	22,815	11,344	410	1,543	2,671	48,187
Total	**51,888**	**32,396**	**2,729**	**16,764**	**13,785**	**109,926**	**82,869**	**27,228**	**–2,043**	**1,873**	**5,375**	**180,974**

Net flows to part II countries	Official aid: Total	Official aid: Bilateral grants	Official aid: Bilateral loans	Official aid: Contributions to multilateral institutions	Other official flows	Private flows: Total	Private flows: Foreign direct investment	Private flows: Bilateral portfolio investment	Private flows: Multilateral portfolio investment	Private flows: Private export credits	Net grants by NGOs	Total net flows
$ millions, 1998												
Australia	1	0	0	1	0	..	..	..	..	..	..	1
Austria	191	143	1	47	0	964	964	0	0	0	6	1,161
Belgium	68	3	0	66	82	16,385	1,128	15,142	0	115	..	16,535
Canada	157	157	0	0	68	34	0	0	0	34	..	260
Denmark	118	113	5	0	189	164	164	0	0	0	..	472
Finland	82	47	4	31	–3	1,407	283	1,130	0	–6	..	1,487
France	823	533	–37	327	0	6,893	2,579	3,723	0	591	..	7,716
Germany	654	391	–152	415	4,485	17,744	5,090	11,638	0	1,016	87	22,969
Ireland	0	0	0	0	0	0	0	0	0	0	..	0
Italy	243	3	0	240	21	3,839	1,028	3,278	0	–467	2	4,105
Japan	132	90	3	39	1,874	3,794	5,778	–675	0	–1,309	..	5,801
Luxembourg	3	3	0	0	0	..	..	..	..	..	..	3
Netherlands	130	4	126	0	212	1,749	2,752	–1,048	0	45	..	2,091
New Zealand	0	0	0	0	0	0	0	0	0	0	..	0
Norway	52	52	0	0	3	92	90	0	0	2	..	147
Portugal	22	0	0	22	3	–22	–22	0	0	0	..	3
Spain	5	5	0	0	0	574	574	0	0	0	..	579
Sweden	105	105	0	0	2	1,284	1,284	0	0	0	..	1,390
Switzerland	76	73	0	4	0	1,387	1,387	..	..	..	17	1,480
United Kingdom	435	122	–1	313	–1	2,848	3,415	–808	0	241	5	3,287
United States	2,726	2,746	–32	12	–20	10,409	8,899	698	0	812	1,438	14,553
Total	**6,024**	**4,589**	**–82**	**1,517**	**6,915**	**69,544**	**35,393**	**33,077**	**0**	**1,075**	**1,554**	**84,038**

Net financial flows from Development Assistance Committee members 6.8

About the data

The high-income members of the Organisation for Economic Co-operation and Development (OECD) are the main source of external finance for developing countries. This table shows the flow of financial resources from members of the OECD's Development Assistance Committee (DAC) to official and private recipients in developing and transition economies. DAC exists to help its members coordinate their development assistance and to encourage the expansion and improve the effectiveness of the aggregate resources flowing to developing and transition economies. In this capacity DAC monitors the flow of all financial resources, but its main concern is official development assistance (ODA). DAC has three criteria for ODA: It is undertaken by the official sector. It promotes economic development or welfare as a main objective. It is provided on concessional terms, with a grant element of at least 25 percent on loans.

This definition excludes military aid and nonconcessional flows from official creditors, which are considered other official flows. (However, refinancing of military aid on concessional terms is included in ODA.) The definition includes capital projects, food aid, emergency relief, peacekeeping efforts, and technical cooperation. Also included are contributions to multilateral institutions, such as the United Nations and its specialized agencies, and concessional funding to the multilateral development banks. In 1999, to avoid double counting extrabudgetary expenditures reported by DAC countries and flows reported by the United Nations, all United Nations agencies revised their data to include only regular budgetary expenditures since 1990 (except for the World Food Programme and the United Nations High Commissioner for Refugees, which revised their data from 1996 onward).

DAC maintains a list of countries and territories that are aid recipients. Part I of the list comprises countries and territories considered by DAC members to be eligible for ODA. Part II of the list, created after the collapse of the Soviet Union to monitor the flow of concessional assistance to transition economies, consists of countries that are not considered eligible for ODA but that nevertheless receive ODA-like flows. To differentiate assistance to the two groups of recipients, ODA-like flows to part II countries are termed official aid.

The data in the table were compiled from replies by DAC member countries to questionnaires issued by the DAC Secretariat. Net flows of resources are defined as gross disbursements of grants and loans minus repayments on earlier loans. Because the data are based on donor country reports, they do not provide a complete picture of the resources received by developing and transition economies, for three reasons. First, flows from DAC members are only part of the aggregate resource flows to these economies. Second, the data that record contributions to multilateral institutions measure the flow of resources made available to those institutions by DAC members, not the flow of resources from those institutions to developing and transition economies. Third, because some of the countries and territories on the DAC recipient list are normally classified as high income, the reported flows may overstate the resources available to low- and middle-income economies. High-income countries receive only a small fraction of all development assistance, however.

Net disbursements of ODA by some important donor countries that are not DAC members are shown in table 6.8a.

Table 6.8a

Official development assistance from non-DAC donors

Net disbursements ($ millions)

	1994	1995	1996	1997	1998
OECD members (non-DAC)					
Czech Republic	25	..	..	..	16
Greece[a]	122[b]	152[b]	184	173	179
Korea, Rep.	140	116	159	186	183
Poland	..	..	..	..	19
Turkey	58	107	88	106	..
Arab countries					
Kuwait	555	384	426	373	278
Saudi Arabia	317	192	327	235	288
United Arab Emirates	100	65	31	..	..

Note: China also provides aid but does not disclose the amount.

a. Greece became a member of DAC in December 1999.

b. Comprises total aid disbursements to both part I (official development assistance) and part II countries (official aid).

Source: OECD.

Definitions

• **Official development assistance** comprises grants and loans, net of repayments, that meet the DAC definition of ODA and are made to countries and territories in part I of the DAC list of aid recipients. • **Official aid** comprises grants and ODA-like loans, net of repayments, to countries and territories in part II of the DAC list of aid recipients. • **Bilateral grants** are transfers in money or in kind for which no repayment is required. • **Bilateral loans** are loans extended by governments or official agencies that have a grant element of at least 25 percent and for which repayment is required in convertible currencies or in kind. • **Contributions to multilateral institutions** are concessional funding received by multilateral institutions from DAC members in the form of grants or capital subscriptions. • **Other official flows** are transactions by the official sector whose main objective is other than development or whose grant element is less than 25 percent. • **Private flows** consist of flows at market terms financed from private sector resources. They include changes in holdings of private long-term assets by residents of the reporting country. • **Foreign direct investment** is investment by residents of DAC member countries to acquire a lasting management interest (at least 10 percent of voting stock) in an enterprise operating in the recipient country. The data in the table reflect changes in the net worth of subsidiaries in recipient countries whose parent company is in the DAC source country. • **Bilateral portfolio investment** covers bank lending and the purchase of bonds, shares, and real estate by residents of DAC member countries in recipient countries. • **Multilateral portfolio investment** records the transactions of private banks and nonbanks in DAC member countries in the securities issued by multilateral institutions. • **Private export credits** are loans that are extended to recipient countries by the private sector in DAC member countries for the purpose of promoting trade and are supported by an official guarantee. • **Net grants by NGOs** are private grants by nongovernmental organizations, net of subsidies from the official sector. • **Total net flows** comprise ODA or official aid flows, other official flows, private flows, and net grants by NGOs.

Data sources

The data on financial flows are compiled by DAC and published in its annual statistical report, *Geographical Distribution of Financial Flows to Aid Recipients,* and the DAC chairman's annual report, *Development Co-operation.* Data are available to registered users from the OECD website at www.oecd.org/dac/htm/online.htm.

6.9 Aid flows from Development Assistance Committee members

Net flows to part I countries	Net official development assistance							Aid appropriations		Untied aid	
	$ millions		% of GNP		annual average % change in volume[a]	Per capita of donor country[a]		% of central government budget		% of total ODA commitments	
	1993	1998	1993	1998	1992–93 to 1997–98	$ 1993	$ 1998	1993	1998	1993	1998
Australia	953	960	0.35	0.27	–0.3	63	60	1.3	1.0	41.9	92.8
Austria	544	456	0.30	0.22	–2.6	71	57	0.7	..	44.8	68.6
Belgium	810	883	0.39	0.35	–0.8	83	86	0.0	..	..	50.0
Canada	2,400	1,691	0.45	0.29	–3.9	82	60	1.6	1.4	61.9	34.5
Denmark	1,340	1,704	1.03	0.99	3.8	271	322	2.5	3.0	..	81.4
Finland	355	396	0.45	0.32	–5.6	83	77	1.2	1.2	59.0	78.6
France	7,915	5,742	0.63	0.40	–5.7	140	98	..	..	31.5	66.8
Germany	6,954	5,581	0.35	0.26	–4.7	87	68	..	..	47.9	86.5
Ireland	81	199	0.20	0.30	19.8	25	55	..	..	..	..
Italy	3,043	2,278	0.31	0.20	–12.7	58	40	0.4	..	43.1	63.9
Japan	11,259	10,640	0.27	0.28	–0.8	81	91	1.3	..	83.9	93.6
Luxembourg	50	112	0.35	0.65	18.2	134	259	..	..	..	94.0
Netherlands	2,525	3,042	0.82	0.80	2.3	170	194	..	3.1	..	85.9
New Zealand	98	130	0.25	0.27	3.9	37	42	0.4	0.6	..	..
Norway	1,014	1,321	1.01	0.91	2.7	260	320	1.7	2.3	81.8	89.8
Portugal	235	259	0.28	0.24	–1.2	26	26	..	0.3	63.9	82.6
Spain	1,304	1,376	0.28	0.24	0.3	33	35	0.9	0.9	0.0	26.1
Sweden	1,769	1,573	0.99	0.72	–3.7	225	183	..	..	85.0	79.3
Switzerland	793	898	0.33	0.32	–2.1	119	125	3.1	2.8	91.4	71.7
United Kingdom	2,920	3,864	0.31	0.27	0.6	60	63	1.2	..	35.2	79.6
United States	10,123	8,786	0.15	0.10	–8.3	42	32	1.4	0.7	37.4	28.4
Total	**56,486**	**51,888**	**0.30**	**0.24**	**–3.6**	**72**	**64**	**1.3**	**1.2**	**56.4**	**72.3**

Net flows to part II countries	Net official aid						
	$ millions		% of GNP		annual average % change in volume[a]	Per capita of donor country[a]	
	1993	1998	1993	1998	1992–93 to 1997–98	$ 1993	$ 1998
Australia	6	1	0.00	0.00	–39.2	0	0
Austria	389	191	0.21	0.09	–13.2	50	24
Belgium	81	68	0.04	0.03	–10.3	8	7
Canada	80	157	0.01	0.03	0.2	3	6
Denmark	175	118	0.14	0.07	–1.0	35	22
Finland	38	82	0.05	0.07	12.8	9	16
France	606	823	0.05	0.06	7.5	11	14
Germany	2,416	654	0.12	0.03	–25.6	30	8
Ireland	9	0	0.02	0.00	–49.0	3	0
Italy	242	243	0.02	0.02	–2.9	5	4
Japan	530	132	0.01	0.00	–20.7	4	1
Luxembourg	7	3	0.05	0.02	–16.7	19	6
Netherlands	272	130	0.09	0.03	–20.5	18	8
New Zealand	1	0	0.00	0.00	–47.1	0	0
Norway	74	52	0.07	0.04	–5.2	19	13
Portugal	13	22	0.02	0.02	5.3	1	2
Spain	87	5	0.02	0.00	–46.2	2	0
Sweden	41	105	0.02	0.05	–5.1	5	12
Switzerland	93	76	0.04	0.03	–4.6	14	11
United Kingdom	285	435	0.03	0.03	1.6	6	7
United States	1,647	2,726	0.03	0.03	15.4	7	10
Total	**7,092**	**6,024**	**0.04**	**0.03**	**–4.5**	**9**	**7**

a. At 1997 prices.

Aid flows from Development Assistance Committee members 6.9

About the data

As part of its work, the Development Assistance Committee (DAC) of the Organisation for Economic Co-operation and Development (OECD) assesses the aid performance of member countries relative to the size of their economies. As measured here, aid comprises bilateral disbursements of concessional financing to recipient countries plus the provision by donor governments of concessional financing to multilateral institutions. Volume measures, in constant prices and exchange rates, are used to measure the change in real resources provided over time. Aid flows to part I recipients—official development assistance (ODA)—are tabulated separate from those to part II recipients—official aid (see *About the data* for table 6.8 for more information on the distinction between the two types of aid flows).

Measures of aid flows from the perspective of donors differ from aid receipts by recipient countries. This is because the concessional funding received by multilateral institutions from donor countries is recorded as an aid disbursement by the donor when the funds are deposited with the multilateral institution and recorded as a resource receipt by the recipient country when the multilateral institution makes a disbursement.

Aid-to-GNP ratios, aid per capita, and aid appropriations as a percentage of donor government budgets are calculated by the OECD. The denominators used in calculating these ratios may differ from corresponding values elsewhere in this book because of differences in timing or definitions.

For many European countries, adoption of the 1993 United Nations System of National Accounts has led to an apparent increase in the size of their GNP. As a result ratios of aid to GNP have fallen. DAC is reviewing the extent to which this phenomenon has affected measures of aid performance.

The proportion of untied aid is reported here because tying arrangements require recipients to purchase goods and services from the donor country or from a specified group of countries. Tying arrangements may be justified on the grounds that they prevent a recipient from misappropriating or mismanaging aid receipts, but they may also be motivated by a desire to benefit suppliers in the donor country. The same volume of aid may have different purchasing power depending on the relative costs of suppliers in countries to which the aid is tied and the degree to which each recipient's aid basket is untied. Thus tying arrangements may prevent recipients from obtaining the best value for their money and so reduce the value of the aid received.

Figure 6.9

Aid fell as a share of GNP for almost all donors between 1993 and 1998

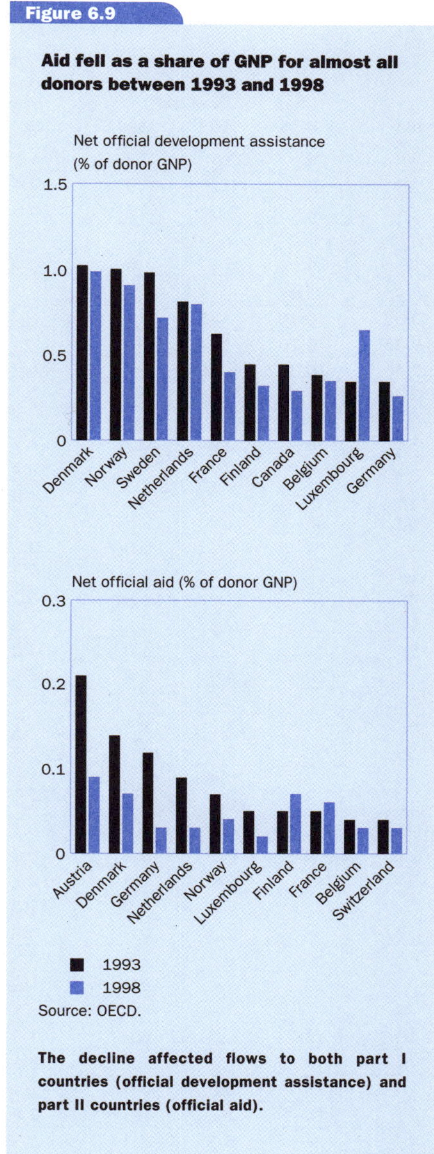

Source: OECD.

The decline affected flows to both part I countries (official development assistance) and part II countries (official aid).

Definitions

• **Net official development assistance** and **net official aid** record the actual international transfer by the donor of financial resources or of goods or services valued at the cost to the donor, less any repayments of loan principal during the same period. Data are shown at current prices and dollar exchange rates. • **Aid as a percentage of GNP** shows the donor's contributions of ODA or official aid as a share of its GNP. • **Annual average percentage change in volume** and **aid per capita of donor country** are calculated using 1997 exchange rates and prices. • **Aid appropriations** are the share of ODA or official aid appropriations in the donor's national budget. • **Untied aid** is the share of ODA that is not subject to restrictions by donors on procurement sources.

Data sources

The data in the table appear in the DAC chairman's report, *Development Co-operation*. The OECD also makes its data available on diskette, magnetic tape, and the Internet. Data are available to registered users from the OECD website at www.oecd.org/dac/htm/online.htm.

6.10 Aid dependency

	Net official development assistance and official aid		Aid per capita		Aid dependency ratios							
					Aid as % of GNP		Aid as % of gross domestic investment		Aid as % of imports of goods and services		Aid as % of central government expenditures	
	$ millions		$									
	1993	1998	1993	1998	1993	1998	1993	1998	1993	1998	1993	1998
Albania	266	242	84	73	22.0	7.8	164.0	49.7	33.4	25.5	..	26.6
Algeria	348	389	13	13	0.7	0.9	2.4	3.0	3.4	3.3	..	..
Angola	291	335	28	28	9.0	8.2	20.8	22.2	7.6	5.7	..	..
Argentina	227	77	7	2	0.1	0.0	0.5	0.1	0.8	0.1	0.7	..
Armenia	109	138	29	36	5.4	7.3	50.5	38.4	37.0	13.4	..	..
Australia												
Austria												
Azerbaijan	22	89	3	11	0.5	2.3	..	5.8	2.5	3.6	..	8.6
Bangladesh	1,372	1,251	12	10	4.0	2.8	21.9	13.2	29.3	15.2	..	..
Belarus	186	28	18	3	0.7	0.1	1.7	0.5	4.3	0.3	..	..
Belgium												
Benin	288	210	56	35	13.9	9.2	88.9	53.4	37.4	25.9	..	..
Bolivia	564	628	80	79	10.2	7.5	59.4	36.6	34.2	25.2	40.9	33.5
Bosnia and Herzegovina[a]	32	876	8	232	..	..	..	..	..	..	..	..
Botswana	130	106	93	68	2.9	2.3	11.7	10.6	6.4	3.5	8.0	..
Brazil	201	329	1	2	0.0	0.0	0.2	0.2	0.4	0.3	0.1	..
Bulgaria	115	232	14	28	1.1	1.9	6.9	12.9	1.9	3.6	2.4	5.7
Burkina Faso	467	397	49	37	22.9	15.5	115.2	53.8	66.1	49.0	99.0	..
Burundi	217	77	37	12	22.5	8.8	141.8	95.9	70.1	40.7	71.3	..
Cambodia	306	337	30	29	15.2	11.9	106.2	78.3	50.3	24.9	..	..
Cameroon	545	424	44	30	4.9	5.1	27.7	26.5	20.6	15.9	30.8	..
Canada												
Central African Republic	171	120	54	34	13.3	11.6	129.1	83.8	54.4	43.9	..	..
Chad	225	167	36	23	15.4	10.0	157.3	65.9	48.2	30.2	..	..
Chile	176	105	13	7	0.4	0.1	1.5	0.5	1.2	0.4	1.8	0.6
China	3,257	2,359	3	2	0.8	0.3	1.7	0.6	3.1	1.3	8.4	..
Hong Kong, China	30	7	5	1	0.0	0.0	0.1	0.0	0.0	0.0	..	..
Colombia	85	166	2	4	0.1	0.2	0.6	0.8	0.6	0.8	1.2	1.0
Congo, Dem. Rep.	178	126	4	3	2.1	2.0	112.7	22.3	10.4	5.5	9.3	..
Congo, Rep.	123	65	51	23	7.5	3.9	21.8	9.4	7.1	3.7	12.5	..
Costa Rica	97	27	30	8	1.3	0.3	4.3	0.9	2.6	0.4	4.9	..
Côte d'Ivoire	764	798	60	55	8.5	7.8	88.5	39.9	19.2	15.8	..	30.2
Croatia[a]	..	39	..	9	..	0.2	..	0.8	..	0.3	..	0.4
Cuba	44	80	4	7	..	..	..	..	..	..	..	..
Czech Republic	100	447	10	43	0.3	0.8	1.0	2.7	0.5	1.2	0.8	2.3
Denmark												
Dominican Republic	–4	120	0	15	0.0	0.8	–0.1	2.9	–0.1	1.2	–0.2	..
Ecuador	236	176	21	14	1.7	1.0	7.8	3.6	5.2	2.2	10.8	..
Egypt, Arab Rep.	2,395	1,915	43	31	5.3	2.2	31.3	10.4	15.0	8.4	14.3	..
El Salvador	397	180	73	30	5.7	1.5	30.7	9.1	15.7	4.0	..	..
Eritrea	67	158	20	41	13.2	20.6	108.2	59.6	24.2	26.6	..	..
Estonia	42	90	28	62	1.1	1.8	4.0	5.9	3.4	1.8	9.2	5.3
Ethiopia	1,089	648	20	11	17.7	10.0	122.6	54.4	79.8	33.7	..	..
Finland												
France												
Gabon	101	45	97	38	2.6	0.9	10.3	2.5	4.0	1.8	..	..
Gambia, The	85	38	82	31	23.5	9.3	110.4	49.5	28.9	11.1	..	..
Georgia	101	162	19	30	3.1	3.1	51.4	40.5	10.0	10.7	..	36.3
Germany												
Ghana	617	701	38	38	10.5	9.3	46.5	40.8	26.9	23.0	49.2	..
Greece												
Guatemala	212	233	22	22	1.9	1.2	10.8	7.7	6.7	4.4	..	..
Guinea	408	359	65	51	12.9	10.3	77.0	47.3	40.4	34.1	..	56.1
Guinea-Bissau	92	96	88	82	41.3	50.0	125.2	410.5	88.1	130.4	..	..
Haiti	123	407	18	53	6.8	10.5	140.0	98.3	40.6	39.4	..	..
Honduras	336	318	63	52	9.9	6.2	28.8	20.0	19.6	10.6	..	..

Aid dependency 6.10

	Net official development assistance and official aid $ millions		Aid per capita $		Aid dependency ratios: Aid as % of GNP		Aid dependency ratios: Aid as % of gross domestic investment		Aid dependency ratios: Aid as % of imports of goods and services		Aid dependency ratios: Aid as % of central government expenditures	
	1993	**1998**	**1993**	**1998**	**1993**	**1998**	**1993**	**1998**	**1993**	**1998**	**1993**	**1998**
Hungary	166	209	16	21	0.4	0.5	2.2	1.4	1.0	0.7	0.8	1.0
India	1,458	1,595	2	2	0.5	0.4	2.5	1.6	4.2	2.5	3.3	2.5
Indonesia	2,013	1,258	11	6	1.3	1.5	4.4	9.6	4.6	2.3	7.6	7.5
Iran, Islamic Rep.	140	164	2	3	0.2	0.1	0.6	0.9	0.6	1.0	0.8	0.3
Iraq	182	115	9	5	..	..	..	..	..	..	..	..
Ireland												
Israel	1,266	1,066	241	179	2.0	1.1	7.6	5.2	4.2	2.5	4.2	2.2
Italy												
Jamaica	100	18	40	7	2.6	0.3	7.2	0.9	3.3	0.4	..	..
Japan												
Jordan	308	408	79	89	5.8	7.1	15.0	22.1	6.3	7.2	17.3	..
Kazakhstan	14	207	1	13	0.1	1.0	0.3	5.4	0.3	2.6	..	..
Kenya	909	474	35	16	19.9	4.2	103.2	28.3	36.8	12.1	61.2	..
Korea, Dem. Rep.	14	109	1	5	..	..	..	..	..	..	..	..
Korea, Rep.	–41	–50	–1	–1	0.0	0.0	0.0	–0.1	0.0	0.0	–0.1	..
Kuwait	1	6	1	3	0.0	0.0	0.0	0.2	0.0	0.0	0.0	0.0
Kyrgyz Republic	94	216	21	46	2.2	13.1	18.6	69.3	18.6	23.0	..	..
Lao PDR	202	281	46	57	15.2	23.0	..	89.6	42.1	43.7	..	..
Latvia	33	97	13	40	0.6	1.5	6.8	6.6	2.6	2.4	..	4.6
Lebanon	144	236	37	56	1.9	1.4	6.6	5.0	2.6	..	8.2	4.3
Lesotho	142	66	77	32	12.9	6.2	27.1	17.2	14.8	6.4	39.8	15.0
Libya	4	7	1	1	..	..	..	..	..	..	..	..
Lithuania	62	128	17	34	1.0	1.2	5.3	4.9	2.6	1.9	10.9	3.9
Macedonia, FYR[a]	3	92	2	46	0.1	3.7	0.8	16.2	..	4.4	..	..
Madagascar	363	494	29	34	11.3	13.4	94.0	99.0	37.4	40.1	54.8	..
Malawi	495	434	54	41	22.3	24.4	157.5	187.8	73.7	36.8	..	..
Malaysia	92	202	5	9	0.2	0.3	0.4	1.0	0.2	0.3	0.6	..
Mali	363	349	39	33	13.6	13.1	62.3	62.0	40.5	36.0	..	..
Mauritania	325	171	148	68	37.2	18.0	156.6	82.3	47.6	33.9	..	..
Mauritius	26	40	24	34	0.8	1.0	2.6	3.9	1.2	1.4	3.8	4.4
Mexico	422	15	5	0	0.1	0.0	0.5	0.0	0.5	0.0	0.7	..
Moldova	28	33	7	8	0.6	2.0	1.1	8.0	..	2.5	..	..
Mongolia	125	203	53	79	24.0	20.6	80.3	75.7	28.9	29.9	..	85.0
Morocco	712	528	28	19	2.8	1.5	11.8	6.6	7.1	4.2	7.8	..
Mozambique	1,179	1,039	79	61	61.3	28.2	440.2	130.7	89.2	75.8	..	..
Myanmar	101	59	2	1	..	..	..	..	7.0	2.0	1.7	..
Namibia	154	180	105	108	5.5	5.7	35.0	30.7	7.8	8.7	14.8	..
Nepal	363	404	18	18	9.5	8.3	41.7	39.0	34.3	24.2	60.5	51.3
Netherlands												
New Zealand												
Nicaragua	319	562	76	117	23.0	31.6	95.5	83.8	25.5	30.8	54.0	..
Niger	344	291	40	29	21.7	14.4	373.6	136.4	65.1	57.4	..	..
Nigeria	279	204	3	2	1.5	0.5	5.6	2.5	2.2	1.3	..	..
Norway												
Oman	47	27	24	12	0.5	..	2.3	..	0.8	..	1.0	0.6
Pakistan	1,004	1,050	9	8	2.0	1.7	9.4	9.7	7.0	6.9	8.3	8.0
Panama	69	22	27	8	1.0	0.3	3.9	0.7	0.9	0.2	3.9	..
Papua New Guinea	305	361	74	78	6.4	10.3	31.7	31.8	13.1	16.8	18.8	..
Paraguay	127	76	28	15	1.8	0.9	9.5	4.2	3.6	1.7	14.2	..
Peru	566	501	25	20	1.4	0.8	7.4	3.3	7.7	3.9	8.9	4.9
Philippines	1,486	607	22	8	2.7	0.9	11.4	4.5	6.6	1.4	14.8	..
Poland	1,031	902	27	23	1.2	0.6	7.7	2.1	4.1	1.6	..	1.5
Portugal												
Puerto Rico												
Romania	167	356	7	16	0.6	0.9	2.2	5.3	2.3	2.6	2.0	..
Russian Federation	2,420	1,017	16	7	0.6	0.4	2.3	2.3	3.8	1.2	..	..

6.10 Aid dependency

	Net official development assistance and official aid		Aid per capita		Aid dependency ratios							
	$ millions		$		Aid as % of GNP		Aid as % of gross domestic investment		Aid as % of imports of goods and services		Aid as % of central government expenditures	
	1993	1998	1993	1998	1993	1998	1993	1998	1993	1998	1993	1998
Rwanda	356	350	47	43	18.3	17.3	125.1	110.1	84.3	70.1	74.7	..
Saudi Arabia	29	25	2	1	0.0	0.0	0.1	0.1	0.1	0.1	..	..
Senegal	500	502	63	56	9.5	10.8	65.4	54.7	27.3	29.0	..	..
Sierra Leone	208	106	48	22	28.9	16.9	348.7	202.3	81.7	48.5	149.8	..
Singapore	24	2	8	1	0.0	0.0	0.1	0.0	0.0	0.0	0.2	..
Slovak Republic	51	155	9	29	0.4	0.8	1.5	1.9	0.6	1.0	..	..
Slovenia[a]	7	40	4	20	0.1	0.2	0.3	0.8	0.1	0.3	..	..
South Africa	275	512	7	12	0.2	0.4	1.5	2.5	1.0	1.4	0.6	1.3
Spain												
Sri Lanka	659	490	37	26	6.4	3.2	24.9	12.3	14.2	6.9	23.6	12.5
Sudan	453	209	18	7	6.5	2.3	..	..	21.4	6.7	..	..
Sweden												
Switzerland												
Syrian Arab Republic	259	156	19	10	1.9	1.0	7.3	3.0	4.3	2.7	3.0	..
Tajikistan	26	105	5	17	0.9	4.9	3.7	..	3.7	13.7	..	..
Tanzania	950	998	34	31	21.8	12.4	80.1	82.8	43.3	39.5	..	..
Thailand	610	690	11	11	0.5	0.6	1.2	2.5	1.1	1.2	3.1	3.3
Togo	97	128	25	29	8.0	8.6	104.9	60.0	17.1	15.5	..	..
Trinidad and Tobago	2	14	1	11	0.0	0.2	0.3	1.0	0.1	0.4	0.1	..
Tunisia	227	148	26	16	1.7	0.8	5.3	2.7	2.9	1.5	4.7	..
Turkey	405	14	7	0	0.2	0.0	0.8	0.0	1.1	0.0	0.9	..
Turkmenistan	25	17	6	4	0.4	0.6	..	..	1.3	1.0	..	..
Uganda	610	471	34	23	19.2	7.0	124.2	46.0	81.7	24.5	..	..
Ukraine	328	380	6	8	0.5	0.9	1.3	4.2	..	1.9	..	..
United Arab Emirates	–10	4	–5	1	0.0	0.0	–0.1	..	..	..	–0.2	0.1
United Kingdom												
United States												
Uruguay	113	24	36	7	0.9	0.1	6.0	0.7	3.4	0.5	2.5	0.3
Uzbekistan	7	144	0	6	0.0	0.7	0.2	3.7	..	4.3	..	..
Venezuela, RB	41	37	2	2	0.1	0.0	0.4	0.2	0.2	0.2	0.4	0.2
Vietnam	252	1,163	4	15	2.0	4.3	9.6	14.9	5.3	8.1	..	..
West Bank and Gaza	179	598	79	219	..	13.8	..	45.8	..	..	..	..
Yemen, Rep.	312	310	22	19	7.0	7.9	34.2	33.4	8.5	9.5	5.7	13.6
Yugoslavia, FR (Serb./Mont.)[a]	..	106	..	10	..	..	..	..	..	..	..	..
Zambia	872	349	103	36	28.9	11.0	177.0	72.6	52.5	20.4	..	..
Zimbabwe	498	280	47	24	7.9	4.7	33.3	25.7	21.3	9.0	26.1	..
World	**62,489 s**	**57,097 s**	**11 w**	**9 w**	**0.9 w**	**.. w**	**.. w**	**.. w**	**.. w**	**.. w**	**..**	**..**
Low income	28,031	24,434	9	7	2.4	1.3	7.6	4.3	9.6	5.5	..	..
Excl. China & India	23,152	20,306	20	16	5.2	4.7	22.1	24.5	15.7	10.7	..	..
Middle income	19,136	17,735	14	12	0.5	0.4	2.1	1.7	2.0	1.1	..	..
Lower middle income	15,320	14,379	19	16	1.1	1.0	4.2	4.5	4.2	2.6	..	..
Upper middle income	3,887	3,516	7	6	0.2	..	..	..	0.7	..	..	..
Low & middle income	59,953	54,742	10	8	1.0	0.7	3.7	2.7	3.8	2.2	..	..
East Asia & Pacific	9,434	8,417	5	4	0.8	0.5	..	..	..	..	..	..
Europe & Central Asia	9,688	8,714	13	14	0.6	0.6	2.3	2.4	2.7	1.4	..	..
Latin America & Carib.	5,249	5,452	10	9	0.3	0.2	1.6	1.0	1.7	0.9	..	..
Middle East & N. Africa	13,038	13,129	21	18	1.3	1.0	5.3	4.7	3.3	..	..	..
South Asia	5,176	5,024	4	4	1.3	0.9	6.3	3.8	8.3	5.0	..	..
Sub-Saharan Africa	17,499	14,186	30	21	5.7	4.1	34.0	22.3	16.9	10.6	..	..
High income	2,316	2,129	..	..	..	..	..	..	..	..	..	..
Europe EMU												

Note: Regional aggregates include data for economies that are not specified elsewhere. World and income group totals include aid not allocated by country or region.
a. Aid to the states of the former Socialist Federal Republic of Yugoslavia that is not otherwise specified is included in regional and income group aggregates.

Aid dependency 6.10

About the data

Ratios of aid to GNP, investment, imports, and public spending provide a measure of the recipient country's dependency on aid. But care must be taken in drawing policy conclusions. For foreign policy reasons some countries have traditionally received large amounts of aid. Thus aid dependency ratios may reveal as much about the donors' interests as they do about the recipients' needs. In general, ratios in Sub-Saharan Africa are much higher than those in other regions, and they increased in the 1980s. These high ratios are due only in part to aid flows. Many African countries saw severe erosion in their terms of trade in the 1980s, which, along with weak policies, contributed to falling incomes, imports, and investment. Thus the increase in aid dependency ratios reflects events affecting both the numerator and the denominator.

As defined here, aid includes official development assistance (ODA) and official aid. The data cover loans and grants from Development Assistance Committee (DAC) countries, multilateral organizations, and certain Arab countries. They do not reflect aid given by recipient countries to other developing countries. As a result some countries that are net donors (such as Saudi Arabia) are shown in the table as aid recipients. (See table 6.8a.)

The data in the table do not distinguish among different types of aid (program, project, or food aid, emergency assistance, peacekeeping assistance, or technical cooperation), each of which may have a very different effect on the economy. Technical cooperation expenditures do not always directly benefit the economy to the extent that they defray costs incurred outside the country on the salaries and benefits of technical experts and the overhead costs of firms supplying technical services.

In 1999, to avoid double counting extrabudgetary expenditures reported by DAC countries and flows reported by the United Nations, all United Nations agencies revised their data to include only regular budgetary expenditures since 1990 (except for the World Food Programme and the United Nations High Commissioner for Refugees, which revised their data from 1996 onward). These revisions have affected net official development assistance and official aid and, as a result, aid per capita and aid dependency ratios.

Because the table relies on information from donors, it is not consistent with information recorded by recipients in the balance of payments, which often excludes all or some technical assistance—particularly payments to expatriates made directly by the donor. Similarly, grant commodity aid may not always be recorded in trade data or in the balance of payments. Moreover, although ODA estimates in balance of payments statistics are meant to exclude purely military aid, the distinction is sometimes blurred. Under DAC rules concessional refinancing of military aid may be counted as ODA; the definition used by the country of origin usually prevails. The nominal values used here tend to overstate the amount of resources transferred. Changes in international prices and in exchange rates can reduce the purchasing power of aid. The practice of tying aid, still prevalent though declining in importance, also tends to reduce its purchasing power (see *About the data* for table 6.9).

The values for population, GNP, gross domestic investment, imports of goods and services, and central government expenditures used in computing the ratios are taken from World Bank and International Monetary Fund databases. The ratios shown may therefore differ somewhat from those computed and published by the Organisation for Economic Co-operation and Development (OECD).

Aid not allocated by country or region—including administrative costs, research into development issues, and aid to nongovernmental organizations—is included in the world total. Thus regional and income group totals do not sum to the world total.

Figure 6.10

The regional distribution of aid from DAC members has remained much the same

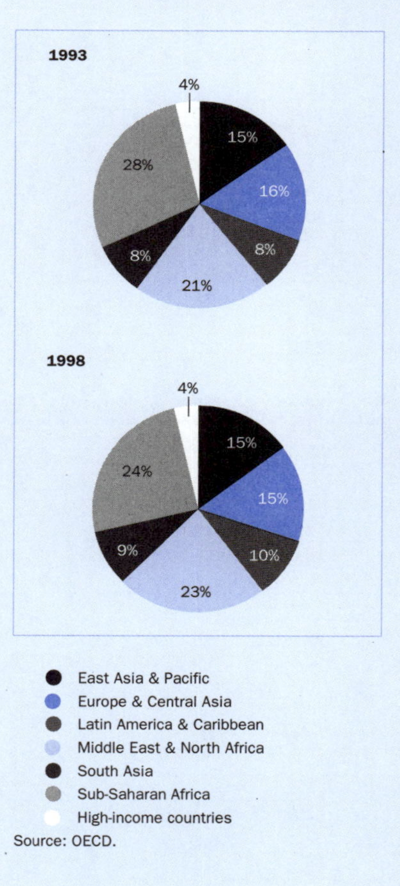

Source: OECD.

Definitions

• **Net official development assistance** consists of disbursements of loans made on concessional terms (net of repayments of principal) and grants by official agencies of the members of DAC, by multilateral institutions, and by certain Arab countries to promote economic development and welfare in recipient economies listed as developing by DAC. Loans with a grant element of at least 25 percent are included in ODA, as are technical cooperation and assistance. • **Net official aid** refers to aid flows, net of repayments, from official donors to the transition economies of Eastern Europe and the former Soviet Union and to certain advanced developing countries and territories as determined by DAC. Official aid is provided under terms and conditions similar to those for ODA. • **Aid per capita** includes both ODA and official aid. • **Aid dependency ratios** are calculated using values in U.S. dollars converted at official exchange rates. See *Definitions* for tables 1.1, 4.9, and 4.14 for definitions of GNP, gross domestic investment, imports of goods and services, and central government expenditures.

Data sources

Data on aid are compiled by DAC and published in its annual statistical report, *Geographical Distribution of Financial Flows to Aid Recipients,* and in the DAC chairman's report, *Development Co-operation.* The OECD also makes its data available on diskette, magnetic tape, and the Internet. Data are available to registered users from the OECD website at www.oecd.org/dac/htm/online.htm.

6.11 Distribution of net aid by Development Assistance Committee members

$ millions, 1998	Total	Ten major DAC donors										Other DAC donors
		Japan	United States	France	Germany	United Kingdom	Netherlands	Canada	Sweden	Denmark	Norway	
Albania	77.7	2.7	14.2	1.8	23.4	0.9	5.5	0.4	1.1	1.7	2.2	23.9
Algeria	121.7	–2.0	..	115.9	4.6	0.2	0.6	0.6	2.8	..	1.5	–2.4
Angola	214.5	17.9	28.8	7.1	11.8	10.6	15.2	2.6	22.5	1.6	23.1	73.3
Argentina	28.9	18.9	0.3	7.5	18.0	0.2	0.2	0.9	0.6	..	..	–17.6
Armenia	62.9	5.5	35.2	2.4	5.1	1.3	8.3	0.2	0.6	0.1	2.3	1.9
Australia												
Austria												
Azerbaijan	35.6	3.5	5.9	3.2	15.3	0.6	2.7	0.2	0.8	..	2.3	1.2
Bangladesh	623.8	189.1	4.0	13.7	65.1	99.0	57.9	53.5	20.0	46.1	29.9	45.6
Belarus	20.8	0.1	3.6	6.9	6.7	0.8	..	0.2	0.5	0.9	0.1	1.2
Belgium												
Benin	144.0	33.0	9.5	28.8	32.4	..	10.1	3.8	..	14.6	–1.1	13.0
Bolivia	416.2	41.4	92.3	12.2	61.9	9.3	67.6	7.2	13.2	18.5	4.0	88.7
Bosnia and Herzegovina	576.9	57.3	216.5	5.1	43.7	3.4	77.2	12.3	24.6	2.5	27.9	106.6
Botswana	73.1	34.0	3.8	0.7	14.2	5.2	4.6	0.2	3.8	1.6	4.2	0.9
Brazil	218.9	104.6	–8.8	4.3	57.7	11.6	18.9	3.4	2.0	0.2	2.1	22.9
Bulgaria	134.4	11.3	7.4	59.4	29.2	4.7	10.3	0.1	0.1	3.4	0.1	8.5
Burkina Faso	226.6	8.9	11.5	64.2	42.1	0.1	34.2	6.1	1.9	30.3	1.6	25.7
Burundi	44.3	..	0.8	5.0	5.0	2.3	4.0	2.6	4.5	..	5.2	14.9
Cambodia	230.6	81.4	32.5	21.4	17.9	9.9	9.3	3.4	14.3	0.7	7.2	32.7
Cameroon	302.9	9.7	7.0	152.8	42.7	6.0	10.4	39.5	..	0.2	0.9	33.9
Canada												
Central African Republic	56.5	14.0	0.3	30.7	7.9	0.9	0.8	0.2	0.5	0.0	0.0	1.2
Chad	74.5	0.3	3.9	42.2	17.1	0.1	1.4	0.2	0.3	..	0.2	8.9
Chile	95.0	32.6	–4.6	11.3	39.6	1.7	5.6	1.1	1.6	..	1.1	5.1
China	1,731.6	1,158.2	0.4	29.8	321.3	55.4	13.2	52.3	10.3	–3.9	11.9	82.7
Hong Kong, China	6.7	2.0	..	3.7	0.9	..	..	0.0	..	..	..	0.1
Colombia	158.9	29.0	48.0	11.8	24.3	4.7	9.7	5.2	3.2	0.0	6.4	16.7
Congo, Dem. Rep.	79.7	0.0	0.1	9.8	2.8	13.5	8.1	6.8	4.2	0.0	2.5	31.8
Congo, Rep.	59.4	0.2	0.1	20.6	13.5	5.5	0.1	3.3	10.8	..	0.5	5.0
Costa Rica	20.4	–4.0	–25.5	2.3	1.5	11.3	15.2	1.8	2.0	7.7	0.4	7.9
Côte d'Ivoire	489.3	40.0	20.8	190.9	35.0	3.5	23.3	45.5	0.2	..	0.2	129.9
Croatia	26.2	0.8	1.7	1.8	–3.4	1.1	0.7	1.0	1.7	1.2	13.6	6.1
Cuba	56.7	8.7	..	2.2	1.7	12.7	2.0	8.9	1.1	0.2	0.9	18.5
Czech Republic	48.8	1.9	0.0	21.2	13.3	2.6	0.1	1.1	0.4	2.4	0.1	5.9
Denmark												
Dominican Republic	60.4	18.3	–2.4	3.2	8.5	0.4	2.5	0.2	0.1	0.2	0.8	28.8
Ecuador	155.1	49.4	4.4	7.1	10.7	3.8	14.3	3.1	2.9	2.8	2.6	54.0
Egypt, Arab Rep.	1,470.8	85.3	810.0	308.0	111.9	12.2	24.1	14.7	1.1	32.1	1.6	69.8
El Salvador	154.4	40.7	40.0	7.4	19.6	0.4	9.5	3.3	5.1	1.6	2.1	24.8
Eritrea	97.7	15.6	20.2	1.2	5.4	1.8	5.3	0.8	2.8	11.3	5.4	28.0
Estonia	35.9	0.3	..	1.9	4.9	0.5	..	0.8	5.7	9.6	2.7	9.5
Ethiopia	364.8	26.1	53.2	10.5	63.5	13.0	36.8	10.9	30.9	3.1	26.7	90.0
Finland												
France												
Gabon	37.4	0.3	1.9	31.6	0.9	..	..	1.7	..	..	0.0	1.0
Gambia, The	13.5	0.6	4.1	0.6	3.6	1.5	0.5	0.3	0.7	0.5	–0.2	1.4
Georgia	74.6	4.6	22.0	0.9	23.2	1.8	11.0	0.2	1.3	..	2.3	7.4
Germany												
Ghana	374.5	149.0	34.3	4.6	32.1	64.6	21.8	17.0	0.7	35.3	1.1	14.2
Greece												
Guatemala	181.6	36.5	33.1	3.4	24.2	0.4	21.4	4.1	11.2	6.9	11.5	29.1
Guinea	148.5	42.3	13.8	54.8	18.1	0.5	0.1	10.7	0.9	0.2	0.1	7.0
Guinea-Bissau	64.7	11.6	10.3	4.4	3.0	..	7.1	0.4	9.2	0.7	0.3	17.8
Haiti	250.9	15.3	82.9	18.3	6.8	0.1	6.0	22.4	0.3	0.0	1.2	97.6
Honduras	190.6	27.0	49.2	7.5	19.9	2.3	17.4	5.4	2.8	1.7	4.7	52.7

Distribution of net aid by Development Assistance Committee members 6.11

$ millions, 1998	Total	Ten major DAC donors										Other DAC donors
		Japan	United States	France	Germany	United Kingdom	Netherlands	Canada	Sweden	Denmark	Norway	
Hungary	79.8	20.1	2.1	44.5	–13.1	5.6	3.4	1.8	0.5	0.8	0.2	14.1
India	915.0	505.0	3.0	–13.4	106.5	186.6	27.0	14.2	16.6	37.7	11.1	20.9
Indonesia	1,243.3	828.5	36.6	24.4	212.8	40.1	–44.6	18.5	0.6	1.5	3.8	121.2
Iran, Islamic Rep.	142.1	48.1	..	10.1	69.7	0.6	2.7	..	..	0.0	0.9	9.9
Iraq	74.6	0.0	0.0	2.1	23.9	6.5	14.3	..	7.5	..	11.5	8.8
Ireland												
Israel	1,055.3	..	1,135.0	16.1	–98.6	0.0	1.0	0.2	1.0	..	..	0.7
Italy												
Jamaica	3.5	11.1	–11.7	–0.8	–5.7	5.9	–0.5	4.4	0.2	..	0.3	0.2
Japan												
Jordan	276.7	44.0	139.9	11.8	51.9	6.7	1.6	2.3	1.2	0.7	1.5	15.2
Kazakhstan	176.5	95.2	61.9	1.9	11.3	3.0	1.3	0.4	0.1	0.2	0.1	1.1
Kenya	275.3	52.6	29.8	3.3	39.0	54.1	29.2	6.7	15.9	10.6	2.5	31.6
Korea, Dem. Rep.	23.5	..	..	0.1	1.8	..	0.2	4.5	4.6	..	4.4	7.9
Korea, Rep.	–49.1	–49.1	–43.8	10.2	27.9	..	0.1	0.8	0.1	0.0	..	4.8
Kuwait	4.9	0.1	..	4.0	0.8	..	..	..	0.1	..	..	0.0
Kyrgyz Republic	79.8	25.2	30.0	3.6	7.0	1.1	2.9	0.3	0.3	2.6	0.3	6.7
Lao PDR	165.7	85.6	7.7	11.7	18.4	0.8	2.5	0.3	12.0	2.2	7.2	17.4
Latvia	47.0	0.3	2.1	3.3	7.5	0.8	0.5	1.3	11.4	10.2	1.8	7.8
Lebanon	73.2	0.8	0.7	39.9	6.5	0.2	3.5	1.7	1.9	..	4.7	13.4
Lesotho	32.5	3.6	2.0	1.1	5.7	8.7	0.5	0.2	0.2	1.4	0.4	8.6
Libya	3.6	0.0	..	0.9	2.2	..	..	..	..	..	0.0	0.5
Lithuania	66.7	1.2	9.3	6.2	8.3	0.5	0.8	2.0	13.5	14.1	3.2	7.7
Macedonia, FYR	31.8	10.6	0.8	0.9	4.3	0.9	7.7	0.4	0.4	1.2	0.2	4.5
Madagascar	333.1	52.0	30.3	68.9	28.7	0.9	3.6	0.1	..	1.1	3.6	143.9
Malawi	203.5	47.4	19.7	0.6	25.5	56.7	4.6	6.9	0.2	22.6	14.3	5.0
Malaysia	198.1	179.1	..	–1.8	5.9	1.7	1.5	3.8	0.6	7.7	0.2	–0.6
Mali	236.2	26.9	28.5	59.7	51.4	1.3	36.1	11.0	0.8	0.8	8.1	11.6
Mauritania	63.5	23.7	2.6	29.6	–2.4	0.7	0.9	0.9	0.3	..	0.3	7.1
Mauritius	19.6	5.7	–0.7	8.1	0.7	1.7	0.1	0.1	..	..	0.0	3.9
Mexico	3.8	–56.3	8.0	10.8	12.8	6.9	3.2	2.5	0.0	0.0	1.0	15.0
Moldova	20.8	0.5	3.8	0.9	2.4	1.6	8.7	0.2	1.0	0.8	..	1.0
Mongolia	141.4	94.0	17.7	2.0	17.0	0.7	1.8	0.2	2.8	2.2	0.6	2.4
Morocco	250.4	39.4	–13.9	198.9	–41.5	0.5	1.8	4.4	0.3	–1.1	0.1	61.4
Mozambique	712.6	40.6	70.5	37.1	85.2	53.0	48.5	12.9	31.9	47.6	49.5	236.1
Myanmar	27.4	16.1	0.3	1.8	1.2	0.6	1.9	0.1	0.3	0.3	2.4	2.6
Namibia	128.7	3.0	13.4	10.6	36.1	6.4	9.7	0.3	12.5	8.3	11.0	17.4
Nepal	212.7	56.9	16.9	3.2	24.5	28.0	11.5	5.8	1.1	22.9	8.8	33.1
Netherlands												
New Zealand												
Nicaragua	313.3	29.0	65.5	14.7	49.6	1.8	26.0	2.7	19.8	28.5	16.8	58.8
Niger	144.6	11.4	10.8	66.1	20.5	1.5	7.8	2.0	..	3.5	1.6	19.5
Nigeria	34.2	–10.9	3.8	3.0	14.1	17.4	1.5	0.9	0.4	0.3	0.2	3.6
Norway												
Oman	19.8	8.1	10.3	0.7	0.4	0.1	..	..	..	..	..	0.1
Pakistan	534.7	491.5	–40.7	9.1	–21.2	46.4	16.8	16.1	2.0	–0.2	5.3	9.6
Panama	22.4	9.1	–13.7	0.3	3.1	0.6	0.2	0.7	0.0	0.2	..	21.8
Papua New Guinea	311.9	47.3	0.9	0.5	3.0	..	1.3	0.1	0.3	..	0.2	258.3
Paraguay	55.7	21.0	1.8	0.6	12.1	0.0	0.1	0.2	0.9	..	0.9	18.2
Peru	381.5	80.1	121.0	21.3	50.4	5.7	36.5	15.6	3.1	3.1	2.1	42.6
Philippines	528.0	297.6	27.3	24.4	45.4	5.0	19.8	14.5	3.9	–3.6	2.4	91.3
Poland	470.9	2.5	30.2	76.6	65.5	17.0	8.7	116.8	11.4	17.8	0.6	123.8
Portugal												
Puerto Rico												
Romania	175.0	9.3	2.0	102.1	31.6	8.0	4.3	1.5	0.5	5.1	0.0	10.6
Russian Federation	870.6	3.3	458.4	82.1	82.3	54.8	70.9	14.1	21.2	17.9	31.8	33.7

6.11 Distribution of net aid by Development Assistance Committee members

$ millions, 1998	Total	Ten major DAC donors										Other DAC donors
		Japan	United States	France	Germany	United Kingdom	Netherlands	Canada	Sweden	Denmark	Norway	
Rwanda	209.0	9.0	23.0	27.9	20.6	20.6	29.0	10.1	9.9	2.1	8.8	48.0
Saudi Arabia	14.7	9.2	..	3.6	1.9	..	..	..	..	..	..	0.1
Senegal	289.0	33.6	14.1	142.3	34.7	1.1	14.1	12.3	0.7	5.2	1.2	29.7
Sierra Leone	53.2	1.2	13.2	1.4	1.9	14.2	2.3	0.6	3.8	0.1	4.0	10.5
Singapore	1.3	2.3	..	4.0	–5.3	0.2	..	0.2	..	..	..	0.0
Slovak Republic	38.8	2.1	4.1	11.0	6.6	4.6	..	1.1	0.2	1.7	0.0	7.5
Slovenia	5.6	0.8	0.0	0.9	0.0	1.0	0.0	0.0	0.0	0.1	..	2.9
South Africa	420.7	30.8	83.0	36.7	42.1	54.1	42.0	10.4	31.1	32.0	22.0	36.4
Spain												
Sri Lanka	282.3	197.9	–0.6	0.4	19.0	13.6	13.2	2.2	12.9	0.7	13.2	9.9
Sudan	150.2	0.2	13.2	3.9	17.1	31.0	26.7	7.5	10.4	1.2	19.1	19.9
Sweden												
Switzerland												
Syrian Arab Republic	82.9	50.0	..	12.0	17.1	0.2	1.2	0.2	0.1	..	1.0	1.3
Tajikistan	40.0	0.4	25.2	0.0	3.3	2.4	1.9	0.2	1.1	..	0.8	4.7
Tanzania	769.0	83.4	29.4	7.5	109.9	158.6	80.3	7.0	59.8	69.6	44.6	118.9
Thailand	675.7	558.4	7.4	6.5	45.3	4.3	4.4	5.6	3.6	12.3	1.6	26.3
Togo	66.1	11.0	1.5	31.6	11.8	2.0	0.2	0.3	0.1	..	..	7.7
Trinidad and Tobago	–2.3	1.5	0.1	0.5	–4.6	–0.2	0.1	0.3	..	..	..	0.0
Tunisia	102.0	29.2	–21.1	90.4	–1.8	0.4	–0.8	1.8	0.4	..	0.2	3.3
Turkey	–80.7	–30.4	–72.6	28.6	–12.1	1.3	2.8	–1.3	1.0	–0.2	0.8	1.4
Turkmenistan	8.2	4.4	2.5	0.3	0.5	0.4	0.0	0.1	..	..	..	0.0
Uganda	383.9	23.9	35.8	2.9	28.3	105.6	35.3	3.5	9.7	70.8	31.3	36.9
Ukraine	270.9	0.7	139.2	20.5	36.3	15.0	28.9	13.8	2.1	2.8	0.2	11.5
United Arab Emirates	3.5	0.1	..	2.0	0.9	..	0.5	..	..	..	..	0.0
United Kingdom												
United States												
Uruguay	19.4	3.9	0.5	1.5	10.7	0.4	0.3	0.8	0.4	..	0.0	1.0
Uzbekistan	123.3	103.0	4.3	2.2	11.9	0.8	0.2	0.1	0.5	..	..	0.3
Venezuela, RB	21.4	3.2	0.5	6.0	4.7	0.5	0.3	0.8	0.1	..	..	5.3
Vietnam	712.6	388.6	–9.6	66.2	54.8	7.3	23.2	9.2	33.7	40.9	7.9	90.5
West Bank and Gaza	..	46.3	75.4	16.7	30.6	8.9	22.3	0.3	16.0	5.4	40.1	70.1
Yemen, Rep.	166.8	62.4	7.1	10.0	31.3	2.1	46.2	0.2	0.8	5.3	0.0	1.6
Yugoslavia, FR (Serb./Mont.)	93.4	0.0	6.4	3.2	34.2	0.2	6.4	1.5	5.6	0.4	10.6	24.9
Zambia	256.5	33.6	12.1	10.4	50.0	33.4	22.5	7.8	13.9	17.9	31.8	23.1
Zimbabwe	216.3	26.8	24.2	–0.8	15.9	36.7	28.0	4.6	19.7	23.3	13.8	23.9
World	39,632 s	8,647 s	8,702 s	4,680 s	3,730 s	2,253 s	2,263 s	1,364 s	1,145 s	1,133 s	1,002 s	4,713 s
Low income	15,218	4,937	982	1,379	1,870	1,222	833	463	439	583	454	2,057
Excl. China & India	12,572	3,274	978	1,363	1,442	980	793	397	412	549	431	1,954
Middle income	11,780	2,553	2,497	1,700	1,296	376	667	305	259	231	253	1,644
Lower middle income	10,198	2,227	2,499	1,316	1,031	318	611	164	227	188	221	1,396
Upper middle income	1,736	327	–2	431	264	146	55	141	32	43	31	266
Low & middle income	37,405	8,598	7,545	3,867	3,820	2,163	2,124	1,361	1,143	1,133	1,002	4,648
East Asia & Pacific	6,617	3,810	270	274	803	151	48	128	96	65	63	910
Europe & Central Asia	5,004	360	2,154	495	491	172	276	171	150	129	126	480
Latin America & Carib.	3,876	553	1,094	175	466	220	331	127	96	79	91	645
Middle East & N. Africa	10,171	1,486	2,935	1,393	796	512	648	522	358	309	235	976
South Asia	2,717	1,462	–17	15	207	383	155	97	65	123	79	147
Sub-Saharan Africa	9,175	933	1,111	1,563	1,038	813	666	315	377	427	408	1,524
High income	2,032	41	1,148	764	–92	1	138	1	1	0	..	29
Europe EMU												

Note: Regional aggregates include data for economies that are not specified elsewhere. World and income group totals include aid not allocated by country or region.

Distribution of net aid by Development Assistance Committee members 6.11

About the data

The data in the table show net bilateral aid to low- and middle-income economies from members of the Development Assistance Committee (DAC) of the Organisation for Economic Co-operation and Development (OECD). The DAC compilation includes aid to some countries and territories not shown in the table and small quantities to unspecified economies that are recorded only at the regional or global level. Aid to countries and territories not shown in the table has been assigned to regional totals based on the World Bank's regional classification system. Aid to unspecified economies has been included in regional totals, but not in totals for income groups. Aid not allocated by country or region—including administrative costs, research into development issues, and aid to nongovernmental organizations—is included in the world total; thus regional and income group totals do not sum to the world total.

In 1999 all United Nations agencies revised their data to include only regular budgetary expenditures since 1990 (except for the World Food Programme and the United Nations High Commissioner for Refugees, which revised their data from 1996 onward). They did so to avoid double counting extrabudgetary expenditures reported by DAC countries and flows reported by the United Nations.

Because the data in the table are based on donor country reports of bilateral programs, they cannot be reconciled with recipient country reports. Nor do they reflect the full extent of aid flows from the reporting donor countries or to recipient countries. A full accounting would include donor country contributions to multilateral institutions and the flow of resources from multilateral institutions to recipient countries as well as flows from countries that are not members of DAC. In addition, the expenditures countries report as official development assistance (ODA) have changed. For example, some DAC members providing aid to refugees within their own borders have reported these expenditures as ODA.

Some of the aid recipients shown in the table are themselves significant donors. See table 6.8a for a summary of ODA from non-DAC countries.

Definitions

• **Net aid** comprises net bilateral official development assistance to part I recipients and net bilateral official aid to part II recipients (see *About the data* for table 6.8). • **Other DAC donors** are Australia, Austria, Belgium, Denmark, Finland, Ireland, Italy, Luxembourg, New Zealand, Portugal, Spain, and Switzerland.

Data sources

Data on aid are compiled by DAC and published in its annual statistical report, *Geographical Distribution of Financial Flows to Aid Recipients,* and in the DAC chairman's report, *Development Co-operation*. The OECD also makes its data available on diskette, magnetic tape, and the Internet. Data are available to registered users from the OECD website at www.oecd.org/dac/htm/online.htm.

Figure 6.11

The flow of aid from DAC members in 1998 tended to reflect regional interests and relationships

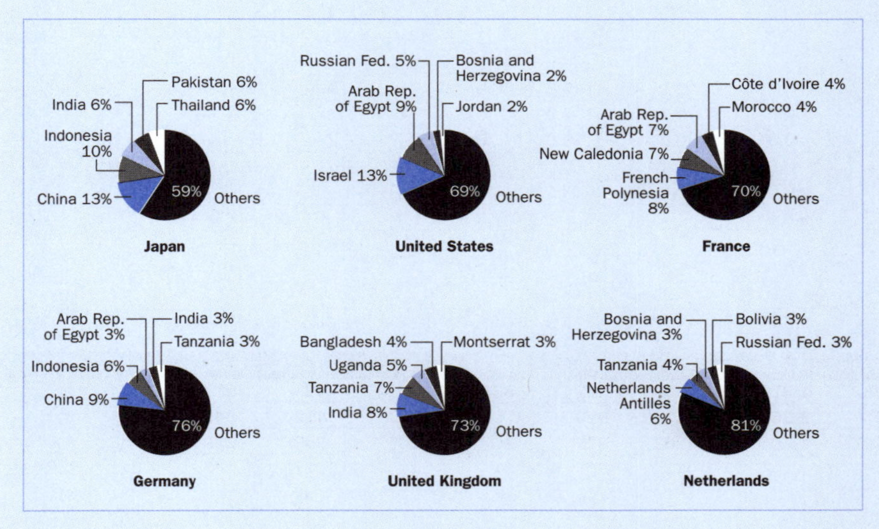

Source: OECD.

This figure shows the distribution of aid from the top six donors to their top five recipients in 1998. Among the top recipients many are middle-income economies—and some are high income.

6.12 Net financial flows from multilateral institutions

$ millions, 1998	International financial institutions							United Nations					Total
	World Bank		IMF		Regional development banks								
	IDA	IBRD	Concessional	Non-concessional	Concessional	Non-concessional	Others	UNDP	UNFPA	UNICEF	WFP	Others	
Albania	62.8	0.0	8.0	–1.2	..	..	5.7	2.7	0.6	1.1	0.3	1.0	81.1
Algeria	0.0	–152.0	..	–91.6	..	42.7	291.7	0.5	0.5	1.0	0.7	5.1	98.7
Angola	35.8	0.0	..	..	0.0	0.7	0.0	7.6	2.2	4.9	2.7	1.4	55.3
Argentina	0.0	1,678.4	..	–656.9	–1.9	66.9	0.0	0.6	0.1	1.6	..	8.9	1,097.6
Armenia	42.9	–0.2	51.3	–0.6	..	..	5.3	2.7	0.4	1.1	..	1.5	104.3
Australia													
Austria													
Azerbaijan	20.6	0.0	19.8	21.4	..	..	21.7	1.3	0.7	1.0	..	0.1	86.7
Bangladesh	290.4	–4.4	–102.3	134.5	181.4	1.5	25.4	20.8	6.9	14.4	16.1	4.7	589.4
Belarus	0.0	3.6	..	–24.3	..	..	9.8	0.7	0.0	0.0	..	1.3	–9.0
Belgium													
Benin	15.6	0.0	–5.3	..	5.0	0.0	6.5	4.5	2.6	1.7	4.3	3.4	38.2
Bolivia	81.9	–12.8	5.0	0.0	85.8	–62.3	–34.8	0.7	1.4	2.1	4.4	2.6	74.1
Bosnia and Herzegovina	134.9	0.0	..	32.9	..	..	..	5.0	0.2	2.4	..	0.9	176.2
Botswana	–0.5	–12.9	..	..	2.8	–8.9	–3.3	0.6	0.5	1.4	..	1.3	–18.9
Brazil	0.0	245.0	..	4,617.8	0.0	1,318.3	4,150.0	0.9	2.4	6.4	..	55.7	10,396.3
Bulgaria	0.0	176.4	..	127.9	..	..	5.5	1.4	..	..	..	2.0	313.1
Burkina Faso	52.5	0.0	15.1	..	12.0	–1.9	–6.0	4.9	1.2	2.6	6.4	2.0	88.8
Burundi	18.5	0.0	–8.7	0.0	3.8	–4.1	–0.4	5.3	1.3	1.9	..	1.5	19.0
Cambodia	19.2	0.0	–1.4	..	28.0	..	0.1	9.8	6.7	3.6	3.6	1.4	71.0
Cameroon	73.7	–65.3	73.3	–16.3	12.5	–13.6	–25.7	1.6	1.0	1.7	1.0	2.3	46.1
Canada													
Central African Republic	–3.4	0.0	5.8	–7.6	–0.5	–1.7	–0.3	5.8	0.5	1.9	0.3	4.4	5.0
Chad	14.7	0.0	7.1	–7.0	18.6	..	–4.1	5.7	1.2	2.5	2.8	1.3	42.7
Chile	–0.7	–34.5	..	0.0	–1.0	–42.8	0.6	1.3	0.2	1.8	..	2.0	–73.2
China	553.8	1,078.0	0.0	0.0	..	622.0	1.5	14.4	1.3	17.5	10.5	7.4	2,306.4
Hong Kong, China	..	..	..	..	..	..	..	0.0	..	..	..	0.2	0.1
Colombia	–0.7	–47.7	..	..	–12.2	149.8	210.6	2.4	0.4	2.6	1.6	2.7	309.4
Congo, Dem. Rep.	0.0	0.0	–0.2	–0.5	0.1	0.0	0.0	13.8	0.2	9.5	..	7.3	30.1
Congo, Rep.	–0.4	–3.3	0.0	–0.8	0.0	–3.6	0.0	0.7	0.7	2.1	..	2.4	–2.3
Costa Rica	–0.2	–20.6	..	0.0	–11.1	9.9	16.9	0.3	0.2	0.8	0.0	14.1	10.3
Côte d'Ivoire	189.7	–139.5	168.1	0.0	55.5	–38.1	–23.9	2.2	1.2	3.3	0.8	10.9	230.2
Croatia	0.0	91.5	..	–8.9	..	..	53.3	1.1	..	0.2	..	0.3	137.5
Cuba	..	..	..	..	..	..	..	1.0	0.6	1.3	2.5	2.3	7.8
Czech Republic	0.0	–20.8	..	0.0	..	..	–130.0	..	..	..	..	2.0	–148.8
Denmark													
Dominican Republic	–0.7	–6.3	..	25.2	11.5	13.9	5.7	2.6	1.3	1.4	4.6	4.4	63.7
Ecuador	–1.1	5.9	..	–67.1	–3.8	88.0	154.3	1.9	1.3	1.7	3.6	3.1	187.8
Egypt, Arab Rep.	39.3	–66.9	0.0	0.0	13.4	–63.1	67.3	3.3	1.5	4.7	3.8	7.0	10.3
El Salvador	–0.8	6.7	0.0	0.0	–7.0	84.5	–10.8	1.8	0.6	1.3	4.9	1.2	82.3
Eritrea	6.3	0.0	..	..	6.4	..	18.6	8.7	1.5	2.0	..	1.4	44.9
Estonia	0.0	10.3	..	–25.4	..	..	–0.6	0.3	0.0	..	..	0.2	–15.1
Ethiopia	51.4	0.0	16.2	0.0	27.7	–1.6	4.3	15.9	1.8	12.8	16.1	19.6	164.3
Finland													
France													
Gabon	0.0	–2.7	..	–22.6	0.2	2.5	–1.0	0.3	0.4	0.4	..	1.2	–21.3
Gambia, The	1.7	0.0	–0.2	0.0	4.4	–1.1	8.7	2.2	0.3	1.3	2.6	1.5	21.3
Georgia	52.9	0.0	37.7	–0.9	..	..	6.0	5.8	0.2	1.5	..	1.3	104.3
Germany													
Ghana	244.8	–4.1	6.1	–33.3	13.2	–15.0	1.0	6.0	4.7	3.2	1.5	3.3	231.3
Greece													
Guatemala	0.0	13.8	..	0.0	–1.8	100.0	15.9	4.4	0.5	1.8	4.2	0.8	139.7
Guinea	61.1	0.0	22.6	0.0	17.8	–32.7	27.7	6.5	0.8	2.5	1.2	21.1	128.6
Guinea-Bissau	4.8	0.0	2.6	0.0	8.5	–0.4	–0.8	1.7	0.3	1.5	1.0	1.1	20.2
Haiti	34.0	0.0	0.0	–5.3	47.1	..	–0.5	10.0	2.7	2.1	2.8	0.8	93.6
Honduras	62.0	–48.2	–1.8	64.4	31.6	–0.6	–24.1	2.8	1.1	1.3	5.3	3.7	97.4

Net financial flows from multilateral institutions 6.12

$ millions, 1998	International financial institutions							United Nations					Total
	World Bank		IMF		Regional development banks								
	IDA	IBRD	Concessional	Nonconcessional	Concessional	Nonconcessional	Others	UNDP	UNFPA	UNICEF	WFP	Others	
Hungary	0.0	–802.3	..	–161.1	..	..	–178.2	0.4	..	..	..	2.1	–1,139.1
India	578.5	–307.4	–390.2	..	..	490.5	–14.9	9.9	8.3	29.9	12.3	8.5	425.3
Indonesia	–21.1	479.1	..	5,772.2	–1.3	873.9	49.5	4.9	5.4	7.1	1.9	5.3	7,177.0
Iran, Islamic Rep.	0.0	–22.0	..	..	..	..	–28.7	0.9	2.0	2.0	1.6	13.9	–30.3
Iraq	..	..	..	..	..	..	..	16.5	0.8	2.5	3.3	5.2	28.2
Ireland													
Israel	..	..	..	..	..	..	..	..	..	..	..	0.5	0.5
Italy													
Jamaica	0.0	–40.6	–16.9	..	–4.7	22.5	–3.2	0.5	0.0	1.0	0.0	1.1	–40.4
Japan													
Jordan	–2.4	–27.4	..	22.8	..	..	181.5	0.7	0.2	1.3	3.1	78.7	258.5
Kazakhstan	0.0	210.8	..	114.9	20.8	114.5	18.1	1.4	1.1	1.8	..	1.0	484.3
Kenya	108.2	–65.9	–62.5	0.0	7.0	–16.3	–15.2	8.0	1.6	5.4	8.6	19.4	–1.7
Korea, Dem. Rep.	..	..	..	..	..	..	..	5.0	0.6	1.3	1.2	1.6	9.7
Korea, Rep.	–3.5	2,875.0	..	5,155.8	..	1,678.3	0.0	1.0	0.2	..	..	1.0	9,707.8
Kuwait	..	..	..	..	..	..	..	0.0	..	..	..	1.0	1.0
Kyrgyz Republic	65.5	0.0	14.6	–11.6	43.3	..	9.3	2.1	0.9	0.8	..	0.8	125.5
Lao PDR	23.7	0.0	–6.4	..	61.7	..	4.8	4.5	0.8	1.7	1.3	0.9	93.0
Latvia	0.0	78.2	..	–24.8	..	..	16.8	0.3	0.1	..	..	0.6	71.1
Lebanon	0.0	38.4	..	..	..	..	51.8	1.8	0.4	1.9	0.1	51.7	145.9
Lesotho	12.5	–1.1	0.0	–4.9	3.1	–2.5	0.8	2.5	0.1	1.3	2.0	0.9	14.7
Libya	..	..	..	..	..	..	..	..	..	..	..	3.4	3.4
Lithuania	0.0	57.1	..	–28.0	..	..	27.3	0.6	0.0	..	..	0.7	57.8
Macedonia, FYR	28.9	39.2	12.3	–2.3	..	..	–5.3	0.3	..	1.1	..	1.5	75.8
Madagascar	64.5	–1.5	–13.9	0.0	7.7	–6.5	–2.8	4.3	2.4	3.7	2.2	2.0	62.1
Malawi	119.7	–9.7	0.7	–8.6	14.6	4.7	–3.2	9.7	3.2	2.9	0.8	2.4	137.1
Malaysia	0.0	208.4	..	0.0	0.0	1.0	–5.3	0.5	0.1	0.6	..	1.5	206.7
Mali	39.0	0.0	3.0	0.0	16.7	0.0	3.4	9.8	1.8	3.5	2.6	1.7	81.4
Mauritania	21.1	–1.8	–6.9	0.0	6.3	–5.6	–8.1	1.6	0.8	1.6	2.0	1.7	12.8
Mauritius	–0.6	–6.1	0.0	0.0	–0.4	–2.1	12.2	0.4	0.3	1.0	..	0.8	5.4
Mexico	0.0	25.9	..	–1,063.3	–2.8	290.3	0.0	0.7	2.0	2.4	..	10.5	–734.3
Moldova	2.3	25.6	..	–64.0	..	..	2.3	..	0.1	0.7	..	0.9	–32.2
Mongolia	16.7	0.0	–1.3	0.0	31.9	..	2.0	2.3	1.5	1.0	..	1.8	55.9
Morocco	–1.4	–7.6	0.0	0.0	4.4	53.5	154.5	2.0	4.6	2.1	0.4	3.5	215.9
Mozambique	127.8	0.0	9.7	..	64.2	–5.8	9.7	14.6	3.9	7.0	3.2	2.3	236.6
Myanmar	0.0	0.0	0.0	0.0	0.0	0.0	–2.3	16.7	1.0	6.6	..	2.6	24.5
Namibia	..	..	..	..	..	..	..	0.8	1.8	1.7	..	2.6	6.8
Nepal	51.9	0.0	–6.6	0.0	87.7	0.0	2.3	7.7	6.6	4.6	9.3	7.9	171.4
Netherlands													
New Zealand													
Nicaragua	103.5	–8.9	22.8	0.0	95.4	–6.2	0.0	2.2	2.2	1.6	8.8	1.1	222.5
Niger	42.8	0.0	19.8	–7.5	15.7	0.0	5.1	4.4	3.6	4.3	5.7	1.7	95.5
Nigeria	133.8	–226.8	..	..	10.0	–60.3	0.0	12.9	3.5	14.4	..	4.4	–108.0
Norway													
Oman	0.0	–4.0	..	..	..	..	–4.1	..	..	1.3	..	1.4	–5.4
Pakistan	172.0	–66.8	51.1	–28.5	236.1	96.0	96.3	8.2	4.3	10.3	8.5	15.0	602.3
Panama	0.0	65.1	..	27.3	–6.5	110.4	1.3	0.9	0.3	0.9	0.3	1.5	201.6
Papua New Guinea	–2.4	–15.2	0.0	–4.1	2.8	8.5	1.8	1.3	0.7	1.1	..	1.4	–4.1
Paraguay	–1.5	14.7	..	..	16.7	43.1	–1.3	0.3	0.6	1.2	..	0.8	74.6
Peru	0.0	207.1	..	–145.3	–6.6	170.0	–38.1	2.0	2.0	2.1	4.5	7.5	205.2
Philippines	6.5	–94.8	0.0	651.4	21.3	152.5	0.4	6.4	3.5	4.1	..	2.8	754.0
Poland	0.0	–22.6	..	0.0	..	..	0.0	..	0.1	..	..	2.9	–19.6
Portugal													
Puerto Rico													
Romania	0.0	84.3	..	–125.2	..	..	–38.1	0.7	0.4	1.0	..	2.4	–74.5
Russian Federation	0.0	1,160.3	..	5,326.8	..	..	4.1	..	0.2	0.3	..	8.2	6,499.9

6.12 Net financial flows from multilateral institutions

$ millions, 1998	International financial institutions							United Nations					Total
	World Bank		IMF		Regional development banks								
	IDA	IBRD	Concessional	Non-concessional	Concessional	Non-concessional	Others	UNDP	UNFPA	UNICEF	WFP	Others	
Rwanda	61.6	0.0	13.8	0.0	14.3	0.0	4.7	9.7	0.9	1.3	4.6	1.1	111.9
Saudi Arabia	..	..	..	..	..	..	..	–0.4	..	..	..	11.1	10.7
Senegal	73.8	–5.5	9.1	–21.0	19.0	–15.6	7.3	1.9	1.0	2.3	2.5	4.1	79.0
Sierra Leone	18.6	–0.8	0.0	15.7	4.3	0.0	–3.6	4.1	0.6	2.0	2.5	2.2	45.6
Singapore	..	..	..	..	..	..	..	..	..	..	..	0.2	0.2
Slovak Republic	0.0	–1.7	..	–67.5	..	..	88.2	..	..	..	..	1.5	20.5
Slovenia	..	..	..	..	..	..	..	0.2	..	..	..	2.2	2.4
South Africa	0.0	0.0	..	–416.8	..	..	..	3.7	0.7	1.6	..	4.7	–406.1
Spain													
Sri Lanka	83.6	–5.8	–81.9	0.0	105.8	0.0	–0.8	5.4	1.7	1.6	0.5	2.8	113.0
Sudan	0.0	0.0	0.0	–57.2	0.0	–1.3	0.0	5.9	2.5	5.8	12.3	11.5	–20.5
Sweden													
Switzerland													
Syrian Arab Republic	–1.5	–21.6	..	0.0	..	..	1.1	1.1	2.7	1.3	5.4	25.0	13.4
Tajikistan	37.9	0.0	54.7	10.2	..	..	17.4	4.5	0.4	0.6	0.3	0.5	126.5
Tanzania	84.7	–12.1	10.7	0.0	53.4	–2.5	–0.2	13.3	3.7	7.0	1.1	3.2	162.2
Thailand	–2.3	319.2	0.0	678.4	–1.6	493.2	70.3	2.1	0.1	2.0	1.6	5.3	1,568.2
Togo	39.3	0.0	3.3	0.0	3.6	–0.1	11.4	2.5	1.0	1.7	..	1.9	64.5
Trinidad and Tobago	0.0	7.1	..	–4.2	–0.1	12.3	–2.7	0.2	0.0	..	..	0.6	13.3
Tunisia	–2.1	–36.5	..	–49.7	..	–14.4	–6.5	0.9	1.3	1.3	–0.1	1.2	–104.7
Turkey	–5.9	–365.8	..	–223.4	..	..	–142.9	1.0	1.3	1.8	..	6.0	–727.9
Turkmenistan	0.0	2.4	..	..	..	..	15.5	0.5	0.7	0.6	..	0.3	20.0
Uganda	104.6	0.0	–12.2	0.0	47.0	–8.0	–14.7	12.5	6.0	4.7	14.8	21.4	176.2
Ukraine	0.0	384.7	..	277.4	..	..	42.9	0.4	0.5	0.1	..	3.7	709.7
United Arab Emirates	..	..	..	..	..	..	..	–0.1	0.0	..	..	0.7	0.5
United Kingdom													
United States													
Uruguay	0.0	65.3	..	154.9	–1.7	99.2	1.2	0.4	0.3	0.9	..	2.0	322.6
Uzbekistan	0.0	13.0	..	0.0	0.5	1.4	51.0	1.6	1.5	1.8	..	0.5	71.4
Venezuela, RB	0.0	8.0	..	–445.7	–1.3	440.3	109.8	1.0	0.4	1.2	..	3.0	116.7
Vietnam	253.1	0.0	0.0	–77.9	117.7	0.0	16.7	14.0	5.5	7.2	11.4	2.0	349.7
West Bank and Gaza	..	..	..	..	..	..	..	..	..	1.9	4.1	154.0	159.9
Yemen, Rep.	110.7	0.0	59.7	12.2	..	..	–19.8	5.8	0.8	3.3	1.3	5.7	179.7
Yugoslavia, FR (Serb./Mont.)	0.0	0.0	..	..	..	..	..	..	..	..	..	..	..
Zambia	39.4	–21.1	0.0	0.0	11.4	–15.5	–8.0	5.9	1.6	2.4	2.7	5.5	24.3
Zimbabwe	28.2	–3.3	–19.0	9.7	4.6	–17.7	18.3	3.2	1.0	1.5	..	2.2	28.7
World	4,816 s	6,831 s	–26 s	19,259 s	1,728 s	7,193 s	5,468 s	609 s	216 s	490 s	270 s	980 s	47,834 s
Low income	4,311	587	21	5,702	1,469	1,811	217	408	127	261	211	275	15,400
Excl. China & India	3,178	–183	411	5,702	1,469	699	231	378	113	211	187	243	12,638
Middle income	505	6,244	–46	13,557	258	5,382	5,251	103	48	91	58	567	32,017
Lower middle income	514	2,258	–46	6,305	266	1,514	1,224	90	39	65	58	392	12,679
Upper middle income	–9	3,986	0	7,252	–7	3,869	4,027	13	9	26	0	175	19,340
Low & middle income	4,816	6,831	–26	19,259	1,728	7,193	5,468	608	216	490	270	974	47,826
East Asia & Pacific	848	4,849	–9	12,176	289	3,828	135	85	32	57	32	62	22,383
Europe & Central Asia	443	1,124	198	5,142	64	116	–93	35	10	23	1	60	7,123
Latin America & Carib.	288	2,126	1	2,502	241	2,912	4,601	43	25	44	48	161	12,992
Middle East & N. Africa	144	–300	60	–103	19	19	688	129	45	149	24	431	1,306
South Asia	1,181	–384	–530	106	615	588	118	70	29	68	48	43	1,952
Sub-Saharan Africa	1,912	–584	254	–565	499	–268	19	247	74	149	117	216	2,070
High income	0	0	0	0	0	0	0	1	0	0	0	6	7
Europe EMU													

Note: The aggregates for the regional development banks, the United Nations, and total net financial flows include amounts for economies that are not specified elsewhere.

Net financial flows from multilateral institutions 6.12

About the data

This table shows concessional and nonconcessional financial flows from the major multilateral institutions—the World Bank, the International Monetary Fund (IMF), regional development banks, United Nations agencies, and regional groups such as the Commission of the European Communities. Much of these data come from the World Bank's Debtor Reporting System.

The multilateral development banks fund their nonconcessional lending operations primarily by selling low-interest, highly rated bonds (the World Bank, for example, has a AAA rating) backed by prudent lending and financial policies and the strong financial backing of their members. These funds are then on-lent at slightly higher interest rates, and with relatively long maturities (15–20 years), to developing countries. Lending terms vary with market conditions and the policies of the banks.

Concessional, or soft, lending by the World Bank Group is carried out through the International Development Association (IDA), although some loans by the International Bank for Reconstruction and Development (IBRD) are made on terms that may qualify as concessional under the Development Assistance Committee (DAC) definition. Eligibility for IDA resources is based on GNP per capita; countries must also meet performance standards assessed by World Bank staff. Since 1 July 1998 the GNP per capita cutoff has been set at $925, measured in 1997 using the Atlas method (see *Users guide*). In exceptional circumstances IDA extends eligibility temporarily to countries that are above the cutoff and are undertaking major adjustment efforts but are not creditworthy for IBRD lending. An exception has also been made for small island economies.

The IMF makes concessional funds available through its Enhanced Structural Adjustment Facility (ESAF), the successor to the Structural Adjustment Facility, and through the IMF Trust Fund. Low-income countries that face protracted balance of payments problems are eligible for ESAF funds.

Regional development banks also maintain concessional windows for funds. According to the DAC definition, concessional flows contain a grant element of at least 25 percent. (The grant element of loans is evaluated assuming a nominal, market interest rate of 10 percent. The grant element of a loan carrying a 10 percent interest rate is nil, and for a grant, which requires no repayment, it is 100 percent.) In the *World Development Indicators* loans from the major regional development banks—the African Development Bank, Asian Development Bank, and Inter-American Development Bank—are recorded according to each institution's classification. In some cases nonconcessional loans by these institutions may be on terms that meet DAC's definition of concessional.

In 1999 all United Nations agencies revised their data to include only regular budgetary expenditures since 1990 (except for the World Food Programme and the United Nations High Commissioner for Refugees, which revised their data from 1996 onward). They did so to avoid double counting extrabudgetary expenditures reported by DAC countries and flows reported by the United Nations.

Figure 6.12

The top 10 recipients of financial flows from United Nations agencies

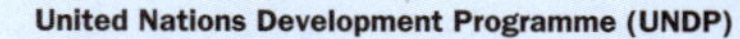

United Nations Development Programme (UNDP)

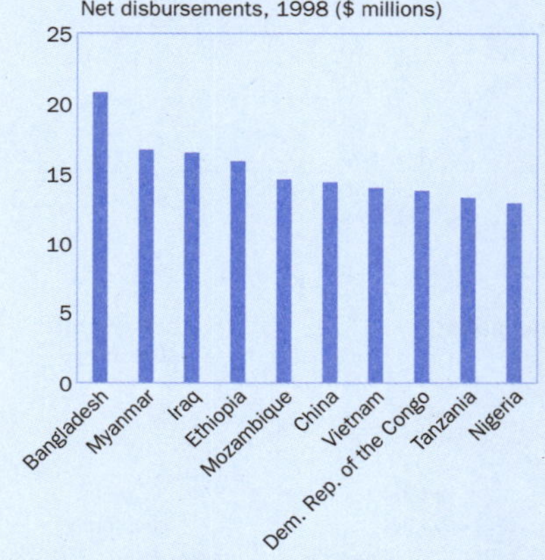

United Nations Children's Fund (UNICEF)

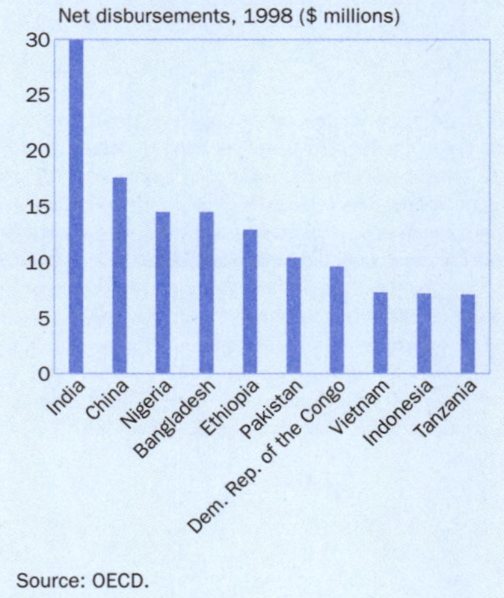

Source: OECD.

Several countries are in the top 10 for both organizations.

Definitions

• **Net financial flows** are disbursements of loans and credits less repayments of principal. • **IDA** is the International Development Association, the soft loan window of the World Bank Group. • **IBRD** is the International Bank for Reconstruction and Development, the founding and largest member of the World Bank Group. • **IMF** is the International Monetary Fund. Its nonconcessional lending consists of the credit it provides to its members, principally to meet their balance of payments needs. It provides concessional assistance through the Enhanced Structural Adjustment Facility. • **Regional development banks** include the African Development Bank, based in Abidjan, Côte d'Ivoire, which lends to all of Africa, including North Africa; the Asian Development Bank, based in Manila, Philippines, which serves countries in South Asia and East Asia and the Pacific; and the Inter-American Development Bank, based in Washington, D.C., which is the principal development bank of the Americas. • **Others** is a residual category in the World Bank's Debtor Reporting System. It includes such institutions as the Caribbean Development Bank, European Investment Bank, and European Development Fund. • **United Nations** includes the United Nations Development Programme (UNDP), United Nations Population Fund (UNFPA), United Nations Children's Fund (UNICEF), World Food Programme (WFP), and other United Nations agencies such as the United Nations High Commissioner for Refugees, United Nations Relief and Works Agency for Palestine Refugees in the Near East, and United Nations Regular Program for Technical Assistance. • **Concessional financial flows** cover disbursements made through concessional lending facilities. • **Nonconcessional financial flows** cover all other disbursements.

Data sources

The data on net financial flows from international financial institutions come from the World Bank's Debtor Reporting System. These data are published in the World Bank's *Global Development Finance 2000*. The data on aid from United Nations agencies come from the DAC chairman's report, *Development Co-operation*. Data are available to registered users from the OECD website at www.oecd.org/dac/htm/online.htm.

6.13 Foreign labor and population in OECD countries

	Foreign population[a]				Foreign labor force[b]		Inflows of foreign population			
	thousands		% of total population		% of total labor force		Total thousands[c]		Asylum seekers thousands	
	1990	1997	1990	1997	1990	1997	1990	1997	1990	1997
Austria	456[d]	733	5.9	9.1	7.4	9.9	..	..	23[e]	7
Belgium	905	903	9.1	8.9	..	7.9	51	49	13	12
Denmark	161	250	3.1	4.7	2.4	..	15	..	5	5
Finland	26	81	0.5	1.6	..	..	7	8	3	1
France	3,597[f]	3,597[f]	6.3	..	6.2	6.1	102[g]	102	55	21
Germany	5,343[h]	7,366	8.4	9.0	7.1	..	842	615	193	104
Ireland	80[i]	114[i]	2.3	3.1	2.6	3.4	..	..	0	4
Italy	781[j]	1,241[j]	1.4	..	..	..	..	..	5[f]	2[f]
Japan	1,075[k]	1,483[k]	0.9	1.2	..	0.2	224	275	..	..
Luxembourg	113	148	29.4	34.9	45.2	55.1	9	10	0	0
Netherlands	692	678	4.6	..	3.1	2.9	81	77	21	34
Norway	143[l]	158	3.4	3.6	2.3	2.8	16	22	4	2
Portugal	108[m]	175[m]	1.1	1.8	1.0	1.8	..	..	0	0
Spain	279[n]	609[n]	0.7	1.5	0.6	1.1	..	..	9[f]	5[f]
Sweden	484	522	5.6	6.0	5.4	5.2	53	33	29	10
Switzerland	1,100[o]	1,341[o]	16.3	19.0	18.9	17.5	101	73	36	24
United Kingdom	1,723	2,066	3.2	3.6	3.3	3.6	..	237	38[p]	42

	Foreign-born population[q]				Foreign-born labor force[r]		Inflows of foreign population			
	thousands		% of total population		% of total labor force		Total thousands		Asylum seekers thousands	
	1990	1997	1990	1997	1990	1997	1990	1997	1990	1997
Australia	*3,753*	*3,908*	*22.3*	*21.1*	*25.7*	24.8	121	86	4[s]	9[s]
Canada	*4,343*	*4,971*	*16.1*	*17.4*	*18.5*	18.5[t]	214	216	37	23
United States[u]	19,767	25,779	7.9	9.7	9.4	11.6	1,537	798	74	80

a. Except for France, Ireland, Portugal, Spain, and the United Kingdom, data are from population registers. Unless otherwise noted, they refer to the population on 31 December of the years indicated. b. Data include the unemployed except for Italy, Luxembourg, the Netherlands, Norway, and the United Kingdom. Data for Austria, Germany, and Luxembourg are from social security registers, those for Denmark from the register of population, and those for Norway from the register of employees. Data for Italy, Portugal, Spain, and Switzerland are from residence or work permits. Figures for Japan and the Netherlands are estimates from national statistical offices. For other countries data are from labor force surveys. c. Data are from population registers except for France (census), Ireland and the United Kingdom (labor force survey), Japan and Switzerland (register of foreigners), and Italy, Portugal, and Spain (residence permits). d. Annual average. e. Data do not include de facto refugees from Bosnia and Herzegovina. f. Data are from the 1990 population census. g. Excludes accompanying dependents. h. Data refer to the Federal Republic of Germany before unification. i. Estimated from the annual labor force survey. j. Data are adjusted to take account of the regularizations in 1987–88 and 1990 and regularization programs in 1995–96. k. Data refer to registered foreign nationals, who include foreigners staying in Japan for more than 90 days. l. Includes asylum seekers whose requests are being processed. m. Includes all foreigners who hold a valid residence permit. n. Data refer to foreigners with a residence permit. Those with permits for fewer than six months and students are excluded. o. Data refer to foreigners with an annual residence permit or with a settlement permit (permanent permit). p. Data are adjusted to include dependents. q. Data are from the latest population census. r. Data are from labor force surveys except for Canada and the United States, for which data are from the latest population census. s. Data refer to principal applicants and do not include dependents. t. Data are from the latest population census. u. Data refer to the fiscal year (October to September).

Foreign labor and population in OECD countries 6.13

About the data

The data in the table are based on national definitions and data collection practices and are not fully comparable across countries. Japan and the European members of the Organisation for Economic Co-operation and Development (OECD) have traditionally defined foreigners by nationality of descent. Australia, Canada, and the United States use place of birth, which is closer to the concept used in the United Nations' definition of the immigrant stock. Few countries, however, apply just one criterion in all circumstances. For this and other reasons, data based on the concept of foreign nationality and data based on the concept of foreign-born cannot be completely reconciled. See the notes to the table for other breaks in comparability between countries and over time.

Data on the size of the foreign labor force are also problematic. Countries use different permit systems to gather information on immigrants. Some countries issue a single permit for residence and work, while others issue separate residence and work permits. Differences in immigration laws across countries, particularly with respect to immigrants' access to the labor market, greatly affect the recording and measurement of migration and reduce the comparability of raw data at the international level. The data exclude temporary visitors and tourists (see table 6.14).

OECD countries are not the only ones that receive substantial migration flows. Migrant workers make up a significant share of the labor force in Gulf countries and in southern Africa, and people are displaced by wars and natural disasters throughout the world. Systematic recording of migration flows is difficult, however, especially in poor countries and those affected by civil disorder.

Figure 6.13

The nationalities of the foreign population in OECD countries in 1997 reflected traditional ties and recent events

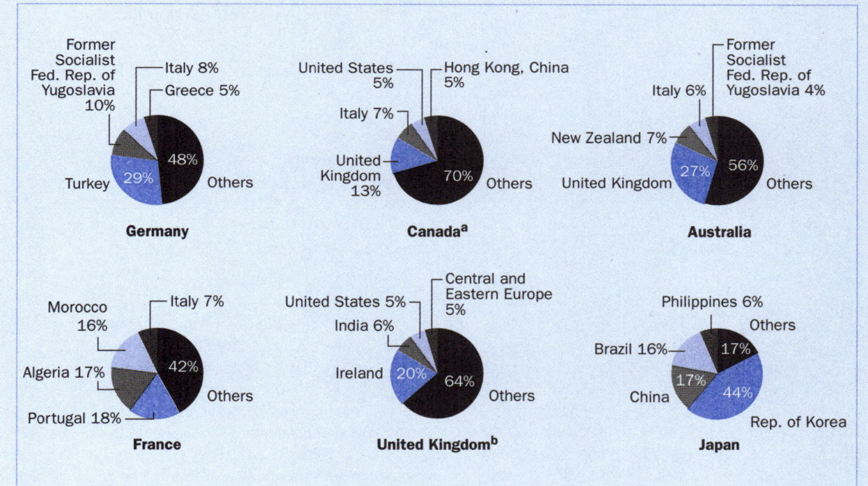

a. Data refer to 1996.
b. Data refer to 1998.
Source: OECD.

A country's stock of foreign population grows through the arrival of immigrants over many years. It reflects the geographical and cultural connections between countries as well as political and economic events.

Definitions

• **Foreign (or foreign-born) population** is the number of foreign or foreign-born residents in a country. • **Foreign (or foreign-born) labor force as a percentage of total labor force** is the share of foreign or foreign-born workers in a country's workforce. • **Inflows of foreign population** are the gross arrivals of immigrants in the country shown. The total does not include asylum seekers, except as noted. • **Asylum seekers** are those who apply for permission to remain in the country for humanitarian reasons.

Data sources

International migration data are collected by the OECD through information provided by national correspondents to the Continuous Reporting System on Migration (SOPEMI) network, which provides an annual overview of trends and policies. The data appear in the OECD's *Trends in International Migration 1999*.

6.14 Travel and tourism

	International tourism				International tourism receipts				International tourism expenditures			
	Inbound tourists thousands		Outbound tourists thousands		$ millions		% of exports		$ millions		% of imports	
	1980	1998	1980	1998	1980	1998	1980	1998	1980	1998	1980	1998
Albania	4	27	..	18	..	54	..	18.3	..	5	..	0.5
Algeria	946	678	698	*1,377*	115	20	0.8	0.2	333	*40*	2.7	*0.5*
Angola	..	52	..	*3*	..	8	..	0.2	..	*70*	..	*1.3*
Argentina	1,120	4,860	..	5,522	345	5,363	3.5	17.2	1,791	2,111	13.6	5.5
Armenia	..	32	..	..	..	10	..	2.8	..	45	..	4.6
Australia	905	4,167	*1,217*	3,161	967	7,335	3.8	10.2	1,749	5,388	6.5	6.9
Austria	13,879	17,352	3,525	*13,263*	6,442	11,184	24.2	11.8	2,847	9,511	9.5	9.8
Azerbaijan	..	170	..	*232*	..	125	..	12.4	..	170	..	7.0
Bangladesh	57	172	..	992	15	51	1.7	0.9	16	198	0.6	2.5
Belarus	..	355	..	*969*	..	22	..	0.3	..	124	..	1.4
Belgium	3,777	6,179	9,565	7,773	1,810	5,437	2.6	2.9	3,272	8,842	4.4	4.9
Benin	39	152	..	*420*	7	33	3.1	6.1	4	7	1.0	0.9
Bolivia	155	434	..	298	40	174	3.9	12.8	52	172	6.2	7.8
Bosnia and Herzegovina	..	100	..	..	..	15	..	..	..	..	..	..
Botswana	236	740	..	*460*	22	175	3.4	7.6	17	126	2.1	5.0
Brazil	1,271	4,818	427	4,598	1,794	3,678	8.2	6.3	1,160	5,731	4.2	7.7
Bulgaria	1,933	3,000	*759*	*3,059*	260	437	2.8	7.9	..	221	..	3.8
Burkina Faso	38	140	..	..	6	39	2.9	9.9	32	*32*	5.5	*5.0*
Burundi	34	14	..	16	22	1	..	1.4	17	12	..	7.0
Cambodia	..	576	..	41	..	157	..	19.3	..	13	..	1.0
Cameroon	86	135	14	..	62	40	3.3	1.7	82	*107*	4.5	*5.2*
Canada	12,876	18,837	*12,833*	17,648	2,284	9,393	3.0	3.8	3,122	10,755	4.4	4.5
Central African Republic	7	20	..	..	3	6	1.5	4.1	18	*39*	5.5	*16.2*
Chad	7	11	..	*10*	3	10	4.2	3.0	14	*24*	17.6	*4.6*
Chile	420	1,757	*379*	1,351	166	1,062	2.8	5.6	195	943	2.8	4.4
China	3,500	25,073	..	8,426	617	12,602	*3.6*	6.1	*66*	9,205	*0.3*	5.5
Hong Kong, China	1,748	9,575	916	4,197	1,317	7,083	5.1	3.4	..	..	..	..
Colombia	553	841	781	*1,140*	357	939	6.7	7.0	250	1,124	4.6	6.4
Congo, Dem. Rep.	23	32	..	..	22	2	0.9	*0.1*	38	*7*	1.6	*0.5*
Congo, Rep.	48	44	..	..	10	3	1.0	0.2	29	*51*	2.8	*3.7*
Costa Rica	345	943	*133*	330	87	829	7.3	12.1	62	445	3.7	6.4
Côte d'Ivoire	194	301	..	*5*	79	108	2.2	2.1	270	237	6.5	5.7
Croatia	..	4,112	..	..	..	2,733	..	31.9	..	600	..	5.6
Cuba	101	1,390	*7*	55	40	1,626	..	..	..	..	..	..
Czech Republic	..	16,325	..	..	..	3,719	..	11.0	..	1,869	..	5.4
Denmark	1,619	2,073	..	4,972	1,337	3,211	*5.6*	5.1	1,560	4,462	*5.8*	7.5
Dominican Republic	383	2,309	257	354	168	2,142	13.2	28.6	166	254	8.7	2.8
Ecuador	243	511	..	330	91	291	3.2	5.8	228	241	7.7	3.8
Egypt, Arab Rep.	1,253	3,213	1,180	*2,921*	808	2,564	12.9	19.0	573	1,153	6.3	5.3
El Salvador	118	542	464	868	7	125	0.6	4.6	106	*75*	9.1	*1.9*
Eritrea	..	188	..	..	..	91	..	70.4	..	..	..	..
Estonia	..	825	..	1,659	..	534	..	12.8	..	133	..	2.8
Ethiopia	42	91	25	140	11	11	1.9	1.1	5	46	0.6	2.5
Finland	1,273	1,858	*291*	4,743	677	1,631	4.0	3.2	544	2,063	3.1	5.3
France	30,100	70,000	7,930	18,077	8,235	29,931	5.4	7.7	6,027	17,791	3.9	5.2
Gabon	17	192	..	..	17	8	0.7	0.3	96	*178*	6.5	*8.2*
Gambia, The	22	91	..	..	18	33	27.2	12.5	1	*16*	0.6	*5.7*
Georgia	..	317	..	433	..	423	..	58.7	..	262	..	18.2
Germany[a]	11,122	16,511	22,473	82,975	6,566	16,429	2.9	2.6	20,599	46,939	9.1	8.0
Ghana	40	335	..	..	1	274	0.1	13.8	27	24	2.3	0.8
Greece	4,796	10,916	1,374	1,935	1,734	5,182	21.3	*25.4*	190	1,756	1.7	*5.2*
Guatemala	466	636	178	391	183	394	10.6	11.3	183	157	9.3	3.1
Guinea	..	99	..	..	..	1	..	0.1	..	27	..	2.8
Guinea-Bissau	..	..	..	..	..	..	..	..	..	..	..	..
Haiti	138	150	..	..	65	58	21.3	12.1	41	37	8.5	3.6
Honduras	122	318	..	202	27	164	2.9	6.9	31	61	2.7	2.2

Travel and tourism 6.14

	International tourism				International tourism receipts				International tourism expenditures			
	Inbound tourists thousands		Outbound tourists thousands		$ millions		% of exports		$ millions		% of imports	
	1980	1998	1980	1998	1980	1998	1980	1998	1980	1998	1980	1998
Hungary	9,413	15,000	5,164	12,317	160	2,504	*2.5*	9.8	88	1,205	*0.9*	4.4
India	1,194	2,359	1,017	3,811	1,150	3,124	10.2	6.6	113	1,713	0.7	2.9
Indonesia	527	4,606	635	*2,200*	246	4,045	*1.2*	7.4	375	2,102	*3.0*	4.8
Iran, Islamic Rep.	156	1,008	428	*1,354*	54	441	0.4	3.1	1,700	153	10.6	0.9
Iraq	1,222	51	443	..	170	13	..	..	..	..	..	..
Ireland	2,258	6,064	669	*3,053*	472	3,252	4.9	4.5	742	2,374	6.2	3.8
Israel	1,116	1,942	513	2,983	903	2,656	10.4	8.3	533	2,376	4.6	6.6
Italy	22,087	34,829	*23,994*	14,327	8,213	29,809	8.4	9.6	1,907	17,579	1.7	6.5
Jamaica	395	1,225	..	..	242	1,197	17.7	35.4	12	198	0.9	5.0
Japan	1,317	4,106	5,224	15,806	644	3,742	0.4	0.9	4,593	28,815	2.9	7.9
Jordan	393	1,256	720	1,347	431	853	36.5	23.5	301	451	12.5	8.7
Kazakhstan	..	..	..	..	..	289	..	4.3	..	*445*	..	*5.4*
Kenya	372	894	..	*350*	220	283	11.0	9.9	33	147	1.2	4.0
Korea, Dem. Rep.	..	130	..	..	..	..	..	..	..	..	..	..
Korea, Rep.	976	4,250	339	3,067	369	5,890	1.9	3.8	350	2,069	1.4	1.8
Kuwait	108	79	*230*	..	377	207	1.7	1.8	1,339	2,517	13.6	19.1
Kyrgyz Republic	..	59	..	32	..	7	..	1.2	..	*4*	..	*0.5*
Lao PDR	..	200	..	..	..	80	..	16.4	..	23	..	3.8
Latvia	..	567	..	1,961	..	182	..	6.0	..	305	..	7.8
Lebanon	..	631	..	1,650	..	1,285	..	70.7	..	..	..	..
Lesotho	73	150	..	..	12	24	13.3	9.7	8	13	1.7	1.4
Libya	126	32	95	*650*	10	18	0.0	..	470	143	3.7	..
Lithuania	..	1,416	..	3,241	..	460	..	9.1	..	292	..	4.6
Macedonia, FYR	..	..	..	..	..	..	..	..	..	..	..	..
Madagascar	13	121	..	*35*	5	92	1.0	11.1	31	119	2.9	10.5
Malawi	46	205	..	..	9	8	2.9	1.4	10	17	2.1	1.3
Malaysia	2,105	5,551	1,738	25,631	265	2,456	1.9	3.4	470	*2,478*	3.5	*2.7*
Mali	27	83	..	..	15	50	5.7	7.8	20	29	3.8	3.1
Mauritania	..	..	..	..	7	21	2.8	5.3	17	43	3.8	9.1
Mauritius	115	558	33	143	45	503	7.8	18.5	27	194	3.9	7.1
Mexico	11,945	19,810	3,322	9,803	5,393	7,897	23.8	6.1	4,174	4,268	15.1	3.1
Moldova	..	20	..	*35*	..	4	..	0.5	..	..	..	..
Mongolia	195	135	..	..	..	35	..	6.5	..	45	..	6.7
Morocco	1,425	3,243	578	1,359	397	1,745	12.3	17.5	98	424	1.9	3.7
Mozambique	..	..	..	..	..	..	..	..	..	..	..	..
Myanmar	38	201	..	..	10	35	1.9	2.1	3	27	0.4	1.0
Namibia	..	560	..	..	..	288	..	17.9	..	88	..	4.6
Nepal	163	435	*23*	*110*	52	124	23.3	11.2	26	78	7.1	4.7
Netherlands	2,784	9,320	6,749	12,860	1,668	6,803	1.8	3.0	4,664	11,174	5.1	5.6
New Zealand	465	1,485	454	1,166	211	1,726	3.3	10.9	534	1,405	7.7	8.9
Nicaragua	..	406	..	422	22	90	4.4	11.8	..	70	..	4.2
Niger	20	19	..	10	3	18	0.5	5.4	18	25	1.9	5.2
Nigeria	86	739	..	..	48	142	0.2	1.4	780	1,567	3.9	11.7
Norway	1,252	2,829	246	3,120	751	2,212	2.8	4.0	1,310	*4,496*	5.5	*8.6*
Oman	60	612	..	..	..	112	..	*1.4*	..	*47*	..	*0.8*
Pakistan	299	429	104	..	154	98	5.2	1.0	90	352	1.6	2.7
Panama	392	431	*113*	211	167	379	4.9	4.7	56	176	1.7	2.0
Papua New Guinea	40	67	..	*63*	12	75	1.2	3.6	18	52	1.4	2.8
Paraguay	302	350	..	498	91	710	13.0	18.2	35	249	2.7	5.8
Peru	373	833	127	*577*	208	878	4.5	11.7	107	429	2.7	4.1
Philippines	1,008	2,149	461	1,817	320	2,413	4.4	6.5	105	1,950	1.1	4.9
Poland	5,664	18,780	6,852	49,328	282	7,946	1.8	18.3	357	4,430	2.0	8.5
Portugal	2,730	11,295	..	*2,425*	1,147	4,853	17.2	14.0	290	2,535	2.9	5.6
Puerto Rico	1,639	3,396	2,758	1,250	619	2,233	..	..	400	874	..	..
Romania	3,270	2,966	1,711	6,893	324	260	2.7	2.7	73	451	0.5	3.5
Russian Federation	..	15,805	..	11,711	..	6,508	..	7.4	..	8,279	..	11.2

6.14 Travel and tourism

	International tourism				International tourism receipts				International tourism expenditures			
	Inbound tourists thousands		Outbound tourists thousands		$ millions		% of exports		$ millions		% of imports	
	1980	1998	1980	1998	1980	1998	1980	1998	1980	1998	1980	1998
Rwanda	30	2	..	..	4	19	2.4	17.0	11	17	3.4	3.5
Saudi Arabia	2,475	3,700	..	..	1,344	1,462	1.3	3.3	2,453	..	4.4	..
Senegal	186	352	..	..	68	178	8.4	13.5	45	*53*	3.7	*3.4*
Sierra Leone	46	50	..	..	10	57	3.6	51.1	8	*2*	1.7	*0.9*
Singapore	2,562	5,631	..	3,745	1,433	5,162	5.9	4.0	322	*3,224*	1.3	*2.2*
Slovak Republic	..	896	..	414	..	489	..	3.8	..	475	..	3.1
Slovenia	..	977	..	..	..	1,117	..	10.0	..	575	..	5.0
South Africa	700	5,898	*572*	*3,080*	652	2,738	2.3	7.9	756	1,842	3.4	5.6
Spain	22,388	47,749	18,022	13,203	6,968	29,737	21.7	18.7	1,229	5,005	3.2	3.2
Sri Lanka	322	381	138	518	111	231	8.6	4.1	34	202	1.5	3.0
Sudan	25	39	..	200	52	8	6.7	1.3	*74*	30	*3.9*	1.5
Sweden	1,366	2,568	2,941	11,422	962	4,189	2.5	4.1	1,235	7,723	3.1	8.7
Switzerland	8,873	10,900	4,451	*12,213*	3,149	7,815	6.5	6.5	2,357	7,126	4.5	6.6
Syrian Arab Republic	1,239	1,267	*1,189*	2,750	156	1,190	6.3	24.1	177	580	3.9	12.1
Tajikistan	..	511	..	..	..	..	..	..	..	..	..	..
Tanzania	84	450	..	150	20	570	2.7	49.8	20	493	1.4	20.9
Thailand	1,859	7,843	497	1,412	867	5,934	10.9	9.0	244	1,448	2.4	3.0
Togo	92	94	..	..	13	15	2.4	2.2	22	*19*	3.2	*2.3*
Trinidad and Tobago	199	347	206	250	151	201	4.8	6.9	140	67	5.8	2.1
Tunisia	1,602	4,718	478	1,526	601	1,557	18.4	18.4	55	168	1.5	1.8
Turkey	921	8,960	1,795	4,601	327	7,809	9.0	14.3	115	1,754	1.4	3.2
Turkmenistan	..	300	..	357	..	192	..	31.3	..	*125*	..	*8.9*
Uganda	36	238	..	..	5	142	1.5	22.4	18	*137*	4.1	*8.3*
Ukraine	..	6,208	..	*10,326*	..	5,407	..	30.7	..	4,482	..	23.8
United Arab Emirates	300	2,184	..	..	..	562	..	..	..	..	..	..
United Kingdom	12,420	25,745	15,507	50,872	6,932	20,978	4.7	5.6	6,893	32,267	5.1	8.4
United States	22,500	46,395	22,721	*52,735*	10,058	71,250	3.7	7.6	10,385	56,105	3.6	5.1
Uruguay	1,067	2,163	640	654	298	695	19.5	16.4	203	265	9.5	5.9
Uzbekistan	..	272	..	..	..	21	..	0.7	..	..	..	..
Venezuela, RB	215	837	747	524	243	1,233	1.2	6.5	1,880	2,427	12.4	12.2
Vietnam	..	1,520	..	168	..	86	..	0.7	..	..	..	..
West Bank and Gaza	..	..	..	..	..	..	..	..	..	..	..	..
Yemen, Rep.	39	88	..	..	24	84	..	4.9	53	83	..	3.0
Yugoslavia, FR (Serb./Mont.)	..	283	..	..	..	35	..	..	..	..	..	..
Zambia	87	362	..	..	20	75	1.2	7.1	57	*59*	3.2	*4.6*
Zimbabwe	243	1,984	326	*123*	38	158	2.4	6.2	140	127	8.1	4.6
World	266,338 s	634,659 s	158,991 s	442,737 s	101,399 s	439,969 s	4.6 w	6.3 w	102,144 s	365,243 s	4.8 w	6.1 w
Low income	8,348	45,439	2,121	14,957	3,193	23,731	3.3	6.0	2,528	17,191	3.1	5.0
Excl. China & India	3,654	17,877	1,104	2,720	1,426	8,005	2.0	5.8	2,415	6,273	3.6	5.0
Middle income	62,781	198,850	33,235	161,250	19,673	107,275	4.5	8.8	20,343	56,498	5.1	5.2
Lower middle income	21,407	75,412	9,147	38,237	7,001	44,533	5.0	10.2	5,751	26,408	4.0	6.7
Upper middle income	41,374	123,438	24,088	123,013	12,672	62,742	4.2	8.0	14,592	30,090	5.6	4.3
Low & middle income	71,129	244,289	35,356	176,207	22,866	131,006	4.3	8.1	22,871	73,689	4.8	5.2
East Asia & Pacific	10,546	52,938	3,678	40,661	2,849	34,197	3.9	5.6	1,584	17,008	2.1	4.0
Europe & Central Asia	21,205	97,306	15,522	92,965	1,353	40,185	2.9	12.0	633	25,102	1.4	7.7
Latin America & Carib.	22,886	51,623	9,907	27,911	11,314	34,549	9.3	9.0	11,343	20,416	8.8	5.0
Middle East & N. Africa	11,096	22,267	4,620	8,632	4,260	11,714	2.3	9.9	6,323	3,297	4.6	..
South Asia	2,086	4,182	1,259	5,358	1,492	3,941	8.6	5.6	283	2,585	0.9	2.9
Sub-Saharan Africa	3,310	15,973	370	680	1,598	6,420	1.9	7.3	2,705	5,281	3.7	6.4
High income	195,209	390,370	123,635	266,530	78,533	308,963	4.7	5.8	79,273	291,554	4.8	6.3
Europe EMU	113,018	221,946	68,933	141,098	42,198	139,375	5.8	6.5	42,121	123,813	5.6	6.2

a. Data prior to 1990 refer to the Federal Republic of Germany before unification.

Travel and tourism 6.14

About the data

The data in the table are from the World Tourism Organization. They are obtained primarily from questionnaires sent to government offices, supplemented with data published by official sources. Although the World Tourism Organization reports that progress has been made in harmonizing definitions and measurement units, differences in national practices still prevent full international comparability.

The data on international inbound and outbound tourists refer to the number of arrivals and departures of visitors within the reference period, not to the number of people traveling. Thus a person who makes several trips to a country during a given period is counted each time as a new arrival. International visitors include tourists (overnight visitors), same-day visitors, cruise passengers, and crew members.

Regional and income group aggregates are based on the World Bank's classification of countries and differ from those shown in the World Tourism Organization's *Yearbook of Tourism Statistics*. Countries not shown in the table but for which data are available are included in the regional and income group totals. World totals are calculated by the World Tourism Organization and include all reporting countries as well as countries not separately reported on by the organization. Thus world totals may differ from the sums of the group totals.

Figure 6.14

More and more tourists are from developing economies

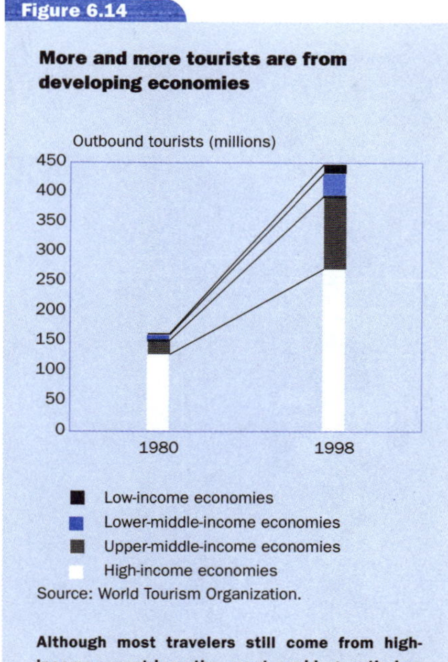

Source: World Tourism Organization.

Although most travelers still come from high-income countries, the most rapid growth has been among travelers from the poorest countries. The number of tourists from these countries increased by 600 percent between 1980 and 1998.

Definitions

• **International inbound tourists** are the number of visitors who travel to a country other than that where they have their usual residence for a period not exceeding 12 months and whose main purpose in visiting is other than an activity remunerated from within the country visited. • **International outbound tourists** are the number of departures that people make from their country of usual residence to any other country for any purpose other than a remunerated activity in the country visited. • **International tourism receipts** are expenditures by international inbound visitors, including payments to national carriers for international transport. These receipts should include any other prepayment made for goods or services received in the destination country. They also may include receipts from same-day visitors, except in cases where these are so important as to justify a separate classification. Their share in exports is calculated as a ratio to exports of goods and services. • **International tourism expenditures** are expenditures of international outbound visitors in other countries, including payments to foreign carriers for international transport. These may include expenditures by residents traveling abroad as same-day visitors, except in cases where these are so important as to justify a separate classification. Their share in imports is calculated as a ratio to imports of goods and services.

Data sources

The visitor and expenditure data are available in the World Tourism Organization's *Yearbook of Tourism Statistics* and *Compendium of Tourism Statistics, 1993–97*. The data in the table were updated from electronic files provided by the World Tourism Organization. Export and import data are from the International Monetary Fund's *International Financial Statistics* and World Bank staff estimates.

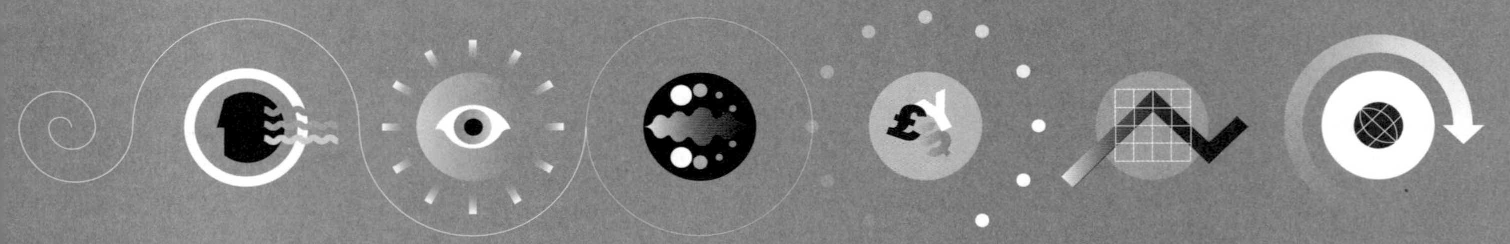

Statistical methods

This section describes some of the statistical procedures used in preparing the *World Development Indicators.* It covers the methods employed for calculating regional and income group aggregates and for calculating growth rates, and it describes the World Bank's Atlas method for deriving the conversion factor used to estimate GNP and GNP per capita in U.S. dollars. Other statistical procedures and calculations are described in the *About the data* sections that follow each table.

Aggregation rules

Aggregates based on the World Bank's regional and income classifications of economies appear at the end of most tables. These classifications are shown on the front and back cover flaps of the book. This year's *World Development Indicators,* like last year's, includes aggregates for the member countries of the European Monetary Union (EMU). Members of the EMU on 1 January 2000 were Austria, Belgium, Finland, France, Germany, Ireland, Italy, Luxembourg, the Netherlands, Portugal, and Spain. Other classifications, such as the European Union and regional trade blocs, are documented in *About the data* for the tables in which they appear.

Because of missing data, aggregates for groups of economies should be treated as approximations of unknown totals or average values. Regional and income group aggregates are based on the largest available set of data, including values for the 148 economies shown in the main tables, other economies shown in table 1.6, and Taiwan, China. The aggregation rules are intended to yield estimates for a consistent set of economies from one period to the next and for all indicators. Small differences between sums of subgroup aggregates and overall totals and averages may occur because of the approximations used. In addition, compilation errors and data reporting practices may cause discrepancies in theoretically identical aggregates such as world exports and world imports.

Five methods of aggregation are used in the *World Development Indicators:*

- For group and world totals denoted in the tables by a *t,* missing data are imputed based on the relationship of the sum of available data to the total in the year of the previous estimate. The imputation process works forward and backward from 1995. Missing values in 1995 are imputed using one of several proxy variables for which complete data are available in that year. The imputed value is calculated so that it (or its proxy) bears the same relationship to the total of available data. Imputed values are usually not calculated if missing data account for more than a third of the total in the benchmark year. The variables used as proxies are GNP in U.S. dollars, total population, exports and imports of goods and services in U.S. dollars, and value added in agriculture, industry, manufacturing, and services in U.S. dollars.
- Aggregates marked by an *s* are sums of available data. Missing values are not imputed. Sums are not computed if more than a third of the observations in the series or a proxy for the series are missing in a given year.
- Aggregates of ratios are generally calculated as weighted averages of the ratios (indicated by *w*) using the value of the denominator or, in some cases, another indicator as a weight. The aggregate ratios are based on available data, including data for economies not shown in the main tables. Missing values are assumed to have the same average value as the available data. No aggregate is calculated if missing data account for more than a third of the value of weights in the benchmark year. In a few cases the aggregate ratio may be computed as the ratio of group totals after imputing values for missing data according to the above rules for computing totals.
- Aggregate growth rates are generally calculated as a weighted average of growth rates (and indicated by a *w*). In a few cases growth rates may be computed from time series of group totals. Growth rates are not calculated if more than half of the observations in a period are missing. For further discussion of methods of computing growth rates see below.
- Aggregates denoted by an *m* are medians of the values shown in the table. No value is shown if more than half of the observations for countries with a population of more than 1 million are missing.

Exceptions to the rules occur throughout the book. Depending on the judgment of World Bank analysts, the aggregates may be based on as little as 50 percent of the available data. In other cases, where missing or excluded values are judged to be small or irrelevant, aggregates are based only on the data shown in the tables.

Growth rates

Growth rates are calculated as annual averages and represented as percentages. Except where noted, growth rates of values are computed from constant price series. Three principal methods are used to calculate growth rates: least squares, exponential endpoint, and geometric endpoint. Rates of change from one period to the next are calculated as proportional changes from the earlier period.

Least-squares growth rate. Least-squares growth rates are used wherever there is a sufficiently long time series to permit a reliable calculation. No growth rate is calculated if more than half the observations in a period are missing.

The least-squares growth rate, *r,* is estimated by fitting a linear regression trend line to the logarithmic annual values of the variable in the relevant period. More specifically, the regression equation takes the form

$$\ln X_t = a + bt,$$

which is equivalent to the logarithmic transformation of the compound growth equation,

$$X_t = X_o (1 + r)^t.$$

Statistical methods

In this equation X is the variable, t is time, and $a = \ln X_0$ and $b = \ln(1 + r)$ are parameters to be estimated. If b^* is the least-squares estimate of b, the average annual growth rate, r, is obtained as $[\exp(b^*) - 1]$ and is multiplied by 100 to express it as a percentage.

The calculated growth rate is an average rate that is representative of the available observations over the entire period. It does not necessarily match the actual growth rate between any two periods.

Exponential growth rate. The growth rate between two points in time for certain demographic indicators, notably labor force and population, is calculated from the equation

$$r = \ln(p_n/p_1)/n,$$

where p_n and p_1 are the last and first observations in the period, n is the number of years in the period, and ln is the natural logarithm operator. This growth rate is based on a model of continuous, exponential growth between two points in time. It does not take into account the intermediate values of the series. Nor does it correspond to the annual rate of change measured at a one-year interval, which is given by $(p_n - p_{n-1})/p_{n-1}$.

Geometric growth rate. The geometric growth rate is applicable to compound growth over discrete periods, such as the payment and reinvestment of interest or dividends. Although continuous growth, as modeled by the exponential growth rate, may be more realistic, most economic phenomena are measured only at intervals, a case in which the compound growth model is appropriate. The average growth rate over n periods is calculated as

$$r = \exp[\ln(p_n/p_1)/n] - 1.$$

Like the exponential growth rate, it does not take into account intermediate values of the series.

World Bank Atlas method

In calculating GNP and GNP per capita in U.S. dollars for certain operational purposes, the World Bank uses a synthetic exchange rate commonly called the Atlas conversion factor. The purpose of the Atlas conversion factor is to reduce the impact of exchange rate fluctuations in the cross-country comparison of national incomes.

The Atlas conversion factor for any year is the average of a country's exchange rate (or alternative conversion factor) for that year and its exchange rates for the two preceding years, adjusted for the difference between the rate of inflation in the country and that in the G-5 countries (France, Germany, Japan, the United Kingdom, and the United States). A country's inflation rate is measured by the change in its GNP deflator.

The inflation rate for G-5 countries, representing international inflation, is measured by the change in the SDR deflator. (Special drawing rights, or SDRs, are the IMF's unit of account.) The SDR deflator is calculated as a weighted average of the G-5 countries' GNP deflators in SDR terms, the weights being the amount of each country's currency in one SDR unit. Weights vary over time because both the composition of the SDR and the relative exchange rates for each currency change. The SDR deflator is calculated in SDR terms first and then converted to U.S. dollars using the SDR to dollar Atlas conversion factor. The Atlas conversion factor is then applied to a country's GNP. The resulting GNP in U.S. dollars is divided by the midyear population for the latest of the three years to derive GNP per capita.

When official exchange rates are deemed to be unreliable or unrepresentative of the effective exchange rate during a period, an alternative estimate of the exchange rate is used in the Atlas formula (see below).

The following formulas describe the calculation of the Atlas conversion factor for year t:

$$e_t^* = \frac{1}{3}\left[e_{t-2}\left(\frac{p_t}{p_{t-2}} \Big/ \frac{p_t^{S\$}}{p_{t-2}^{S\$}}\right) + e_{t-1}\left(\frac{p_t}{p_{t-1}} \Big/ \frac{p_t^{S\$}}{p_{t-1}^{S\$}}\right) + e_t\right]$$

and the calculation of GNP per capita in U.S. dollars for year t:

$$Y_t^{\$} = (Y_t/N_t)/e_t^*,$$

where e_t^* is the Atlas conversion factor (national currency to the U.S. dollar) for year t, e_t is the average annual exchange rate (national currency to the U.S. dollar) for year t, p_t is the GNP deflator for year t, $p_t^{S\$}$ is the SDR deflator in U.S. dollar terms for year t, $Y_t^{\$}$ is the Atlas GNP in U.S. dollars in year t, Y_t is current GNP (local currency) for year t, and N_t is the midyear population for year t.

Alternative conversion factors

The World Bank systematically assesses the appropriateness of official exchange rates as conversion factors. An alternative conversion factor is used when the official exchange rate is judged to diverge by an exceptionally large margin from the rate effectively applied to domestic transactions of foreign currencies and traded products. This applies to only a small number of countries, as shown in *Primary data documentation*. Alternative conversion factors are used in the Atlas methodology and elsewhere in the *World Development Indicators* as single-year conversion factors.

Primary data documentation

The World Bank is not a primary data collection agency for most areas other than living standards surveys and debt. As a major user of socioeconomic data, however, the World Bank places particular emphasis on data documentation to inform users of data in economic analysis and policymaking. The tables in this section provide information on the sources, treatment, and currentness of the principal demographic, economic, and environmental indicators in the *World Development Indicators.*

Differences in the methods and conventions used by the primary data collectors—usually national statistical agencies, central banks, and customs services—may give rise to significant discrepancies over time both among and within countries. Delays in reporting data and the use of old surveys as the base for current estimates may severely compromise the quality of national data.

Although data quality is improving in some countries, many developing countries lack the resources to train and maintain the skilled staff and obtain the equipment needed to measure and report demographic, economic, and environmental trends in an accurate and timely way. The World Bank recognizes the need for reliable data to measure living standards, track and evaluate economic trends, and plan and monitor development projects.

In November 1999 representatives of the World Bank, the International Monetary Fund, the Organisation for Economic Co-operation and Development, and the United Nations came together with policymakers and statisticians from developing countries to discuss means of improving the quality of statistics and increasing the capacity of developing countries to use statistical information effectively in setting development policies. A consortium of interested organizations and government agencies has been established—Partnership in Statistics for Development in the 21st Century, or Paris21. The objective of Paris21 is to increase the resources available for training, technical assistance, and reform of statistical systems in developing countries. More information on Paris21 can be found on the consortium's website (www.paris21.org).

Primary data documentation

	National currency	Fiscal year end	National accounts					Balance of payments and trade			Government finance	IMF special data dissemination
			Reporting period[a]	Base year	SNA price valuation	Alternative conversion factor	PPP survey year	Balance of Payments Manual in use	External debt	System of trade	Accounting concept	
Albania	Albanian lek	Dec. 31	CY	1993[c]	VAP		1996	BPM5	Actual	G		
Algeria	Algerian dinar	Dec. 31	CY	1980	VAB			BPM5	Actual	S		
Angola	Angolan adjusted kwanza	Dec. 31	CY	1997	VAP	1991–98		BPM4	Actual	S		
Argentina	Argentine peso	Dec. 31	CY	1993	VAB	1971–81	1996	BPM5	Actual	S	C	S*
Armenia	Armenian dram	Dec. 31	CY	1994[c]	VAB	1990–95	1996	BPM5	Actual	G		
Australia	Australian dollar	Jun. 30	FY	1989	VAP		1996	BPM5		G	C	S
Austria	Austrian schilling[b]	Dec. 31	CY	1983	VAP		1996	BPM5		S	C	S
Azerbaijan	Azeri manat	Dec. 31	CY	1998[c]	VAP	1987–98	1996	BPM4	Actual	S		
Bangladesh	Bangladesh taka	Jun. 30	FY	1990[c]	VAP	1971–75	1993	BPM5	Actual	G		
Belarus	Belarussian ruble	Dec. 31	CY	1990[c]	VAB	1987–98	1996	BPM5	Actual	G	C	
Belgium	Belgian franc[b]	Dec. 31	CY	1990	VAP		1996	BPM5		S	C	S
Benin	CFA franc	Dec. 31	CY	1985	VAP	1992	1993	BPM4	Actual	S		
Bolivia	Boliviano	Dec. 31	CY	1990	VAP	1960–85	1996	BPM4	Actual	S	C	
Bosnia and Herzegovina	Convertible mark	Dec. 31	CY	..	..			BPM5	Estimate			
Botswana	Botswana pula	Jun. 30	FY	1986	VAP		1993	BPM5	Actual	G	B	
Brazil	Brazilian real	Dec. 31	CY	1995	VAB		1996	BPM5	Preliminary	S	C	
Bulgaria	Bulgarian leva	Dec. 31	CY	1990[c]	VAP	1985–92	1996	BPM5	Preliminary	G	C	
Burkina Faso	CFA franc	Dec. 31	CY	1985	VAB	1992–93		BPM4	Actual	S	C	
Burundi	Burundi franc	Dec. 31	CY	1980	VAB			BPM5	Actual	S		
Cambodia	Cambodian riel	Dec. 31	CY	1989	VAP			BPM5	Actual	S		
Cameroon	CFA franc	Jun. 30	FY	1980	VAB	1970–98	1993	BPM5	Preliminary	S	C	
Canada	Canadian dollar	Mar. 31	CY	1992[c]	VAB		1996	BPM5		G	C	S*
Central African Republic	CFA franc	Dec. 31	CY	1987	VAB			BPM4	Actual	S		
Chad	CFA franc	Dec. 31	CY	1995	VAB			BPM4	Estimate	S	C	
Chile	Chilean peso	Dec. 31	CY	1986	VAP	1993–98	1996	BPM5	Actual	S	C	S
China	Chinese yuan	Dec. 31	CY	1990	VAP	1987–93	1993	BPM5	Preliminary	S	B	
Hong Kong, China	Hong Kong dollar	Dec. 31	CY	1990	VAB		1993	BPM4		G		S*
Colombia	Colombian peso	Dec. 31	CY	1994	VAP	1991–94	1980	BPM5	Estimate	S	C	S*
Congo, Dem. Rep.	New zaire	Dec. 31	CY	1987	VAP	1993–98		BPM5	Estimate	S	C	
Congo, Rep.	CFA franc	Dec. 31	CY	1978	VAP	1993	1993	BPM4	Estimate	S		
Costa Rica	Costa Rican colon	Dec. 31	CY	1966	VAP		1980	BPM4	Actual	S	C	
Côte d'Ivoire	CFA franc	Dec. 31	CY	1986	VAP		1993	BPM5	Estimate	S	C	
Croatia	Croatian kuna	Dec. 31	CY	1997[c]	VAB		1996	BPM5	Actual	G	C	S*
Cuba	Cuban peso	Dec. 31	CY	..	..					S		
Czech Republic	Czech koruna	Dec. 31	CY	1995[c]	VAP		1996	BPM5	Preliminary	G	C	S
Denmark	Danish krone	Dec. 31	CY	1990	VAB		1996	BPM5		G	C	S
Dominican Republic	Dominican peso	Dec. 31	CY	1990	VAP		1980	BPM5	Actual	G	C	
Ecuador	Ecuadorian sucre	Dec. 31	CY	1975	VAP		1996	BPM5	Estimate	S	B	S
Egypt, Arab Rep.	Egyptian pound	Jun. 30	FY	1992	VAB	1965–91	1993	BPM5	Actual	S	C	
El Salvador	Salvadoran colone	Dec. 31	CY	1990	VAP	1982–90	1980	BPM5	Actual	S	B	S
Eritrea	Eritrean nakfa	Dec. 31	CY	1992	VAB			BPM4	Actual			
Estonia	Estonian kroon	Dec. 31	CY	1995[c]	VAB	1990–95	1996	BPM5	Actual	G	C	S
Ethiopia	Ethiopian birr	Jul. 7	FY	1981	VAB	1989–98	1985	BPM5	Actual	G	B	
Finland	Finnish markka[b]	Dec. 31	CY	1990	VAB		1993	BPM5		G	C	S
France	French franc[b]	Dec. 31	CY	1980	VAP		1996	BPM5		S	C	S
Gabon	CFA franc	Dec. 31	CY	1991	VAP	1993	1993	BPM5	Actual	S	B	
Gambia, The	Gambian dalasi	Jun. 30	CY	1987	VAB			BPM5	Actual	G	B	
Georgia	Georgian lari	Dec. 31	CY	1994[c]	VAB	1990–98	1996	BPM4	Actual	G		
Germany	Deutsche mark[b]	Dec. 31	CY	1991	VAP		1996	BPM5		S	C	S
Ghana	Ghanaian cedi	Dec. 31	CY	1975	VAP	1973–87		BPM5	Actual	G	C	
Greece	Greek drachma	Dec. 31	CY	1990	VAB		1993	BPM4	Estimate	S	C	
Guatemala	Guatemalan quetzal	Dec. 31	CY	1958	VAP	1985–86	1980	BPM5	Actual	S	B	
Guinea	Guinean franc	Dec. 31	CY	1994	VAB		1993	BPM5	Estimate	S	C	
Guinea-Bissau	CFA franc	Dec. 31	CY	1986	VAB	1970–86		BPM5	Preliminary	S		
Haiti	Haitian gourde	Sep. 30	FY	1976	VAP	1991–97		BPM5	Preliminary	G		
Honduras	Honduran lempira	Dec. 31	CY	1978	VAB	1988–89	1980	BPM5	Actual	S		

	Latest population census	Latest household or demographic survey	Vital registration complete	Latest agricultural census	Latest industrial data	Latest water withdrawal data	Latest survey of scientists and engineers engaged in R&D	Latest survey of expenditure for R&D
Albania	1989	LSMS, 1996	Yes	1995	1990	1995		
Algeria	1998	PAPCHILD, 1992		1973	1996	1990		
Angola	1970			1964–65		1987		
Argentina	1991		Yes	1988	1993	1995	1995	1995
Armenia	1989		Yes		1991	1994		
Australia	1996		Yes	1990	1997	1995	1996	1996
Austria	1991		Yes	1990	1997	1995	1993	1997
Azerbaijan	1999		Yes			1995		
Bangladesh	1991	DHS, 1996–97		1977	1997	1990	1995	1995
Belarus	1989		Yes	1994		1990	1996	1996
Belgium	1991		Yes	1990	1997	1980	1996	1995
Benin	1992	DHS, 1996		1992	1981	1994	1989	1989
Bolivia	1992	DHS, 1998			1995	1990	1996	1990
Bosnia and Herzegovina	1991		Yes		1991			
Botswana	1991	DHS, 1988		1993	1985	1992		
Brazil	1991	DHS, 1996		1996	1994	1992	1995	1996
Bulgaria	1992	LSMS, 1995	Yes		1996	1988	1996	1996
Burkina Faso	1996	DHS, 1998		1993	1997	1992		1997
Burundi	1990				1991	1987	1989	1989
Cambodia	1998					1987		
Cameroon	1987	DHS, 1998		1972–73	1996	1987		
Canada	1996		Yes	1991	1997	1990	1995	1997
Central African Republic	1988	DHS, 1994–95			1993	1987	1990	
Chad	1993	DHS, 1996–97				1990		
Chile	1992		Yes	1997	1997	1990	1994	1996
China	1990	Population, 1995		1996	1996	1993	1996	1997
Hong Kong, China	1996		Yes		1995		1995	
Colombia	1993	DHS, 1995		1988	1996	1996		1982
Congo, Dem. Rep.	1984			1990		1994		
Congo, Rep.	1984			1986	1988	1987		1984
Costa Rica	1984	CDC, 1993	Yes	1973	1997	1997	1996	1991
Côte d'Ivoire	1998	DHS, 1998		1974–75	1997	1987		
Croatia	1991		Yes		1992	1996	1996	1996
Cuba	1981		Yes		1989	1995	1995	1989
Czech Republic	1991	CDC, 1993	Yes	1990		1995	1997	1997
Denmark	1991		Yes	1989	1997	1995	1997	1996
Dominican Republic	1993	DHS, 1996		1971	1984	1994		
Ecuador	1990	LSMS, 1995		1997	1996	1997	1997	1997
Egypt, Arab Rep.	1996	DHS, 1997	Yes	1989–90	1997	1993	1991	1996
El Salvador	1992	CDC, 1994		1970–71	1997	1992	1992	
Eritrea	1984	DHS, 1995						
Estonia	1989		Yes	1994		1995	1997	1997
Ethiopia	1994	Family and fertility, 1990		1989–92	1996	1987		
Finland	1990		Yes	1990		1995	1995	1997
France	1999	Income, 1989	Yes	1988	1997	1995	1996	1997
Gabon	1993			1974–75	1982	1987	1987	1986
Gambia, The	1993				1982	1990		
Georgia	1989		Yes			1990	1991	
Germany			Yes	1993		1990	1995	1997
Ghana	1984	DHS, 1993		1984	1995	1970		
Greece	1991		Yes	1993	1997	1990	1993	1993
Guatemala	1994	DHS, 1997	Yes	1979	1988	1992	1988	1988
Guinea	1996	SDA, 1994–95		1989		1987	1984	1984
Guinea-Bissau	1991	SDA, 1991		1988		1991		
Haiti	1982	DHS, 1994–95		1971	1996	1991		
Honduras	1988	CDC, 1994		1993	1997	1992		

Primary data documentation

	National currency	Fiscal year end	National accounts					Balance of payments and trade			Government finance	IMF special data dissemi-nation
			Reporting period[a]	Base year	SNA price valuation	Alternative conversion factor	PPP survey year	Balance of Payments Manual in use	External debt	System of trade	Accounting concept	
Hungary	Hungarian forint	Dec. 31	CY	1994[c]	VAB		1996	BPM5	Actual	S	C	S
India	Indian rupee	Mar. 31	FY	1993	VAB		1985	BPM5	Estimate	G	C	S
Indonesia	Indonesian rupiah	Mar. 31	CY	1993	VAP		1993	BPM5	Preliminary	S	C	S*
Iran, Islamic Rep.	Iranian rial	Mar. 20	FY	1982	VAB	1980–98	1993	BPM5	Actual	G	C	
Iraq	Iraqi dinar	Dec. 31	CY	1969	VAB					S		
Ireland	Irish pound[b]	Dec. 31	CY	1990	VAB		1996	BPM5		G	C	S
Israel	Israeli new shekel	Dec. 31	CY	1995[c]	VAB	1998	1996	BPM4		S	C	S*
Italy	Italian lira[b]	Dec. 31	CY	1990	VAP		1996	BPM5		S	C	S
Jamaica	Jamaica dollar	Dec. 31	CY	1986	VAP	1995–97	1993	BPM5	Estimate	G		
Japan	Japanese yen	Mar. 31	CY	1990	VAP		1996	BPM5		G	C	S*
Jordan	Jordan dinar	Dec. 31	CY	1985	VAB		1993	BPM5	Actual	G	B	
Kazakhstan	Kazakh tenge	Dec. 31	CY	1993[c]	VAB	1987–95	1996	BPM5	Actual	G		
Kenya	Kenya shilling	Jun. 30	CY	1982	VAB		1993	BPM5	Actual	G	B	
Korea, Dem. Rep.	Democratic Republic of Korea won	Dec. 31	CY	..	..			BPM5				
Korea, Rep.	Korean won	Dec. 31	CY	1995	VAP		1993	BPM5	Estimate	S	C	S
Kuwait	Kuwaiti dinar	Jun. 30	CY	1984	VAP			BPM5		S	C	
Kyrgyz Republic	Kyrgyz som	Dec. 31	CY	1995[c]	VAB	1985–95	1996	BPM5	Actual	G		
Lao PDR	Lao kip	Dec. 31	CY	1990	VAB	1960–89	1993	BPM5	Preliminary			
Latvia	Latvian lat	Dec. 31	CY	1995[c]	VAB	1987–95	1996	BPM5	Actual	S	C	S
Lebanon	Lebanese pound	Dec. 31	CY	1994	VAB		1996	BPM4	Actual	G		
Lesotho	Lesotho loti	Mar. 31	CY	1980	VAB			BPM5	Actual	G	C	
Libya	Libyan dinar	Dec. 31	CY	1975	VAB		1993	BPM5		G		
Lithuania	Lithuanian litas	Dec. 31	CY	1993[c]	VAB	1987–95		BPM5	Preliminary	G	C	S
Macedonia, FYR	Macedonian denar	Dec. 31	CY	1996[c]	VAP	1992–98	1996	BPM5	Actual	G		
Madagascar	Malagasy franc	Dec. 31	CY	1984	VAB		1993	BPM5	Preliminary	S	C	
Malawi	Malawi kwacha	Mar. 31	CY	1978	VAB		1993	BPM5	Preliminary	G	B	
Malaysia	Malaysian ringgit	Dec. 31	CY	1978	VAP		1993	BPM4	Preliminary	G	C	S
Mali	CFA franc	Dec. 31	CY	1987	VAB		1985	BPM4	Actual	S		
Mauritania	Mauritanian ouguiya	Dec. 31	CY	1985	VAB			BPM4	Actual	S		
Mauritius	Mauritian rupee	Jun. 30	CY	1992	VAB	1998	1993	BPM5	Actual	G	C	
Mexico	Mexican new peso	Dec. 31	CY	1993[c]	VAP	1994–98	1996	BPM5	Actual	G	C	S*
Moldova	Moldovan leu	Dec. 31	CY	1996	VAB	1987–95	1996	BPM5	Actual	G		
Mongolia	Mongolian tugrik	Dec. 31	CY	1986	VAP	1993	1996	BPM5	Preliminary		C	
Morocco	Moroccan dirham	Dec. 31	CY	1980	VAP		1983	BPM5	Actual	S	C	
Mozambique	Mozambican metical	Dec. 31	CY	1995	VAB	1992–95		BPM5	Actual	S		
Myanmar	Myanmar kyat	Mar. 31	FY	1985	VAP			BPM5	Actual	G	C	
Namibia	Namibia dollar	Mar. 31	CY	1990	VAB			BPM5	Estimate		C	
Nepal	Nepalese rupee	Jul. 14	FY	1985	VAB	1973–98	1993	BPM5	Actual	S	C	
Netherlands	Netherlands guilder[b]	Dec. 31	CY	1990	VAP		1996	BPM5		S	C	S*
New Zealand	New Zealand dollar	Mar. 31	FY	1990	VAP		1996	BPM4		G	B	
Nicaragua	Nicaraguan gold cordoba	Dec. 31	CY	1998	VAP	1970–98		BPM5	Actual	S	C	
Niger	CFA franc	Dec. 31	CY	1987	VAP	1993		BPM5	Actual	S		
Nigeria	Nigerian naira	Dec. 31	CY	1987	VAB	1971–98	1993	BPM5	Estimate	G		
Norway	Norwegian krone	Dec. 31	CY	1990[c]	VAP		1996	BPM5		G	C	S
Oman	Rial Omani	Dec. 31	CY	1978	VAP		1993	BPM5	Actual	G	B	
Pakistan	Pakistan rupee	Jun. 30	FY	1981	VAB	1972–98	1993	BPM5	Actual	G	C	
Panama	Panamanian balboa	Dec. 31	CY	1982	VAB		1996	BPM5	Actual	S	C	
Papua New Guinea	Papua New Guinea kina	Dec. 31	CY	1983	VAP		1980	BPM5	Actual	G	B	
Paraguay	Paraguayan guarani	Dec. 31	CY	1982	VAP	1982–88	1980	BPM5	Actual	S	C	
Peru	Peruvian new sol	Dec. 31	CY	1979	VAP	1985–91	1996	BPM5	Actual	S	C	S*
Philippines	Philippine peso	Dec. 31	CY	1985	VAP		1993	BPM5	Actual	G	B	S
Poland	Polish zloty	Dec. 31	CY	1992[c]	VAP	1978	1996	BPM5	Actual	S	C	S
Portugal	Portuguese escudo[b]	Dec. 31	CY	1990	VAP		1996	BPM5		S	C	S
Puerto Rico	U.S. dollar	Dec. 31	CY	1954	VAP		1993					
Romania	Romanian leu	Dec. 31	CY	1993	VAB	1987–96	1996	BPM5	Actual	S	C	
Russian Federation	Russian ruble	Dec. 31	CY	1997	VAB	1989–94	1996	BPM5	Estimate	G	C	

	Latest population census	Latest household or demographic survey	Vital registration complete	Latest agricultural census	Latest industrial data	Latest water withdrawal data	Latest survey of scientists and engineers engaged in R&D	Latest survey of expenditure for R&D
Hungary	1990	Income, 1995	Yes	1994	1997	1995	1997	1996
India	1991	National family health, 1992–93		1986	1997	1990	1994	1994
Indonesia	1990	Socioeconomic, 1998		1993	1997	1990	1995	1994
Iran, Islamic Rep.	1991	Demographic, 1995		1988	1997	1993	1994	1994
Iraq	1997			1981	1997	1990	1993	
Ireland	1996		Yes	1991	1996	1995	1995	1995
Israel	1995		Yes	1983	1997	1997	1992	1997
Italy	1991		Yes	1990	1994	1993	1995	1997
Jamaica	1991	LSMS, 1994	Yes	1979	1996	1993	1986	1986
Japan	1995		Yes	1990	1997	1992	1996	1996
Jordan	1994	DHS, 1997			1996	1993	1989	1989
Kazakhstan	1999	DHS, 1995	Yes			1993		1997
Kenya	1989	DHS, 1998		1981	1989	1990		
Korea, Dem. Rep.	1993					1987		
Korea, Rep.	1995			1991	1997	1994	1996	1996
Kuwait	1995		Yes	1970	1995	1994	1997	1997
Kyrgyz Republic	1989	DHS, 1997	Yes			1994	1997	1996
Lao PDR	1995					1987		
Latvia	1989		Yes	1994	1996	1994	1997	1997
Lebanon	1970			1970		1994		1980
Lesotho	1996	DHS, 1991		1989–90	1985	1987		
Libya	1995	PAPCHILD, 1995		1987	1997	1995	1980	1980
Lithuania	1989		Yes	1994		1995	1996	1995
Macedonia, FYR	1994		Yes		1996		1995	
Madagascar	1993	DHS, 1997		1984	1988	1990	1994	1995
Malawi	1998	DHS, 1996		1981	1997	1994		
Malaysia	1991		Yes		1996	1995	1996	1994
Mali	1987	DHS, 1995–96		1978		1987		
Mauritania	1988	PAPCHILD, 1990		1985		1990		
Mauritius	1990	CDC, 1991	Yes		1996	1974	1992	1992
Mexico	1990	Population, 1995		1991	1995	1998	1995	1995
Moldova	1989		Yes			1992	1997	1997
Mongolia	1989				1995	1993	1995	
Morocco	1994	DHS, 1995		1962		1991		
Mozambique	1997	DHS, 1997				1992		
Myanmar	1983			1993		1987		
Namibia	1991	DHS, 1992		1960	1994	1990		
Nepal	1991	DHS, 1996		1992	1996	1994	1980	1980
Netherlands	1991		Yes	1989	1996	1990	1996	1996
New Zealand	1996		Yes	1990	1997	1995	1995	1995
Nicaragua	1995	DHS, 1998		1963	1997	1998	1987	
Niger	1988	DHS, 1998		1980	1996	1990		
Nigeria	1991	Consumption and expenditure, 1992		1960	1992	1990	1987	1987
Norway	1990		Yes	1989	1997	1985	1997	1997
Oman	1993	Child health, 1989		1979		1991		
Pakistan	1998	LSMS, 1991		1990	1997	1991	1990	1987
Panama	1990			1990	1997	1990	1986	1986
Papua New Guinea	1989	DHS, 1996				1987		
Paraguay	1992	DHS, 1990; CDC, 1992		1991	1997	1987		
Peru	1993	DHS, 1996		1994	1994	1992	1997	
Philippines	1995	DHS, 1998		1991	1997	1995	1992	1992
Poland	1988		Yes	1990	1997	1995	1995	1996
Portugal	1991		Yes	1989	1997	1990	1995	1995
Puerto Rico	1990		Yes	1987	1995			
Romania	1992	LSMS, 1994–95	Yes		1993		1993	1995
Russian Federation	1989	LSMS, 1992	Yes	1994–95	1995	1994	1997	1996

Primary data documentation

	National currency	Fiscal year end	National accounts					Balance of payments and trade			Government finance	IMF special data dissemination
			Reporting period[a]	Base year	SNA price valuation	Alternative conversion factor	PPP survey year	Balance of Payments Manual in use	External debt	System of trade	Accounting concept	
Rwanda	Rwanda franc	Dec. 31	CY	1985	VAB	1994	1985	BPM5	Actual	G	C	
Saudi Arabia	Saudi Arabian riyal	Hijri year	Hijri year	1970	VAP		1993	BPM4	Estimate	G		
Senegal	CFA franc	Dec. 31	CY	1987	VAP		1993	BPM5	Preliminary	S		
Sierra Leone	Sierra Leonean leone	Jun. 30	CY	1990	VAB	1971–79	1993	BPM5	Actual	G	B	
Singapore	Singapore dollar	Mar. 31	CY	1990	VAP		1993	BPM5		G	C	S*
Slovak Republic	Slovak koruna	Dec. 31	CY	1993[c]	VAP		1996	BPM5	Actual	G		S
Slovenia	Slovenian tolar	Dec. 31	CY	1993[c]	VAB		1996	BPM5	Actual	S		S*
South Africa	South African rand	Mar. 31	CY	1995	VAB			BPM5	Preliminary	G	C	S*
Spain	Spanish peseta[b]	Dec. 31	CY	1986	VAP		1996	BPM5		S	C	S
Sri Lanka	Sri Lankan rupee	Dec. 31	CY	1982	VAB		1993	BPM5	Actual	G	C	
Sudan	Sudanese pounds	Jun. 30	CY	1982	VAB	1980–91		BPM4	Estimate	G		
Sweden	Swedish krona	Jun. 30	CY	1990	VAB		1996	BPM5		G	C	S
Switzerland	Swiss franc	Dec. 31	CY	1990	VAP		1996	BPM5	Estimate	S	C	S*
Syrian Arab Republic	Syrian pound	Dec. 31	CY	1985	VAP	1970–98	1993	BPM5	Estimate	S	C	
Tajikistan	Tajik ruble	Dec. 31	CY	1997[c]	VAP	1987–98	1996	BPM4	Actual	G		
Tanzania	Tanzania shilling	Jun. 30	FY	1992	VAB	1981–98	1993	BPM5	Actual	G		
Thailand	Thai baht	Sep. 30	CY	1988	VAP		1993	BPM5	Preliminary	G	C	S*
Togo	CFA franc	Dec. 31	CY	1978	VAP		1993	BPM5	Actual	S		
Trinidad and Tobago	Trinidad and Tobago dollar	Dec. 31	CY	1985	VAB		1993	BPM5	Estimate	S		
Tunisia	Tunisian dinar	Dec. 31	CY	1990	VAP		1993	BPM5	Estimate	G	C	
Turkey	Turkish lira	Dec. 31	CY	1994	VAB		1996	BPM5	Actual	S	C	S*
Turkmenistan	Turkmen manat	Dec. 31	CY	1987[c]	VAP	1990–98	1996	BPM5	Actual	G		
Uganda	Uganda shilling	Jun. 30	FY	1991	VAB	1980–98		BPM4	Actual	G		
Ukraine	Ukraine hryvnia	Dec. 31	CY	1990[c]	VAB	1987–98	1996	BPM5	Actual	G		
United Arab Emirates	U.A.E. dirham	Dec. 31	CY	1985	VAB		1993	BPM4		G	B	
United Kingdom	Pound sterling	Dec. 31	CY	1990	VAB		1996	BPM5		G	C	S*
United States	U.S. dollar	Sep. 30	CY	1992	VAP		1996	BPM5		G	C	S
Uruguay	Uruguayan peso	Dec. 31	CY	1983	VAP	1993–98	1996	BPM5	Actual	S	C	
Uzbekistan	Uzbek sum	Dec. 31	CY	1997[c]	VAB	1991–98	1996	BPM4	Actual	G		
Venezuela, RB	Venezuelan bolivar	Dec. 31	CY	1984	VAP		1996	BPM5	Estimate	G	C	
Vietnam	Vietnamese dong	Dec. 31	CY	1989	VAP	1991	1993	BPM4	Estimate	G		
West Bank and Gaza	Israeli new shekel	Dec. 31	CY	1994	VAP		1993					
Yemen, Rep.	Yemen rial	Dec. 31	CY	1990	VAB	1990–97	1993	BPM5	Estimate	G	C	
Yugoslavia, FR (Serb./Mont.)	Yugoslav new dinar	Dec. 31	CY	..	VAP	1996–98	1985		Estimate	S		
Zambia	Zambian kwacha	Dec. 31	CY	1994	VAB	1990–92	1993	BPM5	Actual	G	C	
Zimbabwe	Zimbabwe dollar	Jun. 30	CY	1990	VAB		1993	BPM5	Actual	G	C	

Note: For an explanation of the abbreviations used in the table see the notes.

a. Also applies to balance of payments reporting. b. European Monetary Union member currency linked to the euro. c. Country uses the 1993 System of National Accounts methodology.

Primary data documentation

	Latest population census	Latest household or demographic survey	Vital registration complete	Latest agricultural census	Latest industrial data	Latest water withdrawal data	Latest survey of scientists and engineers engaged in R&D	Latest survey of expenditure for R&D
Rwanda	1991	DHS, 1992		1984	1986	1993	1995	1995
Saudi Arabia	1992	Maternal and child health, 1993		1983		1992		
Senegal	1988	DHS, 1997		1960	1996	1990	1996	1997
Sierra Leone	1985	SHEHEA, 1989–90		1985	1986	1987		
Singapore	1990	General household, 1995	Yes		1997		1995	1995
Slovak Republic	1991		Yes		1994	1995	1996	1995
Slovenia	1991		Yes	1991	1996	1994	1996	1996
South Africa	1996	DHS, 1997			1996	1990	1993	1993
Spain	1991		Yes	1989		1997	1996	1997
Sri Lanka	1981	DHS, 1993	Yes	1982	1997	1990	1996	1985
Sudan	1993	DHS, 1989–90			1997	1995		
Sweden	1990		Yes	1981	1997	1995	1995	1995
Switzerland	1990		Yes	1990	1996	1995	1996	1996
Syrian Arab Republic	1994	PAPCHILD, 1995		1981	1997	1993		1997
Tajikistan	1989		Yes	1994		1994	1993	
Tanzania	1988	DHS, 1996		1995	1997	1994		
Thailand	1990	DHS, 1987		1988	1997	1990	1996	1996
Togo	1981	DHS, 1998		1983	1997	1987		1994
Trinidad and Tobago	1990	DHS, 1987	Yes	1982	1997			1984
Tunisia	1994	PAPCHILD, 1994–95		1961	1997	1996	1997	1997
Turkey	1997	DHS, 1993		1991	1997	1997	1996	1996
Turkmenistan	1995		Yes			1994		
Uganda	1991	DHS, 1995		1991	1996	1970	1997	1996
Ukraine	1991		Yes			1992	1995	1995
United Arab Emirates	1995				1981	1995		
United Kingdom	1991		Yes	1993	1997	1995	1996	1996
United States	1990	Current population, 1997	Yes	1987	1997	1995	1993	1997
Uruguay	1996			1990	1996	1990	1987	1987
Uzbekistan	1989	DHS, 1996	Yes			1994	1992	
Venezuela, RB	1990	LSMS, 1993	Yes	1997–98	1996	1970	1992	1992
Vietnam	1989	DHS, 1997		1994		1990		1985
West Bank and Gaza	1997	Demographic, 1995		1971				
Yemen, Rep.	1994	DHS, 1997		1982–85		1990		
Yugoslavia, FR (Serb./Mont.)	1991		Yes	1981	1996		1995	
Zambia	1990	DHS, 1996		1990	1997	1994		
Zimbabwe	1992	DHS, 1994		1960	1997	1987		

Primary data documentation notes

• **Fiscal year end** is the date of the end of the fiscal year for the central government. Fiscal years for other levels of government and the reporting years for statistical surveys may differ, but if a country is designated as a fiscal year reporter in the following column, the date shown is the end of its national accounts reporting period. • **Reporting period** for national accounts and balance of payments data is designated as either calendar year basis (CY) or fiscal year (FY). Most economies report their national accounts and balance of payments data using calendar years, but some use fiscal years, which straddle two calendar years. In the *World Development Indicators* fiscal year data are assigned to the calendar year that contains the larger share of the fiscal year. If a country's fiscal year ends before June 30, the data are shown in the first year of the fiscal period; if the fiscal year ends on or after June 30, the data are shown in the second year of the period. Saudi Arabia follows a lunar year whose starting and ending dates change with respect to the solar year. Because the International Monetary Fund (IMF) reports most balance of payments data on a calendar year basis, balance of payments data for fiscal year reporters in the *World Development Indicators* are based on fiscal year estimates provided by World Bank staff. These estimates may differ from IMF data but allow consistent comparisons between national accounts and balance of payments data. • **Base year** is the year used as the base period for constant price calculations in the country's national accounts. Price indexes derived from national accounts aggregates, such as the GDP deflator, express the price level relative to prices in the base year. Constant price data reported in the *World Development Indicators* are rebased to a common 1995 base year. See *About the data* for table 4.1 for further discussion. • **SNA price valuation** shows whether value added in the national accounts is reported at basic prices (VAB) or at producer prices (VAP). Producer prices include the value of taxes levied on value added and collected from consumers and thus tend to overstate the actual value added in production. See *About the data* for table 4.2 for further discussion of national accounts valuation. • **Alternative conversion factor** identifies the countries and years for which a World Bank–estimated conversion factor has been used in place of the official (IFS line rf) exchange rate. See *Statistical methods* for further discussion of the use of alternative conversion factors. • **PPP survey year** refers to the latest available survey year for the International Comparison Programme's estimates of purchasing power parities (PPPs). • **Balance of Payments Manual in use** refers to the classification system used for compiling and reporting data on balance of payments items in table 4.17. BPM4 refers to the fourth edition of the IMF's *Balance of Payments Manual* (1977), and BPM5 to the fifth edition (1993). Since 1995 the IMF has adjusted all balance of payments data to BPM5 conventions, but some countries continue to report using the older system. • **External debt** shows debt reporting status for 1998 data. *Actual* indicates that data are as reported, *preliminary* that data are preliminary and include an element of staff estimation, and *estimate* that data are staff estimates. • **System of trade** refers to the general trade system (G) or the special trade system (S). For imports under the general trade system, both goods entering directly for domestic consumption and goods entered into customs storage are recorded, at the time of their first arrival, as imports; under the special trade system goods are recorded as imports when declared for domestic consumption whether at time of entry or on withdrawal from customs storage. Exports under the general system comprise outward-moving goods: (a) national goods wholly or partly produced in the country; (b) foreign goods, neither transformed nor declared for domestic consumption in the country, that move outward from customs storage; and (c) nationalized goods that have been declared from domestic consumption and move outward without having been transformed. Under the special system of trade exports comprise categories a and c. In some compilations categories b and c are classified as reexports. Direct transit trade, consisting of goods entering or leaving for transport purposes only, is excluded from both import and export statistics. See *About the data* for tables 4.5 and 4.6 for further discussion. • **Government finance accounting concept** describes the accounting basis for reporting central government financial data. For most countries government finance data have been consolidated (C) into one set of accounts capturing all the central government's fiscal activities. Budgetary central government accounts (B) exclude central government units. See *About the data* for tables 4.13–4.15 for further details. • **IMF special data dissemination** shows the countries that subscribe to the IMF's Special Data Dissemination Standard (SDDS). *S* refers to countries that subscribe; *S** indicates subscribers that have posted data on the Internet. (Posted data can be reached through the IMF Dissemination Standard Bulletin Board at dsbb.imf.org.) The IMF established the SDDS to guide members that have, or are seeking, access to international capital markets in providing economic and financial data to the public. The SDDS is expected to enhance the availability of timely and comprehensive data and therefore to contribute to the pursuit of sound macroeconomic policies. It is also expected to contribute to the improved functioning of financial markets. Although subscription is voluntary, it commits the subscriber to observing the standard and to providing information to the IMF about its practices in disseminating economic and financial data. • **Latest population census** shows the most recent year in which a census was conducted. • **Latest household or demographic survey** gives information on the surveys used in compiling household and demographic data presented in section 2. PAPCHILD is the Pan Arab Project for Child Development, DHS is Demographic and Health Survey, WFS is World Fertility Study, LSMS is Living Standards Measurement Study, SDA is Social Dimensions of Adjustment, CDC is Centers for Disease Control and Prevention, and SHEHEA is Survey of Household Expenditure and Household Economic Activities. • **Vital registration complete** identifies countries judged to have complete registries of vital (birth and death) statistics by the United Nations Statistics Division and reported in *Population and Vital Statistics Reports*. Countries with complete vital statistics registries may have more accurate and more timely demographic indicators. • **Latest agricultural census** shows the most recent year in which an agricultural census was conducted and reported to the Food and Agriculture Organization. • **Latest industrial data** refer to the most recent year for which manufacturing value added data at the three-digit level of the International Standard Industrial Classification (revision 2 or 3) are available in the UNIDO database. • **Latest water withdrawal data** refer to the most recent year for which data have been compiled from a variety of sources. See *About the data* for table 3.5 for more information. • **Latest surveys of scientists and engineers engaged in R&D and expenditure for R&D** refer to the most recent year for which data are available from a data collection effort by UNESCO in science and technology and research and development (R&D). See *About the data* for table 5.12 for more information.

Acronyms and abbreviations

Technical terms

BOD	biochemical oxygen demand
btu	British thermal unit
CD-ROM	compact disc read-only memory
CFC	chlorofluorocarbon
c.i.f.	cost, insurance, and freight
CO_2	carbon dioxide
COMTRADE	United Nations Statistics Division's Commodity Trade database
CPI	consumer price index
cu. m	cubic meter
DHS	demographic and health survey
DMTU	dry metric ton unit
DOTS	directly observed treatment, short-course strategy
DPT	diphtheria, pertussis, and tetanus
ESAF	Enhanced Structural Adjustment Facility
FDI	foreign direct investment
f.o.b.	free on board
FYR	former Yugoslav Republic
GDP	gross domestic product
GEMS	Global Environment Monitoring System
GIS	geographic information system
GNI	gross national income
GNP	gross national product
ha	hectare
HIPC	heavily indebted poor country
HIV	human immunodeficiency virus
ICD	International Classification of Diseases
ICRG	International Country Risk Guide
ICSE	International Classification of Status in Employment
IFCG	International Finance Corporation Global index
IFCI	International Finance Corporation Investable index
IMR	infant mortality rate
IP	Internet Protocol
ISCED	International Standard Classification of Education
ISIC	International Standard Industrial Classification
kg	kilogram
km	kilometer
kwh	kilowatt-hour
LIBOR	London interbank offered rate
M0	currency and coins (monetary base)
M1	narrow money (currency and demand deposits)
M2	money plus quasi money
M3	broad money or liquid liabilities
mmbtu	millions of British thermal units
mt	metric ton
MUV	manufactures unit value
NEAP	national environmental action plan
NGO	nongovernmental organization
NPISH	nonprofit institutions serving households
NTBs	nontariff barriers
ODA	official development assistance
PC	personal computer
PPP	purchasing power parity
PWT	Penn World Tables
R&D	research and development
SAF	Structural Adjustment Facility
SDR	special drawing right
SITC	Standard International Trade Classification
SNA	United Nations System of National Accounts
SO_2	sulfur dioxide
SOPEMI	Continuous Reporting System on Migration
sq. km	square kilometer
STD	sexually transmitted disease
TB	tuberculosis
TFP	total factor productivity
ton-km	metric ton-kilometers
TSP	total suspended particulates
UN5MR	under-five mortality rate

Organizations

ADB	Asian Development Bank
AfDB	African Development Bank
APEC	Asia-Pacific Economic Cooperation
CDC	Centers for Disease Control and Prevention
CDIAC	Carbon Dioxide Information Analysis Center
CEC	Commission of the European Community
DAC	Development Assistance Committee
DRS	World Bank's Debtor Reporting System
EBRD	European Bank for Reconstruction and Development
EDF	European Development Fund
EFTA	European Free Trade Area
EIB	European Investment Bank
EMU	European Monetary Union
EU	European Union
Eurostat	Statistical Office of the European Communities
FAO	Food and Agriculture Organization
G-5	France, Germany, Japan, United Kingdom, and United States
G-7	G-5 plus Canada and Italy
GATT	General Agreement on Tariffs and Trade
GAVI	Global Alliance for Vaccines and Immunization
GEF	Global Environment Facility
IBRD	International Bank for Reconstruction and Development
ICAO	International Civil Aviation Organization
ICCO	International Cocoa Organization
ICO	International Coffee Organization
ICP	International Comparison Programme
ICSE	International Classification of Status in Employment
ICSID	International Centre for Settlement of Investment Disputes
IDA	International Development Association
IDB	Inter-American Development Bank
IEA	International Energy Agency
IFAC	International Federation of Accountants
IFC	International Finance Corporation
ILO	International Labour Organization
IMF	International Monetary Fund
IRF	International Road Federation
ITU	International Telecommunication Union
IUCN	World Conservation Union
LME	London Metals Exchange
MIGA	Multilateral Investment Guarantee Agency
NAFTA	North American Free Trade Agreement
NATO	North Atlantic Treaty Organization
NSF	National Science Foundation
OECD	Organisation for Economic Co-operation and Development
PAHO	Pan American Health Organization
UIP	Urban Indicators Programme
UN	United Nations
UNAIDS	Joint United Nations Programme on HIV/AIDS
UNCED	United Nations Conference on Environment and Development
UNCHS	United Nations Centre for Human Settlements (Habitat)
UNCTAD	United Nations Conference on Trade and Development
UNDP	United Nations Development Programme
UNECE	United Nations Economic Commission for Europe
UNEP	United Nations Environment Programme
UNESCO	United Nations Educational, Scientific, and Cultural Organization
UNFPA	United Nations Population Fund
UNHCR	United Nations High Commissioner for Refugees
UNICEF	United Nations Children's Fund
UNIDO	United Nations Industrial Development Organization
UNRISD	United Nations Research Institute for Social Development
UNSD	United Nations Statistics Division
USAID	U.S. Agency for International Development
WCMC	World Conservation Monitoring Centre
WFP	World Food Programme
WHO	World Health Organization
WIPO	World Intellectual Property Organization
WTO	World Trade Organization
WWF	World Wide Fund for Nature

Credits

This book has drawn on a wide range of World Bank reports and numerous external sources. These are listed in the bibliography that follows this section. Many people inside and outside the World Bank helped in writing and producing the *World Development Indicators*. This note identifies those who made specific contributions. Numerous others, too many to acknowledge here, helped in many ways for which the team is extremely grateful.

1. World view

was prepared by Sulekha Patel and K. M. Vijayalakshmi. K. Sarwar Lateef wrote the introduction with contributions from Sulekha Patel and Eric Swanson. Masako Hiraga assisted in the preparation of tables and figures. The introduction drew heavily on the World Bank's *Global Economic Prospects 2000*. Ideas and suggestions were provided by Shaohua Chen, Martin Ravallion, Giovanna Prennushi, and Michael Walton. Substantial assistance in preparing the data for this section was received from Yonas Biru, who prepared the estimates of GNP in PPP terms. Jamie Bartram and Jose Hueb assisted with the data on access to water and sanitation, which also appear in sections 2 and 3.

2. People

was prepared by Sulekha Patel and Masako Hiraga in partnership with the World Bank's Human Development Network, its Development Research Group, and the Gender Anchor of its Poverty Reduction and Economic Management Network. Thomas Merrick suggested the theme for the introduction, and Eduard Bos wrote it with substantial input from Sulekha Patel. Contributions to the section were provided by Eduard Bos (demography, health, and nutrition), Martin Rama and Raquel Artecona (labor force and employment), Shaohua Chen and Martin Ravallion (poverty and income distribution), and Lianqin Wang and Ayesha Vawda (education). Comments and suggestions were also received from Thomas Merrick, Jean Baneth, and Eric Swanson at various stages of production.

3. Environment

was prepared by M. H. Saeed Ordoubadi in partnership with the World Bank's Environmentally and Socially Sustainable Development Network and in collaboration with the World Bank's Development Research Group and Transportation, Water, and Urban Development Department. Robin White of the World Resources Institute, Laura Battlebury of the World Conservation Monitoring Centre, and Christine Auclair of the Urban Indicators Programme, United Nations Centre for Human Settlements, made important contributions. Amy Heyman assisted with research and data preparation. John Dixon, Kirk Hamilton, Nwanze Okidegbe, and Michael Ward provided invaluable comments and guidance. The World Bank's Environment Department and Rural Development Department devoted substantial staff resources to the book, for which we are very grateful. Saeed Ordoubadi wrote the introduction to the section with valuable comments from John Dixon, Kirk Hamilton, Nwanze Okidegbe, Bruce Ross-Larson, and Michael Ward. Other contributions were made by Susmita Dasgupta, Craig Meisner, and David Wheeler (water pollution), Jan Bojö (government commitments), and Kirk Hamilton and Lisa Segnestan (genuine savings). The team received valuable comments from Jean Baneth, Simone Cecchini, Borut Repansek, and Patrice Kado Wadja.

4. Economy

was prepared by K. M. Vijayalakshmi and Eric Swanson in close collaboration with the Macroeconomic Data Team of the World Bank's Development Data Group, led by Robin Lynch and Soong Sup Lee. Swaminathan Aiyar prepared the introduction to this section with advice from Milan Brahmbhatt and Peter Fallon. Substantial contributions to the section were provided by Barbro Hexeberg and Michael Ward (national accounts), Azita Amjadi, Amy Heyman, and Jong-goo Park (trade), Yonas Biru (structure of consumption and relative prices in PPP terms), Gloria Reyes and Ibrahim Levent (external debt), and K. M. Vijayalakshmi (balance of payments and OECD national accounts). The national accounts and balance of payments data for low- and middle-income economies are gathered from the World Bank's regional staff through the annual Unified Survey under the direction of Monica Singh and Mona Fetouh. Maja Bresslauer, Mona Fetouh, Raquel Fok, Soong Sup Lee, and Monica Singh worked on updating, estimating, and validating the databases for national accounts. The national accounts data for OECD countries were processed by Mehdi Akhlaghi. We are grateful to Wladimir Tislenkoff and Jorgen Richtering at the World Trade Organization for providing data on trade in goods and commercial services, to Tetsuo Yamada for help in obtaining the United Nations Industrial Development Organization (UNIDO) database, and to Jean Baneth for helpful comments.

5. States and markets

was prepared by David Cieslikowski in partnership with the World Bank's Finance, Private Sector, and Infrastructure Network, its Poverty Reduction and Economic Management Network, and the International Finance Corporation. Amy Wilson helped prepare the data for this section. David Cieslikowski and Bruce Ross-Larson drafted the introduction to the section with substantial inputs from Michael Crawford, Robert Watson, and Amy Wilson. Other contributors included Carol Gabyzon (privatization data), Graeme Littler (stock markets), Yonas Biru (relative prices and PPP conversion factors), Mariusz Sumlinksi (private investment), Maria Concetta Gasbarro and Michael Minges of the International Telecommunication Union (communications and information), Louis Thompson (transport), Thomas Hatzichronoglou of the Organisation for Economic Co-operation and Development (OECD) and Sunil Mani of the United Nations University Institute for New Technologies (science and technology), and Michael Ward for overall comments.

6. Global links

was prepared by Eric Swanson with assistance from Amy Heyman. Swaminathan Aiyar prepared the introduction with valuable input from Will Martin. Substantial help in preparing the data for this section came from Azita Amjadi and Aranus Batkevicius and John Toye of the United Nations Conference on Trade and Development (UNCTAD) (trade), Aki Kuwahara of UNCTAD and Jerzy Rozanski (tariffs), Betty Dow (commodity prices), Shelly Fu, Ibrahim Levent, and Gloria Reyes (financial data), and Jean-Pierre Garson and Cecile Thoreau of the OECD (migration). We wish to acknowledge the considerable assistance of Jean-Louis Grolleau, Yasmin Ahmed, and Rudolphe Petras of the OECD, who provided data on aid flows, and Antonio Massieu and Rosa Songel of the World Tourism Organization.

Other parts

The maps on the inside covers were prepared by the World Bank's Map Design Unit. The *Users guide* was prepared by David Cieslikowski. *Primary data documentation* was coordinated by K. M. Vijayalakshmi, who served as database administrator. *Statistical methods* was written by Eric Swanson. *Acronyms and abbreviations* was prepared by Estela Zamora. The index was collated by Richard Fix.

Systems support

Mehdi Akhlaghi was responsible for database management and programming tables. Tariqul Khan was responsible for programming database updates and aggregations. Soong Sup Lee provided valuable systems support. Estela Zamora provided assistance in updating the databases.

Credits

Administrative assistance and office technology support

Estela Zamora provided administrative assistance. Office technology support was provided by Nacer Megherbi and Shahin Outadi.

Design, production, and editing

Richard Fix coordinated all aspects of production with the Communications Development Incorporated team led by Terry Fischer. Bruce Ross-Larson edited the section introductions and provided overall direction to the design and planning process. We would like to thank the design team of Peter Grundy and Tilly Northedge, the production team of Garrett Cruce, Megan Klose, and Laurel Morais, and the editing team led by Alison Strong and including Daphne Levitas.

Client services

The Development Data Group's Client Services Team, led by Elizabeth Crayford, contributed to the design and planning of the books and helped coordinate work with the Office of the Publisher. The help of Natasha Rodriguez in responding to numerous client queries over the past year is gratefully acknowledged.

Publishing and dissemination

The Office of the Publisher, under the direction of Dirk Koehler, provided valuable assistance throughout the production process. Jamila Abdelghani and Randi Park coordinated production, and Alan Donovan and Maya Brahmam supervised marketing and distribution. Lawrence MacDonald of Development Economics and Geoffrey Bergen and Phillip Hay of External Affairs managed the communications strategy, and the regional operations group headed by Paul Mitchell helped coordinate the overseas release.

The Atlas

Production was managed by Richard Fix with guidance from David Cieslikowski and Elizabeth Crayford. The preparation of data benefited from the work on corresponding sections in the *World Development Indicators*. William Prince assisted with systems support and production of tables and graphs. Greg G. Prakas and Jeffrey Lecksell from the World Bank's Map Design Unit coordinated map production.

World Development Indicators CD-ROM

Design, programming, and testing were carried out by Reza Farivari and his team: Azita Amjadi, Ying Chi, Elizabeth Crayford, Sathyanarayanan Govindaraju, Yusri Harun, Tariqul Khan, Angelo Kostopoulos, and Nacer Megherbi. Masako Hiraga produced the social indicators tables; Aslam Ansari and Masako Hiraga produced the education tables. William Prince coordinated production and provided quality assurance.

Client feedback

We are also grateful to the many people who took the trouble to provide comments on our publications. Their feedback and suggestions have helped us to improve this year's edition.

Bibliography

Aggarwal, Mita. 1995. "International Trade, Labor Standards, and Labor Market Conditions: An Evaluation of the Linkages." Working Paper 95-06-C. U.S. International Trade Commission, Washington, D.C.

Ahmad, Sultan. 1992. "Regression Estimates of Per Capita GDP Based on Purchasing Power Parities." Policy Research Working Paper 956. World Bank, International Economics Department, Washington, D.C.

———. 1994. "Improving Inter-Spatial and Inter-Temporal Comparability of National Accounts." *Journal of Development Economics* 44:53–75.

Ahrens, J. 1999. "Governance and the Implementation of Technology Policy in Less Developed Countries." Paper presented at the United Nations University Institute for New Technologies international workshop The Political Economy of Technology in Developing Countries, Brighton, England, 8–9 October.

American Automobile Manufacturers Association. 1998. *World Motor Vehicle Data.* Detroit, Mich.

Anker, Richard. 1998. *Gender and Jobs: Sex Segregation of Occupations in the World.* Geneva: International Labour Office.

Armington, Paul, and Yuri Dikhanov. 1996. "Multivariate Normalization of Infrastructure (e.g. Roads) for Comparative Purposes." World Bank, International Economics Department, Washington, D.C.

Azariadis, Costas, and Allen Drazen. 1990. "Threshold Externalities in Economic Development." *Quarterly Journal of Economics* 105(2):501–26.

Ball, Nicole. 1984. "Measuring Third World Security Expenditure: A Research Note." *World Development* 12(2):157–64.

Barro, Robert J. 1991. "Economic Growth in a Cross-Section of Countries." *Quarterly Journal of Economics* 106(2):407–44.

Basant, R., and P. Chandra. 1999. "Building Technological Capabilities in a Liberalizing Developing Economy: Firm Strategies and Public Policy." Paper presented at the United Nations University Institute for New Technologies international workshop The Political Economy of Technology in Developing Countries, Brighton, England, 8–9 October.

Becker, Gary. 1964. *Human Capital: A Theoretical and Empirical Analysis, with Special Reference to Education.* General Series 30. New York: Columbia University Press.

Behrman, Jere R., and Mark R. Rosenzweig. 1994. "Caveat Emptor: Cross-Country Data on Education and the Labor Force." *Journal of Development Economics* 44:147–71.

Bhattasali, Deepak. 1998. "Economic Outcomes and Policies in Sub-Saharan Africa." World Bank, Africa Region, Economic Management and Social Policy Unit, Washington, D.C.

Binswanger, Hans, and Ernst Lutz. 2000. "Agricultural Trade Barriers, Trade Negotiations, and the Interests of Developing Countries." Paper presented at the High-Level Round Table for UNCTAD 10, Bangkok, February.

Bloom, David E., and Jeffrey G. Williamson. 1998. "Demographic Transitions and Economic Miracles in Emerging Asia." *The World Bank Economic Review* 12(3):419–55.

Brown, Lester R., Christopher Flavin, Hilary F. French, and others. 1998. *State of the World 1998.* Washington, D.C.: Worldwatch Institute.

Brown, Lester R., Michael Renner, Christopher Flavin, and others. 1998. *Vital Signs 1998.* Washington, D.C.: Worldwatch Institute.

Brown, Lester R., and others. 1999. *Vital Signs 1999: The Environmental Trends That Are Shaping Our Future.* New York and London: W.W. Norton for Worldwatch Institute.

Bulatao, Rodolfo A. 1998. *The Value of Family Planning Programs in Developing Countries.* Santa Monica, Calif.: RAND.

Caiola, Marcello. 1995. *A Manual for Country Economists.* Training Series 1, vol. 1. Washington, D.C.: International Monetary Fund.

Cassen, Robert, and associates. 1986. *Does Aid Work? Report to Intergovernmental Task Force on Concessional Flows.* Oxford: Clarendon Press.

Centro Latinoamericano de Demografía. Various years. *Boletín Demográfico.* Santiago, Chile.

Chen, Shaohua, and Martin Ravallion. Forthcoming. "Global Poverty Measures 1987–98 and Projections for the Future." World Bank, Development Research Group, Washington, D.C.

Collier, Paul, and David Dollar. 1999. "Aid Allocation and Poverty Reduction." Policy Research Working Paper 2041. World Bank, Development Research Group, Washington, D.C.

Collins, Wanda W., Emile A. Frison, and Suzanne L. Sharrock. 1997. "Global Programs: A New Vision in Agricultural Research." *Issues in Agriculture* (World Bank, Consultative Group on International Agricultural Research, Washington, D.C.) 12:1–28.

Conly, Shanti R., and Joanne E. Epp. 1997. *Falling Short: The World Bank's Role in Population and Reproductive Health.* Washington, D.C.: Population Action International.

Council of Europe. Various years. *Recent Demographic Developments in Europe and North America.* Strasbourg: Council of Europe Press.

Currency Data & Intelligence, Inc. Various issues. *Global Currency Report.* Brooklyn, N.Y.

Daly, John. 1999. "Science and Technology in the World Bank." Strategy Working Paper. World Bank, Energy, Mining, and Telecommunications Department, Washington, D.C.

Dasgupta, Partha. 1993. *An Inquiry into Well-Being and Destitution.* Oxford: Clarendon Press.

Dasgupta, Partha, and Martin Weale. 1992. "On Measuring the Quality of Life." *World Development* 20:119–31.

Demery, Lionel, and Michael Walton. 1997. "Are Poverty and Social Targets for the 21st Century Attainable?" Paper presented at a Development Assistance Committee–Development Centre seminar, Organisation for Economic Co-operation and Development, Paris, 4–5 December.

Demirgüç-Kunt, Aslı, and Enrica Detragiache. 1997. "The Determinants of Banking Crises: Evidence from Developed and Developing Countries." Working paper. World Bank and International Monetary Fund, Washington, D.C.

Demirgüç-Kunt, Aslı, and Ross Levine. 1996a. "Stock Markets, Corporate Finance, and Economic Growth: An Overview." *The World Bank Economic Review* 10(2):223–39.

———. 1996b. "Stock Market Development and Financial Intermediaries: Stylized Facts." *The World Bank Economic Review* 10(2):291–321.

Dixon, John, and Paul Sherman. 1990. *Economics of Protected Areas: A New Look at Benefits and Costs.* Washington, D.C.: Island Press.

DKT International. 1998. *1997 Contraceptive Social Marketing Statistics.* Washington, D.C.

Doyle, John J., and Gabrielle J. Persley, eds. 1996. *Enabling the Safe Use of Biotechnology: Principles and Practice.* Environmentally Sustainable Development Studies and Monographs Series, no. 10. Washington, D.C.: World Bank.

Drucker, Peter F. 1994. "The Age of Social Transformation." *Atlantic Monthly* 274 (November).

Easterly, William. 1999. "How Did Highly Indebted Poor Countries Become Highly Indebted? Reviewing Two Decades of Debt Relief." Policy Research

Working Paper 2225. World Bank, Development Research Group, Washington, D.C.

Euromoney. 1999. September. London.

Eurostat (Statistical Office of the European Communities). Various years. *Demographic Statistics.* Luxembourg.

———. Various years. *Statistical Yearbook.* Luxembourg.

Evenson, Robert E., and Carl E. Pray. 1994. "Measuring Food Production (with Reference to South Asia)." *Journal of Development Economics* 44:173–97.

Faiz, Asif, Christopher S. Weaver, and Michael P. Walsh. 1996. *Air Pollution from Motor Vehicles: Standards and Technologies for Controlling Emissions.* Washington, D.C.: World Bank.

Fallon, Peter, and Zafiris Tzannatos. 1998. *Child Labor: Issues and Directions for the World Bank.* Washington, D.C.: World Bank.

Fankhauser, Samuel. 1995. *Valuing Climate Change: The Economics of the Greenhouse.* London: Earthscan.

FAO (Food and Agriculture Organization). 1986. "Inter-Country Comparisons of Agricultural Production Aggregates." Economic and Social Development Paper 61. Rome.

———. 1996. *Food Aid in Figures 1994.* Vol. 12. Rome.

———. 1999. *State of the World's Forests 1999.* Rome.

———. Various years. *Fertilizer Yearbook.* FAO Statistics Series. Rome.

———. Various years. *Production Yearbook.* FAO Statistics Series. Rome.

———. Various years. *Trade Yearbook.* FAO Statistics Series. Rome.

Feldstein, Martin, and Charles Horioka. 1980. "Domestic Savings and International Capital Flows." *Economic Journal* 90(358):314–29.

Filmer, Dean, Elizabeth King, and Lant Pritchett. 1998. "Gender Disparity in South Asia." Policy Research Working Paper 1867. World Bank, Development Research Group, Washington, D.C.

Fox, James W. 1995. "What Do We Know about World Poverty?" USAID Evaluation Special Study 74. U.S. Agency for International Development, Center for Development Information and Evaluation, Washington, D.C.

Frankel, Jeffrey. 1993. "Quantifying International Capital Mobility in the 1990s." In Jeffrey Frankel, ed., *On Exchange Rates.* Cambridge, Mass.: MIT Press.

Frankhauser, Pierre. 1994. "Fractales, tissus urbains et reseaux de transport." *Revue d'economie politique* 104:435–55.

Fredricksen, Birger. 1993. *Statistics of Education in Developing Countries: An Introduction to Their Collection and Analysis.* Paris: UNESCO.

French, Kenneth, and James M. Poterba. 1991. "Investor Diversification and International Equity Markets." *American Economic Review* 81:222–26.

Gallup, John L., and Jeffrey D. Sachs. 1998. "The Economic Burden of Malaria." Harvard Institute for International Development, Cambridge, Mass.

Gannon, Colin, and Zmarak Shalizi. 1995. "The Use of Sectoral and Project Performance Indicators in Bank-Financed Transport Operations." TWU Discussion Paper 21. World Bank, Transportation, Water, and Urban Development Department, Washington, D.C.

Gardner-Outlaw, Tom, and Robert Engelman. 1997. "Sustaining Water, Easing Scarcity: A Second Update." Population Action International, Washington, D.C.

GATT (General Agreement on Tariffs and Trade). 1966. *International Trade 1965.* Geneva.

———. 1989. *International Trade 1988–89.* Geneva.

Goldfinger, Charles. 1994. *L'utile et le futile: L'économie de l'immatériel.* Paris: Editions Odile Jacob.

Goldstein, Ellen, Alexander S. Preker, Olusoji Adeyi, and Gnanaraj Chellaraj. 1996. *Trends in Health Status, Services, and Finance: The Transition in Central and Eastern Europe.* Vol. 1. World Bank Technical Paper 341. Washington, D.C.

Greaney, Vincent, and Thomas Kellaghan. 1996. *Monitoring the Learning Outcomes of Education Systems.* A Directions in Development book. Washington, D.C.: World Bank.

Haggarty, Luke, and Mary M. Shirley. 1997. "A New Data Base on State-Owned Enterprises." *The World Bank Economic Review* 11(3):491–513.

Hanmer, Lucia, and Felix Naschold. 1999. "Attaining the International Development Targets: Will Growth Be Enough?" Commissioned by the U.K. Department for International Development as a contribution to the *World Development Report 2000/01.* World Bank, Washington, D.C.

Happe, Nancy, and John Wakeman-Linn. 1994. "Military Expenditures and Arms Trade: Alternative Data Sources." IMF Working Paper 94/69. International Monetary Fund, Policy Development and Review Department, Washington, D.C.

Harbison, Ralph W., and Eric A. Hanushek. 1992. *Educational Performance of the Poor: Lessons from Rural Northeast Brazil.* New York: Oxford University Press.

Harrison, Ann. 1995. "Factor Markets and Trade Policy Reform." World Bank, Washington, D.C.

Hatter, Victoria L. 1985. *U.S. High-Technology Trade and Competitiveness.* Washington, D.C.: U.S. Department of Commerce.

Hatzichronoglou, Thomas. 1997. "Revision of the High-Technology Sector and Product Classification." STI Working Paper 1997/2. OECD Directorate for Science, Technology, and Industry, Paris.

Heck, W.W. 1989. "Assessment of Crop Losses from Air Pollutants in the U.S." In J.J. McKenzie and M.T. El Ashry, eds., *Air Pollution's Toll on Forests and Crops.* New Haven, Conn.: Yale University Press.

Hertel, Thomas, and Will Martin. 1999. "Would Developing Countries Gain from Inclusion of Manufactures in the WTO Negotiations?" Paper presented at the World Trade Organization–World Bank conference Developing Countries in a Millennium Round, Geneva, 20–21 September.

Heston, Alan. 1994. "A Brief Review of Some Problems in Using National Accounts Data in Level of Output Comparisons and Growth Studies." *Journal of Development Economics* 44:29–52.

Hettige, Hemamala, Muthukumara Mani, and David Wheeler. 1998. "Industrial Pollution in Economic Development: Kuznets Revisited." Policy Research Working Paper 1876. World Bank, Development Research Group, Washington, D.C.

Hill, M. Anne, and Elizabeth M. King. 1993. "Women's Education in Developing Countries: An Overview." In Elizabeth M. King and M. Anne Hill, eds., *Women's Education in Developing Countries.* Baltimore, Md.: Johns Hopkins University Press.

IEA (International Energy Agency). Various years. *Energy Balances of OECD Countries.* Paris.

———. Various years. *Energy Statistics and Balances of Non-OECD Countries.* Paris.

———. Various years. *Energy Statistics of OECD Countries.* Paris.

IFC (International Finance Corporation). 1999a. *Emerging Stock Markets Factbook 1999.* Washington, D.C.

———. 1999b. *Trends in Private Investment in Developing Countries 1999.* Washington, D.C.

Bibliography

ILO (International Labour Organization). 1990a. *ILO Manual on Concepts and Methods.* Geneva: International Labour Office.

———. 1990b. *Yearbook of Labour Statistics: Retrospective Edition of Population Censuses 1945–89.* Geneva: International Labour Office.

———. 1999. *Key Indicators of the Labour Market.* Geneva: International Labour Office.

———. Various years. *Sources and Methods: Labour Statistics.* (Formerly *Statistical Sources and Methods.)* Geneva: International Labour Office.

———. Various years. *Yearbook of Labour Statistics.* Geneva: International Labour Office.

IMF (International Monetary Fund). 1977. *Balance of Payments Manual.* 4th ed. Washington, D.C.

———. 1986. *A Manual on Government Finance Statistics.* Washington, D.C.

———. 1993. *Balance of Payments Manual.* 5th ed. Washington, D.C.

———. 1995. *Balance of Payments Compilation Guide.* Washington, D.C.

———. 1996a. *Balance of Payments Textbook.* Washington, D.C.

———. 1996b. *Manual on Monetary and Financial Statistics.* Washington, D.C.

———. 1999. *Exchange Arrangements and Exchange Restrictions Annual Report, 1999.* Washington, D.C.

———. Various years. *Balance of Payments Statistics Yearbook.* Parts 1 and 2. Washington, D.C.

———. Various issues. *Direction of Trade Statistics.* Quarterly. Washington, D.C.

———. Various years. *Direction of Trade Statistics Yearbook.* Washington, D.C.

———. Various years. *Government Finance Statistics Yearbook.* Washington, D.C.

———. Various issues. *International Financial Statistics.* Monthly. Washington, D.C.

———. Various years. *International Financial Statistics Yearbook.* Washington, D.C.

Institutional Investor. 1999. September. New York.

Intergovernmental Panel on Climate Change. 1996. *Climate Change 1995.* Cambridge: Cambridge University Press.

International Association for the Evaluation of Educational Achievement. 1997. *Third International Mathematics and Science Study, 1994–95.* Boston, Mass.: Boston College, TIMSS International Study Center.

International Civil Aviation Organization. 1999. *Civil Aviation Statistics of the World: 1998.* ICAO Statistical Yearbook. 23rd ed. Montreal.

International Telecommunication Union. 1999. *World Telecommunication Development Report.* Geneva.

International Working Group of External Debt Compilers (Bank for International Settlements, International Monetary Fund, Organisation for Economic Co-operation and Development, and World Bank). 1987. *External Debt Definitions.* Washington, D.C.

Inter-Secretariat Working Group on National Accounts (Commission of the European Community, International Monetary Fund, Organisation for Economic Co-operation and Development, United Nations, and World Bank). 1993. *System of National Accounts.* Brussels, Luxembourg, New York, and Washington, D.C.

IRF (International Road Federation). 1999. *World Road Statistics 1999.* Geneva.

Irwin, Douglas A. 1996. "The United States in a New Global Economy? A Century's Perspective." Papers and Proceedings of the 108th Annual Meeting of the American Economic Association. *American Economic Review* (May).

Isard, Peter. 1995. *Exchange Rate Economics.* Cambridge: Cambridge University Press.

IUCN (World Conservation Union). 1996. *1996 IUCN Red List of Threatened Animals.* Gland, Switzerland.

———. 1998. *1997 IUCN Red List of Threatened Plants.* Gland, Switzerland.

Journal of Development Economics. 1994. Special issue on database for development analysis. Edited by T.N. Srinivasan. Vol. 44, no. 1.

Kaminsky, Graciela L., Saul Lizondo, and Carmen M. Reinhart. 1997. "Leading Indicators of Currency Crises." Policy Research Working Paper 1852. World Bank, Latin America and the Caribbean Region, Office of the Chief Economist, Washington, D.C.

Kanbur, Ravi. 1997. "Income Distribution and Development." Cornell University, Ithaca, N.Y.

Knetter, Michael. 1994. "Why Are Retail Prices in Japan So High? Evidence from German Export Prices." NBER Working Paper 4894. National Bureau of Economic Research, Cambridge, Mass.

Kunte, Arundhati, Kirk Hamilton, John Dixon, and Michael Clemens. 1998. "Estimating National Wealth: Methodology and Results." Environmental Economics Series, no. 57. World Bank, Environment Department, Washington, D.C.

Lele, Uma, William Lesser, and Gesa Horstkotte-Wessler, eds. 2000. *Intellectual Property Rights in Agriculture: The World Bank's Role in Assisting Borrower and Member Countries.* Washington, D.C.: World Bank.

Levine, Ross, and Sara Zervos. 1996. "Stock Market Development and Long-Run Growth." *The World Bank Economic Review* 10(2):323–40.

Lewis, Karen K. 1995. "Puzzles in International Financial Markets." In Gene Grossman and Kenneth Rogoff, eds., *Handbook of International Economics.* Vol. 3. Amsterdam: North Holland.

Lewis, Stephen R., Jr. 1989. "Primary Exporting Countries." In Hollis Chenery and T.N. Srinivasan, eds., *Handbook of Development Economics.* Vol. 2. Amsterdam: North Holland.

Lovei, Magdolna. 1997. "Toward Effective Pollution Management." *Environment Matters* (fall):52–53.

Lucas, R.E. 1988. "On the Mechanics of Economic Development." *Journal of Monetary Economics* 22:3–22.

Mani, Muthukumara, and David Wheeler. 1997. "In Search of Pollution Havens? Dirty Industry in the World Economy, 1960–95." World Bank, Policy Research Department, Washington, D.C.

Maredia, Karim M., Frederic H. Erbisch, Catherine L. Ives, and Andrew J. Fischer. 1999. "Technology Transfer and Licensing of Agricultural Biotechnologies in the International Arena." *AgBiotechNet* 1(May).

Martin, Will, and Keith Maskus. 1999. "Core Labor Standards and Competitiveness: Implications for Global Trade Policy." World Bank, Development Research Group, Washington, D.C., and University of Colorado, Boulder.

Michalopoulos, Constantine. 1999. "Developing Country Goals and Strategies for the Millennium Round." Policy Research Working Paper 2147. World Bank, Development Research Group, Washington, D.C.

Midgley, Peter. 1994. *Urban Transport in Asia: An Operational Agenda for the 1990s.* World Bank Technical Paper 224. Washington, D.C.

Moody's Investors Service. 1999. *Sovereign, Subnational and Sovereign-Guaranteed Issuers.* December. New York.

Moran, Katy. 1999. "Health: Indigenous Knowledge, Equitable Benefits." IK Notes, no. 15. World Bank, Africa Regional Office, Washington, D.C.

Morgenstern, Oskar. 1963. *On the Accuracy of Economic Observations.* Princeton, N.J.: Princeton University Press.

Murray, Christopher J.L., and Alan D. Lopez, eds. 1998. *Health Dimensions of Sex and Reproduc-*

tion: The Global Burden of Sexually Transmitted Diseases, HIV, Maternal Conditions, Perinatal Disorders, and Congenital Anomalies. Cambridge, Mass.: Harvard University Press.

National Science Foundation. 1998. *Science and Engineering Indicators 1998.* Arlington, Va.

Obstfeldt, Maurice. 1995. "International Capital Mobility in the 1990s." In P.B. Kenen, ed., *Understanding Interdependence: The Macroeconomics of the Open Economy.* Princeton, N.J.: Princeton University Press.

Obstfeldt, Maurice, and Kenneth Rogoff. 1996. *Foundations of International Macroeconomics.* Cambridge, Mass.: MIT Press.

OECD (Organisation for Economic Co-operation and Development). 1985. "Measuring Health Care 1960–1983: Expenditure, Costs, Performance." OECD Social Policy Studies 2. Paris.

———. 1989. "Health Care Expenditure and Other Data: An International Compendium from the OECD." In *Health Care Financing Review.* Annual supplement. Paris.

———. 1996a. *Education at a Glance.* Paris.

———. 1996b. *Shaping the 21st Century: The Contribution of Development Cooperation.* Paris.

———. 1996c. *Trade, Employment, and Labour Standards: A Study of Core Workers' Rights and International Trade.* Paris.

———. 1997a. *Employment Outlook.* Paris.

———. 1997b. *OECD Environmental Data: Compendium 1997.* Paris.

———. Various issues. *Main Economic Indicators.* Monthly. Paris.

———. Various years. *National Accounts.* Vol. 1, *Main Aggregates.* Paris.

———. Various years. *National Accounts.* Vol. 2, *Detailed Tables.* Paris.

———. Various years. *Trends in International Migration: Continuous Reporting System on Migration.* Paris.

OECD, Development Assistance Committee. Various years. *Development Co-operation.* Paris.

———. Various years. *Geographical Distribution of Financial Flows to Aid Recipients: Disbursements, Commitments, Country Indicators.* Paris.

Olson, Elizabeth. 1999. "Drug Groups and U.N. Offices Join to Develop Malaria Cures." *New York Times,* 31 October.

O'Meara, Molly. 1999. "Reinventing Cities for People and the Planet." Worldwatch Paper 147. Worldwatch Institute, Washington, D.C.

Pearce, David, and Giles Atkinson. 1993. "Capital Theory and the Measurement of Sustainable Development: An Indicator of Weak Sustainability." *Ecological Economics* 8:103–08.

Pilling, David. 1999. "In Sickness and in Wealth." *Financial Times,* 22 October.

Plucknett, Donald L. 1991. "Saving Lives through Agricultural Research." *Issues in Agriculture* (World Bank, Consultative Group on International Agricultural Research, Washington, D.C.) 16.

PricewaterhouseCoopers. 1999a. *Corporate Taxes: Worldwide Summaries.* New York.

———. 1999b. *Individual Taxes: Worldwide Summaries.* New York.

Pritchett, Lant. 1996. "Measuring Outward Orientation in Developing Countries: Can It Be Done?" Policy Research Working Paper 566. World Bank, Country Economics Department, Washington, D.C.

Pritchett, Lant, and Geeta Sethi. 1994. "Tariff Rates, Tariff Revenue, and Tariff Reform—Some New Facts." *The World Bank Economic Review* 8(1):1–16.

PRS Group. 1999. *International Country Risk Guide.* December. East Syracuse, N.Y.

Rama, Martin, and Raquel Artecona. 1999. "A Database of Labor Market Indicators across Countries." World Bank, Development Research Group, Washington, D.C.

Ravallion, Martin. 1996. "Poverty and Growth: Lessons from 40 Years of Data on India's Poor." DECNote 20. World Bank, Development Economics Vice Presidency, Washington, D.C.

Ravallion, Martin, and Shaohua Chen. 1996. "What Can New Survey Data Tell Us about the Recent Changes in Living Standards in Developing and Transitional Economies?" World Bank, Policy Research Department, Washington, D.C.

———. 1997. "Can High-Inequality Developing Countries Escape Absolute Poverty?" *Economic Letters* 56:51–57.

Rodrik, Dani. 1996. "Labor Standards in International Trade: Do They Matter and What Do We Do About Them?" Overseas Development Council, Washington, D.C.

Rogoff, Kenneth. 1996. "The Purchasing Power Parity Puzzle." *Journal of Economic Literature* 34:647–68.

Romer, P.M. 1986. "Increasing Returns and Long-Run Growth." *Journal of Political Economy* 94:1002–37.

Ruggles, Robert. 1994. "Issues Relating to the UN System of National Accounts and Developing Countries." *Journal of Development Economics* 44(1):87–102.

Ryten, Jacob. 1998. "Fifty Years of ISIC: Historical Origins and Future Perspectives." United Nations Statistics Division, New York. ECA/STAT.AC.63/22.

Sachs, Jeffrey. 1998. "Globalization and the Rule of Law." Remarks to the 1998 Alumni Gathering of the Yale Law School, New Haven, Conn., 15 October.

———. 1999. "Helping the World's Poorest." *The Economist,* 14 August.

Salter, Ammon J., and Ben R. Martin. 1999. "The Economic Benefits of Publicly Funded Basic Research: A Critical Review." Science and Technology Policy Research, University of Sussex. Draft.

San Martin, Orlando. 1996. "Child Labour and Socio-Economic Development." In Bjorne Grimsrud and Arne Melchior, eds., *Child Labour and International Trade Policy.* Paris: OECD-DNMES Workshop.

Sen, Amartya. 1988. "The Concept of Development." In Hollis Chenery and T.N. Srinivasan, eds., *Handbook of Development Economics.* Vol. 1. Amsterdam: North Holland.

Serageldin, Ismail. 1995. *Toward Sustainable Management of Water Resources.* A Directions in Development book. Washington, D.C.: World Bank.

Serageldin, Ismail, and Wanda Collins, eds. 1999. *Biotechnology and Biosafety.* Washington, D.C.: World Bank.

Shiklovanov, Igor. 1993. "World Fresh Water Resources." In Peter H. Gleick, ed., *Water in Crisis: A Guide to Fresh Water Resources.* New York: Oxford University Press.

South Pacific Commission. 1999. *Pacific Island Populations Data Sheet 1999.* Noumea, New Caledonia.

Srinivasan, T.N. 1991. "Development Thought, Policy, and Strategy, Then and Now." Background paper to *World Development Report 1991.* World Bank, Washington, D.C.

———. 1994. "Database for Development Analysis: An Overview." *Journal of Development Economics* 44(1):3–28.

Standard & Poor's. 1999. *Credit Week.* December. New York.

———. 2000. *The S&P Emerging Market Indices: Methodology, Definitions, and Practices.* New York.

Bibliography

Standard & Poor's DRI. 1998. *Global Risk Service.* Lexington, Mass.

Stiglitz, Joseph E. 1999. "Two Principles for the Next Round—Or How to Bring Developing Countries in from the Cold." Paper presented to a World Trade Organization conference, Geneva, 21 September.

Sunil, Mani. 1999. "Public Innovation Policies and Developing Countries in a Phase of Economic Liberalization." United Nations University Institute for New Technologies, Maastricht.

Syrquin, Moshe. 1988. "Patterns of Structural Change." In Hollis Chenery and T.N. Srinivasan, eds., *Handbook of Development Economics.* Vol. 1. Amsterdam: North Holland.

Taylor, Alan M. 1996a. "International Capital Mobility in History: Purchasing Power Parity in the Long Run." NBER Working Paper 5742. National Bureau of Economic Research, Cambridge, Mass.

———. 1996b. "International Capital Mobility in History: The Saving-Investment Relationship." NBER Working Paper 5743. National Bureau of Economic Research, Cambridge, Mass.

TeleGeography and International Telecommunication Union. 1998. *Direction of Traffic 1997.* Washington, D.C.

Thurow, Lester. 1985. *The Zero-Sum Solution: Building a World-Class American Economy.* New York: Simon and Schuster.

UNAIDS and WHO (World Health Organization). 1998. *Report on the Global HIV/AIDS Epidemic.* Geneva.

UNCTAD (United Nations Conference on Trade and Development). Various years. *Handbook of International Trade and Development Statistics.* Geneva.

UNEP (United Nations Environment Programme). 1991. *Urban Air Pollution.* Nairobi.

UNEP (United Nations Environment Programme) and WHO (World Health Organization). 1992. *Urban Air Pollution in Megacities of the World.* Cambridge, Mass.: Blackwell.

———. 1995. *City Air Quality Trends.* Nairobi.

UNESCO (United Nations Educational, Scientific, and Cultural Organization). 1998. *World Education Report.* Paris: UNESCO Publishing and Bernan Press.

———. Various years. *Statistical Yearbook.* Paris: UNESCO Publishing and Bernan Press.

UNICEF (United Nations Children's Fund). Various years. *The Progress of Nations.* New York: Oxford University Press.

———. Various years. *The State of the World's Children.* New York: Oxford University Press.

UNIDO (United Nations Industrial Development Organization). Various years. *International Yearbook of Industrial Statistics.* Vienna.

United Nations. 1947. *Measurement of National Income and the Construction of Social Accounts.* New York.

———. 1968. *A System of National Accounts: Studies and Methods.* Series F, no. 2, rev. 3. New York.

———. 1990a. *Assessing the Nutritional Status of Young Children.* National Household Survey Capability Programme. New York.

———. 1990b. *International Standard Industrial Classification of All Economic Activities, Third Revision.* Statistical Papers Series M, no. 4, rev. 3. New York.

United Nations Administrative Committee on Coordination, Subcommittee on Nutrition. Various years. *Update on the Nutrition Situation.* Geneva.

United Nations Department of Economic and Social Affairs. 1993. *Report on the World Social Situation, 1993.* New York.

United Nations Economic and Social Commission for Western Asia. 1997. *Purchasing Power Parities: Volume and Price Level Comparisons for the Middle East, 1993.* E/ESCWA/STAT/1997/2. Amman.

United Nations Population Division. 1996a. *International Migration Policies 1995.* New York.

———. 1996b. *Urban Agglomerations 1996.* Wall chart. New York.

———. 1996c. *World Urbanization Prospects: The 1996 Revision.* New York.

———. 1998. *World Population Prospects: The 1998 Revision.* New York.

———. 1999. *World Urbanization Prospects: The 1998 Revision.* New York.

———. Various years. *Levels and Trends of Contraceptive Use.* New York.

United Nations Statistics Division. 1985. *National Accounts Statistics: Compendium of Income Distribution Statistics.* New York.

———. 1991. *The World's Women, 1970–90: Trends and Statistics.* New York.

———. 1993a. *Integrated Environmental and Economic Accounting.* New York.

———. 1993b. *International Trade Statistics Yearbook.* Vol. 1. New York.

———. Various years. *Energy Statistics Yearbook.* New York.

———. Various years. *International Trade Statistics Yearbook.* New York.

———. Various issues. *Monthly Bulletin of Statistics.* New York.

———. Various years. *National Accounts Statistics: Main Aggregates and Detailed Tables.* Parts 1 and 2. New York.

———. Various years. *National Income Accounts.* New York.

———. Various years. *Population and Vital Statistics Report.* New York.

———. Various years. *Statistical Yearbook.* New York.

UNRISD (United Nations Research Institute for Social Development). 1977. *Research Data Bank of Development Indicators.* Vol. 4, *Notes on the Indicators.* Geneva.

———. 1993. *Monitoring Social Progress in the 1990s: Data Constraints, Concerns, and Priorities.* Avebury, England.

U.S. Department of Health and Human Services. 1997. *Social Security Systems throughout the World.* Washington, D.C.

U.S. Department of State, Bureau of Arms Control. 1999. *World Military Expenditures and Arms Transfers 1998.* Washington, D.C.

U.S. Environmental Protection Agency. 1995. *National Air Quality and Emissions Trends Report 1995.* Washington, D.C.

Valdes, Alberto, and Joachim Zietz. 1995. "Distortions in World Food Markets in the Wake of GATT: Evidence and Policy Implications." *World Development* 23:913–26.

Wagstaff, Adam. 1999. "Inequalities in Child Mortality in the Developing World: How Large Are They? How Can They Be Reduced?" World Bank, Human Development Network, Washington, D.C.

Walsh, Michael P. 1994. "Motor Vehicle Pollution Control: An Increasingly Critical Issue for Developing Countries." World Bank, Washington, D.C.

Watkins, Kevin. 1999. *Education Now: Break the Cycle of Poverty.* Washington, D.C. Oxfam International.

Watson, Robert, John A. Dixon, Steven P. Hamburg, Anthony C. Janetos, and Richard H. Moss. 1998. *Protecting Our Planet, Securing Our Future: Linkages among Global Environmental Issues and Human Needs.* A joint publication of the United Nations Environment Programme, U.S. National Aeronautics and Space Administration, and World Bank. Nairobi and Washington, D.C.

WCEFA Inter-Agency Commission (United Nations Development Programme, United Nations Educational, Scientific, and Cultural Organization, United Nations Children's Fund, and World Bank). 1990. *World Conference on Education for All: Meeting Basic Learning Needs—Final Report.* Jomtien, Thailand.

WCMC (World Conservation Monitoring Centre). 1992. *Global Biodiversity: Status of the Earth's Living Resources.* London: Chapman and Hall.

———. 1994. *Biodiversity Data Sourcebook.* Cambridge: World Conservation Press.

Westphal, Larry E. 1999. "Survey of Existing Technology Policies and New Policy Needs: Strategies of Technological Development Reconsidered." Paper presented at the international workshop The Political Economy of Technology Policy in Developing Countries, Isle of Thorns Training Center, Sussex, England, October.

WHO (World Health Organization). 1977. *International Classification of Diseases.* 9th rev. Geneva.

———. 1991. *Maternal Mortality: A Global Factbook.* Geneva.

———. 1996. *Evaluating the Implementation of the Strategy for Health for All by the Year 2000.* Geneva.

———. 1997a. *Coverage of Maternity Care.* Geneva.

———. 1997b. *Monitoring Reproductive Health: Selecting a Short List of National and Global Indicators.* Geneva.

———. 1997c. *Tobacco or Health: A Global Status Report, 1997.* Geneva.

———. 1998. *EPI Information System: Global Summary, September 1998.* Geneva.

———. 1999a. *Global Tuberculosis Control Report 1999.* Geneva.

———. 1999b. *World Health Report 1999: Making a Difference.* Geneva.

———. 2000. *World Health Report 2000.* Geneva.

———. Various years. *World Health Statistics Annual.* Geneva.

WHO (World Health Organization) and UNICEF (United Nations Children's Fund). 1992. *Low Birth Weight: A Tabulation of Available Information.* Geneva.

Willig, Robert. 1998. "Economic Effects of Antidumping Policy." *Brookings Trade Forum 1998.* Washington, D.C.: The Brookings Institution.

Windham, Douglas M. 1988. *Indicators of Educational Effectiveness and Efficiency.* Tallahassee, Fla.: Florida State University, Educational Efficiency Clearinghouse.

Wolf, Holger C. 1997. "Patterns of Intra- and Inter-State Trade." NBER Working Paper 5939. National Bureau of Economic Research, Cambridge, Mass.

World Bank. 1990. *World Development Report 1990: Poverty.* New York: Oxford University Press.

———. 1991a. *Developing the Private Sector: The World Bank's Experience and Approach.* Washington, D.C.

———. 1991b. *World Development Report 1991: The Challenge of Development.* New York: Oxford University Press.

———. 1992. *World Development Report 1992: Development and the Environment.* New York: Oxford University Press.

———. 1993a. *The Environmental Data Book: A Guide to Statistics on the Environment and Development.* Washington, D.C.

———. 1993b. *Purchasing Power Parities: Comparing National Incomes Using ICP Data.* Washington, D.C.

———. 1993c. *World Development Report 1993: Investing in Health.* New York: Oxford University Press.

———. 1994. *World Development Report 1994: Infrastructure for Development.* New York: Oxford University Press.

———. 1995a. *Bureaucrats in Business: The Economics and Politics of Government Ownership.* A World Bank Policy Research Report. New York: Oxford University Press.

———. 1995b. *Private Sector Development in Low-Income Countries.* Development in Practice series. Washington, D.C.

———. 1996a. *Environment Matters* (summer). Environment Department. Washington, D.C.

———. 1996b. *Livable Cities for the 21st Century.* A Directions in Development book. Washington, D.C.

———. 1996c. *National Environmental Strategies: Learning from Experience.* Environment Department. Washington, D.C.

———. 1997a. *Can the Environment Wait? Priorities for East Asia.* Washington, D.C.

———. 1997b. *Confronting AIDS: Public Priorities in a Global Epidemic.* A World Bank Policy Research Report. New York: Oxford University Press.

———. 1997c. *Expanding the Measure of Wealth: Indicators of Environmentally Sustainable Development.* Environmentally Sustainable Development Studies and Monographs Series, no. 17. Washington, D.C.

———. 1997d. *Private Capital Flows to Developing Countries: The Road to Financial Integration.* A World Bank Policy Research Report. New York: Oxford University Press.

———. 1997e. *Rural Development: From Vision to Action.* Environmentally Sustainable Development Studies and Monographs Series, no. 12. Washington, D.C.

———. 1997f. *Sector Strategy: Health, Nutrition, and Population.* Human Development Network. Washington, D.C.

———. 1997g. *World Development Report 1997: The State in a Changing World.* New York: Oxford University Press.

———. 1998a. *Assessing Aid: What Works, What Doesn't, and Why.* A World Bank Policy Research Report. New York: Oxford University Press.

———. 1998b. *1998 Catalog: Operational Documents as of July 31, 1998.* Washington, D.C.

———. 1998c. *World Development Report 1998/99: Knowledge for Development.* New York: Oxford University Press.

———. 1999a. *Fuel for Thought: Environmental Strategy for the Energy Sector.* Environment Department, Energy, Mining, and Telecommunications Department, and International Finance Corporation. Washington, D.C.

———. 1999b. *Greening Industry: New Roles for Communities, Markets, and Governments.* A World Bank Policy Research Report. Washington, D.C.

———. 1999c. *Health, Nutrition, and Population Indicators: A Statistical Handbook.* Human Development Network. Washington, D.C.

———. 1999d. *World Development Report 1999/2000—Entering the 21st Century: The Changing Development Landscape.* New York: Oxford University Press.

———. Forthcoming a. *Poverty Reduction and the World Bank: Progress in Fiscal 1999.* Washington, D.C.

———. Forthcoming b. *Purchasing Power Parities: International Comparison of Volume and Price Levels.* Washington, D.C.

———. Various issues. *Global Commodity Markets.* Quarterly. Washington, D.C.

———. Various years. *Global Development Finance.* (Formerly published under the title *World Debt Tables.*) Washington, D.C. (Also available on CD-ROM.)

Bibliography

———. Various years. *Global Economic Prospects and the Developing Countries.* Washington, D.C.

———. Various years. *World Development Indicators.* Washington, D.C.

World Energy Council. 1995. *Global Energy Perspectives to 2050 and Beyond.* London.

World Food Prize. 2000. "1999 World Food Prize Laureate." www.wfpf.org. 28 February.

World Intellectual Property Organization. 1999. *Industrial Property Statistics.* Publication A. Geneva.

World Resources Institute, International Institute for Environment and Development, and IUCN (World Conservation Union). Various years. *World Directory of Country Environmental Studies.* Washington, D.C.

World Resources Institute, UNEP (United Nations Environment Programme), and UNDP (United Nations Development Programme). 1994. *World Resources 1994–95: A Guide to the Global Environment.* New York: Oxford University Press.

World Resources Institute, UNEP (United Nations Environment Programme), UNDP (United Nations Development Programme), and World Bank. Various years. *World Resources: A Guide to the Global Environment.* New York: Oxford University Press.

World Tourism Organization. 1999a. *Compendium of Tourism Statistics 1993–97.* 19th ed. Madrid.

———. 1999b. *Yearbook of Tourism Statistics.* Vols. 1 and 2. Madrid.

WTO (World Trade Organization). Various years. *Annual Report.* Geneva.

Zimmermann, Klaus F. 1995. "European Migration: Push and Pull." In Michael Bruno and Boris Pleskovic, eds., *Proceedings of the World Bank Annual Conference on Development Economics 1994.* Washington, D.C.: World Bank.

Index of indicators

References are to table numbers.

Index of indicators

Index of indicators

DISTRIBUTORS OF WORLD BANK PUBLICATIONS

Prices and credit terms vary from country to country. Please consult your local distributor or bookseller before placing an order.

ARGENTINA
World Publications SA
Av. Cordoba 1877
1120 Buenos Aires
Tel: (54 11) 4815 8156
Fax: (54 11) 4815 8156
Email: wpbooks@infovia.com.ar

AUSTRALIA, PAPUA NEW GUINEA, FIJI, SOLOMON ISLANDS, VANUATU, AND SAMOA
D.A. Information Services
648 Whitehorse Road
Mitcham 3132
Victoria, Australia
Tel: (61 3) 9210 7777
Fax: (61 3) 9210 7788
Email: service@dadirect.com.au
URL: www.dadirect.com.au

AUSTRIA
Gerold and Co.
Weihburggasse 26
A-1011 Wien
Tel: (43 1) 512-47-31-0
Fax: (43 1) 512-47-31-29
URL: www.gerold.co/at.online

BANGLADESH
Micro Industries Development Assistance Society (MIDAS)
House 5, Road 16
Dhanmondi R/Area
Dhaka 1209
Tel: (880 2) 326427
Fax: (880 2) 8111188
Email: midas@fsbd.net

BELGIUM
Jean de Lannoy
Av. du Roi 202
1060 Brussels
Tel: (32 2) 538 5169
Fax: (32 2) 538 0841
Email: jean.de.lannoy@infoboard.be
URL: www.jean-de-lannoy.be

BOSNIA AND HERZEGOVINA
Book Trading Company "Sahinpasic"
Marsala Tita 29/II
71000 Sarajevo
Tel: (387 71) 21 05 20
Fax: (387 71) 66 88 56
Email: tajib@btcsahinpasic.com
URL: www.btcsahinpasic.com

BRAZIL
Publicacoes Tecnicas Internacionais Ltda.
Rua Peixoto Gomide, 209
01409 Sao Paulo, SP
Tel: (55 11) 259 6644
Fax: (55 11) 258 6990
Email: postmaster@pti.uol.br
URL: www.uol.br

CANADA
Renouf Publishing Co. Ltd.
5369 Canotek Road
Ottawa, Ontario K1J 9J3
Tel: (613) 745-2665
Fax: (613) 745-7660
Email: order.dept@renoufbooks.com
URL: www.renoufbooks.com

CHINA
Chinese Corporation for Promotion and Humanities
15, Ding Hui Dong Li, Kun Lan Hotal
Haidian District 100036
Beijing
Tel: (86 10) 88117711
Fax: (86 10) 88129871
Email: wangjiang99@yahoo.com

China Book Import Centre
P.O. Box 2825
Beijing

China Financial & Economic Publishing House
8, Da Fo Si Dong Jie
Beijing
Tel: (86 10) 6401 7365
Fax: (86 10) 6401 7365

COLOMBIA
Infoenlace Ltda./An IHS Group Company
Calle 72 No. 13-23 - Piso 3
Edificio Nueva Granada
Santafé de Bogotá, D.C.
Tel: (57 1) 255 8783
Fax: (57 1) 248 0808
Email: infoenlace@gaitana.interred.net.co

CÔTE D'IVOIRE
Centre d'Edition et de Diffusion Africaines (CEDA)
04 B.P. 541
Abidjan 04
Tel: (225) 24 6510
Fax: (225) 25 0567
Email: info@ceda-ci.com
URL: www.ceda-ci.com

CYPRUS
Center for Applied Research
6, Diogenes Street, Engomi
P.O. Box 2006
Nicosia
Tel: (357 2) 59 0730
Fax: (357 2) 66 2051
Email: ttzitzim@sting.cycollege.ac.cy

CZECH REPUBLIC
Management Press, NT Publishing, s.r.o.
Nam. W. Churchilla 2
130 59 Prague 3
Tel: (420 2) 2446 2232, 2446 2254
Fax: (420 2) 2446 2242
Email: mgmtpress@mgmtpress.cz
URL: www.mgmtpress.cz

USIS, NIS Prodejna
Havelkova 22
130 00 Prague 3
Tel: (42 2) 2423 1486
Fax: (42 2) 2423 1114
Email: pospisilovaj@usiscr.cz
URL: www.usiscr.cz

DENMARK
Samfundslitteratur
Solbjerg Plads 3
DK-2000 Frederiksberg
Tel: (45 38) 153870
Fax: (45 38) 153856
Email: ck@sl.cbs.dk
URL: www.sl.cbs.dk

ECUADOR
Libri Mundi - Libreria Internacional
Juan Leon Mera 851
P.O. Box 17-01-3029
Quito
Tel: (593 2) 521 606
Fax: (593 2) 504 209
Email: librimu1@librimundi.com.ec

CODEU
Ruiz de Castilla 763, Edif. Expocolor
Primer piso, Of. #2
Quito
Tel: (593 2) 507-383
Fax: (593 2) 507-383
Email: codeu@impsat.net.ec

EGYPT, ARAB REPUBLIC OF
Al Ahram Distribution Agency
Al Galaa Street
Cairo
Tel: (20 2) 578 60 83
Fax: (20 2) 578 68 33

MERIC (Middle East Readers Information Center)
2 Bahrat Aly St.
Building "D" 1st Floor, Apt. 24
Cairo
Tel: (20 2) 341 3824
Fax: (20 2) 341 9355
Email: order@meric-co.com
URL: www.meobserver.com.eg

For subscription orders and publications in French only:
Middle East Observer
41 Sherif Street
Cairo
Tel: (20 2) 392 6919
Fax: (20 2) 393 9732
Email: gfoda@wayout.net

FINLAND
Akateeminen Kirjakauppa
PL 128 (Keskuskatu 1)
FIN-00101 Helsinki
Tel: (358 9) 121 4385
Fax: (358 9) 121 4450
Email: akatilaus@akateeminen.com
URL: www.akateeminen.com

FRANCE
Editions Eska; DJB/Offilib
12, rue du Quatre-Septembre
75002 Paris
Tel: (33 1) 42 86 58 88
Fax: (33 1) 42 60 45 35
Email: offilib@offilib.fr
URL: www.offilib.fr

GERMANY
UNO-VERLAG
Poppelsdorfer Allee 55
D-53115 Bonn
Tel: (49 228) 949 020
Fax: (49 228) 217 492
Email: unoverlag@aol.com
URL: www.uno-verlag.de

GHANA
Epp Books Services
Post Office Box 44
TUC
Accra
Tel: (233 21) 778 843
Fax: (233 21) 779 099
Email: epp@africaonline.com.gh

GREECE
Papasotiriou S.A.,
International Technical Bookstore
35, Stournara Str.
106 82 Athens
Tel: (30 1) 364 1826
Fax: (30 1) 364 8254
Email: gprekas@papasotiriou.gr

HAITI
Culture Diffusion
Mr. Yves Clément Jumelle
5, Rue Capois
C.P. 257
Port-au-Prince
Tel: (509) 23 9260
Fax: (509) 23 4858

HONG KONG, CHINA; MACAU, CHINA
Asia 2000 Ltd.
Sales & Circulation Department
302 Seabird House
22-28 Wyndham Street, Central
Hong Kong, China
Tel: (852) 2530 1409
Fax: (852) 2526 1107
Email: sales@asia2000.com.hk
URL: www.asia2000.com.hk

HUNGARY
Euro Info Service
Hungexpo Europa Haz (Pf. 44)
H-1441 Budapest
Tel: (36 1) 264 8270;
(36 1) 264 8271
Fax: (36 1) 264 8275
Email: euroinfo@euroinfo.hu
URL: www.euroinfo.hu

INDIA
Allied Publishers Ltd.
751 Mount Road
Madras 600 002
Tel: (91 44) 852 3938
Fax: (91 44) 852 0649
Email: allied.mds@smb.sprintrpg.ems.vsnl.net.in

INDONESIA
Pt. Indira Limited
Jalan Borobudur 20
PO Box 181
Jakarta 10320
Tel: (62 21) 390 4290
Fax: (62 21) 390 4289

PF Book
J1. dr. Setia Budhi No. 274
Bandung 40143
Tel: (62 22) 211 149
Fax: (62 22) 212 840
Email: pfbook@bandung.wasantara.net.id

IRAN
Ketab Sara Co. Publishers
P.O. Box 15745-733
Tehran 15117
Tel: (98 21) 871 6104
Fax: (98 21) 871 2479
Email: ketab-sara@neda.net.ir

Kowkab Publishers
P.O. BOX 19575-511
Tehran
Tel: (98 21) 258 3723
Fax: (98 21) 258 3723
Email: kowkabpub@tavana.net

ISRAEL
Yozmot Literature Ltd.
P.O. Box 56055
3 Yohanan Hasandlar St.
Tel Aviv 61560
Tel: (972 3) 5285 397
Fax: (972 3) 5285 397

ITALY
Licosa Libreria Commissionaria Sansoni S.P.A.
Via Duca di Calabria 1/1
50125 Firenze
Tel: (39 55) 648 31
Fax: (39 55) 641 257
Email: licosa@ftbcc.it
URL: www.ftbcc.it/licosa

JAMAICA
Ian Randle Publishers Ltd
206 Old Hope Road
Kingston 6
Tel: (876) 927 2085
Fax: (876) 977 0243
Email: irpl@colis.com

JAPAN
Eastern Book Service (EBS)
3-13 Hongo 3-chome, Bunkyo-ku
Tokyo 113
Tel: (81 3) 3818 0861
Fax: (81 3) 3818 0864
Email: orders@svt-ebs.co.jp
URL: www.svt-ebs.co.jp

KENYA
Legacy Books
Loita House
P.O. Box 68077
Nairobi
Tel: (254 2) 330 853
Fax: (254 2) 330 854
Email: legacy@form-net.com

Africa Book Service (E.A.) Ltd.
Mr. Talat Lone
Quaran House, Mfangano Street
P.O. Box 45245
Nairobi
Tel: (254 2) 223 641
Fax: (254 2) 330 272

KOREA, REPUBLIC OF
Eulyoo Publishing Co., Ltd.
46-1, Susong-Dong
Jongro-Gu
Seoul
Tel: (82 2) 734 3515
Fax: (82 2) 732 9154
Email: eulyoo@chollian.net

Dayang Books Trading Co.
International Division
954-22, Bangbae-Dong, Socho-ku
Seoul
Tel: (82 2) 582 3588
Fax: (82 2) 521 8827
Email: dico3@chollian.net

LEBANON
Librairie du Liban
P.O. Box 11-9232
Beirut
Tel: (961 9) 217 944
Fax: (961 9) 217 434
Email: hsageh@cyberia.net.lb
URL: www.librairie-du-liban.com.lb

MALAYSIA
University of Malaya Cooperative Bookshop, Limited
P.O. Box 1127, Jalan Pantai Baru
59700 Kuala Lumpur
Tel: (60 3) 756 5000
Fax: (60 3) 755 4424
Email: umkoop@tm.net.my

MEXICO
INFOTEC
Av. San Fernando No. 37
Col. Toriello Guerra
14050 Mexico D.F.
Tel: (52 5) 624 2800
Fax: (52 5) 624 2822
Email: infotec@rtn.net.mx
URL: www.rtn.net.mx

Mundi-Prensa Mexico, S.A. de C.V.
c/Rio Panuco, 141 - Colonia Cuauhtemoc
06500 Mexico DF
Tel: (52 5) 533 56 58
Fax: (52 5) 514 67 99
Email: 1015245.2361@compuserve.com

MOROCCO
Librarie Internationale
70, Rue T'ssoule
P.O. Box 302
Rabat (Souissi) MA 10001
Tel: (212 7) 75 01 83
Fax: (212 7) 75 86 61

NEPAL
Everest Media International Services (P.) Ltd.
GPO Box 5443
Kathmandu
Tel: (977 1) 416 026
Fax: (977 1) 224 431

NETHERLANDS
De Lindeboom/
Internationale Publikaties b.v.
M.A. de Ruyterstraat 20A
7482 BZ Haaksbergen
Tel: (31 53) 574 0004
Fax: (31 53) 572 9296
Email: books@delindeboom.com
URL: www.delindeboom.com

NEW ZEALAND
EBSCO NZ Ltd.
Private Mail Bag 99914
New Market
Auckland
Tel: (64 9) 524 8119
Fax: (64 9) 524 8067
Email: WGent%essnz.ebsco@iss.ebsco.com

Oasis Official
P.O. Box 3627
Wellington
Tel: (64 4) 4991551
Fax: (64 4) 499 1972
Email: oasis@actix.gen.nz
URL: www.oasisbooks.co.nz

NIGERIA
University Press Plc
Three Crowns Building Jericho
Private Mail Bag 5095
Ibadan
Tel: (234 22) 411356
Fax: (234 22) 412056
Email: suike@hotmail.com

PAKISTAN
Oxford University Press
5 Bangalore Town, Sharae Faisal
P.O. Box 13033
Karachi 75350
Tel: (92 21) 446307; 449032; 440532
Fax: (92 21) 4547640;449032
Email: usmanm@oup.net.pk

Pak Book Corporation
Aziz Chambers 21
Queen's Road
Lahore
Tel: (92 42) 636 3222; 636 0885
Fax: (92 42) 636 2328
Email: pbc@brain.net.pk

Mirza Book Agency
65, Shahrah-e-Quaid-e-Azam
Lahore 54000
Tel: (92 42) 7353601
Fax: (92 42) 576 3714
Email: merchant@brain.net.pk

PERU
Editorial Desarrollo SA
Apartado 3824
Ica 242, OF. 106
Lima 1
Tel: (51 14) 285 380
Fax: (51 14) 286 628

PHILIPPINES
International Booksource Center, Inc.
1127-A Antipolo St.
Barangay, Venezuela
Makati City
Tel: (63 2) 896 6501
Fax: (63 2) 896 6497

POLAND
International Publishing Service
Ul. Piekna 31/37
00 677 Warsaw
Tel: (48 2) 628 6089
Fax: (48 2) 621 7255
Email: books%ips@ikp.atm.com.pl
URL: www.ips.com.pl

PORTUGAL
Livraria Portugal
Apartado 2681
Rua Do Carmo 70-74
1200 Lisbon
Tel: (351 1) 347 4982
Fax: (351 1) 347 0264

ROMANIA
Compani De Librarii Bucuresti s.a.
Str. Lipscani nr. 26, sector 3
Bucharest
Tel: (40 1) 313 9645
Fax: (40 1) 312 4000

RUSSIAN FEDERATION
Izdatelstvo << Ves Mir >>
Moscow 101831
Tel: (7 95) 917 8749
Fax: (7 95) 917 9259
Email: ozimarin@glasnet.ru
URL: www.vesmir.tsx.org

SENEGAL
Librairie Clairafrique
2, Rue El Hadj Mbaye Gueye
Place de l'Independance
B.P. 2005
Dakar
Tel: (221) 822 21 69
Fax: (221) 821 84 09

SINGAPORE; TAIWAN, CHINA; MYANMAR; BRUNEI
Hemisphere Publishing Services
Golden Wheel Building
41 Kallang Pudding Road, #04-03
Singapore 349316
Tel: (65) 741 5166
Fax: (65) 742 9356
Email: info@hemisphere.com.sg

SLOVENIA
Gospodarski vestnik Publishing Group
Dunajska cesta 5
1000 Ljubljana
Tel: (386 61) 133 83 47
Fax: (386 61) 133 80 30
Email: repansekj@gvestnik.si
URL: www.gvestnik.si/EUROPA/index.htm

SOUTH AFRICA, BOTSWANA
For single titles:
Oxford University Press Southern Africa
P.O. Box 12119
N1 City 7463
Cape Town, South Africa
Tel: (27 21) 595 4400
Fax: (27 21) 595 4430
Email: oxford@oup.co.za

For subscription orders:
International Subscription Service
P.O. Box 41095
Craighall
Johannesburg 2024, South Africa
Tel: (27 11) 880 1448
Fax: (27 11) 880 6248
Email: iss@is.co.za

SPAIN
Mundi-Prensa Libros, s.a.
Castello 37
28001 Madrid
Tel: (34 91) 436 37 00
Fax: (34 91) 575 39 98
Email: libreria@mundiprensa.es
URL: www.mundiprensa.es

Mundi-Prensa Barcelona
Consell de Cent No. 391
08009 Barcelona
Tel: (34 3) 488 3492
Fax: (34 3) 487 7659
Email: barcelona@mundiprensa.es

SRI LANKA, THE MALDIVES
Lake House Bookshop
P.O. Box 244
100, Sir Chittampalam Gardiner Mawatha
Colombo 2, Sri Lanka
Tel: (94 1) 32 104
Fax: (94 1) 432 104
Email: LHL@sri.lanka.net

SWEDEN
For periodicals and serials only:
Wennergren-Williams Informations Service AB
P.O. Box 1305
S-171 25 Solna
Tel: (46 8) 705 9750
Fax: (46 8) 27 0071
Email: mail@wwi.se

SWITZERLAND
Librarie Payot S.A.
Service Institutionnel
Côtes-de-Montbenon 30
1002 Lausanne
Tel: (41 21) 341 3229
Fax: (41 21) 341 3235
Email: institutionnel@payotlibraire.ch

ADECO Van Diermen Editions Techniques
Ch. de Lacuez 41
CH-1807 Blonay
Tel: (41 21) 943 2673
Fax: (41 21) 943 3605

TANZANIA
TEPUSA
The Network of Technical Publications in Africa
P.O. Box 22638
Dar es Salaam
Tel: (255 51) 114 876
Fax: (255 51) 112 434
Email: tepusa@intafrica.com

THAILAND
Centrac International Ltd.
ATTN: Central Books Distribution Co., Ltd.
Sinnrat Bldg. 13th Floor
3388/42-45 Rama 4 Rd. Klong-Teoy
Bangkok 10110
Tel: (66 2) 367-5030-41 X178
Fax: (66 2) 3675049

TRINIDAD & TOBAGO AND THE CARIBBEAN
Systematics Studies Ltd.
St. Augustine Shopping Center
Eastern Main Road
St. Augustine
Tel: (868) 645 8466
Fax: (868) 645 8467
Email: tobe@trinidad.net

UGANDA
Gustro Limited
P.O. Box 9997
Madhvani Building
Plot 16/4, Jinja Road
Kampala
Tel: (256 41) 251467
Fax: (256 41) 251468
Email: gus@swiftuganda.com

UKRAINE
LIBRA Publishing House
Ms. Sophia Ghemborovskaya
53/80 Saksahanskoho Str.
252033, Kiev 33
Tel: (7 44) 227 62 77
Fax: (7 44) 227 62 77

UNITED KINGDOM
Microinfo Ltd.
P.O. Box 3, Omega Park
Alton
Hampshire GU34 2 PG
Tel: (44 1420) 86 848
Fax: 44 1420) 89 889
Email: wbank@microinfo.co.uk
URL: www.microinfo.co.uk

The Stationery Office
51 Nine Elms Lane
London SW8 5DR
Tel: (44 171) 873-8372
Fax: (44 171) 873-8242
Email: chris.allen@theso.co.uk
URL: www.the-stationery office.co.uk/ai/

VENEZUELA, RB
Tecni-Ciencia Libros, S.A.
Sr. Luis Fernando Ramirez, Director
Centro Cuidad Comercial Tamanaco
Nivel C-2
Caracas
Tel: (58 2) 959 5547
Fax: (58 2) 959 5636
Email: lfrg001@ibm.net

VIETNAM
FAHASA (The Book Distribution Co. of Hochiminh City)
246 Le Thanh Ton Street
District 1
Hochiminh City
Tel: (84 8) 829 7638, 822 5446
Fax: (84 8) 822 5795
Email: fahasasg@hcm.vnn.vn
URL: www.tlnet.com.vn/fahasa

ZAMBIA
University Bookshop, University of Zambia
Great East Road Campus
P.O. Box 32379
Lusaka
Tel: (260 1) 252576
Fax: (260 1) 253952
Email: hunene@admin.unza.zm

ZIMBABWE
Academic and Baobab Books (Pvt.) Ltd.
4 Conald Road
Graniteside
P.O. Box 567
Harare
Tel: (263 4) 755 035
Fax: (263 4) 759 052
Email: Academic@Africaonline.Co.Zw

BOOKSELLERS OF WORLD BANK PUBLICATIONS

Prices vary from country to country. Consult your local bookseller for prices and availability.

ARGENTINA, PARAGUAY, AND URUGUAY
Librería Técnica Uruguaya
Colonia 1543, Piso 7, Of. 702
Casilla de Correo 1518
Montevideo 11000, Uruguay
Tel: (598 2) 490072
Fax: (598 2) 41 34 48
Email: ltu@cs.com.uy

CHINA
China National Publications Import
& Export Corporation
16 Gongti East Road
Post Code 100020
Beijing

HUNGARY
Foundation for Market Economy
112 Pf 249
1519 Budapest
Tel: (36 1) 204 2951; 2948
Fax: (36 1) 204 2953
Email: ipargazd@hungary.net

INDIA
Bookwell
Head Office: 2/72, Nirankari Colony
Delhi - 110009
Tel: (91 11) 725 1283
Sales Office: 24/4800, Ansari Road, Darya Ganj
New Delhi-110002
Tel: (91 11) 326 8786, 325 7264
Fax: (91 11) 328 1315
Email: bkwell@nde.vsnl.net.in

JORDAN
Global Development Forum
P.O. Box 941488
Amman 11194
Tel: (962 6) 5537 701
Fax: (962 6) 5537 702

KOREA, REPUBLIC OF
Sejong Books, Inc.
81-4 Neung-dong
Kwangjin-ku
Seoul 143-180
Tel: (82 2) 498 0300
Fax: (82 2) 3409 0321
Email: danielchoi@sejongbooks.com
URL: www.sejongbooks.com

MALAYSIA
MDC Publishers Printers SDN BHD
MDC Building
2718, Jalan Permata Empat
Taman Permata, Ulu Kelang
53300 Kuala Lumpur
Tel: (60 3) 408 6600
Fax: (60 3) 408 1506
Email: mdcpp@2mws.com.my
URL: www.2mws.com.my/mdc

NEPAL
Bazaar International
228 Sanchaya Kosh Building
GPO Box 2480, Tridevi Marg
Kathmandu
Tel: (977 1) 255 125
Fax: (977 1) 229 437
Email: bazaar@mos.com.np

NIGERIA
Mosuro Booksellers
5 Oluware Obasa Street (Near Awolowo Ave.)
P.O. Box 30201
Ibadan
Tel: (234 2) 810-2560
Fax: (234 2) 810-2042
Email: Kmosuro@linkserve.com.ng

POLAND
A.B.E. Marketing
Ul. Grzybowska 37A
00-855 Warsaw
Tel: (48 22) 654 06 75
Fax: (48 22) 682 22 33; 682 17 24
Email: abe@ikp.atm.com.pl

SLOVAK REPUBLIC
Slovart G.T.G. Ltd.
Krupinská 4
P.O. Box 152
852 99 Bratislava 5
Tel: (42 7) 839 471; 472; 473
Fax: (42 7) 839 485
Email: gtg@internet.sk

TAIWAN, CHINA
Tycoon Information, Inc.
Ms. Eileen Chen
5 Floor, No. 500
Chang-Chun Road
Taipei 105, Taiwan
Tel: (866 2) 8712 8886
Fax: (886 2) 8712 4747; 8712 4777
Email: eiutpe@ms21.hinet.net

THAILAND
Chulalongkorn University Book Center
Phyathai Road
Bangkok 10330
Tel: (66 2) 235 5400
Fax: (66 2) 255 4441

Book Link Co. Ltd.
118/4 Ekamai Soi 28
Vadhana
Bangkok 10110
Tel: (662) 711 4392
Fax: (662) 711 4103
Email: bbatpt@au.ac.th

TURKEY
Dünya Infotel A.S.
"Globus" Dünya Basinevi
100, Yil Mahallesi
34440 Bagcilar-Istanbul
Tel: (90 212) 629 08 08
Fax: (90 212) 629 46 89; 629 46 27
Email: dunya@dunyagazete.com.tr
URL: http: www.dunya.com

UNITED ARAB EMIRATES
Al Rawdha Bookshop
P.O. Box 5027
Sharjah
Tel: (971 6) 734 687
Fax: (971 6) 384 473
Email: alrawdha@hotmail.com

World Development Indicators 2000

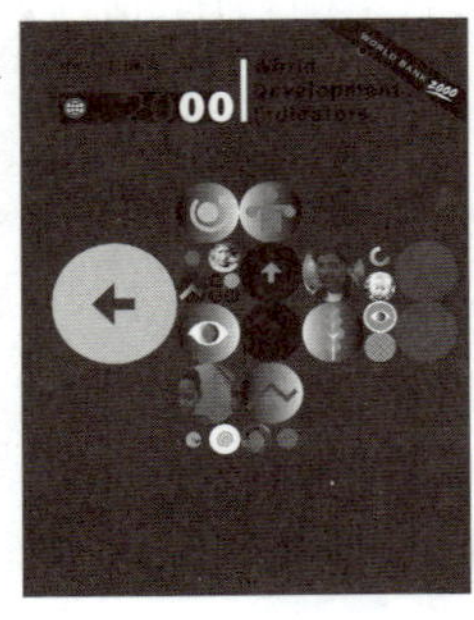

This is the fourth annual edition of the World Bank's flagship statistical reference *World Development Indicators 2000.* This award-winning publication provides an expanded view of the world economy for 148 countries—with chapters focusing on world view, people, environment, economy, states and markets, and global links, as well as introductions highlighting recent research on major development issues. The 2000 edition includes some key indicators for 1999.

April 2000 416 pages Stock no. 14553 (ISBN 0-8213-4553-2) $60.00

Also available on CD-ROM

This comprehensive database contains underlying time-series data for the *World Development Indicators* and *World Bank Atlas*, now covering 1960–1998 for most indicators with some extending to 1999. Powerful features allow you to generate maps and charts and download your results to other software programs.

April 2000 Single user Version: Stock no. 14554 (ISBN 0-8213-4554-0) $275.00
Network Version: Stock no. 14555 (ISBN 0-8213-4555-9) $550.00

This year World Development Indicators is available as a book and single-user CD-ROM package. ***Stock #: 31698 Price: $295.00***

World Bank Atlas 2000

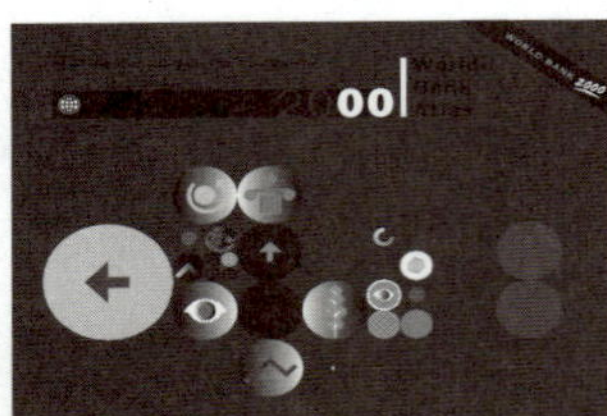

One of the Bank's most popular offerings, the *Atlas* is designed as a companion to the *World Development Indicators*. Tables, charts, and colorful maps address the development themes of world view, people, environment, economy, states and markets, and global links. This easy-to-use book is an international standard in statistical compilations and an ideal reference for office or classroom. Text, maps, and references appear in English, French, and Spanish.

April 2000 64 pages Stock no. 14552 (ISBN 0-8213-4552-4) $20.00

Title	Stock#	Price	Copies	Subtotal
			Subtotal	
			Shipping & Handling	
			Total US$	

Name (Please Print) _________________________

Address _________________________

____

City ____________________ State ____

Zip/Postal Code _____ Phone ___-___-____ Ext. _____

Method of Payment

❑ Enclosed is my check drawn on a U.S. bank made payable to the World Bank

❑ Charge my ❑ Visa ❑ MasterCard ❑ American Express

Credit Card Account Number ________________ Exp. Date __ __ - __ __

Signature _________________________

Customers in the U.S.: Complete this coupon and return to World Bank Publications, P.O. Box 960, Herndon, VA. 20172-0960. To charge by credit card call (800) 645-7247 or (703) 661-1580 or send this completed coupon via fax to (703) 661-1501.

Customers outside the U.S.: Contact your local distributor for information on prices in local currency and payment terms. If no distributor is listed for your country, fax this order form to the number above or mail it to World Bank Publications, P.O. Box 960, Herndon, VA 20172-0960, USA.

***Shipping and handling** charges are $8.00 per order. If a purchase order is used, actual shipping will be charged. For air mail delivery outside the United States, charges are $13.00 for one item plus $6.00 for each additional item.

Institutional customers in the U.S. only

❑ Bill me (purchase order must be included)

❑ Begin standing order.

WD00